The SAG

Public Administration

Concise second edition

SAGE has been part of the global academic community since 1965, supporting high quality research and learning that transforms society and our understanding of individuals, groups, and cultures. SAGE is the independent, innovative, natural home for authors, editors and societies who share our commitment and passion for the social sciences.

Find out more at: **www.sagepublications.com**

The SAGE Handbook of
Public Administration

Concise second edition

Edited by
B. Guy Peters
and
Jon Pierre

 reference

Los Angeles | London | New Delhi
Singapore | Washington DC

Los Angeles | London | New Delhi
Singapore | Washington DC

SAGE Publications Ltd
1 Oliver's Yard
55 City Road
London EC1Y 1SP

SAGE Publications Inc.
2455 Teller Road
Thousand Oaks, California 91320

SAGE Publications India Pvt Ltd
B 1/I 1 Mohan Cooperative Industrial Area
Mathura Road
New Delhi 110 044

SAGE Publications Asia-Pacific Pte Ltd
3 Church Street
#10-04 Samsung Hub
Singapore 049483

Editor: Natalie Aguilera
Editorial assistant: James Piper
Production editor: Imogen Roome
Marketing manager: Sally Ransom
Cover design: Wendy Scott
Typeset by: Cenveo Publisher Services
Printed by: Henry Ling Limited, Dorchester

Library of Congress Control Number: 2012930289

British Library Cataloguing in Publication data
A catalogue record for this book is available from
the British Library

ISBN: 978-1-4462-0050-6
ISBN: 978-1-4462-9580-9 (pb)

MIX
Paper from
responsible sources
FSC
www.fsc.org   FSC™ C013985

Contents

Preface to the Second Edition

Public administration and bureaucracy are as old as government itself, but despite that continuity there is also substantial change. The same is true of the academic study of public administration with its continuing interest in familiar topics such as public finance and accountability, and changing conceptions of management as well as continuing reforms of administration.

This second edition of *The SAGE Handbook of Public Administration* reflects that combination of continuity and change in public administration. It contains a number of the same chapters from the previous edition, although all those chapters have been updated to reflect changes in the discipline and in practice. In addition, there are several new chapters that address emerging issues and changes within the public sector. Every attempt was made to make this second edition a reflection of the state of the art in public administration, just as we believe the first edition was.

We want to thank a number of people who were instrumental in the completion of this second edition. First, we again appreciated the hard work and contributions of our section editors, and of the authors who have produced interesting and important contributions. We have also enjoyed working with our editors at Sage, notably David Mainwaring and Natalie Aguilera. We also should thank our readers who have provided useful feedback about the Handbook and helped in its development.

B. Guy Peters   Jon Pierre
Pittsburgh, PA   Göteborg

About the Editors

B. Guy Peters is Maurice Falk Professor of Government at the University of Pittsburgh, USA, and also Professor of Comparative Governance at Zeppelin University. He was founding co-editor of *Governance* and the *European Political Science Review*. Among his recent publications are *Institutional Theory in Political Science*, 3rd edn, *Interactive Governance: Advancing the Paradigm* (with Jacob Torfing, Jon Pierre and Eva Sørensen) and *Steering from the Centre* (with Carl Dahlström and Jon Pierre).

Jon Pierre is a Research Professor in the Department of Political Science at the University of Gothenburg, Sweden. He is also Adjunct Professor at the University of Pittsburgh and at the Nordland University College in Bodö, Norway. He held a Chair in Politics at the University of Strathclyde between 1996 and 1999. Among his recent publications in English are *Debating Governance* (editor, Oxford University Press, 2000), *Governance, Politics and the State* (with Guy Peters; Palgrave, 2000), *Handbook of Public Administration* (co-editor with Guy Peters; Sage, 2003), *Governing Complex Societies* (with Guy Peters; Palgrave, 2005), *Handbook of Public Policy* (co-editor with Guy Peters; Sage 2006), *Debating Institutionalism* (co-editor, with Guy Peters and Gerry Stoker; Manchester University Press, 2007), *The Politics of Urban Governance* (Palgrave, 2011) and *Interactive Governance* (with Jacob Torfing, Guy Peters and Eva Sörensen; Oxford University Press, 2012). He has also published numerous articles in journals such as *Urban Affairs Review*, *Journal of European Public Policy*, *Journal of Public Administration Research and Theory* and *Journal of Politics*.

About the Authors

Kamran Ali Afzal is a career civil servant with the Government of Pakistan and has served in a range of administrative and policymaking positions over the past 19 years. He earned his PhD in political economy from the University of Melbourne, Australia. He is currently working as a joint secretary in the Finance Division, Islamabad, Pakistan, where he is responsible for medium-term financial planning, drafting annual budgetary proposals, expenditure monitoring and fiscal reforms. His areas of interest include comparative public policy, governance, government accountability structures, public finance and social development.

James Warner Björkman is Professor Emeritus of Public Policy and Administration at the Institute of Social Studies in The Hague, The Netherlands, and has an abiding fascination with South Asia. After a BA summa thesis on the Indian National Congress and a PhD on the politics of administrative alienation in India's rural development programmes, eight of his 15 books address South Asian issues. He has held appointments in the USA, Sweden, England, India, Pakistan, Switzerland, Namibia, Slovenia and Japan.

Marleen Brans is Professor of Public Administration and Policy at the Public Management Institute of the Catholic University of Leuven, Belgium. She is responsible for teaching and training in policy analysis and evaluation, comparative public policy, and administration–citizen interaction. Her research interests include politico-administrative relations, policy analytical capacity of civil service systems, and interactions between government and civil society. She has published in journals such as *Public Administration*, *West-European Politics*, *Journal of Comparative Policy Analysis*, *Halduskultuur*, *International Review of Administrative Sciences*, and *European Political Science*. She is a member of the Accreditation Committee of the European Association for Public Administration Accreditation.

John M. Bryson is McKnight Presidential Professor of Planning and Public Affairs at the Hubert H. Humphrey School of Public Affairs at the University of Minnesota, USA. He works in the areas of leadership, strategic management and the design of engagement processes. He wrote *Strategic Planning for Public and Nonprofit Organizations*, 4th edn (Jossey-Bass, 2011), and co-wrote with Barbara C. Crosby *Leadership for the Common Good*, 2nd edn (Jossey-Bass, 2005). Dr Bryson is a Fellow of the National Academy of Public Administration and received the 2011 Dwight Waldo Award from the American Society for Public Administration for 'outstanding contributions to the professional literature of public administration over an extended scholarly career'.

K. Jurée Capers is a doctoral candidate in the Department of Political Science at Texas A&M University, USA. She was a 2009–2010 American Political Science Association

Minority Fellow. Her research interests lie in the areas of public policy, representation, public management, race and ethnic politics, and education policy. Currently she is working on a project that combines theories of bureaucratic representation, public management and institutional structure, to understand policy implementation decisions, policy outputs and outcomes.

Jørgen Grønnegaard Christensen is Professor in Public Administration at the Department of Political Science, Aarhus University, Denmark. His research covers, among other things, governmental organization, the interaction between politicians and civil servants, civil service reform, governmental regulation and reform as well as the impact of the EU on national administration and policy. He has published widely in journals and books.

Tom Christensen is Professor of Public Administration and Organization Theory, Department of Political Science, University of Oslo, Norway. He is also Adjunct Professor at Uni Rokkan Centre and City University of Hong Kong. His major field of research is comparative public reforms, based on organization theory perspectives. He has published extensively in all the major journals in the field of public administration and he is part of several international research networks and projects. His latest book, co-edited with Per Lægreid, is *The Ashgate Research Companion to New Public Management* (2011).

Mark Considine is Professor of Political Science and the Dean of the Faculty of Arts at The University of Melbourne, Australia. His research areas include governance studies, comparative social policy, employment services, public sector reform, local development, and organizational development. Mark is a Fellow of the Institute of Public Administration Australia (Victoria) and the Australian Academy of Social Sciences.

Paul Craig is Professor of English Law at St John's College, Oxford, UK. His academic field covers European Union law, administrative law, constitutional law and comparative administrative law. His research spans broad areas within these subjects and includes issues of theory, institutional design and legal doctrine. This work is characterised by an inter-disciplinary and contextual focus.

Carl Dahlström is Associate Professor in the Department of Political Science and the Quality of Government Institute, University of Gothenburg, Sweden. He has previously been a visiting scholar at Harvard University, at the Stockholm Centre for Organizational Research and had a fellowship at the Swedish Parliament. His research is mainly concerned with comparative and historical perspectives on public administration, corruption and welfare state policymaking. His papers have appeared in a broad range of peer-reviewed journals, including for example, *Governance* and *Journal of Public Administration Research & Theory*. He is also co-editor of the book *Steering from the Centre: Strengthening Political Control in Western Democracies* (University of Toronto Press), and contributor to handbooks in public administration and political corruption.

Christoph Demmke is Professor of Comparative Public Administration at the European Institute of Public Administration in Maastricht, The Netherlands, and Visiting Professor at the College of Europe. He holds a PhD in Administrative Sciences and has taught comparative public administration at several European universities, national civil service academies and European institutions. He was an Emile Noel Fellow at Harvard Law School and visiting fellow at American University and the University of Georgia. His fields of specialisation are comparative studies of public service reform including human resource management reforms. He has published many books and articles on comparative public service reforms and public-service ethics, among other topics. He has regularly advised the different EU Presidencies in the field of public services reforms and human resource management reforms.

Dionyssis G. Dimitrakopoulos is Senior Lecturer in Politics at Birkbeck College, University of London, UK, where he directs the MSc programme in European politics and policy. He has published extensively on various aspects of the politics of European integration. He is the author of *The Power of the Centre: Central Governments and the Macro-implementation of EU Public Policy* (Manchester University Press, 2008) and the editor of *Social Democracy and European Integration: The Politics of Preference Formation* (Routledge, 2011).

Gavin Drewry is Emeritus Professor of Public Administration at Royal Holloway, University of London, UK, an Honorary Professor in the Faculty of Law at University College London and a Visiting Research Fellow in the Centre for Capital Punishment Studies at the University of Westminster. He is a member of the Council of Administration of the International Institute of Administrative Sciences. In an academic career spanning more than 40 years, he has taught and researched across a very wide range of subjects in political science and public administration. He has a particular interest in the interface between public law and politics and government and has published extensively in that cross-disciplinary area.

Morten Egeberg is Professor of Public Policy and Administration and holds a joint position at the Department of Political Science and at ARENA – Centre for European Studies, University of Oslo, Norway. His academic interests encompass the relationship between organization structure and decision behaviour within national executives as well as in the European Commission and EU agencies. He also studies new patterns of interaction between levels of governance, particularly between the European and the national.

David Feldman, QC, DCL, FBA, is Rouse Ball Professor of English Law, University of Cambridge, UK, a Fellow of Downing College, Cambridge and an Academic Associate at 39 Essex Street, London. From 2002 until 2010 he was a Judge of the Constitutional Court of Bosnia and Herzegovina (Vice-President 2006–2009). He was Legal Adviser to the Parliamentary Joint Select Committee on Human Rights 2000–2004, and has advised several other parliamentary committees. He held posts at the Universities of Bristol (1976–1992) and Birmingham (1992–2000) and the Australian National University (1989), and has been a visiting scholar at the University of Melbourne and the University of Nottingham. He has published extensively in the fields of police powers, administrative law, constitutional law and theory, comparative public law, civil liberties, human rights, the relationship between national and international law, and judicial remedies.

Alan Fenna is Professor of Politics at The John Curtin Institute of Public Policy, Curtin University, Western Australia, specialising in Australian public policy as well as Australian and comparative federalism. He served as President of the Australian Political Studies Association (APSA) in 2009–2010.

Mark Hallerberg is Director of the Fiscal Governance Centre and Professor for Public Management and Political Economy at the Hertie School of Governance in Berlin, Germany.

John Halligan is Professor of Public Administration, University of Canberra, Australia. His current research interests are comparative public governance and management, including public sector reform and political–bureaucratic relationships, with a focus on Anglophone and OECD countries. Recent co-authored books are *Public Sector Governance in Australia* (ANU Press, 2012, forthcoming), *Performance Management in the Public Sector* (Routledge, 2010), *The Centrelink Experiment: Innovation in Service Delivery* (ANU Press, 2008), *Managing Performance: International Comparisons* (Routledge, 2008).

Thomas H. Hammond is Professor of Political Science at Michigan State University, East Lansing, Michigan, USA. He specialises in bureaucratic studies, focusing on theories of information processing and policymaking in hierarchies, and with applications to intelligence agencies and foreign policy decision-making. He also works on theories of political institutions, especially separation-of-powers systems, and on theories of Supreme Court decision-making.

Paul 't Hart is Professor of Public Administration at Utrecht University, The Netherlands, Associate Dean of the Netherlands School of Public Administration and a fellow of the Australia and New Zealand School of Government. He has held prior chairs at the Australian National University and Leiden University. His research and teaching are in executive politics, crisis management, public leadership, accountability studies and policy analysis. He has taught and trained thousands of public officials, mainly in The Netherlands, Australia and Sweden. His recent books include *Dispersed Democratic Leadership* (2009), *The Real World of EU Accountability* (2010) and *How Power Changes Hands* (2011).

Carolyn J. Heinrich, PhD, is the Sid Richardson Professor of Public Affairs at the Lyndon B. Johnson School of Public Affairs, affiliated Professor of Economics and the Director of the Center for Health and Social Policy at the University of Texas at Austin, USA. Dr Heinrich's research focuses on social welfare policy, public management and performance management, and econometric methods for social-programme evaluation.

Rita M. Hilton is a Senior Consultant at the Center for Human Capital Innovation, Alexandria, USA. Her academic training spans the fields of institutional economics and organizational psychology. She was a development economist at the World Bank for 15 years. Since leaving the Bank in 2005 she has built a successful record as an executive coach and consultant focused on helping clients improve organizational effectiveness. She specialises in working with organizations managed by technical experts (e.g., scientists and engineers).

Goran Hyden is Distinguished Professor Emeritus in Political Science at the University of Florida, Gainesville, USA. He has authored many books and articles on African politics and public administration in comparative perspective, and has served as consultant to many international organizations on governance issues.

Patricia W. Ingraham is Founding Dean of the College of Community and Public Affairs at Binghamton University, USA. Formerly a Distinguished Professor of Public Administration at the Maxwell School at Syracuse University, Ingraham has received numerous honours for her teaching and research, including the John Gaus Award from the American Political Science Association, the Dwight Waldo Award from the Society for Public Administration and the Levine Award for Distinguished Research from NASPAA. Ingraham is the editor and author of 14 volumes on governance and numerous scholarly articles. She received her doctorate from Binghamton University and her bachelor's degree from Macalester College.

Philip G. Joyce is Professor of Management, Finance, and Leadership at the Maryland School of Public Policy, USA. He is Editor of *Public Budgeting and Finance*, and a Fellow of the National Academy of Public Administration. Professor Joyce's research mainly focuses on two issues – linkages between performance information and the budget, and the US Congressional budget process. His most recent book is *The Congressional Budget Office: Honest Numbers, Power and Policymaking* (Georgetown University Press, 2011).

Jack H. Knott is the Erwin and Ione Piper Dean and Professor at the Sol Price School of Public Policy at the University of Southern California, USA. He is a scholar in the fields of organization theory, public management and public policy. His research focuses on the impact of institutions and decision-making processes on public policy, with a particular focus on economic, regulatory and monetary policy. He has also done considerable work on government and bureaucratic reform. He is an elected Fellow of the National Academy of Public Administration, USA.

Leonard Kok is CEO of the Department for Economic and Urban Development of the Municipality of The Hague in The Netherlands. His academic background is a masters degree in political science at the University of Leiden and a masters degree in public administration at The Netherlands School for Government in The Hague. He worked for 13 years in the Ministry of Finance, in the last years as Director for Budget Affairs.

Per Lægreid is Professor at the Department of Administration and Organization Theory, Bergen University, Norway, and Senior Researcher at the Uni Rokkan Centre, Bergen. His academic field spans organization theory, institutional analyses, public administration, public management and administrative reforms. He regularly presents his research at international workshops and conferences and publishes extensively in international journals. His recent books include *Government Agencies: Practices and Lessons from 30 Countries* (edited with K. Verhoest, S. van Thiel and G. Bouckaert; Palgrave Macmillan), *The Ashgate Research Companion to New Public Management* (edited with T. Christensen; Ashgate) and *Governance of Public Sector Organizations* (edited with K. Verhoest; Palgrave Macmillan).

Mordecai Lee is Professor of Governmental Affairs at the University of Wisconsin – Milwaukee, USA. He is interested in history and public relations in government and NGOs. His books on American history include *Congress vs. The Bureaucracy* (2011), *Nixon's Super-Secretaries* (2010) and *Institutionalizing Congress and the Presidency: The U.S. Bureau of Efficiency, 1916–1933* (2006). Before joining the academy, he was Legislative Assistant to a Congressman, elected to five terms in the Wisconsin State Legislature and executive director of a faith-based NGO.

Martin Lodge is Professor of Political Science and Public Policy at the Department of Government and the Centre for Analysis of Risk and Regulation at the London School of Economics and Political Science, UK. His key interests are in the fields of executive politics and regulation.

Laurence E. Lynn, Jr is Sid Richardson Research Professor at the Lyndon B. Johnson School of Public Affairs at the University of Texas at Austin, and the Sydney Stein Jr Professor of Public Management Emeritus at the University of Chicago, USA. His previous faculty affiliations have included the John F. Kennedy School of Government at Harvard University, the Irving B. Harris School Graduate School of Public Policy Studies at the University of Chicago, the Manchester (UK) Business School, the George Bush School of Government and Public Affairs at Texas A&M University, and the Graduate School of Business at Stanford University. He spent nearly a decade in senior policymaking positions in the US Federal Government. His most recent books are *Public Management: Old and New*, *Madison's Managers: Public Administration and the Constitution* (with Anthony M. Bertelli), and a textbook, *Public Management: A Three Dimensional Approach* (with Carolyn J. Hill). For his public service, Lynn received the Secretary of Defense Meritorious Civilian Service Medal and a Presidential Certificate of Distinguished Achievement. For lifetime contributions to public administration research and practice, he was selected as a John Gaus lecturer by the American Political Science Association, a recipient of the Dwight Waldo and Paul Van Riper awards by the American Society for Public Administration, and the recipient of the inaugural H. George Frederickson award by the Public Management Research Association.

Helen Margetts is the Director of the Oxford Internet Institute (OII), a department of the University of Oxford, UK, investigating individual, collective and organizational behaviour online. Margetts joined the OII in 2004 as Professor of Society and the Internet, having previously been Professor of Political Science and Director of the School of Public Policy at University College London. Her research focuses on digital governance and politics, investigating the dynamics of online relationships between governments and citizens, and collective action on the Internet. She is the co-author (with Christopher Hood) of *Paradoxes of Modernization: Unintended Consequences of Public Policy Reform* (2010), *The Tools of Government in the Digital Age* (2007) and (with Patrick Dunleavy) *Digital Era Governance: IT Corporations, the State and e-Government* (2006). Her policy reports on digital government for the National Audit Office undertaken with Patrick Dunleavy of the London School of Economics represent the only systematic evaluation of the UK Government's electronic presence. She currently holds an ESRC Professorial Fellowship entitled 'The Internet, Political Science and Public Policy', is Editor-in-Chief of the journal *Policy and Internet* and sits on the Advisory Board of the Government Digital Service in the Cabinet Office.

Kenneth J. Meier is the Charles H. Gregory Chair in Liberal Arts and Distinguished Professor of Political Science at Texas A&M University, USA. He is also a Professor of Public Management in the Cardiff School of Business, Cardiff University, Wales. In addition to his long term interest in questions of representative bureaucracy, he is working on empirical studies of public management (in the USA, the UK, Denmark and The Netherlands), race and public policy, methodological innovations in public administration, and the relationship between democracy and bureaucracy.

Marcia K. Meyers is Professor of Social Work and Public Affairs and Director of the West Coast Poverty Center at the University of Washington, USA. She has published widely on social welfare issues including US anti-poverty and family policy, gender and family care policy, and the implementation of social programmes. With Janet Gornick she co-authored *Families that Work: Policies for Reconciling Parenthood and Employment* and co-edited *Gender Equality: Transforming Divisions of Labor*. She recently co-edited a volume on emerging issues in US social policy, *Old Assumptions, New Realities: Social Policy for Families in the 21st Century*.

Timo Moilanen, MSocSc, is a political scientist specialising in human resource management, and for most of his professional career he has worked at the University of Helsinki, Finland. He has taught human resource management, organizational ethics and research methods at various universities. He has worked for several EU Presidencies in the European Public Administration Network, and carried out projects for several international institutions. He has conducted a number of comparative studies and evaluations on state personnel and employer policy, governing bodies and public-service ethics among the EU Member States.

Donald Moynihan is Professor of Public Affairs at the La Follette School of Public Affairs, University of Wisconsin – Madison, USA. His research examines the application of organization theory to public management issues such as performance, budgeting, homeland security, election administration and employee behaviour. In particular, he studies the selection and implementation of public management reforms. He is a Fellow of the United States National Academy of Public Administration.

Jorge Nef is Professor Emeritus of Development Studies at the University Guelph, Ontario, Canada. His academic field spans political science, international development and human security. He has been very active in conferences relating to international development, public administration and comparative development (especially Latin American studies) He regularly presents his research at international research conferences including LASA, CALACS and the learned societies. He has written edited and co-edited 16 books on political and international issues, and over 120 scholarly articles in refereed journals and in books on issues of human security, technology, and democracy. His most recent books are *Capital, Power and Inequality in Latin America and the Caribbean* (Rowan & Littlefield, 2008) and *The Democratic Challenge* (Palgrave, 2009). His research largely focuses on mutual vulnerability and human security/insecurity.

Vibeke Lehmann Nielsen is an Associate Professor at the Department of Political Science, Aarhus University, Denmark. She has been visiting Research Fellow at RegNet, Australian National University and Texas A&M University. She researches and teaches in regulatory enforcement, compliance, public policy implementation and street-level bureaucratic behaviour. Dr Nielsen has published in international journals including *Public Administration*, *Administration & Society*, *Regulation and Governance*, and *Law & Policy*. She has published the following books in Danish (titles translated from the Danish): *Price of Dialogue: Informal Rules, Asymmetry of Resources and Discrimination in Regulatory Enforcement* (Politica, 2002); and *Implementation of Public Policy* (with Søren Winter; Academica, 2008). With Christine Parker she has edited the book *Explaining Compliance: Business Responses to Regulation* (Edward Elgar, 2011).

Frans van Nispen holds a MPA from Leiden University and a PhD from the Erasmus University of Rotterdam, The Netherlands. He served for several years as policy analyst for the Dutch Government, before he returned to academia. He has been Affiliated Professor at Institute of Public Policy of George Mason University at Fairfax, Virginia and Senior Research Fellow at the Robert Schuman Centre for Advanced Studies of the European University Institute in San Domenico di Fiesole. Currently he is Associate Professor of Public Administration at the Erasmus University of Rotterdam. He has published in various journals, primarily on issues at the interface of policy analysis and public budgeting in a European context. He has done consultancy for the EU, the OECD and the World Bank.

Dele Olowu is an international consultant in public policy and management, institutional analysis and capacity development/management. He has served as Professor of Public

Administration and Public Policy at several universities and graduate centres for public policy and management training in Africa (Ethiopia, Namibia and Nigeria) and also in Europe (Institute of Social Studies, The Hague, now a part of Erasmus University; Maastricht University, Maastricht – all in The Netherlands). His teaching and research span comparative public administration, decentralisation and multi-level governments, roles for state and non-state actors in institution building and development administration.

Laurence J. O'Toole, Jr Is the Margaret Hughes and Robert T. Golembiewski Professor of Public Administration and also Distinguished Research Professor, in the Department of Public Administration and Policy, School of Public and International Affairs, at the University of Georgia, USA. He is also Professor of Comparative Sustainability Studies in the Faculty of Management and Governance, Twente University, The Netherlands. His research interests include policy implementation and public management in networks.

Edward C. Page is Sidney and Beatrice Webb Professor of Public Policy at the London School of Economics and Political Science, UK. His academic field covers comparative public policy and administration. His recent work has examined civil service roles in policymaking. His latest books include *Policy Bureaucracy: Government with a Cast of Thousands* (with Bill Jenkins, 2005), *From the Active to the Enabling State* (edited with Vincent Wright, 2006), *Changing Government Relations in Europe* (edited with Michael Goldsmith, 2010) and *Policy without Politicians: Bureaucratic Influence in Comparative Perspective* (2012).

Martin Painter is Professor of Public and Social Administration, City University of Hong Kong and Director of the Governance in Asia Research Centre. He currently occupies the role of University Coordinator for implementation of the Five-Year Strategic Plan. His research includes autonomy and control in Hong Kong government bodies and the adoption of western models of public management in China and Vietnam. Professor Painter has been awarded several consultancies on public administration reform in Vietnam, working in collaboration with Government of Vietnam agencies and with national and international donors.

Argyris G. Passas is Associate Professor at the General Department of Law of Panteion University of Social and Political Sciences of Athens, Greece. He specialises in public administration and European integration. His most recent book is *National Public Administration and the European Union Policy Process* (2012, in Greek). He has served as an administrator in the European Parliament and has headed the Greek National Centre for Public Administration. He is a special advisor to the Government of the Republic of Cyprus on the training of public servants for the first Cypriot Presidency of the Council of the EU (2nd semester, 2012).

Simona Piattoni is Professor of Political Science at the University of Trento, Italy, where she teaches comparative politics, European politics, multi-level governance and local government. She has worked in the past on clientelism, corruption and regional development and, more recently, on multi-level governance and European democracy. She has published on clientelism, Italy in the European Union, informal and multi-level governance, the Committee of the Regions and, more recently, higher education policy and political representation. She has served on the editorial board of *Rivista Italiana di Scienza Politica*, *Rivista Italiana di Politiche Pubbliche*, *Regional and Federal Studies*, *European Politics and Society* and *European Journal of Political Research*. She is currently Chair of the ECPR (European Consortium for Political Research) and President of CONGRIPS (Conference Group of Italian Politics and Society), a related section of APSA.

Jos C. N. Raadschelders is Professor of Public Administration at the John Glenn School of Public Affairs, The Ohio State University, USA. His research and teaching interests include history of government, comparative government, civil service systems and the nature of the study of public administration. The latter topic was the focus of his most recent book (Oxford University Press, 2011). Between 2006 and 2011 he served as the managing editor of *Public Administration Review*.

Beryl A. Radin is a member of the faculty at the Georgetown Public Policy Institute at Georgetown University in Washington DC, USA. She is the series editor of Georgetown University Press's Public Management and Change book series and the author of a number of books on public management issues. She received the 2012 John Gaus career award from the American Political Science Association for her scholarship involving public administration and political science, as well as several other awards for work involving public management and intergovernmental relations/federalism.

Hal G. Rainey is Alumni Foundation Distinguished Professor in the School of Public and International Affairs at the University of Georgia, USA. His research concentrates on organizations and management in government, with emphasis on change, leadership, incentives, and comparisons of governmental management to management in the business and nonprofit sectors. The fourth edition of his book, *Understanding and Managing Public Organizations*, was published in 2009. Rainey serves as a Fellow of the National Academy of Public Administration. In 2009 he received the Dwight Waldo Award for career contributions to scholarship in public administration. In 2011 he received the John Gaus Award from the American Political Science Association for lifetime scholarly contributions in the joint traditions of political science and public administration.

Bo Rothstein holds the August Röhss Chair in Political Science at University of Gothenburg, Sweden, where he is Head of the Quality of Government (QoG) Institute. He serves as Scientific Coordinator for ANTICORRP – Anti-Corruption Policies Revisited – a five-year research project started in 2012 funded by the European Union and consisting of 21 research groups in 16 countries. He has been a visiting scholar at the Russell Sage Foundation, Harvard University and Stanford University.

Luc Rouban is CNRS Research Director and Professor at Sciences Po (Cevipof), Paris, France. His research focuses on the relationship between politics and public administrations as well as on transformations in the public sector in Europe (the civil service and state reform). He serves in the boards of *Public Administration*, *Public Administration Review*, *Public Management Review*, *Revue Française d'Administration Publique*. Among his recent publications are *Politics in France and Europe* (edited with P. Perrineau; Palgrave Macmillan, 2009).

Fabio Rugge is Professor of History of Political Institutions at the University of Pavia, Italy. His academic interests focus on administrative history in the nineteenth and twentieth centuries, in a comparative perspective. He belonged or belongs to the editorial board of journals like *Jahrbuch für Europäische Verwaltungsgeschichte*, *Public Administration Review*, *Il Politico*. He was a Jemolo Fellow at Nuffield College, Oxford; Humboldt Fellow at the Technische Universität, Berlin; and a Fellow of the Woodrow Wilson Center, Washington DC.

Patrycja Joanna Suwaj is Professor of Law at S. Staszic School of Public Administration, Bialystok, Poland. Her academic interests span public administration, administrative law and public management. She has worked extensively in the area of civil service, anticorruption and conflict of interest research and training. She regularly presents her research at international conferences including NISPAcee (she is a co-ordinator of the Working Group of Civil Service) and EGPA. She is a member of the RENEUAL Network, EAPAA Accreditation Committee and expert for the Polish Accreditation Committee. Since 1999 she has served as the Executive Director of the Polish Association of Public Administration Education (SEAP).

Jean-Claude Thoenig is a Senior Research Director at the French National Center for Scientific Research. He currently is a member of Dauphine Recherche en Management (University of Paris Dauphine). A sociologist and political scientist, he has made relevant contributions in fields such as organization theory, local government, intergovernmental relations, bureaucracy theory, public management and policy analysis. His current research interests deal with the way universities produce academic quality. He favours field and comparative research. He also works on profit-oriented organizations and management.

Paul G. Thomas is Professor Emeritus in Political Studies at the University of Manitoba, Canada where he taught for 40 years. He has written several books and over 200 chapters and articles on various public administration topics. He has served as a consultant to governments in Canada and elsewhere and has been recognised with numerous awards for his contributions to the field.

James R. Thompson is Associate Professor in the Department of Public Administration at the University of Illinois – Chicago, USA, where he teaches courses in public personnel management, information technology and public management. Topics on which he has written include civil service reform, human resource management innovation and organizational change in the public sector.

Theo A. J. Toonen is Dean of the Faculty of Technology, Policy and Management (TPM) at Delft University of Technology, and Professor of Institutional Governance and Public Administration at Delft University of Technology and Leiden University, The Netherlands. He has been Chair of Institutional and Comparative Public Administration in Leiden since 1989 and became Dean of the Faculty of Social and Behavioural Sciences at Leiden University in 2003. In March 2008 he was appointed Dean of the Faculty of TPM at Delft University of Technology. Professor Toonen's research has focused on themes ranging from water management and governance, multi-scaled, multi-level (European) governance, (international) comparative public administration, and public sector and administrative reform to urban and regional government in international perspective. He has been policy advisor to various Dutch Ministers, member of the Independent Dutch National Advisory Committee Water (AcW; 2004–2012), and is currently at the Intergovernmental Financial Relations Council (RfV) and on the board of the StimulanSZ Foundation on Decentralisation and Social Policy.

Tony J. G. Verheijen is Manager of the Governance and Public Sector Management Unit, South Asia Region, World Bank. He has previously held positions in the World Bank as Governance Cluster Leader in the Africa Region and Senior Public Sector Management Specialist in the Europe and CIS region, and has also held advisory and management positions in the OECD and UNDP, as well as teaching positions at the College of Europe, Leiden University, the University of Limerick and the European Institute of Public Administration. His research work has focused on comparative public management and civil service systems, the impact of political and economic transition on state institutions and on managing the challenges of multi-level governance systems. His work has been widely published in both academic and professional literature.

Anchrit Wille lectures at the Institute of Public Administration, Leiden University, The Netherlands. Her research and teaching cover a wide range of key issues in studies of politics and public administration: executive politics, political–administrative relationships, accountability, citizen politics, comparative politics and EU governance. Her work has been published in a number of edited volumes and in scholarly journals. She has co-authored several books. Her recent book *Politics and Bureaucracy in the European Commission* (Oxford University Press, 2013) is on the evolution of accountability and executive politics in the EU.

Søren C. Winter is Professor of Political Science at SFI – The Danish National Centre for Social Research, Copenhagen, Denmark. His research focuses on policy implementation, public management, street-level bureaucracy, performance, regulatory enforcement and compliance. He is currently the principal investigator of a major research project on school management, teaching and student performance sponsored by the Danish Council for Strategic Research. He was a visiting scholar at the University of California at Berkeley in 1993–94 and at University of Washington in 1999.

Jacques Ziller is Professor of European Union Law at the University of Pavia, Italy since 2007. He has long specialised in research and training in the fields of comparative public administration and management and also in the field of European affairs and regional integration. He has been a member of the Steering Committee of the European Group of Public Administration and is a member of the Scientific Council of the German Institute for Research on Public Administration, Speyer.

Introduction: The Role of Public Administration in Governing

B. Guy Peters and Jon Pierre

Enter the bureaucrat, the true leader of the Republic.

(Senator Palpadine, *Star Wars, Episode 1*)

The SAGE Handbook of Public Administration represents an attempt to address the major issues in, and perspectives on, public administration. The Handbook is an international treatment of this subject, with scholars drawn from a wide range of countries and intellectual traditions. Further, although the large majority of the participants in the project are academics, the attempt has been made also to confront issues of practice, and the relevance of academic research to the day-to-day problems of making government programs perform as they are designed to. Public administration is an area of substantial academic activity, but it is also the focus of important practical work, and public servants have a wealth of experience that is important for understanding public administration. No single volume could hope to cover in any comprehensive manner the full range of concerns about public administration, but we have, we believe, illuminated the crucial issues and also provided a starting point for those readers who wish to pursue this field of inquiry and practice more thoroughly.

WHY ADMINISTRATION MATTERS

The most important premise of this Handbook is that public administration matters. There is a tendency among the public, and even among scholars of the public sector, to equate politics and government with dramatic events such as elections, or with the visible conflicts between politicians that shape major policy developments. Those activities are indeed important for governing, but there is a massive amount of activity involved in translating laws and decrees made by politicians into action, and in delivering public programs to citizens. That work is often less visible, but is crucial for making things happen in government. Legislatures and political executives may pass all the laws they wish, but unless those laws are administered effectively by the public bureaucracy, little or nothing will actually happen. The bureaucracy[1] is often the favorite target for newspaper leader writers and for politicians, but without administrators little would happen in government.

Public administrators comprise the bulk of government employment and activity. In the United Kingdom the central government in London has 650 members of the House of Commons, a few hundred members of the House of Lords, a few hundred political appointees in the executive departments, a few thousand judges, but several hundred thousand public administrators. In addition, there are several hundred thousand public employees in local authorities and the devolved governments of Scotland and Wales. The majority of the employees of government are not the paper-pushers one usually associates with public administration but rather are responsible for delivering public services to the public. Many public administrators in central governments are responsible for providing services, but (on average) local and provincial public servants are even more so.

The principal activity of public administration is implementing laws, but there are also a range of other important activities carried on in these public organizations: for example, bureaucracies make policy, and in essence make law. The laws passed by legislatures are often general, and require elaboration by administrators (Kerwin, 1999; Page, 2000). The secondary legislation prepared by the bureaucracy not only makes the meaning of the laws clearer but also permits the application of the expertise of the career administrators to policy. This style of making policy may raise questions of democratic accountability, but it almost certainly also makes the policies being implemented more technically appropriate for the circumstances, as well as making them more flexible. Although even less visible than their rule-making activities, bureaucracies are also important adjudicators.

In addition to writing secondary legislation, administrators also influence policy by advising the politicians formally responsible for making law. Political leaders may have numerous talents but most politicians do not have extensive expert knowledge about the policies for which they are responsible. Therefore, they require assistance in writing laws and setting policy. The senior public bureaucracy has traditionally had a major role in providing their ministers with the needed advice and information (see Plowden, 1984). That role for public administration is, however, under attack as politicians become more distrustful of bureaucrats and want advice from their own politically committed advisors (Peters and Pierre, 2001). In addition, the reforms of the public sector that have been implemented over the past several decades have stressed the role of the senior public administrator as a manager rather than as a policy advisor, and that has altered the career incentives of senior public managers.

We said above that the work of public administration may be less visible than that of other aspects of government, yet at the same time it is the major point of contact between citizens and the state. The average citizen will encounter the postal clerk, the tax collector and the policeman much more frequently than their elected representatives. This contact between state and society has two important consequences for government. One is that the implementation of laws by the lowest echelons of the public service defines what the laws actually mean for citizens. The laws of a country are what is implemented, and lower echelon employees – policemen, social workers, teachers, etc. – often have substantial discretion over how implementation occurs and who actually gets what from government.

The second impact of the lower echelons of government is that these face-to-face interactions often define what government is for citizens. How am I treated by government? Is government fair, efficient and humane or is it the arbitrary and bureaucratic (in the pejorative sense of the term) structure that it is often alleged to be? The bureaucracy is therefore important in creating an image of government in the popular mind. The good news is that evidence about these interactions tends to be rather positive. Citizens in a number of countries report that most of their interactions with government are positive. The bad news, however, is that many of those same citizens still have a generally negative view of government and of the bureaucracy.

PUBLIC ADMINISTRATION AND THE SURROUNDING SOCIETY

Throughout this Handbook, contributors maintain the perspective of the public administration as embedded in the surrounding society. Although this might appear to be a rather obvious point of departure, the approach emphasizes something often forgotten: public administration is an explication of the collective interest and its legitimacy to a significant extent hinges on its ability to play a part in the pursuit of those interests. Much of the recent debate on New Public Management and market-based models of public service delivery, just to give an example, has tended to portray the public bureaucracy as a generic structure. Ironically, however, introducing market-based solutions in public service production has significant effects on the relationship between the public administration and the surrounding society, as we will argue below.

Furthermore, emphasizing the embedded nature of the public administration helps us understand the rationale for creating links between civil society and the public administration, or more generally, links with the state. The governance perspective on the public bureaucracy highlights those links because they are elements of a broader strategy for service production and delivery that is open to a range of means of generating service. By including societal actors in service delivery the bureaucracy enhances its capacity to act and to 'do more for less', as the Gore Report put it.

Finally, the society-centered perspective on the public administration portrays the public bureaucracy as a potential target for group political pressure. The public administration controls vast resources, and operates

frequently at an increasing distance from elected officials; it is also a major source of regulation. All this contributes to making it attractive to a wide variety of societal groups, ranging from trade unions and employers' association to local environmental protection groups and neighborhood organizations. An understanding of the exchanges between the public bureaucracy and its external environment is critical to an analysis of the bureaucracy in a wider sense.

Politics, administration and society

In order to understand how the public bureaucracy relates to society, we need to generate a broader picture of public–private exchanges in society. The triangular relationships between politics, administration and society are, needless to say, manifold and complex. Starting with the politics–administration linkage, most observers of public policy and administration today agree that this is a false dichotomy. The argument coming out of the classic debate between Friedrich and Finer – 'Policies are implemented when they are formulated and formulated when they are implemented' – seems to be a more accurate representation of the current understanding of the politics–administration relationship. If anything, this statement has gained additional currency since the 1940s along with recent administrative reform and structural changes in the public sector. Reforms aiming at empowering lower-level public sector employees and the greater discretion exercised at that organizational level is but one example of recent changes that support Friedrich's argument (Peters, 2001; Peters and Pierre, 2000).

Thus, politics and administration should be thought of as different elements of the same process of formulating and implementing policy. But politics and administration differ in terms of how they relate to society; while both are critical components of democratic governance, 'politics' in the present context is a matter of representation and accountability, whereas 'administration' refers to policy implementation and the exercise of political power and law. Citizens, organized interests, private businesses and other societal actors interact with both politics and administration, albeit for different reasons. Put in a larger perspective, then, we are interested in the nature of the interface between state and society. Leaving aside the input that is channeled primarily through political parties, we now need to look more closely at the linkage between the public bureaucracy and society.

While historically speaking the public administration's main task has been to implement and communicate political decisions to society, one of the key changes that has occurred over the past decade or so has been the increasing opportunities for citizens to have a more direct input into the public bureaucracy. The experiments with *maison services publiques* in France, the concept of *Bürgernähe* in German administrative reform during the 1990s, the emphasis on (even) more transparency in the Scandinavian countries, and the search for different ways to customer-attune public services in the United States all testify to an almost global tendency to reduce the distance (both physical and intellectual) between the bureaucracy and the individual citizen. This pattern, in turn, is evidence of a strong felt need to strengthen the legitimacy of public sector institutions. With some exaggeration it could be argued that while previously that legitimacy was derived from the public and legal nature of the public administration, legitimacy is currently to an increasing extent contingent on the bureaucracy's ability to deliver customer-attuned services swiftly and accurately.

Perhaps the most powerful and comprehensive strategy of bridging the distance between citizens and the public service is found in the various consumer-choice-based models of public service production. The overall purpose here is not so much to bring citizens (now referred to as consumers) physically closer to service producers but rather to empower consumers through market choice. By exercising such choice, consumers can receive public services more attuned to their preferences than would otherwise have been possible. Furthermore, consumer choice sends a signal to the public sector about the preferences of its consumers, which in aggregated form can inform resource allocation. Described in a slightly different way, this model of consumer choice thus provides society with an input on decisions made in the public bureaucracy with the important difference that the input is not funneled through political parties but is rather an instant communication from the individual to the bureaucracy.

Civil society

The role of civil society in the context of public administration takes on many different forms. Perhaps the most conspicuous arrangement of involvement of civil society is the long-established system of so-called laymen boards (*lekmannastyrelser*) in Swedish agencies. But civil society plays many different roles in different national contexts. In much of continental Europe, for example, civil society plays an important part in delivering public – or quasi-public – services. Much of this cooperation between the public administration and civil society takes place at the local level.

The growing interest in governance during the 1990s highlighted these forms of cooperation between the state and civil society. The governance perspective draws on broad strategies of resource mobilization across the public–private border. This is a pattern which has for long been established in the 'corporatist' democracies in Western Europe. As well as the mobilization of resources, a focus on civil society also has a democratic element, with the relationship with groups providing a source of ideas, legitimation and feedback for government from its society. There are real dangers of these ties limiting the autonomy of government, but they can be the means of making administration less remote from the citizens.

Closing the gap: emerging models of administration – citizen exchange

Much of the administrative reform that has been conducted during the past 10–15 years has been implemented against the backdrop of a weakened legitimacy for the public bureaucracy, and, indeed, for the public sector as a whole. The 1980s in particular was the heyday in the belief of the market as an instrument of resource allocation, leaving little support for public institutions. Additionally, the neoliberal elected leaders emerging during that decade – primarily Reagan, Thatcher and Mulroney – made a strong critique of the public sector and its employees part of their political *Leitmotif* (Hood, 1998; Savoie, 1994). As a result, public sector budgets were drastically cut back. Reaffirming the legitimacy for the public sector, it seemed, could only be accomplished by proving that the public sector could deliver services in a fashion not too different from that of private organizations: that is, in close contact between organization and client, with a purpose to provide services adapted to the particular needs and expectations of the individual client. Put slightly differently, the strategy seems to have been that the future legitimacy of public sector institutions should rest less on traditional values like universality, equality and legal security but more on performance and service delivery.

Much of the administrative reform we witnessed during the late 1980s and 1990s was characterized by these objectives. If we look more closely at the points of contact between citizens and the public sector, they can be summarized in two general trends. First of all, there was a clear emphasis on transparency and accessibility. Structural changes in the public bureaucracy aimed at enhancing exchange between individuals and the public sector. Across Western Europe, governments embarked on a decentralization project, partly to bring political and administrative decisions closer to the citizens. In addition, many public service functions were devolved further, and thus closer to the clients.

The other general trend in administrative reform manifested itself in an effort to make exchanges between citizens and the public bureaucracy easier. Obviously, structural changes like decentralization were necessary, albeit not sufficient, for this type of reform. Here, the general idea was to develop less formal and more accessible means of exchange between clients and the public sector employees. So-called one-stop shops were introduced in several countries, frequently on an experimental basis. More recently, we have seen a wide variety of channels into the public sector available to the citizens via the Internet. It is quite likely that we have only seen the beginning of 'e-government'.

Together, these structural and procedural changes have significantly altered the relationships between the public bureaucracy and its clients. There is today a much stronger emphasis on proximity – if not physical, at least technological – between the public sector and clients. More importantly, perhaps, the tenor of these exchanges has tended to change towards a less formal and more service-oriented communication.

The changing role of public administration

Some aspects of contemporary public administration would appear similar to someone working in government decades earlier, while other aspects have been undergoing fundamental transformation. While the changes are numerous, there are two that deserve highlighting. The first, as alluded to previously, is the increasing emphasis on the role of the public administrator as a manager, and the need to apply the managerial tools familiar in the private sector. This drive toward generic management has almost certainly enhanced the efficiency and perhaps the effectiveness of the public sector, but its critics argue that it has also undervalued the peculiarly public nature of management in government, and the need to think about public sector values other than sheer economic efficiency (Stein, 2002).

A second major change in public administration has been the increasing linkage of state and society in the delivery of public services. Government is no longer an autonomous actor in implementing its policies[2] but often depends upon the private sector and/or the third sector to accomplish its ends. This linkage of state and society may enhance the effectiveness and the legitimacy of government but it also presents government with problems of accountability and control. Blending state and society means that public administrators must become more adept at bargaining and governing through instruments such as contracts, rather than depending upon direct authority to achieve the ends of government.

Finally, the bureaucracy is now less centralized and less hierarchical than ever in its recent history. The degree of centralization of the bureaucracy and of government policy has varied by country, but in almost all there is less power now vested in the center than in the past. Just as working with civil society may require a different set of skills than governing alone, so too will working more closely with subnational governments, or with quasi autonomous organizations that are nominally connected to ministerial authority but which may be designed to act more on their own.

A strong bureaucracy in a weak state?

Bert Rockman has observed that 'If one distinguishes between outlays on the one hand and personnel and organizational structure on the other, it may be that the future holds a sizeable public sector, but one that will have less government' (Rockman, 1998: 38). If the New Public Management reform paradigm continues to dominate the orientation of administrative reform we may soon find ourselves with a hollow administrative structure processing huge transfers but with service

provision increasingly conducted under the auspices of market actors, Rockman argues. We have already discussed the changing channels of exchange between the public bureaucracy and its external environment as well as the overarching objectives of the administrative reform that has been conducted during the late 1980s and 1990s.

Rockman is probably too optimistic (or perhaps pessimistic) about the extent to which administrative reform can shrink public employment and the public bureaucracy. We argued earlier that much of our contact with the state is not with elected representatives but with front staff of the public bureaucracy such as police officers, tax collectors, nurses or social workers. There may be some decrease in the number of such personnel, but these functions cannot be automated. Instead, the cutbacks in public employment have been conducted either by transferring entire functions from the state to the market: for example, railway, telecommunications and postal services. The public sector remains a fairly labor-intensive sector, not least because of the nature of the services it delivers.

What is at stake here is the relationship between strength and external orientation. Not least in an historical perspective, the notion of a 'strong bureaucracy' frequently invoked an image of a self-serving and self-referential bureaucracy. A more contemporary definition of a strong bureaucracy is one which swiftly can deliver a wide variety of public services, adapted to the needs of the individual. Furthermore, a strong bureaucracy is characterized by the rule of law. The law-governed nature of the public administration is a safeguard against clientelism, corruption and favoritism. Arguably, there is a potential contradiction between the service-delivery aspect and the law-governed nature of the bureaucracy. The point here is that a public bureaucracy will most likely never be able to compete with private sector companies in terms of flexibility and service but, as we will argue later in this chapter, that is hardly surprising given that public administration was designed primarily according to other objectives.

The strength of the public administration is nearly always a mirror image of the strength of the state. Internal strength is critical to the public bureaucracy's ability to fulfill its role in society regardless of the degree to which the state encroaches society. Also, a strong public bureaucracy is critical to sustain core democratic values like equality, legal security and equal treatment. For these reasons, a strong bureaucracy in a weak state need not be an arrangement that cannot be sustained in the longer term.

MANAGING IN THE PUBLIC SECTOR

We dealt above with one crucial aspect of public administration – its link with society and the political system. We now shift our attention more to the internal dynamics of these organizations (or aggregations of organization), and especially with their management. The reform of public administration over the past several decades has concentrated on the managerial aspects of government, attempting to make government more efficient, effective and economical. These three Es have driven a massive change in the public sector, much of it focusing on the role of the market as an exemplar for good management.

Goodbye to hierarchies?

Much of the administrative reform that has been implemented has been a series of attacks against the hierarchical structure of the public administration. Hierarchies, the dominant argument goes, are rigid and slow, unable to change, inefficient and fail to draw on the professional expertise inside the organization. Furthermore, hierarchical structures are said to be unable to relate effectively to clients and cannot provide customer-attuned services to the public. How valid is this critique? What alternatives are

there to hierarchies? What values and norms are associated with this type of organization? In addressing these questions – and the future of hierarchies in the public administration more in general – we first need to discuss the strengths of hierarchies, given the expectation placed on the public bureaucracy. From that perspective, we can proceed to discuss the extent to which the preferred role of the public administration has changed and how these developments impact on the organizational structure of the bureaucracy.

In most countries, the public bureaucracy found its organizational form at a time when the primary role of these organizations was the implementation of law. Public service production of the scale we know it today did not exist; it is to a very large extent a feature of the latter half of the twentieth century. Hierarchy thus early on became the preferred organizational model as it is an efficient instrument for the implementation of law, a process where values such as uniformity, accountability and predictability are essential. The initial growth of the public sector service production did not significantly challenge the hierarchical structure of the public bureaucracy. These services were rather uniform in character, with little or no flexibility or 'customer-attuning', to quote a contemporary concept. Given the limited and one-way exchange between the public bureaucracy and its clients, hierarchies could prevail. Instead, it was the massive attack on the public sector during the 1980s and 1990s which presented a major threat to the hierarchical structures in the public sector. Hierarchies could not sustain the accumulated challenges from within in the form of drastic budget cutbacks and from clients expecting a higher degree of flexibility. Thus, structure in and of itself became an issue in the administrative reform of the 1990s (Peters, 2001); if the hierarchical nature of public organizations was replaced by some form of flat and flexible organization which accorded greater autonomy to the front-line staff, many of the problems of lacking legitimacy and inefficiency would be resolved, critics argued.

It would be incorrect to argue that the critique concerning the inertia and rigidity in the public bureaucracy is without justification. In some ways, however, that is not the issue. Public organizations were never designed to maximize on efficiency, flexibility and customer friendliness but rather to ensure a uniform and unbiased implementation of the law. Thus, to some extent, the critique during the past couple of decades has employed an irrelevant yardstick for its assessment of public organizations. Moreover, this critique sees only one side of the modern bureaucracy – the service-producing side – and disregards the other side, the exercise and implementation of law. That having been said, it is clear that some relaxation of hierarchy and structure has become critical to the public sector and, indeed, such organizational change is already taking place in most countries.

Does this mean the farewell to hierarchies? As we have pointed out in a different context, hierarchies have more to offer as instruments of governance than is often recognized (Pierre and Peters, 2000). Ironically, some of the problems frequently associated with more flexible and market-like public organizations, such as accountability and a poor responsiveness to the political echelons of government, are often argued to be among the stronger aspects of the hierarchical model. The challenge in the longer term for the architects of government therefore is to design organizations that combine the efficiency and service capacity of decentralized organizations with the uniform and legalistic nature of hierarchical organizations.

Is marketization the answer?

The same arguments that denigrate the role of hierarchies emphasize the importance of markets as an alternative to more traditional forms of organization and management in the public sector. The assumption is that if government were to use the principles of the market, both in the design of individual

programs and in the internal management of government programs, then government will do its job much better. Advocates of the market argue that adopting market principles will make government more efficient, and could reduce the costs of public sector programs to taxpayers.

Although the market has become a popular exemplar for reforming the public sector, there are also a number of critics of the market. Perhaps, most fundamentally, the public sector should not have efficiency as its fundamental value, but rather should be concerned with effectiveness and accountability. Relatedly, market mechanisms may reduce the accountability of public programs by emphasizing internal management rather than relationships with the remainder of the political system. Finally, much of what the public sector does is not amenable to market provision, or they might never have been put into government in the first place, and hence attempting to apply market principles may be mildly absurd. Although an unthinking acceptance of the market is not likely to produce all the benefits promised, there are certainly things to be gained by using some of these techniques. As with so many things in the public sector, the real trick may be in finding the balance between different approaches.

The less politics the better?

There are several circumstances suggesting that the involvement of elected officials in administration is not conducive to maximum performance of the administrative system. The most important argument against too much involvement by politicians in public sector management is that it means not taking management very seriously, or at least not as seriously as electoral considerations. Running large-scale operations, public or private, requires managerial skills and there is nothing in elected office that in and of itself guarantees that the person elected holds those skills. Indeed, the careers of most elected officials rarely involve managing an organization of any significant size. Part of the mantra of administrative reform in the past several decades has been to 'let the managers manage' and that has been in part a claim for a stronger role for public administrators in the governing process.

Clarifying what separates the roles of elected officials and organizational managers in public administration is important (Peters, 1987; Peters and Pierre, 2001). Career officials are expected to provide continuity, expertise and loyalty. Elected officials are expected to provide legitimacy, political judgment, and policy guidance. Bureaucrats are sometimes accused of attempting to monopolize policymaking through their expertise, and their control of the procedures of government, while politicians are accused of micro-management and attempting to politicize the day-to-day management of organizations and personnel. Certainly, public administrators cannot ignore their nominal political 'masters' but they must also be sure to maintain their own rightful position in governing.

APPROACHES TO PUBLIC ADMINISTRATION

We have already pointed out that public administration stands at the intersection of theory and practice. Within this field of study there have from time to time been heated debates over the relative weights that should be assigned to those two ways of approaching the field. The practitioners have seen academics as hopelessly wound up in theoretical debates that had little or nothing to do with actually making a program run successfully. Academics, on the other hand, have seen practitioners as hopelessly mired in 'manhole counting' and incapable of seeing the larger issues that affect their practice.

In addition to standing at the interaction of theory and practice, public administration

also stands at the intersection of a number of academic disciplines, as well as having a distinctive literature of its own. Leaving aside for the time being the literature that can be labeled 'purely' public administration, political science, economics, sociology, psychology, law, management and philosophy, and probably others, have had some influence on the study of public administration. Political science has probably had the longest relationship with public administration, given the importance of the bureaucracy for governing and the fundamental concern in democratic countries about means of holding the bureaucracy accountable to elected officials. That having been said, however, law has been the foundation of public administration in much of continental Europe. More recently, economics and management science have come to play a dominant role in thinking about public administration, as reforms of the public sector have tended to rely upon procedures found in the private sector.

While theory and practice, and an array of academic disciplines, contend for control over the study of public administration, the fundamental point that should be emphasized is that all of these perspectives bring something with them that helps to illuminate administration in the public sector. Political science has emphasized the role of public administration as a component of the process of governing, and has, along with law, also emphasized the importance of enforcing the accountability of the bureaucracy, while philosophy has emphasized the need for an ethical framework for public administrators. Economics has pointed to the role of public administration in taxing and spending decisions, as well as providing a theoretical frame through which to understand bureaucracy (Breton, 1996; Niskanen, 1971). Sociology has brought a long tradition of organizational theory, as well as a concern for the linkage of state and society (Rothstein, 1996). Administrative reforms of the past several decades have placed a substantial emphasis on the similarities of public and private management and there has been a good deal of borrowing from business management to transform government.

WHAT'S SO SPECIAL ABOUT THE PUBLIC SECTOR?

The reader will have noticed by this time that he or she has opened a rather large book containing thousands of words. What about public administration merits this attention, especially when most citizens appear as happy to avoid their own bureaucracy? And could both this attention have been lavished on more general questions of management, not just on administration in the public sector? What indeed is so special about this area of inquiry and, perhaps more importantly, what is so special about this area of human activity?

To some extent the answers to those far from simple questions should be evident from the material already discussed in this introduction. Most fundamentally, public administration is central to the process of governing society, no matter what form that governance may take. Without their public administration, legislatures could make all the laws they wished but unless they were extraordinarily lucky, and the population was extraordinarily cooperative, nothing would actually happen.[3] In Bagehot's terminology, the public bureaucracy is much of the effective part of government, and it is crucial for providing the services that the public expect from their governments.

The absence of public administration is an extremely unlikely occurrence, and the more relevant question is what happens for governing when public administration is not effective, or efficient, or ethical. The various forms of failure of administration each has its own negative consequences for government and society. Almost certainly an unethical and parasitic administration is the worst form of failure, especially in a government that aspires to be democratic and legitimate (see Chapman, 2000). Honesty and accountability

are crucial for building a government that is respected by the public, and may even be central to building an efficient and effective government. A government that is perceived as equitable and fair builds trust, which in turn can make government more effective.

Losses of effectiveness are also important as governments increasingly are being judged by their capacity to deliver, and the contemporary emphasis on performance management provides quantitative indications of how well governments are doing their jobs (Bouckaert and Pollitt, 2003). Despite all the emphasis in the New Public Management, efficiency may be the least important value for the public sector, especially in the eyes of the public. They may mind much more that services are delivered, and that they are delivered in an accountable and humane manner, than they care about the cost per unit of service delivered. This does not mean that public administrators should not care about efficiency, but only that this is not necessarily the dominant value that it has been made to be.

ORGANIZATION OF THE HANDBOOK

The remainder of the Handbook is organized in 14 parts, each having been shaped and edited by a Part Editor. Those editors have each added an Introduction to their section, discussing its contents and relating it to general themes that run throughout the volume. These 14 parts represent the principal dimensions of the literature within public administration, attempting to cover both traditional themes as well as more contemporary managerialist approaches to administration.

NOTES

1   Bureaucracy is often a word of opprobrium, but we are using it here in a more neutral manner, meaning the formal administrative structures in the public sector.

2   The degree of autonomy enjoyed by the public bureaucracy in traditional patterns of governing is often exaggerated, but there has been a marked shift in the involvement of the private sector.

3   A conservative American politician once commented that he should like it if Congress were placed on a cruise ship and had to put all its laws into bottles to float back to land. Only the laws in those bottles that were found would go into effect. Without public administration, governing might be a good deal like that.

REFERENCES

Bouckaert, G. and Pollitt, C. (2003) *Public Management Reform: A Comparative Analysis*, 2nd edn. Oxford: Oxford University Press.

Breton, A. (1996) *Competitive Government: An Economic Theory of Politics and Public Finance*. Cambridge: Cambridge University Press.

Chapman, R.A. (2000) *Ethics in the Public Service for the New Millennium*. Aldershot: Ashgate.

Hood, C. (1998) *The Art of the State: Culture, Rhetoric and Public Management*. Oxford: Oxford University Press.

Kerwin, C. (1999) *Rulemaking*. Washington, DC: CQ Press.

Niskanen, W. (1971) *Bureaucracy and Representative Government*. Chicago: Aldine/Atherton.

Page, E.C. (2000) *Government by the Numbers*. Oxford: Hart.

Peters, B.G. (1987) 'Politicians and Bureaucrats in the Politics of Policy-making', in J.-E. Lane (ed.), *Bureaucracy and Public Choice*. London: Sage.

Peters, B.G. (2001) *The Future of Governing*, 2nd edn. Lawrence: University Press of Kansas.

Peters, B.G. and Pierre, J. (2000) 'Citizens Versus the New Public Manager: The Problem of Mutual Empowerment', *Administration and Society*, 32: 9–28.

Peters, B.G. and Pierre, J. (2001) *Politicians, Bureaucrats and Administrative Reform*. London: Routledge.

Pierre, J. and Peters, B.G. (2000) *Governance, Politics and the State*. Basingstoke: Palgrave.

Plowden, W. (1984) *Ministers and Mandarins*. London: Royal Institute of Public Administration.

Rockman, B.A. (1998) 'The Changing Role of the State', in B.G. Peters and D.J. Savoie (eds), *Taking Stock: Assessing Public Sector Reforms*. Montreal and Kingston: McGill-Queen's University Press, pp. 20–44.

Rothstein, B. (1996) *The Social Democratic State: The Swedish Model and the Bureaucratic Problems of Social Reform*. Pittsburgh: University of Pittsburgh Press.

Savoie, D.J. (1994) *Reagan, Thatcher, Mulroney: In Search of A New Bureaucracy*. Pittsburgh: University of Pittsburgh Press.

Stein, J.G. (2002) *The Cult of Efficiency*. Toronto: Ananasi Press.

PART 1

Public Management: Old and New

edited by Hal G. Rainey

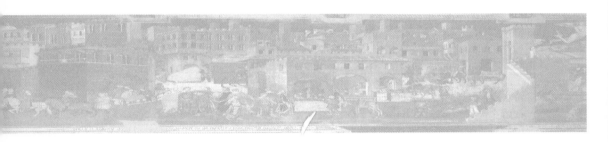

In the past several decades, in nations around the world, the topic of public management has taken on an increased significance in the theory and practice of public administration (e.g., Pollitt and Bouckaert, 2011). One might wonder about this development, since public management and public administration sound synonymous. The authors in this first part of this book illustrate the significance of public management as a topic and its distinctiveness from public administration.

For people in public administration as scholars, and as practicing managers and professionals, this new interest in public management – or renewed interest, as Laurence Lynn will show us in Chapter 1 – has major implications. Scholars note that this worldwide movement has involved increased emphasis on certain patterns and reforms in the management of government agencies and programs (e.g., Christensen and Laegreid, 2007; Pollitt and Bouckaert, 2011). For example, one major implication involves the widespread perception that government needs to give more attention to achieving effective management, often through the adoption of management procedures resembling those of business firms. Kettl (2000), for example, observed that the international movement towards 'public management', including variants of it called 'New Public Management', involves a number of common themes in many nations. These include increasing the productivity of government activities, using economic market or market-like strategies, enhancing attention to citizens as service recipients, decentralizing responsibilities to local governments and to front-line managers, and sharpening accountability for results by focusing more on outputs and outcomes than on processes and structures. As the chapters in this section will show, other scholars interested in public management do not necessarily focus simply on borrowing procedures from business firms; they emphasize enhancing managerial capacities in government through such developments as improved performance measurement and strategic planning.

In addition to these developments in reform and practice, academics have pondered the implications of a public management emphasis for research and intellectual development. Some scholars in public administration employed the public management rubric to express their conviction that their field needs a richer base of theory and empirical research on management skills, responsibilities and procedures akin to that available in the academic fields of business management and organizational analysis (e.g., Perry and Kraemer, 1983). They pointed to the need for more research on how people in management positions in government can carry out their responsibilities and effectively operate their agencies and programs. In related fields such as political science and public policy studies, the prevailing assumption appeared to be that management matters do not matter much – that managerial activities by middle- and upper-level 'bureaucrats' in government simply do not play a significant role in the political system and public policy processes. Still other academics in prestigious schools of public affairs at leading universities also sought to develop the topic of public management, and expressed less concern with the field of public administration than with developing a body of knowledge to support high-level executive leadership in government (Lynn, 1996).

The chapters in this section represent this movement in several ways. Laurence Lynn's chapter provides a rich description of the evolution of the topic of public management and of major current issues in its continuing development. He describes how the major public administration scholars early in the twentieth century concerned themselves with the role of 'management' in the field, often emphasizing its importance in relation to other foci, such as the legal context of administration. He describes how scholars have differentiated between administration and management, and between management in the public and private sectors. This leads him to consider several perspectives on public management: as a *structure of governance*, a 'formalization of managerial discretion intended to enable government to effect the will of the people', as a *craft* or set of

skills applied by public managers and as an *institution* embodying legitimate values and constitutional constraints to which public managers adhere. Lynn also analyzes recent developments, such as a tendency for some scholars to so heavily emphasize the craft perspective that they lose sight of the others. Ultimately, he argues that the main challenge involves maintaining appropriate emphasis on all three of these perspectives simultaneously. Lynn also notes very recent developments in professional association and professional journal activities that pertain to public management.

Carolyn Heinrich then describes and assesses developments in one of the major trends in public management around the world: an increasing emphasis on performance measurement for public organizations and programs. Here again, as she describes, this topic has a classic character, because experts and scholars worked on it in a variety of ways for a very long time. Heinrich provides a historical overview of many of the conceptions and systems of performance measurement that have emerged and evolved since the nineteenth century. In addition, however, she points to new developments in the recent upsurge of emphasis on performance measurement, such as its increasing scope, sophistication and visibility, as well as certain common themes across nations, such as an increase in formal reporting requirements involving comparisons of performance measures to pre-established performance goals and standards. Heinrich goes on to discuss major current issues in performance measurement. These include the challenges of specifying and measuring goals, due to conflicting values and priorities for many public programs and agencies, and the multiple actors and levels involved. With emphasis on the need to provide public managers with information about how their decisions and actions affect performance, she also discusses prospects for addressing such challenges and provides numerous examples of recent models and methods of performance measurement.

As we come to John Bryson's chapter, Lynn has told us that one major reason for increasing interest in public management arises from concern with enhancing the skills and practices that public managers can use proactively to increase agency performance, and to contribute effectively to governance. Heinrich has added valuable description and analysis of one the most important challenges in the pursuit of performance – its conception and measurement. Another of the most important challenges concerns formulation of purposes and of plans for pursuing them, through strategic planning and management. As Bryson tells us, these priorities are 'becoming a way of life for public organizations around the globe'. Bryson, whose book *Strategic Planning for Public and Nonprofit Organizations* is the most widely used and cited book on the topic, provides a highly authoritative description and analysis of strategic planning and management. He describes strategic management systems and models, and current trends in thought and practice of the topic. These include increasing pursuit of speed, inclusion of diverse interests and groups, and systems thinking. Obviously, the analysis of public management and its relation to public administration derives its value not from the parsing of these two rubrics, but from the more fundamental issues involved. As these chapters show, these issues include the institutional and structural context of public management, and the roles, responsibilities, skills and practices it involves. These three authoritative chapters provide description, conceptualization and analysis of clear value to those who think, research and write about public administration, as well as to those charged with carrying out its vital responsibilities in practice.

REFERENCES

Christensen, Tom and Laegreid, Per (eds) (2007) *Transcending New Public Management: The Transformation of Public Sector Reforms*. Aldershot, England and Burlington, VT: Ashgate.

Kettl, Donald F. (2000) *The Global Public Management Revolution: A Report on the Transformation of Governance*. Washington, DC: Brookings Institution.

Lynn, Laurence E., Jr (1996) *Public Management as Art, Science, and Profession*. Chatham, NJ: Chatham House.

Perry, James L. and Kraemer, Kenneth L. (eds) (1983) *Public Management: Public and Private Perspectives*. Palo Alto, CA: Mayfield.

Pollitt, Christopher and Bouckaert, Geert (2011) *Public Management Reform: A Comparative Analysis – New Public Management, Governance, and the Neo-Weberian State*. Oxford: Oxford University Press.

1

Public Management

Laurence E. Lynn, Jr

[H]e liked to organize, to contend, to administer; he could make people work his will, believe in him, march before him and justify him. This was the art, as they said, of managing. ...

Henry James
The Portrait of a Lady

[P]ublic management ... is a world of settled institutions designed to allow imperfect people to use flawed procedures to cope with insoluble problems.

James Q. Wilson
Bureaucracy: What Government Agencies Do and Why They Do It

INTRODUCTION

Public management is the subject of a rapidly growing literature that is international in scope and multifarious in content.[1] The common sense of public management is relatively straightforward. Good public managers are men and women with the temperament and skills to organize, motivate, and direct others toward realizing the complex goals of public policy in a political environment. Few public laws and policies are self-executing, and, in their formulation, all might benefit from managerial insight and experience. Under virtually any political philosophy or regime, then, the achievement of good government requires the responsible and competent use of public authority by a government's managers.

Common sense obscures issues that have been at the heart of public management from its inception as a field of study and practice, however. What if the goals to be achieved and their possible costs and consequences are unclear or in conflict? What if public managers are given insufficient authority, resources, and tools to organize, motivate, and monitor the efforts needed to accomplish those purposes for which they are responsible? How does effective management compare in importance to good policy design, rational organization, adequate resources, effective monitoring, and the approbation of affected publics? What is effective managerial practice and how does it vary across the many contexts in which public management is practiced? How might effective public management be enabled by legislators, executives, and judicial authorities, and how might particular managerial reforms or strategies affect governmental performance?

The objective of public management scholarship is to provide theoretical and empirical foundations for addressing the above questions. In addition, researchers take up the myriad specific issues that arise in organizing and carrying out managerial responsibilities in government departments, bureaus and offices.[2] Theoretical issues include means–ends rationality; the influence of political-legal constraints; appropriate distributions of managerial discretion and allocations of financial and human resources; *ex ante* versus *ex post* controls over administrative behavior; accountability to the public, constituencies, and stakeholders; criteria and methods for measuring, motivating, and evaluating performance; public management reform; and the role of government and governance in democratic societies. Issues concerned more directly with practice include leadership, public service values, evidence-based practice and the determination and promulgation of 'best practices', organizational change and development strategies, and decision making.

It will be useful at the outset to introduce distinctions that are fundamental to the perspective of this chapter. Public administration's classic American literature understood management to be the responsible and lawful exercise of formally delegated discretion by public administrators. In this view, public management is a *structure* of governance (Scott, 1998): that is, a constitutionally appropriate formalization of managerial discretion intended to enable government to effect the will of the people. In contrast, recent literature has tended to view public management as a *craft*: that is, as skilled practice by individuals performing managerial roles. When public managers evince values that are widely held to be legitimate and mindful of public interests rather than narrowly partisan or self-regarding, public management becomes even more an *institution* of constitutional governance (Weimer, 1995; Bertelli and Lynn, 2006). Public management as an institution observes 'rules of practice': that is, *de facto* restraints on or guides to behavior, that ensure their legitimacy within a constitutional, or

de jure, regime. Properly understood, then, public management is structure, craft, and institution: 'management', 'manager', and 'responsible practice' (Hill and Lynn, 2009).

In the initial sections of this chapter, two issues that define the scope of public management as a field of scholarship and practice are discussed: the relationship between 'public administration' and 'public management' and the similarities and differences between 'public management' and 'private management.' With these discussions as background, public management as structure, as craft, and as institution are explored in detail in the following three sections. There follows in the penultimate section a consideration of public management as it relates to the concept of governance. This discussion brings into focus the broader systemic challenges of public management in theory and practice. Summary observations conclude the chapter.

MANAGEMENT AND ADMINISTRATION

When we talk of 'public management' or of 'public administration,' are we talking of the same subject or of different subjects? Arguments to the effect that management and administration are fundamentally different have a long history in American literature, although the distinction often seems arbitrary.[3] Many such arguments relegate management to subordinate, specialized or even stigmatized status. The result is that the structural and institutional aspects of public management which are vital to understanding its significance are overlooked.

Numerous early commentaries either view the two terms as synonymous or regard management as the more general concept.[4] In public administration's first textbook, published in 1926, Leonard D. White rebuked the notion that public law is the proper foundation of public administration. He argued that 'The study of administration should start from the base of management rather than the foundation of law. ...' (White, 1926, p. vii).[5] According to Henri Fayol (1930), 'It is important not to confuse *administration* with *management*. To manage ... is to conduct [an organization] toward the best possible use of all the resources at its disposal ... [i.e.,] to ensure the smooth working of the ... essential functions. Administration is only one of these functions ...' (quoted in Wren, 1979, p. 232). In Roscoe C. Martin's view, by 1940, 'administration was equated with management,' although, he noted, there was comparatively little talk about the 'nature of the craft' (Martin, 1965, p. 8). Paul Van Riper (1990), in assaying mid-to-late nineteenth-century antecedents to Woodrow Wilson's 1887 essay, says: 'Note ... that the words *administration* and *management* have been treated here as synonymous' (p. 8). Observed Dwight Waldo, 'Perhaps as much as any other one thing, the "management" movement has molded the outlook of those to whom public administration is an independent inquiry or definable discipline' (Waldo, 1984, 12).

Yet many public administration scholars have held that, of the two concepts, administration is original and primary, public management is novel and subordinate or specialized. 'Public management as a special focus of modern public administration is new,' say Perry and Kraemer (1983), a view echoed by Rainey (1990, p. 157): 'In the past two decades, the topic of public management has come forcefully onto the agenda of those interested in governmental administration,' perhaps, he suggests, because of the growing unpopularity of government. In their *Public Management: The Essential Readings*, Ott, Hyde, and Shafritz (1991) argue that '*Public management* is a major segment of the broader field of public administration. ... Public management focuses on public administration as a profession and on the public manager as a practitioner of that profession. ...' (p. 1).

Such viewpoints seem to represent a reaction to the opportunistic appropriation of the term 'public management' in the 1970s and 1980s by the newly formed graduate schools of public policy at Harvard University, the University of California, Princeton University, and elsewhere.[6] According to Joel Fleishman, the policy schools' focus on public management originated with Mark Moore's efforts to 'refocus political and organizational analysis into prescriptive subject matter, with a point of view that is decidedly strategic (1990, p. 743). Donald Stokes observed that '[S]trategic political thinking sets off the public manager who is able to *move* an agency from one who plays a custodial role ... [T]he strategic manager sees the small openings presented by the agency's routine to induce change toward an identified goal, step-by-step... .' (1986, p. 55). By 1984, Moore summarized the emerging state of the public management art:

> Our conception of 'public management' adds responsibility for goal setting and political management to the traditional responsibilities of public administration ... . Our conception of public management adds some quintessential executive functions such as setting purpose, maintaining credibility with overseers, marshaling authority and resources, and positioning one's organization in a given political environment as central components of a public manager's job (Moore 1984, p. 2, 3).

In Moore's view, the gist of public management is 'conceiving and implementing public policies that realize the potential of a given political and institutional setting' (1984, p. 3), potential he later termed 'public value' (Moore, 1995). Thus, Moore's view was new – i.e., a departure from traditional conceptions of administration – in that it appeared to disavow interest in the settings for public management and to emphasize its behavioral and psychological aspects.

The newer behavioral approach to public management has tended to become more action-oriented and prescriptive. As such, it says both more and less about public management than traditional conceptions. Briefly, the older view is that public management is the responsible exercise of administrative discretion. The newer conception adds to this what Roscoe Martin called 'the craft perspective': i.e., a concern for decisions, actions, and outcomes and for the political skill needed to perform effectively in specific managerial roles. By emphasizing the strategic political role of public managers *within given political and institutional settings*, however, the newer conception is concerned more with the immediate concerns of executive-level management. In effect (but little noted at the time), the policy-oriented view of public management erased the politics–administration dichotomy that had long dominated traditional public administration. As Robert Behn has put it, 'any emphasis on the perspective of practicing public managers will have a short run focus' (Behn, 1993). A lower priority is placed on the manager's role in developing institutional capacity and in adhering to durable democratic values – that is, to public management as an institution – and on management at middle and lower levels of administration.

Precision concerning the distinction between administration and management is of more than antiquarian interest.[7] Because the concept of public management as the responsible exercise of discretion is at least implied by the intellectual development of public administration as a field, public administration's literature is also a literature of public management. Together, the older and more recent, craft-oriented literatures provide foundations for the structural, craft and institutional aspects of the subject. These three aspects, because they emphasize that practice must conform to constitutional structures and values, supply an analytic framework for evaluating particular public management reform proposals and developments, whether they be those of the Brownlow Report, the New Public Administration, the Blacksburg Manifesto, the US Government Performance and Results Act, the Clinton administration's National Performance Review, or the New Public Management. Of all such proposals, we wish to understand their structural, craft, and institutional implications in order to determine whether they befit constitutional requirements.

One particular argument for distinguishing between administration and management deserves further scrutiny, however. 'Those who define public administration in managerial terms,' argues David Rosenbloom, 'tend to minimize the distinctions between public and private administration' (1998, p. 16). The 'administration,' in this view, conveys respect for the constitutional and political foundations of governance in a way that the term 'management' does not.

PUBLIC AND PRIVATE MANAGEMENT

How alike or unalike are managing in the public and private sectors? Can and should government be more business-like? Is management generic? To the extent that public and private management involve similar temperaments, skills and techniques, the extensive body of ideas and practices relating to corporate success can be applied to the problems of public management, and the public sector can (in principle) draw on the large pool of private sector managers to meet its own managerial needs. To the extent that public and private sectors are different, especially from structural and craft perspectives, the public sector must have people with the knowledge, techniques and skills suited to its unique character.

This issue was addressed with authority at the dawn of public administration as a profession. Argued Frank J. Goodnow in 1893, '[i]n transacting its business [the government's] object is not usually the acquisition of gain but the furtherance of the welfare of the community. This is the great distinction between public and private business' (1893, 1902, p. 10). At a more subtle level, Goodnow argued that 'the grant to the administration of ... enormous discretionary powers' means that '[t]here has ... been a continuous attempt on the part of the people to control the discretion of the administration in the exercise of the sovereign powers of the state' (1893, 1902, pp. 10, 11). In 1926, Leonard D. White added the consideration that the principle of consistency – today, we say equity – governs public administration to an extent not observed in business administration (White, 1926; cf. Stamp, 1923).

The basic elements of the argument that public and private management are fundamentally unlike in all important respects are: (1) that the public interest differs from private interests; (2) that public officials, because they exercise the sovereign power of the state, are necessarily accountable to democratic values rather than to any particular group or material interest; and (3) that the constitution requires equal treatment of persons and rules out the kind of selectivity that is essential to sustaining profitability (Hill and Lynn, 2009, pp. 25–31). Moreover, the extent of the differences (and similarities) between the two sectors has been well documented empirically (Rainey and Chun, 2005).

Some will argue, nonetheless, that an enumeration of such differences is misleading because it obscures important similarities. 'All organizations are public,' argues Barry Bozeman (1987), by which he means that all organizations, whether governmental, for-profit, or non-profit, are affected to at least some degree by political authority. Thus, he argues, '[p]ublic managers can be found in most every type of organization' because public managers are not limited to government employees but encompass 'persons who manage publicness' (p. 146) in any sector. However, one might also argue the converse: that all organizations are 'private' to the extent that they are responsible for tasks that are performed by experts who are governed by professional or technocratic authority rather than by stakeholder interests. These tasks were first recognized by Goodnow (1900, p. 85) as 'the semi-scientific, quasi-judicial, and quasi-business or commercial' functions of administration. As Don Price later warned, however, 'the expert may come to believe that his science justifies exceeding his authority' (1959, p. 492), a pervasive danger in all organizations requiring specialized expertise.

The distinction between public and private management, then, is arguably definitive from structural, craft, and institutional perspectives. The two sectors are constituted to serve different kinds of societal interests, and distinctive kinds of skills and values are appropriate to serving these different interests. The distinctions may be blurred or absent, however, when analyzing particular managerial responsibilities, functions, and tasks in particular organizations. The implication of this argument is that lesson drawing and knowledge transfer across sectors is likely to be useful and should never be rejected on ideological grounds (Rainey and Chun, 2005).

PUBLIC MANAGEMENT AS STRUCTURE

As already noted, the earliest conception of public management was as a structure of governance: that is, a formal means for constraining and overseeing the exercise of state authority by public managers. From a structural perspective, public management involves two interrelated elements: lawful delegation of authority and external control over the exercise of delegated authority. The design of arrangements that balance these elements constitutes the paradigmatic problem of public management viewed as a structure of governance (Bertelli and Lynn, 2001).

Overcoming the reluctance of legislatures and courts to delegate authority to unelected bureaucrats constituted the first challenge to establishing public management as a structure of governance. As early as 1893, Goodnow asserted that 'A large discretion must be given to the administrative authorities to adapt many general rules of law to the wants of the people' (1893, p. 28). He noted further that 'while the main duty of the executive is to execute the will of the legislature as expressed in statutes, ... there is a realm of action in which the executive authority possesses large discretion, and that it looks for its authority not to the legislature but to the constitution' (1893, p. 33). Asked John Dickinson (1927, p. 156),

> if ... we ... imply that the main purpose [of administrative agencies] ... is to adjudicate according to rules, will we not have abandoned the characteristic and special advantage of a system of administrative justice, which consists in a union of legislative, executive, and judicial functions in the same body to secure promptness of action, and the freedom to arrive at decisions based on policy?

Discretion must be controlled, however, and thus a second challenge arose: ensuring adequate legislative, judicial, and public oversight of public management. As legal scholar Ernest Freund put it, '[i]ncreased administrative powers call for increased safeguards against their abuses, and as long as there is the possibility of official error, partiality or excess of zeal, the protection of private right is as important an object as the effectuation of some governmental policy' (quoted by White, 1926). Leonard D. White explored the problem of 'control of the administration' at length in his 1926 textbook. 'The problem,' he argued, 'has gradually developed into that of finding means to ensure that the acts of administrative officers shall be consistent not only with the law but equally with the purposes and temper of the mass of citizens' (1926, p. 419). In Paul Appleby's later view, '[p]erhaps there is no single problem in public administration of moment equal to the reconciliation of the increasing dependence upon experts with an enduring democratic reality' (1952, p. 145).

Delegation and oversight by legislatures and deference to administrators by courts are now accepted features of constitutional governance. Striking the right balance between capacity and control remains a controversial aspect of public management, however. Failure to do so often defeats efforts to achieve public management reform. As Kettl has expressed it (1997), tensions continue to exist between 'making managers manage' (i.e., imposing substantial *ex ante* and *ex post* controls over managerial discretion) and 'letting managers manage' (i.e., holding public managers accountable for their

performance rather than for their compliance with formal rules and procedures). These two strategies, Kettl notes, 'require culture shifts in opposite directions' (1997, p. 449), a reality not always fully appreciated by advocates of public management reform.

PUBLIC MANAGEMENT AS CRAFT

In recent decades, increasing emphasis has been placed on public management as a craft practiced by individuals in managerial roles. An intellectual development of seminal importance to this movement was the appearance in 1938 of Chester Barnard's *The Functions of the Executive* (1968), which laid the groundwork for new perspectives, including that of Herbert Simon, on managerial responsibility. As Frederick Mosher interpreted him, Barnard 'defined administrative responsibility as primarily a moral question or, more specifically, as the resolution of competing and conflicting codes, legal, technical, personal, professional, and organizational, in the reaching of individual decisions' (Mosher, 1968, p. 210).

Barnard clearly influenced John Millett, whose 1954 book, *Management in the Public Service*, constitutes an early example of the craft perspective:

> The challenge to any administrator is to overcome obstacles, to understand and master problems, to use imagination and insight in devising new goals of public service. No able administrator can be content to be simply a good caretaker. He seeks rather to review the ends of organized effort and to advance the goals of administrative endeavor toward better public service (1954, p. 401).

Millett goes on in a manner that prefigures later ideas from the policy schools:

> In a democratic society this questing is not guided solely by the administrator's own personal sense of desirable social ends. The administrator must convince others as well. He must work with interest groups, with legislators, with chief executives, and with the personnel of his own agency to convince them all that a particular line of policy or program is desirable (ibid.).

The newer literature within the craft perspective is based, by and large, on the careful study and analysis of particular cases of managerial experience.[8] As Graham Allison noted in a seminal article, 'The effort to develop public management as a field of knowledge should start from problems faced by practicing public managers' (Allison, 1979, p. 38). The focus of such study is on what managers did or should do in specific settings. A more critical view saw this enterprise as representing an 'ongoing effort to create a new "myth" for public management. ... by emphasizing a political and activist orientation – heroes and entrepreneurs became the stock and trade of its case studies' *at the expense of institutions* (Dobel, 1992, p. 147). Among the numerous examples of this perspective, Heymann's *The Politics of Public Management* (1987), Reich's *Public Management in a Democratic Society* (1990), Behn's *Leadership Counts* (1991), and Moore's *Creating Public Value* (1995) are representative.

Anxious to inspire public officials with the conviction that 'management counts' and with an entrepreneurial, proactive spirit, the craft literature turned heavily to prescription (Lynn, 1996). The best of this literature – e.g., Light's *Sustaining Innovation* (1998) and Bardach's *Getting Agencies to Work Together* (1998) – represents a thoughtful appreciation of the existential challenges of public management and an attempt to deduce best practices from closely observed success stories. Other contributions – e.g., Cohen and Eimicke's *The New Effective Public Manager* (1995) and Haas's *The Bureaucratic Entrepreneur* (1999) – are explicitly didactic and feature numerous prescriptions and principles based on the experiences and reflections of effective practitioners.

Within this genre, many craft-oriented public management scholars have assumed away the structural elements of public management, concerning themselves with the temperamental and psychological aspects of management. This approach leads to a highly reductive view of public management that hearkens back to an earlier preoccupation with leadership traits and managerial personalities. Thus, successful managers are characterized as enterprising or entrepreneurial, disposed to take risks, purposeful, imaginative and intuitive, and inclined to act. Others emphasize simple, generic processes – establishing and reiterating clear goals, managing by walking around – or adhering to unexceptionable principles – develop and focus on a narrow agenda, look for opportunities to act, and the like. Says Behn: 'Most management concepts are simple, and, to have any impact these simple management ideas must be expressible in some pithy phrase' (1988, p. 651). After citing five unexceptionable principles for achieving influence as a manager, Haas asserts: 'Being effective is that simple – and that complicated' (1994, p. 230).

The oversimplifications of its proponents should not discredit the importance of craft as an element of public management. Beyond structural considerations are the behavioral and intellectual challenges that any good manager must take into account. There are, as well, what Barnard called the 'non-logical' aspects that give rise to timely reactions, intuitive insights, and, ultimately, good judgment. From a craft perspective, some public managers are better than others. In general, though, recent empirical research has found that the managerial contribution to governmental performance is significant (Hill and Lynn, 2005; Boyne et al., 2006; O'Toole and Meier, 2011). That significance will be achieved only to the extent that public managers are masters of their craft. Practicing managers, moreover, are more likely to learn craftsmanship from other practitioners, in forums such as those provided by the Kennedy School of Government's Ash Center for Democratic Governance and Innovation at Harvard University, from practitioner-oriented sources such as those listed in Note 2 and from consultancies rather than from academic research.

PUBLIC MANAGEMENT AS INSTITUTION

How, and on behalf of what values, should public managers practice their craft? The answer to this question bears directly on the issue, discussed above, of the feasibility of 'letting managers manage' and the consequences of doing so for constitutional governance.

The appropriateness of intrinsic or self-control by public managers has been a recurring issue since the Friedrich–Finer debate of 1940 (Finer, 1940; Friedrich, 1940). Against Finer's view that public managers should be subject to minute legislative control, Friedrich countered that the best means for ensuring that management is responsive to the polity is the professionalism of the manager. More substantively, Rohr has argued that '[a]dministrators should use their discretionary power in order to maintain the constitutional balance of powers in support of individual rights' (1986, p. 181). Denhardt has urged that public managers commit themselves to 'values that relate to the concept of freedom, justice, and the public interest' (1993, p. 20). Wamsley insists that

> the only possible source of governing impetuses that might keep our complex political system from either a dangerous concentration of power on the one hand, or impotence or self-destruction, on the other, is a public administration with the necessary professionalism, dedication, self-esteem, and legitimacy to act as the constitutional center of gravity (1990, p. 26).

In asserting that public managers 'must resist, thwart, or refuse to implement policy that runs counter to the founding documents or to American regime values', George Frederickson comes tantalizingly close to enunciating a doctrine of administrative nullification (Frederickson, 1997, p. 229).

The notion that public management should be a self-regulated institution evokes the concept of responsibility, another paradigmatic value in traditional public administration. Woodrow Wilson observed that '[t]here is no

danger in power, if only it be not irresponsible' (1887, p. 213). Argued Morstein Marx, '[t]he heart of administrative responsibility is a unified conception of duty, molded by ideological and professional precepts' (1940, p. 251). To Frederick Mosher, '[r]esponsibility may well be the most important word in all the vocabulary of administration, public and private' (1968, p. 7), adding later that responsibility 'would seem to me to be the first requisite of a democratic state' (1992, p. 201).

How should responsible public management be defined? Rohr, Denhardt, Wamsley and others tend to define it in terms of adherence to a liberal political philosophy. Mosher (1968) distinguished between objective responsibility, or answerability for one's actions, a structural perspective, and subjective responsibility, which is akin to identification, loyalty, and conscience, a craft perspective. More specifically, Bertelli and Lynn (2001, 2006) identify in the classic literature of public administration four distinct and demonstrable qualities – accountability, judgment, balance, and rationality – which, they argue, constitute a *precept of managerial responsibility*. When observed in managerial practice, the precept justifies judicial deference when agencies are defendants in litigation and qualifies as a general norm of responsibility. The logic of this precept is as follows.

Accountability has been defined in general terms as 'those methods, procedures, and forces that determine what values will be reflected in administrative decision' (Simon, Smithburg, and Thompson, 1950, p. 513). Accountability is complicated in the United States by the fact that all three branches of government compete for control of public management. Despite this competition, 'no one [branch], nor all three jointly, provide the [public manager] with the totality of the value premises that enter into his decision' (ibid., p. 539). The responsible public manager is not, however, a free agent empowered to act on the basis of whim or ideology: '[m]anagement guided by [the value of responsible performance] abhors the idea of arbitrary authority present in its own wisdom and recognizes the reality of external direction and constraint' (Millett, 1954, p. 403).

After all external direction is taken into account, however, public managers still 'have considerable freedom to decide matters on the basis of their own ethical promptings' (Simon, Smithburg, and Thompson 1950, p. 539). Thus, no combination of mechanisms for enforcing administrative responsibility can extinguish the element of *judgment* from public management. What kind of managerial judgment fulfills a precept of managerial responsibility? Schuyler C. Wallace argued that, apart from 'the primary purpose of Congress in establishing the unit', good judgment makes 'reference to some ideal purpose more comprehensive than that of Congress' (1941, p. 89). The notion of idealism is an unacceptably open-ended standard for judgment, however, because it appears to authorize the public manager to enact political philosophies that may not reflect the will of the polity. More precision is needed.

Because public managers are necessarily accountable to numerous stakeholders in their political environments, one characteristic of good judgment is *balance*. Public managers, argues Morstein Marx, should 'give careful thought to the legislative balance of power, the enunciated or anticipated preferences of the chief executive, and the probabilities of public reactions. Ideally, political and administrative thinking should blend into a joint process' (1959, p. 102). The act of striking a balance is termed 'adjustive activity' by Emmette Redford: 'In the concept of administration as adjustive activity, [public management] is an extension of the political process of adjustment among interests' (1969, p. 188). Thus, public managers must strike a balance among competing interests, political philosophies, and interpretations of fact. The real agenda of public management, say Ott, Hyde, and Shafritz, is 'balancing political, economic, and social concerns for equity, justice, and fairness, as well as integrating perspectives for bettering "the public good"

in complex, highly diverse, competitive, and inequitable environments' (1991, p. xvi).

A second characteristic of good judgment is *rationality*. Marshall Dimock conceptualized managerial discretion as 'the liberty to decide between alternatives' (1936, p. 46). To be responsible, judgment concerning the merits of alternative strategies or actions, whether devised by the public manager or by other stakeholders, should aspire to be logical or rational as well as politically balanced. A rational action is one for which the relationship between the goals and the means for achieving them in the mind of the manager corresponds to the relationship between goals and means for achieving them in reality (or as might be confirmed by independent analysis) (Aron, 1998, p. 121). To be responsible, the public manager must seek out and master arguments and evidence concerning the relationships between means and ends. Inescapable, however, is what Nicholas Rescher termed 'the predicament of reason,' or 'the irresolvable tension between the demands of rationality and its practical possibilities' (Rescher, 1998, p. 169). The fact that the public managers cannot anticipate or calculate all consequences following from their actions, however, does not vitiate the argument for intentional rationality in management decisions.

The institutional perspective on public management might be summarized as follows: the structures of the administrative state constitute an appropriate framework for achieving balance between a jurisdiction's need for administrative capacity to pursue public purposes and citizen control of that capacity (Lynn, 2001). When managerial craft practiced within this framework is guided by a sense of responsibility, public management becomes a primary institution for preserving the balance between the state's capacity to affect the public interest and the citizen's power to hold office holders accountable. The issue was perhaps best stated by Goodnow:

[D]etailed legislation and judicial control over its execution are not sufficient to produce harmony between the governmental body, which expresses the will of the state, and the governmental authority, which executes that will. ... The executive officers may or may not enforce the law as it was intended by the legislature. Judicial officers, in exercising control over such executive officers, may or may not take the same view of the law as did the legislature. No provision is thus made in the governmental organization for securing harmony between the expression and the execution of the will of the state. The people, the ultimate sovereign in a popular government, must ... have a control over the officers who execute their will, as well as over those who express it (1900, pp. 97–98).

As early as 1900, then, the contemporary problem of balancing the competing values of democratic institutions, including the institution of public management, was clearly in view.

PUBLIC MANAGEMENT AND GOVERNANCE

Public management performs its institutional role when public managers conform to lawful constraints, manage responsibly within them, and respond creatively to opportunities for policymaking and structural reform. But public management is not the only institution that preserves balance in a constitutional regime. The capacity to effect the public interest, as Goodnow foresaw, does not reside solely in the executive agencies of government. Nor does the maintenance of control reside solely with legislatures and courts. Capacity and control, and the balance between them, depend upon the actions of executives, legislatures, judicial institutions, and citizens acting in their many capacities. A term for this complex reality is 'governance.' From a public management perspective, governance may usefully be defined as regimes of laws, rules, judicial decisions, and administrative practices that constrain, prescribe, and enable the exercise of public authority on behalf of the public interest (Hill and Hupe, 2009; Lynn, Heinrich, and Hill, 2001).[9]

The broader issue for any self-governing jurisdiction, then, is distributing power

among lawful organizations and institutions so as to establish a balance among competing interests and values. Achieving that balancing is the stuff of partisan politics and, as such, is infused with group interests (Pollitt and Bouckaert, 2000). The task of political actors, argues Terry Moe, is 'to find and institute a governance structure that can protect ... public organizations from control by opponents' (Moe 1995, p. 125). However, as Moe has put it, '[a] bureaucracy that is structurally unsuited for effective action is precisely the kind of bureaucracy that interest groups and politicians routinely and deliberately create' (1995, p. 328). As James Q. Wilson notes, referring to America's constitutional separation of powers, '[t]he governments of the United States were not designed to be efficient or powerful, but to be tolerable and malleable' (Wilson 1989, p. 376). Therein lies the continuing challenge to public management as an institution. As a result of regime restraints and the politics they authorize, the public manager may have to deal with inadequate resources, unreasonable or unrealistic workload or reporting requirements, inconsistent guidance, or missions defined so as to be virtually unachievable.

The consequences for public management of the way governance is organized are ultimately relevant to virtually every regulation, policy, and program. These consequences are discussed most explicitly during debates over administrative reform proposals intended to improve the performance of government as a whole. The popularity of administrative reform at all levels of government in the United States began over a century ago before and during the Progressive era. It has continued through the New Deal's emphasis on planning, the post-war Hoover Commissions, the Planning, Programming, Budgeting System (PPBS), management by objectives (MBO), Zero-Based Budgeting (ZBB) initiatives, and the Reagan administration's Grace Commission. More recent reforms have included the Clinton administration's National Performance Review, the concurrent, Congressionally-initiated

Government Performance and Results Act (GPRA), and the George W. Bush administration's President's Management Agenda and creation of a Program Assessment Rating Tool (PART) (Downs and Larkey, 1986; Pfiffner, 1998; Lynn, 2006; Bruel and Kamensky, 2008). Internationally, these issues have arisen under the rubric of the New Public Management in its many national expressions (Lynn, 2006; Christensen and Lægeid, 2011). To the extent that they are actually implemented, which is often in doubt, these kinds of reforms, intended variously to increase the use of performance measurement in resource allocation, to empower public employees to engage in continuous improvement in public programs and operations, and to mobilize the theoretical advantages of competition and consumer choice to induce greater efficiency, all have major implications for public management as an institution (Pollitt, 2000; Pollitt and Bouckaert, 2011).

Such implications may never be adequately defined, however. They tend to be obscured by partisan claims during the debate preceding adoption. Further, widely accepted standards for evaluating such claims are lacking. Greater clarity concerning the nature of public management as structure, craft, and institution, a purpose of this chapter, will, as suggested earlier, prove helpful in facilitating such evaluations. For example, traditional conceptions of public management respect the desirability of harmonizing law, politics, interests and democratic values. In contrast, customer-oriented managerialism and populist-oriented civic philosophies emphasize power-shifting, and employee, customer/ client, community and citizen empowerment. In doing so, they tend to ignore the inevitability and pervasiveness of the interest-based factionalism foreseen by the authors of *The Federalist*. Many managerial reforms barely acknowledge or actually denigrate the constitutional role of legislatures, courts, and elected executives and the need to anticipate political competition. Proposed reforms of governance which do not exhibit respect for a nation's basic institutions should be regarded with profound suspicion (Lynn, 2006; Kickert, 2008; Pollitt and Bouckaert, 2011).

CONCLUSION

Notwithstanding the vagaries of politics, public management as an institution and public managers as individuals must attempt to do the best that they can under difficult, if not impossible circumstances, even when that means doing little more than 'muddling through' or 'coping' (Lindblom, 1959; Wilson, 1989). Doing the best that they can is unquestionably a matter of craft, which can benefit from training and practice based on the analysis of particular cases, and the shared wisdom and knowhow of practitioners. It is also, and maybe even primarily, a matter of institutionalized, and internalized, values, of public managers being self-consciously guided by a precept of managerial responsibility. The particular character of structure, craft, and institution varies across organizations, levels of government, and countries with different legal and political traditions. Nevertheless, a strong argument can be made for the general relevance of these concepts to effective public management and to successful administrative reform.

In the final analysis, public management is also a matter of common sense. Governments authorize imperfect people to use flawed procedures to cope with insoluble problems. The results of their efforts are remarkably effective given the exigencies of their roles. Responsible public management is indispensable to sound governance.

NOTES

1 As defined in this chapter, public management varies across nations with different legal and political traditions. Useful sources with an American orientation include Tompkins (2005), Rainey (2009), and Heinrich (2010). Public management literature offering a comparative perspective includes Peters (1996),

Pollitt and Bouckaert (2004, 2011), Kettl (2005), Lynn (2005, 2006), Kickert (2008), Schiavo-Campo and McFerson (2008), Bovaird and Löffler (2009), and Christensen and Lægreid (2011).

2 A number of professional associations are now devoted to the academic field of public management. These include the Association for Public Policy Analysis and Management (APPAM), the Public Management Research Association (PMRA), the International Research Society for Public Management (IRSPM), and the International Public Management Network (IPMN). These organizations publish academic journals – the *Journal of Policy Analysis and Management (JPAM)*, the *Journal of Public Administration Research and Theory (JPART)*, the *Public Management Review (PMR)*, and the *International Public Management Journal (IPMJ)*, respectively – and sponsor research conferences, workshops and related activities.

Professional organizations associated with the cognate fields of public administration, administrative sciences, organization studies, and management also take up public management issues. Prominent are the American Society for Public Administration (ASPA), the Academy of Management (AM), the European Group for Public Administration (EGPA) of the International Institute for Administrative Sciences (IIASA) – and journals. Their journals include *Public Administration Review (PAR)*, *Public Administration*, *the American Review of Public Administration (ARPA)*, *Governance*, *Administrative Sciences Quarterly (ASQ)*, the *Academy of Management Review* and the *Academy of Management Journal*. ASPA also publishes 'Government Management Daily,' an on-line newsletter publicizing management news stories, opinions, and analysis. Numerous professional associations and journals in other countries regularly publish journals and hold conferences concerned with public management.

There are also less academic, practitioner-oriented publications. They include *Public Management (PM magazine)*, published by the International City/County Management Association (ICMA); *Governing*, a magazine of politics and policy in Washington, DC; and the publications of the IBM Center for the Business of Government, including a magazine and research reports; these organizations also maintain informative websites. Finally, numerous consultancies and non-academic research organizations, including the National Academy of Public Administration, are supported by grants and contracts and directly assist public managers.

3 The Oxford English Dictionary provides no basis for distinguishing between 'administration' and 'management.' The definition of each refers to the other.

4 Barry Karl (1987) notes that '[f]or American reformers, the term "administration" served to focus a kind of pragmatic attention on the governing process. The term became part of an elite reform vocabulary. ...' (p. 27).

5 'The study of administration from the point of view of management,' White said, 'began with the bureaus of municipal research and was first systematically formulated in the 1920s' (White, 1926, p. viii). An accurate understanding of public administration's intellectual history requires the disentangling of those influences originating in problems of municipal administration, fertile ground for applications of an apolitical 'scientific management', and those originating in problems of national administration, where issues concerning legislative delegation, judicial deference, and managerial accountability were more prominent.

6 As argued in Lynn (1996), public administration scholars would have been justified in claiming that their field had 'owned' the subject of public management for decades. As evidence, in addition to the citations in the text, the journal of the International City Management Association took the title *Public Management* in 1927. In 1940, a volume edited by Fritz Morstein Marx was titled *Public Management in the New Democracy* (Morstein Marx, 1940). John Millett's 1954 book *Managing in the Public Service* hits a strikingly contemporary note (Millett, 1954). A 1955 'classic' in public administration is Catheryn Seckler-Hudson's 'Basic Concepts in the Study of Public Management' (Shafritz and Hyde, 1992).

7 As argued in Lynn (1996), public administration scholars would have been justified in claiming that their field had 'owned' the subject of public management for decades. As evidence, in addition to the citations in the text, the journal of the International City Management Association took the title *Public Management* in 1927. In 1940, a volume edited by Fritz Morstein Marx was titled *Public Management in the New Democracy* (Morstein Marx, 1940). John Millett's 1954 book *Managing in the Public Service* hits a strikingly contemporary note (Millett, 1954). A 1955 'classic' in public administration is Catheryn Seckler-Hudson's 'Basic Concepts in the Study of Public Management' (Shafritz and Hyde, 1992).

8 A more extensive review of this literature is in Lynn (1996, pp. 55–88).

9 According to Pollitt and Bouckaert (2000), the terms 'steering', 'guidance' and 'managerialism' are preferred to 'governance' outside the United States (for an exception, see van Heffen, Kickert, and Thomassen, 2000). The complex interrelationships associated with such terms have also been described by Bouckaert and Pollitt and others in terms of an input/output model.

REFERENCES

Allison, Graham T., Jr (1979) 'Public and Private Management: Are They Fundamentally Alike in All

Unimportant Respects?' *Proceedings for the Public Management Research Conference*, 19–20 November. Washington, DC: Office of Personnel Management, pp. 27–38.

Appleby, Paul (1952) *Morality and Administration in Democratic Government*. New York: Greenwood Press.

Aron, Raymond (1998) *Main Currents in Sociological Thought*, Vol. 2. New Brunswick, NJ: Transaction Publishers.

Bardach, Eugene (1998) *Getting Agencies to Work Together: The Practice and Theory of Managerial Craftsmanship*. Washington, DC: The Brookings Institution.

Barnard, Chester I. (1968) *The Functions of the Executive*. Cambridge, MA: Harvard University Press.

Behn, Robert D. (1988) 'Managing by Groping Along,' *Journal of Policy Analysis and Management*, 8(3): 643–663.

Behn, Robert D. (1991) *Leadership Counts: Lessons for Public Managers from the Massachusetts Welfare, Training, and Employment Program*. Cambridge, MA: Harvard University Press.

Behn, Robert D. (1993). Personal communication with author on 18 April 1993.

Bertelli, Anthony M. and Lynn, Laurence E. Jr (2001) 'A Precept of Managerial Responsibility: Securing Collective Justice in Institutional Reform Litigation,' *Fordham Urban Law Journal*, 29(1): 317–386.

Bertelli, Anthony M. and Lynn, Laurence E., Jr (2006) *Madison's Managers: Public Administration and the Constitution*. Baltimore, MD: Johns Hopkins University Press.

Bovaird, Tony and Löffler, Elke (2009) *Public Management and Governance*, 2nd edn. London: Routledge.

Boyne, George A., Meier, K. J., O'Toole, L. J. Jr, and Walker, R. M. (2006) *Public Services Performance: Perspectives on Measurement and Management*. Cambridge: Cambridge University Press.

Bozeman, Barry (1987) *All Organizations are Public: Bridging Public and Private Organization Theories*. San Francisco, CA: Jossey-Bass.

Bruel, Jonathan D. and Kamensky, John M. (2008) 'Federal Government Reform: Lessons from Clinton's "Reinventing Government" and Bush's "Management Agenda" Initiatives,' *Public Administration Review*, 68(6): 105–126.

Christensen, Tom and Lægreid, Per (2011) *The Ashgate Research Companion to New Public Management*. Farnham, UK: Ashgate.

Cohen, Steven and Eimicke, William (1995) *The New Effective Public Manager: Achieving Success in a Changing Government*. San Francisco, CA: Jossey-Bass.

Denhardt, Robert B. (1993) *The Pursuit of Significance: Strategies for Managerial Success in Public Organizations*. Belmont, CA: Wadsworth.

Dickinson, John (1927) *Administrative Justice and the Supremacy of Law in the United States*. Cambridge, MA: Harvard University Press.

Dimock, Marshall E. (1936) 'The Role of Discretion in Modern Administration,' in John M. Gaus, Leonard D. White, and Marshall E. Dimock (eds), *The Frontiers of Public Administration*. Chicago, IL: University of Chicago Press, pp. 45–65.

Dobel, J. Patrick (1992) 'Review of Impossible Jobs in Public Management,' *Journal of Policy Analysis and Management*, 11(1): 144–147.

Downs, George W. and Larkey, Patrick D. (1986) *The Search for Government Efficiency: From Hubris to Helplessness*. New York: Random House.

Fayol, Henri (1930) *Industrial and General Administration*, translated by J. A. Coubrough. Geneva: International Management Institute.

Finer, Herman (1940) 'Administrative Responsibility in Democratic Government,' *Public Administration Review*, 1(4): 335–350.

Fleishman, Joe L. (1990) 'A New Framework for Integration: Policy Analysis and Public Management,' *American Behavioral Scientist*, 33(6): 733–754.

Frederickson, H. George (1997). *The Spirit of Public Administration*. San Francisco: CA: Jossey-Bass.

Friedrich, Carl Joachim (1940) 'Public Policy and the Nature of Administrative Responsibility,' in C. J. Friedrich and Edward S. Mason (eds), *Public Policy: A Yearbook of the Graduate School of Public Administration, Harvard University, 1940*. Cambridge, MA: Harvard University Press, pp. 3–24.

Friedrich, Carl Joachim (1946) *Constitutional Government and Democracy: Theory and Practice in Europe and America*. Boston, MA: Ginn and Company.

Goodnow, Frank J. (1893, 1902) *Comparative Administrative Law: An Analysis of the Administrative Systems National and Local, of the United States, England, France, and Germany*. New York: G. P. Putnam's Sons.

Goodnow, Frank J. (1900) *Politics and Administration*. New York: Macmillan.

Haass, Richard N. (1994) *The Power to Persuade: How to be Effective in Government, the Public Sector, or any Unruly Organization*. New York: Houghton Mifflin.

Haass, Richard N. (1999) *The Bureaucratic Entrepreneur: How to be Effective in any Unruly Organization*. Washington, DC: The Brookings Institution.

Heinrich, Carolyn J. (2010) 'Public Management,' in Mark Bevir (ed.), *Handbook of Governance*. Thousand Oaks, CA: Sage, pp. 252–269.

Heymann, Philip B. (1987) *The Politics of Public Management.* New Haven, CT: Yale University Press.

Hill, Carolyn J. and Lynn, Laurence E. Jr (2005) 'Is Hierarchical Governance In Decline? Evidence from Empirical Research,'*Journal of Public Administration Research and Theory,* 15(2): 173–196.

Hill, Carolyn J and Lynn, Laurence E., Jr. (2009) *Public Management: A Three-Dimensional Approach.* Washington, DC: CQ Press.

Hill, Michael and Hupe, Peter (2009) *Implementing Public Policy: An Introduction to the Study of Operational Governance,* 2nd edn. Los Angeles, CA: Sage.

Karl, Barry D. (1987) 'The American Bureaucrat: A History of a Sheep in Wolves' Clothing,' *Public Administration Review,* 47: 26–34.

Kettl, Donald F. (1997) 'The Global Revolution in Public Management: Driving Themes, Missing Links,' *Journal of Policy Analysis and Management,* 16(3): 446–462.

Kettl, Donald F. (2005) *The Global Public Management Revolution: A Report on the Transformation of Governance,* 2nd edn. Washington, DC: Brookings Institution.

Kickert, Walter J. M. (ed.) (2008) *The Study of Public Management in Europe and the US: A Comparative Analysis of National Distinctiveness.* London: Routledge.

Light, Paul C. (1998) *Sustaining Innovation: Creating Nonprofit and Government Organizations that Innovate Naturally.* San Francisco, CA: Jossey-Bass.

Lindblom, Charles E. (1959) 'The Science of Muddling Through,' *Public Administration Review,* 19(1): 79–88.

Lynn, Laurence E., Jr (1996) *Public Management as Art, Science, and Profession.* Chatham, NJ: Chatham House.

Lynn, Laurence E., Jr (2001) 'The Myth of the Bureaucratic Paradigm: What Traditional Public Administration Really Stood For,' *Public Administration Review,* 61(2): 144–160.

Lynn, Laurence E., Jr (2005) 'Public Management: A Concise History of the Field,' in Ewan Ferlie, Laurence E. Lynn, Jr and Christopher Pollitt (eds), *The Oxford Handbook of Public Management.* Oxford: Oxford University Press, pp. 27–50.

Lynn, Laurence E., Jr (2006) *Public Management: Old and New.* London: Routledge.

Lynn, Laurence E. Jr., Heinrich, Carolyn J. and Hill, Carolyn J. (2001) *Improving Governance: A New Logic for Empirical Research.* Washington, DC: Georgetown University Press.

Martin, Roscoe C. (1965) 'Paul H. Appleby and His Administrative World,' in Roscoe C. Martin, (ed.),

Public Administration and Democracy: Essays in Honor of Paul H. Appleby. Syracuse, NY: Syracuse University Press.

Millett, John D. (1954) *Management in the Public Service.* New York: McGraw-Hill.

Moe, Terry M. (1995) 'The Politics of Structural Choice: Toward a Theory of Public Bureaucracy,' in Oliver E. Williamson (ed.), *Organization Theory: From Chester Barnard to the Present and Beyond,* expanded edition. New York: Oxford University Press, pp. 116–153.

Moore, Mark H. (1984) 'A Conception of Public Management,' in *Teaching Public Management,* Proceedings of a workshop to Assess Materials and Strategies for teaching Public Management, Seattle, 9–11 May. Public Policy and Management Program for Case and Course Development, Boston University, pp. 1–12.

Moore, Mark H. (1995) *Creating Public Value: Strategic Management in Government.* Cambridge, MA: Harvard University Press.

Morstein Marx, Fritz (1940) *Public Management in the New Democracy.* New York: Harper & Brothers.

Morstein Marx, Fritz (1959) 'The Social Function of Public Administration,' in Fritz Morstein Marx (ed.), *Elements of Public Administration.* Englewood Cliffs, NJ: Prentice-Hall, pp. 89–109.

Mosher, Frederick C. (1968) *Democracy and the Public Service.* New York: Oxford University Press.

Mosher, Frederick C. (1975) *American Public Administration Past, Present, and Future.* Tuscaloosa, AL: University of Alabama Press.

Mosher, Frederick C. (1992) 'Public Administration Old and New: A Letter from Frederick C. Mosher,' *Journal of Public Administration Research and Theory,* 2(2): 199–202.

O'Toole, Laurence J., Jr., and Meier, Kenneth J. (2011) *Public Management: Organizations, Governance and Performance.* London: Cambridge University Press.

Ott, J. Steven, Hyde, Albert C., and Shafritz, Jay M. (eds) (1991) *Public Management: The Essential Readings.* Chicago, IL: Nelson Hall.

Perry, James L. and Kraemer, Kenneth L. (1983) *Public Management: Public and Private Perspectives.* Palo Alto, CA: Mayfield.

Peters, B. Guy (1996) *The Future of Governing: Four Emerging Models.* Lawrence, KS: University Press of Kansas.

Pfiffner, James (1998) 'The American Tradition of Administrative Reform,' in Yong Hyo Cho and H. George Frederickson (eds), *The White House and the Blue House: Government Reform in the United States and Korea.* Lanham, MD: University Press of America.

Pollitt, Christopher (2000) 'Is the Emperor in His Underwear? An Analysis of the Impacts of Public Management Reform,' *Public Management*, 2(2): 181–199.

Pollitt, Christopher and Bouckaert, Geert (2000) *Public Management Reform: A Comparative Analysis*. Oxford: Oxford University Press.

Pollitt, Christopher and Bouckaert, Geert (2004) *Public Management Reform: A Comparative Perspective*, 2nd edn. Oxford: Oxford University Press.

Pollitt, Christopher and Bouckaert, Geert (2011) *Public Management Reform: A Comparative Analysis – New Public Management, Governance, and the Neo-Weberian State*. Oxford: Oxford University Press.

Price, Don K. (1959) 'The Judicial Test,' in Fritz Morstein Marx (ed.), *Elements of Public Administration*. Englewood Cliffs, NJ: Prentice-Hall, pp. 475–499.

Rainey, Hal G. (1990) 'Public Management: Recent Developments and Current Prospects,' in Naomi B. Lynn and Aaron Wildavsky (eds), *Public Administration: The State of the Discipline*. Chatham, NJ: Chatham House, pp. 157–184.

Rainey, Hal G. (2009) *Understanding and Managing Public Organizations*, 4th edn. San Francisco, CA: Jossey-Bass.

Rainey, Hal G., and Chun, Young H. (2005) 'Public and Private Management Compared,' in E. Ferlie, L. E. Lynn and C. Pollitt (eds), *The Oxford Handbook of Public Management*. New York: Oxford University Press.

Redford, Emmette S. (1969) *Democracy in the Administrative State*. New York: Oxford University Press.

Reich, Robert B. (1990) *Public Management in a Democratic Society*. Englewood Cliffs, NJ: Prentice-Hall.

Rescher, Nicholas (1998) *Complexity: A Philosophical Overview*. New Brunswick, NJ: Transaction Publishers.

Rohr, John A. (1986) *To Run a Constitution*. Lawrence, KS: University Press of Kansas.

Rosenbloom, David H. (1998) *Understanding Management, Politics, and Law in the Public Sector*. New York: McGraw-Hill.

Schiavo-Campo, Salvatore and McFerson, Hazel M. (2008) *Public Management in Global Perspective*. New York: M. E. Sharpe.

Scott, W. Richard (1998) *Organizations: Rational, Natural, and Open Systems*, 4th edn. Upper Saddle River, NJ: Prentice-Hall.

Shafritz, Jay M. and Hyde, Albert C. (eds) (1992) *Classics of Public Administration*. Pacific Grove, CA: Brooks/Cole.

Simon, Herbert A. Smithburg, Donald W., and Thompson, Victor A. (1950) *Public Administration*. New York: Knopf.

Stamp, Josiah C. (1923) 'The Contrast between the Administration of Business and Public Affairs,' *Journal of Public Administration*, 1: 158–171.

Stokes, Donald E. (1986) 'Political and Organizational Analysis in the Policy Curriculum,' *Journal of Policy Analysis and Management*, 6(1): 45–55.

Tompkins, Jonathan R. (2005) *Organization Theory and Public Management*. Belmont, CA: Thomson Wadsworth.

van Heffen, Oscar, Kickert, Walter J. M., and Thomassen, Jacques J. A. (2000) *Governance in Modern Society: Effects, Change and Formation of Government Institutions*. Dordrecht, NL: Kluwer Academic Publishers.

Van Riper, Paul P. (1990) 'Administrative Thought in the 1880s,' in Paul P. Van Riper (ed.), *The Wilson Influence on Public Administration: From Theory to Practice*. Washington, DC: American Society for Public Administration, pp. 7–16.

Waldo, Dwight (1984) *The Administrative State*, 2nd edn. New York: Holmes and Meier.

Wallace, Schuyler C. (1941) *Federal Departmentalization: A Critique of Theories of Organization*. New York: Columbia University Press.

Wamsley, Gary L. (1990) 'The Agency Perspective: Public Administrators as Agential Leaders,' in Gary L. Wamsley et al (eds), *Refounding Public Administration*. Newbury Park, CA: Sage.

Weimer, David L. (1995) 'Institutional Design: An Overview,' in David L. Weimer (ed.), *Institutional Design*. Boston: Kluwer Academic Publishers.

White, Leonard D. (1926) *Introduction to the Study of Public Administration*. New York: Macmillan.

Wilson, James Q. (1989) *Bureaucracy: What Government Agencies Do and Why They Do It*. New York: Basic Books.

Wilson, Woodrow (1887) 'The Study of Administration,' *Political Science Quarterly*, 1(2): 197–222.

Wren, Daniel (1979) *The Evolution of Management Thought*, 2nd edn. New York: John Wiley & Sons.

2

Measuring Public Sector Performance and Effectiveness

Carolyn J. Heinrich

INTRODUCTION

The 1990s are widely recognized as a watershed decade for the advancement of performance measurement in the public sector. In *Beyond Machiavelli: Policy Analysis Comes of Age*, Beryl Radin (2000a: 168) observed: 'If there is a single theme that characterizes the public sector in the 1990s, it is the demand for performance. A mantra has emerged in this decade, heard at all levels of government, that calls for documentation of performance and explicit outcomes of government action.' Almost universally, governments in the United States, Canada, Western Europe, New Zealand, Australia, and in countries in Asia, Africa, and Latin America have made performance measurement a core component of public management reforms (Kettl and Dilulio, 1995; Pollitt and Bouckaert, 2000; Behn, 2001). Other elements of public management reforms at this time – reducing 'red tape,' empowering individuals and organizations to streamline processes and devolve decision making, and

incentivizing innovation – were likewise directed at 'getting results.' While the broad objectives of these reforms to promote more 'effective, efficient, and responsive government' are the same as those of reforms introduced more than a century ago, what is new are the increasing scope, sophistication, and external visibility of performance measurement activities, impelled by legislative requirements aimed at holding governments accountable for *outcomes* (Gore, 1993: xxiii; Pollitt and Bouckaert, 2000). The ramifications of reform initiatives that mandate formal, outcomes-based performance measurement in public programs continue to be debated by public management scholars and practitioners, with discourse extending from national legislation such as the US Government Performance and Results Act (GPRA) to local-level performance contracts that aim to 'use market forces to hold the public sector accountable' (Kaboolian, 1998: 191; Laegreid, 2000; Radin, 2000b).

Accountability – to legislative bodies, taxpayers, and program stakeholders – is a primary goal of public sector performance measurement. In *The International Encyclopedia of Public Policy and Administration*, Romzek and Dubnick (1998: 6) define accountability as 'a relationship in which an individual or agency is held to answer for performance that involves some delegation of authority to act.' By this definition, accountability compels some measure or appraisal of performance, particularly of those individuals and agencies with the authority to act on behalf of the public. A historical review of public sector performance measurement shows that the majority of initiatives have focused on holding agencies or executive administrators accountable for *financial* performance or efficiency. Behn (2001) describes 'accountability for finances' as a 'rules, procedures and standards' form of accountability. The New Public Management (NPM) and other recent reform initiatives, which ostensibly differ from earlier approaches in their promotion of a 'customer service' focus, 'market-driven management,' and accountability for 'results,' are also still concerned with 'saving money' and 'productive and allocational efficiencies' (or a government that 'costs less') (Kaboolian, 1998; Terry, 1998; Pollitt and Bouckaert, 2000).

If, however, the legacy of public management reform is likely to be a 'stronger emphasis on performance-motivated administration' that advances the art of public management, as Lynn (1998: 232) suggested, then public sector performance measurement has to involve more than accounting for finances and 'answering for performance.' As John Kamensky (1993: 395) exhorted, 'there have been enough paperwork exercises in government.' We need measures that will inform and be used by public managers, not only 'accountability holders' such as legislators and oversight agencies, to guide them in improving service quality and results.

This begs the question: What information is most useful for public managers striving to improve government performance? For example, how do public managers under GPRA in the United States use the information from annual program performance reports that compare measured performance with performance goals? Simply knowing that they have achieved or failed to achieve target objectives or standards is not likely to aid public managers in understanding *why* performance is at the level it is or *how* managers can effect change. As Hatry (1999: 6) observed: 'A major purpose of performance measurement is to raise questions; it seldom, if ever, provides answers by itself as to what should be done.'

The types of questions public managers can answer depend critically on the types of performance information that are collected. Kamensky (1993) and Hatry (1999), for example, distinguish among categories of performance information that include: (1) input information (e.g., resources and staff), (2) process information (e.g., workload and job complexity), (3) efficiency information (e.g., productivity and unit costs), (4) outputs (products and services delivered), (5) outcomes (in relation to intermediate or end goals), including quality assessment, and (6) impact information. In an ideal performance measurement system, the full range of information – from inputs to outcomes or impacts – would be used by public managers in a logical flow, linking performance monitoring (of ongoing processes, efficiency, and outputs) to performance evaluation (of program outcomes and/or impacts) to *performance management*: that is, using performance information to guide program planning and improve future performance (Osborne et al., 1995).

Supported by public management reforms and aided by advances in information technology, some performance management activities are progressing toward this ideal, providing public managers with more information about how and the extent to which programs are contributing to outcomes or impacts (Abramson and Kamensky, 2001). Recent work by Moynihan (2008) argues for more 'interactive dialogues' to support more effective use of performance information, including the use of strategic planning, learning forums, dialogue routines, and related approaches that encourage the view that documentation of performance is not an end but rather a means for engaging in policy and management change. At the same time, governments worldwide are now attaching higher stakes to the achievement of performance outcomes through the growing use of performance-contingent pay, organization-wide performance bonuses or sanctions, and competitive performance-based contracting (Heinrich, 2007). This trend hastens the need to improve the quality of performance information collected and the efficacy and judiciousness with which it is used to guide public managers in decision making.

This chapter focuses largely on these 'state-of-the-art' performance measurement approaches, although a broader range of performance measurement activities and processes are also discussed. In the following section, an interdisciplinary review of public sector performance measurement approaches is presented, integrated with a discussion of literatures on performance measurement and management/organizational effectiveness. The 'state of the art' is described next, including challenges and prospects for improving performance measurement systems and increasing their usefulness to public managers at all levels of government. The concluding section summarizes major points and discusses the prospects for continuing advances in public sector performance measurement.

A CHRONOLOGICAL REVIEW OF LITERATURES AND SYSTEMS OF PERFORMANCE MEASUREMENT

An interdisciplinary review of historical and contemporary conceptions of performance measurement highlights the diversity in disciplinary perspectives and approaches to this subject. Human resource management scholars, for example, trace the origins of performance measurement to the development of employee rating forms based on

psychological traits by industrial psychologists in the 1800s (Scott, Clothier, and Spriegel, 1941). The US Federal Civil Service has used these types of performance ratings, narrowly focused on individual performance, since at least the late 1800s (Murphy and Cleveland, 1995).

A more generic view of public sector performance measurement, also originating in the late 1800s, can be traced to scholars and experts who called for the government to become more rational and efficient like the private sector. This perspective emerged early in the writings of Woodrow Wilson (1887), who proposed a new 'scientific' or more 'business-like' approach to administration, and was later elaborated by members of the 'scientific management' movement in the early 1900s. Scientific management promoted the careful analysis of workers' tasks and work arrangements, with the objective of maximizing efficiency by 'planning [work] procedures according to a technical logic, setting standards, and exercising controls to ensure conformity with standards' (Taylor, 1911; Thompson, 1967: 5). The 1910 Taft Commission on Economy and Efficiency, one of the first of a series of major US commissions aimed at improving the executive management and performance of government, was significantly influenced by scientific management ideas. Shades of the rational and technical logic of scientific management are also evident in more recent performance measurement initiatives such as GPRA, Next Steps, and Taiwan's Research, Development and Evaluation Commission, which require agencies to develop strategic plans for achieving specific, quantitatively measurable goals, and annual performance reports that compare actual performance with performance goals or standards.

By the 1930s, scholars of 'administrative management,' such as Gulick and Urwick (1937), were shifting public discussion from the micro-level design of efficient work tasks and procedures to the structure of large administrative systems. The writings of administrative management influenced major government reform proposals, including the report by the 1936–37 Brownlow Committee on Administrative Management. Like scientific management, these reforms centered on improving government efficiency, yet the Brownlow Committee Report also made a point to distinguish administrative management from scientific management, declaring that 'administrative efficiency is not merely a matter of paper clips, time clocks, and standardized economies of motion ... [but] must be built into the structure of government just as it is built into a piece of machinery' (1937: 16). The structural reforms proposed by the committee called for the delegation of power within hierarchical structures to managers with 'administrative expertise.' As Feldman and Khademian (2000: 152) observed, 'that expertise would be exercised within rules, regulations, and administrative structures established by political overseers and top managers.' Performance measurement activities of the administrative management era primarily involved auditing of inputs and outputs and fiscal accountability at department or higher-organization levels where control was centralized and administrative decisions were checked (Rosenbloom, 1986).

At the same time, the organization theorist Chester Barnard (1938), in a defining work that diverged from the administrative management perspective, was urging greater attention to the integral role of incentives in organizations (e.g., money, status, power, autonomy) and the 'social character' of cooperative systems. Barnard suggested that individuals' social interactions and awareness of their relative positions in a 'hierarchy of rewards' would be more influential motivators of performance than clear channels of hierarchical authority and rule-based processes for producing outputs (Pfeffer, 1990).

Into the 1940s and following World War II, however, Barnard's ideas about the importance of social relations and incentives in formal organizations were still having little appreciable influence on government performance management. Instead, ongoing

concerns about the size and efficiency of government led to two more major commissions – the First (1947–49) and Second (1953–55) Hoover Commissions – to 'promote economy, efficiency, and improved service in the transaction of the public business ...' (The Hoover Commission Report, 1949: xiii). The commissions' reviews of the organizational structure and performance of the US executive branch reflected the former President Hoover's beliefs, adhering to some principles of scientific management, that 'management research technicians' should advise policy and executive agency decisions (Moe, 1982). The series of reforms that followed in the 1960s and 1970s, including the Planning, Programming, Budgeting System (PPBS), Zero-Based Budgeting (ZBB), and management by objectives (MBO), promoted the application of technical and legal expertise in objective, 'systems analysis' of the efficiency of public programs. These reforms were readily embraced by other central governments as well, including the adoption of PPBS by Canada's Department of National Revenue, the Netherlands in its Government Accounts Act of 1976, and by the Department of Education and Science in England.

The MBO approach, advanced by Drucker (1954) and later adopted by the Nixon administration, departed from administrative and scientific management approaches, however, by prodding performance measurement systems to involve both organization- and individual-level performance measures. The MBO approach is still in used in many public and private organizations to link *organizational* planning for financial, technical, and strategic performance goals with *employee* actions and objectives through their input in participatory processes, feedback from management, and financial rewards allocated on the basis of measured organizational progress. Unlike the top-down, rules-based focus of administrative management, which social psychologists had criticized by for its 'mechanical view' of individuals, MBO sought to coordinate objectives at top and lower organizational levels and to give explicit consideration to employees' under-standing of goals and rewards for improving performance (Campbell et al., 1970).

Still, while attractive to government reformers at first, the limitations of PPBS, MBO, and ZBB that required managers to narrowly define and measure progress toward financial, technical, and strategic perform-ance goals became more evident over time. Thompson (1967: 4–6) described these types of performance measurement systems as 'closed-system' strategies. In a closed or rational model system, there are a relatively small number of variables for managers to control, and they can reliably predict their relationships. Goals and production tasks are known, organizational objectives are verifia-ble, resources are available, and employees are responsive to incentives (i.e., self-interest dominates) (Simon, 1957). As a result, they are more likely to be effective when managers are able to achieve clarity, consensus, and consistency about organizational goals such as economic performance or efficiency in service delivery. MBO-type approaches to perform-ance measurement are more commonly used today by local governments, where budgetary accountability and service efficiency are focal public priorities (Rivenbark, 2001).

As dissatisfaction with these rational model approaches to performance evaluation was growing, organization and management theories were evolving toward more open, adaptive system models that assumed, instead of closure, 'that a system contains more variables than we can comprehend at one time, or that some variables are subject to influences we cannot control or predict.' (Thompson, 1967: 6). Thompson (1967) cited the study of 'informal organization' as an example of an open-system approach, and referring to Barnard's (1938) work, described variables such as cliques, social controls based on informal norms, and status that influence the performance and 'survival' of organizations. These open-system and con-tingency theories – that relate organizational structures and functioning to their contexts or environments – broadened the array of

variables viewed as important in managing organizational performance and measuring the contributions of public managers to organization outcomes.

Perhaps the most prominent example of a more open, adaptive system approach to per-formance analysis that emerged at this time was W. Edwards Deming's Total Quality Management (TQM) system. Deming (1986) challenged the 'narrow, simple-minded' focus of rational 'management by the numbers, management by MBO' approaches on bot-tom-line cost and efficiency targets and urged managers to instead strive for and measure *quality* (Walton, 1986; Kelly, 1998: 202). Quality-focused (TQM) systems feature long-term commitment by top managers to con-tinuous quality improvement, full involvement by employees at all organizational levels, and a shared 'vision' of quality, a customer orien-tation, and the 'systematic collection and analysis of data' that are expected to indicate where potential for quality improvement lies (Halachmi, 1995: 266). Acknowledging the challenges of assessing quality – i.e., the higher level of knowledge and information that are required to evaluate and manage per-formance in terms of quality and the impor-tance of factors outside the control of employees – Deming strongly advocated the use of statistical analysis to understand the causal influence of systemic and situational/environmental factors on performance.

The influence of TQM ideas and their focus on quality or results, in conjunction with the decline of systems more narrowly aimed at increasing outputs and efficiency such as PPBS, were accelerating the advance of public sector performance measurement toward outcomes-based measurement sys-tems. In the early 1980s, for example, under the Reagan administration's New Federalism, the US Job Training Partnership Act (JTPA) introduced a performance measurement system that has been described as a 'pioneer' of outcomes-based performance management (Barnow, 2000).[1] The JTPA performance measurement system was distinct in its focus on program outcomes (e.g., job placements and trainee earnings) rather than outputs (e.g., the number of persons trained), the use of budgetary incentives for managers based on *outcomes*, and the linking of performance measures across federal, state, and local governments. It also incorporated the use of regression models with performance data to statistically adjust performance standards for local population characteristics and economic conditions.

Another example of a public sector performance management system that was working to infuse quality management principles and moving toward a focus on results, or 'value for money' (VFM), was the United Kingdom's Financial Management Initiative (FMI) of 1983. As Osborne et al. (1995: 20) explain, VFM was assessed by measuring 'economy, efficiency and effectiveness,' but with 'an explicit concern with organizational structures and processes likely to lead to the 'three Es'; of 'management' as opposed to 'administration' as the task of senior staff in the public sector; and of decentralization, especially of budget holding, as an integral dimension of organizational design.' Both Reagan's and Thatcher's initiatives incorporated at least three of the four public management reform principles that were emerging in the 'reinventing government' and NPM reforms of the 1990s: (1) measure results, (2) put the customer in the driver's seat, (3) introduce a market orientation, and (4) decentralize (Gore, 1993).

This light probing of the history of performance measurement and public management reforms shows the progression of public sector performance measurement away from a more rational or technical focus on work procedures and process efficiency and a top-down, hierarchical approach to accountability for organization inputs and outputs, and toward more participatory, multilevel systems that consider a broader range of factors affecting performance while maintaining an explicit focus on the outcomes or results of programs. Barbara Romzek (1998) has more generally described these emerging approaches to performance measurement as systems of *professional* accountability. Professional accountability, as Romzek (1998: 204) explains, defers to the discretion of managers 'as they work within broad parameters, rather than on close scrutiny to ensure compliance with detailed rules and organizational directives.' The broad parameters in public sector performance measurement systems of the twenty-first century are outcomes, and a central challenge for public managers is to effectively use the different types of information obtained through performance measurement activities to better understand the link between their own actions and these more broadly-defined organizational goals and outcomes.

THE STATE OF THE ART IN PERFORMANCE MEASUREMENT: CHALLENGES AND PROSPECTS

As the introduction and preceding review suggest, there are some important commonalities across local and national boundaries among evolving public sector performance measurement systems. The more prominent features include: (1) performance measures focused on quality, outcomes or results, (2) formal report requirements for comparing actual performance with performance goals or standards, (3) multiple levels of performance accountability in decentralized programs, and (4) market-oriented provisions such as financial/budgetary incentives for performance, as in the JTPA program, and plans to use performance information to promote continuous improvement and increased citizen ('customer') satisfaction. It is also clear, however, that public managers are still struggling with how to make the 'state-of-the-art' systems work.

Challenges

One challenge public managers confront in broadening performance measures beyond more straightforward, bottom-line targets (e.g., efficiency) to a focus on outcomes are problems in reaching a consensus – at all levels of organization and management – on clearly defined, verifiable public objectives. In a review of agency performance plans, the US Government Accounting Office (US GAO, 1999: 6) stated that 'mission fragmentation and program overlap are widespread across the federal government.' Sometimes the multiplicity or fragmentation of goals are inherent in originating legislation, making it more difficult for public managers to get staff and stakeholders to think about how their diverse activities are related to a common outcome. The JTPA legislation, for example, stated that programs should serve 'those who can benefit from, and are most in need of' employment and training services. Heckman, Heinrich and Smith (2002) established empirically the tradeoff between these equity and efficiency goals in JTPA programs, showing that targeting those most in need (the bottom 20 percent of the skill distribution) significantly lowered the value-added gains from program participation.

Behn (2001) contends that public managers can 'jump this hoop' and avoid goal conflicts by choosing vague, uncontroversial, inconsequential, or easily attainable goals (effectively repudiating the requirement). In Lindblom's (1959: 576) classic work on 'the science of muddling through,' he notes that 'much of organization theory argues the virtues of common values and agreed organizational objectives,' but when administrators cannot agree on values or objectives, the preservation of a diversity of views and fragmented decision making, where some parts of the organization provide a check on others, is an acceptable strategy for managing complex policies and problems.

Agencies' choices for performance objectives have important implications, however, for the complex task of determining quantitative measures of performance goals. If objectives are broadly or vaguely defined, or if multiple goals are in conflict, it will be more challenging to specify accurate and informative measures. For example, the US Department of Veterans' Affairs Veterans Health Administration defined its goal to 'improve the health status of veterans' and identified performance measures of cost reductions per patient and the number of patients served to evaluate progress (US GAO, 1999: 23). The disparities between this health quality goal and the input/efficiency performance measures used are glaring. Alternatively, Anne Khademian (1995) concluded in her study of the US Federal Deposit Insurance Corporation (FDIC) that a clear mandate about organizational objectives, i.e., the solvency of the Bank Insurance Fund, and an explicit measure of organizational performance toward that objective, were important motivators and guides for agency professionals and managers who facilitated key changes to lead the agency out of crisis.

In the case of the FDIC, the measure of the Bank Insurance Fund's solvency was directly related to the central organizational goal of protecting the health of banks; as Khademian (1995: 19) explains, 'to the extent that failures can be prevented through effective examination and supervision, the fund will remain sound.' In their discussion of performance outcome measures, Gormley and Weimer (1999: 9) point out that 'direct measures of outcomes require no relational theories as they are operationalizations of conceptualized values.' As measures become more distant from outcomes, associated through hypothesized relationships and proxy or scalar variables (e.g., test scores for school performance, mortality rates for healthcare services), verification becomes more complex and the degree of uncertainty in performance analysis increases.

An additional challenge for public managers is that performance requirements may contribute to what Bouckaert (1993: 403) describes as the 'time-shortening disease,' which 'makes the organization focus on the short instead of on the intermediate or long run.' Agency executives report that it is especially difficult to translate their long-term missions or strategic goals into annual performance goals and to predict the level of results that might be achieved over a shorter-term (US GAO, 1997a; Next Steps Report, 1998). John Ahearne, a former high-ranking official in the energy field, described GPRA's performance requirements as disastrous for the US Department of Energy's nuclear waste clean-up programs, as they can shift managers' attention to short-term goals that will likely impede progress toward longer-term clean-up and environmental health objectives (decades into the future).

If shorter-term performance objectives and their measures are strongly correlated with longer-term program goals and impacts, public managers might avoid this dilemma. Research on public programs suggests, however, that one is likely to err in assuming a positive correlation between short-term measures and long-term organizational performance. In their studies of federal job-training programs, Heckman, Heinrich, and Smith (2002) and Barnow (2000) showed that short-term performance measures of participants' employment rates and earnings levels following program discharge were at best weakly (and sometimes negatively) related to longer-term employment and earnings impacts estimated using experimental data. Burghardt and Schochet (2001) of the US National Job Corps Study compared impact estimates from an experimental study of education and earnings outcomes across Job Corps centers rated as high, medium, and low performers by the Job Corps performance measurement system and found that the Job Corps performance measurement system failed to distinguish between more and less effective centers. In addition, studies of school effectiveness have found that some teachers respond to performance requirements based on student test scores by 'teaching to the test,' or even worse, by cheating (e.g., changing student answers on exams), with likely negative implications for students' longer-term educational success (Gormley and Weimer, 1999; Koretz, 1999; Jacob and Levitt, 2003). Jacob and Levitt (2003) found that the observed frequency of teacher cheating responded strongly to even

small changes in incentives, highlighting some of the risks that high-powered incentive systems can induce.

At least one US GAO report (1997b) has suggested supplementing performance data with impact evaluation studies to obtain a more precise understanding of program effects and to verify (or disprove) relationships between short-term measures and long-term goals. The National JTPA and Job Corps Studies are examples of these types of evaluations. A primary advantage of experimental impact evaluations is their potential to identify causal linkages and the 'unique contribution' that an organization makes to outcomes (Hatry, 1999; Bloom, Hill and Riccio, 2003). A disadvantage is that multi-site experiments are frequently costly and potentially disruptive to program operations. While they are unlikely to generate the timely, regular feedback that public managers require to produce performance reports and make adjustments (in budget allocations, service strategies, management practices, etc.) to improve performance, they do provide an important check on the performance measurement systems routinely used (as in the case of the Job Corps program).

Another issue embedded in this discussion is the level of accountability and analysis in performance measurement systems. In organization science and public administration literatures, a conventional view distinguishes 'top-down' and 'bottom-up' approaches to performance accountability. The government of New Zealand, for example, only holds officials at the top (policymaking) level accountable for program outcomes, exempting public managers and personnel in operating departments from performance requirements (Hatry, 1999). Bottom-up approaches, alternatively, focus on performance management activities originating at a lower level that have emergent properties at higher levels. TQM, for example, has been described as a bottom-up approach to improving organizational performance, where individual TQM training, work behaviors, and social interactions combine at a lower level and emerge over time to influence organizational outcomes. The fact is, however, that in a majority of organizations, performance analysis is likely occurring at more than one level of organization. As DeNisi (2000: 121) explains, performance measurement is 'both a multilevel and a cross-level phenomenon'; either explicitly (as in the JTPA performance measurement system) or informally, public managers at multiple levels of organization measure performance, and activities and responses at one level are likely to have effects at other levels. Bouckaert (1993: 38) describes this as a 'top-down and bottom-up interaction.' He argues that the more the bottom and middle management are involved in performance measurement activities, the greater their commitment to them.

The challenge for public managers and researchers is to ascertain and understand the effects, multilevel and cross-level, planned and unintended, occurring in performance measurement systems. In studies of the implementation of GPRA, for example, Radin (2000b) and Mintzberg (1996) conclude that rather than freeing public managers to focus on results, the performance requirements have increased administrative constraints, elevated conflict among multiple levels of program management, and engendered distrust between agencies and legislators about gaming of measures. In their study of the JTPA program, Courty and Marschke (2004) showed empirically how some local program managers chose to 'game' the federal performance standards in order to increase their agencies' measured performance in ways independent of actual performance. Given the limited or indirect influence that public managers commonly have on organizational outcomes and the difficulties of separating out effects of multiple layers of policy and management, managers' desire to manipulate performance measures in ways that will improve their *measured* but not *actual* performance is understandable, if not acceptable.

Finally, researchers and practitioners are beginning to grapple with another challenge,

the dynamics of performance incentive systems. It is most often the case that policymakers or other incentive system designers begin with an imperfect understanding of workers' or organizational capabilities for achieving performance goals or their means for influencing measured performance (Heinrich and Marschke, 2010). Over time, in the implementation of performance measurement systems, they learn about behavioral and organizational responses that may suggest the need for modifications to system incentives. For example, achievement test scores have long been used in public education by teachers, parents, and students to evaluate individual student achievement levels and grade progression, based on the belief that test scores accurately reflect student mastery of tested subjects and that increases in test scores correlate with learning gains. However, with higher stakes (primarily sanctions) attached to student performance levels under state and federal accountability initiatives (such as the US No Child Left Behind Act of 2001), researchers have documented some unintended responses (e.g., teaching to the test, shifting resources, and cheating by teachers on these tests) that have undoubtedly reduced the correlation between test scores and students' *true* achievement gains (Jacob and Levitt, 2003; Jacob, 2005).

Awareness or the realization of unintended behaviors that distort measured outcomes and incentives for performance improvement does not imply that a performance measurement system should be discarded. Critics of the expanded use of performance measures in areas such as education and social services have yet to identify alternative (and readily available) measures that are less noisy or prone to distortion. Rather, policymakers and public managers need to recognize that the systems they design and implement will need regular monitoring of worker/organization responses (at multiple levels of organization as necessary) and adjustments, e.g., replacing or modifying performance measures, over time. In addition, ongoing research on the implementation and effects of performance management systems is needed to generate knowledge for policymakers and public managers that will inform and guide their efforts to improve system design and effectiveness, across a wide range of federal, state, and local organizations that are increasingly using performance measures.

Prospects

A central theme of this chapter is that rather than simply documenting performance outcomes, public sector performance measurement activities and research should help public managers to understand how their own policy and management decisions are linked to outcomes and the systemic and situational factors that might constrain or intervene in these relationships to affect performance. Along these lines, Laurence E. Lynn, Jr (1998: 236), deliberating the 'legacy' of the New Public Management, urged a 'theory-based research agenda' that addresses questions about how and to what extent institutions, leadership, and management influence government performance or 'the creation of effective, accountable democratic states.' Rainey and Steinbauer (1999) reviewed the literature on government effectiveness and also called for a more theoretical approach to research on government performance: in particular, theories linking the organization, management, resources, and external stakeholders of agencies to their effectiveness. As Bouckaert (1993) implores, 'performance measures have to contribute to the maintenance or to the development of the organization itself.' The theoretical 'building blocks' for this undertaking exist; the corresponding challenge is to integrate the intellectual contributions of multiple disciplines in analytical frameworks that will produce, on an ongoing basis, useful information and insights for public managers.

Context, Process, and Level of Analysis

A major concern about performance accountability, public managers profess, is that their responsibility is not commensurate with their authority (Mintzberg, 1996). As Lynn, Heinrich, and Hill (2001) note, public policies and programs are being administered through increasingly complex, decentralized governance structures, including networks, collaborations, and partnerships among public, nonprofit and for-profit organizations. In accounting for performance across 'diverse and dispersed' administrative entities and service units, many of which may operate in varying social, political, and fiscal contexts, public managers need to achieve a tenable balance between demands for analytical rigor and accuracy in performance measurement and political and practical limitations on what is feasible to measure in complex governing systems. Furthermore, if results are publicized and agencies are rewarded or penalized for performance, then performance standards have to take into account the ability of agencies or managers to effect change and contribute to improved outcomes or program value added.

One strategy promoted in some public management reform circles is to adopt a narrower focus on a single, relatively straightforward measure of performance such as a scalar measure of client/citizen satisfaction. Described as 'bottom-up accountability,' holding governments accountable to citizens (voters) is seen as 'replicating the virtues of the marketplace' (Gormley and Weimer, 1999: 198). In fact, the National Academy of Public Administration has explicitly called for a greater focus on customer or citizen surveys as a gauge of government performance (Van Ryzin, 2004), and the use of customer satisfaction measures as leading indicators of public sector performance is proliferating in Europe (Workshop on Statistical Methods for Performance Analysis, Cassino, Italy, 2006). It is implicitly assumed in the use of these measures, explain Callahan and Gilbert (2005) and Kelly (2005), that citizens will recognize improved services and government performance and that this will be reflected in higher measured levels of customer (or citizen) satisfaction. This approach also assumes that public managers can ignore context and levels and that citizens are sufficiently informed to provide reliable feedback. Research on the determinants of citizens' attitudes and their evaluations of public activities and services, however, shows 'considerable ambivalence and volatility in their preferences ...' and 'inconsistent evaluations of services and taxes,' reflecting their own conflicting attitudes, values, and perspectives (Beck, Rainey, and Traut, 1990: 71–72). Furthermore, empirical research has confirmed that performance and satisfaction may be conceptually distinct constructs in some contexts (Churchill and Surprenant, 1982). As Kelly elaborates, unlike private sector transactions, public sector service provision involves some degree of legal coercion (i.e., taxation) and may not always be equitable. Thus, regardless of service quality, citizens who are required to pay for services that they do not consume or do not want may report low levels of satisfaction. Thus, public managers are not likely to get a clear picture of whether or not government performance is improving simply by tracking citizen satisfaction ratings.

At another extreme, scholars might collaborate with public managers to construct and apply multidisciplinary, theory-based models of organizational performance that fully account for all potential interrelationships within and between organizations, employee and client/citizen characteristics, and intervening political and environmental factors. For example, sociologists and social psychologists identify contextual factors such as organizational complexity, coordination, climate, culture, and values, competition among or within functional units, and individual member characteristics, cognitive and social behaviors that affect performance (Marcoulides and Heck, 1993; Murphy and Cleveland, 1995). Political scientists highlight the influence of legislative mandates and coalitions, bureaucratic discretion and control, political ideology and values, and other dynamics of political processes. Economists focus on the role of information

asymmetries, transaction costs, monetary incentives, and competition, among other variables affecting public sector performance management (Dixit, 1999). In formulating a model to evaluate performance, including a broad range of variables at multiple levels of government organization or structure, one would confront many obvious conceptual and methodological challenges.

In view of these formidable challenges, public administration/management scholars, along with public managers, have been striving to elucidate a constructive 'middle ground' for public sector performance measurement. While there is no singular strategy or archetype that all public managers might adapt and use, there are a number of well-articulated theoretical and analytical models that executive administrators might draw upon in developing more effective systems for measuring and managing government performance. The differing capabilities and needs for collecting and analyzing performance data among government agencies performing different functions at different levels of government also has implications for the strategy or approach to performance measurement they might use. The models discussed below explicitly consider context, process, levels of analysis, and the data available to public managers in measuring performance and evaluating the relationship of management to outcomes.

Models for public sector performance measurement and their application

Hatry (1999) presents a 'logical model' of 'relevant factors' in a performance measurement system – one that links inputs, activities, outputs, and outcomes – and describes the relationships among these different types of performance information. His very simple model does not formally identify the influence of context or environmental factors or the relationships among performance measures across different levels of government or analysis. However, he calls for public managers to obtain 'explanatory information' along with their performance data – from qualitative assessments by program personnel to in-depth program evaluations that produce statistically reliable information – to interpret the data and identify problems and possible management or organizational responses.

In their 'revised rationalist model of performance assessment' that acknowledges the 'bounded rationality' of public managers, political interests, and other contextual and catalytic influences, Osborne et al. (1995) incorporate the same basic elements as Hatry's model but develop a more complex, formal model or framework for understanding the role and influence of Hatry's 'explanatory' factors. Like Hatry's model, their framework depicts the types and purposes of different performance monitoring/measurement activities and performance indicators and data required for measures.[2] They also identify different levels and frequency of monitoring/measurement in public programs and combine the different types of performance information with three levels of measurement – the project/team level, program level, and strategic (local or national senior management) level – to construct a multidimensional 'matrix-framework' for assessing performance that recognizes different types of monitoring/measurement will occur at different levels. In applying their model in a study of the British Social Programme of the Rural Development Commission, they recounted the dearth of information for all types of monitoring and measures and the challenges of integrating performance assessment practices at multiple levels into a 'holistic framework of performance management' (Osborne et al., 1995: 30). The main strength of their model for public managers lies in its use for conceptually organizing and planning a system of performance data collection.

In an approach that moves closer toward program evaluation in explaining performance, Mead (2003) describes 'performance analysis' as a strategy that aims 'to relate the practices of programs to measures of performance.' The performance studies he sets forth as exemplars involve statistical modeling to associate program features with

performance outcomes, while controlling for demographics, economic conditions, and other contextual factors. Mead urges researchers to use field interviews with program administrators to gain an in-depth understanding of how programs operate and to guide the development of hypotheses for statistical analysis. Public managers who possess this information would need to develop operational definitions and measures of administrative practices, organizational capacity, and other program-level variables that could be monitored and used in statistical analysis. In Mead's generally conceptualized statistical model for evaluating performance, the dependent variable is a program-level performance indicator. His approach is probably best regarded, as he describes it, as a quantitative *process* research methodology applied at a specific level of analysis.[3]

Mead's approach to statistically modeling the processes and practices of programs and their relationship to performance measures is taken a step further in a multilevel, organizing framework for performance analysis advanced by Lynn, Heinrich, and Hill (2001). Their framework delineates a hierarchy of relationships (across multiple levels of government) among: legislative and political choice (i.e., responsibilities for implementing public law), governance structures, management strategies, core technologies and organizational functions, outcomes, and client/citizen assessments. Heinrich and Lynn (2000) describe a number of applications of this framework – in studies of public school performance, welfare and job-training program outcomes, and healthcare services outcomes – that use a multilevel statistical modeling strategy to identify causal relationships within and across hierarchical levels of government and in a broader environmental context, while recognizing the potential influence of unmeasured factors on performance analysis findings. Bloom, Hill, and Riccio (2003), for example, completed a multilevel re-analysis of data from the multisite Job Opportunities and Basic Skills (JOBS) evaluation. In analyzing the effects of program management, services, economic environment, and client characteristics on the earnings of welfare-to-work clients across local offices, they found that *management choices and practices* related to goals, client–staff interfaces, and service strategies had substantive, statistically significant effects on client outcomes and impacts.

Some public managers and scholars interested in following a more advanced analytical and statistical approach to performance analysis might be constrained by the data requirements and costs associated with data collection and analysis. The best data typically available to public managers for *ongoing* performance analyses are administrative data that are regularly and consistently collected in support of an organization's functions. Administrative data commonly include detailed information about clients of public programs, their progression through program services, and outcomes, and the marginal costs of collecting data across multiple programs, sites or fiscal years are generally low.

For example, many of the larger school districts in the United States are developing longitudinal data systems that enable them to conduct value-added analyses and other diagnostic and policy-relevant evaluation research with the ultimate goal of improving student achievement. The basic concept of a 'value-added' approach to performance analysis is simple and appreciated by many educators: it measures the *productivity or contributions* of teachers and schools to student achievement. The analytical methods for producing evidence on value added, however, are not uncomplicated; they adjust for student selection bias, track student achievement over time and allow for decay effects of interventions, and they explicitly address the issue of measurement error in student achievement. The value-added approach is also sometimes described as a growth curve analysis and may be implemented using a multilevel modeling approach. In its application to the study of student achievement, a three-level model is commonly used to estimate at level one, within-student achievement over time; at level two, student achievement growth as a function of student characteristics and student participation in interventions; and at level three, the estimated effects of any school/policy interventions on student achievement as a function of school characteristics and the environment.

Studies that compare the use of experimental data (for estimating program impacts) with regularly collected administrative data on program operations and outcomes generate encouraging findings for public managers about the potential for using administrative data in performance management (Heinrich, 2002; Hill, 2006). Hill and Heinrich both find that relying on administrative data to generate information about *how* to improve program performance is not likely to misdirect managers away from program impact goals, although particular estimates of the magnitude of outcomes may differ from those of the size of impacts. If governments with administrative data systems are able to incorporate data fields that describe management policies and processes across sites or local service locations, public managers might more effectively use administrative and performance data to understand the effects of different policies and approaches to managing and delivering government services.

Finally, the 'interactive dialogue model of performance information use' advanced by Moynihan (2008: 95) is relatively unique in its description of the assembly and use of performance information as a form of 'social interaction.' The basic assumptions of his model – that performance information is ambiguous, subjective, and incomplete, and that context, institutional affiliation, and individual beliefs will affect its use – challenge the rational suppositions underlying most of the other performance management models discussed here. While performance management reforms have emphasized what he describes as the potential 'instrumental benefits' of performance management, such as increased accountability and transparency of government outcomes, Moynihan suggests that elected officials and public managers have been more likely to realize the 'symbolic benefits' of creating an impression that 'government is being run in a rational, efficient and results-oriented manner' (2008: 68). As noted earlier, Moynihan advocates more practical uses of performance information in strategic planning, forums for discussion about results, and other approaches that encourage an 'interactive dialogue' and support more effective use of performance information and organizational learning.

The models for performance management highlighted here, and their applications in measuring and managing public sector performance, are clearly moving toward more in-depth investigations of *how* outcomes are produced and how this knowledge can be used to improve public sector performance. As Hatry (1999: 8) explains, 'performance measurement can be considered a field of program evaluation,' where program evaluations 'not only examine a program's outcomes but also identify the *whys*, including the extent to which the program actually caused the outcomes.' As the time and costs involved in these performance measurement/ evaluation approaches continue to decline with advances in information technology, their recognition as viable strategies for improving the quality and usefulness of performance information available to public managers (and the resulting performance outcomes) is likely to grow.

CONCLUSION

Distinct from the 1990s public sector theme calling for documentation of explicit government outcomes, this chapter elaborates another theme: calling for performance *management* that goes beyond documentation of outcomes. It advocates the collection and use of performance information that will aid public managers in understanding *how* their decisions and actions are linked to outcomes, what environmental or contextual factors might limit or increase their effectiveness as

managers, and how this information can be used to improve future performance.

The historical review of performance measurement and organizational effectiveness literatures showed that scholars and managers have long recognized the influence of a range of organizational, individual-level, and contextual factors on organizational performance. Until recently, the analytical challenges of separating out the role and effects of policy and management from other factors were beyond the technical capabilities of performance analysis. With advances in data collection and storage, theory and statistical modeling, and computing capacity, we have an obligation to increase our understanding of the contributions public managers can make to organizational performance and what realistic expectations for results are, given the context and environment in which they operate.

The examples of models for performance measurement described in this chapter suggest an ambitious path for future research and performance measurement activities, while also recognizing that the differing functions, levels, capabilities, resources, and objectives of government organizations will influence the strategy or approach to performance measurement they use. Where resources for performance management are fewer, initial goals for using performance data may have to be modest, following an approach like that outlined by Hatry (1999). In North Carolina, for example, local governments cooperate in data collection activities that allow for the production of comparative measures of service efficiency and fiscal performance. Local government officials then participate in dialogues that encourage the sharing and discussion of information about 'explanatory factors' – management practices, service processes, and local environment and population characteristics – to help them to understand differences or disparities in observed performance. While there is no formal modeling of relationships between possible explanatory variables and performance measures, the project has established a support structure for the types of discussions that may continue to advance the use of performance data across sites and in a broader management context. As Rivenbark (2001: v) comments, 'The cities and counties that participate in the North Carolina project do not endure the challenges of data collection, cleaning, and reporting simply to produce a report. They participate with the belief that performance measurement and benchmarking are the catalysts to service or process improvement.'

The importance of work that has been done in recent decades, in the context of public management reforms, to advance the use of government administrative data and to link these data across programs or to other databases with economic/environmental/contextual data (e.g., local labor market information data) should not be underestimated. In their discussion of organizational 'report cards,' Gormley and Weimer (1999) described a number of examples of national, state, and local government organizations that collect data regularly and 'transform' them into information that can be interpreted by external audiences and used to assess and improve performance. At the same time, this chapter also addressed some of the continuing challenges and tradeoffs in performance measurement between: comprehensive or broadly-defined goals and precision of measures; short-term, measurable objectives and long-term program goals; and more simple, direct approaches to documenting and understanding performance outcomes versus more complex statistical strategies for performance analysis that aim to identify performance drivers or the causal influences of systemic and environmental factors on performance. Public managers and scholars will have to decide how to continue balancing these tradeoffs, guided by the performance management questions they are addressing, the data available to them, and their capacity for analyzing data.

In the face of these challenges and complexities, we, as a public, also need to acknowledge that some quantitative performance measures will be indicators at best and not highly accurate or informative measures of a program's value or effectiveness. Our demands for performance documentation should focus more on what public managers can learn about *how* to improve performance and less on the precise measurement of performance levels or 'bottom-line' outcomes.

NOTES

1 Because of the comparatively long tenure of outcomes-based standards in the JTPA program and its distinctively advanced use of statistical analysis in determining performance ratings, I draw additional examples from the JTPA performance standards experience throughout this chapter

2 Among the types of performance monitoring and measures, Osborne et al. include: 'context monitoring' (e.g., of changing socioeconomic and institutional factors); three types of input/process assessment ('strategy', 'progress,' and 'activity' monitoring); 'impact' measures, both quantitative and qualitative, that evaluate performance 'against the highest level objectives and targets'; and 'catalytic monitoring' of influences or impacts on the wider service delivery system, other agencies or people (Osborne et al., 1995: 27).

3 Mead applies his 'performance analysis' approach in a study of welfare reform outcomes in Wisconsin.

REFERENCES

Abramson, Mark A. and Kamensky, John M. (2001) *Managing for Results 2002*. Lanham, MD: Rowman & Littlefield Publishers, Inc.
Barnard, Chester (1938) *Functions of the Executive*. Cambridge, MA: Harvard University Press.
Barnow, Burt S. (2000) 'Exploring the Relationship between Performance Management and Program Impact: A Case Study of the Job Training Partnership Act', *Journal of Policy Analysis and Management*, 19(1): 118–141.
Beck, Paul A., Rainey, Hal G., and Traut, Carol (1990) 'Disadvantage, Disaffection, and Race as Divergent Bases for Citizen Fiscal Policy Preferences', *Journal of Politics*, 52(1): 71–93.
Behn, Robert D. (2001) *Rethinking Democratic Accountability*. Washington, DC: Brookings Institution Press.

Bloom, Howard S., Hill, Carolyn J., and Riccio, James A. (2003) 'Linking Program Implementation and Effectiveness: Lessons from a Pooled Sample of Welfare-to-Work Experiments', *Journal of Policy Analysis and Management*, 22(4): 551–575.

Bouckaert, Geert (1993) 'Measurement and Meaningful Management', *Public Productivity & Management Review*, 17(1): 31–43.

Burghardt, John and Schochet, Peter Z. (2001) 'National Job Corps Study: Impacts by Center Characteristics', Mathematica Policy Research Document No. PR01-45.

Callahan, R. F. and Gilbert, G. R (2005) 'End-User Satisfaction and Design Features of Public Agencies', *The American Review of Public Administration*, 35(1): 57–73.

Campbell, J. P., Dunnette, M., Lawler, E., and Weick, K. (1970) *Managerial Behavior, Performance and Effectiveness*. New York: McGraw-Hill.

Churchill, G. A. and Surprenant, C. (1982) 'An Investigation into the Determinants of Customer Satisfaction', *Journal of Marketing Research*, 19(4): 491–504.

Courty, Pascal and Marschke, Gerald R. (2004) 'An Empirical Investigation of Gaming Responses to Pperformance Incentives', *Journal of Labor Economics*, 22(1): 23–56.

Deming, W. Edwards (1986) *Out of the Crisis*. Cambridge, MA: MIT Institute for Advanced Engineering Study.

DeNisi, Angelo S. (2000) 'Performance Appraisal and Performance Management', in Katherine J. Klein and Steve W. J. Kozlowski (eds), *Multilevel Theory, Research, and Methods in Organizations: Foundations, Extensions and New Directions*. San Francisco: Jossey-Bass.

Dixit, Avinash (1999) 'Incentives and Organizations in the Public Sector: An Interpretive Review'. Paper presented at the National Academy of Sciences Conference, Devising Incentives to Promote Human Capital, Irvine, CA.

Drucker, Peter F. (1954) *The Practice of Management*. New York: Harper.

Feldman, Martha S. and Khademian, Anne M. (2000) 'Managing for Inclusion: Balancing Control and Participation', *International Public Management Journal*, 3: 149–167.

Gore, Al (1993) *Creating a Government that Works Better and Costs Less*. New York: Penguin Books.

Gormley, William T. and Weimer, David L. (1999) *Organizational Report Cards*. Cambridge, MA: Harvard University Press.

Gulick, Luther and Urwick, L. (1937) *Papers on the Science of Administration*. New York: Institute of Public Administration, Columbia University.

Halachmi, Arie (1995) 'Is TQM Ready for the Public Sector?', in Arie Halachmi and Geert Bouckaert (eds), *Public Productivity Through Quality and Strategic Management*. Amsterdam: IOS Press.

Hatry, Harry P. (1999) *Performance Measurement: Getting Results*. Washington, DC: The Urban Institute Press.

Heckman, James, Heinrich Carolyn, and Smith, Jeffrey (2002) 'The Performance of Performance Standards', *Journal of Human Resources*, 37(4): 778–811.

Heinrich, Carolyn J. (2002) 'Outcomes-based Performance Management in the Public Sector: Implications for Government Accountability and Effectiveness,' *Public Administration Review*, 62(6): 712–725.

Heinrich, Carolyn J. (2007) 'False or Fitting Recognition? The Use of High Performance Bonuses in Motivating Organizational Achievements', *Journal of Policy Analysis and Management*, 26(2): 281–304.

Heinrich, Carolyn J. and Lynn, Laurence E., Jr (eds) (2000) *Governance and Performance: New Perspectives*. Washington, DC: Georgetown University Press.

Heinrich, Carolyn J. and Marschke, Gerald R. (2010) 'Incentives and Their Dynamics in Public Sector Performance Management Systems', *Journal of Policy Analysis and Management*, 29(1): 183–208.

Hill, Carolyn J. (2006) 'Casework Job Design and Client Outcomes in Welfare-to-Work Offices', *Journal of Public Administration Research and Theory*, 16(2): 263–288.

Hoover Commission Report (1949). New York: McGraw-Hill Book Company, Inc.

Jacob, Brian A. (2005) 'Accountability, Incentives and Behavior: Evidence from School Reform in Chicago', *Journal of Public Economics*, 89: 761–796.

Jacob, Brian A. and Levitt, Steven D. (2003) 'Rotten Apples: An Investigation of the Prevalence and Predictors of Teacher Cheating', *Quarterly Journal of Economics*, 118(3): 843–877.

Kaboolian, Linda (1998) 'The New Public Management: Challenging the Boundaries of the Management vs. Administration Debate', *Public Administration Review*, 58(3): 189–193.

Kamensky, John M. (1993) 'Program Performance Measures: Designing a System to Manage for Results', *Public Productivity and Management Review*, 16(4): 395–402.

Kelly, Janet M. (2005) 'The Dilemma of the Unsatisfied Customer in a Market Model of Public Administration', *Public Administration Review*, 65(1): 76–84.

Kelly, Rita Mae (1998) 'An Inclusive Democratic Polity, Representative Bureaucracies, and the New Public Management', *Public Administration Review*, 58(3): 201–208.

Kettl, Donald F. and DiIulio, John J. (eds) (1995) *Inside the Reinvention Machine*. Washington, DC: The Brookings Institution.

Khademian, Anne M. (1995) 'Reinventing a Government Corporation: Professional Priorities and a Clear Bottom Line,' *Public Administration Review*, 55(1): 17–28.

Koretz, Daniel (1999) 'Foggy Lenses: Limitations in the Use of Achievement Tests as Measures of Educators' Productivity'. Paper presented at the National Academy of Sciences Conference, Devising Incentives to Promote Human Capital, Irvine, California.

Laegreid, Per (2000) 'Top Civil Servants under Contract,' *Public Administration Review*, 78(4): 879–896.

Lindblom, Charles (1959) 'The Science of Muddling Through,' *Public Administration Review*, 19(1): 79–88.

Lynn, Laurence E., Jr (1998) 'The New Public Management: How to Transform a Theme into a Legacy', *Public Administration Review*, 58(3): 231–238.

Lynn, Laurence E., Jr, Heinrich, Carolyn J., and Hill, Carolyn J. (2001) *Improving Governance: A New Logic for Research*. Washington, DC: Georgetown University Press.

Marcoulides, George A. and Heck, Ronald H. (1993) 'Organizational Culture and Performance: Proposing and Testing a Model', *Organization Science*, 4(2): 209–225.

Mead, Lawrence M. (2003) 'Performance Analysis', in Mary Clare Lennon and Thomas Corbett (eds), *Policy into Action: Implementation Research and Welfare Reform*. Washington, DC: Urban Institute Press, pp. 107–144.

Mintzberg, Henry (1996) 'Managing Government, Governing Management', *Harvard Business Review*, 74(May/June): 75–83.

Moe, Ronald C. (1982) 'A New Hoover Commission: A Timely Idea or Misdirected Nostalgia?' *Public Administration Review*, 42(3): 270–277.

Moynihan, Donald P. (2008) *The Dynamics of Performance Management: Constructing Information and Reform*. Washington, DC: Georgetown University Press.

Murphy, Kevin R. and Cleveland, Jeanette N. (1995) *Understanding Performance Appraisal: Social,* *Organizational, and Goal-Based Perspectives.* Thousand Oaks, CA: Sage Publications.

Next Steps Report (1998). United Kingdom: Cabinet Office.

Osborne, Stephen P., Boviard, Tony, Martin, Steve, Tricker, Mike, and Waterston, Piers (1995) 'Performance Management and Accountability in Complex Programmes', *Financial Accountability and Management*, 11(1): 19–37.

Pfeffer, Jeffrey (1990) 'Incentives in Organizations: The Importance of Social Relations', in Oliver E. Williamson (ed.), *Organization Theory: From Chester Barnard to the Present and Beyond*. New York: Oxford University Press, pp. 72–97.

Pollitt, Christopher and Bouckaert, Geert (2000) *Public Management Reform: A Comparative Analysis*. Oxford: Oxford University Press.

Radin, Beryl A. (2000a) *Beyond Machiavelli: Policy Analysis Comes of Age*. Washington, DC: Georgetown University Press.

Radin, Beryl A. (2000b) 'The Government Performance and Results Act and the Tradition of Federal Management Reform: Square Pegs in Round Holes?' *Journal of Public Administration Research and Theory*, 10(1): 11–35.

Rainey, Hal G. and Steinbauer, Paula (1999) 'Galloping Elephants: Developing Elements of a Theory of Effective Government Organizations', *Journal of Public Administration Research and Theory*, 9(1): 1–32.

Rivenbark, William C. (ed.) (2001) *A Guide to the North Carolina Local Government Performance Measurement Project*. Chapel Hill, NC: Institute of Government, University of North Carolina at Chapel Hill.

Romzek, Barbara S. (1998) 'Where the Buck Stops: Accountability in Reformed Public Organizations', in Patricia W. Ingraham, James R. Thompson, and Ronald P. Sanders (eds), *Transforming Government: Lessons from the Reinvention Labs*. San Francisco: Jossey-Bass.

Romzek, Barbara S. and Dubnick, Melvin J. (1998) 'Accountability', in Jay M. Shafritz (ed.), *International Encyclopedia of Public Policy and Administration*. Boulder, CO: Westview Press.

Rosenbloom, David H. (1986) *Public Administration: Understanding Management, Politics, and Law in the Public Sector*. New York: Random House.

Scott, W.D., Clothier, R.C., and Spriegel, W.R. (1941) *Personnel Management*. New York: McGraw-Hill.

Simon, Herbert A. (1957) *Administrative Behavior*. New York: Macmillan.

Taylor, Frederick Winslow (1911) *The Principles of Scientific Management*. New York: Harper & Brothers.

Terry, Larry D. (1998) 'Administrative Leadership, Neo-Managerialism, and the Public Management Movement', *Public Administration Review*, 58(3): 194–200.

Thompson, James D. (1967) *Organizations in Action*. New York: McGraw-Hill Book Company.

US Government Accounting Office (1999) 'Managing for Results: Opportunities for Continued Improvements in Agencies' Performance Plans', GAO/AIMD-99-215.

US Government Accounting Office (1997a) 'Managing for Results: Prospects for Effective Implementation of the Government Performance and Results Act', GAO/AIMD-97-113.

US Government Accounting Office (1997b) 'Managing for Results: Analytical Challenges in Measuring Performance,' GAO/AIMD-97-138.

Van Ryzin, Greg (2004) 'Expectations, Performance and Citizen Satisfaction with Urban Services', *Journal of Policy Analysis and Management*, 23(3): 433–448.

Walton, Mary (1986) *The Deming Management Method*. New York: Pedigree Books.

Wilson, Woodrow (1887) 'The Study of Administration', *Political Science Quarterly*, 2(2): 197–222.

3

Strategic Planning and Management

John M. Bryson

Strategic planning and management are increasingly becoming a way of life for public organizations across the globe. They are being relied upon to deal with the five tasks of: organizing effective participation; creating meritorious ideas for mission, goals, strategies, actions, and other strategic interventions; forging the coalition needed to adopt and to implement the changes; implementing the changes in a timely fashion; and building capacity for ongoing implementation, learning, and strategic change (Bryson, 2011: 39–40). In the process, planning and implementation and strategic and operational concerns are becoming better integrated and sometimes fused.

The chapter is in five parts. The first part presents the basic elements of strategic planning, including its attention to the environment, stakeholders, mission, mandates, strategic issues, and strategies. Strategic planning is the basic building block of strategic management, which is described in the second part. The basic approaches to institutionalizing strategic management systems are presented next. In the fourth section current

trends in strategic planning and management are discussed. Finally, a number of conclusions are presented.

STRATEGIC PLANNING

Strategic planning may be defined as 'a deliberative, disciplined effort to produce fundamental decisions and actions that shape and guide what an organization (or other entity) is, what it does, and why it does it' (Bryson, 2011: 7–8). While many authors have suggested generic strategic planning processes (e.g., Nutt and Backoff, 1992; Bryson, 2011; Ackermann and Eden, 2011), this definition implies that strategic planning is not a *single* thing, but instead is an *approach* (or set of approaches) to responding to circumstances that key actors judge require a considered, collective, and often novel response. As an approach, strategic planning consists of a *set* of leadership roles, concepts, procedures, and tools that must be tailored carefully to situations if desirable outcomes are to be achieved (Johnson et al., 2007; Mintzberg et al., 2009). Poister and Streib (1999), in a review summarizing the field of strategic planning and management, assert that strategic planning:

- is concerned with identifying and responding to the most fundamental issues facing an organization;
- addresses the subjective question of purpose and the often competing values that influence mission and strategies;
- emphasizes the importance of external trends and forces as they are likely to affect the organization and its mission;
- attempts to be politically realistic by taking into account the concerns and preferences of internal, and especially external, stakeholders;
- relies heavily on the active involvement of senior-level managers, and sometimes elected officials, assisted by staff support where needed;
- requires the candid confrontation of critical issues by key participants in order to build commitment to plans;
- is action-oriented and stresses the importance of developing plans for implementing strategies;
- focuses on implementing decisions now in order to position the organization favorably for the future.

Strategic planning for organizations has developed primarily in the private sector. This history has been amply documented by others (Eden and Ackermann, 1998; Mintzberg et al., 2009). In the past 30 years, however, public and nonprofit use of strategic planning has grown dramatically. This experience, and a growing body of literature, have indicated that reasonably rational strategic planning approaches either developed in the private sector, or else strongly influenced by them, can help public organizations, as well as communities or other entities, deal in effective ways with their changing environments (e.g., Barzelay and Campbell, 2003; Boyne et al., 2004; Wheeland, 2004; Poister et al., 2011).

In the United States, for example, a majority of municipal and state governments, most nonprofits, and an overwhelming majority of federal agencies and nonprofit organizations,

make use of strategic planning. Strategic planning has been applied principally to public and nonprofit organizations, but applications to communities have increased substantially as well (Poister and Streib, 1994, 2005; Berman and West, 1998). Other nations – and particularly OECD (Organization for Economic Co-operation and Development) countries – also make use to varying degrees of strategic planning concepts, procedures, and tools for public and nonprofit organizations and communities (eg., Faludi and Salet, 2000; Barzelay and Jacobson, 2009; Mazzarra et al., 2011).

When done well, strategic planning offers a number of benefits. Advocates usually point to five main potential benefits. The first is the *promotion of strategic thinking, acting and learning*. The second is *improved decision making*, while the third is *enhanced organizational effectiveness, responsiveness and resilience*. The fourth benefit is *enhanced organizational legitimacy*. And finally, strategic planning can *directly benefit the people involved* by helping them better perform their roles, meet their responsibilities, and enhance teamwork and expertise. There is no guarantee, however, that these benefits will be achieved. For one thing, strategic planning is simply a set of leadership roles, concepts, procedures, and tools that must be applied wisely to specific situations. For another, even when they are applied wisely, there is no guarantee of success.

Beyond that, strategic planning is not always advisable, particularly for an organization facing an immediate crisis (although every crisis should be managed strategically), or when the organization lacks the skills, resources, or commitment by key decision makers to produce a good plan. Such situations embody what may be called 'the paradox of strategic planning': it is most needed where it is least likely to work, and least needed where it is most likely to work (Bryson and Roering, 1988).

It is important to highlight what strategic planning is *not*. Strategic planning is not a substitute for *strategic thinking, acting, and learning*. It may help people do that, but used unwisely may hinder strategic thinking, acting, and learning. Strategic planning is not a substitute for *leadership*. At least some key actors must be committed to the process or it is bound to fail. Said differently, strategic planning is best seen as a leadership tool, where leadership is broadly conceived to include more than top positional leaders. Strategic planning also is not a substitute for an organizational or community *strategy*. Strategies have numerous sources, both planned and unplanned. Strategic planning is likely to result in a statement of organizational or community *intentions*, but what is *realized* in practice will be some combination of what is intended with what emerges along the way (Mintzberg et al., 2009). Finally, strategic planning is not synonymous with what is called *comprehensive planning* for communities in the United States, or has been called *structure planning* or *strategic spatial planning* in Europe. There may be little difference if the agency doing the comprehensive or structure planning is tied directly to governmental decision makers. However, in practice, there may be three significant differences (Bryson, 2011). First, the plans often are prepared to meet legal requirements and must be formulated according to a legally prescribed process with legally prescribed content. As legal instruments, these plans have an important influence. On the other hand, the plans' typical rigidity can conflict with the political process with which public officials must cope. Strategic plans therefore can provide a bridge from legally required and relatively rigid policy statements to actual decisions and operations. Second, comprehensive or structure or strategic spatial plans usually are limited to less than a government's full agenda of roles and responsibilities. For that reason, they may be of less use to key decision makers than strategic planning, which can embrace all of a government's actual and potential roles before deciding why, where, when, and how to act.

Third, as Kaufman and Jacobs (1987) argue, strategic planning on behalf of a community is more action-oriented, more broadly participatory, more emphatic about the need to understand the community's strengths and weaknesses as well as the opportunities and threats it faces, and more attentive to intercommunity competitive behavior. Thus, typically, strategic planning is more comprehensive than comprehensive planning or structure or spatial planning, while at the same time producing a more limited action focus.

STRATEGIC MANAGEMENT

Strategic *planning* is typically distinguished from strategic *management*. Strategic planning is the cornerstone of strategic management, but the latter is a far more encompassing process, 'concerned with managing an organization in a strategic manner on a continuing basis' (Poister and Streib, 1999, 2005; Poister, 2010). Strategic management links strategic planning and implementation across an organization (or other entity) by adding ongoing attention to budgeting, performance measurement, performance management and evaluation, and to feedback relationships among these elements to enhance the fulfillment of mission, meeting of mandates, and sustained creation of public value.

Poister and Streib (1999) present a framework for thinking about strategic management as a process. The framework incorporates seven elements: values, mission and vision; strategic planning; results-oriented budgeting; performance management; strategic measurement; assessment of the internal and external environment; and feedback relationships among these elements. These elements will be discussed briefly in turn.

Values, mission and vision are seen as a central organizing force for strategic management efforts. If consensus can be achieved on these elements among key stakeholders, the creation and operation of a strategic management system will be far easier than it would be otherwise. If consensus is not possible, then the system no doubt will be looser and less integrated. In fact, because consensus on values, mission, and vision is difficult to achieve in many – perhaps most – circumstances, tightly integrated strategic management systems are not particularly common, and probably should not be pursued in most situations.

Strategic planning can be used to help organizations articulate their values, mission and visions and to develop strategic initiatives to realize them in practice. The initiatives must be resourced properly if they are to be implemented effectively. Results-oriented budgeting is one answer to this challenge and is gaining currency throughout the world. Such an approach begins with the organization's strategic agenda, specifies expected outputs or outcomes for each strategy, program, project, or activity, and then links funding to these elements. This sort of budgeting process can be used to garner adequate resources for specific strategic initiatives and to provide incentives to organizational members and other stakeholders to support the strategic agenda (Osborne and Hutchinson, 2004). On the other hand, if this approach to budgeting encounters political resistance, it may not work (West et al., 2009). Alternatively, using strategic planning to establish the agenda and then relying on incremental decision making informed by a strategic sense of direction can work (Poister et al., 2011).

Performance management involves strategies and mechanisms for assigning responsibility for strategic initiatives to specific units and individuals and holding them accountable for results. For example, management by objectives (MBO) systems are widely used for this purpose. Balanced Scorecard (BSC) approaches are gaining attention globally as another method for translating values, mission and vision into measurable and manageable organizational performance. BSC approaches try to 'balance' attention to financial outcomes with attention to outcomes focused on stakeholders' or customers' concerns, crucial internal processes, and the learning and growth of the organization and its employees (Niven, 2008).

Strategic measurement involves the identification and tracking of valid measures of the organization's performance as it attempts to achieve its strategic objectives. Attending to these measures helps chart progress and success, assess whether budget allocations are appropriate and figure out what to do next. Unfortunately, development of valid and politically supported measures can be very difficult for public organizations and often represents an Achilles heel for strategic management systems; unintended and even perverse results can come from using inappropriate measures (Moynihan, 2008; Soss et al., 2011).

These various elements must be pursued in a context of ongoing internal and external monitoring, assessment, and engagement with key stakeholders or they are unlikely to result in wise or politically realistic information, decisions and actions. Adequate feedback across the various system elements is needed for effective learning, adaptation, and leadership to occur (Moynihan, 2008; Patton, 2008, 2011).

The job certainly is not easy and success is hardly guaranteed. Nonetheless, in the United States and many OECD countries, in particular, powerful forces are prompting public organizations to try, if not to fully embrace, strategic management approaches. These forces include growing demands for public accountability, increased legislative oversight, fiscal conservatism, and professional attention to leadership, improved performance and customer service. The idea of 'managing for results' is a rallying point for public management scholars and practitioners. As Poister and Streib (1999: 323) assert:

[In] public agencies of any size and complexity, it is impossible to manage for results without a well developed capacity for strategic management. Indeed, on a macro level, strategic management, with its emphasis on developing and implementing a strategic agenda, is synonymous with managing for results ... . While treatment of more specific tools, such as strategic planning, performance measurement, quality improvement, work process reengineering, and results-based budgeting, has been more prevalent in the public administration literature, strategic management is the central integrative process which gives the organization a sense of direction and assures a concerted effort to achieve strategic goals and objectives.

Although the implementation of strategic management has its difficulties (e.g., Radin, 2006; Barzelay and Jacobson, 2009), the success of this innovation in the United States, in particular, is a marked improvement over previous related efforts (e.g., the Planning, Programming, Budgeting System, and Zero-Based Budgeting). Clearly, there appears to be something quite different about the current situation. Perhaps it is the cumulative experience of prior reform efforts that has led to greater understanding of how to pursue results-oriented management. Perhaps it is an embrace of the rhetoric of business, the language of customer service, and the ideas of Total Quality Management, along with politicians' and professionals' pursuit of downsizing, reengineering and reinvention (Kettl, 2011). Perhaps it is the rise of a 'results-oriented' discourse, dating to the beginnings of the US version of the New Public Management (Hood, 1991), Osborne and Gaebler's best-selling *Reinventing Government* (1992), Vice President Al Gore's *The Gore Report on Reinventing Government* (1993), Moore's *Creating Public Value* (1995), Osborne and Plastrik's *Banishing Bureaucracy* (1997), or Osborne and Hutchinson's *The Price of Government* (2004). Perhaps it is the rise of a new cadre of political leaders and professional managers who feel free to challenge old shibboleths and homilies about the way things are now and always will be. Whatever the causes, managing for results and public strategic management appear to be embedded in US public administration practice in a way they have not before.

STRATEGIC MANAGEMENT SYSTEMS

Experience suggests that it is relatively easy to get a small group of people – say, five to a few hundred – through a strategic planning process. What is more difficult is to embed strategic thinking, acting, and learning throughout an organization, interorganizational network, or community (i.e., small and large cities, counties, regions, or states). Strategic management systems are one means of inducing and linking strategic thinking, acting, and learning throughout an organization or other entity. The systems are meant to *promote* strategic thinking, acting, and learning in appropriate places at appropriate times, to *control* or *guide* the way strategies are implemented, and to foster sustained creation of public value.

Because organizational strategies typically remain fairly stable for long periods of time and then change rather abruptly (Mintzberg et al., 2009), these systems are usually focused more on strategy implementation than on strategy formulation. The systems are thus mostly organizational arrangements for strategically managing the implementation of agreed-upon strategies. Said somewhat differently, these systems are themselves a kind of organizational (or interorganizational, or community) strategy for implementing policies and plans.

At the same time, the systems do usually embody procedures and occasions for routinely reassessing strategies. It is during the reassessment process that new strategies tend to be 'found' or 'formulated'. These strategies typically are present in nascent or emergent form already in the organization. The strategy reassessment process simply raises them to prominence in an incremental, or otherwise nondisruptive, fashion. The 'new' strategies that these systems produce are thus mainly variations on existing themes, rather than new themes. The really big changes, when they occur, usually are either induced from outside via new mandates, new leadership, significant resource shifts, or drastic environmental changes; or else represent the cumulative minor organizational adjustments to persistent environmental pressures – changes in degree – that lead to changes in kind (Crosby and Bryson, 2005; True et al., 2007; Anderson and Harbridge, 2010).

While it is often important to create and maintain a strategic management system, it is also important to guard against the tendency such systems have of driving out wise strategic thinking, acting, and learning – precisely those phenomena that strategic planning and management (at their best) promote. An important guideline therefore should be that whenever any strategic management system (or strategic planning process) threatens to drive out wise strategic thinking, acting, and learning, efforts should be made to change the system (or process) and get back to promoting effective strategic thinking, acting, and learning.

There appear to be six main types of strategic management systems in the United States and other OECD countries, although every strategic management system that I have seen appears to be a hybrid of the six types. The 'types' therefore refer to dominant tendencies. The types are: the layered or stacked units of management model; strategic issues management models; contract models; portfolio management models; collaboration models; and goal or 'benchmark' models. Each will be discussed briefly in turn.

The purpose of *the layered or stacked units of management model* is to effectively link inside and outside environments through development and implementation of an integrated set of strategies across levels and functions of the organization (Poister, 2010). Often the model is applied through public application of the classic, private sector, corporate style 'goals down – plans up' two-cycle strategic planning process. In the first cycle, there is a 'bottom-up' development of strategic plans within a framework of goals, objectives and other guidance established at the top, followed by review and reconciliation at each succeeding level. In the second

cycle, operating plans are developed to implement the strategic plans. In each cycle efforts are made to explicitly, logically, and persuasively relate levels, functions, and inside and outside environments. The process is repeated each year within the general framework established by the organization's grand or umbrella strategies. Every three to five years these overarching strategies are reviewed and modified based on experience, changing conditions, and the emergence of new strategies that were not necessarily planned in advance. In the United States, the Government Performance and Results Act of 1993 and the Government Performance and Results Modernization Act of 2010 are ambitious attempts to establish a sort of layered or stacked units of management system for each Federal agency and for the Executive Branch as a whole. Charlotte, NC, Hampton Roads, VA, and Miami-Dade County, FL, are well-known US local government examples of this general type of strategic management system.

It is precisely this sort of system that is most prone to driving out strategic thinking, acting and learning, which occurs when the system is underpinned by a belief that the future actually can be predicted accurately, is too detached from the messiness of operational reality and is characterized by excessive centralization of power and formality (Roberts and Wargo, 1994; Mintzberg et al., 2009). Such systems are very likely to be blind-sided by events that cannot be predicted and wreak havoc on existing strategies and plans. The systems therefore must be used with extreme caution, since they can take on a life of their own, promote incremental change when major change is needed and serve only the interests of the leaders, managers and planners who wish to resist – not promote – major change.

Strategic issues management systems are the most common form of institutionalized strategic management system in public organizations. These systems do not attempt to integrate strategies across levels and functions to the extent that layered or stacked units of management approaches do. The reason is that most of the issues are on different time frames, involve different constituencies and politics, and do not need to be considered in the light of all other issues. As a result, issues are not managed comprehensively as a set, but instead are dealt with one by one within an overarching framework of organizational mission and strategic goals or objectives. While each issue is managed relatively separately, it is of course necessary to make sure choices in one issue area do not cause trouble in other issue areas. While many public organizations have several task forces in operation at any one time, fewer go the next step to design and use a strategic issues management system. They do not establish an overall framework of organizational mission, goals or policy objectives, systematically seek out issues to address, or make sure their various issues management activities add up to increased organizational effectiveness. Organizational leaders and managers should thus consider establishing a strategic issues management system, keeping in mind that the resulting centralization of certain key decisions at the top is likely to draw the attention and resistance of those who do not want to see power concentrated in that way or who dislike the resulting decisions.

The *contract model* is becoming an increasingly popular approach to institutionalizing strategic planning and management (Osborne and Plastrik, 1997; Van Slyke, 2006). The contract model is employed for much of the planning and delivery of many publicly financed services in the United States and other OECD countries via either public or nonprofit service providers. The model is also used to institutionalize strategic planning and management in US school districts utilizing site-based management. In this model, there is a 'center' that establishes strategic objectives for the jurisdiction or organization as a whole, negotiates contracts with individual units of management, monitors performance, and ensures the integrity of the system. The contract between the center

and a unit outlines the unit's expected performance, indicates the resources it will receive from the center, lists other support the unit can expect from the center, and describes a review and re-negotiation sequence. Within the framework and legal strictures of the contract, general managers of individual units and their staffs are free to do whatever they think is necessary or desirable to ensure adequate performance. The approach allows both the center and the individual units to focus on what is important for them; both are empowered to do their jobs better. In such a system, there would be a strategic plan for the center and one for each of the units. Key system concerns will include the content and approach embodied in the center's plan, the center's difficulties in acquiring adequate information and the difficulties the center may have in exercising control and ensuring accountability when using a large number of contractors (Osborne and Plastrik, 1997; Frederickson and Frederickson, 2006).

In the *portfolio approach* entities of various sorts (programs, projects, products, services, or providers) are arrayed against dimensions that have some strategic importance. The dimensions usually consist of the attractiveness or desirability of the entity (from high to low) and the capability of the organization or community to deliver what is needed. Portfolio methods are quite flexible, in that any dimensions of interest may be arrayed against one another and entities mapped on to the resulting matrix. Portfolio methods also can be used at sub-organizational and supra-organizational levels as well to assess options against strategically important factors (Nutt and Backoff, 1992; Bryson, 2011). Unfortunately, few public and nonprofit organizations or communities use formal portfolio models, even though many probably use portfolio methods informally. The problem, of course, with use of formal models is that they create comparisons that may be troubling for politically powerful actors.

Collaboration models are used to strategically manage the ongoing work of multi-organizational collaborations. The models typically take one of three forms (Provan and Kenis, 2007):

- *participant-governed networks* are the simplest and involve governance by the network members themselves, not by a separate and unique governance entity;
- *lead organization-governed networks* are more centralized, either because the lead organization is the most powerful or legitimate, or to overcome inefficiencies of shared governance; and
- the third form is the *network administrative organization*, in which a separate administrative entity is set up specifically to govern the network and its activities.

Goal or benchmark models also are much 'looser' than the layered or stacked units of management models and are generally applied at the community, regional, or state levels (Bryson, 2011). They are designed to gain reasonable agreement on overarching goals or indicators (benchmarks) toward which relatively independent groups, units, or organizations might then direct their energies. Consensual agreement on goals and indicators thus provides a weak surrogate for the corporate control exercised in layered models. Nonetheless, when agreement can be reached and support for implementation can be generated, the models can work reasonably well. Besides, in the fragmented, shared-power environments in which most public problems are embedded, the approach may be the only viable approach. For example, most community strategic plans are implemented via goal or benchmark models (e.g., Wheeland, 2004). Large numbers of leaders and citizens typically are involved in the process of goal setting and strategy development. Then action plans outline what each organization might do to help implement the strategies and achieve the goals on a voluntary basis. The State of Virginia has pursued a goal or benchmark model for the state (as a place) called *Virginia Performs* for some time (www.vaperfoms.virginia.gov).

Although there are six general types of strategic management systems, any actual system is likely to be a hybrid of all five types. For example, in the State of Virginia as a place the main model is a *goal or benchmark model*. For individual state agencies, however, there is a *layered or stacked units of management model*, but each would also use explicit or implicit *portfolio* methods as well. Different state agencies rely on a *contract model* to manage relationships with various contractors. To the extent that state agencies are involved in various collaborations, *collaboration models* are be used. Strategic issues that cut across state agencies are handled via a *strategic issues management* approach. The question is simply which type dominates at which level.

Each type of system has characteristic strengths and weaknesses. They each represent a different kind of organizational (or interorganizational, or community) strategy for implementing other strategies that are already agreed upon, at least in broad outline. It is also important to remember that each system embodies a set of arrangements that empowers particular actors, makes particular kinds of issues more likely to arise than others, and particular strategies more likely to be pushed than others. Whenever the environment around the system changes to the extent that the system no longer produces effective strategies, the system itself is unlikely to be able to change enough on its own. Instead, typically, the big changes must be forced from the outside in some way, but also find favor in significant ways inside, or the changes are unlikely to occur without significant and damaging dislocations and distress.

CURRENT TRENDS

A variety of trends are apparent that involve the use of public strategic planning and management. The first is that there is an increased emphasis on organizational and community effectiveness worldwide. People understand that their organizations and communities must be effective if important public purposes and the common good are to be advanced. Three trends are apparent as part of this effort: they involve exploring ways to increase *inclusivity*, the *speed* of the process and *systems thinking*. In other words, many people know that the participation of a variety of different kinds of stakeholders is important, and so is achieving a clearer understanding of the system to be improved and how to improve it. It is also apparent, however, that involving more stakeholders and achieving a better understanding of the system can take a great deal of time, so there is also an emphasis on figuring out how to speed up the process. The final trend involves increasing use of strategic planning and management to help on all three fronts, by fusing planning and implementation, and by attending to strategic and operational concerns simultaneously (Poister, 2010). As a result, the number of concepts, procedures and tools that comprise strategic planning and management is increasing because work in a variety of areas is being incorporated into the theory and practice of the field (see Figure 3.1).

The emphasis on *inclusivity* comes from three sources: the need for information, participation and legitimacy (Suchman, 1995; Thomas, 1995). Information is needed from a variety of sources in order to properly inform action. Participation is needed from key stakeholders in order to build understanding and commitment to collective action. Participation also is an important key to fostering active citizenship, which is of growing interest and emphasis. The renewed emphasis on citizenship comes from several sources: a reaction to the often inappropriate emphasis on 'customers' in public management (Denhardt and Denhardt, 2000), a recognition of the importance of social capital to the achievement of broad public purposes (Putnam, 2000), and a desire to reclaim the full meaning of democracy (Boyte, 2004).

First and foremost, increasing inclusivity means finding ways to include the full range of stakeholders. When a multi-organization or multi-unit response is required, this means an increased reliance on the use of partnerships and collaboration (Agranoff, 2007; O'Leary and Bingham, 2009). The explosive

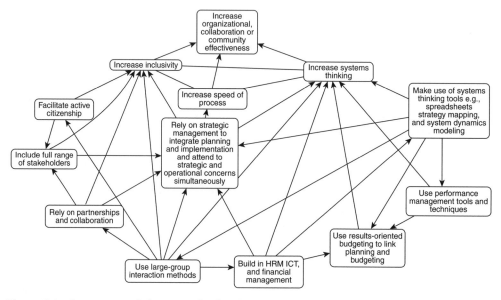

Figure 3.1   Current trends in strategic planning and management

growth of interest in, and use of, large-group interaction methods (Holman, Devane, and Cady, 2007) – such as Future Search (Weisbord and Janoff, 1995), Open Space Technology (Owen, 1997), and Real-Time Strategic Planning (Jacobs, 1994) – also reflects the need to find ways to incorporate large numbers of diverse individuals into the process. Social media open up additional means of being inclusive (e.g., Eggers, 2007; Shirky, 2008). Finally, building in attention to human resource management (HRM), information and communications technology (ICT) and financial management is seen as vital in order to develop viable and self-sustaining 'livelihood schemes' or 'business models' for government organizations (Bryson et al., 2007; Ackermann and Eden, 2011). In the past, when funding typically was more secure, strategic plans were usually prepared without much consideration for their HRM, ICT, and financial management implications; or else separate plans for each function were prepared without adequate attention to the organization's core business. Now it is important that strategic plans and ongoing strategic management reflect the organization or collaborative as an integrated, self-sustaining enterprise. The livelihood schemes or business plans thus become or may be viewed as the core logic animating ongoing strategic planning and management.

The emphasis on *systems thinking* also comes from a number of sources. First, people are increasingly framing their situations in systems terms, and typically at levels that transcend individual organizations (Schon, 1971; Scharmer, 2009). For example, the challenges of elementary and secondary education are being framed in ways that include parents, employers, social services, public health and safety interests, and whole communities. Education generally is seen as an economic development issue, and not just as a matter of personal growth and development. In addition, there is now widespread awareness of the basic elements of the systems view of the world, including attending to the environment, inputs, throughputs,

outputs, and feedback. This awareness facilitates the process of talking in systems terms and increases the expectation that such discourse will occur. And finally, there is awareness that without decent systems thinking there is a high likelihood that the problem will be conceptualized at the wrong level, the wrong problem will be solved, or else the problem will be made worse (Senge, 2006).

Systems thinking is made easier by the increased availability of systems thinking tools, perhaps the most common of which is spreadsheet software (such as Microsoft Excel) loaded onto many kinds of computing devices. Electronic spreadsheets make it possible to develop models of important aspects of systems to understand how they behave in the present and to explore 'what if' scenarios for the future. Beyond that, the use of concept mapping techniques is growing in popularity, including, for example, mind mapping (Buzan and Buzan, 1996) and various kinds of sophisticated strategy mapping (Bryson et al., 2004; Kaplan and Norton, 2004; Ackermann and Eden, 2011). Finally, system dynamics modeling is increasingly widely used (Sterman, 2000). This methodology allows for the creation of very complex quantitative models that can be manipulated to explore the direct and feedback effects over time of numerous policy interventions.

Systems thinking is also assisted by building attention to HRM, ICT, and financial management, using results-oriented budgeting to link planning and budgeting and relying on the range of performance management tools and techniques. The need to accommodate these conceptual pieces of the puzzle is broadly recognized and the development of systems thinking tools and large-group interaction methods now makes it easier to do. While still relatively uncommon, the practice of linking sophisticated systems thinking tools with inclusive participation methods is on the rise.

As noted, the final trend involves *increasing use of strategic planning and management* to help increase *inclusivity*, the *speed* of the process and *systems thinking* by integrating planning and implementation and attending to strategic and operational concerns simultaneously. As a result, strategic planning and management are coming to embrace the entire management process in a way they have not in the past, and the number of leadership roles, concepts, procedures and tools that comprise the field of strategic planning and management is increasing (Poister, 2010). One of the really big challenges these days is figuring out how to be inclusive *and* incorporate systems thinking *and* be quick. Some years ago, Cleveland (1993) described the first part of the challenge as figuring out how to get everyone in on the act and still get some action. The second part of the challenge is figuring out what to do when systems thinking matters. The third part of the challenge is how to do both before it is too late. As noted previously, strategic planning and management must deal with the five tasks of organizing effective participation; creating meritorious ideas for mission, goals, strategies, actions, and other strategic interventions; forging the coalition needed to adopt and to implement the changes; implementing the changes in a timely fashion; and building capacity for ongoing implementation and learning. Inclusion can speed things up when it shortens the time for consultation and re-work. Systems thinking also can speed things up when it leads to prompt and good problem formulation and solution development and to the identification of which stakeholders need to be involved and how. But performing the five tasks well places a real premium on having adequate leadership and management talent and analysis skill on tap, adequate approaches to the strategic planning and management tasks at hand, and adequate institutional designs, relationships and resources available to support the approaches. Identifying or developing models of the talents, skills, designs, and relationships to make strategic planning and management work well in the new circumstances should be high on the academic and practice agendas.

CONCLUSION

First, it should be clear that strategic planning and management represent a range of approaches that vary in their applicability to the public sector and in the conditions that govern their successful use. Second, while any generic approach may be a useful guide to thought and action, it will have to be applied with care in a given situation, as is true of any planning and management process (Johnson et al., 2007). Because every strategic planning and management process should be tailored to fit specific situations, every process in practice will be a hybrid. Third, public sector strategic planning and management are well on the way to becoming part of the standard repertoire of public leaders, managers and planners. Because of the often dramatic changes these people and their organizations confront, we can hypothesize that the most effective leaders, managers and planners are now, and will be increasingly in the future, the ones who are best at *strategic* planning and management.

Fourth, the field of public strategic planning and management is expanding in response to a variety of pressures. As noted in the introduction, people understand that their organizations and communities must be effective if important public purposes and the common good are to be advanced. Increased effectiveness implies a need for increased inclusivity, speed, and systems thinking. Unfortunately, there can be a significant tradeoff between inclusivity and systems thinking, on the one hand, and speed, on the other. Thus, finding ways to enrich and improve strategic planning and management so that gains are made against all three desires simultaneously is and should be an important part of the research and practice agenda.

Along the way, strategic planning and management are incorporating concepts, tools and techniques from a variety of cognate fields. Both the theory and practice are changing to the point that the entire management process is embraced in a way it was not in the past. As a result, planning and implementation and strategic and operational concerns are increasingly fused.

Finally, research must explore a number of theoretical and empirical issues in order to advance the knowledge and practice of public sector strategic planning and management. In particular, strategic planning and management processes that are responsive to different situations must be developed and tested. These processes should: specify key situational factors governing their use; provide specific advice on how to formulate and implement strategies in different situations; be explicitly political; indicate how to deal with plural, ambiguous, or conflicting goals or objectives; link content, process, tools, and techniques; indicate how collaboration as well as competition are to be handled; and specify roles for those involved in the process. Other topics in need of attention include: the nature of strategic leadership; ways to promote and institutionalize strategic planning across organizational levels, functions that bridge organizational boundaries, and intra- and interorganizational networks; and the ways in which HRM, ICT and financial management concepts and technologies can help or hinder the process. Finally, work is needed on how strategic planning and management ought to be pursued in order to strengthen *democratic* institutions, citizenship, responsiveness and accountability. Progress has been made on all of these fronts, but more work clearly is necessary if we are to understand better when and how to use strategic planning and management (Bryson, 2010; Bryson et al., 2010; Poister, 2010; Poister et al., 2010).

REFERENCES

Ackermann, F., & Eden, C. (2011). *Making strategy: Mapping out strategic success.* Thousand Oaks, CA: SAGE.

Agranoff, R. (2007). *Managing within networks: Adding value to public organizations.* Washington, DC: Georgetown University Press.

Anderson, S., & Harbridge, L. (2010). Incrementalism in appropriations: Small aggregations, big changes. *Public Administration Review,* 70, 464–474.

Barzelay, M., & Campbell, C. (2003). *Preparing for the future: Strategic planning in the U.S. Air Force.* Washington, DC: Brookings Institution Press.

Barzelay, M., & Jacobsen, A. S. (2009). Theorizing implementation of public management policy reforms: A case study of strategic planning and programming in the European Commission. *Governance,* 22(2), 319–334.

Berman, E., & West, J. P. (1998). Productivity enhancement efforts in public and nonprofit organizations. *Public Productivity and Management Review,* 22(2), 207–219.

Boyne, G. A., Gould-Williams, J. S., Law, J., & Walker, R. M. (2004). Problems of rational planning in public organizations: An empirical assessment of the conventional wisdom. *Administration and Society,* 36(3), 328–350.

Boyte, H. C. (2004). *Everyday politics: Reconnecting citizens and public life.* Philadelphia, PA: University of Pennsylvania Press.

Bryson, J. M. (2010). The future of strategic planning. *Public Administration Review,* 70(Suppl), S255–S267.

Bryson, J. M. (2011). *Strategic planning for public and nonprofit organizations,* 4th edn. San Francisco, CA: Jossey-Bass.

Bryson, J. M., & Roering, W. D. (1988). Initiation of strategic planning by governments. *Public Administration Review,* 48(November/December), 995–1004.

Bryson, J. M., Ackermann, F., & Eden, C. (2007). Putting the resource-based view of strategy and distinctive competencies to work in public organizations. *Public Administration Review,* 67(4), 702–717.

Bryson, J. M., Ackermann, F., Eden, C., & Finn, C. (2004). *Visible thinking: Unlocking causal mapping for practical business results.* New York: Wiley.

Bryson, J. M., Berry, F. S., & Yang, K. (2010). The state of public strategic management research: A selective literature review and set of future directions. *American Review of Public Administration,* 40(5), 495–521.

Buzan, Tony & Buzan, Barry (1993). *The mind map book: How to use radiant thinking to maximize your brain's untapped potential.* London: BBC Books/Plume.

Cleveland, H. (1993). *Birth of a new world: An open moment for international leadership.* San Francisco, CA: Jossey-Bass.

Crosby, B. C., & Bryson, J. M. (2005). *Leadership for the common good: Tackling public problems in a shared-power world,* 2nd edn. San Francisco, CA: Jossey-Bass.

Denhardt, R., & Denhardt, J. (2000). The new public service: Serving rather than steering. *Public Administration Review,* 60, 549–559.

Eden, C., & Ackermann, F. (1998). *Making strategy: The journey of strategic management.* Thousand Oaks, CA: Sage.

Eggers, W. D. (2007). *Government 2.0.* Latham, MD: Rowman and Littlefield.

Faludi, A., & Salet, W. (eds) (2000). *The revival of spatial strategic planning in Europe.* Amsterdam: Royal Netherlands Academy of Science.

Frederickson, D. G., & Frederickson, H. G. (2006). *Measuring the performance of the hollow state.* Washington, DC: Georgetown University Press.

Gore, Al., Jr (1993). *The Gore Report on Reinventing Government.* New York: Times Books.

Holman, P., Devane, T., & Cady, S. (2007). *The change handbook: Group methods for shaping the future.* San Francisco, CA: Berrett-Koehler Publishers.

Hood, C. (1991). A public management for all seasons? *Public Administration,* 69(Spring), 3–19.

Jacobs, R. W. (1994). *Real-time strategic change: How to involve an entire organization in fast and far-reaching change.* San Francisco, CA: Berrett-Koehler Publishers.

Johnson, G., Langley, A., Melin, L., & Whittington, R. (2007). *Strategy as practice: Research directions and resources.* New York: Cambridge University Press.

Kaplan, R. S., & Norton, D. P. (2004). *Strategy maps: Converting intangible assets into tangible outcomes.* Boston, MA: Harvard Business School Press.

Kaufman, J. L., & Jacobs, H. M. (1987). A public planning perspective on strategic planning. *Journal of the American Planning Association,* Winter, 23–33.

Kettl, D. (2011). *The politics of the administrative process,* 4th edn. Washington, DC: CQ Press.

Mazzara, L., Siboni, B., & Sangiorgi, D. (2011). Strategic planning practices in Italian local governments: What compliance with the European recommendations? *7th Transatlantic Dialogue on Public Administration,* Rutgers University School of Public Affairs, Newark, NJ.

Mintzberg, H., Ahlstrand, B., & Lampel, J. (2009). *Strategy safari: A guided tour through the wilds of strategic management,* 2nd edn. London: Financial Times/Prentice Hall.

Moore, M. H. (1995). *Creating public value.* Cambridge, MA: Harvard University Press.

Moynihan, D. P. (2008). *The dynamics of performance management.* Washington, DC: Georgetown University Press.

Niven, P. R. (2008). *Balanced scorecard step-by-step for government and nonprofit agencies,* 2nd edn. New York: Wiley.

Nutt, P. C., & Backoff, Robert W. (1992). *Strategic management of public and third sector organizations: A handbook for leaders.* San Francisco, CA: Jossey-Bass.

O'Leary, R., & Bingham, L. B. (eds) (2009). *The collaborative public manager.* Washington, DC: Georgetown University Press.

Osborne, D., & Gaebler, Ted (1992). *Reinventing government.* Reading, MA: Addison-Wesley.

Osborne, D., & Hutchinson, P. (2004). *The price of government: Getting the results we need in an age of permanent fiscal crisis.* New York: Basic Books.

Osborne, D., & Plastrik, P. (1997). *Banishing bureaucracy: The five strategies for reinventing government.* Reading, MA: Addison-Wesley.

Owen, H. (1997). *Open space technology: A user's guide,* 2nd edn. San Francisco, CA: Berrett-Koehler Publishers.

Patton, M. Q. (2008). *Utilization-focused evaluation,* 4th edn. Thousand Oaks, CA: Sage.

Patton, M. Q. (2011). *Developmental evaluation: Applying complexity concepts to enhance innovation and use.* New York: The Guildford Press.

Poister, T. H. (2010). The future of strategic planning in the public sector: Linking strategic management and performance. *Public Administration Review,* 70(Special Issue), S246–254.

Poister, T. H., & Streib, G. (1994). Municipal management tools from 1976 to 1993: An overview and update. *Public Productivity and Management Review,* 18(2), 115–125.

Poister, T. H., & Streib, G. D. (1999). Strategic management in the public sector: Concepts, models, and processes. *Public Productivity and Management Review,* 22(3), 308–325.

Poister, T. H., & Streib, G. (2005). Elements of strategic management in municipal government: Evidence after two decades. *Public Administration Review,* 65(1), 45–56.

Poister, T. H., Pitt, D., & Edwards, L. (2010). Strategic management research in the public sector: A review, synthesis, and future directions. *American Review of Public Administration,* 40(5), 522–545.

Poister, T. H., Edwards, L. H., & Pasha, O. (2011). The impact of strategy content and development on performance in public local transit agencies. *Annual*

Conference of the Public Management Research Association, Maxwell School of Citizenship and Public Affairs, Syracuse University, Syracuse, NY, 2–4 June 2011.

Provan, K. G., & Kenis, P. (2007). Modes of network governance: Structure, management, and effectiveness. *Journal of Public Administration Research and Theory*, 18, 229–252.

Putnam, R. D. (2000). *Bowling alone: The collapse and revival of American community*. New York: Simon and Schuster.

Radin, B. A. (2006). *Challenging the performance movement: Accountability, complexity and democratic values*. Washington, DC: Georgetown University Press.

Roberts, N. C., & Wargo, L. (1994). The dilemma of planning in large-scale public organizations: The case of the United States Navy. *Journal of Public Administration Research and Theory*, 4(4), 469–491.

Scharmer, C. O. (2009). *Theory U: Leading from the future as it emerges*. San Francisco, CA: Berrett-Koehler Publishers.

Schon, D. A. (1971). *Beyond the stable state*. New York: W.W. Norton & Company.

Senge, P. M. (2006). *The fifth discipline: The art of practice of the learning organization,* 2nd edn. New York: Doubleday.

Shirky, C. (2008). *Here comes everybody: The power of organizing without organizations*. New York: Penguin.

Soss, J., Fording, R. C., & Schram, S. F. (2011). The organization of discipline: From performance management to perversity and punishment. *Journal of Public Administration and Theory*, 21, 203–232.

Sterman, J. (2000). *Business dynamics: Systems thinking and modeling for a complex world*. New York: Irwin/McGraw-Hill.

Suchman, M. C. (1995). Managing legitimacy: Strategic and institutional approaches. *Academy of Management Review*, 20(3), 571–610.

Thomas, J. C. (1995). *Public participation in public decisions*. San Francisco, CA: Jossey-Bass.

True, J. L., Jones, B. D., & Baumgartner, F. R. (2007). Punctuated equilibrium theory: Explaining stability and change in public policy making, in P. A. Sabatier (ed.), *Theories of the policy process*. Boulder, CO: Westview Press, pp. 155–187.

Van Slyke, D. M. (2006). Agents or stewards: Using theory to understand the government–nonprofit social service contracting relationship. *Journal of Public Administration Research and Theory*, 17, 157–187.

Weisbord, M., & Janoff, Sandra (1995). *Future search*. San Francisco: Berrett-Koehler Publishers.

West, W. F., Lindquist, E., & Mosher-Howe, K. A. (2009). NOAA's resurrection of program budgeting: Deja vu all over again? *Public Administration Review*, 69, 435–447.

Wheeland, C. M. (2004). *Empowering the vision: Community-wide strategic planning in Rock Hill, SC*. Lanham, MD: University Press of America.

PART 2

Human Resource Management

edited by Patricia W. Ingraham

BACKGROUND

In many nations, human resource management (HRM) – personnel or civil service systems in the old terminology – has changed profoundly in the past two decades. From a theoretical perspective, the management of public employees and the institutions of the public service have moved from being treated as mechanistic add-ons to the machinery of government to being viewed as powerful policy institutions in their own right, from bland personnel systems to highly valued human capital management endeavors, and from neutral bureaucracies to active participants in the policy process and targets of policy reform.

In the process, some things about the formerly rigid structure have changed as well. The centralized, rule-bound structures commonly associated with traditional civil service systems are in early stages of morphing into more decentralized, flexible systems. They place greater emphasis on management and leadership than on process and procedure, though process and procedure and the

structures that support them have certainly not gone away. It is well recognized that these structures are not impermeable, but are open to politics, other sectors, and various other environmental influences. While some of the more dramatic reforms were driven by concerns for improved performance and accountability, others emerged from simple economics. Public employees are often the single greatest expense in a ministry or departmental budget; cutting the numbers of public employees is a clear and direct attack on cost. Whether under the flag of reinvention, New Public Management, or budget cutting, human resource management reforms have altered roles, numbers, structures, expectations and rewards of national civil service systems.

The patterns of the changes, however, are difficult to describe tidily. This is clearly demonstrated by the chapters in this section. Discretionary reforms – those granting greater flexibilities to managers and public entities – most often occur in Western industrial nations and Westminster democracies. Other nations in the world – those in Eastern

Europe, for example – continue to struggle to create new structures and institutions to replace the crumbled remains of Communist years. In these cases, the new structures often look remarkably like old bureaucracies. Other nations follow this pattern – many in Latin and South America, for example – and argue that centralized institutions must become a part of the political culture before decentralization can occur. Flexibility and discretion can potentially combat structural dysfunction, reformers from this perspective note, but structure and stability are necessary antecedents to the flexibility reforms blossoming in more developed nations. Blatant corruption and patronage are reasons commonly cited by those who advocate the creation of traditional civil service structures as the first step toward reform.

THEORETICAL PERSPECTIVES FOR ANALYSIS

For much of the past century, Western civil service systems were structured and viewed as technical appendages to the other institutions of government, rather than as institutions in their own right (Bekke et al., 1997). This perspective was based to a large extent on the premise that politics and administration were separable. The reality of contemporary policymaking, however, coupled with the recognition of the power base that control of human resources represents, challenged that premise. Clearly, the separation provided by differences in politics and administration – while real and alluring for its simplicity – masks enormous complexity and leads to myriad problems in the search for change and reform.

MODELS FOR COMPARISON

Despite the complexity and disparity in reform efforts across the world, several patterns or models for managing and leading the human capital of government can be identified. None of the moels is 'pure'; there are numerous variations on a theme, but, overall, there are least four. The first, not surprisingly, is the traditional civil service model: a closed hierarchical system designed to be neutral and to exclude inappropriate political influence, to admit personnel based on testing and expertise, and to reward and dismiss based on merit. It is now commonly noted that protection and process are hallmarks of the traditional model, and that performance is, at best, an afterthought (Ingraham, 1995; Bekke et al., 1997; Pollitt and Bouckaert, 2000). The promise the model delivers is one of stability, efficiency and order.

A variation on the civil service model, but one that does not reject the traditional structures per se, can be termed the strategic human resources model (Kettl et al., 1996). Underpinning this model is the recognition that civil service systems and constraints frequently inhibit governments and their employees from responding to new challenges, but also keep governments from utilizing and rewarding public employees in the most effective way. The model's basic assumption is that the capacity for strategic management resides in the traditional model, but needs to be coaxed out.

Alternative compensation structures, variations on traditional classification structures and some decentralization of authority from a central office to individual agencies are generally included in strategic HR reforms. It is important to note, however, that many of these reforms proceed from the additional assumption that traditional structures can be altered incrementally at the edges to achieve new objectives. It is not unusual, therefore, to find strategic human resource management objectives being pursued from within the old structures. The United States is a leading example of this approach.

A third, more limited model advocated for public employee systems is the human capital model (Walker, 2000). Based on the perception (real in some cases) that governments need to compete for employees in what is fundamentally a 'War for Talent' and expertise, the human capital model urges that human resources be viewed as critical strategic resources to be developed, not as sunk costs to the organization (McKinsey, 1998). This perspective has become more widespread as the demand for more complex technological talents has increased, as third-party government has became more pervasive, and as governments have encountered more and more difficulty in recruiting and retaining qualified employees (OECD Public Management Service, 2001). The human capital model is notable in that it places human resource management at the very center of strategic agency direction and management.

Finally, it is important to note the presence of an enduring influence on public management systems – the private sector. This general model strongly advocates the emulation of private sector techniques in public organizations. Thus, pay for performance, different bargaining authority for public sector unions, greater emphasis on leadership, and much stronger emphasis on overall internal flexibilities and decentralizaation emerged as 'positive' characterisitics of reformed public organizations. Certainly, New Public Management falls squarely into this category.

COMMON CHALLENGES

These general models emerged and persevered as leaders and managers in government faced a set of challenges quite different from those of early civil service years. One of the most important of these was the need to move from pact to performance: that is, from protection of employees and guarantees of security to an emphasis on performance that placed the burden on the employee, not on the government employer. Pay for performance, performance contracts and downsizing were common responses here.

So commonplace as to be nearly inherent in reform discussions, pay for performance is a policy tool whose popularity has not been diminished by very modest success. Other common reforms in those intended to reshape the public workforce – smaller, more flexible core workforces, seasonal or temporary workers, contract employees and even permanent employees who do not view government as their long-term career choice – both shape and are shaped by governments' emerging analysis of workforce needs. This new workforce context has also led to significant challenging of the 'government as model employer' idea. The emerging idea is that government must restructure and redesign many human resource functions so that it can be a competitive employer. Sally Coleman Selden's chapter discusses general patterns and trends in recruiting and retaining a highly qualified and able public service. What are current trends in recruitment, retention and in performance management in nations that have addressed these issues? Selden finds more flexible recruiting tools, a heightened sense of the need to be an effective recruiter, increased use of both recruitment and retention bonuses, a new focus on workforce planning, and a growing awareness of – if not complete adherence to – principles of performance management.

New examinations of the role of public sector unions and collective bargaining are also common reform themes. The 'partnerships' that evolved from reinventing government are one manifestation. James Thompson's excellent chapter provides a rare and very useful summary of the current state of collective bargaining arrangements across the world, detailing the differences among those nations whose political and institutional history allowed consensualist patterns of cooperation between public unions and the leaders and managers of government, and those nations with a fundamentally confrontational labor/management relationship. He asks, 'What is the current practice and future outlook of collective bargaining and unions?'

He examines the potential and the experience with collaboration versus confrontation and explores the potential for the partnership model so favored by reinvention efforts. Finally, he queries: Is a more complete reconfiguration of the relationship between employer and employee either necessary or likely?

An additional challenge underpins all of those just described. As governments subcontract or outsource many of their activities – including core functions, in some cases – they increasingly manage a 'shadow' or 'hollow' workforce (Milward and Provan, 1999). Contract employees are not technically government employees, but responsibility and accountability for the jobs they do often remains with the employees who monitor the contracts – the contract managers of government. Many core human resource management functions are among those on the frequently contracted list: management of retirement benefits is one example. Training provision is also a very frequent contract activity. Managing contractors, particularly when they are providing services that shape the nature and skills of government employees, is an increasingly critical activity. The struggles to balance accountability with the reality of authority and control is manifested to a large extent in the recent attention focused on the roles and responsibilities of public leaders. Senior executive corps, performance contracts, new recruiting patterns and new definitions of how leaders should 'look' are thoughtfully described and critiqued by John Halligan, in a chapter that is an important update to emerging views of public leadership. Halligan explores the nature and characters of several national leadership cadres, identifies and examines models of leadership development and asks the extent to which these models contain fundamental components of learning for effective leadership, such as the capacity to change.

Jørgen Grønnegaard Christensen explores leadership – political and administrative – from other perspectives, examining comparative executive pay through a variety of theoretical lenses. In a far-reaching analysis, he concludes that neither pure market nor pure political explanations suffice to explain variations in executive pay. Neither are there simple categories for the variation. Instead, Christensen finds persistent cross-national differences in countries otherwise alike, and inconsistent developments in countries that are otherwise similar. Concluding that theoretical explanations fall far short of explaining such diversity, he also notes that 'paying for good governance' is a constant policy challenge for all nations, no matter their level of political or economic development. The declining levels of executive compensation in many nations can be attributed, he says, to a lack of political consensus about the value that good learns bring, perhaps even worse, to an exclusion of this issue from political discourse and debate.

Finally, Donald Moynihan looks at developments in overall government performance and governance with an eye toward implications for human resource management. His careful review of research related to the antecedents of performance leads him to conclude that the research may be increasingly rigorous, but this is not necessarily leading to a better understanding of what matters, when and how. Performance management, for example, does not lead to better performance in all cases. For HRM, he notes, '... overall performance systems have promise, but cannot be regarded as a certain contributor to performance.' His thorough and thoughtful discussion of the other variables that can have a potential impact on performance concludes that research in the past decade has altered the way in which we define and consider HRM. Certainly, though there is still a proclivity toward 'one size fits all' practices and potential solutions, there is a new set of 'prove it' challenges.

No brief explanation of the complexities of managing modern public services could cover the subject adequately. In combination, however, the chapters in this section provide both overviews and incisive analysis of broad issues, relevant comparisons and lessons learned thus far – and the long road that is ahead.

REFERENCES

Bekke, Hans, Perry, James, and Toonen, Theo (1997) *Civil Service Reform in Comparative Perspective.* Bloomington, IN: Indiana University Press.

Ingraham, Patricia W. (1995) *The Foundation of Merit: Public Service in American Democracy.* Baltimore, MD: Johns Hopkins University Press.

Kettl, Donald F., Ingraham, Patricia W., Sanders, Ronald P., and Horner, Constance (1996) *Civil Service Reform: Building a Government That Works.* Washington, DC: Brookings Institution.

McKinsey Group (1998) 'The War for Talent', *The McKinsey Quarterly*, 3: 44–57.

Milward, H. Brinton and Provan, Keith (1999) 'How Networks are Governed'. Paper Delivered at the Fifth National Public Management Conference, Texas A&M University, December.

OECD Public Management Service (2001) *Report of the Committee on Public Workforce Issues.* Paris: OECD.

Pollitt, Christopher and Bouckaert, Geert (2000) *Public Management Reform: A Comparative Analysis.* Oxford: Oxford University Press.

Walker, David O. (2000) *Creating Human Capital Value for Government.* Washington, DC: PricewaterhouseCoopers.

4

Identifying the Antecedents to Government Performance: Implications for Human Resource Management

Donald P. Moynihan

INTRODUCTION

To say that public organizations are under more pressure than ever to demonstrate performance is a cliché, but like many clichés it is grounded in reality. As many chapters in this book demonstrate, governments have sought to reform, measure and even privatize services. The central goal of these efforts is to increase government performance. The human resource area is not exempt from such pressures. If the traditional purview of human resource management (HRM) systems were to prevent corruption and instill norms of honest behavior, they are now called upon to be change agents that increase performance.

Where is the field of HRM to find systematic knowledge on the actual predictors of government performance? A nascent empirical literature provides some answers.

This chapter summarizes some of the key findings from this literature, and considers the HR implications that result.

The chapter organizes findings into three broad categories: people (which examines motivation, leadership, and networking efforts), systems (which examines performance management systems, goal clarity, strategic stance, and organizational culture), and rules (which focuses on red tape, centralization, and organizational stability). This review is selective rather than comprehensive, focusing on aspects of the organization subject to the control of HRM systems, and on variables where a critical mass of research offers substantive new findings.

First, however, the basic concept of government performance, as represented in this empirical literature, is examined in greater detail.

THE CONCEPT OF GOVERNMENT PERFORMANCE IN EMPIRICAL RESEARCH

In the late 1990s and early 2000s a number of scholars helped to frame a new research agenda on government performance (Boyne, 2003; Heinrich and Lynn, 2000: Ingraham, Joyce and Donahue, 2003; O'Toole and Meier, 1999; Rainey and Steinbauer, 1999). These works shared some central assumptions. First, government performance was not just a legitimate variable to study, but that it was the most pressing variable for public management scholars; second, there was variation between high- and low-performing public organizations that could be measured; third, that public managers and management variables contributed to performance, and their contributions should be explored via social science research methods.

The emergence of this research agenda parallels the evidence-based policy movement in the broader fields of policy analysis and medicine (Heinrich, 2007). The essential logic for these approaches is the same, in that they demand that academics, analysts, and professionals recommending a certain course of action be able to demonstrate rigorous evidence that such actions make a difference to important outcomes. But while policy and health scholars have a record of employing evaluations and experimental methods to isolate the impact of a particular practice, an equivalent research record does not exist in the field of public management, and researchers there must grapple with some basic problems.

A fundamental challenge is defining and measuring performance. The empirical literature examined in this chapter relies on quantitative studies that in turn depend upon some measure of performance, and a concrete conceptualization of the variable. A basic issue for public organizations is that they pursue multiple goals, and performance is not unidimensional. Just as actual government measures of performance tend to be more attentive to certain values than others (Boyne, 2002), most of the empirical studies of public sector performance utilize one or a very small number of performance indicators that generally focus on effectiveness. If we assume that there are likely to be low or even negative correlations between some competing conceptualizations of performance, factors associated with one aspect of performance may not necessarily be associated with others. For example, the nature or significance of the antecedents of Texas schools performance has been found to vary depending on which particular measure of performance is actually utilized (Meier and Hicklin, 2008; Nicholson-Crotty, Theobold, and Nicholson-Crotty, 2006).

Another basic measurement challenge is a dearth of reliable and comparable indicators across a broad range of organizations. One exception is the policy area of education, where performance indicators such as student exam performance are generally measured in the same way across a range of local governments. Not coincidentally, education is the dominant policy area represented in performance studies, with a particular representation of research utilizing the Texas Education Excellence Project. Other data is more subjective, in that it represents the opinion or aggregation of opinions of a group of individuals. For many studies, indicators of performance rely on perceptual indicators by employees (such as the National Administrative Studies Project, or US federal employee datasets). Such assessments run the risk of an upward response bias, and a common source bias if the independent variables are sourced from the same surveys that collect the dependent variables. In other cases, external stakeholder perceptions are used. The credibility of such data depends upon the independence and rigor of the evaluations. Many UK analyses of local government performance have relied upon assessments completed by the Audit Commission (Andrews et al., 2005). Program performance scores completed by the Bush administration's Office of Management and

Budget for the Program Assessment Rating Tool program have been similarly used (Lewis, 2008), but have been criticized as being partly shaped by partisan preferences (Gilmour and Lewis, 2006).

The underlying message is that the credibility of the research, and the actual antecedents of performance, may vary with the type of measure used. This is true even when using 'objective' indicators. Such indicators have been chosen by actors in the policy process to represents a particular perspective (Moynihan, 2008a), and, as noted above, one objective indicator may result in a different insight about performance than another.

As the above paragraphs suggest, the development of an empirical research agenda on government performance has sought rigor as well as relevance, favoring quantitative techniques and increasingly sophisticated models. This is all to the good in that it has raised the standard of research on the topic. But since no empirical approach is perfect, a concern for methodological nuance also characterizes the field, causing scholars to offer more qualified and less sweeping statements than a previous generation of research.

PEOPLE

HRM systems are ultimately tasked with managing the performance of people. Some studies have sought to link individual characteristics with organizational performance (Brewer and Selden, 2000; Kim, 2005). One obvious problem with this approach is aggregating individual attributes to organizational outcomes. If, for example, we find that individual satisfaction is positively correlated with the same individual's assessment of organizational performance (Kim, 2005), it raises the question of whether the finding tells us that happier employees are more likely to rate their organization better, or that more satisfied employees collectively work to actually make their organizations more

effective. In trying to make the link between individual traits and performance, we focus on factors that enjoy significant theoretical and empirical support. In this section, the roles of individual motivation, leadership, and networking are examined.

Motivation

One aspect of employee behavior subject to consistent theoretical and empirical analysis is motivation. More motivated employees are generally expected to raise the performance of their organization. In public management scholarship the most compelling examination of motivation has been the research literature on public service motivation (PSM). PSM is conceptualized as an individual predisposition toward the public interest and desire to help others, and in its original articulation was hypothesized as being positively associated with performance (Perry and Wise, 1990). A limited number of studies have sought to test this hypothesis, using measures of individual and organizational performance as dependent variables. The results of these analyses vary somewhat, and suggest mediating factors, but in general support the idea that PSM is associated with higher public performance.

Before we examine these studies, why should PSM be associated with performance in a public context? There are a number of reasons. Individuals with high PSM may care more about the basic mission of the organization and hold a desire to help others. As a result, such individuals are likely to work harder toward that mission, going above and beyond role expectations, and be less likely to require pecuniary incentives for their effort (Perry and Wise, 1990).

Brewer and Selden (1998) found higher levels of PSM among whistleblowers in US federal government. This implies that PSM is associated with forms of ethical behavior that help to provide for aspects of performance that are related to good governance, such as transparency and honesty. Naff and Crum (1999) found a positive relationship between US federal employee PSM and employee reports of their most recent federal performance appraisal score. However, using a different model specification, Alonso and Lewis (2001) did not find such a relationship with this data.

Other studies have suggested that there is a link between PSM and individual performance, but that it is at least partly mediated by an individual's perception that their values are shared by their organization. These studies propose that PSM will only motivate individuals to perform better if the employee sees a link between their desire to help others and the work they actually perform. In a study of US organizations, Bright (2007) found that person–organization fit did indeed mediate the impact of PSM on self-reported performance appraisals scores. A study of Dutch civil servants that asked respondents to assess their performance relative to peers also found such a mediating impact, but still found a separate positive effect between PSM and performance even when employees did not feel a strong connection with their work environment (Leisink and Steijn, 2009).

Rather than use measures of self-reported individual performance, some work has sought to link PSM with employee attitudes that have been found to be predictive of performance. PSM has been shown to predict organizational commitment, job satisfaction, and job involvement (Crewson, 1997; Kim, 2005; Leisink and Steijn, 2009; Moynihan and Pandey, 2007a). PSM has also been hypothesized as predicting greater focus on mission (Perry and Wise, 1990; Rainey and Steinbauer, 1999). Two separate studies support this hypothesis: in one study, PSM is associated with mission motivation (Wright, Moynihan, and Pandey, 2012); in another study, PSM predicts the likelihood that individuals will use performance information to make decisions (Moynihan and Pandey, 2010).

A number of studies have sought to test the hypothesis that PSM is positively related to

organizational rather than individual performance, though they are largely limited to measures of employee perceptions of that performance. Brewer and Selden (2000) find that individual self-assessments of PSM are associated with higher employee assessment of organizational performance. Similar findings have been made among Swiss (Ritz, 2009), Flemish (Vandenabeele, 2009), and Korean (Kim, 2005) public employees.

Other research has found that alternative conceptualizations of altruistic behavior generate similar findings. Measures of prosocial motivation have found that employees who are more motivated to help others in their work are more committed, and tend to perform better. One advantage of this work is that has utilized better measures of performance, and some better models (including field experiments) than studies of PSM (Grant, 2008; for a review, see Wright and Grant, 2010).

The practical implication from this research is that public organizations that care about performance should seek to encourage PSM. For example, HRM systems should be designed to select based on PSM, to socialize individuals into expectations, and utilize performance appraisals that reflect PSM; convey the social significance of job and goals; and encourage leaders to promote public service values (Paarlberg, Perry, and Hondeghem, 2008). Such explicit strategies are necessary because public organizations generally do a poor job in explaining the social value of their work (with some exceptions, such as the military). Evidence shows that as individuals spend more time in public organizations, and encounter more red tape, their level of PSM actually declines (Moynihan and Pandey, 2007b).

Leadership

One of the most difficult variables to empirically model and link to government performance is leadership (Ingraham, Joyce, and Donahue, 2003). In large part this is due to the basic difficulty of defining and measuring leadership. While case studies abound, the factors that are characterized as successful leadership in one context might result in failure in another.

Some studies using Texas schools and English local government have found that measures of leadership quality are associated with government performance (Boyne et al., 2010; Hicklin, 2004; Meier and O'Toole, 2002). But it is not always clear what leadership quality means, or what such leaders actually do. Another approach to leadership focuses on how leaders actually work with administrative processes, characterized as integrative leadership (Moynihan and Ingraham, 2004), but Fernandez (2005) finds that leadership desires to change systems may sometimes be counterproductive. Using Texas schools data, he finds that superintendents that promote change are associated with lower school performance.

One potential reason that more progress has not been made in documenting the leadership–performance link is that much of what leaders do, even effective leaders, may only have an indirect effect on performance. Such effects might therefore not be observable in most empirical models, even if they exert a real impact on performance. A series of studies has examined the indirect effects of transformational leadership in public settings. Transformational leadership is perhaps the most popular conceptualization of leadership currently in organization studies, and proposes a leadership style characterized by inspiring employees, identifying the value of organizational goals, and encouraging a culture of innovation. Such characteristics are expected to appeal to the type of intrinsic motivation described in the previous section. In public settings, transformational leadership has been found to increase mission valence and the use of performance data among managers (Wright, Moynihan, and Pandey 2012; Moynihan, Wright, and Pandey, 2012). Using a series of structural equation models, the studies show that the impacts of transformational leadership occur via

mediating variables. For example, transformational leadership does not directly impact performance information use among employees but it does increase goal clarity and a developmental culture, which in turn impact performance information use (Moynihan, Wright, and Pandey, 2012). The implication is that the effects of leadership are easy to overlook, but no less important as a result.

Other studies have sought to understand the impact of leadership by examining the impact of leadership change (Boyne and Dahya, 2002). For example, studies of leadership change in Texas schools and English local government suggest a short-term performance loss when a new executive is hired and the replacement is an outsider to the organization (Boyne et al., 2010; Hill, 2005). Hills's (2005) study of Texas school superintendents finds that as managers gain experience, performance improves, making the long-term impact of succession positive relative to districts that do not experience a change.

Research on English local government shows that the performance impact of change in leadership and top management depends upon the preceding context. Where prior performance is low, the effect of new leaders is likely to be positive, but when performance is already high, new leadership tends to see a reduction in performance (Boyne et al., 2010). Our expectations for leaders should be contingent on context – new leaders can exploit a situation where there is room for improvement, but are more likely to be considered failures when they walk into a situation where performance is already high.

Yet another strategy to understand the impacts of leaders is to examine leadership roles. Some recent studies compare the performance of political appointees with career officials holding similar positions in the US federal government. In one study Lewis (2008) finds that when programs are run by a career professional, they are given higher performance scores by a third party (the US Office of Management and Budget). The main driving factor is that career officials enjoy longer agency-specific experience and longer tenures and both of these factors are associated with higher program performance. In this respect, the findings are consistent with research that has shown that external hires that lack agency-specific experience tend to perform less well (Boyne et al., 2010; Hill 2005). In a related study, Gallo and Lewis (2012) found that appointees who were selected primarily because of their campaign service were associated with lower program performance than appointees selected for non-patronage reasons, or career executives. While political appointments serve important political purposes – such as loyalty, responsiveness, and fulfilling campaign commitments – these studies suggest that they bring a performance cost.

Networking and political support

The findings that political appointees perform less well relative to career managers does not imply that steering clear of politics is the best way to be successful. Indeed, the empirical literature on government performance suggests the opposite. How leaders allocate their time to manage the external political environment is a matter of strategic choice. Political support is associated with higher organizational performance, with a clear implication that leaders should look for ways to increase that support (Fernandez, 2005; Moynihan and Pandey, 2005).

A series of studies have shown that networking with political stakeholders is associated with higher organizational performance, both for schools (Meier and O'Toole, 2003) and policing (Nicholson-Crotty and O'Toole, 2004) in the United States, although Walker et al. (2010) did not find a relationship in the context of UK local government.

Why does networking improve performance? Part of the explanation appears to be that networking is a tool that helps to manage organizational dependence on the environment, and to buffer core operational processes from politics. Some evidence for this

comes from a study that shows that networking matters more for performance in educational organizations that are more dependent on others for financial resources (O'Toole and Meier, 2004). Networking can be a voluntary or coerced act – managers may seek to build networks, or feel compelled to respond to external stakeholders. This distinction matters for how networking relates to performance. Goerdel (2006) found that the positive impact of networking on performance was greater when managers prospectively sought to network rather than when they were reactively responding to the initiatives of others. But it is possible to have too much of a good thing, and at some point networking generates negative returns on performance (Hicklin et al., 2008), and managers would be better off spending their time on other tasks.

PERFORMANCE SYSTEMS

In this section we consider variables related to management systems (especially performance management), while in the following section we examine formal rules.

Performance management

Some models of government performance explicitly focus on the importance of formal management systems (Ingraham, Joyce, and Donahue, 2003). Perhaps the most prominent practical example of how governments have attempted to utilize management systems to improve performance is the popularity of performance management processes. Elected officials might pursue performance systems not because of any conviction that it will improve performance, but because such actions communicate appropriate signals to the general public (Moynihan, 2008a). Under such conditions, the link between formal performance systems and performance is likely to be idiosyncratic rather than systematic, depending on the efforts of individual organizations and managers.

It is perhaps not surprising then that there is only relatively limited evidence of a link between performance management and performance. The best evidence of such a link comes from English local government. In this context, Walker and Boyne (2006) found that as targets are designated as the responsibility for individual managers, and were perceived as achievable, they were associated with higher subjective and objective performance scores. Boyne and Chen (2007) found that performance targets tied to budgetary incentives appeared to increase local school performance: Hanushek and Raymond (2005) offered a similar finding in US settings. Perhaps most compellingly, Walker, Damanpour, and Devece (2011) found that employee perception of the strength of the performance management system was associated with organizational effectiveness (as determined by national auditors), and the impact of management innovations was fully mediated by performance management systems. The analysis serves not only to emphasize the importance of performance management practices in their own right but also to make the point that other efforts to reform government are more likely to succeed if they occur within a functioning performance management framework.

In addition to the relatively limited support that formal performance systems actually improve performance, there is more significant evidence that the type of desired organizational conditions that performance systems are hoped to induce – clear goals, mission-driven strategies, and organizational cultures – are related to performance.

Goal clarity and ambiguity

A well-developed literature on goal theory from organizational studies has documented that individuals with clear and specific goals will be motivated to perform better,

which should in turn increase performance (Wright, 2001). More recent research on the connection, led by Rainey and colleagues, has focused less on the positive impact of goal clarity, and more on the negative impact of goal ambiguity, which is likely to be the more natural condition for public managers who must deal with multiple and conflicting goals (Rainey and Steinbauer, 1999). The two concepts, goal clarity and goal ambiguity, might be considered as alternate sides of the same coin. Goal clarity is expected to increase performance, while goal ambiguity reduces it. Goal ambiguity is defined as 'the extent to which an organizational goal or set of goals allows leeway for interpretation when the organizational goal represents the desired future state of the organization' (Chun and Rainey, 2005a: 2).

Empirical evidence supports the hypothesis that goal clarity and ambiguity are relevant to performance. A study of US state government health and human service managers found that perceptions of goal clarity were associated with higher perceived organizational performance (Moynihan and Pandey, 2005), while a later survey of city government managers found that goal clarity predicts the mission valence and performance information use of employees (Wright, Moynihan and Pandey 2012; Moynihan, Wright, and Pandey, 2012).

Chun and Rainey (2005b) developed a series of measures of goal ambiguity, and found that organizations that scored high on these measures were associated with lower perceived performance in surveys of US federal employees, although the size of the effects were not large. Rainey and Jung (2010) found that federal organizations with higher goal ambiguity also tended to score lower on program performance assessments made by the Office of Management and Budget.

The HRM implications of goal clarity/ ambiguity are similar. Many of these potential solutions to goal ambiguity rely upon the tools of performance management – develop a clear and crisp mission statement; identify a limited number of goals; and establish ex-ante criteria for success. But such actions create their own dangers, primarily the risk of goal displacement: if managers are told to pay more attention to one specific goal, they pay less attention to others that may be no less important. The nature of goal ambiguity seems directly related to the publicness and complexity of a program (Chun and Rainey, 2005a). Organizations that depend more on public funding, are involved more in regulatory activities, and provide more politically salient services can expect greater goal ambiguity (Chun and Rainey, 2005a; Lee, Rainey, and Chun, 2009). At some point efforts to simplify complex programs become counterproductive, and HRM practitioners must use their judgment to know when that point has been reached.

Strategic stance and culture

Performance management systems generally incorporate strategic planning processes, and are intended to engender a mission-based strategic approach that becomes part of the organizational culture. While there is no shortage of recommended approaches to managing strategy, the framework most widely applied to public sector performance is one developed by Miles and Snow (1978). In their typology, prospectors are innovative organizations consistently willing to try new approaches; defenders are conservative organizations focused primarily on efficiency of existing practices; reactors are organizations primarily responding to external pressures. These basic typologies have been widely applied in studies of UK local government, and to a lesser extent in the Texas schools data. In reviewing this body of empirical work, Walker (2010) concluded that prospecting is generally associated with higher organizational performance. To a lesser extent, defending is sometimes linked to performance, but reacting is generally not significant or negatively associated with performance. Studies of multiple performance

indicators from the Texas schools dataset show that the influence of strategic stance depends a good deal on the measure of organizational performance studied.

There is relatively little research on how organizational culture affects performance. In some respects, strategic stance is at least partly a measure of culture, in that it reflects widely accepted employee beliefs about the values of the organization. Moynihan and Pandey (2005) found that a developmental culture (a proactive and innovative culture, similar to a prospector strategic stance) was associated with higher perceived organizational performance. In later studies, developmental culture has also been associated with a willingness on the part of employees to use performance data to make decisions (Moynihan and Pandey, 2010; Moynihan, Wright, and Pandey, 2012), and to overcome red tape (see next section).

The lesson for HRM is that organizational cultures that are more open to change and innovation are associated with strong performance. How to build such a culture is a separate – and daunting – question.

The dark side of performance systems

One cannot complete a discussion of performance systems without considering the possibility of a negative relationship with performance, i.e., such systems have counterproductive and perverse affects that lower effectiveness. In reviewing research on the impact of performance systems, Heinrich and Marschke (2010: 184) note one major reason why they fail:

> the conditions and assumptions under which the simple, rational model for a performance measurement and incentive system model works – organizational goals and production tasks are known, employee efforts and performance are verifiable, performance information is effectively communicated, and there are a relatively small number of variables for managers to control – are stringent, and in the public sector, rarely observed in practice.

For moderately complex programs, performance systems can encourage goal displacement and gaming. One problem with previous studies that have shown that performance management increases performance is that they do not capture 'the dog that didn't bark', that is unmeasured aspects of performance that were not the focus of performance targets or incentives (for an exception, see Kelman and Friedman, 2009). However, a range of empirical studies, mostly in the policy areas of social welfare and education, have revealed the perverse impacts of performance systems (for a review, see Heinrich and Marschke, 2010). It is possible that an increase in performance in one area may be accompanied by a drop in performance in another area, perhaps because the organization devotes more attention and resources to the targeted item (goal displacement), or because there is a simple tradeoff between different aspects of performance, for example, focusing on efficiency might erode quality, or focusing on speed might undermine accuracy. It is also possible that increase in measured performance comes at the cost of integrity of management and measurement processes, and is a function of deliberate gaming (Bohte and Meier, 2000; Jacob and Levitt, 2003).

The risk of perverse behavior appears greatest when performance targets are tied to high-stakes incentives. Such incentives may serve to 'crowd out' the altruistic motivation discussed previously. This may occur via two distinct selection and socialization processes (Moynihan, 2010). As public organizations rely more on performance incentives, they may become less attractive to individuals motivated by altruism, who become less likely to select into, or more likely to exit, public jobs. Those that remain in the public sector may become increasingly accepting of the norm that the value of their work is determined exclusively by financial reward. Since one of the traditional shortcomings of pay-for-performance systems in the public sector is insufficiently large incentives, this danger is not pressing for the core public sector

(Perry, Engbers, and Jun, 2009). However, behaviors consistent with the 'crowding out' hypothesis have been observed in contexts where public services have been contracted out, and contractors utilize high-powered incentives (Heinrich and Marschke, 2010; Soss, Fording, and Schram, 2011).

The general lessons for HRM systems suggest that overall performance systems have promise but cannot be regarded as a certain contributor to performance. Such systems work best under conditions – clear, measurable, and simple goals – unusual to much of the public sector. Whereas performance systems have been shown to increase performance in some instances, they have also been shown to encourage perverse behavior at odds with performance.

STRUCTURE

This section examines the structural allocation of authority from a number of perspectives: red tape, centralization, stability, and rules. Members of the public associate public organizations with an excess of pointless rules and procedures. This view informed public management reformers (especially from the New Public Management school) about the causes, and potential solutions to poor performance, which include decentralizing authority, and reducing rules. Brewer and Walker (2010a) note that international organizations, such as the Organization for Economic Cooperation and Development (OECD), the World Bank, and the International Monetary Fund, have prioritized the elimination of red tape, a policy goal shared by political parties across the ideological spectrum. The empirical evidence, examined below, offers a more complex portrait.

Red tape

Red tape is assumed to be negatively related to performance. Indeed, the basic and widely-used definition of red tape proposed by Bozeman (2000) posits that any rule, process or procedure considered red tape can have no functional value, even as it creates a compliance burden on citizens or employees.

In general, research on red tape rests on measures of employee perceptions of red tape in an organization, or management subsystem, or employee estimates of the time it takes to achieve common tasks such as procurement. This research has generally shown that perceptions of red tape are indeed negatively associated with organizational performance (Brewer and Walker, 2010b; Pandey and Moynihan, 2006; Pandey, Coursey, and Moynihan, 2007).

Some recent work suggests that the effects of red tape on performance is not always negative, but depends upon the measure of performance (Brewer and Walker, 2010b). If performance is understood to be broader than efficiency and effectiveness, red tape is likely to be positively correlated with some aspects of performance. Brewer and Walker (2010b) found that measures of external red tape in English local government were positively correlated with external stakeholder perceptions of performance and equity. Measures of internal red tape had positive impacts on social, economic, and environmental performance.

Another finding is that the effect of red tape on performance seems to depend partly on the type of red tape. Human resource red tape and information systems red tape have been found to be negatively associated with perceived performance, but procurement, budget, and communication red tape were not found to negatively affect performance in the same contexts (Pandey and Moynihan, 2006; Pandey, Coursey, and Moynihan, 2007).

One of the more compelling insights from this research is that organizational culture affects the impact of red tape on performance. Ban (1995) found that organizations with similar rule structures varied in how they responded to these rules. Some had organizational cultures that prioritized

mission, and looked for the most flexible way to apply rules, whereas others were much more rule-bound. While Ban's work relied on case studies of federal agencies, cross-sectional quantitative studies from the United Kingdom and the US state governments point to a similar pattern. In US health and human service agencies, the negative effect of red tape on performance was reduced if an organization had a developmental organizational culture, characterized by innovation and an initiative toward action. Walker and Brewer (2009) found a similar pattern among English local governments, where organizations with a prospecting strategic stance were able to mitigate the negative effects of red tape on performance, whereas more reactive organizational cultures appeared to internalize and magnify the negative impacts of red tape.

Centralization

Consistent with the New Public Management critique of government organizations, there is evidence that workers' experiences of more decentralized structures are associated with higher worker innovation and commitment (Andrews, 2010), and higher perceived organizational performance (Kuvaas, 2008; Moynihan and Pandey, 2005).

However, other research did not find a relationship between centralization and performance (Andrews et al., 2009; Wolf, 1993). In reviewing empirical research on the topic, Andrews (2010) offered a proposition that echoes the discussion of red tape above: the relationship between organizational structure and performance is partly contingent on the other factors – for example, a match between culture and the allocation of authority will facilitate performance.

Stability

Other research in public management lays out explicit assumptions that contrast with the New Public Management advocacy of decentralization, change, and flexibility. The most notable example is O'Toole and Meier's (1999) influential model of public sector performance. At the heart of their model is an assumption that stability is positively associated with performance. While not all stable organizations perform, unstable ones are at an inherent disadvantage. To the extent that managers can buffer environmental shocks, they create a platform for organizational success. The O'Toole and Meier model underpins much of the research on Texas educational outcomes reviewed in this chapter.

Stability can be reflected in terms of an organization's people, budget, or other factors. Turnover of teachers is generally related to lower performance in education (Meier and Hicklin, 2008), and makes organizations less able to battle the negative impacts of external shocks on performance. In another context, Andersen and Mortensen (2010) found that budget stability was associated with higher performance among Danish schools. However, there is also the potential that an excess of stability can become stultifying. Meier and Hicklin (2008) found that for some organizational goals there was a non-linear effect between turnover and performance, suggesting that both too much and too little turnover undermines performance.

Rules

The logic for greater decentralization is that public officials are overly-constrained, and with greater discretion they will make better decisions. But public officials may not always be willing or able to behave in ways conducive to performance when rules are removed. This creates conditions where rules remain valuable. An obvious example to demonstrate the importance of rules is in corrupt organizations and societies, where the removal of rules will likely impede performance (Schick, 1998). Even in non-corrupt settings, rules can prevent public officials

from pursuing incentives to make decisions at odds with long-term performance. In the area of financial management, clear and credible rules constrain the desire of elected officials to make present-day spending commitments that undercut long-term fiscal stability (Hou and Moynihan, 2008; Hou, Moynihan, and Ingraham, 2003).

Rules may also be especially important in conditions where norms of cooperative behavior are not well-established, and trust between actors is low. These conditions appear most likely to occur in networks and contracting arrangements. In the case of networks, more centralized authority arrangements can help ensure cooperation and improve performance under conditions of low trust (Provan and Kenis, 2007). When networks are relatively new, and must respond quickly, standard operating procedures have also been associated with greater network effectiveness because they provide a form of institutional memory (Moynihan, 2008b).

While the move to contract public services reflected the New Public Management belief in flexibility – managers would be freed from traditional constraints in return for meeting performance targets – public agencies have found that the tendency of contractors to exploit incomplete contracts is often best remedied by introducing new rules and constraints (Heinrich and Choi, 2007; Heinrich and Marschke, 2010).

More than in other areas reviewed in this chapter, the findings on how the structural allocation of authority and formal rules matter to performance seems bedeviled by contradictions. Whereas some research seems to suggest that stability and rules engender performance, other research suggests that too much centralization and red tape undermine performance. How to sort out the seemingly inconsistent results? In part, the confusion is partly because of definitional issues, as related but distinct concepts are grouped together in an overly simplistic fashion (a fault that a review chapter such as this is not exempt from). It is also the case that the effects of centralization or red tape seem contingent on other factors, such as culture, the nature of the task, trust between actors, and the incentives that actors have to behave in ways aligned with performance. In addition Rainey and Steinbauer's (1999) proposition that centralization will have a non-linear effect on performance remains plausible. In most cases, performance will be poor in a context where there are few rules and public actors are free to pursue individual incentives. In an administrative state of nature some order is necessary, and rules provide guidance, constraints, and stability. But as organizations, networks, or contracts accumulate more rules, and centralize more authority, they are likely to become calcified, and unable to utilize the performance benefits of innovation and discretion.

CONCLUSION

Even as the field of public administration has been focused on performance, in one form or another, for a relatively long time, it is only in the last decade that we have seen the emergence of a research agenda that actually seeks to link management practices with performance. The results in some respects have been extraordinarily insightful, and have clear implications for HRM. But the research still has limitations that prevent it, at least for now, from being a cure-all for the ills that ail public administration.

On the positive side, the emergence of this research has begun to alter how we understand HRM. Of course, a published article that shows a correlation between such a practice and performance is not, in itself, proof. There are gradations in the persuasiveness of evidence, and few research models are near to being conclusive. The dependant variable may be incomplete or subjective. External controls may be missing. Reverse causality may be an issue.

Even if we were fully convinced of the validity of the studies reviewed, the accumulation of knowledge in some areas seems to have added more to our understanding of the wrinkles of a particular topic, without making our understanding of the big picture clearer. We find that a variable might be significant for one measure of performance, but not for another; it might increase performance for low-performing agencies, but not high ones; that a certain amount of a variable is a good thing, but too much creates negative effects. From the outsider's perspective, the field may appear to be obsessed with interaction terms, contingencies, and non-linear effects. But the findings reflect the complexities of public management. It is clear that there are relatively few universal claims about government performance beyond the very broad ones – people matter, management matters, structure matter. To those, we can add that context matters.

Given the frequent contingencies encountered in this research, we might be especially concerned that a great deal of our empirical knowledge on organizational performance rests upon a handful of studies tied to a particular geographical location, type of public officials, policy area (especially education), and preferences of the researchers involved. This is a real concern, but as much as anything highlights the need for more research in different contexts and using different variables rather than the limitations of existing work.

Even with these issues, there is little doubt this literature has advanced our knowledge of HRM. Within scholarly circles at least, no longer is it good enough to assert that a certain practice makes a difference. The empirical performance literature says 'prove it.' While there were long-standing claims about many of the variables reviewed in this chapter, we now have much more persuasive evidence of how and when they matter to performance.

REFERENCES

Alonso, P. and Lewis, G.B. (2001) 'Public service motivation and job performance: Evidence from the federal sector', *American Review of Public Administration,* 31(4): 363–80.

Andersen, S.C. and Mortensen, P.B. (2010) 'Policy stability and organizational performance: Is there a relationship?' *Journal of Public Administration Research and Theory,* 20(1): 1–22.

Andrews, R. (2010) 'Organizational structure and public service performance', in R.M. Walker, G.A. Boyne, and G.A. Brewer (eds), *Public Management and Performance: Research Directions.* Cambridge, UK: Cambridge University Press, pp. 89–109.

Andrews, R., Boyne, G.A, Law, J., and Walker, R.M. (2005) 'External constraints on local service standards: The case of comprehensive performance assessing English local government', *Public Administration,* 83(3): 639–56.

Andrews, R, Boyne, G.A, Law, J., and Walker, R.M. (2009) 'Centralization, organizational strategy and public service performance', *Journal of Public Administration Research and Theory,* 19(1): 57–80.

Ban, C. (1995) *How Public Managers Manage. Bureaucratic Constraints, Organizational Culture, and the Potential for Reform.* San Francisco, CA: Jossey-Bass.

Bohte, J. and Meier, K.J. (2000) 'Goal displacement: Assessing the motivation for organizational cheating', *Public Administration Review* 60(2): 173–82.

Boyne, G.A. (2002) 'Concepts and indicators of local authority performance: An evaluation of the statutory framework in England and Wales', *Public Money and Management,* 22(2): 17–24.

Boyne, G.A. (2003) 'Sources of public service improvement: A critical review and research agenda', *Journal of Public Administration Research and Theory,* 13(3): 367–94.

Boyne, G.A. and Chen, A. (2007) 'Performance targets and public service improvements', *Journal of Public Administration Research and Theory,* 17(3): 455–77.

Boyne, G.A. and Dahya, J. (2002) 'Executive succession and the performance of public organizations', *Public Administration,* 80(1): 179–200.

Boyne, G.A., James, O., John, P., and Petrovsky, N. (2010) 'Change at the top: Connecting political and managerial transitions', in K. Walshe, G. Harvey, and P. Jas (eds), *Connecting Knowledge and Performance in Public Services: From Knowing to Doing.* Cambridge, UK: Cambridge University Press, pp.128–44.

Bozeman, B. (2000) *Bureaucracy and Red Tape.* Upper Saddle River, NJ: Prentice Hall.

Brewer, G.A. and Selden, S.C. (1998) 'Whistle-blowers in the federal civil service: New evidence of the public service ethic', *Journal of Public Administration Research and Theory,* 8(3): 413–39.

Brewer, G.A and Selden, S.C. (2000) 'Why elephants gallop: Assessing and predicting organizational performance in federal agencies', *Journal of Public Administration Research and Theory,* 10(4): 685–711.

Brewer, G.A. and Walker, R.M. (2010a) 'Red tape: The bane of public organizations', in R.M. Walker, G.A. Boyne, and G.A. Brewer (eds), *Public Management and Performance: Research Directions.* Cambridge, UK: Cambridge University Press, pp. 110–26.

Brewer, G.A. and Walker, R.M. (2010b) 'The impact of red tape on governmental performance: An empirical analysis', *Journal of Public Administration Research and Theory,* 20(2): 233–57.

Bright, L. (2007) 'Does person–organization fit mediate the relationship between public service motivation and the job performance of public employees?' *Review of Public Personnel Administration,* 27(4): 361–79.

Chun, Y.H. and Rainey, H.G. (2005a) 'Goal ambiguity in US federal agencies', *Journal of Public Administration Research and Theory,* 15(1): 1–30.

Chun, Y.H. and Rainey, H.G. (2005b) 'Goal ambiguity and organizational performance in US federal agencies', *Journal of Public Administration Research and Theory,* 15(4): 529–57.

Crewson, P.E. (1997) 'Public-service motivation: Building empirical evidence of incidence and effect', *Journal of Public Administration Research and Theory,* 7(4): 499–518.

Fernandez, S. (2005) 'Developing and testing an integrative framework of public sector leadership: Evidence from the public education arena', *Journal of Public Administration Research and Theory,* 15(2): 197–217.

Gallo, N. and Lewis, D.E. (2012) 'The consequences of presidential patronage for federal agency performance', *Journal of Public Administration Research and Theory,* 22(2): 219–43.

Gilmour, J.B. and Lewis, D.E. (2006) 'Assessing performance assessment for budgeting: The influence of politics, performance, and program size', *Journal of Public Administration Research and Theory,* 16(2): 169–86.

Goerdel, H.T. (2006) 'Taking initiative: Proactive management and organizational performance in networked environments', *Journal of Public Administration Research and Theory,* 16(3): 351–67.

Grant, A.M. (2008) 'Does intrinsic motivation fuel the prosocial fire? Motivational synergy in predicting persistence, performance, and productivity', *Journal of Applied Psychology,* 93: 48–58.

Hanushek, E. and Raymond, M. (2005) 'Does school accountability lead to improved student performance?', *Journal of Policy Analysis and Management,* 24(2): 297–327.

Heinrich, C.J. (2007) 'Evidence-based policy and performance management: Challenges and prospects in two parallel movements', *The American Review of Public Administration* 37(3): 255–77.

Heinrich, C.J. and Choi, Y. (2007) 'Performance-based contracting in social welfare programs', *The American Review of Public Administration,* 37(4): 409–35.

Heinrich, C. and Lynn, L.E., Jr (eds) (2000) *Governance and Performance: New Perspectives.* Washington, DC: Georgetown University Press.

Heinrich, C.J. and Marschke, G. (2010) 'Incentives and their dynamics in public sector performance management systems', *Journal of Policy Analysis and Management,* 29(1): 183–208.

Hicklin, A.K. (2004) 'Network stability: Opportunity or obstacle?' *Public Organization Review,* 4(2): 121–33.

Hicklin, A.K., O'Toole, L.J., Jr, and Meier, K.J. (2008) 'Serpents in the sand: Managerial networking and nonlinear influences on organizational performance', *Journal of Public Administration Research and Theory,* 18(2): 253–74.

Hill, G.C. (2005) 'The effects of managerial succession on organizational performance', *Journal of Public Administration, Research and Theory,* 15(4): 585–98.

Hou, Y. and Moynihan, D.P. (2008) 'The case for counter cyclical fiscal capacity', *Journal of Public Administration Research and Theory,* 18(1): 139–59.

Hou, Y., Moynihan, D.P., and Ingraham, P.W. (2003) 'Capacity, management and performance: Exploring the links', *American Review of Public Administration,* 33(3): 295–315.

Ingraham, P.W., Joyce, P.G., and Donahue, A.K. (2003) *Government Performance: Why Management Matters.* Baltimore, MD: Johns Hopkins University Press.

Jacob, B.A. and Levitt, S. (2003). 'Rotten apples: An investigation of the prevalence and predictors of teacher cheating', *Quarterly Journal of Economics,* 118(3): 843–77.

Kelman, S. and Friedman, J.N. (2009) 'Performance improvement and performance dysfunction: An empirical examination of the distortionary impacts of the emergency room wait-time target in the English National Health Service', *Journal of Public Administration Research and Theory* 19(4): 917–46.

Kim, S. (2005) 'Individual-level factors and organizational performance in government organizations', *Journal of Public Administration Research and Theory,* 15(2): 245–61.

Kuvaas, B. (2008). 'A test of hypotheses derived from self-determination theory among public sector employees', *Employee Relations* 31(1): 39–56.

Lee, J.W., Rainey, H.G., and Chun, Y.H. (2009) 'Of politics and purpose: Political salience and goal ambiguity of US federal agencies', *Public Administration* 87(3): 457–84.

Leisink, P. and Steijn, B. (2009) 'Public service motivation and job performance of public sector employees in the Netherlands', *International Review of Administrative Sciences* 75(1): 35–52.

Lewis, D.E. (2008) *The Politics of Presidential Appointments.* New York: Cambridge University Press.

Meier, K.J. and Hicklin, A.K. (2008) 'Employee turnover and organizational performance: A theoretical extension and test with public sector data', *Journal of Public Administration Research and Theory,* 18(4): 573–90.

Meier, K.J. and O'Toole, L.J., Jr (2002) 'Public management and organizational performance: The effect of managerial quality', *Journal of Policy Analysis and Management* 21(4): 629–43.

Meier, K.J. and O'Toole, L.J., Jr (2003) 'Public management and educational performance: The impact of managerial networking', *Public Administration Review,* 63(6): 675–85.

Miles, Raymond E. and Snow, Charles C. (1978) *Organizational Strategy, Structure and Process.* New York: McGraw-Hill.

Moynihan, D.P. (2008a) *The Dynamics of Performance Management: Constructing Information and Reform.* Washington, DC: Georgetown University Press.

Moynihan, D.P. (2008b) 'Learning under uncertainty: Networks in crisis management', *Public Administration Review,* 68(2): 350–61.

Moynihan, D.P. (2010) 'A workforce of cynics? The effects of contemporary reform on public service motivation', *International Public Management Journal,* 13(1): 24–34.

Moynihan, D.P. and Ingraham, P.W. (2004) 'Integrative leadership in the public sector: A model of performance information use', *Administration & Society* 36(4): 427–53.

Moynihan, D.P. and Pandey, S.K. (2005) 'Testing how management matters in an era of government by performance management', *Journal of Public Administration Research and Theory* 15(3): 421–39.

Moynihan, D.P. and Pandey, S.K. (2007a) 'Finding workable levers: Comparing job satisfaction, job involvement, and organizational commitment', *Administration & Society* 39(7): 803–32.

Moynihan, D.P. and Pandey, S.K. (2007b) 'The role of organizations in fostering public service motivation', *Public Administration Review* 67(1): 40–53.

Moynihan, D.P. and Pandey, S.K. (2010) 'The big question for performance management: Why do managers use performance information?', *Journal of Public Administration Research and Theory,* 20(4): 849–66.

Moynihan, D.P., Wright, B.E., and Pandey, S.K. (2012) 'Setting the table: How transformational leadership fosters performance information use.' *Journal of Public Administration Research and Theory,* 22(1): 143–64.

Naff, K.C. and Crum, J. (1999) 'Working for America: Does public service motivation make a difference?', *Review of Public Personnel Administration* 19(4): 5–16.

Nicholson-Crotty, S. and O'Toole, L.J., Jr (2004) 'Public management and organizational performance: The case of law enforcement agencies', *Journal of Public Administration Research and Theory,* 14(1): 1–18.

Nicholson-Crotty, S., Theobald, N.A. and Nicholson-Crotty, J. (2006) 'Disparate measures: Public managers and performance measurement strategies', *Public Administration Review,* 66(1): 101–13.

O' Toole, L.J., Jr and Meier, K.J. (1999) 'Modeling the impact of public management: The implications of structural context', *Journal of Public Administration Research and Theory* 9(3): 505–26.

O' Toole, L.J., Jr and Meier, K.J. (2004) 'Public management in intergovernmental networks: Matching structural networks and managerial networking', *Journal of Public Administration Research and Theory,* 14(3): 469–95.

Paarlberg, L.E., Perry, J.L., and Hondeghem, A. (2008) 'From theory to practice: Strategies for applying public service motivation', in J.L. Perry and A. Hondeghem (eds), *Motivation in Public Management: The Call of Public Service.* Oxford: Oxford University Press, pp: 268–93.

Pandey, S. K. and Moynihan, D.P. (2006) 'Bureaucratic red tape and organizational performance: Testing the moderating role of culture and political support', in G.A. Boyne, K.J. Meier, L.J. O'Toole, Jr, and R.M. Walker (eds), *Public Service Performance.* Cambridge, England: Cambridge University Press, pp.130–51.

Pandey, S.K., Coursey, D., and Moynihan, D.P. (2007) 'Overcoming barriers to organizational effectiveness and bureaucratic red tape: A multi-method study', *Public Performance and Management Review* 30(3): 371–400.

Perry, J.L. and Wise, L.R. (1990) 'The motivational bases of public service', *Public Administration Review,* 50(3): 367–73.

Perry, J.L., Engbers, T., and Jun, S.Y. (2009) 'Back to the future? Performance-related pay, empirical research, and the perils of persistence', *Public Administration Review,* 69(1): 1–31.

Provan, K,G. and Kenis, P. (2007) 'Modes of network governance: Structure, management and effectiveness', *Journal of Public Administration Research and Theory,* 18(2): 229–52.

Rainey, H.G. and Jung, C.S. (2010) 'Extending goal ambiguity research in government', in R.M. Walker, G.A. Boyne, and G.A. Brewer (eds), *Public Management and Performance: Research Directions.* Cambridge, UK: Cambridge University Press, pp. 110–26.

Rainey, H.G. and Steinbauer, P. (1999) 'Galloping elephants: Developing elements of a theory of effective government organizations', *Journal of Public Administration Research and Theory* 9(1): 1–32.

Ritz, A. (2009) 'Public service motivation and organizational performance in Swiss federal government', *International Review of Administrative Sciences,* 75(1): 53–78.

Schick, A. (1998) 'Why most developing countries should not try New Zealand's reforms', *The World Bank Research Observer,* 13(1): 123–31.

Soss, J., Fording, R., and Schram, S. (2011) 'The organization of discipline: From performance management to perversity and punishment', *Journal of Public Administration Research and Theory,* 21(s2): i203–32.

Vandenabeele, W. (2009) 'The mediating effect of job satisfaction and organizational commitment on self-reported performance: More robust evidence of the PSM–performance relationship', *International Review of Administrative Sciences,* 75(1): 53–78.

Walker, R.M. (2010) 'Strategy: Which strategic stances matter?', in R.M. Walker, G.A. Boyne, and G.A. Brewer (eds), *Public Management and Performance: Research Directions.* Cambridge, UK: Cambridge University Press, pp. 227–52.

Walker, R.M., Andrews, R., Boyne G.A., Meier, K.J., and O'Toole. L.J. Jr. (2010) 'Wake Up Call: Strategic

Management, Network Alarms and Performance', *Public Administration Review*, 70(5): 731–41.

Walker, R.M. and Boyne, G.A. (2006) 'Public management reform and organizational performance: An empirical assessment of the UK Labour Government's public service improvement strategy', *Journal of Policy Analysis and Management*, 25(2): 371–93.

Walker, R.M. and Brewer, G.A. (2009) 'Can managers reduce red tape: The role of internal management in overcoming external constraints', *Policy & Politics* 37(2): 255–72.

Walker, R.M., Damanpour, F., and Devece, C.A. (2011) 'Management innovation, performance measurement, and organizational performance', *Journal of Public Administration Research and Theory*, 21(2): 367–86.

Wolf, P.J. (1993) 'A case survey of bureaucratic effectiveness in US cabinet agencies: Preliminary results', *Journal of Public Administration Research and Theory*, 3(2): 161–81.

Wright, B.E. (2001) 'Public sector work motivation: Review of current literature and a revised conceptual model', *Journal of Public Administration Research and Theory*, 11(4): 559–86.

Wright, B.E. and Grant, A. (2010) 'Unanswered questions about public service motivation: Designing research to address key issues of emergence and effect', *Public Administration Review*, 70(5): 691–700.

Wright, B.E, Moynihan, D.P, and Pandey, S.K. (2012) 'Pulling the levers: Leadership, public service motivation and mission valence', *Public Administration Review*, 72(2): 206–15.

5

Pay and Prerequisites for Government Executives

Jørgen Grønnegaard Christensen

On first consideration it seems a trivial question to ask what government pays its executives and how it does it. The simple answer is that they are paid according to their value on the labor market. The caveat is equally simple. Deviations from the market pattern would be expected only if somebody could exploit his or her political power to contrive a better deal. This chapter shows that both the market and the political power interpretations are far from the reality. However, it is hard to separate the two types of government executives, even if it may seem odd that the settling of the salaries of master and servant are as closely related as is often the case in government.

The market interpretation relies on the assumption that to attract able persons to a government career the government has to pay a price that is competitive with what the private sector pays its executives, allowing for differences in tenure and pension rights. The political power interpretation relies on a similar premise. It presumes executive pay in government to be set by the incumbents, who have both the motive and the opportunity to serve themselves. Much speaks for either interpretation. According to the former, it is hard to imagine a long-term insulation of the public sector from the general labor market, including the market for managerial and leadership talent. It is equally hard to abstract from the fact that, in the end, it is a political decision how and how much the holders of governmental office should be rewarded for their services and that, with this power, they do not have to respond to the constraints of the market.

Both extremes overlook important aspects of political and administrative life. First, elaborate civil service regulations are in place. They establish internal labor markets for the public sector, and even for particular subsectors of government (Wise, 1996). As a result, any competitive exchange with the private labor market, and especially the corporate part, is limited. Second, modern government is democratic government. So, classical political theorists puzzled with the issue of how to provide office holders with proper rewards and incentives. Tocqueville expected democratic competition (and popular envy) to place strict constraints on politicians when they had to determine their own salaries. The implication was a strong trend towards an egalitarian pay system, compressing the governmental pay scale while guaranteing that people in high public office didn't distance themselves too far from the people they ruled (Tocqueville, 1835/1963: 130–134). The Tocquevillian hypothesis thus clearly contradicts the rent-seeking behavior inherent in the political power interpretation.

Third, modern government is highly specialized, and, for the political decision makers, citizens and private business it serves and regulates, the issue is how to ensure its reliable, consistent, professionally competent and equitable operation. This was the concern of Max Weber, another classic theorist. His answer was to combine democracy and the rule of law with a professional civil service. His ideal-type civil servant was recruited on the basis of merit, and a career system with lifelong tenure and a deferred pension at the end of service provided sufficient incentives for civil servants to concentrate on their official duties as specified by general legal rules and their place in the hierarchy. Like Tocqueville, Weber was not overly optimistic about the prospects that his model would succeed. Therefore, the challenge was to create a set of institutions that as far as possible could keep in check bureaucrats bent on usurping political power and a new class of professional politicians making a living off, rather than living for, politics (Weber, 1919/1988).

These classics point to the complexity and tensions involved, but hardly lead to precise predictions as to how much and how government executives are paid. Nor is there much assistance to be gained from modern theories. One theory is Horn's transaction cost theory of public administration. He forcefully argued that to cope with the problems of commitment inherent in demo-cratic policymaking, politicians are inclined to set up a tenured and merit-based civil service providing its members with prospects of promotion and pension (Horn, 1995). Even Horn's elaborate theory is not precise in its predictions of the reward schemes to be expected for administrative executives, not to speak of their political superiors. The situation is no better if we alternatively take recourse to cultural theories that focus on ensuring an appropriate fit between salaries and other rewards in differing organizational and social contexts (Hood, 1994: 67).

PATTERNS TO BE EXPLAINED

Even a scant look at the real world of executive pay in government demonstrates that we are faced with a complex, but fascinating topic. Table 5.1 shows some of the issues involved in a cross-national comparison of the patterns of executive pay in government. The basic distinction concerns the structure of executive rewards: they may consist solely, or to a very great extent, of a taxable salary, the level of which is, in principle, open to the public. Or they may to some, or even a considerable, extent consist of perquisites to the holders of executive office. Such perquisites can consist of cash and be taxable. However, they can also be more substantial (cars, accommodation, traveling, per diem) or immaterial (social status and public esteem derived from the executive position) rewards. Finally, perquisites may be deferred, thus securing future compensation for relative hardships endured while holding public office. The more important such perquisites are, the less transparent the system of rewards is, and the more weight assigned to such perquisites, the less clear the incentives connected with a particular job or career.

One level of analysis involves only comparative statistics. The primary focus is on differences between countries. It reveals considerable differences between countries and political and administrative systems, differences that are not in any way directly related to the wealth of the countries. This holds not only for the countries of the Organization for

Table 5.1 Analyzing the structure of rewards for government executives

Level of analysis	Rewards	
	Pay	Perquisites
Cross-national comparisons	Pay relativities Political vs administrative executives Executives vs MPs Intra-hierarchical differentials Executive pay vs general population	As percentage of direct pay As option for second career outside government
Over-time comparisons	Real-term changes in purchasing power Erosion/improvement in pay relativities	Expansion/restriction of perquisites

Economic Co-operation and Development (OECD) but also for the emerging economies of Southeast Asia (Hood and Askim, 2003; Hood and Lambert, 1994: 34–37). The pattern is even more variegated when pay relativities are included. As Table 5.1 shows, determining the pay relativities requires a series of comparisons, and it is difficult to speak of a consistent pattern of countries falling within distinct categories. Certainly, there are countries where egalitarian modesty dominates and where pay differentials are compressed, whether the standard is relativities within the elite, within the administrative hierarchy or between the executive elite and the general public; this is clearly the case in the Nordic countries. At the other end, Hong Kong and Singapore, for instance, display a uniform pattern of exquisite pay to members of the executive elite, disregarding the standard of comparison.

Actually, the numbers reveal patterns that are specific to each country. Some examples are illuminating. It is quite nearly a general pattern that the pay to political and administrative executives – explicitly and implicitly – is mutually strongly related, and that their pay is related to the pay members of parliament (MPs) receive. But there are conspicuous deviations. So both the members of the New Zealand and Swiss parliaments are poorly paid compared to administrative executives, but when it comes to political executives New Zealand cabinet ministers share the humble lot of their country's MPs. Their Swiss colleagues, however, are comparatively

well-off, as are the country's senior civil servants (Gregory and Christensen, 2004; Klöti, 1994). The implication is that New Zealand and Switzerland resemble Asian countries like Hong Kong, Japan, Singapore, and South Korea rather than the Western countries with which they share cultural and political traits that are otherwise deemed to be important.

The presumption behind the direct pay that governmental executives receive is that it is open. The salaries are decided according to well-specified and well-known procedures, and information on them is available through public accounts and official statistics. Similar transparency is hardly connected with the perquisites that governmental executives receive. The more important such perquisites ('perks'), the more opaque are the systems of rewards. As this happens, sleaze and, at the extreme, the risk of corruption become problems that may negatively affect citizens' trust in government (Ridley and Doig, 1995). For the same reason it is difficult to determine their monetary value. Still, Table 5.2 tries to bring a minimum of order to a phenomenon that, by definition, constitutes the submerged part of the iceberg (Hood and Peters, 1994, 2003).

First, Table 5.2 shows that political executives and, to a lesser extent, top civil servants receive different sorts of allowances. Mostly they are of minor importance and clearly linked to job-related activities. This is the case with allowances for representation and provision of free government cars. The most

Table 5.2 Prevalent types of perquisites for government executives

	In office	Lifetime and/or extended to family	Deferred
Cash allowances and services			
Political executives	Free, chauffeur driven cars; tax free allowances for representation; prevalent in most countries	Common: e.g., in China and in the EU	
Top civil servants	Varying, but smaller	Common: e.g., in China and in the EU	
Add-ons			
Political executives	Political executives holding a parliamentary seat keep their allowance; non-MPs receive a compensation neutralizing the absence of this allowance		
Top civil servants	Bonus and one-off payments; performance-related pay	Side-business allowed to continue after retirement; reimbursed through honorarium	
Accumulation			
Political executives	French 'cumul des mandats'; in other countries ministers are by law obliged to give up other tasks and jobs while in office	Ministers earning a lifelong pension, increasing with the accumulated length of service and coming to payment at retirement, regardless of age	Directorships on boards in government corporations, etc.; exchange of executive staff with law firms and corporate community
Top civil servants	Accumulation of perks for civil servants serving on boards, etc., as government representatives	Civil service pensions regulated according to seniority; retaining pay at replacement	'Descent from heaven' for Japanese top civil servants; French 'pantouflage'; US in-and-outers

conspicuous exception is that in a few systems like China and the European Union (EU), allowances of this kind apply also to family members and that, in the Chinese case, they are for life. The implication is that perks of this kind make up a large share of the Chinese elite's income and, further, that these invisible allowances make the rewards for the country's governmental executives highly inequitable when compared to other countries, even if reformatory steps recently have been taken to downplay the use of perquisites (Burns, 2007).

Second, in particular top civil servants receive monetary add-ons. Different models are used: for instance, the practice of a 13 months' salary in the German and Swiss civil

services, and the confidential practice of handing over closed envelopes to French civil servants who merit a cash benefit; the discretionary one-off payments in the Danish civil service law have a very similar status; the introduction of performance-linked pay has not changed this (Binderkrantz and Christensen, 2012). Civil servants serving ex officio on particular boards and commissions may even continue to hold such posts and the ensuing honoraria upon retirement.

Third, a more important source of rewards is connected with the possibility of accumulating offices. While some countries set strict limitations on this for members of government (e.g., Germany, the Nordic countries, and the EU Commission), 'cumul des mandats' is part of the French political tradition, providing national politicians not only with an extra source of income but also a separate platform for their political career. Top civil servants, as was once the case in Danish central government, may have similar opportunities to accumulate side tasks to which they are appointed by the government, sometimes leaving it to others to pay for their services. Pension schemes have a similar function in a lifetime perspective, although their value depends entirely on the principles regulating their calculation. Finally, in many countries life does not necessarily come to a halt when a career in government ends. In France, as well as Japan and South Korea, a fairly low salary in government paves the way to a later, much more lucrative career in business. In other countries this opportunity is less well integrated into the civil service career system, but former ministers and retired top civil servants have a chance to pursue a second career in the borderland between the public and the private sector.

The rewards of administrative and political executives are often connected. From a classic perspective, derived from either Weber's theory of bureaucracy or Wilson's politics–administration dichotomy, these executive roles are different and should not be blurred. In a comparative perspective, however, they are often difficult to distinguish. Part of the problem lies in an ambiguous conceptualization that is exploited by politicians and bureaucrats alike to institute various ploys against each other (Peters, 2010). Another reason is that empirically the careers of political and administrative executives often converge. This happens when appointments to positions in the administration are made on political grounds, thereby departing from the principles of the merit civil service. Political appointees at the higher echelons of American federal bureaucracy fall within this category, as do the directors-general in charge of the independent agencies of Swedish central government (Lewis, 2008; Christensen and Yesilkagit, 2006). In other European countries like Austria and Belgium a long

tradition of coalition government has led to elaborate procedures for selecting and allocating political appointees to leading positions in the administration (Brans, 1994; Liegl and Müller, 1999). Finally, civil service reforms following recommendations from the EU have not held the Central and East European countries back from a strong politicization of appointments to the higher civil service (Meyer-Sahling, 2011). The other side of the issue is the bureaucratization of politics found in some countries. In democratic France one road to a political career has traditionally been elite training as a civil servant, followed by a career that over time merged into politics (Rouban, 1998). In other, more autocratic countries a similar pattern is evident in that technocrats are indistinguishable from higher civil servants occupying the highest posts in government.

Cross-national comparison has not exactly revealed a consistent pattern and variation is so strong that national idiosyncrasies must be said to prevail. On the surface this is different for changes over time. The Hood and Peters study, covering a number of Western European countries and the USA, revealed a general trend towards erosion of pay to people serving in high public office. This applied not only to political and administrative executives; in particular, members of parliament seemed to suffer a gradual, but constant erosion of their monetary rewards. As the erosion proceeded, the reward systems also became more egalitarian and showed more compressed pay relativities within the governmental hierarchy, combined with a narrowing of income differentials between governmental executives and the general public. But even this pattern is not without exceptions, as demonstrated by the Swiss and, to some extent, the German cases, where members of the elite in comparative terms have been able to uphold their very high earnings (Derlien, 1994; Klöti, 1994). Furthermore, the trend towards erosion is not confirmed when the scope of comparison is expanded to include, for example, Southeast Asia and industrialized and democratic countries like Australia, Japan, and New Zealand (Hood and Askim, 2003).

For those Western countries that experienced a gradual erosion of pay to government executives this raises two questions. The first is whether the trend towards erosion of executive pay has been accompanied by substituting salaried rewards with increased perquisites. No systematic data allows a general answer to this question, but there are sufficient examples to demonstrate that no such logic seems to be at play. First, German politicians, who have otherwise been comparatively well-off, as well as their American colleagues, have experienced difficulties in maintaining their perquisites at a level that kept up with the costs of living. Corporatist Denmark has always had plenty of posts for civil servants on boards and commissions. This is still the case, but where such side activities in the past carried an honorarium, consecutive rounds of perk clearance have led to their eradication. But for both civil servants and political executives such posts represent a kind of deferred perquisite to be enjoyed upon retirement.

The second question is whether the trend towards erosion observed in several Western countries is inescapable. However, the combined effect of civil service and managerial reform has been an increased focus on the role of top civil servants (see Ketelaar, Manning, and Turkisch, 2007; OECD, 2003). Common to this trend is the emphasis on managerial capacity and leadership, the idea that executive pay should reward talent to attract the best and the brightest and that executive pay should be linked to performance. This change in rationale dates back to the late 1980s and early 1990s and is common particularly to Anglo-Saxon and the Nordic countries (see, e.g., Christensen, 2009; Waxin and Bateman, 2009; Wegrich, 2009). Table 5.3 shows, by way of illustration, how this change in rationale has been accompanied by a change in reward structure within the civil service.

First, since the mid 1990s agency heads have regained their position compared to employees. This goes both when their total salary is compared to that of senior clerks and to that of principals in central government service. However, their relative pay is basically constant when compared to the total salary of permanent secretaries, the highest office in central government. Second, Table 5.3 also documents a rather radical change in executive pay structure. Basic salary has decreased while annual one-off payments have increased dramatically when compared to total pay.

ACCOUNTING FOR EXTREME DIVERSITIES

Pay policy for the public sector sounds like a fairly well-defined policy field. This is even more so when, as here, the focus is narrowed

Table 5.3   Pay structure for Danish agency heads (AH) 1996 and 2008

	1996	2008
Pay relativities		
AH/senior clerk	3.1	3.5
AH/principal	2.2	2.6
AH/permanent secretary	0.8	0.7
Pay structure		
Basic salary/total salary	0.65	0.53
One-off payment/total salary	0.04	0.08
N	48	61

Sources: Data kindly provided by The State Employer's Authority.

down to the setting of pay and perquisites for government executives. Still, the descriptive pattern is one of a diversity so extreme that it seems questionable whether there is a consistent pattern of observations. Any viable theoretical account therefore has, apparently, to cope with

1 persistent cross-national differences among countries otherwise alike in economic, institutional and political terms; and
2 inconsistent developments in countries otherwise alike in all relevant respects.

This situation does not exactly make it easy to follow the standard prescription for analytical parsimony through the reliance on one, simple theoretical account. Below I briefly present the complex analytical issues involved. The dismal conclusion is that none of the theories survives an encounter with the real world (Hood and Peters, 1995).

Public choice theory offers a parsimonious account for the setting of salaries and perquisites. Starting from the assumption of individuals rationally pursuing their own interests, those holding the actual positions of public power are expected to see to their own material welfare. This goes for their income in absolute terms and relative position compared to other groups within and outside the public sector. The problem is that most, although not all, government executives in Western countries have had difficulty in upholding their former income in real terms, and further, that for years they experienced an increasing degree of wage compression within the government hierarchy. There is even doubt as to whether people in positions of power actually pursue a policy of increasing their own salary, as witnessed by the politics of setting salaries and allowances for members of parliament.

The obvious caveat is that the pure public choice interpretation does not consider the institutional constraints within which people in high public office operate. One analytic approach follows Alexis de Tocqueville's theory of *democratic institutionalism*. Its causal logic is closely related to public

choice rationalism, but its predictions run counter to it. Instead of striving to improve their personal lots, politicians engage themselves in a competition that over time causes their salaries to spiral down. What is more, if they seek compensation through more or less hidden perquisites they set into motion a devious game that undermines public trust in political office, making it unattractive to people of quality and unaffordable to people without considerable private means. The theory is supported by the trend observed in several Western countries for which we have data. The fact that in these countries the elite has not been able to keep perquisites out of the political debate lends further support to the Tocquevillian interpretation. After all, it is also notable that this development is particular to democratic countries. For countries with more autocratic or technocratic regimes the situation is very different, as witness Southeast Asian countries like Hong Kong and Singapore, and the EU, where the principles of democratic governance are at best highly circumscribed. It is in accordance with the theory that parliamentarians in these countries have not got their share of the spoils derived from high public office.

Still, in a number of Western countries (Australia, Germany, New Zealand, and Switzerland), as well as democratic Japan, members of the executive elite in government have successfully defended their positions in absolute and relative terms. Thus, even if empirically this kind of macroinstitutional theory has a lot of good points, it is unable to stand alone.

A logical extension is modern *rational choice institutionalism*. It shares the actor assumptions of public choice theory with the focus on institutional mechanisms found in Tocqueville's theory of democracy. Furthermore, in spite of its rather narrow focus on an institutionally constrained game, in which elected members of parliament engage, it can easily be expanded to include other strata within the governing elite. However, the gains in realism come at a price. It is impossible from these assumptions to derive any specific predictions as to how and at what level rewards for the executive elite will be set. Any ex ante propositions as to this requires a quite detailed specification of the architecture of the system in question. Still, this analytic strategy presents a way to account for variation among countries that are otherwise alike in democratic terms.

How this may work is seen from two such specifications that have been applied. One prescribes pay and perquisites to be set within a universal bargaining system applied to the entire public sector and may be closely connected to the general labor market. The implication is that the salaries of the governing elite are linked to those of public employees in the lower echelons, and the ensuing prediction is gradual erosion similar to the Tocquevillian pattern described above, but expanded to cover also the executive elites, be they political or bureaucratic. This by and large corresponds to what is found in (for example) the Nordic countries. The other stylized setup presupposes pay and perquisites to be determined through a semi-automatic procedure that is neither coupled to labor market bargaining nor to current political bargaining in parliament. As a result the settling of salaries for the executive elite is highly depoliticized, a fact that protects them against Tocquevillian erosion. Again, this interpretation finds support in the experience of democratic countries like Australia and New Zealand.

This type of rational choice institutionalism basically argues for a strong trend towards stability, and that changes, if they take place at all, will be incremental in relation to the status quo. In this respect it is similar to the different versions of *historical institutionalism*. They all argue that strong path dependencies prevail in public policy. In some cases the causal logic is clearly institutional, with its focus on the transaction costs created by the institutions in place; in other cases, the logic approaches sociological reasoning, emphasizing norms and values shared over time; in yet another version economic logic is translated into politics through

the argument that policies already in place will, as time goes by, engender increasing political returns to the coalition behind them (Pierson, 2004). Yet, historical explanations of this kind lack a precise causal logic and suffer from the scarcity of generalized empirical insights they produce. Their analytical strength lies in their argument that the historical dimension in public policy should not be forgotten, while their Achilles heel is their inherent concentration on unique historical cases and events and their inability to account for radical change and policy reversals (Peters, 1999). Despite such criticisms, history is certainly at play, as both policies and institutions prove to be sticky in any of the countries for which evidence has been available on executive pay and perquisites.

The problem shared by several of the theories reviewed above is that they either predict a gradual, but unidirectional erosion of rewards to the executive elite or a basic stability in the prevailing pattern. The reality is, however, that change, whether it is radical change or incremental changes accumulating to a policy reversal, can be observed in some countries that seemed to follow either a Tocquevillian path or a leveling-down path characteristic of countries where rewards to the governing elite are settled together with other public service salaries. The figures reported in Table 5.3 show how such change has been effected within a relatively short span of time. *Cultural theory* has been brought in to reconcile such reversals of policy. The logic is that policy choices are embedded in a dominant cultural context that defines the values invoked to legitimate specific decisions and choices. They not only define what is appropriate in a particular social or organizational situation but also may frame actor preferences. As a theory, its deficiencies are similar to those found in rational choice institutionalism because in its general form it points nowhere. To derive any predictions from it, it is essential to specify the cultural context within which the analysis is set: for example, an egalitarian or a hierarchical one. As such specifications are by their very nature deemed to be quite vague, it might seem difficult to travel far along this road. Yet, logically, this is one way in which it would be possible to account for non-trivial change and policy reversals.

In *The Art of the State*, Christopher Hood (1999) demonstrated how thinking about governmental organization and public management is heavily dependent on particular modes of reasoning about human motivation and human action in organizational and social contexts. Since the 1990s the public sector in the Western world has experienced a change in basic reasoning concerning its organization and operation. This change is usually referred to as New Public Management (NPM) thinking (Goldfinch and Wallis, 2009). The NPM movement emphasizes the importance of management and leadership over formal structure and of economic incentives operating at the individual level over roles and rules. In addition, it tends to replace the ideal of a Weberian bureaucracy with that of corporate governance. Some countries were highly resistant not only to the rhetoric but also to the design prescriptions contained in the program. This was the case in France, Germany and Norway (Derlien, 1996, 2008; Olsen, 1996; Rouban, 2008). In other countries the ideas gained more ground. Most Western countries have always organized some government activities in state-owned enterprises or government corporations. To the conventional way of thinking about the management of such enterprises, the director received a salary and a pension similar to that of a high-ranking civil servant. With corporatization, the point of reference used for setting the salaries and contractual conditions for members of corporate management has been changed to correspond to those presumably applied in the private business sector.

A similar transformation has taken place within the civil service proper in some countries. This happened when the traditional ideas of civil service tenure, set salary scales and deferred pensions were replaced by the ideas of fixed-term appointments and individual contracts for leading civil servants

(Christensen and Gregory, 2008). In some countries this form of contractualism applies to agency directors and other top civil servants formally operating at arm's length from the political executive, while in the New Zealand model permanent secretaries have become chief executives working on contract with their departmental ministers (Boston et al., 1996; Gregory, 2001). When, as is the case in some countries, such contracts link pay with performance, the question is whether this works out in practice. Both experiments and empirical studies question this link. A study of Danish agency heads concluded that there was no statistically signigicant link between performance as defined in performance contracts and documented in agencies' annual reports and executive pay. Still, there is considerable variation in the one-off payments to agency heads, the implication being that the criteria used by permanent secretaries when deciding who should receive a bonus and, further, how much they deserve deviate from the performance goals stated in agency and executive contracts (Binderkrantz and Christensen, 2012; Weibel, Rost, and Osterloh, 2010).

PAYING FOR GOOD GOVERNANCE

Merit bureaucracy rests on the separation of office from the private property of its incumbents. Civil servants are not only recruited on the basis of their professional merits but also to carry out their job without eyeing their personal interests. This is in contrast to the practice of patrimonial and patronage forms of public administration. In the former, public authority was closely linked to feudal structures of property rights, whereas in the latter the selection of people for public office was linked to one party's conquest of political power at the expense of its political competitors.

Weberian bureaucracy rests on the presumption that a combination of lifelong tenure, a fixed salary and inalienable pension rights shields public bureaucracies and their civil servants from undue political pressure and from corruption. Even a cursory inspection of the indexes that are compiled on a regular basis reveals a relatively low level of corruption in countries that have basically organized their public administration in accordance with the principles of merit bureaucracy, while it is on average much higher in countries where political patronage is still important and political interference into even routine administrative dealings is a daily practice. Hence, the emphasis that the World Bank and academic analysts place on the enactment of civil service reforms in emerging economies as well as in developing countries is very well founded (Geddes, 1994; Nee and Opper, 2009; Nunberg, 1995; World Bank, 1997).

However, recent research questions the validity of a simple causal link between civil service reform along the lines described above and a corruption-free and effective administration. First, the EU made civil service reform a condition for the admission of the Central and East European countries. Still, formal steps to reform have turned out to be a weak guarantee of change and in several of the countries traditional habits of politicization, patronage and corruption coexist alongside seemingly radical reforms designed to implement a Weberian bureaucracy (Meyer-Sahling, 2011; SIGMA, 2010). Second, this is in line with other empirical research questioning the linkage between civil service structure, pay and corruption and more generally administrative behaviour (Rubin and Kellough, 2012; Rubin and Whitford, 2008). Finally, the trend in several Western countries is towards relaxing traditional civil service criteria, pre-eminently the tenure requirement, while upholding basic behavioural norms (Derlien and Peters, 2008).

In bureaucratic theory the focus is on the selection, promotion and rewards for civil servants rather than the level of these rewards. The corollary is that it is the certainty of future income rather than short-term economic gains that provides the incentives

(and the courage) to behave as befits a civil servant. A further corollary is that their pay should be calculated according to formulas that are general, and in addition that formal pay that is taxable and open to public scrutiny, rather than invisible perquisites, should form the core of their rewards.

The conventional logic raises intriguing policy issues. One is whether it is wise to virtually leave the level of rewards paid to civil servants and members of the political executive out of the discussion. This issue that complements and to some extent challenges the conventional civil service logic is in no way unfounded. Above, it was repeatedly noted how Tocqueville expressed concern for the ability of democracies to recruit sufficiently able persons to governing positions because in a democracy it was politically unsustainable to pay them a competitive salary in the long run. The same long-term concern can be raised for the civil service if the politics of settling their salaries lead to a gradual and continuous erosion of their pay.

Here, advocates of NPM reforms have invoked the insights of principal–agent theory, arguing that the incentives of a merit civil service with tenure are poorly engineered. Their argument is that such a system tends to create managers and civil servants who pay little attention to costs and efficiency, and who are in addition not very responsive to the concerns of their clients because their implicit employment contracts do not contain proper incentives. Their solution has been to replace tenure with fixed-term appointments based on individual contracts between the political executive and professional managers. When advocating contractual reforms, they refer to the practices of corporate governance, whose comparative supremacy is claimed to be due to the very incentives tenured civil service fails to provide.

This diagnosis and the prescription that accompanies it has, as also noted above, to some extent been implemented in some, though far from all, OECD countries. In spite of early doubts as to whether the high expectations to performance pay as an effective strategy for better government would actually hold, reform has quite consistently been pursued (cf. Ingraham, 1993; OECD, 2003, 2005). More recent empirical research gives support to these doubts (Binderkrantz and Christensen, 2012; Frey and Osterloh, 2005; Weibel, Rost, and Osterloh, 2010).

THE CONTINGENCIES OF PAY POLICIES

The discussion of patterns of pay and perquisites for government executives revealed a motley pattern of practices. It is unsurprising that given such circumstances it is impossible to boil down the observations to a simple and consistent set of descriptive generalizations. It is equally unsurprising, but nevertheless disappointing, that although a set of sometimes sophisticated analytical tools is at hand, it is equally difficult to account for the variation in a way that allows for consistent predictions, not to mention clear policy recommendations.

Still, having reviewed the literature, certain non-trivial conclusions seem justified. First, it is a fairly well-established fact that general market economics and specific labor market forces only play a minor role in the setting of rewards for political and administrative executives. This mainly political issue is usually dealt with through political procedures and bargaining. But it is worth noticing that economic constraints may be important for the political bargaining that determines the pay of government executives. Second, even if economic forces don't explain the empirical observations, individuals' rational pursuit of material and immaterial rewards cannot be dismissed as valid motivators of individual and collective choices. Constraints on executives are so tight that there are severe limits as to how far they can move to maximize their own rewards. Third, these constraints hardly point in a specific direction. One distinction is that between the macro- and micro-institutional setup. In a macro perspective there seems to be a marked difference with regard to the outcomes of either democratic competition or autocratic seclusion. In a micro-institutional perspective, however, much seems to depend on whether executive pay and perquisites are set according to semi-automatic procedures or integrated into a general bargaining round, politically connecting the regulation of elite rewards to those of public employees at the bottom of the hierarchy. Fourth, these strategic games are embedded in a wider social and cultural context. This will, over long periods, make it politically costly and illegitimate to institute a new policy, but when a change in cultural or ideological context comes about, which has actually happened in this field, the changed context provides new points of reference to be strategically exploited by groups who have considered themselves to be disadvantaged by past pay policies. Finally, when it comes to the policy lessons to be drawn, two conclusions seem justified. One is negative in as far as there is no clear evidence for linking executive pay clearly to either macro-economic performance at the societal level or micro-economic performance at the organizational or policy sector level. The other is positive in that it is far too early to discard merit bureaucracy as unsustainable, even though tenure is under pressure (Frey and Osterloh, 2005). For one thing the experience from the Western democracies seems to be that its adaptive capacity is much higher than certain theories will have it. For another thing, it also seems that the creation of a merit bureaucracy is one of the preconditions for better governance in Third World and emerging democracies and economies, although there is no short-term link between formal reform and performance.

REFERENCES

Binderkrantz, Anne Skorkjær and Christensen, Jørgen Grønnegaard (2012) 'Agency Performance and Executive Pay in Government', *Journal of Public Administration Research and Theory*, 22(1): 31–54.

Boston, Jonathan, Martin, John, Pallot, June, and Walsh, Pat (1996) *Public Management: The New Zealand Model*. Auckland: Oxford University Press.

Brans, Marleen (1994) 'Belgium: Public Office and Private Awards', in Christopher Hood and B. Guy Peters (eds), *Rewards at the Top. A Comparative Study of High Public Office*. London: Sage.

Burns, John P. (2007) 'Civil Service Reform in China,' *OECD Journal on Budgeting*, 7(1): 1–25.

Christensen, Jørgen Grønnegaard (2009) 'Danish Public Management Reform before and after NPM', in Shaun F. Goldfinch and Joe L. Wallis (eds), *International Handbook of Public Management Reform*. Cheltenham: Edward Elgar.

Christensen, Jørgen Grønnegaard and Gregory, Robert (2008) 'Public Personnel Policies and Personnel Administration', in Hans-Ulrich Derlien and B. Guy Peters (eds), *The State at Work, Vol. 2*. Cheltenham: Edward Elgar.

Christensen, Jørgen Grønnegaard and Yesilkagit, Kutsal (2006) 'Delegation and Specialization in Regulatory Administration: A Comparative Analysis of Denmark, the Netherlands and Sweden', in Tom Christensen and Per Lægreid (eds), *Autonomy and Regulation*. Cheltenham: Edward Elgar.

Derlien, Hans-Ulrich (1994) 'Germany: The Structure and Dynamics of the Reward System for Bureaucratic and Political Elites', in Christopher Hood and B. Guy Peters (eds), *Rewards at the Top. A Comparative Study of High Office*. London: Sage.

Derlien, Hans-Ulrich (1996) 'Germany: The Intelligence of Bureaucracy in a Decentralized Polity', in Johan P. Olsen and B. Guy Peters (eds), *Lessons from Experience*. Oslo: Scandinavian University Press.

Derlien, Hans-Ulrich (2008) 'The German Public Service: Between Tradition and Transformation,' in Hans-Ulrich Derlien and B. Guy Peters (eds), *The State at Work, Vol. 1*. Cheltenham: Edward Elgar.

Derlien, Hans-Ulrich and Peters, B. Guy (eds) (2008). *The State at Work, Vols 1–2*. Cheltenham: Edward Elgar.

Frey, Bruno S. and Osterloh, Margit (2005) 'Yes, Managers Should Be Paid Like Bureaucrats', *Journal of Management Inquiry*, 14(1): 96–111.

Geddes, Barbara (1994) *Politician's Dilemma: Building State Capacity in Latin America*. Berkeley, CA: University of California Press.

Goldfinch, Shaun F. and Wallis, Joe L. (eds) (2009) *International Handbook of Public Management Reform*. Cheltenham: Edward Elgar.

Gregory, Robert (2001) 'Transforming Governmental Culture: A Sceptical View of New Public Management', in Tom Christensen and Per Lægreid (eds), *New Public Management. The Transformation of Ideas and Practice*. Aldershot: Ashgate.

Gregory, Robert and Christensen, Jørgen Grønnegaard (2004) 'Similar Ends, Differing Means: Contractualism and Civil Service Reform in Denmark and New Zealand', *Governance*, 17(1): 59–82.

Hood, Christopher (1994) 'The UK', in Christopher Hood and B. Guy Peters (eds), *Rewards at the Top. A Comparative Study of High Public Office*. London: Sage.

Hood, Christopher (1999) *The Art of the State*. Oxford: Clarendon Press.

Hood, Christopher and Askim, Jostein (2003) 'Alike at the Summit?', in Christopher Hood and B. Guy Peter (eds), *Reward for High Public Office: Asian and Pacific Rim States*. London: Routledge.

Hood, Christopher and Lambert, Sonia (1994) 'Mountain Tops or Iceberg Tips? Some Comparative Data on RHPOs', in Christopher Hood and B. Guy Peters (eds), *Rewards at the Top. A Comparative Study of High Office*. London: Sage.

Hood, Christopher and Peters, B. Guy (eds) (1994) *Rewards at the Top. A Comparative Study of High Public Office*. London: Sage.

Hood, Christopher and Peters, B. Guy (1995) 'Erosion and Variety in Pay for High Public Office', *Governance*, 8: 171–194.

Hood, Christopher and Peters, B. Guy (eds) (2003) *Reward for High Public Office: Asian and Pacific Rim States*. London: Routledge.

Horn, Murray J. (1995) *The Political Economy of Public Administration*. New York: Cambridge University Press.

Ingraham, Patricia (1993) 'Of Pigs in Pokes and Policy Diffusion: Another Look at Pay-for-Performance', *Public Adminsitration Review*, 53(4): 348–356.

Ketelaar, Anne, Manning, Nick and Turkisch, Edouard (2007) Performance-based Arrangements for Senior Civil Servants OECD and other Country Experiences. *OECD Working Papers on Public Governance 2007/5*. Paris: OECD.

Klöti, Ulrich (1994) 'Switzerland: Serving the State and Maximizing Income', in Christopher Hood and B. Guy Peters (eds), *Rewards at the Top. A Comparative Study of High Office*. London: Sage.

Lewis, David E. (2008) *The Politics of Presidential Appointments*. Princeton: Princeton University Press.

Liegl, Barbara and Müller, Wolfgang C. (1999) 'Senior Officials in Austria', in Edward C. Page and

Vincent Wright (eds), *Bureaucratic Élites in Western European States*. Oxford: Oxford University Press.

Nee, Victor and Opper, Sonja (2009) 'Bureaucracy and Financial Markets' *Kyklos*, 62(2): 293–315.

Meyer-Sahling, Jan (2011) 'The Durability of EU Civil Service Policy in Central and Eastern Europe after Accession', *Governance*, 24(2): 231–260.

Nunberg, Barbara (1995) *Managing the Civil Service. Reform Lessons from Advanced Industrialized Countries*. Washington, DC: World Bank.

OECD (2003) *Managing Senior Management: Senior Civil Service Reform in OECD Member Countries*. Paris: OECD.

OECD (2005) *Performance-related Pay Policies for Government Employees*. Paris: OECD.

Olsen, Johan P. (1996) 'Norway: Slow Learner – or Another Triumph of the Tortoise?', in Johan P. Olsen and B. Guy Peters (eds), *Lessons from Experience*. Oslo: Scandinavian University Press.

Peters, B. Guy (1999) *Institutional Theory in Political Science*. London: Pinter.

Peters, B. Guy (2010) *The Politics of Bureaucracy,* 6th edn. London: Longman.

Pierson, Paul (2004) *Politics in Time*. Princeton, NJ: Princeton University Press.

Ridley, F.F. and Doig, Alan (eds) (1995) *Sleaze: Politicians, Private Interests and Public Reaction*. Oxford: Oxford University Press.

Rouban, Luc (1998) *La Fin des technocrates?* Paris: Presses de Science Po.

Rouban, Luc (2008) 'The French Paradox: A Huge but Fragmented Public Service', in Hans-Ulrich Derlien and B. Guy Peters (eds), *The State at Work, Vol. 1*. Cheltenham: Edward Elgar.

Rubin, Ellen V. and Edward, Kellough, J. (2012) 'Does Civil Service Reform Affect Behavior? Linking Alternative Personnel Systems, Perceptions of Procedural Justice, and Complaints', *Journal of Public Administration Research and Theory*, 22(1): 121–141.

Rubin, Ellen V. and Whitford, Andrew (2008) ' Effects of the Institutional Design of the Civil Service: Evidence from Corruption', *International Public Management Journal*, 11(4): 404–425.

SIGMA (2010) *Can Civil Service Reforms Last? The European Union's 5th Enlargement and Future Policy Orientations*. Paris: OECD.

Tocqueville, Alexis de (1835/1963) *De la Démocratie en Amérique*. Paris: Union Générale d'Éditions.

Waxin, Marie-France and Bateman, Robert (2009) 'HRM in the Public Sector: Is it Enough?', in Shaun F. Goldfinch and Joe L. Wallis (eds), *International Handbook of Public Management Reform*. Cheltenham: Edward Elgar.

Weber, Max (1919/1988) *Politik als Beruf,* in *Gesammelte Politische Schriften*. Tübingen: J.C.B. Mohr.

Wegrich, Kai (2009) 'Public Management Reform in the United Kingdom: Great Leaps, Small Steps and Policies as Their Own Cause', in Shaun F. Goldfinch and Joe L. Wallis (eds), *International Handbook of Public Management Reform*. Cheltenham: Edward Elgar.

Weibel, Antoinette, Katja Rost, and Margit Osterloh (2010) 'Pay for performance in the public sector. Benefits and (hidden) costs', *Journal of Public Administration Research and Theory*, 20(4): 387–412.

Wise, Lois Recascino (1996) 'Internal Labor Markets', in Hans A.G.M. Bekke et al. (eds), *Civil Service Systems in Comparative Perspective*. Bloomington, IN: Indiana University Press.

World Bank (1997) *The State in a Changing World*. Washington, DC: World Bank.

6

Leadership and the Senior Service from a Comparative Perspective

John Halligan

The leadership of the senior service has undergone substantial change that reflects the era of public sector reform, environmental trends and new thinking about how civil service systems should operate. The environment that was once relatively stable for public organizations has become more competitive, public–private differences have narrowed and the constraints and rules that once dictated much of the character of public organizations have less importance, with the notable exception of those reflecting democratic governance. Senior services have become more open, managerial and generalist and have placed greater emphasis on leadership development.

Nevertheless, there continue to be wide variations within senior services and between country systems. The nature of the senior service and the significance of leadership development vary with administrative traditions, societal factors, institutions and level of reform. Two patterns can be discerned for some purposes: the first, of senior services that have been modernizing within state traditions that are still relatively closed and somewhat impervious to extensive change; and the second, of services that have been more receptive to change, including management and new leadership concepts, and are consequently more open. Leadership frameworks have been developed and tested in a number of countries, and many have established a senior executive corps. For other countries, senior services remain more aligned with administrative traditions that are less sympathetic to these types of change.

The study of leadership in the public sector has also advanced considerably over the last decade reflecting in large part the rapidly changing subject matter and the incorporation of more eclectic and creative theorizing and analysis (compare Boin and Christensen 2008; Raffel et al., 2009; Van Wart, 2005).

A number of leadership issues are salient, reflecting the special character of public organizations, challenges of new leadership demands, the results (often inconclusive) of management experiments and the unresolved tensions between neutral and responsive competence. This chapter reviews these dimensions of the changing approaches to leadership and the senior service within a comparative perspective that recognizes different patterns and the role of institutional factors.

SENIOR SERVICES

Defining the senior service

The senior service comprises heads of ministries, departments, bureaus and agencies within the core civil service (variously known as departmental or permanent secretaries, chief executives, director-generals, etc.) and other senior officials as designated within the central government of each country. The 'higher' components of Anglo-American civil services have ranged from 0.13 per cent to 2.1 per cent, with 1 per cent being suggested as an ideal size (Hede, 1991), but less than 1 per cent has since been reported plus an international trend favouring smaller senior services (World Bank, 2005: 5).

It is important to recognize both the wide variations between country systems and within senior services. A senior service can be expected to comprise a range of generalists and specialists for policy, management, delivery, regulation and technical work. The traditional senior public servant was more likely to have either 'generalist institutional knowledge' or be a specialist in a policy field (OECD, 2008: 73). Today, mainstream public servants may coexist with private sector technocrats and political operatives. Senior officials may have well-defined responsibilities (say policy advice) or combine several elements, including political and administrative/management roles. Professional specialization and defined corps within the civil service contribute to the complexity. The senior service in France has been depicted as 'a heterogeneous category whose

members share neither the same careers nor the same prestige nor the same professional culture' (Rouban, 1999: 65).

The civil service may be more differentiated, with functions associated with specialized organizations that have distinctive cultures. In Britain's agencification phase, approaching 80 per cent of British civil servants were in some form of executive agency. Significant differences were reported between British civil servants and agency chief executives: the former were less disposed to change but more willing to be pragmatic (that is, bending rules to achieve results), while the latter valued control more where it concerned future-oriented activity (Dawson, 2001: 265; Mellon, 2000). There was also considerable variability in the dividing line between middle and senior management, and some senior services have been decapitated compared to others in so far as one or more layers of the most senior positions were assigned to political appointments that may not derive from the civil service. The intermingling of professional civil servants and political appointees may extend to several levels of the senior service (OECD, 2011: 94–95).

Most countries recognize an explicit group of senior public servants, which can extend to legal or formal definition. For a small number of OECD countries, the senior service has a relatively informal basis (e.g. France, Italy, Japan and Norway) (OECD, 2008: 72).

For all these reasons, and the complexity of governmental systems, it is often difficult either to define explicitly the senior service or to characterize it in simple terms. The question has also been posed as to whether there was a US higher civil service in the sense of other systems, and that images derived from several systems could be observed as 'loose groupings of people where the lines of policy, politics, and administration merge in a jumble of bodies' (Heclo, 1984: 8–9). The identification of the senior service is facilitated in reformed systems where classification systems have been simplified and organizational rationalization has occurred, or where a defined senior service exists.

Patterns of senior service

Two patterns of senior service have been identified: those that have been modernized within state traditions, and which may continue to be relatively closed and less responsive to major change; and systems that have been receptive to management change and leadership concepts, and have become increasingly open. Support for the two patterns can be found in the tendency to analyse dimensions of senior services in terms of opposing perspectives: centralized and decentralized approaches to leadership development (OECD, 2001), merit versus patronage in recruitment (Peters, 2010), position versus career recruitment (OECD, 2003), dichotomized characteristics of heads of departments and ministries (Rhodes and Weller, 2001), and two broad conceptions of 'public authority' (based on a distinctive service with rights and privileges) and 'service provision' (based on comparability with the private sector) (Page and Wright, 1999). However, these features of senior services do not necessarily coincide, and the exceptions indicate much greater complexity.

The standard distinction between *Rechtsstaat* (or rule of law) and public interest systems continues to provide the basis for the two patterns. The differentiation is grounded in distinctive administrative cultures and associated structures, with the legal regulation of administration, judicial review and stronger state traditions of the European systems dominating the first, and the greater flexibilities of the Westminster model and the predisposition to private management of Anglo-Saxon countries underlying the second pattern. There are a number of variations on the two patterns, with several smaller European states exhibiting features of both, perhaps forming a third category. There has also been the Korean and Japanese mix of elitism and legalism, and until recently, closed career systems (Kim, 2002; Pierre, 1995; Pollitt and Bouckaert, 2004).

Comparing and managing senior services

The important questions about the senior service centre on its constitution and the provision for the systemic handling of the higher service. The relationship between the conception and the organization of the civil service influences the roles (and potential) of the senior service. Three elements that shape and control the capacity for leadership are the relationship between politicians and bureaucrats, the definition of the senior management role, and the organization of the service.

In terms of relations between politicians and the senior service, three approaches to comparison can be noted. First, a policy role approach seeks to locate responsibilities focusing on politicians and bureaucrats but also on the relative importance of other actors internal and external to government (Aberbach et al., 1981; Peters and Pierre, 2001). Second, several studies focus on political control through either the neutral senior service (the British model), the 'commanding heights' approach (through control of the most senior appointments and/or through political advisers) or politicization of the service through party membership (Page and Wright, 1999). Third, a career approach produces a spectrum of possibilities, ranging from blended careers (France) to separate careers (Anglo countries), with other systems falling between the two. Under the truncated hierarchy (e.g., the United States), the career official is unable to rise to the highest positions in an agency (Peters, 2010).

Comparisons of the organization of senior services can be made in terms of several dimensions. First is whether there is a career service or not and the approach to recruitment is closed or open. Recruitment systems can be divided into the career and position systems (OECD, 2003). A standard traditional system was distinguished by boundaries and career differentiation and distinctiveness. Many systems have opened up positions to external recruitment and have modified (even minimized) the differentiation between public and private sectors. Sweden, for example, has not maintained a career service, and agencies appoint staff to positions that have been publicly advertised. In contrast, the career services of some systems have been closed in the past, with controlled (and often limited) entry from the outside.

Second is the level of commitment to public management, and in particular performance. This may entail reliance on different types of contract and performance incentives and appraisal. It became standard practice to use individual performance agreements for the senior service, but these schemes have not necessarily been sustained in practice.

Third, is the location of responsibility for the management of the senior service: Is it centralized, decentralized or shared? Related questions are the level and mode of integration (including the use or not of a special corps, discussed later), and the relative importance of structure, culture and ethos, and elite recruitment. The several roles include recruitment, training, system maintenance and preservation and enhancement of civil service values. The roles may be divided among one or more central agencies, and between the centre and line agencies. Rule making for the senior service might be expected to be a responsibility of the centre, but agencies may have considerable discretion (OECD, 2003).

The recruitment process for senior civil servants is more centralized than that for other civil servants (OECD, 2011: 92–93). A number of the latter have an operational senior executive service (SES). Senior recruitment may otherwise be relatively decentralized, although standard procedures may exist, and where there is no explicit senior management system, senior officials may nevertheless be subject to special terms and conditions of employment. Central training institutes have been relied on in systems that are otherwise fairly decentralized (such as Germany: OECD, 2001).

Central agencies play a range of systemic roles. The role of the Senior Public Service office in the Netherlands has been to seek greater integration through the senior service, including the development of interdepartmental links and service-wide initiatives (Steen and Van der Meer, 2009). In cases where responsibility for cultivating the senior service was devolved to chief executives of line agencies (e.g. Australia and New Zealand), the central agencies roles were subsequently strengthened.

The final question is oversight of the senior service and promotion of the core values of public service (Ingraham, 1998). Institutional leadership can be provided in the form of either a central agency with systemic responsibilities and/or a specified head of the civil service. The inculcation of values may best be achieved through recruitment, training or role models.

CHANGING CONCEPTIONS OF LEADERSHIP

The scope of the interest here is both with changing conceptions and approaches, as well as with the nature of leaders and leadership qua members of the senior service and relations between appointed and elected leaders (e.g., Peters and Pierre, 2001, 2004), which are picked up in later sections.

Traditional academic questions about leadership fall into two important categories for our purposes here. First, there is the question of what shapes organizational leadership. The familiar option is that it derives from the attributes of unusual individuals in top positions, but another (either an alternative or complementary) position, is that leadership is a product of an organizational context (e.g., the 'density of administrative compe-tence': James March quoted in Doig and Hargrove, 1987: 3). The second question is how significant is leadership? The responses range from positions that leadership is either unimportant (Kaufman, 1981) or change is determined environmentally, to arguments that individual leadership registers an impact (Doig and Hargrove, 1987), and is significant in applying design principles in institution building (Boin and Christensen, 2008; Halligan, 2008). A more inclusive perspec-tive argues for an integrative leadership approach (Van Slyke and Alexander, 2006; Van Wart, 2005) or envisages leadership (adapting Rockman, 1991: 37), as interre-lated with and dependent upon situational factors, administrative culture, institutional forms and the agenda of political leaders.

Questions about the nature of and potential for leadership in a civil service are not settled. One strongly argued case is that civil service leadership remains different from that of business because of constitu-tional and political contexts (do they not *serve* political leaders?), and that even the most senior civil servants cannot be rated as leaders in terms of the business management literature because they are managers or clerks (Performance and Innovation Unit, 2001; Theakston, 1999). Yet some manage-ment studies focus on corporate change across public and private sectors and the types of leader that are associated with dif-ferent tasks (e.g., Stace and Dunphy, 2001; Van Wart, 2005).

There has been movement in conceptions and analysis of civil service leadership. Specific leaders rather than leadership were inclined to be the focus. Leaders were the outstanding individuals who were recognized as having made a significant contribution to public service. Other analyses have taken the form of comparative biography and the linking of case studies of leadership to institutional development and performance (Chapman, 1984; Dutil, 2010; Theakston, 1999, 2000), whether of 'entrepreneurs' who display 'uncommon rationality' (Doig and

Hargrove, 1987) or to the attributes of effec-tive leadership (Riccucci, 2000).[1]

A resurgence of interest in leadership development has been apparent, with the main impetus being the changing environ-ment, which has been to require a new type of leadership (OECD, 2001: 13–15). Several propositions about leadership have become increasingly accepted. First is the recognition that leadership now matters. This largely reflects a substantial shift from traditional administration dominated by the tasks of policy advice to political leaders and process implementation, to acceptance of leadership defined increasingly in management terms and often within a broader governance envi-ronment. This includes leaders being expected to manage down through handling and empowering staff more effectively (e.g., the importance of human relations in the European Union [EU]: Maor, 2000).

Second, there is a better understanding that there are different types of leadership, and that this is a situational question. Recognition of distinctive leadership styles is contingent upon different organizational con-texts and demands. Leadership styles may be defined in terms of the scale of change (incremental to transformational), style of change (ranging from consultative to direc-tive) and commitment to the civil service (e.g., conservator and guardian) (Stace and Dunphy, 2001; Theakston, 1999; Van Wart, 2005).

Third is the more radical position, which reflects the movement from leadership con-ceived in terms of mandarins' attributes to that of acquired skills, which suggests that everyone can become a leader. One expres-sion of this was the assumption by the former head of the British civil service that leaders could be nurtured and skills learned (Wilson, 2000), which implied that leadership could become less exclusive and more inclusive. A related aspect is that leadership applies at several levels. According to OECD, requir-ing leadership 'at all levels is revolutionary in its potential impact, and is an important driver of the move to redefine public sector leadership' (2001: 15). Leading within public organizations has acquired new dimensions and now extends to a range of staff with resource management responsibilities.

New processes have been adopted for leading change and focusing complex organizations. An example was Sue Vardon's use of Kotter's injunction to assemble a 'Guiding Coalition' with sufficient power to lead change to Australia's large multi-purpose delivery agency Centrelink, where a board of 60 or more SES officers regularly met to discuss strategic issues and decide on management directions (Halligan, 2008; Kotter and Cohen, 2002; Vardon, 2000).

CHANGING SENIOR SERVICES

The changing environment and government responses internationally have been well documented (e.g., Ingraham et al., 1999; OECD, 2011; Pollitt and Bouckaert, 2004). The drivers of change can be categorized in several ways. The exogenous impacts of global economic and technological change mean that civil services have to respond more rapidly. As the rate of change increases, so it is argued leadership becomes more important, and responsibility for change has to be broadened organizationally.

The reputation of the civil service has been under greater scrutiny, reflecting *inter alia* declining support for key public and private institutions in many countries, loss of trust in government, and particularly of politicians, and the questioning that arises where a system has been under constant pressure to reform. It has also been recognized (OECD, 2001) that a number of the long-established elite civil services have experienced a loss in popular legitimacy.

Related to this has been the intensifying of pressures on government with greater policy complexity and increasing public expectations for services. Two results are that these pressures are translated into demands for the civil service to deliver, and politicians turn to

other levers where officials are perceived to be inadequate.

While the drivers are common to many countries, the variable responses reflect obstacles to change (e.g., unions, structures and constitutions) and preferences derived from administrative culture and traditions (Painter and Peters 2010; Pollitt and Bouckaert, 2004).

Several broad trends both define the directions in which some services are moving and provide the boundaries for others. Senior services have become rather more open, relying more on generalists, expanding their management roles and (under particular circumstances) cultivating leadership development (OECD, 2001). There has also been a tendency towards greater organizational specialization (e.g., in production and policy advice to ministers) and stronger political direction. However, while the impact of New Public Management may be substantial within a country's public sector, this is often not the case at the senior service level of central government of countries where there is a strong public authority conception of the state (Page and Wright, 1999: 275). The decades of reform have also produced some reinforcement of tradition through neo-Weberianism or retro-administration in other systems.

Roles

The roles of the senior service have evolved over time, but the rate of change has accelerated and responsibilities now differ from those performed under traditional public administration. There is greater consciousness of the tasks of leading in systems operating within management cultures. The infusion of private sector values and techniques has meant a greater emphasis on business planning, being entrepreneurial, performance management and the application of corporate governance principles. Managing externally is now routinely conceived of in terms of customers, clients and stakeholders. These relationships have featured contract management and alliances, collaborations and partnerships within broader governance arrangements.

The policy role of the senior public service has experienced progressive attrition from the traditional position. The rise of managerialism in the 1980s was a reaction against both the emphasis on policy work and the lack of management skills. At the same time, a tendency has been for the political executive to rely increasingly on alternative sources of advice and on their private office staff as conduits for extra-government proposals. As the policy capacity of the ministerial office has been strengthened, the public servant's role has contracted.

With contestable advice, there are more competitors than before: the senior service may no longer be the government's dominant source of advice, although it remains the key advisory voice for the public interest. The policy advisory role may be lost to the civil service, shared with the political executive or diffused across a range of internal and external actors that are competing for attention.

The senior civil servant's role, then, has been transformed over time in a number of ways. In Germany, for example, the decline in opportunities to initiate and champion policies produced gradual changes in 'the profile of the effective senior official from an agenda setter and policy initiator to a political highly sensitive policy coordinator' (Goetz, 1999: 149). A diverse range of roles have been emphasized such as broker, coordinator and fine-tuning of other's policy contributions, but in more challenging environments those of strategic leadership on government reform agenda, effective implementation of policy, collaborating in networks, inter-organizational sharing of accountability and results and crisis mitigation have come to the fore (Barberis, 1998; Horton, 2009; Ingraham, 1998; Mandell and Keast, 2009; OECD, 2011; Van Dorpe and Horton, 2011).

The implications of these changing roles, new relationships and the associated features of careers and profession have important long-term implications for senior services that are discussed later. Here we can note that the US position, where officials have long been largely confined to the roles of manager or technician (but not adviser with direct access to the political executive), begins to look more familiar to other systems (Rockman, 1995).

Leadership characteristics

Most members of the senior service continue to be recruited from within the civil service in OECD countries (and the majority from the same agency), but several draw more on external recruitment (more like 25 per cent compared to less than 10 per cent) (OECD, 1997: Tables 6 and 8).

The age of senior public servants has declined in some countries, but remains stable in others. Seniority continues to be important in a number of countries, particularly in continental Europe. Turnover and tenure were similarly variable. Lawyers continue to predominate overall in continental countries (OECD, 1997; Page and Wright, 1999; Peters, 2001).

There have been significant increases in the proportion of women in senior positions, but the proportion remains below 20 per cent for the majority of OECD countries (with exceptions such as Finland, with around 75 per cent, and Mexico, New Zealand and Portugal exceeding 30 per cent) (OECD, 2001: 28, 2008: 73). The contrasts are most striking with heads of ministries and departments, where some countries have negligible numbers.

The careers of departmental secretaries have been tracked for the past 30 years, with differences being strongest between European and Antipodean countries. The latter recruit them younger, for shorter terms and dispatch them earlier. Of the European countries, France differed from Denmark and the Netherlands in significant respects (Rhodes and Weller, 2001: 232).

Although subject to change in some services, the elite corps has been substantially preserved. In Britain, for example, they have remained fairly constant in terms of collective characteristics (including Oxbridge backgrounds), although more diversity is apparent. They continue to be minister-oriented even if they are now managerially inclined (Barberis, 1998; Horton, 2009). The overwhelming dominance of one university in both Japan and Korea in the education of the upper echelons of their civil services has been possibly unequalled by other OECD countries (Kim and Kim, 1997: 176–178).

The different patterns are indicated by the striking contrasts that exist in the perceptions of higher civil servants: the French regard themselves still as intellectuals rather than managers, while the British secretary is now more inclined to being 'a Manager than a Mandarin' (Dargie and Locke, 1998: 179; Rouban, 1999: 66).

Leadership development

Leadership development has been given more attention in rapidly changing environments, but its significance still depends on state traditions, societal factors, institutional structures and the extent of reform. Many countries have long maintained arrangements for recruiting and cultivating a senior elite. Leadership development is more important where society is diversified, government is decentralized, public administration is less traditional and where comprehensive reform has succeeded incremental change (OECD, 2000: 2).

Two generalized approaches are apparent: either highly centralized or decentralized (OECD, 2001: 19–20). The centralized approach involves high intervention to identify and cultivate potential at an early stage through processes of selection, training and career management. This approach has best been exemplified by the French Ecole Nationale d'Administration (ENA), but has also been apparent in Japan and Korea (although the latter now has provision for limited lateral entry: OECD 2008: 75).

The latest OECD (2011: 92–93) data indicate that France, Israel, Korea and the United Kingdom maintain mechanisms for identifying potential high fliers at an early stage. The decentralized approach is identified with market-driven principles. New Zealand, which used the 'purest form' of this approach, eventually however reviewed its position.[2]

In practice, programs contain centralized and decentralized elements (Maor, 2000). Approaches include the use of comprehensive strategies (e.g., Norway), institutions for leadership development (e.g., Sweden and the United States), targeting high flyers in the fast stream from the beginning of their careers (Singapore and the United Kingdom), and some form of senior executive service. New leadership frameworks have been developed and tested in a number of countries, with increasing emphasis on core competencies (Horton, 2009; Mau, 2009; OECD, 2001).

Senior executive service

A senior executive corps has been another means for developing leadership, although it is designed to serve other purposes as well. Such systems have been focused, with some exceptions, on Anglo-American countries, and may either be termed the senior executive service (SES) or go under another name.

The first group of senior executive services were created in Australia, New Zealand and the United States in the late 1970s and 1980s (as well as some states in the two federal systems). Canada's 'management category' also qualifies, although somewhat differently conceived (Hede, 1991). In these systems the heads of agencies have not been members of the SES, in the US case because they are political positions.

The SES originated in the United States in 1978 as a scheme to develop executive management, accountability and competences reflecting private sector incentives and practices. Standard concepts that have become identified with an SES have been the generalist elite, with an emphasis on performance, capacity for redeployment, appraisal and merit pay. For a variety of reasons, some deriving from the US context, the scheme did not achieve the objectives for mobility, remuneration and becoming a corps of generalist managers operating within a performance culture. The SES was successful politically in that it aided responsiveness. Despite concerns about the fate of the civil service ethos, there is evidence of commitment to core public service values (Aberbach and Rockman, 2000; Ingraham and Moynihan, 2000).

Two contrasting experiences are the Australian and that of New Zealand, the first relatively positive, the second negative. A central component of the Australian reform program was a reformulation of the senior public service as the SES in 1984. Following the existing schemes in the United States and the state of Victoria, the basic principles were the concept of a service-wide executive group that was internally mobile and increasingly invigorated by the recruitment of persons externally, more emphasis on the development of managerial skills and more flexibility for department heads in allocating staff resources (Halligan, 1992). The long-term results of the SES have been reasonably successful, with some mobility, steady infusions of outsiders, a degree of corporate identity and regular use of performance appraisal and (more problematically) performance pay.

A senior executive service was also created in New Zealand to produce a unified set of career professionals, but this objective was not realized under its contractual model within a decentralized system. The SES never developed an ethos and inclusive membership, the problem deriving from the salary ceiling, which meant that in order to attract qualified staff from outside the outsiders had to be employed outside the SES. The SES was soon pronounced a failure, and moribund (Bhatta, 2001), and was subsequently terminated.

The second-generation experiments with the concept of a senior corps, in the United

Kingdom (Senior Civil Service) and the Netherlands (Senior Public Service), moved in this direction in the mid-1990s. Both emphasized mobility and interdepartmental cooperation as well as other standard SES considerations (e.g., expanding management skills). The Dutch model – open, job-oriented and decentralized – moved towards an integrated service with the creation of a Senior Public Service in 1995 for the top three scales. The rationale included the growing policy complexity and internationalization (Steen and Van der Meer, 2009). The advantages of such a system include the integration of 'a loose collection' of officials into a leadership team that shares values and visions for the future of government (OECD, 2001: 27).

LEADERSHIP ISSUES

The long-term impact of trends on the character of public organizations has implications for autonomy, the handling of values and guidance of the senior service, the capacity to approximate business organizations through the new management experiments, and the implications of changing roles. There is a more intense range of challenges involved in leading in competitive environments where governance conditions prevail, alternative providers exist and the arrangements are contestable and diffuse.

First, there is a set of questions that centres on the performance of public officials under different operating environments, such as the legalistic bureaucracy and the managerialized system. It is possible that the increasing emphasis on outcomes will produce insights about comparative performance, at least within the latter category as management systems become more sophisticated. The results are inconclusive about the efficacy of management approaches to public officials who are operating under contracts and conflicting incentives. There has been high investment in performance management systems based on performance agreements in Anglo-American systems (Bouckaert and Halligan, 2008), but lack of analysis of their efficacy. There have been mixed reports about how to measure and reward performance (Ingraham, 1998; OECD, 2003), and a paradox of performance pay has been that it remains popular while not overly successful (Lægreid, 2001).

Second, the results of experiments with new leadership approaches are unclear. Various schemes have been implemented following extensive testing of competencies and there is high commitment to leadership at several levels, but without independent evaluation there continues to be some uncertainty about how well these ideas have transferred to the public sector. There continues to be need for 'an evaluation approach that monitors how well the organization is learning and how well it uses that learning to achieve its strategic objectives.' (Horton, 2009: 375).

This leads to the third point, which is that the demands of political responsiveness have meant the scope for leadership is changing and possibly contracting. Where such demands are intense, the potential for leadership may be limited. This is best show by two types of political role in appointments following elections. For a number of the OECD (2011) countries surveyed in 2010 (including Canada, Denmark, the Netherlands, New Zealand and Norway) there is no turnover of senior civil servants, whereas in the majority of cases there is for the most senior positions, and extending down much further, particularly in Eastern European countries (the Czech Republic, Hungary, the Slovak Republic and Turkey). Relations with politicians are otherwise notable for a range of broadly similar experiences: the senior service had come under mounting pressure from political advisers (e.g., in the UK), politicized (e.g., in France and Germany), or more generally vulnerable and/or subject to short-term responsiveness (in many countries). This relationship has become more ambiguous, and may require that 'communication and facilitation replace unidimensional

direction and leadership' (Ingraham, 1998: 181; also Eichbaum and Shaw, 2010; Halligan, 2001; Matheson et al., 2008; Peters and Pierre, 2004; Rouban, 1999; 't Hart and Wille, 2006).

The importance of these trends and issues raises the question about the character of senior services in the long term. The rebalancing of relationships during recent decades was a reaction by political executives to a period in which senior officials were seen as too independent and influential. But is the redistribution of power part of a cyclical process and is it irreversible? Where the result is excessive political influence, a new imbalance may result, and greater ambiguity in the mediation of relationships.

In this regard, another possibility was suggested by Belgium's attempt at reversing historic patterns. The country had traditionally relied on ministerial cabinets, and had been characterized by high political penetration of the administrative system and a marginalized role for the civil service in policy formulation. It instituted policy boards at the interface between the minister and department in order to strengthen civil servants' role in producing advice (Brans, 2002).

In a number of contexts, debate has occurred about whether trends mean the loss of fundamental elements that define the senior service, or is there too much emphasis on 'growing' leaders as opposed to 'buying' them externally (Ingraham, 2006)? With changes to core relationships, the professional standing of the senior service, conceptions of ministerial responsibility and good governance, the survivability of models is threatened (e.g. Campbell and Wilson, 1995 on Whitehall). The durability of administrative traditions appears to ensure adherence to core values where there is the prospect of system adaptation (Painter and Peters, 2010).

Debate also continues about different views of the role of the senior service and the importance of state traditions (e.g., ranging from guardians of the public interest to political instruments). A fundamental question is the conception of what leadership should be and how it relates to the broader conception of the senior service (Hunt and O'Toole, 1998). Of concern in countries such as the United States has been the lack of institutional leadership that seeks to infuse organizations with value and a sense of the worthiness beyond day-to-day operations. The lament about the lack of a voice to champion higher civil service values has echoes in other systems (Heclo, 2000: 227–228). In these days of responsive servants, the role of the head of the civil service, where such a position exists, may be preoccupied with serving the government's short-term interests rather than the tasks of transmitting and protecting the values of the civil service, and providing a role model (Theakston, 1999).

But perhaps civil service systems have come full circle, as suggested by two cases. The first case, a British study on *Strengthening Leadership* (Performance and Innovation Unit, 2001), adopted a balanced approach to the nature of the civil service, while arguing for the generic features of public sector leadership that arise from an operating environment distinguished by political leaders, accountability, public ethos and cooperation in service delivery. OECD countries report that there is a missing element between the public interest and public service cultures: 'A common complaint is lack of dedication to the underlying values of public service and the interests of the citizens served.' Enhancing public sector leadership is advanced as the means for promoting institutional change in the public interest by espousing fundamental values depicted as 'public spiritedness' (OECD, 2000: 7, 12).

The second case is centred on the roles of Australian departmental secretaries. The relationships between secretaries and ministers have at times been fraught with boundary issues, particularly where there is a tendency for successive governments to claim ownership of the public service. Politicians' lack of strategic focus and 'short-termism' had indicated that an alternative was needed to relying heavily on political direction.

A potentially significant clarification of the secretary's role was the introduction of the stewardship function that is designed for the public service to have 'the capacity to serve successive governments. A stewardship capability must exist regardless of the style of any one Minister or government', and covers financial sustainability and efficient resource management, plus 'less tangible factors such as maintaining the trust placed in the Australian public service (APS) and building a culture of innovation and integrity in policy advice'. Secretaries are to engage together and with the Public Service Commissioner in public service-wide stewardship (AGRAGA, 2010: 5, 47).

CONCLUSION

The senior service provides the front line at which major issues have to be confronted, and the key mechanism for the transmission of change and direction in the administrative apparatus. The constitution of the service assumes a spectrum of forms, but two broad patterns assist with explaining basic variations between systems. Despite these differences, systems are exploring the middle ground where senior services are more managerial and open, leadership is being reviewed and greater balance is sought between central guidance and decentralized implementation.

Senior servants have experienced changes to their status and roles. The special rights and privileges of a separate and distinctive service, and elite status, have become less common. The incorporation of principles from external influences, such as business management, has promoted similarities (and convergence) between the public and private sectors. At the same time, the combination of decentralization, internal differentiation and outsourcing has often diminished the public service ethos and identity.

Those operating at the interface with the political executive have been subjected to heightened demands for performance from political leaders under pressure from resource constraints and expanding public expectations. The managing of ambiguity has become a skill of senior executives operating within political–administrative arrangements that proclaim allegiance to neutrality and professionalism while not sufficiently supporting these principles in practice.

The interest in leadership reflects management thinking and the need to deliver change and performance in the public sector more effectively. The changing conceptions and approaches to leadership development within senior services have reinforced variations among systems according to their commitment, although the common environments and imperatives have been recognized. The reorientation of leadership has moved the emphasis from an inward focus to the external task of managing inter-sector boundaries, such as relationships with business and communities.

There is a renewed interest in core values that define the publicness of services, and of expectations for trust and greater inclusiveness and the role of leaders in promoting them. But it remains unclear whether this will lead to greater senior service identity, distinctiveness and professionalism, for its standing remains contingent on a range of factors: in particular, the stance of politicians ultimately determines whether such aspirations can be realized. The golden age of mandarins and civil service elites is unlikely to be revisited in this era of governance and performance.

NOTES

1 There continue to be important differences between the academic and practitioner formulations, which are more interested in how to cultivate and manage senior officials (e.g. Dawson, 2001; OECD 2001). See Quirk (2011) for a cross-over study.

2 But note that New Zealand has operated one of the most rigorous and systematic performance assessment programs for agency heads, the main function of the central personnel agency, the State Services Commission.

REFERENCES

Aberbach, Joel D. and Rockman, Bert A. (2000) 'Senior Executives in a Changing Political Environment', in James P. Pfiffner and Douglas A. Brook (eds), *The Future of Merit: Twenty Years after the Civil Service Reform Act*. Washington, DC: Woodrow Wilson Centre Press, pp. 81–99.

Aberbach, Joel D., Putnam, Robert D. and Rockman, Bert A. (1981) *Bureaucrats and Politicians in Western Democracies*. Cambridge, MA: Harvard University Press.

AGRAGA/Advisory Group on the Reform of Australian Government Administration (2010) *Ahead of the Game: Blueprint for the Reform of Australian Government Administration*, Canberra: Commonwealth of Australia.

Barberis, Peter (1998) 'The Changing Role of Senior Civil Servants Since 1979', in Michael Hunt and Barry J. O'Toole (eds), *Reform, Ethics and Leadership in the Public Service: A Festschrift in Honour of Richard A. Chapman*. Aldershot: Ashgate.

Bhatta, Gambhir (2001) 'A Cross-Jurisdictional Scan of Practices in Senior Public Services: Implications for New Zealand'. Working Paper No. 13, State Services Commission, Wellington.

Boin, Arjen and Christensen, Tom (2008) 'The Development of Public Institutions: Reconsidering the Role of Leadership', *Administration & Society*, 40(3): 271–297.

Bouckaert, Geert and Halligan, John (2008) *Managing Performance: International Comparisons*, London: Routledge.

Brans, Marlene (2002) 'Abolishing Ministerial Cabinets for Re-inventing Them? Comparative Observations on Professional Advice and Political Control'. Paper for 63 Annual Conference of American Society for Public Administration, Phoenix, Arizona, 23–26 March.

Campbell, Colin and Wilson, Graham K. (1995) *The End of Whitehall: Death of a Paradigm?* Oxford and Cambridge, MA: Blackwell.

Chapman, Richard (1984) *Leadership in the British Civil Service*. London: Croom Helm.

Dargie, Charlotte and Locke, Rachel (1998) 'The British Senior Civil Service', in Edward C. Page and Vincent Wright (eds), *Bureaucratic Elites in West European States*. Oxford: Oxford University Press, pp. 179–204.

Dawson, Malcolm (2001) 'Leadership in the 21st Century in the UK Civil Service', *International Review of Administrative Sciences*, 67(2): 263–271.

Doig, Jameson W. and Hargrove, Erwin C. (1987) '"Leadership" and Political Analysis', in Jameson W.

Doig and Erwin C. Hargrove (eds), *Leadership and Innovation: Entrepreneurs in Government*. Baltimore, MD: Johns Hopkins University Press.

Dutil, Patrice (ed.) (2010) *Search for Leadership: Secretaries to Cabinet in Canada*. Toronto: University of Toronto Press.

Eichbaum, C. and Shaw, R. (eds) (2010) *Partisan Appointees and Public Servants: An International Analysis of the Role of the Political Adviser*. Cheltenham: Edward Elgar.

Goetz, Klaus H. (1999) 'Senior Officials in the German Federal Administration: Institutional Change and Position Differentiation', in Edward C. Page and Vincent Wright (eds), *Bureaucratic Elites in West European States*. Oxford: Oxford University Press, pp. 146–177.

Halligan, John (1992) 'A Comparative Lesson: The Senior Executive Service in Australia', in Patricia W. Ingraham and David H. Rosenbloom (eds), *The Promise and Paradox of Bureaucratic Reform*. Pittsburgh: University of Pittsburgh Press.

Halligan, John (2001) 'Politicians, Bureaucrats and Public Sector Reform in Australia and New Zealand', in B. Guy Peters and Jon Pierre (eds), *Politicians, Bureaucrats and Administrative Reform*. London: Routledge, 157–68.

Halligan, John (2008) *The Centrelink Experiment: Innovation in Service Delivery*. Canberra: ANU E-Press.

Heclo, Hugh (1984) 'In Search of a Role: America's Higher Civil Service', in Ezra N. Suleiman (ed.), *Bureaucrats and Policy Making: A Comparative Overview*. New York: Holmes and Meier, pp. 8–34.

Heclo, Hugh (2000) 'The Future of Merit', in James P. Pfiffner and Douglas A. Brook (eds), *The Future of Merit: Twenty Years after the Civil Service Reform Act*. Washington, DC: Woodrow Wilson Centre Press, pp. 226–237.

Hede, Andrew (1991) 'Trends in the Higher Civil Services of Anglo-American Systems', *Governance*, 4(4): 489–510.

Horton, Sylvia (2009) 'Evaluation of Leadership Development and Training in the British Senior Civil Service: The Search for the Holy Grail?' in Jeffrey A. Raffel, Peter Leisink and Anthony E. Middlebrooks (eds), *Public Sector Leadership: International Challenges and Perspectives*. Cheltenham: Edward Elgar, pp. 360–376.

Hunt, Michael and J. O'Toole, Barry (eds) (1998) *Reform, Ethics and Leadership in the Public Service: A Festschrift in Honour of Richard A. Chapman*. Aldershot: Ashgate.

Ingraham, Patricia W. (1998) 'Making Public Policy: The Changing Role of the Higher Civil Service', in B. Guy Peters and Donald J. Savoie (eds), *Taking Stock: Assessing Public Sector Reforms*. Montreal and Kingston: McGill–Queen's University Press, pp. 164–186.

Ingraham, Patricia W. (2006) 'The Challenge and the Opportunity', *The American Review of Public Administration*, 36: 374–381.

Ingraham, Patricia W. and Moynihan, Donald P. (2000) 'Evolving Dimensions of Performance from the CSRA Onward', in James P. Pfiffner and Douglas A. Brook (eds), *The Future of Merit: Twenty Years after the Civil Service Reform Act*. Washington, DC: Woodrow Wilson Centre Press, pp. 103–126.

Ingraham, Patricia W., Murlis, Helen and Peters, B. Guy (1999) *The State of the Higher Civil Service after Reform: Britain, Canada and the United States*. Paris: OECD.

Kaufman, Herbert (1981) *The Administrative Behavior of Federal Bureau Chiefs*. Washington, DC: Brookings Institution.

Kim, Bun Woong and Kim, Pan Suk (1997) *Korean Public Administration: Managing the Uneven Development*. Elizabeth, NJ and Seoul: Hollym.

Kim, Pan S. (2002) 'Civil Service Reform in Japan and Korea: Toward Competitiveness and Competency', *International Review of Administrative Sciences*, 68(3): 389–403.

Kotter, John P. and Cohen, Dan S. (2002) *The Heart of Change*. Boston, MA: Harvard Business School Press.

Lægreid, Per (2001) 'Transforming Top Civil Servant Systems', in Tom Christensen and Per Lægreid (eds), *New Public Management: The Transformation of Ideas and Practice*. Aldershot: Ashgate.

Mandell, Myrna P. and Keast, Robyn (2009) 'A New Look at Leadership in Collaborative Networks: Process Catalysts', in Jeffrey A. Raffel, Peter Leisink and Anthony E. Middlebrooks (eds), *Public Sector Leadership: International Challenges and Perspectives*. Cheltenham: Edward Elgar, pp. 163–178.

Maor, Moshe (2000) 'A Comparative Perspective on Executive Development: Trends in 11 European Countries', *Public Administration*, 78(1): 135–152.

Matheson, Alex, Weber, Boris, Manning, Nick and Arnould, Emmanuelle (2008) 'Study on the Political Involvement in Senior Staffing and on the Delineation of Responsibilities between Ministers and Senior Civil Servants'. OECD Working Papers on Public Governance 2007/6, OECD, Paris.

Mau, Tim A. (2009) 'Is Public Sector Leadership Distinct? A Comparative Analysis of Core

Competencies in the Senior Executive Service', in Jeffrey A. Raffel, Peter Leisink and Anthony E. Middlebrooks (eds), *Public Sector Leadership: International Challenges and Perspectives*. Cheltenham: Edward Elgar, pp. 313–339.

Mellon, Elizabeth (2000) 'Executive Agency Chief Executives: Their Leadership Values', in Kevin Theakston (ed.), *Bureaucrats and Leadership*. Basingstoke: Macmillan, pp. 200–221.

OECD/Organisation for Economic Co-operation and Development (1997) *Managing the Senior Public Service: A Survey of OECD Countries*. Paris: OECD.

OECD/Organisation for Economic Co-operation and Development (2000) 'Developing Public Service Leaders for the Future'. Background Paper by the Secretariat, HRM Working Party Meeting, Paris, 3–4 July.

OECD/Organisation for Economic Co-operation and Development (2001) *Public Sector Leadership for the 21st Century*. Paris: OECD.

OECD/Organisation for Economic Co-operation and Development (2003) 'Managing Senior Management: Senior Civil Service Reform in OECD Member Countries'. Background Note, 28th Session of the Public Management Committee, 13–14 November, Paris.

OECD/Organisation for Economic Co-operation and Development (2008) *The State of the Public Service*. Paris: OECD.

OECD/Organisation for Economic Co-operation and Development (2011) *Government at a Glance 2011*. Paris: OECD.

Page, Edward C. and Wright, Vincent (1999) 'Conclusion: Senior Officials in Western Europe', in Edward C. Page and Vincent Wright (eds), *Bureaucratic Elites in West European States*. Oxford: Oxford University Press, pp. 266–279.

Painter, Martin and Peters, B. Guy (eds) (2010) *Tradition and Public Administration*. London: Palgrave.

Performance and Innovation Unit (2001) 'Strengthening Leadership in the Public Sector: A Research Study by the PIU'. Cabinet Office, London.

Peters, B. Guy (2010) *The Politics of Bureaucracy: An Introduction to Comparative Public Administration*, 6th edn. London and New York: Routledge.

Peters, B. Guy and Pierre, Jon (eds) (2001) *Politicians, Bureaucrats and Administrative Reform*. London: Routledge.

Peters, B. Guy and Pierre, Jon (eds) (2004) *Politicization of the Civil Service in Comparative Perspective: The Quest for Control*. London: Routledge.

Pierre, Jon (1995) 'Comparative Public Administration: The State of the Art', in J. Pierre (ed.), *Bureaucracy in the Modern State: An Introduction to Comparative Public Administration*. Aldershot: Edward Elgar.

Pollitt, Christopher and Bouckaert, Geert (2004) *Public Management Reform: A Comparative Analysis*. Oxford: Oxford University Press.

Quirk, Barry (2011) *Re-imagining Government: Public Leadership and Management in Challenging Times*. Basingstoke: Palgrave Macmillan.

Raffel, Jeffrey A., Leisink, Peter and Middlebrooks, Anthony E. (eds) (2009) *Public Sector Leadership: International Challenges and Perspectives*. Cheltenham: Edward Elgar.

Rhodes, R.A.W. and Weller, Patrick (2001) 'Conclusion: "Antipodean Exceptionalism, European Traditionalism"', in R.A.W. Rhodes and Patrick Weller (eds), *The Changing World of Top Officials: Mandarins or Valets?* Buckingham and Philadelphia: Open University Press, pp. 228–255.

Riccucci, Norma M. (2000) 'Excellence in Administrative Leadership: an Examination of Six US Federal Execucrats', in Kevin Theakston (ed.), *Bureaucrats and Leadership*. Basingstoke: Macmillan, pp. 17–38.

Rockman, Bert (1991) 'The Leadership Question: Is There an Answer?', in Colin Campbell and Margaret Jane Wyszomirski (eds), *Executive Leadership in Anglo-American Systems*. Pittsburgh: University of Pittsburgh Press, pp. 35–56.

Rockman, Bert A. (1995) 'The Federal Executive: Equilibrium and Change', in Bryan D. Jones (ed.), *The New American Politics: Reflections on Political Change and the Clinton Administration*. Boulder, CO: Westview Press.

Rouban, Luc (1999) 'The Senior Civil Service in France', in Edward C. Page and Vincent Wright (eds), *Bureaucratic Elites in West European States*. Oxford: Oxford University Press, pp. 65–89.

Stace, Doug and Dunphy, Dexter (2001) *Beyond the Boundaries: Leading and Re-creating the Successful Enterprise*, 2nd edn. Sydney: McGraw-Hill.

Steen, Trui and Van der Meer, Frits M. (2009) 'Dutch Civil Service Leadership: Torn between Managerial and Policy-Oriented Leadership Roles', in Jeffrey A. Raffel, Peter Leisink and Anthony E. Middlebrooks (eds), *Public Sector Leadership: International Challenges and Perspectives*. Cheltenham: Edward Elgar, pp. 91–106.

't Hart, P. and A. Wille (2006) 'Ministers and Top Officials in the Dutch Core Executive: Living

Together, Growing Apart?' *Public Administration*, 84(1): 121–142.

Theakston, Kevin (1999) *Leadership in Whitehall*. London: Macmillan.

Theakston, Kevin (2000) *Bureaucrats and Leadership*. Basingstoke: Macmillan.

Van Dorpe, Karolien and Horton, Sylvia (2011) 'The Public Service Bargain in the United Kingdom: The Whitehall Model in Decline', *Public Policy and Administration*, 26: 233–252.

Van Slyke, David M. and Alexander, Robert W. (2006) 'Public Service Leadership: Opportunities for Clarity and Coherence', *American Review of Public Administration*, 36: 362–374.

Van Wart, Montgomery (2005) *Dynamics of Leadership in Public Service: Theory and Practice*. Armonk, NY: M.E. Sharpe.

Vardon, Sue (2000) Centrelink: 'A Three-stage Evolution', in Gwynneth Singleton (ed.), *The Howard Government: Australian Commonwealth Administration 1996–1998*. Sydney: University of New South Wales Press.

Wilson, Sir Richard (2000) 'A New Civil Service'. FDA/ Shareholder Conference, 11 April.

World Bank (2005) *Senior Public Service: High Performing Managers of Government*. Washington, DC: World Bank.

7

Labor–Management Relations and Partnerships: Were They Reinvented?

James R. Thompson

In the aftermath of the 'Great Recession' of 2008–10, the conditions of employment for public sector workers in Western countries became subject to heightened scrutiny. That scrutiny was particularly consequential for public workers at the state level in the United States and in several southern European countries caught up in the European debt crisis of 2010–12.

In the United States, many states faced a fiscal crisis as a consequence of revenue declines attributable to the recession and to the end of federal 'stimulus' assistance. A number of governors looked to reduce the pay and benefits of public workers as one means of addressing budget shortfalls. Policymakers in Republican-dominated states were particularly aggressive in this regard. In Wisconsin, newly-elected Governor Walker secured the approval of a law that limits the scope of bargaining by public employees to wages, restricts raises to inflation, increases the amount employees pay for health insurance and pensions, and gives union members the right not to pay dues (Sulzberger, 2011). Governors in Florida and Tennessee have also targeted the pay and benefits of public employees as a means of reducing expenditures (Simon, 2011). At the national level, President Obama froze the wages of federal workers for two years (Baker & Calmes, 2010).

The pay and benefits of public workers in a number of European countries also became targets for cuts in the aftermath of the 2010 debt crisis. In Greece, the wages of public workers were cut and the retirement age for public workers was increased from 57 to 65, effective in 2013 ('Grim resignation as austerity bites,' 2010). In Ireland, pay cuts for public workers have averaged 15 percent over a three-year period (Brown, 2010). In Spain, public workers went on strike to protest austerity measures, including a 5 percent cut in public sector wages and a freeze in pensions (De La Puente & House, 2010). Although the debt crisis served as the proximate cause of the cuts, also in evidence is a longer-term trend towards the 'deprivileging' of public workers in Western countries.

Public workers were generally advantaged by conditions that prevailed in the postwar era. Many such workers gained the right to organize and were provided with adequate if not liberal levels of remuneration. Specific features of labor–management relations and pay determination practices associated with this model included:

- Statute-based job selection, promotion and pay criteria
- Centralized wage negotiations
- Wage agreements covering whole governments or entire sectors of government
- Retention by governments of the right to unilaterally impose settlements where agreements with employee representatives were not forthcoming
- Limited managerial flexibility on pay matters
- Internal equity as a primary criterion for pay setting
- Pay progression based on seniority

Conditions began to change in the 1970s and 1980s. Politicians in many nations were caught in a squeeze between rising costs associated with expanded social programs and a decline in revenues due to economic recession. Globalizing influences jeopardized industrial competitiveness in many countries, posing threats of job loss and economic dislocation. The public became increasingly amenable to proposals to enhance competitiveness by reducing the size and the cost of the state administrative apparatus. There were simultaneous pressures for improved service from public organizations as a result of enhancements made to product quality in the private sector.

The consequences of these broad secular shifts for human resource management in the public sector were direct; if costs were to be reduced, efficiency enhanced and service improved, changes in employment levels and work practices were required. Consistent with the 'economistic' logic which

underlay these trends, politicians and senior civil servants looked to the private sector for new models of management. One set of market-oriented prescriptions derived largely from the reform experiences of several Anglophone countries, including the United Kingdom, New Zealand, Australia and the United States, was labeled the New Public Management (NPM). Practices associated with NPM include the following:

- 'Hands-on professional management'
- Explicit standards and measures of performance
- Greater emphasis on output controls
- Shift to disaggregation of units in the public sector
- Shift to greater competition in public sector
- Stress on private-sector styles of management practice
- Stress on greater discipline and parsimony in resource use (Hood, 1991)

The NPM model gained broad currency as a consequence of the apparent successes of the early adopters and the endorsement by the Organization for Economic Co-operation and Development (OECD) of the key precepts (Flynn & Strehl, 1996b).

NEW PUBLIC MANAGEMENT AND LABOR–MANAGEMENT RELATIONS

The human resource management (HRM) and labor–management relations (LMR) implications of NPM include the following:

- 'Hands-on professional management' implies at least a partial shift in control over human resource management processes and procedures from politicians to managers.
- The 'disaggregation' of administrative units implies a disaggregation of the civil service and the development of personnel systems 'tailored' to agency mission. To the extent that agencies were provided control over HRM matters, an implication was that collective bargaining would occur at the department/agency level rather than at the government level.

LABOR–MANAGEMENT RELATIONS AND PARTNERSHIPS

- A 'shift to greater competition' and 'greater discipline and parsimony in resource use' imply the privatization of public services, a reduction in the size of the public sector workforce and the containment of public sector wage increases.
- The 'stress on private-sector styles of management practice' is associated with 'greater flexibility in hiring and rewards'. At issue was pay for performance, whereby a portion of the yearly pay increase would be based on individual performance. In most countries, the unions preferred the standardization of pay across job categories.

New public management II

Interest in the NPM approach to reform peaked in the 1990s. With subsequent regime changes and with the consolidation that often follows radical reform, there were modifications to and, in some cases, reversals of NPM-type reforms. For example, there was a sense that the 'disaggregation' of bureaucratic structures that accompanied the creation of executive agencies in the United Kingdom and New Zealand had gone too far. For example, in 2002, the Advisory Committee on the Review of the Centre in New Zealand identified, 'fragmentation and the loss of focus on the big picture that fragmentation can cause' (Advisory Group on the Review of the Centre, 2001, p. 4), as a central structural problem for the new Labor Government to address. In the United Kingdom, Prime Minister Blair issued a call for, 'Joined-up Government,' in which the emphasis was on cross-agency collaboration in contrast to the emphasis of the previous regime on the decentralization of service delivery (James, 2004). Some in the scholarly community concluded that the 2000s represented a, 'post-NPM' era (Goldfinch & Wallis, 2010; Lodge & Gill, 2011).

However, the data seems more consistent with the alternative hypothesis that the NPM model was not so much replaced as refined: That the essence of the NPM model was preserved as is apparent from several late 2000s reviews of the reform status in several

NPM 'exemplars.' A 2007 review of the status of the New Zealand reforms, for example, concludes with the comment that, 'No one has claimed that New Zealand has resiled from a fundamental commitment to the broader principles of NPM, nor has anyone in government openly questioned the soundness of its underlying theory' (Chapman & Duncan, 2007, p. 20). Bach and Winchester (2003, p. 290) comment that in the United Kingdom, the Labour Government, 'accepted most parts of the radical organizational restructuring of the public services introduced under the Conservatives.' Of the industries privatized by the Conservatives, only the railways were renationalized by Labour (Prowse & Prowse, 2007).

The 'NPM II' model that ensued from the regime changes of the late 1990s and early 2000s placed greater emphasis on interagency collaboration and service quality and less emphasis on cost-cutting and operational efficiency than had been the case under NPM I (Bach & Winchester, 2003). One element of the quest to improve service was the use of total quality management techniques accompanied in several countries by partnership arrangements between management and labor.

Under a partnership arrangement, unions and management work collaboratively in addressing issues and challenges in the workplace. The intent is that the relationship between the unions and management become less adversarial. According to Farnham, Hondeghem and Horton (2005, p. 64), 'the central aim of partnership is to seek unity of purpose between the parties, solve problems jointly and work together at central, sector or organizational levels ...'. Prime Minister Blair and the Labour Party put labor–management partnership at the center of its modernization agenda. Bach (2004, p. 16) comments that, 'A central theme of the Labour government's modernisation agenda has been the importance of staff participation and union involvement in workplace reforms ...'. In the United States, President Clinton issued an executive order directing each federal department to create a 'partnership council' (Clinton, 1993). The executive order also provided for the creation of a National Partnership Council within which the leaders of the major federal employee unions could engage in dialogue with officials from the administration. In New Zealand, the Minister of State Services and the Public Service Association entered into a 'Partnership for Quality Agreement' (Goldfinch & Wallis, 2010).

In the discussion that follows, LMR developments in nine OECD countries are tracked in the context of both NPM I and NPM II. The countries are categorized according to (1) NPM exemplars, (2) NPM 'laggards,' and (3) NPM 'in betweens.' Of interest is whether, and to what extent, there is evidence of movement away from traditional, 'closed' civil service models to more open 'market' models which incorporate contracting out, disaggregated structures, and higher levels of discretion for management consistent with NPM doctrine. The focus is on how relationships between governments and organized labor changed as a consequence of these developments. The partnership phenomenon is also of interest: What are the implications of partnership arrangements on labor–management relations and do they represent a fundamental reorientation of the relationship between management and labor? Although developments at the state/regional and local government levels are of interest in some countries, the focus is on developments at the central government level.

CROSS-NATIONAL TRENDS IN LABOR-MANAGEMENT RELATIONS

One of the most widely cited explanations of the NPM phenomenon and of the generally high level of 'ferment' in public management practices over the past two decades is that of economic globalization and the competitive pressures that have been re

leased as a consequence of globalization. One manifestation of this dynamic has been the Maastricht Treaty pursuant to which European countries committed to reducing operating deficits and overall debt loads for purposes of adopting a common currency. Keller (1999, p. 58) comments that, 'the convergence criteria for European Monetary Union created enormous pressure not only to stabilize public employment levels, but to decrease gradually the number of public employees, especially at the local/municipal level, and to introduce public sector reform plans.' Other factors contributing to pressures to curtail the size of – and improve the performance of – the state sector during the 1980s and 1990s included public dissatisfaction with government, the ascension to power of the 'New Right' in several countries, and a perception of poor performance in the critical education and health sectors (Bach, Bordogna, Della Rocca, & Winchester, 1999; Barlow, Farnham, Horton, & Ridley, 1996; Farnham & Horton, 2000).

Reform interventions that adversely impacted public employees included (1) a reduction in the number of public employees as a consequence of the privatization of state-owned enterprises, (2) making some portion of worker pay contingent on performance, (3) providing managers with more discretion over working conditions, (4) disaggregating pay systems to allow pay for different occupations to fluctuate with the market, and (5) increased use of a 'contingent' workforce including temporary and part-time workers. These trends forced unions in many locations to assume a defensive posture, particularly where and when rightist governments have prevailed, as in the United Kingdom in the early and mid-1990s, Australia in the mid- and late 1990s, New Zealand in the mid-1990s, and the United States in the 2000s.[1] As the following review reveals, however, there was substantial variation in the extent to which these practices were adopted consistent with the terms, 'exemplars,' 'laggards,' and 'in betweens'.[2]

New public management exemplars

The United Kingdom, New Zealand, and Sweden are widely regarded as leading examples of the NPM in practice (Hood, 1996; Naschold, 1996). All these nations have made radical changes in governance practices consistent with NPM precepts over the past 20 years and, in each instance, the changes have had major implications for the character and operations of the public workforce. All three nations have taken a two-prong approach to reform, reducing the size of the public sector through the privatization of state enterprises and restructuring the core public sector to provide more operational flexibility at the agency level.

New Zealand

The dominant dynamic in New Zealand during the 1980s was a radical downsizing of the public sector, with the conversion a number of commercial, state 'trading' organizations to autonomous status with a requirement to operate on a for-profit basis. As a result of these changes, public service staffing levels fell from 66,000 in 1983 to 34,500 in 1994 (Boston, Martin, Pallot, & Walsh, 1996b). The trend was reversed in part when the Labour Government (1999–2008) partially renationalized both Air New Zealand and the railway network (Chapman & Duncan, 2007).

Pursuant to the State Sector Act of 1988, service delivery units within the core public sector were provided semi-autonomous status as 'executive agencies.' Although the intent was to provide the chief executive of each agency a high level of discretion in management matters for purposes of improving efficiency and service, the negotiation of employment conditions initially remained under the tight control of the State Services Commission. The State Services Commission (SSC) delegated negotiating authority to the heads of the executive agencies, but the authority had to be exercised in consultation with the SSC and could be withdrawn by the SSC. Furthermore, bargaining outcomes had

to be fiscally neutral (Boston, Martin, Pallot, & Walsh, 1996a).

Despite these changes, many features of the traditional labor relations system were retained. Unions retained exclusive rights to bargain for public sector employees and agency shop provisions with compulsory union membership could be included in employment contracts. In 1991, however, the new National Government enacted the Employment Contracts Act (ECA) which removed privileges enjoyed by the unions. Pursuant to the ECA, agency shop provisions were prohibited and there was a shift from collective to individual employment contracts. The bargaining power of public employees was significantly reduced by the legislation: the New Zealand State Services Commission identified a 6 percent decline in real wages for members of the New Zealand Public Service between 1992 and 1997 (State Services Commission, 1998).

In 2000, the majority Labour Party passed the Employment Relations Act, which restored some of the collective bargaining rights that had been withdrawn by the National Party. According to Farnham, Hondeghem, and Horton (2005, p. 217), 'The legislation obliges employers and employees to conduct employment relations in good faith, ensures improved union rights of access to workplaces and provides that only registered unions can negotiate collective employment agreements.'

Also during this period, the government entered into a partnership agreement with New Zealand's largest public employee union, the Public Service Association (PSA). The Partnership for Quality Agreement (PQA) was intended to provide a means for staff to participate in strategic decisions, with a focus on improving the quality of service provided the public. The umbrella agreement was to be accompanied by agreements between the PSA and agency heads.

The results of the partnership initiative have been mixed, with only 30 percent of agencies participating and with many PSA members 'equivocal about the merits of pursuing partnerships' (Farnham, Hondeghem, & Horton, 2005, p. 222). However, according to Farnham et al. (p. 224), the PQA has, 'facilitated the PSA's participation in several other whole of-government projects that have influenced the trajectory of New Zealand's second-generation reforms ...' including the 2002 'Review of the Centre.'[3]

Sweden

As a proportion of gross domestic product (GDP), the public sector in Sweden has historically been one of the largest in the world. In 2006, government employees constituted 31.6 percent of the total workforce (Ifo Institute for Economic Research, 2011). Facing fiscal difficulties in the early 1990s, the government took steps to both reduce the size of the public sector and to reform administrative practices in ways that could enhance efficiency and effectiveness. Between 1990 and 1996, 13 agencies became public companies, contributing to a reduction of about 18 percent in the number of public employees.[4]

Although Sweden has long had a set of semi-autonomous service delivery agencies, pay determination processes remained highly centralized until 1989 when an agreement was reached between the National Agency for Government Employers (AgV)[5] and the major public sector trade unions to abolish the uniform system of pay grades and replace it with 'a system of individual and differentiated pay of the type that had long applied to salaried employees in the private sector' (Andersson & Schager, 1999, p. 247).

Pursuant to a 'frame agreement' negotiated between the three top public sector trade unions and AgV, each agency or area of government is provided a pay fund from which pay increases for employees are distributed. The frame agreement stipulates the conditions, if any, under which industrial actions are permitted (Nomden, Farnham, & Onnee-Abbruciati, 2003). Wage increases received by the employees in each agency are then settled through local negotiations. Although

the centralized pay and grading system was abolished in 1989, centralized influence over the process remains both in setting the amount of the pay fund (which effectively establishes limits on pay increases) and in stipulations for minimum pay increase guarantees (Bender & Elliott, 2003). According to Roness (2001, p. 181), even though the unions were 'skeptical towards specific proposals for structural devolution ... they have been more concerned with securing jobs and working conditions for their members within the new form of association than with actively opposing the conversions.' Pay rates for public workers are generally set according to the prevailing wages for those in similar occupations in the private sector. Each agency has the option of introducing an individualized pay-for-performance system.

United Kingdom

As in both New Zealand and Sweden, the reforms in the United Kingdom featured a two-prong strategy: first to reduce the size of the public sector through the privatization of state enterprises and second to restructure the core public sector to provide more operational flexibility at the agency level. In the United Kingdom, approximately 800,000 employees were transferred from the public to the private sector as a consequence of the privatization of various state enterprises (Pollitt & Bouckaert, 2004). The total public sector workforce declined by approximately 30 percent between 1981 and 1997 (Winchester & Bach, 1995) and public sector union membership declined from 1.85 million in 1979 to 0.38 million in 2005 (Prowse & Prowse, 2007).

A key structural reform in the United Kingdom was the decentralization of management authority to semi-autonomous service delivery units called 'Next Steps' agencies. As in New Zealand and Sweden, the intent was to induce greater efficiency and higher levels of performance by providing line managers with greater discretion over operational matters. Also, as in New Zealand and Sweden, although pay determination was decentralized, central staff units continued to perform an important oversight and monitoring role.

Although the Next Steps program was initiated in 1988, the Minister for the Civil Service was not authorized to delegate the authority to set pay and working conditions until passage of the Civil Service Act of 1992 and the Conservative Government didn't terminate service-wide bargaining until 1996 (Fredman, 1999; Winchester & Bach, 1995). Since that time, the delegations of authority within the core civil service have been extensive, including

> the prescription of terms and conditions of employment of home civil servants in so far as they relate to the classification of staff, remuneration, allowances, expenses, holidays, hours of work and attendance, part time and other working arrangements, performance and promotion, retirement age and redundancy, and redeployment of staff within and between departments (Fredman, 1999, p. 56).

The intent, consistent with 'strategic human resource management' precepts, was to allow each agency to tailor its human resource policies to its 'business needs.'

The public employee unions have generally opposed the decentralization of pay-setting authorities, in part because of the burden placed on the unions in having to negotiate in multiple venues (Bach et al., 1999). The unions' preference was for centralized collective bargaining or for the use of 'pay review bodies,' according to which the pay of select groups of employees (i.e., the armed services, doctors and dentists, senior civil servants, and judges) have historically been paid (Bach & Winchester, 2003; Bach et al., 1999).

With the accession to power of the Labour Party in 1997, the drive to decentralize pay-setting processes stalled. Pursuant to an agreement between the Labour Government and the unions, the pay of more than 1.5 million civil servants, including doctors, nurses, teachers, prison guards, and allied health professionals is set pursuant to a centralized pay review process (Prowse & Prowse, 2007). Although there is consultation with both

unions and management, the final determination is made by an independent pay review body. Within the National Health Service (NHS), the pay of all employees other than doctors and nurses is negotiated centrally (Bach & Winchester, 2003).

The Labour Government also gained acceptance by the unions for its labor–management partnership program (Danford, Richardson, & Upchurch, 2002). A 2000 umbrella agreement between the government and key public employee unions provided a framework for agreements at the agency level. According to Beale (2005, p. 141) the agreement, 'outlined broad principles of mutual commitment to the success of the organisation, joint management of change, improving public service, greater employee involvement, joint efforts to avoid redundancies, improvements in information technology, training, workplace accommodation and work–life balance, and compliance with employment law.'

Notwithstanding the lofty rhetoric, however, observers have found the results of the partnership effort to have been mixed. For example, Farnham et al. (2005, p. 126) comment that, 'Union officers also expressed "some scepticism" about the extent to which the Cabinet Office could deliver partnership at departmental level,' and they add, 'This major innovation looks at best precarious.' Bach and Givan (2008, p. 528) conclude, 'There is a high level of scepticism, however, about the government's commitment to partnership, reflected in its determination to increase private sector involvement despite widespread union antipathy to this agenda.'

New public management laggards

Bach and Della Rocca (2000) identify France, Germany, and Spain as adherents of a 'traditional' approach to public administration. That the New Public Management has had only a limited impact in these countries is attributable to a variety of factors, including corporatist modes of governance and legally oriented (*Reichstaat*) – approaches to administration.

France

Additional factors identified by Clark (1998) that account for the relatively low level of NPM penetration in France are

- the tradition of a strong state and state direction of the economy ('dirigisme');
- the high social and political status of the civil service and particularly the elite grands corps; and
- a tradition of administrative centralization as evident in the prefectoral system.[6]

Consistent with these elements of the French administrative tradition, pay setting is highly centralized. Negotiations with the seven major public employee unions for employees in the central government, local government, and hospitals are conducted centrally. A common pay grid applies to employees in all three sectors. Although there is a legal requirement to negotiate, the government retains the authority to impose a settlement unilaterally if an agreement is not reached. With the exception of certain categories such as police, public employees have the right to strike.

Despite a generally centralized and rigid set of administrative practices, there have been intermittent attempts to modernize conditions in ways that are consistent with NPM precepts. In 1991, state corporations providing postal and telecommunications services were privatized, resulting in a reduction of public sector employment of approximately 440,000 (Guillotin & Meurs, 1999). There is also provision under French law for employee participation in the determination of some working conditions through a process of 'concertation' (Bazex, 1987).

Clark (1998) and Flynn and Strehl (1996a) describe a series of attempts at administrative modernization. For example, in the late 1980s, Prime Minister Rocard launched a modernization campaign, one element of which was to 'renovate' internal working relationships by devolving management

authority from central ministries to territorial field services through a system of 207 'Centres de Responsabilities' ('responsibility centers' or CDRs) (Clark, 1998; Postif, 1997). Similar to the 'contractualization' of intradepartmental relationships that is now the norm in the United Kingdom, New Zealand, and Sweden, CDR chief executives were to 'negotiate a set of objectives and targets with their parent department, and engage in a dialog about the budget required to deliver those targets' (Flynn & Strehl, 1996a, p. 113). This was extended by a 1995 circular intended to transform the ministries into holding companies 'limited to the functions of policy setting, resource allocation, monitoring and evaluation' (Clark, 1998, p. 107). Citing Fialaire (1993), however, Flynn and Strehl (1996a, p. 118) state that, 'the implementation of the accountability centres has not produced the management freedoms which were expected when they were established,' and that, 'there is, in practice, still a great deal of a priori budgetary control by the Ministry of Finance which has been reluctant to move towards global running cost budgets because such a change would challenge the power of that ministry.' Among the opponents of decentralization have been the grands corps (top civil servants) and the public employee unions. According to Burnham (2000), unions favor the centralized pay-setting process, which serves as 'their main source of power,' and hence are a 'significant cause of inflexibility in human resource management.'

Although the French Government never invoked the term 'partnership,' efforts have been made to enhance the quality of work life for employees and to involve staff in operational decisions. Under the Public Service Renewal Program introduced by Prime Minister Rocard in 1989, employees were provided expanded training opportunities and greater involvement in operational matters through 'service projects.' According to Denis and Jeannot (2005, p. 159), most projects took the form of attempts to improve internal efficiency and to, 'reduce internal divisions between services.' However, participation was at the discretion of heads of service and there is no evidence that the reform program had a systemic impact.

A 2002 white paper recommended the devolution of collective bargaining and the establishment of representative bodies such as works councils, which had been instituted in state hospitals in 1991. According to Denis and Jeannot (2005), the works councils allowed employees other than those representing the unions to address issues such as restructuring and staff training.

Germany

Keller (1999) attributes Germany's low-NPM status to the limited federal role in service provision, a high incidence of representation by civil servants in Parliament, and the highly centralized structure of collective bargaining. Bach and Della Rocca (2000, p. 93) observe that, 'the existence of elaborate rights of co-determination has diluted moves to develop a managerial culture,' and Naschold and Arnkil (1997, p. 285) comment that Germany belongs in a group of countries which have 'rejected results steering … and the selective reduction in the scope of state activity by means of competitive instruments and privatization programs.'

Pay setting continues to be centralized and uniformity of employment conditions prevail for both the civil service (*Beamte*) and non-civil service public employees (*Angestellte* – non-manual and *Arbeiter* – manual). Although civil servants are prohibited from bargaining, other public employees, who comprise approximately 60 percent of the total public workforce, can bargain over pay and working conditions. Employer associations representing all three levels of government bargain with the public employee unions, including the United Services Union and the German Civil Service Union. The agreements negotiated are then binding on employees at the federal, *Länder*, and local government levels (Farnham & Koch, 2005). Non-civil service workers have the right to strike, although it is rarely invoked. Keller (1999, p. 63), citing

Tondorf (1995), comments that, 'this system has been criticized as being highly inflexible because of its purely collective and uniform character, its independence from individual performance on the job and its high degree of job security.'

Despite the predominance of 'administrative rule steering' (Naschold, 1996), however, the influence of NPM ideas is apparent in Germany. Certain natural monopolies such as the postal service and railways have been privatized and, as a result of the Civil Service Reform Law of 1997, 'more weight is given to the idea of performance and merit in the law governing the civil service' (OECD, 1997, p. 55). Labor relations in the public sector, as in the private sector, feature the 'co-determination' of working conditions. With co-determination, staff councils elected by employees have statutory rights of co-determination. 'Measures subject to codetermination that may only be taken with the consent of staff councils include: appointments, transfers, promotions, employment beyond retirement age, establishment and dissolution of social institutions, assessment guidelines, measures to prevent accidents at work and workplace design' (Farnham & Koch, 2005, p. 173).

Reform activities consistent with NPM ideas have been underway at the *Länder* and local levels. The Tillburg model being adopted by some German municipalities includes 'specialized departments' analogous to the New Zealand and United Kingdom-type executive agencies. In some locations, 'workplace-related forms of participation' have led to a 'diminished role for unions' as representatives of workers (Keller, 1999).

Spain

Several features of the Spanish context contribute to the nature of LMR in that country. One is that public administration in Spain, as in the other *Reichstaat* countries, has a legalistic orientation with 'considerable emphasis on regulation and codification of the law to ensure uniformity in the handling of cases' and with lawyers filling many of the top positions in the civil service (Parrado Diez, 1996, p. 260). Similar to France, Spain has a system of administrative 'corps.' Both the general corps, consisting of public employees performing administrative and management duties, and the special corps, such as economists, accountants, diplomats, and professors, largely control processes of recruitment and selection for the Spanish civil service (Parrado Diez, 1996).

The governmental structure in Spain features three levels: the central government, 17 'autonomous communities,' i.e., regional governments, and local authorities. An umbrella law, the Civil Service Reform Measures Act of 1984 (CSRMA), governs LMR at all three levels. CSRMA provides for a Higher Public Services Council (HPSC), which serves as the, 'peak level coordination and consultation body for the public services,' and which includes representatives of both central, regional, and local governments as well as the public employee unions (Jódar, Jordana, & Alós, 1999). The Public Services Coordinating Committee of the HPSC formulates policy relating to workplace conditions for members of the civil service. While a process of negotiation between the government and representatives of the civil servants exists, the openness of the negotiations is constrained by provisions allowing the government to unilaterally set employment terms in case of an impasse (Jódar et al., 1999).

Non-civil service public employees, who make up approximately 50 percent of the workforce of the central government, enjoy full bargaining rights, equivalent to those of private sector employees. Bargaining for these employees is highly fragmented. Although the HPSC determines a general framework for employment conditions, the specifics are worked out by joint councils, including both labor and management representatives in multiple venues according to level of government and sector.

Although the influence of NPM doctrine in Spain has been limited, there have been sporadic attempts at reform. As in a number of other OECD countries, state-owned enterprises have been privatized and legal monopolies eliminated in areas such as telecommunications, air transport, and cigarettes (Jódar et al., 1999). Law 6 of 1997 resulted in the creation of 138 'autonomous bodies,' including 33 percent of civil servants but, as Parrado (2008) notes, these entities were not provided the degree of autonomy accorded the Next Steps agencies in the United Kingdom, nor were they accorded responsibility for pay setting. During the late 1990s, the Ministry of Public Administration promoted the use of quality management tools and techniques, including service charters and quality awards, and in 2002 unions and management agreed to partner for the purpose of improving service quality within the public sector (Lasierra, 2007; Parrado, 2008).

New public management – "in betweens"

Levels of reform activity in Australia, Italy, and the United States have been higher than in France, Germany, or Spain but the results have been less radical than those achieved in New Zealand, Sweden, or the United Kingdom.

Australia

The evolution of the Australian public service over the past 20 years, including its labor–management relations elements, reflects NPM influence. First, there have been, 'very significant reductions in government employment' (Fairbrother & MacDonald, 1999, p. 351) as a result of the privatization of state-owned enterprises, including Aussat, the Commonwealth Bank, Qantas Airlines, and Australian National Railways. Although no use has been made of semi-autonomous service delivery agencies, Australia has been able to decentralize pay-setting authority to management through a variety of mechanisms.

During the period that the Labor Party controlled the government (1983–1992), there was extensive consultation and negotiation over pay and other conditions of federal government employees. The Coalition Government that took power in 1996, however, sought to move from collective to individual contracts and hence to consign unions to the representation of individual employees (O'Brien & Fairbrother, 2000).

Provisions of the Public Service Bill of 1997 were implemented administratively by the Coalition Government subsequent to the failure of passage in the Senate. Consistent with that legislation, authority over personnel and pay matters were substantially devolved to departments. Fairbrother and MacDonald (1999, p. 352) comment, 'The Public Service Bill envisaged that "employment powers (will) rest predominantly with Secretaries (or Chief Executives) and that the primary employment relationship (will be) between the employer and employee at the agency level"' (Public Service and Merit Protection Commission, 1997, p. 14). Under the new system, bargaining occurs at the agency level. 'By 1998, approximately 80 percent of employees within the Australian public service were covered by agency agreements' (Lansbury & Macdonald, 2001, p. 222).

Despite the changes, however, central staff units have continued to play an important role in pay setting. The Department of Workplace Relations and Small Business (DWRSB)[7] has been given a 'watchdog' role to ensure high degrees of procedural uniformity across all federal government employment; any agency-level agreements must receive approval from DWRSB, and agreements must comply with policy parameters on funding, classification, performance management, etc. Agencies are also constrained by their negotiations with the unions to the extent that job classifications, grading, and other employment conditions are specified on a service-wide basis (Bender & Elliott, 2003).

The Labor Government that took office in 2007 initiated a review to evaluate and improve the performance of the Australian Public Service. The results of that review were released in March 2010 in a report entitled *Ahead of the Game: Blueprint for Reform of Australian Government Administration*. Under the heading, 'Clarifying and aligning employment conditions,' the report recommends, 'Strengthen the Australian government employment bargaining framework to ensure that it supports one APS' (Advisory Group on Reform of Australian Government Administration, 2010, p. x). The term 'one APS' connotes a recentralization of some aspects of policy setting and bargaining after the decentralization that occurred under the preceding administration. The report reads as follows: 'Since bargaining of APS wages and conditions was devolved in 1997, wage dispersion has increased significantly ... anecdotal evidence suggests that growing disparity in wages and conditions across agencies has discouraged mobility and reduced the sense of a unified APS' (p. 54). The centralizing intent is apparent from the 'vision,' which includes, 'An APS unified by an enterprise agreement bargaining arrangement that embeds greater consistency in wages, terms and conditions' (p. 54).

Italy

Wage determination in Italy has traditionally been both fragmented and centralized. Separate bargaining was conducted for eight separate sectors, including the central administration (except health and education), national enterprises, local administrations, 'parastatal bodies,' schools, universities, regional and local administrations, and the National Health Service (Nomden et al., 2003). Bargaining between the unions and the state took place centrally and the pay guidelines that resulted afforded little flexibility at lower levels. Pursuant to Act 93 of 1983, all agreements were subject to review by the Council of Ministers for compatibility with budget limitations (Treu, 1987).

In 1993, reforms were instituted as part of the effort to comply with the guidelines for entry into the European Monetary Union.

With legislative decree #29 of 1993, labor relations practices in the public sector were made to conform with those in the private sector. A new agency (ARAN)[8] was created to bargain on behalf of public employers at both the national and local levels. According to Bordogna, Dell'Aringa, and Della Rocca (1999, p. 115), 'the determination of wages and salaries, which in the past was often subject to intervention on the part of the parliament or the administrative courts, is now almost entirely given to the exclusive competence of collective negotiations.' The basic pay for different grades is fixed by national collective agreements for each sector with provision for limited managerial discretion at the local level, including the authority to 'award small lump-sum bonuses on the basis of individual performance' (Bach & Della Rocca, 2000, p. 89). Although the law provided that the unions no longer had to be consulted on matters of recruitment, internal mobility, career development, and training, the unions supported the changes (Bach & Della Rocca, 2001).

In 1998, a new law allowed for a more decentralized system of collective bargaining. According to Keller, Due, and Andersen (2001) the new system resembles that in Sweden to the extent that the agreements negotiated at the national level serve as frameworks within which local bargaining can occur. Topics addressed at the local level include career paths, the allocation of tasks and responsibilities, and the variable portion of employee compensation (Nomden et al., 2003; Ongaro, 2009).

Italy has made intermittent attempts at reform. Consistent with NPM precepts, the 1993 law, 'define(d) the responsibility of public sector management as directed towards achieving measurable results in terms of efficiency and effectiveness, rather than just towards assuring the formal legitimacy of administrative acts …' (Bordogna et al., 1999, p. 115). Also consistent with NPM precepts was a 1998 law that provided for the creation of 'executive agencies' to be steered through performance contracts

(Ongaro, 2009). Although managerial empowerment is implicit in the executive agency model, Bach and Della Rocca (2000, p. 93) caution that, 'the attempts to "empower" management have been constrained by the continuation of an all encompassing framework of administrative and legal regulations with rules defining personnel policies such as recruitment and promotions.'

United States

The nature of the LMR environment in the United States, as in other countries, closely tracks political trends; Democratic administrations have generally engaged in collaborative relationship with the public employee unions, whereas Republican administrations have seen the unions as adversaries. The overall LMR environment is shaped by provisions of the 1978 Federal Service Labor–Management Relations Statute (FSLMRS), which precludes the government from negotiating over pay with most federal employees. As a result, the scope of bargaining is relatively narrow and LMR have been, 'adversarial and often plagued by litigation over procedural matters and minutiae' (US General Accounting Office, 1991, p. 2).

In 1993, as part of the National Performance Review (NPR) reforms, President Clinton issued Executive Order (EO) 12871 of 1993 mandating labor–management partnerships (Clinton, 1993). The executive order, consistent with the emphasis placed by NPR on employee empowerment, created a National Partnership Council consisting of the heads of the major federal employee unions and senior, executive branch officials. Among the charges given the council were to work with the president and vice president on executive branch reform, to oversee the creation of partnership councils within the major federal departments and agencies, and to recommend statutory changes to facilitate better workplace relations.

An evaluation of the partnership program commissioned by the Office of Personnel Management in 2001 found some success indicators; 55 percent of management and union representatives surveyed agreed that their councils were an important decision-making body.[9] Survey results showed that partnerships had resulted in improved labor-management communications, and improved labor relations. However, relatively few participants perceived that partnership had resulted in any significant cost savings or avoidance or improved productivity (Masters, 2001).

LMR under President George W. Bush (2001–09) were highly adversarial. After less than a month in office Bush issued Executive Order 13203, formally revoking Clinton's EO 12871, dissolving the National Partnership Council and rescinding agency directives in support of the order (Bush, 2001). Subsequent to the September 11, 2001 attacks, the Bush administration proposed consolidating 22 agencies with security-related missions into a new Department of Homeland Security. The administration's proposal, eventually enacted, allowed the new department to waive provisions of federal civil service law relating to compensation, performance management, and labor–management relations. A draft of the department's new HRM regulations elicited vocal opposition from the affected unions, in part because of a provision providing that LMR disputes be taken to a management-controlled, department-specific board instead of to the Federal Labor Relations Authority and/or the Federal Services Impasses Panel as provided under FSLMRS (Thompson, 2007). A coalition of unions secured a victory when an appeals court ruled that the administration's proposal did not allow for collective bargaining as stipulated by the law. A similar dispute occurred over a new personnel system for civilians in the Department of Defense. The administration again sought to impose LMR rules that favored management, and again the unions took the administration to court. This time, however, the courts permitted implementation to proceed. In 2007–08, the new Democratic majority in Congress passed legislation revoking the department's authority to waive the provisions of FSLMRS and

returning the department to the pre-2003 LMR status quo.

With the election of President Obama in 2008, the LMR environment became more favorable for the unions. On December 9, 2009, President Obama signed an executive order re-establishing labor–management partnerships with the executive branch (Davidson, 2009) and in 2011, the head of the Transportation Security Administration overturned a ruling by his predecessor by allowing limited collective bargaining privileges for the 30,000+ employees of TSA (Long, 2011). The LMR environment shifted again subsequent to the 2010 elections, a result of which was that the Republicans took a majority in the House of Representatives. Partly in response to Republican demands that federal spending be reduced, President Obama froze the pay of all federal employees for two years.

TRENDS IN LABOR–MANAGEMENT RELATIONS IN OECD COUNTRIES

LMR in the 1990–2010 era have been shaped by several broad trends. The first relates to economic globalization and the competitive pressures released thereby. Proponents of economic liberalization determined that management practices in the public sector were an important determinant of economic performance and that the market logic driving the need for competitiveness should be applied to public bureaucracies. A hallmark of the forthcoming reforms was flexibility. The contention was that the traditional administrative model is centralized, rule-bound, and rigid and that the competitive dynamic demanded more nimble systems and approaches. This, in turn, implied privatization and a decentralization of authority to subordinate levels of the bureaucracy. Results rather than rules were to serve as a means of accountability.

Management practices relating to labor–management relations and pay setting were among those affected. The quest for perform-ance requires that agencies be competitive in the external market for individuals with skill sets required to achieve high levels of performance and that pay rules allow indi-vidual traits and attributes to be considered in hiring and promotion. The economistic logic that underlies NPM further mandates that managers be provided with the authority to use pay as a basis for rewarding and sanc-tioning workers. Allowing variation in pay across agencies, in turn, implies that the rules be set locally, that managers be pro-vided broad negotiating authority, and that employment be contractual rather than statu-tory, with expanded use of a 'contingent' workforce.

Table 7.1 shows the extent of adoption of alternative, labor relations/pay determination practices during the period 1990–2010. As shown, the movement has been fairly extensive, particularly among the NPM exemplars. NPM ideas have gained currency, even among the laggards, as discussed above with regard to the 'Centres de Res-ponsabilities' in France, the Tillburg model in Germany, and attempts at bureaucratic

modernization in Spain, although the degree of actual change was dampened during implementation in each instance.

A second broad dynamic that serves as a counter to the first, is an overarching require-ment for hierarchical accountability that has served as an impediment to radical change in many countries. This was particularly apparent with regard to finances. For exam-ple, although pay-setting authority was purportedly decentralized in the United Kingdom, the Treasury put tight constraints on the use of that authority. White (1999, p. 85) comments that, 'freedom to establish new pay systems is subject to strict central government controls, under which all changes must be cleared by the Treasury. Even pay offers must be cleared before negotiation with the unions commences.' A similar dynamic can be observed in Australia where the coalition government of the late 1990s moved aggressively to implement NPM-type reforms. Fairbrother and MacDonald (1999, p. 352) report that,

> despite the Howard government's professed ambi-tions to create a more decentralized (if not deregulated) approach to industrial relations in the

Table 7.1 Changes in labor–management relations and pay determination practices in selected OECD-member countries, 1985–2000

	NPM "Exemplars"			NPM "In-betweens"			NPM "Laggards"		
	NZ	SW	UK	AS	IT	US	FR	GR	SP
Pay Determination									
pay negotiation; centralized > decentralized	xx	xx	xx	x	x				
pay rules across agencies; uniform > variable	xx	xx	xx	x	x	x			x
basis of pay determination; internal > external equity	xx	xx	x	x					
unit of pay; collective > individual	xx	x	x	x					x
pay progression; seniority > performance	x	x	x	x	x			x	
Employment System									
workforce; permanent/career > flexible/contingent	x	x	x	x	x	x	x	xx	
legal basis of employment; statutory > contractual	x	x			x				
Partnership									
determination of outcomes; unilateral > mutual		x			x		x (1)		
scope of bargaining; narrow > broad		x				x	xx (1)	x	

NZ – New Zealand, SW – Sweden, UK – United Kingdom, AS – Australia, IT – Italy, US – United States, FR – France, GR – Germany, SP – Spain
xx – major emphasis/change, x – minor emphasis/change
(1) Angestellte and Arbeiter (non-civil service workers) only

public sector, the Department of Workplace Relations and Small Business has been given the important 'watchdog' role to ensure high degrees of procedural, if not substantive, uniformity across all federal government employment. Certified Agreements must receive both 'first stage' (i.e. proposal stage) and 'second stage' (i.e. preendorsement stage) approval by the Department before they can go to be voted on by the union membership and/or the staff (DWR&SB, 1998).

A third broad dynamic has to do with the party affiliation of the unions. In most countries the public employee unions are affiliated with Leftist parties and have exerted pressure within the party structure to dampen the extent of change to traditional structures and processes. This dynamic is apparent in a number of countries as follows:

- In Australia where the Labor Government's program of public sector renewal would reverse elements of the Liberal Party's decentralization efforts through greater standardization of employment conditions under the label 'One APS.'
- In New Zealand where the Labor Government passed the Employment Relations Act to restore some of the collective bargaining rights that had been withdrawn under the National Party.
- In the United States where Democratic presidents have supported labor–management partnership and the Republican (George W. Bush) did not. Also, where Democratic members of Congress opposed the imposition of pro-management collective bargaining rules at the Departments of Homeland Security and Defense by the Bush administration.

Notwithstanding these examples however, Leftist parties have often been in a posture of attempting to dampen the impact of NPM-type initiatives promoted by their Rightist adversaries. Thus, key elements of the Next Steps reforms introduced by the Conservatives were retained by Prime Minister Blair in the United Kingdom. Similarly, the essential structure of the reforms in New Zealand have survived several changes in regime.

The dominant trend, accelerated by the 2008–10 recession, is the deprivileging of public employees. As budget deficits have mounted, employee pay and benefits, which comprise the largest element in the budgets of most jurisdictions, have been targeted. Winchester and Bach (1995, p. 41) report that, 'the balance of power between trade unions and employers has shifted decisively in favour of the latter' in the six European countries they studied. Naschold (1996, p. 59) states that, 'in the vast majority of cases the main source of the productivity gains induced by [the modernization program in the United Kingdom] was cuts in staffing levels, cuts in wage levels, and a deterioration in working conditions.'

In the decade of the 2000s, Leftist regimes in a number of countries looked to quality management techniques and partnership as a means of mitigating the otherwise negative consequences of the changes on public employees. For unions, partnership offers a prospect of enhanced influence in the workplace as well as an opportunity for the unions to adopt a pro-reform posture. Danford et al. (2002, p. 1) describe how the Trade Unions Congress (TUC) in the United Kingdom endorsed partnership based on the belief that, 'genuine partnership and co-operation at work can give employees more control over their working lives through the involvement of trade union activists in the development of new working arrangements and the creation of high performance workplaces (TUC, 1999).'

Studies of the partnership experiment in the United Kingdom do not lead to optimistic conclusions about outcomes, however. The potential for co-option is one concern for the unions. Beale (2005, p. 137) comments, with regard to Inland Revenue in the United Kingdom, that partnership

is much more likely to restrain and undermine the militancy of the union than that of the employer. This reality emerges because partnership commits the union substantially to the employer's agenda through a combination of informal relationships and formal agreements – and thus limits the union's ability to act independently.

It is also unclear whether and to what extent consultation with employees was genuine.

Tailby et al. (2004, p. 416) state with regard to partnership at the National Health Service that, 'Our interview and questionnaire survey data suggested that employees were largely unconvinced of the efforts to involve them in organisational decision making.' A concern identified by several analysts is that the success of partnership arrangements is largely contingent on 'personalities'; i.e., partnership can work where both management and union leadership are favorably disposed to making it work but is less likely to succeed otherwise (Farnham et al., 2005).

CONCLUSION

The LMR environment in most Western countries during the period 1990–2010 is best characterized as one of instability. Public employees and their representatives have been on the defensive during much of the era, attempting to preserve elements of the traditional employment model in the face of economic and political conditions that highlighted the vulnerability of that model. The NPM doctrine has been invoked in a number of countries (New Zealand, Sweden, United Kingdom) in ways that advantage employers, for example by bargaining collectively at the agency level either in addition to or in place of central bargaining. With support from Leftist regimes in a number of venues (United States, Australia, United Kingdom), the unions have rallied and have managed to limit disaggregation: for example, in the United States with regard to the Departments of Homeland Security and Defense and within the NHS in the United Kingdom. In question, however, is whether this is a temporary respite from an inexorable deterioration of working conditions in the public sector or a long-term stabilization of the situation.

In some countries, unions have regarded partnership arrangements as an opportunity to redefine their role and to maintain their relevance. The experience with partnerships to date, however, does not afford much confidence of success in this regard. The experience in several countries is that the success of partnership is largely contingent on personalities, and that there has been little systematic impact on LMR generally. For Naschold (1996), a key question relates to the extent to which changes in 'work organization' become a reform focus. Such a focus would provide the unions an opportunity to play a constructive role in partnering with management to, for example, implement a job enrichment strategy. Needed for such a strategy to succeed, however, is an attitude of long-term investment in the workforce, an attitude that, according to Naschold, has been in little evidence.

NOTES

1   Although the reform strategies of Leftist governments in these same countries included similar elements, ways were generally found of mitigating the adverse impact on unions and their members.

2   Hood (1996) categorizes a number of countries as high, medium, or low, 'NPM emphasis.' In general, his categorization tracks that utilized here, with the exception of Australia, which he considers 'high' NPM emphasis, but which is categorized here as an 'in-between,' and France, which Hood categorizes as 'medium NPM emphasis,' but which is considered here to be a laggard.

3   The 2002 Review of the Centre was an effort by the Labour Government to reassess the reforms of the preceding era, particularly with regard to creation of executive agencies.

4   According to the OECD Public Management Service (2000), total public employment in Sweden declined from 1,275,000 in 1990 to 1,044,000 in 1995.

5   AgV stands for Arbetsgivarverket. 'In 1996, the AgV covered 270 different agencies and was entirely financed by membership fees collected from these agencies' (Andersson and Schager, 1999). (See also Bender et al., 2003.)

6   A prefect serves as the central government's representative in each department and 'exercises powers of supervision or prior approval over the decisions of locally-elected politicians' (Clark, 1998, p. 99).

7   Now the Department of Education, Employment and Workplace Relations.

8   ARAN stands for Agenzia per la rappresentanza sindacale nel pubblico impiego.

9   A total of 651 partnership council participants at 54 sites in eight agencies were surveyed (Masters, 2001).

REFERENCES

Advisory Group on Reform of Australian Government Administration (2010). *Ahead of the Game: Blueprint for the Reform of Australian Government Administration*. Canberra: Australian Government Department of the Prime Minister and Cabinet.

Advisory Group on the Review of the Centre (2001). *Report of the Advisory Group on the Review of the Centre*. Wellington, New Zealand: State Services Commission.

Andersson, P. & Schager, N. H. (1999). The reform of pay determination in the Swedish public sector. In R.Elliott, C. Lucifora, & D. Meurs (eds), *Public Sector Pay Determination in the European Union* (pp. 240–284). New York: St. Martin's Press Inc.

Bach, S. (2004). Employee participation and union voice in the National Health Service. *Human Resource Management Journal, 14,* 3–19.

Bach, S. & Della Rocca, G. (2000). The management strategies of public service employers in Europe. *Industrial Relations Journal, 31,* 82–96.

Bach, S. & Della Rocca, G. (2001). The New Public Management in Europe. In C.Dell'Aringa, G. Della Rocca, & B. Keller (eds), *Strategic Choices in Reforming Public Service Employment: An International Handbook* (pp. 24–47). Gordonsville, VA: Palgrave Macmillan.

Bach, S. & Givan, R. K. (2008). Public service modernization and trade union reform: Towards managerial led renewal? *Public Administration, 86,* 523–539.

Bach, S. & Winchester, D. (2003). Industrial relations in the public sector. In P. Edwards (ed.), *Industrial Relations: Theory and Practice* (pp. 286–312). Malden, MA: Blackwell Publishing.

Bach, S., Bordogna, G., Della Rocca, G., & Winchester, D. (1999). *Public Service Employment Relations in Europe: Transformation, Modernization, or Inertia?* London: Routledge.

Baker, P. & Calmes, J. (2010, November 30). Obama declares two-year freeze on federal pay. *New York Times.*

Barlow, J., Farnham, D., Horton, S., & Ridley, F. F. (1996). Comparing public managers. In D.Farnham, S. Horton, J. Barlow, & A. Hondeghem (eds), *New Public Managers in Europe: Public Servants in Transition* (pp. 3–25). London: Macmillan Business.

Bazex, M. (1987). Labour relations in the public service in France. In T. Treu (ed.), *Public Service Labour Relations: Recent Trends and Future Prospects: A Comparative Survey of Seven Industrialised Market Economy Countries* (pp. 83–109). Geneva, Switzerland: International Labour Office.

Beale, D. (2005). The promotion and prospects of partnership at Inland Revenue: Employer and union hand in hand? In M.Stuart & M. Martinez Lucio (eds), *Partnership and Modernisation in Employment Relations* (pp. 137–153). London: Routledge.

Bender, K. A. & Elliott, R. F. (2003). *Decentralised Pay Setting: A Study of the Outcomes of Collective Bargaining Reform in the Civil Service in Australia, Sweden and the UK*. Burlington, VT: Ashgate Publishing Company.

Bordogna, L., Dell'Aringa, C., & Della Rocca, G. (1999). Italy: A case of coordinated decentralization. In S. Bach, L. Bordogna, G. Della Rocca, & D. Winchester (eds), *Public Service Employment Relations in Europe* (pp. 94–129). London: Routledge.

Boston, J., Martin, J., Pallot, J., & Walsh, P. (1996a). Negotiating the employment contract. In J. Boston (ed.), *Public Management: The New Zealand Model* (pp. 225–245). Auckland: Oxford University Press.

Boston, J., Martin, J., Pallot, J., & Walsh, P. (1996b). *Public Management: The New Zealand Model.* Auckland: Oxford University Press.

Brown, J. (2010, November 21). Public sector workers brace for more pain. www.FT.com

Burnham, J. (2000). Human resource flexibilities in France. In D. Farnham & S. Horton (eds), *Human Resource Flexibilities in the Public Services: International Perspectives* (pp. 98–114). London: Macmillan Press.

Bush, G.W. (2001). Presidential Executive Order 13203 Revocation of Executive Order and Presidential Memorandum Concerning Labor–Management Partnerships. Retrieved April 18, 2011, from http://www.archives.gov/federal-register/executive-orders/2001-wbush.html

Chapman, J. & Duncan, G. (2007). Is there now a new "New Zealand model"? *Public Management Review, 9,* 1–25.

Clark, D. (1998). The modernization of the French civil service: Crisis, change and continuity. *Public Administration, 76,* 97–115.

Clinton, W. J. (1993). Presidential Executive Order 12871 Dated 10-1-93, Labor Management Partnerships. Retrieved February 19, 2005, from http://govinfo.library.unt.edu/npr/library/direct/orders/24ea.html

Danford, A., Richardson, M., & Upchurch, M. (2002). "New unionism", organising and partnership: A comparative analysis of union renewal strategies in the public sector. *Capital & Class, 76,* 1–27.

Davidson, J. (2009, August 12). Obama follow's Clinton's lead on creating labor council. www.washingtonpost.com

De La Puente, D. & House, J. (2010, June 9). Spanish workers protest austerity. *Wall Street Journal.*

Denis, J. M. & Jeannot, G. (2005). France: From direct to indirect participation to where? In D.Farnham, A. Hondeghem, & S. Horton (eds), *Staff Participation and Public Management Reform: Some International Comparisons* (pp. 156–167). Houndmills, UK: Palgrave Macmillan.

Department of Workplace Relations and Small Business (now the Department of Education, Employment and Workplace Relations). 1998. Workplace Relations Advice no. 98/4

Fairbrother, P. & MacDonald, D. (1999). The role of the state and Australian public sector industrial relations: Depoliticisation and direct intervention. *New Zealand Journal of Industrial Relations, 24,* 343–363.

Farnham, D. & Horton, S. (2000). *Human Resource Flexibilities in the Public Services.* London: Macmillan Press.

Farnham, D. & Koch, R. (2005). Germany: Limited reforms and restricted participation. In D. Farnham, A. Hondeghem, & S. Horton (eds), *Staff Participation and Public Management Reform* (pp. 168–183). Houndmills, UK: Palgrave Macmillan.

Farnham, D., Hondeghem, A., & Horton, S. (2005). *Staff Participation and Public Management Reform: Some International Comparisons.* Houndmills, UK: Palgrave Macmillan.

Fialaire, J. (1993). Les strategies de la mise en ouevre des centres de responsibilite. *Politiques et Management Publique, 11,* 33–49.

Flynn, N. & Strehl, F. (1996a). France. In N. Flynn & F. Strehl (eds), *Public Sector Management in Europe.* London: Prentice Hall.

Flynn, N. & Strehl, F. (1996b). Introduction. In N. Flynn & F. Strehl (eds), *Public Sector Management in Europe* (pp. 1–20). London: Prentice Hall.

Fredman, S. (1999). The legal context: Public or private? In S. Corby & G. White (eds), *Employee Relations in the Public Services: Themes and Issues* (pp. 53–70). London: Routledge.

Goldfinch, S. & Wallis, J. (2010). Two myths of convergence in public management reform. *Public Administration, 88,* 1099–1115.

Grim resignation as austerity bites. (2010, July 3). *Economist, 396,* 50–51.

Guillotin, Y. & Meurs, D. (1999). Heterogeneity in the French public sector: Some first insights. In R. Elliott, C. Lucifora, & D. Meurs (eds), *Public Sector Pay Determination in the European Union* (pp. 70–113). New York: St. Martin's Press.

Hood, C. (1991). A public management for all seasons? *Public Administration, 69,* 3–19.

Hood, C. (1996). Exploring variations in public management reform of the 1980s. In H. A. Bekke, J. L. Perry, & T. A. Toonen (eds), *Civil Service Systems in Comparative Perspective* (pp. 268–287). Bloomington, IN: Indiana University Press.

Ifo Institute for Economic Research (2011). Online at http://www.cesifo-group.de/portal/page/portal/ifoHome

James, O. (2004). Executive agencies and joined-up government in the UK. In C. Pollitt & C. Talbot (eds), *Unbundled Government: A Critical Analysis of the Global Trend to Agencies, Quangos and Contractualisation* (pp. 75–93). New York: Routledge.

Jódar, P., Jordana, J., & Alós, R. (1999). Public service employment relations since the transition to democracy. In S. Bach, G. Bordogna, G. Della Rocca, & D. Winchester (eds), *Public Service Employment Relations in Europe: Transformation, Modernization or Inertia?* (pp. 164–197). London: Routledge.

Keller, B. (1999). Germany: Negotiated change, modernization, and the challenge of unification. In S. Bach, G. Bordogna, G. Della Rocca, & D. Winchester (eds), *Public Sector Employment Relations in Europe: Transformation, Modernization, or Inertia?* (pp. 56–93). London: Routledge.

Keller, B., Due, J., & Andersen, S. K. (2001). Employer associations and unions in the public sector. In C. Dell'Aringa, G. Della Rocca, & B. Keller (eds), *Strategic Choices in Reforming Public Service Employment* (pp. 71–95). Gordonsville, VA: Palgrave Macmillan.

Lansbury, R. D. & Macdonald, D. K. (2001). Employment relations in the Australian public sector. In C. Dell'Aringa, G. Della Rocca, & B. Keller (eds), *Strategic Choices in Reforming Public Service Employment: An International Handbook* (pp. 216–242). Gordonsville, VA: Palgrave Macmillan.

Lasierra, J. M. (2007). Labour relations in the Spanish public administration in a context of change: The role of context and regulation. *International Journal of Public Sector Management, 20,* 63–74.

Lodge, M. & Gill, D. (2011). Toward a new era of administrative reform? The myth of post-NPM in New Zealand. *Governance, 24,* 141–166.

Long, E. (2011, February 10). TSA administrator defends collective bargaining decision. www.govexec.com

Masters, M. (2001). *A Final Report to the National Partnership Council on Evaluating Progress and Improvements in Agencies' Organizational Performance Resulting from Labor–Management Partnerships.* Washington, DC: US Office of Personnel Management.

Naschold, F. (1996). *New Frontiers in Public Sector Management: Trends and Issues in State and Local Government in Europe.* Berlin: Walter de Gruyter.

Naschold, F. & Arnkil, R. (1997). Modernization of the labour market organization: Scandanavian and Anglo-Saxon experiences in an international bench-marking perspective. In J. Dolvik & A. Steen (eds), *Making Solidarity Work: The Norwegian Labour Market Model in Transition.* Oslo: Scandinavian University Press.

Nomden, K., Farnham, D., & Onnee-Abbruciati, M.-L. (2003). Collective bargaining in public services: Some European comparisons. *International Journal of Public Sector Management, 16,* 412–423.

O'Brien, J. & Fairbrother, P. (2000). A changing public sector: Developments at the Commonwealth level. *Australian Journal of Public Administration, 59,* 59–66.

Ongaro, E. (2009). *Public Management Reform and Modernization: Trajectories of Administrative Change in Italy, France, Greece, Portugal and Spain.* Northampton, MA: Edward Elgar Publishing.

Organisation for Economic Co-operation and Development (1997). *Trends in Public Sector Pay in OECD Countries.* Paris: OECD.

Organisation for Economic Co-operation and Development (2000). Recent Developments and Future Challenges in Human Resource Management in OECD Member Countries Background Paper by the Secretariat. Paris: OECD.

Parrado, S. (1996). Spain. In D. Farnham, S. Horton, J. Barlow, & A. Hondeghem (eds), *New Public Managers in Europe: Public Servants in Transition* (pp. 257–277). London: Macmillan.

Parrado, S. (2008). Failed policies but institutional innovation through "layering" and "diffusion" in Spanish central administration. *International Journal of Public Sector Management, 21,* 230–252.

Pollitt, C. & Bouckaert, G. (2004). *Public Management Reform: A Comparative Analysis,* 2nd edn. Oxford, UK: Oxford University Press.

Postif, T. (1997). Public sector reform in France. In J. Lane (ed.), *Public Sector Reform: Rationale, Trends and Problems* (pp. 209–224). London: Sage Publications.

Prowse, P. & Prowse, J. (2007). Is there still a public sector model of employment relations in the United Kingdom? *International Journal of Public Sector Management, 20,* 48–62.

Public Service and Merit Protection Commission. (1997). The Public Service Act 1997: Accountability in a Devolved Management Framework. Retrieved April 3, 1998 from http://www.psmpc.gov.au/aps/apsact97htmp

Roness, P. G. (2001). Transforming state employees' unions. In T. Christensen & P. Laegreid (eds), *New Public Management: The Transformation of Ideas and Practice* (pp. 173–208). Aldershot, England: Ashgate Publishing.

Simon, R. (2011, April 2). Union battles spread. *Chicago Tribune.*

State Services Commission. (1998). *Assessment of the State of the New Zealand Public Service.* Wellington, New Zealand: State Services Commission.

Sulzberger, A. G. (2011, March 12). Union bill is law, but debate is far from over. *New York Times.*

Tailby, S., Richardson, M., Stewart, P., Danford, A., & Upchurch, M. (2004). Partnership at work and worker participation: An NHS case study. *Industrial Relations Journal, 35,* 403–418.

Thompson, J. R. (2007). Federal labor–management relations reforms under Bush: Enlightened management or quest for control? *Review of Public Personnel Administration, 27,* 105–124.

Tondorf, K. (1995). *Leistungszulage als Reforminstrument? Neue Lohnpolitik zwischen Sparzwang und Modernisierung.* Berlin: Ed. Sigma.

Trades Union Congress (1999). *Partners for Progress: New Unionism in the Workplace.* London: Trades Union Congress.

Treu, T. (1987). Labour relations in the public service in Italy. In T. Treu & Treu (eds), *Public Service Labour Relations: Recent Trends and Future Prospects: A Comparative Survey of Seven Industrialised Market Economy Countries* (pp. 1–47). Geneva, Switzerland: International Labour Office.

US General Accounting Office. (1991). *The Federal Labor–Management Relations Program* (GAO/T-GGD-92-8). Washington, DC: US Government Printing Office.

White, G. (1999). The remuneration of public servants: Fair pay or new pay? In S. Corby & G. White (eds), *Employee Relations in the Public Services: Themes and Issues.* London: Routledge.

Winchester, D. & Bach, S. (1995). The state: The public sector. In P. Edwards (ed.), *Industrial Relations: Theory and Practice in Britain* (pp. 304–334). Oxford: Blackwell Business.

PART 3

Organization Theory
and Public Administration

edited by Tom Christensen

The systematic development of organization theory has traditionally been associated with studies of private organizations, particularly business firms. Studies of public administration, on the other hand, for a long time had no explicit basis in organization theory, even though some pioneering work was done (Scott and Davis, 2006). These studies show clearly that there is a close connection between the practice of public administration and the development of organization theory; in other words, aspects of organization theory have been deployed in the running of public administrations, which in turn has yielded new theoretical insights. Over the past few decades an organization theory more specifically geared to studies of public administration has developed (Christensen et al., 2007; Scott, 2007). This is not a homogeneous field but embraces a number of different theories expounded both separately and in combination. Moreover, it has grown much more complex over time. Having started out with rather simple ideas about 'economic man', 'administrative man' and 'social or cultural man', it has evolved into a complicated pattern of institutional theories in which the original ideas have been further developed and combined in various ways with new ideas.

The introduction to this section provides a brief overview of four main types of public administration organization theory, covered by the four chapters, and reflects on some of the broader questions associated with this field of study. After discussing the different driving forces behind decision-making behaviour – whether individual or organizational/institutional – in public administration, a brief historical outline of the development of the organization theory of public administration is given. The comparative aspect of this type of organization theory is discussed, looking into the dynamic relationship between organization theory perspectives and structural and cultural features of various groups of countries. Finally, and related to the third point, the development of organization theory under New Public Management (NPM) and post-NPM is briefly discussed.

HOW TO DEFINE THE ORGANIZATION THEORY OF PUBLIC ADMINISTRATION?

In a wide and complex body of literature it is not easy to isolate the organization theory of public administration from other kinds of organization theory. One approach is to ask what we want to explain: that is, what are the *dependent variables*? The simplest answer is that we are interested in public decision-making behaviour: that is, the authoritative allocation of responsibility and resources between actors and levels in the political–administrative system. This answer signals that we see the public administration as an integral part of the political–administrative system and that we will therefore also focus on the dynamic relationship between political and administrative actors in a democratic context (March and Olsen, 1989). This is an important distinction from theories that have primarily evolved in the context of private organizations.

A focus on decision-making behaviour may involve studies that aim to produce a theory of political–administrative systems and study their internal life. Such investigations might look at how administrative policies change the internal structure of the civil service – changing such things as the formal structure, recruitment policies and the rights and participation of employees (Egeberg, 1994). Conversely, one might be interested in how different kinds of internal organization result in certain types of public policies, aimed at influencing the environment. A further, rather seldom explored option is to use political science-oriented organization theory and related studies to analyse the societal effects and impact of these decisions and policies. One reason why such studies are rather rare is that they overlap with other research traditions in the fields of sociology, economics, psychology and anthropology.

A further focus might be to analyse the driving forces behind decision making in public organizations using the main perspectives of organization theory: in other words, to ask which *independent variables* can be used to explain features of decision-making processes and their effects. It is possible to divide these explanatory variables into four categories of theories or perspectives – hence, the four chapters in this section. The first chapter, by Morten Egeberg, reviews the tradition of theories and research connected to the seminal work of people like Gulick, March and Simon. This tradition primarily focuses on the importance of formal, normative organizational structures for decision making and on the formal organization of units and roles and also includes elements from social psychology (March and Simon, 1958; Simon, 1945). Decision makers, whether individuals or organizational units, have problems of capacity and with coping with large quantities of information and varieties of premises. Public organizations, therefore, have to be designed or organized in ways that modify these problems. Actors have to select certain decision-making premises and reach 'satisfactory' decisions based on 'bounded rationality'. A decision-making structure of this kind channels attitudes and attention in certain directions, thereby also creating special roles and patterns of contact. One challenge of creating a public administration built on a combination of different principles of specialization is that of coordinating units and roles and balancing their varied decision-making behaviour (Gulick, 1937).

Within this 'formal structure matters' mode of thinking, there are a number of different strands, two of which we will mention here. We use Dahl and Lindblom's (1953) concepts of political–administrative control and 'rational calculation' to define them. The hierarchical version holds that the leaders of a public administration are homogeneous and have tight control over decision-making processes, and that their organizational or means–end thinking is relatively unambiguous: that is, they know what to do and exercise strong control over the means to do it (March and Olsen, 1976). Another version assumes a heterogeneous leadership and actors and different kinds of means–end thinking, resulting in negotiations and compromises. This is what March and Olsen (1983) labelled 'Realpolitik' and Allison (1971) called 'governmental or bureaucratic politics'.

The second perspective on what influences decision-making behaviour, covered by Jack Knott and Thomas Hammond's chapter (chapter 10) in this part, is what can broadly be labelled formal theories. This type of theory is generally based on the premise of rational individual or group actors seeking to advance their own interests through utility-maximizing behaviour. Strictly speaking, this theory is not confined to organization theory, but it has developed in certain ways that allow it to be partly included here. Some formalized models in this theoretical tradition try to explain decisions by rational actors who have more complex decision-making strategies, based partly on institutional factors and formal constraints. Theorists who come under this label are, for example, interested in how formal rules and procedures inside political–administrative bodies shape rational decision-making behaviour, how markets and hierarchies can be blended and how the environment can be made negotiable to modify insecurity (Coase, 1937; Hammond, 1990; Williamson, 1975).

A third branch of organization theory, covered mainly in Jean-Claude Thoenig's chapter, is the cultural–institutional perspective, which is closely associated with Selznick's work (1949, 1957). According to this perspective, public organizations gradually develop into institutions, infusing and adding values to the formal framework. This process of institutionalization and adaptation gradually produces certain informal norms and values that go further in explaining decision-making behaviour than formal norms. Public administrative bodies develop different and unique cultures, characters or 'souls' through this process. This theory combines different types of institutional theories (Peters, 2011): theories of

historical institutionalism (Steinmo et al., 1992), which emphasize historical roots and path dependency, sociological theories of institutionalism, like those represented by Selznick, and theories of normative institutionalism, like March and Olsen's (1989) theory of appropriateness, where public institutions are seen in a broader normative democratic context as integrating, shaping and developing actors on a collective basis.

The fourth type of organization theory in Thoenig's chapter (chapter 9), revolves around the belief that the environment drives decision-making behaviour. Public administration and its actors can, of course, influence their environment as well, but here the focus is on the environment influencing the public administration. This type of theory can be divided into two parts. One is primarily concerned with the 'technical environment', as discussed by Hult, and how the internal organization of the public administration – its structure, function, roles and resource allocation – is dependent on relevant actors in the environment and their demands and organization. Typical theories here are contingency theories and resource-dependency theories (Lawrence and Lorsch, 1967; Pfeffer and Salancik, 1978). The other main type focuses on the 'institutional environment', as also discussed by Thoenig, and stresses that a complex olitical–administrative system creates a demand for some simple 'rules of thumb' (Meyer and Rowan, 1977; Powell and DiMaggio, 1991). These are defined on a macro level through the creation of myths: that is, ideas based on some kind of social-constructivist tradition. It is assumed that certain organizational models, budget or planning systems, types of knowledge, etc., are 'appropriate' for public administrations (March, 1994). A structure of dominance is created for these ideas, often supported by public authority centres or professional groups 'certifying' them, and public organizations have to adapt to them, at least on the surface. Brunsson (1989) emphasizes that the two types of environment and their demands have to be in balance, often in different ways in different organizations, something that strengthens the legitimacy of the public administration. Public leaders have to act, take decisions and deliver services, but they can also gain from 'double-talk': that is, also talking as if they intend to act, even if they have no intention of doing so and no idea of what to do if they run into problems of implementation.

The distinctions between the different types of organization theory implied by the structure of Part 3 of course offer no clear-cut categorization of the different theories, but that is not the purpose here. Theories may combine elements of bounded rationality, culture and myths, like the broad institutional theory of March and Olsen (1989, 1995); they may mix elements of structure and culture with internal and environmental factors, like Selznick (1957) does; or else myth theories may be combined with structural elements, as Brunsson (1989) does. The institutional theories of Pierson (2004) and Thelen (Mahoney and Thelen, 2009) that have been increasingly influential in the last decade are also examples of blending formal and institutional theories.

Another distinction between the theories outlined here is the level on which they focus. The theory of bounded rationality, for instance, often focuses on the micro level and on individual decision makers, while the formal framework in which these actors operate is the organizational or sub-organizational level. Social choice theories have some of the same focus, while cultural theories combine theoretical ideas at the organizational or meso level with elements from the task environment. Environmental theories of a technical nature share the focus on task environment with central cultural theories, while myth theories often focus on phenomena at a macro or organizational field level but relate these to effects and implications on an organizational level.

The theories presented also vary in how they believe public administrative units

become established and change. Bounded rationality and social choice theories both perceive such processes as the result of the intentions of certain actors, such as political and administrative leaders, and as such the result of design and strategy. However, they differ concerning the importance of self-interest and the formal structure that shapes intentions and actions. Cultural theories see change processes as the gradual and incremental evolution of public units, while the theories of both the technical and institutional environment have typical elements of determinism: that is to say public administrations have to adjust to their environment and do not have much leeway. It is also worth pointing out that cultural theories, at least of the Selznick type, mainly emphasize uniqueness, variety and divergence in public administration, while myth theories and certain other environmental theories, like population ecology, often stress isomorphism and convergence, i.e. public administrative units are becoming more similar (Scott and Davis, 2006).

THE DEVELOPMENT OF THEORIES AND THE VARIETY OF TRADITIONS

It is always difficult to describe the development of theory, in this case organization theory for the study of public administration, because theories very seldom appear in neat categories in specific periods. Instead they overlap, sometimes run parallel, disappear, are revived in new versions and so on. Therefore, typologies will always need to bend reality to some extent and post-rationalize. In our case it is also a problem that a strand of theory may develop in one period as a more general theory but be more specifically related to studies of public administration at a later stage. With all this in mind, this section offers a chronology of the four types of theory mentioned.

Early studies of public administration, or political–administrative systems in general, were often oriented towards the judicial–constitutional framework: in other words, to the more formal aspects of such systems (Peters, 2011). However, it was not until Gulick (1937) advanced his theory, based on Weber and Fayol, about the effects of principles of specialization and coordination in public administration, that public administration was associated with any particular organization theory. The breakthrough, in the form of the theory of bounded rationality, came in 1945, with Simon's *Administrative Behavior*, but was also developed by March and Simon (1958) and Cyert and March (1963). What was distinctive about this development was that it combined organization or decision-making theory with political science or political theory. According to March (1997), this tradition was later lost or partly disappeared in the United States, but it has survived in parts of Europe, particularly in Scandinavia (Christensen and Lægreid, 1998).

Scott (2007) sees the roots of institutional theory in the economics of the late nineteenth and early twentieth centuries, in Germany and the United States, and concludes that this theoretical tradition, which questions the simplistic assumptions of a model of economic man by adding the social context of economic processes, had more in common with later sociological and anthropological theories of institutions than with the new institutional economics. With the emergence of the theory of new institutionalism in economics in the late 1930s, many of the traditional institutional factors were disregarded. The empirical focus was also primarily the firm and the market. When formal theories started to be applied to studies of public institutions from the 1970s onwards, seeing them as governance or rules systems, this implied both a theoretical and an empirical extension of new institutionalism in economics and related theories. They did not, however, discard the main premises of the theory regarding the factors driving actors or similarities between the public and private sectors. Studies of public administration

using this approach began during the 1990s (Peters, 2011).

Selznick (1949, 1957) developed his cultural–institutional theory in organizational sociology parallel to the main works on bounded rationality. His work was historically rooted in the theoretical developments of the 1920s and 1930s and specifically connected to the Human Relations School and Barnard's (1938) work but also to contemporary theoretical developments, like Parson's (Scott and Davis, 2006). He embraced the tradition of looking at formal organizations as social systems with complex goals and social needs besides instrumental goals and of stressing the importance of informal norms and integrative features. His work was revived in the 1980s and 1990s, both in organizational sociology and in political science theory, by people like Scott (2007; Scott et al., 2000) and March and Olsen (1989).

Even though influential theorists, like Goffman, and Berger and Luckman, published interesting work in the social–constructivist tradition in the 1960s, it was not until 1977 that Meyer and Rowan (1977), in a pioneering article, formulated a systematic myth theory in organization theory. During the 1980s and 1990s this strand of theory, often labelled the 'new institutionalism', was developed further by many scholars (Powell and DiMaggio, 1991; Scott, 2007) and became more specifically connected to studies of public administration (Brunsson, 1989).

Another, more challenging and perhaps speculative way of looking at the development of the organization theory of public administration is to relate it to the characteristics of the political–administrative structure and cultural traditions in different countries. This can only be done by grouping the political–administrative systems in different countries into some broad categories and indicating possible connections. At the one extreme, the political–administrative system in the United States is characterized by extreme structural and cultural fragmentation and complexity, by a small public sector, by a cultural tradition that caters more to the private sector, efficiency and individual rationality and by greater hostility and mistrust towards politicians and civil servants than elsewhere (Christensen and Peters, 1999). This seems to be reflected in the very complex body of organization theory for public administration generated in the United States, which ignores grand theories of the state and tends instead to emphasize theories like formal theories, which portray strategic actors operating in their own interests in a fragmented system with few integrative features. The emergence of myth theory in the United States can also be seen as a reflection of the fragmented nature of the system: that is, there is a need for symbols capable of integrating the system. The development of organization theory in the United States is, of course, not without collective features, which we find both in theories on organizational rationality and in cultural–institutional theory, but these features are relatively weaker than in, say, the Anglo-Saxon countries that are generally considered to belong to the same type of tradition.

At the other extreme are the features of the political–administrative systems in Scandinavia. These are countries that are much more homogeneous structurally and culturally, attend much more to collective norms and values and less to individual rationality and efficiency, and place greater emphasis on integrating societal groups in public decision making, even though some of these features are slowly beginning to change. These characteristics seem to be reflected in the historically strong position of theories on organizational rationality and cultural–institutional theories. A specifically Scandinavian version of institutional theory has emerged over the past two decades that is characterized by a blend of culture and myth theory (Forsell, 2001). Some Continental European countries have much in common with Scandinavia concerning the structure and culture of the political–administrative system, with strong and centralized states

and an emphasis on collectivity. This is also reflected in the way their theory of the public administration has developed. As Thoenig points out in his chapter (chapter 9), France was rather early in developing a cultural–integrative tradition in organization theory (Crozier, 1964). Unlike the United States, neither Scandinavia nor Continental Europe have a particularly strong tradition of formal theorists working in the field of public administration.

INCREASED COMPLEXITY IN THEORIES AND PUBLIC ADMINISTRATION?

Organization theories of public administration seem in some ways to have grown more complex, both concerning the number of theories developed, the internal differentiation of each theory and the growing number of combinations of different theories. This may reflect the increasing complexity of political–administrative systems and decision-making processes. Civil service systems are more specialized than before, both horizontally and vertically. New and hybrid structures have developed both inside the public apparatus and in its links with the private and societal sectors (Christensen et al. 2007). Traditional political–administrative cultures have been partly transformed and new norms and values have appeared, blending or melding with the old ones. Public decision-making processes currently involve actors with more ambiguous mandates, involve more and different types of actors and there are more connections over time between levels and institutions. Moreover, decisions are more often appealed or changed in the implementation phase, either because of changing conditions or because actors would like to change the content of policies. All this may lead to a more differentiated set of theories that one can combine to understand the workings of public administration.

Another, rather different way of looking at the development of both the theory and practice of public administration is to take New Public Management as a point of departure. NPM has spread all over the world, albeit more in the form of ideas than in practice in some countries, but it is still widely influential. Boston et al. (1996) stress in their book about NPM in New Zealand that there is a close connection between the theories of reform and the actual implementation of reform measures: that is to say the reforms are theory-driven to a large extent. The theories behind NPM in New Zealand and other Anglo-American countries are primarily different versions of formal theories. They stress simplicity much more than complexity, concerning theoretical preconditions, the structure of the political–administrative system, role differentiation between politicians and administrative leaders and the unambiguous chain of command and they attach importance to clear goals and means, efficiency and rationality. An interesting question is whether the simplification of theory also leads to the simplification of practice in the political–administrative system or whether it actually generates more complexity (Christensen and Lægreid, 2001). During the last decade, the trail-blazing NPM countries have experienced post-NPM features with increasing centralization and coordination, modifying and supplementing NPM (Christensen and Lægreid, 2007). This has revived both structural theories based in bounded rationality, but also seen (for example) network-oriented theories emerging.

The example of NPM and post-NPM illustrates how organization theory can lead more directly to certain ways of organizing the public administration. What the coming chapters should ideally do is to cover how the different theories have been applied in studies of political–administrative systems more generally, and public administration specifically. It is beyond our reach to give a comprehensive overview of such studies, so the different chapters instead give representative examples of empirical studies within each theoretical tradition.

REFERENCES

Allison, G.T. (1971) *Essence of Decision. Explaining the Cuban Missile Crisis.* Boston, MA: Little, Brown.

Barnard, C.I. (1938) *The Functions of the Executive.* Cambridge, MA: Harvard University Press.

Boston, J., Martin, J., Pallot, J. and Walsh, P. (1996) *Public Management: The New Zealand Model.* Auckland: Oxford University Press.

Brunsson, N. (1989) *The Organization of Hypocrisy. Talk, Decisions and Actions in Organizations.* Chichester: Wiley.

Christensen, T. and Lægreid, P. (1998) 'Public Administration in a Democratic Context – A Review of Norwegian Research', in N. Brunsson and J.P. Olsen (eds), *Organizing Organizations.* Bergen: Fagbokforlaget.

Christensen, T. and Lægreid, P. (2001) *New Public Management. The Transformation of Ideas and Practice.* Aldershot: Ashgate.

Christensen, T. and Lægreid, P. (2007) 'The Whole-of-Government Approach to Public Sector Reform', *PAR. Public Administration Review*, 67: 1059–1066.

Christensen, T., Lægreid, P., Roness, P.G. and Røvik, K.A. (2007) *Organization Theory and The Public Sector. Instrument, Culture and Myth.* London and New York: Routledge.

Christensen, T. and Peters, B. Guy (1999) *Structure, Culture and Governance. A Comparison of Norway and the United States.* Lanham, MA: Rowman & Littlefield.

Coase, R. (1937) 'The Nature of the Firm', *Economica*, 4 (November): 386–405.

Crozier, M. (1964) *The Bureaucratic Phenomenon.* Chicago, IL: University of Chicago Press.

Cyert, R.M. and March, J.G. (1963) *A Behavioral Theory of the Firm.* Englewood Cliffs, NJ: Prentice Hall.

Dahl, R.A. and Lindblom, C. (1953) *Politics, Economics and Welfare.* New York: Harper and Row.

Egeberg, M. (1994) 'Bridging the Gap between Theory and Practice: The Case of Administrative Policy', *Governance*, 7: 83–98.

Forsell, A. (2001) 'Reform Theory Meets New Public Management', in T. Christensen and P. Lægreid (eds), *New Public Management: Transforming Ideas and Practice.* Aldershot: Ashgate.

Gulick, L. (1937) 'Notes on the Theory on Organizations. With Special Reference to Government', in L. Gulick and L. Urwin (eds), *Papers on the Science of Administration*. New York: A.M. Kelley.

Hammond, T.H. (1990) 'In Defence of Luther Gulick's Notes on the Theory of Organization', *Public Administration*, 68(Summer): 143–173.

Lawrence, P.R. and Lorsch, J.W. (1967) *Organization and Environment: Managing Differentiation and Integration*. Boston, MA: Graduate School of Business Administration, Harvard University.

Mahoney, J. and Thelen, K. (2009) *Explaining Institutional Change: Ambiguity, Agency, and Power*. Cambridge: Cambridge University Press.

March, J.G. (1994) *A Primer on Decision Making*. New York: Free Press.

March, J.G. (1997) 'Administrative Practice, Organization Theory, and Political Philosophy: Ruminations and Reflections of John M. Gaus', *PS Political Science*, 30(3): 689–698.

March, J.G. and Olsen, J.P. (1976) *Ambiguity and Choice in Organizations*. Bergen: Scandinavia University Press.

March, J.G. and Olsen, J.P. (1983) 'Organizing Political Life: What Administrative Reorganization Tells Us About Government', *American Political Science Review*, 77 (2): 281–297.

March, J.G. and Olsen, J.P. (1989) *Rediscovering Institutions: The Organizational Basis of Politics*. New York: Free Press.

March, J.G. and Olsen, J.P. (1995) *Democratic Governance*. New York: Free Press.

March, J.G. and Simon, H.A. (1958) *Organizations*. New York: Wiley.

Meyer, J.W. and Rowan, B. (1977) 'Institutionalized Organizations: Formal Structure as Myth and Ceremony.' *American Journal of Sociology*, 83 (September): 340–363.

Peters, B. Guy (2011) *Institutional Theory in Political Science. The 'New Institutionalism'*, 3rd revised edition. London: Pinter.

Pfeffer, J. and Salancik, G.R. (1978) *The External Control of Organizations*. New York: Harper and Row.

Pierson, P. (2004) *Politics in Time: History, Institutions and Social Analysis*. Princeton, NJ: Princeton University Press.

Powell, W.W. and DiMaggio, P.J. (eds) (1991) *The New Institutionalism in Organizational Analysis*. Chicago, IL: University of Chicago Press.

Scott, W.R. (2007) *Institutions and Organizations*, 3rd edn. Thousand Oaks, CA: Sage.

Scott, W.R. and Davis, G.F. (2006) *Organizations and Organizing: Rational, Natural, and Open Systems Perspectives*. Upper Saddle River, NJ: Prentice Hall.

Scott, W.R., Ruef, M., Mendel, P.J. and Caronna, C.A. (2000) *Institutional Change and Health Care Organizations. From Professional Dominance to Managed Care*. Chicago, IL: University of Chicago Press.

Selznick, P. (1949) *TVA and the Grass Roots*. Berkeley, CA: University of California Press.

Selznick, P. (1957) *Leadership in Administration*. New York: Harper and Row.

Simon, H.A. (1945) *Administrative Behavior*. New York: Macmillan.

Steinmo, S., Thelen, K. and Longstreth, F. (1992) *Structuring Politics: Historical Institutionalism in Comparative Analysis*. Cambridge: Cambridge University Press.

Williamson, O.E. (1975) *Markets and Hierarchies: Analysis and Antitrust Implications*. New York: Free Press.

8

How Bureaucratic Structure Matters: An Organizational Perspective

Morten Egeberg

This chapter analyses the relationship between bureaucratic structure and actual decision behaviour within government. Thus, the chapter does not deal with the role of the executive in the political system, but focuses on how the organizational structure of a government bureaucracy might intervene in the policy process and, eventually, shape its outputs. The relationship is crucial. The extent to which organizations or institutions impact on individual actors' interests and preferences attracts enduring scholarly interest and debate. At the same time, the topic is of great concern to practitioners who want to know how organizational design and redesign could affect agenda setting, coordination, choices and implementation in their ministries or government agencies. Nevertheless, a previous review of relevant literature revealed that our theme has clearly not attained the scholarly attention it deserves (Egeberg, 1999). It appears much easier to find studies on bureaucratic structures, on how such

structures have emerged and on administrative behaviour itself than on the *relationship* between structure and actual decisions (cf., for instance, Derlien, 1992; Farazmand, 1994, 1997; Hesse, 1995; Page, 1995; Bekke et al., 1996; Nelson, 1996; Peters and Wright, 1996; Ferlie et al., 2005; Kettl, 2006).

This chapter's theoretical approach draws heavily on 'bounded rationality' (March and Simon, 1958; Simon, 1965). There are strict limits to the mind's cognitive and computational capacities. Not everything can be attended to simultaneously. Individuals act in an extremely information-rich environment but before information can be used by an individual it must proceed through the bottleneck of attention, meaning that rather few facets of a multi-faceted matter are considered in decision making (Simon, 1985: 302). Thus, since policy makers base their choices on highly simplified models of the world, it becomes crucial to understand the operative selection mechanisms and filters. An organizational perspective highlights the role of a decision maker's *organizational* context in this respect by paying attention to an organization's structure, demography and locus (cf. below).

Theorists seem to agree that organizations and institutions might affect individual actors' strategies. They disagree, however, on how interests and goals themselves are shaped and reshaped. While rational choice institutionalists consider preference formation as exogenous to their models, other institutionalists argue that interests are endogenously forged (March and Olsen, 1996; Peters, 1999). From an organizational perspective, organizations and institutions are capable of endowing individual actors with goals and interests, provided that certain organizational features are in place. What decision makers know and believe is also partly determined by their organizational position (Simon, 1999: 113). Since preference and identity formation are vital aspects of political life, the study of politics and administration cannot rely extensively on approaches that do not accommodate these phenomena into their models.

The next section will present what can be seen as the key variables of an organizational perspective. Although the empirical part of this chapter focuses on the impact of bureaucratic (organizational) *structure*, it is useful to present the other key variables as well, since this provides us with a more solid background for interpreting the observations referred to.

ORGANIZATIONAL KEY VARIABLES

Organizational structure

An organizational structure is a normative structure composed of rules and roles specifying, more or less clearly, who is expected to do what, and how (Scott, 1981). Thus, the structure broadly defines the interests and goals to be pursued, and the considerations and alternatives that should be treated as

relevant. The 'relevance criteria' embedded in role expectations guide search processes, and bias information exposure. Thus, normative structures forge information networks for the development of agendas, alternatives and learning. Since a decision maker is unable to attend to everything simultaneously, and to consider all possible alternatives and their consequences (cf. 'bounded rationality'), it seems to be a perfect match between demands for simplification, on the one hand, and the selection and filter that organizations provide, on the other (Simon, 1965; Augier and March, 2001). The structure can therefore never be neutral; it always represents a mobilization of bias in preparation for action (Schattschneider, 1975: 30).

What reasons then do we have to expect that people will comply with organizational norms when they enter an organization? First, they may feel a moral obligation to comply. Modern cultures, emphasizing impersonal relationships and 'rationalized' codes of conduct in organizational life, assist individuals at separating their private interests from those emerging from their capacity as employees or representatives. Second, they may find compliance to serve their self-interest. Organizations are incentive systems that inform members at lower levels of their potential career prospects, thus inducing them to adapt autonomously to role expectations and codes of conduct. And managers may apply rewards and punishments to achieve obedience. Finally, social control and 'peer review' by colleagues are supposed to minimize deviant behaviour. Thus, these mechanisms do not imply that organizational members give up their private interests when they enter an organization. However, personal policy preferences are, due to compensation, put aside and are thus supposed to be of minor importance in explaining *organizational* behaviour. Even if the mechanisms fail, it could be argued that participants would be unable to define and operationalize their genuine private interests in any meaningful and coherent way. One obvious exception to this could, however, be decision processes that impact more directly on their career prospects: for example, reorganization processes.

I now turn to various dimensions of organizational structure. The *size*, the sheer number of roles that are to be filled, may indicate an organization's capacity to initiate policies, develop alternatives, or to implement final decisions. *Horizontal specialization* expresses how different issues and policy areas, for example transport and environmental protection, are supposed to be linked together or decoupled from each other. Those areas that are encompassed by the same organizational unit are more likely to be coordinated than those belonging to different units (Gulick, 1937). However, in a hierarchy, separation of issues at lower levels only means that coordination responsibility is moved to higher echelons. According to Gulick (1937), there are four fundamental ways in which tasks may be distributed horizontally among units: namely, in relation to *territory*, *purpose (sector)*, *function (process)* or *clientele served*. If, for example, an organization is internally specialized according to the geographical area served, it is expected to induce spatial perspectives and encourage policymakers to pay attention primarily to particular territorial concerns and 'intra-local' policy coherence. In this case, the structure reflects the territorial composition of the system and focuses attention along territorial lines of cleavage. Organizations based on *purpose*, on the other hand, are supposed to foster sectoral horizons among decision makers and policy standardization across territorial units. Functionally arranged bureaucracies are specialized according to affairs such as legal, technical, economic, planning, and so on.

In order to ascertain the basic specialization principle of an organization, one should look at the highest level of the organization. *Vertical specialization* deals with the intended division of labour across hierarchical levels within or between organizations. The structure may express whether *coordination* is supposed to be *hierarchical*

or *collegial*. 'Collegiality' usually means that decisions must be reached through arguing, bargaining or voting rather than through command. Most government organizations are basically hierarchical. However, collegial bodies in the form of committees, task forces, project groups, etc., increasingly seem to complement hierarchical structures. Thus, since organizational units are in this way woven together more densely than before, horizontally as well as vertically, a kind of network administration emerges (Kickert, 1997; Bogason and Toonen, 1998; Rhodes, 2000). Committees usually engage people only on a part-time basis, though (*secondary affiliation*). Most participants remain primarily attached to another organization. Still, committee members may be affected to some extent by being exposed to new agendas, alternatives and actors. We would expect the impact to be less profound, however, than in organizations to which persons have a *primary affiliation*. Finally, an organizational structure may be more *ambiguous* or *loosely coupled* than other structures, thus facilitating innovative behaviour, flexible responses and extensive policy dynamics (Landau, 1969; March and Olsen, 1976; Hood, 1999). Enduring tensions and unresolvable conflicts may also be dealt with more intelligently through ambiguous designs (Olsen, 1997).

Organizational demography

According to Pfeffer (1982: 277), demography refers to the personnel composition, in terms of attributes such as age, gender, ethnicity, nationality, education and length of service within the social entity under study. Such factors are supposed to impact decision behaviour, although the strength of potential effects must depend on characteristics of the organizational structure: for example, how 'demanding' and explicit it is (Meier and Nigro, 1976; Lægreid and Olsen, 1984). In general, except for education, background factors do not seem to have a strong effect on decision behaviour (Suvarierol, 2008;

Christensen and Lægreid, 2009). Even more, a wide variety of socialization experiences are not relevant to policy disputes and thus are unlikely to reveal a representational linkage (Selden, 1997: 65). One may say that the demographic perspective emphasizes the effects that flows of personnel (career patterns) might have on their decision behaviour. Whereas the effects of organizational structure are thought to occur without any socialization of personnel, the impacts of demographic factors are closely related to *socialization*. Socialization usually means that values, norms and role expectations have become internalized in individuals. New recruits arrive 'pre-packed' with images and attitudes acquired over the years in particular social, geographical and educational settings. With increasing length of service in an organization, they may, however, become resocialized. Socialized organizational members *identify themselves strongly* with a particular organization, and are supposed to advocate its interests 'automatically' in the sense that these interests are 'taken for granted'. Arguably, the extent to which an organization must rely on external control mechanisms (incentives and sanctions) depends on the extent to which decision makers have become socialized within that same organization.

Considered as individual attributes, only length of service can, in a strict sense, qualify as a real *organizational* factor among the demographic variables mentioned. However, this becomes different if we instead deal with *proportions* of a given organizational population that come from, for example, different regions or professions. Clusters, or 'enclaves', seem to make it more likely that particular group interests might be pursued (Selden, 1997).

Organizational locus

The physical dimension of organizational life has not been emphasized in the literature (Goodsell, 1977; Pfeffer, 1982: 260–71).

However, most organizations are located in particular places and buildings. First, location and physical space segregate personal lives and their associated role conceptions and identities from organizational roles and identities and may also help to separate various organizational roles from each other where actors have multiple organizational affiliations. Second, physical distance seems to be negatively related to degree of contact and coordination within ministries (Egeberg, 1994). The reason is probably that the contacts most sensitive to physical distance, i.e. unplanned encounters between decision makers, disappear when activities are spread among different ministry buildings. Similarly, the autonomy of government agencies does not seem to depend on whether they are located in the political centre (capital) or not: this is because agencies in the centre also are located at a distance that in practice excludes (unplanned) encounters with ministry personnel (Egeberg and Trondal, 2011a).

METHODOLOGICAL NOTE

The empirical studies used here mainly include research on central government bureaucracies at the national level and how their structures affect *substantive* policy making. However, reference is also made to studies of international administration. 'Substantive policy making' is the kind of policy making most officials are supposed to engage in most of the time. On the other hand, policy making dealing with aspects of the administrative apparatus itself – its structure, personnel composition, physical structure and location – is called 'administrative policy making', but is not considered in this chapter. Neither is how bureaucratic structure might affect citizens' trust in government and the overall legitimacy of the political system dealt with (Olsen, 2005).

Which criteria have been used for selecting the relevant empirical studies? First, to merit inclusion a study must focus explicitly on the relationship between organizational structure and the actual decision behaviour of officials. Second, the study's data sources and the method applied for analysing the data should be clearly stated by the author(s). Third, the observed relationships should be meaningful and understandable theoretically: that is, they should be possible to subsume under one theoretical dimension or another. Government reports on reform evaluation generally fail to meet these criteria. So does some work of social scientists. We could be more conscious of the extent to which statements of an empirical nature are really based on systematic research, or are more loosely founded, or are merely meant to be assumptions. In order to substantiate postulates empirically, scholars often refer to the works of other researchers without separating clearly between research that is 'really' empirical in its character, on the one hand, and works that are primarily of a theoretical or 'impressionistic' nature, on the other.

Research on the relationship between organizational structure and actual decision behaviour seems to have taken place *against the mainstream* of contemporary scholarly work in the field. Volumes and single articles aimed at reviewing the state of the art of public administration research have little to say about the relationship focused on in this chapter (cf. for instance, Derlien, 1992; Farazmand, 1994, 1997; Hesse, 1995; Page, 1995; Bekke et al., 1996; Nelson, 1996; Peters and Wright, 1996; Ferlie et al., 2005; Kettl, 2006). Hood and Dunsire (1981) concluded their 'bureaumetrics approach' book by saying that investigating this relationship was the important *next* step. Fourteen years later, their compatriots Martin J. Smith et al. (1995: 50), in their review of research on British central government, ascertained that many scholars appear content to describe the structural changes and problems with implementation rather than dealing with how these changes affect the internal politics of the departments and the policy process.

Thomas Hammond (1990) argues that one reason for this lack of systematic empirical research on the relationship between bureaucratic structure and actual decision behaviour may be found in Herbert Simon's criticism of the so-called classical school of administrative theory. Thus, the widespread belief that Simon had definitely won the duel in the 1940s may have contributed to the lack of studies on the formal structure and its implications (cf. also Augier and March, 2001). Still, European scholars may have been more focused on structure–behaviour relationships than their American colleagues, who have concentrated more on how individual attributes are linked to organizational performance (Peters, 2011). It should be mentioned, however, that two recent books reporting from large-scale projects on government agencies in several countries focus heavily on structure–behaviour relationships (Lægreid and Verhoest, 2010; Verhoest et al., 2010).

EMPIRICAL EVIDENCE

The impact of horizontal specialization

In theory, structural designs are expected to 'route' information exchange, coordination processes and conflict resolution. Thus, how we draw organizational boundaries should determine which problems and solutions policy makers become aware of, and at which level in a hierarchy various concerns are considered simultaneously, or are allowed to be sheltered from other interests. But do organizational boundaries really matter? Let us first take a look at aspects of *horizontal* specialization.

Studies reveal that contact patterns and exchange of information largely reflect the organizational structure of the administrative apparatus. The flow of information diminishes across organizational boundaries (Lægreid and Olsen, 1984; Larsson, 1986;

Gerding and Sevenhuijsen, 1987; Petterson, 1989). Extensive use of e-mail from the 1990s does not seem to have changed this close relationship between structure and behaviour (Christensen and Lægreid, 2009). Scharpf (1977), in his study of the German Federal Ministry of Transport, found that 'objective' needs for coordination across divisions were recognized by the ministerial bureaucracy itself and reflected in the patterns of information exchange and participation between lower-level organizational units. Further empirical analyses showed, however, that the existing division structure caused serious information deficits and conflicts over substantive policy as well as over jurisdictions. Data indicated that perceived deficits in information supply were four times as likely to occur in interactions across divisions than within divisions; that conflicts over policy substance were more than twice as frequent in inter-divisional interaction; and that conflicts over jurisdiction had a 50 per cent higher probability of occurring in interactions between divisions than within divisions (1977: 62). Scharpf concluded that organizational boundaries may not prevent interaction, but they seem to create semi-permeable walls which impede the flow of information (on the demand side as well as on the supply side) and which reduce the capacity for conflict resolution in the case of substantive and jurisdictional conflict.

The drawing of organizational boundaries *between* as well as within ministries tends to bias the allocation of attention and the formation of preferences and identities (Allison, 1971; Rhodes and Dunleavy, 1995). Broad interministerial interaction is typical for officials affiliated with units like the prime minister's office or the ministry of finance (Campbell and Szablowski, 1979). In general, officials' contacts across organizational units have a strong, positive relationship with their participation in working groups and task forces (Stigen, 1991), and with their ranks (Lægreid and Olsen, 1984; Jablin, 1987).

Strictly speaking, the synchronous research designs of most of the studies dealt with so far make it rather problematic to infer anything about a cause–effect relationship between structure and policy. Fortunately, however, we also find studies in which behaviour has been observed *subsequent to* a reorganization. If behavioural changes can be traced under this circumstance, it is more likely that a cause–effect relationship really exists.

Splitting divisions in a hierarchy means in theory to move processes of coordination and conflict resolution upward in the organization, thus making it more likely that higher-level leadership gets involved. Mergers, on the other hand, are supposed to push such processes downward, thus relieving higher levels of some of their workload (but as a result less insight will be available at the top in this particular issue area). Results from a study of ministerial reorganizations give some support to these expectations. Egeberg (1994) observed that officials affiliated with divisions that had been split experienced less conflict, whereas those in merged divisions tended to experience more conflict. In the first case, conflicts did not disappear they became 'externalized' (they moved upward), whereas in the second case, conflicts were 'internalized' (pushed downward). A study of bureaucratic mergers by Hult (1987) supports these findings. She also discovered that departmental mergers had an impact on the relations with client groups. As more concerns and interests had to be taken care of by the merged unit, external networks became more differentiated, and established 'iron triangles' were challenged and diluted.

In order to illuminate the behavioural consequences of various principles of specialization, European Union (EU) institutions provide an exciting laboratory, and particularly so pertaining to whether a body is structured according to territory or according to a non-territorial principle of specialization, such as sector or function. On the one hand, an inherited intergovernmental order is clearly reflected in the way the Council of Ministers and the European Council is arranged.

The bodies of ministers and heads of government at the top neatly mirror the territorial composition of the system, each member state being represented by an executive politician who also has a national ministry as his or her primary affiliation. Studies show, accordingly, that decision makers mainly upload national preferences, and that patterns of cooperation and conflict tend to follow territorial (national) lines (Hayes-Renshaw and Wallace, 2006). This behavioural pattern is even more striking in the European Council, in which the territorial principle of specialization constitutes the sole principle (Tallberg and Johansson, 2008). On the other hand, the European Commission, the EU's main executive body, is basically structured according to sector and function from the bottom to the top. Thus, executive politicians at the top (commissioners) are in charge of particular sectoral or functional departments (directorates general), and they have the Commission as their primary organizational affiliation. Putting (often) former national ministers into the job as commissioner might then be seen as a critical test of the extent to which organizational structure is able to (re-)shape politico-administrative behaviour in a world most commonly perceived as basically intergovernmental. Studies do indeed indicate that commissioners behave significantly different from ministers in the Council: sectoral and supranational concerns seem to be considerably more emphasized, although national concerns are not absent (Egeberg, 2006; Wonka, 2008). At the administrative level, a departmental structure based on sector or function rather than geography tends to evoke primarily sectoral or functional identities among officials, a pattern also found in international administrations in general (Trondal et al., 2010).

Central governments may be represented at the regional level by sectorally specialized units reflecting the ministry structure, or by integrated government offices (like 'prefects'), reflecting instead the territorial composition of the system. By setting up Government Offices for the Regions (GORs) in the UK, reformers aimed at improving the coordination between the regional offices of Whitehall departments and meeting the demand for a single point of contact, thus counteracting the compartmentalized (sectoral) traditions of the civil service. Research shows that GORs in fact led to greater coordination in the regions and became important mechanisms for developing 'holistic governance' (Mawson and Spencer, 1997; Rhodes, 2000).

The impact of vertical specialization

The *internal* vertical specialization of ministries does matter. Officials' positions are positively correlated with contact with the political leadership, emphasis put on political signals, as well as with their horizontal interactions (Aberbach et al., 1981; Christensen, 1991; Aberbach and Rockman, 2000; Christensen and Lægreid, 2009). Senior officials identify themselves with larger parts of central government than those at lower echelons, who tend to perceive themselves more as section or division representatives (Christensen and Lægreid, 2009). This pattern is not without significance: those with few horizontal contacts and who identify themselves primarily with lower-level units are supposed to consider only a narrow range of problems, solutions and consequences, while those who consider themselves as parts of more overarching entities and have extensive lateral relations are likely to address broader agendas, competing demands and system-wide concerns.

Central government bureaucracies can also be specialized vertically into separate institutions at the national level, for example a ministerial (cabinet-level) department and a central (subordinated) agency (*external* vertical specialization). So-called 'agencification', i.e. entities becoming organized at arm's length from ministerial departments, has been an increasing phenomenon in many countries (Kickert and Beck Jørgensen, 1995; Christensen and Lægreid, 2006). Where such vertical specialization exists, studies indicate that many of the same tasks are performed at both administrative levels; for example, the subordinated agencies engage in policy making by setting goals, preparing budgets, legislation and guidelines, recruiting senior officials and shaping administrative structures (Christensen, 1982; Jacobsson, 1984; Greer, 1994). Policy choices are, however, not unaffected by the organizational context in which they are made. Officials in central agencies, in contrast to their colleagues in cabinet-level departments, exercise discretion comparatively insulated from ongoing political processes at the cabinet level (Wood and Waterman, 1991; Greer, 1994; Christensen and Lægreid, 2001; Egeberg and Trondal, 2009; Bach, 2010; Painter et al., 2010; Verhoest et al., 2010). They have relatively little contact with the political leadership of the ministry, with other ministerial departments than their 'own', and with parliament. When they exercise discretion, they attach most importance to professional and expert considerations, and somewhat less importance to user and client interests. To assign weight to signals from the political leadership of the ministry is their third priority. However, their relative autonomy from the ministerial department implies that they have fewer opportunities to influence decision makers at that level. In ministerial departments, on the other hand, top priority is given to signals from the minister and, also, to expert concerns. Considerably less attention is paid to signals from user and client groups (Christensen, 1982; Beck Jørgensen, 1991; Egeberg and Trondal, 2009).

In general, then, vertical specialization seems to diminish the potential for political steering and control. Studies indicate that this loss of political direction can be partly compensated for by creating an organizational unit in the ministerial department that *duplicates* parts of the work being done in the agency (Jacobsson, 1984; Egeberg and

Trondal, 2009; Verhoest et al., 2010). More drastic, integrating an agency into the ministry, or transforming an agency into a ministerial department ('vertical *de*specialization'), has been shown to enhance the political control over policy (Hult, 1987; Desveaux, 1995). Studies indicate that an agency's size (administrative capacity) may be positively related to its autonomy (Lægreid et al., 2008; Verhoest et al., 2010).

Subordinated and 'independent' agencies sometimes involve collegial structures. Such executive and advisory boards may have representatives from interest groups (clients, users, affected parties, public employees), representatives from political parties and independent experts. Executive boards at the top of agencies seem to balance and reconcile several interests and concerns simultaneously. They are arenas not only for political steering from above but also for the articulation of affected group interests and expert appraisals. The existence of such a board blurs political signals throughout the administrative apparatus, thus providing more agency autonomy (Egeberg, 1994; Painter et al., 2010; Verhoest et al., 2010). A study of a reorganization of the state/central health administration in Kansas that included the removal of the agency's own executive board shows that the agency lost its protection from political processes, previously ensured by the board (Maynard-Moody et al., 1986).

Christensen and Lægreid (2006) have, quite reasonably, questioned the robustness of findings as regards the effects of agencification. What happens if issues become highly politicized; Couldn't that mean that hierarchical control replaces agency autonomy? Studies have in fact documented that political salience tends to enhance ministerial influence over agency behaviour (Pollitt et al., 2004; Christensen and Yesilkagit, 2006; Egeberg and Trondal, 2009; Painter et al., 2010; Verhoest et al., 2010; Egeberg and Trondal, 2011b). However, although political salience and ministerial control over agencies are positively related, this does not seem to annul the original relationship between agencification (vertical specialization) and agency autonomy (Egeberg and Trondal, 2009). (On the consequences of agencification for economy, efficiency and effectiveness, see James and van Thiel, 2011.)

In the era of the so-called 'New Public Management' the external vertical specialization process has been pushed further through creating numerous commercial corporatized agencies (Wright, 1994). Thus, in order to increase efficiency and competitiveness several public services have been organized 'outside' government. One main lesson that can be drawn across countries seems to be that devolution entails a decrease in political steering capacity and authority, and that less attention is given to political considerations in 'decoupled' enterprises (Boston et al., 1996; Pollitt and Bouckaert, 2000; Christensen and Lægreid, 2001; Zuna, 2001). However, as is the case for administrative agencies, the ability to steer public companies politically depends heavily on the extent to which organizational resources are available at the ministerial level (Christensen and Lægreid, 2001).

CONCLUSION

How the executive branch of government is organized is only one factor to be considered in order to explain and understand public policy outputs. The purpose of this chapter has not been to assess the relative importance of different explanations, but rather to identify theoretical components that assign weight to bureaucratic structure, and to systematize empirical findings that shed light on how administrative structure might intervene in the substantive policy processes of central government. Until now, most students of public administration seem to have focused on behaviour and attitudes without relating them explicitly to organizational structure. They also have concentrated on structural descriptions, and on processes preceding

organizational changes. From a scholarly as well as from a practical viewpoint, it is, however, more important to learn about the behavioural and policy consequences of various designs. Dimensions of organizational structure, like size, primary or secondary structure, horizontal and vertical specialization and 'collegialization', are all sufficiently definable theoretically as well as operationally, and are all, at the same time, sufficiently abstract to allow empirical observations to be transferred and aggregated across different contexts.

The dependent variable, substantive policy making, needs greater development. 'Procedural considerations', like importance attached to political loyalty or professional autonomy in this kind of policy making, make sense. The same may be said about substantive concerns derived from the principles of specialization, and about information exchange, actual coordination and conflict resolution that can be linked to different ways of structuring hierarchies. It is possible that the traditional categorization of the policy process into different stages, like formation and implementation, should be revisited. Since the implementation process often departs from already established policy programmes, or a law or regulation, it follows that less leeway is left for the bureaucratic structure to make a substantial difference in this phase than during policy formation. Concerning study designs, synchronous studies of the relationship between organizational structure and policy making within one context should be increasingly supplemented by observations made across time, and also across space.

ACKNOWLEDGEMENTS

I am grateful to Tom Christensen, Johan P. Olsen and Christopher Pollitt for their valuable comments on a previous version of this chapter, and to Tom Christensen for his advice on this revised version.

REFERENCES

Aberbach, J.D. and Rockman, B.A. (2000) *In the Web of Politics. Three Decades of the US Federal Executive*. Washington, DC: Brookings Institution.

Aberbach, J.D., Putnam, R.D. and Rockman, B.A. (1981) *Bureaucrats and Politicians in Western Democracies*. Cambridge, MA: Harvard University Press.

Allison, G.T. (1971) *Essence of Decision*. Boston, MA: Little, Brown.

Augier, M. and March, J.G. (2001) 'Remembering Herbert A. Simon (1916–2001)', *Public Administration Review*, 61: 396–402.

Bach, T. (2010) 'Policy and management autonomy of federal agencies in Germany', in P. Lægreid and K. Verhoest (eds), *Governance of Public Sector Organizations. Proliferation, Autonomy and Performance*. Basingstoke: Palgrave Macmillan.

Beck Jørgensen, T. (1991) 'Moderne myndigheder. Generel profil af danske direktorater, styrelser og statslige institutioner'. Working Paper. Copenhagen: Department of Political Science.

Bekke, H.A.G.M., Perry, J.L. and Toonen, T.A.J. (eds) (1996) *Civil Service Systems in Comparative Perspective*. Bloomington, IN: Indiana University Press.

Bogason, P. and Toonen, T.A.J. (1998) 'Introduction: networks in public administration', *Public Administration*, 76: 205–27.

Boston, J., Martin, J., Pallot, J. and Walsh, P. (1996) *Public Management. The New Zealand Model*. Auckland: Oxford University Press.

Campbell, C. and Szablowski, G.J. (1979) *The Super-Bureaucrats: Structure and Behavior in Central Agencies*. Toronto: Macmillan of Canada.

Christensen, J.G. (1982) 'Den administrative ledelsesfunktion i centraladministrationen', *Nordisk Administrativt Tidsskrift*, 63: 317–47.

Christensen, J.G. and Yesilkagit, K. (2006) 'Delegation and specialization in regulatory administration: a comparative analysis of Denmark, Sweden and the Netherlands', in T. Christensen and P. Lægreid (eds), *Autonomy and Regulation. Coping with Agencies in the Modern State*. Cheltenham: Edward Elgar.

Christensen, T. (1991) 'Bureaucratic roles: political loyalty and professional autonomy', *Scandinavian Political Studies*, 14: 303–20.

Christensen, T. and Lægreid, P. (2001) 'New public management – undermining political control?', in T. Christensen and P. Lægreid (eds), *New Public Management. The Transformation of Ideas and Practice*. Aldershot: Ashgate.

Christensen, T. and Lægreid, P. (2006) 'Agencification and regulatory reforms', in T. Christensen and P. Lægreid (eds), *Autonomy and Regulation. Coping with Agencies in the Modern State*. Cheltenham: Edward Elgar.

Christensen, T. and Lægreid, P. (2009) 'Living in the past? Tenure, roles and attitudes in the central civil service', *Public Administration Review*, 69: 951–61.

Derlien, H.-U. (1992) 'Observations on the state of comparative administration research in Europe – rather comparable than comparative', *Governance*, 5: 279–311.

Desveaux, J.-A. (1995) *Designing Bureaucracies. Institutional Capacity and Large-Scale Problem Solving*. Stanford, CA: Stanford University Press.

Egeberg, M. (1994) 'Bridging the gap between theory and practice: the case of administrative policy', *Governance*, 7: 83–98.

Egeberg, M. (1999) 'The impact of bureaucratic structure on policy making', *Public Administration*, 77: 155–70.

Egeberg, M. (2006) 'Executive politics as usual: role behaviour and conflict dimensions in the college of European commissioners', *Journal of European Public Policy*, 13: 1–15.

Egeberg, M. and Trondal, J. (2009) 'Political leadership and bureaucratic autonomy. Effects of agencification', *Governance*, 22: 673–88.

Egeberg, M. and Trondal, J. (2011a) 'Agencification and location: Does agency site matter?', *Public Organization Review*, 11: 97–108.

Egeberg, M. and Trondal, J. (2011b) 'EU-level agencies: new executive centre formation or vehicles for national control?', *Journal of European Public Policy*, 18: 868–87.

Farazmand, A. (ed.) (1994) *Handbook of Bureaucracy*. New York: Marcel Dekker.

Farazmand, A. (1997) *Modern Systems of Government. Exploring the Role of Bureaucrats and Politicians*. Thousand Oaks, CA: Sage.

Ferlie, E., Lynn Jr, L.E. and Pollitt, C. (eds) (2005) *The Oxford Handbook of Public Management*. Oxford: Oxford University Press.

Gerding, G. and Sevenhuijsen, R.F. (1987) 'Public managers in the middle', in J. Kooiman and K.A. Eliassen (eds), *Managing Public Organizations*. London: Sage.

Goodsell, C.T. (1977) 'Bureaucratic manipulation of physical symbols: an empirical study', *American Journal of Political Science*, 21: 79–91.

Greer, P. (1994) *Transforming Central Government. The Next Steps Initiative*. Buckingham: Open University Press.

Gulick, L. (1937) 'Notes on the theory of organization. With special reference to government', in L. Gulick and L. Urwick (eds), *Papers on the Science of Administration*. New York: Institute of Public Administration, Columbia University.

Hammond, T.H. (1990) 'In defence of Luther Gulick's "Notes on the theory of organization"', *Public Administration*, 68: 143–73.

Hayes-Renshaw, F. and Wallace, H. (2006) *The Council of Ministers*. Basingstoke: Palgrave Macmillan.

Hesse, J.J. (1995) 'Comparative public administration: the state of the art', in J.J. Hesse and T.A.J. Toonen (eds), *The European Yearbook of Comparative Government and Public Administration*. Baden-Baden: Nomos.

Hood, C. (1999) 'The garbage can model of organization: describing a condition or a prescriptive design principle?', in M. Egeberg and P. Lægreid (eds), *Organizing Political Institutions*. Oslo: Scandinavian University Press.

Hood, C. and Dunsire, A. (1981) *Bureaumetrics*. London: Gower.

Hult, K.M. (1987) *Agency Merger and Bureaucratic Redesign*. Pittsburgh: University of Pittsburgh Press.

Jablin, F.M. (1987) 'Formal organization structure' in F.M. Jablin, L. Putnam, K. Roberts and L. Porter (eds), *Handbook of Organizational Communication. An Interdisciplinary Perspective*. Newbury Park, CA: Sage.

Jacobsson, B. (1984) *Hur styrs forvaltningen?* Lund: Studentlitteratur.

James, O. and van Thiel, S. (2011) 'Structural devolution to agencies', in T. Christensen and P. Lægreid (eds), *The Ashgate Research Companion to New Public Management*. Farnham: Ashgate.

Kettl, D.F. (2006) 'Public bureaucracies', in R.A.W. Rhodes, S.A. Binder and B.A. Rockman (eds), *The Oxford Handbook of Political Institutions*. Oxford: Oxford University Press.

Kickert, W.J.M. (1997) 'Public governance in the Netherlands: an alternative to Anglo-American "managerialism"', *Public Administration*, 75: 731–52.

Kickert, W.J.M. and Beck Jørgensen, T. (1995) 'Introduction: managerial reform trends in Western Europe', *International Review of Administrative Sciences*, 61: 499–510.

Lægreid, P. and Olsen, J.P. (1984) 'Top civil servants in Norway: key players – on different teams?', in E.N. Suleiman (ed.), *Bureaucrats and Policy-Making*. New York: Holmes and Meier.

Lægreid, P., Roness, P.G. and Rubecksen, K. (2008) 'Controlling regulatory agencies', *Scandinavian Political Studies*, 31: 1–26.

Lægreid, P. and Verhoest, K. (eds) (2010) *Governance of Public Sector Organizations. Proliferation, Autonomy and Performance*. Basingstoke: Palgrave Macmillan.

Landau, M. (1969) 'Redundancy, rationality, and the problem of duplication and overlap', *Public Administration Review*, 29: 346–58.

Larsson, T. (1986) *Regeringen och dess kansli*. Lund: Studentlitteratur.

March, J.G. and Olsen, J.P. (1976) *Ambiguity and Choice in Organizations*. Bergen: Scandinavian University Press.

March, J.G. and Olsen, J.P. (1996) 'Institutional perspectives on political institutions', *Governance*, 9: 247–64.

March, J.G. and Simon, H.A. (1958) *Organizations*. New York: John Wiley.

Mawson, J. and Spencer, K. (1997) 'The Government Offices for the English regions: towards regional governance?', *Policy and Politics*, 25: 71–84.

Maynard-Moody, S., Stull, D.D. and Mitchell, J. (1986) 'Reorganization as status drama: building, maintaining, and displacing dominant subcultures', *Public Administration Review*, 46: 301–10.

Meier, K.J. and Nigro, L.G. (1976) 'Representative bureaucracy and policy preferences: a study in the attitudes of federal executives', *Public Administration Review*, 36: 458–69.

Nelson, B.J. (1996) 'Public policy and administration: an overview', in R.E. Goodin and H.-D. Klingemann (eds), *A New Handbook of Political Science*. Oxford: Oxford University Press.

Olsen, J.P. (1997) 'Institutional design in democratic contexts', *Journal of Political Philosophy*, 5: 203–29.

Olsen, J.P. (2005) 'Maybe it is time to rediscover bureaucracy', *Journal of Public Administration, Research and Theory*, 16: 1–24.

Page, E.C. (1995) 'Comparative public administration in Britain', *Public Administration*, 73: 123–41.

Painter, M., Burns, J.P. and Yee, W.-H. (2010) 'Explaining autonomy in public agencies: the case of Hong Kong', in P. Lægreid and K. Verhoest (eds), *Governance and Public Sector Organizations*. Basingstoke: Palgrave Macmillan.

Peters, B.G. (1999) *Institutional Theory in Political Science. The 'New Institutionalism'*. London: Continuum.

Peters, B.G. (2011) 'Singing in unison or in harmony?', *Nordiske Organisasjons-Studier*, 13: 67–83.

Peters, B.G. and Wright, V. (1996) 'Public policy and administration, old and new', in R.E. Goodin and H.-D. Klingemann (eds), *A New Handbook of Political Science*. Oxford: Oxford University Press.

Petterson, O. (1989) *Maktens netverk.* Stockholm: Carlssons.

Pfeffer, J. (1982) *Organizations and Organization Theory.* Boston, MA: Pitman.

Pollitt, C. and Bouckaert, G. (2000) *Public Management Reform. A Comparative Analysis.* Oxford: Oxford University Press.

Pollitt, C., Talbot, C., Caufield, J. and Smullen, A. (2004) *Agencies: How Governments Do Things Through Semi-autonomous Organizations.* New York: Palgrave Macmillan.

Rhodes, R.A.W. (2000) 'The governance narrative: key findings and lessons from the ESRC's Whitehall programme', *Public Administration,* 78: 345–63.

Rhodes, R.A.W. and Dunleavy, P. (eds) (1995) *Prime Minister, Cabinet and Core Executive.* Houndmills, Basingstoke, Hants: Macmillan Press.

Scharpf, F. (1977) 'Does organization matter? Task structure and interaction in the ministerial bureaucracy', in E. Burack and A. Negandhi (eds), *Organization Design.* Kent, OH: Kent State University Press.

Schattschneider, E.E. (1975) *The Semisovereign People.* Hinsdale, IL: Dryden Press.

Scott, W.R. (1981) *Organizations: Rational, Natural, and Open Systems.* Englewood Cliffs, NJ: Prentice Hall.

Selden, S.C. (1997) *The Promise of Representative Bureaucracy. Diversity and Responsiveness in a Government Agency.* Armonk, NY: M.E. Sharpe.

Simon, H.A. (1965) *Administrative Behavior. A Study of Decision-Making Processes in Administration Organization.* New York: Free Press.

Simon, H.A. (1985) 'Human nature in politics: the dialogue of psychology and political science', *American Political Science Review,* 79: 293–304.

Simon, H.A. (1999) 'The potlatch between economics and political science', in J.E. Alt, M. Levi and E. Ostrom (eds), *Competition and Cooperation. Conversations with Nobelists about Economics and Political Science.* New York: Russell Sage Foundation.

Smith, M.J., Marsh, D. and Richards, D. (1995) 'Central government departments and the policy process', in R.A.W. Rhodes and P. Dunleavy (eds), *Prime Minister, Cabinet and Core Executive.* Houndmills, Basingstoke, Hants: Macmillan.

Stigen, I. (1991) 'Avbyråkratisering og modifisert forhandling? Om bruk av prosjektorganisasjon i norsk sentraladministrasjon', *Norsk Statsvitenskapelig Tidsskrift,* 7: 173–91.

Suvarierol, S. (2008) 'Beyond the myth of nationality: analysing networks within the European Commission', *West European Politics,* 31: 701–24.

Tallberg, J. and Johansson, K.M. (2008) 'Party politics in the European Council', *Journal of European Public Policy,* 15: 1222–42.

Trondal, J., Marcussen, M., Larsson, T. and Veggeland, F. (2010) *Unpacking International Organisations. The Dynamics of Compound Bureaucracies.* Manchester: Manchester University Press.

Verhoest, K., Roness, P.G., Verschuere, B., Rubecksen, K. and MacCarthaigh, M. (2010) *Autonomy and Control of State Agencies. Comparing States and Agencies.* Basingstoke: Palgrave Macmillan.

Wonka, A. (2008) 'Decision-making dynamics in the European Commission: partisan, national or sectoral?', *Journal of European Public Policy* 15: 1145–63.

Wood, B.D. and Waterman, R.W. (1991) 'The dynamics of political control of the bureaucracy', *American Political Science Review,* 85: 801–28.

Wright, V. (1994) 'Reshaping the state: the implications for public administration', *West European Politics,* 17: 102–37.

Zuna, H.R. (2001) 'The effects of corporatisation on political control', in T. Christensen and P. Lægreid (eds), *New Public Management. The Transformation of Ideas and Practice.* Aldershot: Ashgate.

9

Institutional Theories and Public Institutions: New Agendas and Appropriateness

Jean-Claude Thoenig

INSTITUTION THEORY AND NEW AGENDAS

Since the 1970s public administration institutions as a research domain have increasingly opened up to contributions from other social sciences such as history, political science and sociology of organizations. The domain has become less normative and more empirical, institutions being considered as dependent variables as well as autonomous actors.

New schools of thought have emerged in academic circles. Institutional theory is a label that oversimplifies the fact that such schools are not exactly alike: they do not share the same agenda. The present chapter presents four of such streams: historical institutionalism, sociological institutionalism, new institutionalism, and local order or actor institutionalism. Each develops a more or less specific set of theoretical as well as empirically grounded interpretations. Each also covers major facets of what institutionalization processes are. Political and

administrative machineries experience path dependencies. They are embedded in societal environments. They function like specific social systems. They produce social norms and cognitive references. Therefore interactions between societal change and administrative reform become key issues.

HISTORICAL INSTITUTIONALISM

Historical institutionalism as a theoretical stream emerged in the early 1980s (Hall, 1986) and was labeled as such later (Steinmo, et al., 1992). This perspective defines public administration as part of political life and questions the postulate that the state machinery functions as an undifferentiated whole and as a passive agent. Why are resources and power allocated unequally by the public sector? The essence of politics is competition for scarce resources between groups and issues. It looks much more like a complex set of differentiated institutions, as under-lined by neo-Marxist (Katzenstein, 1978; Evans et al., 1985), neo-corporatist (Anderson, 1979) and organizational theorists (Dupuy and Thoenig, 1985). The UK Treasury, for instance, is fragmented into several policy communities, each gathering public servants and private associations who share conver-gent views or are involved in common prob-lem handling (Heclo and Wildavsky, 1974).

Historical institutionalism considers that outcomes of public policies do not just reflect the preferences or interests of the strongest social forces. They are also chan-neled by existing and past arrangements. Policy choices made in the past shape choices made today. Political and administrative organizations, conventions, and procedures regulating the relationships between eco-nomic actors and the state are therefore path-dependent. Radical and voluntary changes in public administration are to a large extent a hopeless endeavor in such contexts. Existing institutions structure the design and the content of the decisions themselves.

Institutional contexts differ from one country to another, for instance in the real power of the judiciary: this models divergent preferences and interpretations of action by the labor movement organizations (Hattam, 1993). Comparative international approaches, combining in-depth study and longitudinal research, provide a rich set of counter-intuitive observations. They also bring political conflict and social dissent back in, studying a variety of settings in which collective action implies interactions between the public sector and society at large. Some public agencies have more influence than others. They also use loosely coupled procedures that may contradict or conflict. Other institutions such as trade unions, or economic associations of employ-ers or farmers, may also generate public order and political legitimacy (Rose and Davies, 1994). Historical and comparative lenses observe that public institutions influ-ence administrative and socio-political play-ers in two major ways. They offer some degree of predictability about the issues

discussed. And they also define models of behaviors and sets of protocols that are rather stereotyped and ready for immediate use. In other terms, public agencies provide moral and cognitive frameworks that allow their own members, as well as third parties, to make sense of events and to act in specific circumstances. They supply information. They shape the identity, the image of self and the preferences of administrative and political elites.

The implications of such findings are hardly irrelevant. Institutional designs do not reflect intentionality. Criteria used at the time when public policies and organizations were initially designed rapidly vanish. Political stakes and coalition games take over and determine outcomes. A model of punctuated equilibrium posits that public institutions simply respond to changes in the external power balance within society (Krasner, 1984).

Whereas older forms of institutionalism postulated that institutions shape policies and politics, historical or longitudinal approaches underline the fact that politics and policies shape institutions. Public institutions are taken for granted and provide the infrastruc-ture for collective action. Acquiring the status of social conventions, they are never ques-tioned. As social constructs, they resist any incremental change or any reform made by any single actor (Graftstein, 1992).

Although the logic of path dependence and persistence are central to historical insti-tutionalism, developments in this approach have tended to include change more effec-tively. Historical institutionalism did include a means for large-scale change – the concept of 'punctuated equilibrium.' For example, the work of Streeck and Thelen (2005) demon-strates how more gradual changes can alter institutions while maintaining many of the fundamental aspects of those institutions.

SOCIOLOGICAL INSTITUTIONALISM

Selznick's study of the Tennessee Valley Authority was a pioneering step in sociological institutionalism perspectives (Selznick, 1948, 1949).

Public agencies as organizations are considered as institutional actors in as far as their field units appropriate and promote values and interests that are embedded in the local communities in which they operate, and not just as machines implementing goals and values defined by a principal.

A first lesson is that incongruities may exist between the declared ends and those that the agency actually achieves or seeks to achieve. It pursues self-support and self-maintenance goals, as well as productive ends. It turns into a polymorphous system whose struggle to survive induces it to neglect or to distort its goals. Public bureaucracies possess a life of their own and even become active entrepreneurs. People who participate do not act solely in accordance with their assigned roles. Therefore public management is not limited to the art of designing formalized structures, but also considers the way participants are influenced, transformed and completed by informal structures. What happens at the bottom of the hierarchy, in grassroots-level units, matters a lot, in some cases even more than what happens at the top. A public bureaucracy must cope with the constraints and pressures applied by the outside local context in which it operates.

A second lesson is that institutionalization involves processes through which the members of an agency acquire values that go beyond the technical requirements of organizational tasks. No organization is completely free of values: 'to institutionalize is to infuse with value beyond the technical requirements of the task at hand' (Selznick, 1957: 17). It is induced by selective recruiting of personnel, by establishing strong ties or alliances with outside groups through processes such as implicit alliances, sharing common values or cooptation of local partners. Thick institutionalization is achieved when some rules or procedures are sanctified, when some units or members of the public agency become semi-autonomous centers of power and develop their own vested interests, when administrative rituals,

symbols and ideologies exist. Public institutions develop in a gradual manner. They become valued by their members and by outside vested interests for the special place they hold in society.

The real birth or revival of sociological institutionalism occurred in fact about 40 years later (Meyer and Scott, 1983). It endorses some hypotheses already suggested by Selznick. Organizations must cope with the constraints and pressures applied by contexts in which they operate. Nevertheless, it also suggests alternative approaches.

While Selznick emphasized processes such as group conflict and cooptation of external constituencies, the new generation of sociologists downplay their importance. They emphasize the importance of constraints such as conformity and legitimacy imperatives. They also locate irrationality in the formal structure itself, not only in informal interactions such as influence patterns.

While Selznick favored a meso-level perspective and studied a single public agency, the Stanford school is more macro-oriented and hyper-deterministic: ideologies and values that are dominant at a societal level or global level induce institutional uniformity at the meso and at the local level. Wide cohorts of single organizations – defined as organizational fields – are studied to test how they are shaped by external values. The field is examined as a whole, as an activity making rules, and defines an institutional context within which each single organization plots its courses of action: sets of public art museums (DiMaggio, 1991), private and public elementary schools, healthcare programs (Scott and Meyer, 1994).

Compared to historical institutionalism, the sociological perspective defines institutional broadly. Beside formal rules and procedures, it includes symbols, moral models and cognitive schemes. Institutions provide frames of meaning which guide human action and therefore are similar to cultural systems. Institutionalization is a cognitive process that models the sense people give to events or acts. Institutionalized myths are central to explanation. Formal structures should be understood as composed of myths and ceremonies (Meyer and Rowan, 1977), influencing the conduct of public administrators not only by influencing what they have to do but also by shaping the imagination of the actors about alternatives and solutions. Society or culture as a whole determines the acts and non-acts, the structures and the values of the public sector.

Many organizations, whether public or private, adopt formal structures, procedures and symbols that appear identical. Diffusion processes are characterized by institutional isomorphic change (DiMaggio and Powell, 1983). Mechanisms such as coercive isomorphism (change results from pressures exerted by political influence or by outside organizations considered as legitimate), mimetic isomorphism (uncertainty and ambiguity about goals or technology increases the adoption of imitation conducts) and normative isomorphism (the influence of individuals belonging to the same profession or having followed the same educational processes) accelerate similarities. Designing institutions that are radically different from the existing ones becomes an illusion in a world that constrains autonomy of choice and limits action-oriented imagination.

Public organizations, therefore, prefer not to be innovative because conformity reinforces their political legitimacy or improves the social image of their members. Values recognized by their environment drive transformation more than instrumental rationalities increasing efficiency or effectiveness. In the long term, more diversity or competition between alternative organizational models is possible (Kondra and Hinings, 1998).

To explain radical organizational transformation, the concept of archetype is used, referring to a configuration of structures and systems of organizing with a common orientation or underlying interpretative scheme. Evolutionary change occurs slowly and gradually, as a fine-tuning process within the parameters of an existing archetype (Greenwood and Hinings, 1996). Organizational change may also happen swiftly and affect all the parts of the organization simultaneously. It is associated with interactions between exogenous dynamics – or institutional contexts – and endogenous interests, values and power dependencies. Pressures for change are precipitated under two conditions. Inside, group dissatisfaction with accommodation of interests within the existing template for organizing are coupled with values. Outside public agencies, exogenous dynamics exist, pushing for an alternative template. Deinstitutionalization processes occur (Oliver, 1992), in which practices erode or face discontinuity or rejection over time.

NEW INSTITUTIONALISM

New institutionalism as an explicit school of thought finds its origins in a paper published by two political scientists (March and Olsen, 1984).

Government is in the business of forming its environment, not adapting to it. Public administration is driven by societal visions and political projects. Therefore, organizations that handle public affairs should be 'conceptualized as institutions rather than as instruments' (Brunsson and Olsen, 1997: 20). They generate and implement prescriptions that define how the game is played. Who is a legitimate participant? What are the acceptable agendas? Which sanctions should be applied in case of deviations? Which processes would be able to induce actual changes? The way people think, interpret facts, act and cope with conflicts are influenced and simplified by public administration. Do public administration reforms match societal needs? And do they also help and enhance democratic participation?

New institutionalism considers dangerous the very idea that it is possible to reform and control public organizations top down and with a technocratic style. Social science research has to make explicit the less than convincing axioms or hypotheses underlying and legitimizing reforms. New Public Management approaches, for instance, are based on widely accepted postulates inspired by neo-liberal economics – rational choice, agency theory – and that are supposedly generally relevant. Contextualism is a perspective stipulating that politics is a component of society – the mere product of factors such as social classes, culture or demography. Reductionism postulates that political phenomena are mere consequences of individual behaviors: the functioning of a public agency is explainable by the behavior model of the single bureaucrat. Economic utilitarianism implies that conducts of individuals are basically driven by their own selfish interest. Functionalist approaches adopt Darwinian views: historical evolution selects the organizational forms that fit the environmental requirements and kills those that do not. An instrumental perspective claims that the core role political life fulfills is to allocate scarce resources and that it is therefore legitimate to rationalize the criteria of choice governments and budgets use.

The founders of new institutionalism suggest alternative ideas or hypotheses to such perspectives. They question how far organized action can be planned as the product of design or authoritarian will, and to what degree some public order is achievable in pluralistic societies. Public institutions may experience a large degree of autonomy and follow logics of their own, independent of outside influences or requirements. The historical process happens to select organizational forms that are not always efficient. Symbols, myths and rituals have more impact upon political and administrative events than immediate, narrow and selfish economic or power interests.

In other terms, the logic of consequentiality is an illusion. Action in organizations is not to any great extent instrumentally oriented, and only bounded rationality is available. Public administrators make decisions according to some criterion of satisficing. They make tradeoffs between the content of the problem they address and the level of uncertainty they face in real time.

In order to understand how policy making really is processed and handled inside organizations, new institutionalism provides an analytic grid. Empirical observation should consider three fundamental dimensions or aspects: the goals the various units pursue; the way information, opportunities and support are mobilized for action taking; and the choice of decision processes at work. It should identify how far, in a given action set, four main mechanisms may exist: conflict avoidance behaviors; uncertainty reduction processes; problem solving as solutions seeking and finding initiators; and organizational learning dynamics through former experience and rules of attention allocation.

In fact, public organizations function like political arenas. Power issues and power games model their functioning and their policies. Collective goals do not necessarily exist that would provide common references subsuming individual goals or particularistic preferences. Therefore, institutional devices are needed in order to channel opportunistic behaviors and ensure some collective stability.

Two basic socialization mechanisms make behaviors more predictable, provided that they channel the potential risk factor human behaviors represent. One mechanism is induced by organizational routines and by the presence of pre-existing institutions. As underlined by organizational sciences, actors select their conducts according to a logic of appropriateness or conformism (March and Olsen, 1989). The implication is that routines or legacies from the past are powerful sources of integration, and create risk-adverse conditions for collective action. A second mechanism is generated by cognitive patterns and values that are diffused along institutionalization processes. Action mobilizes cultural elements used as frameworks by the various stakeholders. Actors fulfill identities by following rules that they imagine as appropriate to the situation they face and are involved in.

New institutionalism suggests a theory of learning in ambiguous environments. It predicts and explains how and why in a specific action context individuals and organizations try to reach some degree of understanding of the context they face (March and Olsen, 1975). It analyzes why each of them allocates attention, or not, to a particular subject at a given time, and studies how information is collected and exploited (March and Olsen, 1976).

This platform gave birth in 1988 to a research consortium involving American and Scandinavian scholars. More than 30 field studies were conducted on public sector organizations, especially in Sweden and Norway (Christensen and Lægreid, 1998b). Reforms of various kinds were observed, such as introducing corporate strategic planning in the relationships between the national government and state agencies, running a public rail company in a decentralized way and with a strong market orientation, or introducing a three-year budgeting methodology into national government administration and setting up active and participative county councils (Brunsson and Olsen, 1997). Social scientists retained interest in phenomena such as national administrative reform policy (Christensen and Lægreid, 1998a), complex public building projects (Sahlin-Andersson, 1998), decentralization policies in municipalities (Czarniawska and Jørges, 1998), constitutive reforms of the European Union (Blichner and Sangolt, 1998), municipal accounting reforms (Bergevärn et al., 1998) or central government officials (Egeberg and Sætren, 1999).

In this view, public management is the consequence of human activities, not the result of applied techniques. Contrary to what most New Public Management supporters advocate, leaders are not in full control, organizations are not passive, and policy choices are not consensual. Actual administrative reforms, whether successful or not, are characterized by a low degree of simplicity and clarity. Normativity, which should bring order into chaotic reality, is somewhat lacking. No one-sidedness allows a single set of values to be accepted as legitimate. Many promises are made about the future. Nevertheless, the instant production of results

is irrelevant. Public administration organizations cannot be controlled and changed through pure thought based on a so-called abstract rationality. It is easy to initiate administrative reforms, but few are completed (Brunsson and Olsen, 1993). Reformers are prisoners of walls that are to a large extent mental.

Reforms generate more reforms and induce fewer changes and become routinized. Organizational forgetfulness allows acceleration of reforms and helps people accept them. Top-down reforms should be avoided because their relationship with change outcomes is problematic. They paradoxically contribute to stability and prevent change from occurring.

While actual organizational changes are not generated by planned or comprehensive reform, observation suggests that they are abundant. Public administrations as such are not innovation-adverse, but may follow a sequence of transformations reflecting outside factors such as labor market dynamics or inside initiatives informally taken by low-ranking units. Major changes take place without much prior thought and discussion. It is also easier to generate them when reforms are undertaken in non-controversial areas. Hotly debated issues are not subjected to any great change.

Normative institutionalism suggests two main prescriptions for public administration changes to occur. There should be a match between rules, identities and situations: successful reforms are culturally sensitive. And local contexts matter, because they are diverse: importing so-called good practices, mere imitation, is questionable in terms of effectiveness and in terms of legitimacy.

INSTITUTIONS AS CO-CONSTRUCTED LOCAL ORDERS

Are institutional theories able to provide a general theory? So-called critical theories, for instance, use approaches inspired by sociological and historical institutionalisms as substitutes for neo-Marxist interpretations of globalization, as if global or macro factors at work at societal levels would determine any kind of meso or local evolution, including in public administration. Skepticism also abounds about the capacity of new institutionalism to give a grounded analysis of the actual functions and latent roles public bureaucracies fulfill in modern societies and polities.

Revisiting the institutional character of public administration, some alternative schools of thought, in particular in Europe, mix organizational theory inputs with more action-oriented lenses inspired by research practices applied to policy making.

For instance, a research program called actor-centered institutionalism was developed in Germany in the 1970s and 1980s by a sociologist of an organization who had studied policy implementation processes, and who was joined by a political scientist interested in game theory (Mayntz and Scharpf, 1995). In their opinion, institutional factors are not as such direct causes of public practices and norms. They provide negotiation arenas and interaction resources between corporative actors, whether public or private. Various action and actor constellations exist in real life to handle collective issues, as numerous studies on the European Union and Germany underline (Mayntz et al., 1988), demonstrating that more importance should be given to collective action and political bargaining contexts at meso levels.

French scholars addressed the question of how far local orders really matter, not only at an international or at a national level but also at the level of specific organizations or local components. Are institutions as global paradigms able to impose recurrently a similar set of values and action processes across societies? Sociologists and political scientists were influenced by policy analysis inquiry as developed on both sides of the Atlantic. The idea that public institutions may have a thickness of their own inside societies and polities became common sense quite early. Such is

the case with the school of *sociologie des organisations*. It considers institutional phenomena as both independent and dependent variables, as resources, constraints or stakes for the actors involved. Bureaucratic change processes are used as heuristic entry points.

While it is true that bureaucracies are modeled by societal factors such as the education system, national culture patterns or social stratification (Crozier, 1963), that a few corps of public servants trained in exclusive schools such as the ENA and the Ecole Polytechnique control the public agenda of a whole country (Suleiman, 1978) or that they shape in a monopolistic way major policies they also implement themselves (Thoenig, 1987), empirical research suggests that, below the surface, the functioning of public bureaucracies may differ quite markedly. Local orders exist which create heterogeneities in space. In a nation-state such as France, whose founding values incorporate the ideals of unity and equality, and where enforcement is centralized in an authoritarian manner, public institutions are not alike and their bureaucracies function in a centrifugal manner, inducing highly differentiated outcomes across the territory and society.

Local orders matter in administration. Mutual socialization occurs, such a process of cooptation having already been explored by Selznick in his study of the Tennessee Valley Authority (TVA). State prefects think and act like advocates of the interests of their respective geographic and social jurisdiction. Mayors behave as brokers between the state and their constituents. Local agencies of the national ministries are strongly embedded in subnational communities. They get legitimacy from their environment, especially from local elected politicians. It becomes a resource they use to increase their autonomy in relationship with their headquarters in Paris. Informal and stable relation patterns link state agencies to specific environments such as local political and economic leaders (Crozier and Thoenig, 1976).

Public governance all across France is structured and handled by a political and administrative system that is very different from the hierarchical model and which ignores formal division of power between national and local authorities. The machinery of the central state looks like a fragmented organizational fabric: its various subparts cooperate less than each of them cooperates with local environment leaders (Hayward and Wright, 2002). Such cross-regulation practices develop between partners who otherwise perceive each other as antagonistic. They give birth and legitimacy to implicit rules of exchange and to stable interest coalitions with tacit arrangements set during the implementation of national policies. Rigid rules decided in Paris are balanced by flexible arrangements negotiated locally. A secondary norm of implementation, which varies according to time and space and which is perceived as legitimate, prevails over formal conformism and of equality of treatment. State agencies generate exceptions and derogations become local norms. Local polities and politics are shaped in two ways. Bureaucratic ways of doing things more broadly model the cognitions and the expectations of social groups.

Public institutions are just one partner among many who intervene in public affairs. This clearly is the case for regulative policies applied by the state machinery to freight transportation (Dupuy and Thoenig, 1979) or to agricultural affairs (Jobert and Müller, 1988). Each policy domain has a specific system of organized action and functions according to its own logic. Even when some ministry in Paris or some regional public body may play a hegemonic role, its acts and non-acts remain dependent on the presence of other public agencies, firms or voluntary associations. Policy outcomes are highly dependent on initiatives taken by firms or on attention allocated by groups of citizens. At least four different types of functioning seem to coexist in the French public sphere at large: inward-oriented bureaucracies; environment-sensitive institutions; outward-driven organizations; and inter-organizational systems (Thoenig, 1996).

Public administrations also experiences dramatic changes. Central state agencies no longer play a dominant role, governing national as well as local public affairs through the allocation of subsidies and the elaboration of technical rules. A different political and administrative system emerging since the decentralization launched in the early 1980s resulted in massive transfers from the central state to regional and local authorities (Thoenig, 2005). New private, associative or public players, such as the European Commission, get a role in policy making. Public issues coincide less and less with the way subnational territories are subdivided and administrative jurisdictions defined. Collective problems are horizontal and provide uncertain solutions. Cross-regulation gives poor results when the challenge is to identify the nature of collective problems and to set public agendas. State agencies adopt another political integration approach: constitutive policies. New institutional frameworks coordinate the views and mindsets of multiple partners, make them speak a common language and share a common perception about what to do, how, when and for whom. Facing a polity that is fragmented, active and non-consensual, a weakened state uses tools such as institutionalization and institutional design.

Interdependent phenomena are interpreted as results of strategic behaviors of actors operating in power settings. Social regulation – how different actors establish normative arrangements and make their respective logics of action compatible – is key to empirical analysis.

While new institutionalism perspectives favor a vision of democratic order in which responsibility is a consequence of the institution of the individual, citizens are free, equal and discipline-oriented agents, and governance is enlightened and rule-constrained (Olsen, 1998), their continental colleagues are more pessimistic. They adopt a rather cynical or Machiavellian vision of politics. Public institutions are political devices. The essence of politics is power, and individuals behave in an opportunistic way.

Public institutions are action-oriented systems. As specific social arrangements, they are fragile constructs because they are the non-intended outcomes of permanent collective tinkering. Discontinuities in time characterize the essence of public administration and of societal order. The state is more collective and pluralistic: public institutions have no monopoly on public problems and their government. Public affairs are co-constructed.

Public organizations should also be considered as local social orders, as meso or intermediary social configurations, which are neither passive nor intentional, but are constantly reconstructed in terms of social norms and of membership. For instance, the emergence of international standards used as benchmarks for the production of goods is argued to be a form of control as important as hierarchies and markets. People and organizations all over the world seem to follow the same standards (Brunsson and Jacobsson, 2000). For instance, public institutions operating in higher education and research and facing the challenge of international rankings may hardly ignore these standards. A common global order is emerging. Not joining it – not fitting the criteria of academic quality set up by evaluators – is suicidal. Such a global process toward homogeneity is nevertheless far from being obvious or irreversible. Single universities have other options at their disposal to make it in the competition, many of them producing themselves or endogenously local criteria to define academic quality (Paradeise et al., 2009).

CONCLUSION

Institutional theories streams have become leading and widely shared references in public administration (Frederickson, 1999). Because they consider public institutions through three different lenses – as pillars of political order, as outcomes of societal values, and as self-constructed social systems – they offer exciting arenas for academic debates as well as also providing pragmatic or architectonic principles.

The agenda is far from having reached maturity. Major issues still have to be verified and debated. Some empirical phenomena are still open to further research. This is clearly the case, for instance, for international organizations (Schemeil, 2011) and for supranational polities (March and Olsen, 1998; Olsen, 2010). Methodological progress is still required: for instance, a less allusive set of evidence to trace relationships between cognitions and actions, or an in-depth understanding of the collateral effects generated by administrative reforms. Reconciling performance requirements with political support by public opinion, making production of regulations and norms compatible with democratic pluralism, remain in unstable and fragmented worlds' perspectives that institutional theories have still to consider.

REFERENCES

Anderson, C. (1979) 'Political design and the representation of interests', in P. Schmitter and G. Lehmbruch (eds), *Trends towards Corporatist Intermediation*. Beverly Hills, CA: Sage, pp. 145–73.

Bergeværn, L.E., Mellomvik, F. and Olson, O. (1998) 'Institutionalization of municipal accounting – a comparative study between Sweden and Norway', in N. Brunsson and J.P. Olsen (eds), *Organizing Organizations*. Bergen: Fagbokforlaget, pp. 279–302.

Blichner, L.C. and Sangolt, L. (1998) 'The concept of subsidiarity and the debate on European cooperation: pitfalls and possibilities', in N. Brunsson and J.P. Olsen (eds), *Organizing Organizations*. Bergen: Fagbokforlaget, pp. 107–32.

Brunsson, N. and Jacobsson, B. (eds) (2000) *A World of Standards*. Oxford: Oxford University Press.

Brunsson, N. and Olsen, J.P. (eds) (1993) *Organizing Organizations*. Bergen: Fagbokforlaget.

Brunsson, N. and Olsen, J.P. (1997) *The Reforming Organization*. Bergen: Fagbokforlaget.

Christensen, T. and Lægreid, P. (1998a) 'Administrative reform policy: the case of Norway', *International Review of Administrative Sciences*, 64 (4): 457–75.

Christensen, T. and Lægreid, P. (1998b) 'Public administration in a democratic context – a review
of Norwegian research', in N. Brunsson and
J.P. Olsen (eds), *Organizing Organizations*. Bergen:
Fagbokforlaget, pp. 147–70.

Crozier, M. (1963) *The Bureaucratic Phenomenon*.
Chicago, IL: University of Chicago Press.

Crozier, M. and Thoenig, J.C. (1976) 'The regulation of
complex organized systems', *Administrative Science
Quarterly*, 2 (4): 547–70.

Czarniawska, B. and Jørges, B. (1998) 'Winds
of organizational change: how ideas translate
into objects and actions', in N. Brunsson and
J.P. Olsen (eds), *Organizing Organizations*. Bergen:
Fagbokforlaget, pp. 197–236.

DiMaggio, P.J. (1991) 'Constructing an organizational
field as a professional project: U.S. art museums',
in Walter W. Powell and Paul J. DiMaggio (eds),
*The New Institutionalism in Organizational
Analysis*. Chicago, IL: University of Chicago Press,
pp. 267–92.

DiMaggio, P.J. and Powell, W.W. (1983) 'The iron-cage
revisited: institutional isomorphism and collective
rationality in organizational fields', *American
Sociological Review*, 38 (2): 147–60.

Dupuy, F. and Thoenig, J.C. (1979) 'Public transportation policymaking in France as an implementation
problem', *Policy Science*, 12 (1): 1–18.

Dupuy, F. and Thoenig, J.C. (1985) *L'Administration en
miettes*. Paris: Le Seuil.

Egeberg, M. and Sætren, H. (1999) 'Identities in complex organizations: a study of ministerial bureaucrats', in M. Egeberg and P. Lægreid (eds), *Organizing
Political Institutions*. Oslo: Scandinavian University
Press, pp. 93–108.

Evans, P.B., Rueschemeyer, D. and Skocpol, T. (eds)
(1985) *Bringing the State Back In*. New York:
Cambridge University Press.

Frederickson, H.G. (1999) 'The repositioning of
American public administration', *PS, Political Science
and Politics*, 32 (4): 701–11.

Graftstein, R. (1992) *Institutional Realism: Social and
Political Constraints on Rational Actors*. New Haven,
CT: Yale University Press.

Greenwood, R. and Hinings, C.R. (1996) 'Understanding
radical organizational change: bringing together the
old and the new institutionalism', *Academy of
Management Journal*, 21 (4): 1022–54.

Hall, P.A. (1986) *Governing the Economy: The Politics
of State Intervention in Britain and France*. New
York: Oxford University Press.

Hattam, V.C. (1993) *Labor Visions and State Power:
The Origins of Business Unionism in the United
States*. Princeton, NJ: Princeton University Press.

Hayward, J. and Wright V. (2002) *Governing from
the Centre. Core Executive Coordination in France*.
Oxford: Oxford University Press.

Heclo, H. and Wildavsky, A. (1974) *The Private
Government of Public Money: Community and Policy
inside British Politics*. London: Macmillan.

Jobert, B. and Müller, P. (1988) *L'Etat en action*, Paris:
Presses Universitaires de France.

Katzenstein, P. (ed.) (1978) *Between Power and Plenty:
Foreign Economic Policies of Advanced Industrial
States*. Madison, WI: University of Wisconsin Press.

Kondra, A.Z. and Hinings, C.R. (1998) 'Organizational
diversity and change in institutional theory',
Organization Studies, 19 (5): 743–67.

Krasner, S.D. (1984) 'Approaches to the state: alternative conceptions and historical dynamics',
Comparative Politics, 16 (2): 223–46.

March, J.G. and Olsen, J.P. (1975) 'The uncertainty of
the past: organizational learning under ambiguity',
European Journal of Political Research, 3:
147–71.

March, J.G. and Olsen, J.P. (1976) *Ambiguity
and Choice in Organizations*. Bergen:
Universitetsforlaget.

March, J.G. and Olsen, J.P. (1984) 'The New
Institutionalism: organizational factors in political
life', *American Political Science Review*, 78 (5):
734–49.

March, J.G. and Olsen, J.P. (1989) *Rediscovering
Institutions: The Organizational Basis of Politics*.
New York: Free Press.

March, J.G. and Olsen, J.P. (1998) 'The institutional
dynamics of international political orders',
International Organization, 52 (4): 943–69.

Mayntz, R. and Scharpf, F.W. (1995) 'Der Ansatz des
akteurzentrierten Institutionalismus', in R. Mayntz
and F.W. Scharpf (eds), *Gesellschaftliche Selbstregelung und Politische Steuerung*. Frankfurt:
Campus, pp. 39–72.

Mayntz, R., Rosewitz, B., Schimank, U. and Stichweh,
R. (1988) *Differenzierung und Verselbständigung.
Zur Entwicklung gesellschafltlicher Teilsysteme*.
New York: Campus.

Meyer, J.W. and Rowan, B. (1977) 'Institutionalized
organizations: formal structure as myth and ceremony', *American Journal of Sociology*, 83 (2):
340–63.

Meyer, J.W. and Scott, W.R. (1983) *Organizational
Environments: Rituals and Rationality*. London:
Sage.

Oliver, C. (1992) 'The antecedents of deinstitutionalization', *Organization Studies*, 13 (4): 563–88.

Olsen, J.P. (1998) 'Institutional design in democratic
contexts', in N. Brunsson and J.P. Olsen (eds),

Organizing Organizations. Bergen: Fagbokforlaget, pp. 319–49.

Olsen, J.P. (2010) *Governing through Institution Buiding. Institutional Theory and Recent European Experiments in Democratic Organization.* Oxford: Oxford University Press

Paradeise, C, Ferlie, E., Bleiklie, I. and Reale, E. (eds) (2009) *University Governance: Western European Comparative Perspectives.* Dordrecht: Springer.

Powell, W.W. and DiMaggio, P.J. (eds) (1991) *The New Institutionalism in Organizational Analysis.* Chicago, IL: University of Chicago Press.

Rose, R. and Davies, P. (1994) *Inheritance in Public Policy.* New Haven, CT: Yale University Press.

Sahlin-Andersson, K. (1998) 'The social construction of projects. A case study of organizing of an extraordinary building project – the Stockholm Globe Arena', in N. Brunsson and J.P. Olsen (eds), *Organizing Organizations.* Bergen: Fagbokforlaget, pp. 89–106.

Schemeil, Y. (2011) 'Dynamism and resilience of intergovernmental organizations in a world of persisting State power and rising non-State actors', in B. Reinalda (ed.), *The Ashgate Companion to Non State Actors.* London, Ashgate, pp. 237–50.

Scott, W.R. and Meyer, J.W. (1994) 'Environmental linkages and organizational complexity. Public and private schools', in W.R, Scott, J.W. Meyer and associates (eds), *Institutional Environments and Organizations. Structural Complexity and Individualism.* Thousand Oaks, CA: Sage, pp. 137–59.

Selznick, P. (1948) 'Foundations of the theory of organization', *American Sociological Review,* 13 (1): 25–35.

Selznick, P. (1949) *TVA and the Grass Roots.* Berkeley, CA: University of Berkeley Press.

Selznick, P. (1957) *Leadership in Administration.* New York: Harper and Row.

Steinmo, S., Thelen, K. and Longstreth, F. (eds) (1992) *Structuring Politics: Historical Institutionalism in Comparative Analysis.* Cambridge: Cambridge University Press.

Streeck, W. and Thelen, K. (eds) (2005) *Beyond Continuity: Institutional Change in Advanced Political Economies.* Oxford : Oxford University Press.

Suleiman, E. (1978) *Elites in French Society.* Princeton, NJ: Princeton University Press.

Thoenig, J.C. (1987) *L'Ere des technocrates.* Paris: L'Harmattan.

Thoenig, J.C. (1996) 'Public sector organizations', in A. Sorge and M. Warner (eds), *Handbook of Organizational Behavior.* London: Thomson Business Press, Vol. 5: pp. 421–32.

Thoenig, J.C. (2005) 'Territorial administration and political control. Decentralization in France', *Public Administration,* 83 (3): 685–708.

10

Formal Theory and Public Administration

Jack H. Knott and Thomas H. Hammond

Formal theory involves the use of mathematics to develop theories of individuals, groups, organizations and public institutions, and this chapter reviews the application of formal theory to public administration. Formalization can help us in a variety of ways to develop, explore and test theories of public administration (Hammond, 1996). First, formalization forces us to be as explicit as possible about the basic assumptions of our theories. Second, with our initial assumptions made explicit and expressed in some kind of symbolic notation, the rules of mathematics, such as calculus, geometry or probability theory, can then be used to deduce the implications of the assumptions. Third, formalization of a theory can help improve the quality of empirical tests since our formal theory gives us a clearer idea of precisely what should be tested and how to test it. Fourth, the greater capacity for formal theories to be empirically falsified, due to their greater explicitness, makes theoretical improvement more possible. Finally, for studies of especially complex problems only a formal representation, especially via computer simulation, may be able

to capture some of the complexity and yet still allow the theory's implications to be rigorously explored, and thereby made amenable to empirical test.

Over the past three decades, applications of formal theory to public administration have proliferated, and it is impossible to review all the contributions. Hence, in this chapter we can only touch on a few of the contributions that formal theory has made. For example, scholars have used it to explain the existence of public agencies, which may be formed to address inefficiencies in voluntary market exchanges. Formal theory demonstrates that public agencies do not necessarily solve these market failures, and that individually rational choices by agency employees do not necessarily produce rational policies for the agency as a whole. Clarifying the nature of these individual versus agency tensions helps explain the dysfunctional group dynamics identified in earlier sociological and psychological studies of organizational behavior. The emphasis in formal theory on individual preferences and institutional structures has improved our understanding of how agency structure affects agency policy. Additionally, formal theory helps explain why it is difficult to simultaneously pursue such desirable administrative values as accountability, efficiency and decentralization. Moreover, formal theory has contributed to our knowledge of how legislators and executives can gain some control over agencies via the use of administrative procedures and other controls. But formal theory also shows us how agencies can take advantage of asymmetric information and multiple principals to gain autonomy from their would-be overseers.

Formal theory is also well-suited to explain the changes in contemporary social, economic, and political life. Government is increasingly delivered through complex networked relationships and formal and informal contracts. Formal models can help us examine these complex information acquisition, monitoring and compliance imperatives of contemporary governance institutions.

WHY DO PUBLIC AGENCIES EXIST?

Economists were the original developers of formal, mathematical theories in the social sciences, and in neo-classical economics the baseline model of social interactions has long been the competitive market. Hence, a key question asked by economists was this: Why aren't *all* choices made through market exchanges? Several answers have been provided.

Transaction costs

One early answer was provided by Coase (1937), who wanted to explain why economic agents sometimes organize themselves into hierarchically structured firms. His explanation is that under certain conditions hierarchy is more efficient than voluntary market exchange. The reason stems from the costs associated with production processes

requiring multiple transactions among independent suppliers, owners, labor and experts. Economic agents must bear the costs of gathering and evaluating information on their production processes, and must pay the costs of negotiating a contract for each market transaction. Self-interested rational agents will want to minimize these costs. Coase's insight was that when market transactions entail these kinds of costs, central authority can more efficiently coordinate production processes. This authority substituted for the myriad of negotiated contracts in the market.

Coase's work provided an important intellectual foundation for subsequent economic analyses of market failures. It also stimulated economists to examine whether government and public agencies could cope with these failures (Wolf, 1975).

Market failures and public goods

Several different aspects of production and exchange can lead to inefficient outcomes. One kind of inefficient outcome stems from transaction costs. If each street in a city were privately owned, travelers would need to pay a toll at each intersection. One solution to this problem is for the government to own the streets. Such centralized authority would eliminate the transaction costs involved in traveling across town.

A second kind of market failure occurs when transactions impose external effects on third parties. Producers and consumers generally do not take such 'negative externalities' into account when engaging in market exchanges. In judging the overall efficiency of market exchanges, the benefits of market exchanges are reduced by the costs imposed on third parties. In effect, then, since the costs to the producers and consumers are less than the overall costs, this means that the goods involved are overproduced.

A third kind of market failure involves the underprovision of public goods. A defense establishment provides everyone in a country, not just the taxpayers, with national security. Other public goods include clean air, clean water and public broadcasting. Citizens have an incentive not to pay for such a good since they can consume it even if they do not pay for it. Since those producing the public goods are not fully compensated for their production, the goods are underproduced. As a result, governments are often asked to provide these public goods.

A fourth kind of market failure occurs when consumption of a common resource affects others who use the resource. This social dilemma, known as the 'tragedy of the commons', derives from the example given by Hardin (1968) of a village with a common green for grazing cattle. Each herdsman has an incentive to graze as many cattle as possible, but over time the grass on the green is ruined, hurting all the herdsmen. To avoid this kind of dilemma, governments often establish public agencies to regulate use of the commons (Ostrom, 1999).

A fifth kind of market failure occurs when one firm monopolizes an industry. In such a situation, the monopolist can engage in predatory pricing or other practices to prevent competitors from entering the market. Because the monopolist can raise prices to increase profits, this reduces the amount of the good that would otherwise be consumed, thereby causing market inefficiency. Government regulation of monopoly production offers the possibility of avoiding underproduction and overpricing of the good.

Finally, information asymmetries in transactions can also lead to market failure (Greenwald and Stiglitz, 1986). Because consumers often have limited information when making a purchase, they will not know whether the price charged for a product reflects the product's true value to them. Hence, sellers can take advantage of the consumers' ignorance by overcharging for the quality of the product sold. This problem occurs in the purchase of expert services, such as medical care, but can occur even in simpler markets as well, such as the market for used cars (Akerlof, 1970).

Governments often regulate these kinds of transactions through occupational licensing, certification and product quality standards.

In sum, the formal literature describes conditions under which markets fail to operate efficiently. While failures do not necessarily explain the existence of public agencies, citizens often ask governments to create public agencies to perform the necessary tasks. Whether public agencies can perform these tasks more efficiently than private firms is a question that will be discussed next.

INTERNAL ADMINISTRATION

What does formal theory have to say about supervision, control, coordination, motivation, organizational structure and communication in private firms and public agencies? We will consider three problems: team production, principal–agent theory and organizational structure.

Team production

Alchian and Demsetz (1972) argue that contractual arrangements within a firm may be more efficient than those occurring just within the market. When employees work together as a team, they can produce more than when they work separately. This gain from cooperation gives them an incentive to coordinate their activities. A central task of public and private management, therefore, is to help organizations achieve the benefits of team production (Knott, 1993).

One resulting problem, though, is how to allocate any surplus produced by team production (Miller, 1992). Team production often involves tasks that are interdependent, which means that assessing the marginal contribution of each team member is difficult. If information about individual contributions is unavailable, the allocation of the surplus cannot be based on these contributions. Instead, some other allocation rule must be used. The resulting rules for surplus allocation, such as equal sharing or seniority, often produce inefficiency because each member then has an incentive to 'free ride' on others' work.

To produce efficient outcomes the individuals may thus have to act in ways that are contrary to their short-term individual self-interest. Game theory helps us think about this problem. A game is a social interaction in which at least two players have at least two options for choice, and in which the players' choices of one action or another produce benefits or costs for the players (Miller, 1992: 21). The Prisoner's Dilemma (PD) game in particular is at the heart of the problem of team production. The dominant strategy in a PD game is for each team member not to cooperate with coworkers. The resulting outcome, know as a *Nash equilibrium*, comprises a set of choices in which no player can make himself better off by choosing some other option.

However, in a PD this Nash equilibrium is *Pareto suboptimal*: an alternative outcome is possible in which one or more players is better off and no one is worse off. But the two players can only avoid a Pareto suboptimal outcome if they are able to coordinate their choices, and it is often thought that the creation of hierarchy will help solve social dilemmas like the PD: managers should impose an incentive system and monitor the resulting behavior so as to induce individuals to coordinate their activities in ways that produce group efficiency. This function for management is consistent with early work on organizational behavior (Barnard, 1938); so it is to the study of incentive systems that we now turn our attention.

Principal–agent theory

The relation between superiors and subordinates in team production can be generalized to include principals who contract for services and agents who carry out the services (Bendor, 1988). The primary tasks for the principal are, first, to identify agents who are most likely to have the skills to achieve the principal's goals; second, to induce agents to sign a contract with incentives such that the agents find it in their self-interest to pursue the principal's goals; and third, to monitor the agents' behavior in carrying out the contract. Each task involves asymmetric information and conflicts of interest among the contracting parties (Moe, 1984: 754), both of which give the contracting parties incentives to hide their information and actions from each other (Arrow, 1974).

The concepts of 'adverse selection' and 'moral hazard' aid the understanding of hidden action and hidden information. Adverse selection is a major concern in hiring. Since the employer cannot directly observe the skills, values and work habits of applicants, she must rely on indicators such as education or letters of reference. Of necessity, these indicators reflect others' estimates of how the applicant will perform on the job and are frequently unreliable. If the indicators overstate the applicant's value to the organization, the employer may unwittingly hire less qualified applicants.

Moral hazard occurs after an applicant is hired. An employer who cannot costlessly monitor the employee's job performance may have to use indirect, and often unreliable, measures of performance. Employees thus have an incentive to perform well on these proxy measures rather than on the actual goals of the organization; this is what Merton (1940) called 'goal displacement'. Employees also have an incentive to shirk whenever their behavior is not fully observable.

Thus, the social dilemmas that provide the rationale for hierarchy also plague the operation of the hierarchy once it is created. Moreover, incentive systems that induce employees to behave in ways that maximize team efficiency may lead to lower payments to the managers, and for this reason the managers may not implement efficiency-enhancing incentive systems (Miller and Hammond, 1994). In other words, hierarchies appear to suffer from the same conflict between individual self-interest and organizational efficiency that occurs in markets plagued by externalities and the underproduction of public goods (Holmstrom, 1982; Miller, 1992).

A key problem in any hierarchy involves the strategic misrepresentation of information by both principals and agents. In effect, actors often find themselves in a game where revealing the truth about their beliefs and preferences may give others an advantage. There are at least two different kinds of models which have been developed to explain the strategic use of information.

Signaling models focus on the transfer of information between the agents and the principal prior to any action by the principal. In signaling models the principal can modify her beliefs about the effect of a policy, based on the information received from the agents, and then take action accordingly. But the agents are assumed to not necessarily reveal to the principal their true beliefs and preferences or to convey information in an honest and complete fashion. One important implication is that principals will receive better information if the agents have heterogeneous preferences (Gilligan and Krehbiel, 1989). This result supports the public administration literature on redundancy in which principals having multiple heterogeneous agents can gain more reliable information (Bendor, 1985; Heimann, 1997; Landau, 1969).

Models of delegation (Bendor and Meirowitz, 2004; Bendor et al., 2001) also inform the creation and functioning of hierarchies. For example, Epstein and O'Halloran (1999) analyze the behavior of a boss who first receives a report from a subordinate and, then, based on the information in the report, chooses whether to delegate authority for implementation to another agent. Their model provides insight into conflict between executive staff and a line agency. The more the staff shares preferences with the boss, the less likely is the boss to delegate authority to the line agency. The authors also find that if the line and staff in an agency have similar preferences but are distant from the boss, the staff will transmit less information to the boss. The reason is that the more information the staff gives the boss, the less the boss will delegate to the line. If the line and staff are close, the staff prefers more rather than less delegation. Hence, the staff will not transmit as much information.

Information provision and authority delegation often occur in repeated sequences over time. For example, if the subordinate cheats by shirking, the boss might retaliate by more tightly controlling the subordinate's behavior in the next period. Or if the boss cheats by grabbing credit, the subordinate might retaliate by shirking in the next period. These actions might be individually rational for each player but produce Pareto suboptimal outcomes.

Axelrod (1984) has shown that a Tit-for-Tat (TFT) strategy in these repeated games can lead to a cooperative outcome in the long term if the future is important to both players. In a TFT strategy, both the boss and the subordinate would cooperate (delegate, work) in the first period. In further periods, the subordinate would cooperate if the boss delegated and would shirk if the boss controlled. The boss would delegate only if the subordinate worked, and control if the subordinate shirked. Axelrod shows that cooperation is possible in repeated games of this kind, though it is not guaranteed.

Implications for public management
The fact that public agencies are established to deal with market failures, but are themselves subject to many of the social dilemmas that characterize market competition, highlights the challenge facing public officials. Several leadership strategies may help to establish cooperative solutions to the agencies' own social dilemmas.

While managers and employees may each be tempted to engage in self-interested behavior, if one side does behave in a trustworthy, committed, and cooperative way, it makes it easier for the other side to behave in that way as well (Miller, 1992). For example, a credible commitment by management to a cooperative solution signals to employees that they may act efficiently and communicate truthfully without negative repercussions. Recall that Barnard (1938) emphasized the 'moral example' that managers should give to employees, and experiments with TFT strategies in repeated Prisoner's Dilemma games (Axelrod, 1984) further show the potential for cooperation from this kind of behavior.

The popular management literature emphasizes the importance of the motivations of employees and the internalization of norms of cooperation among the members of the team (Bertelli and Lynn, 2003; Brehm and Gates, 1997). Team-building exercises, shared company myths, organizational missions and professional norms may help internalize cooperative behavior by managers and employees. For public agencies, professional core values (Knott and Miller, 1987) can play an especially important role by creating beliefs and expectations about proper behavior (Brehm and Gates, 1993).

Organizational structure

Governments periodically restructure their executive departments. These changes often group formerly separate agencies together or separate formerly integrated departments into smaller agencies (Arnold, 1998; Gulick, 1937; Knott and Miller, 1987). Do these organizational changes in a hierarchy affect the policies chosen by the agencies?

Formal theory is concerned with how individual preferences interact with institutional rules to produce policy choices, and Hammond (1986: 159–61) shows how organizing an agency by geography can produce different policy choices than organizing by function; two different structures populated by individuals with the same preferences can thus produce two different policy choices. Indeed, it may be impossible to design a hierarchy that does not affect policy choices (Hammond and Thomas, 1989).

This logic of preference aggregation in different organizational structures applies to other processes within an organization. At the most general level, hierarchy groups activities, information and people into categories that are then subdivided into subcategories and sub-subcategories (Hammond, 1993). Different groupings may classify information differently, and thus decision makers may learn different things from the aggregated information presented to them. How information is categorized and grouped may thus affect what the agency learns from its environment.

Incompatible design criteria

The public administration literature identifies several different values which organizations may be designed to achieve. For example, Kaufman (1956) focuses on neutral competence, representativeness and executive leadership. Hammond and Miller (1985) demonstrate how a paradox identified by Sen (1970) can illuminate conflicts among various kinds of organizational values. Sen's theorem calls our attention to four desirable organizational principles, but his theorem also shows that while designs can be found which satisfy three of the principles, no organizational design can be guaranteed to satisfy all four.

For example, decentralized organizations may produce Pareto suboptimal decisions (because different division heads do not find it in their interest to cooperate with each other), or exhibit preference cycles (because an agency cannot settle on a final choice but continuously revisits previously rejected options).

Other organizational designs may avoid inefficiency and preference cycles but at the cost of imposing restrictions on the views and beliefs of employees. For example, Herbert Kaufman (1960) showed how recruitment and socialization processes and administrative procedures in the Forest Service created common norms, beliefs and behaviors. Such uniformity of belief has some advantages in a stable environment, but may leave the agency unable to adapt to a changing environment.

Yet another kind of organizational design – the imposition of centralized management – avoids Pareto suboptimality, preference cycles and the uniformity of belief, but the literature on organizational theory and management (Miller, 1992) also emphasizes the hazards of dictatorial management.

The lesson of Sen's theorem is that organizational design consists of choosing which three organizational pathologies one will avoid and which fourth pathology will simply be endured.

EXTERNAL RELATIONS

One of the unique features of public administration is the number and variety of institutions which influence the policy-making process. A government agency head must interact with legislative committees, the chief executive, cabinet departments, the courts, interest groups, contractors, regional offices and state and local governments (Wilson, 1989). Since these institutions possess legal authority or political influence over the agency's activities, dealing with the external environment is a critical dimension of public administration and public management (Bozeman and Straussman, 1990). A number of formal approaches to this critical aspect of public administration have been developed.

Relations with the legislature and the chief executive

An important debate in public administration focuses on whether government agencies exercise independent influence over policy. One scholarly tradition argues that bureaucracy dominates policy making through expertise, secret information and control over implementation (Behn, 1991; Doig and Hargrove, 1987; Lewis, 1980; see also Caro, 1975). A contrary literature suggests that the legislature is able to dominate the bureaucracy (Banks and Weingast, 1992; Lupia and McCubbins, 1994; McCubbins and Schwartz, 1984; McCubbins, Noll and Weingast, 1987; Weingast and Moran, 1983; though, see Moe, 1987). Huber and Shipan (2002) have further enriched this literature by exploring when, why, and how politicians choose to delegate policy decision making to agencies through the crafting of statutes.

Legislators can be seen as principals who have public managers as their agents, and this perspective has generated insights into legislative–agency relationships. Consider the influence of the bureaucracy over public budgeting. Niskanen (1971, 1975) argued that public managers have a monopoly over information on the supply side of the budget, which he defined as the amount of spending required to carry out agency programs. He also argued that public managers know the demand side of the budget, which he defined as the preferences of legislators for spending on government programs. Public managers, he suggested, are able to use this information to propose budget options in the budget process. The legislature finds itself in a weak position to evaluate these options because it has little information about the 'true supply' requirements of the budget; hence, the legislature is forced to simply accept or reject (but not modify) public agency budget proposals. The public managers' monopoly over budget information gives them agenda control in the budget process. For an empirical example, see Romer and Rosenthal (1978).

However, since legislators have authority to pass statutes and otherwise oversee the agencies, legislators possess several means for structuring these relations, which can help prevent the agency from exercising agenda control. For example, legislators can require the reporting of information that reveals agency supply and so they can monitor agency behavior in ways not foreseen by the Niskanen models. These revised models (Bendor et al., 1987; Miller and Moe, 1983) tell a very different story of who controls the budgetary process.

The different means by which legislators can structure these legislative–agency relationships have received considerable attention. Two broad classes of tools have been identified as useful in controlling public agencies (though, see Hill and Brazier, 1991).

First, *ex ante controls* are imposed prior to program design to influence policy choice and implementation. Some of these controls involve hearings, information gathering and 'burden of proof' requirements, and other controls involve administrative procedures that 'stack the deck' in agency decision making by giving some groups the legal right to be involved in selecting and reviewing agency actions (Fiorina, 1982; McCubbins, 1985; McCubbins et al., 1987, 1989).

Second, *ex post controls* are imposed on an agency after the agency has actually implemented a program. The controls are centered on budget and statutory actions to reward or punish agencies for positive or negative performance (Calvert et al., 1987; McCubbins and Schwartz, 1984; Weingast and Moran, 1983).

A related area of research focuses on the politics of agency design, institutional structure, and the appointment of agency leaders. Lewis (2004) looks at the question of Congressional strategies to insulate the agency from future political influences and the impact on the subsequent bureaucratic policy outputs of the agency. He concludes that Congress takes into account preference divergence of the President and the risk of future meddling in agency design. Over time, insulated agencies produce policies better aligned with Congress that are more durable.

Formal theories have also focused on questions of bureaucratic expertise and civil servant competence. Stephenson (2007) posits that the acquisition of expertise by the bureaucracy is maximized when a particular agency is faced with uncertainty about the preferred course of action. Gailmard and Patty (2007) develop a formal model that demonstrates that both effective personnel practices and opportunities to exercise discretion are critical to ensuring bureaucratic capacity. Bertelli (2012) introduces the concept of strategic capacity building. He argues that agencies shape the policy agenda by acquiring expertise in particular areas of interest. Strategic capacity building has important implications for public management in which a diverse set of organizations within and beyond the confines of the traditional state serve public functions.

Multiple principals: political equilibria and agency autonomy

Principal–agent theory, however, has generally overlooked the impact of multiple principals on the autonomy of public managers. As it turns out, though, the fact that multiple institutions may oversee an agency has substantial implications for agency autonomy.

Consider some 'decisive coalition', which consists of the actors (for example, the members of the legislative body and any independent chief executive) who collectively have the authority to overturn agency policies and impose their own. A policy is in equilibrium if there exists no decisive coalition which can replace the current policy with a new one. Define the 'core' as the set of equilibrium policies. Two factors determine the size of the core. The first factor is the number of veto points in the policy-making system (Tsebelis, 1995); a veto point is some institution with the authority to reject a proposal to change policy. An increase in the number of veto points can increase the size of the set of equilibrium policies. The second factor determining the size of the core is the extent of preference heterogeneity among the veto points. If the members of the institutional veto points hold similar preferences, then preference heterogeneity is small, and a small core is the result. In contrast, if preference heterogeneity among the veto points is large, then a large core results. Illustrations of political equilibria in a policy-making system are shown in Calvert et al. (1989), Ferejohn and Shipan (1990), Hammond and Knott (1996), Hammond and Miller (1987), Knott and Hammond (2000) and Krehbiel (1998).

Note that as long as the agency considers only policies that are in the core, the agency can change from policy to policy without fear that any new choice will be upset by some decisive coalition. It follows that the larger the core, the greater the autonomy for the agency: the agency can consider a larger number of policies which are safe from upset by a decisive coalition. However, political equilibrium analysis suggests that for the public manager there may be tradeoffs between autonomy, policy satisfaction and involvement in intense conflicts over policy (Knott and Hammond, 1999).

Political equilibrium analysis also has implications for strategies that public managers might use to achieve their ideal policy. One strategy is persuasion. If a public manager can persuade other actors to change what they consider to be ideal policies, the shape of the core may change enough so that the manager's ideal policy is now within the core; this means she can safely adopt it. Redefining the nature of the policy problem (via 'agenda setting' or 'issue framing' rhetorical techniques) may also change the dimensions of the core, thus altering its shape. Consequently, understanding the shape of the core and the relative strengths of the actors' policy preferences are critical aspects of how a manager should handle the agency's political environment (Knott and Hammond, 1999).

Whitford (2005) demonstrates how attempts by multiple principals to steer bureaucratic activity can damage the agency by causing delays in policy making due to the endless negotiations among the political actors. Krause (1999) shows how the preferences of political principals and the behaviors of bureaucratic agents interact to produce outcomes ranging from bureaucratic manipulation to political domination.

Interest groups

The contributions of formal theory to an understanding of the role of interest groups in public administration stem from Olson (1965); see also Moe (1988). Olson argued that the dispersion of interests across the country gives any one interest little incentive to lobby the government, but he also developed a theory to explain how some groups overcome this collective action problem. If the number of entities affected by a government policy is small and if their impact is large enough, they will be motivated to work together to change government policy.

Olson's theory helps explain special interest policies like cheap bulk mail rates, milk price supports and sugar subsidies (Knott and Miller, 1987). Moreover, associations of citizens concerned about a policy will not be able to gain enough members because of the free-rider problem. However, if these associations provide 'selective benefits' to potential members, such as life insurance, magazines or travel packages, citizens may contribute their money due to the value of these selective benefits.

COSTS AND CRITICISMS OF FORMAL THEORY

The development of formal theories of public administration, like any other research strategy, has some costs (Hammond, 1996). What are some of these costs?

First, because the development of formal theories is often difficult, their scope of application is usually narrower than that of informal theories. Unfortunately, there seems to be a tradeoff between clarity and rigor, on the one hand, and sensitivity to richness, context and nuance, on the other.

Second, formal theorizing requires that particular technical skills be developed, involving various kinds of mathematics or computer languages. The time and effort required to learn these techniques is time that cannot be spent on other research activities.

Third, due to formal theory's technical languages, the audience for its results is sometimes small. Nonetheless, it is possible for formal theorists to do more than they have to date to make their results accessible to a broader audience.

Fourth, it is sometimes argued that formal theories have little connection to real-world politics. However, lack of interest in the real world is not an inevitable trait of formal theorists. Indeed, most formal theorists would agree that formal theorizing cannot take place in an empirical vacuum, since they would otherwise have little idea as to what institutions or processes are worth modeling in the first place.

Fifth, it is sometimes argued that formal theories 'oversimplify reality'. While this is a complex philosophical issue, we would emphasize that every useful theory *must* simplify reality. A theory that is as complex as reality has no scientific value; such a theory could not be tested because testable hypotheses could not be derived from it. So to be useful for scientific purposes, any theory must leave things out. The best test of whether something allegedly important has been left out may be an empirical one: How well does the 'overly simple' theory predict key aspects of the real world, or otherwise account for actual events? If a simple theory works well empirically, then important things may not have been left out after all.

Of course, just because a theory is formalized, however, does not mean it is a good theory. It can be a poor theory in many ways. Ultimately, the test of a good theory, however formulated, is whether it stimulates insight and understanding, and has empirical support.

CONCLUSION

Formal theorizing will never completely replace informal theorizing, nor should it: to the extent that formal theories originate in various kinds of informal theories, reducing the production of informal theories would ultimately reduce the quality and relevance of the formal theories as well. Thus, we would argue that formal and informal theorizing about important problems in public administration, along with empirical testing, rely on each other and improve each other. Neglecting any one of them would only serve to impoverish all of them.

REFERENCES

Akerlof, George A. (1970) 'The Market for "Lemons": Quality Uncertainty and the Market Mechanism', *Quarterly Journal of Economics*, 84: 488–500.

Alchian, Armen A. and Demsetz, Harold (1972) 'Production, Information Costs, and the Economics of Organization', *American Economic Review*, 62: 777–95.

Arnold, Peri (1998) *Making the Managerial Presidency: Comprehensive Reorganization Planning, 1905–1996*. 2nd edn. Lawrence, KS: University Press of Kansas.

Arrow, Kenneth J. (1974) *The Limits of Organization.* New York: Norton.

Axelrod, Robert (1984) *The Evolution of Cooperation.* New York: Basic Books.

Banks, Jeffrey S. and Weingast, Barry (1992) 'The Political Control of Bureaucracies under Asymmetric Information', *American Journal of Political Science*, 36: 509–24.

Barnard, Chester (1938) *The Functions of the Executive.* Cambridge, MA: Harvard University Press.

Behn, Robert (1991) *Leadership Counts: Lessons for Public Managers from the Massachusetts Welfare, Training, and Employment Program.* Cambridge, MA: Harvard University Press.

Bendor, Jonathan (1985) *Parallel Systems: Redundancy in Government.* Berkeley, CA: University of California Press.

Bendor, Jonathan (1988) 'Formal Models of Bureaucracy', *British Journal of Political Science*, 18: 353–95.

Bendor, Jonathan and Meirowitz, Adam (2004) 'Spatial Models of Delegation', *American Political Science Review*, 98: 293–310.

Bendor, Jonathan, Taylor, Serge and Van Gaalen, Roland (1987) 'Politicians, Bureaucrats, and Asymmetric Information', *American Journal of Political Science*, 31: 796–828.

Bendor, Jonathan, Glazer, Amihai and Hammond, Thomas H. (2001) 'Theories of Delegation', *Annual Review of Political Science*, 4: 235–69.

Bertelli, Anthony M. (2012) *The Political Economy of Public Sector Governance*. New York: Cambridge University Press.

Bertelli, Anthony M. and Lynn, Laurence E. (2003) *Madison's Managers: Public Administration and the Constitution*. Baltimore, MD: Johns Hopkins University Press.

Bozeman, Barry and Straussman, Jeffrey D. (1990) *Public Management Strategies*. San Francisco, CA: Jossey–Bass.

Brehm, John and Gates, Scott (1993) 'Donut Shops and Speed Traps: Evaluating Models of Supervision on Police Behavior', *American Journal of Political Science*, 37 (2): 555–81.

Brehm, John and Gates, Scott (1997) *Working, Shirking, and Sabotage: Bureaucratic Response to a Democratic Public*. Ann Arbor, MI: University of Michigan Press.

Calvert, Randall L., Moran, Mark J. and Weingast, Barry R. (1987) 'Congressional Influence over Policymaking: The Case of the FTC', in Mathew McCubbins and Terry Sullivan (eds), *Congress: Structure and Policy*. New York: Cambridge University Press.

Calvert, Randall L., McCubbins, Matthew D. and Weingast, Barry R. (1989) 'A Theory of Political Control and Agency Discretion', *American Journal of Political Science*, 33: 588–611.

Caro, Robert (1975) *The Power Broker: Robert Moses and the Fall of New York*. New York: Vintage Books.

Coase, Ronald (1937) 'The Nature of the Firm', *Economica*, 4: 386–405.

Doig, Jameson W. and Hargrove, Erwin C. (eds) (1987) *Leadership and Innovation: A Biographical Perspective on Entrepreneurs in Government*. Baltimore, MD: Johns Hopkins University Press.

Epstein, David and O'Halloran, Sharyn (1999) *Delegating Powers: A Transaction Cost Politics Approach to Policy Making under Separate Powers*. New York: Cambridge University Press.

Ferejohn, John A. and Shipan, Charles (1990) 'Congressional Influence on Bureaucracy', *Journal of Law, Economics and Organization*, 6: 1–27.

Fiorina, Morris P. (1982) 'Legislative Choice of Regulatory Forms: Legal Process or Administrative Process?' *Public Choice*, 39: 33–66.

Gailmard, Sean and Patty, John W. (2007) 'Slackers and Zealots: Civil Service, Policy Discretion, and Bureaucratic Expertise', *American Journal of Political Science,* 51: 873–89.

Gilligan, Thomas and Krehbiel, Keith (1989) 'Asymmetric Information and Legislative Rules with a Heterogeneous Committee', *American Journal of Political Science*, 33: 459–90.

Greenwald, B. and Stiglitz, J.E. (1986) 'Externalities in Economies with Imperfect Information and Incomplete Markets', *Quarterly Journal of Economics*, 101 (2): 229–64.

Gulick, Luther (1937) 'Notes on the Theory of Organization', in Luther Gulick and Lyndall Urwick (eds), *Papers on the Science of Administration*. New York: Institute of Public Administration, Columbia University.

Hammond, Thomas H. (1986) 'Agenda Control, Organizational Structure, and Bureaucratic Politics', *American Journal of Political Science*, 30: 397–420.

Hammond, Thomas H. (1993) 'Toward a General Theory of Hierarchy: Books, Bureaucrats, Basketball Tournaments, and the Administrative Structure of the National-State', *Journal of Public Administration Research and Theory*, 3: 120–45.

Hammond, Thomas H. (1996) 'Formal Theory and the Institutions of Governance', *Governance*, 9: 107–85.

Hammond, Thomas H. and Knott, Jack H. (1996) 'Who Controls the Bureaucracy? Presidential Power, Congressional Dominance, Legal Constraints, and Bureaucratic Autonomy in a Model of Multi-institutional Policymaking', *Journal of Law, Economics, and Organization*, 12: 121–68.

Hammond, Thomas H. and Miller, Gary J. (1985) 'A Social Choice Perspective on Authority and Expertise in Bureaucracy', *American Journal of Political Science*, 29: 611–38.

Hammond, Thomas H. and Miller, Gary J. (1987) 'The Core of the Constitution', *American Political Science Review*, 81: 1155–74.

Hammond, Thomas H. and Thomas, Paul A. (1989) 'The Impossibility of a Neutral Hierarchy', *Journal of Law, Economics and Organization*, 5: 155–84.

Hardin, Garrett (1968) 'The Tragedy of the Commons', *Science*, 162: 1243–8.

Heimann, C.F. Larry (1997) 'Understanding the *Challenger* Disaster: Organizational Structure and the Design of Reliable Systems', *American Political Science Review*, 87: 421–35.

Hill, Jeffrey S. and Brazier, James E. (1991) 'Constraining Administrative Decisions: A Critical Examination of the Structure and Process Hypothesis', *Journal of Law, Economics, & Organization* 7: 373–400.

Holmstrom, Bengt R. (1982) 'Moral Hazard in Teams', *Bell Journal of Economics*, 13: 324–40.

Huber, John D. and Charles, Shipan R. (2002). *Deliberate Discretion? The Institutional Foundations of Bureaucratic Autonomy.* New York: Cambridge University Press.

Kaufman, Herbert (1956) 'Emerging Conflicts in the Doctrines of Public Administration', *American Political Science Review*, 50: 1057–73.

Kaufman, Herbert (1960) *The Forest Ranger: A Study in Administrative Behavior.* Baltimore, MD: Johns Hopkins University Press.

Knott, Jack H. (1993) 'Comparing Public and Private Management: Cooperative Effort and Principal–Agent Relationships', *Journal of Public Administration Research and Theory*, 3: 92–119.

Knott, Jack H. and Hammond, Thomas H. (1999) 'Public Management, Administrative Leadership, and Policy Change', in Jeffrey L. Brudney, Lawrence O'Toole and Hal G. Rainey (eds), *Advancing Public Management: New Developments in Theory, Methods, and Practice.* Washington, DC: Georgetown University Press.

Knott, Jack H. and Hammond, Thomas H. (2000) 'Congressional Committees and Policy Change: Explaining Legislative Outcomes in the Deregulation of Trucking, Airlines, Banking and Telecommunications', in Carolyn J. Heinrich and Lawrence E. Lynn, Jr (eds), *Governance and Performance: New Perspectives.* Washington, DC: Georgetown University Press.

Knott, Jack H. and Miller, Gary J. (1987) *Reforming Bureaucracy: The Politics of Institutional Choice.* Englewood Cliffs, NJ: Prentice Hall.

Krause, George A. (1999) *A Two-Way Street: The Institutional Dynamics of the Modern Administrative State.* Pittsburgh, PA: University of Pittsburgh Press.

Krehbiel, Keith (1998) *Pivotal Politics: A Theory of U.S. Lawmaking.* Chicago, IL: University of Chicago Press.

Landau, Martin (1969) 'Redundancy, Rationality, and the Problem of Duplication and Overlap', *Public Administration Review*, 29: 346–58.

Lewis, David E. (2004) 'The Adverse Consequences of the Politics of Agency Design for Presidential Management in the United States: The Relative Durability of Insulated Agencies', *British Journal of Political Science*, 34: 377–404.

Lewis, Eugene (1980) *Public Entrepreneurship: Toward a Theory of Bureaucratic Political Power – The Organizational Lives of Hyman Rickover, J. Edgar Hoover, and Robert Moses.* Bloomington, IN: Indiana University Press.

Lupia, Arthur and McCubbins, Mathew D. (1994) 'Learning from Oversight: Fire Alarms and Police Patrols Reconstructed', *Journal of Law, Economics and Organization*, 10: 96–125.

McCubbins, Mathew D. (1985) 'The Legislative Design of Regulatory Structure', *American Journal of Political Science*, 29: 721–48.

McCubbins, Matthew and Schwartz, Thomas (1984) 'Congressional Oversight Overlooked: Police Patrols versus Fire Alarms', *American Journal of Political Science*, 28: 165–79.

McCubbins, Matthew, Noll, Roger G. and Weingast, Barry R. (1987) 'Administrative Procedures as Instruments of Political Control', *Journal of Law, Economics and Organization*, 3: 243–77.

McCubbins, Matthew D., Noll, Roger G. and Weingast, Barry R. (1989) 'Structure and Process, Politics and Policy: Administrative Arrangements and the Political Control of Agencies', *Virginia Law Review*, 75: 431–99.

Merton, Robert (1940) 'Bureaucratic Structure and Personality', *Social Forces*, 17: 560–8.

Miller, Gary J. (1992) *Managerial Dilemmas: The Political Economy of Hierarchy.* New York: Cambridge University Press.

Miller, Gary J. and Hammond, Thomas H. (1994) 'Why Politics is More Fundamental than Economics: Incentive-Compatible Mechanisms Are Not Credible', *Public Choice*, 6: 5–26.

Miller, Gary J. and Moe, Terry M. (1983) 'Bureaucrats, Legislators, and the Size of Government', *American Political Science Review*, 77: 297–322.

Moe, Terry M. (1984) 'The New Economics of Organization', *American Journal of Political Science*, 28: 739–77.

Moe, Terry M. (1987) 'An Assessment of the Positive Theory of "Congressional Dominance"', *Legislative Studies Quarterly*, 12: 475–520.

Moe, Terry M. (1988) *The Organization of Interests.* Chicago, IL: University of Chicago Press.

Niskanen, William A. (1971) *Bureaucracy and Representative Government.* Chicago, IL: Aldine.

Niskanen, William (1975) 'Bureaucrats and politicians', *Journal of Law and Economics*, 18 (December): 617–43.

Olson, Mancur (1965) *The Logic of Collective Action.* Cambridge, MA: Harvard University Press.

Ostrom, Elinor (1999) 'Coping with Tragedies of the Commons', *Annual Review of Political Science*, 2: 493–535.

Romer, Thomas and Rosenthal, Howard (1978) 'Political Resource Allocation, Controlled Agendas, and the Status Quo', *Public Choice*, 33: 27–43.

Sen, Amartya (1970) 'The Impossibility of a Paretian Liberal', *Journal of Political Economy*, 78: 152–7.

Stephenson, Matthew C. (2007). 'Bureucratic Decision Costs and Endogenous Agency Expertise', *Journal of Law, Economics, & Organization*, 23: 469–98.

Tsebelis, George (1995) 'Decision Making in Political Systems: Veto Players in Presidentialism, Parliamentarianism, Multicameralism, and Multipartyism', *British Journal of Political Science*, 25: 289–326.

Weingast, Barry R. and Moran, Mark J. (1983) 'Bureaucratic Discretion or Congressional Control? Regulatory Policy Making by the Federal Trade Commission', *Journal of Political Economy*, 91: 765–800.

Whitford, Andrew B. (2005) 'The Pursuit of Political Control by Multiple Principals', *Journal of Politics*, 67: 29–49.

Wilson, James Q. (1989) *Bureaucracy: What Government Agencies Do and Why They Do It*. New York: Basic Books.

Wolf, Charles, Jr (1975) 'A Theory of Non-Market Failure', *The Public Interest*, 55: 114–33.

PART 4

Administrative History

edited by Jos C.N. Raadschelders

A 'historical approach' in the study of public administration testifies to the degree to which the past exists in the present (Fesler, 1982). At the same time, *a historical approach in the study of public administration recognizes that the present may be embedded in but is not predetermined by the past*. It is in this italicized claim that the inherently historical nature of public administration (both as a study and a field of practice) emerges while clarifying at the same time that it is not bounded by that past. To be sure, this is a Western statement in the sense that Judeo-Christian culture embraces a linear conception of time as 'something' that unfolds from a beginning to a 'final judgment' and where humans can choose which direction to take. In many other cultures, such as in India, history is perceived as '… cyclical within repetitive eons' (Björkman, email to author December 6, 2010; see also Pluciennik, 2004: 20). How a culture views the past influences how it can deal with problems in the present; and it certainly influenced in the past how scholars thought about government and governance.

There are two types of administrative history (Raadschelders, 1998a: 7–8). The first

type, *administrative history in the broad sense*, is concerned with the interaction between government and society at large as well as with processes of state making and nation building (the latter topics are more often studied in political science). Administrative history in the broad sense is relevant because societal developments have consequences for quality and quantity of public service delivery. Students and practitioners benefit from learning how and why government responded to societal change and what consequences this had for the internal structure and functioning of government. The second type, *administrative history proper*, is concerned with the '… study of structures and processes in and ideas about government as they have existed or have been desired in the past and the actual and ideal place of public functionaries therein.' Important in this definition is that not only the topics of mainstream public administration are included (that is, the development of organizational structure and differentiation, of human resource management, of policy, etc.) but also the development of ideas about government and governance in relation to society (which is more often studied within political theory). Administrative history as defined above has the potential to take the study of public administration beyond its traditional instrumental and contemporary focus, thus enriching the understanding of the present (Raadschelders, 2008, 2010: 247–48; Raadschelders et al., 2000).

Having said this, there are some pitfalls that administrative history (that is, when pursued in the context of the study of public administration) should avoid. First, it is not a *l'art pour l'art* exercise that details how 'things' have become. As valuable as such histories are, they are not necessarily what students of public administration and practitioners in government look for. Second, a historical perspective in public administration will not lead to usable knowledge, to use the concept that was coined over 30 years ago (Lindblom and Cohen, 1979). It would be wrong to assume that history provides lessons that can be used to avoid making mistakes now. Each problem has to be considered in its own and unique time and context. History does not repeat itself. Yet, policy and decision makers need not reinvent the wheel and can consider past experiences, without drawing upon misconceived analogies. To prevent the problems that decision makers create when using the past as an analogy for the present, Neustadt and May (1986) developed a set of so-called 'mini-methods' to show where analogies go astray. Third, administrative history should not reconstruct the past in terms of contemporary theories and models. Such an *anachronism* does not do justice to the past in itself, and blinds us to understanding the conceptualizations of decision makers in their own time and place. Fourth, the past should not be interpreted in terms of contemporary outcome. Such *present-mindedness* only results in reconstruction of developmental paths relevant to the present, in which case we lose sight of paths that ended somewhere in the past. In that case, too, decision makers lose potentially valuable information about past policies and reforms.

WHAT MAKES THE STUDY OF ADMINISTRATIVE HISTORY UNIQUE?

There are several features that make administrative history a unique study. First, and like the study of public administration, it is multi- and interdisciplinary, for it must work with theories and concepts from the social sciences and the humanities. Disciplinary approaches can only provide partial insight in the phenomenon of government-in-society.

Second, unlike several of the more disciplinary social sciences, administrative historical research does neither look for law-like generalizations nor work from or strive toward a unifying theory. The strength and the challenge of administrative history is in identifying the impact of general societal trends (for example, secularization, rationalization, industrialization, demographic growth, urbanization and ruralization, scientification, intensification of communication through electronic technologies, etc.) upon the structure and functioning of government and administration at large (for example, the welfare state, bureaucratization) and upon individual public organizations, policies, and offices. If anything, administrative history confronts, sometimes sweepingly, generalizations concerning the world and its regions with more in-depth study of cultural and national traditions.

Third, and related to the second feature, administrative history does not so much study social change as focus on the interplay of continuity, diversity, and change. The continuity of traditions and of local communities provides stability during times of change (at the political regime level). In fact, there has never been a period in history where social change was so total that it eradicated earlier practices and traditions. In emphasizing diversity as well, administrative history helps in recognizing that, for example, such a general trend as bureaucratization has manifested itself in various ways – that is, within particular national and cultural contexts. Thus, administrative history adopts an evolutionary rather than a social change perspective (Nisbet, 1969). The evolutionary perspective draws attention both to inter-generational and intercultural *diffusion of ideas* (for example, political theory) and (administrative) traditions and practices as well as to the phenomenon of *parallel evolution* (where comparable ideas and practices developed more or less independently from one another).

Fourth, administrative history helps preserve collective memory with an eye for present needs. It can serve as a source of understanding and/or reinterpretation of (a) modernity, (b) our time as one of epochal change, and (c) the discourse in public administration. It can and even has served an emancipatory function ('setting the record straight'), for instance, in highlighting the influence of women upon the making of the American welfare state (these four points are mentioned in Raadschelders, 2000: 515).

DEVELOPMENT AND STATE OF THE ART OF ADMINISTRATIVE HISTORY

In the course of the nineteenth century, the study of administrative history emerged in the United States and in Europe as a history of political and administrative institutions from the national down to the local level. In the United States this endeavor was mainly embedded in departments of political science, while in Europe it emerged within the professorial chairs in public administration as they had existed since the early eighteenth century. Intriguingly, the first administrative histories of the world were written by Americans (Duganne, 1860; Wilson, 1889; see Raadschelders, 1997, 2002). Both studies were descriptive in content. From the early twentieth century onward, American scholars adopted theories and conceptualizations from (business) management studies. White's monumental four-volume study (1948–1958) of American administrative history between 1789 and 1901 is an excellent example of this, organizing the analysis around Gulick's

POSDCORB. In Europe, administrative history became largely part of the study of legal history, given the inclusion of the pro-fessorial chairs in public administration into departments of law.

After the Second World War it was within the context of structural functionalism that a variety of scholars published studies on the development of the (early) state. Characteristic for the (old) institutional approach was the development and use of taxonomies. Finer's conceptual prologue to his huge study is a fine example (1997). Somewhat linked to the American managerial focus, studies appeared that were organized around themes specifically relevant to the study of public administration (Gladden, 1972). Until the early 1980s many administrative historical studies were descriptive by nature (see the next section). The emergence of neo-institutionalism since the early 1980s has given the study of administrative history the potential to develop itself on a more theoretical basis. Specifically, historical institutionalism (see Peters, 1999) and its concepts of, for example, path dependency and critical junctures, hold great promise for the further development of administrative history provided that the first is not used to reintroduce a nineteenth-century notion of causality (Raadschelders, 1998b) and the latter does not prohibit the understanding of continuity amidst change.

The study of administrative history is in good shape. At the handbook level, there are at least three studies that provide overviews of the development of government with extensive bibliographic references (Finer, 1997; Gladden, 1972; Raadschelders, 1998a). There are four journals that specifically concern administrative history. The *Journal of Policy History* (JPH) (Cambridge University Press) has been published since 1989. In that same year, the first volume appeared of the international, comparative, multidisciplinary and multi-lingual *Yearbook of European Administrative History* (*Nomos Verlagsgesellschaft*) (YEAH). Both journals contain a wealth of in-depth studies based on research in primary (oral and written) sources. In particular, the forum section in YEAH contains bibliographic articles on the development and state of the art of administrative history in specific Western, Central, and Eastern European countries. The *Journal of Management History* (Emerald Group Publishing Limited) has been published since 1994, and *Management and Organizational History* (SAGE Publications) since 2006. Finally, there are quite impressive national traditions in administrative history. As can be expected, the UK, France, Germany, and Italy lead the way in terms of continuous research throughout the twentieth century. The bibliographic articles that became available in the past two decades (in YEAH, see above), however, indicate that most European countries enjoy a well-developed tradition of study in administrative history. Also, and perhaps a little unexpected, there is quite a tradition in the United States in this area of research, and that goes back further than one might expect (Raadschelders, 2000). The various bibliographies contain references to numerous book- and article-length studies. The major challenge for administrative historians is to make these accessible to large audiences. While many studies are written in English, French, or German, there is even more in other languages. For instance, the *Journal of Korean Public Administration History* is published in Korean. Also, a large portion of studies relevant to administrative history, and perhaps even the majority of them, are generated within other studies than public administration and political science. Notably, scholars of anthropology, law, sociology, and history have contributed greatly to our understanding of the development of government, and many scholars in these fields have seen their work published in the journal *Comparative Studies in Society and History* (Cambridge University Press). Compartmentalization of knowledge, whether for epistemological or more mundane organizational reasons, is certainly a barrier to the multidisciplinary study of administrative history.

METHODS AND CHALLENGES OF ADMINISTRATIVE HISTORY

Methods in the study of administrative history are as diverse as in other topics of interest to social scientists. In view of the 'fringe' status of administrative history in the study of public administration, some questions about methods and challenges need to be raised.

First, how useful and possible are *quantitative-statistical* and/or *quantitative-descriptive methods*? The former are very popular in public administration and political science (given the positivist aspiration to achieve scientific status), but place almost impossible demands upon administrative historians, since consistent time-series that span hundreds of years (for an example on personnel size in four centuries, see Raadschelders, 1994) are very difficult to generate for dependent and – even more – independent variables alike. Historical work relies upon what is available in archives, and the research questions that interest us now may not have been of any concern to those who documented and preserved past decisions and actions of public officials. The administrative historian in Europe will find that the archives hold much, but not enough, while a colleague in the United States will find that, to quote de Tocqueville,

> ... the acts of society [and of government, JR] in America often leave less trace than the actions of a simple family. [...] The only historical monuments of the United States are newspapers [...] ... in fifty years it will be more difficult to gather authentic documents on the details of the social existence of Americans of our day than on the administration of the French in the Middle Ages ... (2000: 198)

A second, and equally challenging, wrench in the attempt to generate time-series of a dependent variable is that they must be grounded in conceptualizations that travel well over time. By way of example, the concept of a politician as we know it (that is, a popularly elected officeholder with an authority and responsibility distinct from that of career civil servants) did not and could not exist before the Napoleonic era.

Perhaps quantitative-descriptive studies hold more promise, which means that we need to be content with nominal time-series. Often, such time-series are merely copied from data-generating institutions such as a national census bureau. When using such data, though, it is necessary to consider the collection rationale. Within public administration (and political science), research aimed at creating new time-series on the basis of primary research in archival sources is rare, perhaps for lack of training in archival research. As a consequence, qualitative-descriptive studies appear to be preferred by administrative historians who were trained in the social sciences.

Second, we need to ask *what* is being compared. Administrative history is a cross-time study (next to the more familiar cross-national, cross-level, and cross-policy studies) that is sensitive to the limits of using contemporary concepts in a historical time and context. There are a variety of studies that concern, for instance, bureaucratization of the public sector or even of society at large. But, as soon as the scholar provides sweeping generalizations with more in-depth observations relating to and illustrations from particular countries, it quickly becomes clear that concepts are not easily commensurable between different countries, and sometimes not even between different policies and levels of government, let alone across time.

Third, *how* can cross-time study be conducted? By way of example, Skocpol and Somers distinguished comparison as *parallel demonstration of theory*, as *contrast of contexts*, and as *macrocausal analysis* (1980). From a scholarly point of view, the third one is intellectually the most challenging and theoretically the most satisfying (see also Mills, 1959: 125). Contrasting contexts is more commonly used, while parallel demonstration of theory attracts attention in view of the emergence of historical institutionalism.

To date, no one has attempted to analyze and 'count' publications in administrative history according to the method employed. It is thus only intuitively that this author suggests that the dominant methods thus far are quantitative and qualitative descriptions of cross-national, cross-level, and cross-policy comparisons of contexts.

OVERVIEW OF PART 4

The three chapters in this part of the Handbook represent the wide range that administrative history roams. In Chapter 11, Mordecai Lee provides an unusual analysis of the development of state and government in the United States. He has conducted administrative history research in the local and federal levels of American government, and has served as a state legislator. In Chapter 12, Fabio Rugge looks at the consequences of increased societal demand for the internal structure and functioning of government itself (that is, administrative history proper). More specifically, he addresses administrative traditions in Western countries, as they still play a role (such as the common law tradition in the UK, the *Rechtsstaat* tradition in continental Europe, and the administrative state tradition in Scandinavia). He holds a professorial chair in administrative history (the only one that I know of) and is an active member of the working group 'History of Government' of the International Institute of Administrative Sciences. The chapters by both Lee and by Rugge show how much the governmental penetration of society and the administrative traditions in government, have made the world as we know it. Indeed, the last remark is not off-base, since Western traditions and models of government disseminated across the globe, especially as a consequence of Dutch, English, French, German, Italian, Portuguese, and Spanish colonization. Hence, both Lee and Rugge chapters emphasize the diffusion of ideas and practices between countries and cultures.

In contrast, in Chapter 13, the final chapter of this section, James Warner Björkman discusses South Asian and Western European ideas about government and governance by comparing Kautilya and Macchiavelli. Doing so, it is possible to develop a sense of the degree to which Western conceptions of democracy and management are not exclusive to the West. Björkman is a comparativist par excellence and has done extensive research in India.

All three authors start their chapters in general, comparative terms and illustrate their observations with developments in a particular geographic setting. Thus, Lee considers the United States, Rugge tackles some European countries in more detail (especially the UK, France, Germany, and Italy), while Björkman draws upon his in-depth knowledge of India when comparing the political theories of Kautilya with those of Machiavelli. Also, each author provides at the conclusion of their chapter some observations about the degree to which remarks and conclusions regarding their specific topic and/or region are generalizable. The ambition of the authors of this section is not to be complete in their account of an aspect of administrative history: rather, it is their desire to show through cross-time and cross-national analysis that historical knowledge is a benefit to students and practitioners alike. Of course, to those reading this Introduction, this is preaching to the converted, but hopefully others will come to recognize that a historical perspective in the study of public administration and in the practice of government is not a waste of time. It may not lead to usable knowledge but will make us aware of the *portée*, to use Montaigne's concept, or reach of our knowledge at present and over time, and – better still – it may make us to 'be lowly wise ...', which Milton claimed in *Paradise Lost* to be the highest form of knowledge (Shattuck, 1996: 29, 72–73). In the same spirit, Jacob Burckhardt wrote more than 150 years ago: '*Wir wollen durch Erfahrung nicht sowohl klug (für ein andermal) als weise (für immer) werden*' (in paraphrased translation: It is through experience that we will not so much aspire to cleverness for the next time, but to wisdom for ever).

The authors of this section accepted with enthusiasm and without reservations the invitation to write, or respectively update, their chapters. I thank them for the time and energy they have put into this project. As far as this Introduction is concerned, it had to be brief but provides the kind of information that enables the interested reader to expand her/his interest in administrative history.

REFERENCES

Duganne, Augustine J.H. (1860) *A History of Governments Showing the Progress of Civil Society and the Structure of Ancient and Modern States.* New York: Robert M. de Witt.

Fesler, James W. (ed.) (1982) *American Public Administration: Patterns of the Past.* Washington, DC: American Society for Public Administration.

Finer, S.E. (1997) *The History of Government from the Earliest Times.* Oxford: Oxford University Press.

Gladden, E.N. (1972) *A History of Public Administration.* London: Frank Cass.

Lindblom, Charles E. and Cohen, David K. (1979) *Usable Knowledge. Social Science and Social Problem Solving.* New Haven, CT/New York: Yale University Press.

Mills, C. Wright (1959) *The Sociological Imagination.* New York: Oxford University Press.

Neustadt, Richard E. and May, Ernest R. (1986) *Thinking in Time. The Uses of History for Decision-Makers.* New York: The Free Press/London: Collier Macmillan.

Nisbet, Robert A. (1969) *Social Change and History. Aspects of the Western Theory of Development.* New York: Oxford University Press.

Peters, B. Guy (1999) *Institutional Theory in Political Science: the "New Institutionalism."* London: Pinter.

Pluciennik, Mark (2004) 'The Meaning of "Hunter-Gatherers" and Modes of Subsistence: a Comparative Historical Perspective,' in Alan Barnard (ed.), *Hunter-Gatherers in History, Archaeology and Anthropology.* Oxford/New York: Berg, pp. 17–29.

Raadschelders, Jos C.N. (1994) 'Understanding the Development of Local Government: Theory and

Evidence from the Dutch Case,' *Administration and Society*, 25(4): 410–442.

Raadschelders, Jos C.N. (1997) 'The Progress of Civil Society: A 19th Century American History of Governments,' *Administration & Society*, 29(4): 471–489.

Raadschelders, Jos C.N. (1998a) *Handbook of Administrative History*. New Brunswick, NJ: Transaction Publishers.

Raadschelders, Jos C.N. (1998b) 'Evolution, Institutional Analysis and Path Dependency: An Administrative History Perspective on Fashionable Approaches and Concepts,' *International Review of Administrative Sciences*, 64(4): 562–582.

Raadschelders, Jos C.N. (2000) 'Administrative History of the United States. Development and State of the Art,' *Administration and Society*, 32(5): 499–528.

Raadschelders, Jos C.N. (2002) 'Woodrow Wilson on the History of Government. Passing Fad or Constitutive Framework for His Philosophy of Governance?' *Administration & Society*, 35(5): 579–598.

Raadschelders, Jos C.N. (2008) 'Administrative History as a Core Dimension of Public Administration.' Foundations of Public Administration series, webpages of *Public Administration Review* at the website of the American Society for Public Administration.

Raadschelders, Jos C.N. (2010) 'Is American Public Administration Detached from Historical Context? On the Nature of Time and the Need to Understand It in Government and Its Study,' *The American Review of Public Administration*, 40(3): 235–260.

Raadschelders, Jos C.N., Wagenaar, Pieter, Rutgers, Mark, and Overeem, Patrick (2000) 'Against a Study of the History of Public Administration: A Manifesto,' *Administrative Theory & Praxis*, 22(4): 772–791.

Shattuck, Roger (1996) *Forbidden Knowledge. From Prometheus to Pornography*. New York: St. Martin's Press.

Skocpol, Theda and Somers, Margaret (1980) 'The Uses of Comparative History in Macrosocial Inquiry,' *Comparative Studies in Society and History*, 22(2): 174–197.

Tocqueville, Alexis de (2000) *Democracy in America* (edited by Harvey C. Mansfield and Delba Wintrop). Chicago, IL/London: University of Chicago Press.

White, Leonard B. (1948) *The Federalists: A Study in Administrative History, 1789–1801*. New York: The Free Press.

White, Leonard B. (1951) *The Jeffersonians: A Study in Administrative History, 1801–1829*. New York: The Free Press.

White, Leonard B. (1954) *The Jacksonians: A Study in Administrative History, 1829–1861*. New York: Macmillan.

White, Leonard B. (1958) *The Republican Era: A Study in Administrative History, 1869–1901*. New York: Macmillan.

Wilson, Woodrow (1889) *The State. Elements of Historical and Practical Politics. A Sketch of Institutional History and Administration*. Boston, MA: D.C. Heath & Co.

11

US Administrative History: Golem Government

Mordecai Lee

go·lem (gŏ′lĕm) *n.* In Jewish folklore, a clod; some-one who is all thumbs, poorly coordinated.
(Rosten, 2001: 129).

In the beginning, there was King George's tyranny. The Founding Fathers looked down in 1776 and saw that it was bad. They said, Let there be independence. And there was. But there was no order. So, in 1789 they said, Let us create a government in our image. And they created a golem of a government, slow-moving, awkward and uncoordinated. The people saw that it was good. They said to the golem, Be fruitful and multiply. And it begat many more golems, until a multitude covered the face of the land, from sea to shining sea. Then, everyone rested. And they lived happily ever after. The end.

Everything else is commentary. Americans don't want efficient and professional government (Wills, 1999). They have gone to great pains for two and a half centuries to assure that. More importantly, this is still true *today*.

The American public sector in the twenty-first century continues to be a lumbering golem. More precisely, thousands of golems, little different in principle from the founding eighteenth-century template. Given that history is a good predictor of the future (Raadschelders, 2010), this is very likely to be correct for the rest of the twenty-first century.

CREATING A PERMANENT TEMPLATE FOR AMERICAN PUBLIC ADMINISTRATION: THE US CONSTITUTION, 1789

The Congress that declared independence on July 4, 1776 was something of an ad hoc body improvising its way. Congress was a decision-making institution that had both executive and legislative powers (and impliedly, judicial as well). It was not under-girded by any governmental infrastructure. The only department was the Continental Army generaled by George Washington. Within a year, the national government was somewhat institutionalized by the signing of the Articles of Confederation. While not formally ratified by the states until 1781, the confederation structure of the Articles governed the activities of the national government on a de facto basis immediately upon signing.

History has generally condemned the Confederation as a failure due to its weakness and lack of major central powers. Still, it is important to emphasize that the Confederation reflected the political consensus at the time. The predominant sense of allegiance by citizens was to their colony-cum-state, not to any unitary national identity. However, it became apparent that the Confederation was *too* weak. It needed to be strengthened. But the significance of what replaced it was, contrary to the conventional narrative, *not* a strong central national government. It was only modestly less weak than the Confederation, but still not too strong, too powerful or too efficient.

The central theme of American administrative history is embedded in the US Constitution, signed in 1787 and, upon ratification, implemented in 1789. This, truly, was 'year zero' in American administrative history. Some common terms characterizing the Constitution only came into use later. Notwithstanding being neologisms, 'separation of powers,' 'checks and balances' and 'judicial review' well summarize the American approach to government. The Constitution created a golem of a government: clumsy, uncoordinated and lumbering. The president had executive power, but the Congress had the power of the purse. The president oversaw the departments, but the Congress had to authorize their existence. The president named the managers of his administration, but Congress had to confirm them. All along, the Supreme Court could insert itself with authoritative interpretations of vague Constitutional terms and could declare any law unconstitutional. This was a premeditated formula for inefficient government and, consequently, inefficient public administration. Civil servants would have three bosses, not one. Bertelli and Lynn called them 'Madison's Managers' (2006) for the chief author of the Constitution (later President), James Madison, although Madison was hoping for better than that.

These principles in the US Constitution subsequently served as the model for all American governments. In today's American public sector, nearly every state has patterned its structure after the federal: hence, 50 state golems of separate elected chief executive officers (governors), legislative branches (state legislatures, 49 bicameral) and judicial branches (usually elected). States also have other independently elected administrative officers, most commonly attorney general, often a state treasurer and a secretary of state. The pattern for incorporated municipalities (about 30,000) is largely similar, with an elected chief executive (mayor), legislative branch (common council or board of aldermen) and judicial branch (municipal court). Like states, many municipalities have other elected administrative officers such as city attorney, comptroller and treasurer.

County government (about 4,700) generally emerged with a unitary body that was both legislative and executive (board of supervisors or commissioners), but recent trends for the higher population ones have been to separate those duties, with about 700 having an elected chief executive officer (county executive). County governments, like state and city governments, also have other elected administrative officers, almost universally sheriff and district attorney, and usually others.

Paralleling the traditional unitary structure of county government are unincorporated township governments (about 16,500) and public school districts (about 13,500). Both usually elect a multiple member body that has legislative and executive responsibilities (town board, school board). Other independent entities in the public sector include tribal governments (about 550) and special purpose districts with taxing powers (about 37,000), some of which are elected, others appointed. The latter were largely a twentieth-century development that gained momentum over time. In 2010, Peters estimated that about 500 new special purpose districts were now being created every year (Peters, 2010: 27). Finally, there is a highly heterogeneous category of quasi-governmental entities, sometimes known by the acronym quangos (Moe, 2001) – numbers unknown.

So, there are roughly 100,000+ autonomous governments in the United States, each exercising the authoritative and compulsory powers of the state. This is golem government in extremis and a sure formula for inefficient public administration. Just about anything an American governmental manager tries to accomplish entails *inter*-governmental relations with other autonomous governments. James Lynn, briefly President Nixon's White House-based supersecretary for community development, testified before Congress that coordination between separate Cabinet departments *within* the federal executive branch was 'extremely difficult' (Lee, 2010: 136). Imagine between *separate* governments.

This government of golems is why it is so hard to conduct public administration in the United States. The structure is *intended* to obstruct efficient management. Simon (1997) suggested that managers could only hope to satisfice in their decision-making, with maximizing truly unrealistic. This is the central theme of the history of American public administration: doing as well as possible under the circumstances; essentially following an expedient path of least resistance; and trying to guide awkward and multiple governments forward. America's much-vaunted ahistorical culture of pragmatism does not apply to its government.

A macro-developmental framework for the rest of the story identifies three main eras: pre-bureaucracy, bureaucracy and post-bureaucracy. Two major historical markers help distinguish them: the 1883 Pendleton Act, creating a national civil service, and the 1978 Civil Service Reform Act, which substantially undid it.

PRE-BUREAUCRACY: SMALL GOVERNMENT WITH A WORKFORCE OF LAYMEN, 1789–1883

After the Constitution went into effect, American administrative development at all levels substantially lagged behind Western Europe. In part, this reflected the widely-shared historical 'lesson' that equated active and thick government with tyranny, or, at least, its potential. That led to the seemingly modest role the Constitution assigned to the president and executive branch. Second President John Adams concluded that the prosperity of the country depended 'very little on anything in my power' (McCullough, 2001: 527). This constrained view was reinforced by the ostensible administrative philosophy of third President Jefferson and his political heirs. Seemingly as a confirmation of that, the federal government had 153 employees in Washington, DC when Jefferson took office and only about double that number three decades later (Balogh, 2009: 112).

However, it would be erroneous to conclude that this administrative apparatus was so modest as to be nearly non-existent or that Jefferson et al. governed as they professed. For example, the Post Office was a major administrative structure. According to John, 'for the vast majority of Americans the postal system *was* the central government' (1995: 4, emphasis in original). It also was a driver of federal funding for transportation infrastructure, such as postal roads. The ongoing need for a military to suppress Native Americans led to relatively major governmental operations. Jefferson also articulated the case for state-sponsored public education (Newbold, 2010). Other major manifestations of government administration included the tax collection system of customs and tariffs, patent registration and foreign relations.

A significant factor in the gradual thickening of government was to support slavery. Usually ignored in American administrative histories, Jefferson was committed to the maintenance of slavery, even if it contradicted his philosophy of limited government (Kennedy, 2003). Slavery necessitated new territory for expansion and an army to clear it of threats, such as from Native Americans who harbored runaway slaves.

Hoffer (2007: 199) called this era the first state, of 'a small, lightly staffed, largely amateur, and highly politicized administrative apparatus.' President Andrew Jackson is most prominently identified as justifying 'rotation in office' rather than any permanent public servants. This was, literally, 'democratic' public administration. He believed that most anyone could hold a position in a federal agency and competently conduct business. Public administration was not so complicated that a layman (they were all men then) couldn't do it.

Later, during the mid-nineteenth century, a 'second state' gradually emerged. It was shaped by the lawyers who dominated politics. They were comfortable with a form of government that somewhat reflected estate administration. Specifically, 'Administration of estates required a light touch ... to sponsor various projects for the good of the estate; ... supervise the assets' use to ensure that they were not wasted [and] ... eliminate the danger of misuse of the assets' (Hoffer, 2007: 7). This gradually expanded the role of government, initially as a *sponsor* of deserved projects, then as a *supervisor* of them, and finally as a *standardizer* of federal actions and national policies. They included creation of a Department of Agriculture (in 1862) to promote productive farming techniques and Land Grant universities tied to agricultural extension programs. States took on expanded roles even earlier, such as New York's construction of the Erie Canal in the 1810s and 1820s (Koeppel, 2009).

Still, this continued to be generically 'small government.' Surveying all levels of government in the South before the Civil War, Blackmon (2008: 61) characterized them as 'unimaginably sparse by modern standards.' Elected officials such as sheriff, district attorney, clerk and treasurer often had no employees. They were one-man government agencies.

No American history can ignore the Civil War (1860–65). Yet, it was such an anomalous event in public administration, that – oddly – little of permanent importance was created during the war. Rather, its *consequences* prompted the need for more administrative capabilities. According to Faust (2008: 268), the aftermath of the war was 'a vast expansion of the federal budget and bureaucracy and a reconceptualization of the government's role. National cemeteries, pensions and records that preserved names and identities involved a dramatically new understanding of the relationship of the citizen and the state.' Notwithstanding these developments in American public administration, Henry Adams described post-bellum Congresses as having 'contempt for matters of mere administration as of trifling importance' (quoted in Wills, 2005: 73). So, at that point, the pell-mell expansion of federal responsibilities was not accompanied by any perception of the need for professionalized public administration.

In the second half of the nineteenth century, the country was in the midst of transforming from rural and agricultural to urban and industrialized. Political machines emerged in those big cities. If immigrants voted for machine candidates, then it would provide them with services and assistance that traditionally were not provided by government. Largely a perversion of what President Jackson envisioned, when machines won elections they gave patronage jobs to their activists. Sometimes 'no show' government jobs, sometimes real but untaxing, their main responsibility was to keep the machine in power by helping it win future elections. The spoils system of rewards and punishment led, of course, to government agencies being staffed sometimes by an incompetent and disincentivized workforce. It also led to the granting of contracts for goods and services based on political graft and kickbacks, often at inflated prices and with shoddy products.

In summary, from the adoption of the Constitution to the late nineteenth century, the United States underwent major demographic, social, economic, geographical, technological and military changes. These inevitably affected the scope and size of all governments. Yet the basic constitutional framework of golem government was fixed. Political leaders responded to new public needs on an ad hoc basis, gave little thought to management issues, and staffed growing government largely with patronage appointments or Civil War veterans. Hence, it was a century of (relatively) small government and democratic administration.

RISING TIDE: THE PENDLETON ACT CREATES A FEDERAL CIVIL SERVICE, 1883

Second only to the Constitution in importance to US administrative history was the establishment of civil service systems. This was, incredibly, a brief moment when public administration was of broad-scale public interest. According to Morris, 'It is difficult for Americans living in the first quarter of the twenty-first century to understand the emotions which Civil Service Reform aroused in the last quarter of the nineteenth. … The fact remains that thousands, even millions, lined up behind the banner, and they were as evangelical (and as strenuously resisted) as any crusaders in history' (2010: 404–405). It was an authentic mass movement that had significant political appeal and greatly influenced legislative and executive decision making.

The corner-turning event at the federal level was the 1883 Pendleton Act, creating a federal civil service. Its origin was the British

Civil Service (Van Riper, 1976: 63–64). (But the sequence was different. In Western Europe, bureaucracy preceded democracy, while in the United States it was the reverse [Nelson, 1982].) The UK's merit-based and permanent workforce was very appealing, as was the clear differentiation between politics and administration, typified by each Cabinet department having a permanent under-secretary who was a civil servant. Ministers would come and go, but the staffing and leadership of the department would not.

In 1880, the National Civil Service Reform League was established to advocate for federal legislation. Its goals were open recruitment; merit-based examination and appointment, so that only qualified applicants were hired; evaluations and promotions based on merit; permanence in office; exclusion of civil servants from the political process (such as mandatory donations); and an independent commission to oversee and implement these goals.

Finally, in late 1882, Congress passed the Pendleton Act creating an authentic civil service system. President Chester Arthur signed it into law in early 1883. As with most major historical developments, there is no single explanation for the success of the reform movement in 1883. Besides the league's lobbying, other factors were public opinion's revulsion at the assassination of President Garfield in 1881 by a disappointed office seeker, partisan competition (Republicans did poorly in the 1882 Congressional elections and wanted to regain public favor), and the inefficiencies of the spoils system – namely, that patronage decisions consumed an inordinate amount of politicians' time and attention. Theriault (2005: 50) concluded that 'public pressure is at least as important in establishing the merit system as spoils system inefficiencies and party politics.'

The adoption of the Pendleton Act in 1883 was a kind of big bang moment, with energy from the center expanding outward long afterwards. First, the act initially covered only 10 percent of the federal workforce (Ingraham, 1995: 27). An indication of how fierce the rearguard resistance by the *ancien regime* was to expanding it, was that half a century later, as part of the recommendations of the 1937 Brownlow Committee, President Franklin Roosevelt still needed to urge expanding the classified service 'upward, outward, and downward to cover practically all non-policy-determining posts.' The death knell for federal patronage finally occurred in 1969, when newly-elected President Nixon decided that local postmasterships would no longer be given to reward party activists, such as those who helped him win election.

Second, the 1883 federal model was gradually adopted throughout the country. The first state was New York, where the idea was pushed by two future presidents, Republican Assemblyman Theodore Roosevelt and Democratic Governor Grover Cleveland (Morris, 2010: 171–172, 179–180). (Later, Roosevelt was a US Civil Service Commissioner, appointed by President Harrison and retained by President Cleveland [White, 2003].) From New York, civil service reform spread to other states, and was also gradually adopted by local governments (Roberts, 1996).

While civil service reform significantly contributed to the professionalization of American public administration, paradoxically, it added to the golemic nature of government. The permanent and professionalized workforce wanted 'their' agency to be successful. Besides job stability and continuity, they also had a *professional* interest in their agency's mission and future. This would include more funding, more programs, independence from political 'meddling,' a positive image in public opinion and active support from external stakeholders: in short, autonomy (Carpenter, 2001). However, autonomy exacerbated bureaucratic politics, subtly encouraging all manner of turf battles and resistance to change imposed from without. Cooperation and coordination were now more difficult than ever. The nascent federal leviathan was becoming more unwieldy, increasingly immune from control by a president, cabinet secretary or Congress.

Another unintended golemic consequence of civil service reform was the increasing cumbersomeness of internal agency operations. All manner of recruitment, appointment, promotion and discipline were regulated by highly detailed personnel policies that had been officially promulgated and had the force of law. Now agency leaders were less able to manage subordinates within the civil service, nearly immune from supervision. New initiatives would die on the vine if long-time and entrenched civil servants decided to wait out the current agency leadership. Political appointees would come and go, while civil servants remained in place permanently. The status quo would now become even harder to change.

BUREAUCRACY: BIG GOVERNMENT STAFFED BY EXPERT ADMINISTRATORS, 1883–1978

Roughly, the Progressive era followed closely upon the Pendleton Act. During that time good-government activists successfully pursued major reforms. They included, roughly in order of importance: the politics–administration dichotomy (Rosenbloom, 2008), efficiency and scientific management (Schachter, 1989), executive-centered government (Rubin, 1994), budgeting (Kahn, 1997), city managers (Stillman, 1974), the short ballot (Hirschhorn, 1997), neutral expertise (Finegold, 1995), reorganization (Arnold, 1998), public reporting (Lee, 2006a; Williams and Lee, 2008), and research bureaus (Lee, 2006b, 2008).

Generally, these were 'masculine' ideas of tough and unsentimental practices intended to make government operate like business. They were generated mostly by men (Stillman, 1998) who were sometimes anti-democratic and authoritarian. Often they were intended to reduce the voting power of the uneducated and supposedly easily led urban ethnic voters and blacks (Lee, 2011a). Furthermore, these reforms were largely process-oriented *methods*. Ostensibly, they were value-free and scientific: they were neither. For these men, government was akin to a machine with many moving parts. Their reforms would be to make the public sector more efficient and cheaper: in short, less golemic from an internal management perspective. However, the central theme of their reforms – making departments more professional and less responsive to elected officials – would make government as a whole more lumbering and less easy to coordinate.

Public administration also had a lesser known, softer, feminine side. In a nearly separate reality, women involved in settlement houses and other charities sought governmental reforms that were more oriented to ends, instead of means, such as social justice, fairness, equality, education, quality of life and opportunity (Stivers, 2000; Schachter, 2010). It is more than a coincidence that the leading theorist for a more cooperation-based form of management was a woman, Mary Parker Follett (Tonn, 2003). Unlike the men, these women believed in democracy's potential benefits to all citizens.

The presidencies of Theodore Roosevelt and Woodrow Wilson during the Progressive era stand out as extraordinary in expanding the scope and responsibilities of the federal government and, especially, a greater role in regulating the political economy. Initiatives included trust-busting, more effective regulation of railroads, greater legitimacy to labor unions, a Federal Trade Commission to assure fair competition, a Federal Reserve System to stabilize monetary policy, a Bureau of the Budget to construct annual presidential proposals for Congress, the Department of Labor, and major expansions of the US Forest Service and national parks.

While the Progressive era faded by 1920, big government was gaining, not losing, momentum. President Hoover came into office in 1929 with a reputation as the 'Great Engineer.' As such, he wanted government machinery to operate more efficiently. In reaction to the stock market crash, and

contrary to a historical image of passivity and dogmatism, he constantly searched for potential federal initiatives to restore the economy that were compatible with his ideology. They included the Reconstruction Finance Corporation and major public works projects such as a dam that was later named after him.

Still, the presidency of Franklin D. Roosevelt (FDR) is appropriately associated with the phenomenal growth of 'big government.' To overcome the Great Depression through Keynesian economics of deficit spending, Roosevelt greatly increased the scope and role of the federal government. Creating an alphabet soup of 'New Deal' agencies, Roosevelt constructed a welfare state to help the 'one-third of a nation ill-housed, ill-clad, ill-nourished.' Reforms included banking and stock regulation, Social Security, full legitimacy for labor unions, farmer production subsidies and unemployment benefits. Then World War II arrived, with increased defense spending and a large standing military.

The United States would never be the same, nor would American public administration. For example, before FDR, social welfare organizations were largely charities funded by donations. Now, nearly every state and county had a public welfare department that administered an array of programs (largely federally financed) to help those in need. More generally, Roosevelt's Brownlow Committee recommended major changes to improve the 'administrative management'of the federal government. Roosevelt believed that the purpose of reorganization was not to save money ('efficiency'), but to improve operations ('effectiveness'). Congress wasn't particularly enthusiastic about *that*, especially about strengthening the presidency vis-à-vis itself.

The permanence of Roosevelt's administrative infrastructure became clear at the beginning of Eisenhower's presidency in 1953. Republican conservatives in Congress had fiercely resisted almost all of Roosevelt and Truman's domestic policies, arguing they were a threat to capitalism, invaded personal freedoms and infringed on the roles of state and local governments. They expected Eisenhower to restore the status quo ante Roosevelt. He didn't. The New Deal stayed in place.

Big government reached its apex during the presidency of Lyndon Baines Johnson (LBJ), who declared a national War on Poverty, believing that the combination of public administration, funding and social science experts could wipe it out permanently. In the 1960s, Bell (2000) wondered if America was on the threshold of the 'End of Ideology,' because all social problems could seemingly be solved. But disenchantment with big government ultimately set in. Banfield (1990) viewed the limited results of the War on Poverty as confirmation that bureaucracy and expertise could not solve deeply rooted urban social problems. Pressman and Wildavsky (1984) tracked what came of some 1960s economic development funding – not much.

Still, Light (2002) made a strong case that such generalizations were too sweeping and pessimistic. Randomly surveying political scientists and historians, he compiled a list of the 50 greatest achievements of the national government in the second half of the twentieth century, rated by degree of difficulty, importance and success. Some were high profile and relatively obvious, such as rebuilding Europe after World War II (1), civil rights (2 & 3), the interstate highway system (7), reducing pollution (11 & 15), containing communism (14) and space exploration (25). Many others, however, were long-term and incremental goals, rarely the subject of public attention. As such, they were largely invisible. They were accomplished by slow and unglamorous, but persistent, bureaucracies. Those public administration successes included reducing disease (4), safer food and drinking water (6), scientific R&D (13), workplace safety (16), reducing hunger (18), expansion of higher education (19), consumer protection (20), arms control (23) and protecting wilderness areas (24). All in

all, some major *accomplishments* by the bureaucratic state, its critics and doubters notwithstanding.

But, by now, bureaucracy was beginning to be perceived as a kind of living and breathing organism that had a life of its own, including immutable behavioral rules (Downs, 1994; Wilson, 2000). Light (1995) wrote of the automatic 'thickening' that happened in federal agencies. That echoed the 1950s' 'Parkinson's Law': that 'work expands so as to fill the time available to do it.' Parkinson light-heartedly suggested this was especially true in public administration, because: 'An official wants to multiply subordinates' and 'Officials make work for each other' (Parkinson, 1957: 4).

Gradually, it became clear to Congresses and presidents of the need to oversee and control the federal leviathan they had created. In a landmark decision, in 1946, Congress enacted the Administrative Procedures Act. This imposed a formal legal-style framework for major decision making within the bureaucracy. Congress followed up with additional rules of the game. Rosenbloom (2000) suggested that this wholly redefined federal management into a *legislative-centered* public administration. Still, despite all of Congress's efforts, it appeared the bureaucracy had the upper hand, even in a showdown with Congress's much vaunted power of the purse (Lee, 2011b).

At the other end of Pennsylvania Avenue, presidents too were seeking ways to herd recalcitrant agencies. Presidents were now engulfed by 'the managerial presidency' (Arnold, 1998). Viewed from the other end of the telescope, they wanted to make the federal bureaucracy more 'presidentialized' (Durant and Resh, 2010).

The vast expansion of the federal government, especially by FDR and LBJ, reflected a high-water mark in US administrative history. It embodied the somewhat naïve American optimism that government could be the solution to social problems and management of the political economy – notwithstanding the Constitution. As a corollary to that, large civil service bureaucracies were viewed as the best vehicle for delivering those solutions. If politicians and politics would just get out of the way, the administrative state would achieve the Good Life. Instead, bureaucracy had become relatively ungovernable and unmanageable. This was a definitive manifestation of golem government, even with its signal accomplishments during the twentieth century.

RECEDING TIDE: THE CIVIL SERVICE REFORM ACT, 1978

President Reagan famously said that 'government is not the solution to our problem; government *is* the problem.' However, the initial effort to undo the rigidities of civil service was by his predecessor, Jimmy Carter. Carter, another engineer, claimed that he had been successful as Georgia's governor partly because of his reforms, such as reorganizing state agencies into a handful of super-departments. By now, the conventional wisdom was that golem government was partly caused by an ossified, bureaucratized and overly autonomous civil service. Actually, it was also partly caused by bureaucrat-bashing politicians who were loading more and more restraints on agency operations.

Carter proposed major changes and Congress agreed, passing the 1978 Civil Service Reform Act. It reduced the scope of civil service positions at the top levels of agencies, creating instead a Senior Executive Service. The thinking was that major policy-making positions should be outside the neutral and permanent civil service. The new law (and accompanying reorganization) abolished the Civil Service Commission, largely replacing it with an Office Personnel Management, a staff agency to the president, not an independent commission. Whistleblowers would now have legal protections from reprisals. Separately, the ban on political activities by federal civil servants (called the Hatch Act) was also largely repealed. In toto, this was not a complete nullification of the Pendleton Act, but it was a rollback of its major principles (Pfiffner and Brook, 2000).

Significantly, the National Civil Service Reform League also changed. It was no longer the guardian of the traditional approach to maximal civil service systems. Instead, it issued a new model civil service law that went against its own earlier orthodoxy. Then, the League endorsed many of the principles in Carter's reform law. The beneficiaries of the status quo, as well as the heirs of the earlier good-government reformers, were horrified. By 1980, the organization collapsed, exactly a century after its founding. The League's implosion symbolized the end of an era in American administrative history.

The 1978 law then influenced major reforms to state and local government civil service systems (Lee, 1979; Bowman and West, 2007). After a century, the belief that professionalized bureaucracy would bring better and more successful government had ebbed. It needed to be substantially reformed, even replaced, everyone agreed. But with what? No one was quite sure. Identifying a problem is easy: solving it is the hard part.

POST-BUREAUCRACY: PUBLIC MANAGEMENT BY EVERYBODY AND NOBODY, 1978–PRESENT

Had golem government died with the 1978 Civil Service Reform Act? No. After all, only a major revision of the US Constitution could truly accomplish that. Still, President Clinton declared, 'The era of big government is over.' Now American public administration was being reformulated. The management of governmental goods and services splayed out in different, even contradictory directions.

Some argued that the way to reduce golem government was to make it operate more like a business, including being more entrepreneurial and risk-taking. 'Down with bureaucracy!'

said the New Public Management movement. It strongly appealed to politicians, regardless of party – but just as long as no agency facilities in their districts were closed or reduced. Another idea was that measuring performance was the only thing that counted. Impliedly, if it couldn't be measured, government shouldn't do it. Technology offered new options as well, with G2C (government-to-customer) e-government having the potential of increasing efficiency. Congressional conservatives were awash with ideas for 'starving the beast,' while moderates simply aimed at taming it: more general management laws, more coordination, more limitations and prohibitions, inspectors general and lots of 'chief' officers in each department, such as for finance, information, and human resources (Stanton and Ginsberg, 2004).

A major idea was to shift from government as the provider of goods and services (by civil servants) to merely the financer, contracting with non-profits and business to deliver them; ibid for routine internal management services, such as security, janitorial services, or contact centers. The main role of the public administrator was as a contract manager (Cohen and Eimicke, 2008). This was sometimes called the hollowing out of the state or networked government. Pressing from the other direction, some reformers called for more citizen participation, more openness and more democratic administration (Stivers, 2008).

Drawing conclusions from poor governmental performance during 9/11 and Hurricane Katrina, Kettl (2009) suggested that effective government management in the future would entail complex partnerships, blended contributions to shared outcomes, information-based action, bureaucracies as holding companies for expertise, fluidity and flexibility, and the development of relationships of trust before crises.

Exactly 30 years after the 1978 Civil Service Reform Act, Roberts reviewed the performance of the Bush II administration. He described significant developments that had greatly 'undercut the power of the executive branch *in the past three decades*,' i.e. since 1978 (Roberts, 2008: 165, emphasis added). Those changes included growing institutional complexity, imposition of additional limits on agency activities by Congress, distrust of the bureaucracy, a fraying ethos of fidelity, and new information and communication technologies. As a result, he concluded, 'the predicament of contemporary governance' was not an imperial presidency, but actually a dysfunctional government, incapable of acting effectively (Roberts, 2008: 174).

Light (2008: 237), too, noted the thirtieth anniversary of the Act by observing that 'Congress and the president have shown little interest at least since the 1978 Civil Service Reform Act in enacting the kind of sweeping reforms' in governance and public administration that were needed. The political system seemed unable to make big decisions; hence, inadequate management of the federal and other levels of government just stumbled forward. Contemporary American government reflected ad hoc, stop-start, flavor-of-the-month fads, path-of-least-resistance and crisis-reacting non-decisions.

A HISTORY OF THE FUTURE

In part, the contemporary argument over improving public management echoed an unresolved argument from the past. Which was the key word in 'public administration': 'public' or 'administration'? Was the governmental (and Constitutional) context relatively minor? Was it essentially like business administration? If so, public ADMINISTRATION. Or, was the different context so crucial that management of a public agency was qualitatively different from business? Sayre quipped that private and public management were 'fundamentally alike in all unimportant respects' (Allison, 1980). So, from that perspective, PUBLIC administration.

The rough answer to this either-or question, it seems, is plainly there to see.

In American culture, 'big is beautiful:' homes, TV screens, food portions and stadia. Americans don't even seem to mind the oligopolies of big business all that much. But there's one thing they definitely *don't* like big – government. Citizens do not think of public administration as a value-adding activity; they only stereotype bureaucrats as wasting time inventing red tape to harass the innocent. It is now a convention to run for office *against* government, as an outsider. Government is bad. If so, then the answer is: ~~public administration~~.

Or, perhaps more precisely, Americans want from government what they want from airlines: cheap prices and high-quality service. The mail should be delivered six days a week, not five. Homeland security should prevent every terrorist attack. Airports should be 100 percent secure, but without any hassles or inconvenience. Zero tolerance for emergency and crisis responses which were less than instantaneous. And – by the way – taxes are too high.

Having it both ways has been reinforced by politicians themselves. Like customer relations, politicians convey that the voter is never wrong. The message is 'Cut government spending, cut my taxes, but don't reduce the services I benefit from.' Will these contradictory impulses of Americans toward government – low taxes and high services – inevitably be joined? Some are sure that a moment of truth is guaranteed, when unsustainability truly becomes unsustainable. Root canal reform may be just around the corner, to be faced after the next election.

But, historically, this does not seem to be the case. It didn't happen with FDR's deficit spending. After Jimmy Carter's televised address on energy policy (the so-called 'malaise speech') urged sacrifice, Americans turned away, preferring the sunny optimism of Ronald Reagan's supply-side economics. Everybody gets what they want. The same holds true when the Bush II tax cuts were extended in 2011, both for the middle class and the wealthy in the face of massive deficits. In a kind of political Gresham's Law,

candidates who promise tax cuts and no reductions in popular programs such as Social Security and Medicare do better than promising only blood, sweat, tears, and toil. Let the good times roll!

So, what is the next chapter of American administrative history? Bet on more of the same. Golem government is here to stay.

REFERENCES

Allison, Graham T., Jr (1980) 'Public and Private Management: Are They Fundamentally Alike in All Unimportant Respects?', in *Setting Public Management Research Agendas: Integrating the Sponsor, Producer and User*. Washington, DC: US Office of Personnel Management.

Arnold, Peri E. (1998) *Making the Managerial Presidency: Comprehensive Reorganization Planning, 1905–1996*, 2nd edn. Lawrence, KS: University Press of Kansas.

Balogh, Brian (2009) *A Government Out of Sight: The Mystery of National Authority in Nineteenth-Century America*. New York: Cambridge University Press.

Banfield, Edward C. (1990 [1974]) *The Unheavenly City Revisited*. Prospect Heights, IL: Waveland.

Bell, Daniel (2000 [1962]) *The End of Ideology: On the Exhaustion of Political Ideas in the Fifties*. Cambridge, MA: Harvard University Press.

Bertelli, Anthony M. and Lynn, Laurence E., Jr (2006) *Madison's Managers: Public Administration and the Constitution*. Baltimore, MD: Johns Hopkins University Press.

Blackmon, Douglas A. (2008) *Slavery by Another Name: The Re-Enslavement of Black People in America from the Civil War to World War II*. New York: Doubleday.

Bowman, James S. and West, Jonathan P. (eds) (2007) *American Public Service: Radical Reform and the Merit System*. Boca Raton, FL: CRC Press.

Carpenter, Daniel P. (2001) *The Forging of Bureaucratic Autonomy: Reputations, Networks, and Policy Innovation in Executive Agencies, 1862–1928*. Princeton, NJ: Princeton University Press.

Cohen, Steven and Eimicke, William (2008) *The Responsible Contract Manager: Protecting the Public Interest in an Outsourced World*. Washington, DC: Georgetown University Press.

Downs, Anthony (1994 [1967]) *Inside Bureaucracy*. Prospect Heights, IL: Waveland.

Durant, Robert F. and Resh, William G. (2010) '"Presidentializing" the Bureaucracy', in Robert F. Durant (ed.), *Oxford Handbook of American Bureaucracy* (pp. 545–568). Oxford: Oxford University Press.

Faust, Drew Gilpin (2008) *This Republic of Suffering: Death and the American Civil War*. New York: Alfred A. Knopf.

Finegold, Kenneth (1995) *Experts and Politicians: Reform Challenges to Machine Politics in New York, Cleveland, and Chicago*. Princeton, NJ: Princeton University Press.

Hirschhorn, Bernard (1997) *Democracy Reformed: Richard Spencer Childs and His Fight for Better Government*. Westport, CT: Greenwood.

Hoffer, Williamjames Hull (2007) *To Enlarge the Machinery of Government: Congressional Debates and the Growth of the American State, 1858–1891*. Baltimore, MD: Johns Hopkins University Press.

Ingraham, Patricia Wallace (1995) *The Foundation of Merit: Public Service in American Democracy*. Baltimore, MD: Johns Hopkins University Press.

John, Richard R. (1995) *Spreading the News: The American Postal System from Franklin to Morse*. Cambridge, MA: Harvard University Press.

Kahn, Jonathan (1997) *Budgeting Democracy: State Building and Citizenship in America, 1890–1928*. Ithaca, NY: Cornell University Press.

Kennedy, Roger G. (2003) *Mr. Jefferson's Lost Cause: Land, Farmers, Slavery, and the Louisiana Purchase*. New York: Oxford University Press.

Kettl, Donald F. (2009) *The Next Government of the United States: Why Our Institutions Fail Us and How to Fix Them*. New York: W.W. Norton.

Koeppel, Gerard (2009) *Bond of Union: Building the Erie Canal and the American Empire*. Cambridge, MA: Da Capo.

Lee, Mordecai (1979) 'Personnel Management in Wisconsin', in Selma J. Mushkin (ed.), *Proposition 13 and Its Consequences for Public Management* (pp. 101–105). Washington, DC: Council for Applied Social Research.

Lee, Mordecai (2006a) 'The History of Municipal Public Reporting', *International Journal of Public Administration*, 29(4–6): 453–476.

Lee, Mordecai (2006b) *Institutionalizing Congress and the Presidency: The U.S. Bureau of Efficiency, 1916–1933*. College Station, TX: Texas A&M University Press.

Lee, Mordecai (2008) *Bureaus of Efficiency: Reforming Local Government in the Progressive Era*. Milwaukee, WI: Marquette University Press.

Lee, Mordecai (2010) *Nixon's Super-Secretaries: The Last Grand Presidential Reorganization Effort*. College Station, TX: Texas A&M University Press.

Lee, Mordecai (2011a) 'History of US Public Administration in the Progressive Era: Efficient Government by and for Whom?', *Journal of Management History*, 17(1): 88–101.

Lee, Mordecai (2011b) *Congress vs. the Bureaucracy: Muzzling Agency Public Relations*. Norman, OK: University of Oklahoma Press.

Light, Paul C. (1995) *Thickening Government: Federal Hierarchy and the Diffusion of Accountability*. Washington, DC: Brookings Institution.

Light, Paul C. (2002) *Government's Greatest Achievements: From Civil Rights to Homeland Defense*. Washington, DC: Brookings Institution.

Light, Paul C. (2008) *A Government Ill Executed: The Decline of the Federal Service and How to Reverse It*. Cambridge, MA: Harvard University Press.

McCullough, David (2001) *John Adams*. New York: Simon & Schuster.

Moe, Ronald C. (2001) 'The Emerging Federal Quasi Government: Issues of Management and Accountability', *Public Administration Review*, 61(3): 290–312.

Morris, Edmund (2010 [2001]) *The Rise of Theodore Roosevelt*, revised edn. New York: Random House.

Nelson, Michael (1982) 'A Short, Ironic History of American National Bureaucracy', *Journal of Politics*, 44(3): 747–778.

Newbold, Stephanie P. (2010) *All But Forgotten: Thomas Jefferson and the Development of Public Administration*. Albany, NY: State University of New York Press.

Parkinson, C. Northcote (1957) *Parkinson's Law: And other Studies in Administration*. Boston, MA: Houghton Mifflin.

Peters, B. Guy (2010) *American Public Policy: Promise and Performance*, 8th edn. Washington, DC: CQ Press.

Pfiffner, James P. and Brook, Douglas A. (eds) (2000) *The Future of Merit: Twenty Years After the Civil Service Reform Act*. Washington, DC: Woodrow Wilson Center Press.

Pressman, Jeffrey L. and Wildavsky, Aaron (1984) *Implementation: How Great Expectations in Washington Are Dashed in Oakland*, 3rd edn. Berkeley, CA: University of California Press.

Raadschelders, Jos C. N. (2010) 'Is American Public Administration Detached From Historical Context?', *American Review of Public Administration*, 40(3): 235–260.

Roberts, Alasdair (1996) *So-Called Experts: How American Consultants Remade the Canadian Civil Service, 1918–21*. Toronto: Institute of Public Administration of Canada.

Roberts, Alasdair (2008) *The Collapse of Fortress Bush: The Crisis of Authority in American Government*. New York: New York University Press.

Rosenbloom, David (2008) 'The Politics–Administration Dichotomy in U.S. Historical Context', *Public Administration Review*, 68(1): 57–60.

Rosenbloom, David H. (2000) *Building a Legislative-Centered Public Administration: Congress and the Administrative State, 1946–1999*. Tuscaloosa, AL: University of Alabama Press.

Rosten, Leo (2001) *The New Joys of Yiddish*. New York: Crown.

Rubin, Irene S. (1994) 'Early Budget Reformers: Democracy, Efficiency, and Budget Reform', *American Review of Public Administration*, 24(3): 229–252.

Schachter, Hindy Lauer (1989) *Frederick Taylor and the Public Administration Community: A Reevaluation*. Albany, NY: State University of New York Press.

Schachter, Hindy Lauer (2010) 'A Gendered Legacy? The Progressive Reform Era Revisited', in Robert F. Durant (ed.), *Oxford Handbook of American Bureaucracy* (pp. 77–100). Oxford: Oxford University Press.

Simon, Herbert A. (1997) *Administrative Behavior: A Study of Decision-Making Processes in Administrative Organization*, 4th edn. New York: Free Press.

Stanton, Thomas H. and Ginsberg, Benjamin (eds) (2004) *Making Government Manageable: Executive Organization and Management in the Twenty-First Century*. Baltimore, MD: Johns Hopkins University Press.

Stillman, Richard J., II (1974) *The Rise of the City Manager: A Public Professional in City Government*. Albuquerque, NM: University of New Mexico Press.

Stillman, Richard J., II (1998) *Creating the American State: The Moral Reformers and the Modern Administrative World They Made*. Tuscaloosa, AL: University of Alabama Press.

Stivers, Camilla (2000) *Bureau Men, Settlement Women: Constructing Public Administration in the Progressive Era*. Lawrence, KS: University Press of Kansas.

Stivers, Camilla (2008) *Governance in Dark Times: Practical Philosophy for Public Service*. Washington, DC: Georgetown University Press.

Theriault, Sean M. (2005) *The Power of the People: Congressional Competition, Public Attention, and Voter Retribution*. Columbus, OH: Ohio State University Press.

Tonn, Joan C. (2003) *Mary P. Follett: Creating Democracy, Transforming Management*. New Haven, CT: Yale University Press.

Van Riper, Paul P. (1976 [1958]) *History of the United States Civil Service*. Westport, CT: Greenwood.

White, Richard D., Jr (2003) *Roosevelt the Reformer: Theodore Roosevelt as Civil Service Commissioner, 1889–1895*. Tuscaloosa, AL: University of Alabama Press.

Williams, Daniel W. and Lee, Mordecai (2008) 'Déjà Vu All Over Again: Contemporary Traces of the Budget Exhibit', *American Review of Public Administration*, 38(2): 203–224.

Wills, Garry (1999) *A Necessary Evil: A History of American Distrust of Government*. New York: Simon & Schuster.

Wills, Garry (2005) *Henry Adams and the Making of America*. Boston, MA: Houghton Mifflin.

Wilson, James Q. (2000) *Bureaucracy: What Government Agencies Do and Why They Do It*, new edn. New York: Basic Books.

12

Administrative Legacies in Western Europe

Fabio Rugge

It is the purpose of this chapter to trace some of the major historical developments that provide the background of today's public administrations. This will be done with the intention of delineating legacies of particular relevance to our contemporary scene.[1]

The account will focus on public administrations in the four largest European countries: France, Germany, Italy and the United Kingdom. This choice is not based on a hierarchical appreciation of the various European traditions. It rather depends on the present state of the art in comparative administrative history (Raadschelders, 1998) – and on the limits set to this chapter, which oblige the author to neglect even some traditionally acknowledged differences between the national cases under review (Heady, 2001; Peters, 1988).

In this chapter no illustration will be provided of the history of the civil service as a social group, nor of the changing features of bureaucratic work. Instead of such 'bureauhistory', special attention will be paid to the governmental penetration of civil society as reflected in the history of the past two centuries.

WHEN IT ALL BEGAN

In contrast to political systems and constitutional arrangements, administrative regimes do not experience that sort of thorough collapses or all-pervading transitions that enable historians to speak of 'new eras' or of 'turning points'.[2] Thus, periodization may become particularly controversial when administrative history is at stake. Nonetheless, no administrative system is isolated from the institutional framework, both political and constitutional, in which it operates. This means that major changes affecting that framework inevitably reverberate on the administrative structures.

Now, the decades prior to 1850 witnessed crucial developments in the sphere of political institutions and the establishment of a new constitutional era. That era had been inaugurated as early as 1787 by the American constitution and, a few years later, by the French revolutionary instruments. Still, the whole first half of the following century had to pass by before a new generation of constitutions spread all over Europe, making constitutional government a permanent feature of most polities.

This great transformation brought about two processes crucial to the development of modern public administration: the end of the so-called 'kingly administrations' (Dreyfus, 2000; Wilson, 1887) and the invention of the politics/administration dichotomy.

As to the first, the adoption of constitutional arrangements entailed that state administration would no longer hinge on the figure of the monarch. And as the state became increasingly depersonalized, the *crown*'s servants were gradually replaced by the *state*'s servants (Jakoby, 1973; Raadschelders and Rutgers, 1996; Rosenberg, 1958) and modern administrative apparatuses developed.

Notwithstanding this restructuring, 'kingly administrations' were not truly superseded until the beginning of the nineteenth century,[3] when new 'princes' arose to claim command over public administration: elected parliaments, speaking in the name of 'the people'. Such a takeover caused relevant changes. In particular, three great administrative issues emerged.

First, just as the 'kingly administration' had served the sovereign's interests, the new 'constitutional administration' was to serve the interests of the 'people', as they were represented in the parliament. Now, in the presence of a liberal-democratic pressure to enlarge the franchise, a proliferation of the represented interests was inevitable in terms both of the issues and of the social groups concerned (Rokkan, 1970). That opened the question as to whether the constitutional administration should take care of those issues and of those social groups through regulative action or through direct intervention. This question, and the solutions given to it, will be addressed later in the chapter.

Secondly, the end of the 'kingly administrations' and the rise of a new constellation of constitutional values meant that any autocratic vein had to be removed from administrative procedures. Administration should no longer act so as to follow to the monarch's arbitrary will, but only according to the law

and *therefore* entirely respecting all individual rights enshrined in the constitution and in the laws.[4]

Finally, a third great issue was brought about by the new constitutional era: the differentiation between politics and administration. This issue will be addressed first.

THE POLITICS/ADMINISTRATION DICHOTOMY

Traditionally, public administration has been conceptualized as distinct from and often as the opposite of politics: its virtuous sister to some, its dull servant to others. The distinction between the two spheres has often been regarded as obvious, their separation as desirable.

Although such a distinction is very problematic in theory and separation has proved more than problematic in practice,[5] no one can deny that these ideas have represented a mighty intellectual pattern, which strongly contributed to shaping modern public administration. For this reason, the pattern and the reality behind it deserve some scrutiny.

First, the separation of politics and administration found a long-lasting anchorage in the doctrine about the separation of powers. According to this doctrine, and to its subsequent adjustments, the executive power, and therefore the administration, must be separated from both the legislative and the judiciary and be exclusively charged with the task of implementing the legislator's will.

Second – and paradoxically – the permanence of some *ancien régime* features fostered the new politics/administration dichotomy. In particular, the persistent influence of the crown over the bureaucracy (for instance, in countries like Prussia) helped permeate administration with a unitary, hierarchical spirit and shape the image of the deferential civil servants (the opposite of the allegedly quarrelsome and treacherous politician).

Third, around the mid-nineteenth century, a new practical factor came to support the politics/administration dichotomy: a growing functional differentiation between the profession of the politician and that of the bureaucrat. For politicians, parliamentary life became more and more demanding, while ministers found it increasingly difficult to deal with the details of state affairs. For civil servants, especially in the high and middle ranks of the bureaucratic pyramid, the complexity and technicality of their work intensified. And the diffusion of the merit system, although the outcome of many other circumstances (and undermined by the persistence of a variety of social privileges) clearly signalled that a certain educational background was required for this kind of work (Cassese and Pellew, 1987; Wunder, 2005).

However, in spite of the three factors just recalled, it would be hazardous to argue that in the past 150 years politics and administration have represented two entirely different enterprises (Rugge, 2007). From the mid-nineteenth century on, at least two major, convergent drives have urged the encroachment of politicians into the administrative arena: the need for loyal cooperation and the exercise of patronage. As an outcome of these two pressures, a sort of politico-administrative continuum has usually emerged, blurring the border between the two spheres. The reasons are clear (Raadschelders and Van der Meer, 1998).

As to the politician's need for loyal cooperation from the side of the civil service, this is an obvious precondition for any effective governmental action. In fact, it was felt to be critical in all parliamentary systems from the very outset of the new constitutional era.

In the United Kingdom, a solution to possible frictions between politicians and bureaucrats was adopted that consisted in the 'neutralizing' of the civil service: whatever the party in power, administration would steadfastly follow its policy. Such an arrangement, based on the acknowledgement of the civil servant's professionalism, is congruent with the politics/administration dichotomy, but removes the conflicting component from it, featuring in fact a sort of fusion of the political and the administrative spheres (Thomas, 1978).

A different tradition prevailed in countries like France and Italy, where the politicization of the public administration became the rule. Basically, this was achieved in two ways. On the one hand, ministerial cabinets were created in order to reinforce the minister's grip over the bureaucracy (Antoine, 1975; Rugge, 1998; Thuillier, 1982). On the other hand, the higher administrative positions were covered through appointment by the government. Such was the case with the prefects – key figures in these two centralized states – whose appointments and transfers very often had clear partisan purposes (Le Clère and Wright, 1973). The politicization of higher civil servants affected Germany too, and it was institutionalized through the figure of the *politischer Beamte* (political civil servant) (Fisch, 2007).

But patronage has been the main breach in the politics/administration dichotomy (although this practice has been traditionally blamed in European political discourse). In particular, the rise of mass parties at the end of the nineteenth and the beginning of the twentieth century reinforced this tendency, creating new stimulants for it. First, mass parties collected and drilled a host of potential seekers of administrative positions. Second, mass parties were based on political creeds, demanding unflinching loyalty. In this kind of polity, ideological affinity between political and administrative officeholders was considered crucial and, indeed, became critical.

The outcome of this change may be observed in its most acute manifestation in the authoritarian regimes of the 1920s and the 1930s. For instance, both Italian Fascism and German National Socialism – the prototypes of that kind of regime in Europe – disclaimed the liberal tenet about the separation between politics and administration; both preached the ideal of a state entirely pervaded by one ideology and commanded by one leader.[6]

However, the two regimes were not equally successful in fulfilling their ideal. In Germany, Hitler's coming to power brought about a far-reaching change (not to say purge) in the higher ranks of public administration; but that did not avoid persistent tensions between the Nazi party and traditional bureaucracy (for instance, as to the recruitment procedures) (Caplan, 1988; Hattenhauer, 1980; Mommsen, 1966; Wunder, 1986). In Italy, the attempt to produce a civil service in 'black shirts' ended up with a tacit compromise (Melis, 1996; Salvati, 1992).

Where Mussolini had a free hand was in those administrative bodies that Fascism itself had created in order to discharge some of the new tasks the state took upon itself throughout the interwar period. In this sort of 'parallel' public administration (see next section), Fascism could place new men with a special reputation for their ideological allegiance to the regime or their administrative talents (Melis, 1996).

Seemingly peculiar to the Fascist regime, this process in fact designs a pattern replicated elsewhere and later on too – in democratic and multiparty systems. Indeed, twentieth-century governments and leading politicians have often enough been confronted with a state bureaucracy they perceived – and sometimes denounced – as sclerotic, incompetent or inefficient. Typically, such complaints had to do with the lack of politic affinity between the civil servants and their political masters or with the resistance put up by the bureaucrats to politicians' encroachments into 'their' administrative territory.

Furthermore, by the end of the twentieth century, political leaders grew often impatient with the traditional type of high officer, and started seeking the support of a more managerial, result-oriented, even spin-doctoring sort of counsellors. Thus the United Kingdom itself, with its tradition of a neutral senior civil service, witnessed the creation of a class of 'political advisers',

challenging the role of the career officers: a politicization practise that, according to some critics, jeopardized the Whitehall standards of non-partisan policy making (Blick, 2004; Theakstone, 2007).

In any event, governments frequently reacted to perceived bureaucratic 'resistance' by circumventing state bureaucracies deemed insufficiently cooperative. Thus, they increasingly resorted – in order to implement their policies – to administrative apparatuses located outside the typical ministerial framework. In pursuing such an 'outflanking strategy', state executives probably responded to a true need for effectiveness as much to their drive for patronage.

THE ROAD TO 'BIG GOVERNMENT' – AND BACK

The creation of administrative structures outside the typical ministries or departments is connected with a well-known phenomenon: the growth of government, i.e. the increase in number and latitude of the socially relevant matters for which government or other public agencies make themselves responsible.

In fact, the idea that the state's responsibility towards society was not limited to 'law and order' was a commonly shared view and an established practice long before the mid-nineteenth century, especially on the Continent. Yet it was neither obvious nor undisputed that further state intervention should mean direct operation of public services rather than regulation of the supplying of those services through private trading or voluntary organizations.

In the years around 1850, the idea of regulative – instead of operative – state intervention probably reached the zenith of its popularity among European ruling classes (although hardly any task already assumed by the state was in those years relinquished to societal actors [Ellwein, 1965]). Also from this point of view as well as from the point of view of constitutional developments, these years may well be considered a turning point, as the regulative approach started yielding to a more operative-oriented philosophy.

From that moment on, the ideals of the minimal state and of the free market began to decline. From the 1880s and 1890s on, the prevalence of the statist tendency became more and more evident and for the century to come practically irreversible (Ashford, 1986). Government grew bigger; and so did public administration. A good piece of evidence of the process is supplied by the figures concerning the public expenditures for civilian purposes.

Table 12.1 shows how, in the four countries considered here, the per capita public expenditure at constant prices grew in the period between 1880 and 1910 (1910 = 100). In the same period, also, the percentage of people employed in the civil service in all levels of public administration increased, especially in the United Kingdom and Germany, as shown in Table 12.2. The figures offered in Tables 12.1 and 12.2 are not totally reliable (also the state's ability to 'count itself' was a product of the development

Table 12.1 Per capita public expenditure, 1880–1910

	1880	1910
France	81	100
Prussia/Germany	48	100
Italy	51	100[a]
United Kingdom	67	100

[a]Year 1912.
Source: Mann (1993: Ch.11); Italy, Cassese (1977); see also Note 7.

Table 12.2 Percentage of total population engaged in all levels of public administration, 1880–1910

	1880	1910
France	1.28	1.42
Prussia/Germany	1.56	2.35
Italy	0.97	0.99
United Kingdom	0.46	2.60

Source: Mann (1993: Ch.11); Italy, Cassese (1977); see also Note 7.

under consideration);[7] nevertheless, they consistently point to an upward trend of the financial and personnel resources wielded by public administrations.

The numerical evidence of the growth of government is supplemented by morphological evidence (Rosanvallon, 1990). The design of public administrations in each country became increasingly differentiated and intricate: new ministries, departments, offices and authorities were established. Sometimes this was the result of a process of functional specialization, sometimes of the necessity to cope with an emergency, sometimes of merely symbolic adjustments.

If we simply look at the central administration and at its typical units – the ministries or the departments – their very name and order of appearance are testimony to the process under scrutiny.

First to appear, often long before the period under consideration, were the ministries for internal and foreign affairs, war and justice – all bound to the state's classical task of preserving the country from internal and external threats – and the ministries of finance or the treasury set out to extract financial resources necessary for discharging the aforementioned task (Mayntz, 1982). But from the 1880s and for the following century, the government's engagement in a number of new fields was institutionalized, supported and displayed by the creation of a host of special ministries.

The path and pace of such a parade of ministries are to a large extent related to the idiosyncrasies of each country's history. Still, a number of departments and other administrative bodies were the result of international events and political movements, which produced cross-national 'generations of ministries'. In 1916 and 1917, with the establishment of the Ministry of Pensions and of Labour, respectively, the United Kingdom inaugurated a wave of homologous institutions like the German *Arbeitsministerium* (1918–19), the Italian *Ministero del lavoro e della previdenza sociale* (1920), the French *Ministère d'Hygiène et de la Prévoyance sociale* (1920). Similarly, at the local government level, in the early twentieth century, utility companies, owned and managed by the municipal corporations (in German *Gemeindebetriebe,* in Italian *aziende municipalizzate*), spread all over Europe.

In sum, from the mid-nineteenth century on, both the figures and the morphology of the administrative complex account for a relentless march towards 'big government'. A discussion of the factors causing this progression lies outside the scope of this chapter. Nonetheless, a couple of those factors may be mentioned while detailing some aspects of the process.

First, there is no doubt that government reacted to direct or systemic pressure to provide the infrastructure necessary for economic development. This meant that an often reluctant state got involved in the provision of important services. The post was a traditional state-operated service; but state railways and telephone were the fruit of the blooming statist season between 1880 and 1914. Germany nationalized its railways from the 1880s, with Prussia as a forerunner in 1879; France, after a timid and almost forced beginning in 1878, purchased a more substantial network from a private company in 1908; the Italian government began to run the entire railway system in 1905 (while the United Kingdom chose the 'regulative option' until 1947). The nationwide telephone systems experienced a similar shift from private to public ownership and operation (France, 1889; Germany, 1892; the UK, 1896–98; and Italy, 1907) (Bertho-Lavenir, 1991).

On a local basis – and in particular in the rapidly expanding cities – transportation means, as well as gas and electricity, were increasingly provided by local authorities all over Europe (see the following section). For instance, at the dawning of the twentieth century, the management of such a key multipurpose resource as water had frequently become a typical town council's business or had been otherwise entrusted to a public (state) authority (Juuti and Katko, 2005; Raadschelders, 2005).

In the policy area considered so far, public administration performed a role that was supportive or propulsive of economic growth. Although conflicts occasionally arose with individual private companies running the mentioned utilities as licensees or grantees, overall industrial and commercial interests benefited from public ownership no less than did the general public.

In another policy area, the role of public administration was of a benevolent and protective rather than propulsive nature. Health care, social insurance and pensions became the terrain of policies that helped relieve poverty, reduce social tensions and enhance living standards (Alber, 1982). In fact, even before the First World War the democratization of the franchise had produced parliaments that were more inclined to legislate in favour of this sort of intervention than had been their predecessors.

It goes without saying that the two policy areas and the two corresponding roles – the propulsive and the benevolent – distinguishable in theory, were not separated at all in practice. Education is a typical case in point. But, also, the control of and/or the support for migration (a phenomenon that had a tremendous impact on European societies in the nineteenth and twentieth century) fall into this ambivalent category of policies and required considerable administrative resources (Peri, 2010).

It should also be noted that, although the commitment of governments was generalized in the course of the statist century, some governments were proactive and others tardier. To take education as an example, once more, as early as 1882 German governmental schools at all levels employed about 115,000 people (Mayntz, 1982); comparable figures were attained in Italy only in 1931. And while in 1902 the UK parliament was ready (some say happy) to put independent School Boards under local authorities' control, the Italian parliament, a few years later (1911), dissatisfied with the way the communes were dealing with primary school matters, enlarged the central government's competence on those matters (De Fort, 1996).

It is generally acknowledged that the First and the Second World Wars provided a spur for further government growth. Moreover, the wars brought about and fostered cooperation between public administration and corporate interests in ways that, with some variations, were to prove permanent.

Admittedly, the preceding account of the march towards 'big government' is to a certain extent one-sided. This account has assumed that the expansion of public administration was the outcome of social pressures originated outside the politico-administrative system. Yet other versions of the same story emphasize that, especially after the rise of mass parties, the growth of government became a vital concern of the politicians, because it was associated with an increase in their power and patronage. Government and public administration then may have grown bigger, independent of social demands or well beyond them (Dunleavy and O'Leary, 1987; Poggi, 1991).

Credit must be lent to this opinion, if only because of the authoritative sources that have generated it (starting with Benjamin Constant, who spoke of the politicians' *esprit de conquête*). However: Did civil servants share their political masters' alleged interest in the growth of government? As a matter of fact, bureaucrats earn their living from bureaucracy: hardly any of those civil servants who made a name as leaders in public administration gained a place in history for having dismantled administrative apparatuses.

Some politicians did. In the early 1980s, British Conservative cabinets made the recurrently voiced demand to reduce government the crucial issue on their agenda. Other European governments followed in their steps. Public welfare administrations were downsized; privatization of public corporations and services was legislated; a regulative rather than operative role for public administration was designed. Such policies have been largely criticized (Clarke and Newman, 1997) and diffusely perceived as a clear

rupture of a well-established European administrative tradition. This rupture also reverberated on the methods and criteria of administrative action (Savoie, 1994). Under the watchword of 'New Public Management' (NPM), an effort has been made to renew the organization and the operation of public administration, basically on the model of the private corporation (Dunleavy and Hood, 1994).

Historical perspective may provide some grounds for de-emphasizing the novelty of both the regulative and the managerial state. As far as regulation is concerned, although partially yielding to direct intervention in the early twentieth century, the regulative paradigm has never ceased to influence the relations between the state and relevant societal actors. And it was often abandoned because it had proven ineffective or costly or both (Rials, 1985).

As to managerialism, it has been the goal of many administrative reformers in the last 100 years: suffice to mention a figure like Henry Chardon (Kuisel, 1981; Pierrot, 1970; Rials, 1977). In any case, subsequent developments showed that NPM, no less than other administrative recipes, had to come to terms with the contexts to which it was applied – and even with its enemy: the traditional bureaucracy (thus, engendering, especially in Continental Europe, new institutional arrangements qualified as 'neo-Weberian' administrative systems) (Pollitt and Bouckaert, 2004; Pollit et al., 2007; Ongaro, 2009).

CENTRAL, LOCAL AND PARALLEL

At the outset of the period under consideration, the design of public administration was a rather simple one. After all, by the end of the nineteenth century, most European states had gone through a process of both unification and centralization, while the march towards 'big government' (with its concomitant process of administrative differentiation) had only just begun. Thus, public administration was still fundamentally state administration and a rather cohering and essential construct.

To be sure, in that construct one could notice differences and inconsistencies, involving, for instance, different ministries called to cooperate in the implementation of one policy, as well as the field services of different ministries operating in the same territorial area. However, differences and inconsistencies of this sort hardly led to real conflicts. On the contrary, conflict was a rather common occurrence in the relationship between central government and local administrations, that relationship offering the most evident instance of division and tension within national administrative systems in the nineteenth century.

At the root of the strains in central–local relations lay the fact that, already in the first half of the century, local governments, especially at the municipal level, had become elective bodies. This had happened in France as early as 1789, during the revolution, but it was a short-lived arrangement. Abolished in 1795, elections of municipal councils were then resumed in 1831. In Prussia, the first German state to adopt communal elections, they were introduced in 1808. In England, elective borough councils were established by the Municipal Corporations Act in 1835 for 178 boroughs and subsequently extended. In the Kingdom of Piedmont, the immediate antecedent of the Kingdom of Italy, elections of municipal councils were enacted in 1848.

As a result, local administrations had become primarily responsive to their own voters and were inclined to set their own policy agenda. Their choices, however, might happen to collide with what central governments would suggest or expect: hence, the aforementioned strain – or unsteady balance – between central government and local self-government, and the former's effort to put the second under tutelage.

To be sure, such state tutelage could be more or less penetrating. But also in England,

whose local liberties were often mythologized on the Continent, restrictions on the use of the boroughs' funds were dictated (especially in 1872) and important tasks were assigned to the boroughs themselves – for example, in the educational field, with the Education Act of 1902 (which entailed that at least 20 per cent of local government spending was absorbed by education) (Ashford, 1980; Bellamy, 1988; Dunleavy, 1984). In countries of the Napoleonic tradition, like France and Italy, interference and control from the central government were normalcy: *maires* and *sindaci* (Agulhon, 1986; Aimo, 1992; Colombo, 2011), the heads of municipal administration, were selected and appointed by the central government, respectively, until 1882/84 in France and 1888/1896 in Italy.[8]

Why then had the nineteenth-century states accepted and even promoted local self-government? What did they need it for? A comprehensive answer to these questions should take into account a larger number of factors. But from the point of view of the administrative historian, the establishment of elective local authorities proceeded from the experience that a centrally ruled public administration was not expedient and possibly not capable of properly implementing all of the (state) public policies.

In addition, local self-government entailed the possibility of mobilizing local elites and involving them in administrative activities on an honorary basis – and that with at least a twofold gain. First, such involvement was likely to enhance local communities' cooperative attitude towards (state) public policies; second, it provided public administration with administrative skills that were relatively rare at that time.

All this implies a systemic relation between central and local administration: they were actually distinct elements of one and the same governance system. In that system, however, the state was the dominating actor. Only at the turn of the century was its position threatened. Cities all over Europe turned into laboratories of new policies and administrative devices (Hietala, 1987).

In the United Kingdom, by the Edwardian period, municipal enterprise had become 'big business', and the Fabian Society was successfully diffusing the gospel of 'municipal trading' (Falkus, 1977; MacBriar, 1966). In Italy, socialists and radicals were governing cities as important as Rome and Milan, while a law passed in 1903 provided legal basis for the mushrooming municipal enterprises. Proactive German burgomasters applied the principles of municipalization and the prescriptions of municipal engineering (*Städtetechnik*) (Hofmann, 1974; Rugge, 1989). Even French *communes*, although under tighter state grip, undertook new important tasks, e.g. in the fields of water provision and sewerage (Cohen, 1998; Rugge, 1992).

In short, municipal government became the cradle of administrative innovations and the expression 'civic renaissance' was forged to characterize this development. But, during the interwar period, the 'civic renaissance' came to a sudden end. War had brought the state to the foreground again. Furthermore, in two countries where municipal activism had been utmost (Germany and Italy), the authoritarian rule reduced local administration to an articulation of the central government and of the party machinery.[9]

Not before the end of the Second World War was the development of local government set in motion again. The most relevant changes, however, did not affect city government: rather, they concerned the intermediate level of administration, i.e. territorial subunits of the state such as regions, departments and the like. In particular, between the 1960s and 1970s, regionalization emerged as an important issue in the political debate of the countries under review (with the partial exception of Germany, with its traditionally established federal fabric) (Meny, 1982).

The practical results of this regionalist upsurge were different. In Italy, a process of devolution of both legislative and administrative tasks to the regions went ahead in the 1970s, in spite of considerable resistance

from the ministerial bureaucracy (ISAP, 1984; Leonardi et al., 1987; Levy, 1996). In France, after the law of 1972 introducing a regionalization *en trompe-l'œil*, substantial decentralization was enacted only in 1982 (Hayward, 1973; Loughlin and Mazey, 1995). In the United Kingdom, a regional movement emerged in the early 1960s, went into hibernation about 15 years later without producing remarkable or lasting outcomes (Regional Economic Planning Councils were established in 1964 and extinguished in 1979), and has only recently revived with major impact.

But the 'pluralism' of the contemporary public administration systems has not only resulted from the creation of new local authorities. In fact, as the state acquired further social and economic powers, these were increasingly vested in public boards or agencies that were neither government departments nor local authorities. A new family of public administrations therefore developed.

The first appearance of this 'parallel' public administration was an occurrence of the interwar period. Pending the First World War, the expansion of state intervention had reached a critical point, making clear that ministerial or departmental administrations were not entirely up to the challenges the conflict had imposed on them. That situation demanded more organizational flexibility, higher capacity to consult and integrate external stakeholders (especially corporate interests) and single mission instead of multi-purpose structures.

An ever-increasing number of authorities, agencies and commissions developed, which were ordinarily created by legislation, and commonly supported by public funds: each acted in one special field, mostly with a national scope (social insurance, health care, education, information, highways, regulation and surveillance on public utilities, etc.) (Rugge, 2000). These parallel administrations, although mostly entrusted to personnel appointed by central government, were indeed neither state nor governmental administrations.

Because of this special position, in French and Italian legal languages these bodies were soon defined as *entités paraétatiques* or *enti parastatali*, respectively, whereas in English they were later described as 'fringe bodies' or 'quangos' (quasi non-governmental organizations) (Yante et al. 2007; Greve et al., 1999; Parliamentary Affairs, 1995). On the Continent, they were considered as part of the public administration system, but they were mostly allowed to operate according to the civil law (that is, as if they were private persons). Since this aspect placed them in a sort of grey zone between the public administration and the private persons, Italian legal doctrine defined these agencies with the somewhat crude but perceptive expression of *enti ermafraditi* (hermaphrodite bodies) (Melis, 1988).

During the interwar period and soon after the Second World War, their growth was relentless and impressive, especially in the economic arena (suffice it to mention the UK's massive nationalization in the aftermath of the war). Here the public/private interpenetration took the form of public corporations, usually created to stabilize key economic sectors, protect sensitive national interests, support the overall development and buttress governmental policies.

As a result of this process, the image of the European administrative system has undergone a profound change: from the state-centred design of the late nineteenth and early twentieth centuries, to a less orderly and almost enthropic pattern: some say, an *administration en miettes* (Dupuy and Thoenig, 1985). In fact, in the new scenario a trend can be observed towards an 'unbundled government': the breaking down of the classical departments and ministries into smaller agencies, performing specific tasks on a contractual basis (the smaller dimension of the agencies and the contractual nature of their relations to government marking the difference between this generation of agencies and those emerging in the first half of the twentieth century) (Pollit and Talbot, 2004).

NOTES

1 An established scholarly tradition has stressed the merit of such approach: from Leonard D. White ('No administrative system can be well understood without some knowledge of what it has been, and how it came to be what it is'; 1955: 13) to the recent historical institutionalist studies (e.g. Pierson, 2004). As for the notion of 'administrative traditions', see Painter and Peters (2010).

2 One can consider Alexis de Tocqueville as the most prominent supporter of this opinion, since he argued that the effects of the Revolution on the developments of French administration had commonly been 'exaggerated' (Tocqueville, 1964).

3 According to Henry Parris, the expression 'permanent civil service' does not apply to the period prior to 1780–1830 (Parris, 1969; see also Harling, 1996). Not before the mid-nineteenth century did the modern concept of 'fonctionnaire' prevail in France (Thuiller and Tulard, 1994: 42).

4 This process is sketched in Rugge (2003: 187–189).

5 For a disclaimer of the 'ancient proverb' about the politics/administration dichotomy, see Peters (1995: 177–178).

6 The attitude of the German regime towards public administration both as a profession and a science is mirrored by the relations between the Berlin establishment and the International Institute of Administrative Sciences in the years 1933–1944 (see Fisch, 2005).

7 Figures drawn from Mann (1993), who offers a convincing discussion of data collected by other authors. Figures concerning Italy are derived from Cassese (1977).

8 For a discussion – also in an historical perspective – of the different models of central–local relations, see Page (1991).

9 A comparison between the local government's path in the Germany and Italy is given in Rugge (2005).

REFERENCES

Agulhon, Maurice (ed.) (1986) *Les Maires en France du Consulat à nos jours*. Paris: Publications de la Sorbonne.

Aimo, Piero (1992) 'La "sciarpa tricolore": sindaci e maires nell'Europa dell'Ottocento', in *Jahrbuch für europaische Verwaltungsgeschichte*, 293–324.

Alber, Jens (1982) *Vom Armenhaus zum Wohlfahrtsstaat. Analysen zur Entwicklung der Sozialversicherung in Westeuropa*. Frankfurt a.M.: Campus Verlag.

Antoine, Michel (ed.) (1975) *Origines et histoire des cabinets des ministres en France.* Geneva: Droz.

Ashford, Douglas E. (1980) 'A Victorian Drama: The Fiscal Subordination of British Local Government', in Douglas E. Ashford (ed.), *Financing Urban Government in the Welfare State.* London: Croom Helm.

Ashford, Douglas E, (1986) *The Emergence of Welfare States.* Oxford: Blackwell.

Bellamy, Christine (1988) *Administering Central–Local Relations 1871–1919. The Local Government Board in Its Fiscal and Cultural Context.* Manchester: Manchester University Press.

Bertho-Lavenir, Catherine (1991) *L'Etat et les télécommunications en France et à l'étranger 1837–1987.* Geneva: Droz.

Blick, Andrew (2004) *People Who Live in the Dark: The History of the Special Adviser in British Politics.* London: Politicos.

Caplan, Jane (1988) *Government without Administration: State and Civil Service in Weimar and Nazi Germany.* Oxford: Oxford University Press.

Cassese, Sabino (1977) *Questione amministrativa e questione meridionale: Dimensioni e reclutamento della burocrazia dall'Unità ad oggi.* Milan: Giuffrè.

Cassese, Sabino and Pellew, Jill (eds) (1987) *Le Système du mérite.* Brussels: Institut International des Sciences Administratives.

Clarke, John and Newman, Janet (1997) *The Managerial State.* London/New Delhi: Sage.

Cohen, William B. (1998) *Urban Government and the Rise of the French City: Five Municipalities in the Nineteenth Century.* New York: St Martin's Press.

Colombo, Elisabetta (ed.) (2011) *I sindaci del re 1859-1889.* Bologna: Il Mulino.

De Fort, Ester (1996) *La scuola elementare dall'Unità alla caduta delfascismo.* Bologna: Il Mulino.

Dreyfus, Françoise (2000) *L'Invention de la bureaucratie: Servir l'état en France, en Grande-Bretagne et aux Etats-Unis (XVIIIè–XXè siècles).* Paris: La Découverte.

Dunleavy, Patrick (1984) 'The Limits to Local Government', in Martin Boddy and Colin Fudge (eds), *Local Socialism? Labour Councils and New Left Alternatives.* London: Macmillan.

Dunleavy, Patrick and Hood, Christopher (1994) 'From Old Public Administration to New Public Management', *Public Money and Management,* 3: 9–16.

Dunleavy, Patrick and O'Leary, Brendan (1987) *Theories of the State: The Politics of Liberal Democracy.* London: Macmillan.

Dupuy, François and Thoenig, Jean-Claude (1985) *L'Administration en miettes.* Paris: Fayard.

Ellwein, Thomas (1965) *Das Regierungssystem Der Bundesrepublik Deutschlands,* 2nd edn. Cologne/Opladen: Westdeutscher Verlag.

Falkus, Malcom (1977) 'The Development of Municipal Trading in the Nineteenth Century', *Business History,* 134–161.

Fisch, Stefan (2005) 'Origins and History of the International Institute of Administrative Sciences: From Its Beginnings to Its Reconstruction after World War II (1910–1944/47)', in Fabio Rugge and Michael Duggett (eds), *IIAS/IISA. Administration & Service 1930–2005.* Amsterdam: IOS Press.

Fisch, Stefan (2007) '"Politische Beamte" und Politisierung der Beamten in Deutschland seit 1800', in Anna Gianna Manca and Fabio Rugge (eds), *Governo rappresentativo e dirigenze amministrative (secoli XIX–XX) – Räpresentative Regierung und führende Beamte (19–20 Jahrhundert).* Bologna–Berlin: il Mulino–Duncker & Humblot.

Greve, Carstens, Flinders, Matthew and Van Thiel, Sandra (1999) 'Quangos – What's in a Name? Defining Quangos from a Comparative Perspective', *Governance. An International Journal of Policy and Administration,* 2: 129–146.

Harling, Philip (1996) *The Waning of 'Old Corruption': The Politics of Economical Reform in Britain, 1779–1846.* Oxford: Clarendon Press.

Hattenhauer, Hans (1980) *Geschichte des Beamtentums.* Berlin: Heymann.

Hayward, Jack (1973) *The One and Indivisible French Republic.* New York: W.W. Norton.

Heady, Ferrel (2001) *Public Administration: A Comparative Perspective.* New York/Basel: Dekker.

Hietala, Marjatt (1987) *Services and Urbanisation at the Turn of the Century: The Diffusion of Innovation.* Helsinki: SHs.

Hofmann, Wolfgang (1974) *Zwischen Rathaus und Reichskanzlei: Die Oberbürgermeister in der Kommunal- und Staatspolitik des Deutschen Reiches von 1890 bis 1933.* Stuttgart/Berlin: Kohlhammer.

ISAP (Istituto per la Scienza dell' Amministrazione pubblica) (1984) *La regionalizzazione.* Milan: Giuffrè.

Jakoby, Henry (1973) The *Bureaucratization of the World.* Berkeley/Los Angeles, CA: University of California Press.

Juuti, Petri S. and Katko, Tapio S. (eds) (2005) *Water, Time and European Cities – History Matters for the Futures.* Tampere, Finland: Tampere University Press, ePublications – Verkkojulkaisut.

Kuisel, Richard F. (1981) *Capitalism and the State in Modern France: Renovation and Economic Management in the Twentieth Century.* Cambridge: Cambridge University Press.

Le Clère, Bernard and Wright, Vincent (1973) *Les Préfets du Second Empire.* Paris: A. Colin.

Leonardi, Robert, Nannetti, Raffaella and Putnam, Robert P. (1987) 'Italy: Territorial Politics in the Post-War Years. The Case of Regional Reform', *West European Politics,* 10 (4): 88–107.

Levy, Carl (ed.) (1996) *Italian Regionalism: Identity, and Politics.* Oxford: Berg.

Loughlin, John and Mazey, Sonia (eds) (1995) *The End of the French Unitary State? Ten Years of Regionalisation in France (1982–1992).* London: Frank Cass.

MacBriar, Alan Mam (1966) *Fabian Socialism and British Politics, 1884–1918.* Cambridge: Cambridge University Press.

Mann, Michael (1993) *The Sources of Social Power: 2: The Rise of Classes and Nation-States, 1760–1914.* Cambridge: Cambridge University Press.

Mayntz, Renate (1982) *Soziologie der iiffentlichen Verwaltung,* 2nd edn. Heidelberg: Müller Juristischer Verlag.

Melis, Guido (1988) *Due modelli di amministrazione tra liberalismo e fascismo: Burocrazie tradizionali e nuovi apparati.* Rome: Ministero per i beni culturali e ambientali.

Melis, Guido (1996) *Storia dell'amministrazione italiana, 1861–1993.* Bologna: Il Mulino.

Meny, Yves (1982) *Dix ans de régionalisation en Europe. Bilan et perspective, 1970–1980: Belgique–Espagne–France–Grande Bretagne–Italie.* Paris: Cujas.

Mommsen, Hans (1966) *Beamtentum in Dritten Reich,* Stuttgart: Deutsche Verlags-Anstalt.

Ongaro, Edoardo (2009) *Public Management Reform and Modernization. Trajectories of Administrative Change in Italy, France, Greece, Portugal and Spain.* Cheltenham: Edward Elgar.

Page, Edward C. (1991) *Localism and Centralism in Europe: The Political and Legal Bases of Local Self-Government.* Oxford: Oxford University Press.

Painter, Martin and Peters, B. Guy (eds) (2010) *Tradition and Public Administration.* Basingstoke: Palgrave Macmillan.

Parliamentary Affairs (1995) *The Quango Debate.*

Parris, Henry (1969) *Constitutional Bureaucracy.* London: Allen and Unwin.

Peri, Arnold (ed.) (2010) *National Approaches to the Administration of International Migration.* Amsterdam: IOS Press.

Peters, B. Guy (1988) *Comparing Public Bureaucracies: Problems of Theory and Method.* Tuscaloosa, AL: University of Alabama Press.

Peters, B. Guy (1995) *The Politics of Bureaucracy.* New York: Longman.

Pierrot, Roger (1970) 'Un réformateur de l'administration au service de la liberté: Henri Chardon', *Revue du Droit Public et de Science Politique en France et à l'étranger,* 4: 925–960.

Pierson, Paul (2004) *Politics in Time: History, Institutions, and Social Analysis.* Princeton, NJ: Princeton University Press.

Poggi, Gianfranco (1991) *The State: Its Nature, Development, and Prospects.* Stanford, CA: Stanford University Press.

Pollitt, Christopher and Bouckaert, Geert (2004). *Public Management Reform: A Comparative Analysis.* Oxford: Oxford University Press.

Pollitt, Christopher and Talbot, Colin (2004) *Unbundled Government: A Critical Analysis of the Global Trend to Agencies, Quangos and Contractualisation.* London: Taylor & Francis.

Pollitt, C., van Thiel, S. and Homburg, V. (eds) (2007) *New Public Management in Europe: Adaptations and Alternatives.* Basingstoke: Palgrave Macmillan.

Raadschelders, Jos C.N. (1998) *Handbook of Administrative History.* New Brunswick, NJ: Transaction Publishers.

Raadschelders, Jos C. N. (ed.) (2005) *The Institutional Arrangements for Water Management in the 19th and 20th Centuries.* Amsterdam: IOS Press.

Raadschelders, Jos C.N. and Rutgers, Mark Roland (1996) 'A History of Civil Service Systems', in A.J.G. M. Bekke, J.I. Perry and Th. A.J. Toonen (eds), *Civil Service Systems in Comparative Perspective.* Bloomington, IN: Indiana University Press, pp. 67–99.

Raadschelders, Jos C.N. and Van der Meer, Frits (eds) (1998) *Administering the Summit.* Brussels: International Institute of Administrative Sciences.

Rials, Stéphane (1977) *Administration et organisation 1910–1930: De l'organisation de la bataille à la bataille de l'organisation dans l'administration française.* Paris: Beauchesne.

Rials, Stéphane (1985) 'Le contrôle de l'état sur les chemins de fer (des origines à 1914)', in M. Brugière (ed.), *Administration et contrôle de l'économie 1800–1914.* Geneva: Droz.

Rokkan, Stein (1970) *Citizens, Elections, Parties: Approaches to the Comparative Study of the Processes of Development.* Oslo: Universitetsvorlaget.

Rosanvallon, Pierre (1990) *L'État en France de 1789 à nos jours.* Paris: Le Seuil.

Rosenberg, Hans (1958) *Bureaucracy, Aristocracy and Autocracy. The Prussian Experience, 1660–1815.* Cambridge, MA: Harvard University Press.

Rugge, Fabio (1989) *Il governo delle città prussiane tra '800 e '900*. Milan: Giuffrè.

Rugge, Fabio (ed.) (1992) *I regimi della città. Il governo municipale in Europa tra '800 e '900*. Milan: Angeli.

Rugge, Fabio (1998) 'Administering the Summit: The Italian Case', in Jos C.N. Raadschelders and Frits Van der Meer (eds), *Administering the Summit*. Brussels: International Institute of Administrative Sciences, pp. 217–226.

Rugge, Fabio (ed.) (2000) *Administration and Crisis Management: The Case of Wartime*. Brussels: International Institute of Administrative Sciences.

Rugge, Fabio (2003) 'Administrative Traditions in Western Europe', in Jon Pierre and Guy Peters (eds), *Handbook of Public Administration*, London: Sage Publications, pp. 177–191.

Rugge, Fabio (2005) 'Die Gemeinde zwischen Bürger und Staat', in Christof Dipper (ed.), *Deutschland und Italien 1860–1960*. München: Oldenburg..

Rugge, Fabio (ed.) (2007) 'La politica e gli alti burocrati. Una traiettoria politica in quattro quadri', in Manca, Anna Gianna and Rugge, Fabio (eds), *Governo rappresentativo e dirigenze amministrative (secoli XIX–XX) – Räpresentative Regierung und führende Beamte (19–20 Jahrhundert)*. Bologna–Berlin: il Mulino–Duncker & Humblot.

Salvati, Mariuccia (1992) *Il regime e gli impiegati. La nazionalizzazione piccolo-borghese nel ventennio fascista*. Turin: Bollati Boringhieri.

Savoie, Peter J. (1994) *Thatcher, Reagan, Mulroney: In Search of a New Bureaucracy*. Pittsburgh, PA: University of Pittsburgh Press.

Theakstone, Kevin (2007) 'The "Whitehall Model". Ministers and Civil Servants in the 20th Century Britain', in Anna Gianna Manca and Fabio Rugge (eds), *Governo rappresentativo e dirigenze amministrative (secoli XIX–XX) – Räpresentative Regierung und führende Beamte (19–20 Jahrhundert)*. Bologna–Berlin: il Mulino–Duncker & Humblot.

Thomas, Rosamund M. (1978) *The British Philosophy of Administration: A Comparison of British and American Ideas, 1900–1939*. London/New York: Longman.

Thuillier, Guy (1982) *Les Cabinets ministériels*. Paris: Presses Universitaires de France.

Thuillier, Guy and Tulard, Jean (1994) *Histoire de l'administration française*. Paris: Presses Universitaires de France.

Tocqueville, Alexis de (1964) *L'Ancien Régime et la Révolution* (1856). Paris: Gallimard.

White, Leonard Dupee (1955) *Introduction to the Study of Public Administration* (1922). New York: Macmillan.

Wilson, Woodrow (1887) 'The Study of Administration', *Political Science Quarterly*, 2 (June). (Reprinted 1941 in *Political Science Quarterly*, 61 (December): 481–506.)

Wunder, Bernd (1986) *Geschichte der Bürokratie* in *Deutschland*. Frankfurt a.M.: Suhrkamp.

Wunder, Bernd (2005) 'Examination Principle and Nobility's Privileges. The Failure of an Elite Change in German Administration', in *Verwaltungseliten in Westeuropa (19./20. Jh.)* (Jahrbuch für Europäische Verwaltungsgeschichte, 17). Baden-Baden: Nomos.

Yante, Jean-Marie et al. (eds.) (2007) *Des Etats dans l'Etat?: autonomie administrative et services publics décentralisés en Europe; States in the State ?: Administrative Autonomy and Decentralized Public Bodies in Europe*. Bruxelles: Archives générales du Royaume.

13

South Asian and Western Administrative Experience: The Past in the Present

James Warner Björkman

By comparing pre-colonial and colonial with post-colonial state administrative traditions, this chapter explores Western and indigenous traditions of governance in order to appreciate the degree to which historical knowledge is a benefit to students and practitioners alike. While generalizations about patterns of administrative change in India may court disagreement, the following discussion derives from having been an 'India-watcher' for almost 50 years, with the built-in biases that such an enterprise entails. Due to its scope and duration over millennia, India should occupy a massive space in the study of administrative history. India, of course, means not just the current nation-state that is one of several successors to the British Raj but the entire subcontinent with its complex history of well over 5,000 years. India's administrative traditions are derived from ancient Hindu kingdoms, medieval Muslim empires, Western (especially British) colonialism and the modern era of independent nation-states.

The twentieth century is the most well known as well as most influential era of administrative practices in India. Its first half spanned the heyday of the British Raj; its second half was characterized by massive efforts for socio-economic development. But the distant past is equally intriguing when viewed as administrative history. In order to explore indigenous traditions of governance that permeate and influence the practice (even the mindset) of public administration in South Asia, comparison is made with one of the most well-known and least admired theorists of Western political thought.

A COLONIAL DUET

Few countries have been so explicitly prepared for independent democratic development as those in South Asia. For nearly a century, the institutions and practice of government had evolved to produce civil and military services that were both experienced and professional. While it would be naïve to suggest that mere administrative apparatus means sound administration or even good governance, shortly after the Raj ended in 1947, Appleby (1953: 8) described India as 'among the dozen or so most advanced governments in the world'. Despite difficulties during the past half-century, public administration in India has demonstrated as much coherence, awareness and balance between tradition and change as most Western nations.

In comparative terms, political organization in India is equally well developed, with competitive elections and multiple parties. Having been founded in 1885, the Congress Party triumphed as a nationalist movement by achieving independence in 1947 and then dominated the party system during the next 40 years by supplying most national and state-level governments. Over the decades, however, internal quarrels plus organizational atrophy (Björkman and Mathur 1996) saw the emergence of many more political parties that, coupled with an increasingly sophisticated electorate, have yielded a new phase of coalitional (that is, non-majoritarian) governments. Without strong central leadership, the importance of public administration has re-emerged, although without its self-confidence of yesteryear.

The British came to South Asia in the sixteenth century in search of commercial trade and their initial administrative practices served mercantile interests. But the East India Company over-reached itself and had to be rescued by the political state from which it had obtained its original commission. From this perspective, the Raj was an accidental empire rather than a purposeful enterprise. Rather than intentionally introducing British administrative practice into India, the Raj inherited a system of administration that had been under way for centuries.

This administrative system was based on geographic areas – specifically the 'district' – that had responsibility for maintaining law and order as well as extracting revenue. Subunits called *tehsils* or *talukas* facilitated

the collection of revenue and the administration of justice, but the district remained the center of action. Despite episodic attempts at reform, revenue units at district and sub-district levels remain the best key to understanding almost all contemporary administrative arrangements in India – including 'development blocks' under the state-managed Community Development Program in the 1950s and its participatory successor called Panchayati Raj (Björkman 1979).

Under the Mughals these administrative areas were assigned to political retainers and allies but, on the demise or removal of these incumbents, the areas reverted to the monarch for reassignment (Moore 1967: 319). Although these areas could be rank-ordered by size and importance, their administrators had no specific training. In the eighteenth-century China trade, however, British merchants observed the value of well-trained Mandarins, and in the early nineteenth century the East India Company introduced specialized training for its apprentice officials by establishing Haileybury College (1806–57). Because recruitment occurred in Britain, the embryonic civil service was dominated by the English but, from 1853 onwards, Indians became eligible as well (Braibanti and Spengler 1963: 31–2).

In a reversal of the usual assumptions of colonial tutelage, Spangenberg (1976) argues that the British experimented with administrative arrangements in India, including specialized training for functionaries, long before bringing those reforms to Britain through the 1854 Northcote–Trevelyan Report and its legislative aftermath. There is modest irony in the argument that the colonial power was itself colonized by administrative practices from its colony – a point that, given considerations of power and status, has not been well publicized. Indeed, the issue of what was borrowed from and/or influenced each partner in the colonial duet – Britain and India – is best described as a symbiotic synthesis that neither can easily recognize nor acknowledge. Yet in many ways the two nations have grown together over some 400 years of interaction.

THE SCIENCE OF POLITY FOR THE PRINCE

While one cannot deny that the pattern of administrative change in India owes much to two centuries of enduring British emphasis on procedural means of attaining equity and probity, the core structure of South Asian administration is equally related to the statecraft enjoined in the *Arthasastra*. The term *artha* signifies 'wealth' and 'the earth which contains mankind'; the term *sastra* or 'science', when affixed to *artha*, designates the 'Science of Polity' because it describes how this earthy realm is acquired and maintained (Shamasastry 1960). Transmitted orally through Sanskrit over millennia, the *Arthasastra* was first transcribed and published in 1909 and attributed to Kautilya, chief advisor to the founder of the vast Mauryan empire that flourished at the close of the fourth century BC. The compendium is a detailed text that documents every aspect of life in Mauryan India: the state and its people, the ruler and officials under him, political economy and foreign policy as well as personal life.

The Mauryan empire was founded by Chandragupta Maurya, commander-in-chief of the last Nanda king of Magadha (modern day Bihar), whom he eventually overthrew. When Maurya's initial conspiracy with Kautilya was discovered, both fled to the Punjab 'where tradition attributes to them a meeting with Alexander the Great' (Bingham et al. 1974: 150) and an exposure to Western ideas. Some 15 years after killing the Nanda king in 322 BC, Chandragupta defeated the Seleucid Greeks (successors to Alexander) and obtained all the lands that Alexander had conquered in India. Given Chandragupta Maurya's conquests in Bengal and Gujarat, his empire over most of the subcontinent lasted for 130 years (Basham 1954: 50–7). At its height the Mauryan empire embraced much of India, with a population of perhaps 100 million people – about as many as lived in Europe 2,000 years later in AD 1600. Yet even after the collapse of the Mauryan empire, Kautilya's manual continued to guide rulers and writers for over 1,500 years (Prased 1928: 245). As Rangaswami Aiyangar (1934: 6) remarks, 'In India more than in many parts of the world the past persists in the present.'

Kautilya's manual is a rich repository of factual information, but its orientation is descriptive, prescriptive and didactic rather than analytical, and its content is predominantly political. Its first book is primarily concerned with how the king must proceed if he is to choose reliable ministers, with how he is to set up and operate effective internal and external spy networks, and how he must guard his internal and external security. Book II deals with political as well as economic regulatory agencies, while the next three books deal with family regulations, criminal justice and public service. The 10 remaining books concern bases of sovereignty, international relations, sources of national distress, invasion, war, the conduct of military operations and international intrigue.

As the manual includes many prevailing customs and rules, the *Arthasastra* represents an attempt to codify Indian laws and customs as Justinian later did under the late Roman empire. It also reflects Brahmanical ethics and ideas about authority as well as the sources of law for the social order. Being aware of the value of propaganda and of the extent of belief in the infallibility of the sacred *Vedas*, Kautilya found in these ideas a powerful source of social stability (Aiyangar 1934: 40–1).

Kautilya was concerned to devise a statecraft that would keep the large Mauryan empire unified, guard its integrity against the intrigues of power-seeking nobles as well as attack from abroad, and prevent the dissolution of the state. Hence, he found it necessary to dismiss unrealistic world-rejecting values and practices that were unfavorable to the functioning of a great empire. While he may be said to have subordinated ethics to politics, Kautilya did not endorse principles that ran counter to the social law and coercive authority of the *Vedas*.

Kautilya's insistence on the importance of coercive authority (physical force) indicates that he conceived of the politico-economic world in essentially Hobbesian terms – as did many ancient authors. It indicates also that he underestimated the self-adjusting homeostatic character of social systems, together with the mechanisms governing their behavior. Yet, the *Arthasastra* contributed to the resolution of the problem of justice because Kautilya's concern was with the rules intended to produce sufficient certainty in various interpersonal relations in order to preserve social stability. His conception of law, although not wholly free of metaphysical content, was essentially empirical and man-made, and his conception of justice consisted in compliance with what the law sanctioned, on the grounds that it promoted the common good (Choudhary 1951: 284–8). In this regard, Kautilya's efforts provide a 'hidden' positive law in contrast to the overt products of Roman law.

Max Lerner's 1950 introduction to *The Prince* and *The Discourses* suggests that 'when [Niccolò Machiavelli] wrote his grammar of power he came close to setting down the imperatives by which men govern and are governed in political communities, whatever the epoch and whatever the governmental structure' (Lerner 1950: xxxiv). To test such a proposition would require extensive scholarship and no satisfactorily definitive conclusion would ever be obtained. However, 'there do arise, from time to time, curious parallels between one period and another' (Muir 1936: 1), so an examination of the theories of another political author totally unrelated to Machiavelli in culture, territory, or time does provide a critical comparison for Lerner's suggestion.

ERA AND AREA IN CONTEXT

Twenty-three centuries ago, almost six times the span of years since Machiavelli wrote, an obscure Indian Brahmin composed a political treatise on government. Although the past does not willingly divulge its secrets, a fortunate discovery near the turn of the twentieth century placed a copy of this treatise in the

hands of modern scholars. This treatise, the *Arthasastra*, and its probable author, Kautilya (also known as Chanakya), will be compared with Machiavelli and his works in order to explore their ahistorical parallels.

Before these political theorists can be compared, the similarities and differences of the disparate eras of each man must be sketched and commentary provided on known biographical information in order to gain a contextual perspective. The political concerns and techniques of each can then be discussed and contrasted, with final attention being paid to the practical results and applications of these theories. It should be noted, too, that both theorists subscribe to a cyclical sense of time that repeats itself or turns back upon itself, rather than the linear sense of time that characterizes Western civilization.

The politics of Europe's Renaissance were unsettled, and the adjective 'chaotic' appropriately characterizes the Italian peninsula that included five major city-states plus other minor principalities. The political kaleidoscope involved the maintenance of a shifting balance of power among the Republics of Venice and Florence, the Kingdom of Naples, the Duchy of Milan and the Papal State. Astute observers perceived that 'political absolutism was the necessary remedy for the chaos and anarchy of internecine strife among the Italian cities' (Elliott and McDonald 1949: 425).

Although the wondrous creations of Italian art held imperial sway in contemporary European culture, other European nations reciprocated with imperialism of a political nature. The kingdoms of France and Spain, through their subsidiary alliances with Milan and Naples, respectively, were intermittently at war over the possession of Italy (Schevill 1936: 463). The Papacy, which during the preceding centuries had been a significant influence in European politics, had become little more than a political football that frequently changed hands through manipulation within the College of Cardinals. The crowning irony of the age was the sack of the sacred and eternal city of Rome in 1527 by that most Holy Roman Emperor, Charles V of Spain. Machiavelli understandably concluded that 'stability was an illusion, life was a flux, nothing is eternal and all must change' (Muir 1936: 138).

During the fourth and fifth centuries before Christ, pre-Mauryan India too was plagued by political division and turmoil. A maze of principalities included some ruled by Greek 'foreigners in the Punjab and the adjoining regions' (Saletore 1963: 51), plus 18 republics in various stages of development (Mishra 2005). This potpourri of states 'represented a bewildering diversity of political and social existence, which necessitated the forging of a delicately balanced system of politico-economic relations among them' (Ramaswamy 1962: 4).

Evidence on the political career of the Brahmin Kautilya is sketchy and he has achieved almost mythological status. German orientalist scholars argued that Kautilya fulfilled a role in the Mauryan empire comparable to Bismarck in Hohenzollern Germany (Mookerji 1914: x). Although occasionally acting as a 'super-advisor' to the new emperor, Kautilya evidently went into semi-retirement after he had replaced the last Nanda ruler with Chandragupta (Ramaswamy 1962: 3). Analogous to the logic of Thomas Hobbes twenty centuries later, the political treatise is an attempted justification of the abolition of 'the anarchy and misrule due to the profligacy and unpopularity of the previous Nanda king, who was unable to discharge the primary functions of government, viz. the protection of the weak against the strong' (Mookerji 1914: xxxiii). Having produced a political handbook for the perpetuation of the newly established regime and beloved by his royal pupil, Kautilya died while reasonably successful in all his endeavors.

Being much closer to ours in time, Machiavelli's life needs little elaboration. Born in 1469 to a Florentine family, he experienced the rule of Savonarola, the vengeful Dominican friar. After the latter's execution, Machiavelli entered public office under the populist Soderini. As secretary to the Second Chancery of Florence, he maintained contact with all the military and diplomatic affairs of the Republic, subjects of immense importance in his later writings (Gauss 1952: 10). In 1512 the aristocratic Medici returned to power in Florence and Machiavelli was dismissed from office, tortured under a false pretext, and banished to his farm until 1526. There he wrote his political analyses, not from the viewpoint of a professional theorist but as 'an active participant in the troubled and unstable political life of his native Florence' (Gauss 1952: 9). *The Discourses* and *The Prince* were written by a miserable, bitter and desperate man who by chance of fate had been exiled from his one true love, the political arena. The books were primarily intended to elicit favor from the politically powerful.

Although Machiavelli was unsuccessful in his goals, Europeans reduced him to a caricature of immorality and evil incarnate. While his suggestions were only operational within a moral void, his greatest offense was to display 'to the world the mechanisms of power which were behind the authority of the rule' (Lerner 1950: xli). Kautilya was likewise charged with having intentions of malicious evil. He 'as much presented a picture of the immoral practices of the kings and Brahmin ministers in the fourth century BC as Machiavelli did of the immoral rulers and Christian statesmen in the fifteen [*sic*] century of his *Prince*' (Saletore 1963: 535). Comparable to Machiavelli's experience, the '*Arthasastra* must have fallen into the hands of unscrupulous pretenders who would extract support for their misdeeds from Kautilyan precepts on statecraft' (Ramaswamy 1962: 5). Political realism dictates a recognition that corrupt conditions and practices had existed long before the respective book was compiled and that the authors had merely observed the facts, utilizing them in a pragmatic manner.

Only brief mention need be made of the fact that Machiavelli represented one more step in the development of Western political thought. To the idealism of Plato, the Stoic republicanism of Cicero, the universalism of Dante, etc., was added the secular realism of Machiavelli. Even advice to tyrants was nothing new, because the fifth book of Aristotle's *Politics* concerns the unemotional preservation of a tyrant's power in order to maintain political order. Yet, Machiavelli never had an explicit theory of the state (Anglo 1969: 272).

Kautilya, too, was preceded by a long chain of political philosophies. Evidence indicates that at least 19 distinct schools of political thought had flourished over the centuries before Kautilya's massive compendium appeared and seemingly terminated all controversies (Saletore 1963: 49). More will be said later about this abrupt ending of speculative thought on politics in India. Ancient Indian political philosophy presupposed 'an inherent propensity of man to encroach on his weaker neighbour, and to be prone to commit acts of disorder and aggression' (Saletore 1963: 68). The continual references to this and other theories of ancient Indian scholars in the *Arthasastra* suggest that the latter political treatise is a compilation and synthesis of earlier thought plus information on the functional operation of government and state machinery (Altekar 1949: 2–3).

POLITICAL CONCERNS AND TECHNIQUES

Idealism/realism

The *Arthasastra* opens with a verse submitting that 'this *Arthasastra* is made as a compendium of almost all the Arthasastras which, in view of acquisition and maintenance of the earth, has been composed by ancient teachers' (Shamasastry 1951: 1). Kautilya selected his political formulas and principles on the basis of past usefulness instead of idyllic formulations (Salatore 1963: 50). This selection of verified principles is characteristic of a modern view of history. Machiavelli, on the other hand, had not 'the faintest conception of the doctrine of evolution; he held the orthodox view that history

returned upon itself, that it was a cycle, and that in studying the past men would learn what was to come in the future' (Muir 1936: 137). The appeal to antiquity for both justification and exemplification is best summed up in his reliance on Titus Livius, the Roman historian, and accounts of the glorious era of the Roman Republic. And yet, the 'search for general rules or principles … [by] reducing the confusing multiplicity of events to compact generalizations … makes the Florentine secretary not so much a historian as a political scientist' (Schevill 1936: 500).

The sometimes derisive, sometimes laudatory terms 'pragmatism' and 'political realism' are trademarks of the cult of Machiavelli. Indeed, Machiavelli was 'of the temper the political idiom of our time terms "realist" [for he combined] a formal deference to "idealism" with contemptuous dismissal of idealist measures in practice' (Steward 1948: 275). He prided himself on the 'stark realism and often the cynicism about human nature that seem to be the hallmark of the experienced diplomat …' (Elliott and McDonald 1949: 19). Undoubtedly, the emphasis on results can be summed up by Machiavelli's view that the 'supreme law of politics is success' (Ferrero 1939: 569). Later, it will be noted that Machiavelli was inconsistent in his supposed rejection of idealism, for he replaced the spiritual 'oughts' of the medieval era with secular 'oughts' of his own.

Kautilya's writings too are permeated by a concern for results and an evaluation of techniques in terms of success. The tenor of the *Arthasastra* is characteristic of 'the work of a consummate politician … who knew very well what to express and what to suppress in writing about contemporary politics' (Mookerji 1914: xxxiv). Many scholars have concluded that 'an idealistic tone [is not] applicable in the case of Kautilya, who was anything but an idealist' (Saletore 1963: 626). Other scholars credit Kautilya with a more flexible approach to political realism and contend that although the state envisaged in the *Arthasastra* was omnipervasive in the political realm, it was probably not a complete reality even under the Mauryas (Basham 1954: 80).

In considering the role that the idealism–realism tension played in the philosophies of both writers, Kautilya more fully comprehended the practical influence that ideals exert on political reality. Machiavelli, an observer of the conditions that immediately preceded the Reformation, failed to realize the political effects of morals and spiritualism (McCoy 1943: 631). Kautilya may have perceived that certain realistic insights should not be committed to writing and therefore paid lip-service to various historical ideals. Ironically, Machiavelli's depth of insight into the political affairs of man may have been the real reason he was not accepted by the Medicis with open arms; he had probed deeply into the realm of Renaissance politics and, in the words of a trite saying, 'knew too much to be trusted'.

As an extension of their realism, Kautilya and Machiavelli each emphasized the importance of empiricism as opposed to rationalism. Machiavelli sets out to discover the system of government possessing the greatest order, the highest efficiency and the probability of longevity (Muir 1936: 137). His devotion to empiricism is remarkably in evidence as he advocates submission to a despot or tyrant as ruler, amazing because of Machiavelli's strong desire for republicanism since the only truly successful portion of his own career occurred under the aegis of the popular-rule Soderini family in the Republic of Florence. However, the social anarchy of his age compelled Machiavelli 'by his clearness of vision and uncompromising rectitude of mind to justify the armed enforcer of laws and the destroyer of parties, the prince' (Schevill 1936: xx). Resolution in accepting the facts of observation and applying them politically is the mark of a committed empiricist.

The Kautilyan *Arthasastra* too is empirically based. Much of our knowledge of Chandragupta's era comes from Kautilya's writing 'which is born only of a living experience of actual problems and contact with

facts' (Mookerji 1914: xliv). Saletore (1963: 281) notes that there is an

> extraordinary thoroughness [in] Kautilya's work; its eminent inductiveness and practical character, its unflinching logic and heedlessness of adventitious moral or religious standards, and its wide range of subjects and interests – which give it a unique combination of features that, in European literature, we find only separately in an Aristotle, a Machiavelli, and a Bacon.

Emphases on the minutiae of organizational government machinery are as central to the *Arthasastra* as are its philosophic justifications.

View of man/worldview

Early Indian political philosophers considered man to be basically evil and 'prone to commit acts of disorder and aggression' – a view shared millennia later by the authors of *The Federalist Papers*. Kautilya subscribed to this view and posited a rudimentary theory of a contractual origin of political society as he explained how the people of India, weary of social anarchy, had voluntarily submitted to a monarch (Basham 1954: 83). But Kautilya also realized that man has a capacity for good and expressed this realization in terms contingent on the activity of the monarch. Thus, if the king were good, the people would be likewise; if he were evil or even passive, the people's base instincts would appear (Shamasastry 1951: 36).

As a harbinger of Hobbes, Machiavelli 'based his theories on the essential baseness of mankind, and on his belief that, left to themselves, men always act from selfish and generally evil motives' (Muir 1936: 76). For the Italian, man was 'an animal driven by the simpler motives of fear, vanity, lust for power, and scheming self-interest … who made the best of brute necessity and by shrewdness and ruthlessness achieved his ends' (Elliott and McDonald 1949: 421). Since Machiavelli had voided himself of moral considerations, the logical procedure in politics was to utilize and maximize these instincts. Yet man, 'when forced to do [otherwise] by law or the conventions of religion' (Steward 1948: 277), could act in the interests of a common good.

This appeal for a transformation in a man when he is cognizant of a common good – in Machiavelli's case the governing of a unified Italy – presents a problem in the interpretation of his writings: not only does he ignore the basically evil view of man's nature and provide a basis for constructive action but also he presents the use of an ideal – the common good – in the philosophy of an avowed realist who had rejected idealism. Here is the aforementioned inconsistency in Machiavelli, who had rejected idealism and had accepted humanity's basic selfishness, yet declared that 'the ideal of a united and triumphant Italy ought to command universal allegiance' (Steward 1948: 277). Certain authors, of course, contend that Machiavelli's conception of a 'common good' is 'purely ornamental' and its only value is symbolic, 'completely emptied of its content' (McCoy 1943: 632). However, the goal of national unity in Italy remained the central doctrine of all Machiavelli's endeavors and this represents an ideal towards which all other efforts are subordinated.

Kautilya also refers to a common good, but apparently with tongue in cheek and completely aware of the emotional appeal of this term. In the pre-Mauryan and Mauryan eras, the monarch was expected 'to be a virtuous ruler devoted heart and soul to the welfare of the people; if he was not such, then gods will punish him' (Altekar 1949: 8–9). As the *Arthasastra* reads: 'The king must regard his own happiness as indissolubly connected with that of his subjects' (Shamasastry 1951: 8). This common good between the ruler and his people, however, is almost sophistical in that, as in the case of Machiavelli, the over-riding concern is with loyalty to the state (Ramaswamy 1962: 30) – not, seemingly, a bad end until one recognizes that normally the benefits will accrue only to those who control the state.

Imperial desires

The emphasis placed on imperialism by the two writers magnifies their respective relationships to the *fait accompli* of political unity from within a plethora of competitive states. Machiavelli, desirous of unifying Italy, decided that since the fragmented political powers remained in flux, a dictatorship was essential (Sturmthal 1940: 79). Thus, he wrote 'for the purpose of eliciting the aid of a strong man in bringing the Italian people out of their condition of political corruption' (McCoy 1943: 629).

On the other hand, the 'Kautilyan strategy of state expansion is much more complicated than the Machiavellian counterpart' (Ramaswamy 1962: 34). Having established a new dynasty, the Brahmin minister faced the necessity of initiating a program of imperialistic expansion to incorporate and to 'mauryanize' the various autonomous or semi-independent principalities across northern India. Therefore, Kautilya recommended two goals for diplomacy: world conquest and world unity. The treatise states that 'the king who is weaker than "the other" should keep the peace; he who is stronger should make war'. This recommendation is compatible with the royal charge to maintain social order domestically; wars are fought on the periphery of the state and divert the attention of the people from their immediate problems.

In its description of facts as well as its advocacy of what needs to be done to govern well, the *Arthashastra* is rigorously analytical. Kautilya describes eight elements of sovereignty in great detail – the king, the minister, the country and so on – and lists the best qualities in each element. He then analyzes the 'circle of states' in which a sovereign finds himself: the neighbor, who is the enemy; the neighbor's neighbor, who is the friend; the rearward enemy; the rearward friend; and each case ascertains whether the friend or enemy is assailable, destructible, a natural friend, an acquired friend and so on. Altogether, Kautilya identifies four primary circles of states, 12 kinds of kings, 60 elements of sovereignty and 72 elements of states. He then lists six possibilities of action and discusses which option is to be selected in a given situation: make peace, make war, observe neutrality, prepare for war, ally with others, or make peace with one while waging war on another. Kautilya categorically recommends that, 'if you are superior you shall wage war, but if you are inferior you shall make peace, meanwhile building up your strength so that you become superior' (Khosla 2010: xii). Book VII is devoted to how to analyze any situation accurately and how to decide the most appropriate policy to choose. Shamasastry (1967) provides extensive detail on the permutations possible among states and actors in this rather utopian description of the Mauryan political system.

As an aside about the 'international' system of states or polities in India before and during the era in which Kautilya wrote his treatise on statecraft, unimpeachable historical information does not exist. However, the Indus valley and the Gangetic plain had a variety of political entities, some of which were conquered by Alexander the Great; others succumbed to the imperial ambitions of the Mauryan monarchs. According to Rangarajan (1992: 28),

> Before the empires arose and after their disintegration, the political map of the subcontinent showed not more than six large kingdoms in the Gangetic plain, various republics in the predominantly hilly areas in the west and the north and a number of smaller kingdoms whose relative independence must have varied with the power of a large neighbour.

In the fourth century BC there were 16 *mahajanapadas* or great races (nations) on the subcontinent, several of which, such as Gandhara, Surasena and Kamboja, are mentioned by Greek sources (Thapar 1966; Mookerji 1988), plus a variety of republics and monarchical states (Ghosal 1962; Mishra 2005).

In public administration, history matters – and comparative study must note that, whatever the contours of their respective eras,

Kautilya and Machiavelli each lived well before the peace treaty of Westphalia ended Europe's exceptionally violent Thirty Years War (1618–1648), a treaty that provided a foundation (however shaky) for international law among sovereign states. Before Westphalia a multiplicity of authorities claimed jurisdiction over a given people and territory: lay rulers like kings and the feudal barons who disputed the authority of kings; ecclesiastical rulers like the Pope or monastic orders not always under papal control such as the Teutonic Knights; city states like Venice and Florence; and commercial alliances like the Hanseatic League that signed treaties with monarchs, raised and used armed forces. This kaleidoscope of authorities constantly encroached on each other's territories and populations to recruit militias and armies, to levy taxes and to appeal to religious loyalty. But after Westphalia, one ruler held power over one territory and its people. Absolute monarchs replaced the representative institutions that had characterized several principalities and kings set about unifying their people, giving them one single set of mutually consistent laws and obligations, and above all creating nations. The idea that peace could be desirable in itself would have been strange to both Kautilya and Machiavelli (Khosla 2010: xxii–xxiii).

Bureaucracy

Centralized state machinery as a mode of government marks the most sweeping variation of the Arthashastran state from the pre-Mauryan political order. The bulk of the treatise is actually more concerned with the minutiae of bureaucratic detail than with either the acquisition or maintenance of power *per se*. The *Arthasastra* is frequently described as more of

> a manual for the administrator than a theoretical work on polity discussing the philosophy and fundamental principles of administration or of the political science. It is mainly concerned with the practical problems of government and describes

its machinery and functions, both in peace and war (Altekar 1949: 5).

Great emphasis is placed upon the prescription of the correct secretariat for government administration, a concern that may be traced back to his long service under the Nandas and, of course, the first Maurya. Kautilya's prescriptions went much further than merely describing the static institutions of government; he also recommended extensive economic planning (Ramaswamy 1962: 27) and continual sampling of public opinion through an internal security system (Basham 1954: 121).

Machiavelli differs substantially from Kautilya on the topic of practical government, for the former's commitment to pragmatism appears solely preoccupied with suggesting the means to obtain power and preserve it. Common, daily functions of government are largely ignored in the *Discourses* and especially in *The Prince*; the greatest elaborations concern the execution of war, the role of the military and the function of diplomacy. Machiavelli probably wrote *The Prince* in a frenzy of activity that made it a bit patchy and disjointed (Hughes 1951: 377). If the recommendations on duplicity, for example, were applied consistently to human affairs, the inevitable effect would be a direct contradiction of the goal sought plus obsolescence of the technique. The closest Machiavelli came to describing the administrative machinery of a unified political state was his blanket proposal that a position be created comparable to that of the ancient Roman *dictator* (Elliott and McDonald 1949: 426–7) and this only for emergencies – like the initial establishment of the state. Machiavelli is concerned neither with the morality of the techniques used to obtain power nor with the specific employment of that power once the initial goal of state unity has been achieved.

Recommendations in the *Arthasastra* for state initiative and the central control of society imply Kautilya's belief in a concept of man's innate abilities similar to Machiavelli's

'virtu'. 'Virtu' does not hinge solely on having a goal in mind towards which to direct one's energies but includes the ability of man to act and to cause that goal to become reality (Muir 1936: 150). This ability, which appears to contain the element of free will, is primarily concerned with how to control and utilize that element of chance and fate called 'fortuna', that 'mysterious … intangible external constraint which comes from above and guides events blindly, as it wills and where it lists' (Chabod 1958: 21).

The centralization of authority prescribed by Kautilya indicates that he regarded the monarchy as the pace-setter for Indian society. The qualities of government, which represents the ruler writ large, will determine whether the base instincts of the populace will be restrained and collective efforts channeled towards a common good. Paralleling the 'mandate of heaven' that underpins the legitimacy of imperial rulers in China and Vietnam (Fitzgerald 1972), Chapter XIX of the *Arthasastra* lays the cause and effect relationship upon the proverbial line: 'If the king is energetic, his subjects will be equally energetic. If he is reckless, they will not only be reckless likewise, but also eat into his works' (Shamasastry 1951: 36). Yet ultimately, Kautilya, like Machiavelli, perceived that the final authority and results rested on the political acquiescence of the populace for 'the character of [a nation's] people determines the destiny of a state more than any other fact of consideration' (Altekar 1949: 27).

Republicanism

Republicanism as a form of government becomes a legitimate alternative to the monarchy when the very structure of political society is ultimately seen to rest upon the 'virtu' of the people. The logical extension of the former premise would be the people can best rule themselves through an egalitarian form of government. Grounded as they are upon empiricism, however, both writers conclude that for their respective societies this solution would be untenable.

Machiavelli becomes particularly enigmatic on the issue of republicanism. His political sympathies, both in his early career and in his theoretical writings, lay with a popular-rule form of government. Not only did he perceive that political power is founded upon the support of the governed (*Discourses* I. 16) but also he declared that, to prevent the public good from being subverted to the enhancement of private advantage, a republic was necessary (Meinecke 1957: 43). The conclusion drawn from the *Discourses* is that the greatest wisdom 'lies in the deliberation of popular assemblies rather than in the edicts of a single man' (Elliott and McDonald 1949: 420). Despite the lip-service paid to the concept of republicanism *if* all political factors were functioning properly, however, Machiavelli persisted in advocating the institution of a tyrant or despot. Total rejection of his republican ideal was avoided by rationalizing that ultimately the deep-rooted prejudices and beliefs of the populace would circumscribe the limits over which even a tyrant may not transgress for fear of deposition (Corry 1943: 289).

Kautilya was much less circumspect about his views toward republics. Northern India in the pre-Mauryan age had several republics with philosophic roots in indigenous philosophies as well as in imported Greek ideals (Ghosal 1962). As the agent of a successful imperialist, however, the Brahmin minister could express his views with impunity. Republics are mentioned in the *Arthasastra* in an unsympathetic manner, although no specific reasons are provided unless it be that they were reluctant to submit to imperialism. Book XI proposes several techniques by which the inherent weakness of factionalism in republics may be intensified and exploited.

While older South Asian philosophies intimate that deliberative legislative bodies were an important element of pre-Mauryan monarchical India as well as in the republics (Altekar 1949: 94–100), the detailed description of Mauryan political institutions includes no mention of such a central legislative body. Interestingly, republics that submitted to Chandragupta retained their internal institutions of government, at least in the early Mauryan era (Altekar 1949: 234–5). Later versions of the *Arthasastra* (transmission, by the way, was orally and verbatim from one generation to the next) omitted the original Kautilyan references to republics, probably because they disappeared with the decline of Buddhism throughout India (Altekar 1949: 10).

Fürstenspiegel

Long before Machiavelli collected and set down his practical observations toward the education of a prince, political scholars of Europe engaged in formulating textbooks for rulers. There was nothing unique, therefore, in Machiavelli suggesting to the Medicis how to execute their tasks of government properly. His production of a 'handbook for rulers' in Renaissance Italy was intended for immediate use. Much later, his compositions were interpreted to provide a more universal application of his principles and recommendations. In fact, one of the most glaring errors Machiavelli committed was his conception of the state as the creation of a single, omnipotent man who could be privately tutored in statecraft (Passerin d'Entrèves 1959: 25). Reiterating a point made several times previously, the proposed education was narrowly confined to the acquisition of political power and not to any long-range utilization of this power once achieved.

The *Arthasastra* also represented a training manual for monarchs, especially in their childhood and adolescence, in order to prevent an improper use of state power (Altekar 1949: 67). But Kautilya realized that the governing of a state, especially an imperial state, was more than a single man could handle efficiently. Therefore, in order to succeed, the *Arthasastra* informs the king that he must be assisted by a cabinet of competent councillors (Shamasastry 1951: 12–14). Furthermore, the inclusion of administrative materials transformed the rather common-place notion of a royal textbook into a manual for statecraft, bureaucracy and administration for the entire Mauryan domain and for an extremely long period of time (Saletore 1963: 50). Even today in certain parts of India, the structure of the village – the dominant form of political organization – closely parallels the suggestions made by Kautilya more than two millennia ago. In short, the Kautilyan *Arthasastra* appears to have been a more practical and universally applicable treatise on government than any of Machiavelli's works.

PRACTICAL RESULTS AND APPLICATIONS

Ironically, although Machiavelli had prepared a reasonably accurate description of the political tenor of the Renaissance, his suggestions for the acquisition and maintenance of power were not readily accepted. Confronted by princely revulsion at this exposé of common political methods and also by the lingering influence of Christianity, Machiavelli's ideas did not enter the mainstream of politics for some 300 years (Gauss 1952: 15). Part of the reason for his failure rested upon himself and his impolitic methods of presentation. A more substantial reason for his rejection was because 'the idea of political regeneration was altogether beyond the capabilities and the wishes of the people and the rulers of that time' (Meinecke 1957: 45). In one sense, his system is only another portion of the rich and varied Western political theory. In another sense, it forms the wellspring for the era of untrammeled nationalism. In the interwar fascistic states where the despotic components of his suggestions came to fruition, political speculation was largely suppressed and/or manipulated. Perhaps, however, Machiavelli made his most significant contribution through his

reintroduction of the conception of politics as an end in itself (Hallowell 1950: 60).

The effect of the Kautilyan *Arthasastra* was quite significant on the activities of Indian political speculation. Although a variety of schools of thought had preceded the Mauryan minister, the appearance of his treatise seemingly resolved all controversies efficiently and effectively (Saletore 1963: 49). In the pre-Mauryan era, the final appeal was to the *dharma* or holy law, but in the system prescribed by the *Arthasastra* imperial decree became supreme. The power of decision making was clearly reserved for the political realm; certain scholars have ascribed this phenomenon to the almost prototypic totalitarianism of the Mauryan empire (Basham 1954: 114). Whatever the reason, previously competitive political philosophies fell into disuse and little political speculation occurred during the centuries following Kautilya (Altekar 1949: 7–9). One wonders what effects a triumphant Machiavellian philosophy might have had on the subsequent political development in the Renaissance, the Reformation, and modern Europe in general.

Whether the system of political realism recommended by Machiavelli and Kautilya in their respective eras actually provides the universal imperatives of Max Lerner remains moot. By almost any definition assigned, political relationships among humankind will remain unstable and, in a certain respect, unpredictable. Yet, at least, conclusions about efficacy, consistency and applicability can be drawn from this topical comparison.

As advocated by Machiavelli, empiricism has become a requisite for the development of political science. Reliance upon observable and verifiable phenomena fulfills a basic requirement for the scientific method. Rejection of idealism, on the other hand, does not appear to be the mark of an astute politician. Although impossible to attain immediately, ideals provide a reference point for the utilization of man's energies, as the example of Kautilya would demonstrate. Machiavelli himself established a certain specific idealist criterion for judging action – namely, success – and on a logical note would appear inconsistent. Much of the motivation for Machiavelli's recommendations stemmed from the desire to promote a common Italian good – unity! The concern shown for a 'common good' would indicate the existence of another ideal for this Renaissance realist.

Promotion or apparent promotion of a commonweal increases the effectiveness and influence of the promoting government; the people, as it were, have a stake in the regime's success. Machiavelli assumed that the unification of his national state would be inherently good and be accepted by all Italians; he misjudged his compatriots on the latter point. Perhaps, comparison of Machiavelli's failure with Kautilya's successes is unfair, for the latter wrote after his goal had been accomplished. Nevertheless, it is obvious in the *Arthasastra* that the Brahmin had persuaded Indians that the most reasonable and productive action on their part was submission to his emperor's state.

Centralization of government, which Machiavelli in general ignored even as Kautilya elaborated, has become a characteristic of modern society. Again, we can only hypothesize that part of Kautilya's success emanated from this emphasis. Government no longer merely presented an arbitrator of man's basically violent nature; sheer maintenance of law and order had expanded into promotion of a complete way of life. Rapid accomplishment of ends became possible as human energies came to be directed by a central agency. Whether the ends accomplished serve the common good is, of course, a different question.

The use of force and fraud is an identifying feature of Kautilya and Machiavelli. Perhaps no better comment can be made on this issue than to mention the speedy demise of *The Prince*'s model ruler, Cesare Borgia. Yet the Mauryan emperors reigned successfully for several centuries and Indian civilization reached an early climax under their aegis. Perhaps the important aspect of force

is not the immediate acquisition of power but its long-range use. Certain countries today insist their lower levels of education, industrial development and political maturity require an authoritative allocation of resources if any progress is to be made. In the long run, force is almost certain to turn upon itself, and hence must be regulated carefully. But its utilization in short-range projects can achieve certain ends rapidly. The question hinges upon the rejection of force as an end in itself and the alternative acceptance of force as the means to some end, some ideal.

Emancipation of politics from the grasp of institutionalized religion represents the greatest advance for the realist position. Ideals are essential to the proper functioning of a political system. But dogma and doctrine, inflexibility and immutability have only dysfunctional roles in the heterogeneous world of politics. In addition, institutions of any kind tend to become ossified and corrupt, especially when they have special vested interests. Until an ideal society is reached, pluralism must be protected in order that truth may flourish where it will, and no single interest should obtain total control of society.

REFERENCES

Aiyangar, K.V. Rangaswami (1934) *Aspects of Ancient Indian Economic Thought.* Benares: Motilal Banarsidass.

Altekar, A.S. (1949) *State and Government in Ancient India from Earliest Times to c. 1200 A.D.* Banares: Motilal Banarsidass.

Anglo, Sydney (1969) *Machiavelli: A Dissection.* New York: Harcourt, Brace and World, Inc.

Appleby, Paul H. (1953) *Public Administration in India: Report of a Survey.* New Delhi: Cabinet Secretariat, Government of India.

Basham, A.L. (1954) *The Wonder That Was India: A Survey of the Indian Sub-Continent before the Coming of the Muslims.* New York: Grove Press.

Bingham, Woodbridge, Conroy, Hilary and Iklé, Frank W. (1974) *A History of Asia: Formation of Civilizations from Antiquity to 1600,* 2nd edn. Boston, MA: Allyn and Bacon.

Björkman, J.W. (1979) *The Politics of Administrative Alienation in India's Rural Development Programs.* Delhi: Ajanta.

Björkman, J.W. and Mathur, Kuldeep (1996) 'India: How a Government Party Decays When Government Swallows Party', in J. Blondel and M. Cotta (eds), *Party and Government: An Inquiry into the Relationship between Governments and Supporting Parties in Western Liberal Democracies.* London: Macmillan, pp. 225–48.

Braibanti, Ralph and Spengler, Joseph J. (eds) (1963) *Administration and Economic Development in India.* Durham, NC: Duke University Press.

Chabod, Federico (1958) *Machiavelli and the Renaissance.* London: Boves and Boves.

Choudhary, Radha Krishna (1951) 'Kautilya's Conception of Law and Justice', *Bihar Research Society Journal*, 37, parts 1 and 2.

Corry, J.A. (1943) 'Machiavellian Politics', *Queen's Quarterly*, Autumn (Kingston, Ontario, Canada: quarterly journal of Queen's University).

Elliott, William Y. and McDonald, Neil A. (1949) 'The Secular State', *Western Political Heritage.* New York: Prentice Hall.

Ferrero, Guglielmo (1939) 'Machiavelli and Machiavellism', *Foreign Affairs*, 18 (April).

Fitzgerald, Frances (1972) *Fire in the Lake: The Vietnamese and the Americans in Vietnam.* London: Macmillan.

Gauss, Christian (1952) 'Introduction to the Mentor Edition', *The Prince.* New York: The New American Library of World Literature.

Ghosal, U.N. (1962) 'Political Organization: The Monarchical States, Republics and Mixed Constitutions', in *Cultural History of India*, Volume 2, 2nd edn. Calcutta: The Ramakrishna Mission Institute of Calcutta.

Hallowell, John H. (1950) *Main Currents in Modern Political Thought.* New York: Henry Holt and Company.

Hughes, Serge (1951) 'The Science of Machiavelli', *Commonweal*, 53 (12 January).

Khosla, I.P. (2010) *Underdogs End Empires: A Memoir.* Delhi: Konarak Publishers Pvt Ltd.

Lerner, Max (1950) 'Introduction', *The Prince* and *The Discourses.* New York: The Modern Library.

McCoy, Charles N.R. (1943) 'The Place of Machiavelli in the History of Political Thought', *American Political Science Review*, 37.

Meinecke, Friedrich (1957) *Machiavellism: The Doctrine of Raison d'Etat and Its Place in Modern History.* New Haven, CT: Yale University Press.

Mishra, Mohan (2005) *Building an Empire – Chanakya Revisited.* New Delhi: Rupa & Company.

Mookerji, Radha Kumud (1914) 'An Introductory Essay on the Age and Authenticity of the Arthasastra of Kautilya', in Narendra Nath Law (ed.), *Studies in Ancient Hindu Polity.* New York: Longmans, Green.

Mookerji, Radha Kumud (1988) *Chandragupta Maurya and His Times.* Delhi: Motilal Banarsidas.

Moore, Barrington, Jr (1967) *The Social Origins of Dictatorship and Democracy: Lord and Peasant in the Making of the Modern World.* Boston, MA: Beacon Press.

Muir, D. Erskine (1936) *Machiavelli and His Times.* London: William Heinemann.

Passerin d'Entrèves, Alexander (1959) *The Medieval Contribution to Political Thought.* New York: Humanities Press.

Prased, Beni (1928) *The State of Ancient India.* Allahabad: Triveni Books.

Ramaswamy, T.N. (1962) *Essentials of Indian Statecraft: Kautilya's Arthasastra for Contemporary Readers.* Bombay: Asia Publishing.

Rangarajan, L.N. (1992) *Kautilya: The Arthashastra.* New Delhi: Penguin Books India Pvt Ltd.

Saletore, Bhasker A. (1963) *Ancient Indian Political Thought and Institutions.* Bombay: Asia Publishing.

Schevill, Ferdinand, (1936) *History of Florence from the Founding of the City through the Renaissance.* New York: Harcourt, Brace and Company.

Shamasastry, R. (transl.) (1951) *Kautilya's Arthasastra*, 4th edn. Mysore: Sri Raghuveer.

Shamasastry, R. (1960) *The Arthasastra*, 6th edn. Mysore: Mysore Government Oriental Library.

Shamasastry, R. (1967) *Kautilya's Arthasastra*, 8th edn. Mysore: Mysore Printing and Publishing House.

Spangenberg, Bradford (1976) *British Bureaucracy in India: Status, Policy and the I.C.S. in the Late 19th Century.* Columbia: South Asia Books.

Steward, H.L. (1948) 'Machiavelli and History', *Queen's Quarterly*, Autumn (Kingston, Ontario, Canada: quarterly journal of Queen's University).

Sturmthal, Adolf (1940) 'The Science of Power', *The Nation*, 150 (20 January).

Thapar, Romila (1966) *A History of India*, Volume 1. London: Penguin Books.

PART 5

Implementation

edited by Søren C. Winter

INTRODUCTION

Implementation research grew out of evalua-tion research. The Great Society policy reforms in USA in the 1960s and 1970s stimulated a lot of evaluation research in order to estimate the effects of the new wel-fare state programs and to suggest improve-ments. Classic evaluation analyses raised the question if it could be documented that a given policy intervention had any effect and, if so, what effect. However, evaluation analysts often became frustrated that most studies actually showed no or little effect (Albæk, 1988). According to the classic interpretation of such findings, the program did not work. It was based on a wrong causal theory. However, gradually, the apparent fail-ures stimulated another interpretation that, possibly, nothing was wrong with the causal theory behind the planned policy interven-tion, but the intervention might not have taken place as intended. This stimulated an interest in studying the relationship between planned and actual interventions and the administrative process in between policy-adoption, delivery-level behaviors and effects.

Most implementation researchers would regard Jeffrey Pressman and Aaron Wildavsky's book *Implementation*, from 1973, as the first piece of implementation research. It was a case study of an economic development program in Oakland California that had been created to stimulate minority employment. However, it failed to do so due to the com-plexity of many actors having to work together. Although the book certainly opened the field, a few pieces of earlier research (e.g., Kaufman, 1960; Murphy, 1971) had actually focused on implementation problems. Pressman and Wildavsky's (1973) guiding research questions were: 'How well was this authoritative mandate (law, regulation, pro-gram, official pronouncement) implemented?' and 'How might it have been better imple-mented?' Later research redefined the ques-tion to focus on achieving the explicit or implicit values in a given mandate rather than its prescriptive details (Bardach, 2001). Accordingly, goal achievement has been the dominating standard and dependent variable for implementation research since the 1970s.

With inspiration from Pressman and Wildavsky and other pioneers, implementa-tion research became one of the fads of political science and policy analysis and reached its peak in terms of number of publi-cations in the mid-1980s. While research published under that explicit label has later decreased (Sætren, 2005), still a substantial amount of research focusing on implementation problems is being published, but often under other labels such as public administration, public management (Boyne, 2004; Meier and O'Toole, 2007), regulatory enforcement (Scholz and Wei, 1986; Kagan, 1994; May and Winter, 2000) and compliance (Winter and May, 2001; Parker and Nielsen, 2012), street-level bureaucracy (Lipsky, 1980), principal–agent theory (Brehm and Gates, 1999), new institutionalism, governance (Bogason, 2000; Lynn et al., 2001), networks (O'Toole, 2000), policy design and instruments (Salamon, 1981, 2002; Linder and Peters, 1989), etc., with several of these labels representing more recent research fads!

In addition, implementation research has later spread to books and journals that are specialized in a particular policy area, such as health policy, with it own implementation journal, *Implementation Science* (see also Fixen et al., 2005), and environmental policy. Sætren (2005) found many more publications under the label of 'implementation' in such policy specialized journals, rather than in core journals in political science, public administration and public policy. However, there seems to be very little relationship between implementation research in the specialized area and political science implementation research in core journals.

Implementation research is part of two subdisciplines of political science: public policy/policy analysis and public administration. Growing out of evaluation research, implementation studies tried to address the basic questions of policy analysis: What are the content, causes and consequences of public policies (Dye, 1976)? Implementation research focused on the consequences of those public policies that have been enacted as laws or other authoritative statutes. However, policy can also be conceived at an operational level as the delivery of public services and enforcement of regulations to citizens and firms. Consequently, implementation

research focuses on the content of such delivery-level behaviors, their causes and consequences. Implementation research has become an established part of public policy research that focuses on different stages of the policy process, such as agenda setting, policy formation, policy design, implementation, evaluation, knowledge utilization, and policy change more generally (Parson, 1995).

However, implementation research also addresses the basic question of public administration research: How is legislation executed? While public administration traditionally had studied formal, institutional and normative aspects of this issue, implementation research offered a fresh empirical, behavioral perspective on execution of laws that fitted well with the behavioral and much more political science-oriented trend in public administration research that started accelerating in the 1970s (Peters, 1978). Implementation research has had a major role in bringing public administration and public policy research together, implying that several scholars have been working in both fields. Joint public administration and public policy programs have been formed at many universities. Other research has been important in that bridging process. The policy perspective has crept into many aspects of public administration research, and new research approaches have contributed as well (e.g., neo-rational, institutionalist, governance, and network approaches); implementation research has certainly played an essential role, too.

THE DIVERSITY OF IMPLEMENTATION RESEARCH

During the barely 40 years of implementation research no general implementation theory has emerged, although many implementation scholars have had the development of such a theory as their ultimate, yet far-sighted objective. The implementation subdiscipline has been characterized by many different approaches, representing different research strategies, evaluation standards, methodologies, concepts, and focal subject areas for research.

One of the major controversies among implementation analysts has been whether implementation should be studied from the top-down as a control problem (Mazmanian and Sabatier, 1981) or from the bottom-up, by focusing first on actors most proximate to the problems to be solved by policies (Hull and Hjern, 1987). Related to that discussion is the proper evaluation standard for implementation studies. While, as mentioned above, goal achievement has been the dominating standard, some bottom-up scholars have suggested focusing on problem solving rather than goal achievement. Problem solving could be defined either from the perspective of the group affected by the problem or from the researcher himself (Elmore, 1982; Hull and Hjern, 1987).

In terms of methodology, implementation analyses have been dominated by single case studies that allow the complex phenomena of implementation to be studied in detail and context. In each case several data sources are often applied, such as text analysis of reports and documents, qualitative interviews and observations of implementers, quantitative data on coverage of the program, target group participation, outputs in terms of delivery behaviors, and outcomes (Yin, 1982). Some scholars even use qualitative or quantitative methods for detailed text interpretation in case studies. Other scholars have called for a replacement of single case studies by comparative and statistical research designs, which can increase the number of observations and control for third variables in order to allow more systematic theory and hypothesis testing and generalization (Goggin, 1986).

Implementation scholars also disagree about the key concepts for implementation research: some want to focus on the implementation *process* as the dependent variable (Lester and Goggin, 1998), while others examine implementation behaviors/output as

the dependent variable (Lipsky, 1980), which is to be explained by process and organizational variables (Mazmanian and Sabatier, 1981; Winter, 1999). Some scholars even include outcomes as dependent variables (Mazmanian and Sabatier, 1981; Hull and Hjern, 1987; May and Winter, 2007; Meier and O'Toole, 2007). According to Peter May (1999), conceptual ambiguity and confusion have severely hampered theory development in implementation research.

Somewhat related to the conceptual disagreement are differences in the subjects that implementation researchers study. Many implementation studies present long lists of variables that might explain variation in implementation. A famous example is Mazmanian and Sabatier's (1981) list of 17 variables. However, implementation scholars tend to focus on different variables and subject matters in their research, e.g., hierarchical structuring, tractability of problems, communication, commitment, political support, resources, interorganizational relations and coordination problems, decision and veto points, discretion at various levels (including discretion by street-level bureaucrats), contexts (including socio-economic conditions and target groups' characteristics), empowerment of target groups, the roles of policy design and instruments, and management in shaping implementation.

AN INTEGRATED IMPLEMENTATION MODEL

One attempt to synthesize and integrate some of the most important and promising variables in implementation research in a common framework of analysis has been presented by Winter (1990; Winter and Nielsen, 2008) in his Integrated Implementation Model (Figure 1). Some of the key factors in that model will be used as the main organizing principle for structuring the division among the following chapters in this implementation part of the Handbook (Part 5).

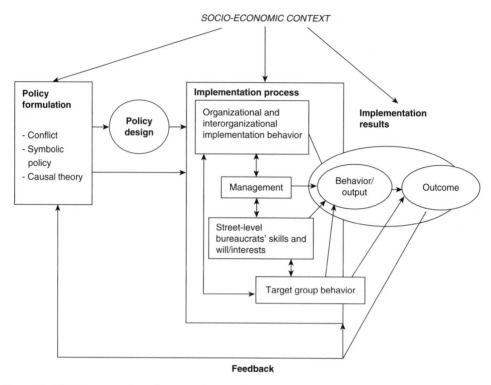

Figure 1   The Integrated Implementation Model

As dependent variable and standard for evaluating the results of the implementation process, the model focuses on both implementation behaviors (outputs) and outcomes in relation to the official policy objectives. This standard is selected from a democratic point of view, as goals formulated in legislatures and in laws have a particular legitimate status and are relevant for holding government accountable.

The first set of factors, which affects implementation results, are the *policy formulation process* and the *policy* design. Too many implementation researchers have erroneously put the whole blame for any lack of goal achievement on implementation. This is in sharp contrast to the early evaluation scholars, who blamed the policy design for any lack of effect; well-designed policies with effective instruments are necessary but not sufficient for improving implementation prospects. Other implementation scholars have ignored or failed to conceptualize the connections between policy formulation, policy design, and implementation.

The roots of implementation problems can often be found in the prior policy formulation process. For instance, conflicts in this process often create a policy that is marked by ambiguous goals as well as an invalid causal theory with a lack of connection between goals and means in the policy design concerned. Sometimes even symbolic policies are adopted to (appear to) address a problem without actually offering the means that could achieve the stated objectives. In addition, as mentioned by Bardach (1977), the conflicts in policy formulation often continue in the subsequent implementation process. Not only conflict but also lack of attention among the coalition partners passing a law can lead to implementation failures (Winter, 1986).

A policy design typically contains a set of goals, a mix of instruments for obtaining these goals, a designation of governmental or non-governmental entities charged with carrying out the goals and an allocation of resources for the requisite tasks (see May, 2012). Policy design and particular policy instruments have received substantial research interest since the 1980s. The basic claim of this literature is that any policy can be disaggregated to one or a mix of a limited number of generic policy instruments. The research interest, however, has not led to agreement on any typology of instruments (Vedung, 1995). One simple classification consists of mandates, economic incentives and information that aim to affect the behavior of either target groups or intermediaries (implementers).

The policy design affects the implementation process and results in various ways. Different mixes of instruments are not equally effective in obtaining a given policy objective. May (2012) finds that policy design is important in affecting the incentives of intermediaries to carry out their requisite tasks, particularly through affecting their commitment and capacity and by signaling desired actions. However, while the validity of the causal theory linking instruments to objectives is certainly important, the research documentation of instrument effects is still meager (however, for another good attempt, see Gunningham and Grabosky, 1998). One reason is that effects of instruments on implementation are often determined by the context, including the political context (as described by May, 2012). Consequently, designing good policies is not a simple, technocratic process like selecting the best types of materials for building a bridge.

The instruments selected may also affect the overall implementation structure and process, as certain instruments favor the formation of particular implementation structures. Mandates aimed at regulating the behavior of target groups normally require a staff for inspecting and enforcing the mandate and a set of sanctions. Information strategies and use of economic incentives such as environmental taxes can sometimes be implemented with fewer staff, although there is no one-to-one relationship between instruments and staff requirements. Some taxes are relatively automatic and easy to collect such as an environmental tax per unit gasoline sold, while others require a substantial staff for inspection and enforcing, e.g., taxing diffuse pollution.

It is important to understand that ineffective policy designs are not always due to lack of knowledge on the part of the policy designers. Policy design of instruments and organizational structure is first of all a political process, in which political actors – both policy proponents and opponents – try to maximize their interests, including selecting an organizational structure that will allow them to maximize long-term control of the implementation process (Moe, 1989).

The next set of factors of the model focuses on how the implementation process affects the results. Implementation processes are characterized by *organizational and interorganizational behaviors* that represent different degrees of commitment and coordination. Interorganizational implementation settings seem to become ever more important, as shown in Laurence O'Toole's Chapter 15: 'Interorganizational Relations and Policy Implementation'. Already, Pressman and Wildavsky (1973) focused on the typical 'complexity of joint action', according to which successful implementation is likely to be negatively related to the number of actors, the diversity of their interests and perspectives, and the number of decision and veto points.

However, O'Toole and Montjoy (1984; O'Toole, in Chapter 15) demonstrated that this insight only applies to certain kinds of interorganizational implementation settings. Decision points are not independent of each other, but successful implementation results can be stimulated by an early agreement on basic understandings, which can promote 'bandwagon effects' in later decisions, and decisions can be merged by crafting 'package deals.'

The implementation prospects also depend on the type of resource dependency among participating organizations. The 'complexity of joint action' is most likely to occur when the implementation process is a chain of sequential relations where one organization is depending on outputs from another as input for its own contribution to implementation. Reciprocal relations where two organizations are depending on each other for inputs may require some coordination but can also decrease the likelihood of veto points because both parties have incentives to cooperate. Pooled relations where multiple organizations can produce and deliver implementation outputs in parallel and independently of each other can produce relatively good implementation results, although coordination may not be optimal. In Chapter 15, O'Toole analyzes interorganizational relations in implementation in more depth, and discusses how interorganizational coordination problems can be reduced by using policy design to increase commitment, build and use a common interest, and facilitate cooperation via exchange.

As the role of management in implementation is easier to describe after discussing the role of street-level bureaucrats, we will first focus on the latter. The behaviors of *street-level bureaucrats* are crucial for the implementation of most policies, and Lipsky's (1980) insights on 'street-level bureaucracy' are included in the Integrated Implementation Model. Street-level bureaucrats make important discretionary decisions in their direct contact with citizens, who tend to define public policies not as crafted in statutes but as delivered to them by street-level bureaucrats. These bureaucrats work in situations characterized by many demands and limited resources. They cope with this situation by rationing services, making biased priorities among cases and clients, controlling clients, and modifying policy goals and client perceptions. According to Lipsky, the coping behaviors of street-level bureaucrats systematically bias the delivery behavior in relation to the policy mandates.

Whereas Lipsky's contribution was important for understanding implementation, the theory needs more specifications of the causal mechanisms that can explain variation in coping behaviors and their consequences (Winter, 2002). The concepts also apply more to social policies than to regulatory policies with target groups who are stronger and less likely to demand more services. In Chapter 14 Winter presents recent attempts to address these problems of conceptualizing and explaining behaviors of street-level bureaucrats, whereas in Chapter 16 Marcia Meyers and Vibeke Lehmann Nielsen analyze the role of street-level bureaucrats in implementation more fully.

As indicated by the above analysis, *management* of street-level bureaucrats is no easy task. The very nature of street-level bureaucrats' practices implies that they exercise considerable discretion in encounters with target groups that are normally not very visible to managers. While bookstands abound with simple recipes for excellent management, these are rarely based on systematic empirical research on public management. The existing evidence is limited and suggests that managing street-level bureaucrats is by no means a simple task, but rather a difficult and complex task.

In a meta-analysis George Boyne (2004) finds surprisingly few studies on effects of management on performance or outcomes. Yet he finds some evidence that management does matter. This has been confirmed by later studies, not least in educational management (Meier and O'Toole, 2007; Andersen and Winter, 2011). However, because such studies measure the direct link between management and outcomes, it is hard to know through what kinds of street-level bureaucratic practices managers can bring about better outcomes. Some causal links are missing. Unfortunately, so far, very few studies have examined the effects of management on street-level bureaucratic behaviors. Most studies indicate that these effects are limited and context contingent. The research challenge is to specify to what extent and how management affects street-level bureaucratic behaviors in given contexts. Such research has just begun, however. Some preliminary findings can be mentioned.

In line with principal–agent theory, managers' influence seems to vary with the visibility of various street-level bureaucratic practices (Winter, 2003). In addition, managers and street-level bureaucrats sometimes experience a multiple principal problem when local politicians are resisting national policies. Thus, the effect of using some goal-directed management tools – such as clear signaling of expectations and recruiting workers with a better fit with the goals of the organization – may depend on whether local policies are supporting or opposing national ones (Winter et al., 2008a).

Finally, management is relational. This implies that the effect of management practices on street-level bureaucratic behaviors may be contingent on the characteristics of individual street-level bureaucrats, including their expertise, motivation and perceptions of the applied management tools. Thus, workers' expertise seems to condition the effect of delegation (May and Winter, 2009), and workers' motivation and perception of economic incentives seem to condition the effect of these incentives (Andersen and Pallesen, 2008). Although the direct and contingent effects of management on the behavior of street-level bureaucrats are often limited, indirect effects must also be taken into account. These include the impact that managers' commitment has on the attitudes of their front-line workers and the way in which managers, by designing or changing organizational structures, can shape bureaucratic attitudes and behaviors (Winter et al., 2008b).

According to the Integrated Implementation Model, also, *target groups* of public policies, i.e., citizens or firms, play an important role, not only on the effects of the policy but also in affecting the behaviors by street-level bureaucrats through citizens positive or negative actions in co-producing public services (Winter and Nielsen, 2008). Finally, the *socio-economic context* forms important

framework conditions for implementation. For example, in employment policies, both the types of employment and training offers and their effects depend heavily on ups and downs in the business cycle.

The Integrated Implementation Model is not a model in the strict sense of a simple causal model. It is rather a framework of analysis presenting key factors and mechanisms that affect implementation outputs and outcomes. For each set of factors, a number of more specific hypotheses can be developed (Winter, 1990; Winter and Nielsen, 2008; see also Chapters 14–16).

As mentioned above, key parts of the model will be used for structuring Part 5 into the following four chapters. In Chapter 14 'Implementation Perspectives: Status and Reconsideration' Søren Winter offers an account of the development of implementation research. The field has been developed across and within three 'generations' of implementation research. Winter also performs a critical examination of the field and focuses on recent promising directions for implementation research. In Chapter 15, Laurence O'Toole analyzes the role of inter-organizational relations in implementation and how these can be affected to improve implementation. Finally, in Chapter 16, Marcia Meyers and Vibeke Lehmann Nielsen give a critical account of the literature on the role of street-level bureaucrats in policy implementation.

REFERENCES

Albæk, Erik (1988) *Fra sandhed til information: Evalueringsforskning I USA – før og nu.* Copenhagen: Akademisk Forlag.

Andersen, Lotte Bøgh and Pallesen, Thomas (2008) '"Not Just for the Money?" How Financial Incentives Affect the Number of Publications at Danish Research Institutions', *International Public Management Journal*, 11(1): 28–47.

Andersen, Simon Calmar and Winter, Søren C. (eds) (2011) *Ledelse, læring og trivsel i folkeskolerne.* Copenhagen: SFI 11: 47.

Bardach, Eugene (1977) *The Implementation Game.* Cambridge, MA: MIT Press.

Bardach, Eugene (2001) 'Implementation, Political', in N.J. Smelser and P.B. Baltes (eds), *International Encyclopedia of the Social & Behavioral Sciences.* Amsterdam: Elsevier Science Ltd.

Bogason, Peter (2000) *Public Policy and Local Governance: Institutions in Postmodern Society.* Cheltenham: Edward Elgar.

Boyne, George A (2004) 'Explaining Public Service Performance: Does Management Matter'? *Public Policy and Administration,* 19(4): 100–117.

Brehm, John and Gates, Scott (1999) *Working, Shirking, and Sabotage: Bureaucratic Response to a Democratic Public.* Ann Arbor, MI: University of Michigan Press.

Dye, T.R. (1976) *What Governments Do, Why They Do It, and What Difference It Makes.* Tuscaloosa, AL: University of Alabama Press.

Elmore, Richard F. (1982) 'Backward Mapping: Implementation Research and Policy Decisions', in W. Williams, R.F. Elmore, J.S. Hall et al. (eds), *Studying Implementation.* Chatham, NJ: Chatham House Publishers, pp. 18–35.

Fixen, D., Naoom, S.F., Blasé, K.A., Friedman, R.M. and Wallace, F. (2005) *Implementation Research: A Synthesis of the Literature.* Tampa, FL: University of South Florida.

Goggin, Malcolm L. (1986) 'The "Too Few Cases/Too Many Variables" Problems in Implementation Research', *The Western Political Quarterly,* 39(2): 328–347.

Gunningham, Neil and Grabosky, Peter (1998) *Smart Regulation, Designing Environmental Policy.* New York: Oxford University Press.

Hull, Christopher J. and Hjern, Benny (1987) *Helping Small Firms Grow: An Implementation Perspective.* London: Croom Helm.

Kagan, Robert A. (1994) 'Regulatory Enforcement', in David H. Roosenbloom and Richard D. Schwartz (eds), *Handbook of Regulation and Administrative Law.* New York: Marcel Decker, pp. 383–422.

Kaufman, Herbert (1960) *The Forest Ranger.* Baltimore, MD: Johns Hopkins Press.

Lester, James P. and Goggin, Malcolm L. (1998) 'Back to the Future: The Rediscovery of Implementation Studies', *Policy Currents – Newsletter of the Public Policy Section of the American Political Science Association,* 8(3): 1–9.

Linder, Stephen H. and Peters, B. Guy (1989) 'Instruments of Government: Perceptions and Contexts', *International Public Policy,* 9(1): 35–58.

Lipsky, Michael (1980) *Street-Level Bureaucracy: The Dilemmas of the Individual in Public Services.* New York: Russell Sage Foundation.

Lynn, Laurence E., Jr, Heinrich, Carolyn J. and Hill, Carolyn J. (2001) *Improving Governance: A New Logic for Empirical Research.* Washington, DC: Georgetown University Press.

May, Peter J. (1999) *Toward A Future Agenda for Implementation Research: A Panelist's Notes.* Prepared for the annual meeting of the Western Political Science Association in Seattle. Department of Political Science, University of Washington.

May, Peter J. and Winter, Søren (2000) 'Reconsidering Styles of Regulatory Enforcement: Patterns in Danish Agro-Environmental Inspection'. *Law and Policy,* 22(2): 143–173.

May, Peter J. and Winter, Søren C. (2007) 'Collaborative Service Arrangements: Patterns, Bases, and Perceived Consequences', *Public Management Review,* 9(4): 479–502.

May, Peter J. and Winter, Søren C. (2009) 'Politicians, Managers, and Street-Level Bureaucrats: Influences on Policy Implementation', *Journal of Public Administration Research and Theory,* 19(3): 453–476.

May, Peter J. (2012) 'Policy Design and Implementation', in B. Guy Peters and Jon Pierre (eds), *The SAGE Handbook of Public Administration.* London, Sage.

Mazmanian, Daniel A. and Sabatier, Paul (1981) *Effective Policy Implementation.* Lexington, KY: Lexington Books.

Meier, Kenneth J. and O'Toole, Laurence J., Jr (2007) 'Modeling Public Management: Empirical Analysis of the Management–Performance Nexus', *Public Management Review,* 9(4): 503–527.

Moe, Terry M. (1989) 'The Politics of Bureaucratic Structure', in John E. Chubb and Paul E. Peterson (eds), *Can the Government Govern?* Washington, DC: Brookings Institution, pp. 267–329.

Murphy, Jerome T. (1971) 'Title I of ESEA: The Politics of Administering Federal Education Reform', *Harvard Educational Review,* 42(1): 35–63.

O'Toole, Laurence J., Jr (2000) 'Research on Policy Implementation: Assessment and Prospects', *Journal of Public Administration Research and Theory,* 10(2): 263–288.

O'Toole, Laurence J., Jr. and Montjoy, Robert S. (1984) 'Interorganizational Policy Implementation: A Theoretical Perspective', *Public Administration Review,* 44(6): 491–503.

Parker, Christine and Nielsen, Vibeke Lehmann (eds) (2012) *Explaining Compliance: Business Responses to Regulation.* Cheltenham: Edward Elgar.

Parson, Wayne (1995) *Public Policy: An Introduction to the Theory and Practice of Policy Analysis.* Aldershot: Edward Elgar.

Peters, B. Guy (1978) *The Politics of Bureaucracy: A Comparative Perspective.* New York: Longman.

Pressman, Jeffrey L. and Wildavsky, Aaron (1973) *Implementation.* Berkeley, CA: University of California Press.

Sætren, H. (2005) 'Facts and Myths about Research on Public Policy Implementation: Out-of-Fashion, Allegedly Dead, But Still Very Much Alive and Relevant'. *The Policy Studies Journal*, 33(4): 559–582.

Salamon, Lester M. (1981) 'Rethinking Public Management: Third-Party Government and the Changing Forms of Government Action', *Public Policy,* 29(3): 256–275.

Salamon, Lester M. (ed.) (2002) *Tools of Government: A Guide to the New Governance.* New York: Oxford University Press.

Scholz, J.T. and Wei, F.H. (1986) 'Regulatory Enforcement in a Federalist System', *American Political Science Review*, 80(4): 1249–1270.

Vedung, Evert (1995) 'Policy Instruments: Typologies and Theories', in M.-L. Bemelmans-Videc, R. Rist and E. Vedung (eds), *Policy Instruments and Evaluation.* New Brunswick, NJ: Transaction Books, pp. 21–58.

Winter, Søren (1986) 'How Policy-Making Affects Implementation: The Decentralization of the Danish Disablement Pension Administration', *Scandinavian Political Studies*, 9(4): 361–385.

Winter, Søren (1990) 'Integrating Implementation Research', in Dennis J. Palumbo and Donald J. Calista (eds), *Implementation and the Policy Process.* New York: Greenwood Press, pp. 19–38.

Winter, Søren (1999) 'New Directions for Implementation Research', *Policy Currents – Newsletter of the Public Policy Section of the American Political Science Association*, 8(4): 1–5.

Winter, Søren C. (2002) *Explaining Street-Level Bureaucratic Behavior in Social and Regulatory Policies.* Paper prepared for the annual meeting of the American Political Science Association in Boston, 29 August to 1 September 2002. Danish National Institute of Social Research, Copenhagen.

Winter, Søren C. (2003) *Political Control, Street-Level Bureaucrats and Information Asymmetry in Regulatory and Social Policies.* Paper presented at the annual meeting of the Association for Public Policy Analysis and Management held in Washington, DC, 6–8 November. Danish National Institute of Social Research, Copenhagen.

Winter, Søren C. and May, Peter J. (2001) 'Motivation for Compliance with Environmental Regulations', *Journal of Policy Analysis and Management*, 20(4): 675–698.

Winter, Søren C. and Nielsen, Vibeke Lehmann (2008) *Implementering af politik.* Copenhagen: Academica.

Winter, Søren C., Skou, Mette H. and Beer, Frederikke (2008a) *Effective Management for National or Local Policy Objectives? Implementing Welfare Sanction Policy in Denmark.* SFI Working Paper Series 14.

Winter, Søren C., Dinesen, Peter T. and May, Peter J. (2008b) *Implementation Regimes and Street-Level Bureaucrats: Employment Service Delivery in Denmark.* SFI Working Paper Series 12.

Yin, Robert K. (1982) 'Studying the Implementation of Public Programs', in W.Williams, R.F. Elmore, J.S. Hall, et al. (eds), *Studying Implementation.* Chatham, NJ: Chatham House Publishers, pp. 36–72.

14

Implementation Perspectives: Status and Reconsideration

Søren C. Winter

Although the field of implementation research is barely 40 years old, implementation has already been analyzed from many different perspectives, representing different research strategies, evaluation standards, concepts, focal subject areas, and methodologies (see Part 5 Introduction). The purpose of this chapter is two-fold.

First, it performs a critical review of some of the major contributions to the literature. This examination follows the development of the field. Commentators have identified three generations of implementation research (Goggin, 1986), which are presented and assessed in the following. These are the pioneers with their explorative case studies, the second-generation studies with their top-down and bottom-up research strategies and synthesis models, and a third generation with more systematic tests based on comparative and statistical research designs. The nice thing about these generations is, however, that as a researcher you can belong to more than one and thus stay alive and even get younger!

Second, based on a critical examination of the development and status of the research field, the chapter suggests ways of moving ahead. Implementation research can be improved by (1) accepting theoretical diversity rather than looking for one common theoretical framework, (2) developing and testing partial theories and hypotheses rather than trying to reach for utopia in constructing a general implementation theory, (3) seeking conceptual clarification, (4) focusing on both outputs (behaviors of implementers) and outcomes as dependent variables in implementation research rather than goal achievement, and (5) applying more comparative and statistical research designs rather than relying on single case studies in order to sort out the influence of different implementation variables.

THE PIONEERS

In several respects, the book *Implementation*, by Pressman and Wildavsky (1973), sets the stage for later implementation research. Most implementation research has focused on implementation problems, barriers, and failures, and this pessimistic view of implementation was already reflected in the subtitle of this seminal work,

> How Great Expectations in Washington are Dashed in Oakland; or, Why it's Amazing that Federal Programs Work at All

In this case study of the local implementation of a federal economic development program to decrease unemployment among ethnic minority groups in Oakland, Pressman and Wildavsky focused on the 'complexity of joint action' as the key implementation problem. In that case – as in many others – federal, regional, state, and local government actors, courts, affected interest groups, private firms, and media had a role and stake in policy implementation. Implementation problems were amplified not only by the many actors but also by the many decision and veto points, which must typically be passed during the implementation process. Although they probably overemphasized the lack of conflict in their case, Pressman and Wildavsky convincingly showed that merely slightly different perspectives, priorities, and time horizons among multiple actors with different missions in repeated and sequential decisions could cause delay, distortion, and even failures in policy implementation.

However, the two authors also demonstrated that failures are not only caused by bad implementation but also by bad policy instruments. Many of the problems in the Oakland case would have been avoided had policy makers chosen a more direct economic instrument that would ex post have tied spending of public expenditures to the actual number of minority workers employed rather than relying on endless ex ante negotiations with affected parties and authorities.

Pressman and Wildavsky (1973) are good representatives for the first generation of implementation studies, which were typically explorative and inductive case studies with a theory-generating aim. Very few central theoretical variables were in focus: in this case, the number of actors and decision points and the validity of the causal theory. Another outstanding example is Eugene

Bardach's (1977) *The Implementation Game*, which placed more emphasis on the aspects of conflict in implementation, seeing implementation as a continuation of the political game from the policy adoption stage, though partly with other actors and other relations among actors. Bardach analyzed the types of games that various actors apply in the implementation process in order to pursue their own interests. However, these games tend to distort implementation from the legislative goals. Among other representatives from what has later been called the first generation of implementation research we find Erwin Hargrove (1975), who called implementation research 'the missing link' in the study of the policy process, and Walter Williams and Richard Elmore (1976).

SECOND-GENERATION MODEL BUILDERS: TOP-DOWN, BOTTOM-UP, AND SYNTHESES

Second-generation implementation studies began in the early 1980s. Whereas the first-generation studies had been explorative and theory generating, the ambition of the second generation was to take the next step in theory development by constructing theoretical models, or rather frameworks of analysis, that could guide empirical analysis. Some of these studies had more optimistic views on successful implementation.

The construction of models and research strategies, however, immediately led to a major confrontation between the so-called top-down and bottom-up perspectives on policy implementation. The predominant top-down researchers focused on a specific political decision, normally a law. On the background of its official purpose, they followed the implementation down through the system, often with special interest in central decision makers. They would typically assume a control perspective on implementation, trying to give good advice on how to structure the implementation process from above in order to achieve the purpose of the legislation and to minimize the number of decision points that could be vetoed.

The best-known and most frequently used (Sabatier, 1986) top-down analysis framework was developed by Mazmanian and Sabatier (1981). It contains 17 variables placed in three main groups, concerning the tractability of the problems addressed by the legislation, the social and political context, and the ability of the legislation to structure the implementation process. This structuring can be made by means of, for example, hierarchy, appointing of authorities and staff with a positive attitude towards the legislation/program, and use of incentives including competition among providers. By adding a long-term perspective of 10–15 years to implementation, the authors show that, over time, start-up problems are often ameliorated by better structuring of the implementation by policy advocates (see also Kirst and Jung, 1982). This gave rise to much more optimistic views of implementation in contrast to the pessimism introduced by Pressman and Wildavsky (1973) and joined by most implementation analysts.

Mazmanian and Sabatier's framework was met by two different kinds of criticism. According to one strand, the model was naive and unrealistic because it overemphasized the ability of policy proponents to structure implementation, thus ignoring the ability of policy opponents to interfere in this structuring process (Moe, 1989). Often policy opponents are able to make policy goals contradictory or ambiguous and to increase their own long-term influence in the implementation process in order to avoid some of the effects intended by policy proponents. Conceptually, the model ignored the politics of policy formulation and policy design (Winter, 1986b).

Another strand of criticism came from the bottom-up researchers who took special interest in 'the bottom' of the implementation system, the place where the public sector – or private providers of public services – meets the citizens or firms. They all emphasized the influence that front-line staff or field workers have on the delivery of policies such as social services, income transfers, and law enforcement in relation to citizens and firms. Field workers are crucial decision makers in these studies, and the disability of politicians and administrative managers to control field workers is emphasized.

Like top-down researchers and also most evaluation researchers, some bottom-up researchers use the official objectives of a given legislation as the standard of evaluation (Lipsky, 1980; Winter, 1986a). Michael Lipsky (1980) developed a theory on 'Street-level Bureaucracy.' It focuses on the discretionary decisions that each field worker – or 'street-level bureaucrat' as Lipsky prefers to call them – makes in relation to individual citizens when delivering policies to them. This discretionary role in delivering services or enforcing regulations makes street-level bureaucrats essential actors in implementing public policies. Indeed, Lipsky (1980) turns the policy process upside-down by claiming that street-level bureaucrats are the real *policy makers*. However, one ironic aspect of the theory is that although he emphasizes the individual role of street-level bureaucrats in implementing public policies, according to Lipsky their similar working conditions make them all apply rather similar behavior. This means that street-level bureaucrats, even across policy types, tend to apply similar types of practices whether they are teachers, policemen, nurses, doctors, or social workers.

Although trying to do their best, street-level bureaucrats experience a gap between the demands made on them by legislative mandates, managers, and citizens, on the one hand, and their limited resources, on the other. In this situation they apply a number of coping mechanisms that systematically distort their work in relation to the intentions of the legislation. They ration services and make priorities between their tasks and clients, e.g., by upgrading easy tasks and cases in which clients make pressure to obtain a benefit or decision, at the expense of complicated, non-programmed tasks and clients that do not press for a decision. Street-level bureaucrats tend to apply few, crude standard classifications for grouping clients and combine these by rules of thumb for the processing of these categories, rather than treating clients individually. To prove successful, street-level bureaucrats tend to apply creaming in favoring relatively resourceful clients and downgrading the weaker clients. Street-level bureaucrats try to gain control over clients in order to make cases simpler to process. As time goes by, street-level bureaucrats develop more cynical perceptions of clients and modify the policy objectives.

Other *bottom-up* researchers go the whole length, rejecting the objective of policy mandates as an evaluation standard. Instead, their analysis departs from a specific problem such as youth unemployment (Elmore, 1982) or small firms' conditions of growth (Hull and Hjern, 1987). In practice it is the researcher himself, who in most cases defines the problem and thereby his evaluation standard. In my opinion this is acceptable if done explicitly, and it can be fruitful if the researcher is able to convince others about the appropriateness of his problem definition.

The next task in Hull and Hjern's *bottom-up* approach is to identify the many actors that are affecting the problem in question and to map relations between them. In these network analyses both public and private actors become essential, and the analyses often include several policies that affect the same problem whether or not it is intended in those policies. For instance, when defining youth unemployment as the focal problem, youth unemployment is affected by a great number of actors such as schools, high schools, educational and vocational training institutions, the social welfare system, employment service, unemployment foundations, and employment providers as well as the social partners (e.g., through fixing of wage rates).

Hull and Hjern (1987) focused on the role of local networks in affecting a given

problem in the implementation process, and they also developed a way of identifying these networks. It is a combination of a snowball method and a sociometric method. Starting with the actors with most direct contact with people exposed to the problem, one gradually identifies more and more actors who are interacting with the first set of actors around the problem, and so on. In this way, this type of bottom-up analysis maps the informal, empirical implementation structure around a given problem, while *top-down* research tends to look at the formal implementation structure related to one particular policy program. According to Hull and Hjern, empirical implementation structures tend to be far less hierarchical than formal ones, and they often cross organizational borders and may include public as well as private actors in forming collaborative networks at the operational level that may even take on an identity of their own relatively independent of their mother organizations. The bottom-up analyses by Hjern and associates, which are important in drawing attention to implementation activities and structures at the local operational level, have given inspiration to later policy network and governance analyses (Bogason, 2000). However, the perspective has more the character of guidelines for an inductive research strategy and methodology than a development of theory and hypotheses that can be empirically tested.

This also applies to Elmore's (1982) 'backward mapping' strategy, which has played an important role in the development of the bottom-up perspective. However, Elmore's perspective is more aimed at helping policy analysts and policy makers in designing sound policies than offering a research strategy and contributing to theory development.

The *top-down* and *bottom-up* perspectives were useful in drawing increased attention to the fact that both top and bottom play important roles in the implementation process, but in the long run the battle between the two approaches was not fruitful. Each tended to ignore the portion of the implementation reality explained by the other (Goggin et al., 1990: 12). Elmore (1985) actually recommends using both forward mapping – which is essentially a top-down analysis – and backward mapping for policy analysis because each tends to offer valuable insights for policy makers. He claims that policy designers need to consider the policy instruments and the resources they have at their disposal (forward mapping) as well as the incentive structure of the target group and street-level bureaucrats' ability to tip the balance of these incentives in order to affect the problematic situation of the target group (backward mapping).

Other scholars have tried to solve the controversy by specifying the conditions where one approach might be more relevant than the other. Sabatier (1986) claims that the *top-down* perspective is best suited for studying the implementation in policy areas that are dominated by one specific legislation, limited research funds, or where the situation is structured at least moderately well. *Bottom-up* perspectives, on the other hand, would be more relevant in situations where several different policies are directed towards a particular problem, and where one is primarily interested in the dynamics of different local situations.

Attempts were also made to synthesize the two models. Richard E. Matland (1995) suggests that their relative value depends on the degree of ambiguity in goals and means of a policy and the degree of conflict. Traditional *top-down* models, based on the public administration tradition, present an accurate description of the implementation process when a policy is clear, and the conflict is low. However, *top-down* models, such as the Mazmanian–Sabatier framework, are also relevant when conflict is high and ambiguity is low, which makes the structuring of the implementation particularly important. In contrast, *bottom-up* models provide an accurate description of the implementation

process when the policy is ambiguous and the conflict is low. When conflict as well as ambiguity is present, both models have some relevance according to Matland.

Other attempts at synthesizing the two approaches were made by the former main combatants. The previous *bottom-up* analyses, which were performed by the circle around Hull and Hjern (1987), focused on actors and activities at the bottom, while in practice their analyses did not rise very high above it. However, in their synthesis proposal – called 'an inductive approach to match outcomes of politics and their intentions' – Hull and Hjern recommend systematic interview analysis of relevant actors from the bottom to the very top, including mapping of implementation activities and structures, the actors' evaluation of the politically determined purposes of the relevant laws and their achievement, and also the actors' opinions on where it goes wrong and analyses of how various policies contribute to solve the *policy problem* in question. Obviously, it would require immense resources to carry out this research strategy, and I am not aware of any such study performed in practice. In addition – as was the case for their bottom-up analyses above – the proposed synthesis suffers from being methodological recommendations rather than theoretically based expectations, which can be tested systematically.

Sabatier (1986) has also suggested a synthesis – the so-called *Advocacy Coalition Framework* (ACF). He adopts 'the bottom-uppers' unit of analysis – a whole variety of public and private actors involved with a policy problem – as well as their concerns with understanding the perspectives and strategies of all major categories of actors (not simply program proponents). He then combines this starting point with top-downers' concern with the manner in which socioeconomic conditions and legal instruments constrain behavior' (Sabatier, 1986: 39). The synthesis applies the framework to explaining policy change over a period of a decade or more in order to deal with the role of policy-oriented learning. It also adopts the top-down style of developing and testing hypotheses as a contribution to theory development. In conceptualizing policy change, Sabatier focuses on government action programs that, in turn, produce policy outputs at the operational level, which again result in a variety of impacts. The focus on legislative mandates as well as outputs and impacts could be potentially relevant for implementation research. In practice, however, the ACF was further developed to focus on policy change in mandates rather than implementation. Although making an important contribution to the public policy literature, Sabatier and his later associate, Jenkins-Smith (Sabatier and Jenkins-Smith, 1993), actually moved the focus of analysis away from implementation towards policy change and formation.

Another kind of synthesis was suggested by Winter (1990; Winter and Nielsen, 2008) in his 'Integrated Implementation Model'. Unlike previous attempts, the purpose here was not to make a true synthesis between *top-down* and *bottom-up* perspectives, but rather to integrate a number of the most fruitful theoretical elements from various pieces of implementation research – regardless of their origin – into a joint model or framework. Its main factors in explaining implementation outputs and outcomes are policy formation and policy design, interorganizational relations, management, street-level bureaucrats' will and capacity, in addition to target group behavior, socio-economic conditions, and feedback mechanisms, cf. Introduction to Part 5 of the Handbook.

THIRD GENERATION: QUANTITATIVE RESEARCH DESIGNS

While the first and second generations of implementation studies have been helpful in directing attention to implementation problems and identifying implementation barriers and factors that might ease implementation, the research had not succeeded in sorting out the relative importance of the explanatory variables. A substantial part of the studies could be criticized as merely presenting – often long – checklists of variables that might effect implementation. Malcolm Goggin (1986) pointed out that because implementation research had been dominated by single case studies, it was plagued by the problem of 'too few cases and too many variables' or by overdetermination, where two or more variables explain variation in the dependent variable equally well. The single case study approach did not allow for any control of third variables. According to Goggin, this problem had hampered the development of implementation theory. He therefore, called for a third generation of implementation studies that would test theories on the basis of more comparative case studies and statistical research designs which could increase the number of observations and allow control for third variables.

Goggin followed up on these recommendations in a study with his associates (Goggin, Bowman, Lester, and O'Toole, 1990). The study was mainly based on a communications theory perspective on intergovernmental implementation, but also included many variables from previous top-down and bottom-up research. The study focused especially on variation among states in the way and extent they implement federal policies in three different social and regulatory policies. The authors tried to encourage further research involving multiple measures and multiple methods, including quantitative methods. Later, Lester and Goggin (1998), in making a status for implementation research, called for the development of 'a parsimonious, yet complete, theory of policy implementation.' They suggested that such a meta-theory might be developed by combining the insights of communications theory, regime theory, rational choice theory (especially game theory), and contingency theories. As a dependent variable for implementation studies, they proposed to focus on implementation processes rather than outputs and outcomes.

A NEW RESEARCH AGENDA

While agreeing with Goggin's (1986) call for using more comparative and statistical research designs based on quantitative methods, I disagree with several of the later methodological and theoretical recommendations made by him and his colleagues. As recognized by one of these authors, O'Toole (2000), to follow the methodological suggestions given by Goggin, Bowman, Lester, and O'Toole (1990) would involve at least outlining a research career's worth of work. It would require applying research designs that involve numerous variables, across different policy types, across 50 states, over at least 10 years, as well as measuring the relevant variables by a combination of content analyses, expert panels, elite surveys, and expert reassessment of the data from questionnaires and interviews. Because such a research strategy is too demanding, less taxing research strategies that can still secure a sufficient number of observations would be more realistic.

Given the many exploratory variables that have already been identified by various implementation scholars, Lester and Goggin's suggested development of a 'parsimonious, yet complete implementation theory' by combining theoretical elements from at least four different theories appear to be a *contradictio in adjecto* and is more likely to lead to theoretical mismatch. Rather than looking for *the* overall and one-for-all implementation theory, we should welcome diversity in both the theoretical perspectives and methodologies applied. Such diversity will give us new insights, some of which may then later be integrated into broader analytical frameworks or models (Mazmanian and Sabatier, 1981; Goggin, Bowman, Lester, and O'Toole, 1990; Winter, 1990). It strikes me, however, as unrealistic to think that many scholars can

agree on applying one common theoretical framework.

Although the general implementation frameworks presented by model builders so far have been helpful in giving an overview of some crucial implementation variables, the generality of such models may in fact be an obstacle for further development of our understanding of implementation. This is because generality inhibits precise specification of variables and causal mechanisms (May, 1999). Consequently, it seems more fruitful to utilize research resources on developing partial theories and hypotheses about different and more limited implementation problems and on putting these to serious empirical tests.

My suggestions for further development of implementation research can be summarized in five points: (1) provide theoretical diversity; (2) focus on partial rather than general implementation theories; (3) seek conceptual clarification; (4) focus on outputs (behavior of implementers – particularly delivery behaviors) as well as outcomes as dependent variables; and (5) use more comparative and statistical research designs (Winter, 1999). While the two first and the fifth points have been developed above, I will elaborate on the other points in the following and illustrate them by recent research.

Need for conceptual clarifications and a focus on both outputs and outcomes as dependent variables

As pointed out by Peter May (1999), most conceptual frameworks in the implementation literature are weakly developed, lacking adequate definitions of concepts and specification of causal mechanisms. The most important issue for the development of implementation research may be to reconsider what constitutes the object of the study. There has been some disagreement in the literature on the term of 'implementation' and on what is the important dependent variable in implementation research (Hill and Hupe, 2009).

One problem is that the concept 'implementation' is often used to characterize both the implementation process and the output – and sometimes also the outcome – of the implementation process. Lester and Goggin (1998) view implementation as a '*process*, a series of subnational decisions and actions directed toward putting a prior authoritative federal decision into effect'. Thereby, they reject focusing on the output of the implementation process as 'a dichotomous conceptualization of implementation as simply success or failure.'

Although agreeing that the success/failure dichotomy is problematic, I suggest that the most important focus of implementation research would not be the implementation process but the outputs of that process in terms of delivery behaviors and the outcomes in terms of change in the behavior or conditions of target populations. As mentioned in the Part 5 Introduction to this implementation section, this would be much more in line with the classic focus of public policy research on the content of policy, its causes, and consequences (Dye, 1976). Implementation output is policy content at a much more operational level than a law. It is policy as it is being delivered to the citizens. Implementation outcomes are the consequences of implementation outputs/delivery behaviors.

The most common dependent variable in implementation research so far has been the degree of goal achievement, whether defined in terms of output or outcome. The first problem, however, is that goal achievement is a fraction. Output in terms of behaviors of implementers or outcome in terms of effects on target population is the numerator, and the policy goal is the denominator. Yet, using a fraction as the dependent variable renders theory building problematic when different factors explain variation in the numerator and the denominator. While the policy formation process is likely to account for variation in goals, the implementation

process is likely to account for variation in delivery behaviors.

Pushing it to extremes, the problem is that any attempt to make generalizations about goal achievement based on analysis of the behavior or outcome of implementers is dependent on the goal variable having a certain value. The generalization may become invalid if the goal changes. Therefore, generalizations about implementation output are extremely relativistic because statements are conditioned by the goals that are formulated. This is problematic when it is recognized that policy makers are often more interested in making decisions on means or instruments than on goals; goals are often invented after decisions on the means have been made in order to legitimize the means adopted, and goals are not always expected or even intended to be achieved.

The second problem of using goal achievement as the dependent variable of implementation research is that such goals can be difficult to operationalize. Much has already been written in the implementation and evaluation literatures about the vagueness and ambiguity of policy goals and the difference between official and latent goals. In addition, while most policy statutes state some kind of goal for the outcome of the policy, many fail to specify goals or standards for the behavior of the implementers.

This is often the case in regulatory policies. For example, the Danish agro-environmental regulation has a general objective of reducing the nitrate pollution of the aquatic environment to a certain level, and it specifies a large number of very specific rules for farmers' behaviors in that respect. However, the only objective or requirement for the implementers – i.e., the municipalities that are in charge of enforcement – is that they inspect farms for compliance with the rules. In this case it is hard to gauge implementation success unless we use the goals for changes in the farmers' behaviors or in the physical environment as the standard. However, from the evaluation and implementation literatures, we also know that other factors than implementation outputs may affect policy outcomes/effects (Rossi and Freeman, 1989).

Whereas the degree of goal achievement at the national level may not be an optimal variable for accumulating research evidence on policy implementation, implementation research has an important task in focusing on and explaining variation in outcomes. For several decades, however, implementation scholars as well as other political scientists have paid far too little attention to explaining variation in policy outcomes and examining the relation between implementation outputs and outcomes. As mentioned above, few implementation scholars have included outcome in their implementation models or framework (Mazmanian and Sabatier, 1981; Elmore, 1982; Hull and Hjern, 1987; Goggin et al., 1990; Winter, 1990).

We do not have a complete understanding of the policy process unless we know how target groups respond to public policies. Despite the fact that 'the authoritative allocation of values for a society' (Easton, 1953) and 'who gets what, when, and how' (Lasswell, 1936) are among the most famous definitions of politics, until the turn of the century very few political science studies focused on how citizens respond to public policies. Some would say that this is the province of evaluation research. However, evaluation is typically characterized by a focus on methods, whereas very little theory development has occurred, especially extremely little political science theory. In political science journals the contrast between many studies of citizens' attitudes and behaviors at the input side of politics and very few outcome studies is striking. Yet, the study of outcomes is as much, if not more, about policy, as are most public opinion studies that relate to the input side of policy.

However, some very promising developments have taken place in the last two decades. First, starting particularly in the 1990s, some law and society and regulation scholars have attempted to explain variation in compliance among citizens (Tyler, 2006) and firms (Parker and Nielsen, 2012) and the role of enforcement (i.e., policy implementation) in shaping compliance (Winter and May, 2001, 2002; May and Winter, 2012). Second, a research agenda on how public management affects the performance of organizations has been initiated around the turn of the century by, in particular, Kenneth Meier, Laurence O'Toole, George Boyne, and their collaborators (Boyne, 2003; Meier and O'Toole, 2007). They use the term 'performance' to indicate valued outcomes, e.g., academic performance of students in schools.

Accordingly, it is fruitful if implementation studies focus on and seek to explain variation in outputs and outcomes and study the relationship between implementation outputs and outcomes. For example, in several countries employment policies of the last decade have demanded that employment agencies and their caseworkers emphasize getting unemployed clients quickly into work in their conversations with such clients and use sanctions for non-compliance in order to increase employment. However, agencies and their street-level bureaucrats typically vary in the extent they deliver such outputs and outcomes. Implementation studies can play an important role in seeking to explain these variations by various implementation factors, such as the role of policy and organizational design (Hill, 2006; Beer et al., 2008; Winter et al., 2008a), interorganizational collaboration (Meier and O'Toole, 2003; Lundin, 2007; May and Winter, 2007), management behaviors, and the attitudes and capacity of street-level bureaucrats (Riccuci, 2005; Winter et al., 2008b; May and Winter, 2009; Schram et al., 2009).

The behaviors of street-level bureaucrats are also important in explaining variation in outcomes (Bloom et al., 2003; Heinesen et al., 2004; Winter, 2005; Baviskar and Winter, 2009; Behncke et al., 2010; Weatherall and Markwardt, 2010; Winter and Baviskar, 2010).

Treating implementation outputs as both a dependent variable – and as an independent variable in explaining variation in outcomes – raises some important considerations on how to conceptualize and categorize the behavior of implementers at different organizational levels, including the crucial level of the individual street-level bureaucrat. One very intriguing question is whether we can find behavioral dimensions and classifications that are universally applicable in all policy areas, or if we should generate concepts and classifications that are different from one policy area to another.

To the extent that a policy statute sets goals or standards for implementation practices – as in the employment policy studies above – it is a relevant task for implementation research both to study the extent to which these standards have actually been met – which is important from a democratic effectiveness perspective (Winter, 1990; Winter and Nielsen, 2008) – and to explain variations in such valued practices. Such findings can be important to policy makers and researchers in that particular policy area. However, some findings on implementation factors that are fostering compliance among implementing organizations and street-level bureaucrats with these standards are also likely to be valid in others settings and policy areas.

Another strategy is to use behavioral concepts that apply to all policy areas, whether these behaviors are mandated or not. Although Meier and O'Toole (2007) in most of their studies of management and performance have studied educational management, their theorizing and concepts on management practices are based on general public management theorizing, and many of their findings are likely to apply to other policies as well. Lipsky's (1980) street-level bureaucracy theory represents an ambitious attempt to offer a universally applicable set of concepts for describing the coping behavior of street-level bureaucrats in all policy areas (see also Winter, 2002). However, several of these coping mechanisms apply better to implementation of social rather than regulatory policies, and a universally applicable classification scheme may suffer from a lack of the precision that a more policy-specific set of concepts could offer.

A middle ground is to use sets of concepts that apply to very broad classes of policies. For example, concepts have been developed that are appropriate to classify the behavior of implementers in almost any kind of regulatory policy (Kagan, 1994). May and Winter (1999, 2000, 2012; Winter and May, 2001) have developed concepts for regulatory enforcement at both agency and individual street-level bureaucrat levels. Agency enforcement choices are conceptualized as (1) tools (use of different enforcement measures: sanctions, information and assistance, and incentives), (2) priorities (whom to target and what to inspect for), and (3) effort (use and leveraging of enforcement resources). The enforcement style of individual inspectors is defined as the character of the day-to-day interactions of inspectors with the target group. May and Winter expect, and verify, in a study of agro-environmental regulation in Denmark, that enforcement style has two dimensions – the degree of formality of interactions and the use of threats and other forms of coercion. They also identify distinct types of enforcement styles among inspectors along these two dimensions (May and Winter, 2000; 2012; see also May and Burby, 1998; May and Wood, 2003).

Whereas relevant concepts for delivery performance/outputs have been developed for regulatory policies, such conceptualizations seem to be underdeveloped in social policies apart from Lipsky's concepts of coping behaviors. Some inspiration can, however, be obtained from the above regulatory policy concepts at agency as well as individual field worker levels. In studies of the implementation of various Danish social policies on employment, integration of refugees and immigrants, and vulnerable children and youth, Winter and collaborators have conceptualized street-level bureaucratic behaviors along the dimensions of coping, formalism/legalism, coerciveness, and professional distance, which seem to be fruitful – both as dependent variables and independent variables explaining variation in outcomes (Winter, 2002; 2005; Heinesen et al., 2004; Beer et al., 2008; Baviskar and Winter, 2009; 2011; Winter and Baviskar, 2010).

One advantage of creating such conceptualization of the behavior of implementers is that it is well suited for testing hypotheses for explaining variation in implementation behavior across time and space. Variables from implementation theory characterizing aspects of the implementation process would be an important basis for the development and testing of such hypotheses. However, another advantage of focusing implementation research on implementation outputs and outcomes as dependent variables is that we can integrate the study of implementation much more with theory on bureaucratic politics as well as organization and management theory. Thereby, implementation research can gain inspiration from these research fields that have a long tradition of studying the behavior of agencies and bureaucrats. In return, these subdisciplines can benefit from implementation concepts that are much more policy relevant than the behavioral variables that have been applied in most bureaucracy and organization theory.

As examples, principal–agent theory and its notion of information asymmetries has been fruitful in examining control problems in service delivery (Brehm and Gates, 1997; Winter, 2003; Winter et al., 2008b). The same applies to classic bureaucracy theory on the role of rule boundedness in shaping street-level bureaucratic behaviors (Winter et al., 2008a). Representative bureaucracy theory has found a renaissance when applied to implementation problems at the street level (Keiser et al., 2002). Network and contingency theories have been important in explaining collaboration in implementation and its effects on outcomes (Meier and O'Toole, 2003; Lundin, 2007; May and Winter, 2007).

The conceptualization of implementation outputs/behaviors is likely to make it much easier to study the relation between implementation outputs and outcomes (May and Winter, 1999; Winter and May, 2001, 2002; Bloom et al., 2003; Baviskar and Winter, 2009; Weatherall and Markwardt, 2010). In such studies delivery-level behaviors/output changes from being a dependent variable in explaining delivery behaviors to being an independent variable in explaining outcomes. However, often, we need different theorizing to explain implementation outputs and outcomes.

As claimed by Elmore (1982, 1985), to change target groups' problematic behavior requires an understanding of the incentives that are operating on these people as well as of how street-level bureaucrats can influence and build on these incentives. For example, in examining Danish farmers' compliance with environmental regulations, Winter and May (2001) map the regulatees' action model and show that compliance is affected by farmers' (1) calculated motivations based on utility and calculating the costs of complying and the perceived risk of detection of violations, (2) normative sense of duty to comply, and (3) social motivations based on adaptation to expectations from significant others. Inspectors signal such expectations through their style of interacting with target groups, including their degree of formalism. However, willingness to comply is not enough if the regulated entities do not have the ability to comply. Thus, awareness of rules and financial capacity increase farmers' compliance. Understanding target populations' motivations and incentives is essential for specifying causal links between implementation behavior and target group responses and for designing smarter policies.

CONCLUSION

Implementation research has made important contributions to public administration and public policy in adding a public policy perspective to public administration, with a strong focus on how policies are transformed during the execution process until the point of delivery – and even after in changing the behaviors of citizens and firms. The research is valuable for our understanding of the complexities of policy implementation. The studies have revealed many important barriers for implementation and factors that may make success more likely.

The research has moved from explorative theory-generating case studies to a second generation of more theoretically ambitious models or frameworks of analysis with top-down and bottom-up research strategies and syntheses. However, while these frameworks presented lists of many relevant variables, the development of theory, specification of causal relations, and tests were still hampered by overdetermination because the common reliance on single case studies did not allow any control for third variables.

Goggin (1986) offered a very valuable suggestion in terms of applying more comparative and statistical research designs to cope with this problem. However, this is hardly enough. There is also a need for more theory development and testing, and the development of partial theories seems more promising than continuing the search for *the* general implementation theory or model.

In addition to methodological improvements and the development of partial theories, we need more conceptual clarification and specification of causal relations in order to increase our understanding of implementation. This includes reconsidering the dependent variable(s) in implementation research. If we return to the classic questions of public policy research formulated by Dye (1976) – i.e., studying the content, causes, and consequences of public policies – the delivery-level behavior/outputs of implementers is policy at its most operational level. Accordingly, I suggest that implementation research should aim at explaining variation in implementing behaviors/outputs and the role of these behaviors in shaping outcomes for target populations.

REFERENCES

Bardach, Eugene (1977) *The Implementation Game.* Cambridge, MA: MIT Press.

Baviskar, Siddhartha and Winter, Søren C. (2009) *The Effects of Casework on Vulnerable Children and Youth.* Paper presented at the XXI World Congress of the International Political Science Association in Santiago, 12–16 July.

Baviskar, S. and Winter, S.C. (2011) *The Relationship between Street-Level Bureaucrats' Attitudes and Their Coping Behavior toward Vulnerable Children and Youth.* Paper presented at the meeting of the Midwest Political Science Association Conference in Chicago, 31 March to 3 April.

Beer, F., Winter, S.C., Skou, M.H., et al. (2008) *Statslig og kommunal beskæftigelsesindsats: Implementering af "Flere i arbejde" før Strukturreformen.* København: SFI: 08:19.

Behncke Stefanie, Frölich, Markus, and Lechner Michael (2010) 'Unemployed and Their Caseworkers: Should They Be Friends or Foes?' *Journal of the Royal Statistical Society*, Series A 173, Part 1, 67–92.

Bloom, Howard S., Hill, Carolyn J., and Riccio, James A. (2003) 'Linking Program Implementation and Effectiveness: Lessons from a Pooled Sample of Welfare-to-Work Experiments', *Journal of Policy Analysis and Management,* 22(4): 551–576.

Bogason, Peter (2000) *Public Policy and Local Governance: Institutions in Postmodern Society.* Cheltenham: Edward Elgar.

Boyne, George A. (2003) 'Sources of Public Service Improvement: A Critical Review and Research Agenda', *Journal of Public Administration Research and Theory*, 13(3): 367–394.

Brehm, John and Gates, Scott (1997) *Working, Shirking, and Sabotage: Bureaucratic Response to a Democratic Public.* Ann Arbor, MI: University of Michigan Press.

Dye, T.R. (1976) *What Governments Do, Why They Do It, and What Difference It Makes.* Tuscaloosa, AL: University of Alabama Press.

Easton, David (1953) *The Political System.* New York: Alfred A. Knopf.

Elmore, Richard F. (1982) 'Backward Mapping: Implementation Research and Policy Decisions', in W. Williams, R.F. Elmore, J.S. Hall et al. (eds). *Studying Implementation.* Chatham NJ: Chatham House Publishers, pp. 18–35.

Elmore, Richard F. (1985) 'Forward and Backward Mapping: Reversible Logic in the Analysis of Public Policy', in K. Hanf and T.A.J. Toonen (eds), *Policy Implementation in Federal and Unitary Systems.* Dordrecht: Martinus Nijhoff, pp. 33–70.

Goggin, Malcolm L. (1986) 'The "Too Few Cases/Too Many Variables" Problems in Implementation Research', *The Western Political Quarterly*, 39(2): 328–347.

Goggin, Malcolm L., Bowman, Ann O'M., Lester, James P., and O'Toole, Laurence J., Jr, (1990) *Implementation Theory and Practice: Toward a Third Generation*. New York: HarperCollins.

Hargrove, Erwin (1975) *The Missing Link: The Study of the Implementation of Social Policy*. Washington, DC: The Urban Institute.

Heinesen, Eskil, Winter, Søren C., Husted, Leif, and Bøge, Ina R. (2004). *Kommunernes integrationsindsats og integrationssucces*. Copenhagen: AKF.

Hill, Carolyn J. (2006) 'Casework Job Design and Client Outcomes in Welfare-To-Work Offices', *Journal of Public Administration Research and Theory*, 16(2): 263–288.

Hill, Michael and Hupe, Peter (2009) *Implementing Public Policy*, 2nd edn. London: Sage Publications.

Hull, Christopher J. and Hjern, Benny (1987) *Helping Small Firm Grow: An Implementation Perspective*. London: Croom Helm.

Kagan, Robert A. (1994) 'Regulatory Enforcement', in David H. Roosenbloom and Richard D. Schwartz (eds), *Handbook of Regulation and Administrative Law*. New York: Marcel Decker, pp. 383–422.

Keiser, Lael R., Wilkins, Vicky M., Meier, Kenneth J., and Holland, Catherine A. (2002) 'Lipstick and Logarithms: Gender, Institutional Context, and Representative Bureaucracy', *American Political Science Review*, 96(3): 553–564.

Kirst, M. and Jung, R. (1982) 'The Utility of a Longitudinal Approach in Assessing Implementation: A Thirteen Year View of Title 1, ESEA', in W. Williams, R.F. Elmore, J.S. Hall et al. (eds), *Studying Implementation*. Chatham, NJ: Chatham House Publishers, pp. 119–148.

Lasswell, H.D. (1936) *Politics: Who Gets What, When, How*. New York: McGraw-Hill.

Lester, James P. and Goggin, Malcolm L. (1998) 'Back to the Future: the Rediscovery of Implementation Studies', *Policy Currents – Newsletter of the Public Policy Section of the American Political Science Association*, 8(3): 1–9.

Lipsky, Michael (1980) *Street-Level Bureaucracy: The Dilemmas of the Individual in Public Services*. New York: Russell Sage Foundation.

Lundin, Martin (2007) 'Explaining Cooperation: How Resource Interdependence, Goal Congruence, and Trust Affect Joint Actions in Policy Implementation', *Journal of Public Administration Research and Theory*, 17(4): 651–672.

Matland, Richard E. (1995) 'Synthesizing the Implementation Literature: The Ambiguity–Conflict Model of Policy Implementation', *Journal of Public Administration Research and Theory*, 5(2): 145–174.

May, Peter J. (1999) *Toward A Future Agenda for Implementation Research: A Panelist's Notes*. Prepared for the annual meeting of the Western Political Science Association in Seattle. Department of Political Science, University of Washington.

May, Peter J. and Burby, Raymond J. (1998) 'Making Sense out of Regulatory Enforcement', *Law and Policy*, 20(2): 157–182.

May, Peter J. and Winter, Søren (1999) 'Regulatory Enforcement and Compliance: Examining Danish Agro-Environmental Policy', *Journal of Policy Analysis and Management*, 18(4): 625–651.

May, Peter J. and Winter, Søren (2000) 'Reconsidering Styles of Regulatory Enforcement: Patterns in Danish Agro-Environmental Inspection', *Law & Policy*, 22(2): 143–173.

May, Peter J. and Winter, Søren C. (2007) 'Collaborative Service Arrangements: Patterns, Bases, and Perceived Consequences', *Public Management Review*, 10(4): 479–502.

May, Peter J. and Winter, Søren C. (2009) 'Politicians, Managers, and Street-Level Bureaucrats: Influences on Policy Implementation', *Journal of Public Administration Research and Theory*, 19(3): 453–476.

May, Peter J. and Winter, Søren C. (2012) 'Regulatory Enforcement Styles and Compliance', in Christine Parker and Vibeke Lehmann Nielsen (eds), *Explaining Compliance: Business Responses to Regulation*. Cheltenham: Edward Elgar, pp. 222–244.

May, Peter J. and Wood, Robert S. (2003) 'At the Regulatory Frontlines: Inspectors' Enforcement Styles and Regulatory Compliance', *Journal of Public Administration Research and Theory*, 13(2): 117–139.

Mazmanian, Daniel A. and Sabatier, Paul (eds) (1981) *Effective Policy Implementation*. Lexington, KY: Lexington Books.

Meier, Kenneth J. and O'Toole, Laurence J., Jr (2003) 'Public Management and Educational Performance: The Impact of Managerial Networking', *Public Administration Review*, 63(6): 675–685.

Meier, Kenneth J. and O'Toole, Laurence J., Jr (2007) 'Modeling Public Management: Empirical Analysis of the Management–Performance Nexus', *Public Management Review*, 9(4): 503–527.

Moe, Terry M. (1989) 'The Politics of Bureaucratic Structure', in John E. Chubb and Paul E. Peterson (eds), *Can the Government Govern?* Washington, DC: Brookings Institution, pp. 267–329.

O'Toole, Laurence J., Jr (2000) 'Research on Policy Implementation: Assessment and Prospects', *Journal of Public Administration Research and Theory*, 10(2): 263–288.

O'Toole, Laurence J., Jr and Montjoy, Robert S. (1984) 'Interorganizational Policy Implementation: A Theoretical Perspective', *Public Administration Review*, 44(6): 491–503.

Parker, Christine and Nielsen, Vibeke Lehmann (eds) (2012) *Explaining Compliance: Business Responses to Regulation.* Cheltenham: Edward Elgar

Pressman, Jeffrey L. and Wildavsky, Aaron (1973) *Implementation.* Berkeley, CA: University of California Press.

Riccucci, Norma M. (2005) *How Management Matters: Street-Level Bureaucrats and Welfare Reform.* Washington, DC: Georgetown University Press.

Rossi, Peter H. and Freeman, Howard E. (1989) *Evaluation*, 4th edn. London: Sage Publications.

Sabatier, Paul A. (1986) 'Top-Down and Bottom-Up Approaches to Implementation Research: A Critical Analysis and Suggested Synthesis', *Journal of Public Policy*, 6(1): 21–48.

Sabatier, Paul A. and Jenkins-Smith, Hank C. (eds) (1993) *Policy Change and Learning: An Advocacy Coalition Approach.* Boulder, CO: Westview Press.

Schram, Sanford F., Soss, Joe, Fording, Richard C., and Houser, Linda (2009) 'Deciding to Discipline: Race, Choice, and Punishment at the Frontlines of Welfare Reform', *American Sociological Review* 74(3): 398–422.

Tyler, Tom R. (2006) *Why People Obey the Law.* Princeton, NJ: Princeton University Press.

Weatherall, C. D. and Markwardt, K.S. (2010) *Caseworker Behavior and Clients' Employability.* Copenhagen: SFI – Danish National Center for Social Research Working Paper Series 04.

Williams, Walt and Elmore, Richard F. (eds) (1976) *Social Program Implementation.* New York: Academic Press.

Winter, Søren (1986a) 'Studying the Implementation of Top-Down Policies from the Bottom-Up: Implementation of Danish Youth Employment Policy', in Ray C. Rist (ed.), *Finding Work: Cross National Perspectives on Employment and Training.* New York: The Falmer Press, pp. 109–138.

Winter, Søren (1986b) 'How Policy-Making Affects Implementation: The Decentralization of the Danish

Disablement Pension Administration', *Scandinavian Political Studies*, 9(4): 361–385.

Winter, Søren (1990) 'Integrating Implementation Research', in Dennis J. Palumbo and Donald J. Calista (eds), *Implementation and the Policy Process.* New York: Greenwood Press, pp. 19–38.

Winter, Søren (1999) 'New Directions for Implementation Research', *Policy Currents – Newsletter of the Public Policy Section of the American Political Science Association*, 8(4): 1–5.

Winter, Søren C. (2002) *Explaining Street-Level Bureaucratic Behavior in Social and Regulatory Policies.* Paper prepared for the annual meeting of the American Political Science Association in Boston, 29 August to 1 September 2002. Danish National Institute of Social Research, Copenhagen.

Winter, Søren C. (2003) *Political Control, Street-Level Bureaucrats and Information Asymmetry in Regulatory and Social Policies.* Paper presented at the annual meeting of the Association for Public Policy Analysis and Management held in Washington, DC, 6–8 November. Danish National Institute of Social Research, Copenhagen.

Winter, Søren C. (2005) *Effects of Casework: The Relation between Implementation and Social Effects in Danish Integration Policy.* Paper presented at the 2005 Research Conference of the Association for Public Policy and Management, Washington, DC, 3–6 November.

Winter, Søren C. and Baviskar, Siddhartha (2010) *Street-Level Bureaucracy and Performance: A Cross-Policy Analysis.* Paper presented at the 2010 meeting of the Midwest Political Science Association, Chicago, IL, 22–25 April.

Winter, Søren C. and May, Peter J. (2001) 'Motivations for Compliance with Environmental Regulations', *Journal of Policy Analysis and Management*, 20(4): 675–698.

Winter, Søren C. and May, Peter J. (2002) 'Information, Interests, and Environmental Regulation', *Journal of Comparative Policy Analysis*, 4(2): 115–142.

Winter, Søren C. and Nielsen, Vibeke Lehmann (2008) *Implementering af politik.* Copenhagen: Academica.

Winter, Søren C., Dinesen, Peter T., and May, Peter J. (2008a) *Implementation Regimes and Street-Level Bureaucrats: Employment Service Delivery in Denmark.* SFI Working Paper Series 12.

Winter, Søren C., Skou, Mette H., and Beer, Frederikke (2008b) *Effective Management for National or Local Policy Objectives? Implementing Welfare Sanction Policy in Denmark.* SFI Working Paper Series 14.

15

Interorganizational Relations
and Policy Implementation

Laurence J. O'Toole, Jr

Policy implementation is an important and arduous task in many kinds of institutional settings. It is clear, nevertheless, that implementation issues are at their thorniest – and most interesting – in interorganizational contexts. This chapter frames the subject of implementation especially as it relates to public administration, with a particular focus on interorganizational settings. The analysis considers how interorganizational relations can influence the implementation process, and what some of the practical implications might be for those who are responsible for trying to manage for policy success.

The first section of the chapter shows that interorganizational settings are both very common and also particularly challenging venues in which to effect implementation success. One implication is that public administrators need to develop an understanding about how to operate in such settings. The section following then begins to offer a way of understanding the interorganizational setting for implementation, and how interorganizational relations can be mobilized for action on behalf of public policy.

Here, the importance of structural relations themselves for implementation action is emphasized. A third section sketches some of the ways that interorganizational cooperation can be encouraged, despite the daunting impediments often faced by implementers. Attention is devoted to factors that may be useful for public administrators to consider in their efforts to improve implementation results, and particular emphasis is given to the efforts that managers can make outward, toward their interorganizational environment, to enhance performance and encourage success.

While scholars can now say a considerable amount about how interorganizational relations shape implementation processes and what managers might do to improve their effectiveness, this chapter provides no 'cookbook' with unambiguous guidance (O'Toole, 2004). The implications offered here, rather, should be considered of heuristic value. While offering guidance, therefore, implementation research nevertheless cannot tell a practicing manager just what to do in all situations.

INTERORGANIZATIONAL SETTINGS FOR POLICY IMPLEMENTATION

Policy implementation almost always requires institutions to carry the burden of transforming general policy intent into an array of rules, routines, and social processes that can convert policy intention into action. This process is the core of what is meant by implementation.

The institutional settings for implementation can vary greatly in many ways (Saetren, 2005). One important distinction is between implementation that can be accomplished by (or through) one organization (Torenvlied, 2000), on the one hand, and implementation that requires the cooperation and perhaps coordination of multiple organizations, or parts of organizations (Winter and Nielsen, 2008, Chapter 4; Oosterwaal and Torenvlied, 2011), on the other. To the extent that implementation can be handled by a single formal organization, much of what is known about public administration in general can be applied to deliver policy results. When public programs need to be executed through actions spanning two or more organizational settings, the capacity for effective action may be enhanced, but the implementation task is more complicated. Impediments to concerted action are greater, *ceteris paribus*, and inducements to work together are typically fewer. Between (or among) organizations, the differing routines and specialized languages, not to mention distinct ways of seeing the world, mean that interorganizational implementation poses particularly daunting challenges. Among other things, such situations call for administrators to supplement what they know about managing within an organization with additional perspectives and options.

Interorganizational relations can be crucial for policy implementation. Two or more ministries of a single government may be tasked with handling a common program. Or so-called 'vertical' intergovernmental programs, such as those involving national and subnational authorities or the European Union with member states (Bauer, 2006), require the development and administration of operations across organizational lines. International organizations also are involved in encouraging domestic implementation action within states (Joachim et al., 2008). 'Horizontal' intergovernmental programs are less obvious but increasingly significant. A set of governments within a large metropolitan area, for example, may jointly administer cooperative programs for transportation, economic development or emergency services (Feiock and Scholz, 2010).

Beyond these types are contracting ties and privatization, and many policy fields in numerous countries now use complicated cross-sectoral implementation arrangements. These may include one or more public agencies linked to for-profit companies and/or non-profit organizations (Koski and May, 2006; Lane and Wallis, 2009). Certainly, the impetus of the 'New Public Management' has further encouraged such developments in some parts of the world (Kettl, 2005). In some nations, public–private patterns for implementation are buttressed by long traditions of social relations – such as the reliance on cooperation among 'social partners' in certain countries of Europe. And many public programs in several parts of the globe now include clients or target groups in the co-production of policy action.

The proliferation of interorganizational connections has become so pronounced that scholars and practitioners increasingly emphasize themes like 'collaboratives' and collaboration (Bardach, 1998; Krueathep et al., 2010) along with the critical role of interorganizational relations in influencing program results. A particularly visible theme in recent years in this regard has been that of 'networks' and network management (for instance, Kickert et al., 1997; Provan and Kenis, 2008; Rethemeyer and Hatmaker, 2008). This last topic is covered more thoroughly elsewhere in this volume, but it is important to recognize the connection between its increasing salience and the interorganizational patterns that typify many implementation settings.

For many implementation managers, the world is a very interorganizational one. Much of the systematic evidence on this point has been developed in Europe and the United States (Hill and Hupe, 2009), although there are few reasons to expect that these parts of the world are especially distinctive in this regard. Indeed, the much-referenced forces of 'globalization' are likely to encourage still more, as interdependencies proliferate.

Research in several countries of Europe shows clearly the importance of interorganizational phenomena for public administration. The works of Butler and Allen (2008), Koppenjan and Klijn (2004) and Lundin (2007) are illustrative; these studies document the complicated realities facing administrators and others in several countries. Data developed in North America are also important (Hall and O'Toole, 2004; Graddy and Chen, 2009; O'Toole et al., 2011).

Systematic studies of policy implementation are among the most telling kinds of evidence. In Europe, social scientists have shown that locally situated managers facing practical challenges like stimulating the growth of jobs and small-business economic activity confront an interorganizational terrain (Hull with Hjern, 1986). In the United States, research has shown that a substantial proportion of the public programs managed by public administrators are interorganizational (O'Toole and Montjoy, 1984; Hall and O'Toole, 2004). At the local and regional levels as well, interorganizational patterns are quite common (see Agranoff, 2007).

Why is the world of policy implementation so structurally complex? One factor has been the increase in the number of public programs crafted to embrace multiple values. When transportation programs focused solely on paving highways and adding lanes of traffic, maximizing the objective of moving vehicles might have seemed relatively easy – an engineering problem to be solved by a department managed in the interests of expanding the highway system. But when such a unit also has to cope with environmental degradation, housing dislocations, noise pollution and other impacts of such a program, implementation problems – and institutional arrangements – become more complicated. A result is the expansion of implementation patterns to embrace additional organizations and concerns.

The sheer expansion of the governmental agenda, furthermore, impels jurisdictional conflicts, overlaps and potential clashes. As the 'policy space' becomes increasingly filled with public programs, it is ever more difficult to operate without touching upon related programs managed elsewhere by governments – often by other departments of the same government. In such circumstances, it makes sense to try to link the operations, or to provide some social infrastructure of mutual consultation and information sharing.

A related issue is that, increasingly, governments are being asked to address problems that cannot be neatly categorized into one niche or another. So-called 'wicked problems' (Rittel and Webber, 1973), which touch upon several arenas and considerations simultaneously, require governmental responses that involve multiple jurisdictions and departments for effective resolution. A consequence is greater cross-boundary institutional links: interdepartmental advisory committees, complex sign-off authorization procedures, multiple veto and approval points, and so forth.

Another influence can be mentioned. Especially for governments facing budgetary stringencies, responses to pressing problems often take the form of 'mandates' directing an array of departments, governments or even outside parties to comply with orders. The purposes can be as varied as civil rights, sustainable development or the enactment of fair labor standards. The consequence can be that many units have additional objectives, and constraints, layered onto existing programs and activities. Such initiatives can constitute a catalyst for the proliferation of interorganizational implementation patterns.

A related stimulus derives from the forces of globalization, especially the impetus toward interorganizational patterning that emerges from the enactment of international agreements in policy fields: from trade, to weapons control, to sustainable develop-ment. Once established, an international agreement can trigger reverberations at the national and subnational levels, as countries try to develop implementation patterns that can induce cooperation and compliance with commitments they have entered into (O'Toole and Hanf, 1992). Oftentimes, the required actions encourage the forging of links across ministries, governments and sectors within a particular country – not to mention ties between national bureaucracies and international secretariats, and transna-tional links between and among cooperating national agencies. The fact that there are thousands of international agreements now in place, and many more on the agenda, sug-gests the importance of this phenomenon. And the European Union, despite emphases on subsidiarity and the lack of a sizeable bureaucracy thus far in Brussels, has also experienced and stimulated multilevel inter-organizational relations (Willems and De Lange, 2007).

Two additional causal factors are directly related to the forces of politics per se. Sometimes managers can handle the techni-cal needs of a policy problem during execu-tion by using a constrained set of actors in implementation, but political imperatives may encourage broadening the involvement to additional parties. The phenomenon is surely common in pluralistic systems, as public managers seek to maintain support for program execution following the enact-ment of policy. The addition of other actors to the 'coalition' involved in program execu-tion can stem criticism and enhance chances for implementation success, even if some of the additional parties are likely to contrib-ute little to the program's performance per se. Of course, interorganizational ties can also increase the chance that complexity and conflict will overwhelm efforts to make things happen. The trick is to promote the building of support while avoiding the ten-dency toward confusion and excessive com-plexity. In more corporatist political systems, there can be little choice. Peak associations of interested parties that are involved during

initial phases of decision making are also explicitly the implementers and co-responsible parties during the latter phases of the process.

The second obviously political influence shaping interorganizational relations and policy implementation is that basic choices have been made, especially in nations with liberal commitments to the protection of a substantial private realm, that limits should be placed on the reach of public authority. A 'solution' during implementation can be for government to commit to problem solving but limit its formal control by opting for more complex, 'partnered' approaches with private firms or not-for-profit organizations. The result is a considerably more compli-cated, networked institutional form.

Of course, there are additional forces, impelling the waves of privatization, con-tracting, and related phenomena. These may include pressures for cost-cutting, ideologi-cal agendas, and weak management capacity in the public sector. In this regard, an irony can be briefly noted. To the extent that gov-ernments commit to contracting and privati-zation out of a concern that they lack internal management capacity, they are likely to be in for a nasty surprise: for public administration in such settings calls for great skill, effort, and capacity – more so, probably, than man-agement in the more traditional situations (Rainey, 2009).

It seems clear, therefore, that the topic of interorganizational relations will remain important for administrators tasked with helping to make policy implementation suc-ceed. Accordingly, it is critical to understand how to make sense of such institutional set-tings to improve prospects for implementa-tion success.

UNDERSTANDING INTERORGANIZATIONAL POLICY IMPLEMENTATION

Generating successful policy implementation means inducing cooperation, and perhaps even coordination, among interdependent actors in the face of impediments. In standard departments or ministries, the incentives to concert action would seem to be three:

- authority (B cooperates with A because B feels it is an obligation to do so);
- common interest (B cooperates with A because B feels that doing so toward the overall objectives would also serve B's own purposes); and
- exchange (B cooperates with A because B receives something else from A, or from elsewhere, that makes it worthwhile to go along).

The formal hierarchy allows public administrators in departments to rely to some considerable extent on authority as an aid to coordination. But administrators working across boundaries typically do not possess this luxury. There may be formal points of authority across disparate departments – the chief executive's office, for instance, or the cabinet – but in practice such authority is almost never invoked. Central officials have little to gain from being dragged into interministerial disputes and typically expect organizations to work out their differences. In addition, the time and authority of even central decision makers is strictly limited and is usually rationed for the most compelling cases. Rare is the implementation manager who can operate informally as an authority figure across organizations. The result is that public administrators who wish to trigger policy implementation while working across organizational borders must turn to other options: finding or stimulating common interest – and its continuing salience – and developing and maintaining sensible exchanges.

Behind these general and rather abstract statements lies a host of possibilities, and also complications. But the main point is that administering policy implementation in interorganizational contexts forces a reconsideration of the basic context of managerial choice, as well as the types and emphases accorded to managerial options. Administrators in interorganizational patterns can never assume support but must work to build it. They typically cannot rely on hierarchical institutional arrangements to congeal agreement, beyond their own formal unit, at any rate. Administrators working to implement in interorganizational settings often have to develop the infrastructure of communication – channels, language, signals, and so forth – to help achieve the objective of policy-oriented cooperation. The interorganizational setting is not a whole new world, for managers have been operating to some extent across boundaries for quite a while. But assuming an interorganizational array means shifting approaches to implementation from those injunctions more typically emphasized.

Public administrators operating in such institutionally complex settings find themselves maneuvering in a world where there are *multiple* points of managerial influence and very different managerial roles across the departments and other units of the policy world. Few moves can be made unilaterally. The task is less one of directing and controlling and more that of assessing contexts of interdependence and seeking to influence these, often in subtle ways, to increase prospects for successful cooperation (see Stoker, 1991).

The implementation challenge faced by public administrators, then, consists of assessing the structural setting itself to determine its strengths and weaknesses for encouraging cooperative effort; and then to tap common interest and exchange, as appropriate and practical, to increase prospects for success. The remainder of this section considers the interorganizational setting itself. The next part of the chapter focuses on the inducements to cooperation that may be available.

Not all patterns of interorganizational relations are created equal. One of the most important aspects of implementation settings is the structure of interdependence required or encouraged among the organizations involved. For it is not the sheer number of units, but their pattern and the way they link to each other, that is most critical.

This point conflicts with an assertion made in one of the most well-known implementation studies, that by Pressman and Wildavsky (1984), who claim that the 'complexity of joint action' is the key impediment to successful implementation. By this term, they mean the number of decision points. Pressman and Wildavsky indicate that as the number of such points required for implementation increases, the chance for action declines. Indeed, they seem to 'demonstrate' this conclusion mathematically.

The contradiction between this deduction and the abundant real-world evidence that success is not only possible but frequent has been dubbed the 'Pressman–Wildavsky paradox' by specialists in implementation. As Bowen (1982), among others, has shown, there are significant flaws in the analysis conducted by Pressman and Wildavsky. In reality, probabilities of agreement among organizations are not impervious to events; agreement on basic understandings at the outset of an implementation process can increase the odds of further agreement later. Organizations can also merge multiple decision points in a single set of negotiations. Bringing all the parties to the table to craft 'package deals' can also dramatically enhance the odds of success. Putting many issues into play simultaneously generates possibilities for tradeoffs. And merging decisions into a more comprehensive set of negotiations reduces the number of separate hurdles (see O'Toole, 2011).

These points suggest that the challenge of generating interorganizational cooperation toward success, even in complicated cases, is not likely to be nearly as uniformly disappointing as the Pressman–Wildavsky analysis suggests. An especially important aspect of complex interorganizational contexts that Pressman and Wildavsky failed to take into account is the structuring among the organizations themselves. Some policy tasks require that organizations – public agencies, say, or an agency along with a few contractors and subcontractors – deal sequentially with the challenge of implementation. In the

purest form of such an assembly-line pattern, one organization delivers outputs to another (which may do similarly to still more organizations down the implementation chain) without in turn receiving outputs from the second organization. Other policy tasks might call on units to work together closely, with the outputs of each serving as inputs for the others on a regular basis. Or perhaps a policy initiative might require several organizations to become active, but each one could act independently of the others. These three different kinds of circumstance fit Thompson's notions of sequential, reciprocal and pooled interdependence, respectively (1967; see also O'Toole and Montjoy, 1984). Of course, in large, complicated interorganizational networks, there may be instances of each of these types of interdependence within the same overall program array.

It should be clear that implementation is affected by the type(s) of interdependence, not simply the number of units or decisions. For example, in a sequential arrangement, a delay or impediment at any place in the chain will mean implementation problems at the point of intended impact. This assembly-line structure of interdependence creates, in effect, potential veto points at each link. Sometimes, interorganizational arrangements for implementation are structured to allow just one of the units involved to exercise potential veto power. This sort of arrangement is sometimes purposely chosen to make sure a particular organization, and its point of view and jurisdiction, are given special weight. An example would be an environmental agency charged with reviewing construction projects and disapproving those with significant adverse impacts.

In sequential arrangements, adding more organizational units in a chain increases the number of possible roadblocks to action. But in other arrangements, for instance in programs that seek to pool the action of multiple organizations, adding units can *increase* prospects for some implementation action. In short, the structure of interdependence among the organizations can make a big difference in what happens. This point can be kept in mind when designing interorganizational patterns for implementation. For example, if reliability is of prime importance, multiple service-providing organizations arrayed in a pooled fashion can increase the probability of success via purposeful redundancy. Note the vast number of organizations assisting the seriously mentally ill in mid-sized US cities (Provan and Milward, 1991); the overall pattern is highly complex, but one result is that fewer clients slip entirely through the cracks. If a particular policy objective or value needs to be ensured in a complicated program setting, creating a veto point unit via sequential interdependence can be effective. If well-integrated action is essential, crafting interunit links framed around reciprocal interdependence can be important. And sometimes structural arrangements can be consolidated or reorganized to reduce coordination demands.

ENCOURAGING INTERORGANIZATIONAL COOPERATION

Recognizing the significance of different interorganizational patterns is one step toward effective implementation. In addition, skillful implementation managers need to find ways of getting organizations to work together toward policy success. Doing so means that implementation managers have to interact with counterparts in other organizations and stakeholders in and outside of government – to build support, negotiate, coordinate, and sometimes fend off disruptive influences. This kind of managerial networking can be expected to be a part of any successful interorganizational implementation, and we address it first. We then turn to the different ways of encouraging cooperative effort during such a process. Inducing implementation success via interorganizational ties typically requires some combination of generating and tapping common

interest, on the one hand, and/or utilizing exchanges to link units in productive ways for purposes of policy. Each of these themes deserves attention as well.

Managerial networking and interorganizational implementation

Implementing programs in interorganizational settings means that managers have to work not only inside their own agency or ministry but also externally to carry out the myriad tasks associated with enhancing cooperative effort. Systematic, quantitative empirical research has shown that managerial networking of this sort can improve performance – boosting the outputs and outcomes of policy. Findings in public education support this claim (Meier and O'Toole, 2001, 2003), as does research on law enforcement (Nicholson-Crotty and O'Toole, 2004). Managerial networking has also been found to improve results for US state agencies charged with managing human resources and also indebtedness (Donahue et al., 2004) and those seeking to implement reforms aimed at 'reinventing government' (Jacobson et al., 2010). In addition, Andrews et al. (2010) find performance-related effects for local authorities in England. Such externally directed efforts can also run the risk of cooptation – thus improving results for the more powerful external actors and clients while doing little or nothing for more marginal stakeholders (O'Toole and Meier, 2004) – but patterns of networking are clearly a regular part of interorganizational implementation.

We turn now to the functions that can be assisted through such interactions.

Building and using common interest

If organizations each care about a policy objective, and if the participation of each is essential for success, their shared interest in the result may be enough to generate effective implementation. This statement is true, and important, but one should be careful to recognize as well the non-trivial impediments to joint action that may still remain. For one thing, different organizations very often have somewhat different goals and perspectives on matters like policy. Even where there are overlaps in interest and priorities, there are also likely to be some discrepancies. Second, one key reason why so much implementation involves interorganizational links is that complicated policy challenges often require consideration by different kinds of units reflecting distinct and partially competing goals. In such cases, which are quite common, it is unrealistic to expect common interest itself to be sufficient. At a minimum, it is likely that even shared goals will be differentially salient in separate units. Third, for a whole set of nitty-gritty implementation details, different organizations will have unique perspectives even if they share a common overall goal. For instance, matters like turf and budgets can trigger conflicts even among strongly committed units.

Even if all relevant organizations share an interest in having the policy succeed, each may be reluctant to commit itself wholeheartedly without knowing that the others are doing so as well. Organizations involved in a complex enterprise, in short, may be cautious about the possibility of 'free riding' among their partners. When numerous organizations are potentially involved in an implementation effort, there may be a problem of collective action, even if there is common interest in the outcome. This issue can be quite vexing. Particularly when levels of trust are low, it may be difficult to get a true interorganizational effort off the ground.

What can public administrators do to assist the process? A number of actions can be helpful.

One possibility is signaling. If different bureaus or departments have similar perspectives on the common endeavor, managers can help by simply making that important fact clear to all involved. The more that all understand that everyone shares the commitment, the less the chance that doubts and second thoughts will arise. A related point is

'framing' (Kahneman and Tversky, 1984): interorganizational efforts are typically complicated. In the real world this complexity may cause doubts to form about the cooperative venture. Questions may arise about whether others are going to be cooperative, or whether differences will overwhelm the potential for success. Managers can help by highlighting the key points of common interest that could get lost from participants' attention amid a welter of detail and uncertainty. Focusing participants' perceptions on the accurate reality that they (mostly) do agree and that they are engaged with others in a valuable activity can help stem hesitation and increase trust (see further comments on this issue shortly).

Similarly, administrators can work to get parties on the record in public and obtain specific commitments to cooperate on certain observable tasks. Commitments on the part of some can facilitate the generation of commitments by others, as the risks of going it alone are substantially reduced. Similarly, iteration can help. Administrators can try to get the action going and keep it moving in relatively predictable, repeated interactions. Doing so reduces coordination costs, increases understanding and predictabililty, and also enhances trust. Moreover, administrators can craft transparent reporting systems, so that all parties can see what the others are up to on issues that matter for them. None of these options really alters the 'natural' line-up of forces among the organizations; instead, the moves are aimed at facilitating the search for stable and cooperative approaches to the joint effort.

Additional steps can also be helpful. Administrators can make efforts to prevent some units from acting as free riders on the efforts of the others – for instance, by monitoring action across multiple units, if all agree. Indeed, all may have an interest in assigning such responsibilities to a particular unit or manager, given the shared interests in cooperative effort. Also, managers of interorganizational implementation can sometimes exercise discretion to design or shift the mix of units involved to ensure a substantial degree of overlap in perspectives; and implementation managers can use the art of persuasion, by finding ways to increase the perceived value associated with cooperative activities.

Cultivating norms supportive of cooperation can also be a valuable step. Such norms, along with respect for the needs of other participants, can be critical as forms of 'social capital' that can pay dividends into the future; and, of course, administrators of programs crossing organizational lines can apply their own influence to help generate regard for those actions supportive of these norms.

Furthermore, administrators can generate increasing amounts of cooperation by delegating large, complicated and potentially risky commitments and decisions into smaller ones. If multiple departments, for instance, are being asked to commit time and substantial resources to a joint enterprise apparently fraught with risks – including the perceived risk that others will not do their part – implementation managers can sometimes make cooperation more feasible by rendering it less risky. By trimming a large commitment into a series of smaller bargains enforced over time, and with at least the potential for withdrawal (or retaliation), the costs of any particular move become less of an impediment, while the benefits of joint cooperation over limited tasks escalate over time. And beyond the direct contributions to achieving the collective task, there is another benefit. Organizations that have learned to work with others and to draw gradually on the contributions of others are very likely to increase their mutual trust. As this shift in expectations develops, additional agreements are easier to strike; the payoffs do not have to be immediate. Successful management of the early stages can contribute to easier policy implementation over the longer haul.

Facilitating cooperation via exchange

Beyond common interest as a kind of inter-organizational 'glue' that can congeal

cooperation toward implementation action, exchange is a social process that can shape implementation in productive ways. Organizations involved in interorganizational implementation typically need things from each other if they are to do their jobs. Just which ones are involved, and how the needs may be distributed, depend on the nature of the policy tasks and the structure of interdependence, a topic discussed earlier. Exchanges between organizations can create sufficient inducements to congeal cooperation. Exchange here refers not simply to the use of funds to produce goods and services, but also to a broad array of types of trades among interdependent units.

The use of funds to cement concerted action, of course, is the most obvious kind of exchange. Often, third-party involvement in service delivery is desired by policy makers, for any of a variety of reasons. Contracting with both such parties is a common instrument for linking organizations and framing the implementation arena, particularly when governments contract in a competitive context. Indeed, a typical element of the 'New Public Management' has been an extensive set of contracting relations across organizations and sectors. Many features of the exchange relations can be designed explicitly into the contracted understanding; and contract elements can be negotiated to try to ensure that incentives match desired behavior and/or outputs. Even here, nonetheless, there is considerable need for skillful public management. Contracts are not self-enforcing; they require talented administration to work well, and no set of incentives, no matter how carefully designed, is completely self-enforcing (Miller, 1992). Some degree of leadership must be employed to congeal support across the units for effective action.

Exchanges among organizations involved in policy implementation can extend considerably beyond formal agreements to trade money for effort or results (Bardach, 1998). Organizations need inputs from their environments on a regular basis, and they seek outlets for their products as well. The inputs can range from political support, to human resources, to information; and the outputs can be of myriad types as well. When implementation requires or encourages inter-organizational cooperation, those concerned about making the process work well are often advantaged by focusing on the kinds of exchanges that have developed, and could be encouraged to develop, among the interdependent units. Central government agencies can offer funding, discretion and information to subnational units, which can often, in turn, regulate or deliver services better than could central authorities within their territory. The success of the subnational effort also benefits the national agency, whose interest is served by smooth flows of funds and delivery of services. And so on.

Exchanges can extend considerably beyond the most obvious kinds of trades. Organizations typically have relatively complex agendas, and often they must deal with each other over many matters and through extended periods. While these facts of life can make negotiating complicated, they also render it more productive. Public administrators involved in policy implementation can use such circumstances to encourage successful policy action. Departments and other organizations are often interdependent on a number of tasks. Even when they are not, it could be that what from one perspective looks like a single (potentially) cooperative endeavor – a joint program or proposal – can also be seen as a stream of interdependent decisions and joint efforts linked together, perhaps via a stream of exchanges.

This complexity can be an advantage, since the separable cooperative actions can be explicitly 'placed on the table' by creative public managers. Exchange might be built across different tasks of interdependent units to facilitate more stable long-term cooperation. In a similar vein, large policy efforts that require management across boundaries can themselves be seen as a substantial set of less overwhelming potentially cooperative efforts. Almost inevitably, different parties

will view the successful completion of these with different levels of salience or enthusiasm – the letting of a contract, the completion of a milestone, the involvement of certain outside interests, the incorporation of certain capital spending items into a larger plan, and so on. These discrete but related foci can offer chances for tradeoffs in the interest of overall success.

Public administrators can contribute to increasing the overall odds of success if they stay alert to such options. Often, the brokering of these possibilities does not happen without active effort on the part of managers focused on the overall effort. Identifying such exchange possibilities, proposing tradeoffs, helping to stipulate the terms of the interorganizational agreement, and then working to monitor and manage information flows so that all relevant parties can see what is happening and whether quid pro quos have remained viable – these kinds of managerial steps may be essential parts of any solutions over the longer term.

Sometimes, exchange can be facilitated by public administrators who can change the set of alternatives for cooperation (and non-cooperation) under consideration. On occasion, simply reminding organizations involved of the 'default option' – the consequences if no agreement is reached – can encourage productive exchange. Particularly if non-cooperation can result in another party (for instance, a higher level of government) enforcing its will on those involved in early stages of implementation, it can be helpful to alert such parties to the consequences of any lack of agreement. Managers can sometimes go beyond this point to identify new and creative options that may have escaped the notice of all other participants. The ability to see stable bargaining alternatives in highly conflictual situations has long been recognized as a key element of skillful diplomacy; and administrative diplomacy is often quite helpful in assisting exchange for interorganizational implementation. Crafting 'new' options, therefore, is often an important element of productive interorganizational relations.

Similarly, shifting the set of organizations involved in an implementation setting can increase the degree of common interest among those in the program, as explained above, and can also facilitate exchange under certain circumstances. Which units ought to be a part of interorganizational implementation is only partially a technical matter. Stoker (1991) has pointed out that it may be possible to involve organizations that have enduring conflicts with each other and yet can find ways of cooperating on a particular program despite the persistence of such differences.

This consideration of exchange as a critical element should not be taken to imply that interorganizational relations are always, or even usually, marked by totally voluntary agreements among organizational units. Despite the reality that formal authority is rarely invoked to force long-term, productive interorganizational cooperation, power relations among interdependent organizations can influence the flow of events during implementation. Resource-dependence theory suggests that those units in possession of critical resources needed by others can be more influential. Units involved in interorganizational implementation tend to try to manage their strategic contingencies to maintain some maneuverability, and certainly, organizations that are crucially important to the other units involved in an implementation effort can be expected to play a particularly significant role in shaping the kind and level of cooperation that develops.

Public administrators located in such agencies may be able to influence implementation processes meaningfully. It is useful for public administrators to be alert for circumstances in which their units are unusually influential; such situations can provide opportunity to institutionalize agreements and understandings in ways particularly favorable to successful implementation action.

CONCLUSION

The implementation of public policy occurs in highly varied settings, but it is clear that, most often, interorganizational cooperation is needed to achieve successful results. The organizations involved include governmental departments and ministries, subnational agencies, non-profit and for-profit units and organizations of target groups – who may even be involved in producing the implementation action. Whether (and how) interorganizational cooperation emerges depends on a number of factors. Substantial impediments may be present, so cooperation must be developed; it cannot be assumed. The pattern of interdependence among the organizations matters, although there is no 'one best' way arrangement for all circumstances. More organizations add capacity and also constraints to any implementation system. Common interest among the units involved can help congeal cooperative action, as can opportunities for exchanges among the participating units. In all these respects, the actions and networking of public managers can be highly consequential.

This chapter has outlined these challenges and opportunities, with particular attention to the role of the administrator. Given the frequently interorganizational context of policy implementation, the importance of such a position is particularly deserving of attention and understanding.

REFERENCES

Agranoff, Robert (2007) *Managing within Networks: Adding Value to Public Organizations.* Washington, DC: Georgetown University Press.

Andrews, Rhys, Boyne, George A., Meier, Kenneth J., O'Toole, Laurence J., Jr and Walker, Richard M. (2010) 'Wakeup Call: Strategic Management, Network Alarms and Performance', *Public Administration Review,* 70 (2): 731–41.

Bardach, Eugene (1998) *Getting Agencies to Work Together: The Practice and Theory of Managerial*

Craftsmanship. Washington, DC: Brookings Institution.

Bauer, Michael W. (2006) 'Co-managing Programme Implementation: Conceptualizing the European Commission's Role in Policy Execution', *Journal of European Public Policy*, 13 (5): 717–35.

Bowen, Elinor R. (1982) 'The Pressman–Wildavsky Paradox ...', *Journal of Public Policy*, 2 (February): 1–21.

Butler, M. J. R. and Allen, P. (2008) 'Understanding Policy Implementation Processes as Self-organizing Systems', *Public Management Review*, 10 (3): 421–40.

Donahue, Amy K., Jacobson, Willow S., Robbins, Mark D., Rubin, Ellen V. and Selden, Sally C. (2004) 'Management and Performance Outcomes in State Government', in Patricia W. Ingraham and Laurence E. Lynn, Jr (eds), *The Art of Governance: Analyzing Management and Administration.* Washington, DC: Georgetown University Press, pp. 125–51.

Feiock, Richard C. and Scholz, John T. (2010) *Self-Organizing Federalism: Collaborative Mechanisms to Mitigate Institutional Collective Action Dilemmas.* Cambridge: Cambridge University Press.

Graddy, Elizabeth A. and Chen, Bin (2009) 'Partner Selection and the Effectiveness of Interorganizational Collaborations', in Rosemary O'Leary and Lisa Blomgren Bingham (eds), *The Collaborative Public Manager: New Ideas for the Twenty-first Century.* Washington, DC: Georgetown University Press, pp. 53–69.

Hall, Thad E. and O'Toole, Laurence J., Jr (2004) 'Shaping Formal Networks through the Regulatory Process', *Administration and Society*, 36 (2): 1–22.

Hill, Michael and Hupe, Peter (2009) *Implementing Public Policy: An Introduction to the Study of Operational Governance.* London: Sage.

Hull, Chris with Hjern, Benny (1986) *Helping Small Firms Grow.* London: Croom Helm.

Jacobson, Willow S., Palus, Christine Kelleher and Bowling, Cynthia J. (2010) 'A Woman's Touch? Gendered Management and Performance in State Administration', *Journal of Public Administration Research and Theory*, 20 (2): 477–504.

Joachim, Jutta, Reinalda, Bob and Verbeek, Bertjan (2008) 'International Organizations and Implementation: Pieces of the Puzzle', in Jutta Joachim, Bob Reinalda and Bertjan Veerbek (eds), *International Organizations and Implementation: Enforcers, Managers, Authorities?* Abingdon, UK: Routledge.

Kahneman, Daniel and Tversky, Amos (1984) 'Choices, Values, and Frames', *American Psychologist*, 39: 341–50.

Kettl, Donald F. (2005*) The Global Public Management Revolution*, 2nd edn. Washington, DC: Brookings Institution.

Kickert, Walter, Klijn, Erik-Hans and Koppenjan, Joop (eds) (1997) *Managing Complex Networks: Network Management and the Public Sector.* London: Sage.

Koopenjan, Joop and Klijn, Erik-Hans (2004) *Managing Uncertainties in Networks: Public Private Controversies.* London: Routledge.

Koski, Chris and May, Peter J. (2006) 'Interests and Implementation: Fostering Voluntary Regulatory Actions', *Journal of Public Administration Research and Theory*, 16 (3): 329–49.

Krueathep, Weerasak, Riccucci, Norma M. and Suwanmala, Charas (2010) 'Why Do Agencies Work Together? The Determinants of Network Formation at the Subnational Level of Government in Thailand', *Journal of Public Administration Research and Theory*, 20 (1): 157–85.

Lane, Jan-Erik and Wallis, Joe (2009) 'Non-profit Organizations in Public Policy Implementation', *Journal of Public Administration and Policy Research*, 1: 141–9.

Lundin, Martin (2007) 'Explaining Cooperation: How Resource Interdependence, Goal Congruence, and Trust Affect Joint Actions in Policy Implementation', *Journal of Public Administration Research and Theory*, 17 (4): 651–72.

Meier, Kenneth J. and O'Toole, Laurence J., Jr (2001) 'Managerial Strategies and Behavior in Networks: A Model with Evidence from U.S. Public Education', *Journal of Public Administration Research and Theory*, 11 (3): 271–95.

Meier, Kenneth J. and O'Toole, Laurence J., Jr (2003) 'Public Management and Educational Performance: The Impact of Managerial Networking', *Public Administration Review*, 63 (6): 675–85.

Miller, Gary J. (1992) *Managerial Dilemmas: The Political Economy of Hierarchy.* Cambridge: Cambridge University Press.

Nicholson-Crotty, Sean and O'Toole, Laurence J., Jr (2004) 'Public Management and Organizational Performance: The Case of Law Enforcement Agencies', *Journal of Public Administration Research and Theory*, 14 (1): 1–18.

Oosterwaal, Annemarije and Torenvlied, René (2011) 'Policy Divergence in Implementation: How Conflict among Decisive Legislators Reinforces the Effect of Agency Preferences', *Journal of Public Administration Research and Theory*, Advance Access published July 12, 2011, doi: 10.1093/jopart/mur037

O'Toole, Laurence J., Jr (2004) 'The Theory–Practice Issue in Implementation Research', *Public Administration*, 82 (2): 309–29.

O'Toole, Laurence J., Jr (2011) 'The EDA in Oakland: A Case That Catalyzed a Field', *Public Administration Review*, 71 (1): 116–20.

O'Toole, Laurence J., Jr and Hanf, Kenneth I. (2002) 'American Public Administration and Impacts of International Governance', *Public Administration Review*, 62 (September): 158–69.

O'Toole, Laurence J., Jr and Meier, Kenneth J. (2004) 'Desperately Seeking Selznick: Cooptation and the Dark Side of Public Management in Networks', *Public Administration Review*, 64 (6): 681–93.

O'Toole, Laurence J., Jr and Montjoy, Robert S. (1984) 'Interorganizational Policy Implementation: A Theoretical Perspective', *Public Administration Review*, 44 (6): 491–503.

O'Toole, Laurence J., Jr, Slade, Catherine P., Brewer, Gene A. and Gase, Lauren N. (2011) 'The Barriers and Facilitators to Implementing Primary Stroke Center Policy in the United States: Results from Four Case Study States', *American Journal of Public Health*, 101 (3): 561–66.

Pressman, Jeffrey L. and Wildavsky, Aaron (1984) *Implementation*, 3rd edn. Berkeley, CA: University of California Press.

Provan, Keith G. and Kenis, Patrick (2008) 'Modes of Network Governance: Structure, Management, and Effectiveness', *Journal of Public Administration Research and Theory*, 18 (2): 229–52.

Provan, Keith G. and Milward, H. Brinton (1991) 'Institutional-Level Norms and Organizational Involvement in a Service-Implementation Network', *Journal of Public Administration Research and Theory*, 1 (4): 391–417.

Rainey, Hal G. (2009) *Understanding and Managing Public Organizations*, 4th edn. San Francisco: John Wiley.

Rethemeyer, R. Karl and Hatmaker, Neneen M. (2008) 'Network Management Reconsidered: An Inquiry into Management of Network Structures in Public Sector Service Provision', *Journal of Public Administration Research and Theory*, 18 (4): 617–46.

Rittel, Horst W. J. and Webber, Melvin (1973) 'Dilemmas in a General Theory of Planning', *Policy Sciences*, 4: 155–69.

Saetren, Harald (2005) 'Facts and Myths about Research on Public Policy Implementation: Out-of-Fashion, Allegedly Dead, but Still Very Much Alive and Relevant', *Policy Studies Journal*, 33: 559–82.

Stoker, Robert P. (1991) *Reluctant Partners: Implementing Federal Policy*. Pittsburgh, PA: University of Pittsburgh Press.

Thompson, James D. (1967) *Organizations in Action*. New York: McGraw-Hill.

Torenvlied, René (2000) *Political Decisions and Agency Performances*. Dordrecht, The Netherlands: Kluwer Academic Publishers.

Willems, P. and De Lange, W. J. (2007) 'Concept of Technical Support to Science-policy Interfacing with Respect to the Implementation of the European Water Framework Directive', *Environmental Science & Policy*, 10: 464–73.

Winter, Søren C. and Nielsen, Vibeke Lehmann (2008) *Implementering af politik*. Copenhagen: Academica.

16

Street-Level Bureaucrats and the Implementation of Public Policy

Marcia K. Meyers and Vibeke Lehmann Nielsen

The democratic control of implementing agents is a perennial public administration concern. Generations of scholars and practitioners have debated the appropriate relationship between the politics of the legislative processes and the administration of the resulting laws. Scholars working with rational choice models have joined the debate, with particular attention to the incentive and contractual structures that align the interests of implementing agents with policy-making principals. Similar concerns have been prominent in the scholarly literature on policy implementation, whether framed as a 'top-down' issue of fidelity to policy-makers' goals or a 'bottom-up' issue of policy adaptation during the implementation process. In recent years scholars have expanded the motivating questions for this field from the study of fidelity, per se, to consider the social construction of policy directives and the impact of the broader social and cultural context on the actions of front-line implementing agents.

In this chapter we consider what is known, how to understand and what remains to be learned, about the role of street-level bureaucrats in policy implementation. We begin with a review of the most commonly discussed characteristics of those front-line workers who function as de facto bureaucratic policy makers. We next consider the questions of whether (and how) policy officials control the discretionary actions of these workers. This leads us to consider the normative questions that motivate concern about hierarchical control, including the implications of the exercise of street-level discretion for democratic accountability, equity, and policy achievement. We briefly review emerging theoretical approaches that integrate theories of institutional, organizational, and individual contingencies and conclude by reflecting on the importance of contextualizing the evaluation of front-line performance to understand the intra- and inter-organizational conditions for policy implementation.

DEFINING THE STREET-LEVEL BUREAUCRAT

In his seminal 1980 study of workers in schools, courts, and welfare agencies, Michael Lipsky defined street-level bureaucrats as 'public service workers who interact directly with citizens in the course of their jobs, and who have substantial discretion in the execution of their work' (Lipsky, 1980: 3). They include teachers, police officers, welfare workers, health and safety inspectors, and other public employees who control access to public programs, deliver service, and/or enforce public laws and regulations. As such, they occupy a unique, and uniquely influential, position in the implementation process.

By virtue of their position at the interface between citizens and the state, street-level bureaucrats are responsible for many of the most central activities of public agencies, from determining program eligibility to

allocating benefits, judging compliance, imposing sanctions, and exempting individuals and businesses from penalties. Because these activities involve direct interactions with citizens, street-level bureaucrats also exercise considerable discretion. In contrast to other production processes, street-level services and regulations require workers to engage in a joint production process with their raw materials; workers can rarely produce desired policy outcomes without the active cooperation of the individuals who are beneficiaries of public services or the targets of public regulations. This interdependence introduces substantial variability and unpredictability into the work of street-level bureaucrats. It increases their need and their opportunities to exercise discretionary judgment and constrains the ability of supervisors to directly observe and monitor their activities.

In Table 16.1 we summarize the job characteristics – and some of the resulting behavioral

Table 16.1   Street-level bureaucrats' job characteristics and their consequences

Job characteristics	Consequence
○ Job responsibilities cannot be fully specified in advance or micro-regulated by superiors	◊ SLBs are able and required to exercise discretion in performance of their jobs
○ Work is part of joint production process(es) that include other actors, including policy targets	◊ SLBs' behaviors and job performance emerge in interaction with other actors, introducing variability and unpredictability
○ On-the job behaviors are difficult to observe or to directly monitor	◊ SLBs have opportunities to interpret policy during delivery and to engage in practices that deviate from those desired by policy makers
○ Goals, priorities, and standards for job performance are often politically contested and the technology for achieving goals may be uncertain	◊ SLBs often experience competing or even contradictory performance demands and may be subject to scrutiny and evaluation by multiple stakeholders with divergent values and expectations
○ Resources available to achieve policy goals are limited	◊ SLBs are required to ration their time, attention, and other resources, often without clear or consistent guidance about priorities
○ Positions in public agencies or publicly authorized non-governmental organizations place them in the position of agents charged to act on behalf of political principals	◊ SLBs manage and are accountable for performing job tasks for which they do not fully determine the goals, content or underlying assumptions
○ Job performance, including specific decisions about cases and clients, have consequences for others	◊ SLBs enact policy, control resources, and construct the terms of social citizenship for individuals who are the targets of policy and/or claimants for government assistance

SLBs– street-level bureaucrats.

consequences – that scholars have identified as common to street-level bureaucrats across policy, institutional, and geographic settings (see also Winter and Nielsen, 2008).

Given their position at the interface of the state and the citizen and their opportunities to exercise discretion, street-level bureaucrats exert influence well beyond their formal authority. They operate, in Michael Lipsky's (1980) term, as bureaucrats who not only deliver but also actively shape policy outcomes by interpreting rules and allocating scarce resources. Through their day-to-day routines and decisions, they *produce* public policy as citizens experience it. Some observers ascribe even more far-reaching influence to street-level workers. Lipsky argues that they act as 'agents of social control' by requiring behaviors of citizens with whom they interact. Vinzant and Crothers (1998: 19) argue for a recasting of street-level bureaucrats as 'street level leaders' whose choices about which outcomes to pursue, and how to achieve them, 'help to define what it means to be a citizen in America.' Maynard-Moody and Musheno (2003: 23) point out that street-level bureaucrats typically reject the term 'street-level bureaucrat,' describing themselves instead as 'citizen-agents who help create and maintain the normative order of society.' Less positively, scholars concerned with issues of oversight and direction of front-line workers draw attention to the potential lack of control and accountability in their work (Moe, 1984; Huber et al., 2001), going so far as to warn about the danger of 'runaway bureaucracies' (McCubbins et al., 1987) when discretion is not controlled.

THE EXERCISE OF DISCRETION AT THE STREET LEVEL

The potential for front-line workers to affect policy as delivered raises obvious questions of democratic control. In his study of Danish farm inspectors, Winter (2000) poses the question: 'Are street-level bureaucrats servants or masters?' The questions of whether, and how, policy-making principals control the discretion of their implementing agents dominated much of the initial empirical research on police, social service workers, health and safety inspectors, building inspectors, and other front-line workers. More recent work has broadened the focus to consider multiple sources of accountability within the contemporary, multi-actor, and often multi-sector context of governance for public programs (Lynn et al., 2000; Hill and Hupe, 2003; O'Toole, Chapter 16 in this Handbook).

Political control

A number of scholars have taken up the question of whether political officials control the discretionary actions of street-level bureaucrats. Several studies using administrative data sets or surveys have found evidence that partisan political power (usually measured as the party composition of local legislatures) explains a significant portion of the variation in the performance of such front-line activities as determining eligibility for disability benefits (Keiser, 1999), granting good cause exemptions to child support cooperation requirements (Keiser and Soss, 1998), and conducting occupational health and safety inspections and imposing penalties (Scholz et al., 1991; Headrick et al., 2002). Two mediating variables have emerged in several studies of the influence of political officials. One variable is the proximity of political officials, with greater influence exerted by officials who are closer to front-line workers, e.g., at the municipal rather than federal level (May and Winter, 2009). A second variable is the clarity and consistency of policy-makers' goals: when policy makers' goals are unclear, contested or contradictory, front-line workers are more likely to make discretionary decisions that favor their own values and beliefs (Meyers et al., 2001; Riccucci et al., 2004; Keiser, 2010).

Because they rely on highly aggregated indicators of street-level behaviors, these studies provide indirect evidence for political control over the actions and decisions of street-level bureaucrats. Research that has been conducted closer to the front lines has identified a number of constraints on the ability of political officials to direct front-line workers. In his study of Danish agricultural inspectors, for example, Winter (2000) concludes that information asymmetries between street-level workers and their supervisors render important aspects of front-line work beyond the control of political executives. He suggests that political principals exert only 'differentiated and limited political control' of street-level bureaucracies. Their control is greatest over actions that are visible, and more limited over less easily observed factors. Studies of front-line workers in social welfare programs have reached similar conclusions about the delivery of social welfare services and policy reforms (Meyers et al., 1998; Lin, 2000; Lindhorst et al., 2009).

In recent years scholars have moved beyond a simple model of political 'top down' vs street-level 'bottom-up' control over policy outcomes to frame the issue in terms of accountability within complex political, institutional, and organizational systems. As Hupe and Hill (2007: 284) argue, the contemporary structure of governance in the public sector places the work of street-level bureaucrats 'in a micro-network or "web" of multiple, both vertical and horizontal, relations.' Traditional forms of hierarchical control and accountability for achieving policy outcomes may be balanced or challenged by other forms of accountability in this web, including, for example, accountability to co-workers for managing work processes and relationships; accountability to peers within and beyond the organization for enforcing professional norms and standards of practice; and accountability to policy targets and other citizens.

Organizational control

Consistent with a model of nested or multiple sources of accountability, many scholars have focused their attention on the role of organization in controlling or directing front-line discretion. At the most basic level, the exercise of discretion by front-line workers has been linked to the structure of the task environment. For example, in their study of the failure of front-line staff to fully implement welfare reforms in California, Meyers and Dillon (1999) describe the 'paradox' that resulted when policy officials exhorted front-line staff to implement new employment-related policies but maintained existing performance-monitoring systems and incentive structures that emphasized eligibility determination tasks.

The extent and direction of front-line discretion has also been linked to organizational and task complexity. Complexity increases the need for discretionary judgments by front-line workers along with the difficulty of overseeing and monitoring their actions. Political efforts to control discretion through the promulgation of detailed rules and procedures often produce the contrary result, forcing front-line workers to selectively apply rules that are too voluminous to enforce in their totality (Simon, 1983). As Maynard-Moody and Musheno (2003: 8) observe: 'Street-level work is, ironically, rule saturated but not rule bound.'

A number of studies have identified resource constraints as a key influence on the extent and direction of front-line discretion. Street-level bureaucrats have been observed to cope with chronically limited time and other resources by rationing services, discriminating in the provision of services to more cooperative clients, and rationalizing program objectives (Pesso, 1978; Lipsky, 1980; Keiser and Soss, 1998; Keiser, 1999, 2010; Winter, 2001). As Brodkin (1997: 24) observes, 'Caseworkers, like other lower-level bureaucrats, do not do just what they want or just what they are told to want. They do what they can.' Ironically, efforts to cope with limited time and other resources may lead to either inconsistent and particularistic treatment of similar clients, or routinized treatment of clients with dissimilar needs (Weatherley and Lipsky, 1977; Pesso, 1978;

Hagen, 1987; Brodkin, 1995, 1997). The importance of resources has been noted also in studies of the regulatory effort of government inspectors (Winter, 2000).

Scholars have expanded the study of resources to consider front-line workers' knowledge. In a study of the local implementation of natural resources (fish stocking) policies in Sweden, for example, Sandström (2011) finds that variation in access to current scientific knowledge resources explained differences in how local officials implemented regulations in the context of complex policy subsystems with conflicting goals. Hill (2003) proposes an even more expansive definition of resources as the 'storehouse of knowledge and practical advice that implementers might turn to for assistance,' including the knowledge and expertise provided by many non-governmental actors such as consultants, academics, journalists, foundations, and professional associations. In a study of community policing practices, she suggests that when street-level bureaucrats make use of such resources their professional practices may improve in advance of (or even in the absence of) policy reforms.

Scholars have also focused on variation in information and communication technology as a significant resource for implementation fidelity. By structuring interactions with clients to conform with data entry protocols and aggregating case-level data that can be used for performance monitoring, the introduction of management information systems would be expected to reduce the discretion of front-line workers and increase consistency across workers and cases (Bovens and Zouridis, 2002). There is some evidence that greater automation in tasks such as eligibility and claims determinations decreases variation in the treatment of clients resulting from street-level bureaucrats' subjective assessments – reducing the opportunities for street-level bureaucrats to act as 'rouge agents' who use discretion to discriminate in their treatment of claimants (Maynard-Moody and Musheno, 2003; Wenger and Wilkins, 2008). As Hupe and Hill (2007) argue, however, when technologies are adopted within the context of

street-level bureaucracies their role is likely to be contested and the consequences for front-line discretion are uncertain. As an example, in a review of four studies of the restructuring of adult social care as part of the shift to new managerialism in the UK, Ellis (2007, 2011) concludes that technologies designed to increase top-down control increased standardization of practices in some setting while 'producing fresh conditions and requirements' for the exercise of front-line discretion in other areas of practice.

Considering the organizational setting more broadly in her study of the implementation of education programs in prisons, Lin (2000) argues that the implementation of new policies is likely to succeed only when the policies are congruent with the organizational context of implementing agencies:

> When policies are bent to purposes other than those that policy makers anticipated … it is not because staff do not understand their work. Instead, it is precisely because they try to make sense of their work, and thus to understand their jobs as a series of related tasks all bent toward the same purpose. This naturally leads them to refer each new policy to the values that are most salient in their organization (Lin, 2000: 162).

The observation that front-line workers seek congruence with existing organizational norms in their exercise of discretion can be extended to consider the influence of the larger context of the organizational networks within which most workers are embedded. In a study of eligibility determinations within the US Social Security Disability Insurance program, for example, Keiser (2010) finds evidence that eligibility workers' decisions were influenced not only by their own beliefs about policy goals and accountability but also by their perceptions of what other actors in the multi-organizational governance network might do. Even if they were not in a hierarchical relationship or direct contact with other actors, workers with greater knowledge about the usual actions of other organizations were more likely to reach eligibility determinations that would be consistent with those actions.

Worker ideology and professional norms

Other scholars argue that street-level bureaucrats are relatively immune to the power of both policy directives and formal organizational incentives. They point, instead, to the influence of individual interests, professional norms, and the processes through which workers construct meaning in their daily work routines.

Numerous public administration scholars have described norms of public service as the most powerful incentive for bureaucratic performance. Some observers of street-level bureaucrats have reached similar conclusions. Examining survey and observational data on bureaucratic behavior, Brehm and Gates (1997) conclude that supervisors exert relatively little influence on the policy choices of bureaucrats, who are largely self-regulating. Bureaucrats 'work' – instead of shirking or sabotaging policy efforts – primarily because they embrace norms of public service and, secondarily, because these norms are shared and reinforced by their fellow bureaucrats.

Scholars have identified various aspects of worker ideology that may be consequential for discretionary behaviors, from their socialization into professional norms to their personal beliefs about policy instruments and targets. Winter's (2001) study of coping behaviors among front-line workers in a Danish social welfare program lends empirical support to the multidimensional role of worker beliefs. His multivariate analyses capture significant, independent contributions from workers' beliefs about their work environment (including perceived workload and adequacy of professional support), their assessment of the potential effectiveness of the policy instruments at their disposal, and their beliefs about target populations.

In a study of front-line workers' engagement with collaborative, interagency activities, Sandfort (2000) describes front-line welfare workers as largely isolated from their external environment and resistant to new policy directives. She concludes that these street-level bureaucrats were guided largely by the shared knowledge and collective beliefs – or schemas – that staff developed to make sense of their day-to-day work. When management initiatives were consistent with these collective schemas, front-line workers found it reasonable to comply with new directives. But when initiatives appeared illegitimate or disconnected from the realities of daily work, workers' collective schemas legitimated workers' pursuit of alternative objectives and definitions of success.

Watkins-Hays (2009a, 2009b) contextualizes the development of workers' individual and shared schemas by focusing on social identity among front-line workers, both their social group memberships outside the organization (e.g., race, gender, class) and their development of professional identities within the organization. These social and professional self-concepts bring what Watkins-Hays calls the missing pieces to models of the implementation of public policies by street-level bureaucrats:

> This limited attention to the evolution of self-conception has caused us to underestimate the degree to which *how* street-level bureaucrats think of themselves – as professionals, members of racial groups, women, men, and community residents – shapes *what* they value, what they emphasize, and how they negotiated distributing the resources of the state to clients (Watkins-Hays, 2009a: 11).

NORMATIVE AND EVALUATIVE QUESTIONS ABOUT STREET-LEVEL DISCRETION

The salience of the question about control depends entirely on normative beliefs about democratic governance and policy delivery. We care about the extent to which policy officials direct and limit the discretionary actions of front-line workers to the extent that we believe it has implications for outcomes such as democratic governance, fair and equitable treatment of citizens, or policy achievement. The belief that these values are best achieved through a top-down, hierarchical model of control is a legacy of early Public Administration theory. A variety of competing perspectives suggest that the exercise of discretion by front-line workers is not only inevitable but also desirable – for promoting democratic control over policy processes, tailoring policies to individual needs, and increasing the effectiveness of policy efforts.

Democratic accountability

The most obvious governance concern is the potential of street-level bureaucrats to undermine the goals of elected officials. Because street-level bureaucrats are neither elected nor appointed by elected officials, they are largely immune to electoral accountability. To the extent that elected officials cannot fully control street-level bureaucrats' day-to-day decisions and actions, citizens have few mechanisms for assessing, much less controlling, their impact on policy. Policy goals may be displaced or distorted when front-line workers focus their energies on managing workloads, coping with job demands, or pursuing their own ideological, policy, or political interests (e.g., Lipsky, 1980; Sandfort, 2000; Winter, 2000). In the language of principal–agent theory, while some street-level bureaucrats may 'work' to achieve policy makers' goals others may 'shirk' by pursuing other objectives or 'sabotage' policy by deliberately undermining the directives of their superiors (Brehm and Gates, 1997).

In other respects the exercise of discretion by street-level workers may actually contribute to democratic accountability by bridging gaps between citizens and elected officials. Local program workers, inspectors, and other front-line workers can serve as one more 'check and balance' on the exercise of power by legislators who are often far removed from the citizens who are the targets of their policies (e.g., Ferman, 1990). The exercise of discretion by front-line workers may promote representative democracy by allowing for local influence on federal rules and bureaucracies (Scholz et al., 1991) and by creating opportunities for those most affected by policies to influence their delivery (Ferman, 1990). Vinzant and Crothers (1998) propose an even more important governance role for 'street-level leaders' whose 'active, accountable, and responsible' work at the interface of citizens, communities, and the state can increase the legitimacy and responsiveness of government agencies.

Equity

A second normative question concerns the implications of street-level discretion for the individuals who are affected by their actions. It is possible that front-line workers use their discretion to the benefit of the citizens with whom they interact, taking individual circumstances into account when allocating benefits, enforcing regulations, applying sanctions, and the like. Street-level bureaucrats are also assumed by many to have professional expertise and knowledge that they can use to the advantage of clients (Vinzant and Crothers, 1998). Studies of welfare workers, rehabilitation counselors, police, and teachers provide numerous examples of the exercise of 'positive discrimination' to assist those individuals that they consider most in need or most deserving of assistance (Goodsell, 1981; Maynard-Moody and Musheno, 2003).

Similar dynamics may create complicit relationships between regulators and the targets of regulation. Gormley (1995), for example, describes 'regulatory rituals' in US childcare arising from a combination of weak state regulations and regulators' unwillingness to punish poor-quality providers by putting them out of business. As he describes, 'the cumulative effect of all these norms is that good and bad providers become virtually indistinguishable, judging from the regulatory agency's output. Inspectors know who has been naughty and who's been nice, that remains their little secret' (Gormley, 1995: 56).

It is equally possible that the exercise of street-level discretion leads to harmful or discriminatory treatment. Street-level bureaucrats in gatekeeping roles have been observed to limit claimants' access to benefits to which they are entitled (Hill and Bramley, 1986) and to discriminate in their treatment policy targets, introducing their own biases into the distribution of public benefits and enforcement of penalties (Lipsky, 1980; Brodkin, 1997; Keiser and Soss, 1998). Brodkin (1997) and others argue that chronic resource limitations, coupled with the difficulty of monitoring the quality of front-line services in public agencies, create conditions in which workers are very likely to deliver government services that are inconsistent and of poor quality. And she notes that this is particularly likely for poor and involuntary 'clients' of the welfare state for whom 'rights are uncertain, 'voice' is risky, and 'exit' means forgoing basic income support' (Brodkin, 1997: 25).

Policy achievement

A third normative question concerns the implications of front-line discretion for the achievement of policy objectives. Street-level discretion introduces considerable uncertainty into the achievement of public policy goals, particularly when the interests of policy makers and workers diverge. Even when they both share a long-term interest in the achievement of policy objectives, in the short-term they usually operate with distinctly different priorities: policy makers to satisfy stakeholder demands for visible results; front-line staff to cope with the problems of managing work; and clients to survive and to manage the social bureaucracies (Lynn, 1993; Lin, 2000; Meyers et al., 2001).

When interests are aligned through policy and organizational design, the attempts of policy makers, front-line workers, and clients to satisfy these short-term objectives may result in achievement of policy officials' goals. Behn (1991), for example, describes successful welfare-to-work programs in which agency managers employed performance measures and incentives (e.g., tracking and rewarding job placements) that aligned workers' interests with those of policy officials (to reduce welfare caseloads) and clients (to obtain stable employment). The attempts of each group to satisfy their own goals can result, however, in implementation that is inconsistent, at best, and incomplete, subverted, or aborted at worst. In these cases, the achievement of policy objectives is partial at most: e.g., routinization of 'individualized' educational plans (Weatherley and Lipsky, 1977), prison education programs that do not provide instruction (Lin, 2000), childcare inspections that become 'regulatory rituals' without sanctions or rewards (Gormley, 1995), or manpower training programs that 'train students for unemployment' by directing them to overcrowded occupations or equipping them with outdated skills (Hjern and Porter, 1981) or that fail to deliver on promises to place them into meaningful training and employment (Winter, 2001).

Much of the empirical research on front-line discretion and policy achievement has relied on detailed case studies of one or a small number of programs. A handful of studies have used multivariate techniques to examine the link between the behaviors of front-line workers and policy achievement by capitalizing on cross-site variation. Findings about the explanatory power of worker behavior from these have been mixed and suggest that results are sensitive to both model specification and to the measurement of the dependent variable.

Riccio and Hasenfeld (1996), for example, find only modest support for their hypothesis that the approach used by welfare-to-work staff influences client participation in employment-preparation activities. When they use a large sample of observations from similar welfare-to-work programs and employ multilevel estimation methods to control for individual- as well as program-level characteristics, Bloom et al. (2001) find substantially stronger client-level effects associated with workers' description of the service approach in their office – such as the degree of personalization.

Multivariate studies also suggest that the same policy and organizational factors may have different effects on different aspects of target group behaviors. May and Winter (2000) find significant but weak effects of agency enforcement tools and inspectors' enforcement styles on perceived compliance of farmers with agricultural regulations. However, May and Wood (2003) find evidence that while building inspectors' enforcement style does not influence homebuilders' compliance with building codes directly, it may do so indirectly through affecting their knowledge of code provisions and cooperation with inspectors.

STUDYING THE STREET-LEVEL BUREAUCRAT IN CONTEXT

The growing body of scholarship on street-level bureaucrats paints a contradictory portrait. In some studies these workers emerge as frustrated and powerless cogs in bureaucratic machines; in others, as self-interested bureaucrats whose coping mechanisms frustrate and distort the policy intentions of elected officials; in still others, as heroic local leaders who translate impersonal policy directives for the benefit of their clients. Detailed case studies of the impact of street-level discretion on policy outcomes ascribe a powerful influence to front-line workers, while efforts to measure this impact using multivariate models have found relatively weak effects.

This contradictory portrait of street-level bureaucrats reflects both the lack of sufficient theory and methods for studying street-level workers and the failure to fully contextualize the evaluation of their performance. As Hjern and Porter (1981) argued over

two decades ago, given the complexity of implementation structures, neither organizational models of hierarchical control nor economic theories of individual incentives fully describe the influences on street-level workers. Scholars have proposed several theoretical frames that may be useful for integrating these factors. While none provide a single unifying theory, two examples suggest promising directors for future work.

One approach focuses on the implementation *process* and the dynamic tension between 'top-down' and 'bottom-up' interests throughout this process. A recent paper by Hasenfeld (2010) provides an example of the integration of structural and political factors in a model of implementation of politically and morally contested policies. His model places worker/client interactions at the center of nested organizational and institutional layers through which political and moral conflicts are passed down from policy makers to policy implementers. The outer layer is the context for the policy design itself, typically crafted by national or local political officials to affirm broad policy principles and moral values. To the extent that these values are contested, political actors buffer themselves from political conflicts by crafting policy designs, to be passed on to implementing agencies, that are often vague, ambiguous or even internally contradictory. Implementing agencies, in turn, operate within the second nested layer of the model, a particular and often local institutional political economy in which multiple interests compete to influence the structures and practices for policy delivery. The decisions, compromises, and accommodations made by actors in the administering agencies in response to dominant interests are passed on, via policy and administrative directives, to organizations that interface with the targets of policy. These organizations also exist within a context of multiple internal and external interests, the third nested layer of the model. These interests influence the strategic choices of organizational actors about the structure and technology of policy delivery – choices that balance, for example, the organization's need to align with dominant values, to mobilize resources, to justify practices ideologies and to satisfy internal and external stakeholders. At the fourth layer of the model, these politically negotiated structures and technologies create the conditions of work in which street-level bureaucrats actually create policy as delivered – from the tasks they are directed to complete to the number and characteristics of clients with whom they interact, the resources at their disposal, and the rewards, penalties, and discretion they experience. Hasenfeld's model suggests that it is through these proximate mechanisms, and the interactions of workers with clients, that larger political and social conflicts are ultimately resolved.

A second, and relatively less-developed conceptual approach to the study of street-level bureaucrats focuses more explicitly on the characteristics of *the street-level bureaucrats themselves* and how they interact with the organizational and institutional settings of their task and agency. Although worker characteristics have been included in empirical studies, they are often interpreted along the single dimension of workers' efforts to control their work environment. More recent work is expanding attention to consider multiple motivations that interact to influence their actions (see, for example, Hill, 2003; Schofield, 2004; May and Winter, 2009).

Working in this emerging area of scholarship, Nielsen (2006 – see also Winter and Nielsen, 2008) provides an example of a conceptual model for street-level bureaucrats' capacity and motivation that draws on theory from organizational learning and human motivation studies. Starting with the assumption that street-level bureaucrats are embedded in organizational and institutional systems, she focuses in particular on the characteristics and experiences of the street-level bureaucrats themselves. In this model the first worker-level factors operate to influence the workers' ability to implement policy, such as knowledge, cognitive abilities, and analytic and emotional intelligence

(Nielsen, 2010). The second worker-level factor that Nielsen proposes is workers' will or motivation to act in ways that go beyond their own self-interest in controlling work demands. She draws on classic motivational theory to suggest features of the organizational and task environment that will compel and/or entice workers to pursue policy goals. From *scientific management*, she considers whether the implementation of policy improves their conditions of work as 'economic (wo)man' – for example, salary, opportunities for promotion or financial bonuses, control over work hours. From *human relations* theory, she identifies factors that align workers' needs as 'social (wo)man' with policy directives, such as improving relations with co-workers, supervisors, and clients. Finally, from *neo-human relations* theory, she suggests factors that are important to workers' interests as 'self-fulfilling (wo)man' – for example, the extent to which implementation of the policy brings professional challenge and the achievement of policy goals is seen to have value and significance. Nielsen argues that both abilities and will are augmented or limited in practice by the regulative, normative, and cultural-cognitive institutions (Scott, 2001) of the organization, thereby recognizing the contingent influence of formal and informal institutions and the power of both policy makers and front-line workers to influence policy 'as delivered.'

EVALUATING OUTCOMES

As scholars theorize about the role of street-level bureaucrats in policy implementation, they face the challenge of articulating clear criteria against which to evaluate their contributions. If street-level bureaucrats are embedded in complex implementation structures that both grant discretionary power and channel the exercise of that discretion, then it is impossible to evaluate their performance without considering the implementation context. This creates considerable difficulties for the analyst who hopes to generalize about the 'success' of implementation or the 'cooperation' of street-level bureaucrats with policy officials' goals. The same front-line decisions and actions that represent cooperation in one implementation context may reflect shirking or even sabotage in another.

Implementation contexts vary across countries and political systems. Hill (1997), for example, contrasts the acute concerns for hierarchical policy control that arise in the highly fragmented and competitive federalist system of the United States with the 'rather gentler and more consensual' debates about national and local collaboration that arise in the more cooperative political systems in Scandinavian countries. Implementation contexts also vary with policy design. Delivering benefits to citizens, for example, raises very different implementation issues than regulating their behavior. Because policies designed to affect the behavior or circumstances of target groups must be co-produced with these targets, the implementation context also varies with characteristics of the target population. And some social problems are simply easier to resolve than others, because the technology is more certain, the desired outcomes are more realistic, or the interests and capabilities of the target population are more consistent with policy goals. Politics and policy designs determine not only what will be done or provided to whom but also the resources and authority that the implementing agencies will have at their disposal, the capacity of the organizational delivery system, the complexity of the inter-organizational network that must cooperate to achieve policy objectives, the density and coherence of the existing policy framework, and other organizational factors.

Given the diversity of implementation contexts, resolving the normative questions of what street-level bureaucrats *should* do, and the empirical questions of what they *do* do have an often-overlooked indeterminacy. As Helen Ingram (1990: 470) suggests,

'the challenge presented to implementers depends very much on the problems passed along to them by policy formulators.' The problems passed on to implementing bureaucracies, and the solutions they adopt, become, in turn, the challenge presented to local agencies and their front-line staff – including the job they are asked to do, the resources they are provided to do it, the rewards for performance, and the penalties for non-performance. If the job of the street-level bureaucrat and his or her capacity to do that job depend on the implementation context, against what criteria do we judge their exercise of discretion?

Recognizing the limited control that many workers exercise over policy outcomes and impacts, some observers suggest that we judge fidelity in terms of street-level behaviors rather than policy outcome (Matland, 1995). Lin (2000), for example, suggests that implementation success be judged on the basis of staff activities that are 'plausibly related' to the achievement of policy objective. Winter, in Chapter 14, also argues for the evaluation of behavioral variables that characterize the *behavior* of implementers. Whether this behavior by implementers brings about desired behaviors among target groups depends on additional variables, including the validity of the underlying causal model, which may be beyond the control of street-level workers.

Activities and performance that reflect fidelity to policy makers' intentions can provide a useful yardstick for evaluation. As Matland (1995 – see also Ingram, 1990) suggests, however, the definition of such actions can still be challenging. Appropriate actions are most easily defined when the intentions of policy officials are clear, consistent, and reasonable in light of agency capacity and expertise. But these implementation conditions are far from certain in democratic societies. Consider the case, quite common in social policy, in which policy-making officials achieve political consensus by adopting ambiguous or even contradictory policy directives. In this case we may judge the activities of front-line workers in terms of their successful negotiation of a clear set of directives. When the technology to achieve desired policy ends is uncertain or unknown, front-line cooperation might be judged by the extent and success of local program experimentation. In still other cases, front-line implementing agents may seek to faithfully pursue policy-makers' interests but fail to achieve policy goals because they are not given the resources, or lack technical capacity, to achieve them. Under these conditions, success and cooperation might be viewed in terms of policy learning, with implementing staff informing decision makers about the mismatch between formal goals and actual capacity. Through a different lens, cooperation under these conditions could be defined as quiet complicity with the non-delivery of bold but essentially hollow promises that policy officials make to their constituents.

In short, in various implementation contexts, we might consider creativity, adaptation, learning, entrepreneurship, experimentation, or even complicity as the appropriate output against which to evaluate the exercise of discretion by street-level bureaucrats. Our failure to acknowledge this indeterminacy can lead us to assign both credit and blame for policy outcomes to street-level bureaucrats when our attention should be directed toward policy designs and other factors in the implementation context. As Hill (1997: 383) observes about the assessment of recent decentralization efforts in Britain: 'The notion of the distinction between policy making and implementation provides a splendid vehicle for shifting the blame – there was nothing wrong with the policy but it was undermined, subverted, and so on.'

REFERENCES

Behn, R. (1991) *Leadership Counts.* Cambridge, MA: Harvard University Press.

Bloom, H.S., Hill, C.J., and Riccio, J. (2001) *Modeling the Performance of Welfare-To-Work Programs: The Effects of Program Management and Services,*
Economic Environment, and Client Characteristics. Working paper. Manpower Demonstration and Research Corporation.

Bovens, M. and Zouridis, S. (2002) 'From Street-Level to System-Level Bureaucracies: How Information and Communication Technology is Transforming Administrative Discretion and Constitutional Control', *Public Administration Review,* 62(2): 174–184.

Brehm, J. and Gates, S. (1997) *Working, Shirking, and Sabotage: Bureaucratic Response to a Democratic Public.* Ann Arbor, MI: University of Michigan Press.

Brodkin, E.Z. (1995) *The State Side of the 'Welfare Contract': Discretion and Accountability in Policy Delivery.* University of Chicago, School of Social Service Administration.

Brodkin, E.Z. (1997) 'Inside the Welfare Contract: Discretion and Accountability in State Welfare Administration', *Social Service Review,* 71(1): 1–33.

Ellis, K. (2007) 'Direct Payments and Social Work Practice: The Significance of "Street-Level Bureaucracy" in Determining Eligibility', *British Journal of Social Work,* 37(3): 405–422.

Ellis, K. (2011) '"Street-Level Bureaucracy" Revisited: The Changing Face of Frontline Discretion in Adult Social Care in England', *Social Policy & Administration,* 45(3): 221–244.

Ferman, B. (1990) 'When Failure is Success: Implementation and Madisonian Government,' in D.J. Palumbo and D.J. Calista (eds), *Implementation and the Policy Process.* New York: Greenwood Press.

Goodsell, C.T. (1981) 'Looking Once Again at Human Service Bureaucracy', *The Journal of Politics,* 43: 763–778.

Gormley, W.T., Jr (1995) *Everybody's Children: Child Care as a Public Problem.* Washington, DC: Brookings Institution.

Hagen, J.L. (1987) 'Income Maintenance Workers: Technicians or Service Providers?' *Social Service Review,* 61(2): 261–271.

Hasenfeld, Y. (2010) 'Organizational Responses to Social Policy: The Case of Welfare Reform', *Administration in Social Work,* 34(2): 148–167.

Headrick, B., Serra, G., and Twombly, J. (2002) 'Enforcement and Oversight: Using Congressional Oversight to Shape OSHA Bureaucratic Behavior', *American Politics Research,* 30(6): 608–629.

Hill, H. (2003) 'Understanding Implementation: Street-Level Bureaucrats' Resources for Reform', *Journal of Public Administration Research and Theory,* 13(3): 265–282.

Hill, M. (1997) 'Implementation Theory: Yesterday's Issue?' *Policy and Politics*, 25(4): 375–385.

Hill, M. and Bramley, G. (1986) *Analysing Social Policy*. New York: Blackwell.

Hill, M. and Hupe, P. (2003) 'The Multi-Layer Problem in Implementation Research', *Public Management Review* 5(4): 471–490.

Hjern, B. and Porter, D.O. (1981) 'Implementation Structures: A New Unit of Administrative Analysis', *Organization Studies*, 2(3): 211–227.

Huber, J.D., Shipan, C.R., and Pfahler, M. (2001) 'Legislatures and Statutory Control of Bureaucracy', *American Journal of Political Science*, 45(2): 330–345.

Hupe, P. and Hill, M. (2007) 'Street Level Bureaucracy and Public Accountability', *Public Administration*, 85(2): 279–299.

Ingram, H. (1990) 'Implementation: A Review and Suggested Framework,' in L. Lynn and A. Wildavsky (eds), *Public Administration: the State of the Discipline*. Chatham, NJ: Chatham House Publishers, pp. 462–480.

Keiser, L.R. (1999) 'State Bureaucratic Discretion and the Administration of Social Welfare Programs: The Case of Social Security Disability', *Journal of Public Administration Research and Theory*, 9(1): 87–106.

Keiser, L. R. (2010) 'Understanding Street-Level Bureaucrats' Decision Making: Determining Eligibility in the Social Security Disability Program', *Public Administration Review*, March/April: 247–257.

Keiser, L.R. and Soss, J. (1998) 'With Good Cause: Bureaucratic Discretion and the Politics of Child Support Enforcement.' *American Journal of Political Science*, 42(4): 1133–1156.

Lin, A.C. (2000) *Reform in the Making: The Implementation of Social Policy in Prison*. Princeton, NJ: Princeton University Press.

Lindhorst, T., Casey, E., and Meyers, M. (2009) 'Frontline Worker Responses to Domestic Violence Disclosure in Public Welfare Offices', *Social Work*, 55(3): 235–243.

Lipsky, M. (1980) *Street Level Bureaucracy: Dilemmas of the Individual in Public Services*. New York: Russell Sage Foundation.

Lynn, L.E., Jr (1993) 'Policy Achievement as a Collective Good: A Strategic Perspective on Managing Social Programs,' in B. Bozeman (ed.), *Public Management: The State of the Art*. San Francisco, CA: Jossey-Bass, pp. 108–133.

Lynn, L.E., Heinrich, C.J., and Hill, C.J. (2000) 'Studying Governance and Public Management: Challenges and Prospects', *Journal of Public Administration Research and Theory*, 10(2): 233–262.

McCubbins, M.D., Noll, R.G., and Weingast, B.R. (1987) 'Administrative Procedures as Instruments of Political Control', *Journal of Law, Economics and Organization*, 3(2): 243–277.

Matland, R.E. (1995) 'Synthesizing the Implementation Literature: The Ambiguity–Conflict Model of Policy Implementation', *Journal of Public Administration Research and Theory*, 5(2): 145–174.

May, P.J. and Winter, S.C. (2009) 'Politicians, Managers and Street-Level Bureaucrats: Influences on Policy Implementation', *Journal of Public Administration Research and Theory*, 19(3): 453–476.

May, P.J. and Winter, S. (2000) 'Reconsidering Styles of Regulatory Enforcement: Patterns in Danish Agro-Environmental Inspection', *Law and Policy*, 22(2): 143–173.

May, P.J. and Wood, R. (2003) 'At the Regulatory Front Lines: Inspectors' Enforcement Styles and Regulatory Compliance,' *Journal of Public Administration Research and Theory*, 13(2): 117–139.

Maynard-Moody, S. and Musheno, M. (2003) *Cops, Teachers, Counselors: Narratives of Street-Level Judgment*. Ann Arbor, MI: University of Michigan Press.

Meyers, M. and Dillon, N. (1999) 'Institutional Paradoxes: Why Welfare Workers Can't Reform Welfare,' in G. Frederickson and J. Johnston (eds), *Public Administration as Reform and Innovation*. Tuscaloosa, AL: University of Alabama Press.

Meyers, Marcia K., Glaser, Bonnie, and MacDonald, Karin (1998) 'On the Front Lines of Welfare Delivery: Are Workers Implementing Policy Reforms?' *Journal of Policy Analysis and Management*, 17(1): 1–22.

Meyers, M.K., Riccucci, N., and Lurie I. (2001) 'Achieving Goal Congruence in Complex Organizational Systems: The Case of Welfare Reform', *Journal of Public Administration Research and Theory*, 11(2): 165–201.

Moe, Terry M. (1984) 'The New Economics of Organization', *American Journal of Political Science*, 28(4): 739–777.

Nielsen, Vibeke Lehmann (2006) 'Are Street-Level Bureaucrats Compelled or Enticed to Cope?' *Public Administration*, 84(4): 861–889.

Nielsen, Vibeke Lehmann (2010) 'Den lille betingede forskel', *Politica*, 42(4): 377–397.

Pesso, T. (1978) 'Local Welfare Offices: Managing the Intake Process', *Public Policy*, 26(2): 305–330.

Riccio, J. and Hasenfeld, Y. (1996) 'Enforcing a Participation Mandate in a Welfare-to-Work Program', *Social Service Review*, 70(4): 516–542.

Riccucci, Norma M., Marcia Meyers, Irene Lurie & Jun Soep Han (2004): 'The Implementation of Welfare

Reform Policy: The Role of Public Managers in Front', *Public Administration Review*, 64(4): 438–448.

Sandfort, J.R. (2000) 'Moving Beyond Discretion and Outcomes: Examining Public Management from the Front Lines of the Welfare System', *Journal of Public Administration Research and Theory* 10(4): 729–756.

Sandström, A. (2011) 'Navigating a Complex Policy System – Explaining Local Divergences in Swedish Fish Stocking Policy', *Marine Policy,* 35(3): 419–425.

Scholz, John T., Twombly, Jim, and Headrick Barbara (1991) 'Street-Level Political Controls over Federal Bureaucracy', *The American Political Science Review,* 85(3): 829–850.

Scott, W. Richard (2001): *Institutions and Organizations*, 2nd edn. Thousand Oakes, London, New Delhi: Sage.

Simon, W.H. (1983) 'Legality, Bureaucracy, and Class in the Welfare System', *Yale Law Journal*, 92: 1198–1250.

Vinzant, J.C. and Crothers, L. (1998) *Street-Level Leadership: Discretion & Legitimacy in Front-Line Public Service*. Washington, DC: Georgetown University Press.

Watkins-Hays, C. (2009a) *The New Welfare Bureaucrats: Entanglements of Race, Class and Policy Reform.* Chicago, IL: University of Chicago Press.

Watkins-Hayes, C. (2009b) 'Race-ing the Bootstrap Climb: Black and Latino Bureaucrats in Post-Reform Welfare Offices', *Social Problems*, 56(2): 285–310.

Weatherley, R. and Lipsky M. (1977) 'Street-Level Bureaucrats and Institutional Innovation', *Harvard Educational Review*, 47(2): 171–197.

Wenger, J. and Wilkins, V.M. (2008) 'At the Discretion of Rogue Agents: How Automation Improves Women's Outcomes in Unemployment Insurance', *Journal of Public Administration Research and Theory*, 19: 313–333.

Winter, S. (2000) *Information Asymmetry and Political Control of Street-Level Bureaucrats: Danish Agro-Environmental Regulation*. Paper prepared for the annual research meeting of the Association for Public Policy Analysis and Management, Seattle, WA (November 2–4).

Winter, S.C. (2001) *Reconsidering Street-Level Bureaucracy Theory: From Identifying to Explaining Coping Behavior*. Paper for the annual meeting of the Association of Policy Analysis and Management held in Washington, DC (November 1–3). Danish National Institute of Social Research.

Winter, S.C. and Nielsen, Vibeke Lehmann (2008). *Implementering af politik*. Aarhus, Denmark: Gyldendal Academica.

PART 6

Law and Administration

edited by Gavin Drewry

Law lies at the heart of both the theory and the practice of public administration. Max Weber (himself a lawyer by his early training, as Jacques Ziller reminds us in Chapter 17) associated the pervasiveness of his bureaucratic model of organization in advanced societies with the rational–legal authority that underpins such societies. Woodrow Wilson's famous essay on 'The Study of Administration' first published in 1887 propounded a working definition of public administration as 'detailed and systematic execution of public law'.[1] Even if this is perhaps a bit of an oversimplification – more applicable in some countries than in others – it is certainly the case that knowledge of the legal framework of administrative systems is crucial to an understanding of the nature and rationale of those systems. In some countries – Germany is a well-known example – civil servants are fully trained lawyers; even in countries where they are not, the practice of public administration requires a good understanding of public law.

Public law is often seen as being necessarily different from private law if only because states are sovereign and governments have to

govern. Public functions and obligations are in many ways intrinsically different from private ones – hence, the fact that governments are often subject to the jurisdiction of constitutional courts; and state bureaucracies are usually subject to regimes of administrative law, of which there are numerous variations – some of them discussed in the chapters that follow – applied in many cases by specialized administrative courts and tribunals (complemented in many countries by ombudsman systems that constitute a parallel universe of administrative justice[2]). And, increasingly, globalization has resulted in a growth in the impact of *international* law, which has both public and private aspects, for example in the domain of human rights. European readers will not need to be reminded of the pervasive significance of European Union Law and of the European Convention on Human Rights.

In one aspect, public law can be seen in this context as having a *restraining* effect – setting the boundaries of what government can legally do. The concept of constitutionalism – based upon a perception that 'a State powerful enough to maintain order may also be strong enough to suppress liberty', and that the machinery of government needs to be equipped 'with brakes as well as a motor'[3] – has been the source of much legal and political science discourse, particularly in the United States. Variants on the idea of a 'rule of law' (the German *Rechtsstaat* sometimes being thus translated) are also relevant to this perception. Also, dispute resolution and redress of citizens' grievances are crucial aspects of judicial review.

But laws and constitutions also have a positive part to play in enabling governments to govern and as providing a *positive* framework for a good public service. In discussing the modern development of administrative law in the United Kingdom, Harlow and Rawlings, in the early editions of their widely-used text, have used the apt metaphor of the traffic signal – showing how a Diceyan 'red light' belief that rampant governments with collectivist ambitions needs to be subjected to the restraints of the ordinary law gave way to a 'green light' perception that law should facilitate and not impede the necessary development and operation of public services; followed then by an inevitable 'forever amber' signal that recognizes law's dual function in this context.[4]

But the distinction between public and private law can never be completely watertight. Public bodies and state functionaries may, in the course of exercising public functions, be liable to private law actions in contract or tort (and/or to criminal prosecutions, for example, for corruption). The line between public and private conduct may be difficult to draw, and the distinctions have become much more problematical as public management reform initiatives have created new contractual and quasi-contractual modes of delivery of public services and hybrid relationships between public and private bodies. The boundary between public and private sector institutions and functions – and hence between public and private law – has become increasingly blurred. A leading treatise on UK judicial review summarized the most

important aspects of recent public service reform and concluded that:

> The legal relationships that arise out of these new forms of service provision are neither wholly 'public' nor 'private'. They involve a complex mixture of regulatory activity on the traditional 'command and control' model, intertwined with regulation based upon contractual-type arrangements between the direct provider of services and the ultimate purchaser, consumer or customer.[5]

In countries that have undergone variants of New Public Management reform, patterns of judicial review (and other mechanisms of accountability) have reflected a continuing struggle to keep abreast of the changes in the machinery of state functions and public services, and to establish a workable line of demarcation between public law, per se, and private law (including the law of contract and tort) as it applies in the context of public functions and state power.

The three chapters that follow explore, from different standpoints, the nature and significance of the interactions between legal systems and public administration. In Chapter 17, Jacques Ziller looks at the development and influence of the two main continental European traditions of public law – the French *principe de légalité* and the Prussian/German *Rechtsstaat*. Both traditions (allied, in the case of post-revolutionary France, with the development of the Napoleonic system of administrative law, and in post-Nazi Germany with a growing concern about constitutional protection of human rights) have been enormously influential across most of Western Europe. Although there have been very big variations in the influence of the two models in different European countries – he dismisses the misleading perception of 'a homogeneous system of law relating to continental European public administration' – both models have resulted in continental public administration systems that are underpinned extensively by law. Ziller also shows that the legal arrangements of many European countries share more characteristics of the common law systems of the UK and/or of the United States than is commonly supposed.

Anglo-American public law traditions are explored by Paul Craig in Chapter 18. The author refutes the claim that administrative law is a recent development in the Anglo-American tradition: it has a long history, rooted in the common law and the development and adaptation of legal remedies by the courts. But although administrative law in the UK and the United States has common roots, there are major divergences, arising substantially from the fact that one country has a codified constitution and an Administrative Procedure Act, while the other has neither; however, the UK has gone down interesting new pathways as a result of its membership of the European Union, and the side-door introduction of European administrative law jurisprudence through authoritative judgments handed down by the European Court of Justice. The chapter discusses, with reference to both countries, the enforcement of 'process rights', the extent of a duty to consult in administrative rule-making and the extent to which courts have refrained (or not) from substituting their own judgment for that of policy makers and administrators.

Finally, in Chapter 19, David Feldman looks more generally at the extent to which law can and should constrain public administration. He examines the functions and characteristics of legal norms in relation to other normative systems, and the part they play in underpinning the legitimacy of democratic systems based on the rule of law. The author discusses the factors that lead administrators themselves to internalize legal norms, and the impact of legal rules and judicial review on the administrative process: 'It would be unreasonable', he concludes, 'to expect law, and judicial review in particular, to provide anything approaching a coherent guide to public administration'. But that conclusion does not mean that either the student or the practitioner of public administration can afford to ignore them. The chapters in Part 6 make that abundantly clear.

NOTES

1 Woodrow Wilson, 'The Study of Administration', *Political Science Quarterly*, 2 (1887), pp. 197–222.

2 Gavin Drewry, 'Ombudsmen and Administrative Law – Bright Stars in a Parallel Universe', *Asia Pacific Law Review*, 17 (2009), pp. 3–25.

3 William G. Andrews, *Constitutions and Constitutionalism*, 3rd edn (Princeton, NJ: Van Nostrand, 1968), p. 9. See also D. Greenberg et al. (eds), *Constitutionalism and Democracy: Transitions in the Contemporary World* (New York: Oxford University Press, 1993).

4 Carol Harlow and Richard Rawlings, *Law and Administration*, 2nd edn (London: Butterworths, 1997), Chs 2, 3 and 4.

5 Lord Woolf and Jeffrey Jowell, *Judicial Review of Administrative Action*, 5th edn (London: Sweet and Maxwell, 1995), p. 165.

17

The Continental System of Administrative Legality

Jacques Ziller

In Continental Europe, until the last quarter of the twentieth century public administration studies were developed in most countries by scholars who had received their main education in law, and by legal practitioners of public administration. For the large part, public administration studies have been primarily a by-product of administrative law. Even Max Weber, the founder of sociology of administration, had been educated as a lawyer before becoming interested in economics and in sociology. This tradition contributes a great deal to a somewhat misleading perception of a homogeneous system of law relating to Continental European public administration – as opposed to an Anglo-American system that would derive its features from common law heritage. A closer look at different countries would reveal a lot of common features between a number of Continental European countries and the United States, other similarities between some Continental European countries and the United Kingdom, and a lot of important differences between one Continental European country and another.[1]

THE GERMAN AND FRENCH MODELS

The two main models of Continental European public administration were developed in Prussia during the eighteenth century and in France at the turn of the nineteenth century, mainly during the time of Napoleon.[2] The Prussian model had an early influence on the Austrian administration, but the attraction of the Napoleonic model has also been important for both countries, as well as for the Netherlands – and thus consequently for Belgium and Luxembourg – Italy and Spain, as well as Denmark and Norway. Only Portugal, Sweden and Switzerland have kept an administrative system with structures very different from the rest of Western Continental Europe.[3] The Prussian tradition of the *Rechtsstaat* and the French tradition of the *principe de légalité* both explain the importance of law for public administration.

The *Rechtsstaat* concept – literally 'legal state', usually translated as 'rule of law' – was developed mainly during the nineteenth century by German writers,[4] as opposed to the *Polizeistaat* – police state which corresponded to autocratic monarchy. The concept has its roots in the Age of Enlightenment, notably in Voltaire's sceptical philosophy which influenced the King of Prussia Frederick the Great and the Austrian Empress Maria Theresa: the sovereign should be bound by rules he established, which have to be stable, known to their subjects and applied in a fair and equal manner by professional judges and administrators. Until the twentieth century it was centred on legal formalism as a safeguard for a stable and fair social order and was closely linked with the existence of a bureaucratic apparatus as the main guarantee of the functioning of the system; it was therefore quite appealing to the European non-parliamentarian monarchies (German countries and the Austro-Hungarian Empire during its most enlightened periods; as well as Nordic countries and to a limited extent the Netherlands). The Nazi period and the perversion of German legal traditions that it fostered led to a deep transformation after World War II. Legal formalism remains important in the perspective of procedural guarantees to the citizen, which have been codified in a general law on administrative procedure in Austria in 1925, followed by Poland in 1928; in a second period, Germany took the lead on codification of administrative procedure in Europe with its law of 1976.[5] The concept has however become a more substantive one, which incorporates the constitutional protection of human rights and non-discrimination, relying on a solid system of judicial protection with a specialised constitutional court – according to the model developed in Austria in 1920 under the influence of Hans Kelsen.[6] This revived concept has had a growing influence in Europe, having met with developments of much the same kind in Italy as a reaction to the fascist period. German constitutional and administrative law has become a major source of inspiration in the transition to democracy in Europe of former autocratic regimes – Greece and Portugal after 1974 and Spain after 1976 – and of former communist countries after 1989.[7]

The *principe de légalité* – principle of legality – is also rooted in the Enlightenment, mainly on Rousseau's theory of democracy, which was adopted and developed by the political personnel of the French Revolution of 1789. Montesquieu's theory of the separation of powers took more time to become part of French tradition: it needed the establishment of a parliamentary regime under the monarchy in 1816–20 and its acceptance by democrats as a feature of the republican regime in the last quarter of the nineteenth century. The concept of *principe de légalité* is mainly based upon statute law as an expression of the general will, linked to the concept of social contract: citizens are only to obey rules that they have accepted through decisions of their representatives. Whereas the idea of *Rechtsstaat* developed independently, and preceded that of democracy in German institutions throughout the nineteenth century, the *principe de légalité* has always been linked to the idea of representative democracy, even if reduced to mere formalism during the autocratic regimes of Napoleon Bonaparte (1799–1814) and Napoleon III (1852–70). From 1848 onwards the concept of legality was directly and permanently linked to universal suffrage, and the Declaration of Human Rights of 1789, which are the three main concepts by which French revolutionary ideas influenced European liberal thinking; at the same time, the Napoleonic system of administration was even more influential, as it impressed on one side liberals, because of its links with the French Revolution, but also on the other side leaders of autocratic monarchies, because of its efficiency. In France the consequences of the principle of legality have been developed mainly by the case law of the *Conseil d'Etat* (State Council), set up in 1799 as the government's legal council, which very soon became the highest appellate body in litigation between citizens and government – i.e. public administration – as government did not depart from its advice. In 1872 it became an independent court, making decisions in the name of the people. As early as the middle of the nineteenth century the case law of the *Conseil d'Etat* was the first developed body of modern administrative law. This body of law therefore has been a source of inspiration for the development of administrative law in most Western European countries and the model of the *Conseil d'Etat* has been used in a – smaller – number of countries for the establishment of supreme administrative courts.[8]

These differences in principle and origins account for a great deal in explaining differences from one European country to the other: the role of endogenous ideas and that of French and German influence differ in time and space. A good understanding of those common features and differences helps in gaining a better overview of the meaning and relevance of the Weberian model of public administration at the turn of the twentieth century as well as a hundred years later.

THE CLOSE LINKS BETWEEN PUBLIC ADMINISTRATION AND STATUTE LAW

The written constitutions of Continental European countries include a set of principles applying to public administration. Sometimes these principles are only vaguely spelt out, as is the case for the constitutions of Belgium of 1832, and also for the French Constitution of 1958; these principles are nevertheless clear, due to their interpretation by courts, as is also the case with the clauses of the US Constitution about the Executive. Sometimes the spelling out of these principles is more precise, as is the case for most constitutions drafted after accession of or return to democracy (Austria 1920, Italy 1947, Germany 1945, Greece 1975, Portugal 1976, Spain 1978, a number of former communist countries in the 1990s) or in a move to rationalization and codification, the most recent examples of which are Switzerland in 1999 and Finland in 2000.

The role of public administration is to apply 'the law' to individual cases. 'The law' amounts to a set of rather abstract general principles that have been written into statute law by the legislature (parliament). Note that throughout Europe (including England) little distinction was made until the seventeenth or eighteenth century between administration and justice as a function, and that applied equally to staffing. The Swedish system of independent administrative agencies has long been an illustration of this lack of differentiation in functions.[9] The same holds true for the Prussian system of career civil service. The separation of judicial and administrative functions had a dominant role in the development of a modern administration, especially in the case of Spain during the sixteenth century and France during the seventeenth century.

The Continental European legal tradition is based partly upon Roman law, with a systematic construction, complemented by systematization in the framework of universities from the thirteenth century onwards. Codification of customary law and case law later developed in several countries, with a main purpose of unifying the law of the land (Denmark 1687, Sweden 1734, Prussia 1794); it also became a tool for social modernization (e.g., French Napoleonic Civil Code of 1804, Austrian Civil Code of 1812, German Civil Code of 1901). This tradition has not only led to an important quantity of written statute law, a feature common to all industrialized countries, but also to a specific way of drafting statute law, different from that of 'common law' countries; it also includes a developed and systematized hierarchy of written law, with at the top the constitution subject to specific rules for amendment and then statute law. According to the drafting tradition best illustrated by the French and German civil codes, statute law is not supposed to go into details, but rather to set up principles and rules according to defined categories. Therefore, statutes have to be complemented by more detailed general regulations (*règlements*, *Verordnungen*) adopted by the executive and providing for a set of specific solutions for predetermined circumstances. In order to apply the law as set up in acts of parliament and regulations to specific real-life cases, legally binding administrative decisions (*actes administratifs, Verwaltungsakte*) of the relevant members of the executive are necessary; the power to adopt them is usually delegated to civil servants on a permanent basis. This hierarchy defines the rules of legality: individual decisions, which have to be taken by the executive in order to apply the law, have to be consistent with general regulations, even if the same authority has the power to adopt both regulations and individual decisions. General regulations have to be consistent with acts of parliament, which in turn have to be consistent with the constitution.

According to both the *Rechtsstaat* tradition and the *principe de légalité*, a public authority can only take a decision with legally binding consequences if it has been duly authorized to do so by law, i.e., formally empowered by the constitution or by statute law. There are very strict rules as to the conditions and limits to delegating decision-making power, for general regulations as well as for individual decisions. The key concept of the Continental European public law tradition is that of competence (*compétence, Zuständigkeit*) – meaning empowerment. As most decisions to be taken in order to implement public policies have legally binding consequences – even if based on a contractual agreement between public administration and a private party – policy making and implementation need statute law as a tool. Any of these decisions is also subject to judicial review by independent courts, who will not only check whether the person who took the decision had legal authority to do so but also whether he or she has duly interpreted and applied the general rules set up by parliament and the executive. Judicial review of the merits of administrative action therefore developed much earlier in Continental Europe – and especially in

France – than on the other side of the English Channel, thus greatly reducing the scope of actions and decisions of public administration which fall outside of law.

The general structures of government at central as well as at local level have to be set down in detailed legally-binding instruments; the same applies not only to autonomous public bodies but also to the internal structures of ministerial departments and departmental agencies. Whereas in all countries only parliament has the power to set up the framework for local government structures, there are important differences from one country to another with regard to the competences allocated by the constitution to different branches of government when it comes to setting up the structures of central government. Whether the basis is laid down in acts of parliament or in government regulations, important procedural rules have to be followed for structural change, a feature that does not facilitate rapid reform in public management. These procedural rules go far beyond parliamentary procedure, as in most countries a number of opinions of consultative bodies have to be sought before government may adopt these types of regulations.

A further aspect of administrative action is that of contractual relationships. A number of Continental European countries, in particular France and Germany, developed at quite an early stage a specific law of public procurements, based on the application of the principle of equality to the tendering procedure. For this reason, public administration has been submitted to quite rigid and explicit procedural rules for contract management. The purpose of those rules has been to safeguard the budget, and guarantee competition. Furthermore, France developed a quite sophisticated law for contracting out public service activities (*concession de service public*) as early as the middle of the nineteenth century and was later imitated by a number of other Continental European countries.

STATUTE LAW IN THE STRUCTURE AND FUNCTIONING OF THE CIVIL SERVICE

The same kind of reasons account for the existence of statutes or regulations setting up the career patterns and working conditions of civil servants. In most Continental European countries parliament has acquired during the twentieth century regulatory power in a field that was traditionally in the competence of the executive; this competence has been transferred to parliament, either through a deliberate mention in the constitution or simply by the fact that parliament decided to legislate on the matter of civil service regulation. Only the Netherlands and Belgium have kept the former system of competence of the executive, derived from the royal prerogative, as far as state civil servants are concerned.

The main reason for this evolution has been the introduction or consolidation of a merit system for the management of civil servants. A number of countries have gone a step further and adopted a general regulation applying to all state civil servants – sometimes also to local government agents. The first country to adopt a general regulation of that kind was Spain in 1852, followed by Luxembourg in 1872 and Denmark in 1899. Italy followed in 1908, the Netherlands in 1929–31 and Belgium in 1937. Germany adopted a first general regulation of this type in 1937 and France in 1941: it was only after the Second World War that for those two countries the concept of a general regulation of the civil service by statute law became linked to the idea of protecting democratic values for all state civil servants.

For about a century there have been two dominating different concepts of the content of civil service regulation in Continental Europe. The first is based on the monarchic tradition, according to which state employees need a specific status due to the fact that they are the servants of the sovereign, to whom they owe a special fidelity and who in turn gives them a special protection; it is best illustrated by Germany. Thus, civil servants are a specific category of state employees, empowered with very specific duties linked to the exercise of public authority. They are subject to rules and employment conditions, which are very different from common labour law. In Germany about 40 per cent of government employees (federal, regional and local) have this position of a civil servant (*Beamter*), whereas the others are submitted to 'ordinary' law, i.e. civil and labour law. This kind of system is also at the basis of civil service regulation in Austria, Denmark or Luxembourg.

The second tradition is linked to the idea of equal access of all citizens to state employment and equal conditions of employment for all government employees. It is best illustrated by France, and followed by a majority of Continental European countries as different as Belgium, the Netherlands, Sweden and Spain. This implies specific rules for recruitment and career, usually different from those of labour law – but not always, as the case of the Netherlands demonstrates. In most other respects, with variations in time and space, the content of civil service regulations need not be very different from that of labour law. In most countries labour law has come closer and closer to civil service law. The fact that government employees enjoy tenure – though this is no longer the case in Sweden or in Italy since a few years ago – should be put in relation to the labour law provisions which tend to protect employees with a contract without time limitation. In practice, however, almost all civil servants tend to enjoy lifetime appointments due to the combination of two factors: (1) government activities are not linked to market performance, and thus government jobs tend to be much more stable than private sector positions, and (2) in most countries unions are quite powerful in public service and have the safeguarding of tenured positions as one of their major goals.

At the end of the twentieth century, a tendency to suppress differences between civil service law and labour law appeared in a number of countries, according to two different formal schemes.[10] The most common trend, followed by Sweden and Finland first, then by the Netherlands, has been to transform the content of civil service regulations – making them similar to labour law – while formally keeping a specific statutory instrument for government employees. A much more radical change – from a formal point of view – has been made in Italy in 1992 and in Portugal in 2008, where the general statute on government employees has been abolished, and where all – state as well as local government – employees are now employed under civil and labour law provisions. Along the same lines, Denmark has been gradually diminishing the category of state employees governed by a specific statute since the 1960s. In all those cases, the change took place at a time when employees in the private sector enjoyed a very high degree of protection as long as their company did not go bankrupt or restructure. A key explanatory factor for the change is also that it allowed a much more important role for trade unions and social dialogue in public administration.

As far as policy making is concerned, a consequence of the principles discussed above is that acts of parliament and regulations are also required, even in cases where they have no binding effects on private parties, in order to allocate responsibilities as clearly as possible. The degree of legal expertise of civil servants varies a lot from one country to another. In the Prussian model, civil servants were considered as part of the legal profession and thus received the same university education as judges and advocates; this is still the case for a big part of German administration. In most other European countries, the number of civil servants having a law degree was quite high, until the last decades of the twentieth century, but this does not mean that they had received a real professional legal training. Typically, a large number of French civil servants educated in the National School of Administration have never studied civil or criminal law, and even less civil or criminal procedure, unlike

their German counterparts. In France, traditionally, about half of the top administrative jobs are occupied by engineers who have been trained first in the *Ecole polytechnique* – created in 1794 and put in charge of training army engineers by Napoleon – than in more specialized *Grandes écoles*, like the schools for *Ponts et chaussées* (bridges and roads), *Eaux et forêts* (waters and forests) or the mines school. This goes together with the monopoly of the *Conseil d'Etat* as legal adviser of the national government and ministerial departments, as opposed to the German system, where almost all top civil servants are traditionally trained as lawyers, and where each section of a ministerial department has legal expertise.

ADMINISTRATIVE LAW IN THE ACCOUNTABILITY SYSTEM OF PUBLIC ADMINISTRATION[11]

Under the influence of Dicey,[12] British scholars and judges long believed that the main purpose of the French system of *droit administratif* was to protect the executive against the public. On the Continent, on the contrary, the French system of judicial review of public administration that developed during the nineteenth century has had a very important influence in the setting up of systems enabling independent scrutiny of the activity of the executive and, especially, public administration.

A key feature of the Continental European systems of administrative law lies in the sophisticated control by independent courts of the exercise of administrative discretion. This goes far beyond reviewing whether public authorities do, indeed, have under statute law the powers they claim to exercise. Through review of legality (*contrôle de légalité – Rechtsmässigkeitskontrolle*), courts have the power to check how public authorities exercise these powers, whether they have chosen the most appropriate means, whether the consequences of an administrative decision do not go beyond what was strictly necessary to achieve the goals set up by legislation (*principle of proportionality*) and whether general principles such as equal treatment and the protection of human rights and civil liberties have been respected by public administration. As a sanction of this scrutiny, the courts have the power to declare an administrative decision to be void and – to an extent that varies from country to country – to impose the content of a decision on the administration. This system was developed in France[13] during the nineteenth century under the very misleading title of *recours pour excès de pouvoir* (remedy for abuse of power – initially corresponding to the common law concept of *ultra vires*), and was then taken up with nationally specific features, usually under the title of 'remedy for review of legality', as in European Community law, or under a number of more specific remedies (*Rechtswege*), like in German law.[14]

A majority of Continental European countries, as different as Sweden, Italy, Germany, Belgium, Greece, France and Portugal, have established a specific system of administrative courts – separate from the so-called *ordinary* courts that deal with civil and criminal litigation. The exception is Denmark (and Norway since its independence) which always had only a single system of courts in charge of administrative as well as civil or criminal litigation. Usually this system of administrative courts is more closely linked to the activities of public administration, although their judges are as independent as so-called *ordinary* judges are. This allows for a specialization of administrative judges that enables them to review much more deeply the activities they are familiar with, and thus allows both for a better protection of citizens against the administration and a better understanding of the needs of policy implementation. Furthermore, in a number of countries, access of plaintiffs to administrative courts is easier and cheaper than to ordinary courts. However, this system is sometimes under suspicion for being too close to public administration and it has the major inconvenience

of generating quite complex and delicate legal debates about the boundary between ordinary and administrative courts' jurisdiction; in a number of cases this leads to considerable delays in legal procedures. These reasons explain why Italy and Greece suppressed their administrative court systems in the second half of the nineteenth century, before reinstalling them at the turn of the century. In the middle of the twentieth century, Spain chose a system of specialized chambers within a unified system of courts, thus hoping to combine the advantages of both systems.

The scope of judicial protection against unlawful or damaging decisions of public administration is not limited to declaring those decisions void. Courts can also allocate damages to be paid by the state budget or local budgets. In a majority of European countries these damages are allocated by civil courts applying general common principles of tort law as stated in the civil code, or principles and mechanisms set up by special legislation for specific public activities. In France, damages have been allocated by administrative courts since 1872 – even since 1806 as far as public works damages are concerned. The French system has allowed for the development of a number of principles unknown to civil tort law, like damages for breach of equality of treatment or damages for the consequences of statutory law – even sometimes for the consequences of acts of parliament. The main feature of these systems of damages[15] is that they are based upon the liability of public institutions as organizations, which is easier to establish and easier to finance than that of individual officials. Their employers can usually, in turn, sue the latter on a disciplinary basis in order to compensate for the damages paid by the institution if the wrongful activity of a specific official was at the basis of the claim.

In France, and later on in most other countries that adopted such a system of administrative law, the administrative courts system has led to building a set of principles to be followed in administrative decision making, or due process in administrative procedure – most of them resting upon judge-made case law. As mentioned earlier, a number of countries have also codified their administrative decision-making procedure during the last quarter of the twentieth century.

European Union (EU) law has been deeply influenced by the Continental European systems of judicial review of administrative action, mainly the French and German system, which accounts for most of the relevant provisions in the Treaty on the Functioning of the European Union. In turn, the European Court of Justice has started to set up a body of principles of European administrative law during the past 25 years which apply not only to European institutions but also to national administrations whenever they implement European law.[16] These principles are geared mainly to a well-functioning and accessible system of judicial remedies against administrative action and are fostering some kind of harmonization of judicial review of administrative action in all EU member states, the United Kingdom included. Some elements of this case law of the European Court of Justice are the basis of the right to good administration, which is guaranteed by Article 41 of the European Union Charter of Fundamental Rights adopted in the year 2000.

LEGALITY AND PUBLIC MANAGEMENT REFORM

In the last quarter of the twentieth century the role of law in public administration came under attack as fostering bureaucracy, especially in the move to New Public Management. The focus on input and procedures – as opposed to the managerial focus on output and achievement – is very often attributed to law itself by critics of bureaucracy as well as by public managers themselves. A comparative study of the role of law in public administration shows that these types of criticism rest upon a double misunderstanding of what

law is today and what Max Weber meant when analysing the systems of public authority a century ago.[17]

Whereas public administration and public management studies easily identify perverse consequences of a too rigid application of the principle of legality, too little attention has probably been paid to what is inherent in the law applying to public administration, and to what is due to the well-intentioned zeal of badly trained administrators who do not differentiate law and detailed written regulation. This might be one of the reasons why there has been a trend in most European countries to increase the number of written regulations that go very deep into details. Too many civil servants whose main task is to write down regulations or general non-binding directives on how to apply the law have not received an appropriate training in drafting statutory law according to the best tradition of Continental codification. Even more civil servants totally underestimate their own margins of manoeuvre in those cases where statute law empowers them with discretionary powers: i.e. the possibility to adapt the application of legal principles to the circumstances of the case. Typically, the French administrative courts have often been led to declare void an administrative decision because its author did not exercise his or her discretionary power on the sole merits of a given case, but blindly applied general directives issued by ministerial departments.

This inflation of written regulation is heavily criticized by politicians and also by a number of public institutions in most Continental European countries. However, the same politicians who criticize it and recommend more deregulation very often contribute to this inflation by the mere fact that they want to present a good record of policy making to their constituents: in a number of Continental European countries this is manifested through attaching one's name to a specific statute. This is why a number of public institutions like the French *Conseil d'Etat* insist on codification, simplification and better drafting of written law rather than on deregulation, a very ambiguous concept even in those countries where the language differentiates between regulation as a function (*Regulierung, régulation*) and regulation as a legal tool (*Regelung, réglementation*).

A number of criticisms addressed to the role of law in public administration seem to derive from confusion between, on the one hand, the law as a set of tools and a limited number of general principles, and on the other, the law of the day as it is set down at a specific moment in a country's legislation. This confusion leads to a very conservative use of law that tends to justify immobility.

In the last decade of the twentieth century it has become fashionable to oppose the Continental tradition of public administration based on law to a tradition of management, sometimes qualified as the 'Anglo-Saxon tradition'. This also rests on confusion between two very different features of British tradition. On the one hand, common law sometimes appears as very flexible to non-specialists, due to a legal culture where statutes do not have the same predominant value in law as in Continental Europe; but in fact formalism is as high on the British side of the Channel, or even more so when it comes to judicial proceedings. On the other hand, the customary principles of the British constitution are also interpreted as corresponding to a tradition of flexible law. Indeed, the principle according to which the Cabinet has all powers under the *royal prerogative* to organize and to manage the civil service has no real equivalent in Continental Europe.

Nevertheless, even detailed written statute law can be changed in order to restructure public administration, as the reforms undertaken in Italy from 1992 to 2000 show, which have introduced in written law most of the elements of the structural reforms introduced into British government on the basis of government papers without legal force, like the 'Next Steps' reports.[18] For a government that has both the will to reform and the political means to do it, the only difference is really a matter of time – a very important factor

indeed for the success of administrative reform. The time factor apart, law as such is not an obstacle to administrative reform, or to the introduction of management: it is a set of tools that can be used well or badly according to the quality of legal education of those who have to set up and implement new modes of management.[19]

NOTES

1 See Rose-Ackerman, Susan and Lindseth, Peter L. (eds) (2011) *Comparative Administrative Law – An Introduction* (Cheltenham: Edward Elgar Publishing).

2 See Wunder, Bernd (ed.) (1992) *The Influences of the Napoleonic 'Model' of Administration on the Administrative Organization of Other Countries* (Brussels: International Institute of Administrative Sciences).

3 See Ziller, Jacques (2001) 'European Models of Government: Towards a Patchwork with Missing Pieces', *Parliamentary Affairs*, 54 (1): 102–19.

4 Especially Gerber (1823–91) and Laband (1838–1918). See Gerber, Carl Friedrich von (1852) *Über öffentliche Rechte* (Tübingen: Laupp); Gerber, Carl Friedrich von (1880) *Grundzüge des deutschen Staatsrechts*, 3rd edn (Leipzig: Tauchnitz); Laband (1876–82), *Das Staatsrecht des deutschen Reiches* (Tübingen: Laupp, vols 1 and 2, 1876 and Freiburg: Mohr, vols 2 and 3, 1882).

5 See Ziller, Jacques (2011) 'Is a Law of Administrative Procedure for the Union Institutions Necessary?', *Rivista Italiana di Diritto Pubblico Comunitario*.

6 Hans Kelsen (1881–1973). A renowned lawyer and academic, one of the Fathers of the Austrian Constitution of 1920, is best known for his 'Pure Theory of Law' – *Reine Rechslehre*. See Kelsen, Hans and Hartney, Michael (1991) *General Theory of Norms* (Oxford: Oxford University Press).

7 See Fromont, Michel (2006) *Droit administratif des Etats européens*. Paris: PUF.

8 See International Association of Supreme Administrative Jurisdictions (IASAJ), at: http://www.iasaj.org

9 See: Ragnemalm, Hans (1991) 'Administrative Justice in Sweden', in Aldo Piras, *Administrative Law – the Problem of Justice*, vol. 1 *Anglo-American and Nordic Systems* (Milan: Giuffré).

10 See Bossaert, Danielle, Demmke, Christoph, Nomden, Koen and Polet, Robert (2001) *Civil Services in the Europe of Fifteen: Trends and New Developments* (Maastricht: EIPA).

11   See Piras, Aldo, (1991–1997) *Administrative Law – the Problem of Justice*, vol. 1 *Anglo-American and Nordic Systems* (Milan: Giuffré) (vol. 1 *Anglo-American and Nordic Systems*; vol. 2 *Western European Democracies*; vol. 3 *Western European Democracies*).

12   Albert Venn Dicey (1835–1922) is famous in a number of Continental European countries as an exponent of the principles of the Rule of Law in Great Britain. See Dicey, Albert Venn (1885) *Law of the Constitution* (London: Macmillan; 9th edn, 1950).

13   See Brown, L. Neville and Bell, John S. (1998) *French Administrative Law*, 5th edn (Oxford: Clarendon).

14   See Singh, Marendra P. (2001) *German Administrative Law in Common Law Perspective* (Berlin: Springer).

15   See Bell, John and Bradley, Anthony W. (1991) *Governmental Liability: A Comparative Study* (London: UKNCCL).

16   See Schwarze, Jürgen (2006) *European Administrative Law*. London: Sweet & Maxwell Ltd; revised edition.

17   Max Weber (1864–1920). His most famous work in this respect is usually know as *Economy and Society* (1920). One of the first translations was Weber, Max, Henderson, A.M. and Parsons, Talcott (1947) *The Theory of Social and Economic Organisation* (Oxford: Oxford University Press). See also Weber, Max and Anderski, Stanislav (eds) (1983) *Max Weber on Capitalism, Bureaucracy and Religion* (London: Allen and Unwin). Max Weber is also famous for his sociology of religions; see his famous work, published in 1905: Weber, Max (1976) *The Protestant Ethic and the Spirit of Capitalism* (London: Allen and Unwin).

18   See: http://www.official-documents.co.uk/

19   Ziller, Jacques (2005) 'Public Law: A Tool for Modern Management, not an Impediment to Reform', *International Review of Administrative Sciences*, 71 (2): 267–77.

Administrative Law in the Anglo-American Tradition

Paul Craig

HISTORICAL FOUNDATIONS

It is a common belief that 'administrative law' is a recent development in the Anglo-American tradition. This is mistaken. The Anglo-American tradition is not premised on the existence of a separate set of courts to adjudicate on public law matters, as is common within civilian jurisdictions. To reason from this premise, to the conclusion that there was, until recently, no administrative law is a *non sequitur*. English law has exercised procedural and substantive controls over the administration for well over 350 years. Three features of this control were of central importance.

First, the history of judicial review was inextricably bound up with the development of remedies as opposed to the creation of new heads of review (Craig, 2000; Henderson, 1963; Jaffe and Henderson, 1956). The elaboration of grounds for review took place within, and was framed by, the evolution of adjectival law. Mandamus was transformed into a general tool for the remedying of administrative error. Lord Mansfield

(*R. v. Barker* (1762) 3 Burr. 1265) gave the seminal rationalization of mandamus. It was, he said, introduced to prevent disorder from a failure of justice, and defect of police. Therefore it ought to be used 'upon all occasions where the law has established no specific remedy, and where in justice and good government there ought to be one'. The evolution of certiorari into a generalized remedy capable of catching a variety of governmental errors occurred later.

Second, it was through the common law that these developments in judicial review occurred. The common law was seen as the embodiment of reason, which could be modified so as to meet the challenges of a new age. Sir Edward Coke and other lawyers 'disapproved of Parliament changing the common law, because they believed that the wisdom of a single Parliament was unlikely to surpass the wisdom embodied in laws shaped by the accumulated experience of many generations' (Goldsworthy, 1999: 119). The same relationship between statute and common law can be seen in the eighteenth century, as exemplified by the work of

Blackstone and Mansfield. Blackstone's *Commentaries* were the pre-eminent statement of the law during this period. They also constituted the main teaching manual for law students in the eighteenth and nineteenth centuries (Lieberman, 1989: 64–5). Blackstone lamented the 'mischiefs' which had arisen from alterations in the law, and laid the blame for this squarely with Parliament, for its passage of imperfect and inadequate legislation. While he acknowledged the importance of certain legislation, such as that concerned with habeas corpus, his general stance was to venerate the perfection of the common law, and regret the manner in which its symmetry had been distorted by ill-conceived legislation. This vision of the common law was inherently conservative and idealistic, as forcefully pointed out by Bentham. The preference for the common law over statute was equally evident in the creative jurisprudence of Lord Mansfield.

Third, the courts did not reason on the basis of any rigid dichotomy between public and private law. This did not mean that there was no administrative law until the mid-twentieth century. There was a wealth of case law dealing with all aspects of review, both procedural and substantive, from at least the seventeenth century onwards. It did mean that the constraints were fashioned on the basis of what were felt to be sound normative principles for the exercise of power. Whether the power was public, private or a hybrid of the two could be a factor in this determination, but there was no assumption that the conceptual rationale for such constraints, or the constraints themselves, had to be different depending on how the body was classified.

THE DICEYAN LEGACY AND BEYOND

It was Dicey's dislike of administrative law that cast a shadow over the subject in the early years of this century, at least in the UK,

but also to some extent in the United States. The modern growth of administrative law was directly connected with the extension of governmental functions relating to the poor, the unemployed, trade regulation and the like. It became impossible to separate an evaluation of the agencies applying these laws from a value judgment of the social policies in the laws themselves. Those who disliked such social intervention, including Dicey, tended to view the agencies applying such laws with suspicion (Dicey, 1959). The predominance he accorded to the 'ordinary law', applied by the 'ordinary courts', was a means of controlling these agencies, and of maintaining judicial supervision over the substantive policies they applied. The paramount function of the courts was essentially negative, to ensure that the agency did not make mistakes by exceeding the power granted to it.

These ideas of mistake avoidance and distrust came to be challenged as a direct consequence of changing attitudes towards the social policies which the agencies were applying. Academics such as Robson (1928: xv) approached the study of administrative justice without 'any ready-made assumption that every tribunal which does not at the moment form part of the recognized system of judicature must necessarily and inevitably be arbitrary, incompetent, unsatisfactory, injurious to the freedom of the citizen and to the welfare of society'.

The consequences of this change in attitude were important. Administrative agencies were not now viewed as perfect. However, it was no longer taken for granted that the justice dispensed by the ordinary courts and the ordinary law was necessarily better than that of agencies. Nor was it felt that the sole object of administrative law was to ensure that the agency avoided making mistakes by overstepping its boundaries. A more positive desire that the agency should successfully fulfil the policy assigned to it became the focus of discussion, and the courts were perceived as but one factor in fulfilling this objective (Aman, 1993: Ch. 1; Harlow and

Rawlings, 1997: Chs 1–3). Scholars differed in their approach.

Some advanced an explicitly pluralist vision of democracy, in place of the unitary view espoused by Dicey. They contested the idea that all public power was wielded by the state. Religious, economic and social associations exercised authority. 'Legislative' decisions would often be reached by the executive, after negotiation with such groups, and would then be forced through the actual legislature. Group power was applauded rather than condemned. The all-powerful unitary state was dangerous. Liberty was best preserved by the presence of groups within the state to which the individual could owe allegiance (Laski, 1917, 1919). This vision of political pluralism was complemented by a concern with the social and economic conditions within the state. There was a strong belief that political liberty was closely linked with social and economic equality. The scope of administrative law should not therefore be concerned only with those bodies to whom statutory or prerogative power had been given, but also with other institutions that exercised public power.

Others advanced a more market-based conception of pluralist democracy, which was manifest in governmental policy within the late 1970s and 1980s, both in the UK and the United States (Craig, 1990: Chs 3–4; Stewart, 1975). The market was viewed as the best 'arbitrator' of economic issues, and direct governmental regulation thereof was perceived as necessary only when there was market failure, the existence of which was narrowly defined. The sphere of legitimate governmental action was therefore closely circumscribed. The very fulfilment of the free market vision required, however, a strong central government. Different conclusions were drawn as to the bodies that should be run by the state. Deregulation and privatization were the consequences of this approach. Even where some continuing regulation of a privatized industry was required, the aim of the regulation was coloured by the market-oriented vision.

The purpose was often to prevent an industry with monopolistic power from abusing its dominant position.

Yet others viewed administrative law through the lens of participatory democracy, and republicanism. This was particularly so in the United States, where Sunstein (1985, 1988a) and Michelman (1986) were prominent advocates of this underlying theory as to the purpose of administrative law. They rejected the view that administrative law was simply about the aggregation of interests. Republicanism connoted an attachment to deliberation, political equality, universalism and citizenship. The purpose of politics was not simply to aggregate private preferences, but rather to subject those preferences to scrutiny and review. Discussion and dialogue were central to this process.

DIVERGENT STRAINS WITHIN ANGLO-AMERICAN ADMINISTRATIVE LAW

It is self-evident that there will be points of divergence within the Anglo-American tradition, in terms of doctrine. Two points are, however, of more general importance in this respect.

The first is that doctrine in the United States is developed against the background of a written Constitution and a general statute, the Administrative Procedure Act of 1946 (APA). By way of contrast, there is no written constitution in the UK, and nothing equivalent to the APA. The greater part of UK administrative law has traditionally been judge-made common law. There have, however, been important statutes dealing with particular issues. The Human Rights Act 1998, which came into effect on 2 October 2000, was especially important in this respect. It brought the rights from the European Convention on Human Rights (ECHR) into UK domestic law, and allowed individuals to rely on such rights in actions before national courts (Beatson et al., 2008; Hickman, 2010; Kavanagh, 2009).

The second point is that the UK is a member of the European Union (EU). This has had a marked impact on its administrative law. EU law is binding on the member states in those areas covered by the treaties. Principles of judicial review developed by the European Court of Justice (ECJ) therefore have to be applied by national courts in areas that fall within the remit of the EU (Craig, 2006). These principles will be fashioned by the ECJ, drawing on concepts from member state law. The great majority of states that are members of the EU have civilian legal systems. The consequence is that EU law, developed from these sources, will be binding on the UK. There is therefore a greater interplay between common law and civil law concepts in the UK than hitherto. It should, moreover, be noted that principles of EU law can have a 'spillover impact'. They may be applied by UK courts in areas not covered by EU law in a strict sense, and thus influence the development of the general principles of judicial review (Andenas, 1998; Andenas and Jacobs, 1998; Ellis, 1999; Schonberg, 2000).

DOCTRINE: PROCEDURAL CONSTRAINTS IN ADJUDICATION

Foundations

Academic commentators and courts alike have recognized two rationales for procedural rights in adjudication. They perform an instrumental role by helping to attain an accurate decision on the substance of the case. They can also serve non-instrumental goals such as protecting human dignity by ensuring that people are told why they are being treated unfavourably, and by enabling them to take part in that decision (Galligan, 1996: 75–82; Hart, 1961: 156, 202; Mashaw, 1985: Chs 4–7; Michelman, 1977; Rawls, 1973: 235; Resnick, 1977). These twin rationales for the existence of procedural rights have been recognized by the judiciary

in the UK and the United States (*R.* v. *Secretary of State for the Home Department, ex p. Doody* [1994] A.C. 531, 551; *Goldberg* v. *Kelly* 397 U.S. 254 (1970)).

The foundations of process rights vary. In the United States these rights will normally be grounded in the Constitution or the APA. There is, as seen above, no written constitution or Administrative Procedure Act in the UK. The common law courts have therefore largely developed procedural rights, although statute has had some impact in this area. The applicability and the extent of procedural rights have also been affected by EU law, and by the ECHR.

If an individual is aggrieved by the actions of government, a public body, or certain domestic tribunals or associations, he or she may claim that there has been a breach of natural justice. The phrase 'natural justice' encapsulates two ideas: that the individual be given adequate notice of the charge and an adequate hearing (*audi alteram partem*), and that the adjudicator be unbiased (*nemo judex in causa sua*).

In the eighteenth and nineteenth centuries the *audi alteram partem* principle was applied to a wide variety of bodies. Deprivation of office (*Bagg's Case* (1615) 11 Co. Rep. 93b), and disciplinary measures imposed on the clergy (*Capel* v. *Child* (1832) 2 Cr. & J. 588) were two common types of case to come before the courts. The principle was also applied to private bodies such as clubs, associations and trade unions (*Abbott* v. *Sullivan* [1952] 1 K.B. 189). The generality of application of the principle was emphasized in *Cooper* v. *Wandsworth Board of Works* ((1863) 14 C.B. (N.S.) 180), where the court held that the omission of positive words in the statute requiring a hearing was not a bar since the justice of the common law would supply the omission of the legislature. This was further reinforced by Lord Loreburn L.C., who stated that the maxim applied to 'everyone who decides anything' (*Board of Education* v. *Rice* [1911] A.C. 179, 182).

The breadth of the *audi alteram partem* principle was, however, limited in the first half of the twentieth century. The courts held that a hearing would only be required if the body was acting judicially rather than administratively (*Errington* v. *Minister of Health* [1935] 1 K.B. 249); there was misunderstanding over remedies, particularly the scope of certiorari, which affected the applicability of natural justice; and some courts held that natural justice would only apply to protect rights and not privileges (*Nakkuda Ali* [1951] A.C. 66, 77–78; *Bailey* v. *Richardson* 182 F 2d 46 (1950)).

The principle of natural justice was revived in the UK by the House of Lords in *Ridge* v. *Baldwin* ([1964] A.C. 40), and in the United States by *Goldberg* v. *Kelly* (397 U.S. 254 (1970)). In *Ridge* the House of Lords swept away many of the limitations on the application of the principle which had been imposed by the case law of the early twentieth century. The applicability of natural justice was to be dependent on the nature of the power exercised and its effect upon the individual concerned. In *Goldberg* the Supreme Court was willing to apply Constitutional Due Process to a welfare claimant, and characterized the claimant's interest as being property for the purposes of the Fifth Amendment.

The applicability of procedural protection

The 'trigger' for the applicability of procedural protection varies in common law regimes, depending upon the more precise foundation for the process rights.

Thus, in the United States claimants can base procedural protection on three different sources. If the claim is framed in constitutional terms, it will have to be shown that the claimant has a life, liberty or property interest that has been affected by the agency action. The interpretation of these terms is for the courts, and ultimately for the Supreme Court (*Board of Regents* v. *Roth* 408 U.S. (1972)). A claimant can invoke the APA of 1946. Section 554 will apply to agency adjudication required by statute to be determined on the record after opportunity for an agency hearing. This statutory language has been interpreted in rather different ways by the courts (compare *Seacoast Anti-Pollution League* v. *Costle* 572 F. 2d. 872 (1978), *Chemical Waste Management Inc.* v. *US Environmental Protection Agency* 873 F. 2d 1477 (1989) and *Dominion Energy Brayton Point LLC* v. *Johnson* U.S. Court of Appeals First Circuit (2006)). Where neither the Constitution nor the APA is applicable, an individual may be able to gain limited process rights through the reasoning in *Citizens to Preserve Overton Park* v. *Volpe* 401 U.S. 402 (1971). This provides a basis for the derivation of limited process rights in relation to informal agency action. The process rights must, however, be linked to enforcing substantive limits on the agency's power.

The position in the UK is somewhat different, because there is no written constitution and nothing equivalent to the APA of 1946. The courts have determined the applicability of procedural protection through the common law. The years since *Ridge* v. *Baldwin* saw the development of the duty to act fairly. Some courts regard natural justice as but a manifestation of fairness. Others apply natural justice to judicial decisions, and reserve a duty to act fairly for administrative or executive determinations. As discredited limitations have been discarded, and natural justice has expanded to new fields, fairness is seen as a more appropriate label (*McInnes* v. *Onslow-Fane* [1978] 1 W.L.R. 1520). The courts determine what adjudicative procedures are required in particular areas. In some it may approximate to the full panoply of procedural safeguards, including notice, oral hearing, representation, discovery, cross-examination and reasoned decisions. In others it may connote considerably less. There will be a broad spectrum in between. The courts have therefore exercised control over procedural rights not by rigid prior classification, but rather by admitting that natural justice or fairness applies and varying the content of those rules according to the facts of the case.

The claimant will, none the less, have to show an interest which is sufficient to trigger the applicability of procedural rights. There is therefore an analogy between the UK jurisprudence and that of the US courts when deciding on the applicability of constitutional due process (*Board of Regents of State Colleges* v. *Roth* 408 U.S. 564 (1972)). In the UK the claimant will have to show some right, interest or legitimate expectation to be entitled to procedural protection. The term *right* covers a recognized proprietary or personal right of the individual. The term *interest* is looser than that of right. It has been used as the basis for a hearing even where the individual would not be regarded in law as having any actual substantive entitlement or right in the particular case. This is exemplified by the application of natural justice in the context of licensing, social welfare, clubs, unions and trade associations. The concept of *legitimate expectations* can provide the foundation for process rights in circumstances where the individual does not possess the requisite right or interest in the preceding sense. Thus, the courts have used the concept to protect future interests, such as licensing renewals (*McInnes* v. *Onslow-Fane*). It has also been used when a representation has been made by a public body, where in the absence of the representation, it is unlikely that the substantive interest would entitle the applicant to natural justice or fairness (*A.G. of Hong Kong* v. *Ng Yuen Shiu* [1983] 2 A.C. 629). The existence of a representation, and the consequential legitimate expectation which flows from it, may serve to augment the procedural rights granted to the applicant (*R.* v. *Liverpool Corporation, ex p. Liverpool Taxi Fleet Operators' Association* [1972] 2 Q.B. 299).

The content of process rights: the balancing process

In deciding on the content of process rights the court will balance between the nature of the individual's interest, the likely benefit to be gained from an increase in procedural rights and the costs to the administration of having to comply with such process rights. This is the *Mathews* v. *Eldridge* calculus (*Mathews* v. *Eldridge* 424 U.S. 319 (1976)). The UK courts have reasoned in a similar manner, as exemplified by *Re Pergamon Press Ltd.* [1971] Ch. 388.

It is clear that balancing necessitates not only identification of the individual's interest but also some judgement about how much we value it, or the weight which we accord to it. For example, to take some position, as Megarry V.C. did in *McInnes* [1978] 1 W.L.R. 1520 as to whether the renewal of a licence is a 'higher' interest than an initial application, is not to engage in rigid conceptualism, but is rather a necessary step in reaching any decision.

It is clear also that valuing the other elements in the balancing process, the social benefits and costs of the procedural safeguards may be problematic. This is not simply a 'mathematical' calculus. Deciding what are the relevant costs and benefits is itself a hard task (Mashaw, 1976: 47–9).

Moreover, the existence of judicial balancing should not lead us to conclude that all such balancing is necessarily premised on the same assumptions. The premises that underpin a law and economics approach to process rights may be far removed from those that underlie a more rights-based approach to process: compare Posner (1973) and Mashaw (1985).

The content of process rights: particular process rights

This section will consider, albeit briefly, the most important process rights which applicants commonly claim. The courts will protect the right to *notice* since as, Lord Denning said, if the right to be heard is to be a real right which is worth anything, it must carry with it a right in the accused man to know the case which is made against him (*Kanda* v. *Government of Malaya* [1962] A.C. 322, 337).

In terms of the *hearing* itself, the strict rules of evidence will not normally have to be followed (*Ex p. Moore* [1965] 1 Q.B. 456, *Richardson* v. *Perales* 402 U.S. 389 (1971)). The tribunal is not restricted to evidence acceptable in a court of law; provided that the evidence has some probative value, is relevant and comes from a reliable source, the court will consider it. Where there is an oral hearing, written evidence submitted by the applicant must be considered, but the agency may take account of any evidence of probative value from another source provided that the applicant is informed and allowed to comment on it. An applicant must also be allowed to address argument on the whole of the case. These general principles are, however, subject to the following reservation. The overriding obligation is to provide the applicant with a fair hearing and a fair opportunity to controvert the charge (*R.* v. *Board of Visitors of Hull Prison, ex p. St. Germain (No. 2)* [1979] 1 W.L.R. 1401, 1408–12). This may in certain cases require not only that the applicant be informed of the evidence but also that the individual should be given a sufficient opportunity to deal with it. This may involve the cross-examination of the witnesses whose evidence is before the hearing authority in the form of hearsay.

The provision of *reasons* is of particular importance. Reasons can assist the courts in performing their supervisory function; they can help to ensure that the decision has been thought through by the agency; and they can increase public confidence in the administrative process and enhance its legitimacy. A duty to provide reasons can, therefore, help to attain both the instrumental and non-instrumental objectives which underlie process rights more generally (*R.* v. *Secretary of State for the Home Department, ex p. Doody* [1994] 1 A.C. 531). Reasons may also be required because of EU law, which imposes a duty to give reasons based on Article 296 TFEU (formerly Article 253 EC). The extent of this duty will depend upon the nature of the relevant act and the context within which it was made. The duty is principally imposed upon the EU organs themselves, but it can apply to national authorities where they are acting as agents of the EU for the application of EU law.

The impact of the European Convention on Human Rights

In the UK, process rights are also influenced by Article 6 of the ECHR. Under the Human Rights Act 1998 (HRA), the courts have an obligation to interpret legislation to be in accord with these rights, and acts of public authorities which are incompatible with the rights are unlawful. Section 2 of the HRA provides that the national courts must take into account the jurisprudence of the Strasbourg institutions, although they are not bound by it. Article 6 provides, so far as relevant here, that 'in the determination of his civil rights and obligations or of any criminal charge against him, everyone is entitled to a fair and public hearing within a reasonable time by an independent and impartial tribunal established by law'.

The phrase 'civil rights and obligations' has been interpreted broadly so as to include disputes concerning land use; monetary claims against public authorities; applications for, and revocations of, licences; claims for certain types of social security benefit; and disciplinary proceedings leading to suspension or expulsion from a profession. The European Court of Human Rights (ECtHR) has stressed a number of elements as integral to the requirement of a fair hearing pursuant to Article 6. There must be access to a court. There must be procedural equality, or what is often termed 'equality of arms'. This implies that each party must be afforded a reasonable opportunity to present his case, including his evidence, under conditions that do not place him at a substantial disadvantage in relation to his opponent. There must be some proper form of judicial process, which will often take the form of an adversarial trial where the parties have the opportunity to have knowledge of, and comment on, the observations and evidence adduced by the other side. While there is no express requirement to give reasons, the ECtHR regards this as implicit in the obligation to provide a fair hearing. Reasons do not have to be given for every single point, but they must be sufficient to enable a party to understand the essence of the decision in order to be able to exercise any appeal rights. The requirements of a fair hearing do not have to be satisfied at every stage in the decision-making process. Where an administrative body does not comply with the duty imposed by Article 6 it will have to be subject to the control of a judicial body which does so comply.

DOCTRINE: PROCEDURAL RIGHTS IN RULE MAKING

There are considerable advantages to allowing some form of consultation or participation before rules are made. It enables views to be taken into account before an administrative policy has hardened into a draft rule. It can assist the legislature with technical scrutiny. It is hoped that there will be better rules as a result of input from interested parties, particularly where they have some knowledge of the area being regulated. A duty to consult allows those outside government to play some role in the shaping of policy. In this sense, it enhances participation. It is moreover not immediately self-evident why a hearing should be thought natural when there is some form of individualized adjudication, but not where rules are being made. The unspoken presumption is that a 'hearing' will be given to a rule indirectly through the operation of our principles of representative democracy. Reality falls short of this ideal, both in the UK and in the United States.

It would be mistaken to think that according such participatory rights is unproblematic. It has been argued that the APA provisions on rule making can lead to 'paralysis by analysis', with interest groups

opposed to the proposed rule using all available legal machinery to delay its implementation. Participatory rights can lead to delay and extra cost. However, if all decisions were made by an autocrat they would doubtless be made more speedily. A cost of democracy is precisely the cost of involving more people. Moreover, the argument for increased participatory rights is based, in part at least, upon the idea that the people who are consulted may have something to offer the administrator. The rule that emerges will, it is hoped, be better. Whether this is always so may be debatable, but there is little reason to suggest that the argument does not hold in certain instances. Where it does have validity, then it is far less clear that the granting of such rights will entail an overall increase in cost. If a less good rule emerges where there is no consultation then the total costs may be greater because, for example, the rule fails to achieve its objective.

In the UK the rules of natural justice are not generally applicable to rule making, and in the United States Constitutional Due Process is not applicable in such instances. This is, however, where the legal analogy stops (Ziamou, 2001). In the UK a right to participate in rule making will exist only where Parliament has chosen to grant it under a particular statute. In the United States the Administrative Procedure Act 1946 accords a general right to participate in rule making by the agencies covered by the legislation.

Notice of any proposed rule making is to be published in the Federal Register, including a statement of the time and place of the rule-making proceedings and the terms or substance of the proposed rule. After notice, the agency is to afford interested persons an opportunity to participate in the rule making. There are, in essence, three differing modes of participation, which have varying degrees of formality. Most administrative rules are subject to notice and comment: the proposed rules are published and interested parties can proffer written comments. Other rules are subject to formal rule making – a full trial-type hearing, which can include the provision of oral testimony and cross-examination. Yet other rules are governed by a hybrid process, which entails more formality than notice and comment, but less than the trial-type hearing.

DOCTRINE: SUBSTANTIVE CONSTRAINTS

General approach

It is clearly not possible, within the limits of available space, to set out all the doctrines of substantive review commonly found within the Anglo-American tradition. Certain foundational principles can none the less be enunciated.

The courts will maintain substantive control over agency determinations. The nature of this control varies, depending upon the issue before the court. Thus, courts in the Anglo-American tradition will tend to maintain greater control over the conditions that set the jurisdictional limits for the agency, than they will over agency discretionary choices. The nature of these controls will be examined below. In relation to discretionary determinations, it is generally accepted that it is not for the courts to substitute their view as to how the discretion should have been exercised for that of the agency. The political branch of government has assigned this discretion to the agency, and it is not for the courts to intervene simply because they would, as a matter of first impression, have exercised the discretion differently from the agency. While courts in the Anglo-American tradition accept this dictate, there is considerably more discussion as to how intensive review of discretion should be. The fact that it is accepted that there should not be substitution of judgement does not mean that there is consensus about the intensity of review falling short of this. It would, for example, be possible for the courts to intervene only where there has been some

manifestly unreasonable or arbitrary decision. They could, by way of contrast, exercise greater control over discretionary determinations, albeit falling short of substitution of judgement, through a hard look form of review, through a more exacting test of reasonableness, or through control framed in terms of proportionality. Courts in the UK, United States and elsewhere have grappled with these issues, and have reached differing conclusions as to the proper bounds of control over discretion. The intensity of review has ebbed and flowed over time. The principal factors that have affected the judicial choices have been the courts' perception of their relationship with agencies, their willingness to become involved in technically complex material, and the structural limits imposed by the nature of the review process itself.

It should not, moreover, be thought that courts in the Anglo-American tradition will always be of the same view as to the appropriate limits of judicial intervention. This can be exemplified by considering the contrasting approaches of the courts in the UK and the United States in relation to control over issues of law.

Control over law: a contrast

All agencies established through legislation will be given a statutory remit that defines the scope of their authority. A simple paradigm is an agency established on the following terms: if an employee is injured at work, the agency may grant compensation. Courts will have to decide on the appropriate test for review when it is claimed that the agency adopted an incorrect meaning of the terms employee, injury or work. The test adopted will reflect judicial choice as to the correct balance between agency autonomy and judicial control. Courts in the United States and in the UK have not always been of like mind on this issue.

The leading case in the UK is *Page* v. *Hull University Visitor* ([1993] 1 All E.R. 97).

It was held that Parliament had only conferred the decision-making power on the basis that it was to be exercised on the correct legal basis: a misdirection in law in making the decision therefore rendered the decision *ultra vires*. In general, therefore, any error of law made by an administrative tribunal or inferior court in reaching its decision would be quashed for error of law.

The seminal modern case on this topic in the United States is *Chevron, U.S.A., Inc.* v. *Natural Resources Defense Council, Inc.* (467 US 837 (1984)). The case concerned the legality of regulations made pursuant to the clean air legislation. The Clean Air Act Amendments of 1977 imposed certain requirements on states that had not met the national air quality standards established by the Environmental Protection Agency (EPA). The requirements included an obligation on such states to establish regulatory regimes under which permits would be issued relating to 'new or modified major stationary sources' of air pollution. The EPA promulgated regulations designed to implement the permit requirement and these regulations allowed a state to adopt a plant-wide definition of stationary source. The effect of this was that an existing plant which had a number of pollution-emitting devices could install or modify one piece of equipment without meeting the permit conditions, provided that the alteration did not increase the total emissions from the plant. The state was, therefore, allowed to treat all the pollution-emitting devices within the same industrial grouping as though they were encased in a 'bubble'. It was this construction of the enabling legislation which was challenged by the National Resources Defense Council (NRDC), the argument being that this interpretation was too generous to industrial users.

Justice Stevens gave the judgement of the Supreme Court. He adopted a two-stage approach. First, if the intent of Congress is clear, that is the end of the matter; for the court, as well as the agency, must give effect to the unambiguously expressed intent of Congress. Second, if, however, the court

determined that Congress had not directly addressed the precise question at issue, the court did not simply impose its own construction on the statute, as would be necessary in the absence of an administrative interpretation. Rather, if the statute was silent or ambiguous with respect to the specific issue, the question for the court was whether the agency's answer was based on a permissible construction of the statute. If Congress had explicitly left a gap for the agency to fill, there was an express delegation of authority to the agency to elucidate a specific provision of the statute by regulation. Such legislative regulations were given controlling weight unless they were arbitrary, capricious or manifestly contrary to the statute. Sometimes, the legislative delegation to the agency was implicit rather than explicit. In such a case, a court should not substitute its own construction of a statutory provision for a reasonable interpretation made by the administrator of an agency. The court should defer to the agency's construction whenever a decision as to the meaning or reach of a statute involved the reconciliation of conflicting policies, in circumstances where the agency had particular expertise in the matters subjected to its regulatory remit.

Applying these principles, the court then upheld the contested agency interpretation. It found that Congress did not have any specific intention with regard to the applicability of the bubble concept to the permit programme. Given that this was so, the question was not whether the reviewing court believed that the bubble concept was a good thing within the general context of a scheme designed to improve air quality. It was rather whether the agency's view that the bubble concept was appropriate within this scheme was a reasonable one. Looked at in the light of the objectives of the legislation in this area the court found that it was a reasonable interpretation which sought to balance the needs of the environment and those of business. The NRDC was, said Justice Stevens, seeking to wage a battle over policy in the courts on an issue which Congress had not specifically addressed, having lost that battle in the agency itself: these policy arguments should more properly be addressed to the legislators or administrators rather than the judges. There has been significant academic commentary on the case (Aman, 1988; Farina, 1989; Pierce, 1988; Scalia, 1989; Sunstein, 1988b).

The case law since the *Chevron* decision is itself of considerable interest, as later cases have sought to test the metes and bounds of the principles set out above. There have been cases that give latitude to agency interpretations. There have been many cases where the court comes closer to substitution of judgement, drawing upon that part of the argument in *Chevron* that asserts the primacy of Congressional intent where that can be identified. It is clear moreover that judges possess considerable discretion as to how to characterize a particular case, in the sense of whether it comes within part one or part two of the *Chevron* formula. This is inevitable. What is less readily apparent is that there has been real disagreement among the judiciary as to the meaning that should be ascribed to the two parts of test, especially part one. This is particularly important, as can be appreciated by considering two contrasting views on this issue.

In *Immigration and Naturalization Service* v. *Cardozo-Fonseca* (480 U.S. 421 (1986)), the Supreme Court decided that the meaning of a particular statutory term was clear within the first limb of the *Chevron* test because the court could divine this through the normal tools of statutory construction. This provoked a powerful separate opinion from Justice Scalia. He felt that the approach of the majority would radically undermine the purpose of the *Chevron* formula, given that a court could always then hold that the meaning of a statutory term was clear through the use of 'normal tools of statutory construction'. The approach in the *Cardozo-Fonseca* case can be contrasted with that in *Rust* v. *Sullivan* (111 S. Ct. 1759 (1991)), where Chief Justice Rehnquist gave the leading judgement of the court. His interpretation of the first limb of *Chevron* was markedly different. On his view, a case would only fall under the first limb of the test if the Congressional meaning of the term really was evident on the face of the statute. If this was not so, then the matter would be determined under the rationality part of the formula. This, in turn, provoked a sharp dissent from Justice Stevens, who argued that the majority was construing part one of the test too narrowly.

The contrast between the UK and US jurisprudence throws into sharp relief the judicial choices that are available in this area. The courts can, as in the UK, substitute judgement for that of the agency on all issues of statutory interpretation. This will be so, irrespective of the nature of the issue posed, and the relative expertise of agency and court to resolve it. The courts can, as in the United States, proceed via a two-part test. Issues coming within part one of the *Chevron* test would lead to substitution of judgement by the court for that of the agency. Issues that fall within part two of that test would be subject to control through the medium of the rational basis or reasonableness test. While there is bound to be some disagreement as to which test should be applied in any particular case, this should not be overstated. Substitution of judgement is suitable either where the legislature really has spoken to the issue, or where the challenged decision involves an issue on which the agency does not have any special expertise. In other instances, the rationality test should be applied, particularly in relation to those matters of statutory interpretation that fall within the agency's sphere of competence. It should not, moreover, be forgotten that agency determinations can be struck down even under this latter standard of review.

The choice between the two approaches outlined above has important implications for the more general relationship between agencies and courts. At base, the issue is whether agencies are to have any autonomy over the meaning to be ascribed to their empowering legislation. Under the UK approach, the answer is essentially 'no'. Under the US approach, the answer is a qualified 'yes'. It is clear that different commentators will have differing views as to which of these options is to be preferred, but at least the US jurisprudence enables us to see that there are ways of maintaining control over agency choices short of substituting judgement on each and every occasion.

REFERENCES

Aman, A. (1988) 'Administrative Law in a Global Era: Progress, Deregulatory Change and the Rise of the Administrative Presidency', *Cornell Law Review*, 73: 1101–247.

Aman, A. (1993) *Administrative Law and Process*. New York: Matthew Bender.

Andenas, M. (ed.) (1998) *English Public Law and the Common Law of Europe*. London: Key Haven Publications.

Andenas, M. and Jacobs, F. (eds) (1998) *European Community Law in the English Courts*. Oxford: Oxford University Press.

Beatson, J., Grosz, S., Hickman, T., Singh, R., with Palmer, S. (2008) *Human Rights: Judicial Protection in the United Kingdom*. London: Sweet & Maxwell.

Craig, P. (1990) *Public Law and Democracy in the United Kingdom and the United States of America*. Oxford: Oxford University Press.

Craig, P. (2000) 'Public Law, Political Theory and Legal Theory', *Public Law*, 211–39.

Craig, P. (2006) *EU Administrative Law*. Oxford: Oxford University Press.

Dicey, A.V. (1959) *An Introduction to the Study of the Law of the Constitution*, 10th edn. London: Macmillan.

Ellis, E. (ed.) (1999) *The Principle of Proportionality in the Laws of Europe*. Oxford/Portland, OR: Hart Publishing.

Farina, C. (1989) 'Statutory Interpretation and the Balance of Power in the Administrative State', *Columbia Law Review*, 89: 452–528.

Galligan, D. (1996) *Due Process and Fair Procedures*. Oxford: Oxford University Press.

Goldsworthy, J. (1999) *The Sovereignty of Parliament, History and Philosophy*. Oxford: Oxford University Press.

Harlow, C. and Rawlings, R. (1997) *Law and Administration*, 2nd edn. London: Butterworths.

Hart, H.L.A. (1961) *Concept of Law*. Oxford: Oxford University Press.

Henderson, E. (1963) *Foundations of English Administrative Law*. Cambridge, MA: Harvard University Press.

Hickman, T. (2010) *Public Law after the Human Rights Act*. Oxford: Hart Publishing.

Jaffe, L. and Henderson, E. (1956) 'Judicial Review and the Rule of Law: Historical Origins', *Law Quarterly Review*, 72: 345–64.

Kavanagh, A. (2009) *Constitutional Review under the UK Human Rights Act*. Cambridge: Cambridge University Press.

Laski, H. (1917) *Studies in the Problem of Sovereignty*. New Haven, CT: Yale University Press.

Laski, H. (1919) *Authority in the Modern State*. New Haven, CT: Yale University Press.

Lieberman, D. (1989) *The Province of Legislation Determined: Legal Theory in Eighteenth-Century Britain*. Cambridge: Cambridge University Press.

Mashaw, J. (1976) 'The Supreme Court's Due Process Calculus for Administrative Adjudication in *Mathews* v. *Eldridge*: Three Factors in Search of a Theory of Value', *University of Chicago Law Review*, 44: 28–59.

Mashaw, J. (1985) *Due Process in the Administrative State*. New Haven, CT: Yale University Press.

Michelman, F. (1977) 'Formal and Associational Aims in Procedural Due Process', in J. Roland Pennock and John W. Chapman (eds), *Due Process*. New York: New York University Press.

Michelman, F. (1986) 'Foreword: Traces of Self-Government', *Harvard Law Review*, 100: 4–77.

Pierce, R. (1988) 'Chevron and Its Aftermath: Judicial Review of Agency Interpretation of Statutory Provisions', *Vanderbilt Law Review*, 41: 301–14.

Posner, R. (1973) 'An Economic Approach to Legal Procedure and Judicial Administration', *Journal of Legal Studies*, 2: 399–458.

Rawls, J. (1973) *A Theory of Justice*. Oxford: Oxford University Press.

Resnick, J. (1977) 'Due Process and Procedural Justice', in J. Roland Pennock and John W. Chapman (eds), *Due Process*. New York: New York University Press.

Robson, W. (1928) *Justice and Administrative Law: A Study of the British Constitution*. London: Macmillan.

Scalia, A. (1989) 'Judicial Deference to Administrative Interpretations of Law', *Duke Law Journal*, 511–21.

Schonberg, S. (2000) *Legitimate Expectations in Administrative Law*. Oxford: Oxford University Press.

Stewart, R. (1975) 'The Reformation of American Administrative Law', *Harvard Law Review*, 88: 1667–813.

Sunstein, C. (1985) 'Interest Groups in American Public Law', *Stanford Law Review*, 38: 29–87.

Sunstein, C. (1988a) 'Constitutionalism after the New Deal', *Harvard Law Review*, 101: 421–510.

Sunstein, C. (1988b) 'Beyond the Republican Revival', *Yale Law Journal*, 97: 1539–90.

Ziamou, T. (2001) *Rulemaking, Participation and the Limits of Public Law in the USA and Europe*. Aldershot: Ashgate/Dartmouth.

19

The Limits of Law: Can Laws Regulate Public Administration?

David Feldman

BACKGROUND: SEVEN PROPOSITIONS

Empirical evidence about the relationship between law and public administration is gradually growing, but remains somewhat sketchy. Understanding depends largely on theoretical analyses, fairly small-scale studies of particular administrative bodies or procedures, and anecdotal accounts. Studies have assessed the impact of applications for judicial review,[1] one type of legal procedure, but these form a tiny (though important) part of the law applying to public administration. Other studies have examined the making and applying of rules, including legal rules, as a way of empowering and controlling administration, and have illuminated the conditions under which rules are more or less likely to achieve their drafters' objectives in practice. More recently, however, scholars of administrative justice have increasingly used empirical studies of areas of administration (particularly those affecting individuals) as bases for developing theoretical models which bridge the gap between law and administration. Whilst we still generalize

from insufficient information, we have a more solid foundation than a few years ago.

First, norms are an important aspect of the idea of bureaucratic rationality which the Weberian tradition sees as a hallmark of the modern state, and have a pervasive effect on administration, shaping both the activities undertaken and the way in which they are undertaken (whether aimed at achieving the objectives enshrined in the norms or at frustrating them).

Second, we should not assume that administrators always treat legal norms as having greater authority than other norms, such as guidance and directions issued to or within the organization, and the morality of individual officers. For front-line staff exercising discretion, 'cultural, social, political, psychological, institutional, and doctrinal forces may moderate that discretion'.[2] Legal norms carry special risks and opportunities for administrators, but they do not necessarily have a decisive influence over administrative behaviour.

Third, not all legal norms are judicially enforceable. A legal rule may contain a broad and imprecise standard, such as 'efficiency', which is not likely to be justiciable.[3] For example, section 1 of the UK's National Health Service Act 1977 requires the Secretary of State to promote a 'comprehensive health service designed to secure improvement (a) in the physical and mental health of the people of [England and Wales], and (b) in the prevention, diagnosis and treatment of illness'. The section does not give rise to judicially enforceable obligations to individual patients; it is politically, rather than legally, enforceable. Non-legal norms may be more compelling than legal ones in the administrative setting, through managerial action (performance appraisal affecting pay and promotion prospects, budgetary penalties, or loss of contracts under contracting-out and compulsory competitive tendering regimes) or social pressure (the ethos of the department concerned).[4]

Fourth, virtually all power-conferring rules must be legal, because a non-legal rule cannot make lawful the action of a public authority which interferes with people's legal rights and freedoms. The most significant contribution of law to public administration is, therefore, to empower authorities to do things which would otherwise be unlawful. Other norms restricting how an authority may exercise its powers, to ensure that they are not used arbitrarily or inappropriately, may be non-legal; their formal authority is less important than that they should strike a balance between preserving space for worthwhile discretionary action in pursuit of goals and ensuring that proper respect is shown to people affected.

Fifth, law (in common with other normative systems) may exercise different functions. Even when it is not expected to be judicially enforced, it may have symbolic value when it enshrines basic aspirations, values and objectives of a field of public administration. It may be educational, helping to shape attitudes as well as activities of public authorities: for example, by encouraging respect for people's equality and dignity. Administrative law becomes coercive when it seeks to control excessive, unfair, misdirected or irrational behaviour,

whether prospectively or retrospectively. Judicial review of administrative action is most often concerned with seeking to rectify, retrospectively, improper action. But it is only one of a growing number of mechanisms for enforcing norms governing public administration, including internal review by a public authority, ombudsmen and financial controls.

Sixth, for administrative law to be effective in fostering good administration it must command respect and support from administrators. This requires the substance of the rules to be compatible with the achievement of public objectives, and to be given effect predictably and in ways that take full account of the objectives of the public programme in which the administrators are engaged. In addition, the rules themselves must be in a form which makes them appropriate to the task of regulating decision making and action in the context of the area of public administration in question. Rules have formal qualities which affect their capacity to influence administrative action. As Julia Black has explained,[5] a rule has four dimensions: its content; its mandatory or permissive character; its legal status and any consequence attaching to non-compliance with it;[6] and its structure. The last three of these give rise to its 'rule-type'. The last dimension, the structure of the rule itself, has four aspects: its scope or inclusiveness; its precision or vagueness; the ease with which it can be applied to concrete situations (which Black calls its 'simplicity or complexity'); and its clarity or opacity, in terms of 'the degree to which the rule contains words with well-defined and universally accepted meanings'.[7] There are both tactical and strategic reasons for using particular rule-types, and the use of particular rule-types has certain consequences, independent of a rule's content, for the ability of agencies to formulate and then achieve policy objectives. A rule may fail through being over- or under-inclusive. The search for precision may help to ensure consistency, but only at the cost of increasing the size of the rule-book, reducing the extent to which rules can be internalized, restricting potentially useful discretion, and making it harder for officials to implement policy flexibly. Clarity may make life easier for non-specialists, but create a barrier to the proper deployment of expertise (for example, in the field of medical assessments).[8] If the form of rules (legal or administrative) makes them difficult for administrators to read, comprehend or apply in practice, they are likely to have little influence over day-to-day decision making and practice, although they may still exercise an influence over high-level policy making which settles the general direction of administrative effort.

Finally, legality and respect for rights are two important bases for the legitimacy of all governmental action, and of public administration generally. Democratic foundations of modern government, via the ballot box, provide one source of legitimacy,[9] but this is only a single thread in the rich web of sources of a state institution's legitimacy in civilized society. Other elements include respect for the constitution, law, fundamental rights, international obligations, and members of society as citizens. Robert Baldwin has identified a number of different 'discourses' within which claims to legitimacy may be made. He distinguishes between claims based on 'democratic mandate', 'accountability' or 'democratic voice', 'due process', 'expertise' and 'efficiency', to which one can add claims founded on recognition of the equality and dignity of the citizen. As Baldwin points out, each of these is problematic individually, but together they have justificatory force.[10] They are, of course, capable of pulling in different directions, and not all are equally appropriate for assessing the legitimacy of any one institution or programme of public administration or law.

THE RELATIONSHIP BETWEEN LEGAL NORMS AND PUBLIC ADMINISTRATION

The doctrine of the Rule of Law imposes standards of governmental legitimacy which

complement others, including democratic accountability, representativeness, efficiency, expertise and rights. Most people think that that the power of the state should be principled and consistent, and should normally be accountable by reference to legal standards. This is expected to further two objectives: first, it allows people aggrieved by governmental decisions to secure a review of the decision according to known standards; secondly, lawyers can help to advance good administration and fair, rational, consistent and predictable decision making. Where legal systems include certain fundamental rights, law may restrict what public authorities can lawfully do to people (for example, by prohibiting degrading treatment), and may require actions which affect fundamental rights to be justified according to special criteria.

The unhappy experiences of states where the Rule of Law is not consistently observed show that principles of legality are important elements in creating effective and legitimate government. Nevertheless, it has never been clear how far legal standards can, and should, provide the basis for the day-to-day work of public officials. Several factors may reduce the influence of law on public administration.

First, public administration is goal-orientated. The law may set the goal, require a body to develop a programme to achieve it, and confer the necessary powers. Yet laws often specify the goal in very general terms, and give limited guidance as to how bodies are to use their powers. Those matters are left to the judgement of administrators, who must respond to infinitely variable and often quickly changing circumstances. For example, a law may require a public authority to take steps to reduce the incidence of homelessness by offering advice and support for homeless people, and if necessary by providing housing for them. Legislation may specify the categories of people who are entitled to be helped, and the kinds of help which can be made available from public funds. It may also specify the procedures that are to be followed in making decisions affecting individual homeless people. However, administrators will need to exercise judgement in deciding whether people meet the criteria of eligibility for assistance, and to find ways of accommodating needs to available resources. The social and economic conditions of different areas, including the available housing stock and the calls on it, will vary widely, as will the personal, family and financial circumstances and needs of individual claimants. Administrators will have to decide how best to use their resources to achieve their goals.

In carrying out that task, the resource constraints are likely to be of more central concern to administrators, and are likely to have a stronger impact on their day-to-day behaviour, than the law.[11] At different times and in various contexts, courts have to decide whether resource constraints provide good reasons for not enforcing a legitimate expectation engendered by official acts or statements, or sometimes even impose implied limits on the scope of a body's legal duty.[12] Where judges give more weight to people's rights than to institutions' resource constraints, authorities are forced to rethink the priority of competing claims. (This can apply equally to private law decisions, such as liability of public authorities for negligence.) The balance between competing interests may change, but the rules will always have to be implemented in ways that reflect a judgement about the relative weighting appropriate to competing considerations in the context of a particular set of objectives. Whilst authorities seem generally to try to give effect to court orders,[13] they are less likely to follow a court's interpretation of a relevant law if it is not in harmony with their purpose. A mental health tribunal will not necessarily apply legal rules as interpreted by judges for the purpose of deciding whether it is lawful to detain a mental patient if it would lead to a compulsorily detained patient being released when the medical member of the panel, who has examined the patient, considers that release would be too risky.[14] Where a

public authority seeks to achieve consistency and predictability and to exercise financial control in administering its programmes by providing directives and guidelines for its staff, compliance with them is likely to be monitored continuously through managerial and audit techniques, and may be part of the staff appraisal process. Staff are unlikely to be as conscious of the importance of purely legal rules as they are of the rules and practices of the public authority itself. To put it another way, there are fewer incentives for most staff to internalize legal rules than to internalize administrative ones. One needs to ask whether the relevant people are aware of a norm, and, if they are, how they use it. All norms, once accepted as such by those who have to operate them or are subject to them, can have a variety of effects. A study of police officers found that they treated rules purporting to govern the exercise of their discretion in one of three ways.

'*Working rules* are those that are internalized by police officers to become guiding principles of their conduct. *Inhibitory rules* are those that are not internalized, but which police officers tend to take into account when deciding how to act and which tend to discourage them from acting in a particular way in case they should be caught and the rule invoked against them. *Presentational rules* are the ones that exist to give an acceptable appearance to the way that police work is carried out. Most of the presentational rules derive from the law and are part of a (successful) attempt by the wider society to deceive itself about the realities of policing.'[15]

This is not unique to police officers. For example, where a norm would produce a result that is unacceptable to an official dealing with a case involving a homeless person, there is evidence that the official, if sufficiently experienced, may finesse the norm by way of procedural sleight of hand (in the case of legal norms) or by exploiting the case worker's advantage over the line manager in terms of familiarity with the case (in relation to institutional policies and managerial monitoring).[16] Institutional ethos and organization thus allow non-legal standards and officers' judgement to generate 'working rules'; legal rules are often merely 'inhibitory', followed if they cannot be avoided. There is also strong evidence of case workers presenting cases to superiors in the way most likely to produce the result the case worker wants under the rules, making them 'presentational' rather than 'working' rules for the case worker (although for the superior officer, applying the rules to the story as constructed by the case worker, it may be a 'working rule').[17]

If legal norms are to be 'working rules', individual officials must see them as being useful. Power-conferring rules are useful, even if a power is rarely exercised because using it would compromise other aspects of the job, or prejudice consensual working relationships (such as those between regulators and regulated enterprises) on which success depends.[18] Legal rules which restrict room for manoeuvre tend, by contrast, to be seen as obstacles to be circumvented, or as hoops to be jumped through, unless staff appreciate how the standards which legal rules encapsulate can help them to do their jobs well. This has implications for staff training: a new law often leads to training which produces a high level of legal consciousness within authorities (although much will depend on the structure and ethos of the organization); after a time, however, the authority's priorities change, and the law slips into the background.[19]

Rules demanding pre-decision procedures that demand additional paperwork and time spent in meetings, and come between the official and the objective, are likely to be regarded as 'inhibitory' rather than 'working' rules. For example, social workers may see procedural protection for the rights of parents in childcare investigations in this light. They will then implement the rules most fully where the threat of review is most potent. The perceived threat of review is likely to be heightened where the people affected are well-informed, eligible for legal aid, and so likely to litigate.

An active and well-publicized pattern of decisions by courts might make such 'inhibitory' rules more effective. It is unlikely to make them more accepted, however, unless accompanied by a programme of training and an institutional ethos which emphasizes the inherent or instrumental value of the rules, together with additional resources to cope with difficulties. For a legal norm to be accepted as a working rule, the institutional ethos must also include what Simon Halliday calls 'legal conscientiousness': 'a professional concern with being lawful, which includes both finding out about "what the law is" on a given question, and being concerned to apply that law'.[20] This is likely to be difficult to instil unless the institution is an adjudicatory body, and may be hard to maintain where members of the organization have different professional values.[21] If a body's legal advisers issue strict guidelines and oversee difficult decisions, the letter of the rules may generally be observed, but their spirit will be ignored, because front-line officials will not understand it. The ability and willingness of a public authority to make the right choice for its own circumstances will considerably influence the success of a new body of rules affecting all public authorities, such as the Human Rights Act 1998 (which incorporated the European Convention on Human Rights [ECHR] into UK law) or the duty to enhance racial equality under the Equality Act 2010, in achieving the legislator's objectives and being judged to be legitimate.

Lawyers' input may also reduce the range of options available to elected decision makers, especially if they are risk-averse in relation to legal challenge.[22]

Law can never offer a complete, or even sufficient, set of standards to guide public administration. It can ascribe functions to public authorities, confer powers for those purposes, circumscribe the circumstances in which and purposes for which a public authority may act, provide for lawful expenditure, and lay down procedural standards.

Two questions follow. First, are the principles of administrative law compatible with the values of public administration? Second, are legal rules decisive, or are they ever to some extent negotiable?

Are legal principles compatible with good public administration?

Some of the principles of public law which typically govern public administration, discussed in the two preceding chapters, derive from the principles of legality and constitutionality. Public bodies must stay within their powers, and respect constitutional limits such as the separation of powers and division of functions between central and more local bodies. Institutions must discharge their legal obligations, and use their powers for authorized purposes.

Other limits relate to the manner in which functions are exercised. There are requirements as to procedural due process, designed to ensure that people can participate in decisions affecting them, respecting their dignity and also helping to ensure that decisions are taken as far as possible in the light of all relevant factors and arguments. Further requirements relate to the way in which decisions must be reasoned and communicated to those affected by them and, sometimes, to the public, to ensure that they are not arbitrary or irrational.

Impartiality, probity, professional competence, rationality, consistency, fairness, giving reliable advice and information, and reasonable expedition are both compatible with and benchmarks of good administration. Good administrators try to avoid decisions that are likely to turn out to be ineffective when tested in court. Respecting the limits of one's powers is as much an ordinary part of public administration as finding ways to work within budgetary constraints. Any good administrator recognizes that fairness and rationality are important characteristics of good decision making. These principles provide a discipline which is likely to enhance the quality of decision making and administrative action. In these areas, the law can reinforce desirable administrative practices.

Nevertheless, there may be tensions between the aims of the administration and the ways in which legal standards manifest themselves in practice. The substance of legal rules may inappropriately restrict administrators in pursuing their programmes. Procedural requirements may be so demanding, time-consuming and inflexible as to make it effectively impossible for an authority to use its powers. For example, the (now defunct) Commission for Racial Equality in the United Kingdom had power to initiate formal investigations into suspected cases of discrimination in employment, but courts interpreted statutory preconditions for such investigations so restrictively that the Commission had to limit itself almost entirely to informal investigations, negotiation and education rather than enforcement.[23] Similarly, due-process requirements may make the discharge of functions so time-consuming and resource-intensive as to compromise a body's effectiveness. There may also be a risk of defensive administration:[24] surviving challenge takes precedence over achieving goals, potentially frustrating the institution's objectives. At the other extreme, administrators may consistently fail or simply refuse to give effect to rules, either because they are ignorant of them or because they run counter to their personal, professional and institutional ethos, intuitions or objectives.[25]

This, however, is not peculiar to legal rules. Any procedural rule may inhibit worthwhile, goal-directed activity. Public administration is, or tends to be, an hierarchically organized activity. Within the hierarchy, administrators in superior positions promulgate vast quantities of rules in an effort to ensure that programmes are implemented consistently and in accordance with budgetary and other constraints. Such codes of practice, directives, guidance and advice are as capable as legal rules of stifling flexibility, initiative and dynamism. Whilst one expects them to be better attuned to an institution's functions and organization than general rules made by judges, even sensible procedures may produce dysfunctional results when interpreted in certain ways by other administrators or by courts.

The pursuit of a programme may, then, sensibly be restricted by reference to such considerations as consistency, economy or proportionality. The issue is often who should decide how much weight should be accorded to different considerations. In the UK, with its strong constitutional doctrine of parliamentary sovereignty, where Parliament has spoken unequivocally it will usually be treated as having authoritatively settled such issues through a statutory rule. There is value in having bright-line rules. They enhance certainty and consistency. Sometimes, however, the law (including international human rights law) requires decision makers to give case-by-case consideration to the proportionality of a decision's impact on certain individuals, particularly where it affects fundamental rights.[26]

Where administrators have made such an assessment, a court or tribunal may decline to interfere with it so far as it depends on evaluating evidence or a judgement in a matter on which the administrator has special expertise and experience. Sometimes, as in Canada, courts regard some decision makers as being subject to only limited review, even as to statutory interpretation.

Another way to avoid over-intrusive review of decisions is to replace legal rules with administrative rules or standards which have no, or limited, legal effect, such as value-for-money assessment, the UK Citizen's Charter programme, 'public service guarantees',[27] and codes of practice. That shifts protection from legal values and procedures to administrative ones; audit supplants adjudication. In the context of some activities (such as policing and tax assessment) it may make it difficult to ensure adequate legal protection or the right to be free of arbitrary detention, for to provide for the right to a fair hearing where that applies, as required by

(for example) Articles 5 and 6 of the European Convention on Human Rights.

A tension between constitutional and administrative priorities is seen in other general principles of public law. For example, the rule against sub-delegation is an aspect of the principle of legality which can support good administration but may sometimes make it unworkable, requiring to be relaxed by administrative practice sanctioned by judges.[28] Sub-delegation may be a practical necessity where a power is granted to a minister or a collective body such as a local authority to decide very large numbers of individual cases: for example, in the land-use planning or social security systems.[29] The effect of the principle and of its relaxation may be very different in a new organizational context, such as that of non-departmental public bodies or private enterprises to which public functions have been contracted out.[30] The same is true of the principles of fairness or natural justice, the rule that discretions must not be fettered, the principle that published policies must be consistently applied, and requirements for reasons for decisions. All are generally aspects of good administration, but in particular settings may be capable of hamstringing administrative bodies and interfering with what administrators or politicians regard as necessary or desirable flexibility or consistency.[31]

From the perspective of an outsider, legal rules can aid good administration systemically by highlighting administrative problems and encouraging institutions to reflect on and improve their performance. In practice, most institutions routinely monitor their performance and look for improvements. Judicial review may encourage such reflection. There is evidence from Australia and the United Kingdom of judicial review stimulating internal reassessment of both individual cases and processes.[32] Internal review does not, however, necessarily make use of the same values as judicial review.[33] Much depends on the attitudes of middle and senior managers, and the availability of time and resources to educate front-line officials.

A Canadian study indicates that one should see the relationship between litigation and change in public authorities as dynamic, and focus not on individual cases but on a continuous process whereby courts interrogate public bodies' decision making and the public bodies reconsider and respond by (among other things) developing 'soft law' which progressively shapes the way officials interpret and use their powers.[34]

Legal rules, administrative rules and procedures, and external review of decisions are, on this view, complementary, enhancing the quality of public administration both within organizations and in dealings between administrators and members of the public.

On the other hand, where conditions are not conducive to constructive responses to judicial decisions, the effect may be different. Whereas administrators may accept that the principles of review are not intrinsically inconsistent with the demands of good administration, any kind of review by an external authority may be perceived as a threat, in two ways. First, it affects the finality of decisions, making administration more uncertain and causing delay. This can be particularly awkward in relation to large-scale and complex programmes of public work affecting many people's diverse interests, such as road building or the siting of airports, and partly explains the UK coalition government's current desire to speed up the land-use planning process. Second, public administration is an increasingly professionalized activity whose practitioners see themselves as having distinctive skills. Review by another professional group asserting special authority may be unwelcome. It is also costly, even if that review is exercised only in limited circumstances and according to principles which are generally in harmony with administrative values. In such circumstances, much is likely to be made of those cases in which the courts are considered to have made decisions which, from an administrative standpoint, are dysfunctional.

Athough an organization that sees itself as having shared interests might accept the principles which outside reviewers propound, making those principles an integral part of its operations, an organization that feels threatened is likely to react defensively, protecting its activities from review by sticking formalistically to the rules and repackaging pre-existing arrangements so that they appear consistent with them. This may sometimes lead to a focus on technical details at the expense of the broad merits.[35]

Do legal rules always provide minimum standards below which public administrators must not be allowed to drop, or are the standards ever, or always, to some extent negotiable?

The answer will often depend as much on the nature of the activity in question and the attitude that administrators adopt to their tasks as on the form or substance of the rules and the way they are interpreted and applied by courts. In childcare programmes, the law normally provides that the best interests of a child are to be the paramount consideration. This would appear to require public authorities to give greater weight to the welfare of the child than to the interests of the parents and other members of the family. However, in practice there is a significant area of flexibility. If the child is living with the family, it is likely to be in the child's best interests to accommodate as much as possible the interests of other members of the family. It is not acceptable to subject the child to a real risk of long-term physical or mental harm, and the authorities must act to prevent that. But the law also provides that removing a child from the family should normally be seen as a temporary measure, because it is assumed that all members of the family benefit from (and, under the ECHR Article 8, have a presumptive right to) the enjoyment of their familial relationships. A care plan for a child in local authority care should therefore aim to effect a reintegration of the family where that is possible, offering education and support to achieve it. This leaves a considerable area of judgement within which local authorities must assess the needs of the child as part of the family unit rather than as an individual, negotiating with the family to achieve as safe and nurturing an environment as possible rather than imposing a solution to advance the supposed best interests of the child alone.

Even where an authority is enforcing a legal regime rather than delicately balancing competing or complementary interests, a number of factors may lead to a flexible approach to the task. Take for example the work of environmental health officers. The ultimate objective of the authority is to protect people against unjustifiable threats to health. Resources do not permit officers to police all possible occasions on which there is a threat to ensure that the law is complied with. The most efficient way of achieving the ultimate goal is therefore often to work as far as possible with potential offenders, helping them to develop their own systems for safeguarding public health without making their activities uneconomic. This will tend to mean that officers will regard education, encouragement and negotiation as the best way of relating to people with whom they deal on a regular basis. Enforcement and prosecution will be relatively rarely used against such people, and then only as a last resort, usually only in cases of egregious breaches of rules; more regularly deploying enforcement powers would tend to interfere with the cooperative relationship on which effective protection of the environment depends. Nevertheless, different departments and individual officers may strike a different balance between the use of what Bridget Hutter has called 'persuasive' and 'insistent' strategies, and the existence of an implicit or express threat of legal enforcement at some future time provides a significant incentive for people to respond constructively to officers' exhortations.[36] A similar pattern was found in the 'enforcement' of antipollution law, where to some extent even the permissible level of pollution (and therefore the content of the applicable legal rules) is open to negotiation.[37]

Enforcement by negotiation creates a risk that an overly cosy relationship will develop between people who potentially threaten public interests and those who are supposed to protect the public interest. Such relationships can give rise to at least the appearance of undue flexibility, and the suspicion that developers exercise undue influence over the land-use planning process, waste disposal operators over pollution regulators, and so forth. Nevertheless, authorities can use the threat of legal action to encourage people to cooperate in developing good practice, achieving a reasonable level of compliance and public protection without expending vast resources on policing and prosecuting likely offenders, particularly as the response of criminal courts may be unpredictable. How the balance is struck between use of formal powers and informal encouragement, assistance and negotiation will depend on the nature of the activity, the extent of an authority's resources, the ethos of the authority and to some extent the personalities of individual officers.[38] Disagreement about the appropriate approach to policing of laws against drugs reflects a debate about the proper balance between negotiation and enforcement in that context; to put it another way, about the extent to which the legal rules should be regarded as laying down hard and fast standards in practice.

In other kinds of administrative programmes, such as taxation, social security and criminal investigation, there may be less scope for negotiation. Where an entitlement to money from the state is set out in statute, the public authority would act unlawfully if it paid too little or too much. Where a benefit depends on an assessment or evaluation, such as a judgement about a claimant's degree of incapacity, the judgement is typically made professionally and is not negotiable, although many factual assessments appear to be made on the basis of intuitive judgements as to the claimant's reliability or need, so personal impressions are important.[39] Even so, some needs are likely to be excluded by statutory regulations or authoritative directions, and the priorities between other needs may be set by local management guidelines. In the context of the British welfare state, discretionary Social Fund payments are of this kind: a local office has to stay within its quarterly budget and meet claims so far as possible, taking account of the seriousness of the need and the money remaining in its budget. The apparently discretionary decisions are thus driven principally by rules derived from a variety of sources, some having legal force and others being wholly administrative and budget-driven. It is not possible to distinguish adequately between the effects of rules coming from these different sources, and judicial review's influence may change over time.[40]

Payments due to the state are in a slightly different position. The maximum amount due is set by statute or statutory instrument, but the officials responsible for collecting the money (tax inspectors and tax and social security fraud investigators) typically have discretion to relieve those subject to the charges of some part of the amount due. Sometimes, these remissions are formalized in administrative rules, such as extra-statutory tax concessions published by Her Majesty's Revenue and Customs (HMRC) in the UK and treated by them and by taxpayers just as if they were binding rules of law. In other contexts, they are the subject of negotiation in individual cases: penalties or other payments may be staggered, or remitted in whole or in part, on the grounds of hardship, or because insisting on the full payment at once would drive the payer into insolvency and make it more or less impossible to recover any substantial amount, or as an incentive for a payer to provide information about other activities or other people. In these investigative settings, the relationship between the legal rules and the behaviour of officials is far more like that between regulators and the regulated, described above. Negotiations take place against the background of the often Draconian legal powers

which officials would in practice find it counter-productive to use to the full.

JUDICIAL PROCEDURES AND THEIR EFFECT ON PUBLIC ADMINISTRATION

The impact of legal procedures on public administration is related to the impact of legal rules. We can distinguish between legal proceedings brought by public authorities and those brought against them. An authority's power to bring enforcement proceedings may be used rarely, and may prove counter-productive if the court does not impose a significant penalty. Nevertheless, it can have a significant impact on subsequent negotiations between the authority and offenders. A possibility of a prosecution and uncertainty about the result affects the balance of power between the authority and an offender when they negotiate. The threat of legal proceedings is, perhaps, more influential than their deployment in controlling breaches of legal rules.

Is the same true in relation to the reverse context of judicial review of public authorities? Applications for judicial review are usually retrospective challenges to decisions or actions already taken. The impact of individual cases will, as Hugh Rawlings suggested, usually be sporadic, peripheral and temporary.[41] This lack of consistency and predictability restricts the potential of principles of judicial review to operate as 'inhibitory' rules. To be effective, they will have to achieve 'working rule' status; otherwise, they will be, at best, 'presentational'.

Nevertheless, judicial review can sometimes have a significant effect on an institution. If a point affects a large number of cases, and the authority has adequate systems for ensuring that the lessons from the case are understood quickly by other officials dealing with them, it can lead to a change in practices. For example, the UK Independent Review Service for the Social Fund has systems for ensuring that the relatively few inspectors understand the implications of legal challenges to their decisions.[42] But in larger and less centralized decision-making structures, or institutions where officials' functions are more diversified and where heavy workloads leave little time for training or reading, or in departments staffed largely by temporary staff who are less well inducted into the work of the department than permanent staff, it will be difficult to achieve that level of legal consciousness, let alone legal conscientiousness. In other words, the impact of judicial review on public administration will vary in part according to the nature, staffing, training and organization of the public authority in question. For judicial review to perform an hortatory or educational role, there must be appropriate systems of communication and education between the judges and those whose behaviour they seek to influence.

So far as judicial review seeks to influence administrative activity, it can be seen as performing three different functions: directing, limiting and structuring decision-making. A court may hold that a body has a duty to act in a particular way on the facts of the case, and direct it to comply. *Directing* decision-making in this way usually gives effect to legislative provisions. It may achieve a high public profile and have significant resource implications, especially where the case is one of a number of similar ones and the duty will be costly to fulfil, and to that extent it may affect a wide range of functions which the authority exercises by forcing it to re-examine its priorities.[43] (The same happens following decisions about tort liability of public authorities.) However, this is unlikely to affect day-to-day administrative practices very much. *Limiting* a public authority to keep it within the range of activities, powers or purposes allocated to it by statute can have a greater effect on day-to-day administration, and may make it more difficult to achieve its goals, but can be justified by the principle of legality. *Structuring* decision-making goes further, and has the

greatest potential for affecting administrative practices. It provides principles to guide decision making by providing for fair procedures, and reasoned and reasonable decisions. It is here that judicial review intrudes most closely into the field of good administration, for good or ill.[44] This is why it is not surprising that studies of the effect of judicial review on prison administration have concluded that the effect has been greatest where decisions relate to procedural matters, such as disciplinary procedures and the right to make representations in respect of parole decisions, and far less extensive in relation to the conditions of imprisonment and regimes of prison governance.[45] However, even in relation to 'structuring' decisions, the tendency of judicial review to focus on the facts of a particular case, rather than to examine the matrix of decisions and procedures from which it emerges, may distort judicial appreciation of the context and so limit the usefulness of the case in shaping future decision-making practices.

Where a decision has an impact on the administration, the practical effect will depend on the nature of the decision, and the ease with which the public authority can respond to it. Particularly in the field of 'structuring', the principles of judicial review tend to be very flexible, varying their content with the context. The flexibility of standards of 'procedural fairness' is essential if judicial attempts to fashion principles of general application to the whole of public administration are not to suffer from over- or under-inclusiveness, strangling administrators with impossible demands in some fields while giving inadequate protection to their clients in others; yet it adds to the uncertainty of judicial review, making it difficult for administrators to predict what is required of them, and so reducing the constructive and useful role that judicial review can play in helping authorities to structure their own procedures.[46]

This shows how the impact of judicial review, like the impact of legal rules, cannot be separated from the social and structural context of the public authority that is being reviewed. There are features of judicial review, and of the principles on which it operates, which make it difficult for them to affect administration. Other problems stem from the nature of the organizations subject to judicial review, their receptiveness, the legal consciousness of staff, and their sometimes very limited awareness and memory of judicial review challenges to decisions of other parts, or even their own part, of the organization.[47] The picture is complex, and, for that reason (among others), it would be unreasonable to expect law, and judicial review in particular, to provide anything approaching a coherent guide to public administration. The focus of law is on legality, which (as suggested at the beginning of the chapter) is valuable as a matter of principle and compatible in principle with good administration; but the value of legality may give rise to tension (constructive or destructive in different settings) with goal-driven principles of good administration.

NOTES

1   In this chapter (as in the UK usage) the phrase 'judicial review' denotes mechanisms for challenging the legality or fairness of administrative action, in contrast to the American usage of the phrase to mean challenges to the constitutionality of legislative or executive action.

2   C.E. Schneider, 'Discretion and rules: a lawyer's view', in K. Hawkins (ed.), *The Uses of Discretion* (Oxford: Clarendon Press, 1992), Ch. 2, p. 87.

3   See, e.g., G. Zellick, 'The Prison Rules and the courts', *Criminal Law Review*, 1981, pp. 602–16; 'The Prison Rules and the courts: a postscript', *Criminal Law Review*, 1982, pp. 575–9. However, it is possible for an apparently non-justiciable standard to become justiciable through subjection to judicial interpretation: for example, the adjective 'economic' as a requirement of the public transport system for London was surprisingly given legal teeth in *Bromley London Borough Council* v. *Greater London Council* [1983] 1 A.C. 768, HL.

4   See, e.g., M. Feldman, 'Social limits to discretion: an organizational perspective', in K. Hawkins (ed.), *The Uses of Discretion*, Ch. 5; G. Richardson with A. Ogus and P. Burrows, *Policing Pollution: A*

Study of Regulation and Enforcement (Oxford: Oxford University Press, 1982), pp. 183–90; B.M. Hutter, *The Reasonable Arm of the Law? The Law Enforcement Procedures of Environmental Health Officers* (Oxford: Clarendon Press, 1988), Chs 5 and 6.

5   J.M. Black, '"Which Arrow?": rule type and regulatory policy', *Public Law*, 1995, pp. 95–118.

6   Black refers only to sanctions, but, as H.L.A. Hart, *The Concept of Law* (Oxford: Clarendon Press, 1961), pp. 26–49 demonstrated, not all rules have sanctions.

7   'Universally accepted' seems to refer to acceptance within a particular social culture or sub-culture, such as a given community or a legal or administrative sub-culture within it.

8   For a broadly similar, though less developed, analysis of the formal qualities of rule-types and their relationship to reasons for failure of rules to achieve compliance, see R. Baldwin, *Rules and Government* (Oxford: Clarendon Press, 1995), pp. 7–11, 159–92.

9   See, e.g., J. Griffith, 'Judges and the constitution', in R. Rawlings (ed.), *Law, Society and Economy* (Oxford: Clarendon Press, 1997), p. 308.

10   Baldwin, *Rules and Government*, pp. 41–6.

11   I. Loveland, *Housing Homeless Persons: Administrative Law and the Administrative Process* (Oxford: Clarendon Press, 1995), Ch. 10; M. Sunkin and A. Le Sueur, 'Can government control judicial review?', *Current Legal Problems*, 1991, 44, p. 161.

12   For example, contrast *R.* v. *Gloucestershire County Council, ex parte Barry* [1997] AC 584, HL, with *R.* v. *East Sussex County Council, ex parte Tandy* [1998] AC 714, and *R.* v. *North and East Devon Health Authority, ex parte Coughlan* [2001] QB 213, CA, with *R. (Luton Borough Council and Nottingham City Council and others)* v. *Secretary of State for Education* [2011] EWHC 217 (Admin), and *R.* v. *Department of Education and Employment, ex parte Begbie* [2000] 1 WLR 1115, CA.

13   R. Creyke and J. McMillan, 'The operation of judicial review in Australia', in M. Hertogh and S. Halliday (eds), *Judicial Review and Bureaucratic Impact: International and Interdisciplinary Perspectives* (Cambridge: Cambridge University Press, 2004), pp. 161–89, esp. pp. 172–6.

14   G. Richardson, 'Impact studies in the UK', in M. Hertogh and S. Halliday (eds), *Judicial Review and Bureaucratic Impact: International and Interdisciplinary Perspectives* (Cambridge: Cambridge University Press, 2004), pp. 103–28, esp. pp. 120–3.

15   D.J. Smith and J. Gray, *Police and People in London: the PSI Report* (London: Gower, 1985), pp. 441–2.

16   S. Halliday, 'The influence of judicial review on bureaucratic decision-making', *Public Law*, 2000, pp. 110–15 and 118; and see Loveland, *Housing Homeless Persons*.

17 See, e.g., Halliday, 'Influence of judicial review', at p. 118.

18 This is discussed further below.

19 M. Sunkin and K. Pick, 'The changing impact of judicial review: the Independent Review Service of the Social Fund', *Public Law*, 2001, pp. 736–63; D. Feldman, 'Changes in human rights', in M. Adler (ed.), *Administrative Justice in Context* (Oxford: Hart Publishing, 2010), pp. 97–126.

20 S. Halliday, 'The influence of judicial review on bureaucratic decision-making', *Public Law*, 2000, p. 114. Of course, even legally conscientious authorities are not equally conscientious in relation to all legal rules, as Halliday shows ('Influence of judicial review', pp. 114–15).

21 Examples include social security adjudication and Mental Health Review Tribunals in the UK. See J. Baldwin, N. Wikeley and R. Young, *Judging Social Security: The Adjudication of Claims for Benefit in Britain* (Oxford: Clarendon Press, 1992), Ch. 2; G. Richardson and D. Machin, 'Judicial review and tribunal decision making: a study of the Mental Health Review Tribunal', *Public Law*, 2000, p. 494.

22 L. Bridges, C. Game, O. Lomas, J. McBride and S. Ranson, *Legality and Local Politics* (Aldershot: Avebury, 1987), pp. 106–11; and on the value of legal advice, and its limitations, in avoiding subsequent liability, see *Porter* v. *Magill* [2001] UKHL 67, [2002] 2 WLR 37, HL, at paras. [34]–[40] *per* Lord Bingham of Cornhill, [147]–[148] *per* Lord Scott of Foscote.

23 C. McCrudden, 'The Commission for Racial Equality: formal investigations in the shadow of judicial review', in R. Baldwin and C. McCrudden (eds), *Regulation and Public Law* (London: Weidenfeld and Nicolson, 1987), Ch. 11.

24 See, e.g., M. Kerry, 'Administrative law and judicial review: the practical effects of developments over the last twenty-five years on administration in central government', *Public Administration*, 1986, 64, p. 163; A. Barker, 'The impact of judicial review: perspectives from Whitehall and the courts', *Public Law*, 1996, p. 612; Halliday, 'Influence of judicial review', pp. 118–19.

25 M. Hertogh, 'Through the eyes of bureaucrats: how front-line officials understand administrative justice', in M. Adler (ed.), *Administrative Justice in Context* (Oxford: Hart Publishing, 2010), pp. 203–25.

26 *Manchester City Council* v. *Pinnock* [2010] UKSC 45, [2010] 3 W.L.R. 1441, SC.

27 House of Commons Select Committee on Public Administration, 12th Report, *From Citizen's Charter to Public Service Guarantees: Entitlements to Public Services*, HC 411 of 2007–08.

28 *Carltona* v. *Commissioners of Works* [1943] 2 All ER 560.

29 For a borderline case, see *R. (Chief Constable of West Midlands Police)* v. *Birmingham Justices* [2002] EWHC 1087 (Admin).

30 See M. Freedland, 'Privatising *Carltona*: Part II of the Deregulation and Contracting Out Act 1994', *Public Law*, 1995, p. 21; M. Freedland, 'The rule against delegation and the *Carltona* doctrine in an agency context', *Public Law*, 1996, p. 19.

31 See, e.g., *R. (Bancoult)* v. *Secretary of State for Foreign and Commonwealth Affairs (No. 2)* [2008] UKHL 61, [2009] A.C. 453, HL; *R. (Lumba)* v. *Secretary of State for the Home Department (JUSTICE and another intervening)* [2011] UKSC 12, [2011] 2 W.L.R. 671, SC.

32 R. Creyke and J. McMillan, 'The operation of judicial review in Australia', in M. Hertogh and S. Halliday (eds), *Judicial Review and Bureaucratic Impact: International and Interdisciplinary Perspectives* (Cambridge: Cambridge University Press, 2004), pp. 161–89, esp. pp.176–82; M. Sunkin, K. Calvo and L. Platt, *Does Judicial Review Influence the Quality of Local Authority Services?* ESRC Public Services Programme, Discussion Paper 801 (2008); L. Platt, M. Sunkin and K. Calvo, *Judicial Review Litigation as an Incentive to Change in Local Authority Public Services in England and Wales* (Colchester: University of Essex Institute for Social & Economic Research, 2009).

33 S. Halliday, 'Internal review and administrative justice: some evidence and research questions from homelessness decision-making', *Journal of Social Welfare and Family Law*, 2001, 23, pp. 473–90.

34 L. Sossin, 'The politics of soft law: how judicial decisions influence bureaucratic discretion in Canada', in M. Hertogh and S. Halliday (eds), *Judicial Review and Bureaucratic Impact: International and Interdisciplinary Perspectives* (Cambridge: Cambridge University Press, 2004), pp. 129–60.

35 I. Loveland, *Housing Homeless Persons: Administrqtive Law and the Administrative Process* (Oxford: Clarendon Press, 1995), Ch. 11; M. Sunkin and M. Pick, 'The changing impact of judicial review' *Public Law*, 2001, pp. 736–62, esp. p. 748.

36 Hutter, *Reasonable Arm of the Law*, Chs 4, 5 and 6.

37 Richardson et al., *Policing Pollution*, esp. Chs 5 and 6.

38 On the need to see rules in the context of the social organization of the authority, see M. Feldman, 'Social limits to discretion'.

39 See, e.g., Halliday, 'Influence of judicial review', at pp. 115, 119.

40 M. Sunkin and K. Pick, 'The changing impact of judicial review: the Independent Review Service of the Social Fund', *Public Law*, 2001, pp. 736–63, esp. p. 753.

41 H.F. Rawlings, 'Judicial review and the "control of government"', *Public Administration*, 1986, p. 135.

42 T. Buck, 'Judicial review and the discretionary Social Fund', in T. Buck (ed.), *Judicial Review and Social Welfare* (London: Frances Pinter, 1998).

43 This is particularly likely to be the case in respect of public interest challenges: as to which, see C. Harlow, 'Public law and popular justice', *Modern Law Review*, 2002, 65, pp. 1–18.

44 D. Feldman, 'Judicial review: a way of controlling government?', *Public Administration*, 1988, 66, p. 21.

45 See, e.g., S. Livingstone, 'The impact of judicial review in prisons', in B. Hadfield (ed.), *Judicial Review: A Thematic Approach* (Dublin: Gill and MacMillan, 1995), p. 180.

46 See S. James, 'The political and administrative consequences of judicial review', *Public Administration*, 1996, 74, p. 613; A. Le Sueur, 'The judicial review debate: from partnership to friction', *Government and Opposition*, 1996, 31, p. 8; A.H. Hammond, 'Judicial review: the continuing interplay between law and policy', *Public Law*, 1998, p. 34.

47 See, e.g., Halliday, 'Influence of judicial review', pp. 120–1.

PART 7

Politics and Administration

edited by Carl Dahlström

The reach of her administration limits every ruler. It does not matter if it is an autocratic or democratic regime; if it concerns requests from a monarch or a democratically elected prime minister. Without control of a reasonably effective administration, decisions will not be implemented, and ruler's policy choices are '… nothing but a wish' (Greif 2008: 18). The relationship between politics and administration is therefore at the heart of government.

In a completely efficient system, harmony between politics and administration is perfect, but there are many reasons why this never occurs in the real world. Implementation problems are obviously parts of the explanation, but these issues are dealt with in other parts of this Handbook. Part 7 will instead concentrate on equally important issues connected to politics and administration relations, including questions of political control, bureaucratic politics, and structural design.

Even though empirical studies have denounced it time and time again, thinking around politics and administration often starts from a dichotomy with very distinct tasks for politicians and administrators, respectively. Politics and administration relations

are in such a dichotomy model, structured by hierarchical subordination of administration. Metaphorically, one could say that politics is the mind, while administration is the body of government. The dichotomy model thus holds that policy decisions are made in the political sphere, with strict neutrality for the administration.

The dichotomy model is often associated with classical writings by public administration scholars in the United States, such as Woodrow Wilson's 'The Study of Administration' (1887) and Frank Goodnow's *Politics and Administration* (1900). Some administrative historians have, however, argued that Wilson and Goodnow had a much more nuanced view of politics and administration relations than was later attributed to them (Svara 1998; see also Simon 1947 for an early critique of the model).

Most administrative scholars today see the dichotomy model as unrealistic, and would probably agree that it is safer to assume that the roles of politicians and administrators are fuzzy and that tensions between politics and administration therefore are unavoidable (Peters 2001). There are several reasons for this. First, politics and administration are interdependent. Policy choices are, for example, not developed exclusively in the political sphere, but are also influenced directly by policy advice from the administration and indirectly by the capabilities of the administration (Heclo 1974). Second, the structure of the administration is, among other things, a product of political struggles. Some political forces might even intentionally want to create an inefficient administration (if they do not sympathize with the political goals of the majority in a democratic system) (Moe 1989). Third, the administration (or, more realistically, parts of it, such as for example, strong agencies) might have goals of its own that do not always harmonize with the goals of the ruler. The administration might, for example, want more autonomy or bigger budgets (Niskanen 1971). All this does not make the relationship between politics and administration less important, but certainly less straightforward and more dynamic than sometimes portrayed.

The chapters in this section will address politics and administration relations from three angles. In Luc Rouban's Chapter 21, one controversial but widespread method of influence of the administration is analyzed: namely, politicization of the civil service. He describes how politicization of the civil service has evolved and its consequences, with examples mainly from Europe and North America. Rouban distinguishes between different types of politicization, such as the participation of civil servants in the policy process, partisan control of recruitments to the administration, and political activities by civil servants in unions and as voters. In Chapter 20, Paul 't Hart and Anchrit Wille discuss what is often referred to as bureaucratic politics. Students of public administration have for a long time been aware of the disadvantage rulers have to their administration when, for example, it comes to information and expertise. 't Hart and Wille describe how the administrators sometimes use discretion to make policy, which in their words '… gives the

administration a political quality', and they describe the different forms bureaucratic politics can take.

Before entering the chapters, the reminder of this Introduction will be used to briefly outline how politics influence administration and vice versa. The next section describes two different ways in which politicians might try to control the administration: through recruitments and structural design. That section is followed by a discussion of how administrations influence politics. The examples discussed here include expertise and one form of bureaucratic politics (budgets). In the concluding section some insights from the politics and administration research field are summarized.

HOW POLITICS INFLUENCES ADMINISTRATION

There are many ways in which political leaders can influence agencies or other parts of the public administration, but I will examine only two of them. These two, therefore, only serve as examples. All means of political control should, however, be understood against the backdrop of the constitutional legitimacy for the political institutions. The relationship between politics and administration is structured around the formal superiority for political institutions, such as the parliament and the government, in relation to the public administration. As Withford notes in his chapter, it would be unrealistic to ignore this hierarchical relationship. This sometimes gives the upper hand to political leaders and is, as B. Guy Peters (2001: 237) notes; 'perhaps the ultimate weapon at the disposal of political institutions …'. The reason for discussing recruitments and structure, rather than legitimacy is that most research on politics and administration relations tries to go beyond the formal relationship, and it is results from these studies that we shall explore further.

Recruitments

The question of who controls careers for civil servants and other public sector employees has engaged public administration scholars since the nineteenth century, as well as international organizations such as the Organization for Economic Co-operation and Development (OECD) and the World Bank. As Rouban explains in his chapter, partisan control of recruitments and promotions of civil servants is the most common understanding of politicization of the civil service. (It is, however, not the only understanding of politicization, as Rouban also describes.)

Generally, there are two methods of imposing political control over the civil service using political appointments. The most common method in the Western world is not to directly replace civil servants with political appointees, but rather to add a layer of political appointees to the civil service (see Lewis 2008 and Light 1995 on the US experience). Political appointees within this new layer take on advisory, public relation, or managerial functions, that could otherwise have been carried out by the civil service. In some cases, for example during the Blair government in the UK, political appointees mix these roles and serve as 'spin doctors' involved in policy-making processes, the implementation of policies, and in public relations (Smith 2011). The system with a layer of political appointees has a long tradition in the United States, historically rooted in the so-called 'spoils-system', where party loyalists fill important functions in the executive branch and in federal agencies (Lewis 2008). Another example of a similar strategy is found in Belgium, where ministers in the government have large private offices, so-called ministerial cabinets, which duplicate civil service functions and give ministers a political apparatus to turn to for advice (Brans, Pelgrims and Hoet 2006). There are, however, also examples where political appointments are used directly within the civil service. In Europe this is most common in the Continental countries.

Widespread and direct substitution of civil servants can be found in Southern European countries like Italy, Portugal and Spain, but are even more common on the African continent and in Asian countries such as Japan and India (Painter and Peters 2010).

Politicians want to control the careers of civil servants for many reasons, and I shall point to two common motives identified by Rouban. The first motive is more legitimate than the other. In a democratic society, elected politicians have a legitimate interest in controlling what government organizations do. From a politician's point of view, having party loyalists in agencies, for example, secures that policies are not changed, or in any other way obstructed, on the way from decision to implementation. The basic idea is that neutral competence is not the only important virtue of the civil service in a democratic society. The neutrality should be complemented by responsiveness to democratically elected leaders. From this point of view, political control, even if it is imposed by politicization of the civil service, could therefore very well be advocated.

The second motive has more to do with patronage, and is generally seen as less legitimate. Politicians, in both democratic and autocratic societies, depend on loyal supporters. One way of buying support is obviously to provide goods to supporters, and if the government controls civil service careers this is one important goods. As Rouban notes there are several examples of this, both historically and today, and both in the Western world and in developing countries.

The use of political control of civil service careers has been much criticized. In the British and US context of the nineteenth and twentieth centuries the main issue was the competence of civil servants. Influential reformers thought that, with a professional and meritocratically recruited civil service, a more efficient public administration would be created (Goodnow 1900; Northcote and Trevelyan 1853; Wilson 1887). Recent comparative studies have also shown that in countries with a higher degree of meritocratic recruitment the economic growth is higher and the corruption is lower (Dahlström, Lapuente and Teorell 2011; Evans and Rauch 1999; Rauch and Evans 2000).

Structure

Administrative structure is a broad concept. As Whitford (2012) points out, there are many ways of analyzing what structure is, and what structure does. However, generally, structure refers to the way the relations both between politics and administration and within different parts of the administration are organized. For example, it considers if administrators are insulated from politics (in agencies, for example), or if they are parts of a ministerial organization with political 'bosses'. Or, if a policy area is 'owned' by one or several agencies.

We should probably not think of the design of administrative structures as the product of one – or even a small number of – distinctive decisions. With few exceptions, it is rather a product of incremental processes, including strategic decisions, negotiations between actors involved in both politics and administration, and pure chance. It is therefore futile to look for *one* master plan behind the administrative structure.

However, it is as problematic to analyze the administrative structure, disregarding strategic motives. Without trying to understand the strategic reasons for different parts of the design, we can understand neither its function nor its causes. It seems fairly clear that politicians and administrators as well as interest groups, to some degree, try to use the design of the administration in order to fulfill their own interests.

Whitford (2012) distinguishes among three ways of understanding the role of structure. Maybe the most straightforward of them is what Whitford calls 'structure as political choice', and I will therefore use it as an example here. This analytic idea has been forcefully advocated by Terry Moe, and is very well captured in his chapter 'The Politics of Bureaucratic Structure' (Moe 1989). In the first sentence he states: 'American public bureaucracy is not designed to be efficient' (Moe 1989: 267). According to Moe, its structure is, instead, the product of layers of power games between politicians, administrators and interest groups. Moe argues that since everyone in this process is uncertain of the political realities of tomorrow and has to compromise to some extent, efficiency is not the guiding principle for design. Uncertainty, among other things, makes winners want to protect their achievements by insulating the administration from politics in the future, which is one strategic motive for one specific administrative structure, and political compromise includes opponents who obstruct policy implementation by crippling the administration: for example, by opposing strong central agencies and clear policy goals.

The structure of administration is important since it has policy effects. When concluding his chapter in the 2012 edition of this Handbook, Whitford describes how structure affects policy both directly and indirectly. The effect is direct in the implementation process, but structure also indirectly affects policy as politicians take the existing structure into account when they are suggesting new policies.

HOW ADMINISTRATIONS INFLUENCE POLITICS

If constitutional legitimacy is the 'ultimate weapon' (Peters 2001: 237) available for politicians, information is probably the most important advantage bureaucrats have in relation to the political sphere. It is part of the role of public servants to have knowledge of specific policy areas, or concerning specific organizations, while most politicians are generalists. It was this observation that, already at the beginning of the twentieth century, made Max Weber conclude that: '… the power position of a fully developed bureaucracy is always overtowering' (Weber 1998: 232). One does not need to agree with Weber's drastic conclusion that the administration will always be the stronger part, to realize the importance of information. I will discuss two examples where actors from the public administration might use the information advantage. The first concerns bureaucratic politics, and I will mainly use what 't Hart and Wille label 'budgetary politics' as an example. The second example is closer to policy making and the examples have more to do with policy expertise of the administration.

Bureaucratic politics

't Hart and Wille define bureaucratic politics as a way of understanding different parts of the executive branch as '… stakeholders in their own right'. From this perspective, the interests of, for example, different agencies, departments or political officials affect both policy making and implementation.

Scholars from public administration and economics, associated with the *public choice* perspective, have advocated a view of agencies and other parts of the public administration as organizations interested in maximizing budgets, mostly in order to create 'slack' for the administration. The basic problem addressed by these scholars is why government – in their view – is so big compared to the social optimum. William Niskanen (1971) made a pioneering effort to explain budgetary outcomes from this perspective. He observed that administrators had the upper hand compared to politicians in budgetary processes. The reason for this, according to Niskanen, is that administrators have a huge information advantage that they can use when bargaining the budget. The most important parts of the information advantage are that administrators know the true cost of 'production' as well as the politicians' demand for their services, while politicians do not know the true production costs and have, at least not in a traditionally organized

administration, no other supplier to turn to. The information asymmetry will make it easy for an administration to create 'slack' in every budget, which will therefore diverge from the optimal budget.

Although influential, this perspective on public administration in general and on the budgetary process in particular has been much criticized. Scholars who sympathize with the basic perspective have for example criticized Niskanen (1971) for exaggerating the information advantage for the administration and not taking monitoring devices available for politicians into account (see Bendor and Moe 1985 for their important critique). Aiming more at the foundations of the model, public administration scholars have questioned the basic assumptions. 't Hart and Wille give several examples in their chapter, but the most important one is probably how realistic it is to assume that agencies, or to be more specific, bureau chiefs in the agencies, have an interest in maximizing their budget. Peters (2001) points to several reasons why bureau chiefs do not wish for larger budgets. According to Peters, larger budgets will only lead to larger agencies, with more managerial problems for those at the top, and he therefore concludes that the interest for those individuals managing the agency – and bargaining the budget – should be to minimize personnel problems rather than to maximize budgets.

However, bureaucratic politics is not only about budgets, even though it has probably gained the most attention. As 't Hart and Wille describe in their chapter, it can also be about turfs, policies or organizational credits and blame. What is common in all of these objectives is that bureaucrats act according to their interests in a 'political' way.

Expertise

With expertise, I refer to accumulated knowledge concerning different policy areas or organizations. Experts from the public administration are often used when governments or other policy makers suggest new policies. In his chapter, Rouban writes that all civil servants are 'political' in the sense that they take part in political decisions. As Hugh Heclo (1977) notes, not even political neutrality for the public administration implies passivity for administrators. It is in fact rather the opposite. Heclo (1977) suggests that the basic civil service idea requires that civil servants employed by merit should actively express their views on policy proposals. It is thus inevitable that administrators take part in the political processes to some extent, but there are large variations in how the public administration is involved in political actions.

Generally, the public administrations participate in three different ways: either directly or indirectly in political decisions, or as advisors to the elected politicians.

One example of a direct involvement is the Japanese tradition where the civil service does not limit its role to policy implementation or technical advice, but is considered to be powerful in the policy-making process. Until the end of the 1990s, top civil servants even took part in discussions regarding the Japanese legislature, the Diet, something that would be unthinkable in most other countries (Nakamura 2001).

In Spain, civil servants are indirectly involved in the policy-making process. Spain traditionally has a close connection between the political and administrative elites. The political elite is largely recruited from the Spanish administrative corps (Parrado 2004). It could therefore be argued that the civil service is involved in the policy-making process, although not in the same direct way as in Japan.

A third example, illustrating the advisory functions of the public administration, can be found in Denmark. It is one of the countries in the world with the least number of political appointments in the public administration. This puts the politically elected leaders in a situation where top career bureaucrats are the only ones outside the party organization that they can turn to for advice. Meritocratically recruited civil servants in Denmark therefore play a significant role in the policy-making process as advisors (Grønnegard Christensen 2006).

The role as policy experts, regardless how it is organized, obviously gives the public administration an opportunity to influence politics. For example, Rouban points out that the involvement in the political process has provided a leeway for interest groups allied with parts of the public administration to affect the policy process, as was the case in Japan during the 1980s, or in the agricultural sector in France today. It is also because it is organizing the relationship between politicians, interest groups and administrators that structure is important, which is discussed in Whitford's chapter.

CONCLUSION

Politics and administration relations influence both policy output and policy outcome, and are therefore important for anyone seeking to understand a modern state. If this Introduction has tried to make one main point, it is that while the two groups are distinct enough for it to be relevant to discuss the relationship between them, they are not of different nature. Bureaucrats in the public administration are also playing political games, and politicians try to interfere in the administration through, for example, recruitments and structural design. Chapters 22–24 illustrate the different ways in which political and administration relations have been studied in the past and are studied today. They give instruments for analyzing political components in the administrative structure and in the way that bureaucrats act.

REFERENCES

Bendor, Jonathan and Terry Moe (1985) 'An Adaptive Model of Bureaucratic Politics', *American Political Science Review*, 79 (3): 755–774.

Brans, Marleen, Christophe Pelgrims and Dieter Hoet (2006) 'Comparative Observations on Tensions between Professional Policy Advice and Political Control in the Low Countries', *International Review of Administrative Sciences*, 72(1): 57–71.

Dahlström, Carl, Victor Lapuente and Jan Teorell (2011) 'The Merit of Meritocratization: Politics, Bureaucracy, and the Institutional Deterrents of Corruption', *Political Research Quarterly*, published on June 16 2011 as doi:10.1177/1065912911408109.

Evans, Peter and James Rauch (1999) 'Bureaucracy and Growth: A Cross-National Analysis of the Effects of "Weberian" State Structures on Economic Growth', *American Sociological Review*, 64 (4): 748–765.

Goodnow, Frank J. (1900) *Politics and Administration*. New York: Macmillan.

Greif, Avner (2008) 'The Impact of Administrative Power on Political and Economic Developments', in Elhanan Helpman (ed.), *Institutions and Economic Performance*. Cambridge, MA: Harvard University Press.

Grønnegard Christensen, Jörgen (2006) 'Ministers and Mandarins under Danish Parliamentarism', *International Journal of Public Administration*, 29 (12): 997–1019.

Heclo, Hugh (1974) *Modern Social Policy in Britain and Sweden*. New Haven, CT: Yale University Press.

Heclo, Hugh (1977) *A Government of Strangers. Executive Politics in Washington*. Washington, DC: Brookings Institution.

Lewis, David E. (2008) *The Politics of Presidential Appointments*. Princeton, NJ: Princeton University Press.

Light, Paul (1995) *Thickening Government: Federal Hierarchy and the Diffusion of Accountability*. Washington, DC: Brookings Institution.

Moe, Terry (1989) 'The Politics of Bureaucratic Structure', in John E. Chubb and Paul E. Peterson (eds), *Can the Government Govern?* Washington, DC: Brookings Institution.

Nakamura, Akira (2001) 'Party Members, Elite Bureaucrats and Government Reform in Japan's Changing Political Landscape', in B. Guy Peters and Jon Pierre (eds), *Politicians, Bureaucrats and Administrative Reform*. London: Routledge.

Niskanen, William (1971) *Bureaucracy and Representative Government*. Chicago, IL: Aldine-Atherton.

Northcote, Stafford H. and C. E. Trevelyan (1853) *Report on the Organisation of the Permanent Civil Service*. London: House of Commons.

Painter, Martin and B. Guy Peters (2010) 'Administrative Traditions in Comparative Perspective', in Martin Painter and B. Guy Peters (eds), *Tradition and Public Administration*. New York: Palgrave Macmillan.

Parrado, Salvador (2004) 'Politicisation of the Spanish Civil Service: Continuity in 1982 and 1996', in B. Guy Peters and Jon Pierre (eds), *Politicization of the Civil Service in Comparative Perspective*. London: Routledge.

Peters, B. Guy (2001) *The Politics of Bureaucracy*, 5th edn. London: Routledge.

Rauch, James and Peter Evans (2000) 'Bureaucratic Structure and Bureaucratic Performance in Less Developed Countries', *Journal of Public Economics*, 75: 49–71.

Simon, Herbert (1947) *Administrative Behavior*. New York: Macmillan.

Smith, Martin (2011) 'The Paradoxes of Britain's Strong Centre: Delegating Decisions and Reclaiming Control', in Carl Dahlström, B. Guy Peters and Jon Pierre (eds), *Steering from the Centre: Strengthening Political Control in Western Democracies* Toronto, ON: University of Toronto Press.

Svara, James (1998) 'The Politics–Administration Dichotomy Model as Aberration', *Public Administration Review*, 58 (1): 51–58.

Weber, Max (1998) 'Bureaucracy', in Hans H. Gerth and C. Wright Mills (eds), *From Max Weber: Essays in Sociology*, 2nd edn. London: Routledge.

Whitford, Andrew B. (2012) 'Strategy, Structure and Policy Dynamics', in B. Guy Peters and Jon Pierre (eds), *The SAGE Handbook of Public Administration*. London: Sage.

Wilson, Woodrow (1887) 'The Study of Administration', *Political Science Quarterly*, 2: 197–222.

20

Bureaucratic Politics: Opening the Black Box of Executive Government

Paul 't Hart and Anchrit Wille

POLITICS AT THE BACK STAGE

Bureaucratic politics, a term that came into use in the late 1960s, has become a staple in the analysis of government and public policy. In this perspective an emphasis is placed on 'the process by which people inside government bargain with one another on complex public policy questions' (Destler, 1972: 52; Kaarbo, 1998: 69). Rather than being carefully aligned components of the executive branch of the state, government agencies, departments, and office-holders are better understood as stakeholders in their own right. They all have certain interests to preserve and policy views to promote. These priorities, and the conflicts they some-times spark, influence the formulation and implementation of policy – not on the front stage of public debate and parliamentary discussion but on the back stage of executive processes.

The approach – sometimes also referred to as the governmental politics approach (Stern & Verbeek, 1998) – was developed mainly in the context of foreign and security policy processes, with the US presidential system in mind. Most of its initial empirical applications were centred on it (Rourke, 1984; Clifford, 1990; Kaarbo & Gruenfeld, 1998; Kozak & Keagle, 1998; Stern & Verbeek, 1998), and this tradition continues today (Smith, 2008). From that stronghold, it has fanned out to other US policy domains, such as natural resources management (Kunioka & Rothenberg, 1993; Ellison, 2006, 2009) and other countries such as Chile (Cleaves, 1975), Canada (Simeon, 1972) and China (Lieberthal & Lampton, 1992). In parliamentary systems where parliaments are weak in relation to executives, bureaucrats have potentially even more policy-shaping influence; however, for the most part, the bureaucratic politics approach has played a comparatively minor role in accounts of public policy making within those systems (Rosenthal, Geveke & 't Hart, 1994). Finally, globalization and Europeanization have increased the incidence and the salience of multilevel and intergovernmental politics, creating a niche for studies of bureaucratic politics at those levels and interfaces (Peters, 1992; Pollack, 2003; Koenig-Archibugi, 2004; Boin & Rhinard, 2008).

The bureaucratic politics approach suggests that non-elected bureaucrats driven by divergent views and interests play a pivotal role in the policy process, and that policy choices emanate from opaque interaction and bargaining among multiple executive actors more so than from deliberation in democratically elected bodies. This raises normative questions about political control, bureaucratic accountability and responsiveness, and the legitimation of bureaucratic influence and discretion in a democratic system (see also the other chapters in Part 7 of this Handbook). If government decisions cannot be traced to individual policy makers but, rather, result from a 'many-hands' process of give and take among both elected and unelected leaders, then assigning responsibility and therefore accountability for these activities becomes nearly impossible (Bovens, 1998). Bureaucratic politics, moreover, implies a parochial organization of interests, rather than an overarching national interest (Preston & 't Hart, 1999: 53). It runs counter to pervasive rationalist conceptions of decision making and challenges the longstanding idea of separation between 'politics' and 'administration'. As bureaucratic 'game players', public servants are prone to act at odds with the Wilsonian/Weberian norm of bureaucratic abstention from the 'hurry and strife' of the political.

This chapter starts with a brief outline of the model's origins and core propositions, followed by an overview of the different forms bureaucratic politics might take. It then draws a conceptual map for studying and evaluating bureaucratic politics. Thirdly, it develops some tentative propositions to guide the quest for an explanation of its incidence and intensity. We conclude with an assessment of the contemporary relevance of the approach within the field of Public Administration.

A PRIMER ON BUREAUCRATIC POLITICS

Theorizing about the role of bureaucratic politics took place in several generations of scholarship (Kaarbo, 1998: 69). The intellectual origins of the bureaucratic politics perspective lie in the 1950s when scholars such as Roger Hillsman, Richard Neustadt, and Samuel Huntington developed a view that the conflicting goals and interests of officeholders and agencies inside government affect its decision-making processes. They began to challenge the assumption of classic institutionalists and system theorists who tended to adhere to what has later been described as a 'billiard ball model of the state' as a unitary, cohesive, purposeful actor. They pointed out that there is a behind government, a complex set of informal relationships between the different participants in policy making, in which bargaining, negotiation, pressure and counter pressure, debate, persuading, dissuading and coercion, have a prominent place. The resultant policy process was one of accommodation, of arranging mutual concessions so as to maximize values gained and minimize sacrifice (Payan, 2006: 4).

The next generation, in the late 1960 and early 1970s, attempted to further specify and systematize the relationships between bureaucracies and politics and to offer 'models' for understanding policy making. Among these scholars were George Appleby, Norton Long, Aaron Wildavsky, Francis Rourke, Graham Allison, Morton Halperin and Guy Peters (Kozak & Keagle, 1998). Their work was funded on the new 'canons' of public administration established by the 'giants' from the first generation. The new claim was that bureaucracy makes policy through the exercise of discretion and that the exercise of these responsibilities gives the administration a political quality.

Allison's famous Model III in which he used a governmental politics 'lens' to cast a different and compelling light on the Kennedy administration's handling of the Cuban missile crisis has been widely discussed and needs no further introduction here. This model, along with contributions with and by Morton Halperin (Allison & Halperin, 1972; Halperin, 1974), has become the 'gold standard' of the approach. Rosati (1981: 236ff) extracted from this era four descriptive propositions concerning the structure and the process of decision making inside executive government:

- Proposition 1 concerns the composition of the executive branch: in every policy domain, there are numerous individuals and organizations with various differences in goals and objects.
- Proposition 2 relates to the distribution of power: it states that 'no preponderant individual or organization exists'.
- Proposition 3 describes the decision-making process: policy outcomes are a 'political product' resulting from bargaining between governmental actors.
- Proposition 4 asserts that this process does not stop once a policy has been formally adopted: there are likely to be gaps between policy as designed and policy as implemented.

Bureaucratic politics scholars took a resolutely pluralistic view of the politics that went on inside government: influence was dispersed, no actor was dominant, and decisions emerged by compromise. The idea that – like in the macropolitical arena – some actors might be consistently more powerful than others, a view espoused by many students of power, was never really explored. To students of the executive politics of, for example, parliamentary systems, this pluralist flavour is odd. In their world it is almost a given that some government departments – Treasury, the Prime Minister's office – are more equal than others, and that some departments routinely maximize their internal influence by virtue of their strong alignment with powerful sectoral lobbies – trade unions, farmers, organized business and, more recently, environmentalist coalitions – whose views Cabinet cannot afford to ignore. More generally, the politicking inside government does not necessarily limit itself to pulling and hauling between people or organizational

units occupying similar hierarchical levels. It may, in fact, be linked to the exercise of formal authority by those in superior hierarchical positions (Child et al., 2010: 111) or directed towards the strategic exercise of upward influence by players lower down the ladder. Bureaucratic politics involves constant intragovernmental competition for various stakes or prizes. Based on work of a 'third generation' of scholars on the approach, such as Patrick Dunleavy (1991) and Rod Rhodes (2011), we discern several forms of bureaucratic politics according to what is at stake: money, turf, policies and programmes, or organizational credit and blame.

Budgetary politics

Wildavsky's classic study of the budgetary process inside government discerned two main roles that officials and agencies played in it: they are either 'guardians' of the treasury or 'advocates' of programme spending. Guardians and advocates interact in a complementary way and their roles are to be understood as a whole, their interactions creating a stable pattern of mutual expectations which tend to reduce the burden of calculations for budget participants:

> Administrative agencies act as advocates of increased expenditure, and central control organs function as guardians of the treasury. Each expects the other to do its job; agencies can advocate, knowing the centre will impose limits, and the centre can exert control, knowing that agencies will push expenditures as hard as they can. Thus roles serve as calculating mechanisms (Wildavsky, 1975: 7).

Niskanen (1971) proposed an equally classical rational choice variant of bureaucratic politics which he called the 'budget-maximizing model'. Each bureau or agency (or other governmental subdivision) continually strives to maximize its budget and its authorized manpower, as well as to protect or extend its operating autonomy and discretion in decision making in the area of its assigned responsibilities. The higher is their budget, the higher is the utility of the bureaucrats. Bureaucratic agencies are in competition with each other for budget shares and for personnel allocations as well as for gaining responsibility for spicy new programmes. Often this can be achieved by lobbying for an expansion of the scope of the bureau's responsibilities. Niskanen claimed that rational bureaucrats thereby perversely contribute to state growth and increased public expenditure.

More salient perhaps to the current climate of fiscal contraction was Dunsire and Hood's (1989) study of cutback management. When the money has run out and bureaucrats are told by their political masters to put the brakes on public spending, they likewise compete among themselves on how to distribute the pain. In the ensuing battles some departments are more vulnerable to major fiscal squeezes because of what they do and how they do it. Moreover, internal rivalries and power games between bureaucracies explain how cuts on spending and staffing are not developed equally across the board but more as target cuts on selected areas.

Turf politics

Bureaucratic actors do not simply maximize their budgets; what they are after most of all is work that they prefer to do. Accordingly, they attempt to maximize their competences by acquiring and protecting 'turf' – mandates, autonomy and networks (Dunleavy, 1991). Bureaucrats have institutional self-interests based upon 'where they sit' in terms of their task allocation, technical expertise and alignment with external parties (Allison & Zelikow, 1999; Preston & 't Hart, 1999; Ellison, 2009). Turf politics explains how bureaus or departments are more motivated to carefully guard their own fief than to contribute dispassionately to reasoned analysis of how to achieve the public good, (or, as some would argue, even the government of the day's policy intentions). Tales of entrenched, protracted and quite often dysfunctional turf wars can be found within virtually every

jurisdiction: agriculture versus environment, navy versus army, foreign affairs versus international development, local versus national police, preventative versus curative health, crime-fighting versus community policing arms of law enforcement. This implies that the bureaucratic politics perspective could be especially relevant to study the genesis of policy and administrative reforms (Bowornwathana & Oocharoen, 2010).

Building upon Downs's (1967) unsurpassable pioneering effort, Dunleavy's (1991) bureau-shaping hypothesis offers a theoretical account of the process (see also Bendor & Moe, 1985). He posits that bureaucrats seek to maximize their preferences for their core budgets based on their wish for certain kinds of work. Bureaucrats have preferences for intellectually stimulating, innovative, low-cost policy advice work; they eschew management responsibilities for routine and/ or risky administrative work. Officials are likely to pursue individual and collective bureau strategies to realize these preferences, particularly the use of contracting and passing on work to other parties within the executive (such as arms-length agencies), major internal reorganizations to promote policy work over service delivery and regulatory activities, transformations of internal work practices, redefinition of relations with external partners to enhance policy contacts, competition with other bureaus to protect the scope of interesting work, load shedding, and hiving off and contracting out functions which are seen as undesirable (Dunleavy, 1991: 203–4).

Silo politics

Silos, politics, and turf wars are often mentioned in the same breath. Silo politics is, however, sector-centred. It points to a lack of desire or motivation to coordinate (at worst, even communicate) between entities within or among organizations whose collaboration is needed to effectively address policy issues that transcend the mandates and resources of any single one of them. Bureaucratic silos feature the politics of localized policy frames, segmented problem-solving expertise, bureau-centred advocacy coalitions, and functional managers anxious to protect their own fiefdoms. When silo subsystems' drives to enhance their specific contributing functions is allowed to prevail, this impedes policy coordination and blocks the flows of information needed to make full use of organizational capabilities. Wilensky's (1967) classic study already pointed to the risks of specialization in and between organizations; the message was driven home in a devastating way decades later by the 9/11 investigation. More widely, policy implementation processes are subject to continued adjustment and revision, owing to needs to select particular (mixes of) organizationally rooted policy instruments and align the activities of multiple service delivery nodes (Pressman & Wildavsky, 1984; Salamon, 2002; Hill & Hupe, 2009). This is compounded when actors lower in the hierarchy engage in political agitation from below that is primarily about identity and selfhood rather than achieving policy outcomes (Brower & Abolafia, 1997).

Court politics

The court politics metaphor refers to differentiation and competition between different (clusters of) advisers to senior government leaders, as well as to dynamics of the resultant interaction between leaders and their advisory groups. The Commissioners' cabinets in the EU Commission, the Privy Council Office in Canada, and the Cabinet Office in Britain are all important nodes of court politics (Rhodes et al., 2009; Wille, 2013). The term itself has been revived by Savoie (2008) and Rhodes (2011) but the phenomenon has been the subject of intense study since Machiavelli (e.g. Janis, 1982; Meltsner, 1988; Preston & 't Hart, 1999; Lord, 2003; Keohane, 2010). In presidential systems, court politics is concentrated among top-level appointed officials such as senior advisers and Cabinet secretaries,

agency heads, cronies and sometimes even spouses – all vying for president's attention and support. In parliamentary systems it focuses on the inner circles around prime ministers and Cabinet Ministers, and often involves jockeying among different types of ministerial advisers, and between those advisers and senior bureaucrats. As the number and clout of political advisers to ministers has increased in many parliamentary systems in recent decades, the incidence and importance of the latter type of courts politics has increased correspondingly (Eichbaum & Shaw, 2007; Savoie, 2008).

In the pursuit of power and preferred policies, office-holders treat their offices or bureaus as instrument of their ambition ('t Hart & Rosenthal, 1998). The role of these courtiers is to provide advice, and they need to be able to sense emerging political crises and to have an intuitive sense of what is required to get things done (Savoie, 2008). Political skills rather than bureaucratic skills are important: 'the ability to know when to proceed, when to delay, when to be bold, and when to be prudent; to sense a looming political crisis; to navigate through a multitude of horizontal processes and networks ... these have come to matter a great deal' (Savoie, 2008: 229). In court politics there is a shift from formal hierarchy and decision making (in Cabinet and the civil service) to informal process involving only a handful of actors. This form of bureaucratic politics takes place in more fluid relationships, providing quick and inventive access to the levers of power, with the aim to get things done, to see results, to manage the news and the media, and the political-bureaucratic environment (Rhodes, 2011).

Accountability politics

Accountability politics relates to the questions of responsibility, answerability, and sanctions as executive performance gets evaluated by institutional watchdogs and in the court of public opinion. Particularly when things go conspicuously wrong, the allocation of blame can become a major concern for public officials and agencies. Some argue that the entire design of administrative structures can be analysed in terms of the anticipation of unpleasant accountability encounters – i.e. as blame avoidance (Hood, 2002) and as the provision of lightning rods (Ellis, 1994) – although, conversely, claiming credit in the event of high-profile policy successes can also occur (McConnell, 2010). Accountability politics centres on reputations. Bureau-political 'blame games' mean that executive actors will attempt to minimize political risk by attributing compromised policy outcomes that cannot be explained away by referring to overwhelming exogenous forces to the influence of other officials or bureaus, the lack of adequate resourcing of their own agencies, or – more risky – the distorting influence of their political masters (Bovens & 't Hart, 1999).

Governing through complex organization and networks has made accountability much more complex. There is no single, standard, formal process for establishing policy or coming to decisions, so that it has been extremely difficult to hold these processes and the 'decision makers' to account. Political decisions made by ministers or heads of state are developed and implemented by lower bureaucrats, departmental units or agencies, or even by organizations and actors outside the government. Legal notions of 'collective responsibility' and the often complex causal diagnoses presented by post-mortem inquiries imply a certain indeterminacy, which makes it difficult to assign responsibility for error to a particular individual (Bovens, 1998), thus opening the door to an internal politics of ducking and running for cover among politicians and bureaucrats alike.

ASSESSING THE HEAT OF BUREAUCRATIC POLITICS

Analysing bureaucratic politics requires a detailed breakdown of the policy process: an examining of the key players, structures, and mechanisms in that process; an eye for the inter-organizational and intra-organizational settings; and an interest in how this all influences the policy formulation. The basic unit of analysis is the behaviour of and interaction between key individuals working inside the 'core executive' (Rhodes & Dunleavy, 1995) and even between players inside particular organizational units within that executive (Child et al., 2010: 108). It requires information on what bureaucrats do and think, including Machiavellian manoeuvres they won't be keen to advertise. As Allison (1971) argued, in searching for an understanding of how a strategic decision was reached, one has to put oneself in the place of the various participants and pay attention to the strategic dimensions of relations within and across government organizations.

This task is helped by having some kind of roadmap to grasp a phenomenon that is both contested and elusive (Michaud, 2002). A key starting point is to recognize that bureaucratic politics can take different forms, that it can occur with different levels of intensity, and that (consequently) its effects on the quality of policy making are variable (and not uniformly negative, as many of its standard critiques assert). To capture this variety, Rosenthal et al. (1991) and Preston and 't Hart (1999) have modelled bureaucratic politics as a multidimensional cluster of structure and process variables. Extending their work, we present the following map of the basic ingredients of a bureaucratic politics 'game':

- *Arena structure*: an indication of the number of actors that have access to the venues or channels and decision structures in which policies or choices are regularly made. The number of bureaucratic actors involved in the policy-making arena can vary, and this affects the number of interests and perspectives contending for policy influence.
- *Issue structure*: an indication of the positioning of the interests or views of these actors vis-à-vis the issues at hand. The institutional or organizational affiliation of those actors make that they

can have more or less diverging and conflicting interests. They may be involved in single-shot or ongoing coordination games with one another.

- *Power structure*: an indication of the strength of the power relationships between these actors. Governments are loosely held together alliances where power relationships may be diffuse. No individual organization is preponderant over the others all the time; and no one actor has overriding influence. Influence varies: some institutional hierarchies and networks are fluid, others are more solidly crystallized.
- *Outcome structure*: actors may be politically or operationally more or less required to cooperate with one another even in areas of disagreement. When tightly coupled action is necessary, the stakes of the coordination game are higher.
- *Process climate*: an indication of the degree to which the process varies between more collaborative or more competitive forms of interaction. The policy-making process is fundamentally a *political* process. The various individuals and organizations negotiate, bargain, accommodate, comprise, and give and take in the direction of their policy preferences. Interaction is characterized by continuous 'pulling and hauling' and bargaining between (clusters of) actors.
- *Resolution modality*: decisions are reached by bargaining, negotiation, coalition formations, and compromise building between different parties (individuals or organizations). This compromise formation can vary in time (from slow to fast); in the degree to which the relevant stakeholders (feel) represented in this process of give and take; and in the degree to which different parties accept the outcome being sensitive to their ideas and interests.
- *Post-resolution outcome*: the extent to which the implementation of decisions involves continued

bureau-political manoeuvring, and the degree to which this produces temporal slippage (time gaps and delays between decision making and actual implementation) and content slippage (e.g. post-decisional modification of the content of the policy) of the official policy.

Table 20.1 summarizes the different dimensions of bureaucratic politics. In any particular policy process each of these characteristics may occur to a greater or lesser degree. It should be noted that even with such a systematic conceptual and normative framework as guidance, bureaucratic politics remains notoriously difficult to study and evaluate.

The fact that the 'temperature' of bureaucratic politics can vary has important normative implications. On the one hand, there is extreme bureau-political 'cold' where there is a fast, firm, and entrenched consensus between a fairly limited set of players. This increases the likelihood of policy pathologies associated with a lack of rigorous and balanced vetting of assumptions underpinning preferred policies, even when such policies begin to fail in implementation (see Janis, 1989; 't Hart, 1994, 1998; Preston & 't Hart, 1999). On the other end, there is extreme bureau-political 'heat' of ongoing politicking between a large number of irreconcilably opposed parties that risks policy deadlock or forced imposition of tie-breaking solutions that will continue to be fought by the losing sides during the implementation process, risking major policy slippage

Table 20.1   Climates in bureaucratic politics – empirical dimensions

		Bureau-political consensus seeking (potentially 'too cold')	Bureau-political confrontation (potentially 'too hot')
Structure	Arena structure: No. of actors	Limited	High
	Issue structure: distribution of interests	Aligned	Opposed
	Power structure: distribution of clout	Unicentric	Polycentric
	Outcome structure: need for alignment	Loosely coupled	Tightly coupled
Process	Process climate	Cooperative	Competitive
	Resolution modality	Consensual	Imposed
	Game outcome: policy slippage	Low	High

Source: adapted from Preston & 't Hart (1999) and from Rosenthal et al. (1991).

through bureaucratic rearguard warfare (even against the intent of their political masters).

Although not shown in Table 20.1, it follows from this analysis that there is also a theoretical optimum of 'moderately warm' bureaucratic politics that features helpful levels of diversity, disagreement, and compromise formation. When moderate levels of bureaucratic politics occur – or are actively stage-managed by chief executives (Janis, 1982; George & Stern, 2003) – the virtues of pluralism and competitiveness within the executive branch lead to well-vetted and flexibly implemented policies, produced by ongoing yet respectful deliberation that allows for clarification of values and testing of assumptions: in short, policy-oriented learning.

MOVING THE BUREAUCRATIC POLITICS APPROACH ALONG

The existing literature to date has considerably less to say when it comes to explaining the forms and intensities bureaucratic politics might take (except for largely deductive rational choice accounts such as Bendor and Moe, 1985, which remain largely untested). Existing models that attempt to do so have drawn criticism for their lack of parsimony and the difficulty of putting their complexity to the test. Allison's Model III has, for example, been dismissed as an analytical grab bag (Bendor & Hammond, 1992: 302; Burke, 2009: 508), failing to specify assumptions and produce testable hypothesis. Moreover, what many see as the analytical core of the bureaucratic politics approach, the maxim that 'Where you stand depends on where you sit' – called Miles' Law after the Truman-era bureaucrat who coined the phrase – has been derided for its narrow view of preference formation and for assuming too close a fit between roles and positions and for ignoring the images and beliefs that are shared across role positions ('t Hart & Rosenthal, 1998).

The numerous criticisms lodged at bureaucratic politics have stunted the growth of this area of research. Despite a steady stream of mostly single-case study accounts within a growing number of jurisdictions and sectors, relatively little analytical progress has occurred since the mid-1970s (Kaarbo, 1998: 70). This has led critics like Welch (1998: 210) to argue that the approach 'has not led to an accumulation of useful knowledge of the kind to which its pioneers aspired.' We echo this sentiment, but support Juliet Kaarbo's (1998: 72) observation that it is time to revive and update the bureaucratic politics perspective, because 'it offers not only a much needed alternative view of ... policy making, but also an opportunity for integration of the bureaucratic politics perspectives with other theoretical perspectives' (e.g. group dynamics, inter-group relations, and institutional design). 't Hart and Rosenthal (1998: 236) note that bureaucratic politics may be a useful 'middle range' or mid-level hypothesis that provides the right 'kind of balance between explanatory scope and in-depth process knowledge required or policy-relevant insight into manipulable variables.' In this spirit, we offer a fresh set of empirical propositions for further research:

1 *The more veto points within an administrative system, the higher the likelihood of 'bureaucratic confrontation' (high-intensity forms of bureaucratic politics) within that system* (Bendor & Moe, 1985; Peters, 1998, 2009). Simply put, the larger the number of players required to make decisions or achieve a unified government stance, the bigger the need for actors within the system to be proactive administrative politicians engaged in coalition-building.

2 *Dominant and opinionated political leadership fosters bureau-political consensus in the executive branch; consensual and open-minded leadership fosters bureau-political confrontation* ('t Hart, 1994; Preston & 't Hart, 1999). This proposition rests on considerable evidence from the study of advisory systems and group dynamics inside government. Bureaucrats are programmed to seek and adopt a strong steer from their political masters. As long as these political masters

know and articulate clear priorities and policy preferences, and are able to secure sufficient political backing for them (with the President, in Cabinet, in the legislature, among peak bodies), ambiguity is reduced, the space and appetite for bureaucratic discretion constructed, and thus the scope for bureaucratic politics limited. This is radically different when the political executive is weak in terms of priority-setting, policy preferences, and ability to deliver the goods politically. This creates a vacuum that bureaucrats will need to fill, if only to prevent their territory from being encroached upon by colleagues who are lucky enough to be serving a strong and ambitious political leader.

3 *Bureau-political confrontation is more likely to occur on issues with relatively low levels of political involvement* (Rosati, 1981; 't Hart & Rosenthal, 1998). This proposition assumes that bureaucrats are responsive to politicians and public pressures. When issues are very 'hot' and managed hands-on by the political stratum, bureaucrats will get on with the job and forge workable compromises between themselves quickly in order to 'deliver'. Conversely, when issues are both materially and politically inconsequential, there are few incentives – at least for senior bureaucrats – to engage in the energy-sapping game of bureaucratic politics. It then follows logically that the likelihood and intensity of bureau-politics are at their highest with regard to issues that their political masters do not attend to very much but that nevertheless are important enough to the bureaucrats themselves in terms of turf, budget, and policy commitments.

4 *The forms and intensity of bureaucratic politics varies between systems with or without 'spoils systems'.* In contemporary parliamentary systems with Westminster/Weberian administrative systems, bureaucratic politics is more likely to occur at the bottom and middle levels of the bureaucracy than at the top; in US-style presidential systems with spoils systems, bureaucratic politics is equally likely to occur at all hierarchical levels, but its intensity is likely to be highest at the very top. The spoils system routinely infuses a large number of political appointees into ostensibly administrative positions. This not only blurs the boundaries between the two types of public officials but also provides those appointees with a short-term, partisan achievement motivation that differs markedly from the norms of system-wide loyalty and convivial collegiality among the members of a classical senior executive service, who rotate frequently across departments, whose socialization now is focused on the administrative system as a whole and not their particular parts, and who are mostly set for an entire working life inside the public service (even though they may be working on limited-term contracts). Unlike their counterparts in spoils systems, this 'professionalized' caste of upper mandarins is more likely to 'see the big picture' and 'get along' than to engage in no-holds-barred competitive points scoring for their own departments. Lower down the hierarchy, this is not the case: the attachment to the policy substance is bigger, the sense of perspective smaller, and the ties with sectoral experts and interests stronger, combined with the desire for career advancement through being seen to be capable of achieving conspicuous 'wins' for the department.

Propositions remain ruthless simplifications of what for the most part are complex, variegated, and ambiguous administrative systems and processes. Perhaps the aim to develop causal generalizations – let alone an explanatory theory – about bureaucratic politics is not the most helpful stance to take for students of public administration in the first place. It might be more fruitful to take an interpretive stance, penetrate the real-world realities of administrative budgeting, coordination, project management, and policy preparation in the richest possible ways to help us understand how participants in what we have come to think of as 'bureaucratic politics' make sense of what they do, and why they do it, rather than impute fairly simplistic motivations and behavioural propensities about them. This latter approach will almost certainly generate more readily recognizable and teachable knowledge to future and current administrators. That said, there is no need to choose between these different analytical and methodological stances. The field of Public Administration is best served by efforts to penetrate what goes on inside the executive branch proceeding along both tracks and in constant dialogue with one another.

REFERENCES

Allison, G. T. (1971) *Essence of Decision: Explaining the Cuban Missile Crisis.* Boston, MA: Little, Brown.

Allison, G. T. & Halperin, Morton H. (1972) 'Bureaucratic Politics: A Paradigm and Some Policy Implications', *World Politics*, 24: 40–79.

Allison, G. T. & Zelikow, P. (1999) *Essence of Decision: Explaining the Cuban Missile Crisis*, 2nd edn. New York: Longman.

Bendor, J. & Hammond, T. H. (1992) 'Rethinking Allison's Models', *American Political Science Review*, 86 (June): 301–322.

Bendor, Jonathan & Moe, Terry M. (1985) 'An Adaptive Model of Bureaucratic Politics', *American Political Science Review*, 79: 755–774.

Boin, A. & Rhinard, M. (2008) 'Managing Transboundary Crises: What Role for the European Union', *International Studies Review*, 10: 1–28.

Bovens, Mark (1998) *The Quest for Responsibility: Accountability and Citizenship in Complex organizations.* Cambridge: Cambridge University Press.

Bovens, Mark & 't Hart, Paul (1998) *Understanding Policy Fiascoes.* New Brunswick, London: Transaction Publishers.

Bowornwathana, B. & Oocharoen, O. (2010) 'Bureaucratic Politics and Administrative Reform: Why Politics Matters', *Public Organization Review*, 10: 303–321.

Brower, R. & Abolafia, M. (1997) Bureaucratic Politics: The View from Below', *Journal of Public Administration Research and Theory*, 7 (2): 305–331.

Burke, J. P. (2009) 'Organizational Structure and Presidential Decision-Making', in: George C. Edwards III & William G. Howell (eds), *The Oxford Handbook of the American Presidency.* Oxford: Oxford University Press.

Child, J., Elbanna, S., & Rodrigues, S. (2010) 'The Political Aspects of Strategic Decision Making', in Paul C. Nutt & D. C. Wilson (eds), *Handbook of Decision Making.* New York: Wiley-Blackwell.

Cleaves, Peter S. (1975) *Bureaucratic Politics & Administration in Chile.* Berkeley, CA: University of California Press.

Clifford, J. G. (1990) 'Bureaucratic Politics,' *The Journal of American History*, 77(1): 161–168.

Destler, I. M. (1972) *Presidents, Bureaucrats and Foreign Policy.* Princeton, NJ: Princeton University Press.

Drezner, D. (2000) 'Ideas, Bureaucratic Politics and the Crafting of Foreign Policy', *American Journal of Political Science*, 44: 733–749.

Dunleavy, Patrick (1991) *Democracy, Bureaucracy and Public Choice.* Harlow: Prentice Hall.

Dunsire, Andrew & Hood, Christopher (1989) *Cutback Management in Public Bureaucracies.* Cambridge: Cambridge University Press.

Downs, A. (1967) *Inside Bureaucracy.* Boston, MA: Little, Brown and Co.

Eichbaum, Chris & Shaw, Richard (2007) Minding the Minister? Ministerial Advisers in New Zealand Government', *Kotuitui: New Zealand Journal of Social Sciences Online*, 2 (2): 95–113.

Ellis, R. (1994) *Presidential Lightning Rods.* Lawrence, KS: University of Kansas Press.

Ellison, Brian A. (2006) 'Bureaucratic Politics as Agency Competition: A Comparative Perspective', *International Journal of Public Administration*, 29: 1259, 1262.

Ellison, Brian A. (2009) 'Bureaucratic Politics, the Bureau of Reclamation, and the Animas-La Plata Project Spring, *Natural Resources Journal*, 49: 367–402

George, A. & Stern, E. (2002) 'Harnessing Conflict in Foreign Policymaking: From Devil's to Multiple Advocacy', *Presidential Studies Quarterly*, 32 (3): 484–508.

Halperin, M. (1974) *Bureaucratic Politics and Foreign Policy.* Washington, DC: The Brookings Institution.

Hill, M. & Hupe, P. (2009) *Implementing Public Policy.* London: Sage.

Hood, C. (2002) 'The Risk Game and the Blame Game', *Government and Opposition*, 31: 15–37.

Janis, I. (1982) *Groupthink.* Boston, MA: Little, Brown.

Janis, I. (1989) *Crucial Decisions.* New York: Free Press.

Kaarbo, Juliet (1998) 'Power Politics in Foreign Policy: The Influence of Bureaucratic Minorities', *European Journal of International Relations*, 4 (March): 67–97.

Kaarbo, Juliet & Gruenfeld, Deborah (1998) 'The Social Psychology of Intra- and Inter-Group Conflict in Governmental Politics', *Mershon International Studies Review* (symposium 'Whither Governmental Politics?', edited by E. Stern and B. Verbeek), November, 42: 226–233.

Keohane, N. (2010) *Thinking about Leadership.* Princeton, NJ: Princeton University Press.

Koenig-Archibugi, H. (2004), 'Explaining Governmental Preferences for Institutional Change in EU Foreign and Security Policy', *International Organization*, 58 (1): 137–174.

Kozak, D. & Keagle, J. (eds) (1998) *Bureaucratic Politics and National Security: Theory and Practice.* Boulder, CO: Lynne Rienner Publishers.

Kunioka, Todd & Rothenberg, Lawrence S. (1993) 'The Politics of Bureaucratic Competition: The Case of Natural Resource Policy', *Journal of Policy Analysis and Management*, 12: 700.

Lieberthal, Kenneth G. & Lampton, David M. (eds) (1992) *Bureaucracy, Politics, and Decision Making in Post-Mao China*. Berkeley, CA: University of California Press.

Lindblom, C. E. (1959) 'The Science of Muddling Through', *Public Administration Review*, 19 (2): 79–88.

Lord, C. (2003) *The Modern Prince*. New Haven, CT: Yale University Press.

McConnell, A. (2010), *Understanding Policy Success*, Basingstoke: Palgrave.

Meltsner, A. (1988) *Rules for Rulers*. Philadelphia, PA: Temple University Press.

Nelson, Michaud (2002) 'Bureaucratic Politics and the Shaping of Policies: Can We Measure Pulling and Hauling Games?' *Canadian Journal of Political Science*, 35 (2): 269–300.

Niskanen, W. (1971) *Bureaucracy and Representative Government*. Chicago, IL: Aldine-Atherton.

Payan, T. (2006) *Cops, Soldiers and Diplomats: Explaining Agency Behaviour in the War on Drugs*. Lanham, MD: Lexington Books.

Peters, B. Guy (1992) 'Bureaucratic Politics and the Institutions of the European Community', in: A. Sbragia (ed.), *Euro-politics: Institutions and Policy-making in the 'New' European Community*. Washington, DC: The Brookings Institution, pp. 75–122.

Peters, B. Guy (1998) 'Managing Horizontal Government: The Politics of Co-ordination', *Public Administration*, 76 (2): 295–311.

Peters, B. Guy (2009) *The Politics of Bureaucracy*. London: Routledge.

Pollack, Mark, A. (2003) *The Engines of European Integration: Delegation, Agency and Agenda Setting in the European Union*. New York: Oxford University Press.

Pressman, J. L. & Wildavsky, A. (1984) *Implementation: How Great Expectations in Washington are Dashed in Oakland*. Berkeley, CA: University of California Press.

Preston, T. & 't Hart, P. (1999) 'Understanding and Evaluating Bureaucratic Politics: The Nexus between Political Leaders and Advisory Systems', *Political Psychology*, 20 (1): 49–98.

Rhinard, M. & Boin, R.A. (2007) 'European Homeland Security: Bureaucratic Politics and Policymaking in the EU', *Journal of Homeland Security and Emergency Management*, 6 (1): 1–17.

Rhodes, R. (2011) *Everyday Life in Westminster*. Oxford: Oxford University Press.

Rhodes, R. A. W. & Dunleavy, P. (eds) (1995) *Prime Minister, Cabinet and Core Executive*. London: Macmillan.

Rhodes, R., Wanna, J., & Weller, P. (2009) *Comparing Westminster*. Oxford: Oxford University Press.

Rosati, J. (1981) 'Developing a Systematic Decision-Making Framework: Bureaucratic Politics in Perspective', *World Politics*, 33, (2): 234–252.

Rosenthal, U., 't Hart, P., & Kouzmin, A. (1991). 'The Bureau-Politics of Crisis Management', *Public Administration*, 69: 211–233.

Rosenthal, U., Geveke, H., & 't Hart, P. (1994), 'Beslissen in een competitief overheidsbestel', *Acta Politica*, 309–335.

Rourke, Francis E. (1984) *Bureaucracy, Politics, and Public Policy*, 3rd edn. Boston, MA: Little, Brown.

Salamon, L. M. (ed.) (2002) *The Tools of Government*. Oxford: Oxford University Press.

Savoie, D. (2008) *Court Government and the Collapse of Accountability in Canada and the United Kingdom*. Toronto, ON: University of Toronto Press.

Simeon, R. (1972) *Federal-Provincial Diplomacy: The Making of Recent Policy in Canada*. Toronto, ON: University of Toronto Press.

Smith, M. A. (2008) 'US Bureaucratic Politics and the Decision to Invade Iraq', *Contemporary Politics*, 14: 91–105.

Stern, Eric & Verbeek, Bertjan (1998) 'Whither the Study of Governmental Politics in Foreign Policymaking: An Introduction', *Mershon International Studies Review*, (42) 2: 205–210.

't Hart, P. (1994) *Groupthink in Government*. Baltimore, MD: Johns Hopkins University Press.

't Hart, P. (1998) 'Preventing Groupthink', *Organizational Behavior and Human Decision Processes*, 73 (2): 105–115.

't Hart, P. & Rosenthal, U. (1998) 'Reappraising Bureaucratic Politics', *Mershon International Studies Review*, 42, Suppl 2, 233–240.

Welch, D. A. (1998), 'A positive science of bureaucratic politics', *Mershon International Studies Review* (symposium 'Whither Governmental Politics?', edited by E. Stern and B. Verbeek), November, 42, 210–216.

Wildavsky, A. (1975), *Budgeting*, Boston: Little, Brown

Wilesky, H. (1967), *Organizational Intelligence*, New York: Free Press.

Wille, A. (2013). *Politics and Bureaucracy in the European Commission: The Normalization of the EU Executive,* Oxford: Oxford University Press.

21

Politicization of the Civil Service

Luc Rouban

The politicization of the civil service has been the subject of considerable debate in Western democracies for at least the past two centuries. The matter is of particular importance in the eyes of both civil servants and theorists of the state. For civil servants at the start of the twenty-first century, politicization represents a threat to their professional status and the strategic balance that has gradually been achieved between public administration and politics. For theorists, politicization implies taking into consideration all dimensions of bureaucratic activity. In fact, public administration is, in the broad sense, a political institution. As Charles Levine et al. point out: 'Since administrative activity invariably affects who gets what from government and cannot be value-free, all of public administration is in a sense political. But different observers see politics from different viewpoints' (Levine et al., 1990: 103).

The scope and complexity of the subject explain why there is no general theory or a major 'paradigm' of politicization but instead a series of limited theories that try to handle some of the variables and analyze the case of a few different countries. In political science, relations between bureaucrats and elected officials have mainly been studied in a very broad manner by theories of political development that attempt to explain the historical dynamics which led to the building of modern nation-states or democratic regimes (i.e., Shils, 1960). But these very ambitious and often disputable theories have devoted no attention to administrative sociology. On the other hand, the public policy analysis literature has brought to light the underlying political arrangements of government programs in the welfare state. Unfortunately, the frontiers between academic disciplines have caused public policy analysis to leave research on public administration by the wayside or devote only minor attention to it. The politicization of the civil service is an interdisciplinary matter that remains at the exploratory stage at the dawn of the twenty-first century. Some epistemological precautions must therefore be taken.

Today, it is impossible to study the politicization of the civil service without taking into account the social evolution, political culture and the history of the various countries reviewed. Although major constitutional and political differences exist between the United States and Latin America countries or between European Union and Eastern

European countries, there are also major national differences that may differentiate countries in the same cultural area or sharing similar political regimes. For instance, the very nature of the relationship between the executive branch and senior civil servants is not the same in Australia, Canada and Great Britain, even if these three countries are part of the 'Westminster system' (Campbell and Halligan, 1992). Moreover, the politicization of the civil service is not only a complex phenomenon but also a changeable one that can evolve over time within a single country. For instance, politicization has suddenly accentuated at a rapid pace in France since 1981, whereas it had remained at a fairly low level from 1958 (Rouban, 2001). Any research on the politicization process should include a good assessment of the whole political environment.

Other questions may be pointed out: Is the politicization process based on the government will? Is there any kind of a 'politicization policy'? Politicization can be the result of voluntary action, as was long the case in totalitarian political regimes, or a systemic effect, as is generally the case in Western democracies. Sweeping reforms have been enacted in the nineteenth century to control the politicization of civil servants in the United States (Civil Service Reform Act of 1883) as well as in Britain (Northcote-Trevelyan Report of 1854). It was indeed a matter of containing a phenomenon that no one could or wanted to eradicate totally. The politicization of the civil service could be desirable in the context of the democratization of Western political systems, allowing governments to overcome bureaucratic resistance. So the questions are: What are the boundaries within which the politicization process is politically affordable and profitable? And for whom?

Another problem lies in the lack of a precise definition, not of politicization this time, but of the civil service. First, Western countries do not all use the same defining criteria: in France, teachers are civil servants, whereas they are not in Britain. Second, the legal status of civil servants may vary considerably. As a result, politicization can be on a very unequal scale, and especially, may have a very different meaning from one country to another. In a country with a weak administrative tradition, such as Greece, not until the 1990s was any policy decision made to control the excesses of politicization (Spanou, 1996). Lastly, politicization can spread beyond the civil service strictly speaking into the entire public sector, affecting state-owned companies, agencies with an ill-defined legal status or even corporations or institutions working under government contract. The fact that frontiers between public and private sectors have been somewhat blurred as a consequence of the New Public Management theories and practices since the 1990s allows a number of political jobs to be created that escape the usual legal or political checks.

The subject of politicization therefore raises important questions that touch as much on the nature of administrative models as on the real extent of democracy. The overlapping of these two registers gives rise to many clichés and much confusion. All public administration specialists (see, in particular, Aberbach, Putnam and Rockman, 1981; Peters, 1988; Pierre, 1995) agree on the point that the politicization of the civil service can refer to at least three distinct phenomena: politicization as civil servant participation in political decision making; politicization as control over nominations and careers; and politicization as civil servants' political involvement. These three phenomena can occur in combination.

Below, the three dimensions of politicization will therefore be studied, as well as the theoretical and practical questions they raise.

POLITICIZATION AS PARTICIPATION IN POLITICAL DECISION MAKING

In a first interpretation, politicization is the result of the prevailing balance between the political control that governments exercise over the administrative machinery and civil servants' involvement in the definition and implementation of public policy. The politicization of the civil service is in this case synonymous with participation in political authority. In this sense, all civil servants are 'political' because they are called upon to carry out political decisions, adapt them and explain them: in other words, to accomplish work of a political nature that obviously is not limited to the mere application of legal or economic rules. The fact that civil servants are thinking beings precludes considering them as machines having no freedom of judgment. However, there are a whole range of situations, varying from intelligent interpretation of political decisions depending on the actual circumstances of implementation to technocracy: in other words, a sociopolitical system in which decisions made by bureaucrats replace decisions that should normally be made by elected officials. The problem here lies in the fact that this sort of politicization is more a matter of degree than of qualitative threshold. Most public administration specialists, unlike politicians, consider that it is very difficult to distinguish between making rules and enforcing them, all the more so since Western democracies have produced complex public policies of which the normative effect has more to do with measures of implementation than with the decisions originally made by legislators or the executive branch. Thus, it is possible to slip imperceptibly into technocracy by allowing civil servants more latitude in managing major public policies.

To a certain extent, all industrialized democracies are more or less technocracies, in that the political class is no longer the sole actor in the decision-making process, and the decision is often difficult to identify and localize (Allison, 1971). Specific national situations can be identified. In certain countries, such as Britain, Conservative governments have criticized the fact that senior civil servants were not enough involved in defining public policy and hid behind total political neutrality (Hood, 1998). In France, on the other hand, a majority of politicians both on the Left and the Right have always been wary of technocracy and what they feel to be the excessive power of graduates of the Ecole Nationale d'Administration and the Ecole Polytechnique. In Japan, the senior civil service controlled the entire political process up until the 1980s, orienting economic policy through a tight network of influences in the Diet as well as in industry. In the Japanese case, some scholars have mentioned a true 'iron triangle' interlocking the bureaucracy, the Liberal Democratic Party and the major state enterprises (Johnson, 1982). In the 1990s, state reform thus aimed mainly at reducing the influence of the bureaucracy (Nakamura, 1998). In the aforementioned cases, the 'politicization' of the civil service has only involved the senior civil service, whose role in public policy making also depends on its social status and its history.

The question is a different one in developing countries, because the civil service is almost always the only expertise and advisory resource for governments. In this case, the 'politicization' of the civil service must be interpreted differently, because civil servants are often the only organized social force on which governments can rely. The situation is sometimes also reversed in favor of the public service, especially the military, which may act as the only organized political force in the country. Relations between the government and the civil service in developing countries can be organized according to a variety of models, depending on the relative strength of the political leadership and the social role assumed by the bureaucracy (Cariño, 1991). One model is that of a political domination provided by the party in power, either in democratic conditions (for instance, Corazon Aquino's government at the end of the 1980s in the Philippines), or in the context of an authoritarian regime that can literally organize purges in the civil service or submit it to an extremely restrictive political discipline (this was in particular the case of Korea between 1961 and 1963). In a contrasting model, bureaucracy shares power with the political leaders on the basis of an implicit 'arrangement'. The bureaucracy can then support democratic reforms as long as they allow it to increase its powers (this was Mexico's case in the 1970s). In some cases, civilian bureaucracy shares power with a military-style authoritarian regime (this was the case of the 'guided democracy' in Indonesia under Sukarno's administration between 1959 and 1965).

The respective role of civil servants and elected officials in defining public policy also depends on contextual variables. One essential variable is a minister's capacity to exercise real political leadership over his civil servants and advisors (Savoie, 1999). Some French ministers have complained of being dispossessed of their power by the senior civil servants in their entourage. Conversely, in Britain, senior civil servants have denounced the overly directive role of Margaret Thatcher's government, accusing it of wanting to politicize the senior civil service, or at least make it espouse the Conservative ideology (Hennessy, 1990). There is no doubt that a politician must often assert himself to earn respect from professionals who have expertise and time on their side. Politicization becomes the result of a potentially perilous power struggle that depends as much on the networks on which senior civil servants can rely as on the political or personal legitimacy of politicians. The question of politicization became all the more sensitive in the 1990s, since it raised a fundamental question about the respective roles that should fall to elected officials and civil servants at a time when public administrations seemed to be losing control of the situation in the face of an increasingly fragmented civil society, infatuated with new technologies and prompted to demand ever greater quality from the public service for lower taxes (Rouban, 1999).

Most public administration specialists have thus concluded that politicization cannot be treated in a broad manner but only on a case-by-case basis. Another series of variables in fact has to do with the fragmentation of today's administrative apparatuses. The most autonomous administrations are usually administrations that have a technical or scientific competence, whereas the most vulnerable are those with a fairly low level of expertise. Reinforcing administrative specialization or transforming civil servants into managers can contribute to weakening the political control exercised over these administrations. Some ministerial bureaucracies can also impose their viewpoint on ministers when powerful and well-organized lobbies in their economic sector back them: this is especially the case of the Agricultural Ministry in France. Here, cases of actual fusion of political, economic and administrative powers have been observed, since the minister himself has sometimes been chosen among farmers' union leaders! The same type of situation has been noted in Japan. Politicization in this case leads to a blending of powers. Not only is there no longer a difference between political decisions and administrative decisions but also it is impossible to distinguish between public and private interests. But it is precisely this 'big difference' that has served as the historical basis for liberal democracies. Paradoxically, then, privatization can foster politicization, as exemplified by the New Public Management reform which favored ad hoc appointments on the basis of private contracts in the process of transforming classical bureaucrats into managers eager to reduce costs. By privatizing state services ensuring economic development, and even, sometimes, sovereign functions such as customs or border control, some African states have been able to recover the political control of their economy (Zartman, 1995). We can also interpret Margaret Thatcher's attempt to submit the British administration to private management and subject it to the rules of competition as a means of recovering the political control of an administration regarded as too independent (Bouckaert and Pollitt, 2004).

The strategies deployed in European countries by politicians and civil servants alike to control the process of politicization have been partly transformed by the creation of the European Union. European integration, in fact, has had two main consequences: the first was to weaken the national political classes, which were forced to comply with decisions made in Brussels, particularly in the area of public sector privatization. The second consequence is the reinforcement of administrations, which have become the primary interlocutors for private interest groups in highly technical matters. National civil servants henceforth adapt directives passed by the European Commission to the state or local level in the framework of a multilateral negotiation that politicians cannot fully control.

POLITICIZATION AS PARTISAN CONTROL OVER THE BUREAUCRACY

The second, much more precise and more widespread, meaning of politicization of the public sector refers to government and non-government activities that subject the appointment and career of civil servants to political will. In this case, politicization means that not only a civil servant's activity but also his career depend more on political than professional norms defined by the administrations and ruled by law.

There is considerable confusion surrounding this point. The first misunderstanding has to do with the fact that politicization can be perfectly legal and legitimate, because democratic rule implies that the voters' choices should actually be implemented and not buried under the workings of bureaucracy. This is the whole logic of the spoils system that developed in the United States in the nineteenth century. It is also logical for certain positions to depend on a political choice that takes into consideration the ideas backed by the civil servants, because these positions have a particular strategic importance in the eyes of the government. Generally, these positions are limited in duration and involve

very few senior civil servants who serve as go-betweens for the political realm and the bureaucracy. All Western countries have created 'political positions' to give the executive branch some means of control over public policy.

Another source of confusion comes from the fact that the politicization of appointments does not necessarily imply a lack of professional competence. Politicization generally seems linked to the idea of an amateurish administration. This matter has always been at the heart of the debate in the United States. But in some countries, such as Germany and France, top-level positions are occupied by senior civil servants who are both highly qualified professionals drawing on an old tradition of professional autonomy and highly politicized, as they have been previously involved in political activities as advisors or party supporters. Actually, politicization connotes incompetence mainly when it affects not only appointments but also careers. Politicization can then become a means of showing favor to some political allies to the detriment of others, whatever their level of performance or their merits, or of allowing trade unions to define personnel policies. On a historical level, there is no question that the fight against favoritism was one of the major labor demands of British and French bureaucrats in the nineteenth century. Today, for many developing countries, the only way to fight politicization therefore that is connected with corruption practices, which can harm the country's economy, is to organize a truly professional civil service.

The division between administration and politics is a central organizing principle in all Western political systems. This distinction is of course based on the principles Max Weber put forth in his classical analysis of bureaucratic legitimacy in modern societies (Weber, 1947). The creation of professional bureaucracies in the first half of the twentieth century stems from the simultaneous application of two principles: subordination to a hierarchy and separation of administrative careers from partisan influences. It is perfectly obvious, as many observers have already pointed out, that the separation principle has never been entirely enforced. In fact, an evolution in the interpretations of this principle can be noted: in the early twentieth century it implied that the political authority made decisions and bureaucrats merely carried them out. With the increasing complexity of the welfare system and public interventionism, it has become nearly impossible to distinguish the decision from its implementation and no longer are there any administrative 'details' that cannot be transformed into a real political issue. The separation between the political and the administrative world has created complex possibilities for strategic interplay between the two groups of actors, depending on the circumstances.

The separation principle is therefore probably a myth, but a founding myth allowing all Western political systems to modernize, since it is useful from a functional standpoint. On one hand, it allows civil servants to intervene in policy making in the name of their professional autonomy when political elites are deficient; on the other hand, it allows politicians to remove some decisions from citizens' control by entrusting them to public administrations, contending that they are too technical in nature to be debated publicly. The separation principle thus organizes the relative autonomy of the political and administrative worlds, an autonomy that paradoxically indirectly challenges the principle of accountability on which democratic regimes are based.

On the strictly administrative level, the separation principle should above all be understood as a professional norm on which the merit system can be organized. It is in this perspective that the major theorists of public administration, such as Woodrow Wilson and Frank Goodnow, have championed it. In the late nineteenth century, the professionalization of public administration was associated with the development of scientific management. In his famous 1887 essay, Woodrow Wilson declared: '... the field of administration is a field of business. It is removed from the hurry and strife of politics' (Wilson, 1941: 493).

Therefore, another problem lies in the fact that this professionalization of civil servants has been conceived in very different ways in Western countries. Although professionalization was early on seen in the United States as a means of developing managerial standards, in France and Germany it was principally associated with the development of a vast body of administrative law. In Britain, professionalization implies the independence of civil servants from Parliament but as agents of the Crown, their steadfast obedience to the decisions of the executive branch.

Although all European systems are based on the merit system and equal access to the civil service, recruitment systems are rooted in very different philosophies. For example, even if all Europeans countries organize the recruitment of professional civil servants on the basis of an objective procedure in order to guarantee equality among candidates, the criteria for selection vary considerably: in Germany, the good professional is above all a high-level legal specialist (Derlien, 1990); in Britain, the main quality is found in a generalist who has a feeling for team work; whereas France prefers to measure the general level of education and intellectual brio. The very notion of civil servant does not, therefore, refer to the same type of culture or even the same type of professional practice. Consequently, it is logical that politicization is conceived and especially experienced in a very different manner from one country to another.

In most Western countries, specific rules have been set up to distinguish civil servants who are political appointees from civil servants whose career is entirely subjected to professional norms. In the United States, the corruption fostered by the spoils system, particularly under Richard Nixon's administration, led to reorganizing the senior civil service with the Civil Service Act of 1978, which created the senior executive service (SES). The SES is made up of higher positions, 10 percent of which can be politically appointed. In Germany, the *Politischer Beamter* are distinct from other civil servants: the *Politischer Beamter* can be appointed and revoked on the basis of political considerations but with career guarantees. France distinguishes 'positions at the government's discretion': in other words, a set of approximately 500 higher positions, the holders of which can be appointed and revoked at the government's discretion. Here again, there are, nevertheless, professional guarantees because these positions are mainly occupied by career civil servants who can use particular legal provisions allowing them to return to their original agency after they are revoked. This distinction between political positions and career positions is far more recent in Eastern European countries. In Russia, it did not appear until 1995 because the concept of civil servant, in the Western sense of the term, did not exist (Peters, 2008).

In many countries, politicization occurs through the multiplication of short-term contract positions. In Britain, there has been a marked rise in the number of personal ministerial advisors since the early 1980s. In Australia, the creation of 'ministerial advisers' in the late 1980s has provided a means to avoid politicizing senior jobs along the American model, while reinforcing political control over career civil servants' activities (Campbell and Halligan, 1992). In most Latin American countries, government political advisors are recruited on a contractual basis (Farazmand, 1991).

Growing job instability can also provide governments with a ready means to politicize the civil service. This form of politicization is not used to control an administrations' activity but much rather to hand out jobs to friends of the political party or parties in power, operating a shift from a relationship of *clientela* to one of *parentela* (Peters, 2009). This politicization has especially been observed in the 1970s in Italy, where the Christian Democratic Party was used to distribute local jobs (the *lottizazione* system). This type of politicization is closer to the administrative models of developing countries, where it is above all regarded as a means to make political allies by giving jobs to the unemployed. Political deals of this kind can, nevertheless, be found in the most developed countries, especially at the local level and fairly often lead to the spread of illegal practices. When this occurs, there are no longer any institutional barriers between government agencies and political parties. Such practices, be they clearly illegal or only ethically dubious, have developed sporadically in Europe, especially in Mediterranean countries, but also at the local level in the United States. This type of politicization quickly exhausts the limits of modern public administration theory, for it very often becomes impossible to distinguish in these public positions between what is due to politicization and what is due to personal loyalty. Weber's 'bureaucratic' model thus gives way to his model of 'traditional' authority. Furthermore, ties of personal loyalty appear to play an important role in setting up new administrations in Eastern European countries. In Russia, nearly 65 percent of the administrative management officials in the 1990s were former Communist Party members associated with networks of personal power that ran through major state enterprises such as Gazprom or the bureaucracies of large cities.

Personal loyalty connections are playing a growing role in the internal regulation of most Western bureaucracies in the twenty-first century, allowing the political class to cheat with transparency provisions and public accountability. The pace of this change varies from one country to another, but it signifies clearly that the state summits are privatized. While politicization implies some kind of an institutionalization of relationships inside bureaucracies, or between them and the political sphere, personal connections call for subtle influence on policy making as well as on careers. Such connections may be based upon specific philosophical communities (historically, this has been the case – and it is suspected to be still the case – of Freemasonry) or social ones (such as women, gays, veterans, etc.) looking for specific promotions or reforms. This new pregnancy of 'private' connections requires public administration specialists to be particularly aware of personal networks when studying the relationship between public administrations and politics. Unfortunately, this 'sociological appraisal' is still rare.

Politicization can also be exercised through the creation of specific structures at high state levels, which are charged with ensuring the link between government wishes and the implementation of public policy by professional bureaucracies. The White House Office in the United States, the Cabinet Office in the UK, the Federal Chancellery in Germany, the Prime Minister's Cabinet and the Secretariat General of the Élysée in France insure a very important role in defining and carrying out administrative activity. In general, these top-level administrations have developed considerably in Europe since the end of the 1980s, in small countries such as Denmark as well (Peters, Rhodes, and Wright, 2000). They are usually made up of a few hundred top-level civil servants who are fairly highly politicized, and have connections in the administrative system either through the network of political advisors or ministerial offices. The strengthening of senior administrations is rooted in three factors: first, in Europe, the European integration policy has required the creation of coordinating agencies to harmonize national policy with European programs. Then, most of the national administrations have adopted a subsidiarity model, meaning that ministers and the executive branch have gone from 'doing things' to 'getting things done'. This has resulted in an increased demand for administrations specialized in policy implementation and evaluation, as most major government programs are now handled by a wide range of public and private agencies. Finally, since the early 1980s, most Western governments undeniably have clearly sought to strengthen and centralize their political power in the face of changing societies that have become much more diversified than before. It is highly probable that the 2008 financial crisis accentuated this evolution even more.

It is always fairly difficult for scholars to measure the degree of politicization. We can take into consideration the turnover of staff appointed to 'sensitive' positions or analyze biographies so as to identify political networks within public administrations. The task is, nevertheless, a tricky one because, although it is possible to measure flows, it is impossible to measure intentions or ulterior motives. Interviews must always be interpreted with great caution, as it is obviously rare to find senior civil servants who will assert that their only qualification is to be a friend of the minister! In most cases, politicization can only be demonstrated through historical comparative data showing trends in recruitments and careers.

In the early twenty-first century, politicization seems to have increased in most Western countries. This may appear paradoxical, because so many observers have drawn attention to the development of an economic orthodoxy that would inevitably lead all developed countries to follow the same model of 'good governance' on the basis of a single recipe: decrease in public deficits, tax reductions, better management of public spending, and public policy evaluation. One of the most intriguing questions is: To what extent has the development of this 'good governance' led to new administrative practices? In particular, the effects of the New Public Management on the relations elected officials have with senior civil servants can be examined. Subjecting senior civil servants to managerial norms can just as much reduce their leeway, and thus subject them more to political authority, as it can increase the power they exercise on a daily basis on the running of administrative affairs and thus give them greater autonomy with respect to the government's political considerations. The blend of New Public Management and politicization has not had the same effects in all countries: although senior civil servants are more tightly controlled by the political authorities in Britain, they are now more independent in the Netherlands and Finland. In 'Napoleonic tradition' countries, the same diversity may be observed (Ongaro, 2009).

It is easy to understand that in countries where democracy is fragile, such as in South America, governments try to win over the public service to their cause, especially the military. Civil servants' loyalty to the single party is also a sine qua non condition for survival and prosperity in totalitarian countries like China. On the other hand, it is more difficult to explain the increasing politicization of the civil service in developed countries. One of the most satisfactory explanations seems to lie in the crisis running through representative democracies, characterized by a high abstention rate at elections and the rise in power of a social criticism condemning the political class (but not civil servants) (Perrineau and Rouban, 2009). The political class in most Western countries is constantly threatened by the risk of scandals or challenges to its usefulness, given the growing independence of civil society. In the face of this criticism, the initial reflex is to make the senior civil service even more political: first, by mounting 'political fuses' that will blow in the event of failure; second, by giving the impression that the government is still capable of coordinating public policy and making effective decisions – that is, simply of governing. Paradoxically, the development of pluralistic 'governance' has thus been associated with a greater will to politicize the civil service, directly or indirectly.

Politicization must therefore be conceived in developed countries as the effect of a general evolution of the political system. If governments attempt to better control administrative activity through politicization, there are, nevertheless, limits to this politicization other than legal ones. Management of the civil service by senior administrations has not always been an easy task. For instance, the setting up of the 'administrative Presidency' in the United States under Richard Nixon was thwarted by the fragmentation of the US administrative machinery. Moreover, direct intervention of political authorities in the professional life of civil servants requires daily effort and therefore considerable energy.

Appointments are another means of politicization, but the political choice is usually considerably checked by the need to recruit competent individuals already having a great deal of experience in administrative affairs. If not, a political cast, or a 'government of strangers' (Heclo, 1978) is created, largely rejected by career civil servants. As Ball and Peters point out: 'Although their political "masters" may want to control the bureaucracy, the expertise of the bureaucracy is crucial for effective government and the success of any elected government' (Ball and Peters, 2000: 221). The fact that technical matters having to do with public health or the environment protection are becoming increasingly preponderant in politics reinforces the professional situation of civil servants who can use their expertise to counter the more or less demagogic plans of governments.

Another limit lies in the fact that political parties, particularly in the United States and in France, can be weakened and divided by internal movements. The political choice then must take into consideration the diversity of these viewpoints that are not necessarily reconcilable. In European countries where government are very often elected on the basis of political coalitions (Austria, Belgium, the Netherlands), political positions must also be distributed in proportion to the election results of the various parties, which leads to a sort of 'parliamentarization' of the executive branch.

Lastly, there is a political limit to politicization, particularly in Europe, which has to do with the fact that civil servants inspire more trust among citizens than politicians or governments (Perrineau and Rouban, 2009). A government's legitimacy can thus be seriously threatened if the press can attest to an overly politicized civil service.

POLITICIZATION AS POLITICAL INVOLVEMENT

Politicization of the civil service has a third meaning. In this case, politicization refers to the degree of civil servants' political involvement as citizens and voters. The question is thus the following: Is the civil service a political force?

First, situations can be found in which the ideological commitment of civil servants is a crucial element in setting up a new political system: this was particularly the case in regimes born in Africa in the 1960s following decolonization. On the other hand, in India and Pakistan, public administration served instead as a stabilizing element at the time of Independence. In both cases, the civil service compensated for the lack of a sufficiently developed middle class to offer democratic governments an electoral base. This central position of the public service, particularly that of the military, is obviously a factor of weakness and political dependence: successive *coups d'état* have occurred in both Africa and Latin America, often following conflicts within the very state apparatus. In Europe, the civil service has rarely served as a social basis for major political change.

The fact that civil servants share political convictions obviously plays an essential role in a country's political life but also in the management of its administrations. It is hard for a government to ask civil servants to implement public policies that run counter to their ideological convictions, even if they are called upon to work as perfectly neutral professionals. In France, civil servants constitute the most loyal electorate of the Socialist Party and a majority of senior civil servants share Left values. This does not facilitate the implementation of public management reforms based upon business and competition values (Rouban, 1998, 2007).

Comparative studies have shown that civil servants in Western countries usually maintain an affinity with the Socialists in Europe and the Democrats or the 'Center Left' in North America (Blais and Dion, 1991;

Rouban, 2001). They are more inclined than private sector workers to defend the welfare state and government intervention in economic and social matters. This propensity to defend the 'big government' can be considered perfectly normal among civil servants who are paid out of the state budget. Nevertheless, behind the global figures there are considerable differences that tend to make civil servants' vote and political attitudes vary according to their profession (police officers are usually more to the Right than teachers) and their rank (senior civil servants are more interested in politics than clerical workers). It is also highly tempting to compare globally civil servants to their private sector counterparts. But here again the profession matters more than the legal status of the job, even if civil servants are generally more culturally liberal and less economically liberal than private business workers.

Depending on the country, civil servant politicization can also draw support in trade unionism. Trade union rights are generally acknowledged in all European countries (except for certain categories such as the military), whereas they are far more limited in the United States. Trade unionism can, however, vary in degrees of politicization as well as its power of influence over government decisions. It is fairly highly politicized in Austria, France, Germany, Italy and Spain, where civil service unions are branches of national unions that group workers by political affinity. In Britain, trade unionism has been very profession-oriented, at least until the 2008 financial crisis when it entered the political debate.

Another dimension of civil servant politicization has to do with the legal and social possibilities bureaucrats have of getting involved in political life. Though in Great Britain senior civil servants are barred from participating in political activity at the national level, there are no such restrictions in France, Germany and Spain. As a result, the political class of these three European countries is largely made up of former civil servants, who can easily recover their posts and their rank in public administration if they lose an election. This professional freedom is often considered a privilege with regard to private sector workers, who must give up their job to enter into politics. It is obviously a strong incentive for civil servants to play the political card if their career is at a standstill. On the other hand, the effects of this massive presence of civil servants in the ranks of parliament on political debate should not be overestimated, because former civil servants very soon adapt to the rules of the political game and no longer consider themselves civil servants.

CONCLUSION

Any scholar will find it difficult, if not impossible, to control all the variables that may influence the politicization of the civil service. In most cases, sociology will be called upon to support political science research. In particular, the effect of politicization on civil servants' switch-over to private enterprise needs to be studied, because in some countries, such as France, Japan and the United States, access to senior positions in the administration allows civil servants later to become chief executive officers (CEOs) of major private corporations.

However, two variables seem especially important: on the one hand, the strength of the administrative tradition, which can be measured by civil servants' degree of professional independence or 'corporatism'; and, on the other hand, civil servants' involvement in political life, which can be measured by their capacity for collective mobilization or their presence within political parties. From these two dimensions, a diagram of politicization in the main developed countries can be drawn up (Table 21.1), showing that political involvement of civil servants can very well go hand in hand with a strong administrative tradition (France, Germany and Spain) and that the lack of a strong professional culture does not necessarily imply any particular

Table 21.1 Models of politicization by civil servant involvement in political life and the strength of the professional tradition

	Professional tradition	
Political involvement of civil servants	Low	High
Low	United States, Russia	Australia, Italy, UK
High	Austria, Belgium, Netherlands	France, Germany, Spain, Sweden, Japan

partisan involvement (the United States). It should especially be noted that there is no 'European model' and that the models of politicization do not fit into simple dichotomies, which, for instance, would divide countries of the Northern Hemisphere from those of the Southern Hemisphere, or federal countries from unitary countries.

REFERENCES

Aberbach, J., Putnam, R. and Rockman, B. (1981) *Bureaucrats and Politicians in Western Democracies.* Cambridge, MA: Harvard University Press.

Allison, Graham (1971) *Essence of Decision: Explaining the Cuban Missile Crisis.* New York: Harper Collins.

Ball, Alan R. and Peters, B. Guy (2000) *Modern Politics and Government*, 6th edn. London: MacMillan (1st edn, 1971).

Blais, André and Dion, Stéphane (1991) *The Budget-Maximizing Bureaucrat: Appraisals and Evidence.* Pittsburgh, PA: Pittsburgh University Press.

Bouckaert, Geert and Pollitt, Christopher (2004) *Public Management Reform: A Comparative Analysis*, 2nd edn. Oxford: Oxford University Press (1st edn, 2000).

Campbell, Colin and Halligan, John (1992) *Political Leadership in an Age of Constraint.* St Leonards: Allen & Unwin.

Cariño, Ledevina (1991) 'Regime Changes, the Bureaucracy, and Political Development', in Ali Farazmand (ed.), *Handbook of Comparative and Development Administration.* New York: Marcel Dekker, pp. 731–743.

Derlien, Hans-Ulrich (1990) 'Continuity and Change in the West German Federal Executive Elite

1949–1984', *European Journal of Political Research*, 18: 349–372.

Farazmand, Ali (ed.) (1991), *Handbook of Comparative and Development Administration*. New York: Marcel Dekker.

Heclo, Hugh (1978) *A Government of Strangers?* Washington, DC: The Brookings Institution.

Hennessy, Peter (1990) *Whitehall*. London: Fontana.

Hood, Christopher (1998) *The Art of the State: Culture, Rhetoric and Public Management*. Oxford: Clarendon Press.

Johnson, Chalmers (1982) *MITI and the Japanese Miracle*. Stanford, CA: Stanford University Press.

Levine, Ch., Peters, B. G. and Thompson, Frank J. (1990) *Public Administration, Challenges, Choices, Consequences*. Chicago, IL: Scot, Foresman.

Nakamura, Akira (1998) 'Japan Central Administration at the Crossroads: Increasing Public Demand for Deregulation, Decentralization and De-Bureaucratization', *International Journal of Public Administration*, 10 (21): 1511–1531.

Ongaro, Edoardo (2009) *Public Management Reform and Modernization: Trajectories of Administrative Change in Italy, France, Greece, Portugal and Spain*. Cheltenham: Edward Elgar.

Perrineau, P. and Rouban, Luc (eds) (2009) *Politics in France and Europe*. New York: Palgrave Macmillan.

Peters, B. Guy (1988) *Comparing Public Bureaucracies: Problems of Theory and Methods*. Tuscaloosa, AL: University of Alabama Press.

Peters, B. Guy (ed.) (2008) *Mixes, Matches and Mistakes: New Public Management in Russia and the Former Soviet Republics*. Budapest: Local Government and Public Service Reform Initiative, Open Society Institute.

Peters, B. Guy (2009) *The Politics of Bureaucracy*, 6th edn. London: Routledge (1st edn, 1978).

Peters, B. G., Rhodes R.A.W. and Wright, Vincent (2000) *Administering the Summit: Administration of the Core Executive in Developed Countries*. Basingstoke: MacMillan and New York: Saint Martin's Press.

Pierre, Jon (ed.) (1995) *Bureaucracy in the Modern State, An Introduction to Comparative Public Administration*. Aldershot: Edward Elgar.

Rouban, Luc (1998) *The French Civil Service*. Paris: La Documentation française.

Rouban, Luc (ed.) (1999) *Citizens and the New Governance*. Amsterdam: IOS Press.

Rouban, Luc (2001) 'Politicization of the Civil Service in France: From Structural to Strategic Politicization', in B. Guy Peters and Jon Pierre (eds), *Politicization of the Civil Service in a Comparative Perspective: the Quest for Control*. London: Routledge, pp. 81–100.

Rouban, Luc (2007) 'Public Management and Politics: Senior Bureaucrats in France', *Public Administration*, 85 (2): 473–501.

Savoie, Donald J. (1999) *Governing from the Centre*. Toronto, ON: University of Toronto Press.

Shils, Edward (1960) *Political Development in the New States*. The Hague: Mouton.

Spanou, Calliope (1996) 'Penelope's Suitors. Administrative Modernization and Party Competition in Greece', *West European Politics*, 19 (1): 97–124.

Weber, Max (1947) *The Theory of Social and Economic Organization*. New York: Free Press.

Wilson, Woodrow (1887) 'The Study of Administration', reprinted in *Political Science Quarterly*, 61, December 1941: 481–506.

Zartman, Ira (ed.) (1995) *Collapsed States. The Disintegration and Restoration of Legitimate Authority*. Boulder, CO: Rienner.

Administration and Society

edited by Bo Rothstein

The central question to be addressed in Part 8 of this Handbook is how public support and legitimacy for the public administration is related to its possibilities to conduct its role in society, especially to implement policies according to the intentions of political rulers. Such a society-centered perspective on public administration is broader and to some extent different from the classical 'tool' questions that focus on the possibilities for politicians to steer the bureaucracy according to their intentions. Empirical research in this society-centered approach is relatively young, while the theoretical questions were posed long ago. It should be remembered that both Karl Marx and Max Weber took a stand on this problem. After the fall of the Paris Commune in 1871, Marx wrote that it had become obvious to him that the working class could not simply take over the existing state apparatus and use it for its political purposes; rather, changes in the government machinery would be necessary first. Just what changes would be needed he never specified, for no fourth volume of *Das Kapital* (which was meant to be about the state) was ever written.

Max Weber, the founder of the theory of modern bureaucracy, had a similar view about the relation between society and the state. At a meeting in Mannheim in 1907 with the German Society for Social Policy (the *Verein fûr Sozialpolitik*), he entered into a debate with some conservative scholars about extending the suffrage to the working class. The Conservatives feared that if democracy was introduced, the Social Democrats would come into power and capture the state and use it to pursue their own narrow class interests. Weber argued against this, saying that if the Social Democrats would come into power by such a process of democratization, it would not be they who conquered the bureaucratic state. Quite the contrary, the bureaucratic state would in the long run conquer the Social Democrats. It is safe to say that research about the impact of Social Democracy still ponders on these questions. The problems taken up in Part 8 about, for example, the social and political representation of the public administration and its direct interactions with citizens, thus have a long history in the social sciences.

The four chapters in Part 8 analyze this problem from different theoretical angles. Chapter 22 by Rothstein points at new empirical survey-based research, showing that it is not democratic rights that are the most important factor for creating legitimacy for the political system. Instead, it is citizens' perception of the quality of the public administration that turns out to be the most important factor for creating overall political legitimacy. This may be related to yet another surprising empirical finding: namely, that "quality of government" factors such as control of corruption, the rule of law and an impartial civil service have a much stronger impact on almost all measures of human well-being (population health, literacy, subjective well-being, prosperity) than have countries' level of democracy. These two results from recent empirical research imply that the quality of a society's public administration is more important both for the political system's overall legitimacy and for the well-being of its citizens than have hitherto been the "generally accepted wisdom". This may, in turn, be related to the level of social capital in societies (defined as interpersonal trust and social networks), which are shown to be central ingredients that make the administrative part of the democratic machinery work. Rothstein turns this around, and argues that it may be the case that a well-functioning public administration is an important causal factor for generating social capital.

Chapter 23 by Meier and Capers on representative bureaucracy poses a number of interesting dilemmas on how to make the administration more legitimate by changing the pattern of recruitment. Since bureaucrats are not elected but wield power, the question about their representativeness becomes important. They make the important distinction between passive representation, which is when the bureaucracy statistically has a social, ethnic and demographic background setup that is similar to the population at large, and an active representation, when civil servants are recruited because they have a certain ideological orientation or background that will make their decisions go in a particular direction. One of the dilemmas is how the demand for neutrality and impartiality can come into conflict with the ideas that the different interests should be represented in the recruitment of civil servants. Another problem is, of course, which type of background should be counted as a legitimate reason for bureaucratic representation: here we can think of age, social class, ethnicity, gender, sexual orientation, language, geography, religion and a quite few others. Deciding which of these should be recognized is a politically charged problem in many countries. In international organizations such as the European Union (EU), national representation in the bureaucracy has become standard.

Smith (2012) stresses the importance of street-level bureaucrats. In many ways, these are the direct link between the administration and society and they are thus central for questions about legitimacy. The basis for the theory about the importance of street-level bureaucrats is their discretionary power in making the numerous micro-decisions that mount up to the public policy that is actually implemented. Smith analyses several ways in which many countries during the last two decades have tried to manage their street-level bureaucracies. One of them is the New Public Management (NPM) approach; another one has been to increase the influence by organizations rooted in the surrounding community. The NPM approach has taken most of its intellectual influence from the *logic of exchange* and market ideology, while the community-based approach is rooted in a fundamentally different normative agenda based on theories about *civil society*. While the NPM approach centers on making street-level bureaucrats more responsive by using contracts, voucher systems, benchmarking and competition, the civil society approach stresses the importance of involving user groups such as neighborhood associations or other types of voluntary associations. Smith points out the implications for the relationship between citizenship rights and street-level bureaucracies for both of these different approaches.

The last chapter in Part 8 analyses what the new information and communication technologies (ICT) have meant for changing the interface between the administration and society. Is the Bureaucratic State finally to be replaced by the "Digital State"? In Chapter 24, Helen Margetts contrasts the optimistic and pessimistic views set by the hyper-modernists and anti-modernists, respectively, with the more cynical approach put forward by the postmodernists. None of these predictions have been borne out by the development so far. The new technologies have neither made discretionary judgments by individual bureaucrats less frequent, nor have they created an electronic Leviathan. In many cases, the new technologies empower citizens as much as the administrators, because access to information and documents have become easier and cheaper. The chapter concludes with a discussion of a number of possible future scenarios in this interesting field of public administration development.

REFERENCE

Smith, Rathgeb Steven (2012) 'Street-Level Bureaucracy and Public Policy', In B. Guy Peters and Jon Pierre (eds), *The SAGE Handbook of Public Administration*. London: Sage.

22

Political Legitimacy for Public Administration

Bo Rothstein

From a comparative perspective, systems of public administration vary tremendously in their relation to societal actors and the public at large. One could mention variation in degrees of patronage, clientelism and corruption, patterns of recruitment and the ways in which the bureaucracy coordinates its activities with various civic networks and organized interests. One perennial question in this research is why do some countries have more efficient and/or legitimate systems of public administration than others? One answer may be that this is determined by the amount of trust citizens have in the bureaucracy in their country, region or city. Simply put, it is easier to govern, coordinate, control, steer and/or manage a complicated system if one is trusted by the ones that are supposed to be governed, coordinated, controlled, steered and/or managed. If the legitimacy and trustworthiness of the civil service is low, it will be difficult for them to implement many policies, which in its turn may spur even more distrust between citizens and the administrative agencies.

If, for example, tax bureaucrats are known to be corrupted and/or inefficient, it makes little sense for citizens to correctly report their income/taxes (Bräutigam et al., 2008). They will draw conclusions like (a) most of their taxes will not reach their proper addresses or (b) most other people will get away with cheating the system (Putnam, 1995: 111). Such vicious circles have proven to be hard to break and seem to be determined by long historical trajectories (Rothstein, 2011; Treisman, 2000). Without legitimacy and trust, it is difficult to obtain the economic and political resources necessary for the state to implement policies in a competent way. But citizens who perceive the state as incompetent or untrustworthy are less likely to provide such resources, not to mention political support (Levi, 1998). To use a game-theoretical language, such an inefficient equilibrium is reinforcing and thereby stable (Bendor and Swistak, 1997).

Several prominent social scientists have recently argued that this 'quality of government' or 'good governance' variable is crucial in explaining differences in standard of living and economic growth among nations (Fukuyama, 2011; Norris, 2012; Rodrik, 2007; Smith, 2007). For many developing countries, not to mention the countries formerly belonging to the Soviet bloc, this may be the most difficult problem to solve for consolidating democracy and economic growth (Diamond, 2008; North et al., 2009). As one expert from the World Bank has stated:

> Rampant corruption, frustrating bureaucratic delays, suppressed civil liberties, failure to safeguard property rights and uphold the rule of law, forces communities back on themselves, demanding that they supply privately and informally what should be delivered publicly and formally. Accordingly, in countries where these conditions prevail, there should be little to show for even the most well-intentioned efforts to build schools, hospitals and encourage foreign investments (Woolcook, 2001: 16).

This 'quality of government' factor has recently gotten a fair amount of attention in research outside the traditional areas of public administration studies. The problem is that creating a high-quality public administration requires a fair amount of resources that a low-quality administration is less likely to obtain (North et al., 2009; Rothstein, 2011). This goes against the standard view in neo-classical economics, which is, to quote Nobel Laureate Gary Becker's advice: 'To boot out corruption, root out big government' (Becker, 1997: 210). Available measures on the level of corruption and the level of public spending show that the opposite is true in that the correlation between high levels of public spending and low levels of corruption is positive. One such empirical study, using data from between 60 and 209 countries, concludes: 'We have consistently found that the better performing governments are also larger, and collect higher taxes' (La Porta et al., 1999: 234). The authors' conclusion is that 'identifying big government with bad government can be highly misleading'. But they would not have been economists if they had not immediately added that this result 'does not of course imply that it is often, or ever, socially desirable to expand a government of a given quality'.

The importance of the quality of the public administration for overall political legitimacy has been underscored by Bruce Gilley. Using the World Value Study survey data from 72 countries Gilley came to a quite surprising result for what explains citizens' view if their government have 'the right to rule'. Citizens' perception of the quality of the public administration (ability to control corruption, government effectiveness and respect for the rule-of-law principles) is more important in explaining their perception of their governments' legitimacy than are democratic rights and welfare gains. His conclusion of these results deserves to be quoted: 'This clashes with standard liberal treatments of legitimacy that give overall priority to democratic rights' (Gilley, 2006: 58; cf. Gilley, 2009). The notion that the legitimacy of the public administration is important for the overall legitimacy of a political system is supported by other studies showing that high levels of corruption and other forms of favoritism in the exercise of power have a strong impact on the risk for civil wars (Norris, 2012; Rothstein, 2011). Thus, quite unexpectedly, this research show that the rule-of-law and meritocratic bureaucracy as an organizational form which historically has been associated with Max Weber, has made an interesting 'come-back', not least in research about governance problems in the developing world (Evans and Rauch, 2000). One explanation for this is the availability of better and more reliable cross-country data on various measures of the quality of the public administration (Holmberg et al., 2009). A new, and normatively quite problematic finding, is that while measures of the level of democracy have only weak or no correlations with most standard measures of human well-being, measures of the quality of the public administration are moderately or strongly correlated with measures of population health, poverty, literacy, peace and subjective well-being (Norris, 2012; Ott, 2010; Rothstein, 2011). A result of this type of empirical findings is that the traditional and often widespread critique against 'bureaucracy' has to some extent been replaced by a new kind of appreciation of this specific organizational form based on its predictability, low levels of corruption, impartiality and orientation towards the use of expert knowledge in the making as well as the implementation of public policies (du Gay, 2000; Olsen, 2006).

THEORETICAL ASPECT OF BUREAUCRATIC LEGITIMACY

The reason why legitimacy and trust is central to any system of public administration is simple. Civil servants usually wield political power because there is room for discretion in the decisions they make. And, unlike elected officials, bureaucrats are neither voted in nor can be voted out of office. There are of course public policies that can be implemented by the use of general and precise rules and regulations, in which case the discretionary power of the bureaucracy is very small. For example, universal child allowances, universal tax credits or pensions systems may work in this way, in which case there is hardly any room for bureaucratic discretion, which in its turn makes the problem of citizens' trust and legitimacy for the civil service less salient (Catlaw and Hu, 2009; Rothstein, 1998).

In many other areas that call for state intervention, it is more difficult to use precise laws and regulations. Instead, laws can only be created which state the general aim of the policy while the actual implementation has to be made according to the specific circumstances of the situation of the actual case. Such policy areas are, for example, labor market policy, industrial policy, workers' protection policy and environmental policy. Other areas are tax policy, the legal system (i.e., the police and the courts) and educational policy. In fact, Aristotle himself noted that written laws cannot be applied in all situations, since legislators, 'being unable to define for all cases, ... are obliged to make

universal statements, which are not applicable to all but only to most cases'. Aristotle concluded therefore that 'equity is justice that goes beyond the written law' (Aristotle, cited in Brand, 1988: 42). Thus, we can conclude that the need for situational adjustment in policy areas is often so great in many situations as to render impossible any centralized, uniform decision-making process (Lipsky, 1980). The more dynamic the policy area into which the government wants to intervene is, and the more they have to rely on the judgment of various professional or semi-professional groups such as doctors, environmental specialists or social workers, the greater the problem with discretionary power.

Already, in 1919, the father of bureaucratic theory, Max Weber, stressed the importance of analyzing the state not only as a system of representation but also, and maybe foremost, as a *form of administration*:

> For the state to endure, then, the persons living under its rule must submit to the authority to which the wielders of power lay claim. When and why do they do this? On what bases of internalized legitimacy, and on what outward instruments, do the rulers ground their authority? (Weber, 1919/1989: 28).

Weber's analytical focus was, in the first instance, on the *legitimacy* of the established order (Barker, 1980; Beetham, 1985). How could the governing class most effectively uphold popular respect for its right to rule? The answer lay in ensuring that the governed – the citizens – regarded the exercise of power as *legitimate*. In contrast to most other social theorists, Weber viewed political legitimacy as depending not just on the political system's input side. For Weber, the output side – the implementation of policy by bureaucrats – was at least as important, for it was this side of the state with which citizens came into direct contact, and on which they were dependent. Weber thought, for example, that the state's legitimacy was more dependent on tax collectors' relations with citizens than on whether or not suffrage was universal (Barker, 1980; Beetham, 1985: 265ff). The central idea in Weber's theory of bureaucratic legitimacy was that the strict neutral implementation of codified universal and precise laws would make the decisions of the administration predictable for the citizens. However, Claus Offe has underlined that 'as soon as legal norms become disposable from the standpoint of their suitability for concrete tasks, they lose their capacity to legitimate the choice and fulfillment of these tasks on the basis of any substantive validity' (Offe, 1984: 308).

This problem is especially acute in modern welfare states, because of the extended responsibility they have for the welfare of their citizens: the distribution of child-care places, the placement of patients in the queue for medical operations, support for industries located in sparsely populated parts of the country, and admission to higher education, to vocational training programs or to clinics for drug-abusers. State personnel in such areas must make discretionary decisions *continually* – doing so is part of the day's work for a teacher in a classroom, for instance, or a doctor in an emergency ward. The scope for democratic control through the representative system over decisions of this kind is very slight because such decisions require a specific knowledge of each case. The need for *situational adjustment*, in other words, is so great in many situations as to render impossible any centralized, uniform decision-making process (Friedman, 1981).

The central problem is thus the following: Given that, in many cases, it is necessary to entrust the administrative agencies and/or individual civil servants with large amounts of discretionary power, how can the public, and especially the various 'target groups' to which the policy in question is directed, trust the administrative agencies not to misuse that power? This 'trust in the state' problem is one of the main questions in the burgeoning research on trust as a general social problem (Braithwaite and Levi, 1998; Cook, 2001; Sztompka, 1998). The policy question to

follow is: In what way can the public administration be organized or interact with the surrounding society so as to increase confidence that power entrusted in its hands will not be misused? This is a difficult policy problem because public images of 'the government' seem to have very deep historical roots that are hard to change (Rothstein, 2005). Citizens in contemporary Scandinavia have very different views and images of the concept of 'the government' compared to those in, for example, Romania (Charron et al., 2012).

SOCIAL CAPITAL AND PUBLIC ADMINISTRATION

There are few concepts that have had such a remarkable and instant success in the social sciences as *social capital* (Castiglione et al., 2008; Hooghe and Stolle, 2003; Svendsen and Svendsen, 2009). Although the concept and the theory behind it has a longer history, the credit for making social capital into a very useful and important tool in empirical research goes to Robert D. Putnam. His book *Making Democracy Work – Civic Traditions in Modern Italy*, published in 1993, has had a very substantial impact on political science as well as on many other disciplines such as economics and sociology. It is also a theory that has had a substantial impact on public policy in many countries. Important international organizations such as the World Bank have become interested in the theory, especially on how it can be used to spur democratic development and economic growth in developing countries.

As the title suggests, *Making Democracy Work* presented an empirically grounded theory about what rightfully can be seen as the 'million dollar question' in political science. The answer given by Putnam and his research team was that the amount and quality of a society's *social capital* is the most important cause behind a well-functioning democracy (Putnam, 1993: Ch. 4). Following sociologist James Coleman, the major idea in the social capital theory is that social networks, informal as well as formal, create norms of trust and reciprocity among citizens (Coleman, 1990). These norms are important because it makes it less difficult to solve problems of collective action such as the provision of various forms of public goods. If the stock of social capital in a society or in a group is low, a situation metaphorically known as a *social trap* may occur (Rothstein, 2005). Situations such as these are very common and range from helping to protect the environment by sorting your garbage (or not), to paying your taxes (or not), to giving/taking bribes (or not). It makes no sense to be the only one who sorts your garbage, pays taxes or refrains from corruption if you are convinced that most other citizens cannot be trusted to do the same, because the good that is going to be produced will then not materialize (Ostrom, 1998).

From a public administration perspective it can be noted that many studies show that correlations between 'generalized trust' as measured in the World Value studies and indexes of corruption is high (Rothstein, 2011; Uslaner, 2008). Using cross-national data, it is stated that: 'Trust is relatively strongly correlated with "judicial efficiency", "anticorruption", "growth" and "bureaucratic quality"' (La Porta et al., 1997: 336; cf. Uslaner, 2008). Another study reaches the conclusion that 'at the aggregate level, social trust and confidence in government and its institutions are strongly associated with each other. Social trust can help build effective social and political institutions, which can help governments perform effectively, and this in turn encourages confidence in civic institutions' (Newton, 1999: 12). The problem, however, is the usual one that arises when using aggregate data. We don't know if there is a causal mechanism at the individual level, and we don't know how such a causal mechanism might actually work.

The main thrust of Putnam's argument is that social capital is produced if citizens engage in horizontal voluntary organizations such as choral societies, parent–teacher associations, sports clubs, etc. In this Tocquevillian notion of the good social order, it is a vibrant civil society that generates social capital. In such a society, citizens engage in local grassroots organizations where they learn the noble art of overcoming social dilemmas by getting to know people and learning that they can be trusted. At the aggregate level, Putnam is able to show very impressive correlations between the density of the world of voluntary organizations and democratic efficiency (Putnam, 1993).

Several scholars have questioned this society-centered approach to how social trust is created. Is it agents who already trust other citizens who join organizations, or is it the activity in the organizations that increases trust? Work by Dietlind Stolle and others seems to support the former thesis more than the latter. From her very interesting micro-level data, she concludes that 'it is not true that the longer and the more one associates, the greater one's generalized trust' (Stolle, 1998: 521). Using survey data from 55 countries, Newton and Delhey (2005) conclude that they find no support for the hypothesis that activity on voluntary associations increases social trust. Instead, they find that 'good government is an essential structural basis for trust' (2005: 323).

The major counter-argument to Putnam's societal theory about trust among citizens is that it can also be created 'from above': i.e., from the state. The argument is that governments can realize their capacity to generate trust only if citizens consider the state itself to be trustworthy (Newton and Delhey, 2005; Rothstein, 2011). States, for example, enable the establishment of contracts in that they provide information and monitor legislation, and enforce rights and rules that sanction lawbreakers, protect minorities and actively support the integration and participation of citizens. If the legal and administrative institutions are perceived as fair, just and (reasonably) efficient, this increases the likelihood that citizens will perceive other citizens as trustworthy (Dinesen, 2011;

Levi, 1998; Rothstein, 2005). The causal mechanism at the individual level between the 'quality of public administration' and social trust may hypothetically run as follows:

1 If public officials are known to be corrupted, citizens will infer that even individuals given the responsibility to guard the public interest are not to be trusted, and if they cannot be trusted, then nor can 'most people' be trusted.
2 Following this, citizens will infer that most people cannot be trusted because they are engaged in direct or indirect corruption of these government institutions.
3 In order to 'survive' under such a system, each citizen will find himself forced to engage in corruption, even if it is against his moral orientation. But because citizens cannot trust themselves to behave according to the rules, they are likely to infer that nor are 'other people' likely to play by the rules, and thus they cannot be trusted (Rothstein, 2011).

The causal mechanism I want to specify here is that social trust may run from trust in the quality of government institutions responsible for the implementation of public policies to trust in 'most people'. It makes little sense to trust 'most people' if they are generally known to bribe, threaten or in other ways corrupt the impartiality of government institutions in order to extract special favors. One reason 'most other people' may be trusted is that they are generally known to refrain from such forms of behavior (Putnam, 1993: 111).

More casually, here is a 'true story' that helps to illustrate our argument. *Lonely Planet* is one of the world's largest companies in the guidebook industry. This is how the police are described in its guide to the Yucatan peninsula in Mexico.

> Be advised that the federal police have been implicated in rapes and murders … so don't turn to them for help if you have been assaulted. Obviously, if you survive an attack and go to the police, only to recognize an officer as one of your assailants, he won't be likely to give you the chance to identify him in a court of law.

Thus, in a society where this type of perception of public officials is common, people will also trust other people in general to a much lower extent. If public officials, who are supposed to provide citizens with protection, cannot be trusted then what are the grounds for you to trust people in general? Even visitors from countries where the population is known to have unusually high levels of trust in other people are likely to change their mind about how wise it is to trust other people, let alone the police. In addition, they will of course also feel vulnerable and unprotected, which makes them fear strangers even more. No wonder that the wonderful beaches on the Yucatan peninsula are, to an astonishing degree, being occupied by 'all inclusive resorts', which is the name for 'gated communities' in the tourist industry.

As stated above, public programs can be designed so as to give more or less discretionary power to bureaucrats. For social programs, the more universal they are, the less room for discretion. Selective programs, on the other hand, must be implemented in a case-by-case manner, with considerable amounts of bureaucratic discretion. The difficulty of handling the discretionary power of administrators in selective programs has two important consequences. These consequences are often thought to be opposites, but in fact they are two sides of the same coin: they are the bureaucratic abuse of power, and fraud on the part of clients. Applicants in a selective system, if they are rational, will claim that their situation is worse than it actually is, and will describe their prospects for solving their problems on their own as small to non-existent. The administrators in such a system, for their part, often have incentives from their superiors to be suspicious of clients' claims.

Working with Swedish survey data, Staffan Kumlin divided the population according to if they had had personal contacts with selective welfare state institutions or not (Kumlin, 2004). The analyses show that experience with selective client-based public authorities (such as means-tested social assistance) has a sizeable and significant negative effect on generalized trust. This is not so surprising, given that this category probably belong to the 'have-nots' in Swedish society, who are generally low on trust (cf. Putnam, 2000: 193ff). What is surprising is that the negative impact on social trust from contacts with client-based selective public institutions holds when controlling for not only social class and income but also for membership in voluntary associations, satisfaction with the way that Swedish democracy works, political interest, life satisfaction and trust in politicians (Kumlin and Rothstein, 2005). One reason for the low levels of corruption and high levels of social trust in the Scandinavian countries may thus be that most of their social programs have been universal, not selective.

There are thus good arguments, both theoretical and empirical, for seeing the standard of a nation's public administration not only as caused by the level of social capital in that country but also as a causal factor in its own right behind high or low levels of social trust. As has been argued by Uslaner, people who in surveys report high levels of social trust are likely to think that not only will most other people 'play by the rules' in 'person-to-person' contacts but also they will 'play by the rules' in their contacts with government institutions. It has also been shown that people who in surveys report high levels of social trust also have a stronger confidence in public institutions, particularly in the legal system (Uslaner, 2002: 112). It should be noted that Putnam states a similar causal arrow in his Italian study, when he claims that the regions with the lowest amounts of social capital 'are the most subject to the ancient plague of political corruption' (Putnam, 1993: 111).

As in many other areas in the social sciences, what is cause and effect is often dependent on which time horizon is chosen. Even if Putnam's analysis stresses the importance of citizens' civic engagement and social trust for a well-functioning government

institution, he also recognizes that the causal mechanism is difficult to measure and opens up the possibility that well-functioning institutions may also influence social capital in a society. For example, the strength of various forms of organized crime in the southern Italian regions is, according to Putnam, based on traditional patterns of clientelism, which in turn has been caused 'by the weakness of the administrative and judicial structures of the state, in turn further undermining the authority of those structures' (Putnam, 1993: 146). While the correlation between social trust and corruption at the aggregate level is strong, it is very difficult to discern how it works at the individual level. Is it individuals who are already highly trusting who refrain from engaging in corruption, or is it corruption that breeds distrust?

This has important policy implications, not least when it comes to how to organize international aid to developing countries. One of the key debates in the social capital approach is between a more sociological approach, which argues social trust grows 'from below' when people come together in various voluntary associations, and the political approach, which stresses the importance of government institutions, not least the public administration (Hooghe and Stolle, 2003). If the sociological theory about social capital is correct, then the rich nations should try to find ways to channel aid to voluntary associations who organize people at the grassroots level and thereby increase trust and norms of reciprocity in society. The risk with this strategy is of course not only that the theory can be wrong but also that groups that discriminate on ethnic grounds or use their power to undermine the integrity of government institutions by resorting to clientelism, patronage and outright corruption will benefit from these resources. It could be argued that societies like Rwanda, Bosnia-Herzegovina and Northern Ireland have 'too much social capital' but of the wrong type. There is, as Putnam (2000) recognizes, also a 'dark side' of social capital and it is far from certain that it is at all possible to increase social capital in a society by supporting voluntary associations. The alternative approach would be to give support for increasing the 'quality of government' factor in developing countries. But where in a society where corruption and patronage is ingrained in the administrative culture can you find or create uncorrupted civil servants?

A case in point is Gary Miller's and Thomas Hammond's discussion of the use of the so-called 'city managers' as a successful way to get rid of corrupt party-machine politics in American cities during the interwar period. These were highly trained civil servants known for their high moral standards and for being disinterested, selfless servants of the public good. They had a reputation, that as a rule, they could not be bribed. But as Miller and Hammond state, '(t)o the extent that such a system works, it is clearly because city managers have been selected and/or trained not to be economic actors' (Miller and Hammond, 1994: 23). And, of course, there is then no collective action problem in the first place, because it is 'solved' by blurring the assumption about human behavior on which the model is built. Due to what is known about bureaucratic discretion, the possibility to solve this problem by implementing controls from above is very limited (cf. Brehm and Gates, 1997; Miller, 1992). Miller and Hammond's advice is thus very simple, namely: 'to find out how such disinterested altruistic actors are created, and then reproduce them throughout the political system' (Miller and Hammond, 1994: 24). Well, what more can you say, than 'good luck'. About this standard 'rule of law' solution, Barry Weingast has made a very important comment: namely, that '(a) government strong enough to protect property rights is also strong enough to confiscate the wealth of its citizens' (Weingast, 1993: 287). If a government has the power to establish the institutions to implement a 'rule of law' system, they would abuse that same power to break the 'rule of law' (i.e., infringe on property rights) if acting as agents in game theory are supposed to act. Without some kind of

social norms against such behavior, there is no solution to this problem (Rothstein, 2005).

NEO-CORPORATIST STRUCTURES AND BUREAUCRATIC LEGITIMACY

Another way to ensure legitimacy and trust is to give interest groups direct influence over the implementation process. These interest groups can be very different: from loosely formed networks to centralized national interest organizations (Jensen, 2011; Öberg et al., 2001; Traxler, 2010). The influence that the interest groups are given can also vary from informal consultation to formal representation in the boards of the public agencies in question. In some cases, the implementation of public policies has been entirely taken over directly by interest organizations. Research in this area started in the 1970s under the label 'neo-corporatism', which was launched by Philippe Schmitter in a seminal article in 1974 as an alternative to the pluralist understanding of how modern Western democracies actually operated (Schmitter, 1974).

The neo-corporatist model assumes that representatives from interest organizations that participate in the implementation of government policies are chosen, so that they enjoy the *confidence* of their constituents. A further assumption is that policy implementation is often successful only when the group towards which the policy is directed cooperates willingly. One way to elicit the group's collaboration is to grant the organization representing it an exclusive right to participate in the policy's execution. One of the reasons for allowing such organizational representatives to participate in administration is precisely that they

> are closer to the target group (their members) than state bureaucracies, and they have more intimate knowledge of its situation and concerns. It is likely that this enables them to apply rules less formalistically and to take the specific conditions

of individual cases better into account – which, in turn, tends to increase the acceptance of regulation by those affected by it (Streeck and Schmitter, 1985: 22).

It may be argued that, in addition to its suitability for legitimizing administrative decisions, this neo-corporatist model has one more advantage. The state can organize the representation from societal groups so as to create an arena for negotiation and compromise between different organizations. In the Northern European countries, this has often been the case in the implementation of labor market and industrial policies. By granting representation on administrative bodies to both sides of industry, state leaders hope to encourage decisions marked by compromise rather than confrontation (Lewin, 1992; Öberg et al., 2001). However, this means that in the neo-corporatist model the distinction between politics and administration is virtually erased, because neo-corporatism is characterized precisely by the institutional fusion of policy conception and execution, of political representation and intervention (Cawson, 1986: 185). Scholars in legal sociology and in law have noted that this fusion produces a new legal form, which they have termed 'reflexive law'. Such law does not govern the disposition of material things, but rather regulates the areas of competence of different societal systems, their organizational and institutional structures, and their forms for decision making (Brand, 1988; Lijphart and Crepaz, 1991).

Claus Offe has called attention to a critical distinction in this model: namely, that between different types of interest organizations. Certain organizations, on the one hand, may be said to generate their strength outside the state (Offe, 1986). They may represent producers with a strong market position (e.g., trade unions, employer organizations, and other *producer organizations*) or popular groups held together by strong ideological bonds (ethnic and religious organizations). Other interest organizations, by contrast, arise as a result of political programs, and acquire their revenues almost exclusively

from public sources (e.g., patient associations, pensioners' organizations and student unions). Organizations of the former kind naturally occupy a position of much greater strength as against the state, since they possess resources over which the state has no direct control. They may in fact be so strong as to be able, when dissatisfied, to prevent implementation of the policies in question. Organizations without such resources obviously find themselves in a much weaker position as against the state.

For both the state and the organizations, the efficiency of the neo-corporatist model rests on what seems to be a difficult balancing act. Over time, the organizations may risk losing their members' confidence if they come to be seen as defending the interests of the state first and foremost. The individual representatives may, over time, come to identify themselves more with the bureaucracy than with their organization. Their constituency may then start seeing them as co-opted, transformed into harmless instruments of state policy. Thus, if their collaboration with the state becomes too close, the model will lose its basis for creating legitimacy (Lewin, 1992; Öberg et al., 2001).

Public bureaucracies also sometimes form alliances with powerful interest organizations so as to increase their political clout against politicians who may want to influence them (or shut them down). Such bureaucratic strategies are known to be very effective and an important source of bureaucratic strength. Such alliances, sometimes known as policy networks or 'iron triangles', are known to be very powerful (i.e., the military–industrial complex). While such a strategy may be efficient to increase the administrations' legitimacy with some parts of society and some societal actors, it has also been known to decrease legitimacy within society as a whole (Offe, 1986).

There are certainly several other problems with this model. A central debate is whether or not neo-corporatist arrangements are harmful for democratic ideals or not. On the one hand, there are scholars arguing that such arrangements make it possible for a democratic government to solve important policy questions which could not be handled if interest organizations would not have been given influence over the implementation process. In this argument, inviting interest organizations to the implementation process can extend the democratic scope. The counter-argument is that neo-corporatism harms democratic ideals because they come into conflict with the principle of political equality. Simply put, some citizens (i.e., those who are members of interest organizations) get more influence than others do.

A second debate has to do with economic and managerial efficiency. Extended representation may create shortsighted 'rent-seeking' by interest organizations and bureaucracies, thereby harming the 'general interest' (Lewin, 1992). One or several interest organizations may 'capture' the bureaucracy in which they are represented and transform its operations so that it mostly serves 'special interests'. Contrary to this, there are studies showing that this model actually increases economic efficiency by making it possible to create working compromises between different societal actors for finding solutions to common problems, especially when it comes to industrial policy and the labor market (Katzenstein, 1994; Traxler, 2010).

USING USER GROUPS TO CREATE LEGITIMACY

Another way to increase legitimacy and handle the problem of discretion is to let the citizens who *directly* use a public service exercise influence over its operations (Barnes, 1999; Simmons and Birchall, 2005). We may then say that the service is organized according to the user-oriented model. In some advanced welfare states, the typical areas in which this model is applied are childcare, education, and care of the elderly. In some countries, students at universities have the right to participate in certain decision-making organs. The hope is that services applying the user-oriented model will appear legitimate in the eyes of their users, since, it is thought, users cannot lack confidence in an institution over which they have been able to exercise influence.

The users are those persons (or in the case of children, the parent) that are physically present when a service is provided. This presents the user-oriented model with its first problem – such persons may feel inhibited from criticizing the service in question. Clients may find it difficult, for instance, openly to criticize the staff on which they are dependent for the daily satisfaction of their needs. It is clear that staff persons – who sometimes entertain specific professional notions about how to run things – enjoy an advantage over users. The precise relation between the influence of personnel and that of users is difficult to establish. In some cases, it is not clear who is to be regarded as a user, in what form decisions shall be taken, what areas users have the right to decide over, and what responsibility they bear for their decisions. In some areas, such as sport and cultural facilities, local government agencies sometimes create networks with voluntary associations, who are invited to take part in operating the facilities. In the Scandinavian countries, this model of user influence has been motivated by the need to get more people interested in participating in the representative democratic process (Jarl, 2005).

Several other problems exist with this way of creating legitimacy. For example, it is unclear what should be done in the case of conflicts among users. Should the minority submit to the will of the majority? Yet another problem with this model is that it tends to favor persons with (a) abundant time resources, who are (b) highly interested in influencing the program, and who (c) possess abundant resources in terms of information, education and experience in decision-making organs. In relation to the democratic ideal – that all citizens possess equal worth – this makes the user-group model problematic.

CONCLUSION

It has for long been taken for granted that the most important factor for citizens to perceive their government as legitimate is the extent to which they are in possession of democratic rights for influencing 'Who governs'. Recent empirical research shows that the democratic rights are not the most important factor for creating political legitimacy. Instead, citizens' perception of the quality of the public administration is more important than are democratic rights for creating political legitimacy. This may be related to yet another surprising empirical finding: namely, that 'quality of government' factors such as control of corruption, the rule of law and impartial civil service have a much stronger impact on almost all measures of human well-being than have countries' level of democracy. These two results from recent empirical research imply that the quality of a society's public administration is more important both for the political system's overall legitimacy and for the well-being of its citizens than have hitherto been the 'generally accepted wisdom'. The public administration in a country has different sources of legitimacy: one is, of course, connected to the 'tool' question. As stated by Schmuel Eisenstadt, the central question in this approach is 'whether the bureaucracy is master or servant, an independent political body or a tool, and if a tool, who's interests it can be made to serve' (Eisenstadt, 1965: 171). A bureaucracy that cannot be steered by elected officials will sooner or later get into legitimacy problems. However, this 'legitimacy from above' is not the only and may be not even the most important source of legitimacy for government agencies. Its relation to the surrounding society, individual citizens as well as various interest organizations, may be even more crucial. In this chapter I have pointed out three such sources of 'legitimacy from below'. One is the relation between the public administration and social capital. Although this approach usually has been connected to the importance of civic networks and voluntary associations, it has also important implications for the study of various dimensions of the public administration. First, the 'quality of government' factor may be a result of the amount of social capital in a society. Second, the structure and operations of the civil service may also be a cause behind the level of social trust and social capital in a society. Two other sources of legitimacy have also been discussed: neo-corporatism and systems' user influence. All these three ways of connecting the public administration to the society it is supposed to serve may very well be connected. It may, or may not, be an accidental occurrence that the countries which score highest in surveys about social trust – namely, the Scandinavian countries – are among those where neo-corporatist arrangements (and to a lesser extent, models of user influence) have been most elaborated.

REFERENCES

Barker, Rodney (1980) *Political Legitimacy and the State*. Oxford: Clarendon Press.

Barnes, Marian (1999) 'Users as Citizens: Collective Action and the Local Governance of Welfare', *Social Policy & Administration*, 33: 73–90.

Becker, Gary S. (1997) *The Economics of Life: From Baseball to Affirmative Action to Immigration. How Real-World Issues Affect Our Everyday Life*. New York: McGraw-Hill.

Beetham, David (1985) *Max Weber and the Theory of Modern Politics*. Cambridge: Polity Press.

Bendor, Jonathan and Swistak, Piotr (1997) 'The Evolutionary Stability of Cooperation', *American Political Science Review*, 91 (2): 290–307.

Braithwaite, Valerie and Levi, Margaret (eds) (1998) *Trust and Governance*. New York: Russell Sage Foundation.

Brand, Donald (1988) *Corporatism and the Rule of Law*. Itacha, NY: Cornell University Press.

Bräutigam, Deborah, Fjeldstad, Odd-Helge, et al. (2008) *Taxation and State-Building in Developing Countries: Capacity and Consent.* New York: Cambridge University Press.

Brehm, John and Gates, Scott (1997) *Working, Shirking, and Sabotage. Bureaucratic Response to a Democratic Public.* Ann Arbor, MI: University of Michigan Press.

Castiglione, D., van Deth, Jan W. et al. (eds) (2008) *The Handbook of Social Capital.* Oxford: Oxford University Press.

Catlaw, Thomas J. and Hu, Quin (2009) 'Legitimacy and Public Administration Constructing the American Bureaucratic Fields', *American Behavioral Scientist,* 53 (3): 458–481.

Cawson, Alan (1986) *Corporatism and Political Theory.* Oxford: Blackwell.

Charron, Nichals, Lapuente, Victor et al. (2012) 'Regional Governance Matters: A Study on Regional Variation in Quality of Government within the EU', *Regional Studies* (forthcoming).

Coleman, James S. (1990) *Foundations of Social Theory.* Cambridge, MA: The Belknap Press of Harvard University Press.

Cook, Karen S. (ed.) (2001). *Trust in Society.* New York: Russell Sage Foundation.

Diamond, Larry (2008) 'The Democratic Rollback: The Resurgence of the Predatory State', *Foreign Affairs,* 87 (2): 36–48.

Dinesen, Peter Thisted (2011) *When in Rome, Do as the Romans Do. An Analysis of the Acculturation of Generalized Trust of non-Western Immigrants in Western Europe* (Diss.). Aarhus: Deparment of Political Science, Aarhus University.

du Gay, Paul (2000) *In Praise of Bureaucracy: Weber, Organization and Ethics.* London: Sage Publications.

Eisenstadt, Schmuel N. (1965) *Essays in Comparative Institutions.* New York: Wiley.

Friedman, Kathie V. (1981) *Legitimation of Social Rights and the Western Welfare State.* Chapel Hill, NC: The University of North Carolina Press.

Fukuyama, Francis (2011) *The Origins of Political Order: From Prehuman Times to the French Revolution.* New York: Farrar, Straus and Giroux.

Gilley, Bruce (2006) 'The Determinants of State Legitimacy: Results for 72 countries'. *International Political Science Review,* 27 (1): 47–71.

Gilley, Bruce (2009) *The Right to Rule: How States Win and Lose Legitimacy.* New York: Columbia University Press.

Holmberg, Sören, Rothstein, Bo and Nasiritousi, Naghmeh (2009) 'Quality of Government: What You Get', *Annual Review of Political Science,* 13: 135–162.

Hooghe, Marc and Stolle, Dietlind (eds) (2003) *Generating Social Capital: The Role of Voluntary Associations, Institutions and Government Policy.* New York: Palgrave Macmillan.

Rauch, James E. (2000) 'Bureaucratic Structure and Bureaucratic Performance in Less Developed Countries', *Journal of Public Economics,* 75: 49–71.

Jarl, Maria (2005) 'Making User-boards a School in Democracy? Studying Swedish Local Governments', *Scandinavian Political Studies,* 28 (3): 277–294.

Jensen, Carsten (2011) 'Negotiated Expansion: Left-wing Governments, Corporatism and Social Expenditure in Mature Welfare States', *Comparative European Politics,* 9: 168–190.

Katzenstein, Peter J. (1994) *Corporatism and Change.* Ithaca, NY: Cornell University Press.

Kumlin, Staffan (2004) *The Personal and the Political: How Personal Welfare State Experiences Affect Political Trust and Ideology.* New York: Palgrave Macmillan.

Kumlin, Staffan and Rothstein, Bo (2005) 'Making and Breaking Social Capital. The Impact of Welfare State Institutions', *Comparative Political Studies,* 38: 339–365.

La Porta, Rafael, Lopez-de-Silanes, Florencio, et al. (1997) 'Trust in Large Organizations', *American Economic Review,* 87 (2): 333–338.

La Porta, Rafael, Lopez-de-Silanes, Florencio, et al. (1999) 'The Quality of Government', *Journal of Law, Economics and Organization,* 15 (1): 222–279.

Levi, Margaret (1998) *Consent, Dissent, and Patriotism.* New York: Cambridge University Press.

Lewin, Leif (1992) 'The Rise and Decline of Corporatism', *European Journal of Political Research,* 26 (1): 59–79.

Lijphart, Arend and Crepaz, Markus M. L. (1991) 'Corporatism and Consensus Democracy in Eighteen Countries', *British Journal of Political Science,* 21 (2): 235–256.

Lipsky, Michael (1980) *Street-Level Bureaucracy: Dilemmas of the Individual in Public Services.* New York: Russell Sage Foundation.

Miller, Gary J. (1992) *Managerial Dilemmas. The Political Economy of Hierachy.* New York: Cambridge University Press.

Miller, Gary J. and Hammond, Thomas (1994) 'Why Politics is More Fundamental than Economics: Incentive-Compatible Mechanisms are not Credible', *Journal of Theoretical Politics,* 6 (1): 5–26.

Newton, Kenneth (1999) 'Social and Political Trust in Established Democracies', in P. Norris (ed.), *Critical Citizens. Global Support for Democratic Government.* New York: Oxford University Press, pp. 323–351.

Newton, Kenneth and Delhey, Jan (2005) 'Predicting cross-national levels of social trust: Global pattern or nordic exceptionalism?', *European Sociological Review*, 21: 311–327.

Norris, Pippa (2012) *Democratic Governance and Human Security: The Impact of Regimes on Prosperity, Welfare and Peace*. New York: Cambridge University Press (forthcoming).

North, Douglass C. and Wallis, John J. et al. (2009) *Violence and Social Orders: A Conceptual Framework for Interpreting Recorded Human History*. New York: Cambridge University Press.

Öberg, Per-Ola, Svensson, Torsten, et al. (2001) 'Disrupted Exchange and Declining Corporatism: Government Authority and Interest Group Capability in Scandinavia', *Government and Opposition*, 46: 365–391.

Offe, Claus (1984) *The Contradictions of the Welfare State*. London: Hutchinson.

Offe, Claus (1986) *Disorganized Capitalism: Contemporary Transformations of Work and Politics*. London, Polity Press.

Olsen, Johan P. (2006) 'Maybe it is Time to Rediscover Bureaucracy', *Journal of Public Administration Research and Theory*, 16 (1): 1–24.

Ostrom, Elinor (1998) 'A Behavioral Approach to the Rational Choice Theory of Collective Action', *American Political Science Review*, 92 (1): 1–23.

Ott, Jan C. (2010) 'Good Governance and Happiness in Nations: Technical Quality Precedes Democracy and Quality Beats Size', *Journal of Happiness Studies*, 11 (3): 353–368.

Putnam, Robert D. (1993) *Making Democracy Work: Civic Traditions in Modern Italy*. Princeton, NJ: Princeton University Press.

Putnam, Robert D. (1995) 'Tuning In, Tuning Out: The Strange Disappearance of Social Capital in America', *PS: Political Science and Politics*, 28 (4): 664–683.

Putnam, Robert D. (2000) *Bowling Alone: The Collapse and Revival of American Community*. New York: Simon & Schuster.

Rodrik, Dani (2007) *One Economics, Many Recipes: Globalization, Institutions and Economic Growth*. Princeton, NJ: Princeton University Press.

Rothstein, Bo (1998) *Just Institutions Matter: The Moral and Political Logic of the Universal Welfare State*. Cambridge: Cambridge University Press.

Rothstein, Bo (2005) *Social Traps and the Problem of Trust*. Cambridge: Cambridge University Press.

Rothstein, Bo (2011) *The Quality of Government: Corruption, Social Trust and Inequality in a Comparative Perspective*. Chicago, IL: University of Chicago Press.

Schmitter, Phillipe C. (1974) 'Still the Century of Corporatism?', *Review of Politics*, 36: 34–76.

Simmons, Richard and Birchall, Johnston (2005) 'A Joined-up Approach to User Participation in Public Services: Strengthening the "Participation Chain"', *Social Policy & Administration*, 39: 260–283.

Smith, B. C. (2007) *Good Governance and Development*. New York: Palgrave Macmillan.

Stolle, Dietlind (1998) 'Bowling Together, Bowling Alone: The Development of Generalized Trust in Voluntary Associations', *Political Psychology*, 19 (3): 497–526.

Streeck, Wolfgang and Schmitter, Philippe C. (eds) (1985) *Private Interest Government: Beyond Market and State*. London: Sage Publications.

Svendsen, G. T. and Svendsen, G. L. H. (eds) (2009) *Handbook of Social Capital: The Troika of Sociology, Political Science and Economics*. Cheltenham: Edward Elgar.

Sztompka, Piotr (1998) 'Trust, Distrust and Two Paradoxes of Democracy', *European Journal of Social Theory*, 1 (1): 19–32.

Traxler, Franz (2010) 'The Long-term Development of Organised Business and its Implications for Corporatism: A Cross-national Comparison of Membership, Activities and Governing Capacities of Business Interest Associations, 1980–2003', *European Journal of Political Research*, 49: 151–173.

Treisman, Daniel (2000) 'The Causes of Corruption: A Cross-National Study', *Journal of Public Economics*, 76 (3): 399–457.

Uslaner, Eric M. (2008) *Corruption, Inequality, and the Rule of Law*. New York: Cambridge University Press.

Weber, Max (1919/1989) *The Profession of Politics* (edited, translated, and introduced by Simona Draghici). Washington, DC: Plutarch Press.

Weingast, Barry R. (1993) 'Constitutions as Governance Structures – The Political Foundations of Secure Markets', *Journal of Institutional and Theoretical Economics*, 149: 286–311.

Woolcook, Michael (2001) 'The Place of Social Capital in Understanding Social and Economic Outcomes', *ISUMA – Canadian Journal of Policy Research*, 2 (1): 12–15.

23

Representative Bureaucracy: Four Questions

Kenneth J. Meier and K. Jurée Capers

Representative bureaucracy, a major theoretical concept in public administration, concerns the ability of the bureaucracy to represent the general public. Mosher (1968; see also Pitkin 1967) distinguished between passive representation that focuses on origins and demographic characteristics of bureaucrats, that is, the degree to which they mirror the society (also termed symbolic representation), and active representation when bureaucrats advocate for constituents' interests (also termed substantive representation). Originally, representative bureaucracy hinged on the idea that bureaucracies are reflective of the dominant class in society and no group could be trusted if it is not reflective of such (Kingsley 1944; Krislov 1974). A group of US scholars (Levitan 1946; Long 1952; Van Riper 1958) refocused the theory on the ability of bureaucrats to represent the general public not just the dominant class in society.

This chapter will address four key questions in regard to representative bureaucracy. First, what characteristics should a bureaucracy represent? Second, what factors determine how representative a bureaucracy is?

Third, how might passive representation lead to active representation and greater policy responsiveness? Fourth, does representation influence how effective bureaucracies can be?

WHAT SHOULD BE REPRESENTED?

Before addressing what characteristics bureaucracies should represent, one might first address whether or not bureaucracies should be representative institutions at all. Many argue that representation is best provided to the public by representatives who can be held accountable to citizens through the traditional democratic processes of elections. Representation by bureaucrats, as a result, is controversial and generally opposed by elected officials since they see representation as an infringement on their own political role (see Daley 1984).

Proponents of representative bureaucracy (Long 1952) contend that representation by political institutions is incomplete and often hampered by majority rule provisions that consider some interests and ignore others. A bureaucracy representative of the diverse population and the wide range of preferences and interests unique to this population, advocates contend, is one way to improve democratic representation. Bureaucratic representation provides a means for the interests and preferences of the minority to be represented by allowing the minority to regain the representation lost through the electoral process. The argument continues that bureaucrats, as public officials, are also accountable for the results of their work (Lipsky 1980; Hupe and Hill 2007). They are subject to performance evaluations, loss in funding or budgetary support, and loss of their clientele base, making them equally, if not more, accountable to citizens than public officials.

Although many scholars justify the study of representative bureaucracy by arguing that bureaucracies can be more responsive to the needs of politically under-representative groups, the representativeness of bureaucracies merits study in its own right. A representative bureaucracy is a symbol of openness and equality to citizens. What characteristics should be represented? Any individual has multiple identities – German, immigrant, woman, Lutheran, Hessian, plumber, and so on. Issues of passive representation might deal with the full range of potential identities; but, in practice, a nation's politics defines which identities are likely to be pushed for representation. This means that the identities seeking representation vary across nations and can vary within a nation across time. Ethnicity/race is frequently the variable that demands representation in the bureaucracy. Although the literature is dominated by American scholars who focus on race and ethnicity, ethnic political cleavages are common in a great many countries (e.g., South Africa, Belgium, Columbia, Zambia; see Dresang 1974). Many ethnic identities are tied to indigenous populations as in much of North and South America and Australia. Others exist owing to long-standing conflict and perceived oppression (Serbia, Bosnia, Macedonia, etc.).

Immigration also contributes to additional ethnic conflict and reinforces the distinct identities of the immigrant populations, a process currently playing out in many of the developed countries in Europe, including France, Denmark, Germany, and the United Kingdom. Ethnicity often correlates with religious and language differences, and so representation might focus on a bundle of identities such as in Quebec, Belgium, or Lebanon.

Demands for representation in the bureaucracy also focus on geographic regions (early United States, South Korea), social class (United Kingdom, Thailand, India), disability (numerous countries), and gender (numerous countries). In most cases these cleavages are also strongly linked to political issues about equity, such as political movements for gender equality, the Cholla province issue in South Korea (P. S. Kim 1993; H. Kim 2005) or the economic status of poor, rural areas in Thailand.

Politics will define the identities that are salient. Naff (2007) shows that South Africa's concerns have moved from race to tribal affiliation. This shift is consistent with recent work on other African countries, for example, that shows over a period of time how politics favors some groups rather than others; and, as a result, can have a dramatic impact on ethnic identification (Posner 2006; Habyarimana et al. 2009). Just as national politics and history shape identity salience, so do specific bureaucratic actions. Bureaucracies can emphasize one identity or downplay others in implementing policy, and citizens are likely to recognize this pattern.

WHAT ARE THE DETERMINANTS OF PASSIVE REPRESENTATION?

Empirical studies of the determinants of representative bureaucracy have been dominated by examinations of US bureaucracies and focused on US salient identities – race, ethnicity, and gender. That is unfortunate since it limits our knowledge about both the extent of bureaucratic representation and the determinants of that representation. The nature of these limits can best be illustrated by two overly simplified but polar types – the Weberian rational bureaucracy and the patronage bureaucracy. Weber's (1946) ideal-typical bureaucracy seeks to maximize rationality and, therefore, uses merit or surrogates for merit such as education as a recruitment criterion. Patronage bureaucracies are less concerned with merit and more concerned with loyalty and use that as a recruitment criterion. Neither bureaucracy is likely to be widely represented of the general public simply because neither education nor political loyalty is likely to be evenly distributed in society.

Because there is so little research on patronage bureaucracies, this review of the determinants will focus on the determinants in Weberian-style bureaucracies. Clearly, the most important barrier to representative bureaucracies is the education level of the population (see Subramaniam 1967; Meier 1975: 537). Although bureaucracies are never a microcosm of the population, they approach equality as the population becomes better educated. To the degree that access to education is not equally distributed across the salient identities for representation in a country, bureaucracies will be unrepresentative of the population.

The US empirical research with different studies examining local, state, and national bureaucracies generally finds that the strongest determinant of minority representation in a bureaucracy is the minority population in the jurisdiction. This is essentially a trivial finding since population can be the strongest predictor whether bureaucracies are highly representative or not representative at all; what matters in these cases is the magnitude of the regression coefficient: i.e., whether the group gets 90 percent of the representation needed for equity or only 10 percent.

The political nature of representative bureaucracy is reinforced by the scholarship that shows representation at the bureaucratic level is related to political representation by the same groups. The work has discovered significant relationships in US cities for representation on the city council (Dye and Renick 1981; Eisinger 1982; Lewis 1989) or as the elected chief administrative officer (Stein 1986; Saltzstein 1989) for racial groups. A parallel literature shows similar impacts in US cities for gender (Saltzstein 1986; Sigelman 1976); and, cross-nationally, Whitford, Wilkins, and Ball (2007) find that political representation for women in high ministerial positions is positively related to gender representation in the bureaucracy in 72 countries. Within a bureaucracy, studies show that representation at top administrative levels in the organization is generally the strongest determinant of representation at lower levels for both race and gender (Meier, O'Toole, and Nicholson-Crotty 2004; Goode and Baldwin 2005; Whitford et al. 2007). The implementation of specific policies, such as affirmative action or quotas, to increase bureaucratic representation, is also linked to more representative bureaucracies (Saltzstein 1986; Naff 2007).

A key limit to these studies, in addition to their US orientation, is that they generally are not effective in separating out how much of the representation is determined by the available labor pool and how much is determined by these other factors. Cross-sectional studies on race and ethnicity, in particular, examine jurisdictions with widely varying labor pools, particularly when one considers the educational requirements for bureaucratic jobs. Minority populations are also highly collinear with minority political resources, and few studies seek to separate out these factors.

The avoidance of a second key causality issue also comes up in a set of studies that challenge what is presented as a top-down process of representation: that is, political representation generates representation at high levels of the bureaucracy and this bureaucratic representation produces correspondingly high representation at the street level of bureaucracy. Two studies, both on school systems in the United States, demonstrate that these relationships are reciprocal. While political representation does influence bureaucratic representation, bureaucratic representation also influences the level of political representation (Meier and Smith 1994; Meier and O'Toole 2006).

WHAT IS THE LINK BETWEEN PASSIVE AND ACTIVE REPRESENTATION?

The basic theory for expecting passive representation to generate active representation is fairly simple, but in recent years the theory has been elaborately revised to focus on the specific situations when active representation might occur. Thompson (1976) effectively summarized the early theory between passive and active representation. He highlights the potential barriers to active representation, yet contends that under certain circumstances these barriers may be breached so that passive representation leads to active representation. He concludes that a passive-to-active linkage is possible when groups and institutions recognize and "press" for minority interests; when issues hold obvious ramifications for one's group; and when there is employee mobilization, support, and discretion (Thompson 1976).

Scholars examining this relationship have found mixed support for the argument that passive representation does in fact lead to active representation. Researchers such as Hindera (1993) and Selden (1997) examining passive and active representation linkages in federal bureaucracies have found evidence of such linkages. Researchers have also found evidence of likely linkages within local and state governments (Bradbury and Kellough 2008). Other bureaucratic agencies such as social service providers and school districts have also been used to investigate and support linkages between passive and active representation (Meier 1984; Wilkins and Keiser 2006).

Keiser et al. (2002) attempted to integrate the previous findings on representative bureaucracy and build a full theoretical framework for when passive representation might result in outcomes favorable to the group in question (which they defined as active representation). They identified seven key variables that constitute the core factors affecting the bureaucratic representation process – discretion, organizational mission, organizational socialization, hierarchy, stratification, critical mass, and professionalization.

First, bureaucrats must exercise discretion, and this discretion must overlap with the issues/values that are salient to the identity in question. Many issues that bureaucrats deal with are not related to the relevant identity, and many other bureaucracies, including the patronage ones, have little discretion (see Van Gool 2008). Keiser et al. (2002) provide an elaborate discussion of when an issue becomes salient, focusing on their concern – issues linked to gender. The specifics of their arguments about salience are less crucial here than their basic contention that such issues are defined politically either by the state or by individuals not benefiting from state actions.

Subsequent studies have revealed that the degree of discretion itself varies at different levels within an organization as well as across organizations. Policy discretion linked to representative bureaucracy has been found at lower levels in schools, police forces, and firefighters (Meier and Stewart 1992; Meier and Nicholson-Crotty 2006; Ashworth and Andrews 2010), at mid-management levels in child support enforcement (Wilkins and Keiser 2006), and at upper levels in schools and federal contracting decisions (Theobald 2007; Smith and Fernandez 2010). In each case, bureaucratic discretion worked to alter policy implementation to allow outputs and outcomes favored by a particular group to occur.

Scholars such as Hindera and Young (1998) contend that the link between passive and active representation is conditional. That is, only under certain situations or conditions will passive representation lead to active representation. Hindera and Young's (1998) research shows a dynamic relationship between passive and active representation. More specifically, they find that when minorities are the plurality, majority, or there is a critical mass, the link between passive and active representation varies among the range of bureaucratic environments (Hindera and Young 1998). Unlike the studies focused on finding a link, this study observes challenges to the link and the conditions under which the link is likely to vary. Minorities are expected to represent differently once a critical mass in the bureaucracy is met and surpassed.

Second, bureaucratic agencies are goal-oriented collectives, and so their mission greatly influences whether discretion is relevant to the identity in question. Some agencies are set up to advocate, particularly the clientele agencies in most countries that implement policy in regard to farmers, labor, business, veterans, and others. In other cases, the organization is not set up to directly advocate for individuals; but in the process of making bureaucratic decisions, individual bureaucrats can advocate for a specific group of people or for an individual from that group.

Third, organizational socialization seeks to instill the values of the organization in the individual bureaucrats. Socialization can include training programs, standard operating procedures, incentives for promotion, and even the history of the organization. Much of the orientation, policies, and procedures of the various agencies try to squeeze out the influence of the bureaucrat's individual characteristics and generate uniform decisions via a common acceptance of values. Wilkins and Williams (2008, 2009) demonstrate that some police forces successfully manage to suppress ethnic identities via organizational socialization. While all agencies and public services socialize employees, the extent of socialization varies a great deal. As the degree of socialization increases, the

link between passive and active representation will be attenuated, except in those cases where the agency's mission is to serve the population of the represented group.

Fourth, hierarchy is used by organizations to limit discretion and, therefore, prevent bureaucratic representation. Bureaucratic representation should be enhanced, theoretically, in more decentralized agencies where bureaucrats are allowed greater discretion, allowing them to make decisions in the interests of the represented group. Meier and Bohte (2001) found that representational outputs are enhanced in more decentralized organizations, as did Keiser et al. (2002). Sowa and Selden (2003) show a corresponding result for US state government agencies. A decentralized organization can also cultivate different values in different parts of the organization and thus permit representation across a wider spectrum of interests.

Fifth, stratification concerns the location of the representative group within the bureaucratic hierarchy. As individuals move up the hierarchy in a bureaucracy, they should have a greater ability to affect agency outcomes; therefore, passive representation at the top of the bureaucracy should increase active representation. Theobald (2007) shows that Latino superintendents, the key decision makers for school districts, are able to allocate more funds to bilingual education. Smith and Fernandez (2010) demonstrate that US federal agencies with more minorities in top management positions also allocated a larger percentage of contracts to minority-owned businesses. Keiser et al. (2002), in their study of gender and schools, discovered an interaction effect; while top-level women were not directly associated with better performance by female students, the impact of female teachers was substantially larger when women were well represented in management.

Sixth, many scholars argue that a single isolated bureaucrat is unlikely to have much influence in an organization, and may, in fact, feel uncomfortable advocating the interests of a group. This logic implies that there needs to be a critical mass of bureaucrats who share some identity before any representation will occur, a position first articulated by management theorist Rosabeth Moss Kanter (1993), who postulated that 15 percent was the critical mass. While the argument has intuitive appeal, the evidence of it is mixed and appears to depend on the level of the organization. Work on US schools shows that teachers, lower-level personnel, do not need a critical mass to influence student assignments, discipline, and performance. At the management level, a critical mass is needed; but the level is closer to 25 percent than the 15 percent that Kanter hypothesized. These results held for both racial minorities (Meier and Stewart 1992) and women (Keiser et al. 2002).

Seventh, professionalism is a major alternative source of bureaucratic identity, and it can act counter to other identities. Much of professional training includes sets of values and ways to approach problems; these values and processes rarely allow for such things as race, ethnicity, or similar factors. Professionalism's impact on bureaucratic representation, however, can also act in a different way. Sometimes, professionalism supports advocacy and the resulting development of active representation. Helping professions such as teaching, nursing, and public health often contain a normative commitment to helping disadvantaged clientele in dealing with bureaucracy or other problems (see Guy, Newman, and Mastracci 2008). Professionals are also likely to have more job security and autonomy, which permits them to exercise greater discretion should they opt to do so.

Other theoretical work has raised the issue that existing studies do not actually demonstrate that there is active representation; rather, they have found a correlation between passive representation and bureaucratic outcomes that benefit the represented. With only few exceptions (see Selden 1997; Bradbury and Kellough 2008), the empirical literature deals with collective representation not individual representation in this way.

Meier, Wrinkle, and Polinard (1999), in their study of minority teachers, suggest that the correlation taken as representation can occur for four different reasons.

First, there might actually be active representation: that is, the bureaucrat acts for the client and in the process benefits the client. Second, the representation might occur indirectly because the presence of the minority bureaucrat influences other non-minority bureaucrats to change their behavior. In this case, a bureaucrat does something different, but it is not the bureaucrat who shares the representative trait with the client. Third, the representation might occur through changes in the policies and procedures of the organization. The bureaucratic representatives are likely to play a role in the discussions in the organization and whether or not policies or procedures have institutionalized biases in regard to the represented clientele. The bureaucrat, therefore, represents by advocating for changes in the standard operating procedures of the organization. All three of these processes include some aspects of active representation in the sense of the adoption of a representation role by the bureaucrat (Selden 1997). Finally, the client changes his or her behavior as a result of the characteristics of the bureaucrat. In the education context, this is termed the "role model" effect, but the process can occur outside the education arena (see Meier and Nicholson-Crotty 2006). In this last case, active representation does not occur.

Lim (2006) takes a compatible view and argues for passive representation's other substantive benefits beyond leading to active representation, which he considers "direct source benefits." It may also produce indirect substantive benefits that are overlooked in studies on the linkage between active and passive representation. His theoretical evaluation of the literature suggests that passive representation may lead to behavioral changes for bureaucrats (both minority and non-minority) and clients, leading to greater benefits for minority clients. Therefore, studies on passive representation that do not consider passive representations' independent effects on group benefits may be wrongly attributing benefits to active representation.

Meier and Nicholson-Crotty (2006) test this theory, finding clients and bureaucrats do change their behavior with increases in passive gender representation. Women were more likely to report sexual assaults as the level of passive representation increased via more female police officers (Meier and Nicholson-Crotty 2006). Additionally, they credit having more female officers on a police force to changes in male colleagues' sensitivity to gender issues. Similar to Lim's (2006) argument, their findings also indicate an additional benefit to passive representation without any action from the bureaucrat. Changes in client behavior make passive representation more important and suggest an additional linkage complication to the literature, highlighting passive and active linkages based on observed policy outcomes.

Building somewhat on Lim's (2006) research and Meier and Nicholson-Crotty's (2006) findings, Herman's (2007) research considers how passive representation in the bureaucracy may produce benefits to clients from client action. Clients may decide that having some type of passive representation is enough to change their behavior and opinions toward the bureaucracy (Herman 2007). Specifically, he looks for two ways that passive representation may produce benefits: better communication between the client and the bureaucrat (or bureaucracy) and increasing the likelihood that the client will use the bureaucracy's services – termed "demand inducement," (Herman 2007). He finds that passive representation does produce the expected benefits, but only under certain conditions. The extent that passive representation produces benefits is dependent on a clients' past experiences with the bureaucracy, their need for the bureaucracy's services, and the institutional structure of the bureaucracy; these findings are particularly strong for African-American respondents (Herman 2007).

Theobald and Haider-Markel (2009) also question the literature on the linkage between passive, or symbolic representation in their study's context, and active representation. They consider the symbolic effect that passive representation may have on clients' attitudes toward a bureaucratic agency. Similar to Meier and Nicholson-Crotty (2006) and Herman (2007), their work also notes the effect passive representation may have on clients. By examining the public attitudes on the legitimacy of police actions after their interactions with an officer of the same race or a different race, Theobald and Haider-Markel (2009) find that passive representation influences clients' perceptions and attitudes toward bureaucratic action. Black respondents confronted by Black officers were more likely to view the bureaucrat's action as legitimate.

Additional extensions further probe the passive representation–policy outcome linkage in education. Meier, Wrinkle, and Polinard (1999) conduct research on the effects of passive representation on students' academic performance to determine if the presence of minority teachers will improve the performance of minority students. However, their research moves beyond looking at the benefits of passive representation to also consider the possible negative consequences of greater passive representation for one group and less passive representation for another group. Essentially, they seek to find the range of consequences for passive representation. They find a positive relationship between the percentage of minority teachers and minority students' academic performance. They also find an increase in white students' pass rate as the percentage of minority teachers increases, suggesting a benefit to minority passive representation for whites also, particularly in districts with greater equity.

Similarly, Weiher (2000) also finds a relationship between passive representation and student performance outcomes. He notes that the performance of minority students are "consistently depressed" when there is a shortfall of minority teachers. For Latino students, a decrease in the percentage of Latino teachers could lead to a 14 point decrease in Latino students' performance overall. Black students could experience a 26 point decrease in their performance overall if the percentage of Black teachers decreased (Weiher 2000). Although this research is similar to Meier et al.'s, Weiher uses distinct model specification techniques. He operationalizes minority teacher population by taking the difference between the percentage of Black/Latino teachers and percentage of Black/Latino students, while Meier et al. simply use a combined percentage of Black and Latino teachers. Weiher's measure highlights the "minority teacher shortfall" issue, and it also allows one to see the exact effects for Black and Latinos when not lumped together as a "minority" group.

There have also been less quantitative studies that pose questions of passive representation and representative bureaucracy. Thielemann and Stewart (1996) examine the "demand side" of representative bureaucracy. More specifically, they investigate if there is an actual demand or desire from represented clients for a representative bureaucracy. Thielemann and Stewart (1996) theorize a client's willingness to seek out services, treatments, or preventive measures may depend on who is providing the services, essentially affecting the effectiveness of service delivery. Using survey data of people living with AIDS in Dallas, Texas, they find results suggesting a demand for a more representative bureaucracy (Thielemann and Stewart 1996). Passive representation on the dimensions of race, gender, and sexual orientation mattered; however, representation from service providers compared to service directors mattered more (Thielemann and Stewart 1996). This suggests that active representation matters greatly and possibly more than passive representation; however, passive representation is still relevant to receiving this active representation. As the population of people affected by AIDS becomes more diverse, the demand and

competition for resources and services increases. Consequently, a representative bureaucracy in AIDS services is becoming increasingly important (Thielemann and Stewart 1996). This research is particularly interesting because it checks the relevance of representative bureaucracy in an area where it would seem to matter a great deal – health care. It provides proof to an assumption that is made in nearly every representative bureaucracy service – the services provided by the "representative" bureaucracy are those that the client wants, needs, and would be interested in receiving.

REPRESENTATIVE BUREAUCRACY AND PERFORMANCE: EVALUATING BUREAUCRATIC EFFECTIVENESS

A general perception is that there is a trade-off between representation and organizational performance (Lim 2006). The argument is based on the idea that organizations maximize efficiency and that any deviation from that such as representation will reduce performance. At the same time, if the representativeness of the bureaucracy causes the client to change behavior, then there is a possibility that improvement – particularly in cases of co-production – in results will occur. The relationship between bureaucratic representation and performance was first examined in a study of representative bureaucracy and education in Texas (Meier et al. 1999, 2001). Those articles examined cross-group tradeoffs: that is, whether an increase in minority teachers negatively affected the performance of non-minority students. As part of the analysis, a bold, aggressive hypothesis was put forth that representative bureaucracies would be more effective than non-representative bureaucracies. The hypothesis was supported theoretically by the work of Gary Becker (1993), who argued that discrimination in employment would create inefficiencies for an organization. Meier et al. (1999, 2001) suggested that an unrepresentative bureaucracy would reveal management's preferences for certain types of employees and those preferences would likely result in reduced organizational performance. The empirical study found that not only were White students (non-minorities) not negatively affected by minority teachers, but they actually experienced higher performance with minority teachers than did minority students.

The relationship between representative bureaucracy and organizational performance was taken a step further by David Pitts and his co-authors. Relying on private sector research that indicates more diverse organizations are likely to generate a greater range of ideas and consequently perform better, Pitts (2005) finds that as the bureaucracy more closely mirrors the clientele in terms of ethnic composition, performance does increase. A subsequent analysis (Roch, Pitts, and Navarro 2010) shows that schools with more representative teaching faculties tend to shift from punitive disciplinary policies to more corrective or ameliorative disciplinary policies. The implication of this change in policy is that the organizations are more likely to get positive results in terms of performance. The work on how representative bureaucracy affects the performance of organizations is clearly in its infancy, but sufficient evidence exists to conclude that it is not necessarily the case that bureaucracies must give up performance if they seek to be representative.

CONCLUSION

Although the study of representative bureaucracy has generated a substantial body of work, there remains much to be done. We know something about which identities should be represented, what the determinants of representation are, whether passive representation leads to active representation, and whether bureaucratic representation affects the performance of the organization. Much of

the research is based in the United States, and the bulk of the US research focuses on a single type of organization, public schools. Organizations take many forms and they exist in many national contexts that vary greatly in terms of politics, structures, public activities, and development. The findings based on local school districts in the United States are unlikely to be relevant to all the bureaucracies in all these contexts. As a result, there are numerous opportunities for theoretically informed research, especially outside the United States. Only by taking the study of representative bureaucracy elsewhere can we get definitive answers on when bureaucracies represent and what difference it makes if they do.

REFERENCES

Ashworth, Rachel and Andrews Rhys. 2010. "Representative Bureaucracy and Fire Service Performance: Evidence from England." Unpublished paper, Cardiff School of Business, Cardiff, Wales.

Becker, Gary S. 1993. *Human Capital*, third edition. Chicago, IL: University of Chicago Press.

Bradbury, Mark D. and J. Edward Kellough. 2008. "Representative Bureaucracy: Exploring the Potential for Active Representation in Local Government." *Journal of Public Administration Research and Theory* 18(October): 697–714.

Daley, Dennis. 1984. "Controlling Bureaucracy among the States." *Administration & Society* 15(February): 475–488.

Dresang, Dennis L. 1974. "Ethnic Politics, Representative Bureaucracy and Development Administration: The Zambian Case." *American Political Science Review* 68(December): 1605–1617.

Dye, Thomas R. and James Renick. 1981. "Political Power and City Jobs: Determinants of Minority Employment." *Social Science Quarterly* 62(September): 475–486.

Eisinger, Peter K. 1982. "Black Employment in Municipal Jobs: The Impact of Black Political Power." *American Political Science Review* 76(June): 380–392.

Goode, S. J. and J. Norman Baldwin. 2005. "Predictors of African American Representation in Municipal Government." *Review of Public Personnel* 25(March): 29–45.

Guy, Mary E., Meredith A. Newman, and Sharon Mastracci. 2008. *Emotional Labor: Putting the Service in Public Service*. Armonk, NY: M.E. Sharpe.

Habyarimana, James, Macartan Humphreys, Daniel Posner, and Jeremy M. Weinstein. 2009. *Coethnicity: Diversity and the Dilemmas of Collective Action*. New York: Russell Sage Foundation.

Herman, J. 2007. "Passive Representation and the Client–Bureaucrat Relationship: Communication and Demand Inducement in the Patient–Provider Relationship." Master's thesis, University of Missouri-Columbia.

Hindera, John J. 1993. "Representative Bureaucracy: Further Evidence of Active Representation in the EEOC District Offices." *Journal of Public Administration, Research and Theory* 3(October): 415–429.

Hindera, John J. and Cheryl D. Young. 1998. "Representative Bureaucracy: The Theoretical Implications of Statistical Interaction." *Political Research Quarterly* 51(September): 655–671.

Hupe, Peter and Michael Hill. 2007. "Street-Level Bureaucracy and Public Accountability." *Public Administration* 85 (June): 279–299.

Kanter, Rosabeth Moss. 1993. *Men and Women of the Corporation*. New York: Basic Books.

Keiser, Lael R., Vicky M. Wilkins, Kenneth J. Meier, and Catherine A. Holland. 2002. "Lipstick and Logarithms: Gender, Institutional Context, and Representative Bureaucracy." *American Political Science Review* 96: 553–564.

Kim, H. 2005. "Female Representation in Korean Government Bureaucracy." *Korea Observer* 36(Spring): 69–86.

Kim, P. S. 1993. "Public Bureaucracy and Regionalism in South Korea." *Administration and Society* 25(August): 227–242.

Kingsley, J. Donald. 1944. *Representative Bureaucracy: An Interpretation of the British Civil Service*. Yellow Springs, OH: Antioch Press.

Krislov, Samuel. 1974. *Representative Bureaucracy*. Englewood Cliffs, NJ: Prentice-Hall.

Levitan, David. 1946. "The Responsibility of Administrative Officials in Democratic Society." *Political Science Quarterly* 61(December): 562–598.

Lewis, W. G. 1989. "Toward Representative Bureaucracy: Blacks in City Police Organizations, 1975–1985." *Public Administration Review* 49(May–June): 257–268.

Lim, H. 2006. "Representative Bureaucracy: Rethinking Substantive Effects and Active Representation." *Public Administration Review* 66(March–Apr): 193–204.

Lipsky, Martin. 1980. *Street-Level Bureaucracy*. New York: Russell Sage Foundation.

Long, Norton. 1952. "Bureaucracy and Constitutionalism." *American Political Science Review* 46(September): 808–818.

Meier, Kenneth J. 1975. "Representative Bureaucracy: An Empirical Analysis." *American Political Science Review* 69 (June): 526–542.

Meier, Kenneth J. 1984. "Teachers, Students, and Discrimination: The Policy Impact of Black Representation." *Journal of Politics* 46(February): 252–263.

Meier, Kenneth J. and John Bohte. 2001. "Structure and Discretion: Missing Links in Representative Bureaucracy." *Journal of Public Administration Research and Theory* 11(October): 455–470.

Meier, Kenneth J. and Jill Nicholson-Crotty. 2006. "Gender, Representative Bureaucracy and Law Enforcement: The Case of Sexual Assault." *Public Administration Review* 66(November–December): 850–860.

Meier, Kenneth J. and Laurence J. O'Toole. 2006. *Bureaucracy in a Democratic State*. Baltimore, MD: Johns Hopkins University Press.

Meier, Kenneth J. and Kevin B. Smith. 1994. "Representative Democracy and Representative Bureaucracy: Examining the Top Down and the Bottom Up Linkages." *Social Science Quarterly* 75 (December): 790–803.

Meier, Kenneth J. and Joseph Stewart Jr. 1992. "Active Representation in Educational Bureaucracies: Policy Impacts." *American Review of Public Administration* 22 (September): 157–171.

Meier, Kenneth J., Robert D. Wrinkle, and J.L. Polinard. 1999. "Representative Democracy and Distributional Equity: Addressing the Hard Question." *Journal of Politics* 61(November): 1025–1039.

Meier, Kenneth J., Warren S. Eller, Robert D. Wrinkle, and J. L. Polinard. 2001. "Zen and the Art of Policy Analysis." *Journal of Politics* 63(May): 619–629.

Meier, Kenneth J., Laurence J. O'Toole, and Sean Nicholson-Crotty. 2004. "Multilevel Governance and Organizational Performance: Investigating the Political-Bureaucratic Labyrinth." *Journal of Policy Analysis and Management* 23(Winter): 31–48.

Mosher, Frederick. 1968. *Democracy and the Public Service*. New York: Oxford University Press.

Naff, Katherine. 2007. "Passive Representation in the South African Bureaucracy: A Lot Has Happened, but it's a Lot More Complicated… ." Paper presented at the annual meeting of the American Political Science Association, Chicago, IL.

Pitkin, Hanna. 1967. *The Concept of Representation*. Los Angeles, CA: University of California Press.

Pitts, David W. 2005. "Diversity, Representation, and Performance: Evidence about Race and Ethnicity in Public Organizations." *Journal of Public Administration Research and Theory* 15: 615–631.

Posner, Daniel N. 2006. *Institutions and Ethnic Politics in Africa*. New York: Cambridge University Press.

Roch, Christine H., David W. Pitts, and I. Navarro. 2010. "Representative Bureaucracy and Policy Tools: Ethnicity, Student Discipline, and Representation in Public Schools." *Administration & Society* 42: 38–65.

Saltzstein, Grace H. 1986. "Female Mayors and Women in Municipal Jobs." *American Journal of Political Science* 30(February): 140–164.

Saltzstein, Grace H. 1989. "Black Mayors and Police Policies." *Journal of Politics* 51(August): 525–544.

Selden, S.C. 1997. *The Promise of Representative Bureaucracy: Diversity and Responsiveness in a Government Agency*. Armonk: NY: M.E. Sharpe.

Sigelman, Lee. 1976. "The Curious Case of Women in State and Local Government." *Social Science Quarterly* 56(March): 591–604.

Smith, C. R. and Sergio Fernandez. 2010. "Equity in Federal Contracting: Examining the Link between Minority Representation and Federal Procurement Decisions." *Public Administration Review* 70: 87–96.

Sowa, Jessica E. and Sally C. Selden. 2003. "Administrative Discretion and Active Representation: An Expansion of the Theory of Representative Bureaucracy." *Public Administration Review* 63: 700–710.

Stein, Lana. 1986. "Representative Local Government: Minorities in the Municipal Work Force." *Journal of Politics* 48(August): 694–713.

Subramaniam, V. 1967. "Representative Bureaucracy: A Reassessment." *American Political Science Review* 61(December): 1010–1019.

Theobald, Nick A. 2007. "Muestreme el dinero: Assessing the Linkage between Latino School Superintendents and English Language Learner Program Resources." In R. Espino, D. L. Leal & K. J. Meier (eds), *Latino Politics: Identity, Mobilization and Representation*. Charlottesville, VA: University of Virginia Press, pp. 249–266.

Theobald, Nick A. and Donald P. Haider-Markel. 2009. "Race, Bureaucracy, and Symbolic Representation: Interactions between Citizens and Police." *Journal of Public Administration Research and Theory* 19(April): 409–426.

Thielemann, Greg S. and Joseph Stewart, Jr. 1996. "A Demand-Side Perspective on the Importance of Representative Bureaucracy: AIDS, Ethnicity, Gender, and Sexual Orientation." *Public Administration Review* 56(March–April): 168–173.

Thompson, Frank J. 1976. "Minority Groups in Public Bureaucracies: Are Passive and Active Representation Linked?" *Administration and Society* 8(August): 201–226.

Van Gool, Bas. 2008. "Untouchable Bureaucracy: Unrepresentative Bureaucracy in a North Indian State." PhD dissertation, Leiden University, The Netherlands.

Van Riper, Paul. 1958. *History of the United States Civil Service*. White Plains, NY: Row Peterson.

Weber, Max. 1946. *From Max Weber: Essays in Sociology*. H. H. Gerth and C. Wright Mills, Trans. New York: Oxford University Press.

Weiher, Gregory R. 2000. "Minority Student Achievement: Passive and Social Context in Schools." *Journal of Politics* 62(August): 886–895.

Whitford, Andrew B., Vicky M. Wilkins, and Mercedes G. Ball. 2007. "Descriptive Representation and Policymaking Authority: Evidence from Women in Cabinets and Bureaucracies." *Governance: an International Journal of Policy, Administration, and Institutions* 20(October): 559–580.

Wilkins, Vicky M. and Lael R. Keiser. 2006. "Linking Passive and Active Representation by Gender: The Case of Child Support Agencies." *Journal of Public Administration Research and Theory* 16(January): 87–102.

Wilkins, Vicky M. and Brian N. Williams. 2008. "Black or Blue: Racial Profiling and Representative Bureaucracy." *Public Administration Review* 68(July–August): 654–664.

Wilkins, Vicky M. and Brian N. Williams. 2009. "Representing Blue: Representative Bureaucracy and Racial Profiling in the Latino Community." *Administration and Society* 40(January): 775–798.

24

Electronic Government: A Revolution in Public Administration?

Helen Margetts

The potential for 'electronic government' or 'e-government' to transform public administration has been heralded at various points throughout the past half-century. Even by the 1960s and 1970s, as computers started to appear in government organizations, some public officials and commentators predicted that information technology would bring a 'revolution' to public administration. As increasingly sophisticated information and communication technologies (ICTs) spread across all organizations during the 1980s and 1990s, politicians jostled to claim credit for 'information age government'. By the beginning of the twenty-first century, as use of the Internet became increasingly widespread, claims for the transformative power of ICTs became correspondingly enthusiastic and 'Digital Era Governance', placing ICTs at the centre of public management reform, emerged as a possible new 'paradigm' for public administration (Dunleavy et al., 2005, 2006; Dunleavy and Margetts, 2010). After the financial crisis of 2008, governments

across the world turned to ICTs as a way to save the money required to cut public sectors and repay government debt, with 'digital by default' strategies offering the potential to reduce the costs of interacting with citizens. Earlier ICTs were largely internal to organizations, doing little to enhance interactions with citizens. But the widespread use of the Internet by both society and government has offered real possibilities for change in citizen–government relationships, just as new channels of communication and transaction have transformed the relationship between all kinds of social and commercial organizations and their customers in countries with high levels of Internet penetration.

This chapter briefly reviews early approaches to analysing the impact of ICTs on public administration. Politicians' enthusiasm for ICTs has its source in a particular tradition of political thought: modernization. Computers and communications have long been cited as the key to bringing public administration up to date, just as domestic appliances modernize the home. They were viewed as a force for rationalization, as was Weberian bureaucracy in the first half of the twentieth century. The various approaches can be grouped according to their degree and direction of enthusiasm for the modernizing effect of ICTs, as hypermodernist, antimodernist and postmodernist. Alongside these commentaries lies mainstream public administration, which in general has underplayed or ignored the possible impact of ICTs, even with the advent of the Internet. Fifty years after the first computers appeared in government, this chapter assesses the claims of these writers in light of the more recent history of government ICTs. First, with respect to pre-Internet technologies, largely internal to public administration, and secondly, looking at web-based technologies which offer new opportunities for public agencies to interact with citizens using new technologies. Both types of technology are relevant to the concept of e-government, which includes both 'providing public access via the Internet to Government services' as well as 'harnessing new technology to transform the internal efficiency of government departments' (National Audit Office [NAO], 2002).

APPROACHES TO ICTs AND PUBLIC ADMINISTRATION

Information and communication technologies are clearly associated with modernization, being at the heart of all three 'pillars' of modernization thought (Margetts et al., 2010): offering potential for economic efficiency and rationalization; linking administration to the benefits of scientific and technological advance; and allowing new possibilities for integration and interconnectedness between previously geographically separate organizational units and individuals.

With respect to rationalization in particular, working from the widely held premise that computers are a rationalizing tool, one

possible role for ICTs in public administration would be to provide a strengthening of bureaucratic organization, to 'out-Weber Weber' as Christopher Hood once put it (Hood, 1994). For Weber, the road to modernity through rationality was facilitated by the development of bureaucracy, which would allow the control of the world through calculation, the systematization of meaning and value into an overall consistent, ethical view (Kolb, 1986: 10). ICTs, at first glance, would appear to facilitate this modernization process still further. ICTs allow the formalization of rules and procedures and enhance the scope for increasing rationality into decision making. Ethical schemata are easier to implement using computers: for example, the calculation of quality-adjusted life years in health care has become increasingly sophisticated. Long-accepted problems of rational decision making such as 'bounded rationality' (Simon, 1955) can be tackled, as computers are used to simulate policy alternatives. The way that some writers have perceived the impact of ICTs is directly analogous to Weber's vision of administrative modernization: 'Informatization in public administration is a process of continued modernization' (Frissen, 1995: 8). It is in reaction to this perspective of ICTs as a modernizing force – either positive or negative – that most approaches to the phenomenon of ICTs are based and may be categorized.

For the most enthusiastic of modernists, such a modernizing force would take government beyond mere bureaucratic efficiency. Thus, hypermodernists are technological utopians who see ICTs as the central enabling element of a utopian vision of public administration. A long-standing and popularly influential example is Alvin Toffler, who in a trilogy extending over 30 years (Toffler, 1970, 1980, 1990), revelled in the notion of transition, transformation and revolution. *The Third Wave* would bring a new civilization with the electronics revolution at its technological base, peopled by 'information workers' in 'intelligent buildings' full of 'electronic offices', organized in networks rather than formal hierarchies. Political systems would not be able to cope with this wave of change and by 1990, Toffler claimed, governments would begin to 'bypass their hierarchies – further subverting bureaucratic power' (Toffler, 1990: 255). Management gurus followed Toffler in enthusiastically pronouncing the end of bureaucracy per se, with titles like *Intelligent Enterprise* (Quinn, 1992) and *The End of Bureaucracy and the Rise of the Intelligent Organization* (Pinchot and Pinchot, 1994), based on the premise that technology would challenge the very basis of organizational theory. As use of the Internet rose steeply during the 1990s, this group of writers expanded to form a positive multitude, predicting the end of organizations, both private and public, that did not adapt radically to the Internet age (see, for example, Lord, 2000).

Politicians have been keen to follow this line of thought, seeing Internet-based technologies as a potentially cheap and effective solution to long-standing administrative problems, with the potential to cover any manifesto for administrative reform with a modernist gloss. In the United States during the 1990s, when Al Gore was promising to replace 'industrial era bureaucracy' with 'information age government' as part of the 1994 National Performance Review, Alvin Toffler himself was in the pay of both the Democrats (Clinton and Gore) and the Republicans (Newt Gingrich). At the same time, in the UK, politicians of both Conservative and Labour parties were assuring voters that they were the 'British Al Gore' (Margetts, 1999: xiii) and in 1998, *Information Age Government: Delivering the Blair Revolution* (Byrne, 1998), outlined a cornucopia of benefits to be gained from information technology and castigated the Civil Service for being 'quite unfit' to deliver the Prime Minister Blair's vision of an 'information age' society. By 2005, Blair himself expressed his commitment to ICTs as a way of furthering the modernization dream:

The world is changing around us at an incredible pace due to remarkable technological change ... . Government has to respond to keep up with the hopes and aspirations of citizens and business, to remain efficient and trustworthy. That is why I asked for a strategy on how we can use technology to transform government services (Cabinet Office, 2005).

After the financial crisis of 2008, where most industrialized nations faced a sustained period of state retrenchment and public sector cuts, politicians again turned to ICTs as a way of obtaining public sector efficiency and doing 'more for less'. In the UK in 2010, the new Coalition Government's Digital Champion Martha Lane Fox promised a 'Digital by Default' strategy which would be 'Revolution not Evolution' (Lane Fox, 2010), promising that online service provision would be the default option across public services and arguing that shifting 30 per cent of government service delivery contacts to digital channels would deliver gross annual savings of more than £1.3 billion, rising to £2.2 billion if 50 per cent of contacts shifted to digital (Lane Fox, 2010: 1).

In contrast, an 'antimodernist' stream of writing has seen computers as having an equally transformative but malign effect on public administration, bringing in the 'Control Revolution' (Beniger, 1991) or the 'Computer State' (Burnham, 1983), where massive databanks would be used as instruments of control. Beniger (1991: 388), for example, claimed that 'the progressive convergence of information processing and communications technologies in a single infrastructure of control is sustaining the "Control Revolution" – a concentration of abrupt changes in the technological and economic arrangements by which information is collected, stored and processed'. Other writers saw information technology bringing about the new Leviathan, 'integrating the state through the backdoor of information management' (Lenk, 1994: 313). Others predicted that computers would lead to a 'cyborg world' (Levidow and Robins, 1989) in which 'infotech systems promote new models of rationality, cognition and intelligence', or a 'military revolution' (Goure, 1993). Such views were founded on the pursuit of a logic of total control, both internal and external: 'The military information society involves internalizing a self-discipline, technologies of the self, in ways that come to be seen as normal, rational and reasonable' (Levidow and Robins, 1989: 8). Wright (1998) presented a 'worst case' scenario, where a 'range of unforeseen impacts are associated with the process of integrating these technologies into society's social political and cultural control systems': for example, the 'militarization of the police and the para-militarization of the army as their roles, equipment and procedures begin to overlap' (Wright, 1998: 4). In authoritarian states, technology would strengthen the power of autocratic regimes: for example, through the collection and control of information about subjects and the easy propagation of state propaganda. These views belong to a wider anti-utopian view that also has its roots in the Weberian tradition. Just as Weber feared unbridled bureaucratic domination, Orwell (1954) and Huxley (1932) warned of a rule of impersonal officialdom disastrously strengthened by technological advance. The human 'machine' of Weberian bureaucracy would be delivered first by systematization of human procedures, followed by the replacement of humans with automated machines.

Finally, ICTs have also caught the attention of another group of writers who viewed them as an essential element of postmodern society, fuelling equally radical changes in public administration. Frissen, for example, argued that in a postmodernized public administration 'fragmentation will lead to an emancipation of the bureaucratic organization – beyond central control' (Frissen, 1995: 9). This enthusiastic welcoming of technology to public administration was echoed in other postmodernist analyses: 'where modernist organization was premised on technological determinism, postmodernist organization is premised on technological choices made possible through "de-dedicated" micro-electronics equipment' (Clegg, 1990: 181). These writers were in general

optimistic about the influence of ICTs on public administration, seeing a strong increase in fluidity and flexibility where 'fragmentation will lead to an emancipation of the bureaucratic organization – beyond central control' and 'the pyramidal nature of public administration' changes into 'an archipelago of network configurations' (see Frissen, 1995, 1999). But more pessimistic postmodern observers have characterized the 'military information society' as postmodernist: 'current US Defense policy is creating a post-modern army of war machines, war managers and robotized warriors' (Gray, 1989: 44). In general, however, as with most postmodernist analyses, this group of commentators are stronger and more in agreement in their criticism of the modernist mainstream than on any outline of what a postmodern ICT-based public administration would look like.

In contrast to all the above, for decades the vast majority of writers on public administration ignored the widespread introduction of computers across government, appearing to regard ICTs as a neutral administrative tool, with little or no implications for public administration or policy. Most books on public administration of the 1990s had very little mention of computers or information technology and even textbooks ignored the phenomenon; see, for example, Lynn and Wildavsky (1990) or Rhodes (1997), neither of which has any mention of computers, ICTs or the Internet in its indexes. In the early 1990s, small groups of researchers – most notably the URBIS group at the University of California in Irvine in the United States, the Kassel group in Germany (see Lenk, 1992) and a European group based in the Netherlands (see Snellen, 1994 for a review) and the UK (see for example Bellamy and Taylor, 1998 or Pratchett, 1994) – initiated what might be called a 'critical modern' approach, carefully monitoring and recording the changes at work. But these groups of writers have tended to be somewhat 'ghettoized' within mainstream public administration. Even in the age of the 'dot.com' boom, bust and eventual stabilization of the 1990s and 2000s, when Internet trends were consistently implicated in a high proportion of news headlines, book titles and policy pronouncements, books on public administration remained relatively impervious to the trend. Pollitt and Bouckaert (2004), for example, in a comprehensive analysis of public administration across 10 countries, offer only a couple of (disparaging) references to ICTs. More recently, however, mainstream political scientists have started to focus on ICTs as a crucial area of public administration. Fountain (2001) and West (2005, 2011) have produced influential works on e-government in the United States, taking an institutional approach to ICT-related change. Pollitt (2010) has recently observed the 'central but neglected' role of technological change in public administration. Dunleavy, Margetts and their research team (Dunleavy et al., 2005, 2006: Dunleavy and Margetts, 2010) have developed the Digital Era Governance (DEG) model, which accords ICTs a key role in public policy and administration; they advocate DEG as a new paradigm for public management, overturning New Public Management (NPM) as the dominant paradigm of the 1980s and 1990s. So, at the time of writing, the stage is set for reconsidering the place of ICTs and e-government in administrative history.

THE POLICY IMPACT OF ICTs

This belief that ICTs make no difference to public administration is challenged by the extent to which they are now embedded within all types of organization. In the period from the 1950s onwards, ICTs have pervaded every corner of public administration across OECD (Organization for Economic Co-operation and Development) countries, with real relevance for policy. In virtually all industrialized nations, there are few government offices without a computer, few

administrative operations that do not rely on the processing of a complex network of ICTs and hardly any government agencies without a presence on the Internet. And ICTs now form a significant proportion of the budgets of government agencies. In the United States, expenditure on ICTs (including staff costs, consultancy, hardware and software) had reached around 6 per cent of the federal operating budget by the 1990s. In the UK, ICTs amounted to 11 per cent of running costs by 1995 (Margetts, 1999: 39–40). By the 2000s, most governments of industrialized nations were spending around 1 per cent of gross domestic product (GDP) on their own information systems; in the UK, annual expenditure peaked at around £16 billion and, even after the Coalition Government that came to power in 2010 scrapped several large-scale high-cost projects, still runs at around £14 billion annually.

ICTs have been shown to be policy critical (Margetts, 1998, 1999). Hood and Margetts (2007) illustrate how all the 'tools' of government policy identified by Hood (1983) – nodality, authority, treasure and organizational capacity – are now heavily reliant on ICTs. First, with respect to nodality – the extent to which government is at the centre of information and social networks – ICTs play a clear role, facilitating information channels both within government organizations and between government organizations, private sector companies, voluntary organizations and citizens. With respect to treasure – that is, money or 'fungible chattels' – all moneys processed within governmental organizations have since the 1960s been processed via computer systems. With respect to the legitimate authority that government has by virtue of being government, research suggests (Margetts, 1999) that authority-wielding organizations have been among the most innovative. Police databases with massive search capacity have long facilitated a move towards more pre-emptive policing; more recently, widespread use of closed-circuit television (CCTV), DNA testing and the creation of searchable databases of DNA samples have revolutionized policing strategies. In addition to the heavy reliance now placed upon them in all streams of government activity, ICTs, particularly in the area of law and order, open new policy windows. For example, the electronic tagging of prisoners made possible new policies, such as the early release of prisoners and curfew orders, which forced policy makers to re-evaluate traditional notions of punishment.

For the more general 'organizational capacity' of government, information systems have played a key role in replacing tranches of government bureaucracy; government organizations at the beginning of the twenty-first century can process more transactions more rapidly with less staff than they could before computers were introduced. The computer technologies of the 1970s, mainframe computers designed for heavy transaction loads, were particularly well suited for taking over bureaucratic operations within the largest of government organizations, processing large quantities of dealings with citizens, particularly those processing tax and social security. But these new technologies required new staff with different skills and have introduced new armies of technical specialists into government. In this sense, ICTs have brought a shift in resources from organizational capacity to 'organized expertise' (Dunleavy, 1994; Margetts, 1995; Dunleavy et al., 2006). While, traditionally, government has marshalled its organizational resources through the operation of large-scale bureaucracies, now information technology is used by government to marshal other resources. Bureaucracy has traditionally been viewed as something that government organizations are 'good at', but now such organizations find themselves involved in large-scale and complex ICT-based development tasks, not something that government has a reputation for being good at. The evident difficulty in the design, development and maintenance of information systems engenders a transfer from organizational capacity to organized expertise. All government bureaucracies must now maintain a

division dedicated to the development of new technology-based projects, with new risks and new dangers.

As well as facilitating new and existing policies, ICTs can prevent policies being implemented, can constrain policy development and become a negative feature of public administration. The history of government computing in the UK, in particular, is littered with high-profile projects that have gone wrong and seriously hampered policy implementation. The introduction of computers into the UK Social Security Department involved a number of large-scale projects that ran over budget, took longer than anticipated to implement and resulted in inadequate, inflexible and outdated systems (see Margetts, 1999; Organ, 2003; Dunleavy et al., 2006). In 1998 the UK Passport Agency reached virtual collapse when a new system was introduced at the same time as a new policy requiring children under five to have their own passports was introduced; the resultant backlog brought the Agency to virtual collapse. Throughout the second half of the 1990s, the Arthur Andersen company battled to replace the huge National Insurance system; the new index system failed to work for a year after the old system had been rendered non-operational. Even small agencies traditionally perceived as completely non-technical have long been vulnerable to the failure of ICT systems: in 1989, the UK Foreign and Commonwealth Office was severely incapacitated when its small accounting system crashed disastrously, causing the Office to produce the most serious qualification of a department's accounts that the Comptroller and Auditor General had ever made (Margetts, 1999: 17). In 2012, the introduction of the UK Coalition Government's flagship policy, the Universal Credit, will involve the meshing of the huge, complex and operationally distinct systems of tax and social security agencies, a task so immense that at the time of writing, even when the benefit was months away from being introduced, the system on which it will critically rely was already on the Chancellor's 'at risk' list of projects. In the United States the history of government computing also includes failures in the most crucial of civilian agencies. In the 1970s, the US Social Security Administration (SSA) experienced a major disaster which ground SSA to a halt in implementing a new system for Social Security Income and blackened SSA's reputation (and consequentially, Congressional funding) for managing technology over the next 30 years. The long-running series of projects to modernize the computer systems of the US Internal Revenue Service (IRS) – Tax Systems Modernization – has absorbed spiralling budgets over 30 years, with few tangible benefits, and resulted in a tax system that is increasingly difficult to manage, with some parts of the system still dating back to the 1960s.

It is the problems in managing technology-based projects and the consequent need for organized expertise that has led to one of the key changes brought to public administration by ICTs – that of drawing into government a bewildering array of information technology experts, by now most usually in the form of huge global computer services providers. In the early days of computers, during the 1960s and 1970s, government organizations gained expertise in ICTs through employment of specialist staff or IT contractors on an individual basis. During the 1980s and 1990s, however, the trend was for contracts for IT expertise to become larger and larger. Particularly in the UK and the United States, great tranches of government work were contracted out in this way in the name of 'systems integration'. Almost all departments and agencies in the two governments are involved in a range of partnerships with large global private sector computer services providers. Some of these contracts represent major chunks of public expenditure: for example, the UK Inland Revenue's contract with Electronic Data Systems (EDS) was worth £1 billion over 10 years when it was first signed in 1996. In 2004, the contract was re-tendered and awarded to Cap Gemini for £4.3 million, again for 10 years, with an option to extend it for an additional eight years. The challenge in such mega-contracts was evidenced by the fact that while EDS's

shares stayed the same when its lost contract was announced, Cap Gemini's dropped on news of the award (Dunleavy et al., 2006: 143). The companies that hold such contracts are major new players in public administration. And most of the major disasters with ICTs, some of which were mentioned above, have been linked with a significant partnership between a government agency and a major computer services provider.

The tendency towards private provision of ICTs in government has in some countries been both fuelled and shaped by New Public Management-style change, of which increased contracting and privatization was a key theme. In the UK, where NPM trends were particularly strong, and in the United States, where NPM rhetoric was used by the Reagan administration during the 1980s and during the second Clinton term in the 1990s (and in any case contracting out has been used as an administrative tool throughout the twentieth century), the vast majority of ICT-related tasks have been outsourced. In other countries where NPM trends have been particularly strong, such as Australia and New Zealand, the US and UK patterns of oligopolistic computer services provision to government can also be observed (Dunleavy et al., 2006), with contracts showing a tendency to increase in size, with a concurrent increase in the size of companies able to tender for them. In the UK, research during the early 2000s showed that of the 37 very large-scale government ICT contracts with individual values greater than £50 million covering the period 1990 to 2000, three companies (EDS, ICL and Siemens) held nearly 80 per cent of the contract value (Dunleavy et al., 2006) and a 1997 report produced by the US Embassy claiming that EDS had over 50 per cent of the total UK government IT services business while the government market research firm Kable suggested that this figure was 80 per cent (Dunleavy and Margetts, 2000). In the United States, the market is less concentrated, with the top four companies holding only around 20 per cent of major ICT contracts (Margetts, 1999; Dunleavy et al., 2006), but large global computer services providers have long been major players in both federal and state administrations. Garvey (1993), for example, has illustrated how the newer 'shadow bureaucracy' of 'beltway bandits' – largely ICT-based companies – operates alongside the more traditional 'formal bureaucracy' in Washington. In European countries outside the UK, NPM trends have been far less extreme and these countries have turned less to outsourcing to solve ICT problems. Where it is used, these countries have tended to adopt a different model of contracting, the so-called Rhineland model where contracts are smaller and based on a more consensual style.

Whatever the individual style of a country's contracting regime, computer services providers are major new policy actors in most administrations. Management of long-term ICT contract relationships and large-scale technology projects have become a permanent feature of contemporary public administration. Control of these major new players, many of them global companies with turnovers equivalent to the GDPs of small countries, will remain a continual challenge for government agencies of all kinds, with potential for such companies to influence policy innovation, shape policy development and import policy solutions across national boundaries (see Dunleavy, 1994; Margetts and Dunleavy, 1995).

SO WHO WAS RIGHT?

Although the policy-critical nature of ICTs challenges the low profile accorded to them by public administration literature, the predictions of the hypermodernists have yet to be realized. For the hypermodernists, there have been many disasters and disappointments. There has been no overarching transformation of government through information technology that lends support to, for example, Toffler's claims that technology would bring the end of bureaucracy. The fact that ICT systems up to the 1990s were almost entirely internal to government organizations meant that they did little to change government–citizen relationships in the way that utopian modernists had hoped. Furthermore, the new risks and dangers inherent in the task of embarking upon large-scale, technology-based projects, unforeseen by hypermodernists, remain with government rather than appearing as a temporary 'glitch' in progress to a fully modernized state. Few would claim that the beginning of the twenty-first century saw 'the end of bureaucracy' and it is hard to discern the rise of 'the intelligent organization' from the experience of government agencies with ICTs. There is no guarantee of the promise that ICTs seem to hold for economic efficiency; they have sometimes been associated with rapid productivity growth, but also with static or declining productivity (Carrera and Dunleavy, 2012).

The worst nightmares of the antimodernists also appear unfulfilled. As noted above, the authority-wielding agencies have been innovative in their use of technology. There remains potential for a 'control state', just as bureaucracy presented possibilities for totalitarian states of the past. Computer systems provide new opportunities for governments to take a government-wide approach, but such an approach would have been out of line with all recent administrative trends and, for example, in neither the United States nor the UK have government-wide databases emerged from 50 years of ICT development. The continual pressure to innovate, the opening up of new policy windows and the difficulty of controlling high-technology projects means that technology seems to have introduced new irrationality as well as rationality into public administration. ICTs are revealed by various studies to be as much a control *problem* as a control *solution*. In general, ICT developments take place independently of each other, with transfers between systems remaining surprisingly limited. Furthermore, government holds no monopoly on technological innovation. Technologically sophisticated, control-wielding agencies encourage the tactics of the 'smart citizen', in turn necessitating further (and more difficult to attain) technological efforts from government agencies in a spiral of innovation. For example, as governments developed radar speed guns during the 1980s, companies started to market 'radar-gun detector devices', and so on. Authority-wielding agencies also find themselves under continual pressure to innovate in response to 'smart criminals'. Fingerprinting techniques transformed criminal detection when first developed, but became progressively less useful as criminals became aware of the necessity of wearing gloves or removing prints. DNA testing overcomes that problem – but requires the criminalization of the theft of DNA material, which could lead to criminals leaving false evidence at scenes of crime (*The Times*, 19 March 2002).

In general, therefore, there has been substantive change, but it has fulfilled neither the wildest dreams of the hypermodernists or the worst nightmares of the antimodernists. Up until the 1990s, this change was largely internal to public administration, part of the hidden world of government as bureaucracy. To citizens, it makes little difference whether the passport agency runs massive electronic databases or a large bureaucracy – except that when something goes wrong, it will probably be blamed on 'the computer system' rather than 'it's the rules'. And if the computer system is actually run by EDS or Cap Gemini rather than the UK Department of Employment, Work and Pensions or the US Social Security Administration, then citizens are unlikely to be made aware unless there is some high-profile disaster. Until the 1990s, it was such disasters rather than the clear benefits that ICTs have brought to government organizations that came to the attention of citizens.

THE INTERNET AND E-GOVERNMENT

The 1990s brought a new technological development, with much greater potential to impact upon the citizen–government relationship than earlier ICTs – rapidly rising usage of the Internet across society, particularly in commerce – and a consequently higher profile for information technology in general, with ICTs being widely credited as a key driver of productivity and economic growth, particularly in the United States (see OECD, 2001a). Over 50 per cent of US citizens were using the Internet by 2001, while in Europe the Scandinavian countries led Europe at around 55 per cent (OECD, 2001b: 77). By 2011, Internet penetration in the United States was around 78 per cent, with the UK not far behind, and some Scandinavian countries at over 90 per cent according to some estimates (see internetworldstats.com). In contrast to earlier technologies, the widespread use of the Internet offers more 'real' promise of transformation of the relationship between government and citizen. As noted above, earlier information technologies were largely internal, with few possibilities for external interactions, while web-based technologies can open up organizations to external users. In the private sector, real transformation of some organizations' relationship with their customers have taken place. By 2011, 86 per cent of UK citizens have bought goods or services online, 78 per cent have made travel reservations and 60 per cent have used Internet banking (Dutton and Blank, 2011: 25). And a huge array of new organizations with no shopfront have opened up and developed, such as the Amazon bookstore, and dashed to the frontiers of their markets (in terms of transaction volume if not in profits). The Internet has brought substantive change to the way citizens interact with each other, particularly with the popularity of social media and applications based on user-generated content from the mid 2000s. These technologies have been implicated in a huge range of political, social and economic activity, to the demonstrations and even revolutions of the Arab Spring of 2011, to the riots that spread like fire across London and other UK cities in the summer of 2011. Although the 'dot.com' crash of 2000 stilled the rush for Internet gold (and dampened political enthusiasm for e-government at the time), by 2011 there was no doubt that the Internet had proved a major new channel of communication and transaction by which the majority of citizens in countries with high levels of Internet penetration are interacting with each other and making transactions with a wide range of organizations.

Internet technologies are qualitatively different from earlier information technologies. As well as offering new potential for organizations to become externally facing, they lend themselves to different development styles. Private sector companies at the forefront of electronic commerce use 'build-and-learn' techniques (Dunleavy and Margetts, 1999, 2002; Dunleavy et al., 2007), whereby web-based developments become part of a process of continual organizational learning and customers' reactions – for example, to new web pages or facilities – can be quickly and continually assessed before further developments are made. Social media exacerbate this change, because users of (for example) social networking sites and microblogging sites such as Twitter are used to posting content themselves, so do not expect the same formality of web-based information that they might have done from the printed word in the past. This style contrasts with the 'big bang' approach applied to many of the large long-term government computer projects noted above.

So how has public administration responded to this new challenge? At the height of the dot.com boom, politicians became particularly keen that government should maximize the potential of the new Internet technologies. During the early 2000s, many countries introduced targets for the percentage of government services that would be available on the Internet. The United States was the first, when, as part of the 1994 National Performance Review, Al Gore promised to provide all citizens with electronic access to government by 2000, by connecting every classroom, library, hospital and clinic to a national information infrastruc-

ture. In the UK, in 1997, the then new Prime Minister Tony Blair pledged that by 2002 at least 25 per cent of all government interactions with citizens would be 'electronic' and the *Modernizing Government* White Paper put in place later targets of 50 per cent 'electronic' interactions by 2005 and 100 per cent by 2008 (see Dunleavy and Margetts, 1999, 2002) and this latter commitment was later brought forward to 2005. In Australia, also in 1997, the Prime Minister pledged that by the end of 2001 'all appropriate services' would be available online via the Internet.

Few of these targets were actually met, even by the late 2000s. Indeed, by 2009 only 0.2 per cent of communications with the UK main benefits department, the Department of Work and Pensions, took place electronically (Dunleavy et al., 2009). But as Internet use has become widespread, there has definitely been Internet-driven change across government organizations, to varying degrees across and within governments. By 2002, most governments in OECD countries had developed central portals intending to offer citizens a coherent 'front-end' to government and, by 2011, virtually all governments have some kind of web presence and most run thousands of websites. In the UK, for example, a survey for the NAO showed that 81 per cent of government bodies (92 per cent of Whitehall departments) had a website by the end of 2001 compared with 60 per cent for a similar survey in 1999 (Dunleavy and Margetts, 1999, 2002). Most sites facilitate the e-mailing of officials with queries, basic information about the organization, the downloading of documents and accessing press releases and annual reports. Key civilian agencies in some countries are undertaking major percentages of transactions with citizens online. For example, in Australia, even by 2001, 70 per cent of tax returns were being filed electronically and in the United States, electronic filing had reached 23 per cent by 1999 (Dunleavy and Margetts, 1999) and 60 per cent by 2009, finally nearing the target of 80 per cent originally set in 1998 (*PC World*, 15 January 2009).

Internet-based changes have been associated with greater transparency and a more open style of government, where relationships between citizens and government have qualitatively changed. In the UK, most government publications are now available free online as soon as they are made public, in strong contrast with the pre-Internet era where they had to be purchased with difficulty and at significant expense from Her Majesty's Stationary Office. The HMSO resisted the change, but in an environment where so much web content is free, their strict interpretation of copyright policy proved unsustainable. Many US states have opened up budgetary information to citizens, to varying degrees of accessibility, and many allow citizens to participate in budget-making decisions. From the late 2000s, 'Open data' initiatives have been pursued in several countries, for example the United States, the UK and Australia, where large government data sets are made available for citizens and private companies to use; this has been heralded as a major move towards greater transparency. In the UK, in 2011, the Coalition Government pledged a 'quantum leap' in transparency, with plans for information on schools, hospitals, general practitioners (GPs) and the courts to be published, building on the publication of the salaries of thousands of high-earning civil servants and the mandate that all spending decisions above £500 by local councils be made available online.

However, there is a strong sense in which government use of the Internet has lagged behind the private sector and, indeed, society more generally. Reports commissioned by the NAO (Dunleavy and Margetts, 1999, 2002; Dunleavy et al., 2007) have consistently found that the UK government in particular was lagging behind the private sector. In fact, in spite of the clear potential of web-based technologies, government organizations in countries with high Internet penetration rates have been in general slow, in comparison with the private sector, with voluntary organizations or with society

in general, to capitalize on the possible advantages of the Internet (Margetts and Dunleavy, 2002). Ironically, among liberal democracies it is in some countries where public administration is less developed, such as Estonia and Lithuania, where government agencies have been more innovative in their use of web-based technologies – possibly because they were able to leapfrog over some stages of technological development that occurred while these governments were still under the control of communist administrations and without access to newer technologies. Other countries have been more innovative in their use of different forms of incentivization for using electronic services; Chile, for example, had achieved around 98 per cent penetration of electronic tax filing by 2003, way beyond the figures even aimed at in the United States and UK, by mandating electronic filing and introducing a large network of internet tax cafes, where taxpayers could obtain free advice on both their tax and how to file electronically (Margetts and Yared, 2003).

One possible explanation for the relatively slow development of e-government is that organizations' ability to manage web-based technologies is shaped by earlier experience with earlier ICTs. For this reason, the extent to which governments make use and benefit from web-based technologies seems to be marked by the history of government computing. Cultural attitudes to technology engendered by previous bad experiences with IT projects or procurements can mean that organizations approach web development in a 'fatalist' way (Margetts and Dunleavy, 2002). Previous experience of ICT projects that ran over budget, brought few costs savings or even failed to work altogether can lead to reluctance to invest in web-based technologies. For example, many UK National Health Service (NHS) managers were scared off entering into ICT contracts in the 1990s after a series of high-profile failures and became increasingly reluctant to spend even budgets already allocated. The poor reputation of NHS computing led to an extremely low Treasury threshold for ICT expenditure in the NHS, further exacerbating the problem. Such a background is unlikely to foster an environment in which managers explore possibilities for innovation via web-based technologies. This barrier to e-government is ironic, because web-based technologies tend to be cheaper and easier to develop than earlier technologies.

Another organizational response to previous bad experiences with IT can be a 'hands-off' approach by all staff outside the IT department, because they do not want to have their careers tainted through association with any more disasters. This response will tend to result in almost complete reliance on technical experts to deal with the problems presented by technology. In such an organization, a traditional-style IT department will tend to dominate all the agency's technological developments – including e-government. This hangover from earlier management experience of IT is also unfortunate, because widespread private sector experience has shown that a traditional IT department can be the worst unit to lead an electronic service initiative – partly because such units have a large amount of intellectual capital invested in earlier technologies and may be resistant to the potential of web-based technologies to render their existing expertise and training obsolete. Another approach can be to leave web-based development to whichever computer services provider delivers other ICT developments to the organization – which can be equally problematic. Many of the big companies undertaking government contracts were slow to develop web-based technologies themselves and have hampered those agencies dependent upon major partnerships in their attempts to develop Internet capability.

THE FUTURE OF E-GOVERNMENT

There is nothing inevitable about the interaction of government and technology and the future of web-based government remains open. So will the Internet, finally, bring about the predictions of the hypermodernists, the antimodernists or the postmodernists? The most prevalent model across the IT industry for the development of electronic services in organizations has been the 'stages model' (see Dunleavy and Margetts, 2002). Like the approaches to earlier ICTs discussed above, the stages model is also based on the modernist idea of progression towards some utopian ideal of e-government. It suggests that there is a natural progression from the most basic services – the provision of information and documentation online – to more advanced interactive facilities and transactions online – such as making and receiving payments – through to full 'account management' where a customer's account history is maintained, as in Internet banking. Translated to government, account management would represent an organization storing information about citizens' history of dealings with the agency. Some commentators have used this model to assess progress towards e-government across OECD countries (for example, Accenture, 2001) or at the local government level (SOCITM, 2001). The problem with this model is that there may be no reason why some agencies would need to implement, say, account management: it will depend, for example, upon the activities they undertake. Dunleavy and Margetts (2002) have developed an alternative model which presents a more realistic picture of how agencies might proceed, suggesting that between a basic web-based service and full 'e-government' there are a variety of routes: e-publishing, interactive facilities, electronic transactions and full account management style can either coexist or be developed into a full 'e-government' style of the agency and there is no automatic reason why government strategy should favour any one of these routes over others for all agencies. Instead, each agency should ask: 'Given the type of organization that we are, and the kind of functions that we have, our fundamental mission and role, how far can we and should we move towards fully electronic or digital operations?' (Dunleavy and Margetts, 2002).

In fact, a very different approach to the stages model may be necessary for government to capitalize on the potential of e-government. As noted above, citizens have been more fast-moving and innovative in their use of the Internet and related technologies and applications than government. Indeed, government faces increasing competition for 'nodality' in the Internet era, given increasing competition from information providers of all kinds. Government agencies may even face a net loss of nodality as social, economic and political organizations capitalize on the mobilization and information dissemination and reduced coordination costs that the Internet provides. Most Internet users use search engines when looking for information, and if government sites are not there in the top 10 search results beyond which most users do not stray, they will not be used (Escher et al., 2006). Certainly, government agencies can no longer expect to act as a 'watchtower' with a privileged overview of citizen behaviour, to which citizens automatically come when looking for information. To achieve watchtower status, government agencies will find themselves having to use the channels that citizens use, such as social media sites, to gain insight into citizen behaviour and preferences and to disseminate government-related information. For example, if a health-related agency wanted to seek to gather data from citizen experiences of their own healthcare, which could provide vital (and cheap) information on the quality and robustness of services, they cannot expect just to build a website and wait for citizens to come – they must rather access the applications and platforms where citizens do increasingly express opinions about healthcare, such as social networking sites, micro-blogging sites and discussion forums on popular civic sites such as Mumsnet.

If states do manage to develop their electronic government, placing ICTs at the centre of public management reform and keeping pace with citizens' digital behaviours, finally maximizing the potential that ICTs have so long seemed to promise, then Digital Era Governance may emerge as a new paradigm for public management, as some commentators have suggested (Dunleavy et al., 2005, 2006), replacing New Public Management, the dominant paradigm of the 1980s and 1990s. In the period of public sector austerity and cutbacks that started with the financial crisis of 2008 and is likely to continue for at least a decade, policy makers are clearly turning to the Internet and ICTs as a way to achieve greater efficiency in public services and to conform to cutback regimes. Although an NPM revival might emerge in those countries (such as Greece) where previously it has been little applied, there is little evidence for a pioneering renewal of NPM taking hold (Dunleavy and Margetts, 2010). For DEG, however, the most likely scenario is that there is a period of 'investment pause'. In the UK for example, the Coalition Government introduced a moratorium on IT projects over £100 million early on after election and several large-scale investments, such as the National Programme for IT in the health service, have already been abandoned. In this environment, public sector managers are unlikely to take on responsibility for major IT programmes with enthusiasm and the tendency of e-government to lag behind digital behaviour in society at large, noted above, is likely to be exacerbated, at least in the short to medium term (Dunleavy and Margetts, 2010).

Whatever happens next, electronic government is finally established as a clear theme of public administration. There is no doubt that the presence of ICTs – both inside government and among society more generally – brings a continual source of change to public organizations. This continual pressure for innovation is now felt by all government agencies and challenges the absence of ICT issues from mainstream public administration. But the rationalizing power of ICTs, predicted by those commentators who have concentrated on ICTs, is less evident, either in terms of ending bureaucracy or in strengthening it disastrously. Even in the age of Internet and the dramatic new possibilities offered by web-based technologies for transforming government–citizen and government–business relationships, the influence of ICTs remains unpredictable and uncertain, with a range of viable scenarios for the future. In the sense that no modernist analysis seems to fit, and ICTs remain as a continual source of uncertainty within public administration, perhaps the postmodernists were nearest to being right. It may be that to understand the relationships between public administration and ICTs we need to disregard the modernist assumption that government is embarked on a continuing process of rationalization, modernization and progress towards some paradigm of e-government but steers away from the wide abundance of 'postmodernisms' which have been used to 'try and shape, define, characterize and interpret the indeterminate, pluralistic, ever more globalized period in culture from 1945 on' (Bradbury, 1995: 766). Such an approach might be called 'ante-postmodernism', beyond modernism but before postmodernism. In the 'ante-postmodernist' era, ICTs are a vital and changing part of any organization, introducing new risks and new dangers but also new sources of creativity and innovation.

REFERENCES

Accenture (2001) *e-Government Report.* May.

Bellamy, C. and Taylor, J. (1998) *Governing in the Information Age.* Buckingham: Open University Press.

Beniger, J. (1991) 'Information Society and Global Science', in C. Dunlop and R. Kling (eds), *Computers and Controversy: Value Conflicts and Social Choices.* London: Academic Press.

Bradbury, M. (1995) 'What was Post-Modernism? The Arts in and after the Cold War', *International Affairs,* 71 (4): October.

Burnham, D. (1983) *The Rise of the Computer State.* London: Weidenfeld and Nicolson.

Byrne, I. (1998) *Information Age Government: Delivering the Blair Revolution* (London: Fabian Society).

Cabinet Office (2005) *Transformational Government: Enabled by Technology.* London: Cabinet Office.

Carrera, L. and Dunleavy, P. (2012) *Growing the Productivity of Government Services.* Cheltenham: Edward Elgar.

Clegg, S. (1990) *Modern Organizations: Organization Studies in the Postmodern World.* London: Sage Publications.

Dunleavy, P. (1994) 'The Globalization of Public Services Production: Can Government Be "Best in World"'?, *Public Policy and Administration,* 9 (2): 36–64.

Dunleavy, P. and Margetts, H. (1999) *Government on the Web.* HC 87. London: National Audit Office.

Dunleavy, P. and Margetts, H. (2000) 'The Advent of Digital Government: Public Bureaucracies and the State in the Internet Age'. Paper to the annual conference of the American Political Science Association, Omni Shoreham Hotel, Washington, 4 September.

Dunleavy, P. and Margetts, H. (2002) *Government on the Web II.* HC 764. London: National Audit Office.

Dunleavy, P. and Margetts, H. (2010) 'The Second Wave of Digital Era Governance'. APSA 2010. Annual Meeting Paper. Available at SSRN: http://ssrn.com/abstract=1643850

Dunleavy, P., and Margetts, H., Goldchluk, S., Khan, M.K., Tinkler, J., Towers, E. and Escher, T. (2009) Department for Work and Pensions. Communicating with Customers. Report by the Comptroller and Auditor General, HC 421 Session 2008-2009. London: The Stationery Office.

Dunleavy, P., Margetts, H., Bastow, S., Escher, T., Pearce, O. and Tinkler, J. (2007) Government on the Internet. Report by the Comptroller and Auditor General, HC 529 Session 2006-2007, 13 July 2007. London: The Stationery Office.

Dunleavy, P., Margetts, H., Bastow, S. and Tinkler, J. (2005) 'New Public Management is Dead – Long Live Digital-Era Governance', *Journal of Public Administration and Theory,* 16 (3): 467–494.

Dunleavy, P., Margetts, H., Bastow, S. and Tinkler, J. (2006) *Ditial-era Governance: IT Corporations, the State and e-Governmen.* Oxford: Oxford University Press (revised paperback edition 2008).

Dunleavy, P., Margetts, H., Bastow, S., Pearce, O. and Tinkler, J. (2007) *Government on the Internet: Progress in Delivering Information and Services Online.* Value for Money Study for the UK National Audit Office. London: Stationary Office, HC 529.

Dutton, W. and Blank, G. (2011) *Next Generation Users: The Internet in Britain 2011.* Oxford Internet Institute. Oxford: Oxford University.

Escher, T., Margetts, H., Petricek, V. and Cox, I. (2006) 'Governing from the Centre? Comparing the Nodality of Digital Governments'. 2006 Annual Meeting of the American Political Science Association, Philadelphia, http://papers.ssrn.com/sol3/papers.cfm?abstract_id=1755762.

Fountain, J. (2001) *Building the Virtual State: Information Technology and Institutional Change.* Washington, DC: Brookings Institution.

Frissen, P. (1995) 'The Virtual State: Postmodernization, Informatization and Public Administration'. Paper to the Governance of Cyberspace Conference at University of Teeside, 12–13 April.

Frissen, P. (1999) *Politics, Governance and Technology: A Postmodern Narrative on the Virtual State.* Cheltenham: Edward Elgar.

Garvey, G. (1993) *Facing the Bureaucracy: Living and Dying in a Public Agency.* San Francisco, CA: Jossey-Bass.

Goure, D. (1993) 'The Military-Technical Revolution', *Washington Quarterly*, 16 (4): 175–192.

Gray, C. (1989) 'The Cyborg Soldier: The US Military and the Post-Modern Warrior', in L. Levidow and K. Robins (eds), *Cyborg Worlds: The Military Information Society.* London: Free Association Books.

Hood, C. (1983) *The Tools of Government.* London: Macmillan.

Hood, C. (1994) *Explaining Economic Policy Reversals.* Buckingham: Open University Press.

Hood, C. and Margetts, H. (2007) *The Tools of Government in the Digital Age.* Basingstoke: Palgrave Macmillan.

Huxley, A. (1932) *Brave New World: A Novel.* London: Chatto and Windus.

Kolb, D. (1986) *The Critique of Pure Modernity: Hegel, Heidegger and After.* London and Chicago, IL: University of Chicago Press.

Lane Fox, M. (2010) *Directgov 2010 and Beyond: Revolution not Evolution.* Report to Francis Maude. London: Cabinet Office.

Lenk, K. (1992) 'Informatics and Public Administration: Towards a Research Programme'. Paper to the ESRC/PICT programme on ICTs in Public Administration, National Institute of Social Work, Tavistock Place, London, 12 March.

Lenk, K. (1994) 'Information Systems in Public Administration: From Research to Design', *Informatization and the Public Sector*, 3 (3/4): 307–324.

Levidow, L. and Robins, K. (1989) 'Towards a Military Information Society?', in L. Levidow and K. Robins (eds), *Cyborg Worlds: the Military Information Society.* London: Free Association Books.

Lord, R. (2000) *The Net Effect.* London: Random House.

Lynn, N. and Wildavsky, A. (eds) (1990) *Public Administration: The State of the Discipline.* Chatham, NJ: Chatham House.

Margetts, H. (1995) 'The Automated State', *Public Policy and Administration*, 10 (2): 88–103.

Margetts, H. (1998) 'Computerising the Tools of Government', in I. Snellen and W. van de Donk (eds), *Public Administration in an Information Age.* Amsterdam: IOS Press.

Margetts, H. (1999) *Information Technology in Government: Britain and America.* London: Routledge.

Margetts, H. and Dunleavy, P. (1995) 'Public Services on the World Markets', *Missionary Government: Demos Quarterly*, 7: 30–32.

Margetts, H. and Dunleavy, P. (2002) 'Cultural Barriers to e-Government'. Academic article for the report: 'Better Public Services Through e-government'. London: National Audit Office, 2002, HC 704-III.

Margetts, H. and Yared, H. (2003) Incentivization of e-government. Article to accompany NAO report: 'Transforming the performance of HM Customs and Excise through Electronic Service Delivery'. London: The Stationery Office.

OECD (2001a) *OECD Science, Technology and Industry Scoreboard: Towards a Knowledge-based Economy.* Paris: OECD.

OECD (2001b) *OECD Science, Technology and Industry Outlook: Drivers of Growth: Information Technology, Innovation and Entrepreneurship.* Paris: OECD.

Organ, J. (2003) 'The Coordination of eGovernment in Historical Context', *Public Policy and Administration*, 18 (2): 21–36.

Orwell, G. (1954) *Nineteen Eighty-Four.* Harmondsworth: Penguin.

Pinchot, G. and Pinchot, E. (1994) *The End of Bureaucracy and the Rise of the Intelligent Organization.* San Francisco, CA: Berrett-Koehler Publishers.

Pollitt, C. (2010) 'Technological Change: A Central but Neglected Feature of Public Administration', *Journal of Public Administration and Policy*, 3 (2): 31–53.

Pollitt, C. and Bouckaert, G. (2004) *Public Management Reform: A Comparative Analysis*, 2nd edn. Oxford: Oxford University Press.

Pratchett, L. (1994) 'Open Systems and Closed Networks: Policy Networks and the Emergence of Open Systems in Local Government', *Public Administration*, 72 (1): 73–93.

Quinn, J. (1992) *Intelligent Enterprise*. New York: Macmillan.

Rhodes, R. (1997) *Understanding Governance: Policy Networks, Governance, Reflexivity and Accountability*. Buckingham: Open University Press.

Simon, H. (1955) *Models of Man*. New York: Wiley.

Snellen, I. (1994) 'ICT: A Revolutionising Force in Public Administration?', *Informatization and the Public Sector*, 3 (3/4): 283–304.

SOCITM (2001) *Local e-Government Now*. London: IDEA in conjunction with SOCITM.

Toffler, A. (1970) *Future Shock*. London: Pan Books.

Toffler, A. (1980) *The Third Wave*. New York: Bantam Books.

Toffler, A. (1990) *Powershift*. New York: Bantam Books.

West, D. (2005) *Digital Government: Technology and Public Sector Performance*. Princeton, NJ: Princeton University Press.

West, D. (2011) *The Next Wave: Using Digital Technology to Further Social and Political Innovation*. Washington, DC: Brookings Institution.

Wright, S. (1998) *An Appraisal of Technologies of Political Control*. Luxembourg: Directorate General for Research, European Parliament.

PART 9

Budgeting and Finance: Budget Watcher's Blues

edited by Frans K.M. van Nispen[1]

THE CALL FOR A BUDGETARY THEORY

The appeal of Valdimer Key for a budgetary theory marks the interest in public budgeting in modern history. He clearly referred to a *normative* theory, raising the question: 'On what basis shall it be decided to allocate X dollars to activity A instead of activity B?' (Key, in Hyde & Shafritz 1978: 20). A couple of efforts to develop such a theory failed before Aaron Wildavsky took over the relay baton, issuing the first edition of his seminal *The Politics of the Budgetary Process*, which changed the budgetary landscape almost completely.[2] He argued that the allocation of scarce resources is not a matter of arithmetics or calculation, but a matter of power. On top of that, he claimed that incrementalism offered both the best description of (and prescription for) the budget process, introducing words such as 'base' and 'fair share' that are now common in the vocabulary of budget watchers (Wildavsky 1964).[3] Soon, incrementalism became the dominant theory of public budgeting in America and,

strange enough, also in Europe, where the power of the purse is with the executive rather than the legislative branch of government. Moreover, empirical support was at least mixed, if not to say weak (LeLoup 1978; Rubin 1988).

The incremental nature of the budget was further challenged in the period of economic decline in the 1980s due to the oil crises. It turned out that decrementalism is not simply the mirror image of incrementalism, since the base is under attack (Schick 1983: 23). The various interest groups and stakeholders will fight the spending cuts, giving the budget process a highly political profile. The traditional way of budgeting – across-the-board cuts[4] – did not provide much relief, requiring more targeted spending cuts. Consequently, micro-budgeting was counterbalanced by macro-budgeting (LeLoup 1988), setting norms for the reduction of the budget deficit and/or public expenditures, changing the rules of the game and, noteworthy, the relative strengths of the players of the game.[5] The advocates suddenly faced strong guardians, playing down the upward pressure on the budget. The success and failure of these budgetary reforms and their predecessors like the Planning, Programming, Budgeting System (PPBS) and Zero-Base Budgeting (ZBB) have got much more attention than the design of a grounded theory. Unfortunately, we have to conclude that our insight in the process of public budgeting and cutback management is still anecdotal and fragmented, though we know a lot more than Valdimer Key when he ventilated his call for a budgetary theory.

THE BATTLE ON THE BALANCED BUDGET

The attempt to balance the budget is still relatively young, though James Savage has argued that balance is deeply rooted in American history (Savage 1988). In the mid 1980s the Gramm–Rudman–Hollings (GRH) amendment (1985), creating the sequestration procedure, prepared the ground for a reduction of the budget deficit. The impact may have been modest, but it is quite clear that the more effective spending caps of the Budget Enforcement Act (BEA) would not have passed without the GRH amendment. The movement became only serious when the budget became an issue in the mid-term elections during the first Clinton administration (1994). The *constitutional* amendment, as promoted by the Noble Prize winner James Buchanan (1995), may have failed, but both parties reached a *statutory* arrangement to balance the budget.

A few years later the European countries followed suit when the heads of states and governments came to terms about a target for the budget deficit and a procedure for the reduction of excessive budget deficits at the Maastricht summit (1991). The reference value for the budget deficit, which is one of the standards for the qualification for the Economic and Monetary Union (EMU),[6] was first set at 3 per cent of gross domestic product (GDP) and later, at the Amsterdam

summit (1997), further reinforced to a 'budgetary position close to balance or in surplus'.[7] In addition, the budgetary policy of the European member states is going to be directed by the 'principle of prudent fiscal policy making', introducing numerical rules that basically curb government expenditures in order to avoid windfalls on the revenue side being spent instead of being used for debt reduction. All efforts are geared to fiscal consolidation in order to avoid debt accumulation (OECD 2010a).

BUDGETARY REFORM

The process of budgetary reform has been driven for some time by the New Public Management (NPM) movement inducing, *inter alia*, a revival of performance budgeting. Taking the traditional line-item budget as point of reference, Christopher Pollitt and Geert Bouckaert discern a trajectory of budgetary reform that is completed by the adoption of accrual budgeting (Pollitt & Bouckaert 2004: 69–70). Only a few OECD (Organization for Economic Co-operation and Development) countries have gone through the full cycle as the constraints of both the strict and broad interpretation of performance budgeting (Schick 2003: 101) have become clear. The scope of is basically limited to homogeneous outputs, which are rare in the public sector; the link between inputs and outputs, respectively outcomes is rather weak and there is not much empirical support for the impact of performance information on – either allocative or technical – efficiency (Van Nispen & Posseth 2009). The NPM movement might be over the hill (Dunleavy et al. 2005; OECD 2010b), but what is new on the horizon, beyond performance budgeting?

The financial crisis and, notably, the situation in Greece, mark a crossroad in the field of budgetary reform. On the one hand, the financial crisis is providing a window for change – to quote Barack Obama's Chief of

Staff Rahm Emanuel: 'You never want a serious crisis to go to waste ... (it) is an opportunity to do things you think you could not do before' (Seib 2008) – as illustrated by the creation of a so-called European Semester that allows the European institutions to assess the draft budget and to come up with recommendations before it is submitted to national parliaments. In addition, the European Commission has issued the so-called 'six pack' of proposals for reinforcement of European governance (Van Nispen 2011). On the other hand, the room for budgetary innovation is small, as the financial crisis is absorbing almost the entire intellectual creativity and physical capacity for budgetary reform, to say nothing of overcoming the resistance of the spending departments. The jury is still out. Only time will tell us the outcome of the tradeoff between reform drivers and reform capacity.

THE ORGANIZATION OF PART 9

Chapter 25 by Mark Hallerberg is about the changing role of institutions – more precisely, rules to deal with the principal–agent problem, moral hazard and common pool resources, using empirical data collected for a report commissioned by the Dutch Minister of Finance about the European member states. He concludes that the selection and the effectiveness of institutions may be affected by the characteristics of the political system.

Chapter 26 by Rita Hilton and Phil Joyce takes a historical angle, looking at the current revival of performance budgeting or rather performance-informed budgeting. A survey of the OECD shows that a lot is going on in the field, but that might be only lip service. The authors identify five critical factors, notably that participants must have incentives to use performance information.

Chapter 27 is about the latest trend in budgeting, which has to do with accrual budgeting. It has its roots in accounting and

control rather than in budgeting. The ins and outs are discussed by Leonard Kok, leaning on evidence of a survey of the OECD that records a growing interest. However, one may question the utility, since only a small portion of the budget is applicable for accrual budgeting.

NOTES

1 Frans K.M. van Nispen is affiliated with the Department of Public Administration of the Erasmus University of Rotterdam, the Netherlands.

2 It is hard to find a book on public budgeting without any reference to his work.

3 In all fairness, I should note Verne B. Lewis already mentioned that instrumentalism in his contribution to (the discussion about) a budgetary theory (Lewis 1952).

4 The sequestration introduced by the Gramm–Rudman–Hollings amendment was built upon automatic across-the-board cuts.

5 The incoming Minister of Finance, Zalm, successfully launched a norm, named after him, to curb public spending at the start of the so-called 'purple coalition' in the Netherlands (1994).

6 The other criteria being participation in the Exchange Rate Mechanism (ERM) for more than two years and the reduction of the inflation rates, the interest rates and the public debt.

7 The budgetary policy of the European member states is geared to country-specific medium-term objectives (MTO) requiring a reduction of the underlying structural budget deficit adjusted for the cycle by at least 0.5% of GDP per year.

REFERENCES

Buchanan, James M. (1995), Clarifying Confusion about the Balanced Budget Amendment. Paper presented at a conference of the National Taxpayers Association, Crystal City, VA, May 22.

Dunleavy, P. et al. (2005), New Public Management is Dead – Long Live Digital-Era Governance, *Journal of Public Administration Research and Theory*, (16) September: 467–494.

Key Jr, Valdimer O. (1940), The Lack of a Budgetary Theory, *American Political Science Review*, (34) 6: 1137–1144. Reprinted in: Albert C. Hyde & Jay M. Shafritz (eds) (1978), *Government*

Budgeting: Theory, Process, Politics. Oak Park, IL: Moore Publishing Company, pp. 19–24.

LeLoup, Lance T. (1978), The Myth of Incrementalism: Analytic Choices in Budgetary Theory, *Polity*, 10 (4): 488–509.

LeLoup, Lance T. (1988), From Microbudgeting to Macrobudgeting: Evolution in Theory and Practice, in Irene S. Rubin (ed.), *New Directions in Budget Theory.* New York: State University of New York Press, pp. 19–42.

Lewis, Verne B. (1952), Toward a Theory of Budgeting, *Public Administration Review*, (12) 1: 42–54.

OECD (2010a), Fiscal Consolidation: Requirements, Timing, Instruments and Institutional Arrangements, *OECD Economic Outlook*, Volume 2010/2, Chapter IV. Paris: OECD Publishing.

OECD (2010b), *Public Administration after 'New Public Management': Value for Money in Government*, Vol. 1. Paris: OECD Publishing.

Pollitt, Christopher & Geert Bouckaert (2004), *Public Management Reform: A Comparative Analysis*, 2nd edn. Oxford: Oxford University Press.

Seib, Gerald F. Seib (2008), In Crisis, Opportunity for Obama, *Wall Street Journal*, November 21. At: http://online.wsj.com/article/SB122721278056345271.

html#articleTabs%3Darticle; retrieved October 6, 2011.

Rubin, Irene S. (ed.) (1988), *New Directions in Budget Theory* (wrongly labeled Budget History). New York: State University of New York Press.

Savage, James D. (1988), *Balanced Budgets and American Politics.* Ithaca, NY: Cornell University Press.

Schick, Allen (1983), Incremental Budgeting in a Decremental Age, *Policy Sciences*, (16) 1: 1–25.

Schick, Allen (2003), The Performing State: Reflection on an Idea Whose Time Has Come but Whose Implementation Has Not, *OECD Journal on Budgeting*, 3 (2): 71–103.

Van Nispen, Frans K.M. (2011), Budgetary Coordination in the Eurozone. The Reform of the Stability and Growth Pact. Paper delivered at the 6th ECPR General Conference, Reykjavik, August 25–27.

Van Nispen Frans K.M. & Johan J.A. Posseth (2009), Performance Informed Budgeting in Europe: The Ends Justify the Means, Don't They? San Domenico di Fiesole: EUI/RSCAS, EUI Working Papers, RSCAS 2009/39.

Wildavsky, Aaron (1964), *The Politics of the Budgetary Process.* Boston, MA: Little Brown & Company.

25

Fiscal Rules and Fiscal Policy

Mark Hallerberg

Fiscal rules are increasingly popular – in European Union (EU) member states, for example, the use of fiscal rules has grown from 16 in 1990 to 47 in 2000 to 67 in 2008 (European Commission 2010). Worldwide, according to the International Monetary Fund (IMF), there were 80 countries by 2009 with either national or supranational fiscal rules in place (IMF 2009). In response to the global financial crisis and the euro crisis, countries have added even more rules, such as Germany's debt brake, while allowing other rules to weaken and sometimes removing them entirely.

Formal rules in budgeting are designed to address certain problems. The focus of this chapter therefore is on classifying formal rules according to the problems some rules are meant to solve. It begins with a consideration of the common pool resource problem that develops when spending is targeted to a specific group but the taxes used to pay for them come from general revenues. It then looks at a related issue that can exist when there are multiple levels of government: namely, the moral hazard problem. Lower levels of government are prone to spend more when they expect that higher levels of government are going to bail them out.

The third topic is the "principal–agent" problem. Budgets inevitably involve some form of delegation of authority. The problem arises when the "agent" does not do what the "principal" wants her to do. In practice, the literature discusses problems that arise when voters delegate authority to elected officials, and when elected officials delegate authority to bureaucrats. The final section discusses who chooses fiscal rules. An important question is whether the institutions themselves matter. If persons with preferences for tighter fiscal discipline always choose certain fiscal rules over others, there is a question whether the preferences or the institutions drive the results.

RULES THAT CENTRALIZE THE BUDGET PROCESS: THE COMMON POOL RESOURCE PROBLEM

One of the fundamental problems of budgeting is what is known as the common pool resource (CPR) problem. The "common pool" in a budgeting framework consists of government revenues. Policy makers draw from this pool when they spend money.

The problem arises when policy makers consider fully the consequences of their spending decisions but do not consider fully how their decisions affect the common pool.[1] Theoretical work indicates that under such a situation policy makers will spend more than the case where they consider completely the tax implications of their decisions. In a multi-period framework, the budget deficits of the government will also be larger and governments will carry larger debt burdens (e.g., Velasco 2000; Krogstrup and Wyplosz 2010).

A question to ask is why policy makers do not consider the full tax implications of their decisions. There are two reasons: one that concerns the preferences of decision makers and one that concerns the budget process. First, there may be incentives for policy makers not to consider the full tax burden. Weingast, Shepsle, and Johnsen (1981) provide a nice example from the US Congress. Voters elect Congresspersons in electoral districts where only one candidate wins and the candidate with the most votes is declared the winner. Representatives appeal to voters in their district through budget policy. Voters like additional spending on projects like bridges, new museums, and the like where they live, but they do not like additional taxes. The representative knows that additional spending is financed by a tax base that includes the entire country, not just the electoral district. In the US House of Representatives, where there are 435 members, this means that each Congressperson worries about only 1/435 of the tax burden (assuming that the tax burden is evenly distributed in the country when making budget decisions). Congresspersons will therefore support more spending in their districts than they would if their district alone had to pay for the spending. It should be noted that this type of incentive structure is not limited to the US Congress or even to legislatures – in a Cabinet setting, a Minister of Defense may consider more the benefits of new planes than their cost implications, while a member of a Green Party may worry more about cleaning up toxic waste sites than where the money is coming from to pay for the clean-up.

Whether policy makers who do not have reasons to consider the entire tax burden make decisions that increase the CPR problem is the second issue to consider; this concerns the decision-making process itself. The classic article by Weingast, Shepsle, and Johnsen (1981) details how the CPR problem can encourage "log rolls" among Congresspersons, who make informal agreements among themselves to back each other's spending proposals for their districts. The way Congresspersons vote on spending determines whether the log rolls happen. Note that if bills for spending in districts are voted on sequentially and separately, Congresspersons should vote for no bill but their own. The reason is that other bills simply increase the tax burden on one's voters without providing any tangible benefits. Some sort of institutional rule is needed to maintain log rolls in legislatures with many members. In another work, Shepsle and Weingast (1994) argue that "closed rules" (simple up or down votes on bills with no possibility of amendment) as well as votes on packages of bills in the form of omnibus bills allow log rolls. In settings with fewer decision makers, informal rules to support each other may be all that is necessary for a log roll to function. Drees (1955) argues that in the Netherlands logrolls were simply implicit and required no formal discussion. Von Hagen (1992) finds that full Cabinet votes on budget bids from different ministries encourage log-rolling behavior. The problem can therefore arise in both parliaments and in Cabinets.

It is also possible that the decision-making process itself hides the full tax implications of additional spending. One policy maker may have a mandate only to increase security at airports while another policy maker is given the task to improve air quality. If their budget requests are simply aggregated into the total budget, there will be little consideration of the tax implications of their decisions and the CPR problem will be endemic. This pattern of decision making is referred to as "bottom-up" budgeting. A second possibility is that the policy makers do not know how much others in the government are spending. If all relevant actors understood the true dimensions of their spending decisions they might modify their own behavior. Empirical studies indicate that "fragmented" decision making leads to higher levels of spending and to higher budget deficits than in "unfragmented" systems: see Kontopoulos and Perotti (1999), Volkerink and de Haan (2000), and Wehner (2010) for discussions of OECD (Organisation for Economic Co-operation and Development) countries; see Baqir (2001) for a discussion of fragmentation in US cities.

These two sources of the CPR problem lead to several suggestions for how to solve it, but they all have the following in common – the goal is to assure that the decision taken is one that considers the full tax implications of any spending. A first solution is to assure that an important budget player has reason to care about the entire budget. Finance ministers at the national level and city managers at the local level can serve as this actor. In one of the classic texts on budgeting, Wildavsky (1975) conceives of the finance minister as the "guardian" of the Treasury who keeps the spending of "advocates" (or spending ministers) in check. Building upon this logic, one could argue that the stronger the finance minister, the more fiscal discipline (Hahm et al. 1996). The Inter-American Development Bank (1997), while noting that most Latin American countries have "strong" finance ministers already, nevertheless argues that strengthening the finance minister would lead to higher budget discipline. Measures a government can take to strengthen the finance minister include:

- having the finance minister propose the annual budget;
- requiring that budget negotiations are between the finance minister and a relevant spending minister and not before the full Cabinet; and

- allowing the finance minister to cut spending during the execution of the budget.

The key is to have budget rules that increase the discretionary power of the actor who considers the entire tax burden.

Not all scholars recommend stronger finance ministers in all cases, however. Hallerberg, Strauch, and von Hagen (2009), while noting that stronger finance ministers play a critical in some countries, caution that the coalition structure of governments may make such "strong" ministers impractical. A given coalition partner may not be willing to delegate decision-making powers to one central player who is not from this partner's party, and this unwillingness increases if the parties in government expect to face each other in the next election. Hallerberg, Strauch, and von Hagen (2009) propose an alternative approach for parliamentary democracies with multi-party coalition governments. As part of their coalition agreement, parties should negotiate "fiscal contracts" that provide detailed spending targets for every ministry. In a country like the Netherlands, for example, parties agree to the budget figures before they agree which party should head which ministry (e.g., Bos 2007). This process assures that the actors consider the tax burden of their decisions on the entire coalition. It is also a process that is most successful when a series of rules exist to reinforce the original contract. Rules for what to do when revenues are too high or too low, for example, allow the actors to avoid contract renegotiations that can spell the end of the coalition.

A second solution proposed is that budget processes be "top-down" instead of "bottom-up." Decision makers first decide on a total spending figure in a "top-down"; then they consider how the total should be divided among the different ministries and departments. An agreement first on the total level should lead decision makers to consider tradeoffs among different spending priorities, which would not occur when the process is "bottom-up" (e.g., Ljungman 2009; see also Wicksell 1896, for the earliest exposition).

Many countries have since instituted some form of a top-down procedure: from the Congressional Budget and Impoundment Control Act of 1974 in the United States that required the Congress to pass aggregate spending targets before a vote on specific appropriations (Wildavsky and Caiden 1997) to sweeping budgetary reforms in Sweden in the mid-1990s that require parliament to pass aggregate targets for the following three years (Molander 2000).

Not all scholars agree, however, that a move to a "top-down" approach is helpful. In an influential article, Ferejohn and Krehbiel (1987) argue that politicians that want more spending can simply pad the aggregate figures, and they provide examples where top-down decision making would lead to more spending than a bottom-up approach. In assessing the discussion, it is important to remember the problem that is being solved and to ask whether the process is forcing the actors to consider the entire tax burden when they make decisions. Changes in the budget procedure in Sweden may be instructive. Following a "top-down" logic, the reforms of the mid-1990s introduced a parliamentary vote on aggregates in the spring and more specific votes on budget items in the fall. In summer 2001, and in the face of clear opposition from the Finance Ministry, the parliament voted to move the consideration of the aggregates to the fall, or just before consideration of the specific parts of the budgets. Finance Ministry officials were concerned that this move constituted a de facto return to bottom-up budgeting. The rationale the parliamentary majority used to move the consideration of aggregates, however, was that parliamentarians needed so much information on the budget in spring on individual programs to feel confident enough to vote on the aggregates that, in practice, they were debating the entire budget twice. This argument for the move suggests that simply moving the timing of votes may not be enough to ensure a true "top-down" process. Fiscal outcomes in Sweden during the 2000s, where the country was one of the few

EU members consistently to run budget surpluses, suggest as well that the change in procedure did not lead to weaker fiscal discipline.

RULES ON SUBNATIONAL GOVERNMENTS: MORAL HAZARD

The second issue, known as moral hazard, is closely related to the CPR problem. The argument once again is that policy makers do not consider the full implications of their spending decisions. The root of the problem, however, is different. Instead of an ignorance of a (local) government's own tax burden, the (local) government expects to be able to draw upon a wider (national) tax burden for its financing. It also expects that another government body will bail it out if it gets into trouble. Subnational governments therefore engage in riskier fiscal behavior. For example, Italian regional and local governments routinely ran large deficits in the 1980s with the knowledge that the national government would, and did, rescue them from fiscal insolvency (Bordignon 1999). Fiscal problems at the subnational level have arisen in developing countries as well (e.g., de Mello and Luiz 2000; Rodden 2006). Within the European Union, there is a concern that the introduction of a common currency under Stage III of Economic and Monetary Union (EMU) in 1999 will lead to a moral hazard problem among its states. The argument is that a given state will enjoy the full benefits of additional spending, but will anticipate that its partners will bail it out if it gets in financial trouble. The states participating in EMU would then bear the costs of the bailout.

There are a series of fiscal rules proposed to eliminate the moral hazard problem, but they have one thing in common – they try to make it unlikely that any government can anticipate a bailout. This is more difficult than one may think. The European Union, for example, agreed to a "no bail-out clause" in the Treaty of Maastricht, but most observers, and for that matter most governments, did not consider the clause credible, and the bailouts of Greece (twice), Ireland, and Portugal in 2010 and 2011 indicate that the skeptics in the early years were correct. The reason why is simple – states participating in EMU will likely suffer less from bailing out a country in need than from letting that country go bankrupt. The European Union's "Stability and Growth Pact," which sets minimum budget balances states should maintain unless they are experiencing a serious recession, did not prevent the bailouts nor prevent many member states from running budget deficits larger than 3 percent of gross domestic product (GDP) (Heipertz and Verdun 2010; Hodson 2011).

The EU's requirement that states have certain deficit targets is not new, although the usual arrangement in more traditional national–subnational governmental forms is that the higher-order government imposes some form of budget balance requirement on the lower-level governments. In France and Germany, localities are required to abide by the "golden rule," which means that borrowing in a given year should not exceed total capital outlays (Seitz 1999; see also Rodden 2000). In Sweden, since 2000, local governments are required simply to run balanced budgets. In other states, such as Ireland, Spain, and the United Kingdom, the central government has the (formal) power to limit subnational borrowing.

Unlike in some European countries, where the central government imposes restrictions on local governments, most US states developed balanced budget requirements of their own. These requirements range in practice from an obligation that state governors propose a balanced budget to a ban on state governments carrying over deficits from year to year. Empirical work indicates that not all balanced budget requirements are created equal – only the carryover ban leads in practice to tighter fiscal discipline in the form of higher average surpluses and faster elimination of outstanding deficits (Alt and Lowery

1994; Bohn and Inman 1996). Rattsø (2000) comes to the same conclusion for Norway, where there are formal budget balance requirements but where local governments can carry over deficits from year to year. A usual problems of such rules is that they are too lenient in good times and too tough in bad times (Anderson and Minarik 2006). The provisions for what to do when a rule is violated are also unclear.

A more recent phenomenon is the use of so-called "debt brakes," with Switzerland introducing it in 2004 and Germany in a transition period at the federal level until 2016 and at the state (or Land) level until 2020. In the Swiss case, deviations from the target go into an adjustment account, and if the adjustment account has a deficit of more than 6 percent of last year's spending, it has to be corrected within three years (Bodmer 2006). Similarly, in the German case, if the actual budget outcome varies from the target after adjusting for potential growth, the difference goes into a "control account." If the control account goes over 1.5 percent of GDP, the government then has to repay the amount in a way appropriate to the economic situation (Federal Ministry of Finance 2009.)

There have been several reservations about the use of such limitations in the literature. Eichengreen and von Hagen (1996) argued that no bailout clauses are credible when governments have revenue sources (such as significant tax bases) at their disposal. If revenues come only from central government transfers, central government bailouts are likely because there is no other way for local governments to get out of financial difficulties. Strict rules on subnational governments, therefore, are needed only in cases where subnational governments do not have their own tax bases. Empirically, Eichengreen and von Hagen (1996) examined the circumstances under which upper levels of governments impose debt restrictions on lower levels of government in a sample of 36 countries. They that such restrictions are most common when subnational governments do not have the ability to generate additional revenues through taxes of their own. Sbragia (1996) reinforced this finding in her work on the United States. Most US states limited the borrowing of their communities during the period after the American Civil War, with the restrictions on borrowing often corresponding to a certain percentage of the taxable property base of a given community. These restrictions were meant to assure markets that the locality had enough resources at its disposal to bail itself out of any financial difficulty.

Others suggest that markets can discipline states so that formal rules are not necessary. Someone must lend governments money, and markets will balk at providing finance to states and localities with real default risks. Bird and Tassonyi (2001) found that market pressure plays a significant role in maintaining fiscal discipline in Canadian provinces, even in the absence of formal rules that limit provincial borrowing. Inman (1995) recounted how the city of Philadelphia, Pennsylvania, failed to find buyers for its bonds when bond traders perceived that the city's finances were in disarray. Yet the effects of market pressure do not seem to be consistent across all governments. Willett (2000), for example, indicated that markets tend to respond to fiscal problems relatively late and, when they do respond, tend to overreact and make fiscal corrections more difficult. Mosley (2000) interviewed market participants and found that they pay closest attention to large swings in government policy. Only half of her sample followed government debt levels. This evidence reinforces the impression that markets are not effective at preserving fiscal discipline by themselves, and that effective fiscal rules do serve an important purpose.

There are also concerns about whether such formal restrictions do nothing more than encourage creative accounting. Strauch (1998) found that US states imposing the strictest expenditure limits led simply to a shift from the expenditure to the investment budget. Von Hagen (1991) found that the stringency of expenditure constraints had no effect on total debt. In, 2000, Von Hagen speculated that other studies find significant effects of these limitations because the studies look at state-guaranteed, rather than total, debt. Stringent expenditure constraints lead to a shift from guaranteed to unguaranteed debt instruments. To the extent that these shifts obscure what the government is doing, they may increase the severity of our next issue: namely, the principal–agent problem.

RULES THAT STRENGTHEN ACCOUNTABILITY PRINCIPAL–AGENT PROBLEM

Budgets inevitably involve some form of delegation. Two forms are common in the literature: the first involves voter delegation of authority to elected politicians, whereas the second is from elected politicians to (generally unelected) bureaucrats. The problem arises when the "agent" (or the person delegated authority) does not do what the "principal" (or the delegator of authority) wants her to do. Politicians ignore the directions of voters and spend more money on defense when the electoral mandate seemingly was to improve the environment; bureaucrats hide the true costs of their work so that politicians give bureaucrats more money than it costs to produce a given public good. The general prediction of principal–agent models of budgeting is that the worse the problem, the higher public spending. This is because agent preferences are somehow different than principal preferences. Politicians may, for example, like to spend money on the perks of office such as first-class plane tickets that populations do not want (Niskanen 1971; for a theoretical argument, see Banks 1989). Bureaucrats may not place the same value in finding and eliminating inefficiencies in spending where they exist because they have different priorities for their time.

One solution to the problem is to design a contract between principals and agents that brings the incentives for the agent more in line with what the principals want. This is not that easy, however – contracts can provide perverse incentives (for examples from budgeting, see Kiewiet and McCubbins 1991). Another option is for principals to screen individuals before they select them as agents. Public debates among candidates for office may allow some screening of future politicians. Similarly, the confirmation process for top bureaucrats in some democracies allows the legislature to evaluate whether future heads of departments have preferences that differ greatly from the median in the legislature. Finally, principals may actively monitor agents to learn what the agents are doing.

Monitoring agents is simpler when the actions of agents are observable, and this insight has led to an emphasis in recent years on the benefits of a transparent budget process. A system is transparent when all relevant information on the budget is made available in both a timely and a systematic fashion (OECD 2001: 3). The critical actor then becomes the public. The easier it is for the public to understand what members of the government are doing, the more accountable the public will hold politicians (International Monetary Fund 1998). This accountability tightens the relationship between the first set of principals (public) and agents (elected politicians). It also brings in the public as a monitor to check the second set of principals (elected politicians) and agents (bureaucrats). If agents are doing what principals want, there should be better budget performance.[2]

What budget rules in practice increase transparency? International organizations, such as the IMF, the OECD, and the World Bank, actively encourage governments to increase transparency levels. The IMF has prepared a Manual on Fiscal Transparency that spells out best practices that states should follow. The international organization also encouraged officials from member states to take a voluntary survey that would allow one to assess the level of transparency across different countries. Similarly, the OECD (2001) published a list of "best practices" based on the experiences of its member states.

While emphasizing that some variation across countries should be expected, and for that matter even encouraged, there is general agreement across the international organizations on a set of fiscal practices governments should approximate. The first general category of recommendations concerns the annual budget. States should make budget documents comprehensive, which means that they should include all government revenue sources as well as all expenditures. They should also provide commentaries that explain each part of the budget. The second category concerns assumptions underlying the annual budget. These should be made explicit so that readers can assess for themselves how the budget would change under alternative assumptions. The assumptions should be quite detailed. How many recipients should receive unemployment benefits, the model for making macro-economic forecasts, etc., should be explicit. A third category concerns timing. The annual budget should be presented as one document. It is not possible for someone to get a clear sense of policy tradeoffs if different parts of the budget are presented throughout the year. The government should present the budget with enough lead-time before the end of the current fiscal year so that the legislature can evaluate fully the different parts of the budget.[3] Similarly, the government should develop medium-term budget forecasts that provide estimates of future budgets. It should also publish a series of reports during the execution of the budget that allow persons outside of government to evaluate whether the government is sticking to the budget law. Finally, the international organizations provide a series of technical recommendations on how to increase control and accountability in accounting practices.

Some initial empirical work indicates that increases in the level of transparency that such fiscal rules provide have beneficial effects on fiscal policy. Alt et al. (2001) tested 11 of 76 measures of transparency that appeared in OECD (1999) on spending levels and on budget deficits in 19 OECD countries.[4]

In their empirical analysis, they found that the most transparent states have both lower spending and lower budget deficits than states with lower transparency. Similarly, in a theoretical paper, Milesi-Ferretti (2000) argued that increases in transparency reduce creative accounting often found in countries with formal rules discussed in the previous section. This suggests that a combination of rules that guarantee transparency and that limit spending is beneficial. It should be noted that this emphasis on fiscal transparency accompanies a more general call for greater transparency throughout the economy. The lack of transparency in financial markets and financial institutions may have contributed to the worsening of the Asian financial crisis of the latter part of the 1990s. Fiscal *and* financial rules that increase transparency should consequently be introduced together (Vishwanath and Kaufmann 1999).[5] Alt and Lassen (2006) found that political business cycles are common in countries with lower levels of transparency.

Another way to increase transparency is to bring the level of government closer to voters. There has been a wave of fiscal decentralization around the globe in the past decade, from the creation of regional parliaments with, in Scotland's case, some fiscal powers in the United Kingdom, to an increase in the fiscal responsibilities of states and localities in countries as diverse as Colombia, Russia, Scandinavia, and the United States. One reason for these decentralizations has been to bring the government closer to a people dissatisfied with the provision of public goods at the national level (Tanzi 1999; for a critical review, see Treisman 2007). While decentralization may potentially reduce the scale of the principal–agent problem, the previous section indicated that new difficulties in the form of the moral hazard problem may arise.

Even if the principal has some sense what the agent is doing, there is also a concern whether the agent is meeting the principal's goals. The tasks the agents do may not seem to accomplish much of anything. A poverty reduction program, for example, could spend a lot of money on what seem like worthy projects, but in the end not reduce poverty. This concern has led to what is known as "performance budgeting" or "results-focused management" (OECD 2002). Governments should include both "output" evaluations of performance, or what amount is actually spent, as well as "outcome" evaluations, which consider the impact of the budget on the relevant target group, environment, etc. One way to implement results-focused management is to establish performance contracts that define explicit targets for the government to achieve. In Denmark, for example, since 1992, departments and agencies have agreed to contracts that define targets and required results within a set period of time (Thorn and Lyndrup 2002). In terms of accounting rules, accrual-based accounting facilitates a more accurate consideration of the costs of both outputs *and* outcomes. To date, however, only a few countries within the OECD – such as Australia, Denmark, New Zealand, and the United Kingdom – have accrual budgeting systems (Robinson 2009: 10).

A final issue to consider is a possible difference in the time horizon between voters and politicians.[6] Politicians want to get re-elected, and they therefore prefer fiscal policies that yield immediate electoral payments. Governments may run larger budget deficits in pre-electoral periods in the hope of stimulating the economy. They may also front-load the benefits of a given governmental program in the first year or two after the program passes, while they back-load the costs of a given program into years further in the future. This problem can be the opposite of the re-election incentive, because the politicians expect to lose office. In this case, they are trying to get what they can for their supporters while trying to leave the costs of their policies with their successors (Alesina and Tabellini 1990; Grilli, Masciandaro, and Tabellini 1991).

One proposed solution is to force governments to propose, and, under "normal" conditions, to maintain multi-annual budget programs. Such programs are meant to force governments to think longer term. Under the Stability and Growth Pact, for example, all EU member states must submit a budget program to the European Commission each year that includes five years of data (year −1 to year +3). As noted earlier, such programs also increase transparency. Medium-term expenditure frameworks (MTEFs), in particular, are increasingly common (e.g., Schiavo-Campo 2008). It is doubtful, however, that simply imposing medium-term budget plans will change the incentives politicians face to think short term.

WHO CHOOSES FISCAL INSTITUTIONS?

Another issue concerns what the literature calls the endogeneity of institutions. That is, why do some countries select a given set of fiscal rules while others do not? This question is important. It may be that countries that are predisposed to combat certain types of problems are the ones most likely to adopt fiscal rules that address them. A population that prefers lower taxes, for example, may support a formal rule that limits tax collections, while a population that will support higher taxes will not support the same rule. This line of inquiry begs the question of whether it is the underlying preferences, rather than the formal rules themselves, that are critical.

There has been little work that takes the question of why the use of fiscal rules differs across countries seriously. Baqir (2001), in his study of US city budgeting, hypothesizes that cities with many electoral districts have greater CPR problems and are more likely to choose a strong executive veto to control the problem. Yet he is concerned that some external effect may explain a change both in the presence of an executive veto *and* in the number of districts. To get at this problem, he finds an instrument − the number of streams,

which are likely to be natural boundaries for electoral districts − for one institutional feature he cares about: namely, the number of electoral districts. Once this correction is introduced, he finds both that cities with many districts are more likely to have executive vetoes and that increases in the veto player of the mayor decrease the level of spending.[7] Fabrizio and Mody (2010) suggest that large deficits retard reforms, but that macro-economic imbalances increase the sense of crisis and make reforms more likely.

As mentioned briefly in a previous section, Hallerberg and von Hagen (1999) and Hallerberg, Strauch, and von Hagen (2009) are concerned about the effectiveness of certain types of rules given the presence of other political institutions. Some scholars argue that proportional representation electoral systems, for example, lead to poorer budgetary performance than plurality (or first-past-the-post) electoral systems because proportional representation leads to unstable governments (Grilli et al. 1991), while others contend that multi-party coalition governments lead to larger budget deficits (Roubini and Sachs 1989) because coalition governments cannot make quick changes to budget profiles that one-party governments can. The counter-argument is that these institutions by themselves do not affect the budget; rather, they *do* affect the type of fiscal rules that are most effective in enforcing fiscal discipline. The "strong finance minister" model mentioned before works best under one-party majority governments, which are usually found in countries with plurality electoral systems. Detailed "fiscal contracts" among coalition partners can serve the same purpose of maintaining fiscal discipline in countries with multi-party coalition governments. Hence, underlying factors found in a country's political system may affect both the choice of a given set of fiscal rules as well the effectiveness of those institutions once they are introduced.

Recent scholarship that attempts to correct for the endogeneity question therefore indicates that formal rules still matter, but scholars should continue to explore this issue. More work in this area clearly needs to be done.

CONCLUSION

Fiscal rules have become increasingly popular. They are increasingly viewed as a precondition for fiscal discipline. In Europe, for example, there is a growing consensus that all members of the eurozone should adopt some form of Germany's debt brake. Whether domestic parliaments will pass this type of restriction on their budget is another question, but this chapter tried to make clear the theoretical rationale for such rules.

This chapter reviews three problems that fiscal policy makers commonly face – the common pool resource problem, the moral hazard problem, and the principal–agent problem. It also discusses several proposed solutions in the literature. While the chapter treats the problems separately for expositional purposes, it also indicates that solutions to one problem may affect the severity of other problems. Fiscal decentralization may decrease the principal–agent problem, for example, but increase the severity of a moral hazard problem. Changes in fiscal rules should therefore not be considered in isolation of one another, but rather as a complete package. Only in this way can one assess the true costs and benefits of using one set of fiscal rules over another. This lesson is especially relevant in countries in danger of experiencing sovereign debt crises, but it is pertinent more broadly for all fiscal systems.

On a more academic level, scholars are only beginning to explain why some countries adopt the fiscal rules they do while others do not. There has certainly been progress on this topic over the past decade, but more work should be done, and the recent crises and the responses to them provide plenty of additional data for scholars to use in their analyses.

NOTES

1 This problem is not limited to budgeting situations. The best theoretical discussions are found in Elinor Ostrom's Nobel-prize winning work (see Ostrom 1990).

2 There is a growing literature that considers what actions the government can take to strengthen the role of the public as a watchdog. Freedom of information acts, laws that give the press wide berth to investigate the government and to publish reports as the press sees fit, and guarantees that persons who are critical of the government are not charged easily with treason all improve the ability of the public to monitor the government. This literature is not directly relevant for an chapter on fiscal rules, but it is important for the reader to understand that one cannot simply assume that the public will be able to serve its watchdog function unless other types of "rules" are in place.

3 The OECD suggests that budgets go to the legislature at least 90 days before the end of the fiscal year; see OECD (2001: 4).

4 They include any measure that increases information on the budget in fewer documents; increases the level of independent verification of the government's figures; non-arbitrary language, such as the use of accrual accounting; and more justification of what the government does with budgeting, such as a legal requirement that the government must present an *ex post* report of how it spent the budget.

5 Joseph Stiglitz (2000) provides a good discussion in general of information economics and, more specifically, of the role of transparency as applied to corporate governance.

6 In the central banking literature one talks about a "time inconsistency" problem. The idea is that politicians have different time horizons than their populations. Governments pledge to have low inflation, but before elections they are tempted to push up inflation. Populations anticipate this response, and they factor in higher inflation in their wage demands. A country then gets a suboptimal policy that leads to higher levels of inflation. If the agents delegate the setting of inflation to a (conservative) central bank, the country will experience the optimal policy that leads to lower inflation.

7 See Knight and Levinson (2000) for a similar type of analysis for the US states.

REFERENCES

Alesina, Alberto and Guido Tabellini (1990) 'A Positive Theory of Fiscal Deficits and Government Debt', *Review of Economic Studies*, 57: 403–414.

Alt, James E. and David Dreyer Lassen (2006) 'Transparency, Political Polarization, and Political Budget Cycles in OECD Countries', *American Journal of Political Science*, 50 (3): 530–550.

Alt, James E. and Robert C. Lowery (1994) 'Divided Government, Fiscal Institutions, and Budget Deficits: Evidence from the States', *American Political Science Review*, 88 (4): 811–828.

Alt, James E., David Dreyer Lassen, and David Skilling (2001) 'Fiscal Transparency and Fiscal Policy Outcomes in OECD Countries'. Paper presented at the 2001 American Political Science Association Meetings, San Francisco, CA.

Anderson, Barry and Joseph J. Minarik (2006) 'Design Choices for Fiscal Policy Rules',. *OECD Journal of Budgeting*, 5 (4): 159–208.

Banks, Jeffrey S. (1989) 'Agency Budgeting, Cost Information, and Auditing,' *American Journal of Political Science*, 33 (3): 670–699.

Baqir, Reza (2001) 'Government Spending, Legislature Size, and the Executive Veto'. Paper presented at the 2001 American Political Science Association Meetings, San Francisco, CA.

Bird, Robert M. and Almos T. Tassonyi (2001) 'Constraints on Provincial and Municipal Borrowing in Canada: Markets, Rules, and Norms', *Canadian Public Administration – Administration Publique du Canada*, 44 (1): 84–109.

Bodmer, Frank (2006) 'The Swiss Debt Brake: How it Works and What Can Go Wrong', *Schweizerische Zeitschrift für Volkswirtschaft und Statistik*, 142 (3): 307–330.

Bohn, Henning and Robert P. Inman (1996) 'Balanced Budget Rules and Public Deficits: Evidence from the U.S. States'. NBER Working Paper #5553.

Bordignon, Massimo (1999) 'Problems of Soft Budget Constraints in Intergovernmental Relationships: The Case of Italy'. Manuscript.

Bos, Frits (2007) 'The Dutch Fiscal Framework: History, Current Practice and the Role of the CPB'. CPB Document 150 (July).

De Mello, Luiz R., Jr (2000) 'Fiscal Decentralization and Intergovernmental Fiscal Relations: A Cross-Country Analysis', *World Development*, 28 (2): 365–380.

Drees, W., Jr (1955) *On the Level of Government Expenditures in The Netherlands after the War*. Leiden: Stenfert Kroese.

Eichengreen, Barry and Jürgen von Hagen (1996) 'Federalism, Fiscal Restraints, and European Monetary Union', *American Economic Review*, 86 (May): 134–138.

Fabrizio, Stefania and Ashoka Mody (2010) 'Breaking the Impediments to Budgetary Reforms: Evidence from Europe', *Economics & Politics*, 22 (3): 362–391.

Federal Ministry of Finance (2009) *Reforming the Constitutional Budget Rules in Germany*. Berlin.

Ferejohn, John and Keith Krehbiel (1987) 'The Budget Process and the Size of the Budget', *American Journal of Political Science*, 31: 296–320.

Grilli, Vittorio, Donato Masciandaro, and Guido Tabellini (1991) 'Institutions and Policies', *Economic Policy*, 6: 341–391.

Hahm, Sung Deuk, Mark S. Kamlet, and David C. Mowery (1996) 'The Political Economy of Deficit Spending in Nine Industrialized Parliamentary Democracies. The Role of Fiscal Institutions', *Comparative Political Studies*, 29 (1): 52–77.

Hallerberg, Mark and Jürgen von Hagen (1999) 'Electoral Institutions, Cabinet Negotiations, and Budget Deficits within the European Union', in James Poterba and Jürgen von Hagen (eds), *Fiscal Institutions and Fiscal Performance*. Chicago, IL: University of Chicago Press, pp. 209–232.

Hallerberg, Mark, Rolf Strauch, and Jürgen von Hagen (2009) *Fiscal Governance: Evidence from Europe*. Cambridge: Cambridge University Press.

Heipertz, Martin and Amy Verdun (2010) *Ruling Europe: The Politics of the Stability and Growth Pact*. Cambridge: Cambridge University Press.

Hodson, Dermot (2011) *Governing the Euro Area in Good Times and Bad*. Oxford: Oxford University Press.

Inman, Robert (1995) 'How to Have a Fiscal Crisis: Lessons from Philadelphia,' *American Economic Review*, 85 (2): 378–383.

Inter-American Development Bank (1997) *Latin America After a Decade of Reforms*. Washington, DC: Johns Hopkins University Press.

International Monetary Fund (1998) *Code of Good Practices on Fiscal Transparency – Declaration of Principles*. Washington, DC: International Monetary Fund.

Kiewiet, D. Roderick and Mathew D. McCubbins (1991) *The Logic of Delegation. Congressional Parties and the Appropriations Process*. Chicago, IL: University of Chicago Press.

Knight, Brian and Arik Levinson (2000) 'Fiscal Institutions in US States', in Rolf Strauch and Jürgen von Hagen (eds), *Institutions, Politics, and Fiscal Policy*. Boston: Kluwer, pp. 167–190.

Kontopoulos, Yianas and Roberto Perotti (1999) 'Government Fragmentation and Fiscal Policy Outcomes: Evidence from OECD Countries', in James Poterba and Jürgen von Hagen (eds), *Fiscal Institutions and Fiscal Performance*. Chicago, IL: University of Chicago Press, pp. 81–102.

Krogstrup, Signe and Wyplosz, Charles (2010) 'A Common Pool Theory of Supranational Deficit Ceilings', *European Economic Review*, 54 (2): 269–278.

Ljungman, Gösta (2009) 'Top-Down Budgeting – An Instrument to Strengthen Budget Management'. IMF Working Paper 09/243.

Milesi-Ferretti, Gian Maria (2000) 'Good, Bad, or Ugly? On the Effects of Fiscal Rules with Creative Accounting'. IMF Working Paper #172.

Molander, Per (2000) 'Reforming Budgetary Institutions: Swedish Experiences', in Rolf Strauch and Jürgen von Hagen (eds), *Institutions, Politics, and Fiscal Policy*. Boston: Kluwer, pp. 191–214.

Mosley, Layna (2000) 'Room to Move: International Financial Markets and National Welfare States', *International Organization*, 54 (4): 737–773.

Niskanen, William A. (1971) *Bureaucracy and Representative Government*. Chicago, IL: Aldine Atherton.

Organisation for Economic Co-operation and Development (1999). Document from Alt et al.

Organisation for Economic Co-operation and Development (2001) *OECD Best Practices for Budget Transparency*. Paris: Organisation for Economic Co-operation and Development.

Organisation for Economic Co-operation and Development (2002). *Overview of Results Focussed [sic.] Management and Budgeting in OECD Member Countries*. Public Management Service Publication no. PUMA/SBO(2002)1. Paris: Organisation for Economic Co-operation and Development.

Ostrom, Elinor (1990) *Governing the Commons*. Cambridge: Cambridge University Press.

Rattsø, Jørn (2000) 'Fiscal Adjustment with Vertical Fiscal Imbalance: Empirical Evaluation of Administrative Federalism in Norway'. Manuscript, Norwegian University of Science and Technology, October.

Robinson, Marc (2009) 'Accrual Budgeting and Fiscal Policy', *OECD Journal on Budgeting*, 1: 75–103.

Rodden, Jonathan (2000) 'Breaking the Golden Rule: Fiscal Behavior with Rational Bailout Expectations in the German States'. Prepared for the Workshop European Fiscal Federalism in Comparative Perspective Center for European Studies, Harvard University, November 4.

Rodden, Jonathan (2006) *Hamilton's Paradox*. Cambridge: Cambridge University Press.

Roubini, Nouriel and Jeffrey D. Sachs (1989) 'Political and Economic Determinants of Budget Deficits in the Industrial Democracies', *European Economic Review*, 33: 903–938.

Sbragia, Alberta (1996) *Debt Wish: Entrepreneurial Cities, U.S. Federalism, and Economic Development*. Pittsburgh, PA: University of Pittsburgh Press.

Schiavo-Campo, Salvatore (2008) 'Of Mountains and Molehills: "The" Medium-Term Expenditure Framework'. Paper presented at the Conference on Sustainability and Efficiency in Managing Public Expenditures, Organized by the East–West Center and Korea Development Institute Honolulu, Hawaii, 24–25 July.

Seitz, Helmut (1999) 'Subnational Government Bailouts in Germany'. Center for European Integration Studies (ZEI) Working Paper.

Shepsle, Kenneth A. and Barry R. Weingast (1994) 'Positive Theories of Congressional Institutions', *Legislative Studies Quarterly*, 29: 149–179.

Stiglitz, Joseph E. (2000) 'The Contributions of the Economics of Information to Twentieth Century Economics', *Quarterly Journal of Economics*, 115 (4): 1441–1478.

Strauch, Rolf (1998) 'Budget Processes and Fiscal Discipline: Evidence from the US States'. Center for European Integration Studies (ZEI) Working Paper.

Tanzi, Vito (1999) 'The Changing Role of the State in the Economy: A Historical Perspective', in L.R. de Mello, Jr and K. Fukasaku, *Fiscal Decentralization, Intergovernmental Fiscal Relations and Macroeconomic Governance*. OECD: Paris.

Thorn, Kristian and Mads Lyndrup (2002) 'The Quality of Public Expenditure – Challenges and Solutions in Results Focused Management in the Public Sector. Denmark.' Manuscript, OECD.

Treisman, Daniel (2007) *The Architecture of Government*. Cambridge: Cambridge University Press.

Velasco, Andrés (2000) 'Debts and Deficits with Fragmented Fiscal Decision-making', *Journal of Public Economics*, 76: 105–125.

Vishwanath, Tara and Daniel Kaufmann (1999) 'Towards Transparency in Finance and Governance'. Manuscript, World Bank.

Volkerink, Bjørn and Jakob de Haan (2000) 'Fragmented Government Effects on Fiscal Policy: New Evidence'. Manuscript, University of Groningen.

Von Hagen, Jürgen (1991) 'A Note on the Empirical Effectiveness of Formal Fiscal Restraints', *Journal of Public Economics*, 44: 199–210.

Von Hagen, Jürgen (1992) 'Budgeting Procedures and Fiscal Performance in the European Communities', *Economic Papers*, 96.

Von Hagen, Jürgen (2000) 'Budgeting Institutions and Public Spending'. Manuscript, Center for European Integration Studies, University of Bonn, December.

Wehner, Joachim (2010) 'Cabinet Structure and Fiscal Policy Outcomes',. *European Journal of Political Research*, 49 (5): 631–653.

Weingast, Barry, Kenneth A. Shepsle, and Christopher Johnsen (1981) 'The Political Economy of Benefits and Costs: A Neoclassical Approach to Distributive Politics', *Journal of Political Economy*, 89: 642–664.

Wicksell, Knut (1896) *Finanztheoretische Untersuchungen*. Jena: Gustav Fischer.

Wildavsky, Aaron (1975) *Budgeting: A Comparative Theory of the Budget Process*. Boston and Toronto: Little, Brown, and Company.

Wildavsky, Aaron and Naomi Caiden (1997) *The New Politics of the Budgetary Process*, 3rd edn. New York: HarperCollins.

Willett, Thomas D. (2000) 'International Financial Markets as Sources of Crisis or Discipline', *Princeton Essays in International Finance*, No. 218. Princeton, NJ: Princeton University Press.

Performance-Informed Budgeting: A Global Reform

Rita M. Hilton and Philip G. Joyce

Public sector budgets allocate scarce resources. Because these budgets result from political processes, they will always be surrounded by some degree of contention: whether about content, process, or both. Calls for process improvements typically rise from one of two directions. On a routine basis, dissatisfaction that interested parties may have – either with allocations or outcomes – lead them to propose or "pull" for changes. On a less predictable basis, major economic events or pressures can be a source of pressure or "push" – for adjustment in public budgets. Changes may be focused on the process of deciding on allocations, or it may relate to managing expenditures for efficient outcomes.

Reforms can range from those genuinely intended to promote better use of public resources within sectors, to efforts aimed at gaining political advantage, all the way to those intended to position governments to adapt to economic shocks. An apparently pejorative view is that budget process reform is "a proposal put forth by losers in an attempt to become winners" (Kliman and Fisher, 1995, p. 27). However, in the early

twenty-first century, reform efforts to increase government effectiveness within sectors by introducing more information on actual performance into decisions on allocation of public resources gradually gained currency worldwide. Whether progress on this front was sufficient to position governments to adjust successfully in the face of worldwide economic shocks that began unfolding in 2008 remains an open question. That continued progress in using performance information to allocate public resources would enhance effectiveness is virtually indisputable: whether progress will transpire is a matter of conjecture.

Performance-oriented budget reforms have been attempted across settings, with varying degrees of success, for the past half-century. Despite extensive government expenditures on "information technology" across the world, evidence indicates that routine use of performance information to ensure effectiveness in allocation and execution in public budgets is uneven. So called "performance-based budgeting" is hard to carry out in practice because: it is conceptually difficult; it requires extensive changes in practice; and supporters of the status quo often raise significant barriers to implementation.

This chapter offers an integrative view of the relationship between performance information and government budget processes. The chapter is organized into three broad sections:

- First, we provide a framework for considering the use of performance information in government budgeting. We prefer the term "performance-*informed* budgeting," noting that the relationship between performance and resources has been an abiding concern of budget reformers and that performance information can be used in many ways at many different stages of the budget process. There is no "one way" – and almost any sound effort is better than no effort.
- Second, we discuss preconditions for the use of performance information in government budgeting. We first cover the necessary conditions for effective budgeting in general. Conditions necessary for successful implementation of more sophisticated techniques – i.e., performance-informed budgeting – include clarity of mission, appropriate performance and cost measurement, and presence of incentives for use of information in making budget decisions.
- Third, the chapter reviews the current state of performance-informed budgeting, with a primary focus on practice in the United States (state/local and national governments) and relatively wealthy countries that are a part of the Organisation for Economic Co-operation and Development (OECD) – complemented by information on selected efforts underway in developing countries. As countries strive to deal with post-2008 debt crises, partially by reducing the public footprint, using data on what works and what doesn't to inform allocation decisions would appear vitally important. Failure to use such data essentially guarantees ineffective use of public resources.

USING PERFORMANCE INFORMATION FOR BUDGETING – HISTORICAL AND CONCEPTUAL FRAMEWORK

One of the major criticisms leveled at government budget processes is that they stop short (perhaps far too short) of asking – and

in turn answering – outcome questions. Often the focus is at best on outputs purchased; many questions don't get past inputs. ("How many dollars are flowing into my state, or legislative district?") For this reason, efforts to integrate consideration of results into budget processes have been central to budget reform since mid-twentieth century.

Initiatives – e.g., the Planning, Programming, Budgeting System (PPBS), management by objectives (MBO), etc. – largely failed to deliver on their promise. The early effort of PPBS, for example, "died of multiple causes, any of which was sufficient." (Schick, 1973, p. 148) A comprehensive review of PPBS and other systems at both the national and state levels in the United States (Harkin, 1982) noted that there were several reasons that these reforms tended to fail. First, opposition from key actors who feared reforms might interfere with flow of funds to key electoral constituencies impeded process change. Second, difficulties inherent in the need for diverse stakeholders to agree on programs' goals and objectives interfered with development of valid performance measures. Finally, perceptions that overwhelming amounts of data are required to track performance tended to kill the systems – particularly when practice indicated data were not being used. Indeed, Aaron Wildavsky indicated that the PPBS reform not only failed but also was destined to fail, because "(i)ts defects are defects in principle, not in execution. PPB does not work because it cannot work … it requires ability to perform cognitive operations that are beyond present human (or technical) capacities" (Wildavsky, 1984, p. 199).

The failure of comprehensive PPBS, however, did not extinguish interest in the genre of reform. The logic of budgeting for results is so intuitively appealing that it has remained a primary focus for budget reformers. Efforts in the stream were reinvigorated in the early 1990s: first in OECD countries such as Australia and New Zealand (Holmes and Shand, 1995), then in state and local governments in the United States (Osborne and

Gaebler, 1992; Ho, 2011; Hou et al., 2011), then in the national government in the United States (Joyce, 2011), and finally in the developing world. The continuing thread of process reform efforts, often described under the rubric "performance-based budgeting," aims to explicitly link budget allocation to demonstrated performance.

Measuring government performance requires specifying and quantifying a complex set of relationships that involves inputs (the resources used by government programs), outputs (the activities or work performed by the government organization itself), and outcomes (the broader societal results anticipated as a result of the input–output chain). Efforts to base budgets on measures of performance stem from a variety of motivations which span a spectrum of perspectives:

- At the simplest level, there is a desire to constrain the footprint of public expenditures – How can less expensive or fewer inputs be used to achieve a given output/outcome? This view assumes that relations between inputs, outputs and outcomes are identifiable – or implicitly assumes that outcomes are assured, independent of input mix.
- From a more complex policy perspective, reforms may be motivated by questions regarding the nature of relations between inputs, outputs and outcomes – the question might be how to improve outcomes by changing the input mix. For example, in the education sector, an input-focused process would ask the question "How many teachers do we have?" An output-oriented process would ask "How many days of instruction are we delivering?" An outcome-focused process would ask "How much are students learning?"

An underlying problem with so-called "performance-based budgeting" involves the challenge of clarity. The term is the most common among many different descriptors that are used to refer to the connection – desired and/or intended – of performance information and government resources. There is a risk that the practice of using performance information in budgeting can be understood as promoting the replacement of "political" resource allocation with some algorithm that allocates resources based solely on performance data. It is not, in our view, either desirable or useful to encourage adherence to such a simplistic model. There will always be a political and a judgment-based dimension to allocation of public resources. However, in order to promote effective use of resources, performance information should be on the table and easily accessible to all stakeholders when political decisions are made. For this reason, we prefer to use not the term performance-*based* budgeting, but focus instead on the use of performance information throughout the budget process, or what could be called performance-*informed* budgeting.

Using a scheme first articulated by Joyce and Tompkins (2002) permits a more robust view of the role of performance information in the budget process. We look at the full budget process, recognizing that there are important questions to be asked regarding the availability and use of performance information at each stage of the traditional budget process – i.e., budget preparation, budget approval, budget implementation or execution, as well as audit and evaluation.

Why does taking a more comprehensive view of the process matter? Simply put, most research into "performance-based budgeting" has looked only at selected stages of the budget process. Questions of legislative and central budget office use predominate. Since performance information may be productively employed at other stages of the process – i.e., agency budget preparation, budget execution, and audit and evaluation – such an artificially limited scope of inquiry risks missing important opportunities for applying and capturing the benefits from performance-informed budgeting.

The typology presented in Table 26.1 (from Joyce and Tompkins, 2002) suggested a comprehensive approach to thinking about the connection between performance information and the budget. The table illustrates that there are many possible decision points

Table 26.1 Dimensions of performance measurement in the budget process

Stage of budget process	Measures available	Use of measures to:
Budget preparation: *Agency level*	• Agency strategic planning and performance planning • Cost accounting • Performance (outcome) measures	• Make tradeoffs between agency subunits to allocate funds strategically • Build budget justification for submission to central budget office • Determine overlapping services within agency
Budget preparation: *Central budget office*	• Government-wide strategic planning and performance planning • Cost accounting • Performance (outcome) measures	• Make tradeoffs between agencies to allocate funds strategically • Build budget justification for submission to legislative body • Determine overlapping services between agencies
Budget approval: *Legislative*	• Performance measures, accurate cost estimates, and strategic/performance plans included with budget justifications	• Compare costs to marginal effects on performance during legislative funding process • Make performance expectations clear as part of budget allocation
Budget approval: *Chief Executive*	• Implications of legislatively approved budget for achieving government strategic objectives	• Make decisions on signature, veto, or line item veto/reduction informed by performance implications
Budget execution	• Agency and government-wide strategic plans • Performance (outcome) measures • Cost accounting	• Use spending discretion and flexibility to allocate funds in line with strategic priorities and consistent with achievement of agency performance goals
Audit and evaluation	• Agency strategic goals • Actual performance data • Cost accounting information	• Shift focus of audits/evaluations to include performance questions, rather than only financial compliance

Source: Joyce, P.G. and Tompkins, S. (2002) "Using Performance Information for Budgeting: Clarifying the Framework and Investigating Recent State Experience," Chapter 5 in *Meeting the Challenges of Performance-Oriented Government*, Kathryn Newcomer et al., eds. Washington: American Society for Public Administration, pp. 61–96.

at which performance information can be incorporated into the budget process. At each of these decision points, the twin questions of availability and use are equally relevant. A given government or agency might have or make use of performance information at one stage of the process, independent of what might happen at other stages of the process. For example, agencies might make substantial use of performance information in building the budget, while other actors (central budget offices, legislatures) make little or no use of that information at subsequent stages. Conversely, the failure to use performance data in preparation and approval would not prevent a given agency from exercising discretion to pursuing goals and objectives. At the execution stage, agencies may find themselves reviewing likely relations between

alternate strategies and anticipated results (i.e., applying outcome measures).

NECESSARY CONDITIONS FOR PERFORMANCE-INFORMED BUDGETING

Outlining a framework for understanding the role of performance information in budgeting is not enough. In our view, successful implementation of performance-informed budgeting cannot occur unless two sets of conditions are present. First, certain fundamental institutional and technocratic prerequisites must exist to support effective budgeting and financial management. These prerequisites simply do not exist in all settings at all times.

For example, some are much more likely to be present in OECD countries than in developing ones. It is important not to be too enthusiastic about replicating systems across countries, without due regard to institutional realities. Second, even if institutional and technical prerequisites are in place, it is unwise to underestimate the depth and extent of practical difficulties that can be encountered in implementing performance-informed budget reforms.

Fundamental prerequisites for effective budgeting and financial management

A number of characteristics must be present in order for budgeting and financial management systems to accomplish the most basic functions of allocating and tracking public resources. Several attempts have been made in the United States to try and identify useful financial management practices (Strachota, 1994; Meyers, 1997; Ingraham et al., 2003).

Briefly, these characteristics include:

- *The Rule of Law* – Budgets are assumed to be adopted by duly constituted authorities (legislatures and governors, city councils and mayors, parliaments, etc.).
- *Budget Adherence* – Once agreed to, spending and revenue plans are assumed to be carried out as enacted (or close) – they are not remade in a room by the minister of finance and several close associates. If remade, they should be revised by the same legitimate authorities who made them in the first place.
- *Transparency* – The government should make information about the budget available to the public. In addition, there should be a free press that has access to information on government resources.
- *Publicly Expressed Preferences* – The government should have the capability of collecting information on the preferences of the electorate. In the absence of reasonable information on preferences, it is very difficult for resources to be allocated efficiently.
- *Avoidance of Structural Deficits* – Over a number of years, the budget should bring in sufficient

revenues to match expenditures. This recognizes that financial management is a long-term, rather than a single year, proposition. For example, it is a cause for concern if a government uses non-recurring revenues (transfers from other funds, short-term borrowing) to finance continuing expenditures.

- *Timely Budget Adoption* – Adherence to budget timetables can be an important contributor to effective financial management and government performance. In particular, the failure to adopt budgets by the start of the fiscal year creates massive uncertainty and therefore tends to promote inefficiency. This is a huge problem for the United States, which increasingly engages in ad hoc budgeting, and has only adopted a full budget by the beginning of the fiscal year four times since 1977.
- *Forecasting Competence and Predictability* – Revenues and expenditures need to be estimated accurately. If revenues are chronically over-forecast or expenditures are under-forecast, mid-year corrections are often necessary, and this compromises the ability of program managers and other recipients of government funds to have predictable funding flows.
- *A Functioning Accounting System* – At a minimum, a government or government agency should have the ability to know how much money is available and how much has been spent. Many developing countries, in particular, have a history of being unable to provide even the most rudimentary accounting information. But this problem is not necessarily limited to developing countries.
- *Audit Capacity* – Governments should have the capacity to ensure accountability through effective auditing. First, a "preaudit" capacity should exist – this has to do with controls, up-front, on expenditures to guard against overspending. Second, a "postaudit" capacity should be present – governments should know, after the fact, what money was spent for and (perhaps) what was obtained as a result of that spending.

In our view, these are the basics – the building blocks, if you will – which must be in place if budget reforms are to be implemented. If a government cannot establish these basic prerequisites, chances are slim that a successful, meaningful, marriage of performance information, and the budget can be carried out. Perhaps as importantly, governments without the basic building blocks are probably better served through developing basic budgeting capacity than by embracing more ambitious reforms.

Necessary characteristics for successful performance-informed budgeting

Even if these building blocks are present, it does not mean that performance-informed budgeting is easy – or destined to be uniformly successful. As noted earlier, it is hard to argue against bringing more performance information into government decision processes. Conversely, it is easy to ignore the real constraints that make such reforms difficult to accomplish in practice (across countries, regardless of economic status). There are at least five conditions for successful use of performance information in the budget process, each of which is difficult to achieve.

1 *Public entities need to have an explicit, tractable, mission and coherent associated goals.* Holmes and Shand noted that a key condition for performance management in government is "clarity of task and purpose" (Holmes and Shand, 1995). Strategic planning (preferably government-wide), to the extent that it enables decisions to be made that establish clear evidence-based direction for government programs, is crucial. This is often quite difficult to carry out in practice, particularly in countries like the United States that have a fragmented political structure. It is relatively easier in parliamentary systems, where the majority party or coalition actually runs cabinet ministries.

2 *Valid measures of performance need to exist.* It is hard to measure outcomes in the great majority of public programs, and far easier to measure outputs. For example, the US National Aeronautics and Space Administration (NASA) claimed in the 1990s that the goal of its Space Science Program was to "chart the evolution of the universe from origin to destiny." Quite understandably, NASA had no performance measures that would enable it to determine whether it has met this objective. It did have a great number of output indicators: e.g., number of missions

successfully launched. Beyond conceptual challenges of defining relevant indicators, most public sector organizations resist being held accountable for outcomes, since they are influenced by so many factors that are outside of agency – or even government – control.

3 *Accurate measures – and relevant components – of cost need to be developed.* Connecting resources with results implies knowing how much it costs to deliver a given level of outcome. Most public organizations cannot even track how much it costs to deliver an output, largely because of problems with allocating indirect costs. In such situations, extrapolating from output to outcome cost is simply not feasible.

4 *Cost and performance information need to be brought together for budgeting decisions.* There is no simple decision rule for relating cost and performance in the public sector, at least at a macro level. A simple, but incorrect approach (embraced by some members of Congress in the United States) would be to take money from those who fail to meet performance targets, and give more money to those who meet targets. This tack relies on heroic assumptions, one of them about the causal link between money and results. In fact, for any program, sorting out the contribution of funding versus other factors requires a full understanding of the logical relationship between inputs, outputs, exogenous factors, and outcomes.

5 *Finally, participants in the budget process must have incentives to use performance information.* Successful performance-informed budgeting occurs only when those involved in the budget process move beyond the generation and storage of information, to the use of information. This can only occur if budgetary actors have effective incentives (and resources) to *use* information. In fact, the incentive question is probably the most important one to focus on in determining the likelihood that performance information will actually be used in the various stages of budget decision making.

In short, understanding viability of performance-informed budgeting requires determining the extent to which each of these conditions is met. They are additive, in the sense that failure to identify a strategic direction imperils the development of appropriate performance measures, and the lack of appropriate measures of performance and cost undermines the appropriate use of information for budgeting purposes.

PERFORMANCE-INFORMED BUDGETING IN PRACTICE

By the early 2000s, enhancing the use of performance information in government budgeting processes was getting worldwide attention. High levels of attention and activity, however, did not necessarily translate into progress in achieving advocates' goals for performance-informed budgeting. This next section of the chapter will survey the current state of performance-informed budgeting, and consider this in light of post-2008 debt challenges which are exerting drag on governments worldwide. We selectively survey, in turn:

1 Governments (local, state, federal) in the United States.
2 Other industrialized countries (i.e., OECD membership).
3 A limited subset of developing countries.

The United States

In the United States, efforts to better connect performance information and public budgets started at the state and local government level. It only gradually migrated to the federal level.

State and local governments

States and localities were on the cutting edge of implementing reforms to promote performance measurement in budgeting and share good practices. Local governments, including Sunnyvale, CA, Charlotte, NC, Dayton, OH, and Phoenix, AZ, have been frequently cited as examples of localities in which performance measurement was alive, well, and influential. The best-seller *Reinventing Government* (Osborne and Gaebler, 1992) took many of its anecdotes

from local governments and used them to define principles for other governments/agencies to follow. The United States contains more than 80,000 local government units (of uneven size and purpose), so it is very difficult to generalize about local government practice and experience. Some facts, however, are indicative. In 1996 the International City/County Management Association (ICMA) piloted, and in 1998 formally established, the Center for Performance Measurement. This center – in partnership with members from 35 states, and the District of Columbia – provides consulting, training, and data access services for local governments engaged in performance measurement efforts (Gloo, 2011). A recent case study of the use of performance information by the city of Indianapolis concluded that performance information does influence budgetary decisions, but does so at a program level rather than at the department- or government-wide level (Ho, 2011). Notably, if an accurate reflection of practice, it would seem unlikely that performance information has risen to a level at which it informs local budget reductions. This point is non-trivial, and in light of prevailing economic pressures may not bode well for use of performance-informed budgeting at the local level.

State governments have been quite active in strategic planning and performance measurement, especially in the past 20 years. Statewide initiatives, such as the Oregon Benchmarks or Minnesota Milestones, focused on strategic planning (Broom and McGuire, 1995), as did the subsequent Council on Virginia's Future (Barrett and Greene, 2008). A 1998 study (Melkers and Willoughby) reported that as of 1997, 47 of the 50 states indicated that they had some kind of requirement for strategic planning and performance measurement – which these authors defined as performance-based *budgeting*. This definition appears too broad to convey clear meaning about practice. Nevertheless, the significance of the result is that it indicates just how widespread the movement toward attempting to – or claiming to – measure performance in the public sector had become in the United States. While reports of activity are extensive, assessments of effectiveness are more limited.

The Government Performance Project (GPP) is to date the only comprehensieve study of the use of performance information for budgeting in the US states. This project (funded by the Pew Charitable Trusts) which reported on state government management capacity four times between 1999 and 2008, found a relatively consistent set of states engaged in some variant of performance-informed budgeting. States that routinely migrated to the top of the rankings of state governments included Virginia, Utah, Washington, Missouri, Michigan, and Texas. Success in these states was frequently driven by the use of performance information in the budget process. For example, Washington State's "Priorities of Government" (POG) initiative allowed policy makers, particularly during the development of the Governor's budget, to avoid across-the-board cuts in the early 2000s, and informed a more targeted approach to budget reductions (Barrett and Greene, 2008). Predictably, given the federal structure of US government, evidence indicates that adoption of performance-informed budgeting is uneven at the state level in the United States. A 2001 study of states characterized as leaders in performance-oriented budget reform concluded that "neither the executive branch nor the legislature appear to have systematically used outcome data for budgeting" (Liner et al., 2001, p. 12). Texas and Louisiana proved partial exceptions to this pattern, since the legislature appeared to be incorporating performance targets in the budget. Managers in these six states expressed concern that performance information might be used solely to punish agencies not meeting targets – as opposed to being employed to gain a broader understanding of the factors contributing to agency performance. A number of additional challenges were identified as well, including: the problem of dealing with results that do not

happen until after the budget year; the potentially biasing incentives legislators may have to use performance information; and the difficulties of establishing sound analytics for cases in which multiple agencies share performance measures.

Most recently, extending the work of the GPP, Hou and colleagues (2011) presented comprehensive research on state government practices through a comparative case study of 11 states. This research addressed several important questions, including the extent to which performance information assisted these states in managing budget reductions necessitated by the "Great Recession" of 2008–2010. The authors argue persuasively that the recent recession offers an opportunity to test the robustness of performance budgeting initiatives, by asking whether states used performance information to pursue targeted budget reductions – or, alternatively, whether states failed to use performance information in distributing cuts. While Hou and colleagues found some evidence that performance information was being used to inform budget decision making (for example, in the states of Maryland and Louisiana), the predominant story across case studies of states was that performance information was not necessarily applied "as a budget tool in the present fiscal climate." Utah illustrated the essential dilemma. The state was limited in its ability to reduce funding for low-rated social service programs, as the recession necessitated that the state maintain funding for those programs. There was clear (and increasing) public need for services, and no alternative delivery mechanisms existed. The general conclusion of this study is that performance information was more routinely used in, and influenced budgeting practices in, case study states when the economy was strong. Perhaps, equally significant for performance-informed budget reform efforts, the authors concluded that performance information is more consistently used in management (i.e., the execution phase), rather than in the preparation and/or allocation stages of budgeting.

The federal government

US federal government budget processes have been the subject of reform efforts since at least the 1960s, when the PPBS was the reform du jour (Schick, 1966). During the 1990s, there was renewed emphasis on the marriage of performance information and the budget, culminating in the Government Performance and Results Act of 1993 (GPRA). GPRA requires agencies to develop strategic and performance plans, and to report on actual performance achieved. It also anticipates an eventual move to "performance-based budgeting." The main focus of GPRA in practice was the development of performance information. Limited use was made of that information for management or budgeting in most agencies (Joyce, 2011).

Progress on the fronts of strategic planning, performance measurement and cost accounting was unquestionably made during the Clinton administration. Starting in 2000, the Bush administration attempted to build on those incremental successes by encouraging the use of performance information in the development of the President's budget proposal, and by the Congress in the budget approval process. There were two parts to this effort. The first, embodied by the President's Management Agenda, attempted to rate federal agencies using a "traffic light" scorecard (green, yellow and red) based on criteria in a number of management areas, including one that explicitly focused on the production and use of performance data. The Bush administration graded 26 agencies (the Cabinet Departments, plus other significant operating units, such as NASA, the Army Corps of Engineers, and the Smithsonian) using a scorecard administered by Office of Management and Budget (OMB). Agencies were, each quarter, evaluated according to a set of established criteria on each of these five dimensions, using a "traffic light" system, where "green" meant that agencies complied with all of the criteria, compared to "yellow" or "red," which implied a progressively worse level of performance. There may be some evidence of

progress over the course of the administration. In the performance categories, there were no "greens" in 2001; by 2008, 19 of 26 agencies were assessed as green – however, there is some evidence "grade inflation" may have biased results (Joyce, 2011).

Perhaps the more noteworthy Bush administration initiative was embodied by the Program Assessment Rating Tool (PART). PART took a heavily decentralized approach to program evaluation, assessing more than 1,000 federal programs in four categories. PART functioned through the use of a questionnaire that scored each program based on weighted responses to between 25 and 30 questions, which covered:

1 *Program purpose and design* – Are they clear and defensible? (20 percent)
2 *Strategic planning* – Does the agency set valid annual and long-term goals? (10 percent)
3 *Program management* –Does the agency exercise sound financial management and engage in program improvement efforts? (20 percent)
4 *Program results* – Does the program deliver results based on its goals? (50 percent)

Each program evaluated was eventually "scored" as falling within one of five categories – effective (85–100), moderately effective (70–84), adequate (50–69), ineffective (0–49), and results not demonstrated (if a program lacked adequate measures, it falls into this category regardless of score) (Gilmour, 2006). Again, there was some evidence of progress over the administration's tenure, with the percentage of programs rated effective or moderately effective increasing substantially. The proportion of programs not demonstrating results declined even more. However, evaluations of the PART have presented mixed results. First, it is noted that the "one size fits all" questionnaire approach contributed to a somewhat superficial view of these programs. Second, while there was some evidence that the information was used in the development of the President's budget, the Congress was either apathetic or hostile to the PART effort. Third, both federal agency and budget office personnel questioned whether the results of the initiative justified the resources expended (Joyce, 2011).

The Obama administration discontinued the PART effort, and has instead distributed its attention across at least four separate initiatives over the first three years.

1 The establishment of an infrastructure to assess the impact of the American Recovery and Reinvestment Act (ARRA, or the stimulus bill) on jobs.
2 As demonstration of the administration's desire to cut back on spending, the identification of a list of programs, as part of each of the first three budgets (2010, 2011, and 2012), that it believed should have funding reduced or eliminated because of inadequate performance.
3 The establishment by agencies, with instruction from OMB, of "high-priority performance goals." This approach puts agencies in the driver's seat for defining goals and metrics, reversing the Bush administration's "top-down" efforts to managing agency performance. The Obama administration has unveiled a website (performance.gov) that reports on the experience of agencies in achieving these high-priority goals.
4 A significant commitment, in time and resources, to program evaluation, in part to assist with the identification of what works and what does not; in all, more than 50 program evaluations were funded in the President's fiscal year 2011 and 2012 budgets.

The Obama administration has faced the fiscal conundrum of need to take actions to promote economic recovery – while simultaneously needing to manage increasing levels of debt within a notably polarized political atmosphere. While performance information might be usefully applied to move forward, there is scant evidence that either executive or legislative policy makers are incorporating performance data into debate and decision making. Obama administration performance initiatives have tended to focus on encouraging agencies to selectively evaluate and assess performance of individual programs.

It is almost inevitable, however, that the need to reduce budgets will produce a more robust federal deficit reduction effort than we have seen since the late 1990s (Joyce, 2011).

As a foreshadowing of this, the first three Obama budgets have attempted to reduce funding or terminate a significant number of programs. These proposed terminations, even if they are informed by performance, were not necessarily met with enthusiasm by the Congress. Of the total of $17 billion in proposed terminations for fiscal year 2010, the Congress approved only $6.8 billion (40 percent) of these (Office of Management and Budget, 2011).

As we write this, it is unclear how, and when, the federal government will deal with its expanding debt – and whether performance information will be meaningfully used in the process of constraining and reshaping the US federal budget. In response to the need to approve an increase in the US Treasury's authority to borrow, the Congress created a special 12-person joint (House and Senate) committee tasked with presenting recommendations for reducing the deficit. This committee failed to reach agreement on any plan for reducing the U.S. debt, therefore the question of whether performance information was used is moot at present Going forward, elected officials have (at best) limited incentives to use performance information in allocating public resources. Until there are electoral penalties for failing to make performance-informed decisions, it is naïve to expect Congress to embrace performance-informed budgeting. So, while there is substantial and accumulating evidence that performance information is being used within federal agencies to manage resources after they are received, if the Congress enacts budget cuts without reference to performance information it must be concluded that performance-informed budgeting as a macro-budgetary decision tool remains, at best, unrealized in the United States.

Other OECD countries

The United States is not alone among industrialized countries in attempting performance-oriented budget reform. Many OECD countries are pursuing similar efforts. The general consensus has been, in fact, that other countries have progressed farther, faster than the United States. A 2005 survey, including responses from 28 OECD member countries (Curristine, 2005), revealed some significant patterns of performance-informed budgeting practice in these countries. A brief synopsis of the most significant results (Curristine, 2005) follows:

- Fifty percent of the countries surveyed have developed both output and outcome measures.
- Respondent countries have been working on developing performance measures for a long time, with 77 percent indicating that the first efforts were introduced at least five to 10 years prior to the survey. Furthermore, efforts continue, with 75 percent having introduced a new initiative within the year prior to the survey.
- Involvement of the Ministry of Finance (MOF) differs from country to country. In about 30 percent of countries, line ministries develop measures that must be approved by the MOF; in a slightly larger number of countries the ministries develop their own measures without MOF approval.
- Countries reported that the quantity, quality, and timeliness of data improved in the five years prior to the survey.
- Perhaps, most significantly for our purposes, the survey asked countries to report the extent of the use of performance information for budgeting. The vast majority of countries indicated that performance data were used to inform, but not necessarily determine, budget allocations. Often the information was only one factor informing allocations. Respondents reported that only rarely was performance information compared to targets to determine budget allocations.

The OECD noted, in a later study, that there were many reasons for adoption of performance budgeting systems, including "a financial crisis, growing pressure to reduce public expenditure, or a change in political administration" (Organization for Economic Cooperation and Development, 2008, p. 2). Sweden and Denmark were highlighted as countries adopting performance budgeting in response to an economic crisis (in the late 1980s and early 1990s). In most cases, there appears to be no systematic relationship between performance information and resource allocation in OECD countries. Instead, the focus has typically been on providing incentives for the use of performance information for allocating and managing resources.

Many OECD countries have been engaged in performance-focused reforms. We have only scratched the surface in terms of reviewing the experiences of OECD countries. A detailed review is precluded by space constraints – and the paucity of information available about the extent to which performance information has a role in shaping budgetary responses to unfolding post-2008 fiscal realities facing OECD members. However, the reported experience of two – Canada and Great Britain – can serve to illustrate the potential utility of performance information in shaping budget decisions, particularly in times of austerity.

Canada

The development of the Canadian performance budgeting system coincided with a transition from national budget surplus to a need to reduce budget deficits. In the new expenditure management system, developed by the latter part of the first decade of the twenty-first century, spending is related to transparent results and outcomes, and value for money must be demonstrated. New spending proposals must include clear measures that can be used to judge the success of the program. Existing spending is subjected to strategic reviews over a four-year cycle to ensure that spending is aligned with (1) priorities and (2) goals of efficiency, effectiveness, and economy. These strategic reviews are similar to (in fact were informed by) the US PART process. Programs are divided, as a result of these reviews, into four categories – high priority/high performing (candidates for reinvestment); high priority/low performing (opportunity for improvements in structure or management); low priority/high performing (secondary candidate for reallocation); and low priority/low performing (primary candidate for reallocation). These reviews are being conducted in the context of a commitment by the government to a zero deficit by 2015, which will necessitate spending reductions. Ministries are tasked with applying these reviews to identify sufficient savings for the government to achieve that the zero deficit goal. Thus, in Canada there is an explicit connection between budgetary goals and performance goals (Stacey, 2011).

Great Britain

Great Britain has been engaged in performance-oriented reforms since the late 1980s, when the "Next Steps" program attempted to bring more performance measurement and commercial approaches into government. More recently, under Prime Minister Tony Blair, the UK increased spending and accompanied that with a commitment to public service agreements (PSAs), which were commitments to deliver particular results with that spending. With time, the Blair government reduced some of the higher-priority "promises" to a "pledge card," showcasing Labour Party commitments to: reducing school class sizes; creating fast-track punishment for young offenders; and transitioning more than 250,000 young workers off welfare and into jobs. In total, there were more than 300 targets included in the PSA regime. Every two to three years, new sets of PSAs were created. In the second Blair term, the focus was on strategies to bridge the gap between current and desired performance. For each policy or program, ministries were required to provide evidence of success, and demonstrate constant monitoring that would permit a course correction, if necessary.

Under Prime Minister David Cameron, the formal Blair targets were abandoned: but in reality there has been more continuity than may appear on the surface. Evidence is that the PSA regime did influence budgeting decisions, particularly in the ministries. The post-2008 British austerity program may have provided a new opportunity to focus on performance government-wide, but it is too early to draw conclusions (Kohli, 2011).

The developing country setting

Variation across non-OECD countries is even greater than that within OECD membership. In 2011, 145 countries fall into either the "low-income" or "middle-income" categories, based on gross national income (GNI) per capita (International Bank for Reconstruction and Development Report, 2011). As a group, these countries face greater challenges in public budgeting than high-income countries. By definition, the fiscal constraints and service demands facing these countries tend to be greater than in OECD or high-income countries. Frequent lack of robust financial management systems, and the often ambiguous and confusing goals and incentives faced within this population of countries, make it quite difficult to assess public sector performance routinely.

The poorest developing countries (35 of the 145 countries cited above) often lack many, if not most, of the basic reform prerequisites suggested earlier in this chapter – i.e., adherence to the rule of law; transparent, publicly expressed preferences; absence of structural deficits (excessive debt financing has been a chronic problem for the poorest countries); timely and conclusive budget adoption; basic institutional capacity (forecasting, systems); and availability of data. In some countries, the most basic links between macro realities, revenue flows, and budget documents may not be in place. In other countries, budgeting and financial systems are more fully developed but steps needed to incorporate use of performance information across the budgeting process are more limited – e.g., to improving capacity in certain technical prerequisites (e.g., forecasting, data systems).

In the last 20 years, a variety of developments have simultaneously resulted in conditions that are not only favorable to reform of public budgeting practices but essentially require it. First, the broad-based movement to improve transparency and promote good governance across countries directly addresses some of the key prerequisites for budget reform (i.e., rule of law, timely budget adoption, access to data). Second, a strong trend among donors towards working with developing country policy makers to focus on a viable medium-term economic outlook addresses a most basic pre-requisite: i.e., establishing a framework within which planning is feasible. Third, starting in the late 1990s, there has been a strong push from donors towards monitoring and evaluating development efforts, which places attention squarely on outcomes. Even given this more favorable environment, however, there are still institutional struggles and capacity challenges that make instituting robust reforms difficult. Further, while arguably it is even more important to get value for money where money is scarce, policy makers can view the challenge as simply trying to deal with the latest crisis – and, correspondingly, view resource-intensive institutional reforms as an unaffordable luxury. Institutional reforms require training, and can threaten vested interests.

Nevertheless, government administration and fiscal management in developing countries has been influenced by practice in OECD countries, for two reasons. First, the natural process of learning across countries, especially in the digital age, results in transfer. Second, development programs – whether bilateral or multilateral – focus on assisting developing countries to implement what is viewed as successful experience. Consequently, a patchwork of developing country experience with use of performance information in allocation of public resources is emerging. Time lag is inevitable, and it's too early to judge the success of these efforts, but there is a wide field to watch.

Virtually without exception, budget reform in developing countries is viewed as comprehensive, integrated with policy at the national level as a means towards the general objective of modernizing government.

Selected examples give a sense of the type of reforms promoting the use of performance information in public budgeting in developing countries:

- Ghana, in 1995, launched a Public Financial Management Reform Program (Kusek and Rasappan, 2001). In addition to focusing policymakers' attention on outcomes and promoting buy-in to public expenditure management, the reform was aimed at simply putting key administrative prerequisites in place – i.e., an adequate accounting system, auditing, monitoring, and information management systems.

- In Chile, evaluations have been used to focus the performance discussion across sectors. The early 2000s saw substantial attention to improving the number and the quality of performance indicators. Between 2001 and 2006, the number of indicators increased from 275 to more than 1,500; more importantly, the number of agencies covered by these indicators almost doubled (Guzman, 2008). Perhaps, most significantly, Chile has, since 1997, focused substantial resources on program evaluation. A relatively small number of targeted evaluations (10 to 20) have been done each year. The evaluations can result in various remedial actions, including minor adjustment, management changes, substantial program redesign, or termination (Guzman, 2008, p. 240).

- Guyana's Fiscal Management and Accountability Act (FMAA) 2003, Act Number 20 of 2003 (signed into law on 16 December 2003), lays out the general procedures for the preparation, approval, and execution of the budget in Guyana. Guyana has had a programme budget for more than a decade, and this act requires each agency to prepare "programme performance statements". Specifically, Section 72 of the Act stipulates that each of these statements shall include information on the objectives of each programme, the impacts of the programme, and the strategies employed to achieve them, and the funds provided. Most significantly, the FMAA requires qualitative and quantitative indicators, both in the current year and related to budgetary resources requested from the Parliament (Financial Management and Accountability Act, 2003). In practice, the programme performance statements have included a proliferation of output and workload measures, and these measures have not been related in any systematic way to resources provided or requested. While the Ministry of Finance is committed to the improvement of the system, progress has been slow, in part because of capacity problems in line ministries, Some ministries, such as the Ministry of Health, have made progress in defining appropriate performance measures.

- Thailand adopted a performance-based budgeting system in 1997. The Thai reform started with a pilot project within two agencies in that year, and then was followed by full adoption in 2001. The intent of the reform is to reduce fragmented decision making, where the focus is only on local issues, and increase attention to national priorities and objectives. Overall strategic goals are translated into public service agreements (PSAs) which identify key indicators that can be used to measure each ministry's performance. The Thailand Bureau of Budget (BOB) has used performance information "to allocate resources through various ministries and agencies, and motivate agencies to achieve targeted outcomes" (Srithongrung, 2011, p. 129).

Recent budget reforms in transition economy countries differ from experience in other regions primarily only in starting point. These countries, in particular, face significant challenges in defining and using performance information. Moving from central planning to a more outcome-oriented resource allocation model requires substantial conceptual and practical change. The practice of using standard formulae or 'norms' to calculate input–output relationships can prove difficult to abandon. Countries across the region are at varying stages of reform.

While experience continues to unfold in developing countries, two common lessons can be drawn from the early stages, irrespective of countries' political starting point or relative wealth. First, because measures aimed at incorporating performance information into the process of allocating public resources are not only technical reforms, but have political implications, significant political will is required in order for the reforms to take hold and become effective. Second, because of the stringency of resource constraints – financial and human – in developing countries, attention to selection and

sequencing of manageable reforms is particularly critical.

CONCLUSION

The introduction of more performance information into government budget processes is a laudable goal. It is very difficult, however, to carry out in practice. Five conclusions seem particularly worth keeping in mind as governments continue to struggle with whether – and how – to put performance-informed budgeting into practice, particularly during periods of fiscal stress.

1   Performance-informed budgeting is not a substitute for sound financial management and budgeting practice. Many countries would do well to focus on building basic budgeting capacity before attempting more sophisticated reforms.

2   Even where necessary conditions for good budgeting in general exist, there are certain building blocks for successful integration of performance information into the budget process. Governments need to know where they want to go, they need to have appropriate measures of performance and cost, and they need to create incentives for relating performance information to budget decisions. The incentives to use performance information may be lacking across some or all stages of the budget process.

3   Performance-informed budgeting can pay real benefits, even if it doesn't apparently pay significant dividends. Government budget processes have many stages, and there are many ways to use performance information to improve government effectiveness at each of these stages. Although it seems more difficult (and less likely) for performance measures to be used to inform resource tradeoffs at the policy level, they can be (and are being) used quite successfully for managing resources during budget implementation. Since the management of resources does involve their allocation, this is a potentially significant development.

4   As governments struggle with defining priorities and accomplishing real outlay reductions in the post-2008 economic world, information on the performance of programs and agencies becomes particularly crucial. The more public

sector budgets are squeezed, the more important it becomes for resources to be used in the most effective manner possible. Evidence-driven decision making will likely yield results superior to those of traditional tactics. "Cheese slicer reductions" that cut budgets across the board are inevitably likely to prove less efficient than performance-informed surgical reductions that cut less effective programs from the budget.

5   Furthermore, the development of better performance and cost information can itself spur greater attention to performance, even in places where an input focus has been ascendant. Transparency concerning the relationship between funding and results can shine a light on practices that result in failing to allocate resources toward desired societal ends. Given the level of resources governments devote to IT expenditures, this would seem a minimum benefit to be expected across the globe.

In short, past reforms have frequently been viewed as failures, in part because they have been oversold; Light (1997) suggests that the problem has been too much reform, rather than not enough. We would argue that the failure of these reforms only looks like failure through a faulty lens. If one looks at the experience of governments over the past 40 years, it is more likely that the trend is upward, both in terms of the availability of performance information and the use of that information. Viewed through a lens that differentiates by budget stage and expectations, the continuing wave of reform appears consistent with a general shift in culture and change in budgetary practice that – while operating in fits and starts – has been underway since the middle part of the last century. Evidence about use of performance-informed budgeting over the next 5 to 10 years, as countries move into unanticipated periods of austerity and adjustment, will be the most telling about the long-run prospects of the movement.

REFERENCES

Barrett, K. and Greene, R. (2008) Grading the states: the mandate to measure. *Governing.com*.

Retrieved October 28, 2011, from http://www.pewtrusts.org/uploadedFiles/wwwpewtrustsorg/Reports/Government_Performance/Grading-the-States-2008.pdf

Broom, C.A. and L. McGuire (1995) "Performance-Based Government Models: Building a Track Record," *Public Budgeting and Finance*, 15 (4): 3–17.

Curristine, Teresa (2005) "Performance Information in the Budget Process: Results of the OECD 2005 Questionnaire," *OECD Journal on Budgeting*, 5 (2): 87–131.

Gilmour, J. (2006) "Implementing OMB's Program Assessment Rating Tool." IBM Center for the Business of Government.

Gloo, D. (2011) "Commentary on 'PBB in American Local Government: It's More Than a Management Tool'," *Public Administration Review*, May/June: 402–404.

Guyana (2003) Financial Management and Accountability Act. Act #20.

Guzman, M. (2008) "The Chilean Experience," in M. Robinson (ed.), *Performance Budgeting*. Basingstoke: Palgrave McMillan, pp. 234–247.

Harkin, J.M. (1982) "Effectiveness Budgeting: The Limits of Budget Reform," *Policy Studies Review*, 2 (3): 112–126.

Ho, A. (2011) "PBB in American Local Government: It's More Than a Management Tool," *Public Administration Review*, May/June: 391–401.

Holmes, M. and D. Shand (1995) "Management Reform: Some Practitioner Perspectives on the Past Ten Years," *Governance*, 8 (4): 551–578.

Hou, Y., R. Lunsford, K. Sides and K. Jones (2011) "State Performance-Based Budgeting in Boom and Bust Years: An Analytical Framework and Survey of the States," *Public Administration Review*, May/June: 370–388.

Ingraham, P., P. Joyce, and A. Donahue (2003) *Government Performance: Why Management Matters*. Baltimore, MD: Johns Hopkins University Press.

International Bank for Reconstruction and Development (2011) "Country and Lending Groups." Report. At: www.data.worldbank.org/country_classifications

Joyce, P.G. (2011) "Transparency and Accountability in the Federal Budget: How is the Obama Administration Building on the Legacy of Federal Performance-Informed Budgeting?" *Public Administration Review*, May/June: 356–367.

Joyce, P.G. and S. Tompkins (2002) "Using Performance Information for Budgeting: Clarifying the Framework and Investigating Recent State Experience," in

Kathryn Newcomer et al. (eds), *Meeting the Challenges of Performance-Oriented Government*. Washington, DC: American Society for Public Administration, pp. 61–96.

Kliman, A. and L. Fisher (1995) "Budget Reform Proposals in the NPR Report," *Public Budgeting and Finance*, 15 (1): 27–38.

Kohli, J. (2011) "Budgeting Reforms in the UK." Presentation before the Peterson–Pew Commission on Budget Reform, July 14.

Kusek, J.Z. and A. Rasappan (2001) "Outcomes-Based Budgeting Systems: Experience from Developed and Developing Countries." Special Paper prepared for the World Bank for the Government of Egypt, November.

Light, P. (1997) *The Tides of Reform: Making Government Work*. New Haven, CT: Yale University Press.

Liner, B, H. Hatry, E. Vinson, et al. (2001) *Making Results-Based State Government Work*. Washington, DC: The Urban Institute.

Melkers, J and K. Willoughby (1998) "The State of the States: Performance-Based Budgeting Requirements in 47 out of 50", *Public Administration Review*, 58 (1): 66–73.

Meyers, Roy T. (1997) "Is There a Key to the Normative Budgeting Lock?" *Policy Sciences*, 29 (3): 171–188.

Office of Management and Budget (2011) *Budget of the United States Government; Fiscal Year 2012, Terminations, Reductions and Savings*. Washington: U.S. Government Printing Office.

Organisation for Economic Co-operation and Development (2008*). Performance Budgeting: A User's Guide*. Paris: OECD.

Osborne, D. and T. Gaebler (1992) *Reinventing Government*. Reading, MA: Addison-Wesley.

Schick, A. (1973) "A Death in the Bureaucracy: The Demise of Federal PPB," *Public Administration Review*, 33 (2), 146–156.

Schick, A. (1966) "The Road to PPB: The Stages of Budget Reform", *Public Administration Review*, 26 (4), 243–258.

Srithongrung, A. (2011) "Public Budgeting and Financial Management Performance in Thailand," in C. Menifield (ed.), *Comparative Public Budgeting: A Global Perspective*. Sudbury, MA: Jones and Bartlett Learning, pp. 107–132.

Stacey, B. (2011) "Performance Budgeting in the Government of Canada: Transitioning from Surplus to Deficit Reduction." Presentation before the Peterson–Pew Commission on Budget Reform, July 14.

Strachota, D. (1994) "A Blueprint for State and Local Government Budgeting," *Government Finance Review*, April: 48–50.

Wildavsky, A. (1984) *The Politics of the Budgetary Process*, 4th edn. Boston, MA: Little, Brown, and Company.

Accrual Budgeting in a Comparative Perspective

Leonard Kok

Since the introduction of New Public Management (NPM), there has been increasing emphasis within the public sector on working more like a business. Those who consult *Reinventing Government* (Osborne and Gaebler, 1992) as the handbook of New Public Management, are confronted on almost every page with the agenda for more business-like government. A few examples include a focus upon service delivery, a results orientation, a focus upon client needs, market orientation, etc. It is not surprising that the countries that have attempted to introduce the ideas of NPM in the public sector sooner or later also confront the issue of how the budgetary system, which in many countries is a cash-based budgeting and accounting system, can also accommodate these more business-like goals.

Why is this topic of budgeting and accounting so important? The answer is that budgeting and accounting are at the heart of the administrative process of a government – and this administrative process is also the basis of the power of the purse in representative democracies. The type of budgeting and accounting system may influence the way in which administrations and parliament decide about policy that has budgetary consequences; and almost each policy decision has budgetary consequences.

The two main systems of budgeting and accounting are the cash-based and the accrual system, which is common in the market sector. It is not possible to say that one system is better than the other. It totally depends on the use of the system within the governing bodies. But one thing must be clear: if you want to introduce more entrepreneurial elements in the public sector, a cash system creates many problems and a business-line system will fit much better.

First, a number of central concepts of business accounting are introduced and discussed. This is a general overview and should not be read as a speed course in bookkeeping. Second, a sketch is offered of developments in this area in a number of OECD (Organization for Economic Co-operation and Development) countries. Finally – as a case study – a more detailed description of the experiences of the Netherlands with business accounting is presented. The plans for the implementation of business accounting in the Netherlands has been described by an OECD report (2002) as an example of best practice in the OECD member countries. The Dutch approach illustrates an interesting combination of both strengthening results orientation and also increasing effectiveness, without disrupting the ability to command and control the budget.

OVERVIEW

Concepts

It is desirable first to clarify a number of concepts. This chapter is about business accounting or – as it is often called – accrual accounting. As has already been stated, there were and continue to be a number of countries that have not adopted the accrual principle within their public sectors, and rather continue to conduct their budgetary activities according to the principles of the cash-based system. In the cash-based system, expenditure is deducted in full from the moment when the expenditure is made. A salary payment to a public servant for example would be deducted from the books and would thus affect the budget in the year and month that the payment took place. Similarly, payment for a road would be deducted in the budget at the moment that the expenditure took place. The difference between the salary payment and the expenditure for a new road is that the payment of wages would have to be paid again and again every month, unless of course the employee has stopped working, while alternatively the payment for the road is in principle a one-off expenditure, even though the road would continue to provide services for many years after the payment is made. The accrual principle allows the expenditures that are made today and that will provide benefits over a number of years to be deducted at small amounts over a longer period of time. The expenditure for a road,

for example, would be included in the bookkeeping at the time that the services of the road are used. Due to wear and tear, the road loses value over time and this reduction in value is described by a technical term: depreciation.

The system of depreciation and calculation of expenditure over time is common practice in the private sector, but this system is clearly also much more complicated than the cash-based system of accounting. How do you determine the rate of wear and tear, for example, and thereby also the yearly depreciation of goods? This is more difficult to calculate than the total cash expenditure that is made at the time the road is laid down. The cash expenditure is simply the concrete payment made to the contractor.

The accrual system provides very useful extra information that its user can draw upon in decision making – for example, whether it is financially better to buy or rent an office. In the cash system, buying is always more expensive than hiring because the one-off purchase will be deducted at the time of purchase and thus will always be a greater deduction than the yearly expenditure for renting an office. But the actual costs of purchasing an office are obviously not the same as the purchase price and the cash expenditure that was made at the time of that purchase. To identify the costs of buying an office, it is first of all important to know the reduction in the value of the office that occurs in a year, the depreciation. In addition, there is also another type of costs that need to be considered when buying an office, and that is the financial costs of the purchase or rather the sequestration of one's property. This requires additional explanation. For example, consider that you did not buy the office but instead put the money in the bank; this would have provided you with a financial return in the form of interest. By not putting the money in the bank and receiving this income from the interest, one incurs a capital charge. A requirement of efficient investment decisions is making visible this lost return, or rather the – hidden – costs of the sequestration of one's property.

In order to be able to calculate the capital charges that the public sector is subject to, it is necessary to be able to get an insight into the value of government property and possessions. In business accounting these possessions (and debts) are included in the balance of the bookkeeping. Therefore in addition to the financial overview that is provided by an accrual accounting system, business accounting also provides an overview of possessions and debts. These two aspects of the financial accounts should connect seamlessly. The balance of the accounts will in this respect give insight into the financial position of the organization or the nation. If the balance is compared to the previous year, one is also able to see how the financial position has changed – whether a nation is becoming wealthier or poorer.

Another element of budgeting and accounting for governments is related to the nature of government: there is no market that sets prices, so you need a budgeting system. The budgeting system is the base for providing departments with money. This system must be clear and tight, otherwise it will lead to budgetary problems. A cash system is from this point of view the most suitable system; the only way to manipulate a cash-based system is at the end of the year by shifting cash from one year to another. The ways of manipulating an accruals system are more difficult to understand, but there are many more opportunities: by making provision for spreading out costs, by making reservations, by changing depreciation periods, etc.

These sorts of things must of course be declared in the annual accounts, but that does not make the accounting system more transparent.

Certainly there are also other aspects that are associated with an accrual accounting system and these will be discussed later in this chapter, when the case of the Netherlands is presented. To summarize, Table 27.1 provides an overview of arguments in the debate on cash and accruals.

DEVELOPMENTS IN OECD COUNTRIES

The countries in the OECD that have introduced some kind of accrual accounting system have generally done so in combination with broader management reforms of the public sector. The most interesting OECD countries will be discussed here but, first, information on the systems used by OECD countries is given in Table 27.2 and planned future developments are detailed in Table 27.3.

Full accrual basis

New Zealand

New Zealand is the most renowned example. In 1984, against the background of serious economic problems, fundamental reforms were introduced. In New Zealand, these reforms included both privatization and the reduction of the public sector, as well as increasing the effectiveness, cost consciousness

Table 27.1 Main elements of accounting systems

	Cash-based system	Accruals system
Main characteristic	Shows payments and receipts	Shows profits and losses
What is administered	Cash as it occurs	Spreads costs over years
Main purpose	Treasury information	Information on costs and property
Main advantage	Easy to understand	More information
Main disadvantage	Less information	Complexity
Main risk	End of the year cash manipulation	Manipulation of figures
Budget control	Solid base	More room for manoeuvring

Table 27.2 Accounting basis applied for budget approved by legislature

	Full accrual basis	Accrual basis, except no capitalization or depreciation of assets	Cash basis, except certain transactions on accrual basis	Full cash basis
Australia	X			
Austria				X
Belgium				X
Canada		X		
Czech Republic				X
Denmark			X[1]	
Finland		X[2]		
France				X
Germany				X
Greece				X
Hungary				X
Iceland		X		
Ireland				X
Japan				X
Korea				X
Luxembourg				X
Mexico				X
Netherlands			X	
Norway				X
New Zealand	X			
Poland				X
Portugal				X
Spain				X
Sweden				X
Switzerland				X
Turkey				X
United Kingdom	X[3]			
United States			X[4]	

[1] Denmark – interest expenses and employee pensions treated on accrual basis.
[2] Finland – transfer payments not on accrual basis.
[3] United Kingdom – budget on full accrual basis effective fiscal year 2001–02.
[4] United States – interest expenses, certain employee pension plans, and loan and guarantee programmes on accrual basis.
Source: OECD 2002.

Table 27.3 Plans to move budget to accrual basis

Country	Full accrual basis budgeting to be introduced	Additional accrual basis information to be presented
Canada	X[1]	
Denmark		X
Germany		X
Korea	X[1]	
Netherlands	X	
Portugal		X
Sweden	X[1]	
Switzerland	X[1]	

[1] Under active consideration.
Source: OECD 2002.

and accountability of the public sector. Inside public sector organizations, contracts for goods and services over a five-year period were made between ministers and the responsible managers [Norman 1997; Posseth 2010]. An accrual accounting system was seen as an essential instrument for supporting these contract arrangements. In the first place, accruals promoted the clarification of concrete products and services and, secondly, they made possible the calculation of the costs of these products and services. In New Zealand, a number of big changes and reforms were introduced at the same time: big reductions in government finances were made, a new organizational structure within the public sector was created, a new system of bookkeeping was introduced and the privatization wave swept across a number of formerly government organizations.

Australia

In Australia, the changes have been more incremental. The creation of units within the public sector that were granted more independence (agencies) occurred in combination with the introduction of accruals (Commonwealth of Australia 1999). These reforms were, as in New Zealand, intended to make managers more accountable for their management and to hold them responsible for their results. In order to meet these intentions in a consistent and comparable way, and at the same time to improve the effectiveness, efficiency and performance of these independent units, the information from an accrual accounting system was central.

United Kingdom

Agencies were also created in the United Kingdom, but here the structure of the public sector maintained core departments with a steering role. Only some organizations responsible for the implementation of policy were granted agency status. Reforms to improve the performance of the public sector had already begun in the 1980s (Her Majesty's Treasury 1999). It was quickly recognized that these reforms could be promoted and strengthened by the replacement of the cash-based accounting system with business accounting methods. The latter would also enable comparisons to be made between the public and private sector and it would also promote cooperation, or rather what has been referred to as public–private partnerships. Therefore, in the UK, the process began with making organizations accountable for their financial activities, according to an accrual basis, and since that time accrual budgeting has been introduced. In the UK, this arrangement is referred to as Resource Accounting and Budgeting (RAB).

The objectives of this operation in the UK can be briefly summarized:

- faster and clearer accountability;
- improved implementation of the budget and planning;
- better management of assets and working capital;
- improvement in cost price information;
- improvement in the way decision making and investment decisions are taken; and
- connecting performance, outputs and outcomes.

The arguments in the UK can also be seen in all of the countries that have, in one way or another, been occupied with the introduction of accruals. Table 27.4 presents the accounting basis that OECD countries use at the present time.

Partial accrual basis

The developments in Canada were, although somewhat later, quite similar to Australia. In Canada, improvements in quality and efficiency were also high on the government's agenda.

Some countries, such as the United States and France, have made only partial use of accruals. These countries do not allow accrual information to be primary in the budget (*ex ante*), but, rather, use it as a way to account for financial expenditure (*ex post*). This is an important point because the rules for reporting on an accrual basis originate from the

Table 27.4 Accounting basis applied for consolidated (whole of government) financial statements

	Full accrual basis	Accrual basis, except no capitalization or depreciation of assets	Cash basis, except certain transactions on accrual basis	Full cash basis
Australia	X			
Austria				X
Belgium				X
Canada		X		
Czech Republic				X
Denmark			X[1]	
Finland	X			
France			X[2]	
Germany				X
Hungary				X
Iceland		X		
Ireland				X
Japan				X
Korea				X
Luxembourg				X
Mexico				X
Netherlands				X
Norway				X
New Zealand	X			
Poland			X[3]	
Portugal				X
Spain				X
Sweden	X			
Switzerland				
Turkey				X
United Kingdom				X
United States			X	X[4]

[1] Denmark – interest expense and employee pensions treated on accrual basis.
[2] France – interest expense and certain other transactions treated on accrual basis. Full accrual basis to be introduced.
[3] Poland – employee pensions treated on accrual basis.
[4] United Kingdom – statements on full accrual basis effective fiscal year 2005–06.
Source: OECD 2002.
In the Netherlands this problem – of reporting requirements that at some point could lend accountants influence over what is primarily a political process, the budget, has been resolved in a very creative way. This is discussed in the next section of this chapter. In addition, the IMF and World Bank have shown – against the background of improved transparency and good government – increased interest in administration on an accrual basis.

private sector. Standards for reporting have been developed in the private sector, but it is ultimately accountants that define how the different aspects of this accounting should be included within the budget. In some countries it is deemed acceptable to use these methods in the process of accounting for organizational activities and performance, but not as a way to set up the budget. This is because setting up both the budget and reporting of expenditure according to the rules of accrual accounting involves the transfer of decision-making power to accountants. This effect has led to some countries preferring to maintain a budget organized according to cash-based principles.

In the Netherlands, this problem – of reporting requirements that at some point could lend accountants influence over what is primarily a political process, the budget – has been resolved in a very creative way. This is discussed in the next section of this chapter. In addition, the International Monetary Fund (IMF) and the World Bank have shown – against the background of improved transparency and good government – increased interest in administration on an accrual basis.

THE DUTCH CASE

Since the beginning of the 1990s, the Netherlands has introduced diverse initiatives to promote the results orientation of the public sector and increase its effectiveness (Blöndal and Kromann Kristensen 2002). Over the years a number of instruments have been adopted to make the cash-based system of accounting less rigid (for example, the year-end margin, the savings facility, etc.), and to promote more flexibility in the management rules: for example, through the creation of agencies. (Agencies are government bodies that implement policy and may use business accounting methods.)

At the end of the 1990s, initiatives were introduced to encourage the public sector to become more results orientated. This was primarily promoted by making the budget more transparent, so that, on the one hand, the relation between policy goals and policy results, and on the other hand, that between policy instruments and financial resources, were central (Budget Memorandum 2002). The policy goals and policy results formed the spine of the budget and accounting to the parliament, but it also strengthened the results orientation inside government organizations themselves. The creation of the budget and the yearly accounting reports to parliament are not just loose facades but are concretely related to the results of policy activities within the government. The agencies represent the jewels in the crown of a government that will be more results orientated.

Owing to the introduction of agencies (from 1994), the situation has arisen where two budget systems are used side by side: the cash-based accounting system in the (core) ministries and the accrual accounting system in the agencies. This has been the subject of an increasing degree of criticism from, among others, the Court of Audit in the Netherlands. In 1997 a sketch was drawn of the actual growth in agencies and other organizations that used an accrual accounting system (at the moment there are more than 20 agencies and another anticipated 20 in preparation). Given this growth, it has become logical to allow the national budgetary system to change from a cash-based system to an accrual accounting system (Van den Berg and Kok 2001). Not least because the provinces, local government and businesses all work with (a form of) accrual accounting. Since the end of the 1990s, it has become less a question of whether the public sector would adopt a national accrual accounting budget system and more a question of when this turning point would take place. The pace of this reform is still uncertain.

Goals of an accrual accounting system

The goals behind the introduction of an integral accrual accounting system in the Netherlands are to a large degree equivalent with those identified in the UK:

1 Improvement in (decision making over) efficiency and effectiveness through:
    1 better insight into (integral) costs of policy instead of just having information on cash payments and
    2 improvements in investment decisions by making cash restrictions less important.
2 Improvement in allocation at the Cabinet level.
3 Introduction of a sustainable and unequivocal budget norm.

These goals are briefly discussed below.

Improvement in (decision making over) efficiency and effectiveness of government expenditures

The most important motivation for introducing an accrual accounting system in the Netherlands was the improvement of (decision making over) efficiency and effectiveness of government expenditure. This can be realized in two ways.

Better insight into the (integral) costs of a policy

In the accrual accounting system the integral costs of a policy are made transparent. Costs and cash expenditures can vary from each other: for example, in the investment expenditure. The accrual accounting system delivers information that makes it possible to make more efficient decisions and promote a better command of fixed assets.

Improvement in investment decisions

By working with more integral costs, it becomes possible to make considerations of future costs in investment decisions (life-cycle costs approach). For example, an investment in a road becomes both the cost of building it and the costs of maintaining it. In the current system investments are funded on a 'pay-as-you-go basis'. This encourages cheaper roads that require expensive maintenance to be chosen instead of more expensive roads with cheaper maintenance. In the accrual accounting system these considerations can be looked at differently because there is not a one-off total payment for the road made but rather the structural costs become central. This promotes more efficient decision making.

Improvement in allocation

The second motivation for an integral accrual accounting system is improvement in allocation at the macro level. The new budget system enables a more balanced consideration of investment expenditure versus possible running costs, and also in times when economic and budgetary conditions are tight. There is thus an end to the relative judgement of consumption expenditure when making budget decisions.

A sustainable and unequivocal budget norm

The third motivation for the integral introduction of an accrual accounting system is the realization of an unequivocal budgetary norm. In the Dutch situation a budgetary norm in cost terms was put in place as part of the introduction of agencies. In contrast, the rest of the national public sector used a budgetary norm that was calculated in cash terms. As a result of this distinction, an intended effect arose whereby it became attractive to be selective about which norm to use, depending upon which calculation provided the better outcome (double norm, double morale). With the increasing growth of agencies and other organizations that use an accrual accounting system in the Dutch public sector, this situation is expected to present greater problems in the future. With the introduction of a national budget that is integrated in terms of cost, the possibility of shopping between different budgeting norms is eliminated.

Contours of an accrual accounting system in the national public sector

In the new budgetary system that is based upon accruals, the budget will obtain the new character of a cost budget. This is in contrast to the cash budget that had characterized the previous budgetary system, and it places primary emphasis on costs. Costs can be equivalent to cash expenditure, such as is the case for running costs and expenditures like wages or subsidies, etc. Costs can also be characterized as long-term investments with depreciation costs; this is the case with capital expenditure. Similarly, costs may also consist of interest. In the annual report of a ministry, the accounting of the cost budget is presented and included in the balance of the budget.

Why choose a variant of accrual accounting administration and not a standard type of administration that is used in the private sector? There are two reasons. The first is that government services and production, unlike in the private sector, often lack a clear relationship between costs and benefits. This can be seen, for example, in the (lack of) relationship between tax receipts and defence expenditure. From the receipts perspective, it is therefore not desirable to make a clear relation with costs. There are some exceptions to this example, such as organizations that are set up to cover their own costs. Similarly, it is just as undesirable to speak of profit and loss when considering the state of a department's costs and receipts.

Second, decisions about the national budget are often made against a background of endless social questions that require extra expenditure; therefore it is desirable that a tight budgetary regime is in place. The budget should – to work effectively and also be governable – be able to manage different aspects of expenditure with respect to the cost of policy.

These two explanations also have consequences for the way that the budgetary system in the Netherlands will continue to be constructed. In setting up the budget, the possessions of the state play an important role. Where there is no 'correction from the market place', the 'correction of the budget' is absolutely necessary. In contrast to the (for the most part) flexible reporting conditions of the market sector, within the public sector the reporting should be conducted according to tight budgetary regulations. This applies also to the definition of capital expenditure and the basis upon which it is valued. These two somewhat more technical aspects are further described below.

Defining capital expenditure and the basis of valuation

In an accrual-based budget, the steering accountability regulations and the introduction of a norm for government expenditure are based upon costs. Therefore, it is necessary that the definition of capital expenditure (i.e. expenditure where the cash price and the costs per definition are not the same) is unequivocal and sustainable. The definition of capital expenditure determines which expenditure can be included within the balance and whether that expenditure may be deducted over a period of time. Beside the requirement that the definition of capital expenditure be unequivocal and sustainable,

this definition must also be economically useful, practical and transparent. The European System of National and Regional Accounts '95 (ESR '95) presents a good option in this respect.

In addition, with regard to the issues of the basis for valuation, the ESR '95 has been explicitly chosen as a starting point. This means that, where possible, valuations are calculated according to actual value. Where ministries' own stocks, e.g. TNT Post Group N.V, the calculation of actual worth can be simply made according to the rates on the stock market. However, it is much more difficult to calculate the value of some of the fixed assets of the public sector. In these cases the actual worth is calculated according to an indexed historical cost price. Where it is desirable, fixed assets can also be periodically revalued in order to correct for differences in the actual worth of an asset and its indexed value.

Guarantees in the system

Since it is generally recognized that an accrual administration offers more possibilities for 'budgetary manipulation' than a cash administration, it is necessary to implement and formulate tight regulations. In the Netherlands such regulations have been developed for the national accounts. This is also clearly advantageous from an efficiency perspective. However, the risk exists that in times of prosperity opportunistic demands may be placed upon valuation, depreciation, etc., in contrast to times when there is greater budgetary flexibility. Therefore it is useful to establish an authority that is able to judge the legitimacy of regulations and exceptions. In order to promote reliability and transparency, it is obvious that this authority should be independent.

Implementation

The implementation of an accrual accounting system demands an extensive transformation process. It is therefore important to connect to this process a number of factors, which, if adequately attended to, offer a greater chance that the implementation will be visibly successful. These critical success factors are:

- availability of (expert) personnel;
- adequate provision of information;
- adequate adaptation of the law and regulations;
- valuation of current fixed assets; and
- support from important politicians.

When adequate attention is granted to these factors, the introduction of an accrual administration can contribute significantly to a more effective and transparent public sector. Also, where stringent regulations are chosen to support the budget and accountability more generally, the risks to budgetary control can be avoided.

CONCLUSION

This chapter has examined budgeting and accounting in the government sector, looking at the two main systems, which we can refer to as 'cash' and 'accruals'. In a cash-based accounting system the expenditures and receipts are calculated in the accounts at the moment that the cash is deducted or received. This is simple, but also provides little information. Alternatively, in the accruals system, expenditure and receipts are calculated and included in the budget in the relevant *period* that these transactions take place. We therefore call these expenditures 'costs' and refer to the receipts as 'benefits'. The balance of the costs and benefits at the end of the year is calculated in the balance. The balance is a yearly overview of the possessions and the debts. This system is much more complicated, but it gives much more information. In many OECD countries, there is a transformation from cash systems to more or less accrual standards.

It is not possible to state that one system is better than the other; it depends on the purpose a government has with its budget. A budget system should be appropriate for a government's purpose. This is also the reason why the government of the Netherlands has developed plans for an alternative system, which can be described as a 'third way', between cash and accruals. It combines elements of budget control of cash budgeting with elements of real cost information of an accruals system. It also provides information for better budgetary decision making: it offers more efficiency, as in a private enterprise.

REFERENCES

Blöndal, Jón R. and Kromann Kristensen, Jens (2002) 'Budgeting in the Netherlands', *OECD Journal on Budgeting*, 1 (3): 43–78.

Commonwealth of Australia (1999) 'Fiscal Policy Under Accrual Budgeting'. Information Paper.

Her Majesty's Treasury (1999) *Resource Accounting and Budgeting, A Short Guide to the Financial Reforms*. London: HMSO.

Ministerie van Financiën (2002) 'Eigentijds Begroten (Modernizing the Budget)', in Ministerie van Financiën, *Miljoenennota 2002* (Budget Memorandum 2002). The Hague: Tweede Kamer 28000, nr 1-2, pp. 106–27 (www.minfin.nl).

Norman, Richard (1997) *Accounting for Government*. University of Wellington, Victoria Link Ltd.

OECD (2002) 'Overview of Results Focussed Management and Budgeting in OECD Member Countries'. Paper prepared for an Expert Meeting on the Quality of Public Expenditures, Paris, 11–12 February 2002.

Osborne, David and Gaebler, Ted (1992) *Reinventing Government: How the Entrepreneurial Spirit is Transforming the Public Sector*. Reading, MA: Addison-Wesley.

Posseth, Johan (2010) *Wat koop je ervoor? Over de ervaringen ban Nieuw-Zeeland en Nederland met 'het managen'van veiligheid via de begroting* [Does it pay off? On the experiences of New Zealand and the Netherlands using the budget for 'managing' safety], Delft, The Netherlands: Eburon.

Van den Berg, J.W. and Kok, L.H. (2001) 'Eigentijds Begroten (Modernizing the Budget)', *Openbare Uitgaven*, 33 (5): 211–16.

PART 10

Comparative and International Public Administration

edited by Edward C. Page

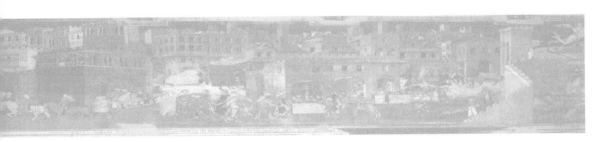

The comparative study of public administration is hardly new. Raadschelders' (1998: 45) analysis of administrative history includes Herodotus, Aristotle and Ibn Khaldun as comparativists. Looking at the modern period only, Weber's ([1920] 1972) analysis of bureaucracy, one of the landmarks in the whole area of public administration and management, is based on a comparative cross-national and historical perspective. And among the early modern social science pioneers in the field one could include Lowell (1896), Otto Hintze ([1911a] 1962), Herman Finer (1932) and Brian Chapman (1959). Yet the field is commonly regarded as something of a laggard when compared to other areas of political science such as the study of elections and parties (see Derlien, 1992).

In Chapter 28, which opens Part 10, Brans helps put this laggard reputation in perspective. The slogan 'compare or perish' underlines the importance of comparative research for explanation, theory development and the generation of practical advice. Despite the major constraints involved in comparison – complexity of subject matter, availability of

data, and definition and specification of data – the field has managed to produce a respectable volume of work, especially if one considers the theory-testing work done on individual countries – a form of comparative analysis aptly termed by Rose (1991) as an 'extroverted case study'. Moreover, as Brans suggests, Derlien's (1992) argument that there is little comparable data covering bureaucracy and administration is not as strong now as it was 20 years ago. What has been missing in comparative public administration is a 'grand theory', to give the field focus and sets of common questions. Instead, the discipline has travelled along two tracks – one reflecting changing practical concerns and the other changes in theoretical concerns in the field.

Perhaps it is no more reasonable to expect comparative public administration to evolve a grand theory than to expect it of public administration as a whole. While the still advancing popularity of public choice perspectives in the discipline as a whole might not itself constitute such a theory, it does offer a method of identifying and analysing diverse issues using an identifiable intellectual toolkit. One or two less than convincing forays aside (Huber and Shipan 2002), the approach has not really made many advances in the comparative study of bureaucracy, and it remains a rather more diverse field. As Brans' discussion of the empirical focus of comparative public administration shows, comparison is a method used to understand key issues and variables (internal administrative structures and processes, politico-administrative relations and relations with civil society) of public administration as a whole. The comparative method in public administration, as elsewhere, is a tool that can be used to analyse substantive questions rather than a field in itself.

Some questions in public administration can, however, only be understood by reference to cross-national experience. One such theme is the increasingly popular question of the development of convergence between administrative systems. Issues connected with Europeanization and globalization, as well as common administrative developments such as New Public Management, have driven this topic along, to use Brans' terms, the policy track. 'New institutionalist' theory, such as the discussion of 'isomorphism' by diMaggio and Powell (1983), has given the whole area of policy transfer a strong impetus in the past decade (see Rose, 1993; Dolowitz and Marsh, 1996).

In Chapter 29, Dimitrakopoulos and Passas point to the apparent paradox that the supranational organization with some direct authority of its own over its members, the European Union (EU), has a rather indirect influence in national administrative development. More direct influence on administrative structures comes from intergovernmental organizations such as the Organization for Economic Co-operation and Development (OECD) and the World Bank. Dimitrakopoulos and Passas show that while such organizations exert different kinds of 'pressures', this says little about responses to such pressures, still less whether they will produce the same response in different nations and thus convergence in administrative systems.

International influence and its impact on the administrative structures and processes in individual states are highly contingent on a wide range of variables that make it impossible to predict growing 'isomorphism' in administrative development.

The range of variables that make administrative systems distinctive and which prevent any confident predictions of a convergence in administrative structures, processes and styles is addressed in Chapter 30 by Martin Lodge. Administrative structures are embedded in national patterns of politics. These patterns are so diverse that attempts to classify and group states with some similar characteristics (such as 'strong' and 'weak' states) can at best be regarded as crude descriptions. To conclude, however, that the diversity and the difficulties involved in making cross-national generalizations make each country unique and comparison impossible is not only pessimistic but also inaccurate.

Lodge shows the range of features of the national political system in which bureaucracies are embedded – historical origins, political institutions and the autonomy and ability of the bureaucratic system to resist political control – can be and have been fruitfully compared. Rather than seeking to imply that bureaucracies fit neatly into 'families' sharing broad characteristics (Page, 1995), Lodge shows that we need more discriminating comparison of the discrete components of national politico-administrative systems. The focus on reciprocal obligations and rewards at the top of the bureaucracy – through conceiving the relationship as a series of variably constructed bargains – offers a means of understanding and ordering a range of the institutional and behavioural characteristics of bureaucracies in developed nations. Bureaucracy scholarship tends to explain changes in such characteristics through broader international trends that point to a reduction of the authority and autonomy of nation-state executives and, consequently, a greater emphasis on negotiation and persuasion than control and hierarchy. Lodge rightly cautions against the simple assumption that hierarchy is on its way out and suggests that longer-established patterns of behaviour could be more durable than we thought.

'Path dependence' is the contemporary term used to describe the way in which inherited politico-administrative structures, processes, constraints and patterns shape national reactions to common issues and stimuli. This of course has been a central notion in administrative history since its inception (Raadschelders, 1998). Lodge shows that path dependence does not involve relinquishing comparison since, if we specify the paths carefully enough, they are comparable. In fact one can go further and suggest that we only know what is a distinctive path if we compare it with others.

To recognize path dependencies should not itself become a theoretical rut. It was conventional at the beginning of the last century to argue that German politico-administrative development was distinctive – that it developed along a monarchical path and in this deviated from much of the rest of Europe, and that policy prescriptions appropriate to states with more liberal paths of development were not appropriate there (Hintze, [1911b] 1962). The fact that Germany's administrative system has for nearly 70 years been entirely integrated in the theoretical, empirical and practical literature on public administration as any other democratic and pluralist system indicates that developmental paths are not straight lines – they cross, merge and in some cases radically change directions.

So is comparative public administration a laggard? There is a growing volume of material that is comparative in Brans' more relaxed definition of the term. There are increased publication outlets for comparative material in the field. Even more encouraging, studies and collections analysing administrative issues using a comparative method tend to include a wider range of countries – while US and West European comparisons still tend to dominate in the literature, increasingly comparative analyses include countries such as Australia, Canada, New Zealand and Japan. There is certainly some way to go before comparative scholars manage to

realize the hopes for much wider comparisons taking in less developed nations. Yet the fact that comparative studies have not yielded one dominant paradigm, or been based upon a common or even widely shared theoretical focus, is more likely to be the result of the pluralism of social science research in general rather than any specific defect in comparative public administration.

REFERENCES

Chapman, B. (1959) *The Profession of Government.* London: Allen and Unwin.

Derlien, H.-U. (1992) 'Observations on the state of comparative administration research in Europe – rather comparable than comparative', *Governance*, 5 (3): 279–311.

DiMaggio, P.J. and Powell, W.W. (1983) 'The iron cage revisited: institutional isomorphism and collective rationality in organizational fields', *American Sociological Review*, 48 (1): 47–60.

Dolowitz, D. and Marsh, D. (1996) 'Who learns what from whom', *Political Studies*, 14 (2): 343–57.

Finer, H. (1932) *The Theory and Practice of Modern Government*, 2 vols. London: Methuen.

Hintze, O. ([1911a] 1962) 'Der Beamtenstand', in Otto Hintze, *Staat und Verwaltung*. Göttingen: Vandenhoeck and Ruprecht.

Hintze, O. ([1911b] 1962) 'Das monarchische Prinzip und die konstitutionelle Verfassung', in Otto Hintze, *Staat und Verwaltung*. Göttingen: Vandenhoeck and Ruprecht.

Huber, J.D. and Shipan, C.R. (2002). *Deliberate Discretion: The Institutional Foundations of Bureaucratic Autonomy*. Cambridge: Cambridge University Press.

Lowell, A.L. (1896) *Government and Parties in Continental Europe*. London: Longmans, Green, and Co.

Page, Edward (1995) 'Administering Europe', in J.E.S. Hayward and E.C. Page (eds), *Governing the New Europe*. Cambridge: Polity Press.

Raadschelders, J.C.N. (1998) *Handbook of Administrative History*. New Brunswick, NJ: Transaction Books.

Rose, R. (1991) 'Comparing forms of comparative analysis' *Political Studies*, 39 (3): 446–62.

Rose, R. (1993) *Lesson Drawing in Public Policy*. Chatham, NJ: Chatham House.

Weber, M. ([1920] 1972) *Wirtschaft und Gesellschaft*, 5th edn.Tübingen: J.C.B. Mohr.

28

Comparative Public Administration: From General Theory to General Frameworks

Marleen Brans[1]

INTRODUCTION ON VALUE, DEFINITIONS AND PROBLEMS OF C.P.A.

'Compare or perish' or the value of C.P.A. for P.A. and p.a.[2]

'Compare or perish' is perhaps too strong a motto for founding the rationale of comparative public administration (C.P.A.) research. However, comparison has since long been acknowledged as the 'very essence of the scientific method' in political science in general and Public Administration (P.A.) in particular (Almond and Powell 1966: 878; Verba 1967; Lijphart 1971; Pierre 1995: 4; Landman 2000; Jreisat 2002).[3] For Dahl (1947: 6) the construction of a science of administration depended upon the success in establishing propositions which transcended national boundaries. This development of concepts and generalizations at a level between what is true of all societies and level between what is true of all societies and

what is true for one society at one point in time and space (Antal et al. 1987: 14; Korsten et al. 1995: 33) takes place along systematic inquiries of cross-national and cross-time similarities and differences. Systematic comparison not only allows for assessing the effects of different environments upon organizational structure and behaviour but also for analysing why organizational structure and behaviour may matter in producing different outcomes that are relevant for society (see Peters 1988: xi).

The theoretical and empirical specification of individual cases in comparative frameworks is not only important for the more ambitious goals of building and testing theories that make us understand and, even more ambitious, predict structures and performances of p.a. in the world. It is multifunctional and not only serves some more modest scientific goals but also less modest practical purposes. At a low level of ambition, the least cross-national comparison can do is reveal, and point at possible exaggerations within the parochial scientific discourse (for instance, on the alleged huge public sector size in the Netherlands and Sweden, or the alleged exaggerated pay of top officials). In such a view, the aims and pretensions of comparative research are reduced to something like putting national results into perspective (Van Deth 1994: 2).

International examples are also important for the practice of p.a., as they enable both researchers interested in practical recommendations and practitioners seeking to adopt them to investigate a broader range of ideas about what constitutes good structure and best practices. Institutional and policy transfer is by no means new (Hood 1995; Raadschelders 2011). In the nineteenth century, institutional transfer, as constitutional consulting, was not merely an academic pastime but actually an export and import business between different nations. To be sure, several authors in the 1960s and 1970s warned against the limits of institutional transfer (see Siffin 1976), mostly associated with the export of administrative technology to the newly decolonized worlds. Their warnings remain valid 40 years later, since the break-up of the Soviet Union and, more generally, processes of globalization have given a new impetus to transfers between different jurisdictions being big business once more, supported by major funding institutions and policy diffusers at the supranational level such as the Organization for Economic Cooperation and Development (OECD), the World Bank and the International Monetary Fund (IMF). Comparative frameworks for understanding political and cultural variables of administrative behaviour and performance beyond listings of best practices is indispensable before considering transfers (Tummala 2000). The same holds for the increased practice of lesson drawing at an intergovernmental level, and peer learning between governments. Successful transfer depends on adapting the lessons learned to the contingencies of administrative systems (Fitzpatrick et al. 2011: 821).

Stringent and relaxed definitions of C.P.A. research

Assessments of the development and state of C.P.A. are strongly dependent on the definition of C.P.A. research. Stringent definitions emphasize uniformity of research approach and structured design. In essence, such definitions call for research in several countries, with data being collected according to a certain regime, guided by a central research question. If not quantitative in nature, cases are chosen according to a most similar systems design (MSSD) or most different systems design (MDSD) or carefully replicated along the relationship between dependent and independent variables in order to control intermediate variables and produce robust evidence or counter-evidence. The goals of such textbook comparative design are most ambitious in that they seek to test hypotheses from certain theoretical perspectives and rule out rival explanations. Such a design already relies heavily on cognitive simplifications of complex realities, which are exactly the subject of research captured by more relaxed definitions, or what Derlien (1992) called weaker variants of C.P.A.. Much comparative research is indeed reported in edited volumes, the cooperative effort of which combines the construction of classifications such as dichotomies or more complex typologies, and contextual description. The extent to which such research is lifted to the level of theory testing will often depend on the strength of editorial hands (see also Page 1995). Such cooperative efforts clearly demand a skilled research management in which editorial rigour is balanced with making allowances for contextual richness.

Another so-called weak variant are secondary analyses, for which monographs and journal articles have provided a mass of information, with the admitted flaw of possible reduced validity: authors are not always explicit which statements are really based on empirical evidence and which are more loosely founded on works that are primarily theoretical and impressionistic in nature (see points of Egeberg 1999: 160 and of Fitzpatrick 2011: 827). Another variant of C.P.A., and by some not perceived at all as part of C.P.A., are single case studies, the material of which returns in the above-mentioned secondary analyses. Some single case studies are themselves theory testing in that they represent unique or critical cases. This implies of course that they use concepts that apply in other countries, or seek to make larger inferences (Landman 2000: 23). Alternatively, they provide the contextual description without which the higher aims of classification and theory testing cannot be reached. Particularly valuable are case studies that seek to decode rather cryptic administrative systems, such as the Chinese one. Contrary to what some observers claim, and following what the comparative sections of major public administration journals contain, single case studies should be considered as part of the larger C.P.A. research enterprise.

Problems and opportunities

C.P.A. research is subject to recurrent criticism. From the late 1960s to date, both in the United States and Europe, assessments of the state of the discipline have not always been enthusiastic, and the sharpness of critiques are to some extent related to the reviewers' explicit or implicit definitions of C.P.A.. Disappointments are greatest among those reviewers with the most ambitious definition of the C.P.A. as a hypothesis-testing enterprise (see Heady 1979: 41; see also Feick 1987). Edited volumes would lack a comparative design and their conclusions on country juxtapositions would remain too impressionistic, depending too heavily on vague notions of differences of political culture (see Derlien 1992; Page 1995). Much of our understanding of the comparative dimensions of p.a. would remain descriptive (Peters 1988: 1–2), and the cumulative capacity to move the mass of case study findings up the hierarchy into meaningful classifications would be insufficient.

Why is it so difficult to move from description onto classification and eventually to theory testing? The reasons are multiple. It is commonplace to refer to the lack of time, money and institutional support. The accepted discourse on the rise and decline of American C.P.A. is telling in this respect (see Riggs 1998). The underlying reasons for the costliness of C.P.A. research are more interesting. They relate to the complexity of the subject matter and the lack of method to reduce this complexity into meaningful typologies and dimensions which allow for a structured set of dependent and independent variables, the relationship between which are conventional building blocks for theory testing.

The subject matter is indeed complex. Public administration is complex and the environment of administrative systems is complex. Even if there is basic agreement on the nature of dependent variables, such as structures, actors and actions of administrative systems (Aberbach and Rockman 1987), they are not easily researched in a comparative perspective. There are many kinds of agencies and actors doing many kinds of things (see Fried 1990: 322), at different levels of government and in different formal settings, which of course challenges researchers to find functional equivalents and use concepts that travel across space (see Pierre 1995: 6–7; Maor and Lane 1999: xiv). Classical examples include the properties of classifying agents as civil servants, or of ministries, departments and agencies into the basic administrative structures of central government, or the many faces of structures that make up local government. In addition, administrative systems are not easily characterized in a general fashion, given that there is much subsystem variability (Aberbach and Rockman 1987: 477, 484). For some features of administration, within-system variance may be greater than between-system variance. Moreover, administrative arrangements are in a constant flux, so concepts should also be able to travel over time. So are their environments, which, irrespective of change, already consist of many possible variables.

Problems of operational definition and measurement hamper singling out the basic dependent variables of administrative systems, and their cross-national and cross-time comparison. Turning the nature of these variables into independent variables for exploring the impact of different institutional arrangements makes things even more difficult: outputs and outcomes are not easily defined and measured either, and are complicated by further problems of data collection.

The availability and reliability of data is indeed a sore point in the development of C.P.A.. Data may be scarce but are also vulnerable to manipulation, as they are often the constructs of the actors and agencies involved (see Fried 1990: 323). For long, there were relatively few independent data sets, particularly when compared to what comparative politics has available for the issues it tends to focus on (Or does comparative politics focus on issues for which data sets are available?). C.P.A. researchers have been generally more eclectic in their use of data, which has the advantage of corroboration from multiple sources of evidence. Some data, however, are legally or ethically warranted, hence embargoed also by researchers, the limited opportunities for replication of which may reduce the validity of their inferences (Gill and Meier 1999: 4–6).

Some critiques go beyond the traditional methodological flaws addressed in reviews and render the prospects for C.P.A. research even bleaker. To be sure, language skills and sensitiveness to translating concepts across cultures have since long been acknowledged as necessary ingredients for cross-national research (Pollitt 2011; Raadschelders 2011). But it is clear that the far-reaching ontological conclusions postmodernists assign to the role of language seriously threaten C.P.A. as a post-positivist endeavour (for an overview of postmodern approaches to P.A., see Heady 2001: 53; see also Pollitt 2011). A further but less existentially threatening source of relativism is related to the alleged process of globalization in general, and European convergence or eurocompatibility pressures in

particular. These forces would reduce the relevance of nation-states as units of analysis, in that their environments are increasingly shared by nations, no longer confined to them (see also Heady 1979: 64).

Leaving aside postmodern relativism, there are many sources of optimism and opportunities for C.P.A.. Moving up from the flaws mentioned above, studies of globalization have not produced indicators of powerful forces for countries to take on similar institutional forms (Chandler 2000: 264). Integration and the loss of sovereignty should not be a break on C.P.A. research in a cross-national context (Korsten et al. 1995: 31–2). Europeanization research, as well as studies of the domestication of international regimes, have shown that national states remain useful contexts of comparative analysis (Sverdrup 2005; Ferraro et al. 2009), given the importance of the path dependency of change, and the meaning major actors keep assigning to national structures and processes.

Globalization does seem to contribute to the rapid spread of information and data, and major policy-diffusing institutions, such as the OECD, the World Bank and the United Nations (UN), have since the 1990s increased their efforts to collect public sector data on and beyond public sector performance. The OECD's *Government at a Glance* (2011) is a recent case in point, but also the OECD PUMA's publications, data and cases warrant special mention here (OECD 1995; see Pollitt 2011). Also through other processes of peer pressure and peer learning, stimulated by both Europe's method of open coordination and national governments' appetite for comparing their performances, many comparative lesson-drawing initiatives have gained ground (see, for instance, the European Network of Public Administration: www.eupan.eu). Of note are also many recent academic initiatives in constructing databases for comparison between nations, organizations, and over time. To name but a few: the Cobra (COST-CRIPO) database on the basis of surveys of agency managers (Verhoest et al. 2011); the longitudinal Norwegian and

Irish databases on structural administrative reforms (Norwegian State Administration Database; Hardiman and MacCarthaigh 2009); or databases on regulatory organizations (Yesilkagit and Christensen 2010), their origin (Levi-Faur 2006; Jordana et al. 2011), or their autonomy (see Braun and Gilardi 2006).

The common comparative drive of supranational institutions, intergovernmental initiatives, and academic collaborative efforts promise to be bear many fruits for the future development of C.P.A.. Yet, keeping in mind that the magnitude in data does not equal the comparability of data, data collection for C.P.A. purposes calls for sustained academic vigilance as to reliability and validity of the multitude of comparative data going around.

The increased data and the bulk of case studies and secondary analyses may not have contributed to a general theory of administrative systems. Leaving aside for now the question whether such general comparative theory of administrative systems is possible or even desirable, an optimistic analysis of C.P.A. research would certainly not miss the following points. First, advances in the comparative documentation and analysis of major subquestions in P.A. are multiple, having produced meaningful typologies and classifications. These include comparative studies on general and senior civil service systems in OECD countries, Central and Eastern Europe and Asia (Bekke et al. 1996; Page and Wright 1999; Verheijen 1999; Burns and Bowornwathana 2001; Raadschelders et al. 2007); local government structures and functions (Martin Harloff 1987); public service delivery systems (Hood and Schuppert 1988); and government agencies (Verhoest et al. 2011). Second, even if not fully comparative by design, we also notice a more informed use of analytical strategies for theory testing. Triangulation (Webb et al. 1966; see Peters 1988: 3), for instance, or running theoretically predicted patterns of rival theoretical lenses through cross-national evidence seems a fruitful strategy to enhance our understanding of certain

administrative phenomena, such as, for instance, local government reorganization (Dente and Kjellberg 1988), decentralization (Page and Goldsmith 1987), public sector pay (Hood and Peters 1994), and public sector reform (Pollitt and Bouckaert 2011). Time series, too, on condition data is available, provide quite straightforward tests of theoretical propositions, as, for instance, in Rose's (1985) study of the growth and decline of big government, or Hood and Peters (1994) on self-interested behaviour in the dynamics of public sector pay. As to the selection of cases, Fitzpatrick et al. (2011) note an increase in purposive sampling, but at the same time a lack of attention for the 'too few cases, too many variables problem' (Goggin 1986). Given the predominance and problems of small N-analysis in the C.P.A. discipline, it is somewhat surprising that the small N-analysis of QCA (Ragin 1989) is still awaiting a broader reception by C.P.A. (www.compasss.org for an overview of applications). The advancements in QCA methods (MSDO/MDSO; crisp set QCA, multi-value QCA and fuzzy set QCA) and software nonetheless offer promising avenues for a more rigorous comparison of a small-to-medium number of cases at macro, meso and micro levels. Besides providing a systematic approach for data exploration and summarizing existing data, the technique could also be fruitful for typology building, theory testing and also for inductive theory formulation . The approach is particularly interesting, as it conceptualizes outcomes as combinations of attributes. It is the very combinations that give social phenomena their unique nature. Searching for the 'net' effect of a certain variable does not make much sense from this perspective, as is also recognized in process tracing (George and Bennett 2005). Configurational methods instead expect that the effect of a certain variable (or 'condition' in QCA vocabulary) might differ depending on the wider context, and that several combinations of conditions can lead to the same outcome (equifinality) (Rihoux and Lobe 2009). Such an approach seems particularly attractive in an age where the contextualization of public administration structures and mechanisms is at the core of much contemporary comparative work (see, e.g., Giauque et al. 2011).

FROM GENERAL THEORY TO GENERAL FRAMEWORKS

Parallel and intersecting tracks of middle-range theory development

The theoretical advancements aided by the above-mentioned research strategies are not situated at the level of grand theory development, attempting broad, cross-cultural explanations and concerned with the definition of clusters of concepts helpful in classifying administrative systems around the world in terms of rich and poor bureaucracies or weak and strong states (see Presthus 1959; Heady 2001: 17). This kind of general systems modelling was at the heart of the American C.P.A. movement in the 1950s and 1960s, with its foreman F. Riggs articulating its strong scientific ambitions, drawing upon structural functional concepts as an alternative for functionalist analysis such as Almond's (Almond and Coleman 1960). The story of the decline of the American C.P.A. movement is partly an institutional story, with references to plummeting funding and the shrinking interest of development agencies in administrative arrangements as levers for social and economic development (see Fried 1990: 326). But the strongest disenchantment derived from unfulfilled scientific promises or the failure to produce a general theory of administrative systems. Several observers advised C.P.A. to move their theoretical efforts from grand theory development of cosmic dimensions (Presthus 1959: 26; Jreisat 1975: 663; both in Heady 2001: 33) to a more incremental production of middle-range theories. It seems this advice was (consciously or not) taken up, since much of the theoretical and conceptual

advancement of C.P.A. developed along subfields within the larger discipline.

At the risk of oversimplification, we document the development of middle-range theory as running along two tracks, at times separated or one catching up with the other, at times intersecting and giving momentum to comparative research in certain subfields. Of these tracks, one is problem driven. Here, theory development seeks to codify, classify and understand structural or behavioural phenomena of public administration or developments in its environment that are politically and socially perceived as problematic or in a state of flux.

First track: problem driven

The problem of the 1980s, following the economic world crisis of the 1970s, and given extra salience by the advent of neo-liberal discourse, was undoubtedly scarcity. The problem of scarcity, and the emerging concerns with efficiency and economy favoured an agenda for comparatively investigating public sector size and growth (see Rose 1985), with a further two-fold spin-off. First, accounting for public sector growth became a focal point in theories on bureaucratic power, which were much influential in modifying the traditional bureaucratic model (see further in text). Second, problems with regard to measuring the size of government called for comparative studies of public sector variance, which was given a further impetus by the downsizing bureaucracy movement towards privatization and deregulation in the late 1980s (Vickers and Wright 1988) and of its effects in the early 1990s (Wright 1994b). Privatization was comparatively noted as a dominant trend, with the public sector becoming leaner and the interactions between public and private actors increasing, one of the results of which was the emergence of a range of new public–private institutional arrangements for service delivery (Hood and Schuppert 1988). The managerialist 'revolution' in several countries further complicated the issue of variance by introducing internal privatization. The widescale practical and political acclaim of the new managerialism triggered off a great deal of comparative research on the variance of administrative reform over time, not only in the Western world but also, gradually, in developing countries (Crozier and Trosa 1992; Wright 1994a; Aucoin 1995; Naschold 1995; Massey 1997; Verheijen 1999; Barzelay 2000; Ongaro 2009; McCourt and Minogue 2001; Pollit and Bouckaert 2011), which so far confirms, against the claims of globalization, the persistence of national administrative traditions. Also personnel policies, particularly performance-based systems and the profile and competencies of the new public managers received comparative attention (see Derlien 1992: 291; Farnham et al. 1996; Lodge et al. 2005).

Meanwhile, administrative reform at other levels of government has established a comparative research tradition for itself. The widescale nature of local government structural reform in the postwar era suggested common causes and efforts to account for cross-national variance and led to fruitful theorizing and operationalization (Sharpe, 1979, 1993; Dente and Kjellberg 1988; Batley and Stoker 1991; see also Page and Goldsmith 1987). Federalism, or more generally devolution, also enjoyed renewed attention, with the unification of (the traditionally already federal) Germany, the federalization of Belgium, regionalization in France, Spain and Italy, devolution in the UK, and the 'new federalism' in the United States (Walker 1995; Keating 2001; Stepan 2001; Swenden 2006).

Much of the administrative reform agenda of the 1980s and early 1990s was concerned with the pursuit of economy and efficiency, and to a lesser extent with effectiveness, the latter receiving more attention from the second half of the 1990s onwards. The concern of politicians to produce policies that make a difference (or that have politicians themselves make a difference) can be viewed as being part of the larger concern to restore declining levels of trust in government (Klingemann and Fuchs 1995; Norris 1999;

Rouban 1999). Real or perceived problems of declining trust have triggered efforts to reaffirm the position of citizens (Pierre 1995: 12–13) and to find ways to create democratic legitimacy that are not elective in character (see Marini 1998: 369; Hendriks 2010). Even the OECD, after having focused for years on managerialist aspects of public administration, started promoting ways to engage citizens in the policy-making process. Systematic research on the different modes of administrative mediation of citizens' perspectives in both policy formulation and implementation is still rather meagre though, and so are structured explorations of the effects the outward-looking behaviour of civil servants will produce for administrative organization and politico-administrative relations.

Meanwhile, quite a bit of comparative research on trust-related issues have materialized. For a long time, corruption was parochially thought to be endemic to the developing world, and looked upon as a sign of immaturity of developing nations. In the United States, the issue surfaced with Watergate, and pushed the issue of administrative ethics on the agenda. In Europe, comparative research on the many faces and causes of corruption only gained real momentum after much reported scandals and sleaze in the late 1980s and early 1990s and subsequent concerns with standards in public life. Maesschalck et al. (2007–8: 7) have identified four strands in international comparative research on administrative ethics: studies on countries' institutional measures to prevent corruption and foster ethical behaviour (e.g. Rohr 2001); analyses of the incidence, process and consequences of corruption and unethical behaviour (e.g. Della Porta and Mény 1997); survey-based studies on public sector values (De Vries 2002) and measurement of ethical decision making in different countries (Stewart et al. 2001); and modelling of causal mechanisms for explaining variation in norms, values and (un)ethical behaviour among various countries.

At the turn of the millennium, the OECD identified the challenges for p.a. associated with the informatization of society as a top priority of governments and also framed the issue of e-government being about government rather than about e- (OECD 2003). The use of new information and communication technologies by government may drastically transform the structures and operations of government and alter government's interactions with civil society. E-government has many faces and the range of concerns for P.A. is broad. How can ICT facilitate governments' capacity to respond to clients and customers? How does e-communication impact on hierarchies within government, on relations between organizations, and on the relations between superiors and subordinates? What does e-government mean for equality of citizens' access? Finally, will the integration of management and policy information systems reinvent rationalist models by increasing the cognitive capacity of government, the limits to which were central in conceptualizing bounded rationality (Simon 1957). The exploration of these questions will no doubt benefit from comparative studies that go beyond listing good practices (Reddick 2010).

We end this overview where we started, with economic crisis. The global financial and economic crisis of the 2010s raises many old and new questions for C.P.A.. Scarcity and budget cutbacks will no doubt reinforce issues of efficient and effective service delivery, if not concerns about minimum service delivery in some cases. In contrast to the 'retreat of the state' crisis of 1970s, the present crisis calls for rearticulating the role of the state, and redressing its regulatory failure.

Second track: discipline driven

The only single most dominant conceptual framework surviving the C.P.A. heyday of the 1950s and 1960s was the bureaucratic one (see Arora 1972; quoted in Heady 1979: 14, 60), either conceived as a checklist instrument or a broader model for comparing the chief structural and functional characteristics of different administrative systems (see Waldo 1964). Middle-range theory development in the C.P.A. discipline was much informed by applications and alterations to the bureaucratic model. Several important developments came from translating generic organization theory to bureaucratic organization and bureaucratic behaviour (see Peters 1989: 7; Joergensen et al. 1998: 500).

Organizational theory did much to articulate the role of environmental differences. Contingency theory, for instance, tried to match characteristics of the environment of organizations and their mode of production to the most appropriate structures. It was criticized, however, for not acknowledging incidences of organizational closure to environmental influences and for over-insulating structural variables from institutional transfer (Peters 1989: 7). Ecology theory, in turn, was interesting in that it offered a perspective on organizational inertia, change and transformation (Kaufmann 1976; see also Hogwood and Peters 1983). Other lasting influences come from organization theory that emphasized cross-national differences in organizational culture. In the United States, Presthus (1959) preceded this development. In Europe, Lammers and Hickson (1979) offered comparative perspectives on organizational cultures. While Crozier's (1963) study on the bureaucratic phenomenon was not comparative by design, and his observations on differences between the French, United States and Soviet bureaucracies were not systematic, the importance of his work should not be underestimated for the development of European C.P.A.. It paved the way for a theoretical and methodological break with administrative sciences, which mainly focused on descriptions of institutions and public law (see Smith 1999).[4] Other influential work from organization theory was produced by Hofstede (1984), whose four dimensions of culture (six in the 2010 edition by Hofstede et al. 2010), offered ways to discern and typify cross-cultural values. In particular, his dimension of power distance has much in common with the often-used dichotomies between Latin and Nordic or

Catholic and Protestant politico-administrative cultures (see, for instance, Page and Goldsmith 1987), and deserves to be integrated in other conceptions of politico-administrative cultures such as the one that distinguishes between Anglo-Saxon, Germanic Rechtstaat, French Napoleonic and the mixed Scandinavian traditions (Rhodes and Weller 2001: 244).

Another important source of modifying the traditional bureaucratic model came from formal theorizing on the dysfunctions and ills of bureaucracy, the public choice tradition of which received much impetus from the bureaucracy-bashing climate that emerged from concerns with the inefficiencies of big government. These accounts (see Peters 1996) of bureaucrats as shirkers, budget maximizers and of bureaucratic monopolies (Downs 1967; Niskanen 1971; Moe 1984) translated concepts from the new organizational economics, primarily principal–agent models. Dunleavy's (1991) bureau-shaping model was original, in that its institutional public choice approach did not draw on principal–agent models. Another influential, empirical study was Allison's (1971), which not only presented a good example of the method of triangulation but also greatly helped in conceptualizing bureaucratic power and politics (Kettl 1993: 412).

These theories seriously challenged the traditional bureaucratic model in two ways. They offered ways to conceptualize bureaucratic power over state policies, and helped viewing bureaucracy as an arena in which conflicts are played out, two neglected issues in the accepted version of the traditional model.[5] The notion of bureaucratization of politics helped revisiting the classic dichotomy between politics and administration, which was, to a great extent unjustifiably, associated with the Weberian bureaucratic model. Meanwhile, other theoretical developments and comparative research came to demonstrate the politicization of bureaucracy. Aberbach, Putnam and Rockman's seminal study (1981) on cross-national variation of bureaucratic roles and Aberbach and

Rockman's (1987) conceptualization of the ways in which politics penetrates bureaucracy further helped to erode the theoretical and empirical claims of the dichotomy. The relationships between policy makers and bureaucrats have become chief variables in the comparative study of administrative systems, both in terms of dependent and independent variables , and in terms of their formal and behavioural manifestations. The four types of politico-administrative relations identified by Putnam and associates, and the fifth type added by Peters (1988), lend themselves to capturing cross-national variation, and also to monitoring shiftings over time (see Golembiewski 1996: 14).

That administration is highly political was also shown by Pressmann and Wildavsky's (1973) empirical study of implementation. Their study was very influential in the development of implementation research in both the United States and Europe (Hanf and Toonen 1985; O'Toole 1986). Whether best understood from a bottom-up or a top-down perspective, the complexities of implementation pointed at the multi-actor character of turning legislation into working programmes, no longer conceptualizing public administration as embedded in a single, monolithic organization (Peters 1989: 8).

This articulation of increased complexity (see Kickert et al. 1997; Teisman 2000) became a focal point in comparative research on networks and found resonance in studies on the implementation of European legislation (Heinelt and Smith 1996; Marsh 1998), and on public–private and public–public arrangements at different levels of government all over the world. The British network approach, which was originally conceived as an account of interest intermediation, moved to accounting for the patchwork organization of the public sector, involving many different public–private actors in different arrangements (Rhodes 1996; Börzel 1998). In Germany, the concept of *Politikverflechtung* of Frits Scharpf and the network studies of his Max Planck School was also much used in examining a whole range of policies (Hanf and Scharpf 1978; Scharpf 1993; Windhoff-Héritier 1993).

Comparative research on policy networks offers strong theoretical perspectives and analytical frameworks, but could still advance in operational definition (see Benz 1999; O'Toole 1997), to analyse network properties in terms of open or closed, and the relationship between their characteristics and their consequences: for instance, in terms of producing private or collective benefits (see Börzel 1998; Pierre 1998).

The involvement of third parties in p.a., whether private sector actors, agencies at different government levels, or groups or individuals from civil society, have emphasized the need to conceptualize public sector diversity, as well as the institutional and societal embedding of the tools of implementation (see Ashford 1978). Classifications of policy instrumentation (Hood 1986; Salomon 2002) are useful here, but also worth mentioning is the great empirical advancement on the properties of organizations, their specialization and co-ordination (Bouckaert et al. 2009; Laegreid and Verhoest 2010; Verhoest et al. 2011), and the articulation of the metagovernance of markets, hierarchies and networks (Meuleman 2008).

Some theory development is cumulative, often building upon sets of empirical studies. But several observers have pointed us out the occurrence of pendulum type development in P.A. theory, with periods of temporary amnesia or blindness for already established theory and evidence or for the wisdom of old masters (Kettl 1993: 408; Hood 1999; Page 1995: 138–9; Golembievski 1996; Holden 1998; Hood 1999). In 1979, Heady (1997: vii), for instance, was doubtful about the longevity or impact of the new public administration movement. He was not able to predict the forcefulness with which the issues at the heart of it would resurface in the new public service movement of the 1990s, in reaction to the alleged normative consequences and the intellectual foundations of the New Public Management. Indeed, NPM should be credited for having

done a great job for P.A.. Not only did it trigger efforts to define its subject matter, or the publicness of public administration, but also it made classic issues such as accountability, control and coordination re-emphasized and sleeping issues awake, such as the role of lower civil servants, and citizen empowerment.

A similar development can be noted in reaction to the intellectual school with which NPM's intellectual tradition is related. In reaction to the public choice 'revolution', the role of institutional arrangements is reconfirmed, which underpins the very rationale of comparative analyses of structural variables. Also, the role of culture, of which individualism is just one variant, is reconfirmed as being important in explaining, for example, different reform trajectories of public sector reform (Pollitt and Bouckaert 2011, Verhoest 2010), or different traditions in public sector pay (Hood and Peters 1994).

General frameworks for C.P.A.

Accounts of problem-driven and discipline-driven theory development for C.P.A. reflect the absence of a single paradigm, a variety of questions, and a variety of approaches. They are one way to structure the discipline and identify the main questions and ways to answer them. But these narratives are no doubt incomplete, and also biased (my own bias being Western European), for other observers may tell a different story, with different sequences and emphases. Another, and possibly more fruitful, way of structuring the discipline of C.P.A., to give it purpose and coherence, is to seek an agreement on what to study, and organize comparative data collection and theory development around core-dependent variables. Such an approach clearly departs from C.P.A. as a grand theory exercise, as it no longer has administrative systems or transformations as wholes as its subjects, but more narrowly defined subjects instead. It has, however, the advantage of allowing for a structured collection of comparative evidence and more feasible in-depth comparative analyses across countries, time and government levels, while not excluding broader theoretical explorations of relations between variables.

The usefulness of such an approach to C.P.A. is recognized by many comparativists, but views differ as to which variables to include. When having acknowledged that grand theory was to be substituted by middle-range theory, some thought progress was best achieved by studying 'the backgrounds, attitudes, and behaviors of bureaucrats and those with whom they interact' (Sigelman 1976: 624, in Heady 2001: 33). This view recognizes the environment in those with whom bureaucrats interact, but it remains quite narrow in that its focus on individuals is behavioural only. In a broader view, Heady (1979, 2001) specifies the environment of public administration by identifying the arena in which bureaucrats interact with others: that is, the broader political system and society in general. He also adds an organizational focus and emphasizes the importance of relying on several levels of analysis for understanding the complexity of public administration (Heady 2001: 34). Maor and Lane (1999) take actors, structures and behaviour as building blocks for comparative public administration, but do not explicitly mention relations with the environment: neither does Peters (1988), for whom the candidate-dependent variables are public employees, public organizations, bureaucratic behaviour and politico-administrative relations. Pierre's approach (1995) to C.P.A. is probably still the most comprehensive, in taking three sets of variables. He adds an explicit focus on the administration's relations with civil society, which in Peter's scheme are not absent but captured under bureaucratic behaviour. The three sets of variables in Pierre's C.P.A. project are the intra-organizational dynamics of bureaucracy, which encompasses such variables as actors, structures and behaviour; politico-administrative relations; and the relations between administration and civil society.

Internal dynamics: actors, structure, behaviour

The building blocks for theory building on the internal dynamics of the public sector are individuals, organization and behaviour. Of these, the first two are the most tangible, although it is acknowledged that the operationalization of public employees and public organizations are not automatic and require careful judgements. The operationalization, classification and explaining of behaviour, however, is more problematic because of the absence of a theoretical paradigm on the nature of human behaviour in general.

The study of the individuals that operate in the public sector has established a research agenda for itself (Peters 1988). The results of comparative civil service studies, either focusing on the civil service in general, or the top, provide a mass of material for secondary analysis. Comparisons of the numbers of public employees, their socio-economic background, and characteristics, the socio-economic conditions of their employment, and more recently their public service motivation (Kim and Vandenabeele 2010), support theory development on public sector employment, recruitment and career patterns in the civil service, and the pays and perks of public office (see e.g. Derlien and Peters 2008). They present answers to central explanatory and normative questions in public administration. The number and nature of public employees serve as indicators for the size of the public sector and the way in which the latter pervades society. The characteristics and background of public employees addressed such issues as the representativeness of the civil service, and the degree of equality, while the level and method of their payment gives insights into the social status of the civil service.

The reasons for comparing organizations and structures as units of analysis are many. Comparing the number and nature of public organizations as more than aggregates of the individuals that operate within them provides a composite picture of the public sector. Comparisons over time and across countries are revealing in that they help to put such issues as the size and modes of public service delivery in perspective, beyond what conventional wisdom might suggest. A focus on organizations as units of analysis also provides perspectives on change and transformation (Kaufmann 1976; Peters 1988; Yesilkagit and Christensen 2010), government priorities (Rose 1985), and the ways in which differences in the environment of administrative system are translated onto the organizational make-up of the state (population ecology). But bringing organizations and organizational structure to the centre of analysis may also serve goals that are more ambitious than explaining public sector size and change only.

As acknowledged in different variants of neo-institutionalism, organizational structures, as composites of culture, path-determining institutions, or equilibrium outcomes will constrain or enable behaviour and strategic interactions within the public domain. This articulation of structure over agency is reflected in studies that address the conditions for effective implementation or in network approaches for understanding complexity, and increasingly also in efforts for understanding the scope and nature of public sector reform (Hood 2001). Comparisons of organizations and structure are thus not only a necessary ingredient for understanding the complexity of the internal dynamics of public sector, or for judgements on the size, diversity, transformation and publicness of the public sector. They are also central building blocks for institutional design, since various structural arrangements of coordination and specialization may produce various outcomes that matter for public administration: trust, information exchange, the smoothness of implementation, professional autonomy, transparency, etc. (see Egeberg 1999).

Together with public employees, organizations and structures are relatively tangible units of analysis, although operational definition and the search for functional equivalents will not always be straightforward, particularly when the boundaries of public and private actors and sectors are blurred. But the third core variable for understanding the internal dynamics of the public sector presents bigger problems of operational definition and data collection, and is more demanding for the interpretation of data and the avoidance of supply and demand side bias. Data on behaviour is less easily accessed and verified, and requires contextual interpretation, which is further complicated by the absence of a behavioural paradigm. An important strand of theory development has chosen to ignore the latter problem, by formally modelling behaviour on the universal assumption of utility maximization. Although such assumptions remain questionable, formal theories of bureaucratic behaviour are useful for C.P.A., in that they provide a vehicle for hypothesis formulation and heuristic tools for structured empirical comparisons. Particularly when used in triangulation with other theoretical perspectives, they may generate explanatory power.

The foci of other, more empirical, theory developments on bureaucratic behaviour reflect the diversity of actions and interactions that public administrators may be involved in. Fruitful theorizing came for empirical work in their behaviour toward clients (street- level bureaucracy, Lipsky 1980), the conversion of decisions into actions (bottom-up and top-down implementation literature), their interactions as superiors and subordinates (management studies), decision making (contending models of rational, incremental, or even irrational decision making) and, more recently, their discretion in secondary legislation (Page 2012 forthcoming). There is no overarching conceptualization of the various ways in which administrators use their discretion, and most available theories cast the nature of discretionary behaviour in negative terms. This is definitely the case for the formal models of bureaucrats as shirkers, budget maximizers or leisure seekers, but also in empirical studies of coping behaviour, policy failures and, more explicitly, even with studies on corruption and ethics. The normative purport of studies of bureaucratic behaviour is apparent, and the importance of comparative approaches for administrative transfer is hence obvious. Comparative analyses of bureaucratic behaviour not only helps to explain how public administration actually functions but also may support informed considerations of what works how under which conditions.

Politico-administrative relations

Consistent with the erosion of the politics–administration dichotomy, the relations between politicians and bureaucrats are now an important set of variables. Their cross-national documentation and investigation of central shiftings over time are important. They are 'at the centre of many issues' (Kettl 1993: 421; see also Golembiewski 1996: 144), the most pressing concern of which is the blending of political control with policy capacity. The bureaucratization of politics or politicization of bureaucracy can take on many faces and produce outcomes that matter for institutional design.

Cross-national comparisons of politico-administrative relations are not simple and require data collection on a number of analytical units. Many advancements, however, have already been made, and the prospects for further advancements are bright. One established way of approaching comparative politico-administrative relations comes from role theory (Aberbach et al. 1981). In this tradition, the attitudes, roles and behaviour are investigated by interviewing large samples of administrative and political elites in a number of countries. These studies have empirically helped to erode the classic dichotomy, provided insights into the different policy roles of administrators, and documented the many faces of politicization of civil servants. The research methodology is robust and deserves application for cases still uninvestigated as well as replication for analysing and theorizing shiftings over time.

An additional way to approach politico-administrative relations is the construction of ideal types, as furthered by Peters (1988), which provides a structured means to empirically identify and classify the interactions between politicians and bureaucrats in such terms as the tone of relations, the likely winners, and the mode of conflict resolution between the two sets of actors. Divergence from idealized patterns of relationships can than be used to refine the models, and give a further theoretical impetus to the future research agenda, as Verheijen's (2001) study of Central and Eastern European cases shows.

Explaining variance of types and hybrids requires careful institutional analysis, and an investigation of a range of variables that impact on the interactions between politicians and civil servants. Such a research programme, however, should not be scary, because many of the candidate variables have already been documented, hence reducing the need for original research. Understanding politico-administrative relations indeed relies on knowledge about civil servants and political executives, and the impact of broader systemic or structural factors. Our comparative knowledge of the background, careers and position of civil servants has advanced greatly, and comparative political science has a lot of data to offer for what we need to know about political executives. Lacking still is a consistent data set on the structural interfaces between the two groups of actors, and more work needs to be done on the role of formal rules and coordination mechanisms through which responsibilities are allocated and interactions structured. These data, together with that on a range of systemic factors such as partitocracy, consensus democracy, majoritarianism or trust, may be combined by applying small N-analysis, from which we expect great progress.

A comprehensive research programme on politico-administrative relations not only challenges the discipline's quest for theory building but also carries great normative appeal for institutional designs that seek to avoid the various negative effects of conflicts over power and policy, ranging from inertia, ineffectiveness to outright policy failure.

The nature of these relations matter greatly for reconciling electoral mandates for political direction with professional policy making, as they present a tradeoff between two classic values for designing institutions and allocating responsibilities between them (Peters 1988: 178).

Relations between public administration and civil society

Parallel with the rise and resonance of the governance debate in the 1990s, a range of buzzwords (re-) emerged such as transparency, consultation and participative or interactive policy making. These and similar concepts serve to highlight the changes or challenges to contact points between public administration and civil society broadly defined. Attention to the relations between p.a. and civil society are not new and neither are certain tools to reduce the distance between them (see Lasswell 1960). Classifications such as weak/strong states, for instance, have been useful in comparing the bureaucratization of society or the penetration of society on the autonomy of the state. Another established research tradition comes from studies that compare differences in trust and consent (Almond and Verba 1965) and more recently of the value of social capital for government performance (Putnam et al. 1994). Approaching the contact points between p.a. and civil society involves disaggregating the relation into several components: tools, direction and subjects. Useful classifications and conceptual frameworks come from political theories on citizenship, communitarianism and discursive democracy, from the literature on policy instrumentation, policy networks and policy-making models, as well as from empirical comparative work on public–private partnerships and the characteristics of the so-called third sector.

The nature and types of contact points seem to vary along with the nature of tools that are employed, the direction of contacts and the subjects with which p.a. renders in contact. Tools for reducing the distance between p.a. and civil society may be legal, when rights are created by freedom of information acts or citizen's charters. They may also be communicative and, for instance, involve enhanced IT-supported information and communication or the use of citizen and client surveys. Contact points may also be anchored in institutions (such as partnerships) or political procedures for access of citizens and groups to one or more steps in the policy cycle. At least as important is the direction of interactions. Information and consultation may be confined to bureaucracy's control over society and the wish to secure effective implementation. Participation, in turn, means more in terms of empowerment, and creates access of citizens and groups beyond the ballot box. A comparative analysis of the relations between p.a. and civil society also involves a narrowing of what is meant by civil society and the third actors that are being engaged. Are the subjects (in less active conceptions, mere objects though) individual citizens, profit-seeking actors or not-for-profit organizations. Cross-national comparison here can benefit from works on conceptions of individual citizens. Interactions will differ if administrations conceive of individuals with whom they interact as customers, clients or active citizens (Sjöblom 1999), giving them different opportunities in terms of choice, dialogue and intervention. As for the operational definition of other subjects too, advancements have been made by work on public–private partnerships (Pierre 1998) or on defining the third sector (Salamon and Anheier 1997).

The normative input from understanding the relationship between p.a. and civil society is obvious, since several important guiding values for institutional design are at stake. Suffice it to refer to the debate on the digital divide that may reduce the distance with government for some but not for a great deal of others, or to the reconciliation of policy co-production by active citizens with electoral policy mandates and accepted standards of representativeness, or to the challenge of steering process towards products.

With these three sets of variables, and a dimension of meta-governance, a comprehensive framework is constructed with which to approach a comparative public administration research agenda that fosters accumulation through structured data collection, the creation of a common language and the development of meaningful theories (Figure 28.1). The agenda can help to identify the need for original research for cases where information is still lacking or in need of updating. The framework is helpful in generating questions about the relationship between the three sets of variables in different governance settings. Generating the questions that are challenging for both theory development and institutional design can also proceed by treating each of the sets of variables as independent variables for the others.

One can for instance explore the impact of the nature and changes within the internal dynamics of p.a. on politico-administrative relations and p.a. contact points with civil society. Public sector personnel and organization are recognized as systemic factors influencing the nature of politico-administrative relations. How then are changes to organizational structure, career paths and the socio-economic conditions of office induced by managerialist reform impacting upon the balance between political executives and civil servants? Comparative designs can test hypotheses on the relaxation or strengthening of political control on policy, or the reduction or increase in the degree of separation between the two sets of players. Does top-level recruitment from outside the bureaucracy, for instance, break into the cosy world of highly integrated interactions between politicians and civil servants and how do political executives deal with the insecurity this may impose upon them? Equally interesting are designs that explore the impact of organizational and behavioural change on the way p.a. interacts with civil society. Do greater pressures for service responsiveness, for instance, lead to different conceptions of citizenship, and what do enhanced particularist client relationships mean for the autonomy and the 'publicness' of bureaucracies?

Comparative designs may also reverse the relationships between these variables. The nature of politico-administrative relations affects the internal dynamics of bureaucracies. It impacts on the behaviour of civil servants in policy making and the various ways in which they apply administrative discretion (Page 2011). It may also determine bureaucratic initiatives for change, and may help account for variance in terms of weaker or stronger vertical integration of politico-administrative elites. The nature

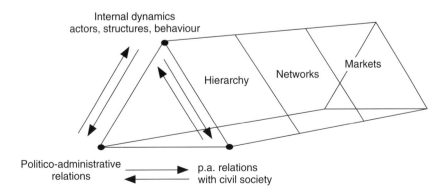

Figure 28.1   General framework for generating and investigating core questions

of politico-administrative relations may thus be conceived as an explanatory factor in accounting for variance in public sector reform. Just as the differential need for political control accounted for various designs of bureaucracies in the nineteenth century (Silberman 1994), differences in politico-administrative relations may help explain who does what kind of public sector reform and why (see Hood 2001).

The contact points of p.a. with civil society, too, may be theorized as affecting bureaucrats' roles and behaviour, as well as the nature of relations between the administrative and political components of bureaucracy. Some of the interesting questions such designs may help to answer are whether the reduction of the distance between p.a. and citizens and groups increases the distance with political executives; what it means for civil servants to do the great split in serving two masters; and how greater access and transparency break up information monopolies and challenge civil servants to act upon competencies other than technical expertise; or what the enhanced involvement of third actors, private or not for profit, means for the publicness of bureaucracies, and its commitment to the common good.

CONCLUSION

There is no grand theory to answer all the central questions of p.a. and P.A.. Such theory is neither possible, nor desirable. The questions are better approached from general frameworks in which the core dependent variables are agreed upon, the required original and secondary collection of evidence feasible, and the theoretical exploration of interconnectedness between variables meaningful. At the same time, such frameworks do not rule out considerations of the wholeness of government, or prevent attempts to classify and explain administrative systems as a whole. The recent past and immediate future of C.P.A. looks bright. At the level of

the discipline, international collaboration and mobility have greatly advanced the collection of data, have improved operational definition and measurement, and have opened up many cases for comparison. At the practitioners' level too, investments in databases have provide fruitful material for academic research. It would be a good development if C.P.A. scholars and c.p.a. practitioners further improved their connections, in order to collectively frame questions for comparison, identify data-collection needs, and increase the reliability of databases. As to methods, C.P.A. scholarship relies on a variety of methods, but has so far failed to embrace QCA. This is surprising, since most research is qualitative and small N, and assigns much meaning to contingencies. Although the number of cases featuring C.P.A. seems to be rising, C.P.A. scholarship should not frown upon further single cases studies, particularly not those that seek to decode rather cryptic administrative systems into a comparative language. Whereas the prospects for C.P.A. research are bright, the practice of p.a. across the world is troubled by crisis. It would be a great achievement for C.P.A. scholarship to move their comparisons to where improvements to p.a. may matter most. Geographically, this means a greater consideration of p.a. in developing countries, and a keen interest in the role of p.a. in democratic innovations in the Arab world. Functionally, this entails a reconsideration of classic domains of modern administration: taxation, internal and external security, justice, and the regulation of markets and banks.

NOTES

1   The author wishes to thank Richard Stillman II and Valerie Pattyn for comments on an earlier draft of this article.

2   This article follows the convention of referring to the academic discipline of Public Administration in upper case and to the practice of public administration in lower case.

'Compare or perish' is translated from the Dutch 'Vergelijk of verga', a provocation to the community of social scientists in 1992 by the Dutch political scientist De Beus regarding the sorry state of comparative research (Korsten et al. 1995: 15).

3   Public Administration is seen here as a subdiscipline of political science.

4   Although having an earlier disciplinary tradition with eighteenth-century cameralism (study of state administration) and polizey studies, European Public Administration was since the late nineteenth century firmly rooted in the discipline of public law (see Rutgers 1994).

5   This is not the place to give a full critique of the assimilation of the Wilsonian dichotomy with Weberian bureaucracy. Suffice it to say that re-reading Weber makes his concepts valid for capturing the intricate relationship between political authority and bureaucratic power, of which the accepted checklist model is but one variant.

REFERENCES

Aberbach, J.D. and Rockman, B.A. (1987) 'Comparative Administration: Methods, Muddles and Models', *Administration and Society*, 18 (4): 473–506.

Aberbach, J.D., Putnam, R.D. and Rockman, B.A. (1981) *Bureaucrats and Politicians in Western Democracies.* Cambridge, MA: Harvard University Press.

Allison, G. (1971) *Essence of Decision.* Boston, MA: Little, Brown.

Almond, G.A. and Bingham Powell, G. (1966) *Comparative Politics.* Boston, MA: Little, Brown.

Almond, G.A. and Coleman, J.S. (eds) (1960) *The Politics of Developing Areas.* Princeton, NJ: Princeton University Press.

Almond, G.A. and Verba, S. (1965) *The Civic Culture: Political Attitudes and Democracy in Five Nations.* Princeton, NJ: Princeton University Press.

Antal, A.B., Dierkes, M. and Weiler, H.N. (1987) 'Cross-National Policy Research. Traditions, Achievements and Challenges', in M. Dierkes, H.N. Weiler and A.B. Antal (eds), *Comparative Policy Research.* Aldershot: Ashgate, pp. 13–31.

Arora, R.K. (1972) *Comparative Public Administration.* New Delhi: Associated Publishing House.

Ashford, D. (1978) *Comparing Public Policies: New Concepts and Methods.* London: Sage Publications.

Aucoin, P. (1995) *The New Public Management. Canada in Comparative Perspective.* Montreal: Institute for Research on Public Policy.

Barzeley, M. (2000) *The New Public Management: Improving Research and Policy Dialogue.* Berkeley, CA: University of California Press.

Batley, R. and Stoker, G. (1991) *Local Government in Europe: Trends and Developments.* Basingstoke: Macmillan.

Bekke, H.A.G.M., Perry, J.L. and Toonen, T.A.J. (eds) (1996) *Civil Service Systems in Comparative Perspective.* Bloomington, IN: Indiana University Press.

Benz, A. 'Bookreview', *Public Administration*, 77 (1): 223–224.

Börzel, T.A. (1998) 'Organizing Babylon – on the Different Conceptions of Policy Networks', *Public Administration*, 76: 253–273.

Bouckaert G., Guy, Peters B. and Verhoest, K. (2010) *The Coordination of Public Sector Organizations. Shifting Patterns of Public Management.* Series: Public Sector Organizations. Hampshire: Palgrave Macmillan.

Braun, D. and Gilardi, F. (eds) (2006) *Delegation in Contemporary Democracies.* London: Routledge.

Burns, J.P. and Bowornwathana, B. (2001) *Civil Service Systems in Asia.* Cheltenham: Edward Elgar.

Chandler, J.A. (ed.) (2000) *Comparative Public Administration.* London: Routledge.

Crozier, M. (1963) *Le phénomène bureaucratique.* Paris : Le Seuil.

Crozier, M. and Trosa, S. (1992) *La Décentralisation: Reforme de l'Etat.* Boulogne : Pouvoirs Locaux.

Dahl, R. (1947) 'The Science of Public Administration: Three Problems', *Public Administration Review*, 7 (1): 1–11.

Della Porta, D. and Mény, Y. (1997) *Democracy and Corruption in Europe.* London: Pinter, pp. 166–180.

Dente, B. and Kjellberg, F. (1988) *The Dynamics of Institutional Change: Local Government Reorganization in Western Democracies.* London: Sage Publications.

Derlien, H.-U. (1992) 'Observations on the State of Comparative Administration Research in Europe – Rather Comparable than Comparative', *Governance*, 5 (3): 279–311.

Derlien, H.-U. and Peters, B.G. (2008) *The State at Work: Public Sector Employment in Ten Western Countries.* Cheltenham: Edward Elgar.

De Vries, M.S. (2002) 'Can You Afford Honesty? A Comparative Analysis of Ethos and Ethics in Local Government', *Administration & Society*, (34) 3: 309–334.

Downs, A. (1967) *Inside Bureaucracy.* Boston, MA: Little, Brown.

Dunleavy, P. (1991) *Democracy, Bureaucracy and Public Choice.* Brighton: Harvester Wheatsheaf.

Egeberg, M. (1999) 'The Impact of Bureaucratic Structure on Policy Making', *Public Administration*, 77 (1): 155–170.

Farnham, D., Horton, S., Barlow, J. and Hondeghem, A. (1996) *New Public Managers in Europe: Public Servants in Transition*. London: Macmillan.

Feick, J. (1987) 'Vergleichende Staats- und Verwaltungswissenforschung', *Jarhbuch zur Staats- und Verwaltungswissenschaft*. Baden-Baden: Nomos, pp. 473–483.

Ferraro, G., Brans, M., Weiqing, G. and Feng, T. (2009) 'An Intra-national Perspective on Regimes Implementation. The Case of Fisheries in China: Keen Conflicts and Hazy Contents', *The Asian Pacific Journal of Public Administration*, 31 (2): 147–169.

Fitzpatrick, J., Goggin, M., Heikkila, T., Klingner, D., Machado, J. and Martell, C. (2011) 'A New Look at Comparative Public Administration: Trends in Research and an Agenda for the Future', *Public Administration Review*, 71 (6): 821–830.

Fried, R.C. (1990) 'Comparative Public Administration: The Search for Theories', in N.B. Lynn and A.B. Wildavsky (eds), *Public Administration: The State of the Discipline*. Chatham, NJ: Chatham House Publishers, pp. 318–347.

George, A. L. and Bennett, A. (2005) *Case Studies and Theory Development in the Social Sciences*. London: MIT Press.

Giauque, D., Ritz, A., Varone, F., Anderfuhren-Biget, S. and Waldner, C. (2011) 'Putting Public Service Motivation into Context: A Balance between Universalism and Particularism', *International Review of Administrative Sciences*, 77 (2): 227–253.

Gill, J. and Meier, K.J. (1999) *Public Administration Research and Practice: A Methodological Manifesto*. Paper at the 5th National Public Management Research Conference, Texas, A&M University, December 1999.

Goggin, M.L. (1986) 'The "Too Few Cases/Too Many Variables" Problem in Implementation Research', *The Western Political Quarterly*, 39 (2), 328–347.

Golembiewski, R.T. (1996) 'The Future of Public Administration: End of a Short Stay in the Sun? Or a New Day A-dawning?', *Public Administration Review*, 56 (2): 139–148.

Hanf, K. and Scharpf, F.W. (eds) (1978) *Interorganizational Policy Making: Limits to Coordination and Central Control*. Beverly Hills, CA: Sage Publications.

Hanf, K. and Toonen, T.A.J. (1985) *Policy Implementation in Federal and Unitary Systems*. Dordrecht: Martinus Nijhoff.

Hardiman, N. and MacCarthaigh, M. (2009) *Breaking with or Building on the Past? Reform of Irish Public Administration 1958–2008*. Dublin: UCD Institute for British Irish Studies Working Paper Series 2009.

Heady, F. (1979) *Public Administration in Comparative Perspective*, 2nd edn. Public Administration and Public Policy/6. New York: Marcel Dekker.

Heady, F. (2001) *Public Administration. A Comparative Perspective*, 6th edn. New York: Marcel Dekker.

Heinelt, H. and Smith, R. (eds) (1996) *Policy Networks and European Structural Funds*. Aldershot: Avebury.

Hendriks, F. (2010) *Vital Democracy: a Theory of Democracy in Action*. Oxford: Oxford University Press

Hofstede, G. (1984) *Culture's Consequences. International Differences in Work-Related Values*. London: Sage Publications.

Hogwood, B.W. and Peters, B.G. (1983) *Policy Dynamics*. Brighton: Wheatsheaf

Holden, M. (1998) *Continuity and Disruption: Essays in Public Administration*. Pittsburg, PA: University of Pittsburg Press.

Hood, C.C. (1986) *Tools of Government*. Chatham, NJ: Chatham House Publishers.

Hood, C.C. (1995) 'Emerging Issues in Public Administration', *Public Administration*, 73 (1): 165–183.

Hood, C.C. (1999) 'British Public Administration: Dodo, Phoenix or Chameleon?', in J. Hayward, B. Barry, and A. Brown (eds), *The British Study of Politics in the Twentieth Century*. Oxford: Oxford University Press, pp. 287–311.

Hood, C.C. (2001) 'Reinventing Government, or Reinventing Politics?', in B.G. Peters and J. Pierre (eds), *Politicians, Bureaucrats and Administrative Reform*. London: Routledge, pp. 13–23.

Hood, C.C. and Peters, B.G. (eds) (1994) *Rewards at the Top. A Comparative Study of High Public Office*. London: Sage Publications.

Hood, C.C. and Schuppert, G.F. (eds) (1988) *Delivering Public Services in Western Europe*. London: Sage Publications.

Joergensen, T.B., Hansen, H., Antonsen, M. and Melander, P. (1998) 'Public Organizations, Multiple Constituencies, and Governance', *Public Administration*, 76 (3): 499–518.

Jordana, J. Levi-Faur, D. and Fernández-i-Marín, X. (2011) 'Global Diffusion of Regulatory Agencies: Channels of Transfer and Stages of Diffusion', *Comparative Political Studies*, 44 (10): 1343–1369.

Jreisat, J.E. (2002) *Comparative Public Administration and Policy*. Boulder, CO: Westview Press.

Jreisat, J.E. (1975) 'Synthesis and Relevance in Comparative Public Administration', *Public Administration Review*, 35 (6): 663–671.

Kaufmann, H. (1976) *Are Government Organizations Immortal?* Washington, DC: Brookings Institution.

Keating, M. (2001) *Nations against the State. The New Politics of Nationalism in Quebec, Catalonia and Scotland*, 2nd edn. London: Palgrave.

Kettl, D.F. (1993) 'Public Administration: The State of the Field', in A.W. Finifter (ed.), *Political Science. The State of the Discipline II*. Washington, DC: APSA, pp. 407–428.

Kickert, W., Klijn, E.-H. and Koppenjan, J.F.M. (1997) *Managing Complex Networks*. London: Sage Publications.

Kim, S. and Vandenabeele, W. (2010) 'A Strategy for Building Public Service Motivation Research Internationally', *Public Administration Review*, 70 (5): 701–709.

Klingemann, H.D. and Fuchs, D. (1995) *Citizens and the State*. Oxford: Oxford University Press.

Korsten, A.F.A., de Jong, P., Bertrand, A.F.M. and Soeters, J.M.L.M. (eds) (1995) *Internationaal vergelijkend onderzoek*. The Hague: VUGA.

Laegreid, P. and Verhoest, K. (eds) (2010). *Governance of Public Sector Organizations: Proliferation, Autonomy and Performance*. Basingstoke: Palgrave Macmillan.

Lammers, C.J. and Hickson, D.J. (eds) (1979) *Organizations Alike and Unlike. International and Inter-institutional Studies in the Sociology of Organizations*. London: Routledge and Kegan Paul.

Landman, T. (2000) *Issues and Methods in Comparative Politics: and Introduction*. London: Routledge.

Lasswell, H.D. (1960) 'The Technique of Decision Seminars', *Midwest Journal of Political Science*, 4: 213–236.

Levi-Faur, D. (2006) 'Varieties of Regulatory Capitalism: Getting the Most Out of the Comparative Method', *Governance*, 19 (3): 367–382

Lijphart, A. (1971) 'Comparative Politics and the Comparative Method', *American Political Science Review*, 682–693.

Lipsky, M. (1980) *Street-level Bureaucracy: Dilemmas of the Individual in Public Services*. New York: Russell Sage Foundation.

Lodge, M., Page, E.C. and Hood, C. (2005) 'Conclusion: Is competency management a passing fad', Public Administration, 83 (4): 853–860.

McCourt, W. and Minogue, M. (2001) *The Internationalization of Public Management. Reinventing the Third World State*. Cheltenham: Edward Elgar.

Maesschalck, J., Jurkiewicz, C. and Huberts, L. (eds) (2007–2008), 'Symposium Introduction: "Transnational Perspectives on Public Sector Ethics"', *Public Integrity*, 10 (1): 7–10.

Maor, M. and Lane, J.E. (1999) *Comparative Public Administration. Volume 1*. Aldershot: Ashgate (The International Library of Politics and Comparative Government).

Marini, F. (1998) 'Foundation under Innovation: Proceed with Care!', *Public Administration Review*, 58 (4): 369–373.

Marsh, D. (ed.) (1998) *Comparing Policy Networks*. Buckingham: Open University Press.

Martin Harloff, E. (1987) *The Structure of Local Government in Europe: Surveys of 29 Countries*. The Hague: IULA.

Massey, A. (ed.) (1997) *Globalization and Marketization of Government Services: Comparing Contemporary Public Sector Developments*. Houndmills: Macmillan.

Meuleman, L. (2008) *Public Management and the Metagovernance of Hierarchies, Networks and Markets. The Feasibility of Designing and Managing Governance Style Combinations*. Heidelberg: Physica-Verlag.

Moe, T. (1984) 'The New Economics of Organizations', *American Journal of Political Science*, 28: 739–777.

Naschold, F. (1995) *The Modernisation of the Public Sector in Europe: A Comparative Perspective on the Scandinavian Experience*. Helsinki: Ministry of Labour.

Niskanen, W.A. (1971) *Bureaucracy and Representative Government*. Chicago, IL: Aldin Publishers.

Norris, P. (1999) *Critical Citizens: Global Support for Democratic Governance*. Oxford: Oxford University Press.

Norwegian State Administration Database: http://www.nsd.uib.no

OECD (1995) *Governance in Transition: Public Management Reforms in OECD Countries*. Paris: OECD.

OECD (2003) *The e-Government Imperative* (*OECD e-Government Studies*). Paris: OECD

OECD (2011) *Government at a Glance 2011*. Paris: OECD.

Ongaro, E. (2009) *Public Management Reform and Modernization: Trajectories of Administrative Change in Italy, France, Greece, Portugal and Spain*. Cheltemham: Edward Elgar.

O'Toole, L.J. (1986) 'Policy Recommendations for Multi-Actor Implementation: An Assessment of the Field', *Journal of Public Policy*, 6: 181–210.

O'Toole, L.J. (1997) 'Treating Networks Seriously: Practical and Research-based Agendas in Public Administration', *Public Administration Review*, 57 (1): 45–52.

Page, E.C. (1995) 'Comparative Public Administration in Britain', *Public Administration*, 73 (1):123–141.

Page, E.C. (2012 forthcoming) *Policy Without Politicians. Bureaucratic Influence in Comparative Perspective.* Oxford: Oxford University Press.

Page, E.C. and Goldsmith, M.J. (1987) *Central and Local Government Relations. A Comparative Analysis of Western European Unitary States.* London: Sage Publications.

Page, E.C. and Wright, V. (1999) *Bureaucratic Elites in Western European States: A Comparative Analysis of Top Officials.* Oxford: Oxford University Press.

Peters, B.G. (1988) *Comparing Public Bureaucracies. Problems of Theory and Method.* Tuscaloosa, AL: Alabama University Press.

Peters, B.G. (1989) *The Politics of Bureaucracy*, 3rd edn. New York: Longman.

Peters, B.G. (1996) *The Future of Governing: Four Emerging Models.* Lawrence, KS: University of Kansas Press.

Pierre, J. (1998) *Partnerships in Urban Governance.* Basingstoke: Macmillan.

Pierre, J. (ed.) (1995) *Bureaucracy in the Modern State. An Introduction to Comparative Public Administration.* Aldershot: Edward Elgar.

Pollitt, C. (2011) 'Not Odious but Onerous: Comparative Public Administration', *Public Administration*, 89 (1): 114–127.

Pollitt C. and Bouckaert, G. (2011). *Public Management Reform: A Comparative Analysis. NPM, Governance and the Neo-Weberian State*, third expanded edition. Oxford: Oxford University Press.

Pressman, J.L. and Wildavsky, A.B. (1973) *Implementation.* Berkeley, CA: University of California Press.

Presthus, R.V. (1959) 'Behavior and Bureaucracy in Many Cultures', *Public Administration Review*, 19: 25–35.

Putnam, R.D. Leonardi, R. and Nanetti, R.Y. (1994) *Making Democracy Work: Civic Traditions in Modern Italy.* Princeton, NJ: Princeton University Press

Raadschelders, J.C.N. (2011) 'Between "Thick Description" and Large – N Studies: The Fragmentation of Comparative Research', *Public Administration Review*, 71 (6): 831–833.

Raadschelders, J.C.N., Toonen, T.A.J. and Van der Meer, F.M. (eds) (2007) *The Civil Service in the 21st Century: Comparative Perspectives.* Houndsmills: Palgrave Macmillan.

Ragin, C.C. (1989) *The Comparative Method: Moving beyond Qualitative and Quantitative Strategies.* Berkeley, CA: University of California Press.

Reddick, C.G. (ed.) (2010) *Comparative E-Government.* New York: Springer.

Rhodes, R.A.W. (1996) 'From Institutions to Dogma: Tradition, Eclecticism, and Ideology in the Study of British Public Administration', *Public Administration Review*, 56 (6): 507–516.

Rhodes, R.A.W. and Weller, P. (eds) (2001) *The Changing World of Top Officials. Mandarins or Valets?* Buckingham: Open University Press.

Riggs, F.W. (1998) 'Public Administration in America: Why Our Uniqueness is Exceptional and Important', *Public Administration Review*, 58 (1): 22–39.

Rihoux, B. and Lobe, B. (2009) 'The Case for Qualitative Comparative Analysis (QCA): Adding Leverage for Thick Cross-Case Comparison', in D. Byrne and C. Ragin (eds), *The SAGE Handbook of Case-Based Methods.* London: Sage Publications, pp. 222–243.

Rohr, J.A. (2001) 'Constitutionalism and Administrative Ethics. A Comparative Study of Canada, France, the United Kingdom and the United States', in T.L. Cooper (ed.), *Handbook of Administrative Ethics*, 2nd edn. New York: Marcel Dekker.

Rose, R. (1985) *Understanding Big Government. The Programme Approach.* London, Sage Publications.

Rouban, L. (ed.) (1999) *Citizens and the New Governance: Beyond New Public Management. Implementation Research as Empirical Constitutionalism.* Amsterdam: IOS.

Rutgers, M.R. (1994) 'De Bestuurskunde als 'Oude' Wetenschap', *Bestuurswetenschappen*, 5: 386–405.

Salamon, L. (2002) *The Tools of Government: A Guide to the New Governance.* New York: Oxford University Press.

Salamon, L.M. and Anheier, H.K. (1997) *Defining the Nonprofit Sector. A Cross-national Analysis.* Manchester: Manchester University Press.

Scharpf, F.W. (1993) *Games in Hierarchies and Networks: Analytical and Empirical Approaches to the Study of Governance Institutions.* Frankfurt: Campus.

Sharpe, L.J. (1979) *Decentralist Trends in Western Europe.* London: Sage Publications.

Sharpe, L.J. (ed.) (1993) *The Rise of Meso-Government in Europe.* London: Sage Publications.

Siffin, W.J. (1976) 'Two Decades of Public Administration in Developing Countries', *Public Administration Review*, 36 (1): 61–71.

Sigelman, L. (1976) 'In Search of Comparative Administration', *Public Administration Review*, 36 (6): 621–625.

Silberman, B.S. (1994) *Cages of Reason. The Rise of the Rational State in France, Japan, the United States, and Great Britain.* Chicago, IL: University of Chicago Press.

Simon, H. (1957) *Models of Man; Social and Rational: Mathematical Essays on Rational Human Behavior in a Social Setting*. New York: Wiley.

Sjöblom, S. (1999) 'Transparency and Citizen Participation', in L. Rouban (ed.), *Citizens and the New Governance: Beyond New Public Management*. Amsterdam: IOS, pp. 15–27.

Smith, A. (1999) 'Public Policy Analysis in Contemporary France: Academic Approaches, Questions and Debates', *Public Administration*, 77 (1): 111–131.

Stepan, A. (2001) 'Toward a New Comparative Politics of Federalism', in A. Stepan (ed.), *Arguing Comparative Politics*. Oxford: Oxford University Press.

Stewart, D.W., Sprinthall, N.W. and Shafer, D.M. (2001) 'Moral Development in Public Administration', in T.L Cooper (ed.), *Handbook of Administrative Ethics*, 2nd edn. New York: Marcel Dekker, pp. 457–480.

Sverdrup, U. (2005) *Implementation and European Integration: A Review Essay*. Working Paper no. 25, ARENA – Centre for European Studies, Oslo.

Swenden, W. (2006) *Federalism and Regionalism in Western Europe: A Comparative and Thematic Analysis*. Basingstoke: Palgrave.

Teisman, G.T. (2000) 'Models for Research into Decision-Making Processes: on Phases, Streams and Decision-Making Rounds', *Public Administration*, 78 (4): 937–956.

Tummala, K.K. (2000) 'An Essay on Comparative Administration', *Public Administration Review*, 60 (1): 75–80.

van Deth, J. (1994) *Comparative Politics in an Incomparable World*. IPSA Paper, Berlin.

Verba, S. (1967) 'Some Dilemmas in Comparative Research', *World Politics*, 1 (20): 111–127.

Verheijen, T. (1999) *Civil Service Systems in Central and Eastern Europe*. Cheltenham: Edward Elgar.

Verheijen, T. (2001) *Politico-administrative Relations: Who Rules?* Bratislava: Nispacee.

Verhoest, K. (2010) 'The Influence of Culture on NPM', in T. Christensen and P. Laegreid (eds), *The Ashgate Research Compendium to New Public Management*. Farnham: Ashgate, pp. 47–65.

Verhoest, K., van Thiel, S., Bouckaert, G. and Laegreid P. (2011). *Government Agencies: Practices and Lessons from 30 countries*. Basingstoke: Palgrave Macmillan.

Vickers, J. and Wright, V. (1988) *The Politics of Privatisation in Western Europe*. London: Cass.

Waldo, D. (1964) *Comparative Public Administration: Prologue, Problems, and Promise*. Chicago, IL: ASPA.

Walker, D.B. (1995) *The Rebirth of Federalism*, 2nd edn. Chatham, NJ: Chatham House Publishers.

Webb, E.J., Campbell, D. T., Schwartz, R. D. and Sechrest, L. (1966) *Unobtrusive Measures*. Chicago, IL: Rand McNally.

Windhoff-Héritier, A. (1993) 'Policy Network Analysis: A Tool for Comparative Political Research', in H. Keman (ed.), *Comparative Politics*. Amsterdam: VU University Press, pp. 143–161.

Wright, V. (1994a) 'Reshaping the State: Implications for Public Administration', *West European Politics*, 17 (3): 102–134.

Wright, V. (1994b) *Privatization in Western Europe: Pressures, Problems and Paradoxes*. London: Pinter.

Yesilkagit, K. and Christensen, J.G. (2010) 'Institutional Design and Formal Autonomy: Political versus Historical and Cultural Explanations', *Journal of Public Administration Research and Theory*, 20 (1): 53–74.

29

International Organizations and Domestic Administrative Reform

Dionyssis G. Dimitrakopoulos
and Argyris G. Passas

INTRODUCTION

This chapter focuses on the role of international organizations as promoters of administrative reform at the national level. Typically, international organizations are placed in one of two broad categories: intergovernmental organizations entail a type of membership whereby the legal autonomy of states remains largely intact primarily because of the subordinate role of the organization's institutional actors; supranational organizations are characterized by an increasing delegation of powers to an autonomous set of institutions whose output penetrates into national legal orders, domestic administrations and operational codes.

As far as the impact of the two types of international organizations upon national administrations is concerned, at first sight, there seems to be a paradoxical relationship. While supranational organizations are typically associated with a more indirect influence on national administrations, some intergovernmental organizations exert a more direct influence.

In supranational organizations – a category that essentially includes the European Union (EU) – the need for reform is an indirect consequence of membership. It stems primarily from the exigencies of (1) the effective participation in policy making and (2) the implementation of common policies. On the other hand, intergovernmental organizations take a different approach. They either

(a) regard domestic administrative reform as a formal *and* functional condition for the effective pursuit of the material advantages that can be gained from an international organization (in this case, loans, etc.,) – this is the case of the World Bank and the International Monetary Fund (IMF) or

(b) foster specific (market-embracing) administrative policies – although they do not necessarily rely on legally binding instruments or other equally coercive mechanisms (Organization for Economic Cooperation and Development; OECD).

The first section of the chapter focuses on the pressures exerted on national administrations as a result of membership of the EU. The second section discusses the responses that have been adopted at the national level. The third section examines the types of reform that are typically promoted by intergovernmental organizations. The final section outlines the main themes regarding the fostering of administrative reforms by international organizations.

Ours is a rather *sceptical* view (Page and Wouters 1995), which highlights – at least in the context of the EU – the conceptual and the empirical limits of the 'convergence thesis': namely, (1) the lack of a specific model (Lippert et al. 2001); (2) the resistance faced by promoters of reform; (3) the persistence of historically defined *national* characteristics; and (4) the inability to distinguish clearly between international organizations and other sources of pressures on domestic administrations. In short, we argue that despite the significant formal and functional pressures exercised upon domestic administrations by the process of European integration, there is no convergence. Rather, domestic administrations have responded through their own standard operating procedures and institutional repertoires (Premfors 1998).[1] These responses exemplify *existing* patterns of success and failure in dealing with public policy issues. In turn, success and failure have clear *national* traits. In other words, the emergence of a shared *European administrative space* (where sovereignty is exercised jointly by increasingly integrated administrations) does not imply one kind of outcome (Heidbreder 2011).

Second, we highlight the fact that pressure for administrative reform varies across international organizations. The idea that our sceptical view regarding 'Europeanization' may apply to the impact of other organizations on domestic administrations as well is appealing. Nevertheless, empirical research is needed before a firm conclusion is reached. Indeed, further comparative analyses of the impact of various types of international organizations on domestic administrations are required in this area.

SUPRANATIONAL ORGANIZATIONS AND NATIONAL ADMINISTRATIONS: THE CHALLENGE OF MEMBERSHIP

Membership of the EU entails a number of challenges for domestic administrations. First, virtually all sections of the domestic central government apparatus are involved in the management of EU-related business. Second, subnational authorities are increasingly involved in the conduct of EU-related business. Third, in procedural terms, the nature of 'EU business' differs radically from traditional international affairs in that it transcends the boundaries between ministerial domains. Indeed, it permeates and affects almost every aspect of the state's operation. Fourth, in substantive terms, the 'product' of this process is legally binding and supersedes domestic legislation, thus significantly affecting the operational capacity of the state and its agents. Furthermore, this product (EU policies) is frequently premised on policy ideas, public philosophies and frames of reference that differ significantly from those that prevail in the domestic arena.

Pressures for reform

The issue of the pressures that national administrations face as a result of the membership of the EU is not new (Wallace 1971, 1973; Davies 1973; Institut International des Sciences Administratives 1990; González Sánchez 1992). One can identify a number of sources of pressure for administrative reform at the national level. They are all inextricably linked to membership of the EU and, therefore, ought to be distinguished from the pressures for reform generated by other international organizations (see infra).

The first pressure stems from the formulation phase of the EU policy process, i.e. the pre-legislative/pre-proposal and agenda/policy-shaping stages, as well as decision taking. This is so because of the intensive involvement of national civil servants therein (Kassim and Wright 1991). In quantitative terms, this type of pressure is demonstrated by the significant number and the duration of the committee meetings that take place in the context of the Council of Ministers and the European Commission (Egeberg et al. 2003: 26). In qualitative terms, this pressure generates two types of functional imperatives: the recruitment and training imperative and the coordination imperative. Both are permeated by the idea that failure to influence the content of EU policies will generate increased adaptation costs, not least because of the legally binding nature of EU law.

National civil servants and the EU decision-making process

Unlike the domestic arena, where key administrative actors share the same frame of reference and policy style, the role of national civil servants in the context of the EU is more complex, not least because of the language barrier, the different – and frequently competing – national policy traditions and frames of reference. This added complexity highlights three types of training-related needs for national civil servants. First, there is an increased need for language training. Second, the nature of the EU decision-making process – in particular the involvement of a variable number of actors and its unpredictable pace – highlights the need for (a) knowledge of the policy styles (and content) that prevail in other member states, (b) advanced knowledge of negotiation skills and techniques and (c) thorough knowledge of 'Community procedures' (Polet 1999). Indeed, the latter is further highlighted by the increasing use of qualified majority voting (QMV). QMV undermines the capacity of individual member states to shape the course of negotiations while also highlighting the need for 'coalition-building'. Third, the EU

is a law-intensive organization. Knowledge of the domain-specific EU (and, ideally, national) policy, legislation and the relevant jurisprudence of the European Court of Justice (ECJ) is an inherent part of the profile of the 'perfect national administrator' who is involved in the management of EU business (González Sánchez 1992; Pertek 1993).

The 'coordination imperative'

This imperative stems from the expansion of the number of national ministries and subnational state actors that are involved in the EU policy process, including the implementation of EU policies. This imperative (Wallace 1971; Davies 1973; Kassim et al. 2000, 2001; Peters and Wright 2001) has a horizontal as well as a vertical dimension. The horizontal dimension concerns the coordinated activity of administrative actors of the same level of (usually central) government that are required to promote a coherent, specific and workable set of policy 'preferences' expressed in a timely manner both in the various levels of the Council of Ministers and in the preparatory meetings organized by the Commission, i.e. in the agenda-setting stage of the EU policy process.

The vertical dimension of coordination refers to the need for the central administrations of the member states to be aware of potential and actual problems regarding the implementation of EU policy at street level and to (1) provide the necessary means for corrective action (in implementation) or (2) devise flexible and pragmatic policies (in policy formulation). This need is further enhanced by the attitude of the Commission that promotes the involvement of subnational authorities in the formulation and, naturally, the implementation of national plans for regional development.[2] Finally, the system of rotating presidencies and the increasing frequency of intergovernmental conferences place additional burdens on national administrations (Kassim 2000: 4–5; Tallberg 2003: 5).

RESPONSES: NATIONAL PATTERNS OF LEARNING?

How did the member states of the EU respond (Debbasch 1987; Mény and Wright 1994; Rideau 1994: 745–864, 1997; Mény et al. 1996; Rometsch and Wessels 1996; Hanf and Soetendorp 1998; Kassim et al. 2000, 2001) to these pressures? Most of the existing literature directly or indirectly emphasizes the changes brought about in national administrations as a result of membership of the EU (see below). Crucially, these changes were produced despite the enunciation by the ECJ of the principle of institutional autonomy (Rideau 1972) whereby the member states are formally obliged to fulfil the obligations that stem from membership of the EU but remain formally free to do so on the basis of their own legal and administrative arrangements. Nevertheless, functional pressures that result from membership of the EU have eroded the formal autonomy of the national administrative systems. Below we discuss the patterns of national administrative reform and the mechanisms that have affected them.

The so-called 'convergence/adaptation' thesis (Mény et al. 1996; Hanf and Soetendorp 1998; Börzel 1999) – also known as the 'Europeanization' thesis – whereby national administrations are *thought* to converge towards a similar structure (or even 'model') as a result of membership of the EU is attractive but not convincing. Arguably, more subtle and theoretically informed analyses of administrative reform at the national level (see Harmsen 1999; Kassim et al. 2000; 2001; Goetz 2001; Page 2003) convincingly highlight the fact that

(a) the *pace* of reform is slow (i.e. incremental change prevails);
(b) the *direction* of reform remains path dependent (i.e. national administrations evolve along the lines of previously *established* patterns); and
(c) *learning* is the mechanism that drives this process whereby member states come to identify the type of pressure that they face but then go on to 'respond' *individually*.

Coordination mechanisms

Both successful and unsuccessful attempts to change the mechanisms whereby central governments coordinate their policies on EU affairs (Kassim et al. 2000; Peters and Wright 2001; Dimitrova and Toshkov 2007) are illustrative of the national patterns of institutional development. Indeed, the French (Lequesne 1993) and the British (Kassim et al. 2000: Ch. 1; Bulmer and Burch 2009) models, which rely essentially on strong central mechanisms that coordinate the increasing number of administrative actors that are involved in the formulation stage of the EU policy process, are widely regarded as the most effective systems of coordination in the EU. Their effectiveness relies on three essential elements, namely

(a) the large number of coordination meetings that bring together proactively a significant number of officials in Paris and London;
(b) the culture of diffusion of information that prevails in these central administrations; and, more importantly,
(c) the establishment of strong mechanisms that provide solutions to conflicts (over competence and policy) between ministerial departments.

Although the British system has been influenced by the French, it essentially relies on the assumptions and the wider logic that permeate the wider Whitehall machinery (Bulmer and Burch 2009). The three aforementioned elements were inherent parts of the manner in which Whitehall departments have managed government business even prior to the accession of the UK to the then EC. Also, the success of the French system accounts for the fact that the British looked at it in the first place. However, the compatibility of the assumptions and logic that permeate the French and the British system of coordination explain why the latter was influenced by the former. The EU-specific mechanisms, in turn, reflect wider similarities in (1) the management of government business in London and Paris (especially the strong core executive) and (2) the two

respective polities (in particular the centralized nature of the two states). Empirical
research on other member states has highlighted the fact that the coordination of
national policies on EU affairs follows 'pre-
existing domestic institutional structures and
values' (Kassim 2000: 26; Kassim et al.
2000, 2001).

The profile of the national civil servants

Incremental and path-dependent changes in
terms of the national structures (and the
interactions that take place therein) are mirrored by the persistence of national patterns
of recruitment to the national civil service.
This is demonstrated by the slow progress
made in the liberalization of access of EU
nationals to the wider public sector of other
member states (Commission of the European
Communities 1988; European Commission
1999). However, as far as senior (policy-
making) posts are concerned, existing patterns of recruitment remain unchallenged
(Burnham and Maor 1995). For example, the
British administration is still dominated
by Oxbridge graduates, the German, Italian
and Greek administrations are still dominated by lawyers, etc., while the procedures
used for the recruitment remain varied
(Ziller 1988).

Furthermore, training and secondment
programmes that are designed to facilitate
the management of EU-related business
at the national level – typically by explaining
how the EU works – have not produced
a *systemic* impact. Discussing the introduction of such programmes in the Scottish
Office, Smith (2001: 162) argues that while
they have

> led to limited cultural change in the sense that
> they facilitated the ability of civil servants
> to develop working practices which met the
> demands of EC/EU membership, *they did not
> herald wider changes in bureaucratic emphasis or
> approach*. In particular, there was no identifiable
> transformation of approach from domestic to

'European' (added emphasis) (see also Christoph
1993: 534).

More importantly, a study of three Whitehall
departments highlights the fact that 'only
limited importance is attached to training
in Eurocratic skills until they are needed'
but the importance of formal training for
language skills has increased (Maor and
Stevens 1997: 541–2).

The limits of the convergence thesis

Kassim, a critic of the convergence thesis,
notes that

> it has an intuitive appeal. Members belonging
> to the same organization are subject to common
> rules, share common obligations and interact with
> common structures. Facing the same demands
> and the same difficulties, it would seem logical to
> suppose that their responses would also be the
> same (2000: 3).

The 'convergence thesis' relies on three cardinal ideas. First, a causal link is thought to
exist between membership of the EU and the
convergence of national administrative systems towards a specific model. Arguably,
there is very little evidence, if at all, to support this view. Although the administrations
of the member states are called upon to perform the same roles, a number of models
continue to exist (Rometsch and Wessels
1996; Kassim et al. 2001). Detailed qualitative case studies of specific countries reveal
that national administrations use their own,
historically defined, standard operating procedures and institutional repertoires so as to
manage the necessities of membership and
remain largely unaltered. This is so because

- they successfully perform their new roles[3] (Harmsen 1999); and
- resistance to change remains strong and implementation is undermined by conflict and the lack
of determined, powerful and resourceful 'fixers'
(Passas 1997).

The second assumption upon which the
convergence thesis is based relates to one

mechanism that is thought to drive convergence: namely, learning. Although learning does occur in national administrations (Olsen and Peters 1996), in the case of EU-related administrative reform, it appears that it concerns the identification of the pressures that stem from membership of the EU rather than the spread of a specific set of ideas as to how one should deal with them.

Third, both the convergence and the related (wider) 'Europeanization' thesis – which concerns the patterns of intergovernmental relations – rely implicitly or explicitly (Börzel 1999) on

1 the idea that the source of the impetus for change, namely 'Europe', is *exogenous* to the member states; and
2 the so-called 'goodness of fit' between national institutions and the EU.

This mode of analysis calls for two comments. On the one hand, it is extremely hard to draw a clear distinction between the effects of membership of the EU and those of other concurrent developments upon national administrations (Christoph 1993: 535; Kassim 2000: 27). Such developments include most notably the advent of New Public Management that is promoted either directly – by organizations such as the OECD (see infra) or indirectly by other organizations and international fora such as the WTO (Kleitz 2001). On the other hand, the logic that underpins the argument about the 'goodness of fit' is inherently static since it ignores the well-documented[4] (Harmsen 1999) capacity of national administrations to perform new tasks by means of their existing standard operating procedures and institutional repertoires, which they modify marginally in an incremental and piecemeal manner. More importantly, it ignores the fact that 'Europe' is not exogenous. Rather, what the EU is and what it does is largely shaped by national civil servants, who (1) manage EU-related business in Brussels, national capitals as well as at the subnational level and (2) are socialized into new or emerging common modi operandi.[5]

INTERGOVERNMENTAL ORGANIZATIONS AND DOMESTIC ADMINISTRATIVE REFORM

Pressures for domestic administrative reform stem from intergovernmental, i.e. more traditional, organizations where the erosion of state power is much less evident. The fundamental difference between the two types of influence is that in the former case, it is an integral element of membership, without necessarily being an area where the EU has a clearly defined, specific and deliberate policy. On the contrary, intergovernmental organizations have a clear policy regarding domestic administrative reform. It focuses on the diffusion of more or less specific neo-liberal principles, ideas and logics that are seen as 'optimal' solutions to 'common problems' such as the quest for operational efficiency, optimal service delivery and accountability.

These pressures exhibit three cardinal features. First, their nature varies across intergovernmental organizations: whereas administrative reform is a *formal condition* for the provision by the World Bank and the IMF of heavily needed financial assistance, the OECD promotes the same kind of reforms through the much more subtle means of the diffusion of ideas, 'best practice' and the provision of advice. Second, these reforms appear to be 'blanket solutions' to seemingly 'common problems'. Finally, they have not led to the homogenization of domestic administrative structures.

The literature on 'isomorphism' that stems from sociological institutionalism and highlights three factors (coercion, mimetism and normative pressures) that are thought to lead to increasingly similar organizational *forms* (DiMaggio and Powell 1983) – as well as *outcomes* (DiMaggio and Powell 1991) – provides a useful organizing principle for the discussion of these pressures.[6] First, *coercive pressures* can be formal and informal. They essentially rely on relations of dependence which are, by definition, asymmetrical. They entail the direct or indirect imposition of either structures or a specific logic that must underpin a set of structures. Second, *mimetism* provides a useful rule of thumb in cases where uncertainty and ambiguity reign. The ambiguity of preferences and a poor understanding of a given context or problem frequently leads decision makers to choose organizational structures and logics that imitate those found in other areas of activity, countries or regions. They do so because these structures are (or are thought to be) successful and legitimate in tackling the same or similar problems. Finally, *normative pressures* essentially rely on professionalization. The latter entails both the formal education of decision makers (i.e. politicians and civil servants) and the establishment of networks of professionals that operate as (1) carriers of a common terminology and approach to problem solving as well as (2) ideas and logics which are meant to resolve common problems.

Our discussion in the next two subsections focuses on two intergovernmental organizations – namely, the World Bank and the OECD – that play a prominent role in the diffusion of policies regarding administrative reform (Jenkins and Plowden 2006) on the basis of the so-called 'New Public Management'. The key characteristics of New Public Management (Aucoin 1990) include (Hood 1991: 4–5) hands-on professional management in the public sector, the introduction of explicit standards and measures of performance, emphasis on output controls, disaggreggation of public sector units and focus on competition and private sector management styles (including a strong emphasis on the disciplined use of resources) in the public sector.

Isomorphism and the diffusion of New Public Management: the case of the World Bank

The key feature of the World Bank's role in the diffusion of New Public Management amongst borrower countries is the conditional nature of the loans: they are disbursed on the condition that specific reforms will be implemented according to a fixed timetable. In particular, the funds that are related to the so-called 'adjustment lending' – typically needed in conditions of extreme financial pressure – are released 'when the borrower complies with stipulated release conditions, such as the passage of reform legislation, the achievement of certain performance benchmarks, or other evidence of progress toward a satisfactory macroeconomic framework' (World Bank 2001d).

The key characteristics of New Public Management are present in the reforms promoted by the World Bank (2001a). Adjustment lending has largely focused on short-term cost-containment measures that were part of a wider effort to limit the public sector in the recipient countries – including the number of public employees, which was construed by the World Bank as an endemic problem (World Bank 2001c), the introduction of performance-orientated budget systems, flexible civil service, increased accountability and fiscal transparency (World Bank 2001a: 46, 48). This process was underpinned by attempts to quantify policy targets as well as service delivery by means of benchmarks, and the use of fiscal performance tests (World Bank 2001c). Moreover, the establishment of semi-autonomous bodies within the public sector was also promoted. These bodies perform tasks previously performed by central government departments in an effort to improve operational efficiency through greater managerial discretion and flexibility as well as operational autonomy from politicians' short-term orientations (typically this is the case of the regulation of industry).

The conditional aspect of loan provision to countries in desperate need for funds exemplifies the importance of *coercive* isomorphism in the transfer of New Public Management through the World Bank. However, this is not the only form of isomorphic pressure exerted by this international organization. Growing criticism of this 'heavy-handed' approach, has led the World

Bank to develop other (much more subtle) forms of (most notably *normative*) isomorphic pressure. This is exemplified by the 'learning programmes' that it runs which focus on themes such as 'decentralization and governance' (entailing the diffusion of knowledge about 'a creditworthy government', 'efficient and client-orientated service delivery' and techniques of public expenditure management'), 'controlling corruption and improving governance' as well as, more importantly, the 'training of trainers' with regard to the implementation of development projects (World Bank 2001b). In addition, the World Bank provides 'analytic and advisory services' to client countries in the form of 'tailored' economic and sectoral programmes, as well as the opportunity for the establishment of 'knowledge networks'.

Isomorphism and the diffusion of ideas and best practices in public management: the case of the OECD

The Organization for Economic Cooperation and Development (OECD) has since 1989 developed a wide range of activities in administrative reform through its Public Management (PUMA) programme directed by the Public Management Committee (and its successor, the OECD's Public Governance Committee), which is composed of senior national officials. Its mission is to facilitate the efforts of member countries, and interested non-member states, regarding good governance and public management (the effectiveness, efficiency, transparency and accountability of public institutions). This objective is pursued through fora for the exchange of ideas, among government top officials, on how to adapt public sector governance to the changing needs of the fast-moving modern world. For that purpose, various materials are produced (studies, comparative analyses, annual reports, etc.) on various policy issues, i.e. public sector budgeting and management (OECD 2002); e-government, knowledge management and

the use of IT; human resources management; regulatory management and reform; territorial governance; ethics and corruption, etc. It also manages a large network of working groups (such as the working party of Senior Budget Officials, working party on Human Resources Management) and shares the results of the existing work with interested non-member countries through the Governance Outreach Initiative.

The reforms promoted by the OECD (Cordova-Novion 2001; Matheson 2001: 6) focus on the enhancement of the managerial autonomy of specialized regulatory bodies as well as the decoupling of policy implementation and advice from policy making. Although the delegation of powers to these bodies is thought to have been 'a largely positive experience', significant problems have arisen (Matheson 2001: 7): the lack of institutional clarity, the inability of central governments to monitor and control these bodies, weaknesses in the governance structure and reporting mechanisms and difficulties in implementing performance management. In particular, these reforms have (1) revealed an increased risk of capture, (2) weakened the efficiency and effectiveness of the public sector and (3) undermined the citizens' trust (Matheson 2001: 8). Nevertheless, the intensity of the pressure for this particular type of reform is exemplified by the fact that the solutions to these problems are sought in the same vein: the quest for a clear division of responsibility between the autonomous institutions and the ministries, the establishment of clear reporting mechanisms, the enhancement of a 'quasi-contractual relationship' and enhanced capacities of audit bodies (Matheson 2001: 9–10).

The OECD's activity in this area relies on continuous interactions between the members of a large group of senior government officials. Thus, it represents an example of normative isomorphic pressure exerted on member states (transfer of ideas, model solutions, best practices, etc., among professionals, knowledge networks/communities).

Indeed, although senior officials of the OECD do not challenge the idea that the same solutions should not necessarily be implemented in differing national contexts, 'modern governance structures in fact are an important determinant of business confidence in all countries participating in the globalised economies' (Kleitz 2001: 3). In other words, these ideas and practices are depicted as being at least more *au fait* with the challenges of modern governance. Hence, even if modifications are needed, they cannot and should not challenge the core principles that underpin the ideas and practices promoted by the OECD.

As far as the *actual* impact of those pressures is concerned, the dominant view highlights the fact that 'no universal practices exist: viability [of reforms] is related to the *political, economic, administrative and social contexts; capacities are as important as the basic setting*' (Cordova-Novion 2001: 14 – our emphasis). The OECD's officials are aware of the role of leadership, professional and technical staff, capacity overload and corruption in the operation of reform programmes (Jenkins and Plowden 2006: 120). In short, the picture is one of diversity rather than homogeneity. Moreover, one can identify other forms of (especially informal) coercive isomorphic pressures in the activity of another OECD group, the SIGMA group (Support for Improvement in Governance and Management in Central and Eastern European Countries), which was established in 1992, as a joint initiative of the OECD and the European Union, to advise transition countries on improving good governance, administrative efficiency and promoting adherence of public sector staff to democratic values, ethics and respect of the rule of law, to build up indigenous capacities at the central governmental level to face the challenges of globalization and to prepare for accession to the EU (OECD/SIGMA 1998).

EU membership is conditional: it depends on the implementation of these reforms.

This programme, in tandem with other EU actions – e.g. the Twinning Programme, benefits from the OECD/PUMA experience and expertise in administrative reform in order to improve results in the pre-accession period. Hence, this joint programme has become an instrument through which the EU exerts coercive isomorphic pressures on the Central and Eastern Europe candidate countries. However, in these countries too, 'reactions and solutions do not converge' (Lippert et al. 2001: 980).

CONCLUSION: RESISTANCE AND CONVERGING PRESSURES

The concept of isomorphism and a significant part of the wider debate about the impact of international organizations on national administrative systems imply, explicitly or not, that membership thereof entails a gradual process of convergence (but see, *inter alia*, Page 2003). In this chapter, we have outlined the sources and nature of these pressures and have linked them to two different types of international organizations.

We have argued that membership of the EU entails a significant *informal* pressure for administrative reform. This concerns primarily – but not exclusively – the need for coordination, the improved training of national civil servants and the *de facto* gradual shift in the balance of power between foreign and 'technical' ministries. On the other hand, intergovernmental organizations exert two kinds of pressure:

1 *Direct* pressures for the adoption of neo-liberal, market embracing reforms. This is typically a condition for the approval of loans and other benefits (World Bank and IMF).
2 *Indirect* pressures: the OECD is an example of an intergovernmental organization that performs the subtle role of a forum for the diffusion of the principles, ideas and norms that permeate market-based reforms.

The distinction between supranational and intergovernmental organizations has provided a useful organizing principle for the discussion of the impact of international organizations upon domestic administrative structures. Nevertheless, there is evidence that the two types of organizations exert increasingly similar pressures. Indeed, the European Union's strategy to embrace the candidate countries of Central and Eastern Europe relies on a set of principles – the 'Copenhagen criteria' – amongst which (1) the capacity to implement the 'acquis communautaire' and (2) the adoption of market economy figure prominently. These are conditions for membership. In that sense, the EU exercises a new type of direct coercive pressure similar to the pressure for reform exercised by the World Bank.[7]

Furthermore, we have argued that existing analyses are much more useful in *identifying pressures* (and the sources thereof), and the *prevailing discourse* regarding administrative reform, than in outlining the *model* towards which national administrative structures and practices are thought to converge. This sceptical view highlights (1) the role of culture (*administrative* culture in particular) that conditions any reform (established patterns of behaviour and accepted lines of resistance) and (2) the idea that reform depends on the timely and effective combination of three cardinal factors: namely, *opportunity* (which is country-specific), the existence of a coherent *strategy* (government goals) and *tactics* (the capacity to mobilize support in an effective manner). In addition, we have argued that there is little empirical evidence to support the 'convergence' thesis: rather, the dominant picture is one of diversity.

NOTES

1   On the issue of human resource management in European central governments, see Meyer and Hammerschmid (2010).

2   The implication (in terms of workload and the need for expertise) for the staff of these authorities is thus evident.

3   A quantitative analysis regarding the UK has revealed a similar pattern (see Page 1998).

4   The same sceptical view has been shown to apply to the wider pattern of intergovernmental relations. Indeed, discussing the case of Germany, Goetz (1995) argues convincingly that European integration has 'tended to affirm, if not reinforce key structural principles of German federalism'.

5   National experts who are seconded to the European Commission have been found to reflect more 'the primacy of departmental and epistemic dynamics' (Trondal et al. 2008: 270).

6   Also, the transfer of Western models to Central and Eastern European countries has been promoted by domestic political elites who have benefited from it (Jacoby 2001). On the case of Brazil, see Imasato et al. (2011).

7   On the example of Turkey, see Sezen (2011).

REFERENCES

Aucoin, Peter 1990. Administrative reform in public management: Paradigms, principles, paradoxes and pendulums. *Governance* 3 (2): 115–37.

Börzel, Tanja A. 1999. Towards convergence in Europe? Institutional adaptation to Europeanization in Germany and Spain. *Journal of Common Market Studies* 37 (4): 573–96.

Bulmer, Simon and Martin Burch 2009. *The Europeanisation of Whitehall: UK Central Government and the European Union*. Manchester: Manchester University Press.

Burnham, June and Moshe Maor 1995. Converging administrative systems: Recruitment and training in EU member states. *Journal of European Public Policy* 2 (2): 185–204.

Christoph. James B. 1993. The effects of Britons in Brussels: The European Community and the culture of Whitehall. *Governance* 6 (4): 518–37.

Commission of the European Communities 1988. Free movement of workers and employment in the public service of the member states – Communication of the Commission with regard to the implementation of article 48 paragraph 4 EEC Treaty, *OJEC*, C 72, 18 March.

Cordova-Novion, Cesar 2001. Regulatory Governance. Paper read at the Conference *Devolving and Delegating Power to More Autonomous Public Bodies and Controlling Them*, Bratislava, 22–23

November, http://www.oecd.org/pdf/M00023000/M00023692.pdf

Davies, John 1973. National governments and the European Communities. *New Europe* 2: 24–8.

Debbasch, Charles, ed. 1987. *Administrations nationales et intégration européenne*. Actes du colloque tenu à Aix, Centre de Recherches Administratives. Paris: Centre Nationale de le Recherche Scientifique.

DiMaggio, Paul J. and Walter W. Powell 1983. The iron cage revisited: Institutional isomorphism and collective rationality in organizational fields. *American Sociological Review* 48 (2): 147–60.

DiMaggio, Paul J. and Walter W. Powell 1991. The iron cage revisited: Institutional isomorphism and collective rationality in organizational fields. In W. Powell and P. DiMaggio (eds), *The New Institutionalism in Organizational Analysis*. Chicago, IL: University of Chicago Press.

Dimitrova, Antoaneta and Dimiter Toshkov 2007. The dynamics of domestic coordination of EU policy in the new member states: Impossible to lock in? *West European Politics* 30 (5): 961–86.

Egeberg, Morten, Günther F. Schaefer and Jarle Trondal 2003. The many faces of EU committee governance. *West European Politics* 26 (3): 19–40.

European Commission 1999. Commission takes further steps against Luxembourg for failing to comply with ECJ ruling in the social field and Spain for discrimination in access to employment in the public service. http://www.europa.eu.int/comm/dg05/fundamri/movement/news/infring_en.htm (26 April).

Goetz, Klaus 1995. National governance and European integration: Intergovernmental relations in Germany. *Journal of Common Market Studies* 33 (1): 91–116.

Goetz, Klaus 2001. European integration and national executives: A cause in search of an effect? In K. H. Goetz and S. Hix (eds), *Europeanised Politics? European Integration and National Political Systems*. London: Frank Cass.

González Sánchez, Enrique 1992. La négotiation des décisions communautaires par les fonctionnaires nationaux: Les groupes de travail du Conseil. *Revue Française d'Administration Publique* 63: 391–9.

Hanf, Kenneth and Ben Soetendorp (eds) 1998. *Adapting to European Integration: Small States and the European Union*. London: Longman.

Harmsen, Robert 1999. The Europeanization of national administrations: A comparative study of France and the Netherlands. *Governance* 12 (1): 81–113.

Heidbreder, Eva G. 2011. Structuring the European administrative space: Policy instruments of multi-level administration. *Journal of European Public Policy* 18 (5): 709–27.

Hood, Christopher 1991. A public management for all seasons? *Public Administration* 69 (1): 3–19.

Imasato, T., P. E. M. Martins and O. P. Pieranti 2011. Administrative reforms and global managerialism: A critical analysis of three Brazilian state reforms. *Canadian Journal of Administrative Sciences* 28: 174–87.

Institut International des Sciences Administratives, ed. 1990. *Les Implications Administratives de l'Intégration Economique Régionale: L'exemple de la CEE. Approche Comparative*, Madrid.

Jacoby, Wade 2001. Tutors and pupils: International organizations, central European elites, and Western models. *Governance* 14 (2): 169–200.

Jenkins, K. and Plowden, W. 2006. *Governance and Nation Building: The Failure of International Intervention*. Cheltenham: Edward Elgar.

Kassim, Hussein 2000. *The National Co-ordination of EU Policy: Must Europeanisation Mean Convergence?* Cahiers Européens de Sciences Po 5/2000. Paris: Presses de la FNSP.

Kassim, Hussein and Vincent Wright 1991. The role of national administrations in the decision-making processes of the European Community. *Rivista Trimestrale di Diritto Pubblico* 31 (3): 832–50.

Kassim, Hussein, Anand Menon, B. Guy Peters and Vincent Wright (eds) 2001. *The National Co-ordination of EU Policy: The European Level*. Oxford: Oxford University Press.

Kassim, Hussein, B. Guy Peters and Vincent Wright (eds) 2000. *The National Co-ordination of EU Policy: The Domestic Level*. Oxford: Oxford University Press.

Kleitz, Anthony 2001. Experience and best practices in achieving regulatory efficiency and open markets. Paper read at the *Regulatory Management and Reform Seminar*, Moscow, 19–20 November, http://www.oecd.org/pdf/M00023000/M00023229.pdf

Lequesne, Christian 1993. *Paris–Bruxelles: Comment se fait la Politique Européenne de la France*. Paris: FNSP.

Lippert, Barbara, Gaby Umbach and Wolfgang Wessels 2001. Europeanization of CEE executives: EU membership negotiations as a shaping power. *Journal of European Public Policy* 8 (6): 980–1012.

Maor, Moshe and Handley Stevens 1997. Measuring the impact of new public management and European integration on recruitment and training in the UK civil service. *Public Administration* 75 (3): 531–51.

Matheson, Alex 2001. The Public Management Service of the OECD (PUMA). Paper read at the Conference *Devolving and Delegating Power to More Autonomous Public Bodies and Controlling Them*, Bratislava, 22–23 November, http://www.oecd.org/pdf/M00023000/M00023675.pdf

Mény, Yves and Vincent Wright (eds) 1994. *La Riforma Amministrativa in Europa*. Bologna: Il Mulino.

Mény, Yves, Pierre Muller and Jean-Louis Quermonne (eds) 1996. *Adjusting to Europe: The Impact of the European Union on National Institutions and Policies*. London: Routledge.

Meyer, Renate E. and Gerhard Hammerschmid 2010. The degree of decentralization and individual decision making in central government human resources management: A European comparative perspective. *Public Administration* 88 (2): 455–78.

OECD 2002. Overview of results-focused management and budgeting in OECD member countries. PUMA/SBO(2002)1, 11–12 February 2002.

OECD/SIGMA 1998. *Preparing Public Administrations for the European Administrative Space*. SIGMA Paper Nr 23.

Olsen, Johan P. and B. Guy Peters (eds) 1996. *Lessons from Experience: Experiential Learning in Administrative Reforms in Eight Democracies*. Oslo: Scandinavian University Press.

Page, Edward C. 1998. The impact of European legislation on British public policy making: A research note. *Public Administration* 76 (4): 803–9.

Page, Edward C. 2003. Europeanization and the persistence of administrative systems. In J. Hayward and A. Menon (eds), *Governing Europe*. Oxford: Oxford University Press.

Page, Edward C. and Linda Wouters 1995. The Europeanization of the national bureaucracies? In J. Pierre (ed.), *Bureaucracy in the Modern State*. Aldershot: Edward Elgar.

Passas, Argyris 1997. L'expérience de la Grèce en matière de réforme de l'administration publique dans la perspective de l'intégration à l'Europe. Séminaire multinational sur l'intégration à l'Europe et la réforme de l'administration publique, 8–10 October 1997, Athènes.

Pertek, Jacques 1993. La formation des fonctionnaires et des juristes aux questions européennes. *Revue du Marché Commun et de l'Union Européenne* 371: 746–53.

Peters, B. Guy and Vincent Wright 2001. The national co-ordination of European policy-making: Negotiating the quagmire. In J. Richardson (ed.), *European Union: Power and Policy-Making*, 2nd edn. London: Routledge.

Polet, Robert (ed.) 1999. *Formation à l'Intégration Européenne*. Maastricht: IEAP.

Premfors, Rune 1998. Reshaping the democratic state: Swedish experiences in a comparative perspective. *Public Administration* 76 (1): 141–59.

Rideau, Joël 1972. Le rôle des Etats membres dans l'application du droit communautaire. *Annuaire Français de Droit International* 18: 864–903.

Rideau, Joël 1994. *Droit Institutionnel de l'Union et des Communautés Européennes*. Paris: LGDJ.

Rideau, Joël (ed.) 1997. *Les États Membres de L'Union Européenne. Adaptation – Mutations – Résistances*, Paris: LGDJ.

Rometsch, Dietrich and Wolfgang Wessels (eds) 1996. *The European Union and Member States: Towards Institutional Fusion?* Manchester: Manchester University Press.

Sezen, Seriye 2011. International versus domestic explanations of administrative reforms: The case of Turkey. *International Review of Administrative Sciences* 77 (2): 322–46.

Smith, James 2001. Cultural aspects of Europeanization: The case of the Scottish Office. *Public Administration* 79 (1): 147–65.

Tallberg, Jonas 2003. The agenda-shaping powers of the EU Council Presidency. *Journal of European Public Policy* 10 (1): 1–19.

Trondal, Jarle, Caspar Van Den Berg and Semin Suvarierol 2008. The compound machinery of government: The case of seconded officials in the European Commission. *Governance* 21 (2): 253–74.

Wallace, Helen 1971. The impact of the European Communities on national policy-making. *Government and Opposition* 6 (4): 520–38.

Wallace, Helen 1973. *National Governments and the European Communities*. London: Chatham House.

World Bank 2001a. *Adjustment Lending Retrospective.* Final report. 15 June, Washington, DC: The World Bank, mimeo.

World Bank 2001b. *Catalogue of Learning Programs: Public Sector Development.* http://WBLN0018.world bank.org/

World Bank 2001c. *Civil Service Reform: A Review of World Bank Assistance.* Sector study Nr. 19599.

Washington, DC: World Bank Operations Evaluations Department.

World Bank 2001d. *World Bank Lending Instruments.* http://www.worldbank.org/whatwedo/svc-lendintro. htm

Ziller, Jacques 1988. *Égalité et Mérite: L'Accès à la Fonction Publique dans les États de la Communauté Européenne.* Bruxelles: Bruylant.

30

Administrative Patterns and National Politics

Martin Lodge

Any assessment of the dynamics between administrative patterns and national politics reflects on a number of perennial debates in the field of executive government and public administration. Foremost, it relates to different conceptions of the roles, functions and relationship between politics and administration. Such distinctions build on Max Weber's diagnosis of the rise of bureaucratic legal rationality, which challenges other types of authority, and Woodrow Wilson's often dismissed distinction between politics and administration (Wilson 1887: 209–11). The dichotomy between politics and administration – where elected politicians decide and professional administrators implement political choices and maintain political authority – continues to attract much interest (Campbell and Peters 1988; Svara 2008). While the normative (liberal democratic) argument and the self-perception of politicians and administrators seem to add weight to the dichotomy, empirical analysis has pointed to an often close, although varying extent of intermeshing between administrative and political levels and roles (Pierre 1995: 207). It is therefore difficult to differentiate clearly between administrative and political functions. While, on the one hand, the two roles are based on different conceptions of legitimization, on the other hand, in terms of functions, both roles substantially overlap.

A second concern relates to the question whether observed or predicted administrative patterns reflect commonalities across territories. For example, claims concerning the 'rise' of bureaucratic rationality and commonality are often used to point to international changes from assumed 'public bureaucracy' towards 'new public management' (Aucoin 1990), 'regulatory' (Majone 1994) and 'post-new public management' states (Christensen and Laegreid 2008; Lodge and Gill 2011). In contrast, studies stressing national or sectoral diversity point to the importance of national institutions and veto points, political and administrative cultures, as well as of sectoral characteristics.

A third concern relates to the nature of administrative or bureaucratic capacity in transposing political preferences and in formulating and adjusting state–society relations: for example, in the diverse interfaces between bureaucracy and society, such as the terms of recruitment and representativeness, administrative coordination and policy responsiveness (Subramaniam 2000: 564–68).

Any attempt to account for the multidimensional complexity of the relationship between national politics and administrative patterns encounters a diversity of approaches. These range from an emphasis of different state and administrative traditions (Bezes and Lodge 2007; Painter and Peters 2010; Meyer-Sahling and Yesilkagit 2011) to discussions as to how the supposed wider societal value shift towards a post-industrial society creates the conditions for different types of citizen demands on administrations (Inglehart 1997, 2008), differences in civil servants' values (Putnam 1974; Aberbach et al. 1981; Aberbach 2003) and the creation of new kinds of 'validation'-type instruments, such as in performance, regulation and risk management (Moran 2003; Radin 2006; Power 2007; Lodge 2008; Roberts 2010). Other accounts focus on the importance of party political concerns, broad institutional factors in exploring the relationship between national politics and administrative patterns (Hall 1986), or the influence of wider political settings in the formal models of legislative delegation to executive and other kind of agencies (Gilardi 2002; Huber and Shipan 2002).

The following attempts to highlight some of the dimensions in which traditional debates on the politics/administration dichotomy continue to inform analysis. It is centered on a discussion of civilian administration in the (European) developed world, given that regions' particular exposure to 'transnationalization' effects. It is therefore less concerned with transition, developmental or military administration.

First, this chapter assesses the different national patterns through which public administration is shaped by its setting within political processes. Second, it explores the impact of national politics and administrative patterns on policy change to highlight the importance of administrative patterns in informing the orientation of political and policy change. Third, the changing nature of the politics–administration relationship is considered, in the light of themes of transnationalization and 'de-hierarchization'. Such developments challenge the traditional conception and study of *national* politics and administration relationships. The conclusion emphasizes the need for a continued exploration of core questions in the way in which the changing nature of national politics interacts with a changing nature of administrative patterns and how consequent interaction effects will have a transformative effect on existing understandings of the relationship between politics and administration.

NATIONAL POLITICS AND ADMINISTRATIVE PATTERNS: CONSTRAINTS AND DISCRETION

Among the most widely discussed themes in public administration are the various means through which relationships between national politics and administrations are patterned. The asymmetric power of bureaucracies, based on expertise and permanence, has traditionally been associated with incomplete political control, leading to self-interested bureaucratic activity, both in terms of shaping and implementing political decisions. The necessities of operating within a legal-rational code, superior resources, professionalization and specialization effects are all said to have led to a 'bureaucratization' of political life (Eisenstadt 1958). Incomplete political control, as suggested in the transaction–cost literature on legislative delegation to administrative bodies, points to 'agency drift', the agent's self-selected activity due to incomplete control by the political principal (McCubbins et al. 1987; Horn 1995). In contrast, the issue of 'political drift', the politically motivated shirking by legislative action at a later time period, points to methods of insulating administrative activity from political intervention, a concern which had already been prominent in nineteenth-century administrative reform debates.

The so-called 'politico–administrative relationship' (Pierre 1995: 207) is an 'informal institution' (Helmke and Levitsky 2004) that is characterized both by formal arrangements and informal understandings. This interest in both the 'contract' and the 'non-contractual conditions' that underpin it, has shaped the interest in different 'role understandings' (Aberbach et al. 1981) and, more recently, Public Service Bargains (Hood and Lodge 2006, drawing on earlier work by Schaffer 1973 and Lipson 1948). At the heart of Public Service Bargains (PSBs) are the explicit and informal understandings that characterize the relationship between public servants and the wider political systems in terms of duties and entitlements (Hood and Lodge 2006: 6; for an account that similarly emphasizes the importance of informal understandings, see Rhodes 2011). Different types of Public Service Bargains can be recognized at various levels of analysis. For example, broad 'trustee'- and 'agency'-type PSBs can be distinguished. The former establishes public servants as a quasi-autonomous part of a wider constitutional settlement, whereas the latter points to a more basic principal–agent relationship in which the 'agent' is expected to do what their political masters ask (within limits). These PSBs emerge in different historical settings, and establish different types of motives and opportunity structures for reform. At the same time, conflict over role understandings, duties and entitlements associated with different PSBs is likely to make conflict over administrative patterns into a feature within political patterns. For example, the creation of executive agencies, whose chief executives are under a 'managerial' agency-type PSB (expected to be capable of performing to fixed targets), is not just an expression of the capacity of national politics to shape the national machinery of government, but potential boundary problems between delegated 'managerial' responsibility and performance, and political responsibility, are likely to influence national politics.

National politics also shape the way in which different PSB dimensions evolve – in turn, these changes can also have direct implications for national politics. The past decade has, for example, witnessed considerable discussion regarding *reward* for high public office (Hood and Peters 1994; Hood, Peters with Lee 2003). On the one hand, the politics of reward for public office is exposed to public pressures, thereby placing a particular 'cap' on the ability of politicians in elected democracies to raise their salaries in transparent ways. On the other hand, these pressures, combined with the supposed managerialist ideas of 'performance pay', have allowed some national public servants to escape the traditional link between politician and public servant pay (such as in the UK and New Zealand), allowing top bureaucrats to increase their relative standing vis-à-vis their own junior staff, but also to decouple their salaries from those of their political masters (for UK: see Lodge 2010: 101–2). The politics of the financial crisis have, however, also affected the reward dimension of the PSB, leading to a further 'de-privileging' of employment safety and pension rights. In addition, pressures were placed on reducing individual performance bonuses (in the UK at least). Wider political criticism of 'perks' traditionally associated as a key part of a bureaucratic over-a-lifetime earning's package have also come under challenge. For example, the possibility to retire early into well-paid positions in business, such as the institutionalized Japanese systems of *amakudari* ('descent from heaven', the post-career employment in businesses close to one's former ministry) and *wataridori* ('migratory birds', the ability to take on a series of positions in retirement) have come under increasing pressure. In the Japanese case, the election of the DJP party in 2009 led to a ban on *amakudari*, although the availability of such positions had declined already over the past two decades in the light of growing public criticism (*Japan Times*, 1 April 2009).

More broadly, reward also points to over-all career expectations and the way in which career progression occurs within the bureaucracy at large, within a single department/agency or *corps*, and/or is based on a system of 'in and out'. Differences have been diagnosed in the degree to which career patterns generate a 'corporate identity'. Substantial differences exist between the US-type 'government of strangers' (Heclo 1977) and agency-based career patterns, the departmentalism of the German federal executive, and the increasingly diversifying 'Whitehall village' (Page 1995: 261–5). Differences further exist in the extent to which public servants originate in similar socio-economic and educational backgrounds, or whether recruitment takes place from a select set of universities and/or social backgrounds (see Goetz 1999; Page and Wright 1999). Questions of reward, finally, also link to politics in terms of 'politicization', defined here as the type of jobs within the bureaucracy that are explicitly 'political', and whose attainment may be more on the basis of a political wheel of fortune than a 'normal' career progression. National differences exist between the 'party-neutral' civil service systems of the UK, Ireland and Denmark and the more party-membership based systems of Austria, Belgium, Greece and Spain (Kickert 2011). The German bureaucracy distinguishes between 'political' civil servants (who exchange access to ministerial top positions with the possibility of being 'resigned' at any time and a good pension) and 'technical' civil servants (who remain the intellectual policy backbone of the federal bureaucracy). Despite nearly two decades of attempting to 'Weberianize' their civil service systems (Meyer-Sahling 2011), post-Communist countries are displaying a considerable 'in and out' system that resembles, to some extent at least, the kind of pattern traditionally associated with the US

federal executive. There, debates about the nature of political appointments (i.e. Are they partisan 'policy' professionals or pure party loyalists?) peaked during the Presidency of George W. Bush. In terms of performance, studies point to an effect of political appointment on agency performance (see Lewis 2007, 2008).

Expectations as to what is regarded as an appropriate level and type of *competencies* represent a second PSB dimension where politics has a direct influence on administrative patterns (Hood and Lodge 2004). Traditional distinctions have been drawn between the largely 'lawyer'-dominated federal bureaucracy in Germany, the more 'generalist' Whitehall public servant tradition (despite its interest in 'professional skills for government' and competency programs, see Hood and Lodge 2005) and other national competency characteristics, such as the French *corps* tradition (Brans and Hondeghem 2005; Ingraham and Getha-Taylor 2005; van der Meer and Toonen 2005; for a comparative perspective on actual civil service work in drafting regulations mostly outside public view and immediate ministerial attention, see Page forthcoming; Page and Jenkins 2005). Political pressures are said to have led to a shift in emphasis from subject-type expertise towards the more managerial 'delivery' kind of skills for 'normal' civil servants. Traditional 'skills' of offering ministers tactical and policy advice are said to be increasingly provided by political advisors and other 'thickened up' political advice units at the top of ministries, whether these are the traditional *Cabinets* (also very prominent in the European Commission), the ministerial *Leitungsstäbe* in Germany (Page and Wright 1999: 277–9), or the rise of politicization in the United States (which peaked in 1980) (Light 1995; Lewis 2008). Donald Savoie has therefore suggested that the past two decades or so have seen (in Canada and the UK at least) the emergence of a 'court government' in which ministers rely on the advice of few personally selected 'courtiers' rather than the 'traditional' civil service machine (Savoie 2003, 2008). Others have diagnosed a growing demand for 'boundary-spanning' skills among top public servants to account for the growing significance of differentiated societies and 'collaborative' forms of governing (Williams 2002).

Changes in demands on skills and competency, as well as in reward patterns, have direct implications on the *loyalty* dimension of PSBs. If rewards are withdrawn and demands on competencies changed, then this has immediate consequences on loyalty understandings as well (and possibly much wider consequences for the quality of democracy; see Suleiman 2003). In particular, it has been argued that these changes have amounted to a 'breaking' of the traditional assumptions that underpinned the relationship between politics and administration, leading, according to some observers in the UK at least, to a deterioration in the quality of government (Foster 2005). Changes towards more 'executive' understandings of loyalty ('deliver or be fired') are, however, said to have gone hand-in-hand with a growing strengthening, if not codification in some jurisdictions, of more traditional 'autonomous' understandings of politico–administrative relationships (see Hood and Lodge 2006), with some arguing that such increased use of 'codification' signifies a 'new era' of post-managerialist public administration (Christensen and Laegreid 2008). More broadly, there has not been a singular trend towards a decline in the status of senior civil servants across countries, with some national bureaucratic elites being able to preserve their status (France, Netherlands, Sweden and Austria) more than others (i.e. Germany and the UK) (see Page and Wright 2007: 238).

PSBs, therefore, centrally define the territory of mutual dependency that characterizes the politico–administrative relationship. PSBs define what is regarded as 'appropriate' or 'cheating', they provide for distinct opportunities to play 'blame games' (Hood 2011) and they are shaped by national politics, while also shaping national politics. The basis for PSBs lies both in the historical

emergence of bureaucracies and the wider political institutional setting.

Turning to origins first, historical developments that shaped the evolution of PSBs (and national administration more generally) have occurred in distinct contexts, primarily driven by the increasing political centralization of emerging states and their need to organize and administer tax collection and the military (Mayntz 1985: 17–32). A prime example is France, with its early development of a centralized administration in the sixteenth century, which after further reforms under Napoleon became an organizational 'template' for Continental European public administration. As in the case of Prussia, this involved the (gradual) centrally driven 'crowding out' of previously existing local patterns of administration, despite the persistence, in certain domains, of corporatist-type governance arrangements. While across the German states bureaucracies were dominant sources for economic and policy reform, England relied largely on self-regulation. Central government only became prominent in the course of industrialization in the nineteenth century, without, however, following the Continental pattern of administrative organization. Similarly, Silberman (1993) has shown that instead of witnessing a unifying march of bureaucratization according to 'legal rationality', bureaucratic development across countries has been diversely path-dependent, set by the way critical institutional design dilemmas were handled at major historical turning points, in particular with regard to senior civil servant recruitment.

Apart from historical trajectories, institutional factors more directly shape both political and administrative patterns. So-called 'macro-level' factors, such as the distribution of functions and responsibilities across levels of government, differences between and among both unitary and federal political systems (making national administration far more pervasive in unitary systems, Page 1995: 259), the nature of the government, whether single party, coalition or consociational, linkages of particular interests to certain political parties, as well as broad access points for lobbying and opposition, are significant in defining the role of national administrations.

At one level, such national differences provide spaces for administrative discretion, and establish different requirements on civil servants' political craft or competency (in addition to technocratic and managerial skills) in understanding and operating within a national political system (Goetz 1997). Thus, national administration in unitary systems faces fewer coordination problems in implementing centrally formulated policy, in contrast to systems, such as Germany's system of 'co-operative federalism' which relies not only on the regional and local delivery of federal policies but also on a large degree of executive-driven bargaining and compromise seeking. Furthermore, apart from different types of interest-group universes and their access to the political system, national systems are also shaped by dominant departments, for example the overarching role of the British Treasury in economic and social policy, as well as by particular sectoral agencies.

At a broader level, political–institutional frameworks also establish the incentives for particular administrative strategies, whether in terms of different types of 'bureau-shaping' activities (Dunleavy 1991), in contrast to 'budget-maximization' (Niskanen 1971), or in terms of the emergence of the 'regulatory state' (Majone 1994, 1997), where budgetary constraints are said to establish an incentive to maximize influence over policy content rather than expenditure. The wider political economy literature has also stressed the importance of the institutional and constitutional framework for explaining regulatory 'commitment' and 'credibility' (Levy and Spiller 1994). Thus, particular administrative patterns are chosen to insulate against particular political influence: for example, by establishing semi-independent regulatory agencies or supposedly autonomous interest-rate-setting central banks.

However, the example of central banks and regulatory agencies highlights the importance of an understanding both of the 'rational' incentives provided by an institutional framework, and of the wider historical and cultural setting of these institutions. Different regulatory institutions (such as the German Federal Office) have enjoyed far more autonomy than legally equivalent institutions (i.e. the German infrastructure regulator) due to its reputation and its ability to manage public perceptions. Elsewhere, too, reputation rather than formal legal arrangement has been key to explaining both the autonomy of particular organizations (Carpenter 2001) and the way in which organizations formulate their decisions (Carpenter 2010; Maor 2010).

ADMINISTRATIVE PATTERNS AND POLICY CHANGE

Closely related to the different institutional settings of public administration have been debates regarding the capacity for change of administrative patterns. Public sector reform provides insights into the dynamics between national politics and administrative patterns. This section therefore considers how political demands for reform are shaped by both political–institutional and administrative patterns.

While for some, administrative and regulatory reforms represent an eventual convergence of forms cross-nationally, others argue that regulatory reforms represent 'catching up' effects, similar themes which are interpreted however in culturally distinct ways or represent persistent diversity due to path dependencies (Hood 2000: 3–4). Research on national administrative reform has therefore stressed the significance of different patterns and reform trajectories (Pollitt and Bouckaert 2011; for an analysis of 'agencification' see James 2003). At the same time, the public sector reform agenda is directed at clarifying (as so often before) the relationship between political control and administrative autonomy, with the so-called 'New Public Management' arguably being directed at both the enhancement of managerial autonomy and the assertion of political control. Furthermore, it addresses questions as to the capacity of political leadership vis-à-vis administrations. For example, Bezes (2001) has stressed the importance of different leadership strategies for explaining different degrees of 'success' in French prime ministerial attempts to reform public administration, distinguishing ineffective 'offensive' strategies (aiming to 'shatter' existing arrangements) and more successful 'defensive' (and internally generated) strategies for administrative reform.

The most prominent accounts for explaining how 'politics matters' in administrative and wider public sector reform have stressed the importance of national political institutions, given that these to a large extent define the extent of political leadership, i.e. the way through which policy is formulated and administered, as well as provides the opportunity structure for those affected to oppose the policy's implementation. It has become popular to argue that the number of veto points in a political system explains the degree of a state's capacity for policy change (Weaver and Rockman 1995). Such accounts have been employed to explain why neo-liberal ideas were so successful in Britain in contrast to other supposedly market-liberal governments in Western Europe in the 1980s and 1990s.[1] For example, differences between public sector reform in the United Kingdom and Germany are linked to different levels of 'reform capacity', with the existence of a unitary state with single party government arguably offering more scope for reform at the UK level, whereas German administrative reform has, for constitutional reasons, primarily occurred at the 'delivery end' of public administration: namely, local government.

Others have concentrated on different types of incentives provided by national political institutional systems. Hall (1986: 273–6)

suggested in the case of Britain that innovation in economic policy was primarily driven by political parties, while Hayward (1976), in his analysis of French and British civil servants, stressed the importance of cultural values, in particular with regard to understandings of the appropriate authority of the state vis-à-vis society, in order to explain differences in civil service engagement in major policy innovation.

Besides this interest in the impact of political institutional frameworks, and wider understandings of the appropriate role of the state vis-à-vis society, for explaining how national politics motivate change in administrative patterns, other accounts regard administrative patterns themselves as crucial in facilitating and constraining innovation. For example, Weir (1989) stresses, in particular, the significance of administrative patterns in terms of recruitment patterns, career promotion and standard operating procedures in order to account for differences in receptiveness to Keynesian ideas. Comparing the 'Keynesian' responses of the 1920s in Sweden, Britain and the United States, Weir and Skocpol (1985) highlight the importance of the 'openness' of the administrative system to external advice and the importance of institutional division of ministerial responsibilities. Apart from different types of prior education (and differences in legal education), it is the type of 'learning on the job' (defined by Weber as *Dienstwissen*) that allows for different degrees of specialization and establishes different patterns of institutional memory (Page 1992: 48). Similarly, Hood (1996) has pointed to the importance of 'second learning' effects from British civil servants moving from one domestic public sector reform to another. While political motivations and preferences are therefore clearly crucial in motivating change, the context of existing administrative patterns is not only likely to shape the extent of reform ambitions and opportunities but also the nature of such policy change, with bureaucracies displaying substantial capacity to internally generate and manage reform processes. Whether, however, these findings will be replicated in the eventual studies of the financial and sovereign debt crises that have affected much of the OECD world since 2008 will require future analysis.

More recent accounts have noted that administrative patterns and national politics are, however, only one part of the relational patterns that shape the way in which market economies develop. In particular, the 'varieties of capitalism' literature has pointed to the significance of patterns within the economy itself that shape the way in which public policies are able to have an effect (Hall and Soskice 2001; Croch 2005; Streeck 2009). This has given rise to distinctions between coordinated and liberal market economies (and, later on, state-led market economies, Schmidt 2009). This literature's concern is with relationships between politics, administrative patterns and policy trajectories – they also highlight the growing significance of continuous change rather than stable continuity intercepted by rare 'critical junctures'. Such concepts include 'drift' (where environmental change paired with non-decision making leads to an increasing qualitative change of the policy intervention), 'layering' (where 'new' polices are added to existing ones), 'displacement' (the removal of old rules and their replacement with new ones), 'conversion' (the use of existing institutions for a different purpose) and 'exhaustion' (breakdown and failure) (Mahoney and Thelen 2010; see also Streeck and Thelen 2005). The unwillingness, for example, of political actors within the US political system to adjust policy is said to have led to 'drift', with considerable consequences in terms of the declining responsiveness of the political system to preferences of the 'median voter' within the United States (see Hacker and Pierson 2010): the 'winner-take-all' economy is, according to Hacker and Pierson, a result of the 'winner-takes-all' character of the political system.

In other words, the relationship between politics and administration is not just one in which politicians with motive face different type of 'opportunity structures' to pursue their strategies. Rather, administrative patterns, given the nature of relationships and participants, shape which options are available. Furthermore, ongoing administrative patterns develop their own politics, for example, through processes defined as drift or layering where the patterns themselves generate items that appear on political agendas.

CHANGING ADMINISTRATIVE PATTERNS AND NATIONAL POLITICS

Existing administrative patterns and the selection of policy instruments are said to be shaped by the dominant national 'policy style' (Jordan et al. 1982). The notion of policy styles refers to a dominant procedural ambition which reflects the preferred choice of instruments and mirrors normative values in how to achieve accommodation. The notion of 'style' in this context relates to national preferences for particular administrative patterns and policy instruments. Similarly, Linder and Peters (1989) suggest that political culture shapes the degree of acceptance of a population to the imposition of particular measures of centralized government intervention. They highlight that particular organizational features are of crucial importance for understanding the appropriateness or non-appropriateness of particular policy choices, which besides reflecting on the internal organizational predisposition towards particular measures also relate to the character of the 'target population' and to the surrounding policy network. For example, Vogel (1986) has pointed to the significance of cultural aspects when comparing the cooperative enforcement style in environmental regulation in Britain with the adversarial process in the United States. The notion, however, that we can distinguish between different 'national' styles has, however, become also increasingly contested, especially in the consideration of how 'risk' is being accommodated in national and transnational policy settings. Debates about whether US approaches towards risk regulation have displayed a less precautionary approach than European ones have pointed to the temporary political origins of much these styles, with some analysis suggesting that there has been a 'flip flop' of approaches over time, whereas others find no dominant 'national' style at all (Wiener and Rodgers 2002; Vogel 2003; Wiener 2003; Kagan 2007). Such debates about national patterns (and other national first-level approximations, such as 'national' varieties of capitalisms) highlight the inherent tensions in seeking to formulate generalizations when faced with domain-specific dynamics (Lütz 2004). Thus, any wider understanding of administrative patterns and their relationship to national politics needs also to include societal actors and their involvement in both the formulation and delivery of policy within particular policy domains or sectors.

Two developments are said to increasingly challenge traditional interaction patterns between national politics and administrative patterns: transnationalization and de-hierarchization. Both developments challenge the centrality of the state and its capacity to act in a 'sovereign' way in its internal or external affairs. On the one hand, national administrations are increasingly exposed to transnational themes, in particular in the context of the European Union, where in some areas national economic regulation merely represents the transposition of EU provisions, especially in internal market and agriculture-related fields (see Müller et al. 2010).

On the other hand, national politics are said to be increasingly required to obtain the consent of particular stakeholders for initiating policy in particular domains. Thus, in the light of increasing difficulties in obtaining societal legitimacy for particular policy measures, new means of legitimization are required which move beyond the traditionally distinct national administrative patterns of interaction with interest groups and associations (see Page 1992: 108–19).

Among these attempts to sustain legitimacy are instruments such as delegation or negotiation, which potentially challenge traditional interaction patterns between administration and societal actors. This section looks first at issues of transnationalization (focusing on EU member states), before turning to issues of de-hierarchization. Both advance the complexity of the relationship between national politics and administrative patterns.

The perceived transnationalization of administrative patterns relates to several commitments through which national states have traded in parts of their formal sovereignty in order cooperate in international or regional agreements, the most prominent being membership of the European Union. While the logic of 'delegation' is often associated with functional dynamics, such as enhanced problem-solving capacity, the impact of membership on national politics and administrative patterns is characterized in cross-national perspective both by commonalities of interests and by diversity of responses.

Membership in the EU requires diplomatic skills and institutional arrangements for effectively representing and negotiating with other member state administrations. It also demands the capacity to transpose and implement transnational provisions and to monitor their implementation. A further aspect is the administration of EU provisions given the European Commission's reliance on national (and subnational) administrations in the execution of its policies. These activities have meant that large areas of national public administration have increasingly come to operate at both the national and the EU level. Wolfgang Wessels (1997) claims that this tendency has led to an 'administrative fusion', with civil servants no longer distinguishing between their national and EU-related activities. Such fusion effects are likely to have increased, given the growing emphasis on the creation of 'regulatory networks' over the past decade. This fusion, however, operates largely within established national administrative and political patterns, thus leading to a Europeanization of policy content and a potential change in the allocation of legal authority, but not necessarily in terms of structure. For example, Bulmer and Burch (2005) point to the absorption and rearrangements of the Whitehall machinery to deal with the requirements of transposition. A similar diagnosis has been made by Goetz (1995) in the case of German federalism. At the policy level, however, the interaction between EU policies and national administrations is leading to a diversity of responses and 'worlds of compliance' due to different degrees of coercion, adaptation pressures and incentive structures (Knill 1998; Héritier et al. 2001; Falkner et al. 2005). Other studies of transposition records (called 'compliance' in the literature) also point to different patterns across and within countries – which suggest no clear relationships between national political and administrative patterns and transposition record (Falkner et al. 2005; Falkner and Treib 2008). In general, the level of adaptation requirements depends on the institutional fit between national administrative patterns, in particular the embeddedness and degree of flexibility of the existing national arrangements, interest mediation, party political preferences and EU measures.

Besides this transnationalization of administrative activity, for national politics, transnationalization of government activity places a constraint on pursuing particular options, either due to the formal requirements of European law or because of the enhanced potential for regulatory competition within the Single Market (Scharpf 1999). The latter is said to limit the ability to impose costly policy options on potentially mobile constituencies. On the other hand, politics at the EU level provide national politics with an additional level to pursue strategies: for example, by allowing them to 'export' particular policy 'solutions' or by aiming to initiate policy change, which would potentially be vetoed at the domestic level.

So far the analysis has assumed that administrative patterns define the activities of *public* administration. However, it is not necessarily a new insight that administration, both in terms of policy formulation and implementation, involves both 'public', 'para-public' and 'private actors': for example, churches in health care, corporatist arrangements between trade unions, employers and governments in macro-economic policy in the 1970s or more recently in 'social pacts' (Avdagic et al. 2011), industry associations in standard setting (Werle 2001) or proposals favoring 'faith-based' policies. The degree to which interest groups influence or dominate administrative patterns depends on the problem constellation, the distribution of costs and benefits (Wilson 1980) as well as on national traditions.

Thus, Wilson (1980) has suggested that the distribution of costs and benefits between affected interest groups largely determines how policy is developed, with a pattern of concentrated costs and diffuse benefits most likely to lead to a 'clientelist' relationship between a particular interest and the responsible bureaucracy. Interaction between interest groups and bureaucracies varies accordingly across sectors, but also across countries. Thus, the United States is arguably characterized by a trend towards 'issue networks', with a strong influence of particular interests in certain domains; in Germany, there is still a reliance on the established associations for consultation and implementation; Sweden has been characterized by technocratic concertation; and in France, the administration is said to stand aloof from the partiality of interest groups. While to some extent this national variation in terms of 'negotiable space' can be explained by the organization of the national interest group universe and the (declining) power of associations over member companies, particular concertation styles and the extent to which political authority is shared are a consequence of historical developments: for example, the (transformed) persistence of guild structures or state–church relations (Crouch 1993).

Despite these historical precedents, political actors are arguably increasingly required, in order to obtain legitimacy for their activities, and to receive the consent of particular actors inside certain policy domains. The primary cause for this perceived increase in need to accommodate domain-based organizations is said to rest in the functional differentiation of society, which challenges the primacy of politics, and in the perceived increase in complexity of policy problems that require involvement of experts. This perceived change in national politics towards negotiation also requires change in administrative patterns and competencies, moving towards an emphasis on coordination and negotiation rather than 'traditional' executive acts, for example, in environmental policy.[2] Thus, political as well as (public) administrative activity is said to be increasingly concerned with interaction and negotiation between political, administrative and large societal organizations (Windhoff-Héritier 1996; Klijn et al. 2010) and requires increased incentive setting and 'tipping of balances' rather than hierarchical acts of government.

Given this increased importance of negotiation as a key political and administrative tool to achieve compliance, increased attention has been paid to administrative and political steering devices that go beyond the 'traditional' tools of hierarchy and market (see also Streeck and Schmitter 1985; Mayntz and Scharpf 1995). These studies point to the considerable self-steering capacity of non-state actors (within and beyond the national level), but they also highlight the residual powers of political and administrative actors to shape these 'decentred' policy settings in which state-based actors play no privileged role.

Nevertheless, besides normative questions which debate the political legitimacy of domain-based governance and the privileged access of partial interests in the context of a further 'de-parliamentarization' of national policy making, less is known about whether and to what extent administrative patterns in terms of governance mechanisms are changing and how deep such changes are, whether these are changing in similar ways and whether these are changing for similar or opposite reasons (see Hood et al. 2004). Furthermore, while it is widely argued that there has been a shift from hierarchical to network and market-type modes of governance, such tendencies also include so-called reverse and mirror-image effects (for UK, see Hood et al. 1999). An historical institutional perspective would suggest that existing administrative patterns and wider political institutional frameworks shape the way in which both political as well as administrative actors operate under these diagnosed changing conditions, what type of responses they prefer and what type of 'new' modes will be regarded as most 'appropriate' and 'functional'.

COMPARING ADMINISTRATIVE PATTERNS AND NATIONAL POLITICS

Arguably one of the key difficulties in comparing administrative patterns is their national and sectoral distinctiveness. This diversity has generated a number of 'varieties', highlighting distinct patterns (see Page 1992 who points to six European varieties). Despite the perceived presence of supposedly 'global' pressures, the supposed convergence of political platforms as well as the rise and fall of doctrinal fads and fashions in administrative design (and subsequent organizational rearrangements), the responses by public administrations have arguably been the replication of diversity rather than emerging convergence, in particular due to immediate 'local' political needs, coupled with the institutional inertia caused by embedded standard operating procedures, strictly guarded distributions of authority, constitutional and historical functions and dominant 'policy styles'.

Across national contexts, similar problems and challenges highlight not so much the dichotomy between politics and administration, but rather relate to problems inherent to the so-called administrative state, which has been defined as a political system largely governed by the bureaucracy but with elected officials ultimately responsible for public policy (Pierre 1995: 207). Nevertheless, how the systems respond to shared concerns and deal with similar issues, for example, the perceived increase of political control attempts over administrations, the way in which administrative and wider public sector reform have been and are continued to be implemented and the operation of both administration and politics at different levels, offer grounds for genuine comparative research. Furthermore, extending the analysis of the relationship between national politics and administrative patterns within the administrative state to issues of policy change, transnationalization and de-hierarchization adds to the challenges to a literature which has evolved from the analysis of relationships within individual states.

As intellectual curiosity moves beyond path dependency (Pierson 2000), the contemporary challenge is to explore the processes of incremental change and challenges to and alterations in informal understandings within supposedly stable patterns. Such changes occur because of the introduction of different logics into administrative practice, the demands of a differentiating society (and media) on public administration and the demands to address 'transboundary crises' (Boin 2009). A further challenge has been the interaction between well-established policy instruments and modes and the import of 'foreign' ideas, such as 'audit' and 'certification', which have challenged traditional exercises of bureaucratic discretion (Lodge and Wegrich 2011). In other words, beyond the 'national' characteristics that derive from long-established relational patterns, there is a diagnosed complexification not just of administrative patterns but also of hybrid policy approaches. The challenge therefore is to explore the causes of national continuities

and discontinuities *and* complexification and differentiation.

This chapter has aimed to point to the increasing difficulty in clearly defining not only the borders between politics and (public) administration in the context of multilevel governance but also to what extent societal actors are part of political and administrative arrangements in diverse areas of policy making and implementation. The challenge for comparative public administration is to combine an awareness of these cross-national trends and tendencies, while at the same time accounting for differences, and locating both in the formal and the historical–cultural context of the particular object of study. A further task is to explore the causes and strategies that sustain particular patterns of public authority. Apart from exploring traditional concerns with regard to public sector recruitment, the receptiveness and interaction between administration and society, implementation patterns and internal administrative arrangements (Subramaniam 2000: 564), such accounts start from commonly observed phenomena (for example, public sector reform or the transposition of legislation) and investigate how and why particular political and administrative factors mattered cross-nationally; or they can utilize particular analytical concepts and 'ideal types' to investigate how different systems process and update their administrative and policy performance 'intelligence', address particular problems of the relationship between politics and administration or aim to 'hardwire' particular administrative design ideas. Such approaches allow for the extraction of salient features of different administrative patterns and the impact of national politics and highlight how they matter. Whereas these suggestions are far from establishing a universal theory of the dynamics between national politics and administrative patterns (and might be an expression of cultural bias), they, nevertheless, inform wider debates within public administration and political science, while being attentive to the changing environment in which the so-called administrative state is supposed to operate.

NOTES

1   It should be noted that prior to the 1980s, the British state was regarded as immobile to change. For example, Hayward (1976: 436) questions whether 'in Britain the undoubted muddle that usually ensues [in decision-making] eventually gets through'. For Moran (2003), the hyper-innovation that characterized the UK since the 1980s is a result of the collapse of the 'old' style club government that shaped policy making in previous generations. The result, for Moran, has been a volatile mixing of old 'club-type' assumptions and 'new' regulatory state arrangements.

2   Such challenges have led to claims that diagnose a shift from the 'welfare state' to the 'regulatory state' (Majone 1997) or the 'supervision state', which is primarily responsible for contextual steering and infrastructure provision and access (Willke 1995). Apart from negotiation, further means of de-hierarchization are arguably the privatization of particular policy functions or the decentralization of executive functions to either lower tiers of government or to agencies (such as so-called quangos). This overall phenomenon has been labeled as a 'hollowing-out' effect.

REFERENCES

Aberbach, J.D. (2003) 'U.S. Federal Executive in an Era of Change', *Governance*, 16(3): 373–93.

Aberbach, J.D., Putnam, R.D and Rockman, B.A. (1981) *Bureaucrats and Politicians in Western Democracies*. Cambridge, MA: Harvard University Press.

Aucoin, P. (1990) 'Administrative Reform in Public Management: Paradigms, Principles, Paradoxes and Pendulums', *Governance*, 3(2): 115–37.

Avdagic, S., Rhodes, M. and Visser, J. (eds) (2011) *Social Pacts in Europe*. Oxford: Oxford University Press.

Bezes, P. (2001) 'Defensive versus Offensive Approaches to Administrative Reform in France (1988–1997): The Leadership Dilemmas of French Prime Ministers', *Governance*, 14(1): 99–132.

Bezes, P. and Lodge, M. (2007) 'Historical Legacies and Dynamics of Institutional Change in Civil Service Systems', in J.C. Raadschelders, T. Toonen and F. van der Meer (eds), *The Civil Service in the 21st Century*. Basingstoke: Palgrave.

Boin, A. (2009) 'The New World of Crises and Crisis Management', *Review of Policy Studies*, 26(4): 367–77.

Brans, M. and Hondeghem, A. (2005) 'Competency Frameworks in the Belgian Governments', *Public Administration*, 83(4): 823–39.

Bulmer, S. and Burch, M. (2005) 'The Europeanization of UK Government', *Public Administration*, 83(4): 861–90.

Campbell, C. and Peters, B.G. (1988) 'The Politics/Administration Dichotomy: Death or Merely Change?', *Governance*, 1(1): 79–99.

Carpenter, D. (2001) *The Forging of Bureaucratic Autonomy*. Princeton, NJ: Princeton University Press.

Carpenter, D. (2010) *Reputation and Power*. Princeton, NJ: Princeton University Press.

Christensen, T. and Laegreid, P. (2008) 'NPM and Beyond – Structure, Culture and Demography', *International Review of Administrative Sciences*, 74(1): 7–23.

Crouch, C. (1993) *Industrial Relations and European State Traditions*. Oxford: Clarendon Press.

Crouch, C. (2005) 'Models of Capitalism', *New Political Economy*, 10(4): 439–56.

Dunleavy, P. (1991) *Democracy, Bureaucracy and Public Choice*. Hemel Hempstead: Harvester Wheatsheaf.

Eisenstadt, S.N. (1958) 'Bureaucracy and Bureaucratization', *Current Sociology* 7(2): 99–124.

Falkner, G. and Treib, O. (2008) 'Three Worlds of Compliance or Four?', *West European Politics*, 46(2): 293–313.

Falkner, G., Treib, O., Hartlapp, M. and Leiber, S. (2005) *Complying with Europe*. Cambridge: Cambridge University Press.

Foster, C. (2005) *British Government in Crisis*. Oxford: Hart Publishing.

Gilardi, F. (2002) 'Policy Credibility and the Delegation to Independent Regulatory Agencies', *Journal of European Public Policy*, 9(6): 873–93.

Goetz, K.H. (1995) 'National Governance and European Integration: Intergovernmental Relations in Germany', *Journal of Common Market Studies*, 33: 91–116.

Goetz, K.H. (1997) 'Acquiring Political Craft: Training Grounds for Top Officials in the German Core Executive', *Public Administration*, 75(4): 753–75.

Goetz, K.H. (1999) 'Senior Officials in the German Federal Administration: Institutional Change and Positional Differentiation', in E. Page and V. Wright (eds), *Bureaucratic Elites in Western European States*. Oxford: Oxford University Press.

Hacker, J. and Pierson, P. (2010) *Winner-Take-All-Politics*. New York: Simon & Schuster.

Hall, P.A. (1986) *Governing the Economy*. Cambridge: Polity Press.

Hall, P.A. and Soskice, D. (2001) 'An Introduction to Varieties of Capitalism', in P.A. Hall and D. Soskice (eds), *Varieties of Capitalism: The Institutional Foundations of Comparative Advantage*. Oxford: Oxford University Press.

Hayward, J.A.S. (1976) 'Institutional Inertia and Political Impetus in France and Britain', *Journal of European Political Research*, 4: 341–59.

Heclo, H. (1977) *A Government of Strangers: Executive Politics in Washington*. Washington, DC: Brookings Institution.

Helmke, G. and Levitsky, S. (2004) 'Informal Institutions and Comparative Politics', *Perspectives on Politics*, 2(4): 725–40.

Héritier, A., Krewer, D., Knill, C., et al. (2001) *Differential Europe*. Lanham, MD: Rowman & Littlefield.

Hood, C. (1996) 'United Kingdom: From second chance to near-miss learning' in J.P. Olsen and B.G. Peters (eds) *Lessons from Experience*, Oslo, Scandinavian University Press.

Hood, C. (2000) 'Paradoxes of Public-Sector Managerialism, Old Public Management and Public Service Bargains', *International Public Management Journal*, 3(1): 1–22.

Hood, C. (2011) *The Blame Game*. Princeton, NJ: Princeton University Press.

Hood, C. and Lodge, M. (2004) 'Competency, Bureaucracy, and Public Management Reform', *Governance*, 17(3): 313–33.

Hood, C. and Lodge, M. (2005) 'Aesop with Variations?', *Public Administration*, 83(4): 805–22.

Hood, C. and Lodge, M. (2006) *Politics of Public Service Bargains*. Oxford: Oxford University Press.

Hood, C. and Peters, B.G. (eds) (1994) *Rewards at the Top*. London, Sage.

Hood, C., Scott, C., James, O., Jones, G. and Travers, T. (1999) *Regulation inside Government*. Oxford: Oxford University Press.

Hood, C., Peters, B.G. with Lee, G. (eds) (2003) *Reward for High Public Office*. London: Routledge.

Hood, C., James, O., Peters, B.G. and Scott, C. (eds) (2004) *Controlling Modern Government*. Cheltenham: Edward Elgar.

Horn, M. (1995) *The Political Economy of Public Administration*. Cambridge: Cambridge University Press.

Huber, J.D. and Shipan, C.R. (2002) *Deliberate Discretion*. Cambridge: Cambridge University Press.

Inglehart, R. (1997) *Modernization and Postmodernization: Cultural, Economic, and Political Change in 43 Societie*. Princeton, NJ: Princeton University Press.

Inglehart, R. (2008) 'Changing Values among Western Publics from 1970 to 2006', *West European Politics*, 31(1/2): 130–46.

Ingraham, P. and Getha-Taylor, H. (2005) 'Common Sense, Competence, and Talent in the Public Service in the USA', *Public Administration*, 83(4): 789–803.

James, O. (2003) *The Executive Agency Revolution in Whitehall*. Basingstoke: Palgrave.

Jordan, G., Gustafsson, G. and Richardson, J. (1982) 'The Concept of Policy Style', in J. Richardson (ed.), *Policy Styles in Western Europe*. London: Allen & Unwin.

Kagan, R. (2007) 'Globalization and Legal Change: The 'Americanization' of European Law?', *Regulation & Governance*, 1: 99–120.

Kickert, W. (2011) 'Distinctiveness of Administrative Reform in Greece, Italy, Portugal and Spain', *Public Administration*, 89(3): 801–18.

Klijn, E.-H., Steijn, B. and Edelenbos, J. (2010) 'The Impact of Network Management on Outcomes in Governance Networks', *Public Administration*, 88(4): 1063–82.

Knill, C. (1998) 'European Policies: The Impact of National Administrative Tradition', *Journal of Public Policy*, 18(1): 1–28.

Levy, B. and Spiller, P. (1994) 'The Institutional Foundations of Regulatory Commitment: A Comparative Analysis of Telecommunications Regulation', *Journal of Law, Economics and Organization*, 10: 201–46.

Lewis, D. (2007) 'Testing Pendleton's Premise: Do Political Appointments Make Worse Bureaucrats?', *Journal of Politics*, 69(4): 1073–88.

Lewis, D. (2008) *The Politics of Presidential Appointments*. Princeton, NJ: Princeton University Press.

Light, P. (1995) *Thickening Government*. Washington, DC: Brookings Institution.

Linder, H. and Peters, B.G. (1989) 'Instruments of Government: Perceptions and Contexts', *Journal of Public Policy*, 9(1): 35–58.

Lipson, L. (1948) *The Politics of Equality*. Chicago, IL: Chicago University Press.

Lodge, M. (2008) 'Regulation, the Regulatory State, and European Politics', *West European Politics*, 31(1/2): 280–301.

Lodge, M. (2010) 'Public Service Bargains in British Central Government', in M. Painter and G.B. Peters (eds), *Tradition and Public Administration*. Basingstoke: Palgrave.

Lodge, M. and Gill, D. (2011) 'Toward a New Era of Administrative Reform?', *Governance*, 24(1): 141–66.

Lodge, M. and Wegrich, K. (2011) 'Governance as Contested Logics of Control', *Journal of European Public Policy*, 28(1): 90–105.

Lütz, S. (2004) 'Convergence within National Diversity', *Journal of Public Policy*, 24: 169–97.

McCubbins, M., Noll, R.G. and Weingast, B.R. (1987) 'Administrative Procedures as Instruments of Political Control', *Journal of Law, Economics and Organization*, 3: 243–77.

Mahoney, J. and Thelen, K. (2010) 'A Theory of Gradual Institutional Change', in J. Mahoney and K. Thelen (eds), *Explaining Institutional Change*. Cambridge: Cambridge University Press.

Majone, G. (1994) 'The Emergence of the Regulatory State in Europe', *West European Politics*, 17: 77–101.

Majone, G. (1997) 'From the Positive and to the Regulatory State', *Journal of Public Policy*, 17(2): 139–67.

Maor, M. (2010) 'Organizational Reputation and Jurisdictional Claims: the Case of the U.S. Food and Drug Administration', *Governance*, 23(1): 133–59.

Mayntz, R. (1985) *Die Soziologie der öffentlichen Verwaltung*, 3rd edn. Heidelberg: C.F. Müller Juristischer Verlag.

Mayntz, R. and Scharpf, F.W. (1995) 'Steuerung und Selbstorganisation in staatsnahen Sektoren', in R. Mayntz and F.W. Scharpf (eds), *Gesellschaftliche Selbstregelung und politische Steuerung*. Frankfurt: Campus.

Meyer-Sahling, J.H. (2011) 'The Durability of EU Civil Service Policy in Central and Eastern Europe after Accession', *Governance*, 24(2): 231–60.

Meyer-Sahling, J.H. and Yesilkagit, K. (2011) 'Differential Legacy Effects', *Journal of European Public Policy*, 18(2): 311–22.

Moran, M. (2003) *The British Regulatory State*. Oxford: Oxford University Press.

Müller, W., Bovens, M., Christensen, J.G., Jenny, M. and Yesilkagit, K. (2010) 'Legal Europeanization: Comparative Perspectives', *Public Administration*, 88(1): 75–87.

Niskanen, W. (1971) *Bureaucracy and Representative Government*. Chicago, IL: Akdine, Atherton.

Page, E.C. (1992) *Political Authority and Bureaucratic Power*, 2nd edn. Hemel Hempstead: Harvester Wheatsheaf.

Page, E.C. (1995) 'Administering Europe', in J. Hayward and E.C. Page (eds), *Governing the New Europe*. London: Polity Press.

Page, E.C. (forthcoming) *Policy without Politicians*. Oxford: Oxford University Press.

Page, E.C. and Jenkins, B. (2005) *Policy Bureaucracy*. Oxford: Oxford University Press.

Page, E.C. and Wright, V. (1999) 'Conclusion: Senior Officials in Western Europe', in E. Page and V. Wright (eds), *Bureaucratic Elites in Western European States*. Oxford: Oxford University Press.

Page, E.C. and Wright, V. (2007) 'Conclusion: The Demystification of High Bureaucratic Office', in E.C. Page and V. Wright (eds), *From the Active to the Enabling State*. Basingstoke: Palgrave.

Painter, M. and Peters, B.G. (2010) 'The Analysis of Administrative Traditions', in M. Painter, and B.G. Peters (eds), *Tradition and Public Administration*, Basingstoke: Palgrave.

Pierre, J. (1995) 'Conclusion: A Framework of Comparative Public Administration', in J. Pierre (ed.), *Bureaucracy in the Modern State: An Introduction to Comparative Public Administration*. Aldershot: Edward Elgar.

Pierson, P. (2000) 'Increasing Returns, Path Dependence, and the Study of Politics', *American Political Science Review*, 94(2): 251–67.

Pollitt, C. and Bouckaert, G. (2011) *Public Management Reform*, Oxford: Oxford University Press.

Power, M. (2007) *Organized Uncertainty*. Oxford: Oxford University Press.

Putnam, R.D. (1974) 'The Political Attitudes of Senior Civil Servants in Western Europe: A Preliminary Report', *British Journal of Political Science*, 3: 257–90.

Radin, B. (2006) *Challenging the Performance Movement*. Washington DC: Georgetown University Press.

Rhodes, R.A.W. (2011) *Everyday Life in British Government*. Oxford: Oxford University Press.

Roberts, A. (2010) *The Logic of Discipline*. Oxford: Oxford University Press.

Savoie, D. (2003) *Breaking the Bargain*. Toronto, ON: University of Toronto Press.

Savoie, D. (2008) *Court Government and the Collapse of Accountability*. Toronto, ON: University of Toronto Press.

Schaffer, B. (1973) *The Administrative Factor*. London: Frank Cass.

Scharpf, F.W. (1999) *Governing in Europe: Effective and Democratic?* Oxford: Oxford University Press.

Schmidt, V. (2009) 'Putting the Political Back into Political Economy by Bringing the State Back in Yet Again', *World Politics*, 61(3): 516–46.

Silberman, B.S. (1993) *Cages of Reason*. Chicago, IL: Chicago University Press.

Streeck, W. (2009) *Re-forming Capitalism: Institutional Change in the German Political Economy*, Oxford: Oxford University Press.

Streeck, W. and Schmitter, P.C. (1985) 'Community, Market, State – and Association?', *European Sociological Review*, 1(2): 119–38.

Streeck, W. and Thelen, K. (2005) 'Introduction: Institutional Change in Advanced Political Economies', in W. Streeck and K. Thelen (eds), *Beyond Continuity*. Oxford: Oxford University Press.

Subramaniam, V. (2000) 'Comparative Public Administration: From Failed Universal Theory to Raw Empiricism – A Frank Analysis and Guidelines towards a Realistic Perspective', *International Review of Administrative Sciences*, 66(4): 557–72.

Suleiman, E. (2003) *Dismantling Democratic States*. Princeton, NJ: Princeton University Press.

Svara, J. (2008) 'Beyond Dichotomies: Dwight Waldo and the Intertwined Politics–Administration Relationship', *Public Administration Review*, 68(1): 46–52.

Van der Meer, F. and Toonen, T. (2005) 'Competency Management and Civil Service Professionalism in Dutch Central Government', *Public Administration*, 83(4): 839–52.

Vogel, D. (1986) *National Styles of Regulation: Environmental Policy in Great Britain and the United States*. Ithaca, NY: Cornell University Press.

Vogel, D. (2003) 'The Hare and Tortoise Revisited: The New Politics of Consumer and Environmental Regulation in Europe', *British Journal of Political Science*, 33: 557–80.

Weaver, R.K. and Rockman, B.A. (1995) *Do Institutions Matter? Government Capabilities in the United States and Abroad*. Washington, DC: Brookings Institution.

Weir, M. (1989) 'Ideas and Politics: The Acceptance of Keynesianism in Britain and the United States', in P.A. Hall (ed.), *The Political Power of Economic Ideas*. Princeton, NJ: Princeton University Press.

Weir, M. and Skocpol, T. (1985) 'State Structures and the Possibilities for "Keynesian" Responses to the Great Depression in Sweden, Britain, and the United States', in P. Evans, D. Rueschemeyer and T. Skocpol (eds), *Bringing the State Back In*. Cambridge: Cambridge University Press.

Werle, R. (2001) 'Institutional Aspects of Standardization – Jurisdictional Conflicts and the Choice of Standardization Organizations', *Journal of European Public Policy*, 8(3): 392–410.

Wessels, W. (1997) 'An Ever Closer Fusion? A Dynamic Macropolitical View on Integration Processes?', *Journal of Common Market Studies*, 35: 267–99.

Wiener, J.B. (2003) 'Whose Precaution after All?', *Duke Journal of Comparative & International Law*, 13: 207–62.

Wiener, J.B. and Rodgers, M.D. (2002) 'Comparing Precaution in the United States and Europe', *Journal of Risk Research*, 5(4): 317–49.

Williams, P. (2002) 'The Competent Boundary Spanner', *Public Administration*, 80: 103–24.

Willke, H. (1995) *Die Ironie des Staates*. Frankfurt: Suhrkamp.

Wilson, J.Q. (1980) 'The Politics of Regulation', in J.Q. Wilson (ed.), The Politics of Regulation. New York: Basic Books.

Wilson, W. (1887) 'The Study of Administration', *Political Science Quarterly*, 2(2): 197–222.

Windhoff-Héritier, A. (1996) Die Veränderung von Staatsaufgaben aus politik-wissenschaftlicher-institutioneller Sicht', in D. Grimm (ed.), *Staatsaufgaben*. Frankfurt: Suhrkamp.

PART 11

Administrative Reform

edited by Theo A.J. Toonen

REFORM

Reform is about bringing about change. More so, reform is about the promise of bringing innovation and, hopefully, improvement. Reform is about becoming better through the removal of faults and errors or by abolishing or correcting malpractice, especially of a moral or political or social kind. Reform is therefore about values and quality. Administrative reform is about the administrative quality, constituted by administrative values, of public sector institutions, of public policy decision-making processes and of public organization and management.

Public administration

We follow the definition of Public Administration provided by the *Blackwell Encyclopaedia of Political Institutions*:[1]

Public administration In the lower case (p.a.) institutional arrangements for the provision of public services; in the upper case (P.A.), the study of those arrangements. 'Institutional arrangements' is a general term to denote the complex of agencies, authorities and enterprises, the formal rule structures, mixes of instruments, and conventions of behaviour which describe the organizational means of public services.

This implies that administrative reform is about improvements suggested or improvements made. Reform is, on the one hand, about PA: ideas, visions, analytical concepts and theoretical promises. The debate on administrative reform is a debate on concepts, models and 'paradigms' of reform: the way to look at and understand actual or proposed reforms; the 'theory' or focus of reform. Reform is, on the other hand, about p.a.: deeds, realizations, empirical developments, actual activities and achievements within a broad spectrum of institutional arrangements for public services delivery. Reform is a debate on the art and nature of the empirical subject matter of administrative reform in any specific context or episode – the p.a. locus of reform.

Generalized studies of the focus of reform – the idea, concept, proposed policy – are more common than detailed and on the ground studies of the locus – implementation and impact – of reform. The latter has often stayed more casuistic and (country) case specific. The internationalization of PA and p.a. is gradually 'reforming' this and

strongly encouraging and enabling comparative studies in public sector and public administration reform. Many studies and reports
claim to address the issue of reform, whereas
actually they concentrate on the pros and
cons or the feasibility of the timely and fashionable concept, approach or 'paradigm' of
reform in any given episode or for any given
cluster of administrative systems or region
of countries. Many criticisms of the public
administration practice are often gauged in
terms of a criticism – or support – of the current paradigm of reform, without studying
and analysing empirically the functional and
operational challenges at hand in any given
system, the degree to which this paradigm
has become a reality or is de facto being
pursued in practice at all.

As a consequence, people often think the
realities of public administration in terms of
a locus of action have changed because the
conceptual language of PA in terms of a
focus of research has changed. Subsequently,
they are often disappointed with the reform,
when research uncovers that reality has
changed less – or differently – than the concept or focus of reform indicated. Because
of the preoccupation with the conceptual
level of reform, it may also be the case that
reform and transformation of public administration goes undetected if the concepts and
language of PA in a given period or country
stay the same. There are still few studies
available, that cover the 'Whole of the
Reforms' – the interrelationship of conceptual reforms, implemented reforms, reform
of government, reform within government,
reform at various levels of government (central, regional, local) – in various countries,
administrative systems or regions over a
longer time span. This is increasingly important, since the debate on administrative
reform from a neo-managerial perspective
now easily covers a continued time span of
three decades, but only addresses one aspect
or domain of administrative reform. From a
PA perspective, public sector or administrative reform is best understood as a long-term,
multidimensional event; certainly not a punctuated equilibrium.

Concept and process

Reform is about content and process.
Different types or visions of reform may be
and have to be distinguished. Yet, there is
no uniformly accepted language, conceptualization or categorization of types of
reform, inside or outside the field of Public
Administration. Many differences in vision
or definition, however, may be attributed to
either differences in a focus on content
of reform or reform movements – in terms
of core values, goals and programmes – or to
differences in a focus on the process
of reform – in terms of the distinction
between (mechanistically) 'planned' versus
(organic) 'emerging' change in many analytical guises – or to conceptual uses of a
specific combination of both.

The underlying debate is not so much
on the difference between 'Change' and
'Reform', as on *the way* administrative systems change. It is a matter of theoretical
choice, rooted in deep historical visions and
doctrines on how administrative systems
change, whether reform is or has to be seen
as a matter of conscious and intentional (central) planning and reorganization, or whether
it is part of more evolutionary, dispersed
and internally dynamic processes of adaptation and transformation. Elements of design,
planning and deliberate choice can be understood from a perspective of reform policy in
a singular governmental or organizational
context, as well as deliberate changes in and
of the structures, processes or procedures of
public sector organizations by the systems –
and systems of systems – of distributed governance that have been emerging, or at least
become more visible with the development
of the inter- and transnational Network
Society. Global and technological developments have required many formerly sovereign national states to implement reforms
which they did not plan for and which are
being designed in the process of participation, as we are witnessing again in events
unfolding in the European Union and the
Arab Spring at the time of writing these
essays (but which both are way beyond the

scope of this part of the Handbook). In the context of global transformation, it is a matter of definition, not 'truth', whether one wants to use a broader, holistic or a more restricted selective and focused understanding of 'reform'. In the latter case, one has to accept that there is much transformation without reform, and much reform without transformation. In the first case, one has to deal with the fact that reform is multileveled, multiscaled, multifaced and close to a never-ending story. There might not be a public management for all seasons; there is a Public Administration for all seasons, which requires permanent adapation to changing historical, technological, economic or environmental circumstances.

Concepts and outcomes

Reform is about promise and performance. Reform, by definition, has to be subject to cycles and fashion. Administrative concepts symbolize administrative practices and policy consequences. Changing governmental, market or third-sector practice often has to start by changing symbols, labels and concepts. Ideas are powerful reform tools. The call for or announcement of 'Reform' is often a highly politicized response to a socially undesired practice, disaster or crisis. The debate on reform is constantly walking the thin line between substantial impact and hollow rhetoric.

Many reform movements and reform efforts are value loaded or have an ideological nature and background. 'Reform' is also a political and economically profitable industry. It is a marketplace for advisers, consultants, academics and politicians alike. Each has the incentive to underscore the innovative, unique and distinct character of the proposed or opposed model of reform. From a broader PA perspective, these different reform movements, reform paradigms, or reform processes do not necessarily contradict each other. They may very well address different and complementary aspects of public sector governance. A mission for PA

theory could be to provide a more balanced and contingent overview of modes and models of reform, their contradictions and complementarities. From a PA point of view, the quality of government is a multifaceted phenomenon, the debate on which has a long history and tradition in the field of both academic Public Administration (PA) as the praxis of government and public administration (p.a.).

ORGANIZATION OF PART 11

Chapters 31–33 try to provide an exploratory overview in a complementary way. Theo Toonen addresses the analytical, conceptual and theoretical aspects – the aspect of conceptual focus – and treats the overall developments in administrative and public sector reform in the Western world from the broader perspective of the field of Public Administration. The next two chapters are more locus oriented. Tom Cristensen and Per Lægreid describe and analyse the reforms in Western Democracies over the past few decades, which implies they have to focus strongly on the New Public Management (NPM) reform movement and the reforms in the aftermath of NPM. Tony Verheijen addresses the development of the reform of public administration in the context of the transitional systems of the post-communist countries in Central and Eastern Europe, which means he has to deal with a holistic reform perspective, where not so much NPM but traditional Continental public administration seems to be in its aftermath. All three chapters try to provide some lessons and directions for the future comparative study of administrative reform in the various meanings of the concept.

NOTE

1 Vernon Bogdanor (ed.), *The Blackwell Encyclopaedia of Political Institutions* (Oxford, 1987), p. 504.

31

Administrative Reform: Analytics

Theo A.J. Toonen

DEVELOPMENTS IN ADMINISTRATIVE REFORM

A superficial glance at reform activities in the 'Western world' over the past two to three decades might easily give the impression that in the 1980s, continued into the 1990s, way into the 2000nds many countries, irrespective of their political and administrative systems, embarked upon a similar type of public sector reform: some sooner, others later. In the first half of the 1990s there was much talk of a 'global paradigm shift' in the approach of government and governance (Aucoin, 1990; Lane, 1993; Chandler, 2000). The concept of a New Public Management (NPM) began to dominate the academic and policy debate on administrative reform for a long time to come.

For right or wrong (Wright, 1994: 109), in much of the literature on reform the case of England of the 1980s, after all these years, still stands out as the unrivalled model in terms of deliberate design, reception and implementation of the neo-managerial types of reform of the late twentieth century. The only other country that seems to meet the English model on equal footing, if not more radically, is New Zealand (Halligan, 1996;

Schick, 1996) – another Westminster-type government system. Now, 20–30 years down the road, however, the NPM reforms should hardly have to serve anymore as the sole analytical yardstick from which to approach the study of administrative reform in the public sector.

The picture started to even out in the course of the 1990s. Those studying public management reforms gradually came to observe the diversity rather than the uniformity of the reform (Flynn and Strehl, 1996: 4; Naschold, 1996; Toonen, 1997; Pollit and Bouckaert, 2000). People working in the tradition of public organization and management studies in Public Administration (PA) came to stress the long-term structural continuities underlying subsequent varieties of public management, old and new (Lynn, 2006). Different countries, administrative systems or institutional contexts, generated different forms and patterns of reform, particularly in terms of actual impact on governmental structure, policy or output. Consensus democracies turned out to pair 'gentle democracy' to performance but were typically slow to reform in the process (Lijphart, 1994, 1999). Many of the Continental systems do have long 'management' traditions, be it that the managers are not 'generalists', but often lawyers or professionals with a technical or engineering background. A professional, no-nonsense, business-like, pragmatic and practical approach to government and administration has for ages been by far the most popular approach within the practice of (Continental) European public administration. The idea was that professionals had to acquire what Max Weber called *Dienstwissen* – generalized but practical rather than theoretical (mba; mpa; mpp) knowledge about how to run – manage – a government.

A business and market-oriented – 'managerial' – approach to government advocated by several government leaders as the way out of the economic and public sector crisis of the 1970s and early 1980s was (1) not new and (2) did not necessarily lead to a preference for markets over governments. A one-to-one relationship between managerial reform and a realized ideological ambition of 'rolling back the state' has still to be demonstrated. The question of *what* government ought to do has to be divorced from the question *how* government manages its affairs. Many countries, particularly the former North-Western European welfare states, did, in varying degrees, roll back the state: not by managerial reform, and not necessarily from an ambition to reduce the power of government in society. More often, budgetary motives and a need to cut back public expenditure in recurrent cycles of growth and austerity provided reason and necessity. Pressures and processes of European integration did the rest. Not only in Europe, the formerly 'sovereign' nation-states of the postwar period were facing strong and international transformational forces by the end of the twentieth century (Kennett, 2008; Camilleri and Falk, 2009). The functional challenges and opportunities of an 'autonomous' change in international economic environment (globalization; Europeanization) and technological context (ICT, informatization, mediatization), required – and enabled – a gradual transformation. Urban regions and their administrative systems entered new

stages of regional and even global competition. This triggered the evolution of new forms of multilevel governance (MLG) across scales of social, political, economic and cultural organization. New forms of interactive, intergovernmental and collaborative public management emerged (Benz, 1995; Peters and Pierre, 2001). The traditional arenas of political action – political parties, national parliaments, local and regional councils – lost much of their former shape, position and meaning in the context of the changing – sovereign – nation-state in its traditional form. This affected political–administrative relationships (Peters and Pierre, 2001). The mission of reform in various countries became to try and reconnect the state to its citizens. A client orientation in public service alone was clearly not sufficient to do the job. New forms of governance and management – regulatory, reflective, participatory and interactive – spurred reform at the various levels within administrative systems. Emerging international notions of human rights, social inclusion and exclusion, sustainability, cost recovery, natural resource scarcity or socially responsible entrepreneurship have become just as important in effectively reforming the nature and content of public management at the operational level of 'the business of government'.

The call for 'reform' in the public sector has hardly weakened over time. Rather than the steady state, administrative reform seems to have become the standard. In the slipstream of a credit crunch, steep global recession and Euro crisis, it has actually gained force again. From a PA perspective, the neo-managerial approach to government and governance has precisely been what it was: a *neo*-managerial approach. Organization and Management studies constitute a strong and classical tradition within the field of PA, as do institutional analysis, policy studies and decision-making analysis. The NPM paradigm over time developed from a locus into a focus of research: an analytical, sometimes implicit and often normatively treated model from which to look at, assess or criticize the advantages and disadvantages of the status quo or ongoing reform processes and – movements. As a consequence, but often unintentionally, observers for a long time seemed happy to overlook historical and spectacular examples of administrative public sector reform. The German unification, the Italian wars on corruption, the French decentralization, Spanish economic consolidation efforts or the early stages of Belgian federalization ('state-reform') at the beginning of the 1990s are just a few examples, not to mention the building of a European Union (EU) with all its reformative consequences (Toonen, 1992). Today, it would be difficult to contest that European integration, for better of for worse, has been one of the forces to bring about more administrative reform at the legal, financial, political and operational levels of government in its region than could possibly be attributed to any managerial or other administrative revolution.

VARIETY OF ADMINISTRATIVE REFORM

Given the changing scenery of international public administration over the past 20–30 years, understanding the variety and dynamics of administrative reform is becoming key. Six different, but interrelated dimensions need to be taken into account: (1) challenges, (2) values, (3) governance, (4) design, (5) power and (6) impact of the reform (cf. Castels and McKinlay, 1979; Hesse and Benz, 1990; Toonen, 2001). These fields do not stand in a linear, but in a complex, internally dynamic relationship. Much like the plane geometry of a Rubic's Cube, a move in the right direction in one domain often creates problems or opportunities in another, giving administrative systems little chance of achieving a stable, permanent equilibrium.

Challenges

Different countries are facing different challenges at different times. The phrase to

'never waste a good crisis' runs the risk of leading to a confusion of crisis and emergency management, on the one hand, with reform or transition management, on the other. The requirements of both tend to run in opposite directions: control vs change, steadiness vs willingness towards 'destructive creativity'. But this phrase refers to a simple truth: without external pressure, chances for effective reform, to even get started, are slim. Hidden reforms are many, but are a neglected area of research. They are usually embedded in the government by anonymous numbers in the rank and file of the administrative system (Page, 2001).

Publicly legitimizing reform facing the vested interest ('stakeholders') of the status quo is an important act. International developments, or 'Europe' (or formerly the *acquis*), have consistently been used to legitimize reform and overcome resistance, until the argument was worn out. Apart from (prevention of) war, by far the most persistent and pressing challenge has been the call for economic reform in the face of recession, crises and ongoing shifts in the world economy. Cutting back expenditure was a major goal of the reforms of the 1980s. It has again become a crucial concern to many countries around the world. Rather than the promise of efficiency and increased productivity implied by the promise of managerial reform, more existential issues of external competition or the very survival of the (financial banking) system, had to be called into arms to get the job done of getting started and getting on with the business of reform.

For seeing the actual reform, in comparative terms, one often has to look at different parts of the system, depending on state of departure and institutional legacies. In systems where government is an instrument of civil society for the provision of public services – the Anglo-American tradition – the managerial levels and approaches within the governmental structure might be a well-advised starting point. In the development of the British welfare state, the non-executant role of central government was translated into strong executive powers for local authorities.

This made them in the 1980s the predictable target for any effort to 'roll back the state'. In other countries, policy domains and their – neo-corporatist relations with – third-sector organizations were the more likely, but no less easy 'victims of reform'. In a Continental welfare state system it makes more sense to have a look at social policy sectors rather than management levels: changes in the volume of public expenditure, welfare schemes, policy savings programs or reduction of social policy entitlements will do the job. The content, visibility and nature of administrative reform are strongly determined by the nature and location of the functional challenges at hand perceived through the eyes of the system, not the observer.

The gradual deployment of previously unknown and non-existent information and communication technologies, social media and knowledge-sharing devices has dramatically reformed the condition of publicness, confidentiality, secrecy, and knowledge and information monopolies, long-time characteristics of public civil service and management of the public sector (Gleick, 2011). Emerging global regional markets have eroded former 'natural' public service monopolies in areas of energy, (public) transportation, telecommunications, mass communications, broadcasting, postal services and public health. The technological development towards light and flexible infrastructure, smart grids, sensing technology and intelligent metering has reformed and will continue to change the landscape of energy production, once dominated by heavy industry and nationalized massive power and energy plants. It will change the future of healthcare delivery, water management and many other domains of traditional public service delivery (Van Santen, Khoe and Vermeer, 2010). This will bring about a host of administrative reforms in terms of institutional arrangements, safety standards, privacy regulation, public accountability, economic governance and managerial strategies within crucial and strategic components

of the public domain (Künneke, Groenewegen and Auger, 2009).

Values

Reform is about changing things for the better. Next to rights and interests, reform is about values, norms and principles. Very often it is not helpful merely to rely on stated goals and purposes. Administrative and public sector reforms are certified domains for sweeping political symbolism and bureaucratic rhetoric. They have to be. Communicative skills are important in many a process of reform. The language differs from era to era. One encounters similar types of goals and values, which, upon close inspection, often reveal quite a different operational meaning. The same political goals and administrative values may give rise to different activities and programs, dependent on time and place.

Different reconstructions of administrative theory (Ostrom, 1973; Henry, 1986 (1975); Toonen, 1983; Bogason and Toonen, 1998) and of administrative argument (Hood and Jackson, 1991) are rather consistent in the type of administrative values, which over time have to be taken into account in judging the administrative quality of government. Hood (1991) has aptly summarized the debate in terms of three 'families' of related administrative core values.

Responsiveness and satisfaction
The first group of values stresses parsimony and economy. It adheres to the mission to 'keep government lean and purposeful'. These values reflect the concern in all organization theory for 'efficiency and productivity'. These values belong to the world of public management. Optimal results have to be produced with given resources and constraints. Given goals have to be achieved at a minimum of organizational cost and effort. These managerial values have been present in the debate on administrative reform ever since modern organization

theory developed at the beginning of the last century.

In this perspective, the administrative organization is easily conceived as a tool of government that needs to be instrumental in achieving given goals. Within the field of PA, this approach has not only been applied to managerial levels. It has also been tried out in reforms to 'rationalize' policy making or reduce and minimize 'transaction costs' – the economist's term for institutionalization, organization and administration. For a long time the focus of efficiency was upon blue-print and organizational structure. What started out as an ambition to rationalize and streamline 'messy' organizational structures in the 1920s and 1930s, and again in the 1960s and 1970s, developed into administrative reform strategies to increase the external *responsiveness* of public service, public management and public administration to the needs of the relevant external environment, rather than reforming structure.

Integrity and trust

The second group of administrative core values, in terms of Hood (1991), comprises fairness, equity and rectitude and relate to the mission 'to keep government honest and fair'. These values refer to the world of public and corporate governance. Processes of governance provide the structure and context in which the 'given' managerial goals (and resources) are defined, standards for managerial performance may be set and evaluation procedures designed, implemented, enforced and publicly accounted for. Without 'good governance', 'strong public management' easily turns against itself or against the public interest. This family of values translates into instrumentalities that have become close to being administrative values in themselves: legality – the Rule of Law – bureaucratic loyalty, unimpeachable behavior and lack of corruption. Democracy is an important institution for political mobilization and social participation, but in many cases started out as a vehicle for openness and transparency of administrative decision

making. The democratic procedures of the administrative state try to secure the validity and fairness of the governance process, respecting justified entitlements, guiding the operation of the system of administrative responsibility and accountability, and seeing to the proper operation and discharge of public duties and responsibilities. Due process and Legimation durch Verfahren are the classic terms.

The administrative values in this category – albeit often less visible to the public – over the past 10 to 15 years possibly triggered more reform in (and of) administrative and managerial practice, than the often acclaimed efficiency measures: the concern for a level playing field, compliance to international rule or procurement procedures, implementation of global standards or care for an impeccable reputation in a globalizing world. The development of modern information and communication technology raised all kinds of new practical questions of confidentiality and political communication, or ethical standards of privacy, transparency and accountability in an age of mass data storage, global social networks and surfing for the 'wisdoms of the crowd'.

Reliability and confidence

These very administrative reforms put the issue of 'administrative cost' and the 'reduction of bureaucracy' back on the central administrative reform agenda of several governments. If not embedded in a proper, underlying institutional system of checks and balances to keep the system vital, governance processes and reforms run the risk of easily turning into a concern for procedure, formalization and 'compliance' as dead ends in themselves. The third set of administrative values for analyzing administrative reform aims to prevent this: robustness, resilience and sustainability. The mission is 'to keep government robust and resilient', which more and more means: innovative and adaptive. Research on 'normal accidents' (Perrow, 1999), emergency and safety learned that a reliable, stable and robust administrative system is not a system that is able to resist change and reform, but which is resilient and able to learn and adapt to meaningful changing circumstances.

This set of values refers to the usually more hidden 'constitutional dimension' of government and administrative reform (Ostrom, 1982; Lane, 1996). For a long time, it was difficult to see what this meant operationally. In the meantime, Europeans have been discovering, both at the EU and member-state levels, that it is nearly as hard to frame a constitution as it is to run one (cf. Woodrow Wilson). With the development of a strongly internationalized 'risk society' (Beck, 1986), the issue of constitutional value has become vastly more concrete, also in practical terms. Whereas the actual impact of, for example, the 'Reinventing Government' Movement or the Gore National Performance Review (1993) is still being disputed (PAR, 1996), in the wake of the 9-11 attacks the formation of a Department for Homeland Security has presented the United States with its own case of an unequivocal, strong, full-blown and operational administrative reform.

The safety of life and limb is still one of the most classic but powerful administrative values to be called upon for reform, not only in the United States. Respect for human rights gradually submerges the traditional 'right of life and limb' as a universal manifestation of good government. With the global scale enlargement of (derivative) financial markets, the emergence of international terrorism, the threat of global pandemics, the worldwide quest for security in food chains, debates on global climate change, natural resource scarcity and the potential of life-changing bio-based technologies, the urgency and visibility of this family of 'constitutional' or institutional design values has been increasing. Vitality, strength, flexibility, entrepreneurship, innovative capacity, strategic asset management and the capability of self-regulation and self-governance within society and administrative (sub)systems have become central concerns

in relation to the quality of *institutional design, redesign and (re)development* and therefore the reform of administrative systems (Toonen, 2010).

Governance

The different value systems constitute interdependent layers of administrative quality within governmental systems (they are summarized in Figure 31.1). There might be no public management, but there is certainly a Public Administration for all Seasons (cf. Hood, 1991). In the long run, administrative reform needs to serve all value families to prevent decline. Seemingly similar reform might therefore serve quite different value systems. There is a huge difference, for example, between whether a privatization program serves to increase the responsiveness and management of public service delivery – as in the Western reforms of the 1980s – or whether it serves the institutional design – the constitution – of a reliable market system, as in the post-Communist countries in the early 1990s (Toonen, 1993), or the bail-out of a country at times of monetary crises in the 2010s.

The sets of values may, in specific situations and contexts, be in conflict and put different demands on specific reform programs: safety vs privacy, speed vs carefulness, reliability vs efficiency. This tension makes administrative reform a highly dynamic process, full of contradictions, conflicts, ambiguity and inherent paradoxes of reform (Wright, 1994; Hesse, Hood and Peters, 2003; Margetts, Perri 6 and Hood, 2010). The existence of conflicting values in government and public administration is the basis of governance. Governance is the process by which natural, technological and social realities have to be mutually adjusted and reconciled (Ostrom, cited in Toonen, 2010). Cases of conflicting public value need to be resolved and decisions accounted for. The emergence of 'governance' (neo-public administration) as a dominant concept in the

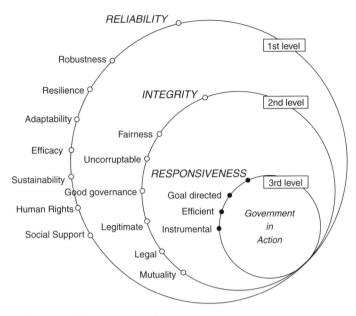

Figure 31.1   Quality in public administration

study of public administration is in itself a byproduct of the transformational processes which surrounded the administrative reform movements in the 1990s and early 2000s. The borders and layers of the state are blurring in a 'network society'. The development of all kinds of public–private partnership and other 'hybrids' in the relationship between state, society and markets raised the question of accountability in distributed systems of government and public service delivery. New regulatory systems for distributed public accountability were introduced in the form of juridification, procurement systems, user boards, independent regulators and overseers, benchmarking techniques, rating, performance contracting, interactive democracy, participative planning and other institutional expressions of administrative reform. Seen over the past 20 years, in many countries, on many occasions, concern for the reform of governance – public accountability – has often been higher on the public and political agenda than reform of public management.

Design

Reform is often presented as the outcome of 'planned' effort, politicized to some degree, and in intent and presentation certainly not incremental in nature. Experience tells a different story. The 'implementation of reform' usually shapes the policy. The nature and impact of the reform is designed in the process. This reflects the deeply rooted theoretical, if not philosophical controversy on how administrative systems change and develop (Leemans, 1970; Rottleuthner, 1988). The empirical study of public administration suggests that administrative reform as a process is best conceived of as somewhere on a continuum between Planned Change (Synoptic, Comprehensive, Rational, Blueprint, Mechanistic, Top down, Centrally Guided, Consciously Designed, Modernizing), on the one hand, and Emerging Strategy (Incremental, Piecemeal, Intuitive, Organic, Mutually Adjusted, Bottom up, Garbage Can, PostModernizing), on the other. A process of negotiated reform turns grand schemes easily into pragmatic and step-by-step processes of change and transformation. Grand-stated ambitions are modified to modest, but sometimes determined and irreversible, changes with large long-term consequences. Effective reform policy is often its own cause. One step leads to the other. If one 'cuts back' policy programs and expenditures long enough, there comes a point at which policy reform spills over into a reform of management structures, on the one hand, or institutional reform, on the other. This may, over time, amount to the wholesale reconstitution of a welfare state (Lane, 1995: 511). New forms of public management presuppose new forms of governance (accountability) (Bouckaert, 1996). These, in turn, require new institutional arrangements or regulatory regimes to frame them.

There are no clear-cut stages in a 'reform-logic'. There are, however, many examples that suggest a certain path dependency constituted by institutional logic. Seen from the early 1980s onwards, France and the UK took quite different trajectories of reform, not only in terms of presentation and the suggestion of continuity of reform. The two countries definitely started to work on the opposite sides of the administrative system, partly because the possibilities of their administrative systems allowed them to start where they did. France started out in the 1980s with an *institutional reform* of regionalization and decentralization. Earlier efforts to reform, modernize and amalgamate a culturally rooted, small-scale, politicized and very traditional local government system had failed. French regions needed not to be developed or (re)designed. They already existed as former administrative units in the abandoned French central planning model of the 1950s. The reform implied that they could be and were 'inflated' with a functional regional and urban development mission and corresponding tasks and budgets. The government soon followed through with a *governance reform*: the democratization of *départments* and regions and the redesign of political (*cumul des mandats*) and administrative intergovernmental relations (position of *préfet*; regional administrative courts; *contrats du plans*). Later in the process, the overall development was backed up by clear attention to the *autogestion*: that is, *management* amounting to managerial innovation of administrative units at various levels within the system (Claisse, 1995). As it turned out, this managerial reform fitted very well within, and actually consolidated, a long-term centralist tradition (Van den Berg, 2011).

The United Kingdom went the other way round. It started out with *managerial reform*, also because the institutional position of central government allowed for it. Unlike in many Continental system, functional local government authority has to be defined – and can be withdrawn – with an Act of Parliament (the *ultra vires* doctrine). The functional managerial reforms (NPM and the agentification and service charters of the Next Steps programs), triggered a subsequent need for governance reform in terms of the coordination of a functionally 'disjointed' administrative system at the regional meso level between central and local government. The *Joint up Government* initiatives were announced. From a PA perspective they are a logical next step towards an effort at *governance reform* in the region. In combination with a difficult but fundamental process of devolution, this has brought the UK system, in terms of regionalization and a structural *institutional reform* of almost constitutional proportions, much closer in step with (other parts of) Europe than any observant in the early 1980s would have held possible, not to speak of desirable (Sharpe, 1993; Toonen, 2001).

The emerging knowledge-based economy (KBE) of the late 1990s and early 2000s was characterized by a drive to a functional – rather than territorial, historical or cultural – new regionalism (Keating, 1998) all over Europe. This reshaped urban landscapes and associated governance structures, irrespective of an ambition at neo-managerial reform, which might or might not be a part of it, both on the Continent as well as in the British Isles (Herrschel and Newman, 2002).

'Britain out of step in Europe'? (Crouch and Marquand, 1989). At best the country has been 'sitting on the fence' at times as European developments are concerned, but from a PA perspective, the long term reform process shows clear signs of convergence. In any case, the example clarifies, that important changes and transformation in administrative structure are easily missed if one wants to restrict the concept of 'administrative reform' to intentional, centrally planned or legislated changes of public management.

Power

Recognizing the need for external pressure, many reforms are induced rather than imposed. There is room for selection and choice. Politics matter. The very notion of reform moved into a more dynamic understanding in terms of differentiated and inherently complex and dynamic processes of adaptation and mobilization within the largely self-governing polycentric administrative systems of the interdependent network society (Ostrom, 1990, 2005). For some, this is a depreciation of 'reform' to 'mere incrementalism' and 'muddling through'. Others see new and emergent 'evolutionary' and 'intelligent' strategies of adaptive transformation, social learning and transition management. An entrepreneurial kind of transformative leadership (MacGregor Burns, 2003) for the common good (Crosby and Bryson, 2005) is required in tackling public problems in a shared-power world. Authenticity, proactivity and communicative skill – framing and personal leadership – rather than centralized power have come to be considered key competencies of reform.

Next to 'governance' as an analytical concept, the rise of the attention for 'leadership' in relation to governance, reform and public administration over the past decade is at least remarkable. Authority cannot be taken for granted anymore. The 'limits of government' have been duly acknowledged. With the changing role of traditional political

institutions in society, the role and characteristics of executive leadership have been changing as well. The administrative icon of the successful reformer is no longer the authoritarian (benevolent) dictator who effectively executes the generalized will of the people. It is the charismatic Steve Jobs'-like public entrepreneur who reforms the system by anticipating the latent demand for change, which quickly becomes manifest when tied into the public, social, or personal senses that awake by giving people things which they were not aware that they needed. Not collective ideology, but personalized vision. Personalized rather than partisan forms of politicization have started to affect the nature of managerial professionalism within the public service in many countries (Toonen, 2001; Suleiman, 2003; van den Berg, 2011).

In the long run, governments can achieve very little in the way of substantial results without broad social support – these days largely addressed under the heading of 'trust' and 'confidence' in government. The power for successful reform is not given anymore by institutional position. Legitimate authority is the combination of power with trust. It has to be earned and accumulated, as 'social capital'. More than client satisfaction, public trust has become accepted over time to be a proven and indispensable resource for governmental support and long-term economic development. In systems theory as well as the Weberian Bureaucracy concept, the three layers distinguished in the administrative value system presented earlier (see Figure 31.1) are sometimes identified as functional legitimacy (responsiveness), procedural legitimacy (integrity) and institutional – regime – legitimacy (reliability). In addition to satisfaction with performance (the value of good management) and trust in public officials (the value of good governance), the group of 'constitutional' administrative values serves to secure the *reliability* of the administrative system in order to secure the *reliance* of citizens and the *confidence* of society in governmental institutions (the value of 'good government' or 'statehood'). An already observed but still rather latent neo-Weberianism in the debate on administrative reform is waiting to be mobilized (Page, 1985; Du Gay, 2000).

Impact

Reforms are often associated with lack of results and undelivered promises. The evaluation of reform, however, is by far the weakest developed step of all of the public sector and administrative reform programs, both from a PA and public administration perspective. Although often called upon, evaluations of reforms are virtually never conducted in a systematic, let alone comparative, way (OECD, 1995: 81; Ingraham, 1996: 262). Evaluative research is more with form and process, than content and impact. Reforms bring about multiple effects, which are appreciated in different ways. Observers and analysts may still see very much what they want to see. It is not only goal-driven behavior which counts. In systems of evolution and complexity, happy surprises count and serendipity matters. There are cases that are internationally recognized to show that attempts to reform, at least for a certain period, may quite well be successful and yield effects. The Japanese model, the Scandinavian model, the New Zealand model, the British model, the Belgian State Reform, Modell Deutschland, the Dutch 'Polder Model', the Wisconsin model, the Tilburg model, the Asian and Celtic Tigers, the 'New Steering Model', or, for a while, the Spanish 'guided organizational development' model as an example of the European modernization strategy, and later again the Swedish, Danish or Finish innovation models, are just a few to mention. Each country seems to be allowed its short moments of glory in the international hall of fame of administrative reform – but often only temporarily. There still looms an already long-standing and largely unaddressed research agenda:

> Addressing problems of global change will require a step change in research on fundamental

questions of governance, economic systems, and the assumptions, beliefs and values underlying human behavior (…). It is insufficient to identify necessary reforms in policies and institutions; research must explore how to catalyze the adoption of those reforms (Reid et al., 2010: 917).

REFERENCES

Aucoin, P. (1990) 'Administrative Reform in Public Management, Paradigms, Principles, Paradoxes and Pendulums', *Governance*, 3 (2): 115–37.

Beck, U. (1986) *Risikogesellschaft: auf dem Weg in eine andere Moderne*. Frankfurt: Suhrkamp.

Benz, Arthur (1995) 'Institutional Change in Intergovernmental Relations: The Dynamics of Multi-Level Structures', in Joachim Jens Hesse and Theo A.J. Toonen (eds), *European Yearbook of Comparative Government and Public Administration*. Baden-Baden/Boulder, CO: Nomos/Westview Press, pp. 551–76.

Bogason, Peter and Toonen, Theo A.J. (1998) 'Networks in Public Administration', *Public Administration*, 76 (Summer): 201–28.

Bouckaert, Geert (1996) 'Overview and Synthesis of the Secretariat'. Paper on Performance Management Practices in Eight OECD Member Countries. PUMA/PAC (95)24.

Camilleri, Joseph A. and Falk, Jim (2009) *Worlds in Transition: Evolving Governance Across a Stressed Planet*, Cheltenham: Edward Elgar.

Castels, F.G. and McKinlay, R.D. (1979) 'Public Welfare Provision, Scandinavia and the Sheer Futility of the Sociological Approach to Politics', *British Journal of Political Science*, 9: 157–71.

Chandler, J.A. (ed.) (2000) *Comparative Public Administration*. London: Routledge.

Claisse, A. (1995) 'La Modernisation Administrative en France: Au delà des Réformes, le Changement', in Joachim Jens Hesse and Theo A.J. Toonen (eds), *The European Yearbook of Comparative Government and Public Administration*. Baden-Baden/Boulder, CO: Nomos/Westview Press, pp. 409–37.

Crouch, Colin and Marquand, David (eds) (1989) *The New Centralism: Britain Out of Step in Europe?* Oxford: Basil Blackwell.

Crosby, Barbara C. and Bryson, John M. (2005) *Leadership for the Common Good; Tackling Public Problems in a Shared-Power World*. San Francisco, CA: Jossey-Bass.

Du Gay, Paul (2000) *In Praise of Bureaucracy: Weber, Organization, Ethics*. London: Sage.

Flynn, Norman and Strehl, Franz (eds) (1996) *Public Sector Management in Europe*. Brighton: Harvester Wheatsheaf.

Gleick, James (2011) *The Information: A History, A Theory, A Flood*. New York: Pantheon.

Halligan, John (1996) 'New Public Sector Models: Reform in Australia and New Zealand', in J.E. Lane (ed.), *Public Sector Reform*. London: Sage.

Henry, Nicholas (1975) *Public Administration and Public Affairs*. Englewood Cliffs, NJ: Prentice Hall.

Herrschel, Tassilo and Newman, Peter (2002) *Governance of Europe's City Regions: Planning, Policy and Politics*. London and New York: Routledge.

Hesse, Joachim Jens and Benz, Arthur (1990) *Die Modernisierung der Staatsorganisation. Institutionspolitik im internationalen Vergleich: USA, Groszbritanien, Frankreich, Bundesrepublik Deutschland*. Baden-Baden: Nomos.

Hesse, Joachim Jens, Hood, Christopher and Peters, B. Guy (2003) (eds) *Paradoxes of Public Sector Reform*. Berlin: Duncker & Humblot.

Hood, Christopher (1991) 'A Public Management for all Seasons?', *Public Administration*, 60: 3–19.

Hood, Christopher and Jackson Michael W. (1991) *Administrative Argument*. Aldershot: Darthmout.

Ingraham, Patricia (1996) 'The Reform Agenda for National Civil Service Systems: External Stress and Internal Strains', in Hans A.G.M. Bekke, James L. Perry and Theo A.J. Toonen (eds), *Civil Service Systems in Comparative Perspective*. Bloomington, IN: Indiana University Press, pp. 247–67.

Keating, Michael (1998) *The New Regionalism in Western Europe: Territorial Restructuring and Political Change*. Cheltenham: Edward Elgar.

Kennett, Patricia (ed.) (2008) *Governance, Globalization and Public Policy*. Cheltenham: Edward Elgar.

Künneke, Rolf W., Groenewegen, John and Auger, Jean-Francois (eds) (2009), *The Governance of Network Industries: Institutions, Technology, and Policy in Reregulated Infrastructures*. Cheltenham: Edward Elgar.

Lane, Jan-Erik (1993) *The Public Sector, Concepts, Models and Approaches*. London: Sage.

Lane, Jan-Erik (1995) 'End and Means of Public Sector Reform', in Joachim Jens Hesse and Theo A.J. Toonen (eds), *The European Yearbook of Comparative Government and Public Administration*. Baden-Baden/Boulder, CO: Nomos /Westview Press, pp. 507–21.

Lane, Jan-Erik (1996) *Constitutions and Political Theory*. Manchester/New York: Manchester University Press.

Leemans, A.F. (1970) *Changing Patterns of Local Government*. The Hague: International Union of Local Authorities.

Lijphart, Arend (1994) 'Democracies: Forms, Performance and Constitutional Engineering', *European Journal for Political Research*, 25 (1): 1–17.

Lijphart, Arend (1999) *Patterns of Democracy: Government Forms and Performance in Thirty-Six Countries*. New Haven, CT/London: Yale University Press.

Lynn, Laurence E. (2006) *Public Management: Old and New*. New York: Routledge.

MacGregor Burns, James (2003) *Transforming Leadership*. New York: Grove Press.

Margetts, Hellen, 6, Perri and Hood, Christopher (eds) (2010) *Paradoxes of Modernisation: Unintended Consequences of Public Policy Reform*. Oxford: Oxford University Press.

Naschold, F. (1996) *New Frontiers in Public Sector Management: Trends and Issues in State and Local Government in Europe*. Berlin and New York: de Gruyter.

National Performance Review (NPR) (1993) *The Gore Report on Reinventing Government*. Washington, DC.

OECD (1995) *Governance in Transition. Public Management Reforms in OECD Countries*. Paris: Organization for Economic Co-operation and Development.

Ostrom, Elinor (1990) *Governing the Commons: The Evolution of Institutions for Collective Action*. Cambridge: Cambridge University Press.

Ostrom, Elinor (2005) *Understanding Institutional Diversity*. Princeton, NJ and Oxford: Princeton University Press.

Ostrom, Vincent (1973) *The Intellectual Crisis in American Public Administration*. Tuscaloosa, AL: Alabama University Press.

Ostrom, Vincent (1982) 'A Forgotten Tradition: The Constitutional Level of Analysis', in J.A. Gillespie and P.A. Zinnes (eds), *Missing Elements in Political Inquiry: Logic and Levels of Analysis*. Beverly Hills, CA: Sage.

Page, Edward C. (1985) *Political Authority and Bureaucratic Power*. Brighton: Wheatsheaf.

Page, Edward C. (2001) *Governing by Numbers; Delegated Legislation and Everyday Policy-Making*. Oxford and Portland, OR: Hart.

PAR (1996) *Public Administration Review*, special issue on 'Reinventing' Public Administration, 56 (3): 245–304.

Perrow, C. (1999) *Normal Accidents: Living with High Risk Technologies.* Princeton, NJ: Princeton University Press.

Peters, B. Guy and Pierre, Jon (eds) (2001) 'Intergovernmental Relations and Multi-Level Governance', special issue of *Policy and Politics,* 29 (2).

Pollitt, Christopher and Bouckaert, Geert (2000) *Public Management Reform: a Comparative Analysis.* Oxford: Oxford University Press.

Reid, W.V., Chen, D., Goldfarb, L., et al. (2010) 'Earth System Science for Global Sustainability: Grand Challenges', *Science,* 330: 916–17.

Rottleuthner, Hubert (1988) 'Biological Metaphors in Legal Thought', in G. Teubner (ed.), *Autopoietic Law: A New Approach to Law and Society.* Berlin: de Gruyter.

Schick, Allan (1996) *The Spirit of Reform: Managing the New Zealand State Sector in a Time of Change.* Wellington: State Services Commission.

Sharpe, L.J. (ed.) (1993) *The Rise of Meso Government in Europe.* London: Sage.

Suleiman, Ezra (2003) *Dismantling Democratic States.* Princeton, NJ : Princeton University Press.

Toonen, Theo A.J. (1983) Administrative Plurality in a Unitary State: the Analysis of Public Organisational Pluralism, *Policy and Politics,* 11 (3): 247–71.

Toonen, Theo A.J. (1992) 'Europe of the Administrations: The Challenges of '92 (and Beyond),' *Public Administration Review,* 52 (2): 108–15.

Toonen, Theo A.J. (1993) 'Analyzing Institutional Change and Administrative Transformation: A Comparative View', *Public Administration,* 71 (1/2): 151–67.

Toonen, Theo A.J. (1997) 'Public Sector Reform in Western Europe: A Paradigm Shift or Public Administration as Usual?', in Joachim Jens Hesse and Theo A.J. Toonen (eds), *The European Yearbook of Comparative Government and Public Administration,* Vol III/1996. Baden-Baden: Nomos, pp. 485–98.

Toonen, Theo A.J. (2001) 'The Comparative Dimension of Administrative Reform', in B. Guy Peters and Jon Pierre (eds), *Politicians, Bureaucrats and Administrative Reform.* London: Routledge, pp. 183–202.

Toonen, Theo A.J. (2010) 'Resilience in Public Administration: The Work of Elinor and Vincent Ostrom from a PA Perspective', *Public Administration Review,* 70 (2): 193–202.

Van den Berg, Caspar (2011) *Transforming for Europe; The Reshaping of National Bureaucracies in a System of Multi-level Governance.* Leiden: Leiden University Press.

Van Santen, Rutger, Khoe, Djan and Vermeer, Bram (2010) *2030: Technology that Will Change the World.* Oxford: Oxford University Press.

Wright, Vincent (1994) 'Reshaping the State: The Implications for Public Administration', *West European Politics,* 17 (35): 102–37.

32

Administrative Reforms in Western Democracies

Tom Christensen and Per Lægreid

INTRODUCTION

Administrative systems have historically always been confronted with a dichotomy between integration, coordination and central capacity, on the one hand, and autonomy, fragmentation and disaggregation, on the other. In this chapter, we examine how the New Public Management (NPM) reform movement and the reforms in the aftermath of NPM, such as whole-of-government reform initiatives, have addressed this challenge (cf. Christensen and Lægreid 2011a). Our focus will be more on administrative reform development in groups of countries than on reforms in single countries.

There is an important distinction between change and reform (Christensen et al. 2007). Whereas change is a broader concept that can be triggered by many different factors and driving forces, reform is a narrower notion that involves elements of design, planning and deliberate choice (Egeberg 2003). Reform is often the result of an active administrative policy designed by political or managerial executives, but also constrained by

polity features, historical–institutional traditions and external pressure (Pollitt and Bouckaert 2011). By administrative reforms we mean deliberate changes in the structures, processes or procedures of public sector organizations undertaken to improve the way they run and, ultimately, aiming to achieve changes in policy and society. In this chapter, we mainly focus on administrative reforms in central government in Western Europe, with a special emphasis on the last decade.

The landscape of administrative reform is often complicated by discrepancies between the world of ideas and the world of practice, which may be loosely coupled (Brunsson 1989). Often it proves more difficult to change how people and organizations act than what they think and believe. If one compares reform policy documents with reform decisions and with reform implementation and results, one tends to see different things (Pollitt 2001).

There is also a tension between a generic and holistic tradition of administrative reforms and a more specific, context-dependent tradition. Whereas the first tends to focus on the common characteristics of formal organizations and downplays the differences between organizations in the public and private sector, the second tends to underline the specific features of public sector organizations (Røvik 2002). The first focuses on convergence and isomorphism and the adoption of private sector organizational forms and management principles by the public sector – i.e. it stresses decontextualization. The second highlights the specific features and contexts that a public sector organization faces, such as having a political leadership at the top of the organization, being multifunctional and often not operating in a market, not to mention the relevance of different cultural contexts. In this chapter we lean more towards the second position than the first, emphasizing contextualization and divergence.

Administrative reforms are typically ambiguous and are rarely streamlined homogeneous reforms with integrated reform means and measures. More typically they are a loosely coupled collection of reform measures that offer a kind of shopping basket from which reform agents can pick and choose sometimes contradictory reform elements with different theoretical foundations (Pollitt 2003). The tensions arising from the hybrid character of NPM, which combines economic organization theory and management theory, are well known (Aucoin 1990). They result from the contradiction between the centralizing tendencies inherent in contractualism and the devolutionary tendencies of managerialism. By advocating both decentralization (let the managers manage) and centralization and incentives (make the managers manage), NPM thus simultaneously prescribes both more autonomy and more central control. A similar kind of diversity, albeit balanced differently, is found in post-NPM reform measures (Christensen and Lægreid 2011b).

Not only within a reform model but also between models there are overlaps when it comes to specific reform means and measures. This is the case, for example, between NPM, neo-Weberian models and New Public

Governance. When one moves from the higher level of large models and paradigms to the lower level of specific reform tools, the menu of techniques is often not very coherent (Pollitt and Bouckaert 2011). Thus, reform strategies are often more characterized by mixed orders, complexity and hybridization than by consistent alternative models of administrative reform.

TRAJECTORY OF REFORMS

Convergence or divergence among countries?

One can argue that some general reform ideas will spread around the world quite easily, while the more specific reform measures will show a pattern of divergence. A quite common stereotype is that Anglo-American countries are NPM front-runners and rather homogeneous in this respect, while Continental Europe and Scandinavia have been more reluctant to take NPM on board, as have the Latin states (Hood 1996).

In terms of the control and organization of public service, NPM represents a global change of paradigm, according to the Organization for Economic Co-operation and Development (OECD 1995), as do post-NPM reform measures (Christensen and Lægreid 2007b). This convergence thesis is, however, contested when it comes to practice rather than just ideas (Pollitt 2001). NPM has led to major changes in the public sector in many countries (Pollitt and Bouckaert 2011), yet the process and content of reforms has not been the same everywhere. Thus, the spread of NPM is a complex process, going through different stages and packaged in different ways in different countries, with each country following its own reform trajectory within a broader framework and starting from different preconditions (Wright 1994; Pollitt, van Thiel and Holmburg 2007). A seven-country study shows that increased specialization, autonomy and proliferation have been counteracted by increased coordination in countries such as the UK, Sweden and the Netherlands, while this has not happened in France or Belgium (Bouckaert et al. 2010). In other words, NPM is not an integrated and coherent set of reforms with a specific starting point and following a specific path towards a common destination (Wright 1994).

There is no clear convergence towards one single organizational form (Pollitt and Bouckaert 2011). On the contrary, the organizational pattern is becoming increasingly complex and hybrid. What we see is a complex combination of old public administration, New Public Management and post-NPM features, often containing elements that point in different directions (Christensen and Lægreid 2007a). NPM ideas have been implemented to different degrees, at different paces and with differing emphases in different countries and sectors. A general finding is that the degree of variation between countries and between policy areas increases when we move away from the world of ideas, talk and policy programs and look at specific decisions, and even more so when we consider the implementation and impact of the reforms (Pollitt 2001). One can argue about whether NPM has led to a convergence of administrative systems in different countries, yet there is much to suggest that ideas and policy programs resemble one another more than the corresponding practices do. One mechanism here is 'double-talk', whereby leaders seek political support by publicly espousing modern principles of government but in fact experience resistance when they try to implement reform measures (cf. Brunsson 1989).

Although different countries present their reforms in similar terms and support some of the same general administrative doctrines, closer scrutiny reveals considerable variation. Pollitt and Bouckaert (2004) distinguish between four groups of NPM reformers: the maintainers, the modernizers, the marketizers and the minimal state reformers.

Nations like the UK, Australia and New Zealand fit the marketizer profile, while the Scandinavian countries, and especially the Continental Europeans, are more sceptical about NPM and therefore conform more closely with the modernizer profile.

Having begun in Britain, NPM gained the strongest hold in the Anglo-American countries (Hood 1996). In Westminster-style parliamentary systems, like Australia and New Zealand, NPM reforms fell on fertile ground and were therefore far-reaching and implemented early (Gregory 2003; Halligan 2007). This was due, on the one hand, to strong external economic and institutional pressure and, on the other hand, to few constitutional and administrative obstacles, a compatible culture and parliamentary conditions that favoured a radical strategy and reform entrepreneurs (Christensen and Lægreid 2001a). By contrast, the Scandinavian countries and some Continental European countries were reluctant to implement reforms. Environmental pressure was weaker, their *Rechtsstaat* culture and strong egalitarian norms were less compatible with the values of NPM, there were more obvious constitutional obstacles and parliamentary conditions often characterized by minority coalition governments made a radical reform strategy difficult to pursue (Christensen, Lie and Lægreid 2007).

Pollitt and Bouckaert (2011) distinguish between two main models. The first group comprises the NPM marketizers – Australia, New Zealand and the UK (as well as the USA below the federal level) – which they label the core NPM group. The UK under Tony Blair was dominated by a reform model that included market orientation, top-down performance management, competition, contestability in providing public services and citizens' choice (Halligan 2011). The second group consisted of the Continental European and Scandinavian modernizers – Finland, France, the Netherlands and Sweden (as well as Belgium and Germany below the federal level). They claim that the latter group of countries represents a distinct reform model labelled the neo-Weberian state. They share a more positive attitude towards the state and a less positive attitude towards private sector models, and underline the role of representative democracy and administrative law. Compared to traditional bureaucracy they are more focused on citizens' needs, citizens' participation, performance and results and professionalization of public service. Citizen orientation and participation are more characteristic of the Northern countries than of France, Italy and Belgium, which are more managerial-oriented modernizers. However, the Scandinavian countries are not only modernizers following managerial and user-responsiveness strategies but also have increasingly adopted competition and marketization strategies while stopping short of major privatization (Foss Hansen 2011). In recent years Denmark and Norway, especially, have followed post-NPM reintegration strategies. Compared with the Northern countries, the Southern ones, whose state traditions are based on the Napoleonic legacy, were latecomers to reforms (Ongaro 2009).

At one end of the spectrum we have slow-moving systems with reluctant reformers, such as federal Germany, while at the other end we have the fast-pace reformers such as the UK. In between we have countries such as the Nordic countries which require time to gather the necessary political consensus for reforms, but where the reforms then have a good chance of long-term survival and successful implementation.

Variations among policy areas

Whether NPM is a kind of generic reform wave, or whether it is primarily suitable for particular public policy areas, is a question that has been debated for some time now. One rather sceptical view is that NPM, with its focus on efficiency, should be used primarily in technically and economically oriented policy areas (Gregory 2003), while in policy areas like education, health, welfare and environment, which are qualitatively different and where it is difficult to quantify and measure goal achievement, it is less easy to apply. What is more, certain norms suggest that these so-called 'soft policy areas' should be protected from – or not exposed to – efficiency-oriented reform measures. This view holds that the use and effect of NPM should vary considerably between different policy areas.

Another way to look at convergence and divergence is to examine the political importance of policy areas. If one assumes that NPM will undermine central political control (Christensen and Lægreid 2001b), political salience may influence the balance between political control and autonomy. The argument then goes that the more important the policy area, the less NPM should be used, because the political leadership will want to have hands-on political control. But political saliency is seldom an objective factor and may change over time.

Many policy areas are characterized by mixed-reform models. In the hospital sector, there has been a convergence among the European states towards managed competition, but the specific NPM reforms have also been challenged by the ideas of a healthcare state and a profession-state perspective (Byrkjeflot 2011). In the university sector, NPM features such as market-based measures, output performance indicators and measurement- and management-based governance models have been implemented in many European countries, but such trends have also been challenged and complemented by reforms aimed at developing networked governance (Bleiklie et al. 2011). Reform of the welfare administration has also produced hybrids. A comparison of German, UK and Norwegian reforms reveals a reform pattern characterized by complexity and hybridization (Christensen et al. 2009). We see a combination of old welfare administration, NPM features, joined-up government measures and partnerships.

BEYOND NPM – POST-NPM, NEO-WEBERIAN MODELS, NEW PUBLIC GOVERNANCE AND WHOLE-OF-GOVERNMENT

The reforms that have emerged during the last decade have been variously labelled as post-NPM, whole-of-government, joined-up government, quality of government, networks, partnerships, etc. In their book on comparative public management reforms, Pollitt and Bouckart (2011) distinguish between NPM, neo-Weberian states and New Public Governance as three major models in contemporary Western European administrative reforms. New Public Governance espouses post-NPM features such as integration, holism, e-government, networks and partnerships (Osborne 2011; Pollitt and Bouckaert 2011). A central question concerns what happens when different reform waves meet each other.

Until the end of the 1990s the general direction of reform was NPM, albeit with much variation among both countries and policy areas. There are now many indications that NPM has stalled and been supplemented by other types of reforms, like post-NPM reform measures that are more preoccupied with increasing central control and coordination inside and across sectors (Christensen and Lægreid 2011b). This does not mean that NPM is dead. It is still very much alive and kicking in many Western European countries. What we see is that reforms are more mixed, combining some elements of NPM with post-NPM reform measures (Pollitt and Bouckaert 2011). This is the case in the Mediterranean countries (Ongaro 2009) in which public management reforms aimed at modernizing had to be reframed in legal terms. In Southern European countries with a legalistic and formalistic tradition and a politicized administration, such as Portugal, Spain, Italy and Greece, public management reforms had a hard time breaking through (Ongaro 2009; Kickert 2011). But there is some evidence of a 'silent' managerial

revolution in these countries in contrast to the 'load' management reforms in NPM countries (Ongaro 2009). In other countries with Napoleonic and legalistic *Rechtsstaat* traditions, such as France and Germany, public management reforms came up against strong legalistic thinking (Kickert 2011). In Germany NPM reforms were not adopted on a large scale at the federal level, and in Belgium the NPM reform movement has been rather weak (Pollitt and Bouckaert 2011). The reform paths pursued in Western Europe have been rather divergent, partly because they had different starting points. Currently, different countries are in different phases of reform and they do not have a shared vision of the future administrative arrangements (Pollitt and Bouckaert 2011). They face different contexts, external and internal constraints, risks and problems and are based on different values and norms.

There is a new generation of reforms emerging under various post-NPM headings, but these are tending to supplement and modify NPM rather than replacing it. The reasons why post-NPM reforms have emerged are complex, but they seem at least partly to be a reaction to a loss of political control and to the fact that NPM has not delivered what it promised in economic terms and has produced proliferation and fragmentation in public administration systems. Added to that, terrorism, pandemics, tsunamis, climate threats and financial recession have created a greater need for control and integration (Christensen and Lægreid 2007b). The strong demands for more central control and capacity and more coordination of sectors, polices and programs are reflected in various new post-NPM reforms.

In the aftermath of the financial crisis, rationalization has risen to the top of the administrative reform agenda in many countries (van Thiel et al. 2012). Mergers and downsizing public sector organizations have become reform tools in countries that have suffered most from the financial crisis, such as Greece, Spain, Portugal and Ireland, but we have also seen this trend in the UK and Germany. Agencies have been reshuffled and merged owing to financial and budgetary concerns but also to counteract a loss of coordination and to meet a need for stronger collaboration.

A main finding in the research in this area is that administrative reforms have not taken place along a single dimension (Pollitt and Bouckaert 2011). In practice we face mixed models and increased complexity. The pace and comprehensiveness of these trends has varied significantly from one country and policy area to another, and reform activities embrace a wide spectrum. Even though NPM has in certain ways produced positive results, it is too early to conclude that the old public administration model is unsustainable. It has considerable capacity to adapt and is both robust and flexible, even after a long period of NPM reforms, and the emerging post-NPM reforms are reintroducing some of the principles of the Weberian state, albeit in new forms.

Typical for the NPM reforms was that the formal structure changed from an integrated to a fragmented one (Lægreid and Verhoest 2010). The formal levers of steering were weakened, the distance to the agencies grew, political signals became weaker, and horizontal specialization increased according to different principles. The post-NPM generation of reforms of the last decade has used formal structures to regain control or to modify the loss of political influence by making public organizations more centralized, complex and varied. Formal structural instruments have been used to modify devolution and vertical specialization, as well as horizontal fragmentation and specialization, especially in Australia and New Zealand, but also in the UK (Gregory 2003, Richards and Smith 2006, Halligan 2007). In contrast to the late 1980s when British government reforms were espousing organizational disaggregation, the recent reforms have been characterized by aggregation and joined-up government (Talbot and Johnston 2007, Halligan 2011). Vertical control and levers of

control are increasingly being applied, while a 'whole-of-government' approach uses new coordination instruments and cross-sector programs and projects to modify horizontal fragmentation.

Whole-of-government initiatives are important for handling the 'wicked issues' that transcend the boundaries between organizational policy areas or administrative levels (Christensen and Lægreid 2007b). NPM reforms primarily addressed the principal–agent issues of how superior bodies could control subordinate organizations within the same ministerial area, but had little to offer when it came to the more pressing question of how to handle problems and tasks that straddle organizational boundaries. The challenge is to find organizational arrangements that can enhance cross-border or intersectoral collaboration and horizontal coordination.

Another element of this post-NPM movement is increased central control. In many countries the agencification process has stalled and the need for central capacity is back on the agenda (Halligan 2007). But whole-of-government, like NPM, is a rather ambiguous and not very coherent reform movement, supplementing rather than replacing NPM measures. The risk of subjecting too many policy areas to overly extensive coordination that uses a lot of resources is evident.

Rather than purifying a single model we need a repertoire of models for political–administrative institutions to face the future challenges of public management, administration and governance. Designing a holistic and integrated public administration is not easy and may not be a good idea either, as research shows that public administration systems actually are a 'mixed' order of partly overlapping, partly contradictory complementary and competing organizational forms and are hence necessarily compound in nature (Olsen 2010). The public administration is multi-functional and has to balance different cultural values and norms in addition to the structural measures.

Complex political–administrative problems require complex solutions. Therefore it is normally not a question of hierarchy, networks or market. The main challenge is how these different elements can be combined and balanced in such a way as to supplement or complement one another. Today we encounter no dominant model. Instead, several key concepts such as NPM, post-NPM, whole-of-government, New Public Governance, networks, partnerships and the neo-Weberian state are on the agenda (Pollitt and Bouckaert 2011).

THE DRIVERS OF REFORM

A broad transformative approach to public reforms contends that when a political and administrative leadership tries to handle and further public reforms it operates in at least three types of contexts: the constitutionally laid down political and administrative structure; the political and administrative culture; and the environment, whether technical or institutional (Christensen and Lægreid 2001a, 2007a). The possibilities for political and administrative executives to carry out an active reform policy are constrained as well as enabled by such factors.

From a structural or instrumental point of view the reforms may generally be seen as conscious organizational design (Egeberg 2003). This perspective is based on the assumption that political and administrative leaders use the structural design of public entities as an instrument to fulfil public goals (Gulick 1937, Weaver and Rockman 1993). According to Dahl and Lindblom (1953), two aspects are important in instrumental decision-making processes and therefore reform processes – social or political control and rational calculation or the quality of organizational thinking. Major preconditions for instrumental design of NPM reforms are that leaders have a relatively large degree of control over change or reform processes and

that they score high on rational calculation or means–end thinking.

One school of thought, based on an instrumental perspective, points to the fact that different countries have different *constitutional features and political–administrative structures* and contends that these factors go some way to explaining how they handle national problems and reform processes (Pollitt and Bouckaert 2011). The polity frames relevant here concern first, whether political and administrative leaders are constrained by constitutional factors that limit their ability to implement reforms decisively and swiftly, or whether they have more leeway. Therefore Anglo-Saxon countries will often, by virtue of their 'elective dictatorship', score high on control potential (Boston et al. 1996).

The second factor is whether the leadership operates within a homogeneous or heterogeneous political–administrative apparatus. A homogeneous apparatus allows leaders to exercise their hierarchical authority more easily, while a heterogeneous apparatus often engenders turf wars and negotiations among leaders and units (March and Olsen 1983).

Another view holds that reforms are primarily a product of the *national historical–institutional context*. The cultural features of public organizations develop gradually in institutional processes, giving institutionalized organizations a distinct character or cultural 'soul' (Selznick 1957). Different countries have different historical–cultural traditions and their reforms are 'path dependent', meaning that national reforms have unique features (March and Olsen 1989). Informal norms and values established in their formative years will influence strongly the paths they follow later on (Krasner 1988). Historical traditions in the state and administration constrain the reform trajectory. Whether countries have a legalistic tradition, a *Rechtsstaat* tradition, a politicized tradition, a consensual and corporatist tradition, an Anglo-American, Napoleonic, Germanic or Scandinavian administrative tradition matters for the reform paths they choose. Traditions are important, but they do not determine reform choices and they need to be understood as one of several factors affecting the way administrative reforms develop (Painter and Peters 2010).

Thus, the cultural context of reform is important (Verhoest 2011). How successfully a reform wave-like NPM is applied in a public organization has a lot to do with cultural compatibility (Brunsson and Olsen 1993). The greater the consistency between the values underlying the reforms and the values on which the existing administrative system is based, the more likely the reforms are to be implemented. Generally speaking, culturally based adaptation tends to be partial and pragmatic.

A third view regards administrative reforms primarily as a response to *external pressure*. This environmental influence can be of two kinds: either institutional or technical (Meyer and Rowan 1977). In the first instance a country may adopt internationally based norms and beliefs about how a civil service system should be organized and run simply because these have become the prevailing, ideologically dominant doctrine diffused all over the world (Czarniawska and Sevon 1996). This diffusion process implies isomorphic elements, creating pressure for similar reforms and structural changes in many countries.

The institutional environment generally involves the development of myths and symbols in the macro-environment of public organizations to a considerable degree. In a complicated world, where political–administrative systems, patterns of actors, problems, solutions and effects are complex and difficult to understand, there is a need to have certain 'rules of thumb'. These are supplied by myths and symbols that evolve and spread between countries, sectors and policy areas. They represent a kind of 'taken for grantedness' concerning which ideas, organizational structures, procedures and cultures are appropriate. Such myths may be provided by international organizations, like the

OECD, the IMF (International Monetary Fund), the World Bank, the WTO (World Trade Organization) and the EU (European Union), but also by national organizations working as reform entrepreneurs (Sahlin-Andersson 2001). The myth theory stresses that myths imported to public organizations remain superficial, functioning as 'window-dressing', enhancing legitimacy without actually affecting practice (Brunsson 1989). In the development of NPM, the group of Anglo-Saxon countries somehow managed to wield ideological hegemony, which led other countries to imitate their reforms; their status was, however, later weakened by post-NPM myths of the late 1990s.

In the second instance, related to the technical environment, administrative reforms may be seen as the optimal solution to widespread technical problems – i.e. they are adopted to solve problems created by a lack of instrumental performance or by economic competition and market pressure (Self 2000). In this instance NPM reforms are adopted not because of their ideological hegemony but because of their alleged technical efficiency (Boston et al. 1996). Quite often, NPM reforms have been initiated or heavily influenced by the technical environment, because of an economic crisis or changing political or administrative pressure. Likewise, post-NPM reform measures develop as a result of anti-fragmentation or efficiency-related arguments.

Summing up, external reform components and programs are filtered, interpreted and modified by a combination of two nationally based processes (Christensen and Lægreid 2001a; Pollitt and Bouckaert 2011). One is a country's political–administrative history, culture, traditions and style of government. The other is national polity features, as expressed in constitutional and structural factors. Within these constraints, political and managerial executives have varying leeway to launch administrative reforms via an active administrative policy.

Studies of NPM reform processes around the world reflect many of the theoretical points outlined (Christensen and Lægreid 2001b, 2007a, Pollitt and Bouckaert 2011). A comparative study of Norway, Ireland and Belgium supports the idea that international pressure for agencification is transformed when it meets state-specific, environmental factors, polity, administrative culture and actor constellations (Verhoest et al. 2010).

THE EFFECTS OF REFORMS

To look at the effects and implications of administrative reforms we need to specify what we mean by effects. Pollitt and Bouckaert (2011) distinguish between operational effects, process effects and system effects. In addition, we may focus on effects on the main goal or on side effects on other goals; on jeopardy or on bonuses (Pollitt 1995, 2003, Hesse, Hood and Peters 2003). The main goal of NPM was to promote different aspects of efficiency. One way to measure efficiency gains is to look at the major macro-economic performance of a country. However, it is not easy to establish whether improvements in performance are the result of NPM, since there are many other factors that play a role. Nevertheless, few studies have demonstrated a favourable macro-economic effect of NPM (Pollitt and Bouckaert 2011).

Another way to look at the effect of NPM on efficiency is to focus on increased service efficiency. Economists often conclude that NPM has increased efficiency, while some political scientists are more sceptical and come up with contradictory findings (Boyne et al. 2003). The latter group also has more of a problem with efficiency studies, pointing to the difficulty of comparing the same services over time, given changes in organization, content, choice and competition.

The evidence-based knowledge about the effects and implications of different administrative reforms is still rather patchy and contested. The means–end knowledge and ability for rational calculation *ex ante* of impacts

and effects of different organizational forms are rather weak among reform agents, as shown by the economic–institutional theoretical background to the trail-blazing reforms in New Zealand (Boston et al. 1996). Fast-pace reforms are often symbol-ridden. Different organizational forms matter and affect the way public organizations operate and work in practice, as shown by the decrease in political control brought about by structural devolution in the NPM reforms, or the increase in central capacity engendered by coordinative post-NPM measures (Christensen and Lægreid 2001b, 2007b). Normally, however, there is no one-to-one relationship between organizational forms and performance. This has to do with the fact that context matters to a great extent, but also with the ambiguity of the performance concept and the problems of attribution.

One implication is that there is a need to go beyond the narrow concept of performance measured in terms of economy and efficiency and to include the broader democratic implications for power relations, trust and legitimacy in the equation. In most democratic systems, values such as impartiality, predictability, rule of law, political loyalty, political control, legitimacy, trust, participation, responsiveness, equity, etc., are also important elements of performance (Christensen et al. 2007). We know less about external political learning and societal effects than about internal administrative effects on efficiency (Olsen 1996). The fundamental purpose of public service is government, not management (OECD 2005). Not only effects on main goals but also side effects and dysfunctions have to be taken into account (Hesse, Hood and Peters 2003).

One line of inquiry asks whether NPM leads to less emphasis on input democracy and more on output democracy (Peters 2011). A related question concerns political control, steering and accountability. The bulk of comparative studies of the effects of NPM reforms seem to stress that the control of the political executive has decreased as a result of NPM reforms (Christensen and Lægreid 2001b,

2007a, Pollitt and Bouckaert 2011). The
'logic of discipline' anchored in the demand
for independent, apolitical bodies did not
work as expected and claims for democratic
accountability have become stronger (Roberts
2010). Concerning responsibility or accountability, NPM studies tend to point to a formalization of the relationship between
political leaders, on the one hand, and managers and the administrative grass roots, on
the other, and to an increase in mistrust
(Christensen and Lægreid 2001b). This represents a change from a more culturally
based relationship, characterized by mutual
respect and common values, to a system
where subordinates are required to account
for themselves and the principal does not
have much trust in the agent.

One international lesson is that most governments do not learn sufficiently from previous administrative reforms in their country
or in other countries. Alleged successes often
have more influence than elements of reform
failure. Therefore, there are a lot of ambigui-
ties in learning from experiences of administrative reforms. And politicians are generally
more interested in launching new reforms
than learning from previous ones, partly
because reforms look more attractive *ex ante*
than *ex post* (Brunsson and Olsen 2003).

An important implication is that one cannot
just graft private sector management tools,
organizational forms and steering mechanisms onto public sector organizations and
expect successful implementation and results.
One reason for this is that public sector
organizations such as central agencies differ
significantly from private sector organizations (Allison 1983). Policy makers may be
well advised not to simply copy new reform
solutions like agency models but instead to
adapt them to local contexts. One implication
of this lesson is that holistic or generic
models have clear limitations. One of the big
flaws of NPM was probably the claim that
there was a clear dividing line between
policy making and formulation, on the one
hand, and policy implementation, on the
other (Kettl 2003).

One conclusion to be drawn is that the
design of the various administrative reforms,
like NPM reforms, may vary considerably
between countries, tasks, sectors and administrative levels and will have differentiated
consequences for effects studies. In some
countries, such as those in Southern Europe,
administrative reforms hardly ever seem to
have had significant effects (Kickert 2011).
Pollitt and Bouckart (2011) underline that
there are multiple difficulties in assessing the
results of administrative reforms, in general,
with government effectiveness especially difficult to evaluate. But it is also difficult to
find concrete proof of money having been
saved, while evidence of efficiency gains is
patchy and incomplete (Andrews 2011). The
same can be said about the effects on citizens' satisfaction and trust, which is a very
complex issue (van de Walle 2011). Some of
the most significant effects may actually
have been in the way we talk about public
sector organizations. The reforms have produced a new discourse and reform climate,
changing attitudes, activities and procedures
more than outcomes. The general conclusion
reached by many studies is that major reforms
are often launched with little or no attention
to evaluation and that 'the international management reform movement has not needed
results to fuel its onward march' (Pollitt and
Bouckaert 2011, p. 58).

CONCLUSION

One important lesson from the comparative
administrative reform movement is the difficulty of drawing general policy recommendations that are valid across countries, policy
areas and over time. Owing to the contextual
variations and different historical–institutional
legacies that different countries face, the
holistic and generic approach has many
limitations.

One important policy recommendation is
that reformers should be preoccupied not
only with the steering capacity and capability

of public sector organizations but also with steering representativeness, legitimacy and trust relations. Gradual reorganization and reform of a more limited scope will more easily allow the broader participation of different stakeholders and potentially increase the legitimacy of the reforms. The main challenge is to find organizational forms that enhance both the representativeness and the capacity of governance. Often there is a trade-off between the two. Reforms intended to enhance one aspect tend to harm the other (Dahl and Tufte 1973).

The big question is whether it is possible to design administrative reforms in a way that strengthens both representativeness and capacity. Experience indicates that this is a difficult task. Input-oriented representativeness and output-oriented effectiveness are both essential elements for democratic self-determination. Input legitimacy of electoral arrangements and output legitimacy of policy service delivery are both important components of sustainable democratic arrangements, and successful administrative reforms in representative democracies have to take both features into account. There has been a shift from input democracy towards output democracy in contemporary reforms, weakening political accountability and strengthening managerial accountability, but this transformation is by no means a panacea for the ills of contemporary democracy. A main recommendation is that one has to go beyond the narrow concept of managerial accountability and address the broader concept of political accountability when reorganizing public sector organizations.

REFERENCES

Allison, G. (1983). Public and Private Managers: Are They Fundamentally Alike in All Unimportant Respects? In J. L. Perry and K. L. Kraemer (eds), *Public Management. Public and Private Perspectives.* Palo Alto, CA: Mayfield Publishing.

Andrews, R. (2011). NPM and the Search for Efficiency. In T. Christensen and P. Lægreid (eds), *The Ashgate Research Companion to New Public Management.* Aldershot: Ashgate.

Aucoin, P. (1990). Administrative Reform in Public Management: Principles, Paradoxes and Pendulums. *Governance*, 3: 115–137.

Bleiklie, I., J. Enders, B. Lepori and C. Musselin (2011). NPM, Governance and the University as a Changing Professional Organization. In T. Christensen and P. Lægreid (eds), *The Ashgate Research Companion to New Public Management.* Aldershot: Ashgate.

Boston, J., J. Martin, J. Pallot and P. Walsh (1996). *Public Management: The New Zealand Model.* Auckland: Oxford University Press.

Bouckaert, G., B. G. Peters and K. Verhoest (2010*). The Coordination of Public Sector Organizations. Shifting Patterns of Public Management.* London: Palgrave Macmillan.

Boyne, G. A., C. Farrell, J. Law, M. Powel and R. M. Walker (2003). *Evaluating Public Sector Reforms.* Buckingham: Open University Press.

Brunsson, N. (1989). *The Organization of Hypocrisy. Talk, Decisions and Actions in Organizations.* Chichester: Wiley.

Brunsson, N. and J. P. Olsen (1993). *The Reforming Organization.* London and New York: Routledge.

Byrkjeflot, H. (2011). Healthcare States and Medical Professions: The Challenges from NPM. In T. Christensen and P. Lægreid (eds), *The Ashgate Research Companion to New Public Management.* Aldershot: Ashgate.

Christensen, T. and P. Lægreid (2001a). A Transformative Perspective on Administrative Reforms. In T. Christensen and P. Lægreid (eds), *New Public Management. The Transformation of Ideas and Practice.* Aldershot: Ashgate.

Christensen, T. and P. Lægreid (2001b). New Public Management – Undermining Political Control? In T. Christensen and P. Lægreid (eds), *New Public Management. The Transformation of Ideas and Practice.* Aldershot: Ashgate.

Christensen, T. and P. Lægreid (2007a). *Transcending New Public Management.* Aldershot: Ashgate.

Christensen, T. and P. Lægreid (2007b). The Whole-of-Government Approach to Public Sector Reform. *PAR. Public Administration Review* 67 (6): 1059–1066.

Christensen, T. and P. Lægreid (2011a). Introduction. In T. Christensen and P. Lægreid (eds), *The Ashgate Research Companion to New Public Management.* Aldershot: Ashgate.

Christensen, T. and P. Lægreid (2011b). Beyond NPM? Some Development Features. In T. Christensen and P. Lægreid (eds), *The Ashgate Research Companion to New Public Management*. Aldershot: Ashgate.

Christensen, T., P. Lægreid, P. G. Roness and K. A. Røvik (2007). *Organization Theory and the Public Sector. Instrument, Culture and Myth*. London and New York: Routledge.

Christensen, T., A. Lie and P. Lægreid (2007). Still Fragmented or Reassertion of the Centre? In T. Christensen and P. Lægreid (eds), *Transcending New Public Management*. Aldershot: Ashgate.

Christensen, T., M. Knuth, P. Lægreid and J. Wiggan (2009). Reforms of Welfare Administration and Policy – A Comparison of Complexity and Hybridization: An Introduction. *International Journal of Public Administration*, 32: 1001–1005.

Czarniawska, B. and G. Sevón (eds) (1996) *Translating Organizational Change*. Berlin: De Gruyter.

Dahl, R. A. and C. E. Lindblom (1953). *Politics, Economics, and Welfare*. New York: Harper & Row.

Dahl, R. A. and E. R. Tufte (1973). *Size and Democracy*. Stanford, CA: Stanford University Press.

Egeberg, M. (2003). How Bureaucratic Structure Matters: An Organizational Perspective. In B. G. Peters and J. Pierre (eds), *Handbook of Public Administration*. London: Sage.

Foss Hansen, H. (2011). NPM Scandinavia. In T. Christensen and P. Lægreid (eds). *The Ashgate Research Companion to New Public Management*. Aldershot: Ashgate.

Gulick, L. (1937). Notes on the Theory on Organizations. With Special Reference to Government. In L. Gulick and L. Urwin (eds), *Papers on the Science of Administration*. New York: A. M. Kelley.

Gregory, R. (2003). All the King's Horses and all the King's Men: Putting New Zealand's Public Sector Back Together Again. *International Public Management Review*, 4 (2): 41–58.

Halligan, J. (2007). Reform Design and Performance in Australia and New Zealand. In T. Christensen and P. Lægreid (eds), *Transcending New Public Management*. Aldershot: Ashgate.

Halligan, J. (2011). NPM in Anglo-Saxon Countries. In T. Christensen and P. Lægreid (eds). *The Ashgate Research Companion to New Public Management*. Aldershot: Ashgate.

Hesse, J. J., C. Hood and B. G. Peters (2003). Paradoxes in Public Sector Reform: Soft Theory and Hard Cases. In J. J. Hesse, C. Hood and B. G. Peters (eds), *Paradoxes in Public Sector Reform*. Baden-Baden: Nomos.

Hood, C. (1996). Exploring Variations in Public Management Reform of the 1980s. In H. A. G. M.

Bekke, J. L. Perry and T. A. J. Toonen (eds), *Civil Service Systems*. Bloomington, IN: Indiana University Press.

Kettl, D. (2003). Contingent Coordination: Practical and Theoretical Puzzles for Homeland Security. *American Review for Public Administration*, 33 (3): 253–277.

Kickert, W. J. M. (2011). Public Management Reforms in Continental Europe: National Distinctiveness. In T. Christensen and P. Lægreid (eds), *The Ashgate Research Companion to New Public Management*. Aldershot: Ashgate.

Krasner, S. D. (1988). Sovereignty. An Institutional Perspective. *Comparative Political Studies*, 21 (1), 1988: 66–94.

Lægreid, P. and K. Verhoest (eds) (2010). *Governance of Public Sector Organizations. Proliferation, autonomy and performance*. London: Palgrave Macmillan.

March, J. G. and J. P. Olsen (1983). Organizing Political Life. What Administrative Reorganization Tells us about Government. *American Political Science Review*, 77: 281–297.

March, J. G. and J. P. Olsen (1989). *Rediscovering Institutions: The Organizational Basis of Politics*. New York: The Free Press.

Meyer, J. W. and B. Rowan (1977). Institutionalized Organizations: Formal Structure as Myth and Ceremony. *American Journal of Sociology*, 83 (September): 340–363.

OECD (1995). *Governance in Transition*. Paris: OECD.

OECD (2005). *Modernizing Government. The Way Forward*. Paris: OECD.

Olsen, J. P. (1996). Norway: Slow Learner – or Another Triumph of the Tortoise? In J. P. Olsen and B. G. Peters (eds), *Lessons from Experience*. Oslo: Scandinavian University Press.

Olsen, J. P. (2010). *Governing through Institution Building*. Oxford: Oxford University Press.

Ongaro, E. (2009). *Public Management Reform and Modernization: Trajectories of Administrative Change in Italy, France, Greece, Portugal and Spain*. Cheltenham: Edward Elgar.

Osborne, S. (2011). Public Governance and Public Services: A 'Brave New World' or New Wine in Old Bottles? In T. Christensen and P. Lægreid (eds), *The Ashgate Research Companion to New Public Management*. Aldershot: Ashgate.

Painter, M. and B. G. Peters (eds) (2010). *Traditions and Public Administration*. London: Palgrave Macmillan.

Peters, B. G. (2011). Responses to NPM: From Input Democracy to Output Democracy. In T. Christensen and P. Lægreid (eds), *The Ashgate Research*

Companion to New Public Management. Aldershot: Ashgate.

Pollitt, C. (1995). Justification by Works or by Faith. *Evaluation,* 1 (2): 133–154.

Pollitt, C. (2001). Convergence: The Useful Myth. *Public Administration,* 79 (4): 933–947.

Pollitt, C. (2003). *The Essential Manager.* Maidenhead: Open University Press.

Pollitt, C. and G. Bouckaert (2004). *Public Management Reform. A Comparative Analysis,* 2nd edn. Oxford: Oxford University Press.

Pollitt, C. and G. Bouckaert (2011). *Public Management Reform: A Comparative Analysis – NPM, Governance and the Neo-Weberian State,* 3rd edn. Oxford: Oxford University Press.

Pollitt, C., S. van Thiel and V. Homburg (2007). *New Public Management in Europe. Adaptation and Alternatives.* Basingstoke: Palgrave Macmillan.

Richards, D. and M. Smith (2006). The Tensions of Political Control and Administrative Autonomy: From NPM to Reconstituted Westminster Model. In T. Christensen and P. Lægreid (eds), *Autonomy and Regulation: Coping with Agencies in the Modern State.* Cheltenham: Edward Elgar.

Roberts, A. (2010). *The Logic of Discipline.* Oxford: Oxford University Press.

Røvik, K. A. (2002). The Secrets of the Winners: Management Ideas that Flow. In K. Sahlin-Andersson and L. Engwall (eds), *The Expansion of Management Knowledge – Carriers, Flows and Sources.* Stanford, CA: Stanford University Press.

Sahlin-Andersson, K. (2001). National, International and Transnational Construction of New Public Management. In T. Christensen and P. Lægreid (eds), *New Public Management. The Transformation of Ideas and Practice.* Aldershot: Ashgate.

Self, P. (2000). *Rolling Back the State. Economic Dogma & Political Choice.* New York: St. Martin's Press.

Selznick, P. (1957). *Leadership in Administration.* New York: Harper & Row.

Talbot, C. and C. Johnson (2007). Seasonal Cycles in Public Management: Disaggregation and Re-aggregation. *Public Money and Management,* 27 (1): 55–56.

Van Thiel, S., K. Verhoest, G. Bouckaert and P. Lægreid (2012). Lessons and Recommendations for the Practice of Agencifications. In K. Verhoest, S. van Thiel, G. Bouckaert and P. Lægreid (eds), *Government Agencies in Europe and Beyond: Practices and Lessons from 30 Countries.* Hampshire: Palgrave Macmillan.

Van de Walle, S. (2011). NPM: Restoring the Public Trust through Crating Distrust? In T. Christensen and P. Lægreid (eds), *The Ashgate Research Companion to New Public Management.* Aldershot: Ashgate.

Verhoest, K. (2011). The Relevance of Culture for NPM. In T. Christensen and P. Lægreid, (eds), *The Ashgate Research Companion to New Public Management.* Aldershot: Ashgate.

Verhoest, K., P. G. Roness, B. Verschuere, K. Rubecksen and M. MacCarthaigh (2010). *Autonomy and Control of State Agencies: Comparing States and Agencies.* Basingstoke: Palgrave Macmillan.

Weaver, B. K. and B. A. Rockman (1993). Assessing the Effects of Institutions. In R. K. Weaver and B. A. Rockman (eds), *Do Institutions Matter? Government Capabilities in the United States and Abroad.* Washington, DC: The Brookings Institution.

Wright, V. (1994). Reshaping the State. The Implications for Public Administration. *West European Politics,* 17: 102–137.

33

Comprehensive Reform and Public Administration in Post-Communist States

Tony J. G. Verheijen

The post-Communist states of Central and Eastern Europe and the former Soviet Union provide a microcosm of the problems inherent in comprehensive public administration reform processes. The group of states discussed in this chapter now range from (new) European Union (EU) member states candidate states to fragile states that have slid to extreme levels of poverty and have fallen back to the level of economic development of the lower strata of the developing countries. All these states share a common inheritance of the pre-1990 systems of governance as far as systems of public administration are concerned. '"... all the same, public administration across these (post-socialist) countries is more notable for similarities than differences both in its shortcomings and the stages of reform (Rice, 1992:117). Although already questionable at the time (Toonen, 1993:165), this common denominator has become increasingly less relevant as time has gone by. Yet, they all, including the EU member states, have faced lasting and significant challenges in putting in place

modern and professional systems of state administration.

As late as in 2002 the focus of discussions on this group of states was still largely on ways of overcoming the inheritance of the past in explaining the limited success achieved in building professional and performing public administration systems at that point in time. A decade later the divergence that has emerged between administrative development in these states overshadows what remained of previous communalities. For the EU member states of Central and East Central Europe, reforms stalled after they ensured admission to the EU. The officially voiced commitment to establishing merit-based civil service systems (as part of the 'European Administrative Space') was soon after entry replaced by a return to the heavily politicized realities of the early 1990s. A World Bank assessment of administrative development in the EU-8 (without Bulgaria and Romania) confirmed the reversal in earlier trends. What is more, it questioned the very paradigm of applying conventional civil service models to states that appear to have developed an entirely different political approach to civil service systems (World Bank, 2007). An OECD study published two years later draws similar conclusions (OECD, 2009). Yet, at the same time, in the EU candidate states of the Western Balkans a more traditional 'western like' approach to civil service development has continued to prevail.

The move away from traditional – professional, depoliticised, law based – European civil service systems does not mean that the systems are non-performing now. In fact, the adaptability of especially the Baltic States after the global financing crisis has shown otherwise, as well as their often solid performance inside the EU (World Bank, 2007). Arguably, the experience of Central and East European EU member states (and candidate states) shows above all that states with a different philosophy and approach to systems of public administration can co-exist within the EU system. This is a notion that has previously often been rejected.

While EU member States and candidate states function in the EU's realm, other post-Communist states do not. States like Russia and Kazakhstan have firmly subscribed to performance management as the starting point for administrative development and at this point are better compared with other BRICS than with EU member states. Some of the smaller states, such as Georgia and Armenia, have followed a similar track, with mixed success. On the other side of the prism, reforms in Ukraine and Belarus have become directionless. They have fallen victim to the political challenges that these states face. Among the Central Asian states, Kyrgyzstan and Tajikistan have fallen back to the realities of fragile developing states, with stop-and-go reforms.

All in all, more than 20 years after the start of transition, diversity among post-Communist states has become a microcosmic reflection of what one tends to witness globally: first, a challenge to previously firmly established notions of 'first best' solutions, derived from notions of best practise in building merit-based public service systems. Second, a strong emphasis on performance-based management as a guiding principle for administrative development. Third, a general scepticism of public sector based solutions to economic development.

The following sections will review some of the previous trends in civil service and administrative reform underlying this pattern. On the basis of this some lessons and overall conclusions can be drawn for the study of civil service systems and administrative reform.

THE STARTING POINT: A NEED FOR COMPREHENSIVE CHANGE

In order to understand process and approaches to reform applied in Central and Eastern Europe, it is important to first reflect on the nature of the task – the challenges – that states in the region faced. There are two important issues to be considered in this respect. The first relates to the nature, the reform processes. It is important to be aware of the comprehensive and holistic nature of reform that needed to be undertaken. In addition, it is important to consider the type of reform process that states needed to engage in: given the legacy of the previous systems, a process of developing a new type of administrative system, rather than 'reforming' what existed was needed. This, while international advice and demands focused often on traditional ways of conducting 'reform'.

The second issue is the context of the reform process, in particular the ideological environment of public administration development in the region, which has been far from conducive to success.

The need for holistic and developmental approaches

Following the start of the transition, the states involved were left with with a post communist legacy of administrative systems that were both irrelevant and inadequate for providing the framework-setting role that systems of public administration are expected to perform in a market economy. The systems of public administration as they functioned in the previous system of governance were at best an 'implementation machine' for decisions taken by the Communist Party apparatus. At worst they had been a means of suppression of citizens by the state. In this respect systems of public administration in post-communists countries were fundamentally different from and hard to compare to, for instance, systems in Southern European states before the transition and regime change in the late 1970s (Verheijen, 1995). A fundamental reorientation of the role of the administration in relation to citizens and in relation to politics was therefore required. The reform of policy processes is of particular importance in this respect. To remedy the lack of policymaking capacity was much more important than the managerial reforms international consultants early in the transition process meant to focus on. With lacking policies, there was little management to conduct.

Second, the role of systems of public administration under the previous regime was one of at least direct control of economic processes and in most economic areas direct, in house delivery of goods and products. The state apparatus, basically, a collection of state enterprises, with little or no, leave alone meaningful general governmental bureaucracy in the western European sense of the word (Toonen, 1993). A complete overhaul of the structure and functions of the state administration was needed.

Third, the notion of a professional civil service, which was different from the private sector both in terms of legal framework and of organization, had been eliminated in most states, with the exception of Yugoslavia. There this notion at least formally remained in place until the late 1980s. This has fundamental implications for the 'usability' of the staff that was in place when the transition

started. It required the definition of a new legal framework as well as a new training and socialization system.

These three reform requirements can only be successfully addressed if reform processes are defined and actually perceived in a holistic manner, and built on integrated strategies and approaches. In addition, the emphasis in addressing the systemic problems of the system of the public administration in the region needed to be developmental rather than reformist. The required reforms implied that systems be developed and built up, rather than existing systems were restructured and reorganised. For a short while in the early stages of the transformation, consultants and observers – ready for the 'Big Bang' and 'Rebuilding the Boat in the Open Sea' (Elster, 1993) – meant that it was just a matter of pushing back the state, to allow the market to 'free' itself. Soon it became clear that creating a market based economy did not happen by itself, which presupposed something of an effective governmental regulatory system, and did not in itself resolve the fundamental issues facing this group of states.

The context of public administration development in post-Communist states

For context, it is important to observe, that the start of the transition in the post-communist era coincided with a period in which neo-liberal concepts of public administration were dominant in thinking about the state and the public sector. More importantly, neo-liberal views were predominant in those countries from which initially inspiration was drawn, especially the USA and the UK, and when post-Communist states faced multiple priorities in difficult economic conditions. Hence reforming the state was not initially considered critical and the option to let it 'wither away' seemed attractive to the new political elites. And this in administrative systems where, for example, effective tax systems and revenue management did not exist, because the state enterprises formerly served as the main source of government revenue (Rice, 1992). The dominant – neo-liberal and managerial – focus of the international reform movement became more important than an empirical assessment of the functional, institutional and operational needs of the locus of reform, which the post-Communist state experience actually constituted and presented to the world. Given this focus – a 'modern market and management oriented paradigm' – it is not surprising that – traditional – public administration development was not considered a priority. Later on, in the second half of the 1990s, different views on the role of the state started to prevail. In addition, EU conditionality was defined also in terms of administrative capacities. Priorities started to shift, but by then further and some would argue almost irreversible damage had already been done both to systems of public administration and to their reputation in society.

It is here that we find the origin for the diverging paths that have emerged since. This ranges between more self-confident new EU member states that assert their prerogative to build systems that suit the political (politicized) context in which they function, to the focus on performance-based management that has prevailed in other states, outside of the EU's realm, as a response to pressures from society and the business community for a more service oriented and less intrusive civil and public service. Finally, administrative development in fragile states such as Kyrygstan, Tajikistan and, arguably, Turkmenistan is better compared to similar developmental contexts. There is a growing volume of work on institutional development in fragile and conflict-affected states, well summarized on the 2011 World Development Report on conflict affected and fragile states (World Bank, 2011). Critical issues for fragile states are to get some basic service delivery going and to ensure that justice and security systems function in a way as to build at least a minimum level of state credibility, without which a return to conflict is highly

likely. Moving to 'standard' level of institutional capacity in such context is, based on comparative analysis likely to take 20+ years. Hence a fundamentally different and long term approach to institutional development is called for.

THE REFORM PROCESS: DIVERGING TRACKS

The prevailing conditions in post-Communist states required an overall, holistic and developmental approach to public administration and civil service. In reality the actual history of the development of public administration has been one of piecemeal and ill-sequenced attempts to reform existing systems, often and sometimes pragmatically driven by (temporary) external conditionality.

The limited impact of holistic strategic approaches

A comprehensive approach to public administration development needs a strong strategic underpinning. Without a strategic vision, possibly embodied by a strategic document and related implementation plan, it is unlikely that comprehensive change can be brought about. Following an additional phase of muddling through and system deterioration, a more strategic approach started emerging from the middle of the 1990s. In part, this was a response to the administrative capacity requirements for EU accession, which were put on the agenda in 1996, and in part it was due to a series of domestic political changes in the mid 1990s that led to a change in the debate on public administration reform.

Strategic approaches adopted included, for instance, the Hungarian government's Public Administration Modernization Strategy (1995), which had a strong managerial approach, the Bulgarian government strategy for 'creating a modern system of public administration', adopted in 1997 and revised in 2001, and the Slovak government strategy on decentralization and modernization of the public administration (1999). Strategic approaches were also put in place in Latvia and Lithuania, but proved to be short-lived. The politicized context of both countries and frequent changes in governing coalitions negatively affected the durability of reform strategies. Hence, regardless of the 'carrot' of EU accession, consistent medium term reform processes were not put in place. Administrative reform remained in most cases a once off/single government undertaking.

The notion that a strategic underpinning for administrative development was required vanished in Central and East European states with EU accession. After 2004 administrative reform processes were put on the back-burner, only to re-emerge on the agenda after the 2008 financial crisis that significantly affected the Baltic States and Hungary in particular. The fiscal crisis that followed, forced countries into broad budget cuts, including salary reductions and public sector lay offs. While some of the budget cuts were implemented across the board, Latvia in particular used the fiscal crisis as an opportunity to address the wild growth of public sector institutions that had emerged during the EU accession process. The urgency of the crisis did not allow for a more strategic reflection on administrative reform, but helped in a practical sense in addressing some of the unresolved structural problems that had remained on the agenda after EU accession. Romania initiated a similar functional review based process in 2009, which will be discussed in the section on reforming administrative structures.

While administrative reform came to a halt in new EU member states following accession, the middle to the last decade saw a step up in reform activity in the Western Balkans. This included the adoption of strategic public sector reform documents in the 2004–2005 period in Serbia, Montenegro, Croatia and Bosnia-Herzegovina. Among those, the Serbia and Montenegro approaches

proved to be relatively durable. The fundamental difference between these documents and those that emerged in Central Europe, the Baltic States and Bulgaria in the late 1990s is that the approach opted for in the former Yugoslav states is one of relative confidence in the suitability of public sector solutions to resolving of critical developmental problems these states faced at that time. This, in contrast to the more public sector-sceptic approaches prevailing in central and east central Europe.

A different and more strategic approach to public sector reform emerged in Russia and Kazakhstan, which in each instance showed the tension between pressure for performance (as part of developmental dilemmas) on the one hand and intransigent and vested interest based public service systems on the other. Nowhere did this come out as clearly as in Russia. The country combined a very traditional approach to civil service reform (in the 2002 civil service reform program) with an innovative and performance oriented administrative reform concept, adopted in 2004 (World Bank, 2006). The tension between performance management practices and highly formalized (and relatively inflexible) civil service systems has remained part of the Russian reform process and has hindered reform progression, as shown, for instance, in a recent evaluation of performance management in Russia (World Bank, 2011). Kazakh reform processes showed a similar tension between a traditional civil service model, based on job security and gradual career progression, and a reform orientation based on performance principles, which requires a degree of flexibility in staffing and rewards. In the meantime, strategic reform processes were also initiated in Tajikistan and Kyrgyzstan in the early part of the last decade, focused on stabilizing and professionalizing public administration systems.

Considering the starting point, and the need for a radical overhaul of public sector management systems in all post-Communist states, the record of strategic, centrally driven reform processes is far from convincing. With few exceptions, strategic approaches to reform failed to take hold as political leaders neither showed the appetite nor the interest in investing in the systematic development of public sector management systems. As a result, the contribution of the public sector to development and transformation is in most countries deemed to be limited, and in some seen as negative. With limited respect and support from society, civil service systems in most of these states remain relatively marginalized and unable to attract the right skills and ability to make a difference.

Civil service reform: from legalistic approaches to rejection of formal models

An important element in the overall administrative reforms, have been efforts to establish or form professional civil services systems, preferably based upon law, following the example of the classical tradition in western states. This came as a reaction to observations like 'Governments have apparently not conceived of their employees as a bureaucracy-wide civil service' (Rice, 1992:21). Approaches to the development of civil service systems have moved from an initially legalistic approach, akin to that prevailing in most continental European states, to a diverse set of models, many of which at this point show little difference with general labor code arrangements. A large part of post Communist states, and in particular the new EU member states, no longer have a distinct legal regime government public sector employees.

To a large extent the demise of 'reform by legislation' is due to the negative perception of civil service laws both among politicians and the general public, and in particular in Central Europe. Numerous attempts to craft and adopt suitable legislation to govern civil service systems were made, many of which were an element of EU membership preparation. However, few of the pieces of legislation that emerged had the necessary local ownership required for laws to be durable.

At the time of EU accession, all but one of the 'EU-8' had some form of civil service legislation on the books, with the Czech Republic being the only country where no formal framework was operational. All laws adopted were molded by EU membership requirements, which emphasized stability and impartiality of the public service, as well as a high degree of permanency. This can be explained both by the 'old' EU member states' traditions as well as by the overriding concern from the side of both member states and the European Commission to have reliable and stable partners in EU decision making. Creating a Law that enshrines such principles was and is still seen as one of the best ways of guaranteeing stability and reliability.

The legal frameworks that were put in place in Central and Eastern Europe largely met EU requirements as they put varying levels of restrictions on political appointments, enshrined merit based recruitment and promotion systems, with formal oversight by civil service management institutions and strong employment guarantees. As noted above, this went against the grain of political tendencies in all these states, which advocated public service models close to private sector models, with a high degree of discretion for political leaders to appoint and dismiss staff. As a result, most civil service systems in place in Central and East Central Europe unravelled in the initial years of EU membership, and by 2007 very few states had even a semblance of a formalized civil service system in place (World Bank, 2007, OECD, 2009). However, regardless of the obvious move away from traditional European models, and the resulting limited stability in staffing and low levels of institutional continuity, the new member states have not underperformed to the extent that might have been feared. While absorption capacity of EU funds (and their appropriate use) has been an issue (World Bank 2007), their performance is not significantly worse than that of the weaker traditional member states. And where many states on the Southern fringe of Europe, having traditional civil service laws in place, have found it difficult to reform frozen systems, the flexibility in public sector systems in the Baltic States in particular made it easier for these states to adapt in the face of the 2008 fiscal crisis and arguably emerge out of it much stronger than some of the old member states. Hence, 20 years after the start of the transition, Central and East Central European states have evolved towards a civil service model that bears little resemblance to continental European practise.

As in the case of strategic plan approaches, discussed above, Central/East Central European states have largely become a separate model, with civil service systems that enjoy little protection from changes in political office holders and hold relatively little attraction as employers. It is difficult to assess what are the underlying factors explaining the reluctance to invest in civil service systems. It is often explained as a feature of the political culture that was formed based on a strong anti-state rhetoric, combined with an affiliation with states that share a less formalized approach to public sector management.

However, what is more difficult to explain is why the path of these states has diverged so significantly from the Western Balkans and parts of the former Soviet Union, where formalized, law-based civil service systems remain the rule. Where Central/East Central European states moved to dismantle much of the created civil service architecture in the middle of the last decade, new legal frameworks formalizing civil service systems were put in place in former Soviet states and the Western Balkans. While this has created tensions between performance orientation and formalized civil service systems in some states, as highlighted in the previous section, in none of these cases has the law-based civil service model been abandoned at this point. Even in fragile states like Kyrgyzstan and Tajikistan, a law-based organization of the

civil service system remains in place. Among the post-Soviet states, the only state that can be associated with the Central/East Central European model is Georgia, which has a laissez faire approach to civil service development that bears some similarity to pattern described above. Similarly, in the Western Balkans law-based civil service systems also continue to prevail. This is often described as a result of the 'Yugoslav exception' on the pre-transition models of civil service,[1] the significantly more formalized civil service models of Serbia, Croatia, Macedonia and Montenegro bear little resemblance to the models that have emerged throughout Central/East Central Europe.

Hence, the pre-occupation with legal frameworks that dominated much of the civil service reform debate between 1995 and 2003 has been replaced with a set of strongly varying models, ranging from relatively marginalized and political civil service systems among the new EU member states, to formalized, law-based models in the Western Balkans and much of the former Soviet Union, with systems in some of the latter living in uneasy cohabitation with performance driving public management reforms.

Designing administrative structures: a re-emerging issue

While patterns in the establishment of formal civil service systems diverge significantly, there is a strong commonality among virtually all states discussed here when it comes to organizational and management reforms. Functional review-based reorganization processes, while having lost much credibility globally, remain a common aspect of public administration development processes in Central/East Central Europe and post-Communist states. They have made a strong come-back in recent years since they are being perceived – for right or wrong – as a suitable instrument to address remaining dysfunctionalities (and high cost) in public administration systems.

Analysis from the early part of the last decade (UNDP, 2001, World Bank 2005) highlighted the strong remaining deficiencies in public sector organization and management across the region, including:

- the lack of a clear conception of the role of the state;
- leftover elements of previous systems remained in place, expanding public sector systems to an unsustainable level;
- mechanical and technical approaches to public administration prevailed, with low priority assigned to strategic thinking;
- intra- and inter-sectoral coordination systems were not functioning; and
- public administration systems remain opaque, with a lack of clarity in lines of accountability.

As late as 2002, this complex set of interrelated problems had not been fully addressed by any state in the region, for a number of reasons.

First, there is the multi-faceted nature of structural reform. Structural reform involves the re-definition of the role and position of ministries, their subordinated organizations and the core executive unit.[2] This is of particular importance in Central and East European states, since the core executive units of the administration under the previous regime used to 'shadow' line ministries and play a dominant role in the process of policy coordination. Policy processes were therefore 'top heavy', based on coordination at the top, and ultimately controlled by the Communist Party. Core executive units also tended to manage large numbers of subordinated institutions. Ministries in turn had direct responsibility for the management of a plethora of subordinated bodies, including often state enterprises and other institutions that in a market economy either belong in the private sector or, at the very least, in the 'third' sector.

A second element of complexity is the need for radical change in accountability systems, which has both institutional and cultural implications. In the past, accountability lines were directed towards the leading political party. Changing a system based on a single hierarchy with single accountability lines to a complex governance system of distributed accountability among various 'centres' to which institutions report is a highly difficult task.

Early attempts to address at least some elements of structural reform were made in Poland and Hungary in the mid-1990s. Poland carried out a substantial reform of the Council of Ministers' administration, with the objective of creating a small-core Prime Minister's Office, among others, by, 'pushing down' coordination tasks into the administration. In Hungary attempts were also made to 'slim down' the Prime Minister's office. However, these partial reforms proved to be insufficient for driving the necessary deep systemic change.

Initial approaches to come to a more comprehensive way of addressing reforms emerged in the late 1990s. One method applied was the use of framework laws to regulate the role and function of the different institutions in the administration and to rationalize their operation. For instance, in Bulgaria a Law on Public Administration was adopted in 1998, defining the type of institutions that can exist in the state administration, and their relations of accountability. Other states, such as Latvia and Lithuania, took similar initiatives. Further east, Kazakhstan and Kyrgyzstan have both been engaged in processes to reform administrative structures and rationalize accountability systems, using a step by-step approach. Functional review processes were used in each of these cases to flesh out more effective and accountable public management models. In later reform processes, such as the Russian administrative reform program, functional reviews became the norm as instruments to help streamlining administrative systems and increasing a service orientation. As noted earlier, Romania and Latvia are among EU member states to have recently applied functional reviews in their efforts to address growing fiscal deficits.

Functional review processes initially were often externally driven as 'prescriptions' for the delivery of budget support by IFIs, and focused largely on sector reorganization. In a next phase, the EU required sector reorganization as a condition for the use of agricultural subsidies, as well as for structural and cohesion funds. However, the use of functional reviews as reorganization instruments were also driven by political considerations and the realization that across-the-board staff cuts, which were often applied in the face of budgetary crises, neither resolved fiscal problems, nor helped in resolving issues of organization and performance (UNDP, 2001). Hence, while functional reviews and related organizational reform processes have lost credibility in other parts of the world (in particular in Africa and Asia) they remain the instrument of choice for designing organizational reforms in post-Communist states. This might be due to the way in which this instrument was used, which in Europe and the CIS was less externally imposed than in other parts of the world, and hence gave the instrument less negative 'baggage', allowing judgement on merit rather than ideology.

REFORM IN POST-COMMUNIST STATES: LESSONS?

The limited academic writing on public administration reform in post-Communist states uses a variety of explanations for the relative failure of reforms (Nunberg, 1998; Verheijen and Coombes, 1998). Apart from the difficult legacy of history, which was already mentioned above and is well documented, there are four further reasons why reforms have generally failed to produce results:

1 lack of political consensus on reforms;
2 the problem of reform design;
3 the changing and often contradictory signals of external organizations; and
4 a genuine political belief that continental European models of civil service are not appropriate for states undergoing rapid change.

The relative importance of these reasons for reform failure is important for the understanding of what may be achieved in the future and through what means. This is potentially of broader relevance, as the rejection of a traditional European civil service model by European states is a new phenomenon.

Lack of consensus: political polarization and a lack of continuity

Political consensus (or the long-term continuity of one political force) and consistency in reforms policies are generally considered to be key conditions for successful administrative reform. These conditions have not been met in large parts of Central and Eastern Europe and the former Soviet Union. In states where there is political consensus or where one political force dominates the political scene, there has often been a remarkable lack of consistency in administrative development policies. To take the argument one step further, in Central/East Central Europe there is often consensus on what is not suitable (protected and 'permanent' civil service systems), though not on what the alternative should look like.

As an aggravating factor, political party systems remain highly polarized, even 20 years after transition. While the former ex-Communist–former Opposition dichotomy has been mostly replaced with Nationalist/conservative–Liberal poles which are often a re-invention of the former, continuity in policies remains very low. Interestingly, this appears to affect economic policies much less than administrative development. The combination of general aversion to the continental European civil service model and low continuity in polarized political systems therefore logically prevents the formulation and implementation of long-term policies to stimulate administrative development.

States in the eastern part of the former Soviet Union have a much higher degree of political stability. Paradoxically, this has created better conditions to build long-term and consistent administrative reform policies. Russia and Kazakhstan stand out as the main examples, but cases like Armenia and Azaerbaijan have equally seen relatively consistent reform patterns. The 10-year process of administrative and civil service reform in Russia and the almost fifteen year process in Kazakhstan have started to show meaningful results, though downward accountability to citizens remains an issues to be addressed. Similarly, Armenia has been involved in a consistent process of reform since 2001, widely seen as having significantly contributed to economic development and growing foreign investment. While more volatile than in CIS states, reform processes in the Western Balkans lack the general aversion agains continental European models that appears to prevail in much of Central/East Central Europe. The systems emerging there are more likely to resemble public administration practices in 'old' Central Europe.

The problem of reform design

Lack of sound judgement in reform design is the second reason for the lack of progress in administrative development. The over-reliance on legislation as the main reform instrument, which is not surprising taking into account the legalist tradition of most of the states discussed here and the EU's insistence on 'reform by law', an overemphasis on civil service reform and the lack of attention to the reform of administrative structures and processes are all key to an understanding of the lack of success in administrative reform. The history of administrative development in post-Communist states provides a textbook illustration that legislation is not an appropriate reform tool on its own. Furthermore, it proves that the development of civil service systems cannot succeed without the necessary accompanying structural reform measures, which in turn need to be based on a well-elaborated assessment of organizational structures and capacities.

The role of international actors

At first glance, external pressure to carry out administrative reform seems to have been considerable. The EU is the main organization to have important political leverage in a majority of the states discussed here. EU membership conditions include the creation of a stable, professional and accountable administration,[3] which should provide incentives to Central and East European governments. However, the EU has been far from consistent in the signals it has sent to the candidate states (Dimitrova, 2001; Verheijen, 2000), and has no instruments to deal with member states, which means that once accession is granted, direct influence on administrative reform processes disappears.

Other institutions, in particular the OECD, the World Bank and the IMF, have also advocated giving more priority to administrative development. The former two organizations have often worked on behalf of the EU in supporting administrative reform, both through technical assistance (the OECD SIGMA program) and direct management of support programs, such as for instance the EU's delegation of the management of the comprehensive functional review program in Romania to the World Bank. External influence is much less direct in states further East. Reforms in Russia, Kazakhstan, Armenia and Azerbaijan are driven more by arguments of economic competitiveness (and for Russia and Kazakhstan comparison with other Middle Income Countries) than by external influence through the EU or IFIs. In the former two states, the role of external actors is limited mainly to technical advice and knowledge sharing.

Lessons learned?

There are various lessons to be drawn from the diverse experience of administrative reform and development in post-Communist states. First, those involved in administrative reform processes have often underestimated the deeply rooted nature of the problems the public administration systems in the region are facing. An over-simplification of proposed recipes for change, combined with a general indifference on the side of politicians, largely explain the failure of the first decade of reform. Where political institutions were reformed and started to operate, administrations were left behind. Second, even when and where the diagnosis of the problems in the systems was correct, and politicians could be convinced that reform was after all really needed, the medicines applied were not the right ones, or at least they were not applied in the right sequence. Designing and adopting civil service legislation without attacking the root causes of the problems in the administration first has proved to be a highly inadequate reform strategy, all the more so because the right of interference in appointments and promotions has been one thing that politicians have in most cases refused to give up.

The not-so-exciting truth remains that convincing political leadership remains the key condition for progress to be made. Definitely there is a much greater understanding in the region of the need and complexity of administrative reform than there was initially, as seen both in the examples from the Western Balkans and from some of the CIS states. Reforms initiated in Russia, Kazakhstan and some of the other CIS states also show that such processes can be successfully driven by internal actors. The dilemma for analysts remains with the new EU member states. While progress in streamlining structures and management systems has been made, and, in some cases, innovations in public management (including through e-government) have been introduced, civil service systems continue to lag both in terms of quality and stability. While political leaders have been clear in expressing what they do not want, a model of civil service beyond the current world of politicization and continuous change has not yet emerged. This now sets the new EU member states firmly

apart from both the 'old' EU and its predominant model of law based civil service, which to a large extent also applies to the Western Balkans, as well as from the blend of traditionalism and performance that has emerged in the more advanced states of the CIS. 'Reconvergence' towards traditional European public administration models appears an unlikely scenario at this point, though a debate on what kind of administrative system these states do want to establish has gained some urgency following the dire crisis experience in this part of the region.

NOTES

The opinions and analysis presented in this chapter represent the personal views of the author only and do not constitute in any way the official view of the World Bank.

1 Yugoslavia retained a distinct civil service system (as opposed to a general labour code regime) until the early 1980s and therefore had a civil service system more comparable to the continental European model, unlike in other post-Communist states.

2 For instance, Chancelleries, Prime Minister's Offices, Cabinet Offices or Councils of Minister.

3 As defined in the so-called SIGMA baseline criteria (World Bank, 2007).

REFERENCES

Dimitrova, A. L. (2001) 'Governance by Enlargement? The Case of the Administrative Capacity Requirement in the EU's Eastern Enlargement'. Paper presented at the ECPR General Conference, 6–8 September 2001, University of Kent at Canterbury.

Elster, Jon (1993) 'Constitution-making in Eastern Europe: rebuilding the boat in the open sea', *Public Administartion: An International Quarterly* (Special Issue on Administrative Transformation in Central and Eastern Europe (J. J. Hesse (ed.)), 71 (1/2) (Spring/Summer), pp: 169–219.

Nunberg, B. (1998) *The State After Communism.* Washington, DC: World Bank.

OECD (2009) *Society at a glance 2009: OECD Social Indicators.* OECD: Paris.

Rice, M. (1992) 'Public Administration in Post-Socialist Eastern Europe', *Public Administration Review*, 52 (2): 116–125.

Toonen, Theo A. J. (1993) 'Analysing Institutional Change and Administartive Transformation: A Comparative View', *Public Administartion: An International Quarterly* (Special Issue on Administrative Transformation in Central and Eastern Europe (J.J.Hesse (ed.)), 71 (1/2) (Spring/Summer), pp. 151–169.

UNDP (1997) *The Shrinking State*. New York: UNDP/RBEC.

UNDP (2001) *Rebuilding State Structures, Methods and Approaches*. Bratislava: UNDP/RBEC.

Vass, L. (2001) 'Civil service Development and Politico-Administrative Relations in Hungary', in T. Verheijen, (ed.), *Politico-Administrative Relations, Who Rules?* Bratislava: NISPAcee, pp. 147–75.

Verheijen, T. (1995) *Constitutional Pillars for New Democracies*. Leiden: DSWO Press.

Verheijen, T. and Coombes, D. (1998) *Innovations in Public Management*. Cheltenham: Edward Elgar Publishers.

Verheijen, T. (1999) *Civil Service Systems in Central and Eastern Europe*. Cheltenham: Edward Elgar.

Verheijen, T. (2000) *Administrative Capacity Building for EU Membership: A Race against Time?* WRR Working Paper 109. The Hague: WRR.

Verheijen, T. (2001) *Politico-Administrative Relations, Who Rules?* Bratislava: NISPAcee.

Verheijen, T. (2007) 'Independent Civil Service Systems: A Contested Value?', In Florian Grotz and Theo A.J. Toonen (eds), *Crossing Borders: Constitutional Development and Internationalisation*. Berlin: De Gruyter: 249–267.

World Bank (2005) *Increasing Government Effectiveness: Approaches to Administrative Reform in the Russian Federation*, Report by Yelena Dobrolyubova, Gord Evans, Nick Manning, Neil Parison, Yuliya Shirokova. Moscow, May.

World Bank (2006) *Institutional Reform in Russia: Moving form Design to Implementation in a Multi-level Governance Context*. Poverty Reduction and Economic Management Unit, Report Number. 35576-RU, June.

World Bank (2007) *The Limits of Innovation? EU-8 Administrative Capacity in the New Member States*. Poverty Reduction and Economic Management Unit, Report Number. 36930-GLB, December 2006.

World Bank (2011) *World Development Report 2011: Conflict, Security, and Development*. New York: World Bank.

Public Administration in Developing and Transitional Societies

edited by Goran Hyden

Part 12 of the Handbook highlights the issues associated with administering public services in societies undergoing economic and political reform. Although such reforms tend to be ongoing in all regions of the world, including industrial societies, their implications and outcomes differ from region to region largely because of differential legacies of state–society relations. They differ also among countries within a single region. Thus, it is important to point out from the outset that the authors in Part 12 are understandably unable to cover everything. We have made a decision to try to capture the essence of what has occurred in each region in recent years and, wherever appropriate, point out some of the more salient differences that exist in each region. There are obvious gaps that the critical reader may discern. For instance, we do not cover the issues of public administration associated with the countries in East Asia and the Middle East, or those that specifically pertain

to the many small island countries around the world.

Public administration in developing countries was once referred to as 'development administration', implying that there is something special about administering development. Although the term is still in use, it has lost its analytical specificity. Thus, in Part 12, we do not specifically discuss development except to the extent that shifting perceptions of the concept bear on how public administration in developing and transitional societies has been affected and reformed in order to correspond to these shifting notions.

More specifically, the chapters in Part 12 highlight both similarities and differences in the way public administration has evolved in recent decades, partly in response to historical legacies and changing domestic conditions, partly as a result of fresh ideas having been introduced from the outside. The two principal challenges that seem to come out of the individual contributions are (1) the task of emancipating public organizations from their embeddedness in social and political circumstances that curtail their performance, and (2) the exercise of finding models and instruments of reform that really work in developing or transitional societies. In this brief introduction, I shall place these issues in a broader and comparative context and highlight important points that the four authors in Part 12 of the Handbook make.

STATE–SOCIETY RELATIONS

A prevalent attribute of the state in developing and transitional societies is the discretionary power that is associated with occupying public positions. This may be most apparent at the top level where heads of state or cabinet ministers use their position of authority to make decisions that are often against even the faintest sense of public good. A similar type of discretion is also evident at lower echelons in the government hierarchy. Members of the public often find it difficult to obtain services or decisions from 'street-level' bureaucrats without first paying them a bribe. The point that the authors make in Part 12 is that this kind of behaviour is not just incidental but part of a system that they call 'patrimonial' or 'neo-patrimonial'. It is a significant feature of public administration in Africa, Latin America and South Asia and even in Central and Eastern Europe, where the pressures to abandon it have been strong, and it continues to be an issue. In making this point, they echo an argument that is quite common in the literature on politics and administration of developing and transitional societies (see, for example, Riggs, 1964; Clapham, 1982; Migdal, 1988; Bratton and van de Walle, 1997).

One can take this point as support for the position that missing in these societies is a culture that prioritizes legality and rationality in the sense that Max Weber described modern bureaucracies (Weber, 1947). Politicians are to blame for not allowing legal-rational forms of organizations

to evolve. Nef (Chapter 35), in discussing Latin America, and Olowu (Chapter 34), in examining Africa, see politicians as the root of the problem. Although Suwaj (Chapter 36) does not give this observation the same weight as the other authors, there is evidence in parts of the region that she covers – Central and Eastern Europe – of the same kind of tension between organizational ideals, on the one hand, and societal values, on the other. Given that the authors come to this conclusion from very different vantage points, this is interesting in itself. The considerably longer state tradition in Asia has not evolved beyond patrimonialism; nor has the now quite old post-colonial state in Latin America. As Olowu points out with reference to Africa, the absence of a state tradition on the Continent translates into not only patrimonialism but also immobilism, or inadequate executive capacity. Eastern and Central Europe, according to Suwaj, manifests similar features, although there is variation, with Central European countries generally having developed a better functioning public administration system than other countries in the region.

In order to fully understand how public administration in developing and transitional societies compares with that of industrial societies, it may be helpful to distinguish public administration systems along two parameters, the first dealing with executive capacity, the second with adherence to rules, or legality. With regard to the former, systems can be placed along a continuum from 'strong' to 'weak'; with regard to the latter, along a continuum from 'firm' to 'soft'. Drawing on the contributions made here and the literature at large, it is possible to use the matrix in Figure 1 to locate public administration systems in different parts of the world.

REFORM LESSONS

The second issue of special significance in Part 12 concerns the reform efforts. The history of reform is long in developing

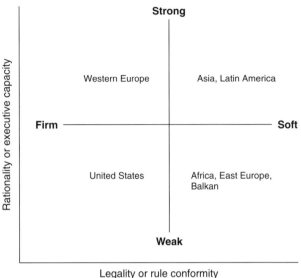

Figure 1   Typology of public administration systems

and transitional societies, but the results are very meagre. Ever since 'development administration' was invented by Western organization theorists in the 1960s as the preferable way of conceiving of the role of public services in promoting national development, the story has been rather dismal. As Schaffer (1969) noted over 40 years ago in one of the first assessments of this movement, bureaucracy is not really suited for tasks that involve coping with change. Because of its rule orientation, it tends to look inwards rather than outwards; it is better at maintaining law and order than promoting social or economic development. In short, there is a poor 'fit' between bureaucracy and development.

A similar situation seems to prevail with regard to more recent efforts to reform the public services. The New Public Management (NPM) approach that has accompanied structural reforms aimed at reducing the size of the public service has encountered criticism for lack of suitability to the conditions in developing and transitional societies. The contributors to Part 12 indicate the problems of implementing NPM in their respective regions. The early enthusiasm that

it had, especially in Central and Eastern Europe has since vanished. Much of the criticism comes from within the public service itself, but the scepticism can be found also in political circles. Much of this has to do with the fact that NPM was part of a broader reform package that was introduced – sometimes imposed upon – developing and transitional societies in the 1990s on the assumption that economic policy changes need the support of administrative reform in order to be sustainable.

The points made in Part 12 raise an issue that previous analysts of public administration have often returned to: Is administrative reform best carried out from within or does it need the 'push' from outside? Earlier studies, for example, by Montgomery (1987), have come to the conclusion that managers and administrators in developing societies are not different from those in Europe or North America. They hold most of the same values. The problem with studies of this type, however, is that they rely on interviews with managers without seeing them in their operational context. As Hofstede (1991) emphasizes, if administrators are studied in their cultural context, significant differences do occur because they are induced or forced to behave in ways that may differ from their own values. They simply cannot avoid the pressures of the societal culture in which they live – and work. Hofstede does not rule out the possibility of change from within, but he is sceptical of the idea that large-scale training programmes, in combination with organizational restructuring, whether along the lines of NPM or any other approach, will produce the expected results. Henderson (1990) suggests that globalization is bringing people and societies closer together; hence the importance of greater emphasis also on internationalization of the effort to build stronger public administration systems. While the chapters in Part 12 do not rule out the prospect for change, they are all cautious, if not outright critical, in their evaluation of the inputs from the outside.

Administrative reform is likely to be both slow and incremental. Public administration systems will continue to be pulled in opposite directions – both forward and backward. There is little room for a 'big bang' approach to progress. Suwaj's study of Central and Eastern Europe confirms that even in those countries where the old system literally collapsed and a new one had to be built from scratch, the legacy of the past continues to hang over the present. If one disaggregates the story that the four chapters in Part 12 tells, it is possible to argue that public administration in developing and transitional societies is being caught in a triangular hold where influences come from political sources

in the shape of patrimonialism, from within professional civil service cadres in the direction of routinization of rules, and from international consultants and finance institutions in the form of the urge to adopt NPM. Table 1 summarizes the principal differences between these three approaches and indicates the long distance that often exists between practice and reform promise.

It is significant that at least in the Central and Eastern European countries there is a search for a new model of administration that incorporates many of the core values of the classical Weberian model, yet is revised in order to serve contemporary governance needs. This search is pursued with a view to locating the system in a legal culture that is the basis for how governments function in Europe. In this respect, the current efforts are not as bold or radical but rather pragmatic and cautious. There is less evidence that something similar is happening in Africa, Latin America and South Asia, but experience with reform in these places may call for something along those lines: a reform effort that takes into consideration cultural values rather than brushing them off as obstacles.

CONCLUSION

In a book similar to this published over 20 years ago (Dwivedi and Henderson, 1990), Gerald and Naomi Caiden argued in a concluding chapter that comparative studies

Table 1   Sources of pressure within public administration systems in developing and transitional societies

Dimension/source	Patrimonialism	Routinization	New Public Management
Organizational objective	Power maintenance	Law and order	Development
Service rationale	Ruler	Rule	Result
Organizational structure	Patriarchal	Hierarchical	Team-based
Operational mode	Discretionary	Mechanistic	Organic
Staff orientation	Upward	Inward	Outward
Career system	Favoritist	Fixed and closed	Flexible and open
Handling of wrongs	Blaming others	Reward and Sanctions	Learning lesson

of administration abound, but comparative administration barely progresses (Caiden and Caiden, 1990: 396). This is not the place to enter into an argument with their position, but it seems that one reason for such a conclusion is that public administration theorists tend to assume that their particular theory has universal value and application. Their ambition is to accommodate all systems of public administration under a single theory or model. The empirical reality of developing and transitional societies defies such an approach, as the authors in Part 12 point out. A more inductive approach, for example, which acknowledges that public administration systems are subject to competing pressures from several sources, seems a more realistic and helpful approach, whether the objective is purely academic or practical in terms of offering prescriptive advice.

REFERENCES

Bratton, Michael and van de Walle, Nicolas (1997) *Democratic Experiments in Africa*. New York: Cambridge University Press.

Caiden, Gerald and Caiden, Naomi (1990) 'Towards the Future of Comparative Public Administration', in O.P. Dwivedi and Keith M. Henderson (eds), *Public Administration in World Perspective*. Ames, IO: Iowa State University Press.

Clapham, Christopher (1982) *Private Patronage and Public Power*. New York: St Martin's Press.

Dwivedi, O.P. and Henderson, K.M. (eds) (1990) *Public Administration in World Perspective*. Ames, IO: Iowa State University Press.

Dwivedi, O.P. and Mishra, D.S. (2012) 'Challenges of Culture and Governance in South Asian Public Administration', in B. Guy Peters and Jon Pierre (eds), *The SAGE Handbook of Public Administration*. London: Sage.

Henderson, Keith M. (1990) 'Rethinking the Comparative Experience: Indigenization versus Internationalization', in O.P. Dwivedi and K.M. Henderson (eds), *Public Administration in World Perspective*. Ames, IO: Iowa State University Press.

Hofstede, Gert (1991) *Cultures and Organizations*. London: McGraw-Hill.

Migdal, Joel (1988) *Strong Societies and Weak States*. Princeton, NJ: Princeton University Press.

Montgomery, John D. (1987) 'How African Managers Serve Development Goals', *Comparative Politics*, 19 (2): 347–60.

Riggs, Fred (1964) *Administration in Developing Countries: The Theory of Prismatic Society*. Boston, MA: Houghton-Mifflin.

Schaffer, Bernard (1969) 'The Deadlock of Development Administration', in Colin Leys (ed.), *Politics and Change in Developing Countries*. Cambridge: Cambridge University Press.

Weber, Max (1947) *The Theory of Economic and Social Organization* (ed. T. Parsons). London: Unwin Books.

34

Public Administration in Africa: Deepening Crisis Despite Reform Efforts

Dele Olowu

A strong state apparatus based on a Weberian-type of public administration has historically proved to be the best guarantee for turning policy aspirations into social and economic development. Forming an integral part of modernization the rise of such type of public administration in Western Europe and North America occurred simultaneously with industrialization, urbanization and the institutionalization of a capitalist economy in the late nineteenth century. This is the time when they abandoned a patronage-based system of administering public affairs in favor of one in which merit, compliance with formal rules and accountability to publicly elected officials became key components.

African countries were exposed to this system in colonial times but it was never institutionalized in a manner that survived political independence. In fact, nationalist leaders called it into question because it was viewed as too conservative for their development ambitions. The first generation of political leaders in these countries wanted to have

a direct control of the state apparatus, an orientation that encouraged the evolution of a patronage-based system of administration. Officials were promoted to senior positions based on personal loyalty, whether it was based on kin, old-boy networks or other narrow criteria. There was little trust in the public institutions that had been inherited from the colonial powers. Thus, very early after independence, public administration in most African countries began to suffer from a crisis of confidence.

Ever since the 1960s public administration in Africa has been the subject of reform efforts. The first generation of these reforms in the 1970s focused on making it more developmental by changing its structures and procedures. Western management consultants offered advice on how to make administration more attuned to the needs of social and economic development, borrowing best practices from developed societies. African civil servants were provided with pay incentives to adopt these new principles and procedures. Some progress was recorded but, unfortunately, this effort was not sustained partly due to the political context but also because in the 1980s African governments were increasingly being pushed to abandon development administration in favor of a market-based approach in which the role of the state would be much less significant.

A second generation of reforms of African public administration emerged in the 1990s until the early 2000s. These reforms took much inspiration from New Public Management (NPM) and encouraged a comprehensive revamping of the system. They aimed at making public services in African countries at one and the same time more efficient, effective and market or service-oriented. Public–private partnerships, executive agencies, citizen charters and other institutional mechanisms that had been tried out in other parts of the world formed the core of these reform efforts.

This overview of public administration in Africa, while bearing in mind its legacies in past years focuses on its more recent experience. It is divided into three sections. The first section discusses the changing international environment in which African countries find themselves and the implications for public administration. The second section deals with challenges facing efforts to reform the public services in these countries. The third section addresses some of the measures that give hope that, despite a deepening crisis, there is scope for improvement.

THE CHANGING ENVIRONMENT OF PUBLIC ADMINISTRATION

The development policies of African countries have increasingly become tied to global plans and agendas. This is apparent with regard to who sets the targets for development and who decides how development should be achieved. African development is currently assessed in terms of the global

Millennium Development Goals (MDGs) and of governance in terms of global standards of 'good governance'. At the same time, new international actors are increasingly influencing development in Africa; China and India are among the most important.

Development and service delivery

African economies have emerged out of the global crisis much better than other countries or regions. Still, there are two key indicators of a growing systemic performance crisis of these economies. The first is the likelihood that African countries will not achieve the Millennium Development Goals (MDGs), a number of eight specific targets agreed to by the United Nations in September 2000 with the objective of halving world poverty by 2015. Table 34.1 shows that of the 53 countries in the region, only 6 (11.3 percent) can be regarded as doing well in terms of having good prospects of attaining the targets. By 2010, five years to the finish line, they had already achieved four of the seven targets that relate to developing countries. Another nine countries can be added to the list that had achieved three of the seven targets, making a total of 15 or 28.3 percent of the countries in the region. The list is worrisome on closer inspection. First, most of the countries in the better segment are either from North Africa or having small populations. The more highly populated countries, especially in sub-Saharan Africa, such as Nigeria, Sudan, Democratic Republic of Congo and Angola are at the other end of the table – regressing or off-track. Second, while sight must not be lost of a few countries that have done well in the region, such as Ethiopia, Gabon, Gambia, Malawi and Eritrea, a majority of the countries (38 out of 53 or 72 percent) are in the last three columns – not so good/ poor performance or off-track. Thirdly, most of the countries performing well with regard to the MDGs, as we shall see later, fail the governance test and have become politically unstable.

Table 34.1   Millenium Development Goals score card – African Economic Outlook 2010

Good-4/7 Targets (6)	Fair-3/7 Targets (9)	Not so Good-2/7 Targets (20)	Poor-1/7 Targets (7)	Mostly Off-track/ Regressing (11)
Ethiopia	Algeria	Benin	B/Faso	Angola
Gabon	Cape Verde	Botswana	Cameroon	Chad
Gambia	Comoros	Burundi	C/Divoire	DRC
Libya	Egypt	Djibouti	E/Guinea	G/Bissau
Morocco	Eritrea	Ghana	Mozambique	Niger
Tunisia	Malawi	Kenya	Togo	Nigeria
	Namibia	Lesotho	Guinea	Somalia
	Rwanda	Liberia		Sudan
	Mauritius	Madagascar		Swaziland
		Mauritania		CAR
		Mali		Congo
		S/Principe		
		Senegal		
		Seycheles		
		S/Leone		
		S/Africa		
		Tanzania		
		Uganda		
		Zambia		
		Zimbabwe		

Source: OECD (2010).

This also brings us to another troubling development in the region: the growing infrastructure decay, with perhaps the exception of the North African subregion. A recent study systematically showed that the better economic performance of the countries of North Africa (Algeria, Egypt, Libya, Morocco and Tunisia) is traceable to the former's higher stock and quality of their public infrastructures. Whereas the size and quality of infrastructures in North Africa were higher (per capita) and have shown increase in the last 15 years between 1991 and 2005, the size and quality of infrastructures in other parts of Africa have declined. According to this study, 'in 1991–5, the level of infrastructure quality in North Africa, Southern Africa and West Africa was higher than that in South Asia. By 2001–5, only North Africa showed a higher level of infrastructure quality than South Asia' (Calderon 2009: 7). On the whole, North Africa is followed by Southern Africa, with Central Africa being the last region in terms of infrastructure. The

study showed that there is indeed a robust positive relationship between infrastructure stock and economic growth. The study further showed that increases in stock and quality of infrastructures stimulate a concomitant amount of economic growth. Unfortunately, most of the development plans and frameworks in many countries of Africa are centered on social (especially basic education, health) rather than the hard economic infrastructures that were focused in this study – namely, electricity, roads and telephones.

It is also significant that a relationship exists between infrastructure quality and public service quality, as demonstrated in Table 34.2. Generally, countries or regions with good-quality infrastructure also tend to have a higher level of management capacity in their public services.

Many of the factors that facilitate the growth of a Weberian-type of public administration, therefore, are still missing in African countries. The conditions in which public services can grow and become more

Table 34.2   African aggregate infrastructure stock and quality, compared with public management quality

Regions	Infra Stock* 2005	Infra Quality* 2005	Infra Quality 2010**	Public Mgt Quality 2010**
North Africa	0.7 (1)	0.2 (1)	45 (1)	68 (1)
West Africa	−0.8 (3)	−0.7 (3)	19 (4)	60 (3)
East Africa	−1.6 (5)	−1.9 (5)	20 (3)	52 (5)
Southern Africa	−0.2 (2)	−0.6 (2)	35 (2)	63 (2)
Central Africa	−1.2 (4)	−1.8 (4)	17 (5)	55 (4)
Africa	−0.75	−1.1		
East Asia	1.9	1.7		
West Europe	2.1	1.9		

Source: Calderon (2009, Fig.1) for Infrastructure (*); Mo Ibrahim Indicators (2010) for Public Management (**)
Note: Infrastructures include telephones, electricity, total roads.
Public management measures extent to which public service is structured to effectively and ethically design policy and deliver services.

service-oriented are not in place to the same extent that they are elsewhere where public sectors reforms have been attempted with a view to improving efficiency, effectiveness and service delivery. This is also true when checking the political conditions that tend to affect development.

Unraveling governance reforms

By the 1990s, the consensus was already fairly well established that governance was the main challenge confronting African countries (World Bank 1989: 60). A number of governance improvement programs were instituted by African governments, with strong support from development partners or donors. These governance reforms have unraveled in many countries in the region. Electoral democracy has not really translated into real democracy as the power of money, ruling parties and the armed forces have continued to be dominant in many countries even though they have diminished somewhat compared with the pre-reform era. A review of national elections conducted from 2004 to 2008 showed few leadership or regime changes. In Libya and Swaziland, there have been no changes for over four decades. Democratic change was quickly reversed in Mauritania and Niger, where the military

intervened. In a number of other countries, elections have been marred by violence (some of the most publicized cases occurred in Ethiopia, Kenya and Zimbabwe in relatively recent times), alleged and verified vote rigging and other forms of corruption of the electoral process and the absence of a level playing field for all participants. Though the OECD (2008) gives a glowing report of how 'more and more countries ... were legitimizing their governments through universal elections', it also noted, in particular, low turn-out rate and slightly increased instability even in traditionally stable countries and the very high level of violence associated with demonstrations of social dissent.

Until the Arab awakening in 2011, many of the countries in the region implemented democratization that enabled the ruling parties and oligarchs not only to remain in office but also to plan to transform their respective regimes to an hereditary monarchy, as they plotted to hand power over to younger family members. Democratic Republic of Congo (Kabila) and Togo (Eyadema) had gone down this path and other countries such as Egypt and Libya in the north were only biding the appropriate time to announce their plans along these lines. In other countries, such as Ethiopia and Eritrea, opposition parties are either formally proscribed or are prosecuted and persecuted.

In Ethiopia, most of the opposition candidates who won votes in the 2005 elections were rounded up as traitors and many had to flee the country. Even in countries where the opposition is given some space, as in Tanzania and Uganda, the ruling parties are accused of manipulating elections. Out of the 50 of all 54 countries in the region for which data was available, only eight countries were regarded by Freedom House, a global organization that rates all countries according to their enjoyment of political and civil rights, as 'totally free' in terms of political rights and civil liberties enjoyed by the country's citizens. These few were the countries that scored between 1 and 2.5 on Freedom House's scale. The majority of the countries were classified as either partly free (23) or not free (19), with scores ranging from 3.0 to 7.0 for a total of 42 countries, nearly 80 percent of the continent as shown in Table 34.3.

It is noteworthy that most of the countries recording good performance in respect of MDGs – e.g. Ethiopia, Gabon, Eritrea

and most of the North African countries in Table 34.1 – are to be found in the Not Free or Partially Free columns of Table 34.3. The last two sections speak to the economic and political context in which public administration functions. Predictions on performance in these two areas – economic and political – are not very encouraging. The United Nations Economic Commission for Africa report (2010) from its surveys in 35 countries in 2005 and 2009 found that corruption was one of Africa's most serious three national problems – the others being poverty and unemployment. It reported that corruption indicators dipped further in 2009 compared to 2005. Overall, there was only minimal (2 percent) governance improvement in the sample countries between 2005 and 2009.

New global actors

One of the more interesting developments on the African continent in recent years has

Table 34.3 State of African democracy – 2010

Free (1–2.5)	Partially Free (3–5)	Not Free (5.5–7)
Cape Verde – 1.0	Lesotho – 3	Algeria – 5.5
Ghana – 1.5	Senegal	Angola
Benin – 2.0	Seychelles	Congo
Mauritius	Sierra Leone	Côte d'Ívoire
Namibia	Comoros – 3.5	Egypt
South Africa	Liberia	Gabon
Botswana – 2.5	Malawi	Mauritania
Mali	Mozambique	Rwanda
	Tanzania	Cameroon – 6.0
	Zambia	Democratic Republic of Congo
	Burkina Faso – 4.0	Swaziland
	Guinea Bissau	Tunisia
	Kenya	Zimbabwe
	Morocco – 4.5	Chad – 6.5
	Niger	Guinea
	Nigeria	Equatorial Guinea – 7
	Togo	Eritrea
	Uganda	Somalia
	Central African Republic –5.0	Sudan
	Djibouti	
	Ethiopia	
	Gambia	
	Madagascar	

Source: Freedom House.

been the growing presence of other global actors and a shift away from dependence merely on aid. Africa's economic fundamentals have been changing in terms of investment, aid and trade with Western countries. For instance, sub-Saharan Africa's (SSA)'s exports to China increased at an annual rate of 48 percent between 2000 and 2005, 2.5 times as fast as the rate of the region's exports to the United States and 4 times as fast as the rate of exports to the European Union (EU). Africa's trade with the EU (its traditional trading partner) has dropped by half , so that Asia now buys about as much as the United States and the EU. And within Asia, China and India have eclipsed Japan and South Korea, buying 10 percent and 3 percent, respectively, of all of Africa's exports. Whereas this trade initially concentrated on the oil-exporting nations of Angola, Equatorial Guinea, Nigeria, Democratic Republic of Congo and Sudan, the economic boom of these two dominant Asian countries has included a number of other commodities, especially cotton and food. Africa is also importing capital goods from these two countries that are helping to bolster the competitiveness of the continent's fledgling assembly industries that produce goods for international markets. Moreover, the direct investments of these countries on the continent have also increased (Broadman, 2008).

It is instructive that China and India, which were once poor countries, invested heavily in boosting the capacity of their respective local and national governments over a period of time. There are important lessons that Africa can learn from this experience. Both countries' efforts at transforming their central government civil services and modernizing their local governments are well researched (Kohli 2001; Shah 2006; Chan & Ma 2011). They clearly took their cue from the astounding economic and bureaucratic reform trajectory of the Asian tigers. The lessons are that when global, big-push reforms are not feasible, it pays to focus on incremental change targeted at evolving a performance-oriented permanent

bureaucracy at the top as a part of the national strategy (what some refer to as strategic performance management [SPM]). It also involves enhancing the capacity of local governing elites, revitalizing local governance (Commonwealth Secretariat 2009; Olowu 2010).

In highlighting the lessons of how Chinese local governance enhances innovative service delivery and local economic development, Shah (2006: 165) concluded that 'a stronger role for local government in public expenditure has helped to promote foreign direct investment, improve efficiency in public resource allocation and foster economic growth'. It also helped to alleviate poverty, stimulated greater effort to levy and collect taxes, and stimulated private enterprises and state-owned enterprise (SOE) reform. Furthermore, decentralized governance has helped to build trust between citizens and the state by helping public officials to focus on 'results-based accountability to citizens' as it created incentives to improve local public services and responsiveness to local preferences' (ibid.).

These lessons are important for Africa as she engages in a triple transformation – *capitalist, democratic and demographic* – with her people moving in ever larger and growing numbers from rural to urban communities (Kapstein 2009). Focus on the challenges to public administration reforms will provide further insights into why these changes in the environment are important.

THE CHALLENGES TO IMPROVING PUBLIC ADMINISTRATION

The main challenges to improving public administration in Africa are a combination of external and domestic variables. Because the countries on the continent are so dependent on foreign aid from other countries, they are also likely to find themselves with little choice but to accept prescriptions issued by these external donors. This is especially apparent in the reform context, where the donors have insisted on large-scale and comprehensive reforms that have proved quite inappropriate. A second set of challenges is the lack of human resources to effectively manage the public service. African countries fall short of training enough cadres, and many of those who have been educated to the appropriate higher level either leave the country or move to the private sector. A third challenge can be found in the limited revenue base that these countries have, and thus the limited opportunity they have to develop a public administration with roots in local communities.

Inappropriate reforms

The reforms of the public service in recent years have been premised on NPM principles. These reforms have made some important gains in Africa but their core premises have also unraveled. In particular, the approach to funding the state and the reforms, premised on donor aid, has been challenged. Related constructs such as budget support, country ownership which were the underpinnings of the Paris Declaration of 2005 have come under increased scrutiny. Key unresolved issues include pay and productivity improvement efforts in the public service linked to wider governance changes.

In Paris in 2005, the rich countries undertook to raise the level of donor support to approach the 0.7 percent level of gross domestic product (GDP) as their contribution to ensuring the actualization of the MDGs. Donors and recipients, alike, undertook to promote national leadership and ownership of the development process, the strengthening of country systems and institutions and procedures for managing development resources that are effective, accountable and transparent. They identified some mechanisms for actualizing these: notably, medium-term expenditure frameworks (MTEFs), budget support mechanism to deliver aid, harmonizing assistance to partner countries

to promote complementarity, collaborative behavior and use of common arrangements that simplify procedures and ensure mutual accountability systems for development results in partner and donor countries.

The question is how far these new measures have really engaged the economic, political and institutional crises prevailing in African countries. Judging from the literature and practical experience gathered in these countries, the following four issues stand out as remaining challenges.

The first is that institutional and political systems take time to change, as they reflect wholesale human behavior and they require sustained incentives to change. Chang (2003: 115) notes that it took the now developed countries (NDCs) several decades, and in some cases centuries, to develop what are referred to as the core good governance institutions, i.e. universal suffrage (democracy), bureaucracy, judiciary, property rights regimes, corporate governance and financial regulations, from the time when they perceived their need for them. Moreover, the experience of these NDCs also shows that there is no single model of democracy. For instance, each country has chosen the democratic model that is most consistent with her political culture: majoritarian or consociational (Lijphart, 1984). Specifically, with respect to the bureaucracy, Chang points out:

> Although some of the changes advocated by NPM may be useful in fine-tuning what is basically a Weberian bureaucracy that already exists in the developed countries, the more relevant question for most developing countries is how their bureaucracies might attain even the most basic 'Weberian-ness' (Chang 2003: 78).

This is also the task which the NDCs were confronted with in the earlier days of their development. Bureaucratic reform in Germany (Prussia) took place between 1713 and 1860, in Britain from 1780 to 1834 and in the United States from 1883 to 1933; the centenary of the reforms was celebrated as late as 1993 (Schiavo-Campo & Mcferson 2008). By contrast, reform proponents give a much shorter time for radically transforming specific public institutions. No one of course expects that new countries would spend a centenary to transform their public institutions but the prevalent reform paradigm also assumes a social and political reality that does not exist.

The second issue is the economic and financial policy set-up, which is grounded in the Poverty Reduction Strategy Paper (PRSP) framework. The latter is seen as a restoration of state-led development and planning processes that were abandoned in the wake of Structural Adjustment Programs (SAP). The donor support that goes with PRSP also offers a financial life line to many African countries that were no longer able to generate funds for capital or development expenditures (Doe 1998). PRSPs also connect well to the MDGs, country ownership and systems development.

PRSPs, however, are criticized for their ambitious expectations, as well as their operational methods. First, donor behavior has often been at odds with the country ownership agenda. Several donors are still reluctant to channel substantial funds through budget support for the medium term, preferring instead annual project support that is neither harmonized with other donors nor with the country PRSPs. Second, whereas many donors would readily fund retrenchment, they are reluctant to fund pay raise or incentive increase for understandable reasons. Nevertheless, a few experiments, introduced in Tanzania as the Selected Accelerated Salary Enhancement Scheme (SASE) and in South Africa as the Senior Management Service (SMS) show that such reforms, if well targeted, are not only politically feasible but also economically sustainable (Stevens & Teggemann, 2004; Cameron 2010). Third, critical institutions are excluded from the PRSP process. Legislatures, decentralized organs and civil society organizations are overlooked; yet these are institutions that are critical to poverty reduction at national and local levels (Narayan et al. 2001; Barkan 2009). It is significant that in most countries

of the world, local governments deliver five of the seven MDG target services (Narayan et al. 2001; Millet et al. 2006).

PRSPs have been introduced for the convenience of the donors as much as for the benefit of their African partner countries. In the context of the relations between donors and recipients, these instruments have become controversial for several reasons. One is that the effort emphasizes reforms on the public expenditure but not the revenue side. The PRSPs have typically been accompanied by another institutional innovation – the medium-term expenditure framework – which is an attempt to reconcile multi-year outcome-based plans with annual budgets that reflect clear policy priorities. PRSPs and MTEFs are natural bedfellows because the objective of the latter is to ensure that only high-priority programs are funded. Furthermore, MTEF offers an instrument for correcting some of the most serious weaknesses of many African government expenditures (unclear government priorities, poor execution of policies and programs, misallocation and regressive expenditures) in that it enables a shift to be made in spending priorities. But technical problems make MTEF a near impossibility: lack of timeliness of budget submissions and approvals; unrealistic and changing revenue estimates; and poor cash forecasting and inability to prevent expenditure commitments from exceeding authorized limits on cash outlays. Budgetary discipline is often lacking and the problems associated with budget support have only aggravated matters (Alfarez 2010).

Development assistance continues to labor under the same old constraints, and these continue to weaken recipient country systems' capacity, especially in Africa (UNCTAD 2006).[1] First, aid remains largely uncoordinated and unpredictable in spite of the exhortations to harmonization and higher, sustained aid levels. The actual aid delivered is often less than commitments made. Second, aid is still largely focused on projects, with parallel agencies, and is increasingly bilateral. Indeed, many donor countries do not subscribe in principle to budget support and use of poor country systems, etc. Only 26 percent of all aid to 14 African countries went to budget support in 2004 and only 20 percent of all bilateral aid. Multilateral aid has increased in recent times compared to the past decade, due in large part to debt relief, but it is still less than 30 percent of all aid. Third, aid is going increasingly to social sectors. While this is understandable because of their connection to PRSPs and MDGs, it also takes support away from development and growth objectives and sectors, especially agriculture and industry, in particular SMEs. Some wonder whether the underlying causes of poverty are really being addressed. Social spending as a proportion of technical cooperation in SSA rose from about 50 percent (1992–1996) to 70 percent (2000–2004) while the share of economic infrastructure fell from 7 to 4 percent within the same period. Furthermore, most SSA PRSPs attach no importance to higher education (discussed below).

All of these have invidious implications for public administration capacity. The problems are not exclusively the donors. Africa's own partnership framework, the New Partnership for African Development (NEPAD), expects that the bulk of resources to finance the resource gap of US$64 billion per annum (about 65 percent of all resources required) to bring development performance to an expected 7 percent GDP growth would come from outside the continent (Maloka 2002: 493).

Human resource challenges

The first human resource challenge to prevailing reform is that the demand for and supply of high-quality human (technical) resource skills have fallen over time for the civil services of most African countries. In the era of globalization, such indigenous skills are moving into countries where they can attract the highest pay incentives. This is further complicated by the fact that due to a number of factors – aging populations, new technologies, mobility of multi-national businesses and finance, etc. – rich countries are attracting skills from the developing world with immigration programs for professionals and skilled labor. There is now a clear consensus that the resulting brain drain has an impact on poverty reduction efforts in poor countries.

Under certain conditions, brain drain could become brain gain. For instance, if the sending countries received in return huge remittances – some countries like the Philippines and Cape Verde receive over 20 percent of their GDP from remittances, higher than the development aid to these countries – such remittances can actually stimulate the economy. This works, however, only if recipient country governments provide the environment for individual citizens to invest their earnings from remittances in productive and not consumption expenditures.

Public services in poor (African) countries thus confront a dilemma: they need their scarce skills, but given the erosion and compression of salaries paid to scarce skills in the public service, there is both internal and external migration of such skills – out of the public service and out of the country, respectively (Kapur & McHale 2005).

A second issue compounds the one above – the decline of the higher educational system. Many African countries have not been able to invest in higher education, preferring to focus scarce financial resources on basic education (Bloom et al. 2006). This is further aggravated by the fact that many African national governments have reneged on an earlier commitment to meritocratic recruitment into public service in favor of patronage, ethnic balancing and politicization (Olowu & Erero 2009, Cameron 2010). Hence, on both the supply and demand sides, scarce skills have become difficult to attract and/or retain. Whereas other developing countries lost only 10–30 percent of their skilled talents that were trained in Western countries in 1990, Africa, the worst affected among the world's regions, lost 75 percent of its tertiary educated work force, followed by Asia/Pacific (52 percent), Latin America (48 percent) and Eastern Europe (20 percent) (Lowell & Findlay 2001). Little wonder that the United Kingdom Commission for Africa (2005) lamented that the continent spends an estimated US$4 billion annually to recruit some 100,000 skilled expatriates who replace some 70,000 African professionals or managers that leave annually to work abroad.

Another human resource management challenge arising from years of salary compression, as politicians pursue egalitarian goals at the expense of a quality civil service, has been the tendency for salaries of people in the lower cadres of the civil and public service to be higher than those paid to counterparts in the private sector while the salaries of those with expertise stagnate. The result is an excess of staff – whose data are poorly and corruptly kept, leading to a large number of ghost workers – in the junior and generalist cadres but scarcity and huge vacancies in the superior and highly skilled cadres.

Yet another important challenge that is readily evident in most African countries is the tendency for scarce skills to concentrate in the central government headquarters and in the largest cities, whereas the real needs for civil servants exist in the rural communities – for health, agriculture, education or small-scale and rural industrialization. It is common to find a lot of officials at the headquarters with little or nothing to do, while the health clinics and field administration systems lack essential staff. Remuneration and other reward systems, and the absence of effective monitoring systems of excessively centralized governments, further aggravate the situation. The result is that basic services are lacking in the rural communities, which further drives away good staff. For most countries, the local government systems remain weak in spite of several rounds of decentralization or local government reforms (Wunsch & Olowu 1995; Olowu & Wunsch 2004; Dickovick & Rield 2010; Olowu et al. 2010a).

In Ghana, for instance, the 1989 local government reform was a bold policy initiative that empowered semi-autonomous district assemblies (or local governments) to handle their own finances and human resources. These key resources have remained in the central government under both military and civilian governments – on the ostensible reason that local governments and decentralized agencies lack capacity (Ayee 2004). Early successes of local government reform that incorporated financial and human resources management devolution in Uganda and Tanzania have also been reversed recently by their respective central governments. In Nigeria, huge resources (almost 30 percent of the country's revenue sources) have been poured regularly into the country's revitalized local government system since the early 1990s, but the poor accounting and the culture of corruption at that level – as in all levels of government – has not allowed these resources to translate into critical skills or the desired development (Olowu et al. 2010b) Tanzania has had a similar experience (Tidemand & Msami 2010).

By contrast, in most industrialized countries (and the industrializing nations of the world), the local state has a substantial responsibility for the services that are used by citizens – from basic services like education and health, which must be tailored to community needs, to infrastructures such as water, roads, utilities, to planning and land use management, etc. In sample OECD countries, the local state is responsible for almost 30 percent of total government expenditures (TGE) and 12.8 percent of the GDP – some spend as much as 60 percent of total government expenditure, while it ranges from 61 percent (Canada) to 12 percent (Portugal). A survey of local governments in OECD countries found that even though local governments have suffered attrition in the Western world since the 1980s as a result of private sector-like innovations (the New Public Management), their operations remain sizeable (Kersting et al. 2009) Whereas other developing countries in Asia and Latin

America have begun to enhance the capacities of their local state, only a few countries have gone beyond paying lip service to the development of the local state in Africa (World Bank 2004; Schiavo-Campo and McFerson 2008; Kersting et al. 2009; ILO 2001; Olowu et al. 2010a).

The local state cannot, however, be nurtured and developed, except by an intelligent and highly motivated national public service that appreciates the strategic importance of devolving some of its own responsibilities to other institutional actors so that it can be more effective in its critical tasks of strategic planning, policy development, monitoring and coordination. Unfortunately, compared to other countries, African public services have fallen behind in terms of number and quality of their public officials – at national and local levels – in stark contrast to presumptions that African public services are oversized or too large. The available data shows that whereas African governments had 2 percent of their population employed in government (0.9 percent in the central government and only 0.3 percent in local government), OECD countries had 7.7 percent (2.5 percent in local government as against 1.8 percent at the national level). OECD is followed by Eastern Europe (6.9 percent), Middle Eastern and Northern African countries (3.9 percent) and Latin America and Asia (3.0 percent and 2.6 percent, respectively) (Schiavo-Campo 1998). Moreover, most of the African countries' efforts at devolution reforms are oblivious of the fact that the continent is one of the fastest urbanizing parts of our planet.

A final human resource management challenge is how to connect pay to performance. Available (IMF) statistics show that African civil services have suffered in particular from wage erosion and wage compression (Schiavo-Campo 1998; Schiavo-Campo & McFerson 2008). Some of the public sector reforms have sought to address these problems using technical or political approaches. For instance, Uganda raised compression ratios from 5 percent to 28 percent between 1992 and 2001 but fell back again to 20 percent. Similar gains were lost by Tanzania, Ghana, Burkina Faso and Senegal. Only two countries recorded sustained decompression – Botswana and South Africa (Kiragu & Mukandala 2005; Cameron 2010). Technical approaches tended to focus on economic variables such as a living or minimum or market wage. Inevitably, political factors complicated the implementation of these technical approaches. Political considerations include the relative power of the government, the influence of civil society and media groups and, especially, of trade unions (Kiragu & Mukandala 2005; see also Olowu 2010 for a full review of pay levels, wage bills and decompression for analysis of their sample of eight countries drawn from different regions of the continent).[2]

On the whole, besides monetization (tried especially in Eastern and Western Africa), most of the countries have had to abandon the economic rationality models and settle for politically driven patronage approaches. They are thus not able to raise and sustain salary levels that can guarantee the attraction and retention of quality civil servants, especially where it matters most – at the highest levels. And since a skilled civil service is key to state developmental and governance reform outcomes, their economies wallow in poverty. The quality of the civil service, the economy and politics further degenerates.

Wage issues are thus problematic not only because of their political nature but also because of economic and fiscal considerations. But critical data for the systematic empirical analysis of existing pay structures and pay-setting practices, including systematic evidence on public–private pay differentials, have also been important. In particular, relevant data on the pay–employment nexus, in terms of the the the willingness of governments to trade-off real wage levels against higher levels of public service employment, are not readily available (Valentine 2006).

Limited resource mobilization

Behind the human resource challenges is the fiscal challenge. Many African countries are heavily dependent on aid to finance both recurrent and capital expenditure. Those that are not dependent on aid rely on mineral or agricultural exports. The effect of windfall natural resource gains and aid are the same on the national public administration system, as ably summarized by Dambisa Moyo. First, both set of countries are susceptible to theft and have provided practically unlimited opportunities for personal wealth accumulation and self-aggrandizement (Karl 1997; Moyo 2010: 48). The only difference is that while efforts are being made through the Extractive Industries Transparency Initiative (EITI) in natural resource -rich countries, little effort is made to question the corruption inspired by aid. Second, aid fosters more aid, as it fuels corruption and nations quickly descend into a vicious cycle in which aid props up corrupt governments that interfere with the rule of law and resist public sector reforms aimed at transparency of civil institutions and protection of civil liberties. These, in turn, make domestic and foreign investments unattractive, reduce economic growth and jobs and increase poverty levels.

In this regard, an important issue in most SSA countries is the ability to mobilize domestic resources. The OECD (2010: 13) notes that many countries in the region collect as little as half of their potential and that when resource-related taxes are excluded, most of the countries in the region fall into low-tax effort countries with some of them collecting as low as US$11 per capita. The poor or sometimes non-existing collection of urban property taxes in many of Africa's rapidly growing cities is the most obvious illustration of the problem (Olowu et al. 2010). The same reasons for the poor performance of the allocative function can be adduced for the non-performance of the other economic functions of all governments – distribution and stabilization – inability to attract and retain the critical skills required

for performing these tasks and the absence of political structures and incentives that make these imperative.

It is in this sense that taxation is regarded as an important and under-rated entry point in the sense well-designed taxes could increase revenues, refocus government spending on public priorities, improve democratic accountability and help to consolidate stable institutions. The origins of representative government are intimately connected to the evolution of taxation. While aid's share of GDP in Africa increased fivefold between the 1960s and 1990s and the number of aid recipients increased from only 21 in 1998 to 29 by 2006, there are concerns that high levels of aid such as those create incentives for donors and recipient governments that discourage building capable and responsive states. The IMF adjudged that 71 percent of African countries receiving more than 10 percent of GDP in aid in 1995 were also in the group of countries to have made a less than expected tax effort. Higher aid levels were associated with larger declines in the quality of governance and lower taxation as a proportion of GDP (Brautigam 2008). The OECD made a case for improving taxation levels in Africa as a goal of economic and governance improvement policy in 2010.

The overall result of the above challenges – poor service delivery and inadequate or irrelevant reforms – has been Africa's descent into a fourth world. Africa is home to 70 percent of all the least developed countries and perhaps the countries designated by the World Bank as LICUS (Low Income Countries under Stress). Over half (57 percent) of the world's fragile states are in Africa. Most of these states are in conflict or just coming out of one (African Development Bank 2006). In such situations, improved public management is practically impossible in the short run, except stimulated and supported by non-governmental, community-based and faith-based agencies (Fass & Desloovere 2004; Trefon 2010).

Although this chapter so far has argued that the crisis of the state has deepened, the same crisis has also instigated a raft of fresh efforts aimed at improving state and public sector performance. These efforts are the subject of the remainder of this chapter.

SCOPE FOR IMPROVEMENT

There are a number of factors that need to be considered finally as part of this assessment of the state of public administration in Africa: (1) the change of the political opportunity structure; (2) the emergence of regional African initiatives to improve governance; (3) a renewed emphasis on finding ways of decentralizing authority; (4) the rise of new public–private partnerships; and (5) the growing use of political economy analysis.

First, the critical and growing importance of dissent outside of the state and the ruling party – even in parts of the continent thought to be beyond such restiveness, especially among the northern African countries – has opened up opportunities for building reform coalitions comprising internal and external agents.

Generally, too much reliance has been placed in the past on the state in tackling the challenge of development and democratization. The last few years have demonstrated that governance reform cannot be carried out by agents of the state working with international development actors. Much more reliance must be placed on building coalitions between reformers within and outside the state. It is this factor that resulted in the differential outcome of popular protests in Northern African countries (and other Arab nations): the role of the army in Egypt and Tunisia in bringing about some kinds of political reform compared with their roles in Gadhafi's Libya and other Northern African countries that witnessed sustained street protests (see Goldstone 2011). However, this is not limited to North Africa. Transitions have happened in countries of West Africa (notably Niger and Sierra Leone) and also on the east coast (Tanzania, Kenya, and even in

Sudan, where several years of fighting were finally resolved in favor of a referendum that paved the way for the new nation of South Sudan). This lesson is not only applicable at the national level. Even at the local level, analysis of decentralization programs in the continent have underscored the importance of coalitions to ensure that devolutionary decentralization is not reversed, as has been the case in many countries in the region (see Ndegwa & Levy 2004; Olowu et al. 2010a).

Second, since the early 2000s an impressive effort has been made by Africa's leaders to improve the architecture of governance through strengthening regional and subregional supranational structures, especially in view of the relatively small size of African states, to tackle several social and economic challenges they confront. These initiatives have had implications for the national public administration systems in a number of ways. The most obvious is the change from the Organization of African Unity (OAU) into an African Union (AU) on July 9, 2002, with specific and clear visions for economic and political renewal at national level. The Partnership for African Development (NEPAD) program and new implementing organs aimed at revitalizing democracy and development on the continent followed this change.

Perhaps best-known example of the latter is the African Peer Review Mechanism (APRM), founded in 2003 with the aim of enforcing AU's Declaration on democracy, political, economic and corporate governance. The APRM process subjects the political institutions (including the public service) of a country to intense scrutiny from several fronts – financial, administrative, structural and political context, etc. A total of 30 of the 54 AU members have acceded to it and, of this, 13 have submitted themselves to the APRM process. The process stresses the responsibility of national governments and other stakeholders, especially civil society actors, to ensure and monitor the domestication and adherence to the standards and conventions set up in the four thematic areas of the APRM: democracy and political governance; economic governance and management, corporate governance; and socioeconomic development. Earlier, in 2001, African Ministers of Public Service had adopted a charter on the African public service. After a series of meetings, this draft was proposed as a charter on the values and principles of public service and administration to be incorporated into the APRM. In July 2003, a set of similar standards for fighting corruption had been articulated and adopted.

Another illustration of the increasing power of supranational initiatives is the growing clout of subregional bodies. Several of these regional economic communities (RECs) had remained weak and ineffective for many years since their founding in the 1990s for a variety of reasons. However, in July 2007, the AU rationalized these bodies into eight. Two of the eight RECs – namely, the Common Market of Eastern and Southern Africa (COMESA) and the Economic Community of West African States, (ECOWAS) – have become important players in their respective sub-regions in the areas of free trade, free movement of persons and goods and conflict resolution. ECOWAS has been particularly successful in resolving conflicts within and between countries in her subregion. The continent is still quite far from her aspirations towards free trade area, common market, central bank and monetary union and a single currency (now targeted for 2032) but these two subregional entities have received positive reviews (*Economist* 2011; Bassett & Straus 2011). The main challenge is to fully institutionalize and indigenize these initiatives, especially in view of the fact that most of them, such as APRM, are funded mainly by development partners.[3] For instance, many countries have not engaged APRM due to the requirement that each participating country must pay US$100,000. For the countries that have engaged the process, it has impacted favorably on the implementation of key governance and PA reforms and refocused national attention on MDGs (Herbert & Grudz 2008).

Third, several African countries have also been compelled by internal and external dynamics to devolve the centralized state structure and rebuild from below as they reconstitutionalize the state. Africa has one of the lowest indices of decentralization compared to other countries of the world, even though it is the fastest urbanizing continent that requires strong municipal governments and there is strong demand for devolution among her citizens (Kapstein 2009; Little & Logan 2009). A number of them have followed the good practice of including subnational governments in their new constitutions – Nigeria, South Africa, Uganda, Ghana and Kenya, to mention only a few, while others, especially in Eastern and Northern Africa are likely to follow (Tanzania, Tunisia, Egypt and Libya). It has also emerged, however, that the obstacles to devolution have been underestimated. Capacity is perhaps one of the most important issues, but this is not just capacity at the local but also at the national level to design, promote and sustain devolution (Wunsch 2002; Awortwi 2011). This may explain why a number of countries have initiated, not full-blown devolution, but asymmetric decentralization that focuses efforts in some specific sectors before undertaking a general or comprehensive national devolution – e.g. selectively in health, education and water and sanitation sectors in Tanzania, Ghana and Botswana. Some other countries have also settled for partial devolution, whereby cities with resources and potential actors to agitate and defend local autonomy are opened to devolution ahead of rural areas where deconcentration continues to prevail. This is the agenda that is being implemented in Mozambique and is also being practiced effectively in other countries in the region – e.g. Botswana, Ghana and some Francophone countries like Senegal. The idea of one size fits all for all localities is giving way to differentiation.

Fourth, one of the more successful reforms of the African state has been the creation of executive agencies (EAs). Perhaps the most notable and successful in many countries has been the semi-autonomous revenue agencies (SARAs). Their success stories have led to a wholly new area of research in the region – the islands of excellence (Roll 2010). The downside is that the success of these agencies may compromise strong country systems, as attention and resources are focused on these few islands, although much also depends on the reform design as they relate to SARAs. One longitudinal study of SARAs in 45 African countries from 1972 to 2005 confirmed that tax reform efforts substantially raised tax incomes, and that these reforms impacted favorably on the wider public administration system, but that this was not sustained after 1996. The authors suggested that the success of SARAs might have actually undermined overall public administration systems, as SARAs were separated from the rest of the civil service in terms of work conditions and the protection from political interference (Prichard & Leonard 2010: 669). The Zambia Revenue Authority (ZARA) provides one of the best illustrations of the successes and frustrations of these organs in Africa. ZARA's success enabled her to uncover fraudulent activities by multi-national companies operating in that nation's copper sector. One of these, Mopani Copper Mines, a subsidiary of Swiss Glencore International which owns 50 percent of the world's global copper market, was accused by ZARA's auditors to have overestimated its operating costs, underestimated production volumes and breached arm's-length principles – all in that company's bid to avoid taxes. The privatization process (lauded by the World Bank in the 1990s as one of the most successful, with 282 entities sold), was discovered to have involved large-scale corruption, involving several multinationals and public officials and a complete lack of transparency. According to a recent review, even relevant ministries and Members of Parliament were not allowed access until a copy of the agreements was leaked to the press (Sharife 2011).

Global Financial Integrity (GFI) reported that the bulk of illicit capital flight from Africa is often siphoned not only by rogue regimes but also by corporations through 'underpricing, overpricing, misinvoicing and making completely fake transactions, often between subsidiaries of the same MNC and companies formed offshore to keep property out of the sight of the tax collectors' (Sharife 2011). GFI estimated that Africa lost over US$854 billion between 1970 and 2008 through such illicit financial flows (Economic Commission for Africa 2010: 13).

Another important area of focus has been public–private partnership (PPP) for *producing* public services that state institutions are authorized to *provide* (Ostrom 1996, Adamolekun 2011). PPP has become an important element in efforts to enhance the capacity of the state. Infrastructures constitute one of the most important areas of development on the continent. Many countries have found that by opening their telephone services to private entrepreneurship, the huge telephony divide between the rich and poor countries has all but vanished. Today, Africa has become one of the fastest-growing cell (mobile) phone users. Similar successes have been recorded in agriculture, water, electricity, gas, etc. (Kapstein 2009).

One of the neglected areas of PPP is the role that non-governmental organizations generally and, especially, faith-based organizations (FBOs) would play in PPP. Whereas colonial authorities and immediate post-independence governments at various levels (e.g. in the mobilization for universal primary education in the Western region of Nigeria 1955–1963) patronized FBOs in building and sustaining basic social infrastructures on a partnership basis, several of Africa's indigenous political leaders since the 1970s have sought to keep these organs out for a variety of reasons: divisiveness, non-inclusiveness and the distaste of foreign and other domestic social partners against any kind of religious engagement. There have been some positive changes in this regard, especially in the post-SAP period.

FBOs have re-emerged in many countries in their traditional areas of service delivery – basic education, basic health, water and rural roads. Moreover, they have also moved to new areas in higher education, policy advocacy and strong partnerships that have been developed between state and FBOs to tackle human rights problems, fight corruption and HIV/Aids in the region (Marshall 2011; Olowu 2011). The important lesson here is the need to strengthen the regulatory capacity of the national and local state organs in relating to both private and non-governmental organizations, including FBOs.

A fifth and final emergent development to touch on is the growing importance and relevance of political economy (PE) analysis to public administration. Much of public sector management analysis related to reform has in the past focused on what happens within the public service or even possibly within the state. Since the state is itself a subset of the larger political and economic forces operating within society, such analyses have been partial at best. Increasingly, there is a growing interest in understanding the PE of public administration reform as critical for reform institutionalization and indigenization. A PE analysis would identify the main drivers of the reforms as well as the restraining forces limiting their impact within and outside the public service. In particular, PE would analyze the political domestic and international context of reform and seek to understand the most potent forces conducive to reforms. On the basis of such an analysis, much more pertinent intervention can be articulated in the form of reforms (Eaton et al. 2010).

A recent PE analysis for understanding why reforms in one East African country had stalled highlighted the main drivers of reforms as being (1) political will from the top leadership, (2) the incentives structure motivating the bureaucrats responsible for implementing reforms, (3) the influence of development partners and (4) the demand from service-users and civil society organizations. The PE then examined these drivers and considered also the restraining forces limiting their impact, in order to recommend how best development partners might support public sector reform in the medium-term. Of the four key drivers identified above, the influence of the development partners was found to have remained strong in recent years, whereas the lack of strong leadership from the top, reflecting a lack of political will, absence of incentives linked to performance for officials, combined with the low level of demand from service-users, have been major constraints.

The PE found that some factors had made the political context more fluid recently than before. Within the domestic context, these included the emergence of an effective opposition, a strong media, an increasingly vibrant civil society, the growing political awareness of the urban population, and the fractures within the ruling party that very recently displaced a powerful anti-corruption faction. The dynamic impact of membership of the East African Community, as well as citizen protests on the streets of Kampala and Nairobi, together with the wave of popular uprisings across North Africa, were identified as factors operating within the international arena (World Bank 2011).

CONCLUSION

A review of the last five decades of political independence by most of the African states reveals deep fault lines in their state and public administration structures, processes and performance. It is doubtful whether current efforts at reforms of governance and of the administrative systems are effectively tackling several of the key challenges identified. These include:

- a serious deficit of trust, transparency and effective accountability to citizens;
- growing loss of loss of critical and managerial skills within state organs;
- excessive reliance on external resources for modeling and financing both capital and recurrent

elements of development and of the state administrative machinery;

- an over-centralized state system;
- policy processes that are delinked from relevant global and indigenous knowledge as tertiary institutions have declined in quality; and
- the weak regulatory capacity of state institutions in working with foreign and indigenous private sector and non-governmental organizations.

Given these factors, it would have been a miracle if overall performance of most of the African states and their administrative systems would have been any different from lackluster.

The above account makes a compelling case for a multidimensional and multilevel national leadership development in state as well as non-state bodies that have capacity to engage in a continuing policy dialogue with the national government organs to collaborate, compete and contract in tackling societal challenges. This is the polycentric constitutional architecture that recognizes multiple centers of power that interact as autonomous agents for overall societal development and management. There are signs that emergent political systems in the continent may grow in this direction – creating multiple, democratic autonomous spaces of action.

In sum, investing heavily in developing a national higher civil service that is knowledgeable and professional, highly motivated and well paid, non-corrupt and positioned to interact with other key societal stakeholders in analyzing policy and strategizing for development must be a priority for countries in the region that wish to overhaul and modernize their public administration systems. Such high-quality leaders at national and local levels of government would be matched by leaders from other sectors: private and non-governmental sectors, but also in the community and other non-conventional organizations such as FBOs – as they interact in the governing and administrative processes over time. Such a design worked in Africa in the immediate post-independent period and is working in some of the most dynamic developing nations of the world, as reviewed earlier in this chapter.

NOTES

1 United Nations Conference on Trade and Development (UNCTAD) (2006) *Economic Development in Africa: Doubling Aid: Making the Big Push Work*. Geneva: United Nations.

2 The countries selected included Benin, Burkina Faso and Senegal (all Francophone West African countries) and Botswana, Ghana, Uganda and Tanzania (English-speaking East, South and West African countries).

3 Of US$17.3 million contributions for APRM in 2007, 10.5 million (61 percent) came from development partners.

REFERENCES

Adamolekun, L. (2011) *Public Administration in Africa, second and updated edition*. Ibadan: Evans.

African Development Bank (AfDB) (2006) *Proposals for Enhancing Bank's Group Assistance to Fragile States in Africa*. Tunis: OPRC.

Alfarez, R.C. (2010) 'The Rise of Budget Support in European Development Cooperation: A False Panacea', *FRIDE Policy Brief*, No. 31, January.

Awortwi, N. (2011) 'An Unbreakable Path? A Comparative Study of Decentralization and Local Government Trajectories in Ghana and Uganda', *IRAS*, Vol. 77, No. 2, pp. 347–378.

Ayee, J. (2004) 'Ghana: Top Down Initiative', in D. Olowu & J. Wunsch (eds), *The Challenge of Democratic Decentralization*. Boulder, CO: Lynne Rienner, pp. 125–154.

Barkan, J. (2009) *Emerging Legislatures in Emerging African Democracies*. Boulder, CO: Lynne Rienner.

Bassett, Thomas J. & Scott, Straus (2011) 'Defending Democracy in Cote d'Ivoire', *Foreign Affairs*, Vol. 90, No. 4, pp. 130–141.

Bloom, D., D. Canning & K. Chan (2006) *Higher Education and Economic Development in Africa*. Harvard: Harvard University Press.

Brautigam, Deborah (2008) 'Taxation and Governance in Africa', Development Policy Outlook, No.1. AER Online, pp.1–13.

Broadman, Harry (2008) 'China and India Go to Africa', *Foreign Affairs*, March/April, pp. 95–124.

Calderon, Cesar (2009) Infrastructure and Growth in Africa. Policy Research Working Paper No. 4914. Washington, DC: World Bank.

Cameron, R. (2010) 'Redefining Political–Administrative Relationships in South Africa', *International Review of Administrative Sciences*, Vol. 76, No. 4, pp. 676–701.

Chan, H. & J. Ma (2011) 'How are they Paid? A Study of Civil Service Pay in China', *International Review of Administrative Sciences*, Vol. 77, No. 2, pp. 294–321.

Chang, Ha-Joon (2003) *Kicking Away the Ladder: Development Strategy in Historical Perspective*. London: Anthem Press.

Commonwealth Secretariat (2009) *Background Paper: Strategic Performance Management in the African Public Service Sector*. London: Commonwealth Secretariat.

Dickovick, T.J. & R.B. Rield (2010) *Africa Comparative Decentralization Assessment*. Washington. DC: USAID.

Doe, L. (1998) 'Civil Service Reform in the Countries of the West African Monetary Union', *International Social Science Journal*, No. 155, pp. 125–144.

Eaton, David, Kai Kaiser & Paul Smoke (2010) *The Political Economy of Decentralization Reforms: Implications for Aid Effectiveness*. Washington, DC: World Bank.

Economic Commission for Africa (2010) 'ECA Develops 'Regional Anti-Corruption Program', *African Governance Newsletter*, Vol. 1, No. 1, March, p.13.

The Economist (2011) Special Supplement on 'Taming Leviathan: A Special Report on the Future of the State', London, March 19.

Fass, S.M & G.M. Deslovere (2004) 'Chad: Governance by the Grassroots', in D. Olowu & J. Wunsch (eds), *Local Governance in Africa: The Challenge of Democratic Decentralization*. Boulder, CO: Lynne Rienner, pp. 155–180.

Goldstone, J.A. (2011) 'Understanding the Revolution of 2011', *Foreign Affairs*, May/June, Vol. 90, No. 3, pp. 8–16.

Herbert, J. & Steven Grudz (2008) *The African Peer Review Mechanism: Lessons from the Pioneers*. Johannesburg: South African Institute of International Affairs.

International Labor Office (2001) Impact of Deentralization and Privatization on Municipalization JMMS/2001; Geneva, ILO.

Kapstein, Ethan (2009) 'Africa's Capitalist Revolution: Preserving Growth in a Time of Crisis', *Foreign Affairs*, Vol. 84, No. 4, pp. 119–128.

Kapur, Devesh & John McHale (2005) Give Us Your Best and Brightest: The Global Hunt for Talents

and Its Impact on the Developing World. At: www.globaldevelopment.org

Karl, Terry (1997) *The Paradox of Plenty*. Berkeley, CA: University of California Press.

Kersting, N., J. Caulfield, R. Nickson, D. Olowu & H. Wollmann (2009) *Local Governance Reform in Global Perspective*. Berlin: VS Verslag fur Socialwissenschaften.

Kiragu, K. & R. Mukandala (2005) *Politics and Tactics in Public Sector Reforms: The Dynamics of the Public Service Pay in Africa*. Dar es Salaam: University of Dar es Salaam.

Kohli, A. (ed.) (2001) *The Success of India's Democracy*. Cambridge: Cambridge University Press, pp. 103–106.

Lijphart, A. (1984) *Democracies: Patterns of Majoritarian and Consensus Government in 21 Countries*. New Haven, CT: Yale University Press.

Little, Eric & Carolyn Logan (2009) 'The Quality of Democracy and Governance in Africa: New Results from Afrobarometer, Round 4', Afrobarometer Working Paper No. 118.

Lowell, L.B. & A.M. Findlay (2001) *Migration of Highly Skilled Persons from Developing Countries: Impact and Policy Responses*. Geneva: International Labor Office.

Maloka, Eddy (2002) Africa's Development Thinking since Independence – A Reader. Pretoria: Africa Institute of South Africa.

Marshall, K. (2011) 'Development and Faith Institutions: Gulfs and Bridges', in Gerrie ter Haar (ed.), *Religion and Development: Ways of Transforming the World*. London: Hurst & Co, pp. 27–54.

Millett, Karin, Dele Olowu & Robert Cameron (eds) (2006) *Local Governance and Poverty Reduction in Africa*. Tunis: Joint Africa Institute.

Mo Ibrahim Foundation (2010) At: www.moibrahim foundation.org/index (data on public management).

Moyo, D. (2010) *Dead Aid: Why Aid is not Working and How There is Another Way for Africa*. London: Penguin.

Narayan, D. R. Chambers, M. Shah & P. Petesch (2001) *Voices of the Poor*. New York: Oxford University Press.

Ndegwa, S. and B. Levy (2004) 'The Politics of Decentralization in Africa: A Comparative Analysis', in B. Levy & S. Kpundeh (eds), *Building State Capacity in Africa: New Approaches, Emerging Lessons*. Washington, DC: World Bank, pp. 283–321.

Olowu, D. (2010) 'Civil Service Pay Reforms in Africa', *International Review of Administrative Sciences*, Vol. 76, No. 4, pp. 632–652.

Olowu, D. (2011) 'Faith Based Organizations and Development: An African Indigenous Organization in Perspective', in Gerrie ter Haar (ed.), *Religion and Development: Ways of Transforming the World*. London: Hurst & Co, pp. 55–80.

Olowu, D. & E.J. Erero (2009) 'Institutional Assessment of the Nigerian Federal Civil Service Commission', Department for International Development (DFID), London.

Olowu, D. & J. Wunsch (2004) *Local Governance in Africa: The Challenge of Democratic Decentralization*. Boulder, CO: Lynne Rienner.

Olowu, D., N. Awortwi & A. Akinyoade (2010a) *Cases in African Decentralization: Botswana, Cameroon, Ghana, Mozambique and Tanzania*. London, Commonwealth Secretariat.

Olowu, B., R. Suberu, J. Erero & R. Soetan (2010b) *Comparative Assessment of Decentralization in Africa: Nigeria* In-country Assessment Report. Washington: USAID.

Organization for Economic Cooperation and Development (2008) African Economic Outlook 2008. Paris, OECD.

Organization for Economic Cooperation and Development (2010) African Economic Outlook 2010, Paris, OECD.

Ostrom, E. (1996) 'Crossing the Great Divide: Co-Production, Synergy and Development', *World Development*, 24, No. 6, pp.1073–1087.

Prichard, W. & D.K. Leonard (2010) 'Does Reliance on Tax Revenues Build State Capacity in Sub-Saharan Africa?', *International Review of Administrative Sciences*, Vol. 76, No, 4, pp. 653–675.

Roll, Michael (2010) *Pockets of Effectiveness and Public Sector Performance in Developing Countries*. Lagos.

Schiavo-Campo, S. (1998) 'Government and Pay: The Global and Regional Evidence' *Public Administration and Development*, Vol. 18, No. 5, pp. 423–478.

Schiavo-Campo, S. and H.M. McFerson (2008) *Public Management in Global Perspective*. New York: M.E.Sharpe.

Shah, Anwar (2006) *Local Governance in Developing Countries*. Washington: World Bank.

Sharife, Khadja (2011) 'Zambia: Copper – Charity for Multinationals', Pambazuka News, June 2. At: www.allafrica.com.

Stevens, M. & S. Teggemann (2004) 'Comparative Experience in Public Sector Reform in Ghana, Tanzania and Zambia', in B. Levy & S. Kpundeh (eds), *Building State Capacity in Africa*. Washington: World Bank, pp. 43–86.

Tidemand, P. & J. Msami (2010) The Impact of Local Government Reforms in Tanzania, 1998–2008. Dar es Salaam, Special Paper 10/1

Trefon, T. (2010) 'Administrative Obstacles to Reform in the Democratic Republic of Congo', *IRAS*, Vol. 76, No. 4, pp. 702–722.

United Kingdom Commission for Africa (2005) Our Common Interest: Report of the Commission for Africa, London, HMSO.

United Nations Conference on Trade and Development (2006) Economic Development in Africa: Doubling Aid: Making the Big Push Work. Geneva: United Nations.

Valentine, T. (2006) *Reforming Pay in the Tanzanian Public Service: Successes, Limitations and Challenges*. Dar es Salaam: ESRF.

World Bank (1989) Sub-Saharan Africa: From Crisis to Sustainable Development. Washington, DC: World Bank.

World Bank (2004) World Development Report. Oxford: Oxford University Press.

World Bank (2011) A Political Economy of Crosscutting Public Sector Reforms in Tanzania: Policy Paper. Washington, DC: World Bank.

Wunsch, J. (2002) 'Decentralization, Local Governance and Recentralization' in Africa', *Public Administration and Development*, Vol. 23, pp. 175–178.

Wunsch, James & Dele Olowu (eds) (1990/1995) *The Failure of the Centralized State*. Boulder, CO: Westview Press.

35

Public Administration and Public Sector Reform in Latin America

Jorge Nef

This chapter intends to provide a general overview of Latin America's public sector restructuring in the context of the broader economic, social and political changes in the past three decades. The term 'administrative reform' may evoke a universal phenomenon, yet its circumstances, outcomes and effects are region- and country-specific and are conditioned by the current pattern, as well as legacy, of state–society relations. Most analysts of public administration studying the region view administrative systems as inseparable from politics: administrative changes have to be studied as driven by particular political interests and with specific political implications for the relationship between state and society.

Six basic questions are addressed. First, what changes can be noticed in administrative structures, culture and behavior in Latin America as a result of economic and political reforms in the past decades? Second, to what extent do the administrative systems increasingly present legal-rational characteristics? Third, is public administration becoming more efficient and/or effective in delivering services as a consequence of the above-mentioned reforms? Fourth, are government agencies becoming more (or less) client- or service-oriented? Fifth, what is happening to public probity and, more specifically, to corruption? Finally, to what extent does public administration contribute to national and regional development?

Despite the great diversity among the countries, there are sufficient structural commonalities (Burns, 1998: 71) as to configure an identifiable set of nations, especially by contrast to the developed states of North America. Conventionally, Latin America has been seen to encompass 18 Spanish-speaking countries, as well as Brazil and Haiti. It does not include the 'newer' microstates of the Caribbean, which are also members of the same regional body, the Organization of American States (OAS). To build a 'model' that portrays Latin American public administration as a whole with rigor and precision is a daunting task. Yet, it is possible to sketch a general outline of the structural, behavioral and attitudinal traits present in the various executive agencies across the region. These agencies comprise diverse national administrations in the central government, functionally decentralized agencies and territorially decentralized units, such as state and local governments. It is important to recognize too that the public and the private sectors, and their cultures, tend to intersect, especially at the level of the power elite (Mills, 1957).

THE HISTORICAL LEGACY

Public administration in the region has experienced induced transformations since the days of colonial rule. It has passed through protracted phases of nation building (1850s to 1880s), early institutionalization (1880s to 1930s), bureaucratization (1930s to 1970s) and authoritarianism (1970s to the mid 1980s). In the latter phase, technocratic and militaristic values dominated the relationship between state and society. However, in the past 20 years, a transition to limited democracy has reduced to some extent the influence of what some call the 'praetorian guards', or bureaucratic autocrats. In conjunction with formal democratization, neoliberal economic reforms have further reshaped the role of the state: it has been downsized, while reducing its past centrality in socio-economic development. In addition to these challenges, the public sector has also confronted emerging social movements and a more complex and transnationalized type of political and economic context.

Any profound understanding of public administration in Latin America must by necessity explore the long run cycle (Braudel, 1980). Moreover, the study of administrative reform and change is, by its very nature, historical analysis, where the past is always

present. The New World was born as a dependency of Madrid and Lisbon (Jaguaribe, 1964). An imitative and ritualistic administration emerged. Even, the seemingly 'modern', yet schizophrenic, patterns of administrative behavior of today's Latin America can be traced back to a colonial tradition of obedience without compliance (Moreno, 1969).

Independence in the early 1800s was more the result of European conflicts and big-power politics than widespread nationalism and liberal ideas among New World aristocrats (Keen, 1992). Emancipation did not result by and large from bourgeois revolutions and homegrown ideas of liberty, equality, civil rights or effective citizenship. The severance of colonial ties, though difficult and violent, maintained almost intact the property and privilege of the same landed oligarchy who profited from colonialism.

Constitutional and legal forms transplanted from Europe and North America were often a measuring rod of 'modernity' by imitation, not a substantial rendering of a public service. Government jobs constituted mostly rewards for loyalty to a faction in power, or to members of the ruling classes, not the manifestation of a neutral, representative and responsible bureaucracy. Even, when efforts at the professionalization of the civilian and military cadres of the state began in the 1880s, this seemingly non-partisan body of state employees was at best an elitist stratum to which ordinary people had little access. Bureaucratic and authoritarian traditions intersected in a political and social order that was patrimonial at its core and only superficially legal-rational. Equally embedded, and seemingly contradictory traditional attitudes towards authoritarianism, formalism, patrimonialism and venality coexisted with more universalistic orientations as distinct cultural layers within this incipient state class. The ideological amalgam described here was particularly noticeable among one of the most typical factions of the Latin American middle classes: the officer corps (Nun, 1968).

The administrative state

The precarious social contract resting upon the export economy, as discussed above, collapsed with the Great Depression. The consequence of the catastrophic 1929–34 economic recession on the Latin American state was twofold. On the one hand, and virtually in all of the states, the role of the military as conflict managers and enforcers of last resort (and as ultimate protectors of elite privilege) was enhanced. On the other hand, in the relatively more developed countries (such as Argentina, Brazil, Uruguay, Chile and Mexico), the dramatic downturn expanded the mediating and brokerage function of a middle class-controlled and relatively autonomous state to arbitrate social conflict by means of economic management. Thus, to the early law and order, educational and social and welfare functions of the state, a new mission was added: economic development. A technocratic and productivity-oriented bureaucracy emerged side by side with the more traditional patrimonial and legal-rational central and local administration. This 'state of compromise' with strong populist overtones manifested itself in the creation of numerous parastatals with broad functions in planning, regulating, financing and covering fields as diverse as energy, industry, transportation and marketing. It also meant a Keynesian policy of induced development, known as Import Substitution Industrialization (ISI) (Furtado, 1976). In the lesser-developed countries, however, the civil service remained ineffectual and mostly prebendary, while the commanding heights of the state were in the hands of military rulers. But even the above-mentioned state of compromise was short-lived. As chronic deficit financing, inflation and paralysis signaled the exhaustion of induced development policies, tensions between labor and business increased, this time in the context of the Cold War. Lower-class defiance grew in scope and intensity. Populism of the kind espoused by ISI was simultaneously under attack by both ends of the ideological spectrum. Political and administrative immobilism, deadlock and hyperinflation fed on each other. Crises of legitimacy affected the relatively more institutionalized administrative states, while those under protracted military rule faced crises of domination (Cox, 1982) – the inability of the repressive apparatus to control by force.

In the context of UN First Development Decade, the US-sponsored Alliance for Progress (1961), a reaction to the Cuban revolution, belatedly attempted to stabilize the region by means of a Marshall Plan-like development assistance. Development administration and administrative development (Pérez-Salgado, 1997) were part of a strategy using modernization as counter-insurgency (Nef and Dwivedi, 1981). Foreign aid, professionalization and development planning played an important role in a broad effort at refurbishing the administrative cadres of Latin America. Under USAID (United States Agency for International Development) sponsorship, increasing numbers of Latin American students and trainees were exposed to American ways. Western European assistance followed a similar course. Money was also pouring in to carry on domestic programs on educational, agrarian and tax reforms, and also for the training and rationalization of the civil service under the principles of Scientific Management, Program Budgeting and Organization and Methods. These civil service reforms were predicated under the logic of induced development ('development administration') and the supremacy of the bureaucratic model ('administrative development'). More important, however, were the modernization and retooling of the security apparatus, both military and police, along national security and counter-insurgency lines (Barber and Ronning, 1966). While the reforms of the civil service, though extensive modernization, remained largely unfocused, 'technical' and piecemeal, the thoroughgoing transformation of the security apparatus had an enormous and long-term systemic impact. With the failure of liberal reformism, the officers and their US-made National Security Doctrine would occupy center stage to secure the maintenance of the domestic and regional status quo.

Despite rhetoric, the military regimes of the 1970s were objectively not only parasitic but also instrumental in undermining the precarious economic and political sovereignty of the Latin American nations. The 'managers of violence' also proved to be incompetent conflict and development managers in the long run (Burns, 1986). Yet, they succeeded in radically restructuring the nature of the Latin American state, as well as the latter's relations with both civil society and the Inter-American system. The US-sponsored transitions to democracy in the 1980s, and the so-called Washington consensus (Vilas, 2000), occurred in the context of these profound alterations (Black, 1998).

While military rule floundered in the midst of staggering debt burdens and mismanagement, critics within the West began to perceive such regimes as a liability for the survival of their economic and political interests, as clearly outlined in the liberally minded blue-ribbon Linowitz Report of 1975 (*Time Magazine*, 1977), commissioned by President Carter. A carefully orchestrated transition to restricted democracy, superintended by the regional superpower, ensued (Nef, 1998). This 'return' had strict limits and conditionalities. On the whole, it maintained the socio-economic and political forces that had benefited from decades of military rule, while excluding radical and popular sectors. The exiting security establishment was to be both the warrantor of the process and the central authoritarian enclave, or insurance policy, of the new institutional arrangement. This 'low-intensity' democracy (Gil et al., 1993) also preserved the basic neoliberal economic agendas of the authoritarian era. Chief among these legacies was a 'receiver state', whose prime goal was to manage fiscal bankruptcies and facilitate International Monetary Fund (IMF)-inspired structural adjustment packages (Vilas, 1995).

Incomplete transition, restricted democracy and the receiver state have had significant effects upon the administrative systems in Latin America. Privatization, budget cuts, downsizing, deregulation and denationalization – especially in the social and developmental areas – have reduced the scope and function of the state. As profit and personal gain, on the one hand, and the national interest, on the other hand, get blurred in the new ideological domain, the notion of public *service* became increasingly irrelevant. Furthermore, as the status and income levels of civil servants has sunk, and with a thriving illegal economy, such as the one centered in the drug trade (Lee, 1988), systemic corruption has been on the rise, reaching the highest levels of government and administration. Under these circumstances, externally induced efforts to make public administration more accountable, responsible, universalistic, effective, service-oriented and less corrupt tend to become as formal and ineffectual as the development administration prescriptions of the 1960s.

THE STRUCTURAL CONTEXT OF PUBLIC ADMINISTRATION

The historical continuities and discontinuities discussed above have resulted in the coexistence of numerous and often incongruous traits. These include foreign and domestic influences, attempted and failed reforms and persistent crises. The aforementioned legacy manifests itself into three deep and interconnected structural contradictions.

The first contradiction is the persistent and unresolved tension between expanding social expectations and shrinking economic capabilities. For all the talk about Latin America's emerging markets and reinsertion in the global economic order, the region is still affected by extreme vulnerability and weak and unstable growth. Most important, even in the instances of economic expansion, disparities are persisting and widening.

The second tension is that between the 'haves' and 'have-nots'. Constricted generation of surplus, compounded by extreme forms of wealth and income inequality, has reduced the possibilities for consensual conflict management. In fact, Latin America exhibits the paradox of being simultaneously the most favorably endowed region of the globe in terms of the balance of resources to population and the worst in income distribution. While contemporary social conflict does not outwardly present the subversive characteristics of the revolutionary confrontations of the Cold War, social unrest has not subsided. As its underlying causes persist, so does its intensity, irrespective of the changing manifestations of mass–elites relations. This proclivity for disequilibria connects to the third systemic tension: that between the formality of sovereignty and the reality of dependence. The Latin American nation-states are penetrated political systems, with ever-more precarious control over actors, events and policies. Their economic foundations are still built upon a skewed and exogenous mode of development, with boom and bust cycles, compounded by massive debt burdens, current conditionalities and rapid transnationalization. In addition, external constituencies – political, military and economic – are essential to maintain adequate support (Easton, 1957) in systems whose internal legitimacy is weak.

Both public disillusionment with government and the increasing meaninglessness of the restricted democracies are ubiquitous. If the state cannot maintain political and economic sovereignty, protect the life and well-being of its citizens, safeguard democratic rights and assure participation – in brief, provide for human security – its very reason for existence becomes problematic. Furthermore, as the prevailing neoliberal ideological and policy packages reduce the state's role to that of protecting business interests, there is little room for a public sector, no matter how efficient, effective or transparent. The New Public Management (NPM) formula, with its corollaries of privatization, downsizing, deregulating, localizing and outsourcing, in the absence of a strong and legitimate political order and community, has potentially destabilizing effects. Moreover, without a pre-existing cohesive and vigorous civil society, administrative modernization is simply a means to a vacuous end.

ADMINISTRATIVE CULTURE

Public servants' attitudes towards public service in the region are embedded in an alienated set of orientations towards public life reflective of the prevailing social tensions. This administrative culture constitutes a rational adaptation and functionalization of conflicting traits present in the context of public organizations. A sketchy interpretative profile of these predispositions would suggest a superimposition of various cultural 'layers'.

Seen from afar, the administrative culture of Latin America presents significant universalistic and achievement-oriented traits. After all, Latin America is squarely in the domain of Western culture. The drive for efficiency, effectiveness, technological innovation and probity by means of public management is pervasive in theory and discourse. Yet in practice, the core component of Latin America's administrative culture is defined by the persistence of ascription and influence peddling. Primary groups, especially extended families and friends, play a fundamental role in social life, even in the allegedly 'modern' confines of urban and corporate life. The endurance of patrimonialism, friendly connections (*'amiguismo'*) and 'godfatherhood' (*'compadrazgo'*) are manifestations of this built-in particularism. So is the overall level of inwardness, lack of transparency and distrust of strangers surrounding the performance of public functions.

The Latin American state classes have been, since their origins, a 'status officialdom' (Morstein-Marx, 1963: 63), derived from their possession of official titles.

A bureaucrat (even a white-collar employee in a private corporation) or a military or police officer, irrespective of the discredit in which the service may find itself, is a 'somebody'. In a hierarchical social order, being middle class confers a degree of respectability and recognition. This accounts for the extreme formalism present in administrative behavior. Ritualism, hyper-legalism and the codification of language in deductive law (rooted in Civil and Roman Law) makes the behavior and expectations of officials depend upon detailed and often Kafkaesque interpretations of norms. There is a fundamental double standard: a public 'facade' for outsiders and a private zone of exceptionality for insiders (Riggs, 1967). The same applies to the use of time: delays, waiting and slowness are selectively used to define the importance of the relationship and delineate power and hierarchy.

Under the mantle of formalism described above, paradoxically, there is a high degree of operational autonomy. Formalism and particularism ostensibly clash. The former becomes a mechanism for avoiding responsibility, or for justifying dynamic immobilism and aloofness. The flip side of this contradiction is that it transforms the role of the civil servant into one of dispensing personal favors as well as facilitating exceptions from existing norms. Such exceptionalism gives rise to recurrent nepotism, corruption, patronage and abuse.

The official's perception of the relations between state and society is influenced by the weak brokerage and associational representation for most of the public vis-à-vis the government. This enhances an almost 'natural' form of corporatism and authoritarianism (Malloy, 1977). Moreover, the recognition of an entrenched, elitist socio-economic structure enhances a self-perception of autocracy, where public functionaries act as mediators and arbiters of social conflicts (Heady, 1984), but with extremely limited accountability. There is a profound schism between 'insiders' and 'outsiders'. Clientelism, patrimonialism, the ubiquitous use of 'insider privilege',

exceptionalism, and the persistence of episodes of military intervention, reinforce the aforementioned characteristics. Though the white-collar military and civilian state classes are not part of the landed, financial and commercial oligarchy, public officials dwell in the confines of the elites and a few of them are able to ascend into the upper crust. Their connection with essentially undemocratic practices and governments makes the functionaries prone to assume an attitude of arbitrariness and disregard for the public. This demeanor towards the outsiders, especially the lower strata, is pervasive not only in government but also in the private sector.

Most administrative structures and processes in Latin America, irrespective of the level of territorial or functional operation, are heavily concentrated at the top. The institutional mold is one of centralism (Véliz, 1980). Most states are unitary; only Mexico, Venezuela, Brazil and Argentina have limited forms of federalism. Moreover, the attempts at territorialization and localization do not necessarily make administration more accountable, democratic and 'closer to the people'. This centralism is even more manifest with regards to the pattern of executive–legislative relations. Without exception, the form of government is one of presidential dominance, where the legislature is a weak instrument for checks and balances. Parliamentary control and parliamentary supremacy, concepts generated in the US presidential and the British parliamentary systems, are not significantly entrenched. Nor is there a word for 'accountability' in the lexicon. Only in recent years the word '*responsabilización*' has been coined, but many authors still prefer to use the English idiom. The administrator's values, behavior and expectations tend to reflect a view of 'things public' defined by high levels of concentration of power. Decisions normally flow up to the 'top'; so does responsibility (Campos, 1967). Though operational autonomy – as mentioned – is not uncommon, propensity to delegate is rather infrequent. Therefore, it is extremely difficult to attain coordination. This, in turn, enhances the propensity to further concentrate authority.

The ideological 'software' of the Latin American public sector is the result of an ongoing process of immersion, acculturation and socialization, whose structural drivers are both implicit and induced. Reform projects and other innovations, originated in the realm of international technical cooperation, are adopted to the extent that they fit pre-existing cultural molds. Thus, diverse views of administration coexist but do not necessarily fuse into a cultural synthesis. The primary vehicles for reproducing administrative culture are, at their most basic levels, the family, the educational system, peer groups and direct experience with the public service. As indicated earlier, the fundamental class identification of civil servants is with the middle strata. There is a sort of circular causation: the middle strata produce employees, while becoming a white-collar worker confers the attribute of middle classness. Class distinctions are very important in Latin America, social identity being a function of ancestry, neighborhood, education, tastes, gender, ethnicity and discourse. The educational system, especially at its secondary and tertiary levels, is quite exclusive and discriminating. High school and university education are in general the points of entry for employee roles. More specific training may occur at the post-secondary levels either in public service schools or in university careers geared to administrative postings. Academic curricula in these educational institutions are connected to law, business and economics, and also to a very narrow view of public administration. All these professions are characterized by a strong and largely uncritical social engineering orientation. Beyond programmatic declarations, few countries have developed an administrative class, in the sense understood in North America, the UK and Continental Europe (Heady, 1984). Many observers point at Costa Rica, Uruguay and Chile as possible examples approaching the model of a 'neutral', 'effective' and relatively more transparent bureaucracy. But even these exceptional cases appear problematic when closely scrutinized.

In the case of the military, officer academies at the secondary and post-secondary levels give specificity to a distinct body of doctrine and *ésprit de corps*. National security and counter-insurgency doctrines define a predominantly antidemocratic, ultraconservative and outward-looking view of the world, heavily dependent upon ideological and material support from the North. In fact, the officers and their external constituencies exercise a kind of relational control, or 'metapower' (Baumgartner et al., 1977) over the domestic political process. Underneath a veneer of nationalism, the security apparatii act as occupying forces of their own countries. Civilian and military roles are sharply divided, with military professionalism being largely defined by the control over the instruments of force, institutional autonomy, verticality, rigidity, secrecy, high transnational integration, institutional arrogance, isolation and corporate identity, as 'Sentinels of the Empire' (Black, 1986). With the shrinkage of the developmental function of the state, by design and by default, security management, combined with the above-mentioned receivership, have evolved into the most ostensible functions of the state (Nef and Bensabat, 1992). With the Cold War over, the content of national security has been redefined to fit other concerns: 'wars' on drugs, 'terrorism', or whatever justifies the paramountcy of the institutional interests of the security forces.

ORGANIZATIONAL FEATURES

A primary feature of organizational life is the already-mentioned coexistence, side by side, of patrimonial and bureaucratic tendencies. In this sense, the administrative machinery of the state often reproduces a neocolonial world view, and cannot be seen as an effective, let alone legitimate, instrument for policy implementation. It is also a pivotal, albeit highly fragmented, socio-political actor with a multiplicity of latent functions related to the maintenance of the socio-political order. Another organizational trait is organizational syncretism: from an 'archeological' point of view, Latin America's public administration presents a complex overlay of actually existing structures and practices. Some of these can be traced as far back as the colonial and post-independence period; others are the outcroppings of more recent reorganizations, policy orientations and hemispheric or transnational political allegiances.

Most significant within this organizational legacy is the presence of numerous agencies and activities inherited from the Keynesian administrative state. In the relatively more developed Latin American countries the scope and depth of state involvement was impressive decades ago. It included mass education, health, social security, housing, popular credit, marketing boards and commercial monopolies, public utilities (especially electricity, water and sewage), mass transportation (trains, sea transport and airlines), strategic industrial enterprises (cement, steel, hydrocarbons, petrochemicals, aeronautics) and in some instances even the film industry. In Chile, Costa Rica, Uruguay, Brazil, Mexico and, to a lesser extent, Venezuela, there existed national development corporations to finance and hold numerous state enterprises, or semi-private ventures financed with government funds or credit. Though many of these entities and activities have been either privatized or eliminated under the policies of structural adjustment, a good number still persist. Successful state corporations, like Mexico's oil monopoly PEMEX, Costa Rica's power and telecommunications monopoly INE, or Chile's Copper Corporation CODELCO, have been spared the privatizing wave. In numerous cases, either the pace of liberalization has been too slow or the institutional and symbolic entrenchment of the corporations too strong to privatize.

A third ostensible trait – already touched upon when discussing culture – is the strong influence of legalism in every aspect of organizational life. There is an elaborate and quite similar body of public law – both constitutional and administrative – as well as abundant jurisprudence regulating virtually every aspect of Latin American bureaucracy. Legalism and formalism are terms virtually synonymous with public administration. Government entities are formal organizations whose origin, mission, instrumentalities and *modus operandi* are explicitly prescribed by law; and this is particularly strong in societies where notary publics have to certify every action or intent; something that Jaguaribe (1968: 144) has referred to as 'cartorialism' (literally, 'notarial state').

A fourth important characteristic is the high autonomy of the military and security apparatus. (The only exception is Costa Rica, which does not have a military force.) The armed bureaucrats are, for all intents and purposes, a virtual state within the state. Furthermore, there are numerous authoritarian enclaves throughout the non-military public service – inherited from the times of bureaucratic authoritarianism – that remain outside the realm of effective political control. In some instances, like Chile's main state copper mining conglomerate, CODELCO, a substantial part of the proceeds (10 percent of revenue until 2011) have gone directly to the military. In other cases (Brazil and Chile), the military are integrated into 'military–industrial complexes' of their own, which include the highly profitable area of international arms sales.

A fifth, significant and enduring characteristic of Latin American public administration is the formal cohabitation of two administrative systems, one central and the other decentralized. The central, or 'fiscal' apparatus is made of ministries, agencies and services, under the helm and budgetary control of the Chief Executive. These units are usually departmentalized by major purpose and operate under the general provisions of public service legislation. The other is the decentralized sector, constituted by the semi-autonomous control and regulatory agencies, functionally decentralized services, state enterprises and corporations of many kinds. A distinct component of the 'autonomous' sector is territorially decentralized and involves local government and administration. Decentralized bodies are chartered in special legislation that grants them relative operational, statutory, budgetary and personnel independence from the central agencies, and in some cases they operate under the provisions of private law. Until recently, the distribution of personnel between these two sectors was roughly similar, while in the budgetary area, the decentralized sector's share was slightly higher than that of the central administration. However, in recent years there have been some significant changes. Functional decentralization has been steadily replaced by privatization, deregulation and downsizing. Meanwhile, under the banner of localization, territorially decentralized agencies (in particular municipalities) have increased in numbers, functions and importance (see Table 35.1).

A final characteristic is the institutionalization of a myriad of newer horizontal functions, in addition to the more conventional horizontal operating systems – that is, planning, budget, financial and personnel management, and legal and accounting controls (for example, the Comptroller General's office). Most of these new agencies are coordinating units, cutting across the more conventional vertically departmentalized ministries and government agencies. Some of these newer structures deal with emerging issues such as the environment, privatization, export promotion, interaction with the civil society (that is, 'the public'), or gender equity. Other integrated functions are those pertaining to administrative and institutional reform itself. Since the 1990s, almost all the governments in the region have embarked on the implementation of strategic plans for the modernization of the public sector.

To accomplish this mandate, presidential-level agencies and commissions have been established. In some cases, such as in Argentina, an Under-Secretariate of Public Management and Modernization has been created, along with an office to fight corruption. Mexico, under the PAN administration of President Fox, initiated a similar program of its own. In most countries, inter-ministerial and inter-agency committees, charged with computerization and technological innovation, quality control, program evaluation, user satisfaction, performance assessments and de-bureaucratization have been in existence for at least two decades. An example of this arrangement is Chile's Inter-ministerial Committee for the Modernization of the

Table 35.1   A comparison of national, functionally and territorially decentralized administrations in a number of countries in the 1990s indicates the following variations

Country	(A) National admin.		(B) Functional		(C) Local		% change (A)	% change (B)	% change (C)
	1991	1997	1991	1997	1991	1997	1991–97	1991–97	1991–97
Argentina	534	462	242	51	1159	1317	−13.5	−89.0	13.6
Chile	120	134	56	37	23	23	11.7	−32.3	0.0
Costa Rica	127	133	6	3	6	8	4.7	−50.0	33.3
Nicaragua	89	81	15	11	41	47	−9.0	−26.6	14.6
Venezuela	238	197	99	28	193	208	−17.3	−71.8	2.3

Figures refer to thousands of civil servants and are in absolute values. If they were calculated as a proportion of population, or economically active population, declines would be larger and increases smaller. The 'Local' comprises municipal, or provincial, or both, depending upon the data available. The term 'Functional' relates to parastatal state enterprises.
Source: CLAD/SIARE website: http://www.clad.org/siare_isis/perfiles/inicio.html; and http://www.clad.org/siare_isis/tamano/estadistica.html (accessed February 5, 2011).

State, which has a broad mandate and is housed in the strategic Ministry of the Secretary General of Government.

A feature of the current approach to administrative modernization, unlike the 'rationalization' efforts under the rubric of development administration of the 1960s, is that it uses a broader definition of the public sector. Besides central agencies, the object of reform encompasses local governments, the judiciary and the drive towards privatization. Most countries, notably Brazil, Argentina, Bolivia, Chile, Colombia, Panama, Ecuador and the Dominican Republic, have created agencies and formulated plans to transfer and download governmental functions at the communal level. These regional development offices and under-secretariats are also mandated to enhance administrative skills and build managerial capabilities in local government. In addition, a great deal of effort has been devoted to modernizing the judiciary, simplifying procedures and attempting to give more agility and transparency to the judicial process, one identified by external observers as being not only slow but also corrupt. Finally, the issue of transferring public ownership to the private sector has been addressed. This is a major ideological and fiscal tenet of the institutional reforms contained in the conditionalities attached to debt relief. The discourse behind this practice refers to a 'leaner but meaner' state, where regulation and leadership replaces direct ownership or management. To this effect, all the countries have established mechanisms (in the form of commissions) to expedite the privatization process.

THE DYNAMICS OF REFORM: PROCESSES AND EFFECTS

Administrative change in Latin America has been for the most part either externally induced, or heavily assisted by external actors (Wharlich, 1978). Colonial reforms, the desire of local elites to modernize, the presence of international missions and consultants (like the Kemmerer Commission in the 1920s), development administration (Crowther and Flores, 1984), and today's New Public Management with structural adjustment programs (SAPs) are all cases in point. The instances of administrative reform from within have been fewer, piecemeal, heavily localized and mostly reactive to deep discontinuities. One such instance was the already-mentioned development of the post-First World War welfare state with limited social security and medical coverage, which preceded its counterparts in Europe and North America by at least a decade (Mesa-Lago and Witte, 1992). The other was Import Substitution Industrialization in the 1930s, the only experience to become codified and theorized upon in the works of United Nations Economic Commission for Latin America and the Caribbean (ECLAC) and other regional agencies. A third example has been the rare attempts at radical reorganization resulting from revolutionary changes, such as in Cuba (1960s), the generally aborted Sandinista experiment in Nicaragua (1980s), as well as populist attempts in Venezuela, Ecuador and Bolivia two decades later. Rhetoric aside, these experiences have been largely improvisations in the face of dramatic international conjunctures and nearly impossible odds. Rene Dumont (1970) has referred to this style of management as 'creative chaos'. Finally, a most remarkable exception is the set of micro experiences in autonomous mobilization, such as the Christian Base Communities in Central America and Brazil, the now-defunct Popular Economic Organizations in Chile, the self-managed urban communities in Peru (Nef, 1991) and the still-vital Landless Rural Workers' Movement (MST) in contemporary Brazil (Robles, 2000; MST, 2001).

The common denominator of all administrative reform in Latin America, whether internally or externally induced, is its distinct political character (Marini Ferreira, 1999). Such reforms, irrespective of the technical language in which they are couched, in the last analysis strengthen, weaken, consolidate or challenge existing power relations. Furthermore, they all operationalize in organizational and managerial terms a broader political, social and economic project.

Administrative modernization in the 1990s has been predicated in a very different domestic and international environment – and programmatic objectives – from those of the structural reforms of the 1960s. The policy framework for international cooperation present in the West today (and a decade ago) was, and continues to be, distinctively neoliberal, not Keynesian. The Southern Common Market (MERCOSUR), North American Free Trade Agreement (NAFTA) and the proposals for a Free Trade of the Americas (FTA) are part of the new regional environment. Markets, rather than planning and government intervention, are seen as central, though paradoxically this policy switch is contingent upon strong state enforcement. Latin America came out of the Cold War through a transition to a limited and not very transparent form of democracy brokered by external agents. The countries were also saddled with enormous and unmanageable debt burdens. The international financial community and its bodies used debt management to impose stringent conditionalities. The latter included a number of measures for attaining macroeconomic equilibrium via debt reduction, open-market policies and institutional reforms.

It is precisely in the context of these structural adjustment policies that the bulk of the prescriptions for the current administrative reform have to be seen. The administrative corollary to the neoliberal package contained in the SAPs is fundamentally the New Public Management paradigm (Ormond and Löffler, 1999). The latter is well known in the United States through the work of Osborne and Gaebler, *Reinventing Government* (Jones and Thompson, 1999). Yet, its lineage can be traced back to the Right-leaning administrative reforms in the 1980s in the United Kingdom, New Zealand, Australia and Canada, which materialized in what was then

called a 'neoconservative' agenda. Its administrative corollary has been a movement from civil service to public management (Bonifacio, 1995). Downsizing government, making it publicly more accountable and transparent, turning it into a more efficient mechanism for delivering services on its own or in partnership with private and/or voluntary organizations are not purely isolated measures to secure 'better' administration. They are all manifestations of a broader neoliberal ideological rationale (Nef and Robles, 2000). The role of the state under this model is mainly subsidiary; that is, its main directive is to protect the functioning of the market, and private property. The basic 'social contract' is post-Fordian, in the sense that it reduces and fragments the role of workers in the system of labor relations, enhancing instead the uncontested hegemony of capital, both foreign and domestic. The notion of popular and national sovereignty is replaced by the sovereignty of capital. This manifests itself in regressive labor, taxation and welfare policy.

Over the past two decades, there has been a redefinition of the role of the state throughout Latin America, as in most of the globe, along the lines mentioned above. This has manifested itself in a transition between two models. One was the Keynesian 'administrative state', whose central mission was the attainment of national development. The other is the 'receiver' state, whose principal role is the management of structural adjustment and whose subsidiary role is the implementation of palliative development. Such development refers to targeted programs to address the plight of those who fall by the wayside as a result of orthodox economic policies, by means of micro-credit, capacity building and the like. This transformation, as mentioned earlier, came on the heels of the bureaucratic authoritarian restructuring of the 1970s and was largely facilitated by it.

Since the 'return to democracy', there has been a reduction in the scope and size of the public sector (Table 35.2), which has been accomplished by closures, privatization of many activities – especially in

Table 35.2   A comparative table, calculated on the basis of data provided by CLAD, between 1987 and 1998–99, indicates a declining trend in civil service employment, vis-à-vis the economically active population (EAP)

Country	Civil service (× 1000)			% EAP		
	1987	1998–99	% change	1990	1999	% change
Argentina*	1.973	1.829	−7.3	14.53	12.23	−26.0
Venezuela	975	374	−61.7	—	—	—
Mexico*	3.751	4.422	17.8	19.46	18.38	1.0
Costa Rica*	272	146	−46.4	13.95	11.20	−19.8
Chile	215	172	−20.0	2.09	1.60	−44.9
Panama	157	136	−13.3	—	—	—
Uruguay*	272	230	−15.5	18.12	16.14	−11.00

*Observations for Argentina are 1991–97: for Mexico, 1990–96; Costa Rica, 1990–98; and Uruguay, 1995–98.
Source: CLAD 2001: http://www.clad.org.ve//siareweb ; CLAD February 2011: http://www.clad.org/siare_isis/perfiles/inicio.html and
http://www.clad.org/siare_isis/tamano/estadistica.html (both accessed February 5, 2011).

public utilities, health, social security and education – and also by outsourcing in the private sector. A myriad of private entities have emerged to take on these downloaded public functions with captive clienteles and low elasticity: Pension Management Funds (Administradoras de Fondos de Pensiones [AFPs]), 'health service' entities (like Health Management Organizations), sanitary services firms and the like.

The record of privatization has shown mixed results, ranging from greater quality and rationalization of service, to more effective costing and profitability, to situations of exclusion and manifest decline in the quality, coverage and accessibility. In some cases, it has given an impetus for modernization, improved standards and generated sources of new investment, and even cheaper and better products (for a while this was the case in telecommunications). However, in many others (as in power utilities) it has spearheaded, at best, speculative appropriations at the public expense and widespread fraud. Downsizing the civil service has led to a proliferation of personnel on limited service contracts and a large quantity of private consultants. It has also meant a resurgence of patrimonialism (Robin, 1995). It is not uncommon to see a parallel structure to the officially downsized agencies, made of contractual and external personnel. More often

than not, this 'temporary' structure evolves into a persistent clientele conditioned to the ups and downs of patronage politics. Loss of employment, labor vulnerability and declining incomes, as in the case of school teachers and other civil servants, has had a generalized deleterious effect on service quality and human security in the region.

Fiscal management, rather than reorganization, has moved to the center stage of public administration. On the one hand, the financial base for public programs has been significantly reduced; on the other hand, budgetary processes have been streamlined. Budget cuts have been geared to attaining fiscal balance, facilitating the management of structural adjustment policies. Institutionally, this has translated into the primacy of the ministries of finance as the key actors and regulators of the administrative process. These ministries increasingly represent the paramountcy of the central banking authorities and the international financial institutions, such as the IMF, the World Bank or the Inter-American Development Bank.

In addition to the macro issues of privatization and fiscal management, the administrative reform under NPM has had some remarkable achievements, especially when it comes to the 'micro' and efficiency-oriented aspects of administration. Of all the activities implemented, the most clearly successful

have been the efforts to streamline procedures, de-bureaucratize and computerize
services. The quality and time of service rendered to customers has clearly improved in
many of the countries. This applies especially to licenses, certificates, filing income
taxes and a reduction of red tape. More substantial structural reforms have met with less
success, ranging from limited accomplishments (such as localization), to mere cos-
metic changes, to complete ineffectiveness,
or worse. This realization has prompted some
participants and analysts of the reform process in Latin America to call for a redefinition
of NPM principles along the lines of a more
socially oriented version of institutional
reform. Many point at the European social
democracies, and Anthony Giddens' *Third
Way* (Giddens, 1998) as an alternative to the
economic and ideological orthodoxy of neoliberalism. In this sense, CLAD's own document, 'A New Public Management for Latin
America' (CLAD, 1999), constitutes a call to
reconstruct an administrative paradigm. It
proposes a 'third way' of implementing market reforms with a human face: putting people
first, revitalizing civil society and emphasizing a more active and democratic state.

CONCLUSION

This interpretative and tentative exploration
makes it possible to hypothesize on the relationships between administrative culture,
structure and functions sketched above and
the larger social and political order. It has
also suggested some conjectures regarding
the dynamic relationship between such patterns and strategies of reform, which can be
summarized in six propositions.

1. The administrative systems of Latin
America reflect the distinctiveness and
complexity of the various national realities
and the common regional trends. The latter
include persistent dependence, the perpetuation of rigid and particularistic social

structures, chronic economic vulnerability,
weak and unstable growth, social marginali-
zation, low institutionalization and acute
social polarization. The above translates into
high levels of ambiguity and uncertainty.
Administrative change in the region is conditioned more by these circumstances than
by the declared goals of 'technical' reform.
Ostensibly, structural transformations have
taken place, yet administrative culture and
behavior have persisted, producing syncre-
tistic adaptations rather than profound
reorganizations. The political economy of
reform has been characterized by a bias for
the maintenance of the domestic and regional
status quo.

2. The administrative systems in Latin
America, unlike other peripheral areas, have
long exhibited the formal attributes of
bureaucracy, and successive reforms have
entrenched these traits. Yet, under the circumstances described here, the presence of
'legal-rational' characteristics do not constitute substantive indicators, let alone predictors, of responsiveness, effectiveness or
democratic accountability. Rather, the formality of the legal-rational model often hides
the reality of a 'mock' bureaucracy (Gouldner,
1954), where complex procedures and technical trappings are geared to a dysfunctional
mixture of issue non-resolution and non-
issue resolution. Public administration in
Latin America has been distinctively derivative. As a reflection of an entrenched center–
periphery regional and global order, it has
tended to follow vogues, recipes and solutions manufactured in the developed societies. In this sense, it has been exogenous in
its motivations, problem identification and
prescriptions (Crowther and Flores, 1984).
The tendency to define problems and questions from the vantage point of rather standard answers and solutions has provided for a
rather mechanistic and acritical approach.
The scientific and technological institutions
in the region have been more interested in
reproducing the prevailing modes of social
engineering than addressing larger contextual – and politically contentious – issues.

Technical cooperation has not fared any better.

3. In the past two decades there have been ostensible improvements in 'de-bureaucratizing', 'de-cluttering', reducing waiting times and cutting down red tape. This has been accompanied by deregulation, a reduction of the size of the civil service and a transfer of many public functions into private agencies. The incomplete transition to democracy of the 1980s, debt crises and structural adjustments have altered the content and instrumentalities of public policy (Nef, 1997). The region's administrative systems have been directly affected by current circumstances and challenges derived from a concerted effort at modernization along the lines of the prescriptions of Western governments and international agencies. However, this alteration has not resulted substantively in greater efficiency, let alone effectiveness to 'get things done' for the public; nor does it seem to effect a deep transformation of administrative practices and behavior.

4. The same applies to the question of administrative responsiveness to public demands. In a narrow technical sense, the transformation of the recipient into a 'client' – as has been attempted in numerous reforms – does not alter substantially the intrinsic quality of the service. A key problem in Latin America is the absence of citizenship in the public arena. The irony is that, while social demands on the public sector to tackle mounting problems and to provide more services are growing, the state apparatus is shrinking. What is happening instead is a revolution of rising frustrations resulting from the inability of the political systems and their bureaucracies to tend to the most basic problems people face in their daily lives.

5. In this, the inability to control corruption is indicative, and indeed the very logic, of the current prescriptions. Administrative practices in Latin America are immersed in a larger cultural matrix, containing values, behaviors and orientations towards the physical environment, the economy, the social system, the polity and culture itself. Corruption in Latin America is not only public: it is systemic. A predatory attitude towards resource extraction (often fueled by the foreign debt), possessive individualism, amoral familism, a weak civic consciousness and a tendency to imitate 'the modern', configures a conservative mind-set with ethical double standards. This also engenders irresponsibility and a lack of capacity (and will) to anticipate and make strategic policy shifts. Administrative reforms promoting privatization, a smaller role for the state, deregulation, downsizing, outsourcing and formal decentralization have failed to address the fundamental issues of inequality, lack of democracy and abuse that underpin the region's administrative structures and practices. They may have also encouraged official corruption (Robin, 1995).

6. Historically, the administrative experience of Latin America has been molded by numerous failed attempts at modernization and cyclical crises. This has resulted in a protracted condition of institutional underdevelopment. It has also contributed to perpetuating a self-fulfilling prophecy of immobility (Adie and Poitras, 1974). Without political and institutional development, addressing real issues such as poverty, unemployment or lack of effective citizenship, administrative reforms – even couched in the current rhetoric of public sector modernization – are mere epiphenomena (Martner, 1984). The contribution of the current reform vogue to development – and democracy – are mostly marginal, as the protection of market forces, not development (let alone democracy), is its prime directive.

Any profound administrative reform involves both structural and attitudinal (as well as value) changes. Efforts at administrative restructuring, 'modernization' and the like, need to address first, either directly or indirectly, the nature of administrative culture and the issue of democracy, or rather lack of democracy, in the region. Administrative culture is something heterogeneous, dynamic and syncretic. But, above all, culture is an agent, not an impediment for change (Maturana and Varela, 1980). It contains the seeds to bring about a critical awareness (Freire, 1971) of the multiple contextual factors – environmental, economic, social, political and ideological – that affect public policies and administration. The contradiction between liberalism and democracy (Macpherson, 1977) lies at the core of the governance problem of Latin America. Administrative modernization without real political democratic reform, beyond purely formal facades, is an interesting but often fruitless exercise.

REFERENCES

Adie, Robert and Poitras, Guy (1974) *Latin America. The Politics of Immobility.* Englewood Cliffs, NJ: Prentice-Hall, pp. 250–71.

Barber, William and Ronning, Neale (1966) *Internal Security and Military Power: Counterinsurgency and Civic Action in Latin America.* Columbus, OH: Ohio State University Press, pp. 217–45.

Baumgartner, Thomas, Burns, Tom and DeVille, Philippe (1977) 'Reproduction and Transformation of Dependency Relationships in the International System. A Dialectical Systems Perspective', *Proceedings of the Annual North American Meeting of the Society for General Systems Research*, pp. 129–36.

Black, Jan (1998) 'Participation and the Political Process: The Collapsible Pyramid,' in Jan Black (ed.), *Latin America. Its Problems and Its Promise. A Multidisciplinary Introduction.* Boulder, CO: Westview Press, p. 226.

Black, Jan (1986) *Sentinels of the Empire: the United States and Latin American Militarism.* New York: Greenwood Press.

Bonifacio, José Alberto (1995) 'Modernizacion del servicio civil en el contexto de la reforma estatal', *Revista centroamericana de Administracion Publica*, Nos 28 and 29 (January–June): 5–26.

Braudel, Fernand (1980) 'History and the Social Sciences: the *longue durée*', in Fernand Braudel, *On History.* Chicago: University of Chicago Press, pp. 25–54.

Burns, E. Bradford (1986) *Latin America. A Concise Interpretative History*, 4th edn. Englewood

Cliffs, NJ: Prentice–Hall, pp. 96–101, 134–53, 313–24.

Burns, E. Bradford (1998) 'The Continuity of the National Period,' in Jan Black (ed.), *Latin America. Its Problems and Its Promise. A Multidisciplinary Introduction.* Boulder, CO: Westview Press, pp. 70–6, 77–8.

Campos, Roberto de Oliveira (1967) 'Public Administration in Latin America', in Nimrod Raphaeli (ed.), *Readings in Comparative Public Administration.* Boston, MA: Alwyn and Bacon, pp. 286–7.

CLAD's Scientific Council (1999) 'A New Public Management for Latin America'. CLAD Document in *Revista del CLAD, Reforma y Democracia*, No. 13 (February).

Cox, Robert (1982) 'Gramsci, Hegemony and International Relations: An Essay on Method', *Millennium: Journal of International Relations*, 12 (2): 162–75.

Crowther, Win and Flores, Gilberto (1984) 'Problemas latinoamericanos en administración pública y dependencia de soluciones desde Estados Unidos', in Gilberto Flores and Jorge Nef (eds), *Administración Publica: Perspectivas Criticas.* San José, Costa Rica: ICAP, pp. 59–89.

Dumont, Rene (1970) *Cuba. ¿es socialista?* Caracas, Venezuela: Tiempo Nuevo SA.

Easton, David (1957) 'An Approach to the Analysis of Political Systems', *World Politics*, 9 (3): 384–5.

Freire, Paulo (1971) *Pedagogy of the Oppressed.* New York: Herder and Herder.

Furtado, Celso (1976) *Economic Development of Latin America*, 2nd edn. Cambridge: Cambridge University Press, pp. 107–17.

Giddens, Anthony (1998) *The Third Way: the Renewal of Social Democracy.* Cambridge: Polity Press; Walden, MA: Blackwell.

Gil, Barry, Rocamora, Joel and Wilson, Richard (1993) *Low Intensity Democracy: Political Power in the New World Order.* London: Pluto Press, pp. 3–34.

Gouldner, Alvin (1954) *Patterns of Industrial Bureaucracy.* Glencoe, IL: The Free Press, pp. 117–30.

Heady, Farrel (1984) *Public Administration. A Comparative Perspective*, 3rd edn. New York: Marcel Dekker, pp. 174–221, 338–42.

Jaguaribe, Helio (1964) *Desarrollo económico y desarrollo político.* Buenos Aires: EUDEBA, pp. 122–9.

Jaguaribe, Helio (1968) *Political Strategies of National Development in Brazil.* Palo Alto, CA: Stanford University Press, p. 144.

Jones, Lawrence and Thompson, Fred (1999) 'Un modelo para la nueva gerencia publica: leciones de los sectores publico y privado', *Revista del CLAD. Reforma y Democracia (Caracus)*, 14 June (electronic version, pp. 1–26).

Keen, Benjamin (1992) *A History of Latin America*, 4th edn. Boston, MA: Houghton-Mifflin, pp. 158–62, 182–3.

Lee, Rensselaer W. (1988) 'Dimensions of the South American Cocaine Industry', *Journal of Interamerican Studies*, 30 (3): 87–104.

Macpherson, Crawford Brough (1977) *The Life and Times of Liberal Democracy*. Oxford: Oxford University Press.

Malloy, James (1977) 'Authoritarianism and Corporatism in Latin America: the Modal Pattern', in James Malloy (ed.), *Authoritarianism and Corporatism in Latin America*. Pittsburgh, PA: Pittsburgh University Press, pp. 3–19.

Marini Ferreira, Caio, Marcio (1999) *Crise e reforma do estado: uma questão de cuidadania e valorização do servidor'*. Rio de Janeiro: Escola Nacional de Administração Pública, pp. 1–37.

Martner, Gonzalo (1984) 'El papel de la reforma administrativa en la estrategia del desarrollo', in Bernardo Kliksberg (ed.), *La reforma de la administración pública en América Latina. Elementos para una evaluación*. Alcalá de Henares, Spain: Instituto Nacional de Administración Publica, p. 62.

Maturana, Humberto and Varela, Francisco (1980) *Autopoiesis and Cognition. The Realization of the Cognitive*. Boston and Dordrecht: T. Reidell. (Boston Studies in the Philosophy of Science, Vol. 42.)

MercoPress (2011) 'Piñera Submits Bill to Repeal Financing Military with Copper Exports', August 17.

Mesa-Lago, Carmelo and Witte, Lothar (1992) 'Regímenes previsionales en el Cono Sur y en el area andina', *Nueva Sociedad*, No. 122 (November–December): 19–34.

Mills, C. Wright (1957) *The Power Elite*. New York: Oxford University Press, pp. 3–29.

Moreno, Francisco José (1969) *Legitimacy and Stability in Latin America. A Study of Chilean Political Culture*. New York: New York University Press, pp. 34–7.

Morstein-Marx, Fritz (1963) 'The Higher Civil Service as an Action Group in Western Political Development', in Joseph LaPalombara (ed.), *Bureaucracy and Political Development*. Princeton, NJ: Princeton University Press, p. 63.

MST (Landless Rural Workers Movement) (2001) Manifesto, 'Fundamental Principles for the Social and Economic Transformation of Brazil', *Journal of Peasant Studies*, 28 (2): 153–61.

Nef, Jorge (1991) 'Development Crisis and State Crisis: Lessons from Latin American Experience', in O.P. Dwivedi and P. Pitil (eds), *Development Administration in Papua New Guinea*. Boroko: ADCOL-PNG, pp. 10–33.

Nef, Jorge (1997) 'Estado, poder y sociales: una visión crítica,' in Raúl Urzúa (ed.), *Cambios sociales y política públicas en América Latina*. Santiago: Andros, pp. 233–62.

Nef, Jorge (1998) 'The Politics of Insecurity,' in Jan Black (ed.), *Latin America. Its Problems and its Promise. A Multidisciplinary Introduction*. Boulder, CO: Westview Press, pp. 239–40.

Nef, J. and Bensabat, R. (1992) '"Governability" and the Receiver State in Latin America: Analysis and Prospects', in Archibald Ritter, Maxwell Cameron and David Pollock (eds), *Latin America to the Year 2000. Reactivating Growth, Improving Equity, Sustaining Democracy*. New York: Praeger, pp. 171–5.

Nef, J. and Dwivedi, O.P (1981) 'Development Theory and Administration: A Fence Around an Empty Lot?', *The Indian Journal of Public Administration*, XXVIII (1): 42–66.

Nef, Jorge and Robles, Wilder (2000) 'Globalization, Neoliberalism and the State of Underdevelopment in the New Periphery', *Journal of Developing Societies*, XVI (1): 27–48.

Nun, José (1968) 'A Middle-Class Phenomenon: The Middle-Class Military Coup,' in James Petras and Maurice Zeitlin (eds), *Latin America: Reform or Revolution? A Reader*. Greenwich, CT: Fawcett, pp. 145–85.

Ormond, Derry and Löffler, Elke (1999) 'Nueva Gestión Pública ¿Que tomar y que dejar?', *Revista del CLAD. Reforma y Democracia*, No. 11 (February): 141–72.

Pérez Salgado, Ignacio (1997) 'El papel de la cooperación técnica internacional en el proceso de modernización del Estado y la gestión en América latina', *Revista del CLAD. Reforma y Democracia*, No. 8 (July): 247–70.

Riggs, Fred (1967) 'The Sala Model: An Ecological Approach to the Study of Comparative Administration', in Nimrod Raphaeli (ed.), *Readings in Comparative Public Administration*. Boston, MA: Alwyn and Bacon, pp. 415–16.

Robin, Theobald (1995) 'Globalization and the Resurgence of the Patrimonial State', *International Review of Administrative Sciences*, 61 (3): 424.

Robles, Wilder (2000) 'Beyond the Politics of Protest: The Landless Rural Workers Movement of Brazil',

Canadian Journal of Development Studies, XXI (3): 657–91.

Time Magazine (1977) 'Latin America: Good Neighbors Again?', *Time Magazine* 178 (7): January 3.

Véliz, Claudio (1980) *The Centralist Tradition of Latin America*. Princeton, NJ: Princeton University Press.

Vilas, Carlos (1995) 'Economic Restructuring, Neoliberal Reforms, and the Working Class in Latin America,' in Sandor Halebsky and Richard Harris (eds), *Capital, Power, and Inequality in Latin America*. Boulder, CO: Westview Press, pp. 137–63.

Vilas, Carlos (2000) 'Más allá del Consenso de Washington? Un enfoque desde la política de algunas propuestas del Banco Mundial sobre reforma administrativa', *Revista del CLAD. Reforma y Democracia*, No. 18 (October): 25–76.

Wharlich, Beatriz (1978) 'The Evolution of Administrative Science in Latin America', *International Review of Administrative Sciences*, No. 12: 70–92.

Website

Further references on Argentina: http://www.clad.org/siare_isis/innotend/calidad/calidargentina.html#1

36

Public Administration in Central and Eastern Europe

Patrycja Joanna Suwaj

INTRODUCTION

The purpose of this chapter is to provide an overview of the public administration landscape in Eastern and Central Europe, with a brief comparison with other countries that were previously under Soviet rule in Asia. The chapter is organized so as to provide a historical background of the countries in the region and trace the roots of contemporary public administration in the various periods that precede the fall of Communism and Soviet rule. It then proceeds to look at the reform efforts that began in the 1990s and concludes by identifying what the results have been on the ground.

Defining the region is itself worth an introductory discussion. References to Eastern Europe tend to vary in regard to what they refer to. For instance, the United Nations' Statistics Division includes the following countries: Belarus, Bulgaria, the Czech Republic, Moldavia, Poland, Romania, Russia, Slovakia, Ukraine, and Hungary. Other definitions include all the countries of what was once called "the Eastern Bloc",

i.e. all countries in Europe controlled by the Soviet Union, and therefore including the Baltic states. Central Europe is easier to define, since it is almost always referring to the four countries – Czech Republic, Hungary, Poland and Slovakia – that make up the Visegrad Group. For the purpose of this chapter, the distinction is made between the countries of Central and Eastern Europe (CEE countries) and those others that were under direct Soviet rule.

THE HISTORIC LEGACY OF PUBLIC ADMINISTRATION

The foundational code of present-day political systems in Europe dates back to the eighteenth-century doctrine of the Age of Enlightenment. The first of these is the principle of sovereignty of the people. It stands in opposition to absolute monarchy, as well as the principle encoded in the Soviet system where the vanguard party was elevated to the position of guardian and leader of the working class masses. As Izdebski and Kulesza (2004: 66–67) underline, there has always been a close link between the idea of the sovereign nation, on the one hand, and the postulates of political democracy, on the other.

The second principle is the idea of the rule of law, which stands in contrast to the police state, based on arbitrary use of authority. The state ruled by law is inseparably connected to the idea of a sovereign nation. In such a country a subject becomes a citizen and the law also binds authority, thereby giving citizens guarantees of respect for their rights and protection from lawlessness of authority. Authority is always limited, even when the will of citizens democratically legitimizes it.

The third principle is the postulate that individuals should be allowed and guaranteed to fulfil their freedoms. For this reason, the sovereign nation must establish constitutional and other procedural guarantees. Since the end of the Second World War, these rights and guarantees have been extended to the extra-territorial level, notably through international and regional conventions and other types of accords negotiated through the United Nations and other relevant bodies.

The fourth principle is the separation of power between the different branches of government: the executive, legislative and judicial. These three branches should keep each other in check and be horizontally accountable to each other.

The French Revolution gave practical expression to these Enlightenment ideas by initiating development of countries and public institutions, directed at implementation of the above postulates. This initial attempt on the European continent, however, did not succeed immediately. It took almost 150 years before these principles became institutional practice in Europe and another 50 years before they were fully adopted in Central and Eastern Europe.

The historical legacy of what happened in these latter countries includes the principles of totalitarian rule which began in Russia through the October Revolution of 1917 and spread to Central and Eastern Europe after the Second World War when the Soviet Union was able to extend its control westwards following Hitler's defeat. The totalitarian state aims at complete subordination of the individual to its commands. Thus, there are no independent courts, churches, trade unions, media or other institutions that are present in democratic society. The vanguard party based on strong internal discipline rules without fetters.

This system, called democratic centralism, was enforced in varying degrees throughout the region but was generally characterized by the following four types of subordination (Kudrycka, Peters and Suwaj 2009):

- *Organizational subordination.* Close hierarchical subordination of lower-level bodies to higher-level ones was at the center of the system. The practical existence of real and independent territorial self-government, therefore, was discontinued. This subordination (dependence) existed also in others spheres.
- *Personal subordination.* Elections to positions of authority either did not exist or were fiction. There were no competitive candidates; in practice, people were assigned to public offices by way of Party nominations. Retaining formal elections (like, e.g., in Poland) was in reality an act of political correctness and their results were falsified anyway. Personal assignment on territorial levels depended only on the governing party – besides, all members of councils as other key persons performing public function were nominated following this way. Not educated but obedient and easy to manipulate persons were appointed to high positions.
- *Competence subordination.* This meant that even if formally some decision-making competences were delegated to subnational levels, decisions were taken on the central level and were dependent on the official nomenclature anyway. Deciding about public matters that concerned local or regional level was in the hands of the central government and the central party, which from a formal point of view should have been beyond the government structure.
- *Financial subordination.* Local and regional levels were also financially dependent on decisions of the Communist Party. Local budgets were a part of the central budget where division

of financial means took place in the supreme bodies. Central grants composed the lion's share of local incomes, while possibilities to decide on financial resources at the local level were very limited. The community did not own property within its territorial boundaries; nor did its local government body. Buildings and other types of property were owned by the state and only administered by the local administration.

Michal Illner (1999: 12) has portrayed the Soviet system in the following way:

> Public administration and self-government were amalgamated into a single system based on the ideology of democratic centralism. According to this ideology, no contradictions could, by definition, arise between the "real" interests of the state and the interests of its territorial subsystems because they were all supposed to express the interests of the working class. A single political and administrative body – the local version of the soviets – was, therefore, made responsible for advocating both local and central interests.

The common feature of administration in CEE countries in Communist times was accepting nearly every agenda concerning public life with a simultaneous lack of skills in satisfying social needs in a proper way. After the nationalization of industries, communication, and banks as well as agricultural reform, socialization of commerce, the introduction of the public economy of accommodation, and a common medical service as part of the social health service, it was extended to incorporate new fields of economic activities into a planned economy (Błaś, Boć and Jeżewski 2003: 21). As a result, the following tasks of state administration were singled out in the literature on socialism:

- traditional regulating and disciplinary tasks as an original sphere of administrative activity of the country, ruling the people with orders and bans executed by state recourses;
- tasks in the sphere of socialized economy, which were carried out through the dominance of the socialized means of production of basic economic processes, notably economic plans,

recommendations and orders for the nominated managerial personnel; and
- tasks manifest through providing with services by the country on a massive scale in order to satisfy essential human needs.

As some authors underline (e.g. Elander 1995: 6–7; Illner 1999: 12–13), it is interesting to reveal some examples of contradictions that appeared between the official ideological model promoted during Communist times and its real nature. One such example would be "the erosion of territorial government by economic organizations". Vertically organized and controlled by the central authorities, enterprises frequently influenced decisions about local issues. For this reason, they can even be referred to as centers of power, which often possessed considerably more money than the local administration. What is more, they were responsible for public sector tasks that pre-empted the responsibility of local administration. As Illner (1992: 42) indicates, "in some places, enterprises even became the main sponsors of local development, making territorial authorities ultimately dependent on them. The political and economic relevance of territorial government was thus undermined not only by centralism but also by the increasing strength and patronage of economic organizations". When the transition to a market economy and liberal democracy took place, these powerful enterprises – which employed too many people, where staff were paid whether or not they worked and management was very incompetent – became a real problem and burden for these countries.

This degenerated model of central guidance affected not only the contemporary shape of administration but also it distorted the attitudes of people. For the inhabitants of the countries that fell under Soviet control, it became a norm to circumvent the law. Virtually every issue which lay in the competence of the bureaucracy (whether it was planning permission, admitting a child to a pre-school, medical and nursing service in hospital, or a trip abroad), required not only the ability to negotiate or to persuade but also having contacts in the governing party. Jan Boć (2003: 291) referred to this phenomenon as "letaprivation" (from French "*l'Etat privée*"). Nepotism, unequal treatment, an excessive development of power, widely spread corruption – these are the elements of mundane life of that time.

The legacy of totalitarian rule in CEE countries survived until the end of the 1980s and the beginning of 1990. What is more, some of those features are still problematic for these countries, such as suffering losses by state enterprises in Poland, or deeply rooted corruption in the majority of post-Communist countries. In Belarus, almost all features of the Soviet system have been retained under the strong influence of President Lukashenka's regime.

The fall of 1989, called the Autumn of Nations in Central and Eastern Europe, resulted in the breakdown of the Soviet empire and changed the historical path of these countries. Poland is an instance of a country where taking over the government and building a new democratic country was conducted in a peaceful way; the two people who are ascribed the most merit for this matter were the initiator and the leader of the independent self-governing trade union "Solidarity", Lech Walesa, and the superior of the Roman Catholic Church at the time, Pope John Paul II.

The various measures introduced before 1991 generally resulted in weakening of the Communist Parties in the countries which were under the influence of the USSR. The genesis of the Autumn of Nations dates back to 1980s; that was the time when Solidarity was formed in Poland, opposition movements grew stronger, and the first attempts of introducing reforms in socialist countries were made (including *perestroika* and *glasnost* in the USSR). Round Table Talk in Poland as well as the opposition's success in parliamentary elections in 1989 became a model for similar transformations in the remaining countries of socialist CEE countries, especially in Hungary, Czechoslovakia,

the German Democratic Republic, Bulgaria, Romania, and Albania.

As a consequence of the Autumn of Nations, the Warsaw Pact was finally dissolved. In addition, all the units of Red Army were withdrawn from the CEE countries. The withdrawal was connected with a nuclear disarmament, which extensively increased security not only in Europe but also in the whole world. An indirect effect of the Autumn of Nations was the breakup (much of it in a bloody fashion) of Yugoslavia, but also the peaceful division of Czechoslovakia into the Czech Republic and Slovakia.

The main point is that the dramatic events at the end of the 1980s resulted in the overthrow of the totalitarian political system and a restoration of freedom of speech and democracy in the former countries of the Communist Block. At the same time it raised popular expectations about higher levels of prosperity that proved not so easy to meet.

REFORM EFFORTS IN THE 1990s AND AFTER

Various international institutions and experts argued that the public administration in CEE countries required as quick a rearrangement as possible, because it was the condition under which political transformations aiming to strengthen democracy and the market economy could be made. The need for rapid changes mainly concerned:

- abandoning central planning as well as the command and divided system of economy management;
- beginning the process of privatization and re-privatization;
- restricting functions and influences of government administration;
- introducing different forms of civil law not only by administration but also within administration;
- keeping the powerful influence where needed; at the same time, partly abandoning delivering

public services by the state itself (free of charge) and implementing equivalent benefits (partly or wholly paid);

- acquiring a fresh attitude towards management of public affair; and
- restoring a self-governing administration.

The transformation entailed measures that could build on institutional patterns that had existed in pre-Communist times. As Illner (1999: 14–15) shows, this was particularly true for self-governing traditions in Central Europe that had been in place before:

Aside from the legacies of the Communist system, the older, pre-communist traditions of public administration also played some role in the 1990 reforms. Territorial government has quite a long history in all three Central and Eastern European countries (Poland, Czechoslovakia and Hungary) and the pre-communist system has been an inspiration for reformers. In the territories that belonged to the former Austro-Hungarian monarchy (the Czech Lands, Hungary and Galicia), modern territorial administration was founded in 1862. With modifications, this system was maintained in both countries until 1945, and it served again as the point of reference for recent reforms. In Poland, which until 1918 was partitioned between its three neighbouring imperial powers, elements of the Austro-Hungarian, Prussian and Russian legal systems coexisted after reunification until the 1930s, and here the Austrian and the German systems of Territorial administration were the largest inspiration for the reforms of 1990.

At the same time, it should be pointed out that not all countries shared a similar legacy. For instance, Bulgaria, Latvia, Romania, Slovakia and Slovenia did not have developed traditions of self-governance before Communist rule (Rydlewski 2007).

Generally since 1989, CEE countries have been involved in a fundamental transition, consisting of three paths connected and interrelated to each other: (1) introducing democracy and democratic state institutions; (2) shifting to a market system; and (3) moving towards integration into the European Union (EU) (e.g. Fournier 1998a). This does not mean that the countries have

followed a single path. Models differ from each other in scope of timing, processing and content of taken reforms and the process has been dependent on internal political, social or cultural conditions.

As researchers of transformation and reform periods notice, it is possible to organize the analysis along different lines. Bouckaert, Nakrošis and Nemec (2010) make their distinction based on the political legacy. Thus, they refer to two groups of countries that embarked on public administration reforms. The first is composed of the countries of Central Europe and the Baltic states – countries that made efforts to join the EU. The second group are countries which were previously under direct Soviet rule. Péteri and Zentai (2002) make a different distinction, where the point of reference is the moment when public administration reforms really began and showed an impact on the political and administrative systems. According to these authors, Hungary and Poland started political and institutional changes at a relatively high speed: political, legislative and structural reforms were implemented in two to three years. This quick start was followed by almost a decade of slower process reforms. Bulgaria and Latvia belong to the second group, where after the initial revolutionary political changes (independence, new constitution) the actual public sector reforms were delayed. After several years of stagnation, structural reforms and the modernization of local governments were started only in the late 1990s. In the third group of countries – Croatia and Slovakia – not only did the basic structural changes start only after a significant delay but also they were unable to launch any comprehensive reforms in the first decade of transition.

In this chapter we will accept the geographic division as the basis for discussing the reform programs since the early 1990s. The main focus will be on Central and Eastern Europe, followed by a briefer discussion of what was done in the countries formerly under direct Soviet rule.

Reforms in Central and Eastern Europe

The first period of reforms in the CEE countries in the early 1990s concentrated on building systems of public administration based on democratic foundations. Reforms in these countries were relatively similar and they took their lead from the same OECD (Organization for Economic Co-operation and Development) source. The advice emphasized the importance of transformation of public institutions if a democratic system of governing and market economy is to be successfully achieved and as fast a change as possible.

The reform programs benefitted from significant financial, organizational and expert support from the United States and Canada. Support from the OECD and organizations like the Open Society Institute enabled the realization of projects focused on building capacity and institutions. These foreign technical assistance programs played critical roles not only in design and introduction but also during the implementation of reforms.

Initially, democratization meant establishing new constitutional provisions transferring power to elected representatives, laws protecting freedom of opinion and expression, the establishment of a multi-party system and the possibility for the electorate to replace those in power. The following steps towards democracy also required the creation of a legally constituted state, acting under the rule of law and with the elimination of arbitrary use of public power, openness and transparency promotion or systemic fight with corruption. It therefore presupposed a thorough transformation of the system of governance; government was no longer at the service of a party or class. Public administration in the new democratic dispensation represented the permanence, continuity and regularity of the state, as well as implementation of the policies of the government in power. Administration is not only neutral execution of policy but also a constitutional safeguard. Civil servants are

protected from partisan influences, at least in the sphere of legal guarantees. Other measures included the introduction of impartial control procedures, channels for interaction with the public at large, and the decentralization of authority (Fournier 1998a).

The process of economic transformation was based on similar actions for building a market economy. Market reforms meant mostly the necessity of abandoning the central planning and command-and-quota system of economy management in favor of private initiatives. These elements were included in a new legal and administrative framework. Privatization of state-owned enterprises, trade and price liberalization, establishment of mechanisms supporting markets through taxation and bank restructuring were at the center of these reforms. In fact, government departure from direct production of goods and services required wholesale transformation of the public law, duties, structures and personnel of national public administrations and their regional agencies (Fournier 1998a). Despite debates on the speed of reforms and forms of privatization during this early stage of economic transition, the basic institutions of a market economy were established and the process had been completed by the end of the decade (Péteri and Zentai, 2002). The cost of this transformation, however, was high. General government expenditures decreased and unemployment rose, although the effects were less serious in Hungary and Poland.

The domestic political context and, especially, the stability and persistence of the ruling political regime were major elements that significantly facilitated or hindered the administrative reform processes. Party systems took time to stabilize, and coalition arrangements were often feeble. Major legislative and institutional reform measures were subject to not only political deliberations but also to bargaining processes in which the professional clarity and coherence of proposals frequently got lost (Péteri and Zentai 2002). For example, in Bulgaria the Leftist parties supported decentralization to the lowest possible level, while the Rightist political party favored the region as the basic unit of economic development (Djildjov 2002). Shifts in political power, e.g. as a result of elections, also influenced the pace and direction of reforms. In Poland the model of new territorial administration had been prepared in 1992,[1] but it was implemented only in 1998 when forces sympathetic to this particular model got back into power. In Slovakia and Croatia, the radical shift from the previous political regime in 1998 and 2000, respectively, opened up the possibility of designing and launching fresh decentralization programs (Péteri and Zentai 2002).

The other factor that significantly influenced the reform processes in Central and Eastern Europe was the desire in these countries to join the European Union. This process began in the late 1990s and was completed in the early 2000s. The incorporation of CEE countries in the EU was the fourth wave of enlargement and was generally deemed to be the most challenging (Metcalfe 1998). Questions were being asked whether these countries would be able to meet the Copenhagen Criteria and develop the management capacities needed to sustain governmental performance as a member state. The process had been made even more difficult as the threshold of membership requirements had moved up even further since the relatively easy incorporation of Austria, Finland and Sweden.

The task of integrating the CEE countries was further complicated by the fact that EU itself had a significant "management deficit", which urgently need to be resolved. Because of internal institutional deficiencies and weaknesses and the need to deal with them, candidate countries in the early 2000s were negotiating to join a system which would be changed in some quite unpredictable ways by their incorporation within it (Metcalfe 1998).

The EU's own assessment of the 10 candidate CEE countries[2] in 1997 pointed to many shortcomings that had to be tackled before,

or as part of, the accession process (Fournier 1998a). The main observations were:

Political Institutions. The assessment was on the whole favorable, since seven of the 10 countries were considered as already meeting the conditions laid down in Copenhagen. Two others (Bulgaria and Romania) were "on the way" to meeting these conditions. In only one country, Slovakia, was the situation considered to be unsatisfactory. The situation of minorities was considered to be satisfactory on the whole, although cases where improvement was needed were mentioned, particularly as regards the Russian-speaking population in the Baltic states, the Hungarian minority in Slovakia, and gypsy populations in Central and Southern Europe.

Justice. There were specific comments on the situation in some countries: for example, regarding the independence of judges in Slovakia; penal procedure in Bulgaria; the definition of the powers of the prosecutor-general in Lithuania; and judicial control of prosecutors' activities in Romania. For a number of countries (Bulgaria, Poland, Slovakia and Slovenia), the role played by the constitutional court or its equivalent was assessed favorably. On the whole, however, the Commission remained highly circumspect in its evaluation of the ability of these countries' judicial systems to apply the Community *acquis*[3] in the medium term.

Local Government. In 1997 all countries had already introduced local autonomy at the level of municipalities, but only some had an intermediate level between the municipal and central level, a matter that was described but not criticized. The Commission stressed, however, the need for decentralized authorities to achieve greater financial autonomy and mentions excessive financial dependence on central government in a number of countries, notably Bulgaria, the Czech Republic, Poland and Romania.

Administrative Reform. This proved to be an area of special concern since all countries needed to design and implement a coherent overall plan of administrative reforms. Although reforms had been made in some countries like Poland, Hungary, Lithuania and Slovenia, by 1997 there was no real reform momentum in the region. It only began in earnest in 1999 following the EU candidacy assessment, and in many countries, including Poland, has yet to be completed today.

Central Administration. The Commission only mentioned the role of central government sparingly, observing that it is too weak in Slovakia, which slows down strategic decision making. Bulgarian ministries needed basic reform, while in Latvia the effectiveness and cohesiveness of the various ministries was highly uneven, and in Estonia they were considered to be too small and overloaded. The administrative structures devoted to coordinating European affairs were on the whole looked on in a favorable light in almost all countries. As regards procedures, it was recommended that Slovenia improves coordination procedures between ministries. Romanian civil servants were reported to have shown an unwillingness to assume responsibility, while in Bulgaria, there was a need for greater transparency in the handling of public affairs.

Civil Service. Few countries had introduced specific legislation governing the civil service in 1997. Hungary had done so in 1992, and amended it in 2001. Latvia did it in 1994, with a new law adopted in 2000. Estonia and Poland followed in 1996. It should be noted that Poland introduced a new law on the civil service three more times: in 1998, 2006 and 2008.

Fighting Corruption. Almost every CEE country suffered from widespread corruption, the exception being Slovenia, where there was no evidence of significant corruption in the civil service. The recommendations concerning improved effectiveness of the judicial system and the police and weeding out corruption in the civil service, therefore, were very much stressed in the Commission report. The inclusion of corruption as an issue of key importance for EU accession implies that there exists an anti-corruption framework that is already binding on EU member states and to which candidate states must conform. In fact no such framework exists, or at least not in a formal sense, and it is clear that the corruption issue arose only in the context of extending accession rights to the CEE countries (Suwaj 2005).

Reforms in the countries of the former soviet union

Whether the collapse of the Soviet Union is blamed on the failure of President Gorbachev's *perestroika* and *glasnost* program or on something else, it was a multidimensional process, and it is difficult to set it in unambiguous, chronological time frames, in contrast to the formal process of the collapse, which was officially started by Russia declaring its independence.

The collapse of the Soviet Union led to the establishment of 15 new countries.[4] The patterns of reform vary among these countries and progress has been more uneven than in the CEE countries. As Bouckaert, Nakrošis, and Nemec (2011: 11) point out, "the contents and timing of reforms is individual and depends on the country-specific internal and external environment." These authors indicate that the reforms that were carried out, for example, in the Ukraine, where in fact they started relatively early (1991–97), were chaotic not only in the socio-economic sphere but also in the sphere of the organization and functioning of the country. In spite of the fact that many different legal acts attempting to reform the system were prepared, growing political destabilization considerably restricted not only the success of those reforms but also even the chance to introduce them. A similar lack of stability characterized the reforms also in Kyrgyzstan and Armenia (the conflict between Armenia and Azerbaijan lasted until May 1994). Admittedly, Armenia managed to rebuild basic government institutions later in the 1990s, but fundamental reforms of public administration and civil service were not carried out until the end of the decade (Lucking 2003). Compared to those countries, Kazakhstan comes out positively. The 1997 "Kazakhstan 2030" blueprint was adopted and served as a guide for consistent reform efforts, including an increase of government's effectiveness, introduction of up-to-date information technologies, elimination of bureaucracy in government organs and restriction of state intervention in the economy.

Russia is perceived as a country in which reforms were systematically inhibited or even blocked by the people representing the preceding system. As a result, essential reforms have started late. A Civil Service

Act was passed by the State Duma in 2004, a civil service bureau was established in 2007, and in 2009 Russian President, Dmitry Medvedev, signed a decree to reform the civil service system between 2009 and 2013 as a part of a drive against corruption. Because these reforms are recent, it is difficult to assess their consequences and impact (Obolonskij 2009; Bouckaert, Nakrošis and Nemec 2011).

Europeanization tendencies in the countries of the former USSR are visible in chosen areas and the process is slowly advancing, notably in the Ukraine. They are manifest, for example, in the endeavor to adjust the education standards in the area of public administration at university level and applying for European accreditation given by European Association for Public Administration Accreditation (EAPAA). As stated by the European Commission on the subject of EU enlargement: "At the moment there are no access negotiations with Ukraine, Moldova or Georgia. All resolutions concerning such perspective would have to be taken unanimously by all member states".

RESULTS OF THE REFORMS

It is possible to distinguish between three separate periods of public administration reform based on what has been done in the past 20 years. The first period was characterized by constitutional reforms which radically changed the political system as a whole and brought fundamental democratic instruments (Ágh 2009). In reality, this transformation was a far-flung civilizing project, reconstructing the grounds for how the state and the economy function. The results from this initial wave vary from country to country. It can be deemed especially successful in Poland because it has not only been sustained in later phases but also resulted in big material and cultural gains. Since the reforms were initiated in that country, the gross

domestic product (GDP) has increased 10 times while Polish salaries have increased 16 times. As Ágh (2009) points out, the reforms in the initial phase paved the ground for a political, economic and social transformation, which together with the task of nation building, have characterized the whole period since 1990.

A second period began in the late 1990s and included the transfer of responsibilities to local governments, moving towards reformed social assistance systems, where both local and national governments had a new role, as well as developing transparent regulatory mechanisms (Péteri and Zentai 2002). These second-generation reforms are necessary in all democratization processes in order to move on to the tasks of institutionalizing and fine-tuning the reforms. The main components of the second-wave reforms are the institution-building initiatives aimed at good governance and increasing citizen inputs into the policy-making process. The quest for good government includes the creation of a more professional civil service, the modernization of local government, judicial reforms and the establishment of a more constructive dialogue with civil society. This task of institution building has been especially crucial in order to create the social capacity for Europeanization (Ágh 2009).

The third period may be best described as the post-accession time. Discrepancies between institutional and policy harmonization have been noticed by the European Commission, because as Ágh (2009) points out: "the legal harmonization showed the implementation gap between the formal rules and non–adequate practices". Two processes, which at a first glance are simultaneous and lead to institutional changes and changes in scope of policies, have not been equally easy to implement. Institutional changes have been "hard" criteria and put under stronger scrutiny when compared to "soft" and more complicated changes in the matter of policies. Policy transfer has come to the fore much more in the post-accession period, and it has been closely connected with the second wave of institutional reforms aimed at completing the democratic institutionalization (Ágh 2009).

Changes have occurred in CEE countries as the effect of access to the EU has made them institutionally similar to Western European countries. Fournier (1998b) pointed out the following determinants as characteristic for Western Europe and, today, they are also largely incorporated into the governance systems of CEE countries:

1. Central Organisation and Decision-Making
1.1 a constitution guaranteeing the right of the people to replace those in power, the separation of powers, and the rule of law;
1.2 a government organisation providing for effective co-ordination among the ministries and a sound link with budgeting, giving the Prime Minister sufficient authority to assume the political leadership of the country;
1.3 procedures to ensure a co-ordinated policy-making and implementing process including procedures for producing laws and regulations, ensuring that these are proper from a legal and technical standpoint and making it possible to assess their financial, economic and social impact;
1.4 an organisation of ministries whereby Ministers and policy staffs are freed from day-to-day implementation of policies and can instead concentrate on devising policies, drafting statutes and overseeing their implementation;
1.5 a public sector which, in the areas in which it operates, is given specific tasks to fulfil with a degree of management autonomy, within the framework of clearly laid out legal structures.

2. Territorial Administration, and Relations with Citizens and Economic Actors
2.1 a certain degree of decentralisation which, depending on the country, can apply at one or more levels with varying responsibilities and powers;
2.2 interaction between the national government's territorial services institutions and local/regional authorities, making it possible to implement public policy effectively throughout the country;
2.3 a set of rules, sometimes laid out in a code of administrative procedures, governing relations between citizens and their government, including obligations to ensure equal access to public services, to justify decisions

and respect time requirements, to conduct proceedings in which all parties have a right to notice and an opportunity to be heard, to provide for remedies and appeals, etc. (for instance through an Ombudsman-type institution).

2.4 a set of rules and guidelines providing for ongoing communication between the government and civil society and its components, including NGOs and unions.

3. Means of Action and Control
3.1 a professional civil service, governed by laws, with hiring and promotion based on human resources management policies (including merit, skills, motivation, stable work force), loyally implementing government policy.
3.2 a set of rules and ethical guidelines, guaranteeing the accountability of public institutions and the reliability of administrative acts, including priorities governing the ethical behavior of public servants;
3.3 budget and tax authorities which can ensure that taxes are collected and that public funds are correctly managed and efficiently spent;
3.4 internal and outside institutions responsible for monitoring administrative decision making, respected by civil servants and safeguarding against corruption;
3.5 ready access by citizens and business to a court system with procedures providing for the prompt and final settlement of disputes including, where appropriate, the development of capacities to address economic, administrative and other special areas.

The period after the accession of CEE countries to the EU has been characterized by a slower pace of reforms and dealing with challenges based on growing social expectations, financial crisis and political games that tend to accompany every election. Another feature of the post-accession period is the inclination to fall back on "trendy" approaches, notably the embracing of New Public Management (NPM). Estonia is a case in point, where NPM has been adopted to the point where it is seen as "over-idealizing" the private sector (Randma-Liiv 2008; Bouckaert, Nakrošis and Nemec 2011: 17). Key companies, e.g. the railways, were privatized in a wave of selling state property in the early 2000s although in the case of the railways it was returned to state ownership some years later. Randma-Liiv (2008) points out that this tendency to over-idealize the private sector and the free-market economy continues in many of the CEE countries.

A recent comparative study of public administration and management reforms in these countries found significant variation in the types and orientation of reforms (Bouckaert, Nakrošis and Nemec 2011). Based on classifications of reforms done by Coombes and Verheijen (1997) and Pollitt and Bouckaert (2004), it was possible to arrange countries according to three types of reform: (1) radical, (2) mixed and (3) incremental. The majority of CEE countries – Hungary, Latvia, Lithuania, Slovakia and Romania – fall into the mixed type of reforms. Hungary is an example where the legal and organizational frames of a *Rechtsstaat* (rule of law) were established in the early 1990s and shortly after that the country faced implementation of managerial methods and techniques in the public sector (Jenei, 2008). Estonia is the best example of a country attempting radical reforms. As Bouckaert, Nakrošis and Nemec (2011) point out, a characteristic attribute of the Estonian reforms was the desire "to jump straight into having modern management systems without previously establishing a solid base – the classical hierarchically structured public administration". The key aim of Estonian administration was not building solid democratic fundamentals, but to increase the effectiveness of public institutions. Hence, as authors of the report point out, the consequence of implementing the reforms was a reduction of the state's role and contribution to development of ideas based on "minimum state" (Bouckaert, Nakrošis and Nemec 2011: 18). Poland and the Czech Republic represent the incremental type. For example, in 2006 the Czech government proposed the introduction of changes along NPM lines, yet afterwards withdrew from taking any drastic steps in that direction. So far, in Poland there has been no crucial interest in the approach of NPM, and its impact on reorganization of public administration has been minimal.

The idea of borrowing practices from the private sector for transfer to the public sector – a core principle of the NPM – seems to lose its grip on the field in the CEE countries. New approaches are emerging: for example, governance, which pulls public administration away from economistic thinking and towards a greater concern with its relation to law and politics. There is also a growing interest in promoting a return to the source and roots of European legal culture. Because of its reluctance to adopt NPM methods, Poland is a leader in helping these new ideas emerge.

Creating the legal and organizational frames for a *Rechtsstaat* is a first step in this direction but, as Jenei (2008) argues, it does not necessarily mean a state functioning along classical Weberian principles only. In countries like those of Central and Eastern Europe where the respect for law is still quite low, there is a danger of over-legislation and over-regulation, and thus a risk to efficiency and effectiveness in service delivery. There is also a risk of increased corruption in these circumstances.

It seems from the experiences in the CEE countries so far that neither NPM nor Weberian principles alone will bring about improved public management. Each approach has its protagonists, but none is absolutely right. It is in this context that the idea of a neo-Weberian state has gained ground among both theorists and practitioners. The outcome of the lively debate that has ensued suggests that putting some key Weberian elements of a neo-Weberian state approach into place is a prerequisite for subsequent success with public management reforms (see, e.g., Pollit and Bouckaert 2004; Hajnal and Jenei 2008; Jenei 2008; Potůček 2008; Randma-Liiv 2008; Nemec 2010). In short, what is needed is a balanced and pragmatic approach.

The final issue concerns the extent to which reproducing new approaches to public administration and management is being secured through training and educational institutions. Although the influences from the West are undeniable, teaching and research in the post-Communist countries still falls behind America and Western Europe. For instance, few public administration programs in CEE countries have achieved accreditation from the EAPAA. For example, in Poland there are some 200 programs, but only one of them – Bialystok School of Public Administration – has obtained such accreditation. Furthermore, a review of the literature indicates that there are relatively few researchers interested in public administration. There is no real tradition of research in public administration. The best researchers are found in adjacent fields such as economics, law and political science. It is not clear, therefore, how far local researchers will contribute to new thinking in the public administration field in these countries.

CONCLUSION

The political, administrative and economic reforms in the CEE countries have proceeded far enough that there is no longer a possibility of return to what prevailed in Communist days. Political democracy and some form of market economy are taken for granted. Both democracy and market economy have their weaknesses in many of these countries and they lag behind Western Europe with regard to such issues as combating corruption. Yet, access to and membership in the European Union has given the countries reasons for embarking on reforms that otherwise would not necessarily have happened.

At the same time, it is clear that the momentum for reform was driven by the conditions associated with EU membership and once the countries had been accepted in the European Union, the pace of reform slackened. The pressure was no longer there to the same extent. Analysts began talking about "drifting" away from the original goals of reform (Hughes, Sasse and Gordon 2004; Goetz 2005; Bouckaert, Nakrošis and Nemec 2011). In addition, the high expectations that political leaders, as well as ordinary citizens,

held about social and economic improvement did not materialize as fast as anticipated. It became increasingly difficult to sustain the drive to reform public management.

This does not mean that improving the system of public administration has ceased. The need for it is there and politicians realize how much is at stake for their own credibility if government institutions fail to deliver in a convincing manner. The issue today, therefore, is not so much the need for reform but how to go about it. The days of ideological conviction and enthusiasm, driven notably by beliefs in the NPM model, are gone. There is a return to the basics, i.e. the legal and administrative culture that is historically associated with the countries in Europe. Max Weber is being revisited, even though his ideas are not reinstated lock, stock and barrel, but rather in a selective fashion. Many theorists in the region nowadays embrace the concept of a neo-Weberian state, implying that reforms won't work unless they rest on a solid organizational foundation that reflects the core Weberian principles.

While this chapter has tried to identify the principal features of public administration in Central and Eastern Europe, it has also pointed to differences among countries in the region. It is important to recognize that while they share much in common as a result of their exposure to Communism and the desire to become members of the EU, they do follow separate tracks both in terms of direction and intensity of reforms. For example, Pridham (2008) while comparing ongoing changes in Latvia and Slovakia, on grounds of EU political membership conditions, noticed that while Latvia continues pre-accession reforms in respect to its anti-corruption policy, Slovakia has difficulties with processing judicial system reforms.

This also means that some countries have fared better than others when it comes to improving the management and administration of public services. Meyer-Sahling (2011), while analyzing the situation of the civil service (and its professionalization) in after accession to the European Union, emphasizes three paths of change that in his opinion proves the lack of a single pattern. The first path is a continuation of civil service reforms, characteristic for the Baltic states. The second case is constituted by those countries in which changes depart from pre-accession assumptions and end in reform backsliding – the Czech Republic, Poland, Slovakia and Slovenia being cases in point. Authors of a 2007 World Bank Report evaluating administrative capacity of CEE countries two years after accession to the European Union came to similar conclusions. In regard to performance management in government, policy coordination and human resource management, Lithuania and Latvia were classified as the lead countries, while Poland, the Czech Republic and Slovakia were classified as weak. Hungary is pointed out by Meyer-Sahling as an ambiguous case which represents a combination of successful civil service reforms with simultaneous departure from them.

It would be wrong, therefore, to conclude by suggesting that there is a special CEE approach to public administration reflecting its historical legacies. Countries in the region are increasingly exposed to ideas from other places and in a competitive global context they have little choice but to respond to new challenges by adopting approaches that work. What does make the CEE countries worthy of a special chapter is clearly the specific circumstances under which they have had to embark on reforms.

NOTES

1 Michal Kulesza, Jerzy Stepien and Jerzy Regulski – authors of the early 1990s reforms – are to be remembered as great Polish reformers.

2 The candidate countries were Poland, the Czech Republic, Slovakia, Slovenia, Hungary (the Central European countries), Bulgaria, Romania (South-East Europe) and Lithuania, Latvia and Estonia (North-East Europe).

3 The EU acquis refers to the accumulated legislation, legal acts and court decisions which constitute the body of European Union law. The term means "that which has been agreed upon".

4 The countries are Armenia, Azerbaijan, Belarus, Estonia, Georgia, Kazakhstan, Kyrgyzstan, Lithuania, Latvia, Moldova, Russia, Tajikistan, Turkmenistan, Ukraine and Uzbekistan.

REFERENCES

Ágh, A. 2009. "Politics and Policy in East-Central Europe in the Early 21st Century: Synergies and Conflicts between Policy Regimes and Political Systems." *The NISPAcee Journal of Public Administration and Policy*, II (1): Summer.

Błaś, A., J. Boć and J. Jeżewski (eds) 2003. *Administracja publiczna*. Wrocław: Kolonia Limited.

Boć, J. 2003. "Kadry." In: A. Błaś, J. Boć and J. Jeżewski (eds), *Administracja publiczna*. Wrocław: Kolonia Limited.

Bouckaert, G., V. Nakrošis, and J. Nemec 2011. "Public Administration and Management Reforms in CEE: Main Trajectories and Results." *The NISPAcee Journal of Public Administration and Policy*, IV (1): Summer.

"Central Europe" – The Future of the Visegrad Group 2005. *The Economist*, 14 April.

Coombes, D., and T. Verheijen 1997. *Public Management Reform: Comparative Experience from East and West*. Brussels: European Commission.

Djildjov, A. 2002. "Methods and Techniques of Managing Decentralization Reforms in Bulgaria." In: G. Peteri (ed.), *Mastering Decentralization and Public Administration Reforms in Central and Eastern Europe*. Budapest: OSI/LGI.

Dimitrova, A. 2010. "The New Member States of the EU in the Aftermath of Enlargement: Do New European Rules Remain Empty Shells?" *Journal of European Public Policy*, 17 (1).

Elander, I. 1995. *Between centralism and localism: On the development of local self-government in post-socialist Europe*. Paper presented at conference, Democratization and Decentralization: Four Years of Local Transformation in Central and Eastern Europe, Krakow, 2–6 August.

Fournier, J. 1998a. "Governance and European Integration — Reliable Public Administration." SIGMA Paper No. 23, OECD.

Fournier, J. 1998b. "Administrative Reform in the Commission Opinions Concerning the Accession of the Central and Eastern European Countries to the European Union." SIGMA Paper No. 23, OECD.

Goetz, K.H. 2005. "The New Member States and the EU: Responding to Europe." In: S. Bulmer and C. Lequesne (eds), *The Member States of the European Union*. Oxford: Oxford University Press.

Hajnal, G., and G. Jenei 2008. "The Study of Public Management in Hungary." In: W. Kickert (ed.) *The Study of Public Management in Europe and the US*. Routledge: London and New York. pp. 208–233.

Hughes, J., G. Sasse, and C.E. Gordon 2004. "Conditionality and Compliance in the Eu's Eastward Enlargement: Regional Policy and the Reform of Sub-National Governance." *Journal of Common Market Studies*, 42(3): 523–551.

Illner, M. 1999. "Territorial Decentralization: An Obstacle to Democratic Reform in Central and Eastern Europe?" In: J.D. Kimball (ed.), *The Transfer of Power. Decentralization in Central and Eastern Europe*. Budapest: LGI.

Illner, M. 1992. "Municipalities and Industrial Paternalism in a 'Real Socialist' Society." In: P. Dostal, M. Illner, J. Kara, and M. Barlow (eds), *Changing Territorial Administration in Czechoslovakia: International Viewpoints*. Amsterdam: University of Amsterdam, Charles University and the Czechoslovak Academy of Sciences.

Izdebski, H. and M. Kulesza 2004. *Administracja publiczna*. Warszawa: Liber.

Jenei, G. 2008. "A Post-Accession Crisis? Political Developments and Public Sector Modernisation in Hungary". *The NISPAcee Journal of Public Administration and Policy*, I (2): Winter.

Kudrycka, B., B.G. Peters and P.J. Suwaj 2009. *Nauka administracji*. Waraszawa: Wolters Kluwer.

Lucking, R. 2003. "Civil Service Training in the Context of Public Administration Reform." *A Comparative Study of Selected Countries from Central and Eastern Europe, and the Former Soviet Union (1989 to 2003)*. UNDP BiH of the United Nations Development Programme.

Metcalfe, L. 1998. "Meeting the Challenges of Accession." SIGMA Paper No. 23, OECD.

Meyer-Sahling, J.H. 2009. *The Sustainability of Civil Service Reforms in Central and Eastern Europe: Five Years after Accession*. SIGMA Paper No. 44, OECD.

Meyer-Sahling, J.H. 2011. "The Durability of EU Civil Service Policy in Central and Eastern Europe after Accession." *Governance: An International Journal of Policy, Administration, and Institutions*, 24: April.

Nemec, J. 2010. "New Public Management and Its Implementation in CEE: What Do We Know and Where Do We Go?" *The NISPAcee Journal of Public Administration and Policy*, III (1): Summer.

Obolonskij, A. 2009. *Gosudarstvennaja sluzba*. Moscow: Delo.

Péteri, G. and V. Zentai 2002. "Lessons on Successful Reform Management." In: G. Péteri (ed.), *Mastering Decentralization and Public Administration Reforms in Central and Eastern Europe*. Budapest: OSI/LGI.

Pollitt, C., and G. Bouckaert 2004. *Public Management Reform: A Comparative Analysis*, 2nd edn. Oxford: Oxford University Press.

Polska 2030. wyzwania rozwojowe. 2009. http://www.premier.gov.pl/files/file/Dokumenty/PL_2030_wyzwania_rozwojowe.pdf

Potůček, M. 2008. "The Concept of the Neo-Weberian State Confronted by the Multi-Dimensional Concept of Governance." *The NISPAcee Journal of Public Administration and Policy*, I (2): Winter.

Pridham, G. 2008. "The EU's Political Conditionality and Post-Accession Tendencies: Comparison from Slovakia and Latvia." *Journal of Common Market Studies*, 46 (2): 365–387

Randma-Liiv, T. 2008. "New Public Management versus the Neo-Weberian State in Central and Eastern Europe." *The NISPAcee Journal of Public Administration and Policy*, I (2): Winter.

Rydlewski, G. 2007. *Systemy administracji publicznej w państwach członkowskich Unii Europejskiej*. Warszawa: Elipsa.

Sedelmeier, U. 2006. "Europeanisation in New Member and Applicant States." *Living Reviews in European Governance*. At: http://europeangovernance.livingreviews.org/Articles/lreg-2006-3

SIGMA 1998. *Preparing Public Administrations for the European Administrative Space*. SIGMA Paper No. 23, OECD.

Suwaj, P.J. 2005. "Preventing Corruption and Conflict of Interest: Necessity or Fashion? Case of Poland." In: G. Jenei, A. Barabashev and F. van den Berg (eds), *Institutional Requirements and Problem Solving in the Public Administrations of the Enlarged European Union and Its Neighbours*. Bratislava: NISPAcee.

Tiersky, R. 2004. *Europe Today*. Lanham, MD: Rowman & Littlefield.

World Bank 2007. *EU-8: Administrative Capacity in the New Member States – The Limits of Innovation?* Washington, DC: World Bank.

PART 13

Accountability

edited by Paul G. Thomas

Accountability has always been a central concern of both the study and the practice of public administration. This key concept has also been elusive and controversial, with theoretical debates underway almost constantly. In the realm of practice, critics have seldom been hard-pressed to find fault with existing accountability arrangements and procedures, regardless of the type of political and bureaucratic system under examination. Because accountability is such a highly prized political and administrative value, the usual assumption has been that there can never be too much of it. Accordingly, there has been a reluctance to acknowledge that accountability must, at times, adjust to, compromise with and even yield to other important political and administrative values, such as representation, responsiveness, efficiency, equity and legitimacy. Only recently has there been some concern expressed that an insistence on ever-stricter accountability must not be allowed to trump other cherished values, including trust, innovation and productivity (Thomas, 2009).

While controversy swirls around the concept of accountability, there is a core meaning on which most commentators agree. Accountability is best understood as a formal relationship governed by a process. As a relationship it involves a person or an organization negotiating with others the performance of certain tasks and/or responsibilities, ideally based upon certain agreed-upon expectations and standards. Those persons and organizations who are assigned responsibility are obliged to answer for their performance and it is usually assumed that they are potentially subject to penalties for non-performance or the beneficiaries of rewards for successful performance. The sanctions and rewards that underpin accountability relationships can be tangible and/or symbolic. Loss of office, demotion or reduced autonomy are examples of tangible penalties, while the assignment of blame, guilt, humiliation and loss of reputation represent more symbolic penalties. The potential impact of such psychological costs on the thinking and behavior of public officials should not be underestimated (Thomas, 2008).

For accountability to be fairly enforced requires that the responsible persons or organizations be given the capacity to deliver results through some combination of authority, resources, control over events and, in general, a supportive environment. Accountability also assumes that the authoritative party in the relationship has an obligation to monitor performance to ensure compliance with assigned directions and expectations. Accountability breakdowns can occur, not only because individuals and organizations fail to perform but also because authorizing persons and/or institutions lack the will and/or capacity to provide direction and/or scrutiny of performance. In summary, accountability represents both a constraint and an opportunity. While it limits freedom of action and requires justification of behavior, it also entails the delegation of authority and resources that empower persons and organizations to act. Robert Behn (2001) neatly captures the balance between delegation and checking, with his comment that accountability means "trust but verify".

The meaning of accountability has consistently widened over the years. The term is now used to describe situations where the core features of an authoritative relationship and a formal process of enforcement, with the potential for penalties and rewards, are not necessarily present. Certainly the public not longer sees accountability in strictly legal, organizational and procedural terms. For them, accountability is now a broader moral and ethical construct that is achieved only when public officials, both elected and appointed, serve with the commitment to do the right thing in the right way. Reflecting its ubiquitous prominence in public debates, accountability is now used at different times to describe: a general subjective sense of responsibility, the upholding of professional values and standards even in the absence of external scrutiny, a demonstrated responsiveness to particular clients or the community at large, and/or the requirement for openness, genuine democratic dialogue and public participation in governance.

The expansion of the meaning of accountability has caused a number of academic commentators to develop interpretative frameworks and typologies to compare how accountability is enacted in various contexts. Resisting this tendency, other academics have called for more precision and consistency in the use of the term, insisting that it should be reserved for those situations where an authoritative relationship exists (Mulgan, 2000). Some writers have argued that the aims and means of accountability should not be conflated and confused. For example, transparency is a highly prized value, but on a strict interpretation it is a means to achieve ultimate democratic accountability rather than an end in itself.

In a democratic state, the five key accountability relationships are between:

- citizens and elected politicians;
- politicians in executive roles and the senior public service;
- the legislature and ministers;
- senior public servants and the legislature; and
- public servants and the community.

Depending upon the political system involved, there may be a more or less direct accountability relationship between the bureaucracy and the legislature and/or the public at large. The emergence of a wide variety of accountability approaches has somewhat obscured and displaced the central importance of these key traditional accountability relationships.

Inside and outside of government, the sources of accountability, both formally and informally, have become more numerous. The sources include the constitution, laws, executive–legislative relationships, the organizational arrangements for various public bodies, administrative policies, rules and procedures, reporting requirements and access to information rules, contracts with other governments and private organizations, access to the courts and judicial rulings, the activities of pressure groups, scrutiny by the media, public debates and, the ultimate accountability mechanism, regular, free and fair elections.

All of these mechanisms shape and reinforce, to some not easily measured extent, an internalized subjective sense of responsibility and accountability which is supposed to motivate and guide public office holders, whether they are elected politicians or appointed public servants. The rules and behavioral norms of accountability are deeply rooted in particular societies and even particular policy communities. National differences in terms of history, constitutional arrangements, political processes and political/administrative cultures can have a profound impact on how accountability is understood and practiced. Theoretical debates may have raged over the meaning of accountability, but the practical meaning of the concept is determined mainly by how power is distributed and exercised under the constitution and through the political process within each political system.

In most democratic societies, government officials recognize that they are facing more extensive, diverse and demanding accountability expectations, but many believe that in practice the essence of accountability has not changed all that much. For them, accountability still comes down to a process of naming, blaming and shaming. If anything, the reliance upon "public shaming" as an accountability tool has increased since the first edition of the Handbook appeared and there exists a major research challenge of determining how well such devices work alone or in combination with other, more traditional approaches to accountability.

The widespread public suspicion and cynicism towards governments written about in the first edition seems to have increased, particularly as reflected in media coverage and in general political debates. Accountability mechanisms have increased in number in most jurisdictions, but the prevailing public perception remains that governments are not sufficiently accountable and that no one pays a serious price when misdeeds or errors occur. Governments are blameworthy, but the avoidance of blame is seen by many citizens to be the standard operating practice. Most of the public suspicion and blame is targeted at politicians, but public servants come in for their own share of criticism.

In response to public disillusionment and to revelations of wrongdoing, governments have tended to layer new accountability requirements on top of existing accountability mechanisms, usually without much attention to why existing devices have failed. The spread of whistleblower protection laws is an example of this trend. There is both a remedial and a symbolic aim behind the proliferation of such accountability measures. They are meant both to correct problems and to offer the assurance to the public that such problems will not recur. The result has been to create – over time – multiple criteria, institutions, processes and reporting requirements intended to strengthen accountability. Ironically, an unintended consequence of having so many accountability requirements may be even greater confusion in a given situation about who is accountable to whom, for what and with what consequences.

Focusing responsibility and accountability within government has become more difficult by reason of the wider trends within the governance processes. The underlying assumption of the practice of accountability (as opposed to the emerging theories) remains that identifiable individuals and institutions have independent, reasonably complete and predictable control over actions and outcomes. However, this is now widely recognized not to be an accurate description of the realities of public sector decision making. The external and internal environments in which most public sector organizations operate have become complicated, interdependent, turbulent and unpredictable. Activities undertaken by individual public organizations and governments as a whole have become more collaborative in nature, whether that collaboration occurs across programs, departments, governments or with other institutions within society. In an era of joined-up, networked or partnership-based governing, no one individual or institution is completely in charge of decision making and/or in control of the outcomes. Under these conditions the traditional, vertical, straight line and individualistic interpretation of accountability fits less and less with the reality of a horizontal, interconnected and collective approach to problem solving (Considine, 2002; Wilkins, 2002).

Governments and academics have made some headway in developing interpretations and meaningful models of accountability that take account of the new environmental conditions and approaches to governing. A decade ago, Behn (2001) called for the development of a shared "360-degree" approach to accountability based on a "compact of mutual collective responsibility". Such an approach would be primarily cultural and values based rather than legal and procedural. It would require reciprocal obligations and trust among institutions and individuals. It would involve acceptance of collective responsibility, risk and accountability and the abandonment of "scapegoating" when something goes seriously wrong. Behn was not suggesting that we scrap existing legal and organizational approaches, but he does acknowledge their limits.

Under the influence of public choice thinking, which included the so-called principal–agent problem, governments have focused mainly on legislative/regulatory approaches to prescribe appropriate behaviors by politicians and public servants and they have established more oversight bodies to expose wrongdoing. This has led to polarized debates over laws/sanctions versus values/education as alternative routes to integrity and accountability in public offices. Some commentators have argued that such debates pose a simplistic, false dichotomy and that governments must recognize that the two approaches to the prevention of wrongdoing and the achievement of "right doing" can be mutually complimentary and reinforcing.

A shift to more of a collective, cultural approach to accountability faces the difficulty that ideas of individual fault, blame, liability and punishment remain at the heart of popular understanding of what accountability should mean in practice. There is therefore the need to develop accountability mechanisms for the collaborative arrangements that have become so common in the public sector. Some progress has been made on this challenge over the past decade: there

is growing emphasis on the delineation of roles and responsibilities, the creation of shared management structures, dispute resolution mechanisms for when collaborating entities disagree, better defined performance expectations, more careful monitoring and measurement of performance and more public reporting on results. Ideally, such arrangements/processes will enable authorizing bodies and the public to keep track on what is happening within the framework of the new partnership and networked relationships that have become so popular in the public sector.

Unfortunately, the evidence from many jurisdictions around the world suggests that the shift in emphasis away from accountability as compliance/blame and toward accountability for results/learning has been anything but smooth or complete. In legislatures, opposition parties focus mainly on negative evidence and interpretations of government performance. Governments usually react defensively and engage in "spin" to present the most positive performance story possible. The media have become a more important source of accountability, but the focus of their coverage is mainly on the mistakes, abuses and deficiencies in government performance. Most citizens pay no direct attention to accountability reports published online or tabled in legislatures, so their perceptions of government are shaped mainly by the polarized, theatrical debates within legislatures and the mainly negative media coverage that flows from such events.

In terms of more meaningful accountability for results, there is also the complication that most performance measures/reports represent "dumb data" that does not speak for itself or says different things to different people. Despite progress toward specifying accountability requirements in advance and in more detail, the result will always likely involve "fuzzy accountability" (akin to fuzzy logic) that sacrifices a measure of prescription in order to take advantage of the expertise, discretion and judgment that is needed from the bureaucracy to solve complex problems. Moreover, the challenges of attribution for explaining why desired results were, or were not, obtained have increased as a result of the interdependence among factors in the congested world of policy making and the related collaboration that takes place among different actors and institutions in the design and delivery of programs (Wilkins, 2002). In short, a neat, logical, strictly evidence-based approach will never (and should never) completely supplant "politics" as the primary means to achieve democratic accountability and hopefully responsiveness to citizens.

Having multiplied the number and types of accountability mechanisms in the last decades of the twentieth century we are left without a good understanding of the interactive and cumulative impact on the thinking and acting of public officials arising from the thick web of laws, rules, guidelines, reporting requirements and oversight bodies. At times politicians and public servants may face conflicting accountability requirements and expectations. A certain amount of overlap and redundancy in a particular accountability system can provide protection against untoward events because the breakdown in one mechanism might be compensated by the effectiveness of another. Only recently has there been emerging work on practical theory on how to design different accountability structures, procedures and standards for different types of action by an increasingly diverse range of organizations that comprise the kaleidoscopic world of the modern public sector (Jarvis and Thomas, 2009).

OVERVIEW OF PART 13

Three insightful and stimulating chapters offer different perspectives on the controversies that swirl around accountability in the twenty-first century.

In the hardback edition of this Handbook, Robert Gregory (2012) leads with an extensively revised version of his chapter from the first edition of the Handbook. Two cases from the past and the present serve as "bookends" to frame his analysis and to demonstrate how accountability has become an ever more variegated and contentious concept. He synthesizes the conceptualizations and analyses of leading scholars to illustrate how debates over accountability have become more complicated, sophisticated and intense in response to changes in the so-called real world of governance and governing.

Gregory maintains his argument from the first edition that we need to be more careful in our use of contentious terms like accountability, responsibility, answerability and morality. Acknowledging the simplification involved, he argues that formal objective accountability should be distinguished from informal, subjective responsibility. Most of the debates over accountability focus mainly on answerability, the obligation to give an account to an authorizing person or organization, and this diminishes the attention given to the morality and ethics of government actions and inactions. In short, answerability may contribute to reflective, values-based behavior, but offers no guarantee that individuals and institutions will examine the moral implications of their choices.

Scholars may have identified more multiple, potential meanings of responsible and accountable behavior, but Gregory argues that in practice its meaning is inherently political and comes out of the shifting power dynamics of governing under changing conditions. He notes the growing insistence in all political systems that politicians and bureaucrats must answer for their decisions and pay a significant price for abuses of authority or when serious mistakes occur that could have been prevented. He contrasts the different ways that accountability is enforced, or not enforced, in presidential–congressional versus cabinet–parliamentary systems of government. Throughout his analysis, he references many different types of accountability: political, administrative, professional, cultural, prospective, retrospective, process-based versus results-based, tight/strict versus loose/weak and others. More institutions and procedures have been created in the movement for greater accountability. The role of the media as a source of accountability and the efforts by governments to create positive political narratives are recognized to be prominent, recent trends.

Gregory was one of the first commentators to warn of the dangers for accountability from the rise of New Public Management (NPM) thinking. NPM ideas do not enjoy the same ascendancy they had when the first edition of the Handbook appeared, but they have an ongoing residual impact on the dynamics and challenges of accountability. According to Gregory, the technocratic and mechanistic propensities of NPM based on artificial dichotomies between policy and operations or outputs and outcomes continue to produce perverse effects, the most important of which is a neglect of debates over what is the right, moral and ethical action to take in complicated factual cases where more than one fundamental value is at stake. Gregory concludes that the challenges of accountability will never be resolved permanently, but coping with them will require what has been called "responsible accountability".

In Chapter 38, Mark Considine and Kamran Ali Afzal focus on the implications of markets and networks for the theory and practice of accountability. Recognizing the impossibility of defining accountability in the abstract to the satisfaction of all commentators, they adopt a pragmatic conceptualization based on three dimensions. The "political" dimension goes beyond elections, parties, legislatures, etc., to include bureaucracies and judicial bodies. The "institutional" dimension involves the web of interdependent and interactive public bodies that comprise government and which gives rise to legal, administrative, professional and personal forms of accountability. The "resource" dimension refers to the taxing and spending authority of governments, which was the original focus of accountability debates that over time broadened out to include other dimensions of government performance. By disaggregating the general concept of accountability in this way, it is possible, the authors maintain to identify the accountability implications of the movement away from traditional top-down governing approaches towards newer governance approaches in which power, initiative, risk and accountability are shared between state and non-state actors and institutions.

Based upon previous research by Considine and his colleagues, three broad governance orientations are identified: the traditional "procedural" approach; a more recent "enterprise" approach arising out of NPM; and, finally, a "networked" approach that reflects the reliance on third parties to design and deliver policies and programs. Put simply, procedural governance relies primarily on legal instruments; enterprise governance relies upon both external markets and market-type mechanisms within government; and network governance combines technological and cultural components to establish and maintain a diverse array of collaborative relationships involving state and non-state actors and institutions.

NPM and the new governance arrangements have both benefits and costs when it comes to accountability. However, the authors argue forcefully and persuasively that accountability has been much compromised by the shift to governance based on markets and networks. They claim the shift has hollowed out the competencies of the state, sacrificed equity considerations to a preoccupation with efficiency and productivity, undermined both substantive and procedural fairness in government decision making, dispersed authority to third parties, created thereby serious problems for the assignment of responsibility and blame when things go wrong, and failed to provide tools to enforce accountability within the new multicentric world of governance.

In their final section, Considine and Ali Afzal concentrate on how to strengthen the institutional and resources dimensions of accountability, with a particular focus on building accountability regimes in emerging democracies. Concentrating on attempts to rehabilitate the traditional political avenues of accountability, they argue, may be futile, even dysfunctional. Instead, they suggest reform efforts in developing democracies should concentrate on giving citizens more direct control and influence over the numerous institutions and actors who comprise the congested world of modern governance. On the institutional front, they call for such reforms as a clearer delineation of objectives of policies and the assignment of responsibility for outcomes and the balancing of the past, present and future in designing institutional reforms, and the promotion within bureaucracies of a public service ethos which recognizes that neutrality and detachment are not the same as accountability. In terms of the resource dimension, authoritarian governments must become more transparent and answerable for their taxing and spending decisions. In addition, Western governments must formulate more sophisticated aid policies which promote sound governance arrangements while not creating undue dependence and further blurring the accountability picture.

In Chapter 37, Christoph Demmke and Timo Moilanen examine the connection between ethics and accountability in both the study and the practice of public administration. As a starting point, they note that whereas accountability is mainly about external relationships and processes of control, ethics involves mainly internalized, subjective forms of restraint and self-control within organizational cultures based on the values and motivations which are meant to guide individual public servants.

When public administration first emerged as an academic field and a vocation, ethical behavior was understood in the Weberian terms of following directions from politicians who made the value judgments about the use of power for public purposes. Over the past century there has been a steady increase in the number and complexity of the values and ethical dilemmas facing public servants. In the turbulent, interconnected, pluralistic and disorderly world of twenty-first century governance, what qualifies as responsible and

ethical administrative behavior has become highly problematic and controversial in many different ways. In addition, as the public has grown less deferential, more suspicious and less trusting towards public officials – mainly politicians but also public servants – the demands for greater accountability and higher ethical standards have increased. The result has been a proliferation of new, and the strengthening of existing, accountability and ethical rules which are meant to regulate and guide behavior in the public sector.

Demmke and Moilanen note that most countries have adopted codes of *rules, conduct* and *ethics* (the three labels are often used interchangeably) to prevent wrongdoing and to promote "right doing". Of these three, types of codes those labeled codes of ethics tend to be the most general in content and weakest in terms of enforcement mechanisms. According to the authors, there are theoretical paradoxes and potentially unforeseen consequences in practice arising from the adoption of such codes and other accountability initiatives that form part of a worldwide movement to reassure the public that there is integrity in government. For example, in the category of paradoxes, there is a seeming contradiction between the spread of accountability/ethical rules enforced by oversight bodies within government and the more general rhetorical support (and to a lesser extent actual action) for less regulation, bureaucracy and red tape when it comes to controlling private sector behavior. One of the unforeseen consequences of more internal regulation and enhanced scrutiny of administrative behavior may be to discourage the experimentation and risk taking that is seen by many to be necessary in the public sector of the twenty-first century.

For the future, the authors predict new, more widespread value conflicts within the policy and administrative processes, which means that public servants will have to be more aware of the principles/values of right and wrong within the public sector, have self-knowledge and be reflective about their actions and inactions, and be capable of reasoning ethically in complicated factual situations when one or more fundamental principles/values are in conflict. In terms of policies, structures and processes, governments will have to move beyond the prevailing "bad person" approach to "policing" wrongdoing and adopt more sophisticated educational and cultural approaches to the promotion of integrity.

These brief summaries cannot adequately capture the breadth, depth and nuances of the three chapters that follow. The authors have done a highly commendable job in making it clear that the challenges and paradoxes of accountability will only increase in the future. Accountability is best understood and approached not as a problem to be solved but rather as a condition to be continuously monitored in the light of changing external circumstances, institutional arrangements and power relationships. Accordingly, we must promote political, administrative and citizen cultures of accountability that allow for learning and improvement.

REFERENCES

Behn, Robert D. (2001) *Rethinking Democratic Accountability*. Washington, DC: Brookings Institution.

Considine, Mark (2002) "The End of the Line? Accountable Governance in the Age of Networks, Partnerships, and Joined-Up Services", *Governance*, 15 (1): 21–40.

Gregory, Robert (2012) "Accountability in Modern Government", in B. Guy Peters and Jon Pierre (eds), *The SAGE Handbook of Public Administration*. London: Sage.

Jarvis, Mark and Paul G. Thomas (2009) "The Limits of Accountability: What Can and Cannot be Accomplished in the Dialectics of Accountability". Paper presented to a conference honoring Professor Peter Aucoin. Halifax: Dalhousie University, November 2009.

Mulgan, Richard (2000) "Accountability: An Ever-expanding Concept?" *Public Administration*,78: 555–574.

Thomas, Paul G. (2008) "The Swirling Meanings and Practices of Accountability in Canadian Government", in K. Rasmussen and D. Siegel (eds), *Power, Professionalism and Public Service: Essays in Honour of Kenneth Kernaghan*. Toronto: Institute of Public Administration of Canada/University of Toronto Press, pp. 43–75.

Thomas, Paul G. (2009) "Trust, Leadership and Accountability in Canada's Public Services", in O.P. Dwivedi, Tim Mau and Byron Sheldrick (eds), *The Evolving Physiology of Government: Canadian Public Administration in Transition*. Ottawa: University of Ottawa Press, pp. 212–245.

Wilkins, Peter (2002) "Accountability and Joined Up Government", *Australian Journal of Public Administration*, 61 (1): 114–119.

37

The Pursuit of Public Service Ethics – Promises, Developments and Prospects

Christoph Demmke and Timo Moilanen

INTRODUCTION

Ethics and accountability are of paramount importance for the functioning of democratic governance. Still, both concepts are also fashionable and blurry concepts which are used in numerous ways in various contexts (Bovens 2007, 448). In general, accountability can be seen as a system of external control, while ethics can be understood as a system of internal control. This mirrors the commonly used distinction between compliance approach and integrity approach used in administrative ethics (Paine 1994; OECD 1996). The compliance approach emphasizes the importance of external controls on behavior, favoring formal and detailed rules and procedures. Behavior which is in line with the rules is considered correct, whereas the violation of rules is considered unethical and penalized. The integrity approach focuses on internal controls, i.e., self-control exercised by each public servant. This approach relies on a person's own capacity to make the right moral choices, which is supported through codes of ethics, training, leadership and professional and fair human resources (HR) policies aiming to translate ethical standards into actual behavior. However, these two approaches should not be considered mutually exclusive, and in practice they should be combined and considered complementary. Still, this dichotomy has prevailed, and alternative conceptualizations are rare (see Maesschalck 2004).

Accountability can be defined as "a relationship between an actor and a forum, in which the actor has an obligation to explain and to justify his or her conduct, the forum can pose questions and pass judgment, and the actor may face consequences" (Bovens 2007, 450). Accountability is generally understood as legal accountability: if the actor has not adhered to legal rules and regulations, a court of law will punish the actor. However, there are also other accountability forums leading to different forms of accountability, such as political accountability (e.g., minister to parliament, representative to electorate), administrative accountability (e.g., officials to audit office), professional accountability (professionals to supervisory bodies) and social accountability (e.g., agencies to civil interest groups). More and more, public officials are subject not only to legal accountability but also to administrative and professional accountability as well, including also the ethical aspects of their behavior.

For a long time, opinions prevailed that civil servants were linked to the authority of the state and could not be compared to other public employees or employees in the private sector. They were offered a public law status in order to bind them to the state and to the law and not to an individual interest. Public law status has its origin in the French Revolution, aiming to establish and guarantee a democratic society based on the principles of the French Revolution (Schulze 2004, 39). In Germany, the introduction of the public law status was inspired by the philosopher Friedrich Hegel. Hegel's idea of the civil servant and the state as such was conceptualized as a Leviathan which stood above the society and citizens. Its main role was to protect the society by using rules to achieve fairness and to balance the diverging egoistic interests within the society.

The most influential definition of bureaucracy comes from Max Weber. In his well-known lecture on Politics as a Vocation in 1919, he defined the role of the public officials as follows:

> The honor of civil servant is vested in his ability to execute conscientiously the order of the superior authorities, exactly as if the order agreed with his own conviction. This holds even if the order appears wrong to him and if, despite the civil servant's remonstrances, the authority insists on the order. Without this moral discipline and self-denial, in the highest sense, the whole apparatus would fall to pieces.

According to Weber, the essence of administrative behavior is to follow legally given orders. Following this, at a minimal level, administration was considered to be good and ethical if it achieved the implementation

and enforcement of the existing laws and policy goals of the government of the day. Moreover, ethically good or acceptable behavior was also defined in terms of law obedience, impartiality and standardization. The purpose of rule orientation was also to achieve fairness and equity, to implement the merit principle, to allocate rights to citizens and to protect public employees against arbitrary administrative decisions.

The above-mentioned traditional Weberian approach can be called the *ethic of neutrality* (Thompson 1985). In reality, administrators are not neutral machine-like cogs. Moreover, trends towards the delegation of more responsibilities to managers have also increased individual decision-making powers. Weber also overestimated the dominance of rational behavior in organizations and neglected the role and importance of emotions at the workplace, which is still widely underresearched in the public sector (Cropanzano et al. 2010, xiii).

In sum, traditionally, the compliance approach has predominated within government. Obedience to authority is the cornerstone of the traditional bureaucracy and this concept is still alive and doing well in many countries. From the ethical point of view, following the law or superior's orders is usually not problematic. It is still a very relevant guideline for public officials, as it highlights the importance of the rule of law and loyalty to democratically elected government. However, the problem with the Weberian concept is that as an ethical guideline it is simply too narrow for today's multilevel governance.

The era in which obedience, hierarchical decision making and treating all persons in the same way meant treating everybody fairly is not anymore the paradigm of our times (Menzel 2011, 122). The key phenomena of modernity are assumptions about universal values, absolute values, bureaucracy and rationality. Contrary to this, postmodernism is a term in which "fundamental assumptions are being discredited as final and absolute. Assumptions about some kind of objectively real and universal human nature, or natural law, or absolute values and ultimate truths [...] no longer hold ...." (Cooper 2006, 45). Still, in today's discussions on public values, assumptions are often made that one universal set of values exist (van der Wal & van Hout 2009) and that public values should be safeguarded against private sector values despite the fact that research indicates that values differ according to different organizations (van Thiel & van der Wal 2010). Moreover, distinctions between public and private values are more difficult to define. It seems the future will be dominated by more value conflicts and new emerging values. How do civil servants know which values and standards they should follow? In most countries, the state has codified a set of official values and standards of conduct for its public officials.

DEFINITION OF OFFICIAL VALUES AND STANDARDS OF BEHAVIOR: ETHICS CODES

In the field of ethics, rules and codes are still, by far, the most important instruments. During the last 15 years many countries have introduced new rules and regulations to prevent unethical behavior and to promote good behavior. Today a well-written and well-implemented ethics code is seen as a useful instrument that clarifies the values and standards of official behavior to the extent that no administration can afford to function without a code.

For analytical purposes it is useful to make a distinction between a code of ethics, a code of conduct and a code of rules and regulations (van Wart 2003, 333–334). A code of rules and regulations refers to legislative acts and other official regulations, setting clear behavioral expectations and disciplinary consequences. For example, in Finland the Administrative Procedure Act defines the fundamental principles of good administration such as the legal principles of equal

treatment and impartiality and it regulates the conflict of interests (grounds of disqualification). It is important to notice that in some languages, such as German, the term code (*der Kodex*) cannot be used in the context of legislation, as code refers to informal guidelines without sanctions, so its usage matches with the code of conduct and the code of ethics.

A code of ethics, on the other hand, discusses the ethical principles of official behavior. For example, in the UK, the Committee on Standards in Public Life has defined Seven Principles of Public Life (selflessness, integrity, objectivity, accountability, openness, honesty and leadership) which apply to all aspects of public life. These principles are not statutory, but many public bodies have incorporated them into their internal standards as codes of conduct. Codes of ethics are typically rather abstract and short documents (one to two pages). They are often used to announce fundamental principles, but they usually do not provide detailed rules or advise on how to adopt these principles in practical situations. For example, most codes of ethics state that transparency or openness is a core value, but they do not provide guidelines on, for instance, how open civil servants can be towards the public on matters that are still under preparation. Unlike a code of rules and regulations, a code of ethics cannot be enforced, although some countries like Australia, Canada and New Zealand make adherence to a code of ethics a condition of employment which means that there can be consequences of varying degrees of severity for violation of the code. Sometimes, a code of ethics is also called a values statement (Boatright 2008).

A code of conduct lies in between these two poles: it contains mid-level norms that set both aspirational values and expectation values, and therefore, the level of abstractness varies from moderately abstract to moderately concrete. A code of conduct can be seen as an extended code of ethics that transforms principles into practice. Most of the ethics codes used by professional associations are codes of conduct outlining not just general principles but detailed standards of behavior: for example, see the American Political Science Association's code of conduct (Guide to Professional Ethics in Political Science [APSA 2008]). In Europe, a good example for a public service code of conduct is the voluntary, non-legally binding "Ethics Framework for the Public Sector" (EUPAN 2004; see also Bossaert & Demmke 2005). It reflects the basic common values and standards which the European Union (EU) member states consider important for the proper functioning of their public services. It comprehensively discusses the general core values, specific standards of conduct, actions to safeguard integrity and measures on handling situations where there have been possible violations of ethics. The code of ethics is associated with the "high-road" or integrity-based ethics regime, whereas the code of rules and regulations is associated with the "low-road" or compliance-based ethics regime.

The distinctions made between a code of ethics, a code of conduct and a code of rules and regulations is a heuristic device, but in practice these terms are often used interchangeably. A clear majority of the Organization for Economic Co-operation and Development (OECD) and EU member states have introduced codes of ethics and/or codes of conduct (Moilanen & Salminen 2007; OECD 2000). Although these tools are not mutually exclusive and can be used simultaneously, the code of conduct generally includes the core values, thus eliminating the need for a separate values statement. These tools can be used on many levels: there may be a general code of conduct, branch-specific codes of conduct and agency-specific codes of conduct. General codes apply to all public servants working in the central state administration, whereas branch-specific codes apply to officials working in a particular branch or sector of government, such as the judicial branch. Agency-specific codes apply only to the public officials of a particular organization in question. Exactly what kind of ethics

codes should be used depends on the legal, cultural and administrative context. If a country suffers from serious problems such as corruption, then a code of rules and regulations is probably the right solution, containing stronger deterrent tools to prevent misbehavior (e.g., police investigates, court of law decides penalties). However, if the country wants to change its administrative culture towards more openness and better service, i.e., to create aspirational values, then a code of ethics or a code of conduct should be given priority.

Still, the question remains open as to the effectiveness of these instruments. In particular, codes of ethics and codes of conduct may take different forms. In addition, they differ as to the subjects dealt with. They are often suited to fight mild forms of misbehavior and are in many ways a direct response to a dynamic and changing civil service environment which calls for clearer guidance. One of the main weaknesses of codes of ethics and codes of conduct is that in most cases they are characterized by weak enforcement mechanisms. This means that, on the one hand, they are more vulnerable to non-observance and violations, and, on the other hand, their successful implementation depends to a large extent on the existence of an environment of trust and an ability to ensure the organizational adherence to the code.

THE INCREASE OF ETHICS REGULATION

Ethics policies often follow a fairly simple logic: the more public and media scrutiny, the more discovered political scandals and conflicts of interests, the more failure is attributed to too little control, not enough monitoring and not enough law (Anechiarico & Jacobs 1998, 12). Calling for new rules and standards is in most cases an easy response to a complex challenge. Consequently, there are more rules, procedures and monitoring procedures in place than ever before. In the meantime, "achieving an ethos of honesty and transparency becomes the Holy Grail" (Gay 2006, 107). As Stark (2000, 264) states: "We now prophylactically prohibit all officials from entering into an ever-increasing number of specified, factually ascertainable sets of circumstances because they might lead to inner conflict". This trend towards more law, rules, standards and monitoring runs counter to one of the most important reform trends: the reduction of administrative burdens and bureaucracy. So far, no country has removed, reduced or abolished ethics standards, as deregulating ethics policies would be highly unpopular.

On the contrary, many ethics reforms are launched with great media support about increased ethical standards. For example, the European Commission (EC) rewrote its code of conduct after the fraud allegations involving the French Commissioner Edith Cresson that eventually led to the resignation of the Santer Commission in 1999 (Cini 2007, 27–57; 108–121). Many new member states that entered the European Union in 2004 have an impressive arsenal of laws, standards and codes which are more detailed compared to most former EU-15 countries. Still, those EU member states with less rules in force tend to have lower corruption levels than those with more rules; however, that should be no argument for removing ethics policies. Even to the contrary: more rules and standards are no guarantee for more effectiveness. However, abolishing rules could easily raise public and media suspicion and contribute to lower levels of public trust (Demmke et al. 2008).

Ethics experts face many difficulties in answering whether ethical challenges are increasing, decreasing – or both? Another development is also striking: whereas the media and the wider public call for the introduction of more rules and standards in the field, more experts discuss the potential negative effects of more standards, processes and rules, pointing, for example, to the fact that public discussions on ethics pay too little attention to the impact of ethics policies on administrative procedures, disclosure and monitoring requirements, costs and civil rights. Moreover, there is very little evidence on the nature of (the growing number of) specialized bodies and ethics committees that oversee and investigate conflicts of interest, misconduct and corruption. The latter is a truly opaque field and merits further research. Overall, literature on the challenges and paradoxes of ethics is still fairly recent.

In fact, experts in the field of ethics comment on the effectiveness of instruments in the field very differently and represent an even broader spectrum of views. In the field of conflicts of interest, some argue that more and better post-employment policies are necessary, whereas others think that this will hamper mobility between the public and private sector. Again, others believe that a public register of interests (or reporting system) is necessary, whereas opponents say that requiring the filing and review of confidential reports would sufficiently prevent financial conflicts of interests. Some believe that public scrutiny is having a too strong impact on privacy rights.

EFFECTS OF ETHICS RULES ON ETHICAL BEHAVIOR – MORE RULES, MORE EFFECTIVENESS?

There have been three distinct trends in the ethics literature in the last decade. The first is a surge in ethics literature which focuses on scandals and the failures of politicians and public officials and, consequently, decreasing trust levels. A second trend is a sort of reaction to the many reforms, policies and instruments which were introduced as a response to the scandals. Here the focus is mostly on whether we now have "too much" or "too little" ethics rules. Ultimately, the argument goes that while costs associated with increased monitoring, oversight and control have risen, it has not, to this point at least, translated into higher trust levels and less ethical violations. A third trend is the broadening and diversification of the whole discussion. For example, whereas more experts discuss ethics in the context of good governance policies, others are interested in the institutionalization of ethics, the effects of different ethics instruments and social justice perceptions as a result of administrative reforms.

One of the greatest strengths of research in the field of public sector ethics lies in the diversity of those who are interested in the topic. Where else could we find more management scholars, public administration experts, psychologists, political scientists, moral philosophers, organizational sociologists and behavioral economists? In the meantime, this literature covers a wide array of fields, ranging from the design of ethics infrastructure to workplace ethics. For a long time the field was dominated by US and Canadian scholars (Menzel 2005), but during the last years European scholars have also become more active (Lawton & Doig 2006).

Still, the increasing interest in public service ethics has not necessarily produced more clarity and consensus on the effectiveness of ethics policies, the right choice of policy instruments and the best organizational design of the systems. Moreover, although in theory most experts agree on the importance of ethical leadership, little empirical evidence exists on whether leadership is actually supporting ethical behavior or whether it is an obstacle for an effective policy. Yet, it is also "not clear what types of rewards or penalties work best to create incentives for responsible and accountable behavior, including the search for improvement" (Jarvis & Thomas 2009, 11). Many studies still focus on the input side: for example, introduction of new rules, standards, codes of ethics and ethics instruments. Only few discussions take place on the "output" side and the impact of reform policies on workplace behavior, the added value and the effectiveness of ethics policies.

For example, the principle of proactive disclosure is becoming more important in achieving greater transparency and openness in conflicts of interest policies (Fung et al. 2007). The public availability of disclosed information by top decision makers is seen as important to ensure accountability and reinforce trust in government (OECD 2011, 203). The popularity of public disclosure seems due to the clear message it sends to the public that the government is committed to openness and transparency. Despite the popularity of this instrument, discussions on the pros and cons of registration obligation and obligation to register financial interests remain the subject of vivid discussions within the countries and the different institutions. First evidence shows that declarations and registers work only if requirements (as to what must be declared) are clear and known. Second, there must be a means to monitor these declarations and registers effectively (and independently). Third, there must be credible sanctions for non-compliance. If all of this does not exist, it will be difficult to detect wrong, misleading or partial information. On the other hand, financial disclosure policies and registers must be designed in such a way that the collection, storage and management of detailed financial disclosure forms will not cause a new "conflicts of interest" bureaucracy. Thus, the most important questions concern what should be declared, whether (or not) the declarations should be made public, whether (or not) independent bodies should have the power to monitor the registers and whether (or not) there should be sanctions for non-compliance (Demmke et al. 2008).

Also cost–benefit tests of other ethics policies have only rarely been carried out. Overall, there is very little research on the organizational aspects of ethics (Hoekstra et al. 2010; Thompson 2004). How do you institutionalize different effective ethics policies within different organizations? What do we know about good practices and ways to best organize ethics policies? In the following, we discuss the state of affairs as regards the different pros and cons of strict ethics policies.

Positive aspects of rules and standards in the field of ethics

One may argue that the rise in regulations and of expectations in the field of ethics is to be welcomed since it reflects more critical and more mature citizens' attitudes towards authorities. In fact, media and citizens tolerate unethical behavior less than before. For good reasons: people expect holders of public office and public officials to have very high standards of integrity because they have considerable power, influence and decision-making discretion. Because of this, standards of integrity must be set at high levels.

A study by Gaugler (2006, 108) in Germany shows that the higher the prestige and the position of a holder of public office, the more companies and organizations seek to establish contacts and to offer board memberships to them. Accordingly, former cabinet members frequently assume important positions or functions in companies and organizations after they have left office. In recognizing this, it seems appropriate that specific rules and standards should regulate the behavior of holders of public office and of top public servants. Also, supporters of more and better ethics rules in the field of registering financial assets claim that rules and standards are important because holders of public office and top officials "hold positions of such importance and such accountability that the public can claim a reasonable right to know some of the details of their personal finances and the potential conflicts those might create" (Mackenzie 2002, 168).

Other experts claim that strict rules, standards and management instruments in the field of ethics bring a number of benefits for public sector organizations. First and foremost, opportunities for corruption will be reduced. Detailed policies and procedures for identifying, disclosing and managing conflicts of interest mean that accusations of bias can be dealt with more easily and efficiently. Detailed prohibitions can be highly effective. Some authors suggest that ethics laws that had a major impact on legislative process are those that ban or limit gifts "(…) from lobbyists or their principals, or laws that simply require their disclosure. In most states these laws have reduced gift giving and gift taking" (Saint-Martin & Thompson 2006, 172).

A truly transparent system will also demonstrate to the public and to citizens and groups who deal with the organization that its proper role is performed in a way that is fair and unaffected by improper considerations. In particular, the often cumbersome requirements for transparency and declaration of information reveal important information to the public. The existence of strict transparency requirements and monitoring mechanisms may not automatically improve public trust. However, unclear ethics codes and lack of codes may raise suspicion and contribute to higher levels of distrust. Thus, integrity, openness, and loyalty to the public interest are a necessary condition in increasing public trust (Feldheim & Wang 2003, 73). Partisans in favor of more or better rules do not always pretend that more rules and standards will decrease corruption and conflicts of interest. However, additional standards may deter public officials and holders of public office from questionable behavior.

A stronger focus on ethics policies may also raise awareness for the importance of ethical rules and policies amongst public officials. A recent study indicated that many public employees in the European Union considered that ethics rules are better known than before (Demmke & Moilanen 2010). On the other hand, public employees believe that the national public services have become more transparent, customer- and citizen-oriented, people are dealt with in friendlier ways, etc.; even more, many public employees believe that ethical violations are decreasing and ethical attitudes have improved. Rules and standards also contribute to transforming cultures. One example is the British code of ethics, Seven Principles of Public

Life, which has become a well-known ethics code also on the international level. The popularity of these principles may have also convinced other countries to adopt centralized codes of ethics.

Finally, the process of elaborating ethics codes can have important educational effects at the organizational level:

> It would be unfortunate if the emphasis on a code of ethics as a product obscured the value of the process by which a code is developed and subsequently revised. This process is a time of critical self-examination by both individual members and the profession as a whole. The profession must institutionalize a process whereby its moral commitments are regularly discussed and assessed in the light of changing conditions both inside and outside the profession. The widespread participation of members in such an effort helps to reinvigorate and bring into sharp focus the underlying values and moral commitments of their profession (Frankel 1989, 112–113).

Critical approaches towards ethics rules

Critics argue that more ethics rules do not necessarily provide an efficient response to the decline of public trust and integrity issues but may cause even more cynicism regarding public and political institutions. The problem is that the expansion of ethics regulations and more public discussions about the need for more and better ethics rules, especially in the field of conflict of interest, have not contributed to a rise in public confidence in government. In fact, the calls for more ethics rules may even have the opposite effect. More "ethics regulations and more ethics enforcers have produced more ethics investigations and prosecutions. ... Whatever the new ethics regulations may have accomplished ... they have done little to reduce publicity and public controversy about the ethical behavior of public officials" (Mackenzie 2002, 112).

Despite the increasing number of rules and regulations, politicians continue to promise ever higher ethical standards as a means of securing votes. Therefore, ethics measures are often introduced by politicians with an eye on the perceived problem of decreasing public trust in the own political class. The intention of increasing public trust, however, is rarely met in reality. Therefore, most ethics experts are indeed of the opinion that more rules, even if well managed, may not automatically build more trust. Contrary to this, new rules may decrease public trust "by generating a sense that all lawmakers are fundamentally untrustworthy" (Rosenson 2006, 137).

Even among those who favor a public disclosure system, they do not agree on what information filers should disclose. For example, some argue that filers should be required to report the identities of their assets but not their values, under the assumption that the magnitude of the financial interest is irrelevant to the question whether it creates an actual conflict of interest. Others believe that the value of an asset is a critical predictor of whether it will cause a conflict of interest (cf. OGE 2004). Moreover, differences should be taken into account between public officials who exercise important state functions and other public officials (Fleming & Holland 2002). The call to regulate post-employment issues more strongly for members of the government and not for ordinary public officials also stems from these differences.

As Behnke writes (2005, 3), the risk is that

> in spite of the individual rationality of these strategies, the collective irrationality lies in the fact that ever more transparency, ever higher standards and tighter regulations create ever more violations of ethical rules, more scandals and more investigations, thus undermining the legitimacy of the institution and destroying public trust and creating collective costs that far outweigh the individual benefits.

In the field of ethics, the emphasis has been excessively on scandals and stopping wrongdoing. We argue that this regulatory top-down approach to integrity in government must advance beyond the "bad person" model of law and policy. Instead, we should look at the social psychology of organizational life and the capacity of individuals and leaders to understand and to be critical of their own behavior.

THE EFFECTS OF EXTERNAL FACTORS ON ETHICS

Public management reforms

Public discussions on public service reforms are not without paradoxes. In their seminal book on public management reforms, Pollitt and Bouckaert (2011, 164) present the history of public management reforms as a history of trade-offs, limits, dilemmas, paradoxes and contradictions. In the field of ethics, Frederickson (1997, 2005) has argued that corruption and unethical behavior in government are on the rise because of attempts to run government organizations as though they were businesses. At the same time, Bovens and Hemerijck (1996) concluded that the scandals that have attracted media exposure in recent years and given rise to public debate on integrity include activities and techniques that are relatively new in the public sector: specifically, privatization, introduction of market techniques, pay that conforms to the market, outsourcing of tasks and services, and commercial activities performed by civil servants or public agencies. Such issues all relate to the trend of introducing business- or market-like approaches into government. In one of the few existing empirical studies, Kolthoff (2007) concluded that New Public Management reforms may even lead to less integrity violations.

Today, also, discussions on good governance policies focus on the positive effects (and much less on the negative or unintentional effects), although evidence is rising that many good governance policies are also paradoxical. For example, while people call for less administrative burdens, administrative simplification and deregulation, they are also asking for new laws and rules in the fight against terrorism, data protection, climate change, corruption, conflicts of interests, citizen rights, anti-discrimination and diversity. Another paradoxical feature of the current reform discussion is the discrepancy between the reform speed in some public sector reform areas and the reform inertia in other areas. For example, whereas the introduction of new ethics policies and accountability mechanisms are high on the agenda, the evaluation of the effectiveness of ethics and accountability instruments has been neglected.

In fact, ethical requirements imposed onto government, administrations and public officials are continuously increasing. It seems that never before have governments and public authorities invested as much in the fight against corruption, the establishment of ethical infrastructures, ethics training and in the adoption of new rules in order to curb corruption levels, fight against discrimination and – more generally – in order to improve ethical cultures and ethical behavior. The extent of ethics has consistently broadened over the years, covering an ever-growing number of issues. At the same time, public management reforms also produce new ethical challenges.

Despite the complex link between public management reforms and ethics, in the meantime public officials are not only required to avoid ethical violations but also even the appearance of unethical conduct, as this is feared to undermine public trust. Thus, ethics is not a win–win policy. While there are often calls for heads to roll when things go wrong "those who wield public power can readily be punished for the one per cent of things that go wrong while being deprived of praise for the ninety-nine per cent of things that go right" (Gregory 2003, 558).

Perception of organizational justice

The term "organizational justice" refers to the extent that employees perceive administrative practices, administrative reforms and HR policies as fair in their outcome. Organizational justice theories have also been linked to health issues. Experts often make a distinction between distributive justice, procedural justice and interactional justice. For many years, researchers have attempted to find out why employees behave ethically or unethically in the workplace. Most have accepted the distinction offered by Kish-Gephart et al. (2010) as to the influence of individual characteristics, moral issue characteristics and organizational characteristics. In particular, the social environment in which public employees operate has been shown to relate to important output variables. Many ethics experts have analyzed whether particular dimensions of the social context have connections with the attitude and behavior of individual employees. For example, many studies have shown the impact of multiple organizational contexts on ethical behavior. For example, employee's perceptions on ethical climate, ethical culture and leadership styles have been related to employees' attitudes and behavior (Kish-Gephart et al. 2010).

Impact of the financial crisis

Fairness perceptions can strongly influence the individual behavior and have a good or bad impact on individual and organizational performance (De Schrijver et al. 2010). Thus, people are naturally attentive to the justice of events and situations in their everyday lives, across a variety of contexts. Individuals react to actions and decisions made by organizations every day. With the coming of the financial crisis, ongoing restructuring processes are taking place in many economies on a global scale. Voluntary and involuntary redundancy, reform of retirement schemes, workplace transfers and the reduction of salaries do not only affect conditions of employment but also they have an impact on workplace ethics. For example, in the European Union, public employees have

seen their salaries and social benefits being reduced, especially in Greece, Ireland and Latvia. Furthermore, recruitments are frozen and promotions stopped. How does this affect the ethical behavior of these people? So far, there is also very little evidence of the impact of the financial crisis on workplace behavior.

From what is known, compensation and benefit reductions and adjusted work schedules, which have a direct impact on an employee's personal finances, life, and livelihood, are most likely linked to increases in misconduct, disengagement and less work commitment. Cost-cutting reforms are also linked to reduced rates of employee commitment and disengagement. Overall, economic pressures, budgetary cuts, the reduction in salaries and promotion opportunities may result in more stress, competition and a general decline in organizational culture. In these situations, issues such as fairness, courtesy and impartiality may be at risk. This, again, can result in more ethics violations such as stealing, misconduct at work, unwelcome behavior, etc. Moreover, job satisfaction and organizational commitment is found to be negatively associated with overall perceptions of organizational and procedural injustice (for example, in the case of injustice, unprofessional performance assessments and unfair recruitment decisions) (Greenberg 2010; Menzel 2010; Schminke 2010).

In the European Union, the financial crisis has also supported speedier reforms of the traditional employment status (lifetime tenure, full-time employment) under the flexicurity agenda. As a consequence, more states are confronted with growing inconsistencies as regards the employment of public employees in civil service positions. This has led to the fact that several member states apply different employment relationships in the same sectors, sometimes for the same professions and for employees who are working in the same office. Here, little is known on the fairness perceptions and ethical behavior of civil servants, public employees and employees under short-term contracts. Do the different categories of staff show different behavior patterns because of different employment statuses?

However, the financial crisis may also have positive effects on public service ethics. It is even possible that during hard times when an organization's well-being or its whole existence may be at risk, the management talks more about the importance of high standards in order to guide the organization through the crisis. It may also be that some are less inclined to commit misconduct when management is on high alert.

CONCLUSION

During the current decade public service ethics has received more attention than ever before. There has been enormous activity to create new ethics codes. However, there is a need to be cautious in interpreting this development. There are no good reasons for assuming that the number of new legal norms, codes of ethics and codes of conduct would lead to better public service ethics as such. The situation may in fact be more complex. In some countries, fundamental principles and basic standards might already be explicitly defined in the legislation, such as in the Civil Service Act. Furthermore, if there is no coordination between the codes set at the different levels of government (i.e., general, branch-specific and agency-specific), codes might be overlapping and even contradictory, thus creating confusion rather than offering any clear guidance. There also seems to be different interpretations with regard to what constitutes a code of conduct. Many countries seem to consider that a document cannot attain the status of code of conduct unless it has been passed by the parliament (law) or accepted by an authority such as the Council of the State (directive or a decision in principle) or State Employer's Office (staff regulations), whereas some countries use documents that have not been officially

authorized but which have a de facto status of a code.

In most cases, the code of conduct restates and elaborates the values and principles already embodied in legislation. This is useful since the relevant values and standards in many countries are scattered in numerous legal documents, which makes it difficult to locate the information and to understand the general idea of public service. If properly used, legislation and codes complement each other effectively. In fact, a code of ethics and a code of conduct can be seen as two steps in the development of official ethics. As a first step, member states often begin by identifying their core values and promoting them by announcing a statement of core values (code of ethics). After this, as the discussion on public service ethics advances, the state is ready to introduce more systematic and detailed guidelines in the form of a code of conduct. We anticipate that there might well be a third step in the development, and that is to take the codes of conduct down to the agency level in order to provide more specific and useful guidelines for practical situations that vary between different agencies. This enables a bottom-up approach to codes which probably leads into stronger commitment. The downside is that this approach increases discrepancies that may fragment the public service ethics if not coordinated.

The expansion of the national ethics system poses new challenges and questions. If in the past there were seen to be regulatory gaps and a lack of enforcement, the more recent concern is that some governments have gone overboard in building an elaborate ethics apparatus that reflects the prevailing negative assumptions about the motivations and capabilities of both politicians and public servants. Today, trying to be ethical in every sense of the word, could mean that public organizations and their leaders end up pleasing no one. In reality, work in the public sector is more individual, value-laden, emotional, pluralistic, unpredictable and therefore contentious than is allowed for in a dichotomous "too much"/"too little" (Jarvis & Thomas 2009).

Our present understanding of ethics seems to be more and more paradoxical: on the one hand, there have never been so many regulatory activities, reforms and studies in this field; on the other hand, scientific evidence about the effectiveness of the different reforms, measures and regulatory strategies is still lacking. Unfortunately, to date, the debate on the effectiveness of ethics policies has been conducted in polarized terms, with the proponents of the two perspectives often distorting the positions of the other side and talking past one another. Mostly, pros and cons are exchanged in rather general terms and with general arguments. In fact, what is needed is a rational discussion about every single instrument and policy.

For example, Hesse et al. (2003) have presented a useful matrix to assess the various effects reforms may have. First, the impact of reform measures on major goal achievements can be positively or negatively effective or ineffective. Second, reforms may have an impact not only on the main goal but also over some other goals. In other words, they may have positive or negative side effects, or they may not have side effects at all. From these combinations, it is possible to construct a ninefold table describing nine different effect combinations. Applying this analytic framework to the field of ethics may also help to bring in a more rational discourse.

So far, developments within the political and administrative systems have expanded the meaning and the practical expression of the concept of ethics. Today, governments invest in ethics policies more resources than ever before. In many cases governments have institutionalized ethics infrastructures as a reaction to political scandals in a rather ad-hoc, hasty and fragmented way. At the same time, modern public management reforms have contradictory effects in the field of ethics and on the behavior of public officials. The field of mobility policies is just one example: whereas more member states promote and support more mobility between

the public and the private sector and remove legal, political and technical obstacles to cross boundaries, they are becoming increasingly aware about the consequences such as potentially conflicts of interest, new value dilemmas, threats to the classical public service ethos and the need to regulate post-employment.

Notwithstanding the differences between countries, they share a central characteristic: ethics policies have been largely scandal- not value-driven. This means that decision makers largely react to media attention and to the grand issues like corruption and conflicts of interest. In fact, ethical challenges can be found in many areas which receive less attention. Therefore, more empirical and conceptual studies and more non-ideological considerations in the field of ethics are badly needed if we are to better understand ethical promises, challenges and limitations. Still, there is no objective answer to whether we have too many or too few ethics rules or what the precise impact of ethics is on trust, democracy, effectiveness, efficiency, performance and behavior.

REFERENCES

APSA (2008) *A Guide to Professional Ethics in Political Science.* American Political Science Association, http://www.apsanet.org/media/PDFs/ethics-guideweb.pdf (2.4.2012).

Anechiarico, Frank & Jacobs, James B. (1998) *The Pursuit of Absolute Integrity: How Corruption Control Makes Government Ineffective.* Chicago and London: University of Chicago Press.

Behnke, Nathalie (2005) *Ethics as Apple Pie – The Arms Race of Ethical Standards in Congressional and Presidential Campaigns.* Paper presented at the joint conference of EGPA and ASPA "Ethics and Integrity of Governance: A Transatlantic Dialogue" in Leuven, June 2005. http://soc.kuleuven.be/io/ethics/paper/Paper%20WS5_pdf/Nathalie%20Behnke.pdf (2.4.2012)

Boatright, John R. (2008) *Ethics and the Conduct of Business.* Englewood Cliffs, NJ: Prentice Hall.

Bossaert, Danielle & Demmke, Christoph (2005) *Main Challenges in the Field of Ethics and Integrity in the*

EU Member States. Maastricht: European Institute of Public Administration.

Bovens, Mark (2007) "Analysing and Assessing Accountability: A Conceptual Framework", *European Law Journal*, 13 (4): 447–468.

Bovens, Marc and Hemerijck, Anton (1996) Het verhaal van de moraal: een empirisch onderzoek naar de sociale bedding van morele bindingen, Amsterdam/Meppel: Boom.

Cini, Michelle (2007) *From Integration to Integrity. Administrative Ethics and Reform in the European Commission.* Manchester: Manchester University Press.

Cooper, Terry L. (2006) *The Responsible Administrator*, 5th edn. San Francisco, CA: Jossey-Bass,

Cropanzano, Russell, Stein, Jordan H. & Nadisic, Thierry (2010) *Social Justice and the Experience of Emotion.* London: Routledge Academic.

Demmke, Christoph & Moilanen, Timo (2010) *Civil Services in the EU of 27 – Reform Outcomes and the Future of the Civil Service.* Frankfurt: Peter Lang.

Demmke, Christoph, Bovens, Mark, Henökl, Thomas & Moilanen, Timo (2008) *Regulating Conflicts of Interest for Holders of Public Office in the European Union.* Maastricht: European Institute of Public Administration.

De Schrijver, Annelies, Delbeke, Karlien, Maesschalck, Jeroen & Pleysier, Stefaan (2010) "Fairness Perceptions and Organisational Misbehaviour: An Empirical Study", *American Review of Public Administration*, 40 (6): 691–703.

EUPAN (2004) *Main Features of an Ethics Framework for the Public Sector.* Proposed by the Dutch EU Presidency and adopted by the Directors General responsible for Public Administration in the Members States and the Institutions of the European Union in their 43rd meeting in Maastricht. Also published in Bossaert & Demmke (2005), pp. 253–267.

Feldheim, M.A. & Wang, X. (2003) "Ethics and Public Trust", *Public Integrity*, 6 (1): 63–75.

Fleming, Jenny & Holland, Ian (2002) "Motivating Ethical Conduct in Government Ministers", *Public Integrity*, 5 (1): 69–84.

Frankel, Mark. S. (1989) "Professional Codes: Why, How, and with What Impact?", *Journal of Business Ethics*, 8 (2–3): 109–115.

Frederickson, H. G. (1997) *The Spirit of Public Administration.* San Francisco, CA: Jossey-Bass.

Frederickson, H. G. (2005) "New Manageralism: An Axiomatic Theory". In H. G. Frederickson & R. K. Ghere (eds), *Ethics in Public Management.* New York: M.E. Sharpe, pp. 165–183.

Fung, Archon, Graham, Mary & Weil, David (2007) *Full Disclosure. The Perils and Promise of Transparency.* Cambridge: Cambridge University Press.

Gaugler, M. (2006) *Bundestagsabgeordnete zwischen Mandat und Aufsichtsrat.* Saarbrücken: VDM.

Gay, Oonagh (2006) "Comparing Systems of Ethics Regulation". In Denis Saint-Martin & Fred Thompson (eds), *Public Ethics and Governance, Volume 14: Standards and Practices in Comparative Perspective.* Netherlands: JAI Press, pp. 93–107.

Greenberg, Jerald (2010) *Insidious Workplace Behavior.* London: Routledge.

Gregory, Robert (2003) "Accountability in Modern Government". In B. Guy Peters, & Jon Pierre (eds), *Handbook of Public Administration.* London: Sage Publications, pp. 557–568.

Hesse, Joachim, Hood, Christopher & Peters, Guy (eds) (2003) *Paradoxes in Public Sector Reform: An International Comparison.* Berlin: Duncker & Humblot.

Hoekstra, Alain, Kaptein, Muel & van de Burg, Deniece (2010) "Het institutionaliseren van integriteit: de organisatie van de integriteitsfunctie binnen lokale overheden verkend", *Bestuurs Wetenschappen*, 64 (5): 54–73.

Jarvis, Mark D. & Thomas, Paul G. (2009) "The Limits of Accountability: What Can and Cannot be Accomplished in the Dialectics of Accountability?". Paper presented at Dalhousie University, Halifax, November 11–13, 2009.

Kish-Gephart, Jennifer, Harrison, David. A & Trevino, Linda K. (2010) "Bad Apples, Bad Cases, and Bad Barrels: Meta-analytic Evidence about Sources of Unethical Decisions at Work", *Journal of Applied Psychology*, 95 (1): 1–31.

Kolthoff, Emile (2007) *Ethics and New Public Management. Empirical Research into the Effects of Businesslike Government on Ethics and Integrity.* Den Haag: Boom Juridische Uitgevers.

Lawton, Alan & Doig, Alan (2006) "Researching Ethics for Public Service Organizations: The View from Europe", *Public Integrity*, 8 (1): 11–33.

Mackenzie, G. Calvin (2002) *Scandal Proof. Do Ethics Laws Make Government Better?* Brookings Institution, Washington D.C.

Maesschalck, Jeroen (2004) "Approaches to Ethics Management in the Public Sector. A Proposed Extension of the Compliance–Integrity Continuum", *Public Integrity*, 7 (1): 21–41.

Menzel, Donald C. (2005) "Research on Ethics and Integrity in Governance: A Review and Assessment", *Public Integrity*, 7 (2): 147–168.

Menzel, Donald C. (2010) *Ethics Moment in Government, Cases and Controversies.* Boca Raton, FL: CRC Press.

Menzel, Donald C. (2011) Ethics and Integrity in the Public Service. In Menzel, Donald C. & White, Harvey L. (eds) *The State of Public Administration: Issues, Challenges, and Opportunities* (pp. 108–125). New York: M. E. Sharpe.

Moilanen, Timo & Salminen, Ari (2007) *Comparative Study on the Public-service Ethics of the EU Member States.* Ministry of Finance, Research and Studies. Helsinki: Edita Prima Ltd.

OECD (1996) *Ethics in the Public Service. Current Issues and Practice.* Public Management Occasional Papers No. 14. Paris: OECD Publishing.

OECD (2000) *Trust in Government: Ethics Measures in OECD Countries.* Paris: OECD Publishing.

OECD (2011) *Government at a Glance 2011.* Paris: OECD Publishing.

OGE (2004) "Evaluating the Financial Disclosure Process for Employees of the Executive Branch". Report to Congress, Office of Government Ethics. Washington, DC.

Paine, Lynn Sharp (1994) "Managing for Organizational Integrity", *Harvard Business Review*, 72 (2): 106–117.

Pollitt, Christopher & Bouckaert, Geert (2011) *Public Management Reform. A Comparative Analysis*, 3rd edn. Oxford: Oxford University Press.

Rosenson, B.A. (2006) "The Costs and Benefits of Ethics Laws". In Denis Saint-Martin & Fred Thompson, (eds), *Public Ethics and Governance: Standards and Practices in Comparative Perspective*, Vol. 14 (pp. 135–155). Oxford: Elsevier JAI Press.

Saint-Martin, Denis & Thompson, Fred (eds) (2006) *Public Ethics and Governance: Standards and Practices in Comparative Perspective*, Vol. 14. Oxford: Elsevier JAI Press.

Schminke, Marshall (ed.) (2010) *Managerial Ethics: Managing the Psychology of Morality.* New York: Routledge.

Schulze, Hagen (2004) *Staat und Nation in der europäischen Geschichte*, 2nd edn. Munich: Beck.

Stark, Andrew (2000) *Conflict of Interest in American Public Life.* Cambridge, MA: Harvard University Press.

Thompson, Dennis F. (1985) "The Possibility of Administrative Ethics", *Public Administration Review*, 45 (5): 555–561.

Thompson, Dennis F. (2004) *Restoring Responsibility: Ethics in Government, Business, and Healthcare.* Cambridge: Cambridge University Press.

van Thiel, Sandra & van der Wal, Zeger (2010) "Birds of a Feather? The Effect of Organizational Value Congruence on the Relationship between Ministries and Quangos", *Public Organization Review*, 10 (4): 377–397.

van der Wal, Zeger & van Hout, E. Th. (2009) "Is Public Value Pluralism Paramount? The Intrinsic Multiplicity and Hybridity of Public Values", *International Journal of Public Administration*, 32 (3–4): 220–231.

van Wart, Montgomery (2003) "Codes of Ethics as Living Documents", *Public Integrity*, 5 (4): 331–346.

Weber, Max (1991) *From Max Weber: Essays in Sociology.* London: Routledge.

38

Accountability in an Age of Markets and Networks

Mark Considine and Kamran Ali Afzal

Beginning in the early 1980s, the structure, objectives, and operation of the public sector have experienced unprecedented change, not just in the Western industrialized nations, but to a considerable extent also in the developing world. In broad terms, the traditional hierarchical organization of the public sector appears to have given way to structures characterized by markets and, more recently, by networks comprising state and private sector actors, not-for-profit agencies, community bodies and citizens. Even though scholars like Bevir and Rhodes (2006a, 2006b) do not find any inevitability in the perceived drive from hierarchies to markets to networks in the sense that the public sector structures which emerge in any state are the outcome of the interaction between, on the one hand, its institutional, societal and ideological heritage and, on the other, the nature of the dilemmas faced by state actors, many academics and practitioners in the field have viewed the new countenance of the public sector as a paradigm shift from *government* to *governance without government*. Considine and Lewis (2003a), for instance, find empirical evidence of two distinct governance orientations among the bureaucracies of Australia,

New Zealand, the United Kingdom and the Netherlands – *enterprise* governance and *network* governance; and they find both to be very different from the coexisting *procedural* (or traditional) governance orientation.

This chapter focuses on the implications of markets and networks for public accountability. The first section explains the concept of public accountability as understood in democratic polities; the second section reviews, very briefly, the basic tenets of the New Public Management (NPM) and network governance; the third and fourth sections examine, respectively, the effects of NPM and network structures on public accountability; the fifth section discusses how accountability might be strengthened in contemporary public sector settings; and the sixth section concludes.

THE CONCEPT AND CONTOURS OF PUBLIC ACCOUNTABILITY

Public accountability has a broad spectrum of meaning, with implications that vary with context; its characteristics, criteria and parameters also elude precise definition (Behn, 2001; Dunn, 1999; Halligan, 2001; Sinclair, 1995). However, the central postulate of public accountability is much less ambiguous. In classical construction, this postulate can be understood as the obligation of those who hold public office to safeguard the public interest (e.g., Waldo, 1956; Wilson, 1887); and its contemporary meaning remains much the same – 'a belief that persons with public responsibilities should be answerable to "the people" for the performance of their duties'(Dowdle, 2006: 3). It is, therefore, comprehensible that the focus of public accountability should be on its processes and outcomes, rather than on its definition (Fearon, 1999). A pragmatic way of studying the accountability process is to conceptualize it in terms of the principal–agent framework, where the agent is responsible and/or authorized to act on behalf of the principal in accordance with the principal's preferences or interests, in the expectation of being rewarded or punished on the basis of some, often preconceived, performance criteria, including the outcomes of public action (Fearon, 1999; Maravall, 1999). The processes of public accountability, nevertheless, are shaped by the overall political, institutional and fiscal structures of the state. This observation suggests that the paradigm of public accountability in any state may be seen as having three basic dimensions, to which we now turn in some detail.

Political regimes: The political dimension

Democratic regimes, despite their many imperfections, tend to be more accountable to citizens than any other type of regime (Diamond, 1999, 2008; Manin, Przeworski & Stokes, 1999a), even when we conceive of democracy in its minimalist sense (Przeworski, 1999). Representative democracy – the most popular form of contemporary democracy – does not, of course, have any legally binding mechanism that can

ensure the accountability of representatives (agents) to citizens (principals), but in classical configuration, the election process embedded in representative democracy, whether comprehended in terms of the mandate model or the sanction model, operates as the primary mechanism that tends to ensure, despite its shortcomings, the accountability of representatives to citizens (Diamond, 2008; Maravall, 1999; Przeworski et al., 1999). This understanding of the centrality of the election mechanism to democracy has been more recently validated by a number of incisive empirical studies included in Maravall and Sánchez-Cuenca (2008). Collectively, these studies show that even though a number of factors like ideology, ethnicity, class interests, information gaps and internal party organization mediate the ability of voters to control governments, leaders and parties, both those in the political executive and those in the legislature, cannot escape political accountability to voters, who can and do hold them accountable for policies pursued and performance shown.

Administrative and judicial institutions: the institutional dimension

Political accountability to citizens, however, is not the only dimension of public accountability in democracies: all other public bureaucracies and their employees must also be accountable to citizens for public action or inaction. Even though the Wilsonian politics–administration dichotomy sustained by a neutral Weberian bureaucracy remains the traditional public sector ideal, it has long been accepted that the bureaucratic domain is not limited to the implementation of public policies and that bureaucracies often mould policy decisions also (Behn, 1995, 2001; Moore, 1994; Waldo, 1948). Thus, the question of the ability of citizens to hold their political representatives accountable becomes only one part of a bigger story. Fortunately, however, the structures of democratic accountability extend the control of citizens, through their representatives in legislatures, over non-representative public sector organizations also. This link in the chain of accountability is indirect and complex, but owing to the more formal procedures available to legislatures, as well as lesser information asymmetries, the ability of legislatures to control bureaucracies tends to be greater than the ability of citizens to control legislatures.

In parliamentary democracy, the chain of political accountability runs from citizens to the legislature, to the cabinet,[1] to ministers, to senior bureaucrats, to subordinate civil servants[2] (Laver & Shepsle, 1999; Sinclair, 1995). The first link in the chain – the accountability of the legislature to the citizens – tends to be institutionalized by the election process. The second link – the accountability of the political executive to the legislature – is institutionalized differently in cabinet–parliamentary political systems compared to presidential–congressional systems. In cabinet–parliamentary systems there is, in theory, and to a lesser extent in practice, the ability of the legislature to move a motion of 'confidence' or 'no confidence' with respect to an individual minister or the cabinet[3] (Laver & Shepsle, 1999). Concentration of power in the hands of the prime minister and the cabinet, combined with party solidarity and party discipline in the legislature, means that 'no confidence' motions seldom succeed. This, however, also means that prime ministers and cabinets are subject to party control and accountable within party hierarchies. In presidential regimes, the legislature seems in theory to have weaker control over the executive as compared to parliamentary regimes. But, because the executive is directly elected, it is also directly accountable to the citizens and, in the United States, the leading presidential–congressional system, the facts of divided government and decentralized political parties mean that the legislature is a powerful political force in shaping policy and holding executives accountable.

The third link in the chain is the control of the bureaucracy by the government, which

is created by the institutionalized accountability of the heads of government departments (who in most cases are senior civil servants) to their ministers. The accountability of civil servants to the government, and through the government to the legislature and citizens, constitutes the political accountability of the bureaucracy, and lies at the very heart of democratic accountability (for example, Dunn, 1999; Sinclair, 1995).

Theorists such as Behn (2001), Halligan (2001) and Sinclair (1995) identify several other traditional forms of accountability, the more significant of which are administrative, legal, professional and personal. Drawing from these theorists:

Administrative accountability is structured primarily by the internal hierarchical relationships of responsibility and answerability of public functionaries that exist within government departments as well as the accountability relationships of the departments themselves within the organizational structure of government. The broader scope of administrative accountability, however, also includes external governmental administrative institutions such as the ombudsman, the Auditor-General and parliamentary committees. In effect, administrative accountability defines the traditional form of institutional answerability of public agencies and their bureaucracies.

Legal accountability refers to the horizontal answerability of all public functionaries before courts of law, statutory bodies, or other regulatory agencies, and is implemented through formal laws, rules or codes of conduct.

Professional accountability relates to civil servants' sense of responsibility emanating from loyalty to the ethos of their service cadre or profession, which might include time-honoured values like 'probity, a care for evidence and respect for reason, the willingness to speak truth to power ... equity and fairness, constant and careful concern for the law and for the needs and procedures of Parliament, and concern for democracy' (Woodhouse, 1997: 34). Such unwritten value systems are expected to be an integral part of a civil servants' character.

Personal accountability of public officials arises from their principles and moral values as individuals, and tends to be configured by the belief system of the society in which they live as well as by their organizational culture.

In terms of the ability of citizens to hold public actors accountable, the latter forms of accountability (i.e. other than political accountability) tend to be as important – if not more – as mainstream political accountability.

When political accountability is ineffective, for instance when governments or legislatures act in an unrepresentative manner, administrative institutions and their bureaucracies may become safety mechanisms to align public policy with the public interest. In strict constitutional terms, it is not part of the formal role of core public services to safeguard democratic accountability in such a manner, but the weakness of political mechanisms has led to the emergence of innovative auxiliary administrative agencies serving both legislatures and citizens, such as ombudsmen and integrity commissioners, intended to promote and uphold fundamental public sector values like fairness, propriety and accountability. Similarly, independent and impartial judiciaries can force both aggrandizing governments and their bureaucracies to become responsive to citizens' interests. Of course, courts cannot directly align public decision making by politicians and bureaucrats with citizens' preferences, but by providing firm disincentives against laxity, improbity or corruption, or the disregard of codes or rules, or the neglect of due processes in matters of the public interest, to say the least, and sometimes even by simply ensuring free and fair elections, they can create an environment that induces governments and bureaucracies to act in the best interest of citizens. This, in fact, explains why democracies establish formal codes of law, rules and conduct, and create independent and transparent judicial institutions to implement them. Rather, there cannot be a concept of liberal democracy without the rule of law and the judicial institutions that establish it (Behn, 2001; Considine, 2005; Diamond, 1999, 2008; Diamond & Morlino, 2005; O'Donnell, 2005).

Modes of resource mobilization: the resources dimension

Resource mobilization, whether through taxation, mineral rents or foreign aid, also tends to create accountability relationships for governments. These resource-based accountability structures may not be as formally institutionalized as is, for instance, political accountability created by the election process, or as legally enforceable as often is, for example, the codified administrative accountability of bureaucracies; but even so, they can exert a powerful influence through political and administrative institutions. Each of these modes of resource mobilization imposes a different set of accountability relationships on governments, which largely derives from:

- the nature of the actors who yield resources;
- the implicit or explicit understanding between these actors and the governments on the use of the resources yielde; and
- the extent to which these actors can formally or informally induce governments to abide by their mutual understanding.

Taxation, for instance, can be expected to make governments more accountable to citizens than any other mode of resource mobilization, since paying taxes not only tends to vest a right in taxpayers to have a say in the manner in which the proceeds from the taxes are spent but also strengthens the right of the broader citizenry to demand answers from their governments. As Brautigam (1992: 11) notes: '[w]hen government revenues and spending are dependent on successfully negotiating direct taxation of citizens, domestic pressure builds to enforce accountability for the use of those revenues.' This tax–accountability nexus has deep roots in history: the Magna Carta and the call to arms for the American War of Independence, 'no taxation without representation,' define merely two of the many critical junctures that pushed absolutism onto trajectories of representative and accountable political organization. On the other hand, mineral rents (Anderson, 1987; Clark, 1997;

Karl, 1997; Shambayati, 1994) and foreign aid (Collier, 2000, 2007; Feyzioglu et al., 1998; Knack, 2001; Smith, 2007) reduce the dependence of governments on citizens, and thereby undermine the ability of citizens to demand accountability from state actors.

THE NEW PUBLIC MANAGEMENT AND NETWORK GOVERNANCE

The New Public Management does not refer to a single cohesive theory of public administration; it would be more appropriately described as a broad group of connectable ideas inspired by private sector management practices and introduced over the last three decades or so, first in advanced industrialized nations such as the United States, the United Kingdom, Australia and New Zealand, and then more generally around the world (Ferlie et al., 1996; Frederickson & Smith, 2003; Kettl, 2000; Nolan, 2001; Peters, 2001). The objective behind core NPM practices was mainly to acquire the productive efficiency and cost-effectiveness of the private sector by adopting not only the managerial practices of private sector organizations but also their norms, values, routines and even organizational structures. New Public Management's focus on the *customer* or *client*, for instance, does not merely reflect altered practices; rather, it signifies a paradigm shift. In fact, NPM is structured upon an ideological foundation that does not appear to consider any aspect of the public sector to be intrinsically different from the private sector and which normatively prescribes the adoption of private sector values and standards in public sector organizations (Beckett, 2000; Peters & Pierre, 1998). In the initial phases, referred to in the literature as *managerialism* or *corporate governance*, the focus was largely on meeting quantified performance targets, achieving stipulated benchmarks and satisfying the clients of public organizations along

private sector lines. In the subsequent phases, referred to as *post-managerialism*, *contractualism*, or *market governance*, the focus shifted to cost-effectiveness; decentralization, disaggregation and deregulation; and downsizing, privatization and outsourcing (Ferlie et al., 1996; Frederickson & Smith, 2003; Nolan, 2001; Peters, 2001). In contemporary public sectors, both phases of NPM now appear to have created a hybrid, which Considine and Lewis (2003a) term *enterprise governance*. But even enterprise governance manifests many varied shades of the New Public Management, describing a mosaic of private sector orientations, rather than their blend.

On the other hand, policy development and service delivery networks that now dominate public sector operations, particularly in the advanced industrial democracies, are no less nuanced: they exhibit many different shapes, forms and purposes, and cut across contemporaneously existing hierarchies and markets (Considine, 2002b, 2005; Considine & Lewis, 2003b). These networks, which Peters and Pierre (1998: 225) term 'amorphous collections of actors', can also adopt many different modes of multilevel collaboration, partnership, or joining up between different state actors and levels of government, public sector agencies, private enterprises, third-sector voluntary organizations, interest groups, community representatives and even individual citizens. Network governance has been encouraged in part because the interdependence, cooperation and reciprocal trust between state and civil society actors lying at its basis is seen to compensate somewhat for NPM's disregard of public sector values. But there are several other factors also. More significant amongst these are

- globalization of socioeconomic policies;
- the expanding role of international organizations and financial institutions;
- the rise of regional trade and cooperation;
- the introduction of modern administrative practices that advocate more self-regulation of

institutions rather than their direct control by governments (Skogstad, 2003; Sørensen, 2002); and

- the need for increased collaboration between public and private sector agencies to achieve common objectives as well as possibilities of greater synergy from joint efforts by various state actors (Considine, 2002a).

ACCOUNTABILITY IMPLICATIONS OF THE NEW PUBLIC MANAGEMENT

Where changes in the public sector paradigm – many of them fairly radical – instigated by the New Public Management have conflicted with conventional public sector structures, prerogatives, objectives and norms, including the traditional foundations of public accountability, it is also true that in the process NPM reforms have created new rationales and channels for accountability. For instance:

- The concept of managerial accountability, supported by quantitative techniques of evaluation, may have strengthened accountability in the public sector, particularly in terms of performance, by providing supplementary quantitative evaluation tools to accountability holders (Moore, 1995).
- Where NPM has increased the efficiency of programmes, it has helped rescue aspects of public service organization from claims that the older bureaucratic norms were more sensitive to local conditions and stakeholder concerns. In an age where business interests and economic performance is much valued by citizens and elites, performance-driven accountability of public organizations must be taken seriously. The question then becomes an empirical one from the perspective of accountability: those elements of NPM that increase responsiveness, tailoring of services and efficiency, in fact, reflect the enhanced accountability of state institutions to citizens and elites, while those that push services out to contractors, who might care little for creating public value and seek only to maximize profits, have the opposite impact.
- Disaggregation and decentralization have strong potential to make public agencies more

accountable to citizens. Devolution of state authority brings decision-making arenas closer to stakeholders; but more importantly, fiscal decentralization, which in most cases accompanies administrative decentralization, augments the ability of citizens to demand accountability and responsiveness from the state by bringing taxpaying groups closer to state agencies responsible for appropriating and apportioning public revenues.

On balance, however, public accountability appears to have been much compromised by the New Public Management. For one, NPM-inspired practices have relieved the state from some of its core responsibilities and obligations, *hollowed out* its competencies, and have, thus, confused the right of the citizenry to demand responsiveness from state actors. Similarly, in concentrating narrowly on the cost-efficiencies of private providers of public services, NPM has sometimes crowded out considerations of equity and fairness, thereby weakening the claims of public servants to be the upholders of any special ethical or normative role in society. In the same vein, by giving precedence to performance and efficiency in terms of outputs and costs over considerations of procedural propriety (Beckett, 2000; Hedley, 1998), NPM has reduced the accountability of public sector agencies with reference to formally defined rules, codes and processes designed to uphold conventional public sector values. The NPM discourse views such regulatory or procedural requirements as red tape, sources of organizational rigidity and impediments to efficiency and output-based performance (Lane, 2000; Osborne & Gaebler, 1992; Walsh, 1995). But where the significance of performance-based accountability cannot be underestimated, it is equally indefensible to ignore, in the public domain, dimensions of accountability grounded in institutional processes and formal procedures that have been devised to ensure due diligence, promotion of the common weal and protection of the public interest. These process or activity norms are apt to get lost in a pure performance model, especially one that sees regulation as a potential threat to efficiency. An obvious example would be the British National Health System (Wilkinson, 1995) where it has been argued that pressures for performance have sometimes undermined equity in access and considerations of treatment.

Effective accountability, leading from citizens to state actors, is critical from two distinct, but interrelated, aspects (Considine, 2005):

- It is essential if public policies are to achieve the goals for which they have been designed: this can be called the 'functional' aspect.
- It tends to ensure that shared values and common perceptions remain the final arbiters of public policies: this can be termed the 'ethical' aspect.

From either aspect, effective accountability requires that responsibility be assignable to real actors, be they individuals or organizations. This, however, may not be easy, for it entails the ability to distinguish the contribution of each actor to a public policy or programme, or as Hardin (1996: 126) notes: '[w]ho is how much responsible for which part of what?' In the case of functional accountability, it may not be necessary to assign responsibility precisely, as long as anomalies can be understood and improvements made. Ethical accountability, on the other hand, is a different matter, for individuals at fault need to be identified and sanctioned in commensuration with their role. From this vantage point, whereas both the organizational and individual form of contribution–identification may be possible in a traditional public sector setting, neither form appears attainable in the complexity created by overlapping vertical and horizontal domains and channels of responsibility.

Even more importantly, in an entrepreneurial public sector, the authority to hold people accountable derives not from formal rules and codified procedures but from contracts linking service providers to managers, and managers to government departments. Unfortunately, however, the implementation

of contracts is seldom as straightforward as that of rules and codes. Even the most carefully worded contract clauses lend themselves to different interpretations, which are often used by defaulters to their advantage. Further compounded by radical initiatives like outsourcing policy formulation and even privatizing public authority, the outcome has not only been a more complex framework of control, responsibility and accountability but also, very often, a vague one (Christensen & Lægreid, 2001). The many additional, mostly competing, channels of responsibility, have left the lines of accountability between citizens and legislatures, ministers and departmental secretaries, and even senior bureaucrats and field managers, neither straight nor continuous (Ciborra, 1996; Considine, 2002a, 2005). An even greater concern is that the expanded interaction between state actors and private entrepreneurs in settings of dispersed accountability has increased the potential for connivance, collusion and corruption (Considine & Lewis, 1999). On the other hand, weak disclosure protection laws, where they exist, are hardly an inducement for potential whistleblowers to identify malpractices in the conduct of government or breaches of public trust (Thomas, 2011).

When default cannot be appropriately identified and sanctioned, accountability loses its *deterrent effect*, or, in other words, its ability to align public action with the public interest. This may be a pithy issue even for developed nations, but for the developing world, where the integrity of judicial systems and quasi-administrative adjudicating forums is often suspect, NPM-driven reforms have warped the orientation of public institutions in many respects. Even more challenging in the context of public accountability is NPM's supposition that the customer represents the citizen. Certainly, the customer focus in the public sector is useful to the extent that it generates incentives for public agencies to improve the quality of their services to clients, but customers cannot be equated with citizens, for citizens are the owners (Frederickson, 1992).

This distinction has a crucial bearing on the question of accountability. The final consumers of public programmes are not those who obtain only private value as clients of public agencies but the citizens through their representatives in government, who derive public value from public action (Alford, 2002; Moore, 1995); and it is the public value of public policies, as determined by citizens, which is the primary rationale for the accountability of public actors to citizens. Public and private values of public action will frequently move in the same direction, but it is not uncommon for the self-interest of a select group of customers of any public agency to diverge from the public interest. In the latter eventuality, accountability to the customer can only detract from considerations of the common good ascertained by citizens.

ACCOUNTABILITY IMPLICATIONS OF NETWORKS

Network governance has not merely expanded the horizontal dimensions of accountability but also has complicated its linkages by producing many secondary, and even tertiary, extensions. State coordination is now based upon pluricentric steering rather than unidirectional instruction, for networks require the government official to both fulfil the formal mandate of office *and* move beyond traditional hierarchies to forge cooperative, collaborative and quasi-market alliances with other state and non-state actors (Considine, 2002a, 2005). And with the domain and authority of public agency having become multidimensional, it is no longer possible to understand accountability simply as compliance with rules and procedures or as operating within a small set of horizontal linkages. It is now more pertinent to conceive of it as navigational competence – or the appropriate utilization of authority to traverse across a vast domain of multiple relationships and multifaceted structures in the quest for the most advantageous route to achieving

objectives (Considine, 2002a, 2005). In fact, where the New Public Management banished the neutral bureaucrat in favour of an entrepreneurial public official, network governance has moved even beyond by requiring a mediating and facilitating public service (Sørensen, 2002). This puts the public, including services users, at a disadvantage if office holders are unwilling or unable to clearly explain the basis upon which they seek to 'bend' programme procedures in order to increase performance. Undeniably, the new role of bureaucracies as facilitators of collaborative action seems to blend better with the new public sector environment (Box, 2002) as compared to their conventional responsibilities embedded within the framework of political accountability, but common purposes as well as reliable accountability mechanisms are prerequisites for successful cooperation even within networks (Van Dijk & Winters-van Beek, 2009); and the assortment of vertical and horizontal relationships that networks produce can, in fact, make objectives ambiguous and render questionable the relevance of agency-based accountability (Considine, 2002a, 2005).

Public accountability has, of course, never been without its layers, with actors being simultaneously accountable before legislative committees and lateral legal or quasi-legal establishments, and even directly to the public, in addition to being answerable within hierarchical chains of command. But until recently, the domain for accountability was mostly confined to the jurisdiction of a single ministry or public organization, where actors had clear areas of responsibility and obligation. Network governance has, however, rendered organizational boundaries irrelevant within an intricate web of accountability, which is itself plagued with gaps and inconsistencies (Considine, 2002a, 2005). Even worse, the blurred identities of public, private and civil society actors, and their overlapping mandates across loose networks, make accountability an elusive task: it may not be easy to identify defaulting state actors, much less their default; while in the case of private and third-sector actors, an additional handicap is often the absence of tools, or even the authority, to hold them accountable. It is, therefore, rather unsurprising that Rhodes (1997: 5) should lament that '[s]elf-steering interorganizational policy networks confound mechanisms of democratic accountability focused on individuals and institutions.'

On the other hand, supranational actors may complicate accountability nexuses even further by becoming part of networks. This appears to be true, for instance, in case of the European Commission (EC) in the context of the European Union (EU), and institutions like the World Bank, the International Monetary Fund (IMF) and several others in the context of the developing world. The inclusion of supranational bodies in national governance structures may not only weaken the ownership of policy objectives by national actors, as Van Kersbergen and Van Waarden (2004) suggest, but it may also distort the concept of public accountability as we have understood it until now. For instance, how far can ministers (or even public servants), as the same authors question, be held responsible for decisions flowing down from supranational authorities, and how far can they be answerable for actions taken by networks that often lie beyond their direct jurisdictions and which may comprise more private than public actors?

Nevertheless, it is not that accountability within networks is always ineffective; rather, it is a question of approach. While in traditional governance, accountability is often a legal strategy centred on compliance, and in enterprise governance it is mostly an economic strategy predicated on performance, in network governance it is more of a cultural strategy, or a matter of organizational convergence based on core public sector values (Considine, 2002a, 2005). Not just this, even if network accountability cannot be grounded in the hierarchical political control of citizens over public agencies through legislatures, citizens and community groups may, in fact, be able to control public action less circuitously through direct participation in networks. From this perspective, networks can

be considered as the practical manifestation of participatory or deliberative democracy, predicated on a more direct notion of public accountability than is the case in representative democracy, with public action becoming rooted in the participation and trust of the citizenry (Chambers, 2003; Papadopoulos, 2000; Skogstad, 2003). There are, however, several caveats. For one, the question of mandate and responsibility must always remain in the public domain (Considine, 2002a, 2005). Second, as Häikiö's (2007) Finnish case study shows, the inclusion of citizens in networks will not always make public policies responsive to the common good, since personal interests may often take precedence. Similarly, the possibility of elite or interest group capture, or the exclusion of the less-organized segments of society, or even the inclusion of unrepresentative and unaccountable groups, cannot be eliminated from networks either (Skogstad, 2003). Not just this: network governance also tends to produce friction and rivalry between national legislatures, subnational governments, local bodies, semi-public institutions and private agencies over questions of representation, authority and accountability (Sørensen, 2002).

Thus, as in the case of enterprise governance, network governance has, on the whole, left public sector accountability somewhat disturbed.

BUILDING ACCOUNTABILITY IN AN AGE OF MARKETS AND NETWORKS

As discussed in the preceding two sections, NPM practices and network governance have some very significant implications for public accountability. These implications can be serious, even in advanced democracies, but in the developing world – where basic democratic structures for citizens to hold governments accountable are frequently either non-existent or very weak – they can cripple the authority of citizens over state institutions. The first requirement in the age of markets and networks is, therefore, to develop democracy. Much has been said in the literature on how to develop and sustain democracy, as well as the many hurdles expected; and keeping in mind the limited scope of this chapter, it should suffice to say that electoral democracy alone cannot make public actors accountable to citizens – for this it would be necessary to infuse in nations the spirit of democracy. The remainder of this section concentrates on how to strengthen the institutional and resources dimensions of accountability.

The institutional dimension

Even though the formal structures of administrative and legal accountability of the bureaucracy remain intact, they have, as explained above, been conflicted and complicated in many ways by the adoption of NPM practices and the emergence of governance networks. It may no longer be possible, either in the developed world or across developing states, to define accountability merely as 'the following of rules or as honest communication with one's superiors.' Admittedly, '[d]oing these things might be part of an accountability process, but they are not on their own sufficient conditions for establishing real responsiveness' (Considine, 2005: 213). Nevertheless, while considering the potential modes to strengthen the accountability of public actors to citizens in a constantly changing public sector environment, especially in the developing world, worrying over the diminishing control of legislatures, ministers or senior civil servants in purely hierarchical structures may only be retrogressive. If the authority and responsibility of state agencies have now become multidimensional and spread over multiple relationships (Considine, 2005), so must we structure the chains of accountability that link them back to citizens. If NPM and network governance have created common domains and shared mandates for institutions, and if governance now comprises not just public and quasi-public organizations but also their private

and civil society appendages, then the framework of obligations and accountability must also be expanded beyond the traditional linkages (Considine, 2005). Clearly, when accountability involves a multiplicity of actors and several pathways, it becomes more relevant to conceive of it as a *chain of elements* that determines the responsiveness of individual and organizational actors (Considine, 2005). And it is this chain that needs to be strengthened. This can be done, for instance, by (Considine, 2005):

- spelling out unambiguously the objectives behind public policies and programmes, including the identification of the targeted beneficiaries and earnestly rendering all government operations open for public scrutiny, irrespective of whether they are performed by public sector agencies or contractors;
- rendering public interventions and their outcomes open to public scrutiny in a manner that also enables observers to understand the link between the two;
- enabling any individual or group dissatisfied by any public intervention to seek redress from some administrative or legal forum that has authority over the agencies responsible for the intervention;
- ensuring that individuals or organizations responsible for any failings are expeditiously held accountable and sanctioned in proportion to their responsibility; and
- making interventions open to revision, alteration or even rollback where they do not meet the accountability requirement.

The chain of elements will, of course, need to be given new linkages in response to evolving public sector environments, extended into emerging dimensions, and carefully embodied in institutional design. The vertical structure of accountability in contemporary public sector contexts can be reinforced, for example, by expanding the role of parliamentary committees and coordinating departments; and the horizontal dimension can be strengthened by expanding the role of courts, audit departments, anticorruption agencies and ombudsmen. However, given the diversity and intricacy in the horizontal spread of new governance, improving horizontal accountability will be the more daunting task, requiring not just bold, but also innovative, initiative and reform. In addition, the chains of horizontal accountability for market or competitive environments will need to be different from those developed for collaborative and cooperative networks (Considine, 2005). In the case of networks, the supervisory role of networks' centres will also have to be made more formal; and in the case of markets, the accountability of private sector service providers to core government departments will have to be made less ambiguous, more stringent and more enforceable, with not just private agencies being made liable for public action but also the individuals working for them. Most importantly, both in the case of markets and networks, effective rules, procedures and structures will need to be devised to keep in the public realm the question of the public interest, the obligation to protect it and the authority to hold actors accountable for default.

While reforming and innovating on institutional structures, continuity or any potential break from it in terms of institutional design will need to be explicitly factored in. Pollitt (2008), for instance, presents several convincing reasons why the continuing influence of past institutional structures can have definitive significance for institutional reform, and why it may be necessary to 'govern *with* the past, not *against* it [emphasis original]' (p. 161). According to Pollitt (2008: 161–168):

- Elements of the past place limits on future possibilities, and a complete truncation from the past may be very difficult, if not entirely impossible;
- A reference to the past helps in revealing the windows of opportunity for radical or transformational change as well as elements that can be used to legitimize reform;
- Some elements of the past are always valuable, but also fragile, making a deliberate and careful effort for their preservation necessary during reformation; and finally,
- Past experiences frequently provide wise counsel for the future.

The choice, Pollitt (2008: 181) goes on to conclude, is rather clear: 'We can recognize the reality of long linkages over time, and adapt our policies and institutions to allow for them, or we can blunder forwards without either rearview mirrors or forward vision much beyond the end of the ship's prow.' This admonition is all the more relevant for the developing and transitional states, which as Peters (2001: 164) advises, require administrative systems that come 'as close to some of the traditional ideals of probity and equality as possible.' This, of course, raises the question of what would be the core characteristics of such a system. Many really; but more prominently, three aspects are crucial.

The politics–administration dichotomy
Even though the politics–administration dichotomy is invoked mostly to protect policy making from bureaucratic incursions, it is grounded as much in the need to shield policy implementation from political interference as it may be in the principle of excluding the bureaucracy from the domain of politics. Not only is this understanding of the dichotomy in conformity with the Wilsonian conceptualization but also it has been even more emphatically resurrected in Osborne and Gaebler's (1992) insistence on separating steering from rowing and in NPM's dictum to *let managers manage*. Restricting political interference in service delivery assumes much greater importance in the less developed countries, where public services hold critical value for the poor, while political interference – usually driven in these countries by clientelism – tends to divert public provision towards the more affluent and politically influential groups. Thus, in any reform of developing world administrative structures aimed at strengthening accountability of public agencies to the citizenry and protection of the public interest, preservation of the administrative autonomy of individual public servants will remain of critical value.

Bureaucratic neutrality

Partly rooted in the politics–administration dichotomy, and yet distinct from it, is the ethic of bureaucratic neutrality. This is a concept of neutral competence or professionalism, which, as Asmerom and Reis (1996: 8) explain, 'does not mean that top-level civil servants cannot or should not be involved in the articulation of public policy.' Rather, as these scholars suggest, '[t]he expectation that they will render these services from a non-partisan position is the crux of the matter (p. 9).' In the same vein, bureaucratic neutrality also requires that public servants remain equally impartial and non-partisan when implementing public policies (Caiden, 1996).

It would, of course, be erroneous to expect civil servants to be sterile in terms of personal beliefs, political inclinations or other ideological proclivities that individuals can be expected to possess. But neutrality does require their professional conduct to conform to expected standards of impartiality and detachment. Such a concept of neutrality should not be confused with democratic unaccountability to the political representatives of citizens. Far from it, it means that it is civil servants' institutionally embedded knowledge, insight and experience as well as an unbiased concern for the public interest – not any personal or political consideration – that should inform the policy advice that they offer to political representatives as well as guide their implementation of public policies. In fact, it may not be incorrect to visualize bureaucratic neutrality as a concept akin to Rawls' (1971) *veil of ignorance.* Undeniably, the New Public Management appears to have rejected the virtues of neutrality by encouraging the political alignment of the senior echelons of bureaucracy with the political party in power. But in a paradigmatic sense, this political alignment is envisaged more along ideological, rather than partisan, lines; and even in this dimension, any political bias in civil servants' conduct which might affect their professional judgement remains unacceptable. Professional

neutrality is even more important for the bureaucracies of the less developed world, where civil servants often become attached to political parties – even when they have no ideologically affiliation with them – merely for personal benefits. Such political loyalties very often lead them to disregard the public interest, or even violate rules and law, in favour of the interests of the ruling party or of individual politicians in power, placing a wedge between public agencies and their accountability to citizens.

The ethos of public service

Institutional design based on the principles of the politics–administration dichotomy and bureaucratic neutrality subsumes the existence of a high-quality bureaucracy inspired by time-honoured norms and values of public service such as:

- unwavering allegiance to the profession, and dedication to duty;
- impartial application of rules and law;
- concern for fairness and equity;
- commitment to the protection of the public interest and promotion of the common weal;
- high standards of personal integrity and probity; and
- a sense of being accountable for the preservation of professional ethics.

While the bureaucracy of one developed state may be nearer to these ideals than that of another developed state, the bureaucracies of the developing world are generally far removed from them. In many less developed states, bureaucracies are corrupt, inefficient and motivated more by self-preservation than any consideration of the public interest. In these settings, structuring administrative institutions that afford bureaucratic autonomy and neutrality requires, in the first instance, the development of efficient and accountable bureaucracies capable of sustaining these principles. Indeed, without bureaucracies inspired by a strong public service ethos, bureaucratic institutions in the less developed world would neither have the potential to promote the common weal in the policy-making process nor be able to utilize their authority in citizens' best interest at the implementation level by conforming to the wishes of political representatives where they are democratically accountable to citizens, or by protecting the public interest where the links in the chain of democratic accountability are weak.

An interesting question, however, is: How far would it be possible to infuse the public service ethos into bureaucracies? Woodhouse (1997), for instance, views this ethos as something more in the nature of a *genetic code* that is passed on from one generation of civil servants to the next, and which cannot be converted into memorizable rules. Again, there cannot be any definite answers. But where the wisdom of Woodhouse's (1997) construction – as well as the inherent responsibility of one generation of civil servants to the next that this construction implies – cannot be disputed, it also cannot be denied that a framework of rules that enforces the intent of the public service ethos will contribute significantly in keeping under check any negative genetic mutations in civil servants' ethics.

A focus on developing the civil service ethos means, in particular, that the issue of corruption will be centre stage in public service reform. In the less developed world, corruption – whether financial, political or moral – remains both a cause and an effect of weak public accountability, and eradicating it is a key requirement of good governance (Kaufmann et al., 2009; Smith, 2007). Unfortunately, as is evident from the World Bank's *World Governance Indicators 1996–2010*, despite concerted efforts by international development agencies and country governments, corruption in many developing states actually appears to have worsened. Even where there has been some improvement, it has been mostly marginal, and in most cases also ephemeral. This is, nevertheless, rather unsurprising, since corruption is rooted in multidimensional social, political, cultural and economic factors (Smith, 2007; Tarling, 2005) and any

superficial efforts that do not address its underlying causes can yield no more than transient outcomes. As such, not only will policies to eradicate corruption need to be implemented with a clear understanding that the pace of success will generally be painfully slow but also they will need to focus beyond improving the internal environment of institutions and take into account their external sociocultural context which sets limits on the extent to which corruption can be controlled in any society.

On the other hand, as noted in the first section, strong judiciaries are the linchpin of the rule of law in any civilized society as well as the guarantors of the right and ability of citizens to hold public actors accountable. Under democratic structures, the ability of the judiciary to implement laws and dispense justice impartially is preserved mainly through its independence from the executive and by providing some mechanism for vertical accountability within judicial hierarchies. Some notion of external accountability – usually to the legislature – might also accompany, but it is generally kept weak so as not to allow it to impinge upon judicial independence. The initial appointment of judges in the higher judiciary is, of course, largely a political process; but once appointed, constitutional protections tend to ensure the immunity of judges from executive authority. The precise mechanisms vary across states, particularly between presidential and parliamentary systems, but they appear to be working well in the established democracies of the developed world. The story in the developing world's weak and unstable democracies is, however, very different. In many cases, judiciaries in the less developed states are merely compliant extensions of executive authority and are often used to legitimize exploitation by authoritarian regimes, in particular the illegal acts of military despots. This has been especially true in Africa, in Latin America and in many of the Asian states, where the dynamics of institutional symbiosis often make judiciaries scripture-citing accomplices in despotic usurpations.

The question then is how to ensure judicial independence in countries where democracy is fragile and where judiciaries are susceptible to capture by the executive, or, worse still, where they tend to collude in undemocratic rule. What is required in such instances, is not just judicial independence, but also a rigorous check on the actions of judges. And clearly, this has to be a check that moves beyond internal mechanisms of accountability or the weak accountability of judiciaries to legislatures: it has to be one that creates an effective incentive for judges not to submit, either voluntarily or involuntarily, to executive control. If properly structured, this notion of judicial accountability would reinforce, rather than compromise, judicial independence. Care would, of course, need to be taken that the structure of judicial accountability is not so stifling that it compromises judicial independence; for even though there appears to be no inherent contradiction between judicial accountability and judicial independence to the extent that both seek judicial impartiality (Voigt, 2008), the structures of judicial accountability and judicial independence need to be in proper balance to make judiciaries impartial (Domingo, 1999; Nicholson, 1993).

The resources dimension

Low taxation and the consequent weak accountability of governments to citizens in their capacity as taxpayers is another problem that needs to be addressed, particularly in the context of mineral-rich states as well as those that rely on foreign aid. In the case of mineral-rich states, neither citizens nor their governments could be expected to have any incentives to enhance the level or base of taxation. Citizens, in any case, cannot be expected to willingly relinquish any part of their incomes without the expectation of being compensated by equivalent benefit through the provision of public goods. And the governments of these states do not have any incentive to generate resources from taxation for at least three reasons:

- they may not need additional revenues because of the large amounts of mineral rents they usually command;
- they may not want to become unpopular with citizens by raising taxes when they might be able to raise any additional revenues through non-tax channels; and
- they would not want to provide citizens any additional reason to hold them accountable for their spending decisions.

Thus, by not taxing their citizens, rentier states block the development of 'the organic expectations of accountability that emerge when states make citizens pay taxes' (Diamond, 2010: 98). From a public accountability point of view, this situation creates a perverse inertia that is perhaps nowhere starker than in the authoritarianism of the Arab oligarchies of the oil-rich Middle East and North Africa, which survives mostly unabated in spite of the *Arab Spring*. The expected long-run availability of mineral wealth to most oil-rich states – and the extent of international credit that they can raise on the basis of this expected availability – often gives their governments great financial power, and thus appears to have so far prevented the development of any Magna Carta- or Boston Tea Party-like situation, or even of any gradual variant.

A more feasible alternative that can potentially break the inertia is the democratization of these authoritarian regimes. For instance, perhaps the most important reason why the United Kingdom and Norway have not been reduced to unaccountable petro-states is their enduring democratic traditions, which had taken firm root in both states much before the discovery of oil. With the democratization of oil-rich authoritarian states, one might expect their governments to become more accountable and responsive to citizens' long-term interests and also to *sow the oil* through responsible public policies for economic expansion that might outlast the mineral deposits. With economic expansion, the tax base of these states is also bound to expand; and with increased taxation, the ability of citizens to demand accountability from their governments would also increase. Democratizing oil-rich authoritarian regimes, however, is going to be a path riddled with obstacles and complexities, and would require, more than anything, sincere commitment from established democracies (Diamond, 2010).

Moving beyond the context of oil-rich states, the ability of the international development community to enhance the tax-driven accountability of governments to citizens appears to be greater in the case of those low-taxation states that are reliant on foreign aid. In fact, not only is enhanced taxation often a condition imposed by many international financial agencies and bilateral donor governments for continued aid, but a framework of good governance under which tax reforms are one of the main components is also being increasingly stipulated (Smith, 2007; World Bank, 2000, 2003). This broader paradigm of governance reforms can prove more effective in enhancing revenues from taxation than a focus merely on increasing the tax levels or expanding the tax base. For instance, by curtailing corruption, good governance can potentially also reduce tax evasion (which is often facilitated by conniving collecting departments) as well as enhance the willingness of citizens to pay taxes following reduced pilferage by spending departments and citizens' realization that taxes do not end up in private coffers.

The predicament, however, is the actual ability of donors to impose or cajole good governance in recipient countries, especially when foreign aid itself can lead to a deterioration in accountability rather than an improvement. A reliance on aid can, for instance, expand the scope of corruption, partly relieve governments from answerability on expenditures, reduce incentives to improve cost-efficiencies and even drain talented civil servants into aid-sponsored projects (Knack, 2001; Smith, 2007; World Bank, 2000). This situation can be further

compounded by the reluctance of aid agencies to discontinue financial assistance, despite the unresponsiveness of recipient governments to good governance requirements, because they themselves might have organizational interests in meeting disbursement targets (Collier, 2000, 2007) or because they apprehend the adverse impact that a termination of aid can have on groups already living in abject poverty (Gibson et al., 2005). Similarly, Smith (2007) cites several instances where Western governments continued to directly assist not just regimes with dismal governance records but even those that were guilty of oppression and large-scale human rights violations, simply for their own strategic geopolitical or economic interests. This clearly remains an area of concern and needs even more vigorous attention.

CONCLUSION

The New Public Management and network governance have had a deep impact on traditional notions and mechanisms of public accountability. In many spheres accountability has been conflicted, and in many others it has been rendered ambiguous. This does not mean, however, that traditional structures of public accountability have become irrelevant. Parliaments still monitor the performance of public agencies and hold them accountable for both probity and outcomes; judiciaries still want to see laws implemented and rules followed; bureaucracies still enforce answerability within hierarchies; and citizen groups still view public officials responsible for public programmes, even if services are delivered through private contractors. Clearly, the public sector cannot focus on efficiency alone, and public sector performance and outcomes must inevitably be evaluated against core public sector values such as justice, fairness and equity (Van Thiel & Leeuw, 2002), since an unqualified focus on quantification will always have the inherent danger of compromising public sector concerns for probity, traditional public sector values and procedural propriety (Considine & Painter, 1997).What is required, then, is the strengthening of these structures where they have become weak, their realignment where they have become distorted and their redefinition where they have become vague. However, where traditional hierarchies have acquired lateral appendages, public accountability will have to be reinforced through additional horizontal avenues. On the other hand, those elements of market and network structures that can help make public agencies more accountable to citizens will also need to be incorporated in formal institutional design.

NOTES

1   In terms of the principal–agent construct, the legislature is the principal and the cabinet is the agent.
2   In this case, the cabinet is the principal and the bureaucracy is the agent.
3   When moved by the government, the motion is referred to as a motion of 'confidence', and when moved by the opposition, it is referred to as a motion of 'no confidence'.

REFERENCES

Alford, J. (2002) 'Defining the Client in the Public Sector: A Social-Exchange Perspective', *Public Administration Review*, 62(3): 337–46.

Anderson, L. (1987) 'The State in the Middle East and North Africa', *Comparative Politics*, 20(1): 1–18.

Asmerom, H. K. & Reis, E. P. (1996) 'Introduction', in H. K. Asmerom & E. P. Reis (eds), *Democratization and Bureaucratic Neutrality*. New York: St. Martin's, pp. 3–19.

Beckett, J. (2000) 'The "Government Should Run Like a Business" Mantra', *The American Review of Public Administration*, 30(2): 185–204.

Behn, R. D. (1995) 'The Big Questions of Public Management', *Public Administration Review*, 55(4): 313–24.

Behn, R. D. (2001) *Rethinking Democratic Accountability*. Washington, DC: Brookings Institution Press.

Bevir, M. & Rhodes, R. A. W. (2006a) *Governance Stories*. New York: Routledge.

Bevir, M. & Rhodes, R. A. W. (2006b) 'The Life, Death and Resurrection of British Governance', *Australian Journal of Public Administration*, 65(2): 59–69.

Box, R. C. (2002) 'Pragmatic Discourse and Administrative Legitimacy', *American Review of Public Administration*, 32(1): 20–39.

Brautigam, D. (1992) 'Governance, Economy, and Foreign Aid', *Studies in Comparative International Development*, 27(3): 3–25.

Caiden, G. E. (1996) 'The Concept of Neutrality', in H. K. Asmerom & E. P. Reis (eds), *Democratization and Bureaucratic Neutrality*. New York: St. Martin's, pp. 20–44.

Chambers, S. (2003) 'Deliberative Democratic Theory', *Annual Review of Political Science* 6(1): 307–26.

Christensen, T. & Lægreid, P. (2001) 'New Public Management: The Effects of Contractualism and Devolution on Political Control', *Public Management Review*, 3(1): 73–94.

Ciborra, Claudio U. (1996) *Teams, Markets, and Systems: Business Innovation and Information Technology*. Cambridge: Cambridge University Press.

Clark, J. (1997) 'Petro-Politics in Congo', *Journal of Democracy*, 8(3): 62–76.

Collier, P. (2000) 'Conditionality, Dependence and Coordination: Three Current Debates in Aid Policy', in C. Gilbert & D. Vines (eds), *The World Bank: Structure and Policies*. Cambridge: Cambridge University Press, pp. 299–324.

Collier, P. (2007) *The Bottom Billion: Why the Poorest Countries Are Failing and What Can Be Done about It*. Oxford: Oxford University Press.

Considine, M. (2002a) 'The End of the Line? Accountable Governance in the Age of Networks, Partnerships, and Joined-up Services', *Governance*, 15(1): 21–40.

Considine, M. (2002b) 'Joined at the Lip? What Does Network Research Tell Us about Governance?', in M. Considine (ed.), *Knowledge Networks and Joined-Up Government: Conference Proceedings*. Melbourne: University of Melbourne, Centre for Public Policy.

Considine, Mark (2005) *Making Public Policy: Institutions, Actors, Strategies*. Cambridge: Polity Press.

Considine, M. & Lewis, J. (1999) 'Governance at Ground Level: The Frontline Bureaucrat in the Age of Markets and Networks', *Public Administration Review*, 59(6): 467–80.

Considine, M. & Lewis, J. (2003a) 'Bureaucracy, Network, or Enterprise? Comparing Models of Governance in Australia, Britain, the Netherlands, and New Zealand', *Public Administration Review*, 63(2): 131–40.

Considine, M. & Lewis, J. (2003b) 'Networks and Interactivity: Making Sense of Front-line Governance in the United Kingdom, the Netherlands and Australia', *Journal of European Public Policy*, 10(1): 46–58.

Considine, M. & Painter, M. (eds) (1997) *Managerialism: The Great Debate*. Melbourne: University of Melbourne Press.

Diamond, L. (1999) *Developing Democracy: Toward Consolidation*. Baltimore, MD: The Johns Hopkins University Press.

Diamond, L. (2008) *The Spirit of Democracy: The Struggle to Build Free Societies Throughout the World*. New York: Times Books, Henry Holt and Company.

Diamond, L. (2010) 'Why Are There No Arab Democracies?', *Journal of Democracy*, 21(1): 93–112.

Diamond, L. & Morlino, L. (2005) 'Introduction', in L. Diamond & L. Morlino (eds), *Assessing the Quality of Democracy*. Baltimore, MD: The Johns Hopkins University Press and the National Endowment for Democracy, pp. ix–xliii.

Domingo, P. (1999) 'Judicial Independence and Judicial Reform in Latin America', in A. Schedler, L. Diamond & M. F. Plattner (eds), *The Self-Restraining State: Power and Accountability in New Democracies*. Boulder, CO: Lynne Rienner, pp. 151–75.

Dowdle, M. W. (2006) 'Public Accountability: Conceptual, Historical, and Epistemic Mappings', in M. W. Dowdle (ed.), *Public Accountability: Designs, Dilemmas and Experiences*. Cambridge: Cambridge University Press, pp. 1–29.

Dunn, Delmer D. (1999) 'Mixing Elected and Nonelected Officials in Democratic Policy Making: Fundamentals of Accountability and Responsibility', in A. Przeworski, S. Carol Stokes and B. Manin (eds), *Democracy, Accountability, and Representation*. Cambridge: Cambridge University Press, pp. 297–325.

Fearon, James D. (1999) 'Electoral Accountability and the Control of Politicians: Selecting Good Types versus Sanctioning Poor Performance', in A. Przeworski, S. Carol Stokes and B. Manin (eds), *Democracy, Accountability, and Representation*. Cambridge: Cambridge University Press, pp. 55–97.

Ferlie, E., Ashburner, L., Fitzgerald, L. & Pettigrew, A. (1996) *The New Public Management in Action*. Oxford: Oxford University Press.

Feyzioglu, T., Swaroop, V. & Zhu, M. (1998) 'A Panel Data Analysis of the Fungibility of Foreign Aid', *The World Bank Economic Review*, 12(1): 29–58.

Frederickson, H. G. (1992) 'Painting Bull's-eyes around Bullet Holes', *Governing Magazine*, October.

Frederickson, H. G. & Smith, K. B. (2003) *The Public Administration Theory Primer*. Boulder, CO: Westview Press.

Gibson, C. C., Andersson, K., Ostrom, E. & Shivakumar, S. (2005). *The Samaritan's Dilemma: The Political Economy of Development Aid*. Oxford: Oxford University Press.

Häikiö, L. (2007) 'Expertise, Representation and the Common Good: Grounds for Legitimacy in the Urban Governance Network', *Urban Studies*, 44(11): 2147–62.

Halligan, John (2001) 'Accountability', in C. Aulich, J. Halligan & S. Nutley (eds), *Australian Handbook of Public Sector Management*. Crows Nest, NSW: Allen & Unwin, pp. 174–85.

Hardin, Russell (1996) 'Institutional Morality', in R. E. Goodin (ed.), *The Theory of Institutional Design*. Cambridge: Cambridge University Press, pp. 126–53.

Hedley, T.P. (1998) 'Measuring Public Sector Effectiveness Using Private Sector Methods', *Public Productivity and Management Review*, 21(3): 251–8.

Karl, T. L. (1997) *The Paradox of Plenty: Oil Booms and Petro-States*. Berkeley, CA: University of California Press.

Kaufmann, D., Kraay, A. & Mastruzzi, M. (2009) 'Governance Matters VIII: Aggregate and Individual Governance Indicators, 1996–2008'. World Bank Policy Research Working Papers No. WPS 4978.

Kettl, D. F. (2000) *The Global Public Management Revolution: A Report on the Transformation of Governance*. Washington, DC: Brookings Institution Press.

Knack, S. (2001) 'Aid Dependence and the Quality of Governance: Cross-Country Empirical Tests', *Southern Economic Journal*, 68(2): 310–29.

Lane, Jan-Erik (2000) *The Public Sector: Concepts, Models, and Approaches*, 3rd edn. London: Sage (1st edn, 1993; 2nd edn, 1995).

Laver, Michael & Shepsle, Kenneth A. (1999) 'Government Accountability in Parliamentary Democracy', in A. Przeworski, S. Carol Stokes & B. Manin (eds), *Democracy, Accountability, and Representation*. Cambridge: Cambridge University Press, pp. 279–96.

Manin, B., Przeworski, A. & Stokes, S.C. (1999a) 'Introduction', in A. Przeworski, S. Carol Stokes & B. Manin (eds), *Democracy, Accountability, and Representation*. Cambridge: Cambridge University Press, pp. 1–26.

Maravall, José M. (1999) 'Accountability and Manipulation', in A. Przeworski, S. Carol Stokes and B. Manin (eds), *Democracy, Accountability, and Representation*. Cambridge: Cambridge University Press, pp. 154–96.

Maravall, J. M. & Sánchez-Cuenca, I. (2008) *Controlling Governments: Voters, Institutions, and Accountability*. New York: Cambridge University Press.

Moore, M. H. (1994) 'Public Value as the Focus of Strategy', *Australian Journal of Public Administration*, 53(3): 296–303.

Moore, Mark H. (1995) *Creating Public Value: Strategic Management in Government*. Cambridge, MA: Harvard University Press.

Nicholson, R. D. (1993) 'Judicial Independence and Accountability: Can They Co-Exist?', *Australian Law Journal*, 67(6): 404–26.

Nolan, Brendan C. (ed.) (2001) *Public Sector Reform: An International Perspective*. New York: Palgrave.

O'Donnell, G. (2005) 'Why the Rule of Law Matters', in L. Diamond & L. Morlino (eds), *Assessing the Quality of Democracy*. Baltimore, MD: The Johns Hopkins University Press and the National Endowment for Democracy, pp. 3–17.

Osborne, David & Gaebler, Ted (1992) *Reinventing Government: How the Entrepreneurial Spirit is Transforming the Public Sector*. Reading, MA: Addison-Wesley.

Papadopoulos, Y. (2000) 'Governance, Coordination and Legitimacy in Public Policies', *International Journal of Urban and Regional Research* 24(1): 210–23.

Peters, G. B. (2001). *The Future of Governing*, 2nd edn. Lawrence, KS: University Press of Kansas.

Peters, G. B. & Pierre, J. (1998) 'Governance without Government? Rethinking Public Administration', *Journal of Public Administration Research & Theory*, 8: 233–44.

Pollitt, C. (2008) *Time, Policy, Management: Governing with the Past*. Oxford: Oxford University Press.

Przeworski, A. (1999) 'Minimalist Conception of Democracy: A Defense', in I. Shapiro & C. Hacker-Cordón (eds), *Democracy's Value*, New York: Cambridge University Press, pp. 23–55.

Przeworski, A., Stokes, S. C. & Manin, B. (eds) (1999) *Democracy, Accountability, and Representation*. Cambridge: Cambridge University Press.

Rawls, J. (1971) *A Theory of Justice*. Cambridge, MA: Belknap Press of Harvard University Press.

Rhodes, Roderick A. W. (1997) *Understanding Governance: Policy Networks, Governance, and Accountability*. Buckingham, Philadelphia, PA: Open University Press.

Shambayati, H. (1994) 'The Rentier State, Interest Groups, and the Paradox of Autonomy: State and Business in Turkey and Iran', *Comparative Politics*, 26(3): 307–31.

Sinclair, A. (1995) 'The Chameleon of Accountability: Forms and Discourses', *Accounting, Organizations and Society*, 20(2–3): 219–37.

Skogstad, G. (2003) 'Who Governs? Who Should Govern? Political Authority and Legitimacy in Canada in the Twenty-first Century', *Canadian Journal of Political Science*, 36(5): 955–73.

Smith, B. C. (2007) *Good Governance and Development*. Houndmills, Basingstoke, UK: Palgrave Macmillan.

Sørensen, E. (2002) 'Democratic Theory and Network Governance', *Administrative Theory and Praxis*, 24(4): 693–720.

Tarling, N. (ed.). (2005). *Corruption and Good Governance in Asia*. Abingdon, UK: Routledge.

Thomas, P. G. (2011) 'Problems with Canada's Public Servants Disclosure Protection Act', *Optimum: The Journal of Public Sector Management*, 41 (1): http/www.optimumonline.ca/print.phtml

Van Dijk, Jan & Winters-van Beek, Anneleen (2009) 'The Perspective of Network Government: The Struggle between Hierarchies, Markets and Networks as Modes of Governance in Contemporary Government', in A. Meijer, K. Boersma & P. Wagenaar (eds), *ICTs, Citizens and Governance: After the Hype!* Amsterdam: IOS Press.

Van Kersbergen, K. & Van Waarden, F. (2004) '"Governance" as a Bridge between Disciplines: Cross-disciplinary Inspiration Regarding Shifts in Governance and Problems of Governability, Accountability and Legitimacy', *European Journal of Political Research*, 43(2): 143–71.

Van Thiel, S. & Leeuw, F. L. (2002) 'The Performance Paradox in the Public Sector', *Public Performance and Management Review*, 25(3): 267–81.

Voigt, S. (2008) 'The Economic Effects of Judicial Accountability: Cross-Country Evidence', *European Journal of Law and Economics*, 25(2): 95–123.

Waldo, Dwight (1948) *The Administrative State: A Study of the Political Theory of American Public Administration*. New York: Roland Press.

Waldo, Dwight (1956) *Perspectives on Administration*. Tuscaloosa, AL: University of Alabama Press.

Walsh, Kieron (1995) *Public Services and Market Mechanisms: Competition, Contracting and the New Public Management*. Houndmills, Basingstoke, UK: Macmillan.

Wilkinson, M. J. (1995) 'Love is not a Marketable Commodity: New Public Management in the British

National Health Service', *Journal of Advanced Nursing*, 21: 980–7.

Wilson, W. (1887) 'The Study of Administration', *Political Science Quarterly*, 2(2): 197–222.

Woodhouse, D. (1997) *In Pursuit of Good Administration: Ministers, Civil Servants, and Judges.* Oxford: Clarendon Press.

World Bank (2000) *Reforming Public Institutions and Strengthening Governance: A World Bank Strategy.* Washington, DC: The World Bank.

World Bank (2003) *Reforming Public Institutions and Strengthening Governance: A World Bank Strategy Implementation Update.* Washington, DC: The World Bank.

PART 14

Intergovernmental Relations

edited by Martin Painter

Once upon a time, the field of intergovernmental relations was confined principally to the study of central–local relations within a national system of government. The units of study were mostly national, regional and local general-purpose government bodies (along with their constituent units). A major subdivision of the field was between central–local relations in unitary states and intergovernmental relations in federal states. Institutional features such as financial arrangements and formal structures were the primary concern. But times have changed: intergovernmental relations as a field has widened in scope and new perspectives have been introduced.

Institutional analysis in various forms remains central, but increasingly policy processes and policy effects have been at centre stage. Rather than being too concerned with institutional mapping based on distinctions drawn from different models of intergovernmental relations – especially the federal versus non-federal divide – policy analysts viewed the field as a case of the complexities of policy making in a multi-organizational context. For example, Pressman and Wildavsky (1973) in their study of the intricacies of public programme implementation

drew attention to multi-organizational complexity as a general phenomenon, not to the significance of levels of government as a particular form of complexity. While they were acutely conscious of the institutional context of American federalism, this was not the primary focus. They were concerned with the policy failures that resulted from 'falling between the gaps'. On the other hand, Deil Wright (1983) focused primarily on intergovernmental relations (or IGR) as its own field of study – 'the multiple, complex, and interdependent jurisdictional relationships found in the United States'. IGR studies in this vein are also very often concerned with the complexities of intergovernmental policy implementation, but they relate these to problems of 'intergovernmental management' (Agranoff 1986).

Increasingly, however, institutional and policy studies have come closer together with their mutually reinforcing foci on the policy effects of supposedly malfunctioning institutional arrangements and of organizational complexity more generally. With the growth of government in the twentieth century, the field of IGR became an increasingly significant one for scholars of public administration, as it was apparent that the practical complexities of public policy – for example, the interdependence of problems and sectors, with their 'spillovers' and 'externalities' – increasingly resulted in an intergovernmental dimension to most public policy issues. Global trends such as growing urbanization, the pace of technological change and rapid depletion of ecosystem services have resulted in new spatial dimensions to policy problems, with consequences for existing arrangements in the division of powers and functions both between levels of government and also across borders. In the latter part of the century, the reordering of spatial relations and policy problems increasingly took on a supranational or global dimension, calling into question the most fundamental building block of systems of intergovernmental relations, the nation-state itself (Elazar 1998), and hence challenging state-centric views of government and politics (Rosenau 2000). This, in turn, spawned the burgeoning field of 'multi-level governance', of which more below.

Conceptual and theoretical developments in the field have tended to be uneven and fragmentary, with different traditions and approaches overlapping, but evolving in parallel. In the United States, intergovernmental relations is close to being coterminous with the study of federalism, which draws on diverse fields, including political theory (Ostrom 1987), studies of political culture (Elazar 1994) and public finance (Oates 1972). From a very different starting point, theories of intergovernmental competition based on economics have been influential (Breton 1996). In another set of parallel studies, theorists of 'polycentric government' have combined constitutional analysis, public choice theory and game theory in the study of collective good problems, with a strong preference for multiple, locally constituted systems of self-rule (McGinnis 1999). In Europe, the study of central–local relations was for long dominated by legal and institutional approaches, but in the 1980s in the UK and elsewhere it took on board ideas and concepts both from the American study of

IGR and also from the realm of organization theory, in particular interorganizational analysis (Rhodes 1988). Network analysis later became a significant strand in the field (Kickert et al. 1997). In recent times, the complexities of relations across and between levels of government within the European Union have stimulated new conceptual and empirical analysis, drawing on interorganizational and network theories, as well as connecting back with the field of implementation studies in the public policy literature and more widely with theories of inter-state cooperation and conflict in international relations. Political scientists in Europe faced with the many complexities and novelties of politics and policy making in the European Union, coined the name 'multi-level governance' or MLG for short (Jordan 2001; Enderlein et al. 2010).

Both parts of this neologism are equally significant for understanding the scope and significance of this body of work. 'Multi-level' draws attention to the existence of many layers of actors, not just those formed by superior and subordinate levels of government. By not using the term 'government' or 'governmental', the new terminology also draws attention away from formal governing entities as the principal actors. The term 'governance' pointed to the growing significance of non-governmental participants in the governing process. Indeed, this was also being remarked on by scholars of more traditional fields of intergovernmental relations. Some who came to a 'governance' view of government did so from a background of studying central–local relations in particular policy sectors (Rhodes 2000: 60–2), where non-government actors intimately concerned with a sector were increasingly key players in seeking joint solutions to cross-jurisdictional problems. Again, studies of processes of public policy making and implementation, rather than of formal–legal aspects of public administration, were influential in this change of perspective. The idea that the policy process was an orderly one focused on a set of identifiable, authoritative decision makers ('government') was for the most part not helpful. Stories of intergovernmental relations were about overlapping spheres of influence, power and resource sharing, collaboration and negotiation. In such contexts, unofficial, 'informal' channels were often the most important, while there was a continuous blurring of the lines between 'government' and 'non-government' in the complex patterns of alliances and boundary-spanning political stratagems that emerged. Students of intergovernmental relations were regularly describing a world of partnerships, collaboration and networks. And, as in other areas where the term 'governance' has become a common part of the lexicon, its growing use in studies of intergovernmental relations was also associated with concerns for accountability and democratic control. Some scholars have highlighted the legitimacy problems arising from informal networking arrangements between public officials and 'civil society', and questioned the extent to which these can substitute for traditional forms of political accountability, warning of the 'democratic deficits' that can result (Peters and Pierre 2004). This concern echoes a long-standing worry expressed in many institutional studies of federalism, where the burgeoning formal and informal machinery for handling intergovernmental relations tends to create a shadowy world of collaboration, far removed from scrutiny or accountability.

In sum, the field of intergovernmental relations has been increasingly concerned with a problematic arising from the increasingly rapid dissolution of the boundaries that define the 'spaces between'. Under the MLG scenario, as the boundaries dissolve, so the entities within them (governments) purportedly become weaker and less stable. This has all the features of a vicious cycle. The space between not only expands but also becomes increasingly empty of government, weakening policy capacity in the face of a growing burden of cross-jurisdictional policy dilemmas and failures. Some scholars see networking, partnerships and innovative

cross-jurisdictional MLG institutions and instruments as an inexorable trend in response to these issues, challenging the formal institutions of the nation-state while providing a solution to the problems of complexity. Other scholars have argued that the enthusiasm for MLG has overstated the extent to which non-state actors have risen in significance, overstating their role and effectiveness and understating the continuing centrality of the state (Bell and Hindmoor 2010).

In Part 14 of the Handbook, the three contributors reflect three of the major traditions or strands in this increasingly wide-ranging field of study. In Chapter 39, Beryl Radin draws on and brings together the rich traditions of American scholarship in intergovernmental public policy implementation and intergovernmental management. This approach draws heavily on policy case study findings, building up a systematic depiction of the complex variety of the instruments of intergovernmental relations and the political stratagems they represent. In Chapter 40, Allen Fenna situates his discussion within the institutional tradition, with a concern for the specific character of intergovernmental relations in federal states, focusing in particular on performance dilemmas and policy effects. Finally, In Chapter 41, Simona Piatonni surveys the evolving theoretical and empirical study of multi-level governance in Europe, with particular concern for whether the novel ways of filling the growing intergovernmental gaps with multi-level governance arrangements will solve, rather than exacerbate, mounting problems of legitimacy.

REFERENCES

Agranoff, Robert J. (1986) *Intergovernmental Management.* Albany, NY: State University of New York Press.

Bell, Stephen and Hindmoor, Andrew (2010) *Rethinking Governance: The Centrality of the State in Modern Society.* Cambridge: Cambridge University Press.

Breton, Albert (1996) *Competitive Governments: An Economic Theory of Politics and Public Finance.* Cambridge: Cambridge University Press.

Elazar, Daniel J. (1994) *The American Mosaic: The Impact of Space, Time, and Culture on American Politics.* Boulder, CO: Westview Press.

Elazar, Daniel J. (1998) *Constitutionalizing Globalization: The Postmodern Revival of Confederal Arrangements.* Lanham, MD: Rowman & Littlefield Publishers.

Enderlain, Henrik, Walti, Sonja and Zurn, Michael (2010) *Handbook on Multi-level Governance.* Cheltenham: Edward Elgar.

Jordan, Andrew (2001) 'The European Union: An Evolving System of Multi-level Governance … Or Government', *Policy and Politics,* 29(2): 193–208.

Kickert, W., Klijn, E.H. and Koppenjan, J.F.M. (1997) *Managing Complex Networks: Strategies for the Public Sector.* London: Sage Publications.

McGinnis Michael D. (1999) *Polycentric Governance and Development: Readings from the Workshop in Political Theory and Policy Analysis.* Ann Arbor, MI: University of Michigan Press.

Oates, Wallace E. (1972) *Fiscal Federalism.* London: Harcourt Brace Jovanovich.

Ostrom, Vincent (1987) *The Political Theory of a Compound Republic: Designing the American Experiment,* 2nd edn. Lincoln, NE: University of Nebraska Press.

Peters, B. Guy and Pierre, Jon (2004) 'Multi-level Governance and Democracy', in Ian Bache and Matthew Flinders (eds), *Multi-level Governance.* New York: Oxford University Press, pp. 75–89.

Pressman, Jeffrey L. and Aaron Wildavsky (1973) *Implementation.* Berkeley and Los Angeles: University of California Press.

Rhodes, R.A.W. (1988) *Beyond Westminster and Whitehall: The Sub-central Governments of Britain.* London: Unwin-Hyman.

Rhodes, R.A.W. (2000) 'Governance and Public Administration', in John Pierre (ed.), *Debating Governance: Authority, Steering and Democracy.* Oxford: Oxford University Press.

Rosenau, James N. (2000) 'Change, Complexity and Governance in a Globalizing Space', in John Pierre (ed.), *Debating Governance: Authority, Steering and Democracy.* Oxford: Oxford University Press.

Wright, D.S. (1983) 'Managing the Intergovernmental Scene: The Changing Dramas of Federalism, Intergovernmental Relations and Intergovernmental Management', in W.B. Eddy (ed.), *The Handbook of Organization Management.* New York: Marcel Dekker.

39

The Instruments of Intergovernmental Management

Beryl A. Radin

This is a topic that has changed quite dramatically over the past several decades. If this Handbook had been published three decades ago, the discussion of instruments of intergovernmental management would have been a very straightforward and relatively simple exposition, for at that point it would be assumed that intergovernmental management focused almost entirely on vertical relationships between levels of government and, occasionally, on horizontal relationships. The metaphor 'picket fence federalism' – alliances between program specialists or professionals that transcend the level of government in which they serve – captured this set of relationships in the US setting (Wright, 1988: 83).

The initial literatures that developed this frame of reference assumed that traditional approaches to institutional authority would remain. The first writings on intergovernmental management did not focus on changes in systems, structures, policies or programs. However, they did highlight management

activities that effectively blended politics and administration by focusing on public managers – including program and policy professionals – in the policy process. While much of this literature highlighted the role of national governments, it increasingly moved toward a flatter and less top-down approach. In fact, at least some of the literature accentuated a bottom-up, more collegial approach to these relationships. But as fiscal issues preoccupied intergovernmental players, the discussion often moved away from protection of authority to budget issues. This was particularly true in the United States during the Obama presidency.

It also became clear that many of the behaviors described in federal systems were also found in unitary political systems. In the United Kingdom, for example, researchers have described the distinctive interests in cities and the national state (Gurr and King, 1987). Many of the dynamics that stem from social, economic and political changes in unitary systems are very similar to the dynamics traditionally associated with federalism. And the reality of coalition governments in parliamentary systems has spanned behaviors in unitary systems that have some attributes of federal systems (particularly when political parties are linked to geographic areas).

Fuzzy boundaries between public and private entities, the development of non-governmental organizations (especially civil society groups) and creation of networks have indicated that intergovernmental management can occur in both unitary and federal systems. In a sense, globalization has created increased complexity in an already complicated set of issues.

Three sets of changes have occurred that are crucial to understanding the contemporary context of intergovernmental management:

- an increase in boundary-spanning activities;
- the new management skills required as a result of the boundary-spanning changes; and
- the international expression of these changes.

AN INCREASE IN BOUNDARY-SPANNING ACTIVITES

The landscape of the public sector that is in place at the beginning of the twenty-first century appears to be quite different from that found several decades earlier. Several aspects of this changed landscape have contributed to the context for intergovernmental management.

Shifting policy boundaries

In the early period of intergovernmental management, relationships could be established that followed clear demarcations of policies and programs. Rural policy, for example, was defined as a part of agricultural policy and the relationships across levels of government were found within that policy sphere. By the end of the twentieth century,

however, many countries found that rural policy was no longer defined solely within the agriculture sphere. Rather, it involved sectors including economic development, health, education, housing and infrastructure. Education, for example, became less the purview of education specialists than an issue of concern to a broader group of decision makers and citizens. Deference to professionals in many areas decreased. Similar movement out of a single-policy world has been found in other areas, such as drug policy, crime and welfare.

Shifting views about the role of government

There have been quite dramatic changes in the way that both citizens and governments themselves think about the role of government in democratic societies. The traditional hierarchical bureaucratic structures with powers concentrated at the top of organizations have been subjected to criticism; criticism not only about the structure of government but also its span of powers has contributed to what has been called the 'hollowing' of government. This has led to a shrinking of the direct role of public agencies in actually delivering services to the public as well as a diminution of the span of responsibilities of the public sector. Privatization and contracting out have become increasingly common, utilizing public funds but relying on for-profit or non-profit entities to deliver services. The 'hollowing out' argument points to a number of changes, including transfer of functions, loss of expertise and the breakdown of traditional relationships (Frederickson and Frederickson, 2006).

Interdependence between levels of government

Since the earlier recognition of the need for management of programs across jurisdictions and sectors, more and more policies have exhibited characteristics of interdependence between levels of government. This means that multiple levels of government are involved simultaneously in increasing numbers of programs and policies and that a single level of government rarely has single power and influence over the way that programs are designed, funded, managed and delivered.

Public–private interdependence

The changes that have occurred in the reach and structure of government have made it obvious that the activities involving intergovernmental management do not end with players only from the public sector or government agencies. Rather, management of public sector programs involves a wide range of players from both the for-profit and nonprofit sectors. They come to the policy table with their own agenda and imperatives. In some cases, the representatives from the for-profit sector have had minimal experience with the limited authority and constraints placed on public sector officials. Reciprocally, the public sector officials have not had experience with players who have value orientations that are different from those in the public sector.

A focus on performance

The concern about performance is closely linked to the reinvention movement popularized in the United States by Osborne and Gaebler (1992), and, more broadly, to the global New Public Management (NPM) movement (Barzelay, 2001). The reinvention movement accentuates the importance of measuring results, highlighting outcomes rather than inputs, processes, or even outputs. It focuses on the benefits derived from the use of public sector funds and seeks to establish a framework that moves away from incremental decision making in which budgets are created largely on the basis of past

allocation patterns. It has been used as a way to counter the public's disillusionment with government as well as the government-bashing that has been employed by political figures at all ends of the political spectrum. But while the concern about performance is pervasive, it is not expressed consistently; it takes many different forms and is attached to efforts at all levels of government (Radin, 2006).

NEED FOR NEW MANAGEMENT SKILLS

Managers have found that the traditional 'command and control' paradigm, accentuating the authority of the individuals at the top of the hierarchy, did not provide an adequate framework to deal with the major issues found in the intergovernmental debate in the United States and in other countries. Neither did it capture the tension between national and local governmental units in unitary systems. An approach has developed around intergovernmental relations that emphasizes the importance of bargaining, compromise and networking as essential processes of decision making. This highlights a movement away from a 'sorting-out' of intergovernmental roles to a focus on the development of interorganizational networks that include both governmental and non-governmental actors. It involves the acceptance of the independent and separate character of the various members; avoidance of superior–subordinate relationships; interfacing of political and career actors; inclusion of appropriate specialists when needed to focus on technical issues; and agreement to abide by tasks and goals (Agranoff, 1986). It also includes recognition of the use of informal relationships even when structural centralization appears to dominate (Gurr and King, 1987; Rhodes, 1988).

This approach also draws on the policy notion of issue networks. This concept, developed by Hugh Heclo, is viewed as a 'web' of largely autonomous participants with variable degrees of mutual commitment or dependence on each other. Heclo (1979) focuses on the hybrid interests that provoke such alliances and comprise a large number of participants who move in and out of the network constantly. The issue network approach provides a way to include various interests in a process, cutting both horizontally (across multiple issues) as well as vertically (down the intergovernmental chain). It also establishes a framework that is responsive to the transient nature of policy coalitions, with various networks established for a particular situation but dissolved when that situation changes.

While this approach has intrigued intergovernmental scholars, it has not been used extensively in the world of practice. Intergovernmental dialogue continues to be characterized by a focus on separate programs, policies or organizations and a search for clarity and simplicity in the delineation of roles and responsibilities. This has been reinforced not only by a concern about efficiency in government but also by a focus on the role of government in the broader economy (Painter, 1997). There is a pattern of borrowing both practices and values from the private sector.

systems and public–private relationships; others move to more centralized control systems, creating tensions for intergovernmental management.

The concern about performance is one aspect of the NPM movement. Performance measurement initiatives have taken on the characteristic of a movement across the globe (Radin, 2006). Yet another aspect of the movement highlights the importance of empowering those who actually deliver services. This has been a problem in the United States, where many of the national programs involve intricate intergovernmental relationships. Thus, managers in national government agencies have struggled with ways to structure these relationships. National government agencies are balancing two competing imperatives. On the one hand, they are attempting to hold third parties accountable for the use of the national government monies but, on the other hand, they are constrained by the political and legal realities that provide significant discretion and leeway to the third parties for the use of these national government dollars. In many ways, the performance movement at the national government level collides with strategies of devolution and a diminished national government role.

NEW PUBLIC MANAGEMENT: THE INTERNATIONAL EXPRESSION OF THESE CHANGES

Many of the shifts that have been described above affecting intergovernmental management have coincided in time with the development of the NPM movement. While this movement is not composed of a well-defined set of principles and practices, a number of the behaviors that have been associated with it do have implications for intergovernmental management because they appear to shift the balance between central governments and subnational jurisdictions. Some of these developments emphasize decentralized

INSTRUMENTS OF INTERGOVERNMENTAL RELATIONS

The increase in boundary-spanning activities, the need for new intergovernmental management skills and the emergence of NPM globally – in particular, the upsurge of performance management – can all be seen in action through the choice and application of tools or instruments of intergovernmental relations. New demands have been placed on intergovernmental managers. This is especially true when attempting to link the relationship between budget and fiscal issues to concern about the effectiveness of programs. These demands require managers to think about a repertoire of instruments that might be used in different situations. The available tools have emerged from many different sources and are best understood in the context of specific governmental structures and specific policy areas. Four broad categories of instruments are of particular interest:

- structural;
- programmatic;
- research and capacity building; and
- behavioral.

See McDonnell and Elmore (1987), Salamon and Lund (1989) and Salamon (2002) for other approaches to classifying tools or instruments.

Structural

Structural matters have to do with formal roles and relationships; patterns of authority and leadership; rules, policies and regulations; and mechanisms for differentiation and integration of formal roles, tasks and relationships. In some cases, the actual structure of the public service may actually provide the setting for intergovernmental management. This is the case in India, where the design of the Indian Administrative Service is itself an instrument of federalism (Radin, 1999).

Reorganization
Formal roles and relationships are shaped and reshaped in the design and redesign of organizations. Patterns of authority and leadership are disrupted and re-established. Redesign, or reorganization, is a tool frequently employed in government as a means of responding to changing needs and priorities. Reorganizations can bring together programs that seem to be related, thus affecting horizontal intergovernmental relationships. However, reorganizations cannot settle these issues. Reorganization can be approached on a grand scale (as was the case in the United States with President Nixon's Ash Commission, charged with studying the

organization of the national government) or on a more incremental base (as was the case with President Carter's Reorganization Project inside the Office of Management and Budget). These issues continued during the Clinton administration through the National Performance Review and reoccurred in an inchoate form during the Obama administration. Frequently, attempts are made to create mega-departments, assuming that these centralized bodies will improve efficiency of government operations and service delivery. In the United States, some state-level reorganizations have been spawned by national government incentives. In the 1970s, several states created departments of behavioral health or departments of substance abuse, believing that they would be in a better position to take advantage of national government grant funds targeted at comprehensive approaches to those issues. In the United Kingdom, increasing centralization by the Thatcher government reduced local discretion over budgetary allocations and restructured local government (Gurr and King, 1987).

Commissions
Commissions are structural tools which can be used for any number of intergovernmental purposes. They are frequently a tool of horizontal integration but often appear to shift power to a centralized level. While some may view commissions as a coordination tool, they are likely to operate at a symbolic level that makes coordination difficult. This is particularly true in large federal systems where coordination across programs and across levels of government is difficult.

Coordination
Coordination and efficiency are the bywords of the structural approach. Coordinating mechanisms are tools for structural integration – the integration of units differentiated by function or level or geography. Implicit in attempts at reorganization is the assumption that increased coordination and efficiency

will make it easier to manage both horizontal and vertical intergovernmental relationships.

In practice, coordination is often transparent. It is easy to say it is being done, but its tangible products are illusive. While interagency coordination has costs, it does not necessarily require new appropriations, or particular budgetary line items. Unlike reorganization, coordination doesn't run the risk of alienating political constituencies, and it is difficult for one to argue that coordination is unnecessary or seriously detrimental to major interests. Applied properly as intergovernmental tools, formal mechanisms of interagency coordination can strengthen horizontal relationships. At the same time they can both strengthen a higher level of government's capacity to hold lower levels responsible for program performance and empower actors at those lower levels so that they can improve performance.

Premiers or governors meetings, bringing together the political leaders of states or provinces (as found in Australia and Canada), are sometimes used as a coordination device. The Council of Australian Governments was created in 1992 to bring together state and central government officials to work on specific problems that required joint action (Painter, 2001). Scharpf has noted that coordination efforts can involve negative coordination (causing gridlock and lowest common denominator outcomes) (Scharpf, 1997: 112–114).

Deregulation

Rules, policies and regulations are instruments for controlling intergovernmental relationships; they are instruments for increasing accountability and decreasing autonomy. Consequently, deregulation swings the pendulum in the other direction. Mandates are impediments imposed on lower intergovernmental actors from above through regulatory mechanisms. Mandates are removed through deregulation and are relaxed or removed through ad hoc experiments such as waiver procedures or regulatory negotiation, or the creation of new coordinating mechanisms

(Radin et al., 1996; Radin, 1998, 1999, 2001). When crises occur, however, it is common to call for re-regulation of practices that appear to have contributed to the crisis situation.

Devolution and decentralization

These are structural tools with which the national government may delegate power to the states or with which states may delegate power to local governments. When used, then, devolution and/or decentralization shift the pendulum toward autonomy. President Nixon's New Federalism in the United States was an attempt at devolution and a reaction to many of the centralizing tenets of Johnson's Creative Federalism. This effort provided decentralization within national government departments to field units and a general preference for relying on general-purpose governments and elected officials rather than program specialists (Walker, 1995: 105).

Devolution took the form of general and special revenue sharing and attempts by President Nixon to impound national government funds as a way to eliminate program resources. Proponents of devolution are quite willing to trade accountability to the national government for discretion on the part of state and local officials. Decentralization has been employed in much the same manner by some states in an effort to manage intergovernmental relationships. Use of this tool involves passing authority (some would say 'passing the buck') to local units of government. In some instances, when states are given national government mandates without resources, they simply pass the mandates on to local government. This coping mechanism shifts the burden of the intergovernmental dilemma but it clearly does not solve it.

Regulation and oversight

Regulation is itself a structural intergovernmental tool, even though the degree to which the national government exercises oversight with respect to its state and local grantees is, in part, a political/ideological matter. In the Nixon, Reagan and Bush administrations in the United States, for example, the operative ideology was minimal national government involvement and maximum state and local responsibility. Attention to regulation did resurface during the Obama administration, responding to problems that were linked to earlier deregulation decisions. Block grants and revenue sharing carry with them fewer strings than conditional grants.

Oversight can occur at the input, process or output side of programs. Input requirements generally specify the form and elements of the program design, leaving little discretion for the program implementers. Process requirements include elements such as citizen participation or planning requirements that are built in to insure accountability. Output and outcome requirements tend to rely on evaluation as an accountability tool.

Evaluation requirements are imposed by either legislative or administrative mandate. Depending on where one sits, evaluation can be looked at as a management tool which is necessary for intelligent decision making or as an unwarranted intrusion on management discretion. Evaluation requirements are often used to assure that grant recipients are able to justify the expenditure of funds. Not only are these requirements sometimes built into programs but also recipients are often required to pay for them with grant funds. However, evaluation can also facilitate additional autonomy on the part of state and local grantees. If evaluation is related to performance rather than input or process (that is, focus on outcomes and program impacts), grantees may be given more discretion as to the way they produce those outcomes and impacts.

Process requirements can include citizen participation and planning approaches. Citizen participation requirements provide an opportunity for a form of accountability that is imposed early in the life of a program. While some may view them as a constraint, others view them as an opportunity to improve programs and avoid unnecessary conflict in their implementation. The idea of consulting with parties who will be affected by decisions is consistent with the general notion of

empowerment: it empowers program clients as well as program operators.

Planning requirements can also be used as a form of process accountability. Like other requirements, they can be viewed as a set of constraints or as an effective instrument for intergovernmental management. Planning processes allow a jurisdiction to identify its current status, its goals and its strategy for change. This requirement might stipulate that the process will occur openly, with ample opportunity for input from those affected by plan implementation. If plans are written to reflect the real status of the jurisdiction (rather than as compliance documents), they can both increase autonomy and ensure accountability.

Programmatic instruments

This second category of instruments employed to deal with the intergovernmental dilemma involves the application of resources and redesign of programs and grant types. From the national government perspective, the intention has been to make it easier for states, provinces, localities or regions to attack social and economic problems by providing them with the resources to do so. In many instances, these resources have emerged as a result of lobbying by states and localities. While this approach was the most common response to newly identified problems, limited resources make it less commonly used. In fact, programmatic requirements may be imposed on third parties without funding from the national government. Various grant forms such as competitive project grants, formula grants, matching grants and block grants are still used as tools today.

The shift toward broader-purpose grants
Highly specific categorical grants are the most restrictive but also the most targeted type of national government funding. These grant forms – particularly project grants – require potential eligible recipients to submit

applications under guidelines specified by national government grantor agencies. Depending on the area, states continue to have discretion in this process. In some cases, applications from local units of government (or the private sector) must be reviewed and receive favorable recommendations from state agencies prior to submission to the national government grantor.

In the United States, block grants in law enforcement, employment and training, community development and social services were enacted which strengthened the hand of state and local officials in their dealing with national government grantors. While these approaches appear to be fairly radical approaches to intergovernmental management, they resulted in rather incremental changes in the system because the existing procedures were well entrenched and not easily modified.

Partnerships

As Peters has noted, partnership involves two or more actors, at least one of which is public; each participant is a principal; there is an enduring relationship among the actors; and each of the participants brings something to the partnership and a shared responsibility for outcomes of their activities (Peters, 1998: 12–13). As intergovernmental tools, partnerships generally involve setting priorities and providing incentives at higher levels of government and letting others take action to achieve them. It means less reliance on service delivery through public bureaucracies and more utilization of public–public or public–private partnerships. Partnerships involve national government, state and local governments and the private sector in a variety of activities.

While states and localities have traditionally been partners in the intergovernmental arena, this approach focuses on the creation of specific partnership forms in response to the tensions inherent in the intergovernmental dilemma. Osborne and Gaebler (1992) pointed out that under partnership schemes governments share or trade services

or contracts with one another for specific services. Additionally, information, ideas and other resources may be shared in partnerships. Creating partnerships involves reframing the intergovernmental dilemma at the national government level. This approach attempts to define accountability and, at the same time, do more to empower states and localities so that they can be full partners in the federal system. This is often easier to promise than to deliver.

Collaborations

Collaborations may involve the granting of national government funds to a set of state or local agencies (or a combination of public and private actors that cross jurisdictions as well as roles) conditional upon their ability to work together and share resources. Often collaboration is based on recognition that no single agency or system of services can effectively respond to the myriad of needs presented by those in or at risk for a particular service. Interagency collaboration envisions that partners will relinquish total control of resources in favor of the group process, pooling resources and jointly planning, implementing and evaluating new services. This programmatic approach overlaps with structural instruments in that it indicates recognition by national government, state and local officials that old structures must give way to new ones if intergovernmental problems are to be solved.

Research and capacity-building instruments

The third category of intergovernmental instruments involves 'empowerment'. As fiscal issues have become more important, there have been fewer resources available in this area. Implicit in this empowerment notion is the idea that steps may have to be taken to build increased management capacity at all levels if empowering is to have a chance of succeeding. So, empowerment is an empty exercise if it does not also include the tools that the newly empowered need to get the job done. Specific tools in this category include research, the collection, storage and dissemination of information and training, and other forms of capacity building.

Research

Research is an indirect tool of intergovernmental management aimed at helping people understand problems and issues, options and consequences. To the extent that public policy research is cross-cutting, it can aid those promoting interagency coordination. To the extent that research produces useful knowledge which is in turn utilized below the national government level, it can increase the negotiating power, and thus the autonomy of state and local intergovernmental actors.

The provision of information

National and state governments often serve as clearinghouses for those seeking information on just about anything. This information is expected to improve inter-agency coordination and strengthen state and local discretion.

Capacity building

This is one of the most widely used tools of intergovernmental management. Generally, it involves efforts by the national or state governments to strengthen the capabilities of state or local officials to manage programs on their own Central governments often provide substantial technical assistance to officials at lower levels, and that they have been doing so for some time is often overlooked. This assistance can be in the form of grants or contracts which provide for training and skill building in the areas of program design, planning and evaluation, to name just three.

There are two ways in which capacity building and the strengthening of state and local expertise in specific program areas is an intergovernmental management tool. First, it makes sense for the grantor to insure that grantees who are given additional discretion have the skills and abilities necessary to manage the grants. Second, it helps to insure

accountability through development of management skills that facilitate compliance with national grant requirements.

Behavioral instruments of intergovernmental relations

The traditional view of the national official's dilemma is whether to allow more or less autonomy or to impose more or less accountability. Accountability can be framed in a narrow fashion, holding grantees accountable for inputs and processes. However, looking at the situation through a wider lens suggests that accountability should be for performance, and autonomy means that grantees are empowered and given the tools they need to accomplish that performance. This broader view of accountability requires attention to individual and group processes of communication and to processes of conflict management.

Conflict management

No matter what metaphor is used to describe the intergovernmental system, there is evidence of conflict. The issue, then, is not to attempt to avoid or suppress conflict but, rather, to prevent unnecessary conflict and to manage the conflict that does occur toward productive ends (Buntz and Radin, 1983).

Conflict prevention in an intergovernmental context calls for attention to building consensus among actors in particular programmatic or policy areas. Actors are urged to identify and overcome barriers like the language and jargon of different program cultures and resistance to change among agency staff.

Conflict management might involve taking a negotiated approach to the promulgation of rules and regulations, as opposed to a 'decide, announce and defend' approach. The US Environmental Protection Agency (EPA) has engaged in a process of negotiated rule making referred to as 'reg-neg'. Regulatory negotiation involves affected parties and the agency in an orderly process of debate and discussion over proposed regulations. This consultative approach produced environmental regulations which were acceptable to all. It enabled the EPA to move away from the 'decide, announce and defend' approach, which landed it in court more often than not. However, the negotiation process was time consuming and thus had limited application.

Individual communication

Closely connected to the consensus building/ conflict management notion is the idea of improving communications between levels of government as a way to manage the accountability/autonomy dilemma. Effective intergovernmental relationships in an environment of resource scarcity and political uncertainty demand openness in interactions across governments. They demand national officials who can listen, delegate, manage conflict and build consensus. The 'command and control' method of communicating from national to state and local levels is not viewed as an adequate way to manage intergovernmental relations.

Group communication

Hearings are among the time-honored and formal means of group communication in policy development. Hearings provide a forum for representatives of groups inside and outside of government to take positions and express their views. They also provide a means for governmental actors to collect information and shape ideas that later become policy. Hearings can be traditional and formal, or of the town-meeting type. If one reframes the intergovernmental dilemma and looks at it as an opportunity rather than a problem, hearings can be another way to build consensus. If one looks at these issues in a narrow sense, hearings can be viewed as a way to exert national influence.

None of these four categories of intergovernmental tools or instruments is a panacea. Intergovernmental actors must look at issues from a number of different perspectives simultaneously. Structural, programmatic, educational and behavioral approaches are each appropriate under the right set of circumstances. While one might search for rules of thumb that make particular instruments more or less appropriate in particular situations, the determination to adopt one or several of these approaches appears to be highly idiosyncratic to particular countries and to specific situations.

A SPECIAL CASE: DEALING WITH PERFORMANCE

As highlighted in the first section, the global adoption of performance management notions and techniques has been one of the defining aspects of recent developments in intergovernmental management. Drawing mainly on US experience, this discussion highlights six different approaches that have been taken recently within national agencies to deal with issues of performance and intergovernmental management. Some performance approaches have been devised as a result of legislation and others through administrative action. All are struggling with the tension between national agency accountability and devolution and discretion provided to state and local agencies. These approaches include performance partnerships, incentives, negotiated measures, building performance goals into legislation, establishment of standards and waivers (Radin, in Posner and Conlan, 2008).

Performance partnerships

Over the past several decades a number of national agencies have adopted, or at least explored, the possibility of moving categorical programs into performance partnerships. These partnerships have become increasingly popular as agencies realize the limitations of their ability to achieve desired changes in complex settings. While partnerships between various agencies and government have been around in some form for some years, the performance orientation of the contemporary effort is new. The image of the partnership is one in which partners discuss how to combine resources from both players to achieve a prespecified end state. This end state is expected to be measurable in order for a partnership to be successful.

The design of a performance partnership addresses what some have viewed as one of the most troubling problems faced by national managers: lack of control over outcomes. While the managers may have control over inputs, processes and outputs, they cannot specify end outcomes. Performance partnerships may involve agreements between national officials and state or local agencies; they may be ad hoc or permanent.

This process is not without problems. The General Accounting Office (GAO) in the United States highlighted a number of what they called 'technical challenges':

- an absence of baseline data to use as the basis for measuring improvements;
- the difficulty of quantifying certain results;
- the difficulty of linking program activities to results; and
- the level of resources needed to develop a high-quality performance measurement system (US GAO, 1999) .

The experience of US EPA with performance partnerships illustrates some of the problems that are intrinsic to this performance strategy and agreement form. The individual negotiation between the national agency and (in this case) states is likely to result in variability of agreements across the country. In fact, to some, the individual tailoring of agreements is the strength of the mechanism. However, others are concerned that this variation results from differential treatment of jurisdictions.

The strategy is often attractive to national agencies charged with the implementation of programs that involve policy sectors that do not have well-established data systems or even data definitions. In such settings, it is difficult to establish and to garner data for the performance measures required to achieve the expectations of the approach.

Incentives

Incentives seek to induce behavior rather than command it. But bureaucrats and politicians tend to be attracted to direct regulation, since they believe that incentives also require governmental intervention and therefore involve regulation. The reality of fiscal scarcity, however, has raised questions about whether the incentives are effective or actually may produce perverse effects that do not lead to increased performance. To some degree, however, incentives have been at play in the past in a number of national programs through matching fund requirements. When the national government offers funds as an incentive to induce states or provinces to provide their own funds, the matching requirements do serve an incentive function. In many cases, however, performance expectations are not usually made explicit, particularly in programs carried over from the past.

There are a number of dilemmas involved in using an incentive strategy. It is difficult to ascertain the direct relationship between the behavior of the state or local government and specific outcomes. In addition, complex programs have an array of program goals and expectations and it is not easy to achieve agreement on performance standards. Some critics of the incentive strategy argue that state or local jurisdictions will attempt to game the system and develop policies that may meet the performance measures rather than achieve the basic expectations of the legislation. Others argue that this already occurs and so the situation is not much different than it has been in the past.

Negotiated performance measures

One of the most common complaints by state and local governments in the United States is that the national government imposes a set of requirements as to the use of its funds that do not meet the needs of the non-national jurisdiction. Indeed, this is one of the arguments used to justify the transformation of categorical program grants into block grant efforts. Block grants have proved to be one of the most difficult grant forms on which to impose performance requirements. It has been problematic for national officials to balance the flexibility of the block grant (allowing states and localities to meet their own particular needs) with a desire for greater accountability for the use of those funds.

However, there are times when it is possible to achieve agreement on performance measures when certain conditions are met. Programs that are not politically volatile or do not have a widely disparate set of expert opinions are appropriate for this process. In addition, prior work and data systems can lay the foundation for consensus on many outcome and process objectives: measures can recognize and separate objectives over which grantees exercise influence and control from those that depend on external factors beyond their control. But even when these conditions are present, the negotiation process is time consuming and requires an investment of staff and resources by national agencies.

Building performance goals into legislation

Various pieces of legislation in the United States have been crafted with attention to performance goals. In these cases, the legislation represented a move from an emphasis on input or process requirements to a focus on performance outcomes. Further refinements of these requirements were established by both national departments through the regulations development process. In drafting legislation, Congress has assumed that the core indicators reflect common practices across the country and that data systems are available to report on achievement of the goals. However, the experience over the past decade has indicated that this is not as simple as was once believed, particularly if the goals are defined by the national government and imposed on third parties (Frederickson and Frederickson, 2006; Radin, 2006; Moynihan, 2008).

Establishment of standards

In some cases, the role of the national government has been to establish performance standards that are meant to guide the behavior of state, provincial or local governments. At least, theoretically, these standards are to be voluntary and the ability of a state or locality to conform to them is not tied to eligibility for specific national dollars. The national role in this strategy may involve the development of the standards, provision of technical assistance, and at times could include payment for meeting these norms and guidelines.

The Clinton administration's proposal for the development of a voluntary national test in reading and mathematics was an example of this approach. The response to this proposal, particularly by some governors and educational leaders, illustrates the types of problems that may emerge from this strategy. Although several governors were supporters of this administration proposal in 1997, others expressed concern. A number of states already had test systems in place and did not want to replace their existing performance accountability systems with the national approach. Still others were uncomfortable with the content of the tests, particularly their accuracy and validity in measuring achievement and their substantive scope. Passage of the 'No Child Left Behind' program during the Bush administration turned the voluntary standards into requirements; these generated controversial responses across a range of actors that led to federal-level administrative decisions to effectively waive the enforcement of those requirements.

This proposal also uncovered another problem that is likely to be confronted whenever the standards strategy is employed: fear that the information gathered through these assessments has a life of its own and will be used inappropriately. This is particularly problematic because the information that is collected was meant to illustrate achievement at the individual level. Questions of privacy and information security have been raised and were not answered to the satisfaction of critics.

Waivers

Authority to grant waivers to state or local governments for specific programs has been in place for many years. While the waiver authority has been viewed as a way to meet the unique needs of individual states, it has also been closely tied to a research and development strategy, providing latitude to non-national jurisdictions to experiment with new ways to deliver services. In the United States the waiver has been touted as a way to move beyond process or input requirements and, instead, to give states and localities the opportunity to devise their own approaches to achieve specific outcomes. The waiver authorization has usually been defined in the context of specific programs and the criteria for granting the waivers are established within the authorizing legislation or implementing regulations. Certain requirements (such as civil rights requirements or filing performance information) cannot be waived.

This authority has been employed extensively in the United States in several program areas, particularly involving welfare, Medicaid, and the Job Training Partnership Act. Waivers have been used to allow states to establish their own approach and to eliminate or modify input or process requirements. Many of the waivers require the proposed modification to be budget neutral. For some, the waiver process is a mechanism that can be used to make a case for policy change. However, there are concerns that the waivers produce a situation where nobody will be watching, monitoring, or holding those granted the waiver accountable.

CONCLUSION

Managers and management strategists must be sensitive to differences among policies

and programs, differences among the players involved, the complexity of the worlds of both the national and non-national agencies involved, and the level of goal agreement or conflict. Focusing on a variety of approaches suggests that government-wide approaches are not particularly effective. The process of defining instruments should be devised in the context of specific programs, sensitive to the unique qualities surrounding those initiatives.

As this process unfolds, there are a number of elements that should be considered by those who seek to develop approaches that are sensitive to intergovernmental concerns. While there is not a template that can be used to determine the appropriate approach for a particular situation, the following checklist provides a framework for such a determination (Gawande, 2009):

- determining who is responsible for establishing the implementation effort;
- assessing whether the current system actually affords implementers the opportunity to redefine goals to meet their own needs;
- determining the type of policy involved (it may be more difficult to deal with redistributive policies than with distributive or regulatory policies);
- assessing the current policy instrument used to implement a program;
- determining whether the decision makers involved are general-purpose government officials or program specialists;
- determining the extent of the national role or presence in the program area (for example, the level of funding involved);
- determining the level of risk for non-compliance as perceived by both parties;
- determining whether sanctions are available for non-performance;
- assessing the history of past oversight relationships (collegial or conflictual); and
- determining the level of diversity of practices across the country.

While the information gleaned from this checklist will not always lead to a specific instrument, it will provide a rough outline for program and policy officials to use to think about the range of approaches that might make sense in a particular situation. The determination of a particular instrument calls on intergovernmental managers to exercise creativity and care as they confront the multiple pressures that are a part of the reality of the current intergovernmental landscape.

REFERENCES

Agranoff, Robert (1986) *Intergovernmental Management: Human Services Problem-Solving in Six Metropolitan Areas.* Albany, NY: State University of New York Press.

Barzelay, Michael (2001) *The New Public Management: Improving Research and Policy Dialogue.* Berkeley, CA: University of California Press.

Buntz, C. Gregory and Radin, Beryl A. (1983) 'Managing Intergovernmental Conflict: The Case of Human Services', *Public Administration Review*, 43(5): 403–410.

Frederickson, David G. and Frederickson, George H. (2006) *Measuring the Performance of the Hollow State.* Washington, DC: Georgetown University Press.

Gawande, Atul (2009) *The Checklist Manifesto: How to Get Things Right.* New York: Picador Publishing.

Gurr, Ted Robert and King, Desmond (1987) *The State and the City.* Chicago, IL: University of Chicago Press.

Heclo, Hugh (1979) 'Issue Networks and the Executive Establishment', in A. King (ed.), *The New American Political System.* Washington, DC: American Enterprise Institute for Public Policy Research, pp. 87–124.

McDonnell, Lorraine M. and Elmore, Richard F. (1987) *Alternative Policy Instruments.* Philadelphia, PA: The Center for Policy Research in Education.

Moynihan, Donald P. (2008) *The Dynamics of Performance Management: Constructing Information and Reform.* Washington, DC: Georgetown University Press.

Osbourne, David and Gaebler, Ted (1992) *Reinventing Government.* Reading, MA: Addison-Wesley.

Painter, Martin (1997) 'Reshaping the Public Sector', in B. Galligan, I. McAllister and J. Ravenhill (eds), *New Developments in Australian Politics.* Melbourne: Macmillan, pp. 148–166.

Painter, Martin (2001) 'Policy Capacity and the Effects of New Public Management', in T. Christenson and P. Laegreid (eds), *New Public Management: The Transformation of Ideas and Practice.* Aldershot: Ashgate, pp. 209–230.

Peters, B. Guy (1998) '"With a Little Help from Our Friends": Public–Private Partnerships as Institutions and Instruments', in J. Pierre (ed), *Partnerships in Urban Governance: European and American Experience.* New York: St Martin's Press, pp. 11–33.

Radin, Beryl A. (1998) 'Bridging Multiple Worlds: Central, Regional and Local Partners in Rural Development', in J. Pierre (ed.), *Partnerships in Urban Governance: European and American Experience.* New York: St Martin's Press, pp. 140–162.

Radin, Beryl A. (1999) 'Bureaucracies as Instruments of Federalism: Administrative Experience from India', in I. Copland and J. Rickard (eds), *Federalism: Comparative Perspectives from India and Australia.* New Delhi: Manohar Press, pp. 85–112.

Radin, Beryl A. (2001) 'Intergovernmental Relationships and the Federal Performance Movement', in Dall W. Forsythe (ed.), *Quicker, Better, Cheaper: Managing Performance in American Government.* Albany, NY: Rockefeller Institute Press, pp. 285–306.

Radin, Beryl A. (2006) *Challenging the Performance Movement: Accountability, Complexity, and Democratic Values.* Washington, DC: Georgetown University Press.

Radin, Beryl A. (2008) 'Performance Management and Intergovernmental Relations', in P. L. Posner and T. J. Conlan (eds), *Intergovernmental Management for the 21st Century.* Washington, DC: Brookings Institution Press and National Academy of Public Administration, pp. 243–262.

Radin, Beryl A., Agranoff, Robert, Bowman, Ann O'M., et al. (1996) *New Governance for Rural America: Creating Intergovernmental Partnerships.* Lawrence, KS: University Press of Kansas.

Rhodes, R. A. W. (1988) *Beyond Westminster and Whitehall: The Sub-central Governments of Britain.* London: Unwin–Hyman.

Salamon, Lester M. (ed.) (2002) *The Tools of Government: A Guide to the New Governance.* New York: Oxford University Press.

Salamon, Lester M. and Lund, Michael S. (1989) 'The Tools Approach: Basic Analytics', in L. M. Salamon (ed.), *Beyond Privatization: The Tools of Government Action.* Washington, DC: The Urban Institute Press, pp. 23–50.

Scharpf, Fritz (1997) *Games Real Actors Play: Actor-Centered Institutionalism in Policy Research.* Boulder, CO: Westview Press.

US General Accounting Office (1999) *Environmental Protection: Collaborative EPA–State Effort Needed to Improve New Performance Partnership System.* GAO/RCED-99-171.

Walker, David B. (1995) *The Rebirth of Federalism: Slouching Toward Washington.* Chatham, NJ: Chatham House.

Wright, Deil S. (1988) *Understanding Intergovernmental Relations*, 3rd edn. Pacific Grove, CA: Brooks/Cole.

40

Federalism and Intergovernmental Coordination

Alan Fenna

INTRODUCTION

Federalism is a distinct governmental form with its own particular impact on public administration and policy and programme coordination between governments. In particular, it is a system where intergovernmental relations and coordination occur within a constitutionally structured relationship between central governments and the constituent units. At the same time, no two federations are the same, and each tends to operate in its own distinctive manner. This follows from differences in approaches to the division of powers and the form of government; as well as the degree to which there is an underlying federal society. The degree of entanglement between levels of government in contemporary federations puts a premium on cooperation and coordination that is accomplished through a variety of institutions and processes and which spans political and administrative spheres. Attempts to characterize these realities have generated a range of concepts, including cooperative federalism, collaborative federalism, administrative federalism, regulatory federalism, coercive federalism, executive federalism, pragmatic federalism, adaptive federalism, opportunistic federalism, conditional federalism, and much more.

THE CHARACTER OF FEDERALISM

Intergovernmental coordination is a challenge in all political systems, but particularly so in federal ones. Even the most unitary of states delegate responsibility for certain functions to local or regional jurisdictions and some unitary states do so to a substantial degree. Federal systems are distinctive, though, in two important regards:

- by having two constitutionally guaranteed levels of government with assigned powers and their own citizen bodies to whom they are accountable;
- by carrying the normative assumption that 'federalness' is a quality to be preserved for a range of purposes it serves or benefits it can deliver.

Federalism and its governments

The first of these considerations means that the central axis of federal systems is between the central government and the constituent units – the states, provinces, *Länder*, cantons, or howsoever those units are termed. The constitutionally privileged status of the constituent units reflects the premise of federalism that it is about the recognition of separate political communities (Levy, 2007). There are of course many other vertical intergovernmental relationships in federations: between central governments and their territories; between the constituent units and their local governments or special purpose jurisdictions; and between central governments and local governments and special-purpose jurisdictions. Constitutionally, however, these are relationships of superior and subordinate as in a unitary state.

Federalism and its benefits

The second consideration means that federal systems have a presumption in favour of action by the constituent units rather than by the central government. The federal character of the union, as embodied in an ongoing significance and autonomy for the constituent units, is widely seen as being valuable for the potential it holds to deliver certain benefits. These are chiefly: protecting regional diversity and responding to regional differences in policy preferences; optimizing the role of local knowledge in policy design and implementation; increasing the scope for policy experimentation and learning; and enhancing constitutional safeguards of liberal democracy by dispersing power.

Given the normative claims made about federalism, intergovernmental coordination in systems of divided jurisdiction always raises questions about the scope for legitimate diversity; local experimentation and policy learning; and the clarity of accountability. While received wisdom has held that these benefits will spontaneously flow from having a federal order, doubts have regularly been expressed about how likely that is and, in general, it seems that such benefits may well be undersupplied. In their notion of a 'constitution of democratic experimentalism', Dorf and Sable (1998) have argued that such potential can be reinvigorated by a central government that encourages and provides support for experimentalism among the constituent units and facilitates the drawing of lessons and dissemination of learning. Traditional federal thinking, however, is disposed to be sceptical about the capacity for such restrained benevolence on the part of central governments (e.g. Filippov et al., 2004; Bednar, 2009).

Structuring intergovernmental relationships

The manifold vertical and horizontal relationships exist in a complex web of rules and norms, the overarching framework for which is provided by fundamental law, or the constitution. This is a factor that is characteristically of much greater significance for intergovernmental relations within federal systems than in unitary ones. Within that framework operate laws of the central government and constituent units, many of which play a role in the relationships of cooperation and conflict between the different levels and governments. However, this captures by no means all of the practical reality of intergovernmental relations, which is made up of formal but non-judicial instruments such as intergovernmental agreements; extensive structured practices and behavioural norms; and a range of informal practices and working relationships.

VARIETIES OF FEDERALISM

While a number of generalizations applicable to most or all federations can be made, the considerable variety of federal types and experiences does impose limits. Federations differ significantly in their constitutional design; in the type of representative democracy they are organized around; and in their underlying societal characteristics. Considerable diversity exists even within the core of established OECD (Organisation for Economic Co-operation and Development) federations that is made up of the United States, Switzerland, Canada, Australia, and Germany. Diversity increases once the list is extended to India, Belgium, Spain, Brazil, Ethiopia, or even the 'quasi-federation' of the European Union (EU).

Constitutional design

In constitutional design a clear difference is evident, first of all, between the general approach employed in the Anglo federations and that taken in the Continental. The US model of 'legislative federalism', applied with variation in both the Canadian and Australian systems, assigns global responsibility for policy domains to the respective level of government. By contrast, the German model of 'administrative federalism' assigns a broad policy-making authority to the central government and leaves responsibility for implementation and administration to the constituent units (Brecht, 1945; Hueglin and Fenna, 2006: 69–72). This is often described in the German tradition as 'executive federalism' (*Vollzugsföderalismus*) because national laws are 'executed' by the subnational units. This is also to be found in Swiss federalism, whose particularly effective operation seems to be related to the way this approach dovetails with other aspects of Swiss political practices and culture (Armingeon, 2000).

The US model originally envisaged a 'coordinate' or 'dual' system, where some concurrency would occur, but on the whole, each level would operate autonomously in its own sphere. By contrast, the German model involves an 'interlocked' form of governance, or *politikverflechtung,* comprising both prescribed revenue sharing and integrated

decision making (Scharpf et al., 1976; Halberstam and Hills, 2001; Gunlicks, 2003, 2005; Kropp, 2010). A necessary correlate of dividing powers on the basis of function rather than domain is strong and direct representation for the constituent units in the law-making processes of the central government. Following historical practice, the German constitution sought to achieve this via the *Bundesrat* (Federal Council) composed of delegates representing the *Länder* executives – an approach echoed in the operation of the EU.

In the legislative federations, the division of powers was set in some sort of stone by enumerating a list of policy domains over which the central government was granted an authority to legislate. In the US and Australian cases, this was an exhaustive list. The US and Australian State governments, meanwhile, were granted an ostensibly broad grant of 'residual' power, with no specific domains being identified. In addition to enjoying identified powers, the national legislatures in these two federations were granted an explicit 'supremacy' in those instances where any overlap should occur.

Different again is the approach to dividing powers that has taken shape in the quasi-federal EU. It was the novel and indeterminate character of the EU that gave rise to the concept of multi-level governance and discussion continues about how best to characterize this case of 'treaty federalism' (Hueglin, 2000) or 'post-modern confederation' (Majone, 2006:147; Menon and Schain, 2006; Laursen, 2011). While under the treaties the EU has been assigned certain powers, the archetypal EU approach has been to substitute a procedural rule – *subsidiarity* – for a substantive assignment or allocation (van Hecke, 2003; Hueglin, 2007). The 'federal project' in Europe is, among opinion leaders and governments, still a minority view, because it entails surrendering too much de jure sovereignty by the constituent nation-states; at the same time, the crisis in the Eurozone in 2011 led to calls for much more de facto coordination and policy capacity at the centre in order to solve the euro's problems.

Form of government

Federations differ not just in the design of their federal arrangements, but, quite separately, in the degree to which they take parliamentary or presidential forms and have strong or weak second chambers. Whereas the United States was established on a federal and presidential basis, with a strong second chamber, Canada was established on a federal and parliamentary basis, with a formal rather than real second chamber. Indeed, in combining federalism with presidentialism, the United States is anomolous, with the leading federations being parliamentary in nature (though Switzerland is difficult to categorize). A number of comparative studies conclude that presidentialism is a key variable in explaining distinctive characteristics of intergovernmental coordination in the United States (Radin and Boase, 2000; Kelemen, 2004; Bakvis and Brown, 2010; Simeon and Radin, 2010). Australia is different again in combining federalism, parliamentarism and strong bicameralism, whereas Germany is distinctive in having a second chamber, the *Bundesrat*, that is designed primarily to operate as a house of the states.

Societal characteristics

One of the chief rationales for federalism is to provide constitutional assurance for particular cultural or ethnic minorities or regional interests. The extent to which such a 'federal society' exists will have a major impact on the functioning of the federal system. In particular, those federations with a clear language division – notably Switzerland and Canada – will have built-in tendencies towards the maintenance of a decentralized structure, while those such as the United States and even more so Australia, without such a division, will not have the same

centrifugal pressure (Erk, 2007; Fenna, 2007a). It also creates a *de facto* asymmetry in federal systems such as Canada's, with Québec often opting for special arrangements rather than participating in joint schemes with the other jurisdictions.

EVOLUTION OF FEDERAL SYSTEMS

The Anglo federations' original conception of the two levels of government functioning in parallel rather than in tandem soon gave way as the role of government increased and existing governmental tasks that had once been strictly local in their scope developed strong externalities or spillover effects and assumed a national dimension. As Conlan and Posner (2008: 3) point out, this has reached the stage in the United States where, being 'a critical front line in the national homeland security initiative', even something as truly local as fire brigades are the subject of national policy making. The consequence of these trends is that, for the United States, 'the major public problems and policy responses of recent years are overwhelmingly intergovernmental in nature' (Conlan and Posner, 2008: 2).

Coordinate to 'cooperative'

For many years this centralization was an incremental process, but the real turning point was the Great Depression. From that point on, the Anglo federations became decidedly more centralized and entangled (Clark, 1938; Wallis and Oates, 1998). In the United States, the turning point was 1937, when the Supreme Court was obliged to reconsider its views on the New Deal legislation (Corwin, 1950). Instances of 'cooperation' in all federations can be traced much further back (Elazar, 1962), but the situation by the mid-twentieth century was qualitatively different (Scheiber, 1980). Fundamentally, that process reflected changing economic and social conditions (Peterson, 1995). It may also have occurred partly in response to the democratic and policy deficiencies of subnational governments in the 1950s and 1960s (Parkin, 2003: 104; Bowman and Kearney, 2010: 5; though cf. Teaford, 2002). Meanwhile, a somewhat analogous transition to cooperative federalism may be occurring in the EU (Schutze, 2009). It is an evolving historical process where new modes both supersede and layer themselves over old modes in a 'sedimentary' process (Conlan, 2008).

Instruments of centralization

Central governments greatly expanded their role through some combination of legislative assertion and fiscal leverage. The rise of income tax as the primary revenue source positioned central governments to capture revenue well in excess of their normal expenditure needs. This provided the basis for conditional grant programmes (in the US 'categorical grants-in-aid') whereby central government funding bought potentially extensive influence over policy domains within the formal jurisdiction of the constituent units. In a number of cases, conditional grants have allowed national governments to circumvent a constitutional division of powers that corresponded only poorly to modern economic conditions and social demands.

The second main vehicle for centralization has been expansive interpretation of enumerated powers, conspicuous in both the US and Australian federations in particular. In the United States, this has manifested itself since the early 1970s in Congressional 'preemption', whereby Congress partially or wholly occupies a field previously assumed to be the responsibility of the states (Zimmerman, 2005; Buzbee, 2009).

Using its spending power and its expansively interpreted enumerated powers, the US government has been notable for the extent to which it has imposed so-called mandates on the states. While 'mandate' might normally refer to the granting of authority, in this context it is rather the opposite: the imposition of a requirement. Dubbed 'regulatory federalism', this practice seeks to regulate state and local government action in line with national policy decisions (ACIR, 1983). The tendency, over time, for the spending power lever to be replaced in the United States with direct orders that create 'unfunded mandates' has made such interventions increasingly contentious (Posner, 1998, 2008). Centralization seems to be secular trend that continues regardless of partisanship (Fenna, 2007a; Posner, 2007).

Concessions to federalism

The United States, where directive or regulatory federalism is most pronounced, has developed some compensatory mechanisms, notably in the system of 'waivers' allowing states to deviate from imposed requirements. In line with the normative underpinnings of federalism, this practice should restore or even enhance the potential for experimentation and learning (Weissert and Weissert, 2008).

COOPERATIVE FEDERALISM IN PRACTICE

The omnibus term for the overlapping and entangled state that the Anglo federations had reached by the latter twentieth century has been 'cooperative federalism'. It is 'a term that covers a multitude of sins from genuinely mutual adjustment, policy coordination and collaborative arrangements; to vertical competition between levels of government; to full-blown centralization through coercion and unilateral interventionism' (Fenna, 2007b: 175). Rather than carrying any necessary implication of mutualism or harmonious coordination, it refers simply to the fact of governments working and functioning together (Elazar, 1991: 69) and indeed may well be a 'euphemism' (Sawer, 1969: 123). In some analyses, cooperative federalism was originally characterized by mutualistic relations that called for more attention to administrative coordination (CIR, 1955) and indeed continued to grow and evolve as the happily 'pragmatic' adjustment of an old constitution to new conditions (Glendening and Reeves, 1977; Hollander and Patapan, 2007). In other views, these originally mutualistic patterns soon gave way to more blatantly coercive ones (Kincaid, 1990) and the 'opportunistic' exploitation by central governments of the dominant fiscal and constitutional position they enjoy in the federation (Conlan, 2006).

Power of the purse?

The extensive use of conditional grants to create new roles for national governments in areas of subnational jurisdiction has continued in Australia and the United States, but sharply declined in Canada (Bakvis and Brown, 2010). In many ways the tied grant remains a powerful tool for incorporating the US and Australian states into national policy frameworks (Cho and Wright, 2007). However, the effectiveness of this instrument in directing states and holding them accountable remains a live question given everything from distance to data-collection limitations (e.g. Handley, 2008; Nugent, 2009; Ramamurthy, 2012). Although Pressman and Wildavsky's (1973: 161) famous study of policy implementation gone badly awry indicted much more than just federalism, it did endorse the view that a system of divided jurisdiction 'not only permits but encourages the evasion and dilution of federal reform' (quoting Murphy, 1971: 60). How much this is a function of federalism specifically, or more generally of multiple levels of government, and the overlapping hierarchies that result, is another question (e.g. Hupe, 2010).

Performance monitoring and benchmarking

The difficulties caused by overlapping and entanglement generate, in turn, the periodic, almost inevitable, enthusiasm for 'new federalism'. This is typically not 'new' at all, but an attempt to restore some element of the *status quo ante* by returning fiscal capacity, policy responsibilities, or administrative autonomy to the constituent units through such mechanisms as block grants or devolution of policy-making responsibility.

The most recent wave of such reform has been characterized by an attempt to implement performance monitoring and management regimes shifting the emphasis from input and output controls to outcomes assessment. This is more novel, and in one view represents a major step towards a constitution of democratic experimentalism (Metzenbaum, 2008). In less sanguine views, performance management in itself is fraught with difficulties of data quality, perverse incentives, output–outcomes relationships and more. Combined with the challenges of federalism it becomes a truly heroic objective (Radin, 2006, 2008). These developments are most evident in those federations, notably Australia and the United States, with stronger central governments (Gamkhar, 2002; Fenna, 2008, 2012) – the US government's 'No Child Left Behind' policy being the most salient example (Manna, 2011). Indeed, the use of performance management techniques across levels of government is more characteristic of unitary regimes with their clear hierarchy of authority between central government at the national level and general- or special-purpose authorities at the local level exercising merely delegated (and hence revocable) powers. This has been particularly so in the UK (Downe, 2008).

At the other end of the spectrum is the European Union's Open Method of Coordination (OMC), which seeks to use benchmarking as a technique to disseminate 'best practice' among a diverse range of member states across a wide range of policy areas. With little or no authority in a number of social policy and other fields where comprehensive national policy frameworks already exist, and no major revenue sources to fund extensive grant programmes, the EU has had little choice but to employ 'soft law' devices. These focus on a highly consultative and iterative practice of indicator development, performance reporting and qualitative peer review (e.g. Heidenreich and Bischoff, 2008; Sabel and Zeitlin, 2010; Tholoniat, 2010). These methods correspond admirably with the ethos of federalism but raise questions of efficacy.

Collaborative arrangements

The increasingly entangled nature of intergovernmental relations in the legislative federations creates a need for coordination that is inherently challenging, given the assumptions of separate and parallel operation that informed their design. The challenge is arguably more acute in the United States, given the separation of powers and the nature of the US public service (Kettl, 2006; Bouckaert et al., 2010). Both Australia and Canada have long-standing practices of high-level intergovernmental relations, referred to as 'executive federalism' for the way they occur largely to the exclusion of the respective legislative bodies (e.g. Simeon, 1972). These comprise meetings of portfolio ministers in regular 'ministerial councils' as well as summit-like meetings of the heads of government and, of course, the attendant work of officials from each jurisdiction's public service. This is more structured in Australia, where heads of government meetings have been regularized as COAG, the Council of Australian Governments. While COAG cannot be said to have a formal institutional existence, it has become a well-established practice since Australian intergovernmental relations entered a decidedly more collaborative phase in the early 1990s (Painter, 1998). That collaborative spirit has waxed and waned since, tending to grow when positive-sum issues

are prominent and shared partisanship dominates (Carroll and Head, 2010; Fenna and Anderson, 2012) but even then the Commonwealth is almost inevitably the dominant partner (Anderson, 2008; Jones, 2008).

Similar collaborative practices are also evident in other parliamentary federations, including both Canada and Germany, although their degree of development varies (Cameron and Simeon, 2002; Inwood et al., 2011; Lhotta and von Blumenthal, 2012). The Canadian First Ministers' Conference is seen – by contrast with COAG – as the 'weak link' in the intergovernmental chain (Papillon and Simeon, 2004). In Germany, both informal and formal heads of government meetings (the *Ministerpräsidentenkonferenz*, MPK) are well-established practices, as are ministerial councils. Much noted has been the role senior officials play in directing German intergovernmental relations behind the scenes – the 'brotherhood of technocrats' (Lhotta and von Blumenthal, 2012).

Driven by the same need to work out collaborative solutions to challenges that span levels of government, these federations have also come to rely increasingly on formal intergovernmental agreements (IGAs) that spell out in contractual detail the commitments of the respective governments. Not being made pursuant to any constitutional provision, and with parliaments generally lacking the authority to bind themselves in that way, they have little or no juridical force (Poirier, 2004). However, this has not prevented them from being respected in practice. In Switzerland, Germany and the United States, IGAs are predominantly horizontal in nature and enjoy some form of constitutional recognition. Such agreements allow spillover problems in such areas as pollution to be addressed without abnegating responsibility to national authority (Rabe, 2008; Lhotta and von Blumenthal, 2012). In Germany, their binding character is ensured through the constitutional doctrine of *bundestreue*, or 'federal faithfulness'.

As was noted over half a century ago (CIR, 1955) if not earlier, the great centralization of policy making has placed a premium on administrative coordination between levels of government. This leads to what in a general sense may be called 'administrative federalism', or the reality that much of that coordination occurs through a process of bargaining and negotiation between officials in the respective governments or agencies (Agranoff and McGuire, 2004). In this regard, the legislative federations have assumed characteristics similar to the administrative federations, with constituent units often responsible for implementing national policies. Administrative federalism in this more technical sense is thus now to be found in a variety of circumstances (e.g. Schwager, 1999). The term has, however, accumulated a range of meanings. It has, for instance, been used to describe the unusual situation found in India where, as a consequence of origins in a unitary state, the civil service is integrated between the two levels of government (Maheshwari, 1992). In yet another twist, the term has also been used to describe the US practice whereby decisions about the practical workings of the division of powers between the two levels of government may be delegated to a particular agency for resolution. Debate in that literature focuses on whether, in bypassing the political process, such delegation buttresses or undermines federalism (Galle and Seidenfeld, 2008; Metzger, 2008; cf. Logan, 2010).

ENVIRONMENTAL POLICY

Few policy domains have more clearly epitomized the transition to 'cooperative' federalism than environmental policy. Traditionally an exclusively local matter, the environment has rapidly become the subject of national policy making since the 1960s and early 1970s – with the US Clean Air Act of 1970 as bellwether. Not surprisingly, this has been more evident in the United States than Canada where limits on the assertion of national authority are greater (Harrison, 2000;

Winfield and Macdonald, 2008; Weibust, 2009). Widespread spillovers, both material and non-material, make local control problematic – as does the strong possibility that local environmental protection is adversely affected by competitive federalism and its promotion of a 'race to the bottom' (Saleska and Engel, 1998; Engel and Rose-Ackerman, 2001; Schwab, 2006; Andreen, 2009; Weibust, 2009). While this view is not universally accepted (Oates, 1997; Esty and Geradin, 2001; Revesz, 2001), it is reflected in prevailing policy directions. In the United States, this has followed the pattern of administrative federalism akin to the German model, with national regulations specifying regulatory minima and states tasked with implementing, administering and, if they wish, augmenting.

The German model has been judged particularly effective in environmental governance, although rather more for the way it creates effective coordination by integrating the *Länder* into the national policy-making process than simply for its functional division of powers (VanNijnatten, 2000). In practical terms, the strong national role in American environmental policy brings about a dynamic relationship of negotiation and compromise between state authorities, national authorities, and regional offices of national authorities (Scheberle, 2004). Complexity and entanglement, duplication and overlap may well reflect the reality of environmental policy, with its multiple dimensions carrying highly varying footprints, and provide a suitably 'adaptive' response (Adelman and Engel, 2009). It may also provide a degree of insurance against mismanagement by one level or the other (Hollander, 2010). Where, for instance, one level of government seems paralysed – as in the case of national climate change policy in the United States – some states and local governments may voluntarily occupy the temporarily vacant policy space, in the process engaging with transnational policy networks of competition and coordination (Rabe, 2008). Quite what metaphor best captures the reality of such interactive over-lapping continues to be discussed (Schapiro, 2009).

DISASTER MANAGEMENT

Some federations, such as Australia and the United States, happen to be particularly prone to natural disasters, and such events may well provide a particular stress test for systems and practices of intergovernmental coordination (Landy, 2008) – as equally may disasters of human making (Birkland and DeYoung, 2011). In such circumstances, the question of the respective roles of the different governments arises – as, when things go wrong, does the question whether federalism obstructs effective disaster management. One potential problem is that different governments will fail to coordinate preparation and action sufficiently. Federalism compounds the already challenging nature of service delivery in a disaster, where systems are placed under great pressure and when the capacity for effective *intra*-governmental coordination is already itself being tested. Another problem is that federalism may create perverse incentives for lower-order governments to under-invest in preparation – effectively, a moral hazard problem.

The destruction of New Orleans by Hurricane Katrina in 2005 gave rise to much criticism and soul-searching in the United States about the governmental response in general, and the intergovernmental dimension of that response, in particular. Was federalism to blame for the 'disaster within a disaster' (Menzel, 2006: 810)? In general, the answer arising from official reports and academic analysis is 'no': the main source of the problem was ineptness *within* the respective governments rather than between them. Most particularly, analyses point to failures of preparation, orientation and coordination within the US government and its main relevant agencies (Kweit and Kweit, 2006; Birkland and Waterman, 2008). There is also

the consideration, as the White House report put it, that 'Hurricane Katrina was the most destructive natural disaster in U.S. history' (Townsend, 2006: 5) and New Orleans is so precariously situated as to be almost unprotectable (Derthick, 2007). It remains the case, though, that federal systems do place a premium on coordinated systems for contingencies (Kweit and Kweit, 2006).

Underlying the practical challenge of ensuring effective vertical coordination between levels of governments as well as effective horizontal coordination within the respective governments is the possibility that the logic of federalism contributes to dysfunctional free-riding behaviour by individual jurisdictions. Given public expectations in situations of natural disaster, lower-order governments can safely assume that they will be rescued by the national government, and thus have less incentive to plan adequately and invest sufficiently in avoiding or managing the problem themselves (Goodspeed and Haughwout, 2012).

CONCLUSION

The impossibility of making a legislative division of powers work today as designed has given rise to techniques and instruments of intergovernmental coordination in the first-generation federations of the United States, Canada and Australia. Through a variety of devices, and with varying degrees of coerciveness, these systems have generated ways in which formerly local matters have been subjected to national policy making. At the same time, administration in what has come to be generically known as 'cooperative federalism' has often been left to the subnational authorities, and thus there has been, in some respects, a significant convergence with those systems based on a functional division of powers. Nonetheless, as federations, they remain distinctive for the way that those adaptive developments must operate within the confines of a governing constitutional order and thus reflect an ongo-ing relationship of competing powers.

REFERENCES

ACIR (1983) *Regulatory Federalism: policy, process, impact and reform.* Washington, DC: Advisory Commission on Intergovernmental Relations.

Adelman, David E. and Engel, Kirsten H. (2009) 'Adaptive Environmental Federalism', in W. W. Buzbee (ed.), *Preemption Choice: the theory, law, and reality of federalism's core question.* New York: Cambridge University Press, pp. 277–99.

Agranoff, Robert and McGuire, Michael (2004) 'Another Look at Bargaining and Negotiating in Intergovernmental Management', *Journal of Public Administration Research and Theory,* 14(4): 495–512.

Anderson, Geoff (2008), 'The Council of Australian Governments: a new institution of governance for Australia's conditional federalism', *University of New South Wales Law Journal,* 31(2): 493–508.

Andreen, William L. (2009) 'Delegated Federalism versus Devolution: some insights from the history of water pollution control', in W. W. Buzbee (ed.), *Preemption Choice: the theory, law, and reality of federalism's core question.* New York: Cambridge University Press, pp. 257–76.

Armingeon, Klaus (2000) 'Swiss Federalism in Comparative Perspective', in U. Wachendorfer-Schmidt (ed.), *Federalism and Political Performance.* London: Routledge, pp. 112–29.

Bakvis, Herman and Brown, Douglas (2010) 'Policy Coordination in Federal Systems: comparing intergovernmental processes and outcomes in Canada and the United States', *Publius,* 40(3): 484–507.

Bednar, Jenna (2009) *The Robust Federation: principles of design.* Cambridge: Cambridge University Press.

Birkland, Thomas and Waterman, Sarah (2008) 'Is Federalism the Reason for Policy Failure in Hurricane Katrina?', *Publius,* 38(4): 692–714.

Birkland, Thomas A. and DeYoung, Sarah E. (2011) 'Emergency Response, Doctrinal Confusion, and Federalism in the Deepwater Horizon Oil Spill', *Publius,* 41(3): 471–93.

Bouckaert, Geert, Peters, B. Guy and Verhoest, Koen (2010) *The Coordination of Public Sector Organizations: shifting patterns of public management.* Basingstoke: Palgrave Macmillan.

Bowman, Ann and Kearney, Richard (2010) *State and Local Government,* 8th edn. Boston, MA: Wadsworth.

Brecht, Arnold (1945) *Federalism and Regionalism in Germany: the division of Prussia.* New York: Oxford University Press.

Buzbee, William W. (ed.) (2009) *Preemption Choice: the theory, law, and reality of federalism's core question.* New York: Cambridge University Press.

Cameron, David and Simeon, Richard (2002) 'Intergovernmental Relations in Canada: the emergence of collaborative federalism', *Publius,* 32(2): 49–71.

Carroll, Peter and Head, Brian (2010) 'Regulatory Reform and the Management of Intergovernmental Relations in Australia', *Australian Journal of Political Science,* 45(3): 407–24.

Cho, Chung-Lae and Wright, Deil S. (2007) 'Perceptions of Federal Aid Impacts on State Agencies: patterns, trends, and variations across the 20th century', *Publius,* 37(1): 103–30.

CIR (1955) *A Report to the President for Transmittal to the Congress.* Washington, DC: Commission on Intergovernmental Relations.

Clark, Jane Perry (1938) *The Rise of a New Federalism: federal–state cooperation in the United States.* New York: Columbia University Press.

Conlan, Tim (2006) 'From Cooperative to Opportunistic Federalism: reflections on the half-century anniversary of the Commission on Intergovernmental Relations', *Public Administration Review,* 66(5): 663–76.

Conlan, Timothy J. (2008) 'Between a Rock and a Hard Place: the evolution of American federalism', in T. J. Conlan (ed.), *Intergovernmental Management for the Twenty-First Century.* Washington, DC: Brookings Institution, pp. 26–41.

Conlan, Timothy J. and Posner, Paul L. (eds) (2008) *Intergovernmental Management for the Twenty-First Century.* Washington, DC: Brookings Institution Press.

Corwin, Edward S. (1950) 'The Passing of Dual Federalism', *Virginia Law Review,* 36(1): 1–24.

Derthick, Martha (2007) 'Where Federalism Didn't Fail', *Public Administration Review,* 67(S1): 36–47.

Dorf, Michael C. and Sable, Charles F. (1998) 'A Constitution of Democratic Experimentalism', *Columbia Law Review,* 98(2): 267–473.

Downe, James (2008) 'Inspection of Local Government Services', in H. Davis and S. Martin (eds), *Public Services Inspection in the UK.* London: Jessica Kingsley, pp. 19–36.

Elazar, Daniel J. (1962) *The American Partnership: intergovernmental co-operation in the nineteenth century United States.* Chicago, IL: University of Chicago Press.

Elazar, Daniel J. (1991) 'Cooperative Federalism', in Daphne A. Kenyon and John Kincaid (eds), *Competition among States and Local Govern-ments: efficiency and equity in American federal-ism.* Washington, DC: Urban Institute Press, pp. 65–86.

Engel, Kirsten and Rose-Ackerman, Susan (2001) 'Environmental Federalism in the United States: the risks of devolution', in D. C. Esty and D. Geradin (eds), *Regulatory Competition and Economic Integration: comparative perspectives.* New York: Oxford University Press, pp. 135–53.

Erk, Jan (2007) *Explaining Federalism: state, society and congruence in Austria, Belgium, Canada, Germany, and Switzerland.* London: Routledge.

Esty, Daniel C. and Geradin, Damien (2001) 'Regulatory Co-Opetition', in D. C. Esty and D. Geradin (eds), *Regulatory Competition and Economic Integration: comparative perspectives.* New York: Oxford University Press, pp. 30–48.

Fenna, Alan (2007a) 'The Malaise of Federalism: com-parative reflections on Commonwealth–state rela-tions', *Australian Journal of Public Administration,* 66(3): 298–306.

Fenna, Alan (2007b) 'The Division of Powers in Australian Federalism: subsidiarity and the single market', *Public Policy,* 2(3): 175–94.

Fenna, Alan (2008) 'Commonwealth Fiscal Power and Australia Federalism', *University of New South Wales Law Journal,* 31(2): 509–29.

Fenna, Alan (2012) 'Adaptation and Reform in Australian Federalism', in P. Kildea, A. Lynch, and G. Williams (eds), *Tomorrow's Federation: reforming Australian government.* Leichhardt, NSW: Federation Press.

Fenna, Alan and Anderson, Geoff (2012) 'The Rudd Reforms and the Future of Australian Federalism', in G. Appleby, N. Aroney and T. John (eds), *The Future of Australian Federalism: comparative and inter-disciplinary perspectives.* Cambridge: Cambridge University Press.

Filippov, Mikhail, Ordeshook, Peter C. and Shvetsova, Olga (2004) *Designing Federalism: a theory of self-sustainable federal institutions.* Cambridge: Cambridge University Press.

Galle, Brian and Seidenfeld, Mark (2008) 'Administrative Law's Federalism: preemption, delegation, and agencies at the edge of federal power', *Duke Law Journal,* 57(7): 1933–2023.

Gamkhar, Shama (2002) *Federal Intergovernmental Grants and the States: managing devolution.* Cheltenham: Edward Elgar.

Glendening, Parris N. and Reeves, Mavis Mann (1977) *Pragmatic Federalism: an intergovernmental view of American government.* Pacific Palisades, CA: Palisades Publishers.

Goodspeed, Timothy and Haughwout, Andrew (2012) 'On the Optimal Design of Disaster Insurance in a Federation', *Economics of Governance,* 13(1): 1–27.

Gunlicks, Arthur B. (2003) *The Länder and German Federalism.* Manchester: Manchester University Press.

Gunlicks, Arthur B. (2005) 'German Federalism and Recent Reform Efforts', *German Law Journal,* 6(10): 1283–95.

Halberstam, Daniel and Hills, Roderick M. (2001) 'State Autonomy in Germany and the United States', *Annals of the American Academy of Political and Social Science,* 574(11): 173–85.

Handley, Donna Milam (2008) 'Strengthening the Intergovernmental Grant System: long-term lessons for the federal–local relationship', *Public Administration Review,* 68(1): 126–36.

Harrison, Kathryn (2000) 'The Origins of National Standards: comparing federal government involve-ment in environmental policy in Canada and the United States', in P. Fafard and K. Harrison (eds), *Managing the Environmental Union: intergovern-mental relations and environmental policy in Canada.* Kingston, ON: School of Policy Studies, Queen's University, pp. 49–80.

Heidenreich, Martin and Bischoff, Gabrielle (2008) 'The Open Method of Co-ordination: a way to the Europeanization of social and employment poli-cies?', *Journal of Common Market Studies,* 46(3): 497–532.

Hollander, Robyn (2010) 'Rethinking Overlap and Duplication: federalism and environmental assess-ment in Australia', *Publius,* 40(1): 136–70.

Hollander, Robyn and Patapan, Haig (2007) 'Pragmatic Federalism: Australian federalism from Hawke to Howard', *Australian Journal of Public Administration,* 66(3): 280–97.

Hueglin, Thomas O. (2000) 'From Constitutional to Treaty Federalism: a comparative perspective', *Publius,* 30(4): 137–53.

Hueglin, Thomas O. (2007) 'The Principle of Subsidiarity', in Ian Peach (ed.), *Constructing Tomorrow's Federalism: new perspectives on Canadian govern-ance.* Winnipeg, MB: University of Manitoba Press.

Hueglin, Thomas O. and Fenna, Alan (2006) *Comparative Federalism: a systematic inquiry*. Peterborough, ON: Broadview Press.

Hupe, Peter L. (2010) 'The Thesis of Incongruent Implementation: revisiting Pressman and Wildavsky', *Public Policy and Administration*, 26(1): 63–80.

Inwood, Gregory J., Johns, Carolyn M. and O'Reilly, Patricia L. (2011) *Intergovernmental Policy Capacity in Canada: inside the worlds of finance, environment, trade, and health*. Montreal and Kingston: McGill–Queen's University Press.

Jones, Stephen (2008) 'Cooperative Federalism? The case of the Ministerial Council on Education, Employment, Training and Youth Affairs', *Australian Journal of Public Administration*, 67(2): 161–72.

Kelemen, R. Daniel (2004) *The Rules of Federalism: institutions and regulatory politics in the EU and beyond*. Cambridge, MA: Harvard University Press.

Kettl, Donald F. (2006) 'Managing Boundaries in American Administration: the collaboration imperative', *Public Administration Review*, 66(S1): 10–19.

Kincaid, John (1990) 'From Cooperative to Coercive Federalism', *Annals of the American Academy of Political and Social Science*, 509(1): 139–52.

Kropp, Sabine (2010) *Kooperativer Föderalismus und Politikverflechtung*. Wiesbaden: VS Verlag.

Kweit, Mary Grisez and Kweit, Robert W. (2006) 'A Tale of Two Disasters', *Publius*, 36(3): 375–92.

Landy, Marc (2008) 'Mega-Disasters and Federalism', *Public Administration Review*, 68(S1): 186–98.

Laursen, Finn (ed.) (2011) *The EU and Federalism: polities and policies compared*. Farnham: Ashgate.

Levy, Jacob T. (2007) 'Federalism, Liberalism, and the Separation of Loyalties', *American Political Science Review*, 101(3): 459–77.

Lhotta, Roland and von Blumenthal, Julia (2012) 'Intergovernmental Relations in the Federal Republic of Germany', in J. Poirier and C. Saunders (eds), *Intergovernmental Relations in Federal Countries*. Montreal and Kingston: McGill–Queen's University Press.

Logan, Wayne A. (2010) 'The Adam Walsh Act and the Failed Promise of Administrative Federalism', *George Washington Law Review*, 78(5): 993–1013.

Maheshwari, Shriram (1992) *Problems and Issues in Administrative Federalism*. New Delhi: Allied.

Majone, Giandomenico (2006) 'Federation, Confederation, and Mixed Government: a EU–US comparison', in A. Menon and M. Schain (eds), *Comparative Federalism: the European Union and the United States in comparative perspective*. New York: Oxford University Press, pp. 121–48.

Manna, Paul (2011) *Collision Course: federal education policy meets state and local realities*. Washington, DC: CQ Press.

Menon, Anand and Schain, Martin A. (eds) (2006) *Comparative Federalism: the European Union and the United States in comparative perspective*. New York: Oxford University Press.

Menzel, Donald C. (2006) 'The Katrina Aftermath: a failure of federalism or leadership?', *Public Administration Review*, 66(6): 808–12.

Metzenbaum, Shelley H. (2008) 'From Oversight to Insight: federal agencies as learning leaders in the information age', in T. J. Conlan and P. L. Posner (eds), *Intergovernmental Management for the Twenty-First Century*. Washington, DC: Brookings Institution Press, pp. 209–42.

Metzger, Gillian E. (2008) 'Administrative Law as the New Federalism', *Duke Law Journal*, 57: 2023–109.

Murphy, Jerome T. (1971) 'Title I of EASA: the politics of implementing federal education reform', *Harvard Educational Review*, 41(1): 35–63.

Nugent, John D. (2009) *Safeguarding Federalism: how states protect their interests in national policymaking*. Norman, OK: University of Oklahoma Press.

Oates, Wallace E. (1997) 'On Environmental Federalism', *Virginia Law Review*, 83(7): 1321–29.

Painter, Martin (1998) *Collaborative Federalism: economic reform in Australia in the 1990s*. Melbourne: Cambridge University Press.

Papillon, Martin and Simeon, Richard (2004) 'The Weakest Link? First Ministers' Conferences in Canadian Intergovernmental Relations', in J. P. Meekison, H. Telford and H. Lazar (eds), *Canada: the state of the federation 2002 — reconsidering the institutions of Canadian federalism*. Montreal and Kingston: McGill–Queen's University Press, pp. 113–40.

Parkin, Andrew (2003) 'The States, Federalism and Political Science: a fifty-year appraisal', *Australian Journal of Public Administration*, 62(2): 101–12.

Peterson, Paul E. (1995) *The Price of Federalism*. Washington, DC: Brookings Institution.

Poirier, Johanne (2004) 'Intergovernmental Agreements in Canada: at the crossroads between law and politics', in J. P. Meekison, H. Telford and H. Lazar (eds), *Canada: the state of the federation 2002 — reconsidering the institutions of Canadian federalism*. Montreal and Kingston: McGill–Queen's University Press, pp. 425–62.

Posner, Paul L. (1998) *The Politics of Unfunded Mandates: whither federalism?* Washington, DC: Georgetown University Press.

Posner, Paul L. (2007) 'The Politics of Coercive Federalism in the Bush Era', *Publius*, 37(3): 390–412.

Posner, Paul L. (2008) 'Mandates: the politics of coercive federalism', in T. J. Conlan and P. L. Posner (eds), *Intergovernmental Management for the Twenty-First Century*. Washington, DC: Brookings Institution, pp. 286–309.

Pressman, Jeffrey L. and Wildavsky, Aaron (1973) *Implementation: how great expectations in Washington are dashed in Oakland; or, why it's amazing that federal programs work at all; this being a saga of the Economic Development Administration as told by two sympathetic observers who seek to build morals on a foundation of ruined hopes*. Berkeley, CA: University of California Press.

Rabe, Barry G. (2008) 'Regionalism and Global Climate Change Policy: revisiting multistate collaboration as an intergovernmental management tool ', in T. J. Conlan and P. L. Posner (eds), *Intergovernmental Management for the Twenty-First Century*. Washington, DC: Brookings Institution, pp. 176–205.

Radin, Beryl A. (2006) *Challenging the Performance Movement: accountability, complexity, and democratic values*. Washington, DC: Georgetown University Press.

Radin, Beryl A. (2008) 'Performance Management and Intergovernmental Relations', in T. J. Conlan and P. L. Posner (eds), *Intergovernmental Management for the Twenty-First Century*. Washington, DC: Brookings Institution Press, pp. 243–62.

Radin, Beryl A. and Boase, Joan Price (2000) 'Federalism, Political Structure, and Public Policy in the United States and Canada', *Journal of Comparative Policy Analysis*, 2(1): 65–89.

Ramamurthy, Vijaya (2012) 'Tied Grants and Policy Reform in Public Hospitals and Schools', in P. Kildea, A. Lynch and G. Williams (eds), *Tomorrow's Federation: reforming Australian government*. Leichhardt, NSW: Federation Press.

Revesz, Richard L. (2001) 'Federalism and Regulation: some generalizations', in D. C. Esty and D. Geradin (eds), *Regulatory Competition and Economic Integration: comparative perspectives*. New York: Oxford University Press, pp. 3–29.

Sabel, Charles F. and Zeitlin, Jonathan (eds) (2010) *Experimentalist Governance in the European Union: towards a new architecture*. New York: Oxford University Press.

Saleska, Scott R. and Engel, Kirsten H. (1998) '"Facts are Stubborn Things": an empirical reality check on the theoretical debate over the race-to-the-bottom in state environmental standard-setting', *Cornell Journal of Law and Public Policy*, 8(1): 55–62.

Sawer, Geoffrey (1969) *Modern Federalism*. London: C. A. Watts & Co.

Schapiro, Robert A. (2009) 'From Dualism to Polyphony', in W. W. Buzbee (ed.), *Preemption Choice: the theory, law, and reality of federalism's core question*. New York: Cambridge University Press, pp. 33–53.

Scharpf, Fritz W., Reissert, Bernd and Schnabel, Fritz (1976) *Politikverflechtung: theorie und empirie des kooperativen Föderalismus in der Bundesrepublik*. Kronberg: Scriptor.

Scheberle, Denise (2004) *Federalism and Environmental Policy: trust and the politics of implementation*, 2nd edn. Washington, DC: Georgetown University Press.

Scheiber, Harry N. (1980) 'Federalism and Legal Process: historical and contemporary analysis of the American system', *Law and Society Review*, 14(3): 663–722.

Schutze, Robert (2009) *From Dual to Cooperative Federalism: the changing structure of European law*. New York: Oxford University Press.

Schwab, Robert M. (2006) 'Environmental Federalism', in W. E. Oates (ed.), *The RFF Reader in Environmental and Resource Policy*, 2nd edn. Washington, DC: Resources for the Future, pp. 109–14.

Schwager, Robert (1999) 'The Theory of Administrative Federalism: an alternative to fiscal centralization and decentralization', *Public Finance Review*, 27(3): 282–309.

Simeon, Richard (1972) *Federal–Provincial Diplomacy: the making of recent policy in Canada*. Toronto, ON: University of Toronto Press.

Simeon, Richard and Radin, Beryl A. (2010) 'Reflections on Comparing Federalisms: Canada and the United States', *Publius*, 40(3): 357–65.

Teaford, Jon C. (2002) *The Rise of the States: evolution of American state government*. Baltimore, MD: Johns Hopkins University Press.

Tholoniat, Luc (2010) 'The Career of the Open Method of Coordination: lessons from a "soft" EU instrument', *West European Politics*, 33(1): 93–117.

Townsend, Frances Fragos (2006) *The Federal Response to Hurricane Katrina: lessons learned*. Washington, DC: White House.

van Hecke, Stephen (2003) 'The Principle of Subsidiarity: ten years of application in the European Union', *Regional and Federal Studies*, 13(1): 55–80.

VanNijnatten, Debora L. (2000) 'Intergovernmental Relations and Environmental Policy Making: a cross-national perspective', in P. Fafard and K. Harrison (eds), *Managing the Environmental*

Union: intergovernmental relations and environmental policy in Canada. Kingston, ON: School of Policy Studies, Queen's University, pp. 23–48.

Wallis, John Joseph and Oates, Wallace E. (1998) 'The Impact of the New Deal on American Federalism', in M. D. Bordo, C. Goldin and E. N. White (eds), *The Defining Moment: the Great Depression and the American economy in the 20th century.* Chicago, IL: University of Chicago Press, pp. 155–80.

Weibust, Inger (2009) *Green Leviathan: the case for a federal role in environmental policy.* Farnham: Ashgate.

Weissert, Carol S. and Weissert, William G. (2008) 'Medicaid Waivers: license to shape the future of fiscal federalism', in T. J. Conlan and P. L. Posner (eds), *Intergovernmental Management for the Twenty-First Century.* Washington, DC: Brookings Institution Press, pp. 157–75.

Winfield, Mark and Macdonald, Douglas (2008) 'The Harmonization Accord and Climate Change Policy: two case studies in federal–provincial environmental policy', in H. Bakvis and G. Skogstad (eds), *Canadian Federalism: performance, effectiveness, and legitimacy.* Don Mills, ON: Oxford University Press, pp. 266–88.

Zimmerman, Joseph F. (2005) *Congressional Preemption: regulatory federalism.* Albany, NY: State University of New York Press.

41

Multi-level Governance and Public Administration

Simona Piattoni

INTRODUCTION

Multi-level governance (MLG) has become the code word for a number of interrelated developments in public administration that find their clearest manifestation in the context of European integration. The first development (recorded by the governance literature – whether multi-level of otherwise) is that effective policy making requires that many actors outside of central government, both private and public, work together. The second development is the continuous redefinition of the territorial articulation of European states, whether unitary or federal, aimed at establishing an efficient division of labor between governmental levels. The third dynamic is connected to the process of European integration, which tries to weld together different traditions of territorial management and thus ends up upsetting existing political and administrative models. Each of these developments poses a distinct challenge to the public administration of European states and points to a number of theoretical puzzles in conventional political science. MLG, then, is not simply coterminous with intergovernmental relations (IGR) but, while sharing some of the same basic concerns denoted also by this term (Ongaro, 2010), points to debates that uniquely characterize European nation-states and the process of European integration.

Analyzing MLG draws attention to the historical record of state development and to normative concerns regarding the quality (and the changing nature) of democracy. History warns against oversimplifying the developmental trajectory of the European territorial state, while normative concerns temper the enthusiasm for novel governance arrangements that fly in the face of conventional and tried models of democracy. At the same time, these developments open up new vistas onto the meaning of democracy in post-sovereign, post-national and, perhaps, post-territorial states.

This chapter is organized as follows: first, it offers a recapitulation of the developments that changed perceived notions of government and resulted in the increased use of the term governance and, second, a review of the debate on the adoption and diffusion of multi-level governance arrangements in Europe. 'Conventional wisdom' attributes these developments to the quest for greater efficiency but here it will be argued that MLG is driven by the highly political attempt to find policy-making arrangements that can be perceived as not only efficient but also legitimate. The following sections illustrate how MLG fits uneasily with the different state traditions present in Europe, so that no single member state has a clear advantage over others when it comes to implementing European Union (EU) legislation, and how it differs across policy areas. The conclusion is that MLG is a constant work in progress rather than an already defined 'new political order' and that whatever destination is eventually reached will depend on the capacity of political and policy leaders to project MLG arrangements, and the policies made through them, as legitimate.

WHENCE MLG?

The pedigree of the concept can be traced back to three concomitant, but independent developments in public administration. The first has to do with the expansion of welfare state services in West European states particularly in the first postwar period (1950s to 1970s). As West European states took on increasing welfare tasks, service delivery became more and more complex. In an attempt to boost efficiency, several administrative solutions were experimented with, from the creation of general-purpose meso-governmental levels in charge of several services simultaneously to the creation of single-purpose functional organizations directly controlled by central departments (Radin, 2003). This led to a drive towards the rationalization of territorial jurisdictions and the standardization of public services. As a partial response to the resulting excessive bureaucracy, new ways of delivering services were attempted, thus giving rise to a growing involvement of non-governmental and civil society organizations in the formulation and implementation of welfare policies.

The second development, closely connected to the first, was the heightened attention to developmental issues. World War II left a legacy of uneven destruction and development that could not be tolerated in the political mood of the postwar period. All West European states adopted economic development programs, paying attention both to lagging (mostly agrarian) regions and to declining (mostly industrial) regions. For the sake of regional planning and policy implementation, unitary states created administrative or planning regions, thus contributing to a generalized drive towards a 'meso-level in Europe'(Rokkan et al., 1987; Sharpe, 1979, 1993). Some states embarked on rationalization drives, collapsing municipal governments into larger units that ended up resembling the regional governments that were simultaneously created in others. The consequence was to create a new group of meso-level administrative and political actors who attached new meaning to territorial entities engineered for efficiency reasons. In some cases, this top-down *regionalization* got intertwined with bottom-up *regionalism* (Keating, 1996, 1998) – an independent revival of regional and local identities, arising from the upsurge of post-material values and a search for more authentic territorial identities (the so-called right to roots).

The third development derived, paradoxically, from the failure or declining effectiveness of the measures just described in the more turbulent economic context of the 1970s. Two oil crises imposed heavy restructuring on European industries in advanced regions, suggested the rescaling of industry-centered developmental plans in formerly agrarian regions and, more generally, imposed cost reductions on welfare provisions. In an interesting reverse drive for efficiency – now directed at containing costs and reducing services – central governments resorted to three different management strategies, which are synthetically captured by the terms hierarchy, network and market (Streeck and Schmitter, 1985; Wollmann, 2003). The hierarchical solution – the creation or consolidation of meso governments that could preside over multiple services delivery but presumably also over service containment – was adopted by centralized Continental states (notably, France and Italy). The networked solution – the creation of concertative arrangements among representatives of state, social partners and civil society organizations at various territorial levels – was preferred by both unitary and federal North European countries with solid neo-corporatist traditions (Scandinavian countries and Continental 'consensus' democracies such as Germany and the Netherlands). The market solution was embraced by neo-liberal countries that, wary of either administrative or political meso-level institutions, preferred to impose the economic discipline of market-like mechanisms onto single-purpose administrative units directly subordinate to central government.

The influence of entrenched national administrative and political traditions was evident throughout. Both in times of expansion and in times of contraction, each polity banked on its own strengths and tinkered with its own administrative system without fundamentally departing from it. Still, common traits were discernible, as all three solutions entailed closer collaboration between public and private actors and the rescaling of the territorial articulation of the nation-state to meet the economic and social challenges of the day: the essence of multi-level governance. These partly distinct and partly convergent trends were further affected by the process of Europeanization.

A vast literature has developed which studies the ways in which member states' institutions, policies, procedures and, even more generally, actors' cognitive maps change under the impact of the process of European integration (Börzel and Risse, 2003; Radaelli, 2003). While fairly general propositions have been developed indicating that the amount of change is correlated with the degree of fit or misfit between national and European 'ways of doing things' (Green-Cowles et al., 2000), more detailed analysis reveals the distinctive difficulties that each member state encounters in adapting to common or convergent policies and standards. Thus, in addition to responding to common growth and crises during the post-war period in distinct but parallel ways, West European states further overhauled their administrative practices and territorial organization under the impact of the process of European integration.

MLG: THE THEORETICAL CORE

The term 'multi-level governance' was coined by Gary Marks in a seminal article (Marks, 1992) aimed at describing the distinctive type of policy making that characterized EU structural policy. Marks suggested that, in certain policy areas such as cohesion policy and environmental policy, European policy making was no longer dominated by national governments: supranational and subnational actors had become crucially important as well. He described this 'new political order', or 'emerging political disorder', as 'a complex, multilayered, decision-making process stretching beneath the state as well as above it' (Marks, 1992: 221). This multi-level vision of EU policy making was contrasted to the state-centrist vision – in both the neo-realist and liberal intergovernmentalist versions – that saw central governments as firmly in control. In addition, he noted that 'extremely wide and persistent variations' (Marks, 1992: 221) structurally characterized EU policy making across policy areas. In practice, Marks argued that while EU decision making could no longer be characterized as a 'neat, two sided process involving member states and Community institutions', it was at the same time difficult to say precisely which 'new political order' was replacing the state-centric one (Hooghe and Marks, 2003).

The MLG concept was increasingly applied both in EU studies and beyond in many subfields of political science, public policy and political economy (Bache and Flinders, 2004; Conzelmann and Smith, 2008; Enderlein et al., 2010; Hooghe and Marks, 2001). But if MLG captured important dynamics in the 'business of rule' (Poggi, 1978), it did not yet point to a distinct developmental trajectory that could indicate what was driving it and where it was heading: while it was a 'compelling metaphor' (Rosamond, 2000), MLG was still 'ill-theorized' (Benz, 2000).The debates that ensued as a reaction to Marks' initial provocation can help to flesh out MLG's theoretical core (but see also Hooghe and Marks,1996; Marks, 1993, 1996; Marks et al., 1996). Three main debates unfolded, touching three distinct directions of change and three sources of challenge to the nation-state. By looking at the answers provided by these debates – none of them fully satisfactory if taken in isolation – we should be able to capture the theoretical core of MLG.

The first debate revolved around the idea that *regions*, rather than states, were the most efficient level at which economic production and service delivery could be organized (Cox, 1997; Storper, 1997). Regions were also supposedly more authentic communities, which commanded genuine allegiance and pristine attachment among their citizens; hence, regional government was potentially more democratic (Loughlin, 1996; Rokkan and Urwin, 1982, 1983). The second debate had to do with the increasing role that subnational and transnational *societies* played in setting the political agenda and in implementing solutions. It was theorized that parliamentary democracies, based on territorially defined communities, were inherently unable to identify the problems and the solutions of the day, and that policy networks (whether forming spontaneously, facilitated by the state, or created by the European Union) were better able to deliver governance solutions (Andersen and Burns, 1996; Smismans, 2004, 2006). The third debate reasserted the

centrality of the nation-state and basically denied any loss of relevance, sovereignty and control on the part of nation (and member) states. Far from being superseded by transnational social groups and outflanked by sub-national authorities, *nation-states* were supposedly still able to orchestrate European integration in the direction, though not necessarily to the degree, that best fitted their needs and were equally able to steer subnational authorities into doing what they (central governments) decided (Hoffmann, 1966; Moravcsik, 1993, 1998).

These three debates reveal many challenges to the nation-state and its public administration. These challenges to the unity, specificity and autonomy of the nation-state could be thought of as coming from below (from subnational levels of government and society), from within (from private and public interests and from for-profit and non-profit organizations) and from the top (from supranational institutions) (Piattoni, 2010: 1–13).

The challenge from below

A rich literature on regionalism – on the resurgence of regional economies and identities – had anticipated many of the themes that were later also captured by the notion of multi-level governance (Jeffery, 1997b; Keating, 1988, 1998). Spurred in part by the observation that Fordist production was being replaced by flexible specialized production in Marshallian industrial districts (Piore and Sabel, 1984) and in part by the observation that lesser-spoken languages and regional identities (or sub-state nations) were experiencing a revival (Anderson, 1994), the literature on regionalism boomed in the 1970s and 1980s. In a probably overzealous enthusiasm for the regional phenomenon, some scholars lent credibility to the claim that regions were destined to replace states as the most meaningful level of political organization (Hooghe, 1995, 1996; Hooghe and Marks, 1996; Jeffery, 1996, 1997a; Keating et al., 2003). Marks (1992) himself seemed to support the vision of a dawning 'Europe of the Regions'.

The claim that regions could replace states as the political unit on which Europe (and the European Union) could be based is naïve, and, as such, it has been extensively criticized (Anderson, 1991; Jeffery, 2000; Keating, 2008; Rhodes, 1974; see also the entire *Regional & Federal Studies* 17(5) 2008 issue). However, the underlying fallacy – that an 'optimum scale' of government can indeed be identified and engineered into existence (Oates, 1972) – still enjoys wide circulation (see, for example, Jordan, 2001; Scharpf, 1988). In reality there is no single governmental scale that is 'optimal' for all governmental purposes and functions: there are only territorial jurisdictions that manage to attract enough loyalty to project themselves as viable governmental units. If the 'Europe of the Regions' claim has any value at all, this lies in drawing attention to the highly political, therefore contestable, nature of this project and certainly not to the intrinsic efficiency and optimality of any one level of government (Piattoni, 2010: Ch. 2).

The challenge from within

The debate on the relevance of civil society for policy making also anticipated some of the themes later captured also by multi-level governance. One strand in the literature records the widespread retrenchment from the welfare state since the early 1970s. 'From cradle to grave' did not sound all that cozy any more, particularly given the high levels of taxation that it implied and the overly bureaucratic services that it delivered. The reaction against it took different forms: for example, in Denmark and Norway, the formation of political parties protesting against the 'excessive intrusion' of the state; in countries like the UK and the United States, the dismantling of many welfare services and the adoption of market-like mechanisms (Piattoni, 2010: 6).

A second strand highlighted the upsurge of (transnational) social movements pressing for civil rights, opposing nuclear power, mobilizing in favor of the environment, protesting against xenophobia and, in general, claiming greater and more open political participation (Keck and Sikkink, 1998). Parallel to this transnational mobilization in favor of 'public interests' was the mobilization of society in favor of 'private interests', i.e., in favor of more liberal markets and greater self-regulation on the part of business (Sandholtz and Stone-Sweet, 1998).

The myth of the 'self-regulating society' is common to these arguments. In public administration, this suggested various strategies: from the involvement of all potential stakeholders in policy making to the promotion of forms of self-regulation on the part of industries, professions and corporations. Co-governance (Kickert et al., 1997), organic governance (Andersen and Burns, 1996) and supranational governance (Smismans, 2004) are some of the terms coined to indicate these developments. Authoritative pages have been written about the transformation of governance as a consequence of the increased self-awareness of civil society (Peters, 2001; Peters and Pierre, 2003; Pierre, 2000; Pierre and Peters, 2000) and inspiring visions of self-governing networks have been supplied (Rosenau and Czempiel, 1992). This debate captures the challenge that derives to the state from an increasingly self-aware society that demands direct involvement in policy making. However, it is doubtful that self-regulating societies could replace nation-states in their entirety.

The challenge from above

In a challenge to state-centrist approaches that took intergovernmental bargains as the events to be explained, Marks instead focused on the day-to-day relationships between EU functionaries, governmental actors, subnational representatives, lobbyists and social activists. By adopting this 'actor-centered' approach, Marks (1993) could note the existence of a thick web of relationships ('multi-level governance') that escaped institutional conventions and defied existing hierarchies. The heart of the controversy with state centrists (Bache, 1999; Hoffmann, 1966; Pollack, 1995) revolved around the continued capacity of member states to 'keep the gates' to the inter- and supranational levels and to regulate how societal actors and subnational authorities could relate to Europe. Even when such actors were busy lobbying European institutions, the assumption of state centrists was that they were pushing forward a national agenda and that they were keeping within limits set by the state. For state centrists, all international cooperation takes place (by definition) at the behest and in the interest of member states. But determining which decisions occur in the interest of the member states and which developments create a supranational order that ends up, perhaps unexpectedly, constraining them is an empirical matter.

Hooghe and Marks (2003) confronted the question of what type of order might replace the unraveling state. For them, MLG comes in two fundamentally distinct types: Type I MLG is based on a limited number of general-purpose territorial jurisdictions that resemble federalist polities; Type II MLG is the haphazard juxtaposition of overlapping special-purpose, functional jurisdictions. Membership in Type I MLG is stable and exclusive and the typical mode of participation is voice. Membership in Type II MLG is fleeting and intersecting and the characteristic mode of participation is exit. Real-life MLG structures normally straddle these two ideal-types: worlds strictly coinciding with either extreme are highly improbable. Still, a world of Type I MLG would be congenial to scholars that propound the relevance of regional governments and the staying power of territorial jurisdictions more generally, while a world of Type II MLG is not so distant from what the proponents of the self-regulating society have in mind. What is missing from this analysis is a sense

of direction: Which of these two types is going to prevail? Will mixes endure? Hooghe and Marks' answer is that the contemporary EU can be described as a 'layered network of Type II arrangements of varying institutional durability, fixity and geographical scope which are broadly coordinated by (a) relatively durable institutional arrangements among sets of national governments and (b) a small number of Type I international organizations' (Hooghe and Marks, 2010: 23). Type II jurisdictions normally coexist with Type I jurisdictions in the same overarching polity and will most likely keep doing so (Hooghe and Marks, 2003: 238).

Clearly neither solution, Type I nor Type II MLG, is self-evidently more 'efficient' (Marks and Hooghe, 2000). The other contributions to this section of the Handbook amply demonstrate that many solutions are tried by member states, depending on their administrative tradition and on the values prevalent in their polity and society, but that none is unquestionably superior to any other. Federal (Type I MLG) solutions attempt to capitalize upon the theoretically greater coordination capacity of general-purpose territorial jurisdictions that can aim at internalizing most significant externalities in the production and delivery of social and developmental services. Typically, they must then coordinate with lower-level jurisdictions and seek, at these lower levels, the involvement of civil society. Similar solutions have given rise to what is known in the United States as 'picket-fenced federalism', with few large general-purpose jurisdictions connected with one another through coordinating committees, or to what in Canada is known as 'executive federalism', where cross-provincial coordination is sought through high-level agreements among provincial executives (Painter, 1991). Functional (Type II MLG) solutions are tried mostly in unitary states. Single-purpose jurisdictions can there more easily be tied into a centralized system of political control and can be more easily reined in by economic

imperatives (such as profit making or breaking even). However, single-purpose jurisdictions are also more easily captured by the
clienteles that they are supposed to service or
regulate and generate externalities that may
affect the production and delivery of other
services. In order to compensate for these
sources of inefficiency, Type II MLG solutions require the activation of coordinative
and negotiated solutions that do not differ
very much from the solutions implemented
in Type I MLG arrangements. In no case,
however, are these negotiated solutions spon-
taneous and self-regulating, but they are
rather interstitial correctives to long administrative traditions and engineered reforms.

Under what conditions will MLG arrangements spread and become dominant across
the EU? Do all European member states
embody MLG in the same way and to the
same extent? The next section further develops MLG's theoretical core and charts the
cross-country and cross-policy variation in
MLG arrangements. The main argument is
that MLG arrangements will further spread
and stabilize into a new political order only
insofar as they will be perceived as legitimate, which is in itself a 'contentious concept' that can be settled only politically.

CROSS-POLICY VARIATION IN MLG

Multi-level governance arrangements have
not appeared in equal degree across all policy
sectors. Some policies have a clear territorial
dimension and hence lend themselves more
immediately to becoming grounds for MLG
experimentation. Territories are characterized by physical and cultural peculiarities
which induce their citizens to prefer certain
policy solutions to others. Territory is not
just a 'space' in which any type of economic
and social activity can theoretically take
place, but it is a 'place' endowed with specific natural resources and charged with particular cultural meanings. These conditions
give rise to special policy preferences that

local political classes can promote in order to
command electoral consensus: the essence of
democracy and the foundation of self-rule.
Also, civil society organizations – voluntary
organizations, transnational social movements, non-governmental organizations,
public-private partnerships, professional
organizations – claim 'self-rule' rights in
specific fields and create self-regulating
policy networks on the basis of which they
can command prestige and obedience from
their members.

Examples of policies with a clear territorial dimension include:

- developmental policies, especially if linked to
  primary sectors such as agriculture, fishing, and
  mining;
- environmental policies, for which local conditions determine sensitivity to one or the other
  type of pollutant or suggest different environmental strategies;
- transport policies, which create different problems and call for different solutions (for example,
  Alpine and transborder regions are affected by
  international traffic to an extent unknown to
  maritime regions, which may rather suffer from
  being peripheral and difficult to reach); and
- higher education policy, for which the territorial
  dimension is becoming increasingly relevant, particularly as the creation of knowledge-intensive
  skills demands the pooling together of different
  educational strengths that are located in different places sometimes across national borders.

Whether these policies areas are better tackled through territorially specific instruments
or through national or supranational sector-
specific tools –Type I or Type II MLG
arrangements, respectively – is also a question of prevailing scientific and political
conviction. Until the 1970s, developmental
issues were tackled through demand-side
policies and did not differentiate across territories. Economic theory postulated that
different economic activities would be created according to the relative factor endowment – the comparative advantage – of any
given area, and that free trade would slowly
equalize factor remuneration throughout. It
was only when the effect of economies of

scope and the ensuing theory of increasing returns could be modeled that the effect of territory (Marshallian districts) and historical path dependency could be theorized. Similarly, environmental issues can be tackled through regulatory policies that impose the same standards across territories for each type of pollutant or can be addressed through more flexible tools that take into account the vulnerability of given areas to specific pollutants. Policy tools will be rather different, as will be the actors mobilized and the type of MLG arrangements thus created. Finally, higher education has traditionally been a policy in which, with the exception of federal states, national standards have been uniformly imposed as a way of consolidating and preserving national identities. It is only since national cultures, languages and identities have been challenged and knowledge has become a factor of production in its own right that higher education has become a policy area in which, at the same time, both international and localized solutions can be devised. So, while some policies are more easily tackled through Type I MLG arrangements, they might also be tackled through Type II MLG arrangements (Piattoni, 2010: Part II).

If policy issues can be tackled through standardized solutions that apply uniformly across territories and require the direct involvement of general-purpose institutions (hierarchy), through differentiated regulations uniquely tailored to the specificities of given territories and societies (networks), or through market-like mechanisms that require the active involvement of the receivers of the policies (market), what makes any one of these solutions preferable to the others? No one policy solution is uniquely or obviously more efficient, provided that the limitations and externalities produced by each solution are compensated through coordination among levels of government or between public and private actors. The choice will then depend on the prevailing scientific convictions and political preferences, hence on the success of different public and private actors – political and policy entrepreneurs – in winning the argument for one or the other type of solution.

CROSS-NATIONAL VARIATION IN MLG

The diffusion of MLG arrangements is also uneven across states and poses different challenges to different member states. All European member states have implemented administrative and territorial reforms under the pressure of the three developments described above and all have introduced some form of meso administrative or political level. These new arrangements were constrained significantly by national administrative traditions, yet they involved also new departures. Despite resistance and path dependency, both France and the UK reformed their territorial administration in response to the stimuli described in the beginning of this chapter – the desire to implement far-reaching welfare and developmental policies, crisis management, and changes in economic and social thinking – and both submitted to the pressures stemming from the EU to create meso-level institutions to manage the structural funds. France created regions spanning across several *départements*, which, however, remained in charge of most aspects of structural policy (Smith, 2003), while the UK created Government Offices for the Regions that were steered from the center by national government officials and manned with local functionaries drawn from various civil society associations. Neither France nor the UK introduced merely perfunctory changes: in both cases, institutions created for one purpose began to mobilize material and immaterial resources well beyond the original intentions. In the rather diverging MLG configurations that arose, true innovations were introduced that put existing practices and cognitive frames under strain.

A similar, and even more telling, story can be told of a country that was already endowed with a system of multi-level governance: Germany. The peculiarities of German cooperative federalism have been recounted a number of times (Benz, 1998, 1999, 2000; Scharpf, 1988), but they are worth recalling as they have become paradigmatic of the difficulties that can bewitch federalist (Type I MLG) institutions. German federalism is dubbed 'cooperative' because cooperation must be sought between the federal government and the *Länder* if most policies are to be decided and implemented. In selected policy areas, German *Länder* have veto power and can therefore extract nice rewards for their consent. Because the decision-making rule is 'all in or none in' (Painter, 1991), unanimity is required. This leads to very lengthy and cumbersome joint decision-making processes (*Politikverflechtung*) which, once they have produced a decision, are extremely difficult to undo (Scharpf's 'joint decision trap'). The joint decision trap does not always snap: it all depends on the nature of the decision, on the partisan alignment of the two chambers (*Bundestag* and *Bundesrat*) and on the economic conjuncture (Benz, 1999). Decisions are toughest when they are of the zero-sum type, when the two chambers are dominated by opposed parties, and when the economic conjuncture is unfavorable. Under these circumstances, poorer or more vulnerable *Länder* will withhold their consent and the temptation for the federal government will be to buy consensus with increased institutional powers to all *Länder*. This shift in bargaining level gives the federal government momentary respite and buys needed policy decisions, but ties further the rope around its neck (Benz, 1999). Europeanization has given the German federal government greater space for maneuver, since many framework decisions are taken through co-decision by governmental representatives in the Council and by the European Parliament, institutions to which *Länder* have no immediate access. It also triggered the reaction of the *Länder* to obtain a number of safeguards in order to protect their domestic privileges in Brussels (hence, the 'Europe of the Regions' initiative). They did obtain representational rights in the Council and the creation of a Committee of the Regions that makes the voice of subnational authorities heard in EU policy making (in an advisory capacity). However, German *Länder* have been thus almost put on a par with other, less powerful subnational authorities and have been forced to try and influence EU policy making through lobbying as if they were single-purpose Type II jurisdictions. What this story shows is that a Type I MLG institutional setting, such as German cooperative federalism, does not necessarily fit well with EU MLG configuration because *in Europe Type I and Type II jurisdictions are de facto equalized*. A similar story could be told of corporatist countries in which societal Type II jurisdictions had to fight back and recoup the policy-making powers enjoyed at home or of unitary states in which categorical associations have found themselves relatively disempowered by EU MLG.

Italy's trajectory is in part similar to that of France: being also a post-Napoleonic state, the original imprint of the Italian state was unitary. The central state interacted with its citizens in the periphery through provincial offices headed by prefects, much like in French *départements*, and self-government was limited to the municipal level. The republican constitution of 1948 introduced the regions, self-governing intermediate tiers charged with developmental and policy coordination policies. The planning vocation of these regions was strengthened in the 1960s, but it was only in the 1970s that welfare distribution (and later welfare containment) was entrusted to them. In the 1980s they became the obvious referent of the European Union for the implementation of the reformed structural funds and it was at this point that the differential capacity of regional political classes started to emerge (Bukowski et al., 2003). The regions began to acquire political meaning: later developments – the creation and success of regional parties claiming for greater autonomy and devolution – gave political teeth to these institutions and moved

Italy onto a path of progressive devolution if not outright (and until now still incomplete) federalization. In the Italian case, Europeanization served to strengthen and accelerate a process that was already in the making and that now seems irreversible (even though far from complete; Hooghe et al., 2010). In this case, too, EU MLG upset established equilibriums and projected the state onto a reform path that would have probably not unfolded precisely in this way had it not been for the process of European integration.

CONCLUSION: MLG LEGITIMACY

In the end, the specific MLG solution which is adopted depends very much on the legitimacy that Type I or Type II jurisdictions command in each country and on which type of solution appears to be more efficient for any given policy issue. Type I jurisdictions constitute an intermediate level of administrative and political power that challenges the unity of the national state and leads to requests for greater political and institutional empowerment. Type II jurisdictions constitute insulated sub-governments that may challenge the universalism of the state; tensions between different single-purpose jurisdictions typically lead to requests for greater policy and budgetary empowerment on the part of specialized agencies and their clienteles. Type II MLG arrangements are more typical of unitary, liberal states that focus more on the output and outcome side of politics, while they are seen with suspicion in unitary post-Napoleonic states that emphasize the input side of politics and are wary of the creation of intermediate bodies between state and citizens. Liberal states are more likely to rely on the power of financial incentives (block grants, matching funds, etc.), while post-Napoleonic states are more likely to rely on the power of legal and procedural requirements. The tug of war between the national and the subnational level is not necessarily about acquiring ampler powers or competences, but is determined by the specific goals of the actors that get mobilized at these levels.

Both Type I and Type II MLG arrangements are successful only insofar as they are backed by the will and vision of political and policy leaders who mostly belong either to the territorial subnational level or to the societal infranational level. In liberal states, Type II MLG leaders do not strive to create and maximize the institutional power of some subnational level of government, an objective which they correctly perceive beyond their reach and which they probably also deem ultimately wasteful. They are interested in maximizing control over given policy areas: the power to co-determine policy objectives and to reap the economic benefits that derive from their implementation. In post-Napoleonic states, Type I MLG leaders are not necessarily interested in acquiring responsibility over all types of regulatory policies, as they correctly anticipate that their citizens might be happier to abide by national or international standards when it comes to industrial or environmental regulation. They rather attempt to strengthen the legislative and institutional power of the subnational government to which they belong and are interested in maximizing the fiscal and spending powers of their level of government and to reap the electoral benefits that derive from both.

What is, rather, a common and surprising development is the de facto equalization of Type I and Type II MLG arrangements engendered by Europeanization, a development that challenges the distinctiveness of the state in addition to its sovereignty and unity.

REFERENCES

Andersen, Svein S. and Burns, Tom R. (1996) 'The European Union and the Erosion of Parliamentary Democracy: A Study in Post-Parliamentary

Governance', in S.S. Andersen and K.A. Eliassen (eds), *The European Union: How Democratic Is It?* London: Sage, pp. 227–67.

Anderson, Jeffrey (1991) 'Skeptical Reflections on a Europe of the Regions: Britain, Germany and the ERDF', *Journal of Public Policy*, 10(4): 417–47.

Anderson, Perry (1994) 'The Invention of the Regions, 1945–1990'. EUI Working Paper 94/2.

Bache, Ian (1999) 'The Extended Gate-Keeper: Central Government and the Implementation of EC Regional Policy in the UK', *Journal of European Public Policy*, 61: 28–45.

Bache, Ian and Flinders, Matthew (eds) (2004) *Multi-Level Governance*. Oxford: Oxford University Press.

Benz, Arthur (1998) 'From Cooperative Federalism to Multi-Level Governance: German and EU Regional Policy', *Regional & Federal Studies*, 10(3): 505–22.

Benz, Arthur (1999) 'From Unitary to Asymmetric Federalism in Germany: Taking Stock after 50 Years', *Publius: The Journal of Federalism*, 29(4): 55–78.

Benz, Arthur (2000) 'Two Types of Multi-Level Governance: Intergovernmental Relations in German and EU Regional Policy', *Regional and Federal Studies*, 10(3): 21–44.

Börzel, Tanja and Risse, Thomas (2003) 'Conceptualizing the Domestic Impact of Europe', in K. Featherstone and C.M. Radaelli (eds), *The Politics of Europeanization*. Oxford: Oxford University Press, pp. 57–80.

Bukowski, Jeanie, Piattoni, Simona and Marc, Smyrl (eds) (2003) *Between Europeanization and Local Societies. The Space for Territorial Governance.* Lanham, MD: Rowman & Littlefield.

Conzelmann, Thomas and Smith, Randall (eds) (2008) *Multi-Level Governance in the European Union. Taking Stock and Looking Ahead.* Baden-Baden: Nomos.

Cox, Kevin (ed.) (1997) *Spaces of Globalization. Reasserting the Power of the Local.* New York: The Guilford Press.

Enderlein, Hendrik, Wälti, Sonja and Zürn, Michael (eds) (2010) *Handbook on Multi-Level Governance.* Cheltenham, UK: Edward Elgar.

Green-Cowles, Maria, Caporaso, James A. and Risse, Thomas (eds) (2000) *Transforming Europe: Europeanization and Structural Change.* Ithaca, NY: Cornell University Press.

Hoffmann, Stanley (1966) 'Obstinate or Obsolete? The Fate of the Nation-State and the Case of Western Europe', *Daedalus*, 95(3): 862–915.

Hooghe, Liesbet (1995) 'Sub-National Mobilization in the European Union', *West European Politics*, 18(3): 175–98.

Hooghe, Liesbet (ed.) (1996) *Cohesion Policy and European Integration. Building Multi-Level Governance.* Oxford: Clarendon Press.

Hooghe, Liesbet and Marks, Gary (1996) '"Europe with the Regions": Channels of Regional Representation in the European Union', *Publius: The Journal of Federalism*, 26(1): 73–91.

Hooghe, Liesbet and Marks, Gary (2001) *Multi-Level Governance and European Integration.* Lanham, MD: Rowman & Littlefield.

Hooghe, Liesbet and Marks, Gary (2003) 'Unraveling the Central State, but How? Types of Multi-Level Governance', *American Political Science Review*, 97(2): 233–43.

Hooghe, Liesbet and Marks, Gary (2010) 'Types of Multi-Level Governance', in H. Enderlein, S. Wälti and M. Zürn (eds), *Handbook on Multi-Level Governance.* Cheltenham, UK: Edward Elgar, pp. 17–31.

Hooghe, Liesbet, Marks, Gary and Schakel, Arjan (2010) *The Rise of Regional Authority. A Comparative Study of 42 Democracies.* London: Routledge.

Jeffery, Charlie (1996). 'Regional Information Offices in Brussels and Multi-level Governance in the EU: A UK–Germany Comparison', *Regional & Federal Studies*, 6(2): 183–203.

Jeffery, Charlie (1997a) *Sub-National Authorities and European Integration. Moving Beyond the Nation-State.* Birmingham: University of Birmingham Press.

Jeffery, Charlie (1997b) *The Regional Dimension of the European Union. Towards a Third Level in Europe?* London: Frank Cass.

Jeffery, Charlie (2000) 'Sub-National Mobilization and European Integration: Does It Make Any Difference?', *Journal of Common Market Studies*, 38(1): 1–23.

Jordan, Andrew (2001) 'The European Union: An Evolving System of Multi-level Governance… or Government?', *Politics & Policy*, 29(2): 193–208.

Keating, Michael (1988) *State and Regional Nationalism. Territorial Politics and the European State.* New York: Harvester Wheatsheaf.

Keating, Michael (1996) 'The Invention of Regions: Political Restructuring and Territorial Government in Western Europe'. ECPR Joint Sessions, Oslo, 29 March to 3 April.

Keating, Michael (1998) *The New Regionalism in Western Europe. Territorial Restructuring and Political Change.* Cheltenham, UK: Edward Elgar.

Keating, Michael (2008) 'A Quarter Century of the Europe of the Regions', *Regional & Federal Studies*, 17(5): 629–35.

Keating, Michael, Loughlin, John and Deschouwer, Kris (2003) *Culture, Institutions and Economic Development: A Study of Eight European Regions.* Cheltenham, UK: Edward Elgar.

Keck, Margaret and Sikkink, Kathryn (1998) *Activists beyond Borders: Advocacy Networks in International Politics.* Ithaca, NY: Cornell University Press.

Kickert, Walter J. M., Klijn, Erik-Hans and Koopenjan, Joop (1997) *Managing Complex Networks: Strategies for the Public Sector.* London: Sage.

Loughlin, John (1996) '"Europe of the Regions" and the Federalization of Europe', *Publius: The Journal of Federalism,* 26(4): 141–62.

Marks, Gary (1992) 'Structural Policy in the European Community', in A. Sbragia (ed.), *Euro-Politics. Institutions and Policymaking in the 'New' European Community.* Washington, DC: The Brookings Institution, pp. 191–225.

Marks, Gary (1993) 'Structural Policy and Multi-Level Governance in the EC', in A. Cafruny and G. Rosenthal (eds), *The State of the European Community. Vol. 2, The Maastricht Debates and Beyond.* Boulder, CO: Lynne Rienner, pp. 391–410.

Marks, Gary (1996) 'An Actor-Centred Approach to Multi-Level Governance', *Regional & Federal Studies,* 6(2): 20–40.

Marks, Gary and Hooghe, Liesbet (2000) 'Optimality and Authority: A Critique of Neoclassical Theory', *Journal of Common Market Studies,* 38(5): 795–816.

Marks, Gary, Hooghe, Liesbet and Blank, Kermit (1996) 'European Integration from the 1980s: State-Centric v. Multi-Level Governance', *Journal of Common Market Studies,* 34(3): 341–78.

Moravcsik, Andrew (1993) 'Preferences and Power in the European Community: A Liberal Inter-Governmentalist Approach', *Journal of Common Market Studies,* 31(4): 473–524.

Moravcsik, Andrew (1998) *The Choice for Europe: Social Purpose and State Power from Messina to Maastricht.* Ithaca, NY: Cornell University Press.

Oates, Wallace (1972) *Fiscal Federalism.* New York: Harcourt Brace Jovanovich.

Ongaro, Edoardo, Massey, Andrew, Holzer, Marc and Wayenberg, Ellen (eds) (2010) *Governance and Intergovernmental Relations in the European Union and the United States: Theoretical Perspectives.* Cheltenham, UK: Edward Elgar.

Painter, Martin (1991) 'Intergovernmental Relations in Canada: An Institutionalist Analysis', *Canadian Journal of Political Science,* 24(2): 269–88.

Peters, B. Guy (2001) *The Future of Governing,* 2nd edn. Lawrence, KS: University Press of Kansas.

Peters, B. Guy and Pierre, Jon (2003) 'Introduction: The Role of Public Administration in Governing', in B. G. Peters and J. Pierre (eds), *Handbook of Public Administration.* London: Sage, pp. 1–9.

Piattoni, Simona (2010) *The Theory of Multi-Level Governance. Conceptual, Empirical and Normative Challenges.* Oxford: Oxford University Press.

Piore, Michael and Sabel, Charles (1984) *The Second Industrial Divide. Possibilities for Prosperity.* New York: Basic Books.

Pierre, Jon (ed.) (2000) *Debating Governance: Authority, Steering, and Democracy.* Oxford: Oxford University Press.

Pierre, Jon and Peters, Guy (2000) *Governance, Politics and the State.* Houndmills: Macmillan Press.

Poggi, Gianfranco (1978) *The Development of the Modern State. A Sociological Introduction.* Stanford, CA: Stanford University Press.

Pollack, Mark (1995) 'Regional Actors in an Inter-Governmental Play: The Making and Implementation of EC Structural Funds', in J. Richardson and S. Mazeyeds (eds), *The State of the European Union, Vol. 3. Building a European Polity?* Boulder, CO: Lynne Rienner, pp. 361–90.

Radaelli, Claudio (2003) 'The Europeanization of Public Policy', in K. Featherstone and C.M. Radaelli (eds), *The Politics of Europeanization.* Oxford: Oxford University Press, pp. 27–56.

Radin, Beryl (2003) 'The Instruments of Intergovernmental Management', in B.G. Peters and J. Pierre (eds), *Handbook of Public Administration.* London: Sage, pp. 607–18.

Rhodes, R.A.W. (1974) 'Regional Policy and a "Europe of the Regions": A Critical Assessment', *Regional Studies,* 8: 105–14.

Rokkan, Stein and Urwin, Derek (eds) (1982) *The Politics of Territorial Identity. Studies in European Regionalism.* London: Sage.

Rokkan, Stein and Urwin, Derek (1983) *Economy, Territory, Identity: Politics of West European Peripheries.* London: Sage.

Rokkan, Stein, Urwin, Derek, Aarebrot, Frank H., Malaba, Pamela and Sande, Terje (1987) *Centre–Periphery Structures in Europe.* Frankfurt: Campus Verlag.

Rosamond, Ben (2000) *Theories of European Integration.* New York: St. Martin's Press.

Rosenau, James N. and Czempiel, Ernst-Otto (eds) (1992) *Governance without Government. Order and Change in World Politics.* Cambridge: Cambridge University Press.

Sandholtz, Wayne and Stone-Sweet, Alec (eds) (1998) *European Integration and Supranational Governance*. Oxford: Oxford University Press.

Scharpf, Fritz W. (1988) 'The Joint Decision Trap: Lessons from German Federalism and European Integration', *Public Administration*, 66(3): 239–78.

Sharpe, Laurence J. (1979) *Decentralist Trends in Western Democracies*. London: Sage.

Sharpe, Laurence J. (1993) *The Rise of Meso-Government in Europe*. London: Sage.

Smith, Andy (2003) 'Multi-Level Governance: What It Is and How It Can Be Studied', in B.G. Peters and J. Pierre (eds), *Handbook of Public Administration*. London: Sage, pp. 619–28.

Smismans, Stijn (2004) *Law, Legitimacy and European Governance. Functional Participation in Social Regulation*. Oxford: Oxford University Press.

Smismans, Stijn (ed) (2006) *Civil Society and Legitimate European Governance*. Cheltenham, UK: Edward Elgar.

Storper, Michael (1997) *The Regional World: Territorial Development in a Global Economy*. New York: Guilford Press.

Streeck, Wolfgang and Schmitter, Philippe (eds) (1985) *Private Interest Government. Beyond Market and State*. London: Sage.

Wollmann, Hellmut (2003) 'Coordination in the Intergovernmental Setting', in B.G. Peters and J. Pierre (eds), *Handbook of Public Administration*. London: Sage, pp. 594–606.

Index

political responsiveness, senior service 103–104
political rights 547
politics
 administration and society relations 360–362
 administration dichotomy 201–204, 321
 administration involvement 172–175
 civil service politicization 340–350
 comparative public administration 445–454
 implementation research 246–250
 Institutionalization 142, 156–159, 346, 523
 interest groups 22, 174–175
 interorganizational relations 671–675
 Latin America 523, 563–568
 organization theory 346, 523
 reform 495–498
politics-administration dichotomy 201–203, 625
polycentric government 636
population ecology 138
portfolio approach 56
power distance 452
preference aggregation 7
presentational rules 309
Pressman-Wildavsky paradox 256
principal-agent theory
 accountability 406–408
 comparative public administration 481–483, 516
 formal theory 169–178
 implementation research 454
 intergovernmental coordination 600
 internal administration 169–171
Prisoner's Dilemma 169, 171
private management 473, 520, 619
private sector, accountability 619–623
privatization
 accountability 619
 administrative patterns 252, 640
 administrative state 117
 African reform 546–548
 Central and Eastern Europe 582–585
 comparative public administration 119–124
 labor-management relations 117
 Latin America 565–568
problem identification, policy process 574
procedural-based approach 215
procedural fairness 316, 598
procedural policy instruments 125
procedural protection 284
procedural rights 126, 215
professional accountability 37
professionalization 192, 313, 345, 373, 462
professional norms 171, 267
professional socialization 267–268
Progressive movement, USA 5, 192
property taxes 554
proportionality principle 289, 301
Prussian model 283, 288
public administration, legitimacy 357–367
public choice theory 93, 596, 733

public enterprise reform 565–569
public goods 167–168, 170, 361, 408, 628
public interest systems 18, 26, 73, 101, 314, 362
public management 17
 administration comparison 483–491
 as craft 22–23
 governance 8, 26–27
 as institution 24–26
 performance and effectiveness 71–80
 politics 264–266
 as structure 21–22
public participation 117, 158, 196, 300, 342, 361
public policy *see* policy
public-private interdependence 641
Public services bargain 481–486, 566
PUMA program 473

qualified majority voting (QMV) 468
qualitative-descriptive method 183
quality
 see also Total Quality Management (TQM)
 control 36, 39
 of government 353–356
quantitative research, implementation research 58, 229

rational calculation 136, 517, 519
rational choice
 institutionalism 93–94, 144
 organization theory 166–176
rationality 18, 25, 518, 521, 550, 602
 bounded 43
 public management 168–173
 sociological institutionalism 158–160
Realpolitik 137
Rechtsstaat 102, 183, 280, 283–284, 286, 513, 515,
  517, 589
recruitment
 civil service 323–324
 human resource management 73–78
 senior service 105–107
redistributive policies 652
red tape 79–80
reductionism 159
reform 5, 488–492, 495–508
 see also New Public Management (NPM)
 administrative state 61, 67, 81, 391–392
 African crisis 543–548
 analytics 499–508
 capacity 500–501
 developing/transitional societies 500–502,
  524–533
 interorganizational relations 668–673
 Latin America 562–567
 law 290–291
 logic 5
 modes 495–498
 multi-level governance 668–673
 politics 489–493